FEMINIST JURISPRUDENCE

FEMINIST JURISPRUDENCE

◆

EDITED BY

Patricia Smith

New York   Oxford
OXFORD UNIVERSITY PRESS
1993

Oxford University Press

Oxford   New York   Toronto
Delhi   Bombay   Calcutta   Madras   Karachi
Kuala Lumpur   Singapore   HongKong   Tokyo
Nairobi   Dar es Salaam   Cape Town
Melbourne   Auckland   Madrid

and associated companies in
Berlin   Ibadan

Published by Oxford University Press, Inc.
200 Madison Avenue, New York, New York 10016

Oxford is a registered trademark of Oxford University Press

Library of Congress Cataloging-in-Publication Data
Feminist jurisprudence / edited by Patricia Smith.
p.   cm.   Includes bibliographical references.
ISBN 0-19-507397-5
1. Women—Legal status, laws, etc. 2. Sex discrimination against
women. 3. Sex and law. 4. Feminist theory. 5. Feminism.
I. Smith, Patricia, 1956-
K644.Z9F457 1993
346.01'34—dc20   [342.6134]   92-3465

2 4 6 8 10 9 7 5 3 1

Printed in the United States of America
on acid-free paper

For Yuri

Preface

I first assembled these materials in response to students' requests for a course on feminist legal theory. I had wanted to offer such a course for several years before I was able to squeeze it into the curriculum, which is apparently a common problem for feminist topics; we are not yet a regular part of the core. Along with the obvious disadvantages, this provides feminists with the distinct advantage of raising natural questions about what the core curriculum ought to be, and even more fundamental questions about how we organize our categories of knowledge. When I finally did manage to find time for the course, I realized that there was no book that assembled major feminist contributions to legal theory in one collection, so I did what all good college professors do: I assembled a photocopy packet. And this volume, with some rather substantial revisions due to student responses in the classroom, further research and experience on my part, and some very helpful and much appreciated advice from others in the field, is the result.

The course is modeled after a mainstream jurisprudence course, mainly because that is what I am used to teaching, and how I am used to thinking. I have tried to provide background on the traditional approach to the topics in this book in the introduction to each part. Perhaps because of this, several reviewers have suggested that this book could be used for a standard jurisprudence course. Especially if combined with a concise complementary text, such as Murphy and Coleman's PHILOSOPHY OF LAW, it could provide a fascinating foundation for any jurisprudence course, and one that students will find particularly stimulating and timely.

Two standard topics of jurisprudence are not explicitly (or separately) covered in this collection, namely, rights and punishment. This omission is not due to lack of interesting material; it was simply a judgment call in the face of limited space. I was not willing to leave out any of the topics that are included here, and the book would have become unmanageably long if I had included two more sections. There is excellent feminist work available on these topics, some of which is cited in the suggested readings. Other topics also deserve to be considered that I could not include here. Feminists have contributed to the discussion of contracts, torts, divorce and family law, property, and other traditional legal categories, as well as areas of special interest to women. I urge the reader to seek them out, and I have attempted to provide some helpful sources in the suggested readings. Unfortunately, comprehensive coverage is simply impossible, even for the areas I chose to cover, let alone all possible subjects.

The course I organized was a "special topics" jurisprudence course, and since I had been teaching jurisprudence for ten years, it was natural for me to organize it according to traditional philosophical subjects such as freedom, justice, equality, adjudication, and law. What surprised me was the fascinating way feminist work fell into these categories and transformed them. I believe that this book shows that feminist jurisprudence provides some of the most innovative and challenging legal analysis being done today. And more than that, feminist jurisprudence represents the first steps of conceptual change necessary to a cultural revolution that will bring about the end of patriarchy. Feminism is the only intellectual movement that faces that reality squarely. The challenge of women's experience to the traditional topics of freedom, justice, equality, adjudication, and law requires us to rethink these ideas, and to reexamine how they apply to women—if the lives of women have the same value as anyone else's. For example, if freedom, justice, and equality are universal values, what do they mean if they apply to women? If women's lives deserve equal concern and respect, it changes all the traditional patriarchal categories, creating new ones and rearranging the priorities of others. That is what makes feminist analysis exciting, and in fact, makes this collection of interest beyond jurisprudence or women's studies classrooms. The message of this book is a positive one of cultural revolution. Through the range of feminist work, I have tried to demonstrate the pervasiveness of patriarchal influence and some of the implications of its decline.

This book benefited greatly from the suggestions of several contributors and reviewers. I wish I were able to take advantage of more of these suggestions—perhaps in another volume. I would particularly like to thank Peggy Radin and Deborah Rhode for taking time to make valuable suggestions about organization and content, and my colleague Joan Callahan for more help than I could ever articulate gratitude for. I would also like to express my appreciation to Cynthia Read at Oxford University Press for having confidence in this project and others, and to Peter Ohlin for his patience and good judgment. Most of all, I want to thank my husband, Yuri Breitbart, for his continuous support and challenging conversations that keep me alive and growing. All of the errors in this book are definitely his fault.

Lexington, Kentucky   P. S.
1992

Contributors

REGINA AUSTIN
Professor of Law
University of Pennsylvania

ANDREA DWORKIN
Author and Attorney at Law
New York

SUSAN ESTRICH
Robert Kingsley Professor of Law and
   Political Science
University of Southern California

LYNNE N. HENDERSON
Professor of Law
Indiana University, Bloomington

NAN D. HUNTER
Associate Professor of Law
Brooklyn Law School
Director, American Civil Liberties
   Union Projects on Lesbian and Gay
   Rights, and on AIDS and Civil
   Liberties

HERMA HILL KAY
Jennings Professor of Law
University of California, Berkeley

SYLVIA A. LAW
Professor of Law
New York University
Director, Arthur Garfield Hayes Civil
   Liberties Memorial Program

CHRISTINE A. LITTLETON
Professor of Law
University of California, Los Angeles

CATHARINE A. MACKINNON
Professor of Law
University of Michigan

MARTHA MINOW
Professor of Law
Harvard University

LAURIE NSIAH-JEFFERSON
Consultant, Bureau of Maternity
   Services and Family Planning
New York Department of Health

FRANCES E. OLSEN
Professor of Law
University of California, Los
   Angeles

MARGARET JANE RADIN
Professor of Law
Stanford University

DEBORAH RHODE
Professor of Law
Stanford University

ANN C. SCALES
Professor of Law
University of New Mexico

JUDY SCALES-TRENT
Professor of Law and Jurisprudence
State University of New York at
   Buffalo

PATRICIA SMITH
Associate Professor of Philosophy
University of Kentucky

NADINE TAUB
Professor of Law
Rutgers University

KATHLEEN WAITS
Visiting Associate Professor
Albany Law School
Union University

ROBIN WEST
Professor of Law
University of Maryland

JOAN C. WILLIAMS
Associate Professor of Law
Washington College of Law
American University

WENDY W. WILLIAMS
Professor of Law and Associate Dean
Georgetown University Law Center

ELIZABETH WOLGAST
Professor of Philosophy
California State University, Hayward

Contents

FEMINIST
JURISPRUDENCE

♦

Feminist Jurisprudence
and the Nature of Law

What is feminist jurisprudence? One prominent feminist scholar, Catharine MacKinnon, explained that feminist jurisprudence is the analysis of law from the perspective of all women. This provides us with a good point of departure, as it captures the central focus of feminism, which is to attempt to represent women's side of things. Feminist theory recognizes that throughout history and even today, public discourse has been almost exclusively conducted by men from (quite naturally) the perspective of men. That is, the nature of women has been formulated by men, and the interests of women have been determined by men. Historically, women have never been allowed to represent themselves. They have always been represented by men, but this representation has hardly been accurate or fair. Even though it claims to represent all human beings, the fact is that public discourse has left out, silenced, misrepresented, disadvantaged, and subordinated women throughout all of history, relegating them to a single role and reserving the rest of life for men. MacKinnon's explanation underscores this point.

Using her explanation as a definition, however, might create the impression that there is a single perspective of all women, which is certainly false. Not even all feminists hold a single perspective, and not all women, of course, are feminists. But all feminism does begin with one presumption, namely, that a patriarchal world is not good for women. Virtually everyone agrees that the world is, in fact, patriarchal; that is, human societies have always been organized in a hierarchical structure that subordinates women to men. This is simply the observation of a social fact. Until recently it was virtually impossible to imagine the world any other way, and even now a great many men and women think that patriarchy is good, natural, or inevitable. Feminists think that patriarchy (the subjugation of women) is not good, not ordained by nature, and not inevitable.

The rejection of patriarchy is the one point on which all feminists agree. It is also apparently a distinguishing feature of feminism as a school of thought, as no other school of thought focuses on the critique of institutions and attitudes as patriarchal. Only feminism analyzes the patriarchal origin, nature, and effects of human attitudes, concepts, relations, and institutions and criticizes them on that ground. So we might take as a reasonable working definition that feminist jurisprudence is the analysis and critique of law as a patriarchal institution.

This analysis and critique manifests itself in a variety of ways, owing partly to the range of issues it covers and partly to divergence among feminists on virtually all points other than the rejection of patriarchy. Feminists tend to concentrate on issues of particular concern to women, such as equal protection law; discrimination in education, hiring, promotion, and pay; protection of reproductive freedom and other freedoms; protection from rape, sexual harassment, and spouse abuse; regulation of sexual and reproductive services such as surrogate mother contracts, prostitution, and pornography; and patriarchal bias in law and adjudication. But feminist analysis is appropriate to any area, concepts, relations, and institutions of law, and many legal theorists offer feminist critiques of standard legal categories such as contracts, property, and tort law. Clearly, the issues covered by feminist jurisprudence are as wide ranging as the areas covered by law. To appreciate the diversity of feminist jurisprudence, consider the differences among feminist theories.

Feminist Theories

The earliest explicit feminist writing is associated with the liberal tradition, as exemplified by Mary Walstonecraft's eighteenth-century book *A Vindication of the Rights of Women,* by John Stuart Mill's nineteenth-century *Subjection of Women,* and by Betty Friedan's twentieth-century *Feminine Mystique.* The general view is that the subordination of women is caused by the legal and social barriers that block or preclude their access to the public sphere of economic and political life. Liberal feminists demand that liberals follow their own principles of universal human rights. If all human beings are moral equals, as liberals have claimed since at least the seventeenth century, then men and women should be treated equally, which means that no one should be excluded from participating in political, educational, or economic life. Because they followed the classical liberal tradition, the early liberal feminists tended to be very individualistic, arguing for equal rights and equal freedom. They felt that the law should be gender blind, that there should be no special restrictions or special assistance on the basis of sex. Most of the gains made for women's equal rights and freedom in the 1960s and 1970s were made using liberal feminist arguments. The solution to the oppression of women, in this view, is to remove all formal barriers to their equal participation in social, political, and economic life, thus providing equal opportunity for all.

In the 1970s and 1980s some liberal feminists (including Friedan) began to rethink their position, as simply removing formal or legal restrictions did not seem to provide equal opportunity after all. Women still faced a great deal of informal discrimination and an uphill battle against old stereotypes that portrayed them as emotional, incompetent, and passive. Furthermore, even women who did manage to break into the male world of politics, economics, or academic life found themselves faced with a choice of eliminating any personal life whatsoever or working a double day, a choice that men did not have to face. Women found themselves responsible for home and family whether or not they also had a career, and this meant that most women could not compete on an equal footing with men who did not have this responsibility, precisely because it had been delegated to women. In response to this situation, many liberal feminists began to focus more on the socialization of children, the removal of stereotypes, the reorganization of family life, and the restructuring of state institutions to be more supportive of family needs. This change in focus mirrors the difference between classical liberal and modern welfare liberal views, but it is not a real change of position. The view of liberal feminists, whether classical or modern, is still that the solution to the oppression of women is to provide equal opportunity for all. The difference between the two views is in what constitutes equal opportunity.

Radical feminists believe that neither the classical nor the modern liberal view adequately explains women's oppression or provides effective solutions to it. Changing economic structures, eliminating political and educational barriers, and even socializing children will not abolish the subjugation of women so long as society is organized in a patriarchal system. Patriarchy is so pervasive that it structures our thoughts and attitudes, our assumptions and basic institutions, including the family and church. The only way to change the position of women is to change the way we think about gender itself, to reexamine our assumptions about our nature and relations to others. Although radical feminist views vary widely, most do focus on some aspect of the effect that biology has on women's psychology, their lives and their status, to recognize good effects as valuable and to overcome negative ones.

Some radical feminists (such as Adrienne Rich or Mary O'Brien) have concentrated on the significance of women as mothers (as child bearers and rearers), arguing either that women must be relieved of having the sole responsibility for these things or that because women are responsible for them, they must also be in control of them. Others (such as Shulamith Firestone or Kate Millett) look at the ways that gender and sexuality oppress women, for example, through sexual harassment, spouse abuse, rape, pornography, and the use of women as sex objects. Most radical feminists insist that male power or male dominance is the basis of the construction of gender and that this construction pervades all other institutions and ensures the perpetuation of patriarchy and thus the subordination of women. Some have suggested the promotion of androgeny (the appropriation of the full range of traits to both men and women) as a solution to the problem of patriarchy. Others contend that androgeny is not liberating for women and that the goal is, rather, to revalue those characteristics associated with the feminine role, such as nurturing and gentleness. Still others believe that because the feminine role and character have been constructed by patriarchy, women must reconstruct them for themselves—must find their true nature. Overall, in the most general terms, the focus of radical feminism is on the domination of women by men through the social construction of gender within patriarchy. For them the solution to the oppression of women is to reverse the institutional structures of domination and to reconstruct gender, thereby eliminating patriarchy.

Marxist and socialist feminists, however, believe that the construction of gender is not the primary issue. They think that equality for women is not possible in a class-based society established on the basic principles of private property and exploitation of the powerless. According to the Marxists, the oppression of women originated, or at least solidified, when the introduction of capitalism and private property sharply divided the world into private and public spheres of life, relegated women to the noneconomic private sphere, and devalued that sphere, that is, made it worthless in market terms. To relieve the oppression of women, the capitalist system must be replaced with a socialist system in which no class will be economically dependent or exploited by any other. The solution to the oppression of women is to change the economic system so that women will not be economically dependent, marginal, and exploited.

Many modern socialist feminists have nonetheless become dissatisfied with the traditional Marxist approach, as it fails to account adequately for the oppression of women as women rather than as workers, fails to explain the domination of women in the private as well as the public sphere, and fails to provide an analysis of gender and patriarchy.

Some feminists have tried to combine economic (Marxist or socialist) theories with radical theories or psychoanalytical theories that attempt to deal with gender and patriarchy as such. In fact, many modern feminists think that no single theory can account for all aspects of the domination and oppression of women.

Furthermore, some feminists deny altogether the usefulness of general theories in their traditional form. This skepticism or denial of the utility of theory, at least "Grand Theory," is commonly associated with a loose collection of views often called *postmodern* or *French feminism.* The term *French feminism* originated from the fact that most of the early contributors were French (e.g., Helene Cixous and Luce Irigaray) and that most follow the work of French thinkers associated with the postmodern movement, such as Jacques Derrida, Jacques Lacan, and Jean-François Lyotard. In law and jurisprudence, this approach is associated with a movement called *critical legal studies,* with which many postmodern feminists are closely associated. Like most postmodern thinkers, these feminists deny that categorical, abstract theories derived through reason and assumptions about the essence of human nature can serve as the foundation of knowledge. They call such ambitious theorizing *phallologocentric,* meaning that it is centered on an absolute word (*logos*) that reflects a male perspective (*pahllus*). They claim that it is a male approach to believe that a single answer or a single truth can be found that will organize all issues and lead to a single reformative strategy. Above all, postmodern feminism is critical. Often following Derrida, many postmodern feminists use techniques of *deconstruction* to expose the internal contradictions of apparently coherent systems of thought. This has been a useful method of debunking patriarchal structures of thought and social organization, including law. Other postmodern feminists, following Lacan, are interested in reinterpreting traditional Freudian psychoanalysis, with all its implications for biological determinism and the subordination of women.

In addition, many postmodern feminists display attachments to existentialism in terms of their focus on the "Other." Existentialists have always portrayed the Other as a negative status. To be the Other is to be objectified, determined, and marginalized. Simone de Beauvoir considered the fundamental question of feminism to be "why is woman the Other?" She considered the oppression of women to be an expression of their status as the Other, as the sex objectified by men. Postmodern feminists, however, celebrate Otherness. Because they are criticizing the mainstream of thought and society, the "Law of the Fathers" or the "Symbolic Order," there is a positive side to Otherness, as it disassociates itself from the mainstream accepted structures of reality, knowledge, and society: To be Other to patriarchy is not necessarily a bad thing.

In general, postmodern feminists do not offer a single solution to the oppression of women, first, because they do not think that there can be single solutions to anything. Second, to propose a single solution to *the* oppression of women suggests that all women's experiences are alike, that women's oppression is a unitary thing. But real human problems cannot be solved by abstract rules and generalizations. Rather, attacking the oppression of women requires contextual judgments that recognize and accommodate the particularity of human experience. As Deborah Rhode put it, "Such an approach demands that feminists shift self-consciously among needs to acknowledge both distinctiveness and commonality between sexes and unity and diversity among their members." For postmodern feminists there is no single solution and no single oppression of women, but only solutions tailored to the concrete experience of actual people.

One problem with postmodern views, particularly those associated with deconstruction, is that they tend to be better at destroying theories than at building them, which may generate a debilitating skepticism that is not useful to the feminist cause in the long run. One response to this skepticism has been a revitalization of pragmatism within feminism. Pragmatism also subscribes to a postmodern antiessentialist theory of human nature and knowledge. In law it is associated with legal realist theory, which views law as a dynamic process of conflict resolution and focuses on the function of courts to analyze law and legal reasoning. Feminists are drawn to the practical, personal, contextual approach of pragmatism, which coincides with feminist rejection of traditional abstract categories, dichotomies, and the conceptual pretensions of the logical analysis of law.

Finally, a trend sometimes called *relational feminism* in some ways reverses the focus of some earlier theories, especially liberal theories that call for equal rights for women on the ground that men and women are fundamentally similar. Many recent relational feminist writers have been greatly influenced by the work of Harvard educational psychologist Carol Gilligan. In her book *In a Different Voice,* Gilligan hypothesizes that men and women are not fundamentally similar; rather, men and women typically undergo a different moral development. The predominant moral attitude of men she calls the *ethic of justice,* which concentrates on abstract rules, principles, and rights. The predominant moral attitude of women Gilligan calls the *ethic of care,* which focuses on concrete relationships, concern for others, and responsibility. The important thing for Gilligan is to recognize the value of both, and especially not to devalue the ethic of care.

Following Gilligan, many relational feminists have argued that the important task for feminists today is not to fit women into a man's world, not to assimilate women into patriarchy, and not to prove that women can function like men and meet male norms, but to change institutions to reflect and accommodate the value that should properly be accorded to characteristics and virtues traditionally associated with women, nurturing virtues such as love, sympathy, patience, and concern. It is not that women should change to meet existing institutions but that institutions should be changed to accommodate women (or at least the best virtues associated with women). Of course, when put in these terms, most feminists would agree. No feminist thinks that women should be turned into clones of men, and there is increasing concern over what might be lost in the unthinking assimilation of women into male institutions.

The difference between liberal feminists on the one hand and relational feminists on the other represents a split among feminists and others as to whether men and women are fundamentally similar or fundamentally different, particularly in psychological and/ or moral terms. This split is actually an old one that was prominent in the early twentieth century in debates about women's rights. The question is whether women, being basically similar to men, require equal treatment or, being significantly different from men, require special treatment. This question is reflected in many jurisprudential and legal debates today, and each side has its hazards. The deficiency of the liberal view is that treating men and women as exactly alike ignores genuine physical and social differences that tend to disadvantage the vast majority of women. But the deficiency of the relational view is that it can easily be transformed into the old, traditional stereotype of women as biologically domestic and dependent, which perpetuate bias, discrimination, and domination instead of counteracting it. Many feminists now think that this old debate needs to be ended or transcended, but exactly how to do this is not clear. It is clear, however, that the sameness/ difference debate is a snag that has often divided feminists and hindered social progress.

There are (at least) three points that provide some ground for optimism that the old sameness/difference debate may, this time, be overcome. First, for postmodern theorists, the sameness/difference problem is a nonstarter in the first place, because dichotomies like sameness and difference are illusions caused by the flawed structural frameworks that generate them. That is, they rely on a faulty essentialist view of human nature. Insofar as postmodern thinking dominates intellectual life (which it may, at least among feminists, as the antiessentialist view is shared by pragmatists, existentialists, and many Marxists, socialists, and liberals), the sameness/difference problem has already been resolved by an overall critical view that does not recognize an essential human nature.

Second, unlike feminist theories of an earlier era, virtually every feminist theory today challenges male norms. This, for example, is the intended objective of relational feminism, even though it is highly susceptible to abuse or misinterpretation. So the following question has been raised: Even if men and women are different, why should the standard of measure be male? The simple (and accurate) answer, that historically it has always been male, is one explanation, but it is obviously not a justification. Because historical standards relied on historical discrimination, some ground other than history must be found for retaining them. But no other supportable ground has been forthcoming.

Finally, the fact that many feminists see the sameness/difference debate as a misformulation of the problem provides more possibilities for progress beyond it. To see how easy it is to fall into the patriarchal trap, look back to the statement that the question is whether women, being basically similar to men, require equal treatment, or being significantly different from men, require special treatment. What may not be obvious is that this essentially means, Heads I win, tails you lose. That is, it assumes the outcome in advance, for to agree that if women are "different" (i.e., different from men) they will require "special treatment" is to assume a male or patriarchal standard of what normal treatment is. Feminists today reject such a formulation of the problem, and so this question is no longer viewed as the crucial question that must be answered before further steps can be taken. In fact, many feminists now think that it is not even an answerable, or perhaps even a meaningful, question, and some have proposed alternative views. For example, some feminists suggest that it is not difference but disadvantage that should be the goal of legal and social reform; some argue that the focus should be directly on eliminating domination; and some seek common standards of human flourishing and/or pragmatic approaches that can contextualize the problem instead of presuming abstract or essentialist models of human nature or the structure of gender.

We do not need a final unified vision of society and gender, however, to argue against oppression, disadvantage, domination, and discrimination. We do not need to know beforehand the nature of the good society or the ideal person so long as we know what prevents a society from being minimally good or prevents an individual from realizing the basic potentials of personhood. We do not need an ultimate vision when we have not yet met threshold conditions for a minimally just society. Many visions are possible, and many theories are useful. The commitment to foster open dialogue that allows the expression of diverse views and gives particular attention to eliciting views not usually heard is a unifying thread among feminists that attempts to represent the commonality of fundamental values without misrepresenting the plurality of experience.

Some Basic Objections

The acceptance of diversity within feminism has led some critics (and even some feminists) to contend that there is therefore no common feminist perspective. There is no point of view of all women. Feminism can be reduced to those theories that inform its many facets. Liberal feminism is reducible to liberalism; postmodern feminism is reducible to postmodernism; and so on. Thus, it is claimed, feminism provides no new idea, no new theory. It is simply the application of old theories to the particular problem of women's oppression.

This objection is mistaken, however, for several reasons. First, even if it were true of some views (such as liberal feminism or Marxist feminism), it cannot be true of radical feminism, because the centerpiece of radical feminism is the structure of gender or sexual identity itself. Radical feminism starts with the idea of sexism as gender, the idea that gender is socially constructed within a hierarchy that embodies male domination and female subordination. Everything else flows from that. One may agree or disagree with this idea, but it cannot be reduced to another theory.

Furthermore, this core insight now informs all other feminist theories, whose differences are largely differences of emphasis. Nearly all feminists are too eclectic to fit neatly into any one category, and so it is misleading to set up categories or theories as though they worked in that limiting sort of way for feminists. Creating distinct or rigid categories within which to fit particular accounts or limit dialogue is a decidedly antifeminist way of proceeding, as feminists generally oppose this sort of abstract conceptualization without attention to context and detail. Instead, the way to use the general descriptions of the various feminist theories, such as those in the previous section, is simply to note and trace their influences, interactions, and manifestations in the particular views that people offer on specific issues. The function of general descriptions of theories in feminism is clarification and simplification, not limitation or reduction.

Finally, the one thing that unites all feminist theories and distinguishes them from all other theories is that their primary goal is the rejection of patriarchy. No matter what differences there are among these divergent views, and there certainly are many, this one point of reference is always shared. It is an irreducible point, and it distinguishes feminism from all other theories.

Nonetheless, one can argue that if the entire project of feminist jurisprudence is to show that law is patriarchal, it is not intellectually very interesting. How can an entire jurisprudence be supported by the single ground of rejecting patriarchy? But this is a political position, one may contend, not a philosophical one.

The problem with this objection is that it assumes that the recognition and rejection of patriarchy is a small point, when in fact it is a revolutionary one. Likewise, noting that the world is not flat but round is a small point in the sense that it can be stated in a brief and simple sentence, and it is not philosophical in the sense that it is the observation of an empirical fact. But in another sense, it changes everything. Its implications are profound, and exploring some of those implications is of great philosophical interest, and so it is with the rejection of patriarchy.

Thus, the one new thing about feminism (or feminist jurisprudence) is the very fact that it is feminism, that it constitutes a critique of patriarchal institutions from the perspective of women. To put it more generally, it constitutes, at least potentially, a genuine critique of patriarchal institutions, structures, and assumptions from the perspective of a group that is outside those patriarchal structures, institutions, and assumptions, at least in the sense (among other things) that it did not participate in their formulation. This is the first time in the history of civilization that anything like that has been possible at a level that can be taken seriously.

Intellectually, this provides a new basis for an external critique of social structures. In *The Structure of Scientific Revolutions,* Thomas Kuhn explains such external critiques as paradigm shifts that represent revolutionary changes in thinking. Internal critique refines thinking within a framework. External critique rejects the old framework altogether and proposes a new paradigm in its place. External critique is not everything, but it can be extremely useful, especially for spotting assumptions that otherwise go unexamined because they are unnoticed. Internal critique tends to develop and refine details and spot inconsistencies within a structure or framework. External critique can challenge the entire framework, and thus, external critique is also the most threatening and the hardest to understand or accept. It is like Martin Luther saying to the pope, "Why, as a Christian, do I need to be Catholic at all?" Luther's critique is external to Catholicism but still internal to Christianity and, of course, to religion. When Nietzsche declared that "God is dead," his critique was external to the idea of religion. Needless to say, both critiques were viewed with hostility and disbelief by those who were defending the status quo. Similarly, feminist jurisprudence challenges basic legal categories and concepts rather than analyzing them as given. Feminist jurisprudence asks what is implied in traditional categories, distinctions, or concepts and rejects them if they imply the subordination of women. In this sense, feminist jurisprudence is normative and claims that traditional jurisprudence and law are implicitly normative as well.

Because of this, feminist jurisprudence has the potential to offer some of the most intellectually stimulating critiques of legal structures today, and this would be much more readily recognized if it were not so politically and socially frightening. That is the problem with revolutionary critique: It is revolutionary. This means, first, that it is hard to understand or else to take seriously. Revolutionary external critique may sound strange, heretical, irrational, or silly because it starts from a different set of basic assumptions. The most difficult thing in the world for two people (let alone a group of people) to discuss reasonably are differing basic assumptions. They need some common ground to begin the discussion. So the first problem is just to understand the critique or to be able to take it seriously. The elimination of patriarchy would constitute a cultural revolution at least as profound as the Copernican revolution, the Protestant revolution, or the Industrial Revolution. Could anyone living before these revolutions imagine what life or human thought would be like after them? The first response to early feminism was ridicule. People could not imagine the status or role of women being different from what it always had been.

Second, if the critique is understood and taken seriously, it often scares people to death. Why? Why was the pope upset with Luther? Revolutionary critiques are frightening just because they are revolutionary. If they succeed, life will never be the same again. The end of patriarchy will be the end of social life as we know it. And so the critique of patriarchy tends to generate hostility, misunderstanding, ridicule, and fear almost as soon as it is mentioned. Like religion, it is one of the most difficult topics to discuss with, for example, nonbelievers. Accordingly, most feminists discuss the critique of patriarchy primarily with one another, and for good reason. Anyone who speaks of it too much "in public" is considered an extremist (and generally tiresome and ill tempered as well). For these reasons (and some others) many women disassociate themselves from feminism, and most men do not want to hear about it. It is dubbed a women's issue and ignored. And when some feminist takes the critique directly to the patriarchs, so to speak, it tends to be hostilely delivered or hostilely received, or both.

Feminists tend, therefore, to concentrate on more specific issues rather than on the general critique, and there are many good reasons for doing that, in addition to the difficulty of the more general topic. Nevertheless, the critique of patriarchy is the general rationale behind feminism itself and behind all those discussions of more specific topics, such as pregnancy leave, rape, pornography, or child care. That means that all those issues also proceed from different basic assumptions, which in turn can lead to the same problems just mentioned: hostility, ridicule, disregard, and resistance. And this also expresses the progress of so-called women's issues.

All that is understandable, but it is not excusable, nor is it wise. Hostility is misplaced when directed against cultural revolutions, which is what we are talking about here. Cultural revolutions are profound but not violent. Cultural revolution is the discovery (usually after the fact) that everyone or almost everyone has joined a new order (usually without realizing it). It is internally developed rather than externally imposed. When women and men no longer think of women first and foremost as mothers, and secondarily as anything else, then the world will have changed. When women are thought of and think of themselves as primarily self-supporting and not as dependent, the world will have changed. In sum, when women and men actually think of themselves as equals, the world will have changed. In a cultural revolution, what changes is what people think, their basic assumptoins about what is normal. So, cultural revolutions are inevitable because they follow from a change of worldview.

Thus, cultural revolutions should not be confused with political revolutions, which are not necessarily internal and not inevitable. Hostility to political revolutions makes sense. Hostility to cultural revolutions is understandable but relatively useless. To return to my analogy, it really did not do the Catholic church any good at all to reject Martin Luther when the rest of the world was ready for him. At a certain point in time, certain ideas become part of history, and they cannot be reversed. They can be affected, sometimes revised or modestly changed, possibly guided or directed, but not reversed or erased.

This is now the status of the women's movement and feminist thought. It cannot be reversed or erased. The bridges have been burned. This can easily be seen by comparing the lives of women today with those of one hundred years ago. Some of the biggest steps in the revolution have already been taken, as is illustrated by the legal changes in the status of women, which recognize them as independent individuals and equal citizens. Whether the legal system fashions the future from cooperative endeavor or hammers it out of the adversarial system, it will respond to the requirements of social change. To think, therefore, that the rejection of patriarchy is philosophically or intellectually uninteresting is to underestimate the extent or profundity of the change entailed in rejecting it. For philosophers and social analysts to ignore the feminist revolution today, thinking their work is outside it, is like philosophers and social analysts some centuries ago who ignored the Industrial Revolution, thinking that their work was outside it. Basic revolutions such as this touch everything and change assumptions about human nature and human life. Nothing could be more philosophically interesting.

The Pervasiveness of Patriarchy

Obviously, some thinkers reject the idea that the feminist critique is as fundamental or as revolutionary as I am suggesting. Accordingly, the following chapters are intended to represent the breadth of feminist jurisprudence, which in turn illustrates the pervasiveness of patriarchy and the enormity of the change that follows from its rejection. Several important areas are, however, not represented, owing to limitations of space. Of particular note here is the feminist work on reproductive rights, the nature of self-defense, child custody and family law, divorce and property settlement, and the nature and function of rights.

This book is intended to illuminate the extent and subtlety of patriarchy, particularly in regard to an interesting recent phenomenon. Historically, the challenge was to prove that women were entitled to be treated equally with men. That battle is still not completely over, but many people today are convinced that women are entitled to equal treatment. The interesting twist is that although many people do believe that men and women are entitled to equal treatment, they also believe that this goal has already been accomplished in law. Because formal barriers (at least the most obvious ones) have, for the most part, been removed—women can vote, hold office, attend college, participate in business, own property, execute contracts, and so forth—many people think that legal equality has been achieved. So, discrepancies in accomplishments—the wage gap, for example—must be explained by differences in abilities or by social factors that are beyond the purview of law. But the chapters in this volume show that this view is premature. Law is affected by patriarchy in many subtle ways that have not yet been eradicated by the simple change of some obvious sexist barriers like the prohibition of women from voting or owning property. Patriarchy is an all-encompassing worldview, and as an institution of patriarchy, law reflects that worldview as well. But because of its distinctive features as law—its reliance on precedent, which perpetuates the status quo—law is not like an ordinary mirror that instantly reflects the reality before it. Rather, it is like a magic mirror that always reflects a vision that is slightly in the past; that is, it can reflect reality only if reality moves slowly. Transient changes are therefore not reflected. Big changes or fast changes are reflected only after a period of transition. Because law is a somewhat selective, delayed-action mirror, feminist jurisprudence is concerned with correcting the current lag.

Part I of this book addresses the issue of equality as it is central to all other issues raised by feminists. But what equality means is far from clear. Most of the chapters in this part discuss the problem of inequality in the workplace. Unequal treatment in the workplace reflects the patriarchal view of women as primarily homemakers and men as primarily breadwinners. Women are at a disadvantage in the workplace if they are viewed as mainly responsible for the home and family, because this marginalizes them at work and effectively requires them to hold two jobs. Furthermore, the standard of what is normal in the workplace is the ideal worker: a male breadwinner who has no family responsibilities himself. Today, this norm is unrealistic for both men and women and it puts women at a great disadvantage. But is it an issue for law to decide? There are laws prohibiting discriminatory employment practices, and the U.S. Constitution extends equal protection of the laws to all persons. All this requires interpretation, however: What are discriminatory employment practices? What is equal protection of the law? For example, recognizing that women get pregnant and men do not, what does equal treatment require in regard to pregnancy benefits? Should they be covered like any other medical need, or are they different? What does equality require in cases of difference? The point is that even if a society says that it is committed to equality, different conceptions of what equality entails can leave some members of society at a great disadvantage.

Part II explores the nature of harm, extending the point just made about equality. Our society has always been committed to the view that the intentional infliction of harm, coercion, and the restriction of freedom are unjust. These are supposedly the clear cases of actionable claims: physical assault, battery, harassment. But what counts as a harm, or as coercion or restriction, limits what is thought of as unjust. It is surprising to think that what a harm is could be open to interpretation, but it is. Sexual harassment, for example, was not a cause of action until very recently. Although women employees were coerced into sexual relations, it was not recognized as an addressable harm. Indeed, there was no word for it. There was no way to speak of it. It was just the way of the world, like breathing or drowning. Similarly, wife battering was not thought of as a harm; rather, it was discipline. It reflected a patriarchal view of men as heads of households and women as subordinate dependents subject to the chastisement of authority. Rape law also reflects the patriarchal view of personal and sexual relations and in some ways illustrates even more clearly than wife battering and sexual harassment do that the law protects women from men who are strangers but not from men who know them. Accordingly, date rape is not a "real" harm, and spousal rape in many states is an impossibility.

Yet all three areas—sexual harassment, rape, and wife battering—represent areas of incipient change in the law. Even the fact that they are being discussed is a sign of progress. Sexual harassment, wife battering, and date rape all are formally recognized today as actionable legal claims, whereas not long ago, such claims were literally unthinkable. However, discriminatory informal barriers discourage most claims from being filed, and most that are filed are dismissed. The responses of many judges and prosecutors thus leave much to be desired, demonstrating that sexist attitudes are still common and raising the question of how legal procedures could be structured to alleviate the problem.

Part III considers the legal procedures of adjudication. What does it mean to say that the judicial system itself is sexist? Although the law presumes itself to be neutral, feminists argue that the law is not neutral. On the contrary, it is patriarchal, as it embodies the worldview of patriarchy that systematically subordinates women. It uncritically assumes a traditional male standard of what is normal. This is the problem illustrated in workplace norms that ignore the needs of families, or in attitudes toward rape and sexual harassment that define the offense from the perspective of the perpetrator rather than the victim and then try the victim rather than the accused. Many other examples could be given. Law is built on a worldview that presupposes patriarchy as normal, which means that law—the entire legal system—is based on the presumption that men and women are not equal and that women are subordinate to men. And this means that law is not neutral, that it supports a particular, traditional way of life that is now being called into question and that feminists claim is unjust.

This raises the question of what law should do—or what law can do—to address the systemic injustice, the comprehensive bias built into legal, social, and political institutions from the beginning of human association. Obviously, precedent cannot be used to correct it. If patriarchy (or the subordination of women) is now considered unjust (which, of course, many traditionalists would dispute) and the entire legal system is and has always been patriarchal, how can law address this problem? How can law correct its own bias if the bias is systemic? Feminist jurisprudence responds to this question. But it is clear that standard, narrow notions of adjudication cannot deal with systemic injustice because narrow notions of legal reasoning and judicial review preclude the evaluation of the system itself. Judges, it is claimed, are supposed to work within the system, not evaluate it. The impartial application of biased procedures to all cases, however, is a questionable practice. Feminists have made practical suggestions for enhancing the possibility of impartiality on the part of judges, by recognizing the nonneutrality of law and enlisting views that often go unheard. If feminists are right that law is not neutral, then it is not reasonable or just to adhere to old legal methods that limit what counts as a cause of action, what and who can be considered, who can be heard, what can be thought, and what counts as a legal judgment. New methods of legal reasoning must be advanced that can open up the process to provide truly equal access and genuinely equal consideration for all.

Part IV moves from the procedural issues of the judicial process back to particular substantive issues central to the oppression of women. The most fundamental of these is the issue of reproductive freedom, which is a precondition to any other freedom for women. Yet the legal treatment of reproductive freedom demonstrates the unequal treatment of men and women in regard to freedom and reflects the central patriarchal premise of women as primarily reproductive vessels or reproductive property. This is the core issue of the women's movement, and it will cause the greatest fight between progressives and traditionalists. On the one hand, reproductive freedom is the prerequisite for any other freedom or equality for women. On the other hand, reproductive destiny is the focus of the meaning of life for women in the traditional view, and the organizing principle of patriarchy.

In the patriarchal view, women are mothers first and foremost in the service, and for the benefit, of their husbands. This is their biological destiny and the best way for them to fulfill themselves and benefit *man*kind. Throughout all of history, men have controlled the reproductive capacities of women because it is the only crucial ability that women have that men do not have. Furthermore, if women controlled their own reproductive ability, they would also control men's ability to reproduce. So women have been viewed as biologically destined to be mothers in the service of mankind, under the control and protection of men. Legally, men are viewed as free and autonomous, whereas the status of women is much more open to question, especially the status of reproductive rights. It is inconceivable that any issue that comparably affected the basic individual freedom of any man would not be under his control in a free society.

Today, as we approach the twenty-first century, it is a matter of great controversy whether women should be entitled to control their own bodies. Because patriarchy sets the terms of the debate, women are forced to argue for their right to control their own bodily integrity, with the burden of persuasion set against them. The very conception of the identity or nature of women and of fetuses is established by patriarchal religions, customs, and laws. Women are fundamentally mothers, and therefore their pregnancies are blessings. Men are free. Women are determined by their biology. Men are autonomous. Women are "protected," which means that they are regulated. How can the differential treatment be justified? It goes right back to the old sameness/difference debate. Men are the standard of freedom. Women are different. They get pregnant. Therefore they must be protected, which means that they must be controlled. Surely they are not entitled to be in control of their own pregnancies. Feminists are fighting to challenge the assumptions that perpetuate the subordination of women to motherhood and that place the control over motherhood in the hands of a patriarchal state. It may be that this issue illustrates more powerfully than any other the effect of the patriarchal structure of law. It is the core of patriarchy and the greatest challenge that feminists face. The basic legal issue is whether the Constitution protects the reproductive autonomy of women through the right to privacy or the equal protection clause. Feminist support for both views is represented in Part IV.

Part V addresses the commodification of women as sexual or reproductive objects, which reflects the long history of viewing women in these terms. It is not quite as explosive as the issue of reproductive freedom is, but it is very closely related to it. In fact, in some respects it is a broader issue, of which reproductive freedom is a special case. If women were viewed as equal subjects and not as sexual objects, the question of reproductive freedom might not be raised. But the objectification and consequent commodification of women present complex issues of freedom and equality for both men and women. Commodification is a cardinal feature of capitalist society. It is not unique to women, but what is virtually unique to women is their commodification as sex objects. The question is, What is significant about that? Is it worse than other forms of commodification? Or is the special condemnation of it an artifact of patriarchy? Does allowing women to sell themselves as sexual or reproductive objects free them or enslave them? Does it increase their options or seduce them out of better options? Can women sell their reproductive or sexual services without being sex objects themselves? Does banning such sales protect women in the long run, or is it just another mechanism of control and repression? Feminists are not united on these issues, but all do agree that women should not be exploited as a class. All feminists agree that women should be equal and free, but what it means to be equal and free in the context of sexual commodification is one of the most difficult questions that they face. The chapters in Part V discuss the feminist struggles to understand how the equality and freedom of women can be recognized in a society that conditions them to be sex objects.

In the last part, Part VI, we consider what feminists have to say about law and jurisprudence that reflects their project of countering patriarchy as the systematic oppression of women—of exposing the prejudices of patriarchy in law and jurisprudence. The chapters here represent the range and variety of approaches within feminist jurisprudence. What does it mean to say that the legal system is sexist? This is a question that literally could not have been asked less than thirty years ago. In 1971 the *Oxford English Dictionary* defined *sexism* as an archaic seventeenth-century term referring to a run of six cards in a game. In other words, sexism as we understand it today was not a word just thirty years ago. In those days (and notice what a short time that is) sexism could not be thought by ordinary people. Sexism could not be objected to because it could not be spoken; it certainly could not be a legal cause of action. But by 1980 all dictionaries recognized *sexism* as referring to prejudice against women. The appearance of the word is significant, for it means that new questions can be asked, new issues can be raised, and new objections can be formulated. Asking new questions demonstrates true progress of human thought, and shows that the biggest step in the feminist revolution has already been taken. Human thought has already changed. This is not to say, however, that no work is left to be done. The project now is to determine all the implications of that change.

1

On Equality: Justice, Discrimination, and Equal Treatment

Are men and women equal? What does it mean to say that they are or are not? It may help to consider what it means to say that any two things are equal. Sometimes when we say that two things are equal, we mean that they are the same, identical, or interchangeable. Let us call this *material* or *factual* equality. Often courts have referred to equality in this way, but it is a very restricted notion of equality, and it does not actually apply well to human beings, as no two human beings are ever identical. Nevertheless, when courts determine the equality of classes of persons, they are deciding whether those classes are materially the same. This often translates into assumptions (or deliberations) about whether they would function in the same way in certain specified circumstances. This analysis has always caused problems for women because traditional worldviews have always delegated different roles and functions to men and women, as though the roles were defined by nature. That is, men and women have been viewed as materially different—different in their factual character.

Often when we say that two things are equal, we mean that they are of comparable value, that they are worth the same. We mean something like that when we refer to human beings as being equal. When we say that "all men are created equal," we mean that morally speaking, they are of equal worth. Let us call that *moral* equality. Every human life, we say, has the same intrinsic value, but what that amounts to in practical terms has always been a difficult matter, especially when races, sexes, and nationalities have been viewed as materially different.

People frequently claim that they are entitled to equality: to equal opportunities, equal treatment, equal protection of the law, or perhaps even an equal distribution of material goods. These sorts of claims to equality are much like claims to justice. Equal treatment and just treatment may be the same thing. We know that equality and justice are closely connected, but what the connection is has always generated considerable controversy. The old Aristotelian notion of procedural justice enjoins us to treat like cases alike and unlike cases differently in proportion to their differences. According to this formula (which is certainly one of the most widely accepted propositions in the history of philosophy and law), the puzzle of equality has three pieces.

First, we must identify like cases. Are men and women (or Christians and Jews, blacks and whites, rich and poor, or educated and illiterate) relevantly similar or different? This is the question on which most of history has focused. Second, once we have identified who is alike or equal, what does it mean to treat these equals alike? What is equal opportunity, equal treatment, or equal protection of the law? Third, if people can be different but still equal, what does it mean to treat different cases in proportion to their differences? This last question has hardly been discussed at all in traditional legal and philosophical discourse, but it is central to recent feminist discussions of equality.

Consider the first set of issues. We must be able to recognize which cases are alike, and that is not as easy as it might seem. In fact, no two cases, situations, or individuals (except mathematical abstractions) are exactly alike in every respect. So we must decide which features are relevant to our considerations, and those relevant features will then determine whether the cases are equal. For example, some features of men and women are similar, and others are not. We must decide which features are relevant to the case in question and whether those features are similar. Thus, determinations of equality require judgment; they are not self-evident.

Unlike modern societies, ancient civilizations (or even medieval ones) assumed that human beings were not equal, either morally or materially. Aristotle, for example, thought that some men were natural slaves and that all women were inherently inferior to men (except slaves). National origin was also considered a source of superiority and privilege, especially among conquerors. Greeks, for example, considered themselves superior to all others, and Roman citizenship conveyed special protections and rights. Furthermore, discussions in ancient texts regarding the equal citizenship of Athenians or Romans applied only to small groups of wealthy, male landowners. This view assumed both moral and material inequality.

Even the Christian doctrine of universal (moral) equality (the equality of the souls of all human beings as the children of God) was greatly qualified in practice. For example, St. Thomas Aquinas reconciled slavery with Christian equality as being a consequence of sin (an interesting inversion of biblical accounts of the teachings of Christ). The principal points are that ancient and medieval societies were predominantly hierarchical and that notions of equality applied only within classes, not across them. The basic presumption was that human beings are not equal, morally or materially, and so any claims of such equality had to be justified before questions of equal treatment sould be appropriate to consider. For example, if men and women—or aristocrats and peasants or slaves and free people—are morally or materially different, then equal treatment of them will be inappropriate.

It is this presumption (the presumption of *in*equality) that began to change in the seventeenth century, with movements for the recognition of universal or human rights and democratic, constitutional government. In philosophy, Hobbes presumed the natural equality of all men, as did Locke, Rousseau, Kant, and most major thinkers in the Western tradition from that time on (a striking exception being Nietzsche). Even those thinkers, however, did not presume the moral or material equality of men and women.

Still, we should keep in mind that the presumption of equality was true in theory or in rhetoric more than in fact and that it did not mean that all men were to be treated equally. Instead, it meant that unequal treatment had to be justified. That is, it did not deny inequality altogether; it merely shifted the burden of proof. So even though the English law spoke bravely of the rights of all Englishmen, English workers who did not own property were denied the right to vote, because property ownership was considered a relevant difference. Even though the American revolutionaries declared all men to be created equal, their Constitution recognized slavery as a legitimate practice, because blacks were considered relevantly different. Even in the twentieth century, illiteracy was considered a relevant ground for denying basic rights, such as the right to vote. Certain races, nationalities, and classes have always been denied equal rights. And women have always been, and still are, denied equal rights on the ground that they are different and therefore not equal. We may say that all men are created equal, but we do not act as though it were true. Furthermore, we did not even say that women are equal to men until very recently, and even now the claim is highly controversial.

So determining which cases are alike, who are moral equals, and what counts as a relevant difference are difficult matters that have progressed very slowly through human history. Nevertheless, addressing these questions is absolutely crucial to understanding the nature of equality. The traditional view is that unless we can determine which cases are alike, our answers to the other two issues will be futile. As we shall see, many feminists now believe that this position is mistaken, or at least overdrawn.

The second set of issues requires us to figure out what it means to treat like cases alike. In many cases this is a relatively easy task (especially given the way in which the first issue has been handled). Once it has been determined that two cases are alike, they must be treated the same. For example, if two groups, say landowners and nonlandowners, are deemed political equals, then they should have the same political rights: the same right to vote, the same right to a fair trial, the same right to free speech, and so forth. Similarly, if two legal cases are found to be alike, then they must have the same determination according to the same rule of law. Thus, it appears that the difficult question is the first one—which cases are alike. Once that is determined, it is usually not difficult to decide how to treat them alike.

Even so, equal treatment is not always obvious. For more than two decades American courts and legislatures tried to describe what it means to provide equal opportunity or equal protection of the law to all citizens. The consequences of describing wrongly can be profound. For example, for almost one hundred years it was thought that the requirements of equal treatment could be met by providing separate but equal facilities for different races, specifically blacks. Of course, it now appears that this idea was always a sham (as a matter of fact) and that those who proposed it were not actually interested in equality, but only in separation, precisely because they did not really consider the races to be equal at all. Furthermore, given the history and social circumstances in the United States (again, as a matter of fact), separate but equal facilities are thought to be impossible for blacks. That is, it is impossible for separate facilities to be equal, given the dominated history and status of blacks in the United States.

Nevertheless, as a matter of principle, it is not obvious that there is anything inherently unequal about separate facilities. For example, suppose that two different nationalities, say Japanese and Italian, or two different religious groups, say Catholic and Jewish, decided to maintain separate communities (separate schools, neighborhoods, stores, restaurants, etc.) in order to preserve their separate cultures. Whatever problems there might be with doing this, there is not any obvious problem of inequality merely in the fact of separation.

However, two points seem relevant to this apparent acceptability. First, the separation in our hypothetical case is voluntary. As soon as the government is introduced in order to enforce separation, the circumstances are immediately suspicious. Second, when put in terms of different nationalities or religions that wish to preserve their differences, we seem to have moved from like cases to different cases. That is, we seem to have moved from the second set of issues to the third set. The third set of issues asks what it means to treat different cases differently in proportion to their differences.

One interesting thing about this last set of issues is that it has hardly been discussed at all. Philosophers have had little to say about what it means to treat different cases in proportion to their differences. And in law, a determination of difference in the courts has always led to deference to legislative action of any sort. This has always been a particular problem for women.

For example, because women were considered different, they could be banned from universities, libraries, businesses, and professions. It was simply up to the legislatures (which, of course, were composed entirely of men) to deal with such matters as they saw fit. If they felt that it was inappropriate or disruptive for any woman to attend a university or enter a library or a business establishment, they could bar women from the premises. If they felt that it was indecent or "unladylike" for any woman to practice law, or carpentry, or bartending, or medicine, they could deny all women a license to practice, simply on the ground that they are women. Such action in the United States would violate the constitutional rights of men, but because women were considered different, they had no constitutional rights to equal protection of the law. It did no good to appeal to the courts. The courts, assuming that this was not an equal protection issue and thus not a constitutional issue, deferred to the legislatures. Women had few rights of their own, and certainly no right to be treated as equal to men. This view was seldom challenged until the 1970s.

What this shows is that despite the egalitarian movements of the seventeenth and eighteenth centuries and the ever-widening presumption that "all men are created equal," the ancient presumption of inequality was maintained between men and women until well into the twentieth century. Although women gained the right to vote in 1920, their progress toward equality was otherwise sharply limited. Until the 1970s the courts maintained the idea that separate spheres of endeavor for men and women were natural and good. Women should inhabit the private domain of home and family into which the law ought not intrude. Only men should inhabit the public sphere of politics and market. This assumption made women dependent on men and subject to their authority. Thus, hierarchal institutions of patriarchy were maintained as though decreed by nature.

The reaction to this by women, beginning more or less with Mary Walstonecraft in the late eighteenth century, was to argue that women are not relevantly different from men for legal, political, or economic purposes. That is, this argument addressed the first set of issues (the question of which cases are alike). We are the same, women contended, and so we should be treated the same. This argument was generally ignored for two centuries, until the 1970s when the courts began to recognize basic similarities among men and women and consequently to require equal protection of the laws in certain cases in which women were finally recognized to be equal to men. For example, it was recognized that there was no relevant difference between men and women in regard to their ability to administer an estate, and so the legislature cannot make women ineligible to do so. Men and women are the same in this area, and so they must be treated the same. Here equal treatment (the second set of issues) is easily determined once the first set of issues is determined, namely, that men and women are materially alike. Although this development in court analysis is a clear advance over assumptions that women are materially unfit for any professional or intellectual pursuits, it still has its deficiencies.

First, material equality maintains traditional standards of what is normal or good, and given the structure and history of society, those standards are male. So, recent court analysis will protect women only if they meet male norms. It does not evaluate the norms. Women will be protected only if they function in the same way that men do. But the question is, Why should that be the standard of what is normal simply because it has been in the past?

An example will illustrate this point. Until recently it was thought to be reasonable to exclude women from being pilots because many of them are not tall enough to reach the controls. The courts' analysis now recognizes that this also discriminates against all women who are tall enough to reach the controls; thus women cannot be banned as a class. If individual women meet the standard, they cannot be excluded. That is a step in the right direction: At least women cannot be excluded for being women, but only for being smaller than the average man. This shows that the courts now recognize that some women can meet male norms (standards set by men for men), but it does not reevaluate the norms. Recently it has been noticed that pilots in some other countries (such as Japan) have no trouble reaching the controls, even though the average Japanese man is no taller than the average American woman. So the question arises, How do we set the standard for the size of cockpits (or any number of other workplace standards)? Why should the design for cockpits require an operator of five feet ten inches, when that excludes most women and many minority men as well, for no particular reason except that it was done that way in the past? Traditional norms need to be challenged. There is no reason for normal to mean male, or just like male. But the courts' analysis assumes traditional norms instead of examining them.

Second, the courts' analysis ignores social disadvantages caused by patriarchal institutions and a history of sex discrimination. Thus, women are expected to compete with men on an equal footing and also to assume primary responsibility for the home and family. But that is like holding down two jobs while competing with others who are able to concentrate on one job precisely because they reap the benefits of those who are holding two jobs. That is, assuming that pregnancy and child raising is a social benefit, women should not be penalized for providing this service. The cost of preserving the species should be borne by the entire species, not just half of it. Furthermore, historical discrimination and traditional social roles have led to the fact that women are regularly paid less, promoted less often, and channeled into lower-level, subordinate positions more often. But the courts' analysis is not set up to recognize these disadvantages, let alone address them.

Third, in cases in which women are not identical to men, the analysis of the courts (particularly the U.S. Supreme Court) has been useless or detrimental to women because it is based on an initial requirement of material equality to men. For instance, recognizing that only women can get pregnant, what does equal treatment mean in regard to working conditions and benefits? Does equal protection of the law apply here? When faced with these questions, the Supreme Court decided that equal protection of the law does not apply. So, among other things, pregnancy does not have to be covered by state insurance programs, even if all other medical needs are covered. Congress, however, appears to disagree with the Court's approach, having responded to it by specifically instituting the Pregnancy Discrimination Act to protect pregnant women under Title VII of the Civil Rights Act of 1964. This means that as the law currently stands, pregnant women are guaranteed equal treatment by federal law but not by the U.S. Constitution, even though the Constitution says that the law equally protects all persons.

Thus, the Court's analysis assumes unreflectively a male standard of normality, especially in the workplace. It ignores the disproportionate burden of child bearing and rearing on women. And it assumes that equal protection of the law is preconditioned on women's material equality with men. That is, instead of considering what equality requires in cases of difference, it assumes that equality does not apply in cases of difference. This is the same position that the Court has always held. The only new development (within the past twenty-five years) is that instead of assuming, as it once did, that women are necessarily inferior to men or unfit for intellectual, economic, or political pursuits, the Court now recognizes that some individual women can meet traditional norms, the same norms formulated by and for men. This approach uses what has been called an *assimilation model of reform* for promoting equality. It assimilates women to male norms that structure the workplace and the political and legal process on a male model. By failing to consider these norms, it reinforces patriarchy by assuming that it is normal or inevitable. Women are now considered equal to men (by the law) if, and only if, they can function like men. Is that acceptable?

Discussion of this issue has been widespread, generating what has been called the *sameness/difference debate* (also called the equal rights/special rights or the equal treatment/special treatment debate) within feminism. Philosophically, the difference between these two positions is potentially profound. According to the sameness view, men and women are fundamentally similar. What is important about men and women is what they hold in common—perhaps their common humanity, morality, or intellect. Differences are incidental and can be handled by analogy to comparable points or broader categories. No special treatment is called for or justified, only the elimination of unequal treatment. In the difference view, by contrast, differences between men and women are considered significant, fundamental. They must be dealt with on their own terms, not by analogy or assimilation to more general categories. The difference between the two views is the difference between a unified or harmonious view of human nature and a pluralistic view of sex or gender differences. Are men and women basically similar or basically different?

There is also a pragmatic version of this debate within feminism, especially among legal scholars. On the one hand, many feminists argue that whether men and women are basically similar or dissimilar, anything other than equality is too dangerous a risk, because in the long run special allowances have always been, and almost certainly will always be, used against women. So-called protective legislation, for example, was always used to limit and control women, not to free them. And making special allowances perpetuates stereotypes of women as inferior or dependent. For example, even if pregnancy is a serious disadvantage for women in certain areas, if special accommodations are made for it, employers will view women as more expensive or less valuable than men, and so stereotypes of women as primarily mothers and only secondarily anything else will be perpetuated. Women will continue to be viewed as central to home and family and marginal everywhere else. So even pregnancy is better handled by simply including it with other medical conditions common to all workers.

On the other hand, it is argued that ignoring the social disadvantages imposed on women by dominant patriarchal institutions of both family and market impairs women's ability to succeed, by placing them in unfair competition with men who do not have similar disadvantages. Furthermore, treating pregnancy as a disability rather than as an ability misconstrues it, ignores the social contribution that women make in virtue of it, and reinforces a male standard of what is normal. The only reason that pregnancy must be analogized to medical disabilities is that men have no comparable ability. Pregnancy is an abnormality only for men. The average woman, on the other hand, will experience pregnancy about twice in her working career. So if the standard is not male, pregnancy is not an abnormality at all. Recognizing social and biological differences between men and women may risk perpetuating stereotypes, but refusing to recognize them will unjustly ignore burdens disproportionately imposed on women to the advantage of men, will require women to "do it all," and thus will set up the average woman for failure. That is, ignoring differences benefits a few superwomen at the top but makes life more difficult for the average woman juggling an ordinary job and family, with fewer benefits and lower pay than the average man has.

These feminist positions should be distinguished from the historical and current conservative view that men and women, being fundamentally different, ought to inhabit different spheres of life. This view argues that biology dictates that the organization of the family in terms of a male breadwinner and a female homemaker is the proper arrangement for both men and women and provides the best environment for children. A woman's first duty is to her children, and thus she should view herself as primarily a wife and mother and secondarily anything else. By the same token, she is entitled to support and protection in this role. Men, women, and children all are better off when they adhere to these traditional family values.

This view is antithetical to any feminist position and should not be confused with the difference side of the feminist debate. All feminists hold that women are first and foremost human beings who are entitled to choose their own future from the full range of choices available to all human beings. The debate over the sameness or difference of men and women within feminism is about how best to facilitate the freedom and equality of men and women, not to restrict them.

The chapters in Part I are intended to cover the major developments in the feminist debate over the requirements of equality. In the first chapter, "Equality and Difference," Herma Hill Kay discusses the case of pregnancy. She argues that clearly definable biological differences, because they can be clearly limited, should be recognized and accommodated on grounds of equal treatment. Equal treatment, after all, requires that differences be accommodated. Treating unlike cases as though they were alike hardly meets the requirements of equality and justice. However, heeding the lessons of the past, Kay suggests that no other less clearly definable differences should be recognized in law, as they cannot be clearly limited and thus pose dangers of restriction on the very persons who are intended to be equalized. Thus the accommodation model is much like the assimilation model used by the courts, with a few clearly defined and sharply limited exceptions to cover clear physical differences that give rise to pregnancy and the danger of rape. Kay's analysis is pragmatic. She recognizes the deficiencies of the Court's assimilation model of analysis and tries to address them in a narrow and carefully defined way that will avoid the traps set by the protective legislation and special rights analysis of the past.

The next chapter, by Nadine Taub and Wendy Williams, represents the liberal feminist view, which is often claimed by its detractors to be an "assimilation" model. It is, rather, a symmetrical model, accepted within limits by the courts, which represents the liberal notion that men and women should be treated the same. Women should get no special breaks but should face no special obstacles, either. Any supposedly female problem (such as pregnancy) can be handled by analogy to broader common problems (such as medical disability in general). Taub and Williams point out rightly the dangers of legally recognizing differences among classes of people, even if they exist, as in the case of pregnancy. But they go further, trying to explain why their view is not an assimilationist position, as they propose a long-range plan to evaluate norms or institutions by assessing them in terms of the notion of disproportionate impact. If a norm or institution has a disproportionate impact on women, it should be reevaluated.

In the third chapter, "The Family and the Market," Frances Olsen explores the limits of institutional reform, contending that as long as reform efforts to improve the lives and prospects of women are carried out within a worldview that assumes social life is divided between two separate spheres of family and market, those efforts will be sharply limited, not only in practical effect, but also in concept. Olsen suggests that the lives of all individuals might be radically improved if we could reorganize our understanding of relations between male and female and between state and civil society, by transcending the market/ family dichotomy. This also is a symmetrical view, often called an *androgeny* model, because it envisions common standards of excellence for men and women to be devised by utilizing the best of each gender as the best of both.

In "The Emergence of Feminist Jurisprudence," Ann Scales states that nothing less than the radical feminist position, or the *empowerment* model, can address inequality at a structural or cultural level, which is necessary in order to address inequality at its roots. According to this view, legal judgments should be made with an eye toward ending domination. If the issue presented by a case (in a court) or a bill (in a legislature) is one of domination and subordination, the authority should move toward empowering the subordinated group, and specifically women. This is the only way to confront the power of patriarchy, which is the only way to eliminate (rather than merely rearrange) inequality. The empowerment model claims that the sexes, whatever their differences, have been constructed by the subordination of women to men. We cannot know what the sexes would be like without the dynamic of domination and subordination, and so we should forget about trying to evaluate equality and difference and concentrate on eliminating domination.

The last chapter in Part I is Christine Littleton's summary of the equality debate and her discussion of a more moderate version of the radical thesis, which acknowledges the need to address structural problems of patriarchy that entrench inequality, but argues for addressing them in terms of disadvantage rather than domination. Littleton's positive focus, which she labels an *acceptance* model, calls for accepting diversity in all its forms and using law to ensure that diversity is not penalized. This model requires the equal acceptance of cultural differences and concentrates on eliminating the unequal consequences of sex differences, whatever their origin or nature. The idea is to embrace diversity and make difference costless.

One important development that this exploration has generated is that many, perhaps most, feminists now believe that the sameness/difference controversy must be transcended altogether, in the sense that the focus on the first question (who is alike or different) should be shifted to some version of the third question or some combination of the third and second questions (what equal protection requires in cases of difference). Assuming that men and women are moral equals, what norm should be the standard of evaluation? The point is to shift from a male norm, especially the unexamined and often unrecognized assumption of a male norm for equal treatment.

This shift is reflected in various forms in all the chapters in Part I. For example, it can be seen in Kay's struggle to deny the assimilation model of the Court without entrenching the stereotypes associated with special treatment. It motivates Taub's and William's attempt to support and extend the *Griggs* doctrine of disproportionate impact to reevaluating institutions. Similarly, it underlies Scales's view that the real issue is not difference but domination. It is reflected in Olsen's proposal to restructure the institutions of family and market to reflect human needs without patriarchal bias. And it is the basis of Littleton's view that it is not difference among people but disadvantage that should be our concern.

Overall, these chapters represent an advance in the analysis of equality beyond anything done before, and they illustrate one of the greatest theoretical contributions of feminism to jurisprudence. What it means to treat unlike cases in proportion to their differences has never been seriously examined until now. Before this, difference has been used only as a trigger to declare people incompetent, unfit, or unworthy of rights, freedom, or autonomy. Now for the first time we are beginning to consider what the value of equality requires in cases of difference.

1

Equality and Difference:
The Case of Pregnancy

HERMA HILL KAY

Women and men in the United States are entitled to the equal protection of the laws[1] and to freedom from discrimination in employment because of sex.[2] Beginning in the 1970s,[3] the United States Supreme Court has applied the laws that guarantee these rights so as to enable both women and men to gain access to positions and privileges formerly dominated by the other sex. The resulting exchange of power between the sexes reflected in Supreme Court litigation has not been equal, nor has the process of exchange been completed. Men, who hold and historically have held most of the power in American society, have been called upon to concede their exclusive authority in the economically dominant public sphere, while women have been asked to relinquish their priority in the less highly valued private sphere. But I have identified elsewhere[4] a pattern of dual access characteristic of the Supreme Court sex discrimination cases that suggests a mutual desire on the part of both women and men to transcend traditional sex lines.

In ruling upon the legal aspects of this exchange of power, the Supreme Court has attempted to use an assimilationist model of equality drawn from earlier cases challenging race discrimination. I have argued that a model of cross-sex assimilation is useful in those many situations in which women and men share the relevant characteristics that are compared for purposes of measurement.[5] In those few situations where the biological reproductive differences that define the sexes are directly involved, however, I have concluded that the assimilationist model is not useful in achieving legal equality between women and men and that a different model must be developed. This chapter represents a beginning effort to develop an alternative model for thinking about the reproductive difference that has been used to justify the existence of a separate sphere for women: pregnancy. Part I of this chapter will examine two recent cases that raise the question of whether pregnancy, a condition that only women experience, may be treated differently in the employment setting from other physical conditions that all workers may experience. Part II will offer a new analytical approach to conceptualizing the legal significance of biological reproductive conduct, which I call "episodic analysis." My thesis is that episodic analysis will help us to avoid penalizing women as the result of their reproductive behavior and thus permit us to accommodate pregnancy within a legal and philosophical framework that affirms the equality of women and men.

I. Pregnancy at Work: The Disability Cases

A. Background: *LaFleur*, *Geduldig*, and *Gilbert*

Litigation over the treatment of pregnancy at work appeared on the Supreme Court's docket early in its consideration of the meaning of legal equality between the sexes. The first cases, consolidated under the name *Cleveland Board of Education v. LaFleur*,[6] involved mandatory maternity leave policies that excluded pregnant teachers from the classroom, even though they were able and willing to continue working.[7] Plaintiffs challenged the policies as violations of both due process and equal protection.

The courts of appeal gave the equal protection claim a mixed response. In *LaFleur*, a Sixth Circuit majority accepted plaintiff's argument that a mandatory maternity leave rule based on pregnancy was a classification based on sex. Judge Edwards compared the treatment accorded to pregnant teachers with that applied to male teachers suffering from other illnesses or disabilities and held that the pregnant teachers had been denied equal protection.[8] In *Cohen v. Chesterfield County School Board*,[9] the Fourth Circuit split over whether a classification based on pregnancy constituted sex-based discrimination at all. Chief Judge Haynsworth was of the view that no sex discrimination was involved because the regulation "does not apply to women in an area in which they may compete with men."[10] Judge Winter, in dissent, made two points. He argued first that a rule applicable to pregnant teachers affected only women, barring them from working because of their sex. Second, he contended that such a rule treated pregnant women differently from other employees, both male and female, who were absent from work because of elective surgical procedures.[11] The courts of appeal thus disagreed over which groups were being compared for purposes of the equal protection analysis. Chief Judge Haynsworth was clear that the two comparison groups could not be men and women, since "only women become pregnant."[12] Neither Judge Winter nor Judge Edwards clearly affirmed that the two comparison groups were men and women. Instead, both compared women excluded from work because of pregnancy to a group of employees composed of women and men who were absent from work because of other medical conditions. Because both groups contain women, their analysis left open the possibility that the defect in the classification was the exclusion of pregnancy as a covered disability, rather than the exclusion of women because of their sex. An equal protection analysis, however, scrutinizes discriminations based on sex. In the absence of a demonstration that a discrimination based on pregnancy constitutes a discrimination based on sex, the equal protection argument is technically incomplete. One would have thought that the missing connection between pregnancy and sex could easily be supplied. But events proved that assumption to be mistaken.

Justice Stewart, writing for the Supreme Court majority in *LaFleur*, did not resolve the conflict between the Fourth and Sixth circuits over whether a classification based on pregnancy constituted a discrimination based on sex for purposes of the equal protection clause. Instead, he invalidated the school board policies on due process grounds, using an analysis that focused on whether the policies embodied an irrebuttable presumption of physical incapacity to work that unduly penalized the teacher's constitutionally protected decision to bear a child. Justice Powell, concurring in the result, thought that "equal protection analysis is the appropriate frame of reference" but added in a footnote that he did not reach the question "whether these regulations involve sex classifications at all." In his view, the conclusion that the regulations did not rationally further any legitimate state interest was sufficient to decide the case.[13]

Five months later, in *Geduldig v. Aiello*,[14] Justice Stewart confronted the question of the fit between a pregnancy-based classification and equal protection analysis in the context of a state disability insurance program that excluded from coverage disabilities accompanying normal pregnancy and childbirth. He did not discuss in the text of his opinion for the majority whether a classification based on pregnancy constituted a discrimination based on sex. Instead, he compared the condition of pregnancy to other excluded disabilities, primarily short-term disabilities of less than eight days' duration. He concluded that the state could rationally distinguish between those two types of excluded disabilities and covered disabilities in order to preserve the self-supporting nature of the program, its low cost to employees, and the adequacy of its coverage.[15] Justice Stewart examined in a footnote the impact of the state's choice of covered risks on women employees. He denied that the exclusion of pregnancy as a covered disability classified employees by sex. Rather, he asserted, "the program divides potential recipients into two groups—pregnant women and nonpregnant persons."[16] Based on this characterization of the groups being compared, Stewart drew the conclusion that neither Winter nor Edwards had expressed: "While the first group is exclusively female, the second includes members of both sexes." It followed, seemingly inexorably, that the classification did not involve a "discrimination based upon gender as such."[17]

Justice Brennan, in dissent, did not challenge the majority's logic directly. Instead, he argued that the exclusion of pregnancy created one set of rules for males and another for females: "A limitation is imposed upon the disabilities for which women workers may recover, while men receive full compensation for all disabilities suffered, including those that affect only or primarily their sex, such as prostatectomies, circumcision, hemophilia and gout."[18] Justice Stewart's implicit response to this criticism invoked still more formal logic. "There is no risk," he said, "from which men are protected and women are not." True, for men do not risk pregnancy. "Likewise," he added, "there is no risk from which women are protected and men are not."[19] True again, for women are not protected against loss of work due to pregnancy. The suspicion that Justice Stewart saw only the trees while ignoring the forest is implicit in the criticism of one commentator who charged that "the conclusion that pregnancy-based classifications are not in themselves sex-based suggests an exceedingly formalistic view of the problem."[20]

Justice Stewart's view that a classification based on pregnancy is not discrimination based on sex was extended from the context of equal protection analysis to an interpretation of Title VII's prohibition against sex discrimination in employment in *General Electric Co. v. Gilbert*.[21] General Electric's disability plan included benefits for nonoccupational sickness and accidents but excluded disabilities arising during pregnancy. Justice Rehnquist, speaking for the majority, explained that "since it is a finding of sex-based discrimination that must trigger, in a case such as this, the finding of an unlawful employment practice under [the statute], *Geduldig* is precisely in point in its holding that an exclusion of pregnancy from a disability-benefits plan providing general coverage is not a gender-based discrimination at all."[22] He offered Justice Stewart's characterization of the relevant comparison groups as "pregnant women and nonpregnant persons,"[23] this time in the text of the opinion as the centerpiece of the Court's interpretation of Title VII.

Justice Brennan, in dissent, again responded indirectly to the Court's reasoning. He did not confront the Court's denial that the omission of pregnancy was necessarily a discrimination against women because of their sex. Rather, he challenged the Court's assumption that General Electric's plan represented a gender-free actuarial decision about which risks to include, arguing instead that General Electric had a history of past practices that were designed to and did disadvantage pregnant women employees.[24]

Justice Stevens undertook the task of refuting the Court's characterization of the two groups being compared. He rose to the challenge, pointing out in a footnote that

> it is not accurate to describe the program as dividing "potential recipients into two groups—pregnant women and non-pregnant persons." Insurance programs, company policies, and employment contracts all deal with future *risks* rather than historic facts. The classification is between persons who face a risk of pregnancy and those who do not.[25]

Stevens concluded from his characterization that the relevant comparison groups were indeed women and men. "By definition," he pointed out, "such a rule discriminates on account of sex; for it is the capacity to become pregnant which primarily differentiates the female from the male."[26]

Justice Stevens's characterization of the groups being compared provides one possible solution to the logical dilemma posed for traditional equal protection analysis by the absence of a matching male group for pregnant women. His classification does not, however, demonstrate that the respective classes are divided exclusively by sex. While all persons who face a risk of pregnancy are female, the group of those who do not includes women who are infertile and who have been surgically sterilized, as well as men. Moreover, the first group is defined too broadly to be useful in all situations. Thus, the requirement imposed in *LaFleur* of a mandatory maternity leave prior to delivery affected only pregnant teachers, not all teachers who faced the risk of pregnancy. Stevens's characterization, with its emphasis on future risk, is helpful in the context of insurance, but it does not solve the entire range of actual problems associated with reproduction that confront working women.

The Supreme Court's analysis in *Gilbert* rejected the contrary view of Title VII's coverage that had been adopted in the wake of *Geduldig* by six courts of appeal. Pregnant women and their allies, thwarted in their attempt to obtain judicial protection against the exclusion of pregnancy from employer disability programs, turned to Congress for relief.

B. The Congressional Response to *Gilbert:* The Pregnancy Discrimination Act of 1978

A coalition of more than three hundred groups, including labor unions, feminist groups, and some church groups, lobbied for congressional repeal of *Gilbert*. In response, Congress amended Title VII by enacting the Pregnancy Discrimination Act[27] (PDA) which defined the statutory term *sex* to include *pregnancy*. Commentators[28] pointed out that the PDA was intended to overrule the Supreme Court's decision in *Gilbert*. The Court, in *Newport News Shipbuilding & Dry Dock Co. v. EEOC*,[29] acknowledged that the PDA had rejected both the result and the reasoning in *Gilbert*. For statutory purposes,[30] after 1978, the Court conceded that "discrimination based on a woman's pregnancy is, on its face, discrimination because of her sex."[31]

Many feminist lawyers active in the repeal effort interpreted the PDA as mandating that pregnant women be treated the same as other workers.[32] Other observers pointed out, however, that although the PDA ensures that pregnant women workers are equally entitled to any disability coverage the employer may provide for other workers, "less clear . . . is what the PDA requires of an employer who currently offers no disability programs at all, and who refuses to grant pregnancy benefits on the ground that to do so would be to treat pregnancy differently than other disabilities."[33] Specifically, the questions left open are whether Title VII, as amended by the PDA, forbids neutral employment practices with a disparate impact on pregnant women and whether the PDA permits states to require employers to provide job-related incentives to retain pregnant women in the labor force if similar benefits are not mandated for other workers. Such incentives may include, for example, the availability of a reasonable, nonmandatory leave during pregnancy, workplace accommodations, such as facilities for lying down during rest breaks, and the right to return to work following delivery. Two recent cases, discussed in the next section, raise the potential conflict between state and federal law when state statutes impose a duty upon employers to provide a reasonable leave to pregnant employees without regard to whether leaves are available to employees disabled for other reasons and to provide reemployment after delivery. If such laws are not preempted by Title VII, the further question remains whether they violate any relevant state or federal constitutional provisions.

C. *Miller-Wohl* and *California Federal:* An Acknowledgment of Difference

1. *Miller-Wohl*

In 1972, Montana adopted an equal rights amendment to its state constitution.[34] In 1974, the Montana legislature created an interim study group and charged its members with the responsibility of studying existing Montana laws distinguishing between persons on the basis of sex and determining "what changes should be made in these laws to achieve true legal equality of the sexes while preserving for all the people of Montana those essential protections which orderly government provides for its citizens."[35] In responding to this charge, the subcommittee noted its awareness of "the most common criticism of equal rights legislation: that equal rights for men and women would destroy the family and bring chaos to an orderly society and government."[36] The subcommittee sought to meet this criticism by harmonizing the potentially divisive pursuit of equality with the preservation of traditional family life. To that end, it proposed legislation which it believed "would accomplish real sexual equality while encouraging stable and workable family and societal relationships."[37] This approach, applied to the situation of pregnant working women, produced a bill that, as redrafted, was enacted in 1975 as the Montana Maternity Leave Act.[38] The act enabled pregnant women to choose to continue working during pregnancy, to have a reasonable pregnancy leave, to collect any appropriate and available disability benefits; to return to work after delivery, and to be free of retaliation for filing a complaint against an employer who violated the act.[39] The Montana law thus predated the enactment of the PDA. Indeed, the House Committee Report accompanying the PDA cited Montana, along with five other states, as jurisdictions that "specifically include pregnancy in their Fair Employment Practices Laws."[40] Once the PDA became effective, on October 31, 1978, however, the stage was set for a potential conflict between the two laws.

The facts that provided the legal basis for a challenge to the Montana law based on the PDA occurred less than a year after the enactment of the federal provision. On August 1, 1979, the Miller-Wohl Company hired Tamara L. Buley to work as a salesperson in its clothing store in Great Falls, Montana. She missed two and a half days of work during her first week of employment. She thought she had contracted the flu. Instead, as she learned two weeks later, she was pregnant. In its opinion in *Miller-Wohl Co. v. Commissioner of Labor and Industry,* the Montana Supreme Court thus described her condition:

> During the next two weeks she suffered from "morning sickness." She felt nauseated and faint, and as a result missed time from work, had to leave the selling floor for breaks, and spent considerable time in the store bathroom vomiting, and was sent home early on occasion.[41]

Miller-Wohl fired Buley on August 27, 1979. The Montana Supreme Court observed that the employer took this action "undoubtedly because her pregnancy diminished her effectiveness as a sales clerk."[42]

Buley filed a complaint on August 6, 1980, with the Montana Commissioner of Labor and Industry. The Commissioner found that Miller-Wohl had violated the Montana Maternity Leave Act. It ordered Miller-Wohl to reinstate Buley as an employee and provide her with back pay plus penalty of $6,573.60. Miller-Wohl, which had earlier commenced a declaratory judgment complaint in the federal district court, then pressed that court for a determination that Title VII preempted the Montana law. The federal district court ruled against preemption, but its judgment was vacated by the Ninth Circuit for lack of subject matter jurisdiction.

Miller-Wohl then turned to the Montana state courts, petitioning for a review of the commissioner's decision. A lower state court reversed the commissioner's order. Buley and the commissioner appealed that judgment to the Montana Supreme Court, which reversed, reinstating the commissioner's order.

2. California Federal (Cal Fed)

The California legislature amended the California Fair Employment Practice Act in 1978 to define as an unfair labor practice an employer's refusal to allow a female employee to take a leave for a reasonable period of time, not to exceed four months, on account of pregnancy.[43] Unlike the Montana Maternity Leave Act, which had been proposed in response to a charge to implement the Montana Equal Rights Amendment, the California statute was enacted in response to the Supreme Court's decision in *Gilbert.* The amendment broadened the coverage of an existing provision that made it unlawful for governing boards of school districts to discriminate against females because of their pregnancy or to terminate any employee whose temporary disability could not be accommodated because of an employment policy that provided no leave or insufficient leave, if the policy had a disparate impact on employees of one sex and was not justified by business necessity. The attorney general of California argued in a brief filed before a federal district court that the legislative intent underlying the amendment "was aimed at broadening employee protection against adverse impact on the basis of pregnancy."[44]

As in the case of the Montana law, an employer charged with violating the state law challenged the California statute as being in conflict with Title VII. Lillian B. Garland, who worked as a receptionist and PBX operator for California Federal Savings and Loan Association in Los Angeles, took a pregnancy/childbirth disability leave beginning around January 18, 1982. Her baby was born on February 12, 1982. She notified the company on or about April 20, 1982, that she was able to return to work. The personnel department informed her that no receptionist position or similar job openings were then available. After waiting for seven months, Lillian Garland returned to work at Cal Fed as a receptionist on November 22, 1982.

Garland contacted the California Department of Fair Employment and Housing for advice. The department served an accusation on Cal Fed on May 2, 1983, alleging that it was in violation of California law. A hearing on the charge was scheduled for September 15–16, 1983. On August 1, 1983, Cal Fed filed a suit for declaratory and injunctive relief in the federal district court, contending that the California pregnancy leave provision was preempted by federal law. The federal court entered its order on March 21, 1984, granting Cal Fed's motion for summary judgment. The department appealed the judgment to the Ninth Circuit, which reversed.[45]

3. Arguments by the Parties in *Miller-Wohl* and *Cal Fed*

The employers in *Miller-Wohl* and *Cal Fed* made broadly similar statutory arguments. Both characterized the respective state statutes as requiring that they violate Title VII by treating pregnant women more favorably than they treated other disabled employees.[46] Miller-Wohl, but not Cal Fed, also claimed that the state law violated the due process and equal protection clauses of the federal constitution.

The state defendants in the two cases took essentially similar positions. The Montana commissioner contended that the Maternity Leave Act was supplemental, rather than contradictory, to Title VII.[47] In addition, the commissioner sought to uphold the statute against constitutional attack by characterizing it as an affirmative action measure designed to enable women to contribute to society according to their fullest possible potential. The California state defendants argued that the state statute was fully consistent with the goals and objectives of Title VII. In their view, the state statute was designed to ensure equal employment opportunity for women by protecting female employees affected by pregnancy, childbirth, and related medical conditions from the adverse impact of employment policies that provide insufficient disability leave or fail to ensure that women who take disability leave on account of pregnancy have the right to return to the same or similar job within a reasonable period of time. The California defendants relied on *Abraham v. Graphic Arts International Union,* in which the Court of Appeals for the District of Columbia Circuit had held in a case arising prior to the enactment of the PDA that an employer's ten-day maximum leave policy violated Title VII because of its adverse impact on women who became pregnant. In addition, they pointed to passages in the legislative history of the PDA that they interpreted as evidencing congressional approval of the Montana statute and other similar statutes dealing with pregnancy. The California defendants broadly summarized this part of their argument:

> While the legislative history of the PDA reflects Congress' intent that women affected by pregnancy, childbirth or related medical conditions not receive less favorable treatment than similarly situated coworkers, plaintiffs have pointed to nothing in the legislative history which supports their assertion that in enacting the PDA it was Congress' intent to foreclose state legislation which provides pregnant workers with additional protection in order to ensure equality of employment opportunity.[48]

4. Arguments of *Amici Curiae* in *Miller-Wohl* and *Cal Fed*

Feminist and civil rights groups split over the question of statutory interpretation posed in *Miller-Wohl* and *Cal Fed*. Briefs filed in *Miller-Wohl* by a consortium of groups led by the American Civil Liberties Union and in *Cal Fed* by a consortium of groups and individuals led by the National Organization for Women argued that state legislative efforts to provide special benefits to pregnant workers constituted "protective" legislation that was adverse to the long-range interests of women in equal treatment with men. The state statutes were thus prima facie in conflict with the provisions of the PDA, which mandated equal treatment, but the courts could interpret those statutes so as to make their terms consistent with Title VII by ordering that their benefits be extended to all disabled workers.

The California Department of Fair Employment and Housing, a defendant in *Cal Fed,* jointed by two other groups, filed an *amicus curiae* brief before the Ninth Circuit in *Miller-Wohl.* One of those groups, Equal Rights Advocates, Inc., appeared as *amicus curiae* in *Cal Fed* as well. Both briefs argued that the restrictive leave policies maintained by the employers in the two cases violated Title VII because of their adverse impact on pregnant women. Moreover, the state laws were consistent with the PDA in that both state and federal laws were designed to provide equal employment opportunities to pregnant women.

Despite their theoretical disagreement, the two sets of *amici* were divided only narrowly in their proposed outcome in both cases. Each sought to sustain the state statutes against a claim of federal preemption. The ACLU and NOW briefs insisted, however, that the benefits provided by the state statutes must be judicially construed to extend to all workers, not merely to pregnant women. Benefits limited to pregnant workers, they contended, would be preempted by Title VII. Equal rights advocates and its allies believed that the PDA left the states free to enact additional measures to place pregnant workers on an equal basis with all other workers.

5. The Courts Decide

The Montana Supreme Court held that Miller-Wohl violated both the Montana law and Title VII when it fired Tamara Buley because of her pregnancy.[50] It rejected, however, the argument that the PDA preempted state law. Instead, it adopted Judge Hatfield's reasoning, which he had offered to rebut the equal protection argument in the subsequently vacated federal district court judgment in *Miller-Wohl.* Hatfield had argued that the Montana statute did not treat men and women unequally by providing benefits limited to pregnancy. He continued:

> Rather, by removing pregnancy-related disabilities as a legal grounds for discharge from employment, the MMLA places men and women on more equal terms. All workers, male or female, disabled for any reason other than pregnancy are still treated identically. Whether the disability or sickness is one that members of either sex could suffer—such as a broken leg, or hepatitis—or is one that members of only one sex could suffer—such as an ovarian cyst or prostatitis—the MMLA still permits plaintiff to treat workers under its leave policy with equal severity. The MMLA merely makes it illegal for an employer such as plaintiff [Miller-Wohl] "to burden female employees in such a way as to deprive them of employment opportunities because of their different role." *National Gas Company v. Satty,* 434 U.S. 136, 142 (1977).[51]

The Montana Supreme Court thus recognized that the differentness of pregnancy cannot be adequately accommodated in the workplace by treating women the same as men. Its holding is consistent with the view taken in this paper, and developed more fully below, that equality between men and women requires compensating for biological reproductive sex differences that would otherwise handicap women and impede their realization of equal employment opportunity.

The Montana Supreme Court went on to point out that extension to all workers of the benefits provided by the Montana law only to pregnant workers would end any argument that the state law violated Title VII. The court recommended to the Montana legislature that it consider appropriate language to extend the act's coverage.

The Ninth Circuit also rejected the claim of federal preemption in *Cal Fed.* It disposed of Judge Real's assertion that the California statute discriminated against men on the basis of pregnancy as a conclusion that "defies common sense, misinterprets case law, and flouts Title VII and the PDA."[52] Judge Ferguson, writing for the court, characterized the preemption inquiry as a narrow one: the court must decide only whether the pregnancy leave provided by the California statute was "permissible" under Title VII. In an effective rebuttal to those who fear that any judicial recognition of the uniqueness of pregnancy might lead to the uncritical acceptance of other differences as well, to the ultimate disadvantage of women, Judge Ferguson made plain the limits of the holding:

> Because ¹ 12945(b)(2) deals with a condition that is unique to women—pregnancy disability rather than, say, parenting—our decision has no bearing on the lawfulness of state statutes or employment practices that classify on the basis of purportedly sex-linked factors that are actually less biological than stereotypical.[53]

The Ninth Circuit's interpretation of the PDA recognizes that its two clauses are to be read independently. It reasoned that the first clause made the term *pregnancy* a substitute for the term *sex* in Title VII's antidiscrimination mandate, thus enabling Congress to procure "for pregnancy that which it had already procured for sex: a guarantee against discrimination of all varieties, including facially neutral policies with a disparate impact."[54] Contrary to Cal Fed's argument, however, the court refused to read the second clause of the PDA as demanding "pregnancy-neutral policies at all times." Instead, it reasoned that Congress had intended to require at a minimum that pregnant women be treated as well as other employees, but not to prevent the states from requiring more complete maximum coverage.[55]

The Ninth Circuit's view of how pregnancy fits within the framework of an analysis based on equality between men and women is consistent with the approach taken in this chapter. Judge Ferguson put the argument concisely and well in the following passage:

> The PDA does not require states to ignore pregnancy. It requires that women be treated equally. As the preceding discussion shows, the PDA also provides a common-sense test of whether a policy—or a statute—affords equal treatment to women who are pregnant. The measure is whether the policy furthers "Title VII's prophylactic purpose of achieving 'equality of employment opportunities.'" *EEOC v. Puget Sound Log Scaling & Grading Bureau,* 752 F.2d 1389, 1392 (9th Cir. 1985) (quoting *Griggs v. Duke Power Co.,* 401 U.S. 424, 429 (1971)). Thus, equality under the PDA must be measured in employment opportunity, not necessarily in amounts of money expended—or in amounts of days of disability leave expended. Equality in the disability context compares coverage to actual need, not coverage to hypothetical identical needs.[56]

The ultimate authority to interpret an act of Congress rests, of course, with the United States Supreme Court. Litigants in both cases have invoked the Court's power to interpret the PDA. The remaining task of this chapter, in anticipation of that interpretation, is to show how the differentness of pregnancy can be recognized and accommodated within a legal and philosophical framework that affirms the equality of women and men.

II. Equality and Difference

A. An Episodic Analysis of Biological Reproductive Sex Differences

The philosophical claim that all men—or all women—are equal is commonly challenged by the existence of such inequalities as those of intelligence, ability, merit, physical condition, wealth, status, or power. Some philosophers have chosen to respond to challenges of this sort by invoking a generalized ideal of equality that transcends inequalities stemming from the specific differences of the human condition, such as equality of respect owed to all humans,[57] equality of opportunity,[58] or equality of consideration of interests.[59] Others have sought to justify some forms of social and economic inequalities within a theory of justice.[60] With rare exception,[61] these philosophical discussions of equality have been phrased in terms of equality among men, with the term *man* being used in its generic sense to include *woman*. When the specific question is raised about what equality between women and men might mean,[62] the debate focuses on a particular set of differences: the biological differences that define the two classes of male and female. The question then becomes: Given that biological reproductive sex differences exist and may be expected to persist, how can it be argued that men and women are equal?

At least two approaches to this question have been taken. The significance of biological reproductive sex differences can be minimized, or it can be exalted. The first approach holds that although differences of this sort may be acknowledged, no public consequence should turn on whether a person is male or female.[63] Equality between men and women is achieved by removing sex as a consideration of consequence; that is, by making the sexes morally, if not physically, indistinguishable. A second approach identifies biological reproductive sex differences as the basis of sexual identity and uses that identity, in turn, as the foundation for social differences that establish separate sex roles for women and men.[64] This approach would abandon egalitarian models in favor of a bivalent concept of the interests of women and men, to create a sort of "separate but equal" social model for the sexes. Adherents of the first position generally support a vision of the good society in which cross-sex assimilation is the norm and difference is limited as narrowly as possible.[65] Those holding to the second position may support a range of social arrangements, from traditional ones in which women and men occupy separate spheres,[66] to more modern views of an androgynous society in which the spheres converge, preserving the best characteristics of both sexes.[67]

I wish to propose a third, alternative, approach: that we take account of biological reproductive sex differences and treat them as legally significant only when they are being utilized for reproductive purposes. I suggest that biological reproductive sex differences should be recognized as a functional attribute, rather than an inherent characteristic, of sexual identity, and as one that may or may not be exercised. A woman may be distinguished from a man by her capacity for pregnancy, childbirth, and lactation, but she may choose never to utilize that capacity. Is she any less female? A man has the unique capacity to produce and ejaculate sperm. But if he fathers no children, he is still a man. Infertile women and men retain their sexual identity, if not their distinguishing sexual capacity. In our society, salient distinctions are based on sexuality rather than reproductive behavior.[68] Women and men do not exercise their different biological reproductive capacities when they conform to social norms of appropriate interaction, nor do they necessarily do so when they engage in sexual intercourse. Those differences appear only when the reproductive function is manifested through a pregnancy that resulted from the reproductive behavior of both sexes.

This way of looking at reproductive behavior permits us to examine biological reproductive sex differences in a new light. It becomes clearer that reproductive behavior is episodic and temporary. Male reproductive behavior is quite brief in duration; that of females occupies approximately nine months, but its cycle is complete following childbirth. Men and women who are parents are not functionally distinguishable by sex in their capacity to care for the newborn infant, except where breast feeding is utilized as the method of choice for providing nourishment. Some have argued that a cultural preference for females over males in the role of primary nurturing parent produces psychological differences based on sex in children that in turn reinforce existing social patterns of male domination, and have proposed that the recurrent cycle be broken by having males join females in caring for children.[69] Such arguments rest on the assumption that no innate biological traits prevent men from forming primary bonds with infants.

The relevance of this episodic analysis of biological reproductive sex differences for a theoretical model of equality between women and men is that it recognizes that those differences exist but regards them as inconsequential except during the specific occasions on which they are utilized. Upon those occasions, as the result of the union between sperm and egg, pregnant women experience a complex of needs that are different from those of men and, indeed, of nonpregnant women. Pregnant women may be advised to follow a certain diet, to abstain from ingesting particular substances, to avoid identified toxic environments, and to engage in or refrain from specified conduct in order to maximize their chances of delivering a healthy child. And as a consequence of their changing physical condition, pregnant women may be temporarily disabled from work.

The necessary result of a woman's reproductive behavior is that for a limited time and in ways that may vary widely among pregnant women, her condition will be different from that of other persons of both sexes. Is she therefore unequal to those other persons? In particular, is she unequal to a man who has also engaged in reproductive conduct?

I think it is clear that if a woman who is not pregnant is assumed to be equal to a man on some such measure as, say, equality of respect or equality of consideration of interests, her reproductive behavior does not remove or detract in any way from her claim to that sort of equality. A woman may, however, unlike a man who engages in reproductive behavior, be placed at a temporary disadvantage with respect to equality of opportunity. In order to bear a child, she may be temporarily disabled from pursing her own self-interests. If she becomes pregnant more than once, she may face recurrent disadvantages. It appears unjust to place the consequential disadvantages of reproductive conduct only upon women. This unjust result need not follow, however, for a philosophical basis exists for alleviating the temporary disadvantages of pregnancy within a framework of equality.

Philosophers recognize that just as the concept of equality requires that equals be treated equally, so it requires that unequals be treated differently.[70] To treat persons who are different alike is to treat them unequally. The concept of formal equality, however, contains no independent justification for making unequals equal. A different concept, that of equality of opportunity, offers a theoretical basis for making unequals equal in the limited sense of removing barriers which prevent individuals from performing according to their abilities.[71] The notion is that the perceived inequality does not stem from an innate difference in ability, but rather from a condition or circumstance that prevents certain uses or developments of that ability. As applied to reproductive behavior, the suggestion would be that women in general are not different from men in innate ability. During the temporary episode of a woman's pregnancy, however, she may become unable to utilize her abilities in the same way she had done prior to her reproductive conduct. Since a man's abilities are not similarly impaired as a result of his reproductive behavior, equality of opportunity implies that the woman should not be disadvantaged as a result of that sex-specific variation.

As applied to the employment context, the concept of equality of opportunity takes on the following form. Let us postulate two workers, one female, the other male, who respectively engage in reproductive conduct. Assume as well that prior to this activity, both were roughly equal in their ability to perform their similar jobs. The consequence of their having engaged in reproductive behavior will be vastly different. The man's ability to perform on the job will be largely unaffected. The woman's ability to work, measured against her prior performance, may vary with the physical and emotional changes she experiences during pregnancy. At times, her ability to work may be unaffected by the pregnancy; at other times, she may be temporarily incapacitated by it. Ultimately, she may require medical care to recover from miscarriage, or to complete her pregnancy by delivery, or to terminate it earlier by induced abortion. In order to maintain the woman's equality of opportunity during her pregnancy, we should modify as far as reasonably possible those aspects of her work where her job performance is adversely affected by the pregnancy. Unless we do so, she will experience employment disadvantages arising from her reproductive activity that are not encountered by her male coworker.

I will explore some of the legal implications of this theoretical position in the sections that follow. Here, I note a possible objection: the cost of compliance. Cost, however, is a function of social value. As the enactment of Title VII demonstrates, our society has made equality between women and men in the workplace a high priority. At the same time, it has accorded to individual decisions concerning procreation the status of a constitutionally protected fundamental right. Men do not experience a conflict between their right to engage in reproductive conduct and their right to be free of discrimination based on sex at work. Women, however, have experienced such a conflict, and will continue to do so unless pregnant workers are safeguarded from the loss of employment opportunities during pregnancy. The social value of accommodating reproduction and employment opportunities so that women remain free to engage in both activities on an equal basis with men justifies the additional cost of enabling working women to cope with the differential physical and emotional changes associated with pregnancy.

B. Application of Episodic Analysis to Title VII

The episodic analysis of biological reproductive sex differences, particularly pregnancy, suggested in this chapter is consistent with the interpretation of Title VII offered by Judge Ferguson for the Ninth Circuit in *Cal Fed.* Under that interpretation, both "sex" and "pregnancy" are covered by Title VII's prohibition against discrimination, and the test of pregnancy discrimination consists of whether a challenged policy or statute affords the pregnant woman equality of employment opportunity.[72] The analysis offered here shows that pregnancy differs from sex, however, in that pregnancy is an episodic occurrence rather than an immutable trait. The category of pregnant persons is a subclass within the larger category of women. To some extent, the statutory prohibitions are the same for both groups. Neither women nor pregnant persons may be rejected for employment or fired because of their sex or their pregnancy. Per se discrimination based on either sex or pregnancy may be justified, however, by a showing that the statutory bona fide occupational qualification defense[73] applies. If justified by that defense, pregnant workers who cannot perform their jobs may be temporarily removed from hazardous work sites or from jobs where the woman's pregnancy may prevent her from ensuring the safety of customers. Employers must take those measures that may be reasonably necessary to permit pregnant workers to continue working until delivery, in order to avoid discrimination against them. Women returning from pregnancy leave must be allowed to resume their former status as workers. An episodic view of pregnancy requires that any benefits extended to pregnant workers or restrictions imposed on them be tailored to actual medical need resulting from the pregnancy, and not be triggered by stereotypical notions of what pregnant women should or should not do.

This interpretation of Title VII based on an episodic analysis of biological reproductive sex differences will permit pregnancy to be recognized as the normal consequence of reproductive behavior that can and should be accommodated in the workplace. Pregnancy is not itself a disability, although an individual pregnant woman may experience disabling symptoms and may require medical care. If she is temporarily impaired from performing at work up to her normal level of ability, the concept of equal employment opportunity embodied in Title VII requires not only that she remain free of resulting job reprisals but also that she secure compensatory benefits to offset any potential work-related disadvantage. Under this analysis, women will be equal to men in their ability to work and to make reproductive choices.

C. Application of Episodic Analysis to the Constitution

After the effective date of the PDA, discrimination against pregnant persons was illegal in the employment context, but it was not unconstitutional. *Geduldig* remains the governing interpretation of the equal protection clause, and it stands for the proposition that a classification drawn on the basis of pregnancy is not a discrimination based on sex.

An episodic analysis of pregnancy demonstrates the fallacy in the *Geduldig* classification between pregnant women and nonpregnant persons. The legal issue of *Geduldig* was how one consequence of reproductive conduct—pregnancy—should be treated in the workplace for purposes of an employer's disability plan. The Court took as its reference point a group composed of all persons who worked for the employer. But that is not the relevant reference group. Instead, the group should be limited to those persons who have engaged in reproductive behavior while continuing to work. That group is divided into two subgroups, persons who will require medical care and who may at times be temporarily disabled as a result of that reproductive conduct and persons who will not. The first group of persons is exclusively female, while the second is entirely male. Men and women who have not engaged in reproductive behavior are not similarly situated with respect to the work-related consequences of that conduct to persons who have so acted and so are not properly part of the equal protection equation. The *Geduldig* classification was overly broad, because it included within the category of "nonpregnant persons" both women and men who had not chosen to initiate a reproductive episode as well as men who had so chosen.

Moreover, the *Geduldig* line was drawn at the wrong point in the reproductive cycle. By focusing on the consequence of reproductive conduct—pregnancy—the Court ignored the male role in reproduction. Properly rephrased in light of an episodic analysis of biological reproductive sex differences, the legal question in *Geduldig* is whether two persons of the opposite sex who have engaged in reproductive behavior and wish to continue working may be treated differently for purposes of disability coverage. Since the man will not be disabled from work as the result of that conduct, equal protection for the woman requires that she not be penalized if she does become disabled. It follows not only that the pregnant woman must be covered by any existing disability plan applicable to workers generally but also that she must be protected against disability resulting from pregnancy even in the absence of a general disability plan. *Geduldig* results in unequal treatment of similarly situated women and men who have engaged respectively in reproductive conduct. It should be overruled.

It follows from this analysis that for constitutional purposes as well as statutory coverage under Title VII, a discrimination against a woman based on pregnancy is a facial discrimination against her because of her sex. The same intermediate standard of judicial review developed for equal protection sex discrimination cases can be adapted for use in pregnancy discrimination cases. The analysis will, however, be different in pregnancy discrimination cases, because there is no matching group of pregnant males to use for purposes of comparison. Instead, the constitutional test must be applied so as to assure pregnant women equality of opportunity to the same extent as that available to males who have engaged in reproductive conduct. Thus, pregnant women may be treated differently from such males if the result is to prevent a disadvantage that might otherwise follow from their condition. For example, a reasonable leave provided by a state employer to pregnant workers is not only constitutional, it is constitutionally compelled to avoid discrimination by the state against pregnant workers.

An employer's policy, however, may not be facially directed against pregnant workers but may have a disparate impact on them, such as a no-leave or inadequate leave policy. Present equal protection doctrine established in *Washington v. Davis*[74] does not restrict such policies unless the discrimination is intentional. But the very uniqueness of the condition of pregnancy may ameliorate the impact of *Washington v. Davis* in light of a recent modification of its procedural implications. The Court has made clear that "once racial discrimination is shown to have been a 'substantial' or 'motivating' factor behind enactment of the law, the burden shifts to the law's defenders to demonstrate that the law would have been enacted without this factor."[75] This holding should be extended to sex and pregnancy discrimination cases. In pregnancy discrimination cases, it may not be difficult to show, for example, that a state employer's inadequate or no-leave policy was motivated in part by a desire to reduce the cost of pregnancy leave coverage, if only because the practice of differential coverage for pregnancy at work was so widespread before the enactment of the PDA. If such a showing is sufficient to shift the burden on the issue of intent to the employer, the impact of *Washington v. Davis* on pregnancy discrimination cases may be minimized.

D. Episodic Analysis and the "Equal Treatment/Special Treatment" Debate

The episodic analysis as applied to pregnancy may serve as a basis for harmonizing some of the views of the opposing participants in the so-called equal treatment/special treatment debate. For example, episodic analysis highlights how narrowly the dispute is limited. In her excellent defense of the "equal treatment" model, Wendy Williams identifies two propositions as essential to the theoretical framework within which that model was developed.[76] They are, first, "that sex-based generalizations are generally impermissible whether derived from physical differences such as size and strength, from cultural role assignments such as breadwinner or homemaker, or from some combination of innate and ascribed characteristics, such as the greater longevity of the average woman compared to the average man";[77] and, second, "that laws and rules which do not overtly classify on the basis of sex, but which have a disproportionately negative effect upon one sex, warrant, under appropriate circumstances, placing a burden of justification upon the party defending the law or rule in court."[78] Neither of these propositions is in conflict with the episodic analysis of biological reproductive sex differences offered in this paper. I agree with Williams that taken together, these two propositions form the basis of a legal doctrine of equality between women and men that has served both sexes well in breaking down "the legal barriers that restricted each sex to its predefined role and created a hierarchy based on gender."[79] As I have shown elsewhere, this assimilationist view of equality has worked well as a tool against both race discrimination and sex discrimination, where the two groups being compared are not different in any relevant way.[80]

Episodic analysis departs from the "equal treatment" model, however, at the point where Williams claims that her "general framework applies, with minor alteration, to laws or rules based on physical characteristics unique to one sex."[81] In my view, biological reproductive sex differences are not comparable to other traits or characteristics that are shared by both sexes and cannot adequately be analyzed within a framework that turns on differential treatment of two comparable groups.[82] Instead, episodic analysis recognizes that biological reproductive sex differences exist but confines their legal significance to the brief period during which they are utilized. I take it that Williams and I agree that women and men should be deemed equals prior to the time either engages in reproductive behavior. At the moment of conception, sperm and egg play equally important roles. Following childbirth, we both would place equal responsibility for child rearing on men and women who are parents. But, unlike Williams, I insist that during the episode of pregnancy itself the woman's body functions in a unique way. We must recognize that unique function in order to prevent penalizing the woman who exercises it. If confined in this way, the recognition of pregnancy as "unique" will enable the law to treat women differently than men during a limited period when their needs may be greater than those of men as a way of ensuring that women will be equal to men with respect to their overall employment opportunities.

The narrow difference between my approach and that taken by Williams is also emphasized by another consideration. One of the major arguments of proponents of the equal treatment model has been strategic rather than theoretical. It is that ultimately women will be more successful in escaping traditional stereotypical roles if they refrain from seeking special treatment for the uniquely female condition of pregnancy and rely primarily on demands for benefits that can be pressed in common with all workers.[83] Thus, Williams points out that the equal treatment model "separates pregnancy and childrearing and insists that each be independently analyzed,"[84] so that the workplace can be restructured to accommodate parenting as the joint responsibility of working fathers and mothers.

As I have noted above, my analysis, like that of Williams, makes clear that the woman's reproductive cycle ends with childbirth. In those cases where two parents are available to care for the child, episodic analysis carries no implications for how they should assign between themselves the ensuing stage of childrearing. My analysis envisions a bright line between pregnancy and child care that requires the provision of any available child-rearing leave to both parents.[85] More fundamentally, episodic analysis is consistent with a model of equality that acknowledges the reproductive conduct of both men and women while allowing a woman's pregnancy to be recognized and provided for on its own terms. It is thus consistent with the view of proponents of the "special treatment" approach that the best way to enable women to compete on an equal basis with men is to assure them that pregnancy will not hinder their achievements.[86]

Williams has questioned the fairness of a differential approach to pregnancy, using the *Miller-Wohl* case as a vehicle. She asks: "On what basis can we fairly assert, for example, that the pregnant woman fired by Miller-Wohl deserved to keep her job when any other worker who got sick for any other reason did not?"[87] The short answer to this question is that no male worker who had exercised his reproductive capacity lost his job as a result. Episodic analysis supports that brief response and also provides a more complete justification. The point at which that longer justification begins, however, is not when Miller-Wohl was thinking of firing Tamara Buley but, rather, when she was thinking of going to work. Planned pregnancy, unlike other medical conditions, is an episode that is intended to culminate in the birth of a child. A woman who plans both to work and to have children must take account of how she will manage her pregnancy at work. If she knows that her employer has in place a program that will accommodate her pregnancy-related needs, she will be able to enter the work force without fear of encountering obstacles to her decision to bear a child. Such employer programs will encourage women to enter and remain in the job market by mitigating the disadvantages to women caused by pregnancy. Not being fired, of course, is an important part of such a program of accommodation. An employer disability policy that limits the amount of sick leave to very short periods or that has long probationary periods cannot provide the necessary assurance to women that they will not be penalized at work if they become pregnant. Such provisions are, therefore, inadequate for pregnant workers, although they may be justifiable—even if undesirable—when applied to fortuitous sickness or injury suffered by other workers. Although employers and their insurers can predict statistically how many workers will be injured or disabled while at work, individual workers themselves normally do not plan for such disabling events. Therefore, they are not deterred from entering the work force by the anticipation of such risks.

Ruth Bader Ginsburg put the point nicely, although I do not claim that she shares my views on this specific issue. Commenting on some of the pregnancy cases decided prior to the enactment of the PDA, she observed:

> The likelihood that childbirth will occur nowadays normally twice in a working woman's life, and the cost generated by insurance coverage for pregnancy-related physical disability no doubt influenced the Court's decisions—its meandering course and its current position that discrimination based on pregnancy is unlawful "sometimes." If Congress is genuinely committed to eradication of sex-based discrimination and promotion of equal opportunity for women, it will respond to the uneven pattern of adjudication by providing firm legislative direction assuring job security, health insurance coverage, and income maintenance for childbearing women. Women will remain more restricted than men in their options so long as this problem is brushed under the rug by the nation's lawmakers.[88]

I do not believe that enactment of the PDA, unless it is interpreted to permit employers to provide coverage for pregnant workers, regardless of whether other workers are covered for other conditions, has responded satisfactorily to Ginsburg's argument. Such an interpretation would be consistent with the congressional goal of ending discrimination against working women because of their pregnancy. If such an approach is adopted, feminists on both sides of the "equal treatment/special treatment" debate will be free to pursue our common goal of eradicating the pervasive prejudice against working mothers.

Conclusion

The biological fact that only women have the capacity to become pregnant has been used historically to define women as different from men along social, psychological, and emotional dimensions. Those asserted differences, in turn, have served to justify the legal, political, and economic exclusion of women from men's public world. Even now, when the barriers that separate women and men in the work force are breaking down, the uniqueness of pregnancy remains an obstacle to equal opportunity for women.

The nadir of this isolation of pregnancy was reached in modern times by the Supreme Court's distinction in *Geduldig* between pregnant women and nonpregnant persons, an overly broad characterization properly condemned as artificial and demeaning. Yet the Court's flawed perception of the relevant comparison groups contained an element of factual truth, albeit one from which the Court drew the wrong conclusion. Episodic analysis allows us to reclaim the accurate biological fact of sexual reproductive difference and to draw the appropriate legal conclusion that difference requires. The Court's false conclusion was that pregnant persons are not women. That conclusion led to the improper legal result that women were protected against sex discrimination only when they are like men—that is, when they are not pregnant. Episodic analysis reveals the right conclusion: that both men and women engage in reproductive conduct and that women are pregnant persons only for brief and self-contained periods. That insight can give rise to the proper legal result that women continue to be women even when pregnant, and should be provided with legal redress against discrimination based either on their sex or their pregnancy. On both legal and philosophical grounds, the temporary inequality that stems from the condition of pregnancy can and should be accommodated within a framework of equal opportunity for both sexes.

Notes

I am grateful to my research assistant, Mark D. Greenberg, for his help during the preparation of this chapter and to Katherine Bartlett, Jesse Choper, Ruth Bader Ginsburg, Christine Littleton, Andrea Peterson, Robert Post, Deborah Rhode, and Karen Tokarz for commenting on an earlier draft of this chapter. The views expressed here are my own.

1. U.S. CONST. amend XIV.

2. Title VII of the Civil Rights Act, 42 U.S.C. § 2000e *et seq.* (1964); *see also* the Equal Pay Act, 29 U.S.C. § 206(d) (1963).

3. The Supreme Court first construed the provisions of Title VII in a sex discrimination case in Phillips v. Martin Marietta Corp., 400 U.S. 542 (1971); it first invalidated a sex-based classification on constitutional grounds in Reed v. Reed, 404 U.S. 71 (1971).

4. *See* Kay, *Models of Equality,* 1985 U. ILL. L. REV. 39 (1985).

5. *Id.* at 77–78.

6. 414 U.S. 632 (1974). The *LaFleur* opinion also resolved another case reported below as Cohen v. Chesterfield County School Bd., 474 F.2d 395 (4th Cir. 1973), *rev'd sub nom.*

7. The pregnant teachers in *LaFleur* were required to take a maternity leave without pay, beginning five months before the expected date of birth. A teacher on maternity leave was not promised reemployment following delivery, but she was given priority in reassignment. At any event, she was not permitted to resume teaching until the beginning of the regular school semester which followed the date upon which her child attained the age of three months. In *Cohen,* a teacher was

required to leave work four months prior to the expected date of birth, and was guaranteed reemployment no later than the first day of the school year following the date on which a physician certified in writing that she was physically fit for work, if she could assure the board that care of the child would cause only minimal interference with her job responsibilities (*LaFleur,* 414 U.S. at 634–37).

8. LaFleur v. Cleveland Bd. of Educ., 465 F.2d 1184, 1188 (6th Cir. 1972), *aff'd on other grounds,* 414 U.S. 632 (1974).

9. 474 F.2d 395 (4th Cir. 1973) (en banc), *rev'd sub nom.* Cleveland Bd. of Educ. v. LaFleur, 414 U.S. 632 (1974).

10. *Id.* 474 F.2d at 397. Chief Judge Haynsworth elaborated this point at length, *see* 474 F.2d at 397–98, finding it helpful to invoke in aid of his argument the observation of Anatole France that "the law, in its majestic equality, forbids the rich as well as the poor to sleep under bridges, to beg in the streets, and to steal bread," and concluded that "pregnancy and maternity are *sui generis,* and a governmental employer's notice of them is not an invidious classification by sex" (474 F.2d at 398).

11. *Cohen,* 474 F.2d at 400–1.

12. *Id.* at 397.

13. 414 U.S. at 651 (concurring opinion of Justice Powell).

14. 417 U.S. 484 (1974).

15. *Id.* at 495–96.

16. *Id.*

17. *Id.*

18. *Id.* at 501 (dissenting opinion of Justices Brennan, Douglas, and Marshall).

19. *Id.* at 496–497.

20. *The Supreme Court, 1976 Term,* 91 Harv. L. Rev. 1, 244 (1977).

21. General Electric v. Gilbert, 429 U.S. 125.

22. *Id.* at 136.

23. *Id.* at 135 (quoting Geduldig v. Aiello, 417 U.S. 484, at 496–97, n.20).

24. *Id.* at 149–50 (dissenting opinion of Justices Brennan and Marshall).

25. *Id.* at 161 n.5 (dissenting opinion of Justice Stevens) (emphasis in original).

26. *Id.* at 161–62 (dissenting opinion of Justice Stevens).

27. 42 U.S.C. § 2000(e)(k) (1982).

28. *See, e.g.,* Williams, at 193; Note, *Sexual Equality Under the Pregnancy Discrimination Act,* 83 Colum. L. Rev. 690, 691–93 (1983).

29. 462 U.S. 669 (1983).

30. The PDA did not affect the Court's constitutional holding in *Geduldig.*

31. *Newport News,* 462 U.S. at 684.

32. *See, e.g.,* Williams, *The Equality Crisis,* 7 Women's RTs. L. Rep. 175, at 193, 9 (1982).

33. *See* Note, *Sexual Equality,* at 693.

34. Mont. Const. art. II, § 4 provides in part that "neither the state nor any person, firm, corporation, or institution shall discriminate against any person in the exercise of his civil or political rights on account of race, color, sex, culture, social origin or condition, or political or religious ideas."

35. 1974 Mont. Laws, S.J. Res. No. 68. The study group issued an interim report recommending specific legislation, including a provision that ultimately became the Montana Maternity Leave Act. *See* Equality of the Sexes, Appendix 1–11 (Interim Study by the Montana Subcommittee on Judiciary, December, 1974).

36. Equality of the Sexes, at 3.

37. *Id.*

38. Mont. Code Ann. §§ 49———310-49———311 (1983).

39. *Id.* Section 49———310(4) was not part of the subcommittee proposal.

40. H.R. Rep. No. 948, 95th Cong., 2d Sess. 11, *reprinted in* 1978 U.S. Code Cong. & Ad.

News 4749, 4759. The other five states mentioned were Alaska, Connecticut, Maryland, Minnesota, and Oregon.

41. 692 P.2d 1243 (Mont. 1984), *appeal docketed,* 53 U.S.L.W. 3718 (U.S. April 9, 1985) (no. 84–1545) at 1245.

42. *Id.*

43. 1978 Cal. Stat. 4320 § 1, adding Cal. Lab. Code § 1420.35 to the California Fair Employment Practice Act, former Cal. Lab. Code §§ 1410-33. The FEPA was rechaptered and retitled as the Fair Employment and Housing Act in 1980. The provisions of Cal. Lab. Code § 1420.35 were incorporated into the FEHA as Cal. Gov't Code § 12945.

44. Defendants' Notice of Motion and Motion for Summary Judgment; Memorandum of Points and Authorities in Support of Motion for Summary Judgment at 23, California Federal Savings & Loan Ass'n v. Guerra, 34 Fair Empl. Prac. Cas. (BNA) 562 (C.D. Cal. 1984), *rev'd* 758 F.2d 390 (9th Cir. 1985). The legislation as enacted may have gone further than some of its sponsors and supporters intended, if they thought that a purely comparative approach extending already existing benefits to pregnant workers was envisioned. *See* Brief of National Organization for Women as *amicus curiae* at 36–41, California Federal Savings & Loan Ass'n v. Guerra, 758 F.2d 390 (9th Cir. 1985).

45. *Cal Fed,* 758 F.2d 390 (9th Cir. 1985).

46. Complaint of Miller-Wohl Co. at 7, Miller-Wohl Co. v. Comm'r of Labor & Industry, Etc., 515 F. Supp. 1264 (D. Mont. 1981), *vacated,* 685 F.2d 1088 (9th Cir. 1982); Complaint of California Federal Savings & Loan Ass'n at 11, *Cal Fed,* 34 Fair Empl. Prac. Cas. (BNA) 562 (C.D. Cal. 1984), *rev'd* 758 F.2d 390 (9th Cir. 1985).

47. Brief of the Commissioner of Labor and Industry at 1–14, Miller-Wohl Co. v. Comm'r of Labor & Industry, Etc., 515 F. Supp. 1264 (D. Mont. 1981), *vacated,* 685 F. 2d 1088 (9th Cir. 1982).

48. Defendants' Memorandum in Response to Plaintiffs' Motion for Summary Judgment at 12, *Cal Fed,* 34 Fair Empl. Prac. Cas. 562 (C.D. Cal. 1984), *rev'd* 758 F.2d 390 (9th Cir. 1985).

49. Brief of American Civil Liberties Union as *amicus curiae,* Miller-Wohl Co. v. Comm'r of Labor & Industry, 692 P.2d 1243 (Mont. 1984). Other groups joining the ACLU brief were the ACLU of Montana, the National Organization for Women, Montana State NOW, the NOW Legal Defense and Education Fund, the League of Women Voters of the United States, the League of Women Voters of Montana, the National Women's Law Center, and the Women's Legal Defense Fund. Three other Montana groups filed separate *amicus curiae* briefs in support of the Montana statute: the Women's Law Section of the State Bar of Montana, the Montana Human Rights Commission, and the Montana Education Association.

50. *Miller-Wohl,* 692 P.2d at 1251–52. In holding that Miller-Wohl violated Title VII, the Montana Supreme Court seemed to rely both on disparate treatment (*see* McDonnell Douglas Co. v. Green, 411 U.S. 792, 802 (1972)) and disparate impact (*see* Griggs v. Duke Power Co., 401 U.S. 424, 430 (1971)) theories of Title VII violation.

51. Miller-Wohl Co. v. Comm'r of Labor & Industry, 692 P.2d 1243, 1254 (Mont. 1984) (quoting *Miller-Wohl,* 515 F. Supp. at 1266).

52. *Cal Fed,* 758 F.2d at 393 (9th Cir. 1985).

53. *Cal Fed,* 758 F.2d at 395.

54. *Cal Fed,* 758 F.2d at 396.

55. *Cal Fed,* 758 F.2d at 396.

56. *Id.*

57. *See* B. Williams, *The Idea of Equality,* in Problems of the Self 230, 234–39 (1973).

58. *See* Frankel, *Equality of Opportunity,* 81 Ethics 191 (1971). *Compare* Simon, *The Liberal Conception of Equal Opportunity and Its Egalitarian Critics,* in M. Darrogh & R. Blank, at 95–98, *with* Schaar, *Equality of Opportunity, and Beyond,* in Nomas IX: Equality 228,233–36 (1967).

59. *See* Benn, *Egalitarianism and the Equal Consideration of Interests,* in Nomos IX: Equality 61 (1967).

60. *See, e.g.,* J. RAWLS, A THEORY OF JUSTICE 60 (1971).

61. *See* Mill, *On the Subjection of Women,* in ESSAYS ON SEX EQUALITY 123 (A. Rossi ed. 1970).

62. *See* Gould, *The Woman Question: Philosophy of Liberation and the Liberation of Philosophy,* in WOMEN AND PHILOSOPHY: TOWARD A THEORY OF LIBERATION 5 (C. Gould & M. Wartofsky eds. 1980).

63. This position is defended by Alison Jaggar and Richard Wasserstrom. *See* Wasserstrom, *Racism, Sexism, and Preferential Treatment: An Approach to the Topics,* 24 UCLA L. REV. 581, 605–15 (1977); Jaggar, *On Sexual Equality,* 84 ETHICS 275 (1974).

64. This position is defended by Elizabeth Wolgast. *See* E. WOLGAST, EQUALITY AND THE RIGHTS OF WOMEN 25–30, 103–37 (1980).

65. *See, e.g.,* Wasserstrom, at 612–14.

66. *See, e.g.,* De Marco, *Men and Women, Their Difference and Its Importance,* 56 THOUGHT 449 (1981); Brown.

67. *See, e.g.,* Rossi, *Gender and Parenthood,* 49 AM. SOC. REV. 1 (1984).

68. *See* MacKinnon, *Feminism, Marxism, Method, and the State: An Agenda for Theory,* 7 SIGNS 515, 516 (1982).

69. *See generally,* N. CHODOROW, THE REPRODUCITON OF MOTHERING: PSYCHOANALYSIS AND THE SOCIOLOGY OF GENDER (Berkeley: Univ. of Cal. Press, 1978); or D. Dinnerstein, The Mermaid and the Minotaur: Sexual Arrangements and the Human Malaise (NY: Harper & Row, 1976).

70. The point seems to have been made originally by Aristotle. *See* NICHMACHEAN ETHICS v.3. 1113a–13b (W. Ross trans. 1925).

71. *See* Frankel, at 204, advancing a conception of "educational" equality of opportunity, which I have adapted here to fit the case of pregnancy. Frankel's formulation is as follows:

> Equality of opportunity means that men shall not be limited except by their abilities; the advocate of the "educational" conception of equality of opportunity holds that we cannot have real equality of opportunity unless we successfully modify those aspects of the individual's situation which prevent him from performing up to the level of his natural abilities.

72. *Cal Fed,* 758 F.2d at 396.

73. 42 U.S.C.A. § 2000e-2(e).

74. 426 U.S. 229 (1976). *See generally* Segal, *Sexual Equality, the Equal Protection Clause, and the ERA,* 33 BUFFALO L. REV. 85, 114–30 (1984) (arguing that the *Washington v. Davis* standard, as applied to sex discrimination in Personnel Adm'r of Mass. v. Feeney, 446 U.S. 256 (1979), sanctions discriminatory policies by equating equality with facial neutrality).

75. Hunter v. Underwood, 105 S. Ct. 1916, 1920 (1985).

76. *See* Williams, *Equality's Riddle: Pregnancy and the Equal Treatment/Special Treatment Debate,* 13 N.Y.U. REV. L. & SOC. CHANGE 329–31 (1984–85).

77. *Id.* at 329.

78. *Id.* at 330.

79. *Id.* at 331.

80. *See* Kay, at 77–78.

81. Williams, at 331.

82. *See* Kay at 78–87.

83. *See* Williams, at 196–98. This position was reflected in the *amicus* briefs filed in *Miller-Wohl* by the American Civil Liberties Union and in *Cal Fed* by the National Organization for Women.

84. Williams, at 354.

85. Like Williams, I therefore prefer the Swedish model of parental caretaking to the ILO model which limits child care benefits following delivery to mothers. *See* Williams, at 376–78.

86. *See* Note, *Employment Equality,* at 952–55; Note, *Equality in the Workplace: Is That*

Enough for Pregnant Workers 23 J. FAM. L. 401 (1984–85); Johnston, *Pregnancy Leave,* in 1984 YEARBOOK 8, 9 (California Women Lawyers 1984–85); Krieger & Cooney, 515–17; Scales at 435–42; Carey, *Pregnancy Without Penalty,* 1 CIV. LIB. REV. 31 (Fall 1973).

87. Williams, at 196.

88. Ginsburg, *Some Thoughts on Benign Classification in the Context of Sex,* 10 CONN. L. REV. 813, 826–27 (1978).

2

Will Equality Require More Than Assimilation, Accommodation, or Separation from the Existing Social Structure?

NADINE TAUB
WENDY W. WILLIAMS

> Congress has now provided that tests or criteria for employment or promotion may not provide equality of opportunity merely in the sense of the fabled offer of milk to the stork and the fox. On the contrary, Congress has now required that the posture and condition of the jobseeker be taken into account. It has—to resort again to the fable—provided that the vessel in which the milk is proffered be one all seekers can use. The Act proscribes not only overt discrimination but also practices that are fair in form, but discriminatory in operation.
>
> Griggs v. Duke Power Co.[1]

Will equality require more than assimilation, accommodation, or separation from the existing social structure? From our prospective as lawyers who have worked on gender equality issues, the answer is an emphatic yes.

When we became lawyers and went to work for the women's movement in the early 1970s, we came in on the heels of the civil rights movement and, in important ways, lacked the more sophisticated comprehension of our status that blacks and others already possessed. We, and women in general, were struck—seemingly for the first time[2]—by women's bald exclusion from opportunities open to men, and we tended to view the complex of law and practice that treated women differently from men as simple miscalculations of what women's real capacities were and are. The treatment of women under a different set of rules than men seemed merely arbitrary and irrational; the approach was simply to explain, with the use of statistics and examples, that an error had been made. While we spoke of "the role-typing society had long imposed,"[3] we had not yet fully comprehended that the legal structure we saw in 1970 was not the product of misinformed legislative bodies but, rather, the expression of a powerful informing ideology, inherited from the nineteenth century, about the proper allocation of the tasks of the sexes.

Although varying somewhat in both form and content with changes in the organization of work, the essence of this "separate spheres" ideology was remarkably constant, assigning to men the role of breadwinner and family representative in the public world and to woman the role of child rearer and keeper of the home.[4] Each individual law which seemed merely irrational when looked at in isolation, made perfect sense when understood as a brick in a much larger edifice constructed to maintain the sexes in their separate spheres.[5] Underpinning and legitimizing this ideology of the separate spheres for men and women was the belief that women and men are fundamentally different kinds of human beings—physiologically, psychologically, socially, and functionally. Sex difference was not noticed for its own sake. Rather, sexually related differences were marshaled or ascribed to support sexual hierarchy. Woman's was the supportive, complementary, role; she was to provide essential services to a man and his children. She was expected to subordinate her own development and advancement to his. Federal and state law and the rules of the employment world reflected and reinforced these allocations.

Feminist litigators of the 1970s responded to the legal manifestations of the separate spheres ideology by focusing on the assertions of fundamental differences between the sexes and denying the truth or the universality of the assertions. Their insistence that the particular differences emphasized in the old ideology were socially constructed rather than innate and that, in any event, even physical differences were average rather than absolute, was an important step and a good litigation strategy. The approach made it possible to see that because there would always be similarly situated men and women, treating all women as if they were the average woman and all men as if they were the average man surely was unfair to the nonaverage woman and often the nonaverage man as well. The shorthand way of stating this idea was to say that employers and legislators could not rely on generalizations and stereotypes about the sexes. The underlying principle was that the legislature or employer could not use sex as a proxy for characteristics or functions which, though they might predominate in one sex, were not exclusive to that sex. The position was an easy one for courts to accept. Judges could view themselves as cleaning up legislative inaccuracy rather than dismantling a long-standing social policy and thwarting a venerable ideology.

The Supreme Court early on demonstrated its responsiveness to the position advocated by these litigators. In *Phillips v. Martin Marietta Corp.,*,[6] the Supreme Court's first Title VII[7] sex discrimination case, the Court declared that an employer's rule excluding mothers but not fathers of preschool-aged children from certain jobs prima facie violated Title VII. The most dramatic use of this principle, however, came a few years later when the Court held in *Los Angeles Department of Water and Power v. Manhart*[8] that an employer could not charge female employees more than male employees for their pensions, even though the *average* woman lives longer than the *average* man and therefore collects more pension dollars. Justice Stevens wrote for the Court:

> The statute's focus on the individual is unambiguous. It precludes treatment of individuals as simply components of a racial, religious, sexual or national class. If height is required for a job, a tall woman may not be refused employment merely because, on the average, women are too short. Even a true generalization about the class is an insufficient reason for disqualifying an individual to whom the generalization does not apply.[9]

Later in the opinion, he provided the policy argument:

> Even if the statutory language were less clear, the basic policy of the statute requires that we focus on fairness to individuals rather than fairness to classes. Practices that

classify employees in terms of religion, race, or sex tend to preserve traditional assumptions about groups rather than thoughtful scrutiny of individuals. The generalization involved in this case illustrates the point. Separate mortality tables are easily interpreted as reflecting innate differences between the sexes; but a significant part of the longevity differential may be explained by the social fact that men are heavier smokers than women.[10]

It would, of course, have been possible for the Court to rule, as it did in *Phillips* and *Manhart,* that the existence of a sex-based rule always makes out a prima facie case of discrimination, but simultaneously to undermine that position by an expansive reading of the bona fide occupational qualification (BFOQ) exception to Title VII's rule against sex classifications.[11] Yet despite Supreme Court performances that were alternately sloppy[12] and bizarre,[13] the lower courts have firmly and persistently declared that the BFOQ exception to Title VII is to be narrowly interpreted.[14] Average physical differences between the sexes will not constitute a BFOQ; rather, as the Fifth Circuit said in its influential *Weeks* case,[15] the employer, to establish a BFOQ, must show that all or substantially all women (or men) cannot perform the job. The Ninth Circuit went even further in *Rosenfeld,*[16] limiting the availability of the BFOQ to situations where one sex's unique physical characteristics, rather than average physical characteristics, are necessary to job performance.[17]

We also note—though we do not take the time for further elaboration—that the Supreme Court has often produced similar results under the equal protection clause. Thus, in challenges to explicitly gender-based laws, the Court has frequently presumed unconstitutionality, thereby thrusting a relatively heavy burden of justification on the laws' defenders.[18] In this way, the Court has expressed its belief that more often than not the sexes are sufficiently similar that they should be similarly treated.[19]

These well-established statutory and constitutional doctrines have proved powerful tools in righting some substantial wrongs and improving the position of women in the workplace and elsewhere. Nonetheless, an important critique has been levied against existing doctrine. The critique rests on three related points. First, the critics urge, the doctrine promotes the assimilation of women into a predefined male world[20] rather than requiring that that world change in any fundamental way to reflect the needs and wants of both sexes. Second, the doctrine's focus on the individual (often, the critics contend, the atypical woman) has the effect of masking the continuation of a serious and persistent group affliction. The atypical woman attains the right to be treated the same way as men are; the typical woman continues to labor under significant disadvantages. For example, in a workplace whose rules and patterns are based on an assumption that the standard worker has no primary parental obligations, the woman who still carries that burden herself, as the average woman does, faces serious and continuing obstacles to her work force participation. Third, and concomitantly, women's traditional nurturing role, as essential today as ever,[21] is undervalued. Some women, including feminists, may also directly fear the obliteration of group identity that comes with women's assimilation to male norms, an identity which is a source of comfort, pride and community as well as oppression. A different critique of assimilation comes from the right, which identifies a single unisex norm as the threat, with loss of sexual identity, and even heterosexual attraction, the feared consequence of assimilation.

The assimilation critique places the critics themselves in a position polar to what we shall call, for the sake of having a label, the formal equality or individual equality position, typified by *Manhart.* Like the separate sphere ideologists of old, the critics of assimilationists are prepared to advocate that women at times should be dealt with as a group rather than as individuals. This view is informed by the insight that the average woman is often ill served by a structure defined by men with men in mind. Their attack on the separate spheres ideology is leveled against sex-based hierarchy rather than different treatment of the sexes per se: They would ask whether such gender-based laws contribute to the subordination of women or to their empowerment rather than whether they unjustifiably treat women differently than similarly situated men.[22] Hierarchy is, of course, eroded by the formal equality position as well. What the formal equality approach does not directly do, however, is measure the validity or invalidity of sex-based legislation by whether it promotes hierarchy.[23]

The critique of the individual equality model has a powerful appeal. We have accomplished relatively little, it seems to us, if all we can claim is that we have guaranteed for women born tall as the average man or willing and able to adopt traditional male life patterns and habits the right to move into the male world. Surely the critics are right that for the average woman, the male-defined environment is sometimes a procrustean bed. The average woman's material position is rendered more difficult[24] and, in subtle and not so subtle ways, the essential nurturing and homemaking functions traditionally performed by women are devalued by a theory of equality under which women have gained little more than assimilation into the male sphere.

The problem with the critique, which we shall label, again for the sake of having something to call it, the *antihierarchy position,* is that its proponents cannot agree (and, more importantly, would in any event not be the ones to decide) what group-based treatment subordinates women and what group-based treatment empowers them.[25] Furthermore, Justice Stevens's observation in *Manhart*[26] that group treatment tends to reinforce perceptions of difference to the detriment of women seems, as a historical matter, unanswerable. That group treatment for the advantage of women, even when proposed and supported by women, has at best been a mixed blessing is also apparent. One need only recall protective labor legislation for women, such as the maximum hours laws which harmed women at least as much as they helped them. While many employed women viewed the hours laws as helpful, others found themselves excluded from jobs because they, unlike men, could not work the necessary hours. The chief victims of the maximum hours laws were immigrant women, women least able to interject their special perspectives into the political process.[27] The Mann Act, passed to protect women against "white slavery," was, within a short time of its passage, used to prosecute women as well;[28] the statutory rape laws, passed to protect girls and young women from being seduced into prostitution, contributed to the repression of female sexuality and punishment for deviation through the juvenile court system.[29] Indeed, in most of the cases involving discrimination against women upheld by the courts before 1971 (and since, for that matter[30]), laws which treated women differently than men were justified as beneficial to women.

Thus it would seem that not only the moral judgment that women are entitled to be treated as individuals rather than restricted because of their sex, but also the moral judgment that the group to which they belong may no longer be relegated to an inferior position, is better, although manifestly imperfectly, served by the individual, "formal equality," approach. This is so, in large part, because the perspective of predominantly male courts and legislatures on when different treatment is or is not in women's interests will differ from our own. A dual system of sex-based rights and responsibilities, however well intentioned, will preserve hierarchy.[31]

If one's only avenues of escape from the clutches of legal manifestations of the old ideology are the individual treatment/formal equality approach on the one hand or the group treatment/antihierarchy approach on the other, one might well feel compelled to choose the individual treatment route. As we shall argue shortly, the choices are not, however, thus constrained. At least under Title VII, the formal equality approach, which we endorse, is one piece in a larger scheme. Understood in its entirety, that scheme is, we submit, superior to any approach which endorses departures from a rule of gender neutrality.

Before we discuss this larger scheme, however, we must look at an issue which, in the debate just described, generates widespread disagreements today among feminist legal theorcticians and practitioners. A description of it will capture additional dimensions of the debate between those who advocate the antihierarchy approach to sex discrimination and those who subscribe to the individual equality line. That issue is how to approach pregnancy, the one incontestably significant difference between the sexes. Feminist attorneys otherwise in agreement on the general need to pursue a formal equality approach reenact the basic tensions we have just described within the debate over pregnancy; thus, that debate is a microcosm of the whole. One group advocates the position that pregnancy-based discrimination be viewed and treated as sex discrimination in the way the courts have treated other sex-based discrimination under Title VII: Discrimination for or against pregnant workers would constitute a prima facie violation, and the question would then be whether the BFOQ defense can be established.[32] (This was the approach rejected by the Supreme Court in *Gilbert*[33] and instituted by Congress through the Pregnancy Discrimination Amendment to Title VII.[34]) Under this approach, pregnant workers must be treated the same as other workers similar in their ability or inability to work. The other approach insists that pregnancy cannot be compared to anything else.[35] Some of its proponents argue, by analogy to the religious and handicap cases, that special "accommodation" is appropriate and indeed necessary for pregnant women.[36] Without such accommodation, they argue, women's particular needs and burdens are not taken into account.

Again, there is merit in both sides of the argument. Pregnancy is, in important ways, unique. Men are not starkly confronted with a conflict between procreation and employment in the way that women are. Yet at the same time, in the work context, pregnancy can be compared to other physical conditions, and doing so has yielded pregnant workers tangible benefits and protections long denied to them.[37] It also seems to us that there is a long-range attitudinal benefit for both sexes in demythologizing pregnancy by linking it in the work context with conditions that have a comparable effect on ability to work. If pregnancy and childbirth are thus conceptualized as physical events analogous to other physical events, it becomes possible clearly to distinguish the child care and rearing function from pregnancy, teasing those functions free from their inevitable conjunction with the mother so that child care can be viewed as an undertaking possible for either parent.[38]

More fundamentally, the "accommodation" concept seems to us to present built-in dangers and difficulties. As the experience with the concept in the religious and handicapped context shows, the Supreme Court uses the concept in a stingy fashion,[39] imposing almost no requirements on businesses to change their positions for the benefit of religious freedom or employment opportunities for the handicapped. The reason for this, it seems to us, is to be found in the concept of accommodation itself. The idea, in this context, is one of noblesse oblige. It presents itself as a question of how far employers will be required to deviate from "standard" procedures, laid down for their "normal" employees, in order to take account of the special problems of abnormal workers. The employer "accommodates" not because sound business practice suggests that a certain policy is warranted but because it is required to do so for entirely extrinsic social policy reasons. Not surprisingly, courts will not carry such an idea very far, and also not surprisingly, *accommodation* labels the workers to whom accommodation is made as "different," "special" and, in large part, a burden. Provisions meant to upgrade the situation of certain workers by creation of "special rights" become for them a double-edged sword.

Moreover, the "special treatment" of pregnancy position rests on a philosophic base which, for the advocate of sexual equality, has an unfortunate history, one which threatens the very idea of equality. The idea of accommodation—with all its problems—flows naturally from the conception of women's reproductive role as imposing an "extra" burden on our sex from which men are exempted. Equality for women, in their view, requires adjustment to or accommodation of this special burden that women bear. Implicit in their vision is a definition of men as the norm on whom general rules will be based and of women, insofar as they deviate from the norm, as in need of special, additional consideration.

The Supreme Court has relied on such a vision, with detrimental consequences. Early in the century, that vision provided the rationale for protective labor legislation in *Muller v. Oregon.*[40] In recent years, it brought us *General Electric Co. v. Gilbert,* in which the Court found that the exclusion of pregnancy-related disabilities from an otherwise comprehensive disability program did not discriminate against women because pregnancy disabilities are "an additional risk, unique to women,"[41] and *Michael M. v. Superior Court,*[42] in which the Court upheld a law under which teenage boys but not teenage girls could be punished for consensual sexual intercourse, explaining that because pregnancy deterred "young females" from sexual intercourse, while no "similar natural sanction" deterred males, "a criminal sanction imposed solely upon males . . . serves roughly to 'equalize' the deterrents on the sexes."[43]

Yet despite such dangers, when caught in a system where male attributes are in fact treated as the norm, one is tempted to develop principles to justify the occasional accommodations that are made to women's "differences." One feels, once again, on the horns of a dilemma, caught between the demands of individual equality and group needs. On the one hand, it is apparent that traditionally excluded and disadvantaged groups (such as pregnant workers) may require certain reforms in the workplace, such as a leave period sufficient to encompass the recovery period from childbirth or a right to return to the same job. On the other hand, it seems that attempts to recognize and institute special rules for their benefit automatically harms as well as helps them.

Are we, then, doomed forever to oscillate between dualities—group versus individual equality, assimilation versus accommodation, "formal"equality versus "real" equality? Or is there a way to move legal doctrine beyond these dualities to some richer synthesis?

As suggested earlier, we believe there is, and that the answer may lie, at least in part, in revitalizing the *Griggs* doctrine of disparate effects. This may seem a somewhat peculiar idea, given that the Supreme Court seems—far from seeking to flesh out the implications of that doctrine—in a mood to undo it.[44] Nonetheless, when one looks at the dilemma posed above, the importance of a disparate effects doctrine becomes apparent.[45] Equality doctrine as spelled out by the Court in cases such as *Manhart* will result, in most cases, in the invalidation of sex-based employer rules. Employers are thereby restricted to neutral formulations in order to accomplish the goals they originally sought to attain through a sex-based formulation. Sometimes this restriction will cause the employer to reevaluate its stance and result in neutral rules that are fair to both sexes. But if the critics who worry about assimilation of women to male norms are correct, and we believe they sometimes are, what the employer may substitute is a rule which is sex neutral on its face but not at all neutral in the way it affects male and female employees. If the employer is also required to adopt truly neutral rather than merely facially neutral rules, we have, by definition, a powerful corrective to the tendency of formal equality requirements to result only in women's assimilation into a male-defined environment. We have, to rephrase, a doctrine that is explicitly sensitive to group inequality and which is capable of ensuring that the requirement of formal equality is more than a hollow promise.

Moreover, a broader educational benefit may flow from courts' cumulative experience in examining facially neutral rules and the justifications offered to sustain them. Courts, over time, have helped make the point that facially discriminatory classifications are often the "accidental by-product of traditional ways of thinking about females."[46] So, too, the process of evaluating so-called neutral rules may lead courts to expose the widespread and unquestioned use of white male norms as *the* frame of reference in the public sphere.

The immediate benefits of the *Griggs* analysis are well illustrated when that analysis is applied to the problem of pregnancy. Under the formal equality approach, pregnant workers can be treated no worse than others similar in their ability or inability to work. At the same time, they can be treated no better. Special rules to accommodate their special needs are not permitted, in the absence of establishment of a BFOQ, for reasons we have already discussed. If formal equality were the only promise of Title VII, these workers would be left to cope with a workplace structured and defined by the traditional, typical male worker. To the extent their needs could be met by existing benefit structures, formal equality would require that they must be. To the extent their needs could not be met, the law would abandon them to the consequences. Like the stork that Aesop's fox invited to dinner, they would be unable to partake in the meal because the vessel in which it is offered is one out of which they cannot eat.

Disparate effects doctrine addresses the assimilation problem without resorting to an accommodation approach under which special, exceptional rules are created for special needs. Where an employer's rule has a substantially disproportionate effect (and, we must here add, the employer cannot make out the business necessity defense),[47] the relief the court grants is the invalidation of the rule, not just as applied to pregnant workers, but to everyone.[48] The employer is free to meet its needs by adopting a new, more truly neutral rule. In the pregnancy context, this would mean that the remedy for a disability policy that is routinely inadequate to meet the basic leave demands of workers who become pregnant is a leave policy that does meet those needs.[49] In the process, the workplace tilt toward the male model has been readjusted to encompass the needs of the typical woman worker (typical because approximately 85 percent of women workers will be pregnant at some point in their work lives[50]). The tendency of disparate effects theory is to force the employer to modify the male-defined workplace so as to encompass the experience of both sexes. Disparate effects doctrine thus encourages an androgynous[51] rather than male model in the workplace.

There is, of course, resistance to the disparate effects doctrine, stemming, we believe, from three related concerns: the absence of a requirement that "intent" be proved as an element of discrimination, the costs that may result, and the lack of immediately apparent limits on the doctrine's sweep. An intent standard that assures us that the defendants will be asked to make changes only if they have willfully embarked upon a morally unacceptable course sits more comfortably with traditional notions of fairness.[52] Cost concerns are tied to the intent problem: Resistance to imposing costs on employers grows the further one moves from acts consciously motivated by gender bias. The third problem results from the perception that an enormous number of perfectly acceptable rules and laws might have a disparate effect and that the doctrine thus, simply put, jeopardizes too much.[53]

Given these problems, it is hardly surprising that the equal protection clause has been limited by an intent standard narrowly defined[54] and that at least some members of the Supreme Court seem to be trying to bring intent into the *Griggs* doctrine through the back door, at the plaintiff's rebuttal stage.[55] Nevertheless, for the reasons stated, we view the disparate effects approach as crucial to achieving real equality. Thus, irrespective of developments in the equal protection context, every effort must be made to maintain the doctrine's vitality as a matter of Title VII law: Only a true business necessity should be permitted to justify a neutral rule having a disparate impact. To this end, it seems essential to renew the collective understanding that an employer's use of exclusionary "neutral" practices is both unfair and counterproductive from a societal perspective. Historically, this understanding seems most likely to emerge in cases where some awareness, if not conscious exploitation, of facially discriminatory practices can be attributed to the employer. Indeed, the Supreme Court first endorsed disparate impact doctrine under Title VII in a race discrimination case challenging diploma requirements and testing practices that easily evoked our well known and shameful history of *de jure* school segregation. However, as the most obvious forms of intentional discrimination recede into the past, it becomes harder to call upon the sense of injustice associated with those practices.[56]

A number of us working in the women's rights area think that our relatively newly won insights—that our society has been thoroughly organized around sex-based assumptions and that in particular, the workplace has been constructed using male experiences and norms—may provide a way to renew that sense of collective understanding.[57] We start with the perception that the same assumptions, beliefs, predilections, ways of looking at the world that yield overtly sex-based rules also result in rules that are neutral on their face but have a discriminatory effect. The old notion that a household was properly composed of a male breadwinner and a female homemaker manifested itself in bygone days in rules that excluded married women from employment; today it manifests itself more subtly in rules providing benefits to the "primary breadwinner" or head of household. Like machine and tool specifications based on the dimensions of the average male body, no-leave and other personnel policies that fail to take account of child bearing and child rearing needs also reflect the assumptions that only men, indeed, only men in traditionally organized families, belong in the workplace. In short, our hope is that by stressing the common origin of facial discrimination and neutral rules with disparate impact, we can revive a commitment to eliminating real barriers to women's full societal participation. Whether we call this analysis an intent analysis or an effect analysis or something else, the point we wish to convey is that there must be a mechanism, tied to the subtle and sophisticated realities that produce our divided world, sensitive enough to identify and correct for the male model.

In the sex discrimination context, we have spoken of the male model of the typical worker. But the model is, of course, not only male but also white, able bodied, English speaking, and a member of a mainstream religion. The norms which form the basis for the model reflect a variety of assumptions about particular places for particular kinds of people. Each excluded group has its own history. Consequently, the package of assumptions about each group represents its own mix of conscious animus and unquestioned internalized belief systems about appropriate roles.[58] This mix, however, is being transformed by the presence of legal proscriptions on facially discriminatory practices. As many participants in this conference have noted,[59] subtle forms of discrimination now take the place of blatant manifestations of conscious animus. Moreover, segregation and subordination of minorities persist. Under these conditions, norms and expectations are understandably established by the dominant group based on their characteristics and experiences. Thus, even for groups whose histories have been shaped primarily by overt hostility and repression, the problem of internalized and unquestioned assumptions is increasingly important. For this reason, we believe our approach to revitalizing *Griggs* also has value beyond the field of gender equality.[60]

The great virtue of the *Griggs* doctrine, as originally articulated and still applied by many lower courts, was and is that in effect, it creates a substantive presumption: If the plaintiff demonstrates that an apparently neutral rule has a substantially disproportionate racial or gender-based effect, the burden of persuasion shifts to the employer. Significantly, the burden imposed on the employer is to show business necessity for the policy. Thus, the substantive power of the presumption lies not only in the fact that it shifts the burden of persuasion but also, importantly, in its implicit recognition of the intent standard's inability to sort acceptable from unacceptable motives: The employer's defense is not that it did not intend the lopsided effects it created but that its policy was essential to its business. A policy essential to one's legitimate business is both by definition tailored to legitimate business concerns and highly unlikely to rest upon race or gender-based considerations or assumptions.

As critical as we believe it is to preserve *Griggs* intact, we appreciate the possibility that as a practical and political matter, drawing on the common origin of neutral and facially discriminatory exclusionary rules may not suffice to overcome the fear that the disparate impact analysis lacks meaningful limits. Thus, as a secondary approach, we would seek to overcome this concern by identifying acceptable limits. Our perception that overt sex-based classifications and many neutral rules having a disparate negative effect on women flow from the same assumptions, beliefs, ways of looking at the world is also the source of the limiting principle we see as capable of counteracting concerns about the reach of disparate impact analysis. Practices which load the dice in the old ways should be discarded precisely because they do just that. At a minimum, then, those neutral rules which are traceable to, build on, reproduce, or perpetuate the old notions and hierarchies must be justified by a business necessity.[61] Moreover, in keeping with established Title VII principles, the employer should bear the burden of showing that the "neutral" rule at issue did not reflect or perpetuate old hierarchies.[62]

Two illustrations will help describe the contours of this limiting principle. Consider first a fringe benefit policy that affords insurance coverage to an employee's dependents only when the employee is the "head of household." Policies of this sort are particularly egregious when they provide that a woman shall be recognized as head of household only when there is no male present in the household. But even absent an overtly sex-based limitation of this sort, such policies have a disparate impact on women. Further, they reflect and perpetuate the notion that only one income—the male's—is primary, when both incomes are likely to be essential to the family's economic well-being. For this reason, such policies, according to the limiting principle, must be justified by a business necessity. Consider next an employer who institutes a technological advance, such as computerized word processing, that leads to a reduction in jobs held predominantly by women. Here, too, the policy in question disproportionately affects women employees. However, because it is difficult to link the practice with assumptions or notions about women's proper place, it would probably not require special justification.

Will identifying the root of built-in bias suffice to stem fears of limitless disruption of acceptable rules and to justify the imposition of the substantial costs that correcting the dominant model might ultimately entail? Obviously this is a difficult question. We must, at a minimum, stress the fairness of our approach, emphasizing that the refusal to reexamine one's practices so as to eliminate bias is morally quite close to engaging in intentional bad acts.

Cost, however, remains a problem worthy of detailed consideration. We initially thought to respond to the problem of cost by noting that as the workforce reaches 50 percent female, there simply is no justification for acting as if the typical worker is male. This is particularly true when one observes the enormous influx of women into the workplace and recognizes the social significance of that movement.[63] The basic functions performed under the old order—economic support of the family, maintenance of the home, and, crucially important, the care of children—still must be performed. With both parents in the work force it seems elementary that the workplace must be restructured to accommodate the new reality. The state and the private sector will necessarily be implicated in those changes.

But this justification for a renewed or revised *Griggs* doctrine is itself fraught with dangers, because it relies crucially upon numbers. Women make up almost half of the work force. Racial minorities, older people, the handicapped, to give a few examples, do not. At what point are costs considered unjustified because they benefit too small a minority of workers? A striking illustration of the difficulty of this calculation is the federal government's experiment with requiring the installation of lifts on buses to accommodate those confined to wheelchairs.[64] Our model must provide guidelines for determining when costs are justified.

We suggest that numbers don't tell us as much as they might appear to: the benefits of restructuring are not always easily measured in dollars. We have been impressed by the degree to which the search for truly neutral rules and policies results in a broader understanding of common interests and sounder overall policies. The requirement that pregnancies be treated like other disabilities has, for example, led to cretive new approaches to disabilities which benefit a larger class of workers than those who become pregnant.[65] Problems, redefined, can capture broader needs and suggest broader and sounder solutions. As other participants in this conference have noted, revisions in management training, hiring, and promotion procedures to minimize racial bias result in generally more effective and efficient personnel procedures. Those ramps and retooled street corners, created to accommodate the handicapped, serve every person pushing a baby carriage or shopping cart, temporarily on crutches, vision impaired, or restricted by age.

A final note about the employer's burden. Proffered business necessities must be scrutinized to ascertain whether they too incorporate old notions of proper roles. For example, the business necessity proffered to justify a minimum height requirement for airline pilots is usually the seemingly compelling concern that pilots be able to reach the instrument panel. Yet when one considers that cockpit design has been based on male specifications on the assumption that their incumbents will be male and that such design "imperatives" have constituted no barrier in countries in which male pilots have smaller average heights than in the United States, the justification for the rule that excludes so many women from employment is in fact far from compelling.

The concept of alternatives will prove particularly useful to the scrutiny of proffered justifications, and a refurbished *Griggs* doctrine should put great emphasis on that concept. The need to consider the various ways a legitimate goal may be achieved will expose and help overcome the possibly unconsciously made yet biased assumptions that underlie exclusionary practices. Thus, even if an employer's need to accomplish a goal leads to a neutral rule with a disproportionate effect, if there is an alternative way of achieving that goal, one which avoids or mitigates the effect, the employer should be required to employ the alternative. At present, however, despite the tenacity of the *Lorillard*[66] formulation in some circuits, the Supreme Court seems to be moving away from a disparate impact approach that makes the employer's alternatives a key question. Not only has the Supreme Court made the existence of alternatives part of the plaintiff's burden on rebuttal,[67] but its language in certain opinions suggests that the relevance of alternatives may be limited to showing an intent to discriminate.[68] Given the close connection between conscious and unconscious discrimination, this development of the law is indeed unfortunate, and we hope that an awareness of the closeness of that connection will help revive a commitment to this aspect of the *Griggs* formulation as well. It should be clear, then, that we do not mean to advocate that current widely accepted formulations of the *Griggs* doctrine should be abandoned and a test constructed upon our suggestion substituted for it. Rather, our suggestion is meant as an additional rationale for its preservation. If the day does come when *Griggs* is abandoned, we offer our formulation as a principled place to halt the erosion of an effects standard. Moreover, we see in our test the potential for expanding the concept of equality under the equal protection clause and, if ratified, the equal rights amendment.

Finally, faced with an administration less attuned than its predecessors to civil rights concerns and dedicated to appointment of a federal judiciary that reflects its ideological bent, it may well be that the federal courts will no longer be a place to go for vindication of civil rights. Even if that proves to be true, we believe that the effort to revitalize and rearticulate our basic premises is an important one. The perceptions acquired through the civil rights movement, ones which we have tried to describe here, can be the basis for formulating workplace rules, through collective bargaining or other kinds of negotiation with employers, and for providing shape and content to legislation proposed to solve problems with which courts will no longer contend.

Notes

The authors thank Clifford Zimmerman, Rutgers Law School, Class of 1985, for his research assistance.

1. 401 U.S. 424, 431 (1971).

2. We had, as a group, almost no knowledge of the women's movement, a movement whose life extended for more than three-quarters of a century during the century that directly preceded our own. Since then, a women's history movement has blossomed, and our past is being steadily recaptured.

3. Finally picked up by Justice Blackmun in Stanton v. Stanton, 421 U.S. 7, 15 (1975), this phrase, and variations on it, appeared regularly in women's rights briefs in the late 1960s and early

1970s. *See, e.g.,* Brief for Appellants, at 4, 5, 10, 15, 25, Kahn v. Shevin, 416 U.S. 351 (1974); American Civil Liberties Union at 7, 18, 24, 29, 40, Frontiero v. Richardson, 411 U.S. 677 (1973); Brief for Appellants, at 21, 46, Reed v. Reed, 404 U.S. 71 (1971).

4. *See, e.g.,* N. COTT, THE BONDS OF WOMANHOOD: "WOMAN'S SPHERE" IN NEW ENGLAND, 1780-1835 (1977) (describes ideology and content of women's separate sphere); Bradwell v. State, 83 U.S. (16 Wall.) 130, 141 (1872) ("The constitution of the family organization, which is founded in the divine ordinance, as well as in the nature of things, indicates the domestic sphere as that which properly belongs to the domain and functions of womanhood").

Compare G. GILDER, SEXUAL SUICIDE 59 (1973) (Gilder says, for example, "Deprived of his role as provider and protector, the man, like males all over the world throughout human history, will leave. As a general rule of anthropology the likelihood of his presence in the home decreases in direct proportion to the aggressiveness of the woman.") *See also* B. BERGER AND P. BERGER, THE WAR OVER THE FAMILY: CAPTURING THE MIDDLE GROUND (1983). Of course, the "separate spheres" ideology had an economic basis as well. As twentieth-century economic changes rendered the separation of male and female spheres less viable, the numbers of women who perceived themselves harmed by enforced separation grew.

5. *E.g.,* laws creating a preference for men as estate administrators (Reed v. Reed, 404 U.S. 71 (1971)); prohibiting women from tending bar (Sail'er Inn, Inc. v. Kirby, 5 Cal. 3d 1, 485 P.2d 529, 95 Cal. Rptr. 329 (1971)); punishing males but not females under the age of 18 for sexual intercourse (Michael M. v. Superior Court, 450 U.S. 464 (1981)); permitting unwed mothers but not unwed fathers to sue for the wrongful death of their children (Parham v. Hughes, 441 U.S. 347 (1979)); excusing all women from jury service (Hoyt v. Florida, 368 U.S. 57 (1961)); treating women as adults at a younger age than men for civil purposes, but reversing the treatment for purposes of the criminal law (*see, e.g.,* Stanton v. Stanton, 421 U.S. 7 (1975); Craig v. Boren, 429 U.S. 190 (1976); Lamb v. Brown, 456 F.2d 18 (10th Cir. 1972).

Some commentators still view sex discrimination as primarily involving legislative miscalculation. *See, e.g.,* J. ELY, DEMOCRACY AND DISTRUST: A THEORY OF JUDICIAL REVIEW 157, 164 (1980) (prejudice against women usually involves a legislative generalization whose incidence of counter-example is significantly higher than the legislative authority thought it was).

6. 400 U.S. 542 (1971).

7. 42 U.S.C. §§ 2000e to 2000e-17 (1982).

8. 435 U.S. 702 (1978).

9. *Id.* at 708.

10. *Id.* at 709–10.

11. 42 U.S.C. § 2000e-2(e) (1982).

12. The Court said, in Phillips v. Martin Marietta Corp., 400 U.S. at 544, that "the existence of such conflicting family obligations, if demonstrably more relevant to job performance for a woman than for a man, could arguably be a basis for distinction under [the BFOQ section] of the Act." Justice Marshall was sufficiently concerned about the implications of this dictum to file a concurring opinion in which he stated, "When performance characteristics of an individual are involved, even when parental roles are concerned, employment opportunity may be limited only by employment criteria that are neutral as to the sex of the applicant." *Id.* at 547. In other words, rules about absenteeism rather than mothers were required. He pointed out that to hold otherwise would be to permit the BFOQ exception to swallow the rule. *Id.* at 545.

13. Dothard v. Rawlinson, 433 U.S. 321 (1977). The Court, per Justice Stewart, declared that women were rendered incapable of maintaining security, the essential duty of a prison guard in a male maximum security prison, because of their "very womanhood." What Stewart meant to convey by this euphemism is not entirely clear, but he seems to have meant that women, because they were women, would be the "natural" objects of male prisoners' sexual attacks and thus were "inherently" disruptive in the male prison context. Justice Marshall's protest, in dissent, that the majority's approach was based on "'ancient canards'" about women, went unheeded. *Id.* at 343 (*quoting* Phillips v. Martin Marietta Corp., 400 U.S. 542, 545 (1970)).

14. In practice, the one major deviation from this general rule has been in cases where airline flight attendants have challenged rules grounding them as soon as it was discovered that they were pregnant. *See, e.g.,* Burwell v. Eastern Air Lines, Inc., 633 F.2d 361 (4th Cir. 1980) (en banc) *cert. denied,* 450 U.S. 965 (1981).

15. Weeks v. Southern Bell Tel. & Tel. Co., 408 F.2d 228, 235 (5th Cir. 1969).

16. Rosenfeld v. Southern Pac. Co., 444 F.2d 1219 (9th Cir. 1971).

17. *Id.* at 1224–25. Perhaps the Supreme Court's holding in Dothard v. Rawlinson, 433 U.S. 321 (1977), that woman's very womanhood (presumably the possession of a vagina) rendered her unable to perform the job of prison guard because of the inevitable sexual assaults by male inmates was a crude attempt at the *Rosenfeld* approach.

18. The standard for upholding the constitutionality of a statutory classification, announced in a plurality opinion by Justice Brennan in Craig v. Boren, 429 U.S. 190, 197 (1976), was that in sex discrimination cases, the defender of a statute must establish that the governmental objective is "important," and that the sex-based legislation is "substantially related" to the governmental purpose. Some of the justices, however, have never subscribed to the Brennan approach, and their opinions uphold sex-based legislation. *See, e.g.,* Parham v. Hughes, 441 U.S. 347 (1979) (Stewart, J.); Michael M. v. Superior Ct., 450 U.S. 464 (1981) (Rehnquist, J.); Rostker v. Goldberg, 453 U.S. 57 (1981) (Rehnquist, J.). The standards used by the various factions of the Court in sex discrimination cases brought under the equal protection clause are described and discussed in Freedman, *Sex Equality, Sex Difference and the Supreme Court,* 92 YALE L.J. 913 (1984).

19. *See, e.g.,* Kirshberg v. Feenstra, 450 U.S. 455, 461 (1981); Wengler v. Druggist Mut. Ins. Co., 446 U.S. 142, 151 (1980); Craig v. Boren, 429 U.S. 190, 199 (1976).

20. *But see* Kay, *Models of Equality,* 1985 ILL. L. REV. 39 (1985), for an important corrective to this one-way assimilation view. She points out that in the sex cases assimilation has been a two-way street: women have sought to be treated like men in the public sphere, and men have sought equal treatment with women in the family setting. Her observation does not entirely undercut the critics' position, however. Since women still carry most of the burden in the area of child rearing and housework, while they also seek to participate in the public world, the difficulties described in the text below persist; to the extent men engage in child rearing and housework, they too may experience difficulties in a workplace constructed for the traditional man who had no such responsibilities.

21. *See generally* Taub, *From Parental Leaves to Nurturing Leaves,* 13 N.Y.U. REV. L. & SOC. CHANGE 381 (Fall 1985).

22. *See, e.g.,* C. MACKINNON, SEXUAL HARASSMENT OF WORKING WOMEN 101–41 (1979).

23. The basic nondiscrimination principle is, of course, supplemented by affirmative action where appropriate. Notice here that affirmative action is not the same as the group-based treatment advocated by the opponents of assimilation. Affirmative action assumes that the sexes are inherently similar and resorts to group-based treatment solely to overcome an artificial inequality created by discrimination. Affirmative action, in theory at least, self-destructs when the group is brought up to the starting line with everyone else. It is thus an adjunct to the equal treatment, rather than a manifestation of the group treatment, approach. (This is not to say that one of the dangers of group treatment—reenforcement of stereotypes—is not present, but it is minimized by the underlying rationale and limited nature of affirmative action.)

24. To take one urgent example from outside the employment context, to turn women loose after divorce with custody of children and minimal child support, on the theory that they can function as wage earners in the same way men can, is to fail to reckon with women's generally lower wage-earning capacity and the constraints single parenthood places on employment opportunity. Of such difficulties is the "feminization of poverty" constructed. *See* Weitzman, *The Economics of Divorce: Social and Economic Consequences of Property, Alimony & Child Support Awards,* 28 UCLA L. REV. 1181 (1981).

25. Judges and legislators would be the decisionmakers; their record on discerning what benefits and what hurts women is uneven, to say the least. For some recent examples, see Michael M. v.

Superior Ct., 450 U.S. 464 (1981); Kahn v. Shevin, 416 U.S. 351 (1974); Califano v. Goldfarb, 430 U.S. 199 (1977).

This point is elaborated in Taub, *Book Review*, 80 Colum. L. Rev. 1686, 1691–92 and n.16 (1980).

26. *See* note 10 and accompanying text.

27. Landes, *The Effect of State Maximum-Hours Laws on the Employment of Women in 1920*, 88 J. Pol. Econ. 476 (1980) (employment of foreign-born women was reduced by as much as 30 percent in some states; employment of native white women was largely unaffected). The maximum hours laws also caused women in nontraditional jobs to lose those jobs because they could not work the longer hours required of male employees, thereby promoting occupational sex segregation. In addition, the laws probably depressed wages of segregated women's jobs. B. Babcock, A. Freedman, E. Norton, and S. Ross, Sex Discrimination and the Law: Causes and Remedies 36 (1975).

28. *See generally* Note, *The White Slave Traffic Act: The Historical Impact of a Criminal Law Policy on Women*, 72 Geo. L.J. 1111, 1119–22 (1984). Some commentators fear that the pornography-as-civil-rights-violation ordinances, such as that struck down by the federal court in American Booksellers Association, Inc. v. Hudnut, 771 F.2d 323 (7th Cir. 1985), *aff'd*, 106 S.Ct. 1172 (1986), if allowed to stand, will similarly be used against women. *See generally* Duggan, Hunter, and Vance, *False Promises: Anti-Pornography Legislation in the United States*, in Women Against Censorship (V. Burstyn ed., 1985).

29. Walkowitz, *Male Vice and Female Virtue: Feminism and the Politics of Prostitution in Nineteenth Century Britain*, in Powers of Desire 419–38 (A. Snitow, C. Stansell, and S. Thompson eds. 1983); Gorham, *The "Maiden Tribute of Modern Babylon" Re-examined: Child Prostitution and the Idea of Childhood in Late Victorian England*, 21 Victorian Stud. 353, 363, 365 (1978) (describes tension between desire to "protect" young women and to control them); J. Weeks, Sex, Politics and Society: The Regulation of Sexuality Since 1880 81–93 (1981); J. Walkowitz, Prostitution and Victorian Society: Women, Class and the State 17, 247 (1980) (increase in statutory rape age gave police greater summary jurisdiction over poor working women and children).

30. *See, e.g.*, Michael M. v. Superior Ct., 450 U.S. 464 (1981); Kahn v. Shevin, 416 U.S. 351 (1974).

31. See Brown, Emerson, Falk, and Freedman, *The Equal Rights Amendment: A Constitutional Basis for Equal Rights for Women*, 80 Yale L.J. 871, 889–93 (1971), for another articulation of this conclusion.

32. *See, e.g.*, Brief of amicus curiae American Civil Liberties Union et al., Miller-Wohl Co. v. Commissioner, 692 p. 20 1243 (Mont. 1984); Brief of National Organization for Women et al., amici curiae. California Fed. Sav. & Loan Ass'n v. Guerra, Nos. 84–5842 and 84–5844 (9th Cir. Oct. 1984).

33. General Elec. Corp. v. Gilbert, 429 U.S. 125 (1976).

34. 42 U.S.C. § 2000e(k) (1982).

35. *See, e.g.*, Scales, *Towards a Feminist Jurisprudence*, 56 Ind. L.J. 375, 422, 435–37 (1981); Krieger & Cooney, *The Miller-Wohl Controversy: Equal Treatment, Positive Action and the Meaning of Women's Equality*, 13 Golden Gate U. L. Rev. 513, 515 (1983), Note, *Sexual Equality Under the Pregnancy Discrimination Act*, 83 Colum. L. Rev. 690, 707–09 (1983); Law, *Rethinking Sex and the Constitution*, 132 Pa. L. Rev. 955, 1007 (1984); Kay, *Equality and Difference: The Case of Pregnancy*, 1 Berk, Women's L.J. (1985).

36. Krieger & Cooney, at 558–60; Note, *Sexual Equality Under the Pregnancy Discrimination Act*, at 717–19. *Cf.* E. Wolgast, Equality and the Rights of Women 47–49 (1980). Neither Professor Scales nor Professor Law relies on the analogy.

37. *See, e.g.*, Williams, *Equality's Riddle: Pregnancy and the Equal Treatment-Special Treatment Debate*, 13 N.Y.U. Rev. L. & Soc. Change 325 (1985); S. Kamerman and A. Kahn, Maternity Policies and Working Women 50–52, 60–62, 74–76 (1983).

38. A legislative proposal embodying this concept has been introduced in the House of Representatives. HR 2020 (Apr. 4, 1985) 99th Cong., 1st Sess., reintroduced as H.R. 4300, 99th Cong., 2d Sess. (March 4, 1986). Under the proposal, employees would acquire a federal right to return to the same or similar jobs following temporary disability (including pregnancy-related disability) and parents would be entitled to a leave in conjunction with the birth, adoption, or serious illness of a child. CONGRESSIONAL CAUCUS FOR WOMEN'S ISSUES, FACT SHEET ON PARENTAL LEAVE 2 (1984).

39. *See, e.g.*, Board of Educ. v. Rowley, 458 U.S. 176 (1982) (when it passed the Education of the Handicapped Act, Congress did not intend to require a state to maximize the potential of each handicapped child commensurate with the opportunity provided nonhandicapped children but, rather, sought only to provide them with access to a free public education); Southeastern Community College v. Davis, 442 U.S. 397 (1979) (§ 504 of the Rehabilitation Act of 1973 imposes no requirement upon an educational institution to lower or effect substantial modifications of its standards in order to accommodate handicapped persons); Transworld Airlines, Inc. v. Hardison, 432 U.S. 63 (1977) (discharge of employee who refused to work on Saturday sabbath upheld; accommodation requirement of Title VII does not extend to imposing more than de minimis cost on employer).

40. The Court explained, 208 U.S. 412, 422 (1908):

> Though limitations upon personal and contractual rights may be removed by legislation, there is that in her disposition and habits of life which will operate against full assertion of those rights. She will still be where some legislation to protect her seems necessary to secure a real equality of right.

41. 429 U.S. at 139.

42. 450 U.S. at 464 (1981).

43. *Id.* at 473.

44. *See, e.g.*, New York Transit Auth. v. Beazer, 440 U.S. 568, 584–87 (1979); Albemarle Paper Co. v. Moody, 422 U.S. 405, 425 (1975). In both *Beazer* and *Moody,* the majority stated that the plaintiff's rebuttal burden is that of showing that the employer's business necessity defense is a "pretext." The pretext notion has traditionally been associated with the intent standard. *See, e.g.,* McDonnell Douglas v. Green, 411 U.S. 792, 804 (1973); Texas Dept. of Community Affairs v. Burdine, 450 U.S. 248, 254–56 (1981).

45. The mere fact that it is "important," does not, of course, guarantee its acceptance. As part of existing Title VII doctrine, it can be strengthened and rerationalized. But such a doctrine has been squarely rejected under the equal protection clause. Washington v. Davis, 426 U.S. 229, 239–45 (1976). Its resurrection there depends on an argument that such a doctrine is a necessary and proper outgrowth of the equality guarantee of that amendment. Proponents of the equal rights amendment have argued that its central principle is that rights, privileges, duties, and responsibilities of persons should not be assigned on account of sex. Furthermore, they have asserted that this fundamental principle requires recognition that "government policies, practices or laws which classify on some neutral basis but which have a disproportionate negative effect on one sex only are under certain circumstances prohibited." EQUAL RIGHTS AMENDMENT POSITION PAPER (DRAFT) 4–5 (unpub., Fall 1983) (authored by a coalition of feminists; on reserve at the *Rutgers Civil Rights Developments* office). *See also* Segal, *Sexual Equality, the Equal Protection Clause, and the ERA,* 33 BUFFALO L. REV. 85, 130–46 (1984). Suzanna Sherry makes a similar argument with respect to the equal protection clause in *Selective Judicial Activism in the Equal Protection Context: Democracy, Distrust, and Deconstruction,* 73 GEO. L.J. 89, 118–20 (1984). *See also* Eisenberg, *Disproportionate Impact and Illicit Motive: Theories of Constitutional Adjudication,* 52 N.Y.U. L. REV. 36 (1977).

46. Califano v. Goldfarb, 430 U.S. 199, 223 (1977) (Stevens, J., concurring).

47. *See, e.g.,* Dothard v. Rawlinson, 433 U.S. 321 (1977).

48. in *Griggs,* 401 U.S. 424, 436, *Albemarle,* 422 U.S. 405, 435–36, and *Dothard,* 433 U.S. 321,

331–32, the Supreme Court held that facially neutral policies with a disproportionate effect should be struck down.

49. *See* EEOC Guidelines on Pregnancy, 29 C.F.R. § 1604.10(c) (1984) ("Where the termination of an employee who is temporarily disabled is caused by an employment policy under which insufficient or no leave is available, such a termination violates the Act if it has a disparate impact on employees of one sex and is not justified by business necessity"). *See also* Abraham v. Graphic Arts Int'l Union, 660 F.2d 811 (D.C. Cir. 1981).

50. S. Kamerman and A. Kahn, at 5.

51. Androgynous is defined in *Webster's New Collegiate Dictionary* as "having the characteristics or nature of both male and female." The botanical definition captures the image: "having both staminate and pistillate flowers in the same cluster."

52. Concern with the defendant's mental state may, of course, be challenged from society's, as well as from the victim's, perspective. In terms of obtaining the maximum contribution from every member of society, it should matter little whether obstacles encountered by particular groups are the product of conscious animus or unconsciously absorbed bias.

53. *See, e.g.,* Washington v. Davis, 426 U.S. 229, 248 (1976).

54. *See, e.g.,* Personnel Adm'r of Mass. v. Feeney, 442 U.S. 256 (1979); Arlington Heights v. Metropolitan Hous. Corp., 429 U.S. 252 (1977); Washington v. Davis, 426 U.S. 229 (1976).

55. *See* note 44.

56. But of course, note the continued acceptance of certain forms of facial discrimination. *See, e.g.,* Rostker v. Goldberg, 453 U.S. 57 (1981); Michael M. v. Superior Court, 450 U.S. 464 (1981); Geduldig v. Aiello, 417 U.S. 484 (1974). *See* Freedman, *Williams, The Equality Crisis: Some Reflections on Culture, Courts and Feminism,* 7 WOMEN'S RIGHTS L. REP. 175 (1982).

57. *See* EQUAL RIGHTS AMENDMENT POSITION PAPER (DRAFT), at 6–9; *Equal Rights Amendment: Hearings on H.R.J. Res. 1 Before the Subcomm. on Civil and Constitutional Rights of the House Judiciary Comm.,* 98th Cong., 1st Sess (1983) (testimony of Ann Freedman) (copy on reserve at *Rutgers Civil Rights Developments* office); Segal, *Sexual Equality, The Equal Protection Clause, and the ERA,* 33 BUFFALO L. REV. 85 (1984).

58. There is substantial social science literature describing and documenting the existence and functioning of such belief systems. *See, e.g.,* F. J. DAVIS, MINORITY-DOMINANT RELATIONS 44–52 (1978); H. EHRLICH, THE SOCIAL PSYCHOLOGY OF PREJUDICE 20–57 (1973); E. GOFFMAN, STIGMA 5 (1963); G. ALLPORT, THE NATURE OF PREJUDICE 6–15, 33–34 (1954).

59. *See, e.g.,* Pettigrew, *New Patterns of Racism: The Different Worlds of 1964 and 1984,* 37 RUGTERS L. REV./1 CIV. RTS. DEVS. 673 (1985).

60. Congress, when it amended Title VII in 1972 to include public employers, approved of the emergence of the *Griggs* doctrine, explaining its new awareness that "the problem [is] in terms of 'systems' and 'effects' rather than simply intentional wrongs." H. REP. NO. 92–238, 92d Cong., 2d Sess., *reprinted in* 1972 U.S. CODE CONG. & AD. NEWS 2137, 2144. While the point seems both important and correct, we make a somewhat different one (or perhaps offer an explanation for the phenomenon Congress identified): namely, that systems as well as individual rules are infected by a point of view that is both white and male and which fails adequately to incorporate the realities and concerns of nonwhites and women).

61. Our preference would be to maintain the original *Griggs* approach, which simply required that neutral rules with a disparate effect be job related or else eliminated. For equal protection clause purposes, however, we believe that such a test is appropriately tied to the substantive aims of the clause and would constitute a sufficiently tolerable limit on the otherwise open-ended neutral rule doctrine that should be adopted by the court.

62. In her 1983 congressional testimony regarding the proposed federal ERA, Professor Ann Freedman articulated the limiting principle as distinguishing sex discriminatory impact that is "traceable to and reinforces, or perpetuates, discriminatory patterns similar to those associated with facial discrimination." *Hearings,* at 60. *See also* Segal, at 137–42. In the ERA context, however, the

plaintiff would probably bear the burden of showing that the limiting principle had been satisfied. Professor Freedman gave, as an example of a neutral rule that would *not* be invalid under the equal rights amendment, the progressive income tax. Even though the system may have a disproportionate effect on men, who pay a disproportionate share of the income tax, the effect is attributable to their higher average earnings, hardly the result of discrimination against them.

63. The participation rate of women rose from 19.6 percent in 1890 to 59.9 percent in 1980, and the female component of the labor force increased from 17 percent to 43 percent. Golden, *The Female Labor Force and American Economic Growth, 1890 to 1980,* in LONG TERM TRENDS IN THE AMERICAN ECONOMY, S. Engerman and R. Gallman eds. (1985). Indeed, white males now make up less than a majority—49.7 percent—of the labor force; nonwhite males make up 6.8 percent of the labor force; and women of all races constitute the remainder. *Washington Post,* August 30, 1984, at A7, col. 1.

64. *See* American Pub. Transit Ass'n v. Lewis, 655 F.2d 1272, 1278 & n.12 (D.C. Cir. 1981) (court found § 504 of the Rehabilitation Act of 1973 (29 U.S.C. § 794), which prohibits discrimination against the handicapped in any public transit program receiving federal funds, did not authorize the Department of Transportation to issue regulations providing that new bus purchases with federal assistance must include handicapped access, including wheelchair lifts; regulations imposed an "extremely heavy financial burden," between $460 million (DOT estimate) and $4.5 billion (plaintiff's estimate) over 30 years); *compare* Bartels v. Biernat, 427 F. Supp. 226, 232 (E.D. Wis. 1977) (permanent injunction issued to halt purchase of buses, with some federal funding, which were inaccessible to the handicapped in violation of DOT regulations).

65. For example, the "leave in anticipation of disability," negotiated by the Communications Workers of America in its 1979 collective bargaining agreement with the Bell System, allows employees to take a leave for elective surgery, childbirth, and other anticipated disabilities.

66. Robinson v. Lorillard Corp., 444 F.2d 791, 798 (4th Cir. 1971) (a business interest, in order to overcome a prima facie case, must be "sufficiently compelling to override any racial impact; the challenged practice must effectively carry out the business purpose it is alleged to serve; and there must be available no acceptable alternative policies or practices which would better accomplish the business purpose advanced, or accomplish it equally well with a lesser differential racial impact").

67. *See* notes 44 and 57 and accompanying text.

68. *Id.*

3

The Family and the Market: A Study of Ideology and Legal Reform

FRANCES E. OLSEN

A new round of debate has developed regarding the family and family values. Some argue that the family is a reactionary institution and a primary locus for the oppression of women; others extol the sharing within family life and seek to reclaim family values as supportive of democratic and progressive goals. Although this debate is yet unresolved, it is already boring. Admittedly, it can stir strong emotions, but on some level we all know it will not lead to any solution. Rather than join the debate, this chapter examines the terrain upon which the debate has been conducted.

A central concern underlying the debate is the subordination of women to men. Both sides share the goal of equality and independence for women. Repeated efforts at reform have resulted in a significant measure of success, yet the subordination of women continues. Many different factors may help to explain why the reform strategies adopted have had ambiguous and even contradictory effects. One factor that often receives insufficient attention is the ideological foundations of social reforms. In particular, reforms are limited by their premises, by the unexamined assumptions upon which they are based.

One such assumption embodies the radical separation of the market and the family, the idea that the market structures our productive lives and the family structures our affective lives. In the nineteenth century, the family was seen to constitute a separate sphere of activity—a sphere particularly suited to women. "Woman's sphere" may no longer be considered to be just home and family, but we do continue to view the family as something sharply distinct from the market. The vision of the market and the family as a dichotomy—the perception that social life comprises two separate though interdependent spheres—can be described as a structure of consciousness. By structure of consciousness, I mean a shared vision of the social universe that underlies a society's culture and also shapes the society's view of what social relationships are "natural" and, therefore, what social reforms are possible.

In my discussion of the market/family dichotomy, I shall refer frequently to two other dichotomies—the ones between state and civil society and between male and female. The state/civil society dichotomy is crucially related to the complexities of the market/family dichotomy, and the dichotomy between male and female is particularly important both to the ways in which the market/family dichotomy now affects human existence and to our hopes for constructing new ways of thinking about and leading our lives. These three dichotomies are each distinct: None is logically dependent upon another and none necessarily entails another. Nevertheless, deep ties exist among them, and each reflects a way of thinking that entails a radical division of the world. All three dichotomies seem eternal, yet by transcending all three, by reconceiving the relationship between the two elements in each of the three pairs and restructuring our thoughts and lives to create, reflect, and reinforce those reconceptions, we have the greatest possibility for bringing about changes that would significantly improve our individual and collective lives.

I. The Ideology of the Family and the Market

The separate and unequal spheres constituted for men and women had two opposite effects on women: The woman's sphere both constrained women and provided them with valuable opportunities. In the early nineteenth century, as men's work was largely removed to the factory while women's work remained primarily in the home, there came to be a sharp dichotomy between "the home" and "the [workaday] world." This dichotomy took on many of the moral overtones developed in the theological dichotomy between heaven and earth. Often the home was referred to as "sacred," and home life was celebrated as the reward for which men should be willing to suffer in the earthly world of work. The family and home were seen as safe repositories for the virtues and emotions that people believed were being banished from the world of commerce and industry. The home was said to provide a haven from the anxieties of modern life—"a shelter for those moral and spiritual values which the commercial spirit and the critical spirit were threatening to destroy."[1]

At the same time that the home was being glorified, it was being devalued. The woman's sphere was for men "the object of yearning, and yet of scorn."[2] Ann Douglas has pointed out that while men sentimentalized the family and exalted domesticity, they continued to behave in the marketplace as if they believed that "profane," worldly goals represented the greatest good. "It is to their credit that they indirectly acknowledged that the pursuit of these 'masculine' goals meant damaging, perhaps losing, another good, one they increasingly included under the 'feminine' ideal. Yet the fact remains that their regret was calculated not to interfere with their actions."[3]

Further, while the world of the marketplace was decried for being selfish, debasing, and exploitative, it was also admired and esteemed. Self-reliance, progress, modernization—each had positive connotations that were associated with the world of commerce and industry. Rationality, discipline, and a focus on objective reality were considered desirable aspects of the "male" sphere of the market.[4] Moreover, although the values of domesticity were used to criticize the destructiveness of marketplace values and the pursuit of wealth, they nevertheless served to "undercut opposition to exploitative pecuniary standards in the work world, by upholding a 'separate sphere' of comfort and compensation, instilling a morality that would encourage self-control, and fostering the idea that preservation of home and family sentiment was an ultimate goal."[5]

Given this simultaneous glorification and denigration of both the home and the marketplace, it should be no surprise that the sharp split between the two spheres had complex effects upon women. The market/family dichotomy tended to exclude women from the world of the marketplace while promising them a central role in the supposedly equally important domestic sphere. The dichotomy encouraged women to be generous and nurturant but discouraged them from being strong and self-reliant; it insulated women from the world's corruption but denied them the world's stimulation. While the dichotomy tended to mask the inferior, degraded position of women, it also provided a degree of autonomy and a base from which women could and did elevate their status.

Nancy Cott has perceptively noted that rather early in the nineteenth century "domestic occupations began to mean for women what worldly occupations meant for men." The very process of "distinguish[ing] 'home' and 'woman' from 'the world' and 'man' tended to make the two spheres analogous and comparable."[6] This chapter will examine the "analogous and comparable" aspects of the family and the market and the importance that ideas about both have to the status of women and to feminist theory.

◇ ◇ ◇

With the decline of feudalism there arose the dichotomies between the state and civil society and between the market and the family. The free market combined an egalitarian ideology with an individualistic ethic. The private family combined a hierarchical ideology with an altruistic ethic. In both the market and the family, state activity has tended to moderate these characteristics. Welfare state reforms in the market have reduced individualism while promoting a new kind of hierarchy. Regulation of the family has undermined the hierarchical ideology and at the same time promoted individualism.

The market and the family reflect a parallel development with respect to the dichotomy between state and civil society. The ideologies of both the free market and the family tried to legitimate actual inequality by emphasizing the equality of all with respect to the state. Inequality was said to result from the private relations among people and was thus a natural attribute of civil society rather than the responsibility of the state. It is currently asserted that the state is promoting as much equality as it reasonably can in both the family and the marketplace and that any remaining inequality is a private or particularized matter.

The market and the family also relate to each other inversely. While the values of the market provide the basis for a critique of the family, the values of the family provide the basis for a critique of the market. The state intervenes in the market to make it more like the family and in the family to make it more like the market.

Viewed from a perspective that favors democratic, intersubjective relations, these state interventions have two distinct effects. Intervention in the market is desirable insofar as it promotes altruism but is undesirable insofar as it takes the form of the family hierarchy and legitimates and particularizes inequality instead of eliminating it. The state steps in to protect workers; the workers do not assert their own control through local organization and consolidation of power.[7] Similarly, intervention in the family is desirable insofar as it promotes women's claims for greater power and tends to undermine formal family hierarchy; it is undesirable insofar as it promotes individualism and particularizes and legitimates hierarchy rather than eliminates it. Intervention exposes family members to market exploitation. Further, it entails the state's stepping in to equalize the results of family interaction; it does not democratize the family.

II. Ideology and Legal Reform

The dichotomization of market and family pervades our thinking, our language, and our culture. It limits and impoverishes the ways we experience our affective and productive lives, the possibilities we can imagine for restructuring our shared existence, and the manner in which we attempt change.

A wide variety of reforms aimed at improving the lives of women have been undertaken in the last two centuries. The reform efforts discussed in Part II are familiar, as are their successes and failures. Less familiar are the reasons the reforms have not been more successful—the reasons they have damaged as well as improved women's lives. By approaching this issue from the perspective of the dichotomization of market and family, I hope to cast new light on the attempts at reform and their mixed results.

Reformers who have sought to improve the status of women have tried reforming the family either (I) to promote equality within the family or (2) to encourage husbands to behave altruistically toward their wives. Reformers have tried to improve the status of women in the market either (I) by requiring market actors to deal equally with women and men or (2) by making the market more responsive to the needs of women. These four categories of reforms can be described more generally in market/family terms as efforts, respectively, to make the family more like the market, to make the family more like the ideal family, to make the market more like the ideal market, and to make the market more like the family.

Despite its simplicity, this conceptual scheme has considerable descriptive and analytic power. First, the extent to which the four categories capture the broad contours of reform efforts is striking and suggests that insight may be gained from considering such efforts in relation to the dichotomy between market and family. Second, when the reforms are examined from this perspective, a pattern in their successes and failures emerges. The reforms that make the market more like the ideal market or the family more like the ideal family tend to eliminate imperfections in each institution, but as long as we view market and family as a dichotomy, our ideal images of market and family will remain incomplete and unsatisfactory. The failures characteristic of the market sabotage the market reforms, and the failures characteristic of the family sabotage the family reforms.

The reforms that make the family more like the market and the market more like the family likewise do not overcome the dichotomy between market and family but presuppose it. Although these reforms might appear to be a step toward transcending the market/family dichotomy, experience with such reforms suggests a persistent tendency simply to reproduce in each sphere the failures as well as the successes of the other. The market/family dichotomy is left intact; the effect of the reforms is less to overcome the dichotomy than simply to reposition it within each sphere. Thus, the successes of reforms designed to make the family more like the market are the successes of the market: they increase freedom and equality. Likewise, the failures of such reforms are the failures of the market: First, the equality promoted by the reforms is juridical equality, which at best is inadequate and at worst legitimates the unequal results that characterize marketplace equality; second, the reforms are based on market individualism, which discounts communal ties and promotes isolation. Similarly, reforms that use the family as a model to improve the market reflect the flaws as well as the virtues of the family. The reforms are successful insofar as they moderate the destructive effects of market individualism, but the altruism with which they would replace it is deeply tied to hierarchy and is ultimately unsatisfactory.

The link between equality and individualism on one hand, and altruism and hierarchy on the other—a link that plagues reforms of the family and of the market—poses a central problem for efforts to improve the lives of women. The analysis presented in this part does not provide a formula for making reforms more effective, nor does it map out alternative reform strategies. Instead, this part attempts a fresh look at reform efforts from the perspective of the dichotomization of market and family, in order both to understand the nature of the problem and to lay a foundation for transcending it.

A. Strategies for Improving the Status of Women by Reforming the Family

Family reforms aimed at improving women's status tend either to encourage the family to emulate the egalitarianism of the market or to protect the family from the selfish, individualistic tendencies of the market and to encourage husbands to treat wives better.

1. Greater Equality via the Market Critique: (a) Independence and Equality. Blackstone's well-known aphorism about the suspension of the wife's legal existence during marriage[8] found support in early common law provisions that appeared to merge the wife's legal personality into the husband's. Any property to which a woman held legal title passed to her husband upon marriage, and the husband was entitled to any wages the wife earned during the marriage. A married woman could not enter into contracts or execute a will; her husband was responsible for her torts and, if he had been present, for her crimes. A husband was entitled to "chastise" his wife, to rape her, and to force her to stay in his home. Ordinarily a wife could not testify in court against her husband. The husband had complete guardianship rights over the children. Once a woman married, she could not divorce, and only in extreme circumstances would she be authorized to live apart from her husband.

Reformers condemned these provisions for being feudal and oppressive and worked to develop for the married woman a legal personality and existence separate from her husband's. They persuaded courts to qualify the father's superior guardianship rights over his children, to multiply the exceptional circumstances authorizing a woman to separate from her husband, and to receive testimony of wives against husbands in certain situations. Equity courts developed forms of property ownership that enabled wealthy families to establish estates for their daughters. Around the middle of the nineteenth century, several states adopted married women's property acts that allowed women to own property, conduct business, enter into contracts, sue and be sued, and keep any wages they might earn.

Reforms establishing the wife's independent and equal existence have continued to the present day and have benefited women in a number of ways. They have promoted equality for women in marriages by undermining the legitimacy of family hierarchy and the oppressive prerogatives claimed by husbands. At the same time, however, the results of such reforms have often proved detrimental to women. Although the reforms promote equality, they also undermine the altruistic bases of the family and thus leave women open to the kind of individualized, particularized domination characteristic of market relations. The reforms have tended to give women equal rights, but they have not democ-ratized the family.

For example, the married women's property acts did not force the husband to share his power over the family's wealth but instead provided that each spouse owned his or her separate property. Given that women performed vast amounts of unpaid labor while men owned most of the property and earned most of the money, the acts had little effect on the lives of most women. Similarly, when the law declared wives to be equal guardians of their children, this pronouncement did not by itself prevent the husband from making every important decision about the children. The basis for the father's authority changed from juridical superiority to other forms of power, such as financial control and physical force, but the authority nonetheless continued. The mother might no longer be powerless simply because she was a wife, but she might well remain powerless for reasons that would seem more particular to her situation.

Women gained more rights to independence in the marriage, but these rights could isolate women as well as empower them. Rather than force husbands to share their power over the family name and domicile, reforms gave the married woman only the right to retain her own surname and to establish her own domicile.[9] Moreover, by custom and sometimes by law, the father has been permitted to attach his surname to the children of the marriage; a mother's different surname has symbolized the isolation that so often seems to accompany equality for women.[10]

While reformers were trying to establish a separate and equal legal status for married women, they were also struggling to enable women to leave unsatisfactory marriages. After liberalizing the grounds for separation, reformers began working on the grounds for divorce.[11] Legislative reform increased the grounds upon which divorce could be granted, and the new statutes sometimes included vague "catchall" grounds like "incompatibil-ity" or "cruelty." The reforms also tended to make divorce law more gender neutral. Reformers persuaded trial courts to grant uncontested divorces on increasingly scanty evidence and encouraged a liberal policy for recognizing out-of-state divorces granted in jurisdictions with less stringent laws. These reforms have enhanced the ability of women to obtain a divorce and have reduced the need for perjury or forum shopping. During the 1970s, almost every state enacted some form of "no-fault" divorce, which allowed the dissolution of any unsuccessful marriage. The cause of liberalized divorce law has long been strongly associated with the cause of equal rights for married women, in part because men have been more able than women to avoid the devastating effects of an unhappy marriage.

Although these reforms enable women to leave unsatisfactory marriages, they fail to address the economic, social, and emotional impact that divorce has on women. More-over, the reforms do little to help women prevent their marriages from becoming unsat-isfactory in the first place. In fact, the reforms may adversely affect women by increasing the ease with which *men* can get out of marriages and by undermining the power some wives once had when a husband needed his wife's consent and cooperation to obtain a divorce. A man's earning power typically increases during the course of his marriage, while a woman's often remains constant or even decreases. If a couple divorces after twenty years of marriage, the wife is likely to experience a sharp drop in her living stan-dard, despite provisions for alimony, while the husband's living standard often rises.[12] Marital instability may also have a more pronounced social and emotional impact on women than on men: a divorced forty-year-old man occupies a decidedly different posi-tion in society from that of a divorced forty-year-old woman.

(b) Legislation. Reforms tending to establish the husband and wife as juridical equals also tend to "legalize" the relationship—that is, to allow rights to be enforced between husband and wife just as rights are enforced between people in the marketplace. Legalization requires that any deviation from the treatment of husband and wife as strangers be based on their voluntary agreement, not on any state-imposed definition of marriage.[13]

In marriage as in the market, the will of the contracting parties is increasingly considered to be the appropriate basis for their relationship. Contracts between husband and wife are no longer treated as illegitimate efforts to alter terms and conditions of marriage that are properly imposed by the state. Rather, such contracts are seen as valid, if perhaps overly formal, expressions of the agreement between the parties, an agreement that is the essence of marriage. Even if many courts will not enforce a marital contract during marriage, they will usually give some effect to the agreement upon the death of one of the parties or the dissolution of the relationship.

At the same time that contracts between husband and wife have become enforceable, torts and crimes perpetrated by one spouse against the other have become actionable. Reformers have steadily eroded doctrines of intrafamily tort immunity,[14] and what used to be considered the husband's right of "correction" is now recognized as assault and battery.[15] Increasingly, behavior that would be tortious or criminal if committed against a stranger will be so if committed against a spouse. Even if few husbands or wives sue their spouses and interspousal crimes are rarely prosecuted, the removal of the immunities barring such actions represents an important legalization of the husband–wife relationship. In both criminal law and tort law, the state is undertaking to enforce the basic rights of individual women, even against their own husbands.

These reforms are beneficial in two ways. First, legalization serves generally to improve the wife's status and to protect individual women. Wife beating and marital rape, for example, lose some of their social approval and probably take place less often. Second, the reforms that legalize the husband–wife relationship do enable some individuals to negotiate better marriage terms than those provided by the state. People have more options available to them, and they are freer to experiment with new forms of family relationships.

The reforms, however, do not go far enough. The state will enforce individual rights of women, but the position of women in society may make these rights meaningless. For example, a battered wife may be legally entitled to send her husband to jail, but her economic incentive not to do so may be overwhelming. Although the reforms end certain specific kinds of domination, they legitimate others. A wife who does not press criminal assault charges against a battering husband, for example, may be blamed for allowing herself to be a victim. Similarly, as long as a woman can obtain a divorce but does not, she may be said to have consented to whatever abuse she receives from her husband. The husband and wife are treated as if they were equal bargaining partners, even though women are in fact systematically subordinated to men.

Further, although these reforms promote legal equality and individual freedom, they may discourage altruistic behavior. When a relationship is legalized, parties are left to look out for themselves, and unless the contract provides otherwise, the sharing behavior of one party may not be reciprocated by the other. If a marriage may easily be dissolved, whoever sacrifices for the sake of the marriage is taking a greater risk than she or he would be taking for a permanent relationship.

Finally, in the same way that contracts in the marketplace may formalize domination as much as they express the will of the parties, contracts among lovers and friends may reflect and perpetuate the inequalities in their relationships. Similar legal treatment of situations involving married couples and those involving strangers may not promote equality or independence for women. Just as advocates of the welfare state argued that special legislation was necessary to protect the rights of workers and create real equality, so advocates of the regulated family have argued that special provisions are necessary to create real equality in families and to protect the individual rights of family members.

(c) Regulation. Designed to create "real equality" within the family, a number of reforms replace rules of formal juridical equality between husband and wife with regulations that treat relations between married couples differently from relations between strangers; these regulations tend to make the family more like the welfare state market.[16] One of the earliest forms of such regulation was aimed at ensuring that marital contracts expressed the "true will" of the parties. Courts recognizing and enforcing contracts that altered the financial consequences of marriage frequently devised special rules regarding undue influence. Forms of overreaching that would not void a commercial contract might well be found to invalidate a marital contract. Some courts have based their special treatment of marital contracts on openly paternalistic appeals and stereotyped images of conniving men and unworldly women, whereas other courts have held that the marriage relationship imposes certain fiduciary obligations on both spouses.

Another example of such regulation appears in domestic violence statutes that allow a wife to obtain injunctive relief against a battering husband without making the showing normally required for such relief.[17] It is argued that the particular problems of interspousal violence make this sort of special provision necessary. If a married woman is to receive the same protection against violence that she would enjoy if she were not married, the state must take account of the fact that she *is* married.

2. Increased Altruism and Solidarity Through State Regulation. An alternative strategy seeks to reform the family not by making it more like the market but rather by making the family more like the ideal image of the family and enforcing an altruistic ethic. Generally, these reforms tend to widen the separation between the market and the family, and they frequently increase sexual hierarchy. Some of the reforms create financial interdependence within the family; others substitute for a regime of individual rights of family members a strategy of detailed regulation of family behavior on a case-by-case basis.

(a) Financial Dependence. Community property laws,[18] enacted in eight states, have established community ownership both of property gained by the spouses' joint efforts and of wages earned by the husband or wife during the marriage. These laws provide for shared ownership of property by the husband and wife. Whereas the married women's property acts were individualistic, community property laws are altruistic. The shortcomings of community property laws stem from their tendency to undermine equality and promote hierarchy. As originally enacted, most of these laws provided that the husband would manage the property owned by the marital community.[19] A married woman's wages would thus become community property subject to the control of her husband.

Another group of reforms attempted to ensure that the husband would support his family. These reforms sometimes made nonsupport a crime or provided a procedure by which a wife could enforce the husband's support obligations.[20] Some alimony and child support provisions similarly required men to be financially responsible for their families. Statutes were enacted that allowed a widow to take a "forced share" of her deceased husband's estate and thus circumscribed a husband's ability to disinherit his wife.[21] These reforms were successful insofar as they limited the husband's power to abuse the control he exercised, but they were unsatisfactory insofar as they left the husband in control.

Recent reforms of this type tend to impose mutual obligations of support upon both spouses and to prevent either spouse from disinheriting the other. Such a cosmetic change, however, fails to eliminate the ideology of sexual inequality, because merely formal gender neutrality does not address actual conditions of economic dependency.

(b) "Deformalization." The clearest example of "deformalization" as a reform strategy is the family court movement that began at the turn of the century. Family courts were established to deal in an informal and sensitive manner with problems that arise in a family.[22] Frequently, social workers and other "helping" professionals who emphasize adjustment and reconciliation serve on the staffs of family courts. Disputes are to be approached on a case-by-case basis, with resolutions carefully tailored to the particular family. The point is not to protect the individual rights of each spouse against infringement by the other but to use the state apparatus to promote family solidarity.

Deformalization should be recognized as an alternative strategy, different from both delegalization and legalization. The delegalized private family instituted a limited "state of nature" in which the husband, if he was stronger or more powerful, could dominate his wife. Legalization of the family establishes the husband and wife as individuals with rights against each other and places the enforcement mechanisms of the state at their disposal. In both of these strategies, the state avoids making *ad hoc* adjustments in the outcomes of family relations.

Delegalization threatens individual rights by refusing to enforce them, and legalization threatens family solidarity by enforcing individual rights against the family. Deformalization tries to protect family solidarity without destroying individual rights. The anarchy of delegalization is avoided: The state does undertake to protect one spouse from the other. Moreover, because the state does not blindly and impersonally protect abstract rights, the protection is supposed to be less subversive of family solidarity. Rather than require the state to remain formally neutral, deformalization allows the state to make *ad hoc* readjustments in the outcomes of family relations. Thus, deformalization may avoid both the brute-force domination possible in the delegalized private family and the free market domination possible in the modern legalized family.

At the same time, though, the deformalization reform strategy may have adverse effects on women. First, it fails to provide full protection for individual family members because in encouraging agreement between the parties, it may force the weaker party to accept a resolution that gives her far less than she would be entitled to in a formal adjudication. Women who try to deal with battering husbands through the family court system may well find themselves the victims of continued battering. Thus, although the aim of deformalization is altruism and family solidarity, the actual result is too often the perpetuation of hierarchy and domination. Second, deformalization violates notions of the rule of law and may result in *ad hoc* readjustments that are themselves oppressive. The welfare of family members may come to depend upon the uncontrolled discretion of state agencies, with the result that the state may directly dominate family life.

Recent efforts to deformalize family law and family relations share the same pattern of possibility and risk that characterized earlier efforts. Informal dispute settlement mechanisms are sometimes beneficial and sometimes harmful. Community courts may themselves be oppressive and may fail to protect one party from the other. Effective local control of informal dispute resolution reduces both these risks, but deformalization should not be supported a priori.

B. Strategies for Improving the Status of Women by Reforming the Market

Strategies for improving women's status in the market tend to attack the market either for being too much like the family or for being too little like the family. The market is said to be too much like the family in that the inequality of the family is reproduced in the market: The sexual identities that people develop in families[23] and the social meanings attached to maleness and femaleness are carried into the marketplace and undermine its supposedly egalitarian character. One solution pursued by reformers is to bar considerations of gender from the marketplace by preventing sex discrimination—and unequal treatment based on familial roles—in employment and other market activities. Thus, the market is to be insulated from the lives people live in families.

The market is said to be too little like the family insofar as it fails to reproduce the altruistic ethic of the family. Reformers often consider women to be particularly victimized by market individualism. The focal point of their criticism is the social irresponsibility or anarchism of the market; reforms are intended to make the market more responsive to human needs. In particular, these reforms call for an adjustment of the market to account for people's family lives rather than for a radical separation between the market and the family.

1. Eliminating Discrimination Against Women: Making the Market Less Like the Family. Reformers generally conceive of antidiscrimination law as a strategy to enable women to participate in the market as freely and effectively as men do. For women to participate in the market at all, it was necessary first to change the state laws that made women objects in the market or mere agents of their husbands or that barred them from the market.[24] The further project of making women equal participants in the market is the subject of continuing political and legal battles. The market, despite its egalitarian theoretical premises, reproduces the inequality of the family.[25] This reproduction takes place for a number of reasons and through a number of mechanisms. Efforts to combat it are thus also varied in their intentions and their effects.

One reason women are disadvantaged in the market is that some market actors intentionally discriminate against them. Before such discrimination was outlawed, there were frequent efforts to justify it. The justifications ranged from protecting the family[26] and women from the corruption of the market,[27] to protecting men[28] and the market itself from the ill effects said to result from women's participation in the market.[29] These four concerns are generally no longer considered adequate justifications for state policies excluding women from working in the market, but they continue to appear in various forms[30] and in some cases operate to rationalize differential treatment of men and women.

Even when these concerns are rejected as justifications for differential treatment, they are often accepted as explanations for the patterns of pervasive inequality and sexual segregation that continue in the market. Thus, it may be admitted that the market reproduces the inequality of the family but denied that this inequality is caused by intentional discrimination against women. Rather, unequal results in the market are explained as the effect that growing up and living in families has upon the behavior of men and women in the market. These inequalities may be referred to as "sex-blind" discrimination.

There are two general mechanisms by which sex-blind discrimination operates. First, differing family obligations and expectations about men and women prejudice women. Second, the particular upbringings girls receive in families and the roles women have played in the past do in fact leave women ill prepared to succeed in the market, as it is now organized.

An important aspect of both mechanisms is that the market was constructed primarily by men, and the roles available in the market as well as the rewards associated with those roles were created in a sexist and discriminatory environment. It is the interaction between women's behavior and the particular demands of the market that results in sex-blind discrimination against women.

(a) Reforms Designed to Integrate Women into the Free Market. Many antidiscrimination provisions can be explained or justified as efforts to allow women to be assimilated into the free market. Laws barring women from certain professions or forbidding their employment under the same conditions applicable to men clearly restricted the free market; only if such laws were repealed would employers be able to utilize female labor in accordance with the free market ideal. Laws forbidding conscious sex discrimination in employment,[31] education,[32] credit,[33] and housing,[34] as well as laws and regulations prescribing hiring procedures that employers must follow to protect women from such discrimination, can also be viewed as efforts to make the market more like the free market ideal. Three of the four classic reasons for intentional discrimination against women—protecting women from the corruption of the market, insulating the family from market pressures, and protecting men's position in the marketplace—are factors that ideal free market actors would not take into account in purely profit-motivated activity. Only the fourth concern—that women are in general less valuable or less productive in the market—provides a market justification for intentional discrimination. Even that argument, however, is weak support for discriminating against all women. Thus, requiring market actors to abandon their irrational biases against women or their misplaced, altruistic inclinations to protect women, family life, or men can be seen as a way of forcing these actors to behave as rational profit maximizers.

Even affirmative action for women can be justified on free market grounds as a measure to eliminate irrational discrimination against women. First, a target or quota may be set to approximate the number of women who would be hired or promoted in the absence of irrational discrimination; such a quota serves as a proxy for gender-neutral decisions, especially in areas, like academic hiring, that are difficult to police. Furthermore, even when affirmative action is intended to compensate individual women for prior discrimination or to create a sexually integrated marketplace by rewarding women beyond what they individually merit, it is conceived of as a temporary, stopgap measure. It may be seen as a brief departure from the free market system, a departure designed to correct a malfunction caused by irrational, intentional discrimination and to restore free market, profit-maximizing rationality.

Finally, reforms eliminating facially neutral policies that serve to handicap women are sometimes supported as efforts to purify the free market. For example, under the principles established in *Griggs v. Duke Power Co.*,[35] courts have invalidated minimum height, weight, and strength requirements that have a disproportionate impact on women and that cannot be demonstrated to be job related. The very fact that the requirements are not job related suggests that from a free market perspective they are irrational. Courts have also begun to use antidiscrimination law to provide relief for victims of sexual harassment, even though employment policies condoning sexual harassment are, in a technical sense, facially neutral. One explanation for banning sexual harassment is that such behavior does not belong in the marketplace.

The major benefit of reforms that attempt to integrate women into the free market is their tendency to promote freedom and equality for women. Such reforms help to free women from economic dependency on men, expand the career options available to women, and increase the salaries and advancement possibilities of certain groups of women workers. Further, laws requiring equal treatment tend to undermine demeaning and debilitating stereotypes of women and their roles. Finally, antidiscrimination law legitimates women's complaints of unfair treatment and provides women with a vehicle for fighting back against institutions that oppress them.

The reforms, however, do not go far enough toward real equality or empowerment of women. Moreover, they encourage market individualism. Antidiscrimination law does not end the actual subordination of women in the market but instead mainly benefits a small percentage of women who adopt "male" roles. Meanwhile, it legitimates the continued oppression of most women. The reforms maintain the status quo by particularizing and privatizing inequality and encouraging women to blame themselves for their failures in the market.

Antidiscrimination law promotes market individualism and promises each individual woman that she can win success in the market if only she chooses to apply herself. It obscures for women the actual causes of their oppression and treats discrimination against women as an irrational and capricious departure from the normal objective operation of the market, instead of recognizing such discrimination as a pervasive aspect of our dichotomized system. The reforms reinforce free market ideology and encourage women to seek individualistic inward-looking solutions to social problems.

(b) Welfare State Reforms Designed to Help Women. A second common understanding of antidiscrimination law is that it moderates the effects of the free market in order to promote women's equality. If intentional discrimination is considered rational but socially irresponsible, laws against such discrimination can be seen as an effort to counteract the individualistic ethic of the market and to force market actors to behave more responsibly. Similarly, affirmative action can be considered more than just an effort to eradicate irrational discrimination; it can be viewed as a method of combating sex-blind discrimination or even as an attempt to restructure the workplace.

Another category of welfare state reforms designed to counteract sex-blind discrimination seeks to reduce the discriminatory impact that the unequal division of family responsibilities has on women in the market.[36] Probably the most important reform in this category has been the amendment of Title VII[37] to include as sex discrimination most forms of pregnancy discrimination. Enacted after the Supreme Court ruled that antidiscrimination law did not require states or private employers to include pregnancy benefits in otherwise comprehensive medical plans,[38] the amendment is perhaps the paradigmatic reform phrased in neutral terms but recognized as a reform for women. Government training programs for displaced homemakers may also be seen as reforms primarily designed to help women overcome the negative effects of family roles upon women's participation in the market.[39] Neutral phrasing takes on importance with respect to other programs and proposals, such as government subsidies for child care costs, that are generally understood to be programs to help working mothers but that also help working fathers.

These reforms share the advantages of the welfare state. Like other welfare state provisions, antidiscrimination law can promote more than mere formal equality. By recognizing women's subordination, the law can account for and counteract sex-blind discrimination. Because affirmative action acknowledges the common themes in the oppression that each woman suffers, it encourages women to recognize their shared interests and can serve to empower women as a group. The reforms compensate women for their unequal family roles, improve women's market opportunities, and spread to employers and to the government some of the costs of bearing and raising children, costs that would otherwise fall disproportionately on women. Finally, by acknowledging the unfair treatment accorded women, antidiscrimination law can counteract the tendency of both men and women to lay the blame for a woman's failure in the marketplace on the woman herself rather than on a systemic bias against women.

The disadvantages of these reforms are related to the limitations of the welfare state. Although the state claims to promote greater equality, its efforts to do so have been inadequate. Antidiscrimination law helps only a small group of successful women but fails to change the basic pattern of sexually segregated employment and thus ensures that most women will remain in dead-end jobs. Yet the success of a few is used to justify a system that continues to oppress most women. Although the doctrine of affirmative action presupposes prior discrimination against women, affirmative action policies pretend to have ended such discrimination. Affirmative action thus creates another reason for women to blame themselves when they fail in the marketplace. Moreover, although affirmative action may expand women's social roles, it also tends to reinforce the ideology of inequality and to reintroduce problems of paternalism.

2 Forcing the Market to Respond to Human Needs: Making the Market More Like the Family. Reforms that seek to improve the status of women by moderating the individualism of the market often improve conditions for women, but they also reinforce sexual stereotypes, augment hierarchy, and therefore undermine the quality of women's lives. Labor legislation that protects women illustrates well the advantages and drawbacks of this reform strategy. Such legislation, enacted around the turn of the century, often singled out women for special treatment, especially after *Muller v. Oregon*[40] established the validity of laws that would have been unconstitutional under the freedom-to-contract principles of *Lochner v. New York*[41] had they applied to men as well as to women.

Changed social conditions have made it easy in recent years simply to condemn *Muller* for its blatant sexism and offensive stereotyping, but at the time the case was decided, it was recognized that the case itself and the gender-based labor legislation it authorized had more complex and ambiguous implications. On one hand, *Muller* was part of the attack upon the laissez-faire policies associated with *Lochner* and upon the *Lochner* case itself. *Muller* admitted what *Lochner* had tried to deny—that protective labor legislation can benefit workers and society. *Muller* may be seen as part of an effort to make the marketplace responsive to human needs by "delegitimating" certain forms of exploitation and limiting the free reign of market individualism. The protective labor legislation validated by *Muller* directly benefited many of the most exploited women by undermining the autocratic power of employers and by improving women's working conditions.

On the other hand, *Muller* undermined the struggles of women for equality and, paradoxically, even offered support for the *Lochner* free market principle by carving out a limited exception to it based on a view of women's frail physique and unique role in the family. One effect of this exception was to relieve pressure for broader reforms by making laissez-faire more acceptable. Indeed, associating the need for protective labor legislation with the frailty of women offered ideological support for the claim that legislative protection was unmanly. Moreover, protective labor legislation is effective only when its beneficiaries have no choice but to receive the protection; if individual workers or a whole group can waive the benefits, they can compete more effectively in the market, and the protective legislation loses much of its value. As long as employers can hire workers who waive protection, the employers will have insufficient incentive to improve working conditions. Thus, by restricting the protective legislation to women, *Muller* placed women at a competitive disadvantage and achieved the same effect that might have been expected had the states passed gender-neutral labor legislation but allowed men to waive the protection. Protective labor legislation fell victim to the vicious circle characteristic of much reform: If a reform is too limited in its application, it is unlikely to be very effective; because it appears ineffective, its application is less likely to be extended.

Muller illustrates another disadvantage of reforms that try to make the market responsive to human needs: The altruism they pose against market individualism is linked to hierarchy. *Muller* was based on the thesis that women differ from men in important ways, and although the case might have seemed to exalt women, it effectively degraded them by treating the asserted differences as evidence of women's inferiority.

The same basic pattern of possibility and risk illustrated by *Muller* is repeated in other reforms that try to make the market less individualistic. Paid maternity leave requirements, for example, provide an immediate benefit to many women workers because they force employers to moderate profitmaking to accommodate family needs. Yet they create only a minor exception to the normal operation of the market and relieve the pressure for broader reforms that would allow workers to take leaves whenever it might be socially desirable for them to do so. Focusing on maternity leave implies that having babies is the only legitimate reason for temporarily withdrawing from the marketplace. Finally, both blatant and subtle forms of prejudice continue to operate against women who take maternity leave. Maternity leave provisions tend to encourage stereotyping and hierarchy, and thus operate as *Muller* did, though far less offensively.

It might seem that as long as reforms do not single out women as a group, they will not augment hierarchy. Although neutral phrasing does make some difference, it often seems merely cosmetic: The reform is clearly intended for women. Sweeping proposals have been made to grant paid maternity and paternity leaves to parents, to require child care facilities in workplaces, to change career patterns in order to eliminate the pressure to work long hours during the years when people are most likely to be raising young children, to discourage employers from transferring reluctant workers from city to city, and to reduce the disadvantages suffered by people who choose to spend several years out of the work force. If these policies were applied to everyone without exception or opportunity for waiver, nonparents and other people might well denounce them as forced subsidies of the nuclear family.

Alternatively, if market reform laws condition the granting of benefits on voluntary acceptance by the recipients, two problems arise. First, men will generally not choose the benefits, or if they do, they will seem to be adopting a woman's role. Practices rather than specific wording may thus reinforce hierarchy and stereotypes. Additionally, a voluntary program introduces the possibility that both men and women will be penalized for choosing to participate. Provisions designed to enable a parent to commit time to child care, for example, may simply result in a subclass of (primarily female) child caretakers who will be able to participate in the market but who will remain relatively unsuccessful there. Thus, altruism is once again inseparable from hierarchy. It sometimes seems that if women want to be treated well, they must accept second-class status.

C. Summary

Strategies to improve the lives of women by reforming the family have often promoted the equality of women within families and have sometimes encouraged husbands to treat their wives better. Reforms that increase the juridical equality of wives, however, also tend to undermine altruism and foster individual selfishness. Moreover, some of these reforms legitimate actual inequality by individualizing and particularizing it. Reforms that encourage altruistic behavior within the family tend at the same time to encourage and legitimate sex hierarchy within the family. Although some of the reforms might help to democratize the family, none of them is particularly suited to the task.

Strategies to improve the lives of women by reforming the market have often promoted women's equality and have sometimes made the market more responsive to human needs. Reforms that purport to require equal treatment for women, however, often legitimate actual inequality by individualizing and particularizing it. Such reforms also tend to reinforce market ideology and to encourage individual selfishness. Reforms that try to force the market to respond to human needs frequently produce and justify hierarchy in the process. Although any of these reforms may in some cases democratize the market, none of them is particularly suited to the purpose. Both sets of strategies— reforming the family and reforming the market—will sometimes meaningfully improve the lives of women, but none of these strategies should be advocated without qualification: None is adequate for creating democratic, sharing relations among people.

III. Toward a New Vision

Up to this point I have described a particular structure of consciousness—the market/ family dichotomy—and have explored the destructive effects it has on various reform strategies intended to improve the lives of women. As long as our discourse and our thinking remain constrained within this dominant conceptual scheme, we are faced with a kind of stalemate. Like the characters in the story from the first-grade reader, we are trying to build two different playhouses out of the same set of bricks; each effort to improve one aspect of our lives inflicts loss upon some other aspect.

I now examine the possibility of breaking out of this stalemate and speculate upon alternative ways of conceiving and experiencing our affective and productive lives. My aim is simply to begin a conversation about such alternatives.[42] This conversation can be enriched by the speculative thinking of left and feminist theorists. The critique of the state/civil society dichotomy, developed by Karl Marx and others, is useful for understanding the nature of, and the possibilities of overcoming, the market/family dichotomy. Feminist speculation about transcending the male/female dichotomy provides insight into the possibilities and advantages of transcending the market/family dichotomy.

Becoming aware of these dichotomies and recognizing the crippling effects they have upon our lives and upon efforts to improve our lives will not automatically bring about change. The dichotomies are not only a way of thinking: We have in fact come to experience our lives through them. Thus, we must combine our theory with political practice. A better understanding of alternative conceptions of the world can help us to carry out reforms more effectively. The reforms may in turn change the actual conditions under which we live in such a way that our own experiences will affirm and elaborate upon a different view of the market and the family, the state and society, men and women.

A. Feminism and Antiliberal Theory

An important factor in the failure of feminist reforms is their acceptance of a liberal understanding of the state and its relationship to civil society. Criticism of the liberal state and the attack on the state/civil society dichotomy have been important elements of the left attack on liberalism for over a hundred years.[43] Some feminists have participated in this attack: Most feminist reform efforts, however, have taken place against a background of liberal capitalism and have tended to patch up and refine the liberal theory of the state rather than challenge and disintegrate it. The reforms have exposed contradictions within liberalism, but they have not yet led us to develop a feminist theory of the state. One reason the reforms have not been more successful is that they accept as a given the state/ civil society dichotomy and are conceived of as state regulation of some aspect of society or as state creation and enforcement of individual rights for women.

Just as feminist reform theory has failed to be adequately informed by the leftist critique of liberalism, so too has leftist theory failed to respond adequately to feminist critiques of patriarchy. Leftist theorists have frequently ignored gender issues or seen them as matters peripheral to the important issues of social change, as mere reflections of the incomplete or inconsistent triumph of liberal principles. Although leftist theorists acknowledge that women and men do not receive equal treatment, they perceive the oppression of women as just a particular instance of the failure of the liberal state to live up to its ideals; few left thinkers have attempted to examine the significance to liberal thought of the male/female and market/family dichotomies.

Antiliberal theorists have made either of two mistakes in dealing with the family. Some have ignored the family or thought of it only in the context of the lag theory and have thus treated the seeming backwardness of the family as a mere curiosity or as a reason for neglecting the family in theoretical discussions. The family has not been recognized to be integral to the structure of liberalism. Some proponents of antiliberal theory have therefore underestimated the family's importance.[44] Other proponents have placed false importance on the family by celebrating it as a socialist community. When Carl Degler asserts that Marxists have taken the family as their "model of human order" because they see in it the "epitome of true humanity and interrelatedness,"[45] he exaggerates only a little. "The very slogan of Communism—'from each according to his abilities, to each according to his needs'—is," says Degler, "the central principle of family life."

Both of these leftist approaches to the family accept unquestioningly the market/family dichotomy and fail to appreciate the significance of the family as a *structural* element of civil society. The altruistic, hierarchical, private family is an essential element of nineteenth-century ideology. The liberal family is an equally essential element of modern ideology and a structural component of society in the modern corporate welfare state. By failing to address or even notice the dichotomy between the market and the family, most leftist theories assume and thus encourage the continued existence of the dichotomy.

We can learn a great deal by recognizing the relationship between the leftist and feminist contributions and the power of each to enrich the other. The leftist critique of the state/civil society dichotomy and the feminist critique of the male/female dichotomy together inform, and are enriched by, the critique of the market/family dichotomy. Moreover, leftist and feminist speculation about transcending the dichotomies between state and civil society and between male and female suggests the possibility of transcending the market/family dichotomy.

B. Criticizing the Dichotomies

The market/family dichotomy is a human construct that entails the same kind of self-alienation that Karl Marx described in *On the Jewish Question*,[46] his classic essay on the state/civil society dichotomy. Marx perceived that human beings lead a "double life"—one life in the state and a separate life in civil society. He referred to the political state, in which we regard ourselves as communal beings, as the *species-life* of mankind; the political "citizen" is abstract and universal. Civil society, however, is the realm of the particular; each member of civil society is a "private individual," separated from his community and concerned only with his own interests and desires. The dualism between species-life and individual life involves a form of self-alienation, an artificial split of the person into an abstract citizen of the state and an egoistic individual in civil society. According to Marx, the project of human emancipation is to overcome this alienation: the human being may become a species-being by reuniting the abstract universal citizen and the concrete particular individual.[47] We can thus reclaim our own powers as social powers and thereby become complete *and* moral beings.

The dualism between life in the market and life in the family is slightly different from, but even more pronounced than, the dualism between species-life and individual life. We expect the market to achieve the efficient production of goods and services; it is not the arena in which we are supposed to develop our personalities or satisfy human relational wants. Pervasive hierarchy in the market is imposed and justified on grounds of efficiency. The market is the realm of alienated labor. The expression of the desires to develop personality and to interact with others is relegated to the family and simultaneously glorified and devalued. We see the market as a means to an end, whereas we see the family as an end in itself. The market is the arena for work and the production of goods; the family is the arena for most forms of play and consumption. Dividing life between market and family compartmentalizes human experience in a way that prevents us from realizing the range of choices actually available to us. Much of social and productive life seems effectively beyond our control.

The seemingly contradictory desires to be free and to relate with others in a community present an important dilemma of liberal society.[48] In laissez-faire ideology, the market is predominantly associated with freedom, and the family is associated with community. In welfare state ideology, the market is supposed to be controlled by the community (the state), and the family is celebrated as a realm of freedom with which the state should not interfere. It turns out, however, that the liberal dilemma of freedom and community is not resolved by the interplay between the market and the family.

The family has a dual role for both men and women. For men, the family is a realm in which they can expose their "weaknesses," in which they may embrace without shame the values traditionally associated with women. By relating with women in families, men try to reclaim wholeness. Second, the family is a realm in which men can be bosses. In their families men can express competitive values and other values traditionally considered masculine. Men may be compensated in the family for their failures in the marketplace. The home is a haven for men.

The family likewise plays a dual role for women. The home is supposed to be where women belong and where their values are appreciated and allowed free expression. Rather than a haven for women, however, the home has traditionally been a workplace; and now that most women work in the marketplace, the home has become a second workplace. In contrast to the market, where people must often play roles, the family is supposed to be the arena in which people can express their real selves. For many women, however, the contrary is true: It is precisely within the family that they must subordinate themselves and play roles.

The market serves for a few women some of the same functions that the family serves for men. A woman as employee or manager may more acceptably display traits that are considered masculine. The market may offer a socially approved opportunity for women to be rational, objective, and even selfish. In theory, the market frees women from their ascribed roles. In fact, most women are forced into subordinate positions in the market, and their freedom is quite circumscribed.

For men, the market is supposed to be the realm in which masculine values are promoted and rewarded. The market presents images of freedom, rationality, and power. The reality of the market for most men as well as most women is that they are dominated and oppressed by employers exercising arbitrary power over them. In some cases the intercession of seemingly neutral rules will reduce the sense of personal domination, but people are to a great extent the "plaything[s] of alien powers" in the market.[49] Thus, both in the market and in the family, we are all faced with a sense of powerlessness.

In fact, we have created a market that embraces a warped and impoverished notion of freedom, a market characterized by alienated commodity production and a radical loss of the sense of human control over market activities.[50] Although isolated, individual choice is a hallmark of the free market, such choice becomes part of the "objective" forces of supply and demand that are beyond conscious human control. Even in the welfare state market, we underestimate the extent to which we could consciously determine what to produce and how to produce it.

We have also created a family that embraces warped and impoverished notions of community and freedom. The community within a family is hierarchical. Moreover, freedom in the family is largely an illusion. The family is just what we make it—it exists only to please us. We glorify the family's lack of objective purpose; in the family, one is supposed to be free to express personality and to satisfy the human desire to interact with others, but the very attempt to divorce these goals from other purposive or productive activities makes their realization problematic.

We often tend to forget that our present family arrangements and our present market arrangements are of purely human creation. Marx observed that civil society seems natural because it was formed as a by-product of the dissolution of feudal society, at a time when people's self-conscious activity was focused on the political act of forming the state.[51] This is equally true of the modern nuclear family, which is seen as the social form left over from the disintegration of earlier forms of extended families or households. The home is the place where people not recruited into the market are left, and the place to which people return when they finish their work in the market.

Each succeeding political change seems to leave the family a more *natural* entity, a freer expression of human impulses. This process in turn increases the appearance of the family's particularity and of the diversity of family life. Insofar as people consider that the family exists only to serve human emotional wants, that it lacks practical purpose, they believe that it is becoming more pure and familylike.

Most of the time neither our family lives nor our market lives seem fully satisfactory, yet our dissatisfaction with each leads us to romanticize the other in a vicious cycle. To the extent that the freedom of the marketplace turns out to be a sham, people cling to notions of marital felicity and domestic happiness. To the extent that community in the family turns out to be an illusion, people seek refuge in their work. Once we accept the "heartless world" as a given, the value of a "haven" from it seems self-evident. Only by collapsing the facade of a refuge, however, can we lay the foundation for real freedom and community.

C. Transcending the Dichotomies

The dichotomies between state and civil society and between market and family are very much a part of our thinking. Criticisms of the family are often misinterpreted as attacks upon humanization, connectedness, and parenthood, just as criticisms of the market may be misunderstood to be attacks upon efficient production of goods and services. Yet the production of goods and services is a worthwhile goal, just as it is worthwhile to express personality and to satisfy human desires to relate with others. At present, production is carried out primarily by the market, and the opportunity for expressing personality occurs mostly in the family. My argument is that this separation and polarization of functions reinforces the status quo and limits the possibilities of human association.

People who support the market/family dichotomy argue that life will be impoverished if all of it "falls under a single set of terms."[52] The problem, however, is that life all too often is circumscribed by a double set of terms. The market and the family are seen as correlatives, each opposing yet reinforcing the other. But it is my contention that we do not need inhuman environments in order to enjoy human ones, nor do we need unproductive or impractical associations in order to enjoy productive or practical ones. Polarizing the family and the market does not increase the possibilities available to individuals and to the human personality. Instead it reifies the abstractions of "the market" and "the family" and renders us powerless.

Another criticism of efforts to transcend the market/family dichotomy is closely related to liberal criticisms of efforts to transcend the state/civil society dichotomy. Some commentators express the fear that if feminists have their way, families will be abolished and nothing adequate will emerge to replace them. Institutional child care is portrayed as a form of neglect likely to produce children who are unable to form close human attachments and are thus not fully human.[53] Communal or other alternative forms of social life are seen as mere "hollow replications" of the family—weak, frivolous imitations.[54]

This concern is identified with the fear of totalitarianism. Critics contend that the rearing of children outside family structures will lead to oversocialized and conformist adults, people who automatically follow orders that they ought to question and challenge. These commentators view the family as a potential hiding place—a refuge for subjectivity and irrational fancy, a realm antithetical to totalitarian existence.[55] Keeping the family distinct from the rest of civil society, they believe, is crucial to the hopes of maintaining civil society as a separate realm of freedom, a realm not engulfed by the all-powerful state.

The image of Nazi Germany or the cold war image of Soviet Russia is presented as the fearsome alternative to the state/civil society dichotomy. The state controls every aspect of human life; nothing is personal and private; there is no freedom.[56] The state is rational, instrumental, and objective and, at the same time, deeply irrational and frighteningly subjective. Even if a totalitarian state could assume a democratic form, it is argued, the result would be a dictatorship of the masses, and human freedom would be destroyed.

I do not advocate replacing the present dichotomies with an all-powerful state and an all-embracing market any more than I would advocate making women just like men. The state as it now exists must be ended at the same time that civil society as it now exists is ended; and when we transform the contemporary family, we must simultaneously transform the market.

I favor neither a romantic return to a simpler form of life nor a regression to an earlier, undifferentiated world. It would not be a solution to reestablish cottage industries, to have both parents at home working and caring for the children. I am not envisioning an escape from the complications of existing in the world as conscious free-willed beings, nor do I advocate an evasion of the conflict that may be painful but is inherent in human growth. Rather, I have in mind a situation in which conflict can take place more effectively. The dichotomies stunt human growth by avoiding and displacing conflict—conflict within the individual psyche and among people. The problem of externalizing conflict through compartmentalization, and the advantages to be gained by transcending the dichotomies, can be illustrated by an examination of the male/female dichotomy.

The differences between men and women are as natural as starvation, religion, and brutality. Inequality between men and women has existed throughout recorded history and has persisted across widely divergent cultures. So too have starvation, religion, and brutality. That each of these phenomena has been long lived does not mean that any of them is immutable.

We have sometimes viewed gender differences as Malthusians viewed starvation— unfortunate for individual victims, but socially necessary and logically inevitable. At other times, gender distinctions have been recognized to be socially created but, like religion, enormously useful for maintaining social and political stability, and perhaps even good for the common man. Recently, gender differences have been considered analogous to brutality—we can reduce or overcome them to a certain extent, but we can probably never eliminate them altogether, and perhaps the world would be all too homogenous if we could. In any event, it may be thought that the amount of coercion necessary to eliminate completely either brutality or gender distinctions would constitute too great an infringement on human freedom.

1. The Feuerbach Model: The Progress of History. Perhaps the most useful model for capturing the nature of the male/female dichotomy is suggested by atheist Ludwig Feuerbach's description of religion.[57] Feuerbach saw religion as a product of human imagination and God as a projection of human qualities. In Feuerbach's Hegelian language:

> Man—this is the mystery of religion—projects his being into objectivity, and then
> again makes himself an object to this projected image of himself thus converted into
> a subject; he thinks of himself [as] an object to himself, but as the object of an object,
> of another being than himself. Thus here. Man is an object to God.[58]

Feuerbach hypothesized that people project their nature onto the God they create, and in contemplating this God, they perceive their own nature: "Consciousness of God is self-consciousness, knowledge of God is self-knowledge."[59] Through their relationship to God, people reclaim their own nature.

The male/female dichotomy, like religion, is a human construction. The "mystery" of sexuality consists in projecting human qualities separately onto males and females to make each the object of the other. The relationship between the sexes becomes a means by which members of each gender can reclaim their own projected nature. In becoming acquainted with each other, men and women become acquainted with themselves.

Feuerbach believed that the process of projecting human qualities onto God served a useful human purpose. "Man first of all sees his nature as if *out of* himself, before he finds it in himself."[60] The history of religion is the history of the recognition by humans of more and more of their own nature. Each new religion correctly perceives the previous one to be idolatry—the worship of something human as if it were divine.[61] "Man has given objectivity to himself, but has not recognized the object as his own nature: a later religion takes this forward step; every advance in religion is therefore a deeper self-knowledge."[62]

Gender differentiation serves a useful human purpose analogous to that served by religion. The gradual shifts that have taken place in our understanding of maleness and femaleness can be seen as reflections of an historical process resulting in deeper self-knowledge. The historical progress of gender differentiation consists in recognizing that what was previously considered immutable is contingent and subject to human control. The division of human beings into male and female could be judged to have been a useful device for enabling us to become conscious of the wide range of human possibilities. The transcending of the male/female dichotomy would then be the final step in the reclamation of the whole self, the last stage in this historical process.

2. Elaborating on the Model: Complications of Gender. There are several problems with viewing gender differentiation as historic progress. The first problem is shared by Feuerbach's analysis of religion. Feuerbach did not believe that God actually existed, and although his work was part of an argument for the nonexistence of God, it was at the same time premised upon that nonexistence. A contemporary believer would either disagree with Feuerbach or would insist that, although early gods were admittedly human projections, Feuerbach failed to capture the essence of contemporary belief because he made a simple factual mistake regarding the existence of God. Similarly, I am arguing that gender distinctions are historically contingent, and an underlying premise of my argument is that male and female traits are not immutable. Anyone convinced that biology is destiny will be unpersuaded by my argument. Given that people identified as women really do exist and are biologically distinguishable from men, some observers will always argue that perceived differences are real rather than projected.

Just as Feuerbach could never really disprove the existence of God or gods, I cannot disprove the general claim that the differences between women and men are biologically determined rather than the result of projections of the self. It is clear, however, that our understandings of maleness and femaleness have undergone dramatic changes and that previous understandings of biological determinism have therefore been mistaken. Whenever assertions of biological constraints are made in a sufficiently specific context, scholars and researchers are ready to disprove them. But such disproof will never convince the faithful that there do not exist other basic differences between men and women that make it impossible or unwise to transcend the male/female dichotomy. Perhaps the most we can say with certainty is that even if biological constraints exist that may ultimately limit the possibilities for remaking society, we will not be able to determine the part played by such constraints until we have correctly assessed the part played by the social construction of gender roles. At present, I find no evidence that biology prevents us from making major alterations in the relationship between women and men or from transcending the male/female dichotomy.

The application of Feuerbach's historical progress model to gender differentiation is complicated by the presence of factors in the relationship between women and men that are not present in the relationship between human beings and God. First, the relationship between man and woman involves two people and two different projected relationships. There is an actual relationship between a man and a woman that takes place alongside the two projected relationships. The projections that are an integral part of our present gender system interfere with the actual relationship. I refer to this interference with companionship and love and the limitations it places upon the possibilities of human association as *problems of love*. Second, the historical process has been blocked by the reality that men dominate women. Feuerbach's model is based on the projection of positive traits upon God, whereas the traits projected upon women are simultaneously despised and exalted. Thus, the problem of domination that characterizes male–female relations is not present in Feuerbach's picture of religion.

(a) *Problems of Love*. Feminists have long argued that our present gender system, with its inequality and domination, makes true love between the sexes difficult, perhaps impossible.[63] What currently passes for love has been described as "a one-sided pathological dependency of women on men."[64] Men are seen to be strong and powerful, women to be weak and dependent. Additionally, in our present society women are economically and socially dependent upon men. The chief determinants of a woman's status are her acceptance by and associations with men. Under these circumstances, romantic love plays an apologetic role; it mystifies women about their dependency on men and reinforces male hegemony.[65]

Shulamith Firestone builds upon the ideas introduced by John Stuart Mill[66] and others about the harmful effects that sexual inequality has upon the possibilities for love. Firestone explains that healthy love requires mutual self-respect, which is destroyed when neither men nor women regard females to be autonomous, equal beings deserving of respect. Women lack self-esteem and seek to gain identity and worth by being loved by men.[67] Men do not actually respect women but instead generally undervalue them; at the same time, they idealize individual women with whom they "fall in love." Because women know they do not fit this idealized image, they can feel no security in being loved and must fear honest and intimate contact that would reveal their true selves.[68] Thus, Firestone argues, love as we know it is both a delusion and a trap for women. But the solution lies in sexual equality: Among equals there can be meaningful love.[69]

Elizabeth Rapaport has extended Firestone's critique to show how love is transformed into a destructive dependency relationship for men as well as for women. Drawing on Rousseau, she suggests that achieving equality of power and influence between men and women would not by itself solve the problems of love. Love begins with a healthy attraction, a recognition of like sensibilities. But lovers then focus on differences, she argues, because they are seeking to find in their partners the qualities they fear they lack in themselves and are thus in some sense seeking to gain possession of those qualities.[70] They do not choose the partner with whom they have most to share, but rather seek the "preeminent" member of the opposite sex. Each person hoping to be loved must strive to appear to be that preeminent person. Consequently, even if there were equality between men and women, a relationship of dependency might lead to a false presentation of the self as well as to a fear of exposing the real, flawed self. The lover thus loses his or her identity and autonomy.

According to Rousseau, the tendency to love the one who seems most virtuous and most beautiful,[71] combined with the desire to be loved, leads to "emulation, rivalry, and jealousy." If we locate choice in sharing rather than in virtue and beauty, however, quite different results obtain. People will be attracted to each other by how much they have to share. They will focus on what they have, not on what they lack or fear they lack.

Thus, the real issue is not dependency but, rather, one's attitude toward oneself. It is important that one be self-sufficient but not that one be independent. The choice is not between being a complete, independent individual and being dependent and incomplete.

Rapaport contends that healthy love is impossible not only because of the inequality between men and women but also because of the individualist assumptions of liberalism and the actual competitive and hierarchical conditions of capitalist society.[72] Thus, she argues, socialism and women's equality hold the promise of healthy love. Rapaport is correct to reject dependency and autonomy as polar choices. An adult can and should be "autonomous" in the sense of being a full and complete human being. Yet social life is richer than isolation; sharing and intimacy enable a person to enjoy life more fully. To the extent that our social interactions enrich the quality of our lives, we can be said to be "dependent" upon others for this enhanced existence. To have to depend on another to fulfill immediate emotional needs can be a bad thing; to be able to depend on another to enrich one's life is a good thing. To be autonomous means not to need another in order to feel complete; it does not mean that one is incapable of enriching one's life through social interaction.

Socialism and sexual equality together, however, are not enough to rehabilitate love. We must also counter the self-alienation inherent in our present gender system. When we project human traits separately upon men and women, we ensure that we remain incomplete beings. Our attraction for the opposite sex has a quality of urgency because a relationship with a member of that sex is necessary for our own completion. Our present gender system tends to foster relationships based on need rather than desire. To need another to complete oneself is ultimately unsatisfactory; it interferes with the intimate sharing that is possible between human beings, a sharing that leads us to want contact with others.

(b) Problems of Domination. The domination of women by men is self-perpetuating. Women's unfamiliarity with aspects of the world to which they have been denied access has justified their continued exclusion. Menstruation, pregnancy, and childbirth have been made to operate as disadvantages to women and have allowed women to be dominated by men and to need their protection. The degradation of women in the real world was matched by their exaltation in a fantasy world. Women were seen as wonderful and terrible.

The world came more generally to be viewed as a series of complex dualisms—reason/passion, rational/irrational, culture/nature, power/sensitivity, thought/feeling, soul/body, objective/subjective. Men, who have created our dominant consciousness, have organized these dualisms into a system in which each dualism has a strong or positive side and a weak or negative side. Men associate themselves with the strong sides of the dualisms and project the weak sides upon women. In the same way that men simultaneously exalt and degrade women and the family, they simultaneously exalt and degrade the concepts on the weak sides of the dualisms. Nature, for example, is glorified as something awesome, a worthy subject of conquest by male heroes, while it is simultaneously degraded as inert matter to be exploited and shaped to men's purposes. Irrational subjectivity and sensitivity are similarly treasured and denigrated at the same time.[73]

Another important aspect of the way these dualisms are viewed in dominant culture is that the inferior half of any dualism is often seen to pose a constant danger to the stronger half. Man is warned to do battle with the flesh, with nature, even with women. Irrationalism is regarded as something that must be conquered, like nature. The weak sides of the dualisms are simultaneously indispensable and threatening to men.[74]

The limited choices that seem available to women may be described in terms of women's relationship to these dualisms. One feminist strategy accepts the identification of women with their traditional side of the dualisms but tries to deny the hierarchy men have established between the two sides. Another strategy struggles to identify women with the stronger side of the dualisms instead of challenging the devaluation of the side traditionally associated with women. Reformers often adopt both strategies simultaneously. Suffragists, for example, argued not only that women should be allowed to vote because they could be as reasonable and rational as men but also that granting women the vote would benefit society because of women's superior sensitivity to human values. Although neither of these two feminist strategies is necessarily inconsistent with a rejection of the dualisms themselves, such a rejection has not in practice been emphasized.

The traditional identification of women with the weak side of the dualisms—with nature, subjectivity, nurturance—has been a legacy of oppression. Accepting this identification may be tantamount to embracing women's subordinate position. Yet the identification is also a potential source of power and insight. To reject the weak side of the dualisms is to neglect the qualities that women have been allowed to cultivate. Both approaches may be considered to accept, perhaps even to reinforce, the dualisms.

The answer that I endorse is not to reject identification with the strengths and values of women but to recognize the incompleteness of the traditional roles of women and of women's identification with one side of the dualisms. Thus, I would not repudiate the traditional values and roles of women but would refuse to give those values and roles a privileged place. It is the acceptance and the sexualization of the dualisms that is the chief problem. When one side of a dualism is forced upon us, it is not enough to insist upon the right to choose the opposite side. Nor, of course, is it helpful to grab the weak side of the dualism voluntarily before it is forced upon us. We cannot choose between the two sides of the dualism, because we need both. Similarly, we cannot choose between men's roles and women's roles, because both are essential to us. We can never win if we fight for the bigger portion or even an equal portion of a body torn in two; we must prevent the initial destruction.

3. Criticisms and Conclusions. As early as the nineteenth century, feminists became aware of the idea of abolishing sex roles.[75] The rebirth of the women's movement has again brought this idea into popular discourse, and critics have leveled a variety of attacks against what has been loosely labeled *androgyny.* In order to clarify my position, I shall briefly set forth two of these attacks and my response to them.

First, opponents of androgyny warn that the elimination of the present gender system will diminish the possibilities for passion and variety in human association by making everyone boringly the same.[76] It is true that as long as we sexualize dichotomies and constitute ourselves as incomplete beings, we must depend on finding other, correlatively incomplete beings in order to reclaim wholeness. As incomplete beings, we find it threatening to consider the sudden loss of other incomplete beings who are our inverse. It is perhaps for this reason that atheism or the notion of God's being "dead" is so terrifying to some people:[77] They fear that they will forever lose divine traits and remain permanently incomplete. Feuerbach, however, saw that eliminating the belief in God would allow people to recognize that so-called divine qualities are in fact human.[78] With respect also to the division between male and female, whole people do not need correlatives and will find their social wants more readily satisfied by other complete beings. We can recognize that we would not increase diversity by chopping off the right arms of all women and the left arms of all men, yet what some opponents of androgyny argue is no more sensible. Sex roles limit human potential far more than they expand it.

A second objection to androgyny suggests that the union or transcendence of the male/female dichotomy may be undesirable because it would require that women accept what men have been as a part of the wholeness women seek.[79] Instead, this argument runs, women should reject what men have been and find strength in women's culture and the values of our foremothers. My response to this is that most of what is wrong with what men have been is what they have not been. The point is not that the passions are superior to reason, subjectivity to objectivity, nature to culture, and so forth. To reverse the dualisms may secure for women a fairer portion of the divided psyche, but to reject the polarization of the dualistic pairs is to create the possibility of wholeness. Although I share the rejection of much of what men have been (or rather what they have *not* been), I feel that I must also reject much of what women have not been (and thus, in the same sense, what we have been).

When I speak of transcending the male/female dichotomy, I have in mind creating a new referential system for relating men and women to the world, a systemic departure from the ordinary image of male and female as correlatives. This does not mean making women more like men, or men more like women. Rather, it means radically increasing the options available to each individual and, more importantly, allowing the human personality to break out of the present dichotomized system. We have all experienced occasional glimpses of what this might mean—moments of power, sensitivity, and connectedness. We should recognize these fleeting experiences as a source of hope, a foreshadow of the human beings we can become. In some ways women will be *less* like present men, and men will be *less* like present women. Rather than shades of grey as an alternative to all black and all white, I envision reds and greens and blues.

Notes

This chapter is based in part on research supported by the Peter B. Livingston Fund of Harvard Medical School. I wish to express my appreciation to the fund, to the editors of the *Harvard Law Review,* and to the dozens of friends and colleagues who offered helpful comments on earlier drafts. Mary Joe Frug, Chris Littleton, Martha Minow, and James B. White were particularly generous and supportive. Duncan Kennedy enriched my understanding of how helpful one person can be to another. I am grateful for his valuable insights, his numerous critical readings, and his unswerving encouragement. He has provided an example I hope to follow.

1. W. HOUGHTON, THE VICTORIAN FRAME OF MIND, 1830–1870, at 343 (1957) (emphasis omitted).

2. N. COTT, THE BONDS OF WOMANHOOD, 64–70 (1977).

3. A. DOUGLAS, THE FEMINIZATION OF AMERICAN CULTURE, 12 (1977).

4. *See generally* R. TRYON, HOUSEHOLD MANUFACTURES IN THE UNITED STATES, 1640–1860 (1917) (recounting rise of disciplined modes of production); M. WEBER, GENERAL ECONOMIC HISTORY (F. Knight trans. 1927) (same).

5. N. COTT, at 69.

6. *Id.*

7. The family offered the model for safe, contained reform of the market system. Radical proposals would have abolished the dichotomy between state and civil society; a reformist program was

developed that kept this dichotomy in place by utilizing the dichotomy between market and family. In very important ways, the welfare state is paternalistic rather than democratic.

8. *See* I. W. BLACKSTONE, COMMENTARIES, 432—33.

9. Although a wife may choose her own domicile, the husband's choice of job continues to determine where most couples will live. *See* Gillespie, *Who Has the Power? The Marital Struggle,* in FAMILY, MARRIAGE, AND THE STRUGGLE OF THE SEXES, 121-50 (H. Dreitzel ed. 1972). In some two-career families, considerable negotiation does occur, but tradition and men's higher wages combine to increase the husband's bargaining power.

10. Some couples give their children a hyphenated last name composed of both the mother's and the father's surnames. This system would seem to be a considerable improvement over using just the father's surname. Of course, in seven generations someone could have a name composed of 128 surnames connected by 127 hyphens. The results after only three generations, however, might sound very dignified: Frances Elisabeth Olsen-Dige-Sørensen-Andersdatter-Hood-McIntyre-Licht-Pfeifer.

11. *See* W. O'NEILL, DIVORCE IN THE PROGRESSIVE ERA (1967).

12. *See* Weitzman, *The Economics of Divorce: Social & Economic Consequences of Property, Alimony & Child Support Awards,* 28 UCLA L. REV. 1181, 1241-54 (1981).

13. *See* Weitzman, *Legal Regulation of Marriage: Tradition and Change,* 62 CALIF. L. REV. 1169, 1249 (1974).

14. *See* I F. HARPER AND F. JAMES, THE LAW OF TORTS §§ 8.10-.11, at 643-52 (1956); McCurdy, *Torts Between Persons in Domestic Relation,* 43 HARV. L. REV. 1030, 1035-56 (1930).

15. *See* Davidson, *Wifebeating: A Recurring Phenomenon Throughout History,* in BATTERED WOMEN, 2 (M. Ray ed. 1977); Note, at 167.

16. To the extent that welfare state reformers of the market have looked to the family for a model, the welfare state market may resemble the family. Thus, reforms of the family that attempt to make it more like the welfare state market will bear a relationship to reforms that attempt to make the family more like the ideal image of the family. The focus of reforms of the former category is upon recognizing actual inequality of women in order to establish more than mere juridical equality. Reforms that make the family more like the ideal family differ in that they focus on family solidarity rather than equality. The distinction can be illustrated by two different approaches to dealing with wife beating. The welfare state approach gives wives additional rights against their husbands; the family approach attempts to mediate between the spouses, even at the expense of the wife's rights.

17. *See* S. FEDERICI, WAGES AGAINST HOUSEWORK (1975).

18. *See* H. CLARK, § 7.2, at 226 & n.37.

19. *See* Glendon, at 703. Most community property states have recently abandoned this rule and provided for equal management. *See* W. REPPY AND C. SAMUEL, COMMUNITY PROPERTY IN THE UNITED STATES, 205 (1982);

20. *See* H. CLARK, § 6.4, at 192-94; *id.* § 6.5, at 200-06.

21. *See* W. MacDONALD, FRAUD ON THE WIDOW'S SHARE, 21-25 (1960).

22. *See* Arthur, *A Family Court—Why Not?,* 51 MINN. L. REV. 223 (1966); Foster, *Conciliation and Counseling in the Courts in Family Law Cases,* 41 N.Y.U. L. REV. 353 (1966); Kay, *A Family Court: The California Proposal,* 56 CALIF. L. REV. 1205 (1968). For a cogent criticism of family court performance, see Paulsen, *Juvenile Courts, Family Courts, and the Poor Man,* 54 CALIF. L. REV. 694 (1966).

23. For a more sophisticated explanation of the construction of gender within the "ideology of familialism," see M. BARRETT, WOMEN'S OPPRESSION TODAY, 205-16 (1980).

24. The first steps in integrating women into the market were the emancipation of the slaves, a large number of whom were women; the adoption of married women's property acts or community property laws, and the judicial or legislative overturning of statutes barring women from various market activities, such as practicing law or tending bar, *see, e.g.,* Sail'er Inn, Inc. v. Kirby, 5 Cal. 3d 1, 485 P.2d 529, 95 Cal. Rptr. 329 (1971) (striking down state law forbidding women from being

bartenders); Act of Mar. 22, 1872, 1871 Ill. Pub. Laws 578 (guaranteeing all persons freedom in the selection of an occupation; passed in response to the state supreme court's refusal to admit a woman to the state bar, a refusal upheld by the United States Supreme Court in Bradwell v. Illinois, 83 U.S. (16 Wall.) 130 (1873)).

> Slaves represented a large portion of the female work force; thus, their emancipation radically increased the number of women workers participating in the market. The work of black women also had complex ideological effects. On the one hand, it undermined any stereotypic notions that women were incapable of working. On the other hand, it identified work by women with the low status accorded to black women, with the health problems suffered by black slaves, and with the sexual availability forced upon slave women. These complex associations continue to influence the lives of all of us and are discussed in A. DAVIS, WOMEN, RACE & CLASS (1981); B. HOOKS, AIN'T I A WOMAN (1981).

25. *See* C. MACKINNON, SEXUAL HARASSMENT OF WORKING WOMEN, 18–21 (1979); Alexander, *Women's Work in Nineteenth-Century London: A Study of the Years 1820–50, in* THE RIGHTS AND WRONGS OF WOMEN, 59 (J. Mitchell and A. Oakley eds. 1976).

26. Proponents of "woman's separate sphere" argued that the family would suffer if women participated in the market. Market opportunities would tempt women away from their natural roles as wives and mothers. Good wages would make some women unwilling to marry and raise children, and would make others neglectful of their homes and families, rebellious against their husbands' authority, and sexually unfaithful. *See* W. WANDERSEE, WOMEN'S WORK AND FAMILY VALUES: 1920–1940, at 67, 70 (1981).

27. Women themselves, it was argued, would suffer damage by participating fully in the market. Women were said to be physically more vulnerable than men, and women's health was said to be crucial because the perpetuation of the race depended upon women's capacity to reproduce. *See, e.g.,* Muller v. Oregon, 208 U.S. 412, 421 (1908).

28. Discrimination was justified on the ground that it was necessary to protect the market role of men. *See* W. WANDERSEE, at 67, 70 (women workers take jobs away from men). Even when jobs were sexually segregated so that women were not in direct competition with men, employers could save money whenever they were able to convert labor that had been performed by men into "women's work." *Cf.* C. MACKINON, at 11–12 (1979) (by simplifying jobs and breaking them into components calling for less skill, employers create "women's work"). There seemed to some men to be an endless supply of young women who lived with their parents and were thus willing and able to work at wages inadequate to support one person, let alone a family. Women workers were therefore thought to depress wage levels and cause male unemployment.

29. It was asserted that women were worse workers than men were because women were too weak for many jobs, lacked mechanical ability, and were inadequately educated. *See* C. MAC KINNON, at 10–12. Moreover, their psychological makeup—their "natural and proper timidity and delicacy"—ill equipped them for market pursuits. *See* Bradwell v. Illinois, 83 U.S. (16 Wall.) 130, 141 (1873).

30. First, working mothers and "two-career" families are thought to create special problems. Popular books assert that nurturant families and women's equality may be hopelessly incompatible goals. *See, e.g.,* C. BIRD, THE TWO-PAYCHECK MARRIAGE (1979); C. DEGLER, AT ODDS (1980).

Second, both feminists and antifeminists express concern that too exclusive a focus on eradicating discrimination may damage women psychologically or spiritually by encouraging them to adopt the kinds of instrumental rationality and aggressiveness that are rewarded in the market. *Cf.* J. KREPS, SEX IN THE MARKETPLACE, 64–68 (1971);

Third, there is concern that men will be harmed by women's participation in the market. For example, women police officers and firefighters are thought by some to create special problems for their male colleagues, who may feel forced into unsafe situations by their sense of chivalry. *See Wall Street Journal,* February 3, 1958, at 1, col. 1;

Finally, it is still asserted that the market may suffer from women's participation in it. The concern remains that women are psychologically ill prepared for many jobs and occupations. A number of employers also continue to expect that a woman worker will take time off if her child is sick and will quit her job if her husband is transferred. *See* W. WANDERSEE, at 3.

31. *See, e.g.,* Equal Pay Act of 1963, 29 U.S.C. § 206(d) (1976); Civil Rights Act of 1964, 42 U.S.C. §§ 2000e to 2000e-17 (1976 & Supp. V 1981).

32. *See, e.g.,* Education Amendments of 1972, 20 U.S.C. § 1681 (1976).

33. *See, e.g.,* Equal Credit Opportunity Act of 1974, 15 U.S.C. §§ 1691–1691f (1976 & Supp. V 1981).

34. *See, e.g.,* Fair Housing Act of 1968, 42 U.S.C. §§ 3604–3607 (1976).

35. 401 U.S. 424 (1971).

36. Insofar as the family is used to critique the market, the welfare state market may be said to resemble the family, and reforms of the market that make it more like the welfare state will bear a relationship to those that make the market more like the family. The point of the welfare state reforms, however, is to promote equality for women, whereas the chief point of the market reforms is to moderate individualism. The reforms can both promote equality and reduce individualism only to the extent that they begin to transcend the dichotomy between market and family.

37. 42 U.S.C. § 2000e(k) (Supp. V 1981).

38. *See* General Elec. Co. v. Gilbert, 429 U.S. 125 (1976) (title VII); Geduldig V. Aiello, 417 U.S. 484 (1974) (equal protection clause).

39. *See generally* L. SHIELDS, DISPLACED HOMEMAKERS (1981)

40. 208 U.S. 412 (1908).

41. 198 U.S. 45 (1905).

42. None of what I say here is in any sense intended to be a resolution of the dilemmas I have sketched out, nor is it an effort to construct a new system that could become as rigid and oppressive as the market/family dichotomy. Rather, it is meant to be an example of the kind of speculative thinking that we can and should undertake as a first step in a better direction. This endeavor is facilitated by the critique presented in the previous Parts, but the aptness and value of that critique is in no way dependent upon the speculation I engage in here. Criticism or rejection of the direction I suggest should not cast doubt upon my critique. Rather, it should encourage the reader to continue the conversation and to suggest new directions and alternative approaches.

43. For a seminal work, see MARX, *On the Jewish Question,* in WRITINGS OF THE YOUNG MARX ON PHILOSOPHY AND SOCIETY 216 (L. Easton and K. Guddat eds. 1967). Much of the recent legal scholarship criticizing the public/private distinction should be understood as a call to transcend the state/civil society dichotomy. *See, e.g.,* Frug, Cities and Homeowners Associations: *A Reply,* 130 U. PA. L. REV. 1589, 1589–91 (1982); Frug, *The City as a Legal Concept,* 93 HARV. L. REV. 1057 (1980); Horwitz, *The History of the Public/Private Distinction,* 130 U. PA. L. REV. 1423, 1428 (1982);

44. For general treatments of leftist analyses of the family, see M. BARRETT; E. ZARETSKY, CAPITALISM, THE FAMILY, & PERSONAL LIFE (1976).

45. C. DEGLER, at 472.

46. Marx, 30.

47. *Id.*

48. The best statement of this dilemma is in Kennedy, *The Structure of Blackstone's Commentaries,* 28 BUFFALO L. REV. 209, 211–13 (1979).

49. This terminology comes from K. MARX, at 216, 225.

50. *See generally* K. MARX, *Alienated Labor,* in WRITINGS, at 287 (classic discussion of alienated labor).

51. K. MARX, at 216, 240.

52. J. ELSHTAIN, PUBLIC MAN, PRIVATE WOMAN 335 (1981).

53. *See, e.g., id.* at 328–31.

54. *Id.* at 330.

55. *See* C. LASCH, HAVEN IN A HEARTLESS WORLD (1977). subjugation of individual by new forms of coercion).

56. *See, e.g.,* J. F. DULLES, WAR ORPEACE 5–16 (1950) (describing Soviet "enemy").

57. *See* L. FEUERBACH, THE ESSENCE OF CHRISTIANITY (G. Eliot Trans. 1957).

58. *Id.* at 29–30.

59. *Id.* at 12.

60. *Id.* at 13.

61. *Id.*

62. *Id.*

63. For an excellent summary and evaluation of some of these views, see Rapaport, *On the Future of Love: Rousseau and the Radical Feminists,* in WOMEN AND PHILOSOPHY, at 185.

64. *Id.*

65. S. FIRESTONE, THE DIALECTIC OF SEX, 146–48, 165–75 (1970).

66. *See* J. S. MILL, *The Subjection of Women,* in J. S. MILL AND H. T. MILL, at 233–36. ESSAYS ON SEX EQUALITY 89, 99–100 (A. Rossi ed. 1970).

67. *See* Firestone, at 155–56.

68. *See id.* at 149.

69. *See id.;* Rapaport, at 185–86.

70. *See* Rapaport, at 199.

71. *See* J. ROUSSEAU, EMILE, (Everyman ed. 1911) at 175–76, *discussed and quoted in* Rapaport, at 197.

72. Rapaport, at 203–4.

73. *See* C. CHRIST, DIVING DEEP AND SURFACING 25–26, 129–31 (1980).

74. *See id.* at 25.

75. For a review of nineteenth-century feminist views, see W. LEACH, TRUE LOVE AND PERFECT UNION (1980).

76. *See, e.g.,* Elshtain, *Against Androgyny,* 47 TELOS 5, 21 (1981).

77. *See* F. NIETZSCHE, *Thus Spoke Zarathustra,* in THE PORTABLE NIETZSCHE 124 (W. Kaufman trans. 1954).

78. *See* L. FEUERBACH, at xxxviii–xxxix, 20–25.

79. This position has been attributed to Adrienne Rich. *See* C. CHRIST, at 83–84.

4

The Emergence of Feminist Jurisprudence: An Essay

ANN C. SCALES

A hand or something passes across the sun. Your eyeballs slacken,
you are free for a moment. Then it comes back: this
test of the capacity to keep in focus
this
    unfair struggle with the forces of perception

A. Rich[1]

We as lawyers have been trained to desire abstract, universal, objective solutions to social ills, in the form of legal rules or doctrine. Much of the history of feminist jurisprudence has reflected that tradition. It has been a debate, in the abstract, about appropriate rules. This chapter uses the work of several nonlegal authors to illustrate the impossibility of seeing solutions to inequality through that lens of abstraction. This chapter concerns feminist efforts to live with, and ultimately to resist, abstraction itself. It is also a chapter about the power of the way things are: how comfortably we respond in accord with our learned reticence; how easily we leap for shallow solutions; and how such solutions are shifting shadows, constantly testing our capacity to keep in focus, keeping us in fear of being blinded by a brighter light.

Where We've Been

In this country, the engine of the struggle for equality has been Aristotelian: Equality means to treat like persons alike and unlike persons unlike. Under this model, when legal distinctions are made, the responsible sovereign must point to some difference between subjects which justifies their disparate treatment. That was the model in *Reed v. Reed,*[2] the first equal protection case decided favorably in the Supreme Court for women. Under the expert guidance of Ruth Bader Ginsburg and the ACLU Women's Rights Project, the *Reed* Court held that the state of Idaho could not presumptively deny to women the right to administer estates. With respect to such activities, the Court saw that women and men are "similarly situated." That is, no demonstrable difference between the sexes justified treating them differently.

This is what Professor Catharine MacKinnon has called "the differences approach,"[3] and it worked extraordinarily well for Ginsburg and her legions. Indeed, all was going swimmingly until the Court had to face situations where the sexes are not, or do not seem to be, similarly situated—situations involving pregnancy,[4] situations involving the supposed overpowering sexual allure which women present to men,[5] and situations involving the historical absence of women.[6] When the "differences approach" was applied in those cases, the plaintiffs lost. Aristotle would have been thrilled.

Feminist legal scholars have devoted enormous energies to patching the cracks in the differences approach. The debate has been, and continues to be, arduous. Which differences between the sexes are or should be relevant for legal purposes? How does one tell what the differences are? Does it matter whether the differences are inherent or the result of upbringing? Is it enough to distinguish between accurate and inaccurate stereotyped differences? Or are there situations where differences are sufficiently "real" and permanent to demand social accommodation?

In response to these questions, feminists have tried to describe for the judiciary a theory of "special rights" for women which will "fit" the discrete, nonstereotypical, "real" differences between the sexes. And here lies our mistake: We have let the debate become narrowed by accepting as correct those questions which seek to arrive at a definitive list of differences. In so doing, we have adopted the vocabulary, as well as the epistemology and political theory, of the law as it is.

When we try to arrive at a definitive list of differences, even in sophisticated ways, we only encourage the law's tendency to act upon a frozen slice of reality. In so doing, we participate in the underlying problem—the objectification of women. Through our conscientious listing, we help to define real gender issues out of existence. Our aim must be to affirm differences as emergent and infinite. We must seek a legal system that works and, at the same time, makes differences a cause for celebration, not classification.

A new jurisprudence emerges as we cease to conduct the debate in prescribed legalistic terms. The equal/special rights debate, for example, reflects the circularity of liberal legal thinking. The rights formula, described in terms of constitutional fit, presumes a fixed reality of gender to which law must conform. The problem of sexual inequality, however, when understood as systematic domination, is not susceptible to that view. Our past reliance on rights/rule structuring has been disappointing because we have been unable to see the solipsism of the male norm. Our tendency as lawyers to seek comprehensive rules in accordance with that norm is a dangerous learned reflex which defeats feminism's critique of objectification.

The Tyranny of Objectivity

> Male dominance is perhaps the most pervasive and tenacious system of power in history . . . it is metaphysically nearly perfect. Its point of view is the standard for point-of-viewlessness; its particularity the meaning of universality. Its force is exercised as consent, its authority as participation, its supremacy as the paradigm of order, its control as the definition of legitimacy.[7]

Underlying the Supreme Court's ruling in *Reed v. Reed*[8] was a perception that sexism is a distortion of reality. Once the Court made this discovery, it needed to transform its discovery into a legalistic code, to construct an "objective" rule. And here lies the most difficult part of rule making in our system as it is—phrasing the rule so that people believe that the rule is detached, so that it appears to transcend the results in particular cases.

The philosophical basis of such an approach is "abstract universality."[9] In order to apply a rule neutrally in future cases, one must discern a priori what the differences and similarities among groups are. But because there are an infinite number of differences and similarities among groups, one must also discern which differences are relevant. To make this determination, one must first abstract the essential and universal similarities among humans, one must have strict assumptions about human nature as such. Without such an abstraction, there is no way to talk about which differences in treatment are arbitrary and which are justified. Underlying this approach is the correspondence theory of truth: The sovereign's judgments are valid only when they reflect objective facts.[10] Thus, somewhere in the nature of things there must be a list of sex differences that matter and those that do not. Notice, however, that abstract universality by its own terms cannot arrive at such a list. It has no "bridge to the concrete"[11] by which to ascertain the emerging and cultural qualities which constitute difference.

With nothing above ground, abstract universality constructed a dark tunnel to its tainted delusion. It made maleness the norm of what is human, and did so sub rosa, all in the name of neutrality.[12] By this subterranean system, the "relevant" differences have been and always will be those which keep women in their place. Abstract universality is ideology, pure and simple. It is a conception of the world which takes "the part for the whole, the particular for the universal and essential, or the present for the eternal."[13] With the allegedly anonymous picture of humanity reflecting a picture males have painted of themselves, women are but male subjectivity glorified, objectified, elevated to the status of reality. The values of things "out there" are made to appear as if they were qualities of the things themselves. So goes the process of objectification: The winner is he who makes his world seem necessary.

Feminist analysis begins with the principle that objective reality is a myth. It recognizes that patriarchal myths are projections of the male psyche. The most pernicious of these myths is that the domination of women is a natural right, a mere reflection of the biological family.[14] The patriarchal paradigm of the will of the father informs rationality at every historical stage. Professor J. C. Smith points out how that paradigm centrally driven by a need to subjugate woman and all that is womanly, is violently reflected in the myth of Perseus. Perseus was able to slay the female monster Medusa, but only with the goddess Athena guiding his hand. Whereas Medusa was the archetype of a free woman, Athena was the patriarchal stereotype of women, reflecting male needs. Because Athena was not of woman born, she was always for her father's side. She was an avowed servant of patriarchy.[15]

With the advent of the Golden Age, Greek thinkers rejected the Olympian ideal and embraced natural laws susceptible of mathematical formulation. When all that irrationality gave way to objectivity, it would seem that the Greeks could have begun to take equality seriously in civic life. But they never did free their slaves or emancipate their women. Objectivity left them plenty of room for immoral discretion, and they chose a political structure that ensured the survival of male privilege. With the Olympian mythic structure displaced, however, privilege had to be justified some other way, for detached justification is the mechanism of domination. The master must be able to describe the relationship as good in itself (as Olympian-decreed hierarchy seemed good), in order to get the slave to exhibit the regularities being used to justify the relationship. That is the hegemonic method of patriarchy: Its aims are united within a social fabric by assimilating the subordinated classes into the dominant one, and by allying those classes with it.[16]

Plato and Aristotle were hegemonic heroes, not only for their own times, but as models for the future. Their declarations of woman as partial man have been the prototype for all neomythic justifications of domination, from Christianity to Freud, through social Darwinism, and including economic and scientific explanations of the social order.[17] The narcotic influence which objectivity has increasingly exerted over our minds makes us ever less alert to the mythic structure around us.

A legal system must attempt to ensure fairness. Fairness must have reference to real human predicaments. Abstract universality is a convenient device for some philosophical pursuits, or for any endeavor whose means can stand without ends, but it is particularly unsuited for law. Law is, after all, a social tool. It is only extrinsically important. Its actual value depends upon its success in promoting that which is intrinsically valuable. By inquiring into the mythic structure of objectivity, we see that abstract universality explicitly contradicts the ideal of a "government of laws, not men." Our task, therefore, is to construct a system which avoids solipsism, which recognizes that the subjectivity of the lawmaker is not the whole of reality.

A Call for Vigilance

It is imperative for jurisprudence to tap the power of the more radical versions of feminism. An effective contemporary feminist critique must be radical in the literal sense. It must go to the root of inequality. Without extraordinary subterranean vigilance, the radical potential of feminism will be undermined. Like other movements that presage revolutionary change, feminism faces a constant threat of deradicalization.

In her popular book *In A Different Voice,*[18] developmental psychologist Carol Gilligan observed that little girls and little boys appear to grapple with moral problems differently.[19] Boys tend to make moral decisions in a legalistic way: They presume that the autonomy of individuals is the paramount value and then employ a rulelike mechanism to decide among the "rights" of those individuals. Gilligan refers to this as the "ethic of rights" or the "ethic of justice."[20] Girls, on the other hand, seem to proceed by the "ethic of care." They have as their goal the preservation of the relationships involved in a given situation. Their reasoning looks like equity: They expand the available universe of facts, rules, and relationships in order to find a unique solution to each unique problem.[21]

Just as Gilligan's work has the potential to inspire us in historic ways, it could also become the Uncle Tom's cabin of our century. Lawyers are tempted to use Gilligan's work in a shallow way, to distill it into a neat formula. Her thesis is memorable, handy, and easy to oversimplify. Rightly or wrongly, many people feel that such an oversimplified version comports with their experience of the sexes. Moreover, generalizations taken from Gilligan provide accessible analogues to the law/equity split and to the ethical positions competing in any legal dispute. All in all, Gilligan's work tempts one to suggest that the different voices of women can somehow be grafted onto our right- and rule-based legal system.

One in a nonvigilant mode might be moved to think that we could have a system which in the abstract satisfies all the competing considerations: rules, rights, relationships, and equity. This is what I call the *incorporationist* view. Gilligan asserts that as a matter of personal moral development, the ability to integrate the ethics of care with the ethics of rights signals maturity. I think no one would disagree with such a goal in an emotional realm. Emotional and cognitive maturity have, however, come to mean very different things.[22] In the majority culture, emotional maturity does not count as knowledge. The *ad hoc* evaluations we must undertake in the emotional realm cannot be acknowledged elsewhere. Such judgments are not "reliable"; only "objectivity" is reliable. We should be especially wary when we hear lawyers, addicted to cognitive objectivity as they are, assert that women's voices have a place in the existing system. In the words of James Agee: "Official acceptance is the one unmistakable symptom that salvation is beaten again, and is the one surest sign of fatal misunderstanding, and is the kiss of Judas."[23]

Incorporationism presumes that we can whip the problem of social inequality by adding yet another prong to the already multipronged legal tests my students feel they must memorize. Incorporationism suffers from the same lack of vision as the "equal rights/ special rights" debate. Both presume that male supremacy is simply a random collection of irrationalities in an otherwise rational coexistence. Both presume that instances of inequality are mere legal mistakes—a series of failures to treat equals as equals which we can fix if we can just spot the irrationality in enough cases. As Professor MacKinnon has demonstrated, however, from such viewpoints we cannot see that male supremacy is a complete social system for the advantage of one sex over another.[24] The injustice of sexism is not irrationality; it is domination. Law must focus on the latter, and that focus cannot be achieved through a formal lens. Binding ourselves to rules would help us only if sexism were a legal error.

A commitment to equality requires that we undertake to investigate the genderization of the world, leaving nothing untouched. The principles of objectivity, abstraction, and personal autonomy are at risk. In our search, we must look for the deeper causes and consequences of Gilligan's findings. Her work is empirical evidence for what feminist theory has already postulated: A male point of view focuses narrowly on autonomy, on the separation between self and others. That disjunction contains the roots of domination. In the terms of feminist theory, male reality manifests itself by negating that which is nonmale. The male model defines self and other important concepts by opposing the concept to a negativized "other."[25] Male rationality divides the world between all that is good and all that is bad—between objective and subjective, light and shadow, man and woman. For all of these dichotomies (and there are scores more), the goodness of the good side is defined by what it is not.

Whereas the male self/other ontology seems to be oppositional, the female version seems to be relational. The female ontology is an alternative theory of differentiation that does not define by negation or require a "life and death struggle" to identify value in the world. Instead, it perceives relationship as constitutive of the self. It perceives dichotomization as irrational.[26]

Male and female perceptions of value are not shared and are perhaps not even perceptible to each other.[27] In our current genderized realm, therefore, the "rights-based" and "care-based" ethics cannot be blended. Patriarchal psychology sees value as differently distributed between men and women: Men are rational; women are not. Feminist psychology suggests different conceptions of value: Women are entirely rational, but society cannot accommodate them because the male standard has defined into oblivion any version of rationality but its own.[28] Paradigmatic male values, like objectivity, are defined as exclusive, identified by their presumed opposites. Those values cannot be content with multiplicity; they create the other and then devour it. Objectivity ignores context; reason is the opposite of emotion; rights preclude care. As long as the ruling ideology is a function of this dichotomization, incorporationism threatens to be mere cooptation, a more subtle version of female invisibility.

By trying to make everything too nice, incorporationism represses contradictions. It usurps women's language in order to further define the world in the male image; it thus deprives women of the power of naming.[29] Incorporationism means to give over the world, because it means to say to those in power: "We will use your language and we will let you interpret it."

Feminist Method

Feminist thinking has evolved dramatically in the last twenty years, from an essentially liberal attack on the absence of women in the public world to a radical vision of the transformation of that world. The demand for "gender neutrality" which served valiantly in the legal struggles of the seventies has inevitably become a critique of neutrality itself, which proceeds by an admittedly nonneutral method. Explanations of our method usually provoke the charge of nominalism, such is the staying power of the ideal of objectivity. Feminist method would appear to be an easy target for that weapon. Feminism does not claim to be objective, because objectivity is the basis for inequality. Feminism is not abstract, because abstraction when institutionalized shields the status quo from critique. Feminism is result oriented. It is vitally concerned with the oblivion fostered by lawyers' belief that process is what matters.

The next step for theory is therefore to demonstrate that feminist method leads to principled adjudication and a more orderly coexistence. Let us begin by reconsidering Carol Gilligan's results. The little boys' approach divides life into opposing camps. In a moral dilemma, this person or that person shall win, based upon some "essential" difference in their situations. One must be shown to be unworthy and wrong. One must be transformed into the "other."

Perhaps there is something in the paradigm of male infant development which teaches a harsh method of differentiation. Insofar as objectification is taught as the preferred way to see the world, we replicate the emotional substructure of domination. The children are thereby programmed, prepared to fall into the habit of objectification, which is at the heart of woman loathing. As adults, these people may have noble intentions, but it will be too late. At best, they will become incorporationists—people who must coopt the voices of the powerless, who can't let them speak for themselves because, by definition, "the other" is mute.

Compare the problem-solving method used by the little girls. Their habit of expanding the context, of following the connections among people and events, is descriptive of rationality. When given a situation with which to grapple, the girls do not insist upon uncovering an essence of the problem but look, rather, for a solution that is coherent with the rest of experience.

If I am right that the "rights-based" and "care-based" approaches are incompatible, we must make a choice between adjudicative principles. The choice is not, however, between male and female hegemony. The choice is, rather, between a compulsion to control reality and a commitment to restrain hegemony. Do we want a system that brooks no disagreement or one that invites as many points of view as the varieties of existence require? The values of honesty and pragmatism require us to choose the relational model, because only it describes how we as language users actually and responsibly perform according to truly meaningful criteria.

Consider Wittgenstein's explanation of the concept of "games." It is a concept we all use with great success, but what is its "essence?" There isn't one. . . .
Investigation of the world is a matter of communication, and communication can never be made out of context. How we use any concept, whether it be "game" or "domination," cannot depend on some universal essence. By looking around, we have examples—we can grasp the concept. Then we recognize other examples, not because they share any essence, but because of their relational matrix.

> We extend our concept . . . as in spinning a thread we twist fibre on fibre. And the strength of the thread does not reside in the fact that some one fibre runs through its whole length, but in the overlapping of many fibres.[30]

Law, like the language which is its medium, is a system of classification. To characterize similarities and differences among situations is a key step in legal judgments. That step, however, is not a mechanistic manipulation of essences. Rather, that step always has a moral crux. Consider another Wittgensteinian example:

> Someone says to me: "Shew the children a game." I teach them gaming with dice, and the other says "I didn't mean that sort of game." Must the exclusion of the game with dice have come before his mind when he gave me the order?[31]

Imagine this as a legal problem. Shall we indict Wittgenstein for corrupting minors or not? Perhaps he simply made a mistake about what he was supposed to do. It was just a lapse in communication. Or it could be that Wittgenstein had the requisite intent; perhaps he is a lover of corruption. In the first case, shall we say that Wittgenstein was mistaken about the essence of the command, or in the second, that he violated the essence of the command? As the last sentence of the quote implies, the order giver didn't think about the possibility that Wittgenstein would choose dice when the order was given. The essence of the thing does not exist. Our decision does not depend upon whether "dice" falls within the statutory term, or upon any objectively determinable similarity or difference between this game and others. It depends upon a larger context which is not neutral at all.

Law needs some theory of differentiation. Feminism, as a theory of differentiation, is particularly well suited to it. Feminism brings law back to its purpose—to decide the the moral crux of the matter in real human situations. Law is a complex system of communication; its communicative matrix is intended to give access to the moral crux. Finding the crux depends upon the relation among things, not upon their opposition. In any case, imperfect analogies are available; a case is similar or dissimilar to others in an unlimited variety of ways. The scope and limits of any analogy must be explored in each case, with social reality as our guide. This is a normative but not illogical process. Any logic is a norm[32] and cannot be used except with reference to its purposes. Why should that be so hard to perceive, to teach, and to do?

Wittgenstein believed that his work with language was obvious, that he was supplying "observations which no one has doubted, but which have escaped remark only because they are always before our eyes."[33] It would also seem obvious that relational reasoning is law's soul, that law's duty is to enhance, rather than to ignore, the rich diversity of life. Yet this purpose is not obvious; it is obscured by the myth of objectivity which opens up law's destructive potential. Feminism inverts the logical primacy of rule over facts. Feminist method stresses that the mechanisms of law—language, rules, and categories—are all merely means for economy in thought and communication. They make it possible for us to implement justice without reinventing every wheel at every turn. But we must not let means turn into ends. When those mechanisms obscure our vision of the ends of law, they must be revised or ignored. Sometimes we must take the long route in order to get to where we really need to be.

In feminist thought, deciding what differences are relevant for any purpose does not require objectifying and destroying some "other." Feminism rejects "abstract universality" in favor of "concrete universality." The former conjures differences—it elevates some to dispositive principles and defines others out of existence—and makes maleness the norm. The latter reinterprets differences in three crucial ways. First, concrete universalism takes differences to be constitutive of the universal itself. Second, it sees differences as systematically related to each other and to other relations, such as exploited and exploiter. Third, it regards differences as emergent, as always changing.[34]

In the past, two legal choices appeared to resolve claims of social injustice: Law could either ignore differences, thereby risking needless conformity, or it could freeze differences, thereby creating a menu of justifications for inequality. Concrete universality eliminates the need for such a choice. When our priority is to understand differences and to value multiplicity, we need only to discern between occasions of respect and occasions of oppression. Those are judgments we know how to make, even without a four-part test to tell us, for every future circumstance, what constitutes domination.

> Only let us understand what "inexact" means. For it does not mean "unusable."[35]
> One might say that the concept "game" is a concept with blurred edges.—"But is a blurred concept a concept at all?"—Is an indistinct photograph a picture of a person at all? Is it even always an advantage to replace an indistinct picture by a sharp one? Isn't the indistinct one often exactly what we need?[36]

A precise picture of a fuzzy scene is a fuzzy picture. Domination comes in many forms. Its mechanisms are so insidious and so powerful that we could never codify its "essence." The description that uses no formula, but which points to the moral crux of the matter, is exactly what we need.

◇ ◇ ◇

Coping with Equality

The problem of inequality of the sexes stands in complex relation to the problem of survival. Inequality in the sexual division of labor ensures replication of the model of aggression. Pathological aggression accounts for inequality. If these connections are ever to be unpacked, if we are serious about survival, we need a radically more serious approach to equality. Law must embrace a version of equality that focuses on the real issues—domination, disadvantage and disempowerment—instead of on the interminable and diseased issue of differences between the sexes. I endorse the definition of equality proposed by Professor MacKinnon in 1979: The test in any challenge should be "whether the policy or practice in question integrally contributes to the maintenance of an underclass or a deprived position because of gender status."[37] MacKinnon contrasts this to the "differences approach," calling it the "inequality approach." I would call the former "thinking like a lawyer;" the latter, "thinking like a person."

That is not to say that the proposed standard will be easy to implement. It will require us to bring the very best of our humanness to bear. That is a scary proposition. No data yet exist to reassure us on the standard's reliability, and by its own terms, results cannot be predicted without the compilation of records very different from those underlying previously decided cases. The critics appropriately worry, for example, that classifications designed to address the real problems of women (such as pregnancy legislation) will serve to reinforce stereotypes about women's place.[38] The problem for feminist legal scholars, I think, is that we are unsure how to measure what about stereotyping is at issue in a given case. The notion of stereotyping connotes oversimplification, inattention to individual characteristics, lack of seriousness, and invariance. We use the concept of stereotyping without difficulty when the challenged practice is based upon an untrue generalization. All of the connotations of stereotyping are clearly implicated in negative ways. In such cases, both the differences approach and the inequality approach would prohibit the classification.

The inequality approach focuses upon two other sources of feminist discomfort: first, the need for a reliable approach to generalizations which are largely true (either because of biology or because of highly successful socialization) and, second, the need to distinguish between beneficial and burdensome legislation.

Only the inequality approach attempts to reckon with true generalizations. Indeed, in that view, different treatment based upon unique physical characteristics would be "among the *first* to trigger suspicion and scrutiny."[39] In the past, biological differences have been used to show that classifications are not sex based.[40] Thereby, the reasons for having antidiscrimination laws have been seen as the reasons to allow discrimination. The inequality approach unravels the tautology. It makes no sense to say that equality is guaranteed only when the sexes are already equal. The issue is not freedom to be treated without regard to sex; the issue is freedom from systematic subordination because of sex.[41]

The inequality approach would also reach stereotypes which, though not biologically based, have largely made themselves true through a history of inequality. Consider the situation in *Phillips v. Martin Marietta Corp.,*[42] where the company hired males with preschool-aged children but would not hire women in that category. As a variation, suppose the trial court had found that women with small children did in fact have greater responsibilities and therefore were, as a group, less well suited for the jobs in question. Such a finding would correspond to the facts of allocation of child-raising responsibility. The only challenge that will work in this scenario is one from an "exceptional" woman candidate for employment—a woman with preschool-aged children whose job performance will not be impaired by her obligations to them. The policy will be deemed irrational as applied to her.

Compare the inequality approach, which is triggered not by irrationality but by disadvantage. In our scenario, the inequality approach is superior because it reaches the worse injustice: The fact that women who fit the stereotype are precluded from advancement in our economic system. A challenge adjudicated by that standard would succeed on behalf of the unexceptional as well as the exceptional. Employers (and other employees who have carried a disproportionately lower burden in child rearing) would then essentially have to compensate for the benefits they have derived from women's double burden. Such payment should include damages, and court-ordered advancement, day care, parents' leave, and reallocation of workers' hours and rewards. This redistribution of historical burdens and benefits may seem a sweeping remedy, but it is the only one which addresses the reality.

With respect to our second problem, the discernment of genuinely beneficial classifications, suppose that the same company offered a hiring preference for women with school-aged children and provided some relief from the double burden. The offer undoubtedly "reinforces a stereotype," but what shall we make of the fact that the stereotype is in large part—if only contingently and temporarily—true? But true only because women carry a disproportionate burden of the child-caring responsibility in our society. Especially when women can elect to receive the benefits (as opposed to risking stigmatization by them), what is the objection to such a plan? Disadvantage has a way of replicating and reinforcing itself. To oppose the scheme is to be reduced to relying upon a groundswell of exceptional behaviors within the disadvantaged group itself. Historically, however, disadvantaged groups have been forced to rely upon surrogates to better themselves. That has not required that the groups thus assisted conform for all time to the surrogates' perceptions of them (or even to their own perceptions of themselves).

Beneficial classifications, therefore, seem necessary to the ultimate undoing of stubborn stereotypes. It is true that in our history, stereotypical differences, both real and imagined, have served primarily as convenient, "natural" justifications for imposition of burdens. It does not follow, however, that we cannot use differences progressively. Injustice does not flow directly from recognizing differences; injustice results when those differences are transformed into social and economic deprivation. Our task, then, is to exercise our capacity for discernment in more precise ways. Allegedly beneficial classifications, even when they invoke a stereotype, must be measured against what is objectionable in stereotyping. Beneficial classifications, such as the employment preference in our example, will survive under the inequality approach if they do not have those characteristics. Insofar as the employment preference oversimplifies, it is an oversimplification in the service of a profound complexity, as is any well-drafted policy. The preference provides to individuals the opportunity to demonstrate their capacities when the stereotype is set aside. It evinces laudable seriousness toward the problem, especially insofar as the stereotyper takes upon itself some of the burden of the past discrimination. Last, and perhaps most important, it is not invariant. By definition it points to the stereotype for the purpose of undoing it, as an example of how revised present arrangements can relieve centuries of disadvantage. When allegedly beneficial classifications do not have this form or when once beneficial schemes cease to have it, the inequality approach would prohibit them.

Admittedly, the inequality approach would sometimes require that different standards be used for men and women. If that were not so, however, the approach would not be working. Its emphasis is upon enforced inferiority, not sex-differentiated treatment. When the aim is to discover the reality of domination, the standard to be applied depends upon the context. The inequality approach requires an investigation which must delve as deeply as circumstances demand into whether the challenged policy or practice exploits gender status. To worry in the abstract about which standard should be applied at what time is to replicate the fallacy of the differences approach.

In short, the inequality approach means that we have to think more broadly about what we want "equality" to mean. The traditional bases for differentiation between the sexes are socially created categories, given meaning only by assigned biases. We create the relevant comparisons and are free to do so *de novo* in light of social realities. Thus, in the preferential hiring situation, we would say that the right at stake, rather than the right to be treated without regard to sex, is the right not to have one's existence bifurcated because of sex. In the pregnancy situation, it is the right to have one's total health needs taken as seriously as are those of the other sex.

Logic is no obstacle to the implementation of the inequality approach. The obstacles are, rather, perception and commitment. When the fact of judicial manipulation has been so salient in the past, why should we now expect those responsible for implementing the law to be able to see, in any given situation, how women have been disadvantaged? Accustomed as judges are to looking for similarities and differences, they cannot or will not make the assessments of deprivation and disempowerment.

My response to this, on optimistic days, is that we are more persuasive than we believe we are. If judges are supposed to accept guidance, we as practitioners and scholars ought to be able to provide it. There has been some progress, however modest. Our duty is to be vigilant in ensuring that what happens is real progress and to guide the courts through our proposed transformation of adjudication. Four members of the current Supreme Court, for example, seem prepared to listen to a well-reasoned alternative to the plethora of superstructure which plagues constitutional law.[43] The entire Court cries for guidance as to what differences among us mean.[44] I believe we are up to the task.

At less optimistic moments, candor would compel me to admit that implementation of a feminist approach will ultimately depend upon significant changes in judicial personnel. Given what we have experienced, however, I feel comfortable with such an admission. It is time that feminist lawyers spoke openly about the politics of neutrality, instead of pretending that sexism were a legal mistake. We have, for example, squandered over a decade discussing what legal standard could have prevented the outrage of *Geduldig v. Aiello*.[45] But let's face it—the problem in that "analysis" (that no discrimination exists if pregnant women and pregnant men are treated the same) is not that the Supreme Court used the wrong legal standard. The problem was much more serious: It was that our highest court cavalierly allowed California to disadvantage women with respect to their reproductive capabilities. Our highest court endorsed a modern version of a centuries-old method of domination.

We must never forget *Geduldig*. Our Supreme Court got away with it because we allowed the question of pregnancy to be sequestered in our own minds from the question of domination. In our search for a liberal resolution, the real issue remained invisible, and our critique came dangerously close to consent. Our objections can no longer be oblique, for then they are lost. Keeping dissent hidden is an ancient tactic which renders the dissent trivial, abnormal, and disconnected from its roots. Due to the distribution of women in society, this has particularly been the case with feminism. Because each new feminist work or insight appears as if from nowhere, "each contemporary feminist theorist [is] attacked or dismissed ad feminam, as if her politics were simply an outburst of personal bitterness or rage."[46] Trust we must have that we can describe the issues; empowered we must be when our trust is violated.

The proposed inequality standard will not take root overnight. Developments in feminist theory take decades to manifest themselves in law. But it will happen; the difficulty of the process must not stop us from demanding that change or from continuing the tradition that makes it possible.

Feminist Method Revisited

The term *feminist jurisprudence* disturbs people. That is not surprising, given patriarchy's convenient habit of labeling as unreliable any approach that admits to be interested, and particularly given the historic a priori invalidation of women's experience. That long-standing invalidation also causes women, including feminist women, to be reluctant to make any claims beyond the formal reach of liberalism. Further, we are taught to ascribe the legal system's successes to the principle of detachment.

In the understandable rush to render feminism acceptable in traditional terms, it is sometimes suggested that we ought to advertise our insight as a revival of the Legal Realism of the 1930s. We are surely indebted to the Realists for their convincing demonstration that the law could not be described, as the positivists had hoped, as a scientific enterprise, devoid of moral or political content. The Realists' description of the influence of morality, economics, and politics upon law is the first step in developing an antidote for legal solipsism. In the end, however, the Realists did not revolutionize the law but merely expanded the concept of legal process. The Realists did not press their critique deeply enough; they did not bring home its implications. In the face of their failure, the system has clung even more desperately to objectivity and neutrality. "The effect of the Realists was much like the role that Carlyle pronounced for Matthew Arnold: 'He led them into the wilderness and left them there.'"[47]

Feminism now faces the charge leveled at Realism, that it destroys the citadel of objectivity and leaves nothing to legitimate the law. Our response to this state of affairs begins with an insight not exclusive to feminist thought: The law must finally enter the twentieth century. The business of living and progressing within our disciplines requires that we give up on "objective" verification at various critical moments, such as when we rely upon gravity,[48] or upon the existence of others,[49] or upon the principle of verification itself. Feminism insists upon epistemological and psychological sophistication in law: Jurisprudence will forever be stuck in a postrealist battle of subjectivities, with all the discomfort that has represented, until we confront the distinction between knowing subject and known object.

Feminist method is exemplary of that confrontation. The physics of relativity and quantum mechanics demonstrate that nature is on our side: Nature itself has begun to evince a less hierarchical structure, a multidirectional flow of authority which corroborates our description of perception. We warmly embrace the uncertainty inherent in that perceptual model, recognizing the humanity, and indeed, the security, in it. And because we do not separate the observer from the observed, "feminism is the first theory to emerge from those whose interest it affirms."[50] Feminist method proceeds through consciousness raising. The results of consciousness raising cannot be verified by traditional methods, nor need they be. We are therefore operating from within an epistemological framework which denies our power to know. This is an inherently transformative process: It validates the experience of women, the major content of which has been invalidation.

> Feminism criticizes this male totality without an account of our capacity to do so or to imagine or realize a more whole truth. Feminism affirms women's point of view by revealing, criticizing, and explaining its impossibility. This is not a dialectical paradox. It is a methodological expression of women's situation. . . . Women's situation offers no outside to stand on or gaze at, no inside to escape to, too much urgency to wait, no place else to go, and nothing to use but the twisted tools that have been shoved down our throats. If feminism is revolutionary, this is why.[51]

Consciousness raising is a vivid expression of self-creation and responsibility. To Wittgenstein's insight that perceptions have meaning only in the context of experience, feminism would add that perceptions have meaning only in the context of an experience that matters. Consciousness raising means that dramatic eyewitness testimony is being given; it means, more importantly, that women now have the confidence to declare it as such. We have an alternative to relegating our perception to the realm of our own subjective discomfort. Heretofore, the tried and true scientific strategy of treating nonconforming evidence as mistaken worked in the legal system. But when that evidence keeps turning up, when the experience of women becomes recalcitrant, it will be time to treat that evidence as true.

The foundations of the law will not thereby crumble. Though feminism rejects the notion that for a legal system to work, there have to be "objective" rules, we admit that legality has (or should have) certain qualities. There must be something reliable somewhere, there must be indications of fairness in the system, but neither depends on objectivity. Rather, we need to discard the habit of equating our most noble aspirations with objectivity and neutrality. We need at least to redefine those terms, and probably to use others, to meet our very serious responsibilities.

My admission that feminism is result oriented does not import the renunciation of all standards. In a system defined by constitutional norms such as equality, we need standards to help us make connections among norms, and to help us see "family resemblances."[52] among instances of domination. Standards, however, are not means without ends: They never have and never can be more than working hypotheses. Just as it would be shocking to find a case that said, "The petitioner wins though she satisfied no criteria," so it must ultimately be wrong to keep finding cases that say, "Petitioner loses though the criteria are indefensible." In legal situations, a case is either conformed to a standard or the standard is modified with justification. That justification should not be that "we like the petitioner's facts better"; rather, it is that "on facts such as these, the standard doesn't hold up."

The feminist approach takes justification seriously; it is a more honest and efficient way to achieve legitimacy. The feminist legal standard for equality is altogether principled in requiring commitment to finding the moral crux of matters before the court. The feminist approach will tax us. We will be exhausted by bringing feminist method to bear. Yet we must force lawmakers and interpreters to hear that which they have been well trained to ignore. We will have to divest ourselves of our learned reticence, debrief ourselves every day. We will have to trust ourselves to be able to describe life to each other—in our courts, in our legislatures, in our emergence together.

Notes

This chapter is derived from the inaugural lecture in the Dean's Lecture Series, Yale Law School, on April 15, 1985. Thanks to the persons connected with that event, particularly Dean Guido Calabresi, Associate Dean Jamienne Studley, and Ellen Liebman. The text has been expanded and footnotes added with the assistance of Jane Marx.

1. A. RICH, *A Vision (Thinking of Simone Weil).* in A WILD PATIENCE HAS TAKEN ME THIS FAR 50 (1981).
2. 404 U.S. 71 (1971).
3. C. MACKINNON, SEXUAL HARASSMENT OF WORKING WOMEN 101 (1979) (emphasis omitted).
4. Geduldig v. Aiello, 417 U.S. 484 (1974)
5. For an analysis of how the image of "woman as temptress" excuses discrimination, see

Aiken, *Differentiating Sex from* Sex: *The Male Irresistible Impulse,* 7 N.Y.U. REV. L. & Soc. CHANGE 357 (1984). Most illustrative of this phenomenon are Dothard v. Rawlinson, 433 U.S. 321 (1977) (refusal to hire female prison guards allowed under Title VII as bona fide occupational qualification), and Michael M. v. Sonoma County Super. Ct., 450 U.S. 464 (1981) (constitutionality of California's statutory rape law sustained).

6. Rostker v. Goldberg, 453 U.S. 57 (1981) (upholding constitutionality of exclusion of women from draft registration). For the reverse side of this familiar coin, see Personnel Adm'r v. Feeney, 442 U.S. 256 (1979) (upholding Massachusetts veterans' preference for civil service positions).

7. MacKinnon, *Feminism, Marxism, Method, and the State: Toward Feminist Jurisprudence,* 8 SIGNS, 635, 638 (1983) (footnotes omitted). This article was the sequel to MacKinnon, *Feminism, Marxism, Method, and the State: An Agenda for Theory,* 7 SIGNS, 515 (1982).

8. 404 U.S. 71 (1971).

9. Gould, *The Woman Question: Philosophy of Liberation and the Liberation of Philosophy,* in WOMEN AND PHILOSOPHY: TOWARD A. THEORY OF LIBERATION 5–6, 63. C. Gould and M. Wartofsky eds. 1976).

10. For a fuller explanation of correspondence, see B. RUSSELL, THE PROBLEMS OF PHILOSOPHY 126–30 (1959).

11. Gould, at 20.

12. The most striking example is Justice Bradley's concurrence in Bradwell v. Illinois, 83 U.S. (16 Wall) 130 14–42 (1872).

13. Gould, at 21.

14. Smith, *The Sword and Shield of Perseus: Some Mythological Dimensions of the Law,* 6 J.L. & PSYCHIATRY, 235, 239, 240–41. (1983).

15. *Id.* at 260–61.

16. *See* A. GRAMSCI, SELECTIONS FROM THE PRISON NOTEBOOKS OF ANTONIO GRAMSCI, 181–82, 195–96, 246–50 (Q. Hoare & G. Smith trans. & eds. 1971) (discussing dominant groups in general).

17. *See* Smith, at 255–60.

18. C. GILLIGAN, IN A DIFFERENT VOICE (1982).

19. Gilligan does not claim to be making generalizations about either sex or about the origins of the differences observed. *Id.* at 2. Her book is about modes of problem solving which happen in her research to correspond, albeit incompletely, to gender categories. For us to worry about the lack of fit between her observations and those gender groups is to fall back into the fallacy of the "equal rights/special rights" debate. We must resist the pressure to decide, abstractly and irrevocably, what the differences between the sexes might be. For present purposes, I would use Gilligan's results for two working hypotheses. First, given what I have experienced as the expectations imposed upon growing up female, I am always surprised to observe women who do not tend toward conformity to a simplified Gilligan-esque model. The same holds true for my experience with male decision makers. Thus, insofar as law reflects the "rights-based" part of that model, it would seem disproportionately to have excluded women's point of view from participation in its creation and administration. Second, given "objectivity" as the systemic criterion for the validity of decisions, the mode of reasoning associated with femaleness does not and cannot count. Thus, more than mere incorporation of that "female" voice is required.

20. Gilligan, at 25–51, 164, 174.

21. *Id.* at 164, 29.

22. E. KELLER, REFLECTIONS ON GENDER AND SCIENCE 84 (1985).

23. J. AGEE AND W. EVANS, LET US NOW PRAISE FAMOUS MEN, 15 (1941).

24. *See* C. MACKINNON, at 102, 121.

25. These ideas were first articulated in a feminist context by Simone de Beauvoir. S. DE BEAUVOIR, THE SECOND SEX (H. Parshley trans. 1952).

26. The term *self/other ontology* and the distinction between *relational* and *oppositional* ontologies are taken from Whitbeck, *A Different Reality: Feminist Ontology,* in BEYOND DOMINATION: NEW PERSPECTIVES ON WOMEN AND PHILOSOPHY, 64, 69, 76. (C. Gould ed. 1984).

27. C. GILLIGAN, at 173.

28. *See* Harding, Is Gender a Variable in Conceptions of Reality A Survey of Issues, in Beyond Domination, 44–45 (C. Gould ed. 1984).

29. "Naming" is a critical concept to feminism. When we discover what we really think and express it, we give words and the world new meaning.

30. L. WITTGENSTEIN, PHILOSOPHICAL INVESTIGATIONS §§ 66–78, at 31–36 (G. Anscombe trans. 3d ed. 1968).

31. *Id.* at 33 (note without section number).

32. Harding, at 57.

33. I. WITTGENSTEIN, § 415, at 125.

34. Gould, at 27.

35. L. WITTGENSTEIN, § 88, at 41.

36. L. WITTGENSTEIN, § 71, at 34.

37. C. MACKINNON, at 117. Nearly identical standards could be applied to other historically disadvantaged groups.

38. *See* Taub, Book Review, 80 COLUM. L. REV. 1686, 1682–93 (1980).

39. *See* C. MACKINNON, at 118 (emphasis in original).

40. *See, e.g.,* Michael M. v. Sonoma County Super. Ct., 450 U.S. 464, 476 (1981) (upholding statutory rape law that presumes male is culpable aggressor because "consequences of sexual intercourse and pregnancy fall more heavily on the female than on the male"); Geduldig v. Aiello, 417 U.S. 484, 496 n.20 (1974) (disability insurance system did not "exclude anyone from benefit eligibility because of gender but merely removes one physical condition—pregnancy—from the list of compensable disabilities").

41. *See* C. MACKINNON, at 227.

42. 400 U.S. 542 (1971) (per curiam).

43. *See* the concurrence of Justice Stevens (joined by Burger), and the partial concurrence of Justices Marshall, Brennan and Blackmun in City of Cleburne v. Cleburne Living Center, 105 S. Ct. 3249 (1985) (zoning ordinance violative of equal protection clause as applied to prohibition of group home for mentally retarded).

44. *Id.* The *Cleburne* plurality seems to hold that in order for classification to command higher scrutiny, the petitioners must first show that the classification at issue can never be justified. 105 S. Ct. at 3255. Thus, the irrelevance of a classification must be demonstrated before the classification can be shown to be irrelevant. Thus, the Supreme Court has illustrated the truth in MacKinnon's *reductio ad absurdum* treatment of the differences approach: In order to achieve equality you must first be equal. As unfortunate as it may be, the *Cleburne* state of affairs smacks to me more of confusion than ideology.

45. 417 U.S. 484 (1974).

46. A. RICH, Forward: On History, Illiteracy, Passivity, Violence & Women's Culture, in On Lies, Secrets, & Silence: Selected Prose 1966–1978, at 11 (1979).

47. R. STEVENS, LAW SCHOOL: LEGAL EDUCATION IN AMERICA FROM THE 1950s TO THE 1980s, at 156 (1983).

48. *See* T. KUHN, THE STRUCTURE OF SCIENTIFIC REVOLUTIONS 108 (2d ed. 1970) (abandonment by eighteenth-century scientists of attempt to explain gravity reflected "neither a decline nor a raising of standards, but . . . the adoption of a new paradigm").

49. *See* L. WITTGENSTEIN.

50. MacKinnon, *An Agenda for Theory,* at 543. Because feminism emerges from women themselves, we can largely avoid the old quandary of whether revolutionary consciousness arises from the masses or must be prompted by a revolutionary elite. *See* M. BARRETT, WOMEN'S OPPRESSION TODAY: PROBLEMS IN MARXIST FEMINIST ANALYSIS, 88–98 (1980); V. LENIN, WHAT IS TO BE

DONE? 29–53 (1969 ed.). That is not to say that the women's movement has not suffered from elitism. It has, but not due to a theoretical failure; feminism is not plagued with a theory that is "acontextual". *See* MacKinnon, *An Agenda for Theory,* at 527 n.23.

51. MacKinnon, *Toward Feminist Jurisprudence,* at 637, 639.

52. L. WITTGENSTEIN, at 32.

5

Reconstructing Sexual Equality

CHRISTINE A. LITTLETON

Introduction: The Project

> *Like* and *different* are quickening words,
> brooding and hatching.
> *Better* and *worse* are eggsucking words,
> they leave only the shell.
> Ursula K. LeGuin[1]

Feminist critique has illuminated the "male-dominated" or "phallocentric" nature of every social institution it has examined, including law. Critiques of the patriarchal family are by now too familiar to need recounting, and the feminist project has moved on. Feminists have revealed religion as a cultural artifact of the patriarchal conquest of female power; the sciences as "intimately involved in Western, bourgeois, and masculine projects"; and even law as the symbol and mechanism for continuation of male power. Much of the critique has focused on women's absence from, or at least marginal place in, the discourse and thought that has shaped modern social structures.

Although one more criticism of men's domination of the public discourse on equality might not be amiss, that is not the focus of this chapter. Rather, the focus here is on a more insidious and complex form of male domination, which I term *phallocentrism*. A history of almost exclusive male occupation of dominant cultural discourse has left us with more than incompleteness and bias. It has also created a self-referencing system by which those things culturally identified as "male" are more highly valued than those identified as "female," even when they appear to have little or nothing to do with either biological sex. By this process, "to be a man" does not simply mean to possess biologically male traits but also to take on, or at least aspire to, the culturally male. Similarly, social institutions within a male-dominated culture can be identified as "male" in the sense that they are constructed from the perspective of the culturally male. By use of the term *phallocentrism* I hope to capture this perspective—not the perspective of biological males, but the perspective to which the culture urges them to aspire, and by which the culture justifies their dominance.

Language, being a social institution—perhaps even the constitutive social institution—is also subject to feminist critique. While Carol Gilligan's *In a Different Voice* does not deal explicitly with language, it is aptly titled.[2] In uncovering the limitations of Kohlberg's theory of moral development, Gilligan discovered more than the methodological error of constructing a theory of *human* reasoning from a sample of only *male* humans.[3] She also uncovered a "different voice," one that reasons morally in terms of connection and relationship, rather than in terms of separation, hierarchy of values, and abstraction of principles. While this voice was exhibited by more female children than male children, it was by no means limited to one biological sex.

The "French feminists" attack language more explicitly, finding in the disruption of male language the only possible expression of a female voice.[4] Whether the problem identified by feminists is as "simple" as the use of the generic "he" or as complex as the structure of language itself, the reach of feminist critique is toward the phallocentric construction of the medium by which we transmit knowledge, rather than merely toward the sexist word choice of individuals. In all its manifestations, phallocentrism defines the boundaries of acceptable discourse—not only of what can be heard and responded to, but also to some extent of what can be thought, and thus the extent to which women can articulate their own concerns, values, and interests.

Equality, belonging both to law and to language, provides its own case study of phallocentrism. Using feminist methodology's primary questions—"What has been women's concrete experience?" and "What has been left out?"—feminist critique has examined the phallocentrism of equality as both a concept and a form of legal analysis. As a concept, equality suffers from a "mathematical fallacy"—that is, the view that only things that are the same can ever be equal. In legal analysis, courts routinely find women's "difference" a sufficient justification for inequality, constructing at the same time a specious "sameness" when applying phallocentric standards "equally" to men and women's different reproductive biology or economic position to yield (not surprisingly) unequal results for women.

This feminist critique of equality has cast doubt on the merits of another feminist enterprise—the as-yet only partially successful attempt by feminist lawyers to have sex accepted as similar to, and coextensive with, race under constitutional and statutory guarantees of equality. "Equality," which has historically been the rallying cry of every subordinated group in American society, can no longer be embraced unambivalently by feminists.

Equality is enmeshed in, and ensnared by, the very gender system feminists are resisting. But I believe it is capable of having meaning beyond that system. To the extent that it is a social construct, equality can be deconstructed and, at least theoretically, reconstructed as a means of challenging, rather than legitimating, social institutions created from the phallocentric perspective. This possibility is so appealing, so evocative of the yearnings of so many of us, that the project of reconstructing sexual equality must at least be attempted, difficult and fraught with dangers as it appears. Even if we disregard the pragmatic value of equality analysis as one of the few avenues by which concrete experiences of subordination can be translated into legal claims,[5] we should not disregard the relational nature of equality language, its consistent theme of belonging, of somehow "counting" as human.

This chapter attempts a speculative reconstruction of sexual equality that I find appealing. My hope is that others—especially feminists and feminist sympathizers—will find it appealing, too. My proposal is easy to state, somewhat harder to fill with content, and even harder to implement. It is simply this: The difference between human beings, whether perceived or real and whether biologically or socially based, should not be permitted to make a difference in the lived-out equality of those persons. I call this the model of *equality as acceptance.* To achieve this form of sexual equality, male and female "differences" must be costless relative to each other. Equal acceptance cannot be achieved by forcing women (or the rare man) individually to bear the costs of culturally female behavior, such as child rearing, while leaving those (mostly men and some women) who engage in culturally male behavior, such as private law firm practice, to reap its rewards.

◊ ◊ ◊

The parts of this chapter reflect the development of the model of sexual equality as acceptance. The model responds to four separate but interrelated ideas: (1) intellectual development of equality analysis in general, and feminist equality analysis in particular; (2) feminist critique of equality; (3) feminist critique of male power as a system; and (4) the complexity of various sex or gender differences. The chapter's scope is constrained in a number of ways, not the least of which is my use of "the master's tools"[6] in attempting to reconstruct sexual equality. Recognizing these constraints, I accept the task of building theory on the tightrope between incrementalism and utopianism.

We have inherited the forms and content of equality from our fathers, who occupied the available space in the public discourse. Perhaps we can pass on something richer to our daughters.

I. Development of Feminist Legal Theory

◊ ◊ ◊

Feminist legal theory has been primarily reactive, responding to the development of legal racial equality theory. The form of response, however, has varied. One response has been to attempt to equate legal treatment of sex with that of race and deny that there are in fact any significant natural differences between women and men; in other words, to consider the two sexes symmetrically located with regard to any issue, norm, or rule. This response, which I term the *symmetrical* approach, classifies asymmetries as illusions, "overbroad generalizations," or temporary glitches that will disappear with a little behavior modification. A competing response rejects this analogy, accepting that women and men are or may be "different" and that women and men are often asymmetrically located in society. This response, which I term the *asymmetrical* approach, rejects the notion that all gender differences are likely to disappear, or even tthat they should.

A. Symmetrical Models of Sexual Equality

Feminist theorists frequently take the symmetrical approach to sexual equality not as an ideal but as the only way to avoid returning to separate spheres ideology. For example, in her highly compelling defense of symmetry in the law, Wendy Williams warns that "if we can't have it both ways, we need to think carefully about which way we want to have it."[7]

There are two models of the symmetrical vision—referred to here as *assimilation* and *androgyny.* Assimilation, the model most often accepted by the courts, is based on the notion that women, given the chance, really are or could be just like men. Therefore, the argument runs, the law should require social institutions to treat women as they already treat men—requiring, for example, that the professions admit women to the extent they are "qualified" but also insisting that women who enter time-demanding professions such as the practice of law sacrifice relationships (especially with their children) to the same extent that male lawyers have been forced to do.[8]

Androgyny, the second symmetrical model, also posits that women and men are, or at least could be, very much like each other but argues that equality requires institutions to pick some golden mean between the two and treat both sexes as androgynous persons would be treated. However, given that all of our institutions, work habits, and pay scales were formulated without the benefit of substantial numbers of androgynous persons, androgynous symmetry is difficult to conceptualize and might require very substantial restructuring of many public and private institutions.[9] In order to be truly androgynous within a symmetrical framework, social institutions must find a single norm that works equally well for all gendered characteristics. Part of my discomfort with androgynous models is that they depend on "meeting in the middle," while I distrust the ability of any person, and especially any court, to value women enough to find the "middle." Moreover, the problems involved in determining such a norm for even one institution are staggering. At what height should a conveyor belt be set in order to satisfy a symmetrical androgynous ideal?[10]

Symmetry appears to have great appeal for the legal system, and this is not surprising. The hornbook definition of equal protection is "that those who are similarly situated be similarly treated," and many courts, following the Supreme Court's lead, have held that absent a showing of similarity, strict scrutiny is simply inapplicable.[11] Symmetrical analysis also has great appeal for liberal men, to whom it appears to offer a share in the feminist enterprise. If perceived difference between the sexes is only the result of overly rigid sex roles, then men's liberty is at stake too. Ending this form of sexual inequality could free men to express their "feminine" side, just as it frees women to express their "masculine" side.

B. Asymmetrical Models of Sexual Equality

Asymmetrical approaches to sexual equality take the position that difference should not be ignored or eradicated. Rather, they argue that any sexually equal society must somehow deal with difference, problematic as that may be. Asymmetrical approaches include *special rights, accommodation, acceptance,* and *empowerment.*

The special rights model affirms that women and men *are* different and asserts that cultural differences, such as child-rearing roles, are rooted in biological ones, such as reproduction. Therefore, it states, society must take account of these differences and ensure that women are not punished for them. This approach, sometimes referred to as a *bivalent* model, is closest to the "special treatment" pole of the asymmetrical/symmetrical equality debate. Elizabeth Wolgast, a major proponent of special rights, argues that women cannot be men's "equals" because equality by definition requires sameness. Instead of equality, she suggests seeking justice, claiming special rights for women based on their special needs.[12]

The second asymmetrical model, accommodation, agrees that differential treatment of biological differences (such as pregnancy and perhaps breast feeding) is necessary but argues that cultural or hard-to-classify differences (such as career interests and skills) should be treated under an equal treatment or androgynous model. Examples of accommodation models include Sylvia Law's approach to issues of reproductive biology[13] and Herma Hill Kay's "episodic" approach to the condition of pregnancy.[14] These approaches could also be characterized as "symmetry, with concessions to asymmetry where necessary." The accommodationists limit the asymmetry in their models to biological differences because, like Williams, they fear a return to separate spheres ideology should asymmetrical theory go too far.

My own attempt to grapple with difference, which I call an *acceptance* model, is essentially asymmetrical. While not endorsing the notion that cultural differences between the sexes are biologically determined, it does recognize and attempt to deal with both biological and social differences. Acceptance does not view sex differences as problematic per se but, rather, focuses on the ways in which differences are permitted to justify inequality. It asserts that eliminating the unequal consequences of sex differences is more important than debating whether such differences are "real" or even trying to eliminate them altogether.

Unlike the accommodationists, who would limit asymmetrical analysis to purely biological differences, my proposal also requires equal acceptance of cultural differences. The reasons for this are twofold. First, the distinction between biological and cultural, while useful analytically, is itself culturally based. Second, the inequality experienced by women is often presented as a necessary consequence of cultural rather than of biological difference. If, for instance, women do in fact "choose" to become nurses rather than real estate appraisers,[15] it is not because of any biological imperative. Yet, regardless of the reasons for the choice, they certainly do not choose to be paid less. It is the consequences of gendered difference, and not its sources, that equal acceptance addresses.

If, as it appears from Gilligan's studies,[16] women and men tend to develop somewhat differently in terms of their values and inclinations, each of these modes of development must be equally valid and valuable. In our desire for equality, we should not be forced to jettison either; rather, we should find some way to value both. That such different modes do not perfectly correspond to biological sex does not prevent them from being typed socially as "male" and "female," and neither should it prevent us from demanding that they be equally valued. Thus, if women currently tend to assume primary responsibility for child rearing, we should not ignore that fact in an attempt to prefigure the rosy day when parenting is fully shared. We should instead figure out how to ensure that equal resources, status, and access to social decision making flow to those women (and few men) who engage in this socially female behavior.

The focus of equality as acceptance, therefore, is not on the question of whether women are different but, rather, on the question of how the social fact of gender asymmetry can be dealt with so as to create some symmetry in the lived-out experience of all members of the community. I do not think it matters so much whether differences are "natural" or not; they are built into our structures and selves in either event. As social facts, differences are created by the interaction of person with person or person with institution; they inhere in the relationship, not in the person. On this view, the function of equality is to make gender differences, perceived or actual, costless relative to each other, so that anyone may follow a male, female, or androgynous life-style according to their natural inclination or choice without being punished for following a female life-style or rewarded for following a male one.

As an illustration of this approach, consider what many conceive to be the paradigm difference between men and women—pregnancy. No one disputes that only women become pregnant, but symmetrical theorists analogize pregnancy to other events, in order to preserve the unitary approach of symmetrical theory. Such attempts to minimize difference have the ironic result of obscuring more fundamental similarities.

In *California Federal Savings & Loan Association v. Guerra (Cal. Fed.)*,[17] Lillian Garland, a receptionist at California Federal, tried to return to her job after the birth of her child. The bank refused to reinstate her, and she sued under the California Fair Employment and Housing Act (FEHA).[18] That law requires that employees temporarily disabled by pregnancy be given an unpaid leave of up to four months, with guaranteed reinstatement in their original job or its equivalent. The bank in turn sued in federal court, claiming that the FEHA was preempted by Title VII of the Civil Rights Act of 1964,[19] as amended by the Pregnancy Discrimination Act (PDA). The PDA requires only that employers treat pregnancy the same as any other disability. California Federal argued that the PDA prevented California from enforcing its pregnancy disability leave requirements against firms that did not provide these benefits for disabilities unrelated to pregnancy.[20]

In addition to narrow questions of statutory interpretation, *Cal. Fed.* raised more fundamental questions about the meaning of equal employment opportunity for women. Citing the dangers of separate spheres ideology raised by "protectionist" legislation, the national ACLU filed an *amicus* brief arguing that the California law should be struck down and that the remedy should provide for job-protected leave for all temporarily disabled employees, whatever the source of their disability.[21] California feminist groups, such as Equal Rights Advocates, filed on the other side of the debate, arguing that the California law guaranteed equality of opportunity, and was thus consistent with federal law and policy.[22]

Missing in these arguments, however, was any recognition that working men and women shared a more fundamental right than the right to basic disability leave benefits or job protection. The Coalition for Reproductive Equality in the Workplace (CREW) advanced the position that working women and men share a right to procreative choice in addition to an interest in disability leave.[23] In order to ensure equal exercise of procreative rights, it argued, an employer must provide leave adequate to the effects of pregnancy.

> The California statute eliminates barriers to equality in both procreation and employment faced by women who cannot afford to lose their jobs when they decide to become parents. Male employees who become fathers and female employees who become mothers are thus enabled to combine procreation and employment to the same extent.[24]

This form of acceptance, unlike those that analogize pregnancy to disability, emphasizes the basic commonality of procreation as a human endeavor involving both women and men. By recognizing pregnancy as "different" from other causes of disability, it supports efforts to equalize the position of working women and men with respect to this fundamental right.[25]

The foregoing asymmetrical models, including my own, share the notion that regardless of their differences, women and men must be treated as full members of society. Each model acknowledges that women may need treatment different than that accorded to men in order to effectuate their membership in important spheres of social life; all would allow at least some such claims, although on very different bases and probably in very different circumstances.

A final asymmetrical approach, *empowerment,* rejects difference altogether as a relevant subject of inquiry.[26] In its strongest form, empowerment claims that the subordination of women to men has itself constructed the sexes and their differences. For example, Catharine MacKinnon argues:

It makes a lot of sense that women might have a somewhat distinctive perspective on social life. We may or may not speak in a different voice—I think that the voice that we have been said to speak in is in fact in large part the "feminine" voice, the voice of the victim speaking without consciousness. But when we understand that women are forced into this situation of inequality, it makes a lot of sense that we should want to negotiate, since we lose conflicts. It makes a lot of sense that we should want to urge values of care, because it is what we have been valued for. We have had little choice but to be valued this way.[27]

A somewhat weaker version of the claim is that we simply do not and cannot know whether there are any important differences between the sexes that have not been created by the dynamic of domination and subordination. In either event, the argument runs, we should forget about the question of differences and focus directly on subordination and domination. If a law, practice, or policy contributes to the subordination of women or their domination by men, it violates equality. If it empowers women or contributes to the breakdown of male domination, it enhances equality.

The reconceptualization of equality as antidomination, like the model of equality as acceptance, attempts to respond directly to the concrete and lived-out experience of women. Like other asymmetrical models, it allows different treatment of women and men when necessary to effectuate its overall goal of ending women's subordination. However, it differs substantially from the acceptance model in its rejection of the membership, belonging, and participatory aspects of equality.

C. The Difference That Difference Makes

Each of the several models of equality discussed above, if adopted, would have a quite different impact on the structure of society. If this society wholeheartedly embraced the symmetrical approach of assimilation—the point of view that "women are just like men"—little would need to be changed in our economic or political institutions except to get rid of lingering traces of irrational prejudice, such as an occasional employer's preference for male employees. In contrast, if society adopted the androgyny model, which views both women and men as bent out of shape by current sex roles and requires both to conform to an androgynous model, it would have to alter radically its methods of resource distribution. In the employment context, this might mean wholesale revamping of methods for determining the "best person for the job." Thus, while assimilation would merely require law firms to hire women who have managed to get the same credentials as the men they have traditionally hired, androgyny might insist that the firm hire only those persons with credentials that would be possessed by someone neither "socially male" nor "socially female."

If society adopted an asymmetrical approach such as the accommodation model, no radical restructuring would be necessary. Government would need only insist that women be given what they need to resemble men, such as time off to have babies and the freedom to return to work on the same rung of the ladder as their male counterparts. If, however, society adopted the model of equality as acceptance, which seeks to make difference costless, it might additionally insist that women and men who opt for socially female occupations, such as child rearing, be compensated at a rate similar to those women and men who opt for socially male occupations, such as legal practice. Alternatively, such occupations might be restructured to make them equally accessible to those whose behavior is culturally coded *male* or *female.*

The different models also have different potential to challenge the phallocentrism of social institutions. No part of the spectrum of currently available feminist legal theory is completely immune to the feminist critique of society as phallocentric. We cannot outrun our history, and that history demonstrates that the terms of social discourse have been set by men who, actively or passively, have ignored women's voices—until even the possibility of women having a voice has become questionable. Nevertheless, the models do differ with respect to the level at which the phallocentrism of the culture reappears.

Under the assimilationist approach, for example, women merit equal treatment only so far as they can demonstrate that they are similar to men. The assimilation model is thus fatally phallocentric. To the extent that women cannot or will not conform to socially male forms of behavior, they are left out in the cold. To the extent they do or can conform, they do not achieve equality as women but as social males.

Similarly, empowerment and androgyny (an asymmetrical and a symmetrical approach, respectively) both rely on central concepts whose current meaning is phallo-centrically biased. If *power* and *neutrality* (along with *equality)* were not themselves gendered concepts, the empowerment and androgyny approaches would be less problematic. But our culture conceives of power as power used by men, and creates androgynous models "tilted" toward the male. As Carrie Menkel-Meadow put it, the trouble with marble cake is that it never has enough chocolate; the problem with androgyny is that it never has enough womanness.[28] Similarly, empowering women without dealing with difference, like assimilation, too easily becomes simply sharing male power more broadly.

Equality as acceptance is not immune from phallocentrism in several of its component concepts. However, these concepts are not necessarily entailed by the theory and may be replaced with less biased concepts as they reveal themselves through the process of equalization. For example, in discussing employment-related applications of the model, I use the measures already existing in that sphere—money, status, and access to decision making. These measures of value are obviously suspect. Nevertheless, my use of them is contingent. Acceptance requires only that culturally coded male and female complements be equally valued; it does not dictate the coin in which such value should be measured. By including access to decision making as part of the measure, however, the theory holds out the possibility that future measures of value will be created by women and men together. Thus, acceptance strives to create the preconditions necessary for sexually integrated debate about a more appropriate value system.

The various models of equality arise out of common feminist goals and enterprises: trying to imagine what a sexually equal society would look like, given that none of us has ever seen one, and trying to figure out ways of getting there, given that the obstacles to sexual equality are so many and so strong.

The perception among feminist legal thinkers that the stakes in the symmetrical-versus-asymmetrical debate are high is correct. Difference indeed makes a difference. Yet the frantic nature of the debate about difference between the sexes makes the divergent views within feminist legal thought appear as a deadly danger rather than an exciting opportunity. The label *divisive* gets slapped on before the discussion even gets under way.

We need to recognize difference among women as diversity rather than division, and difference between women and men as opportunity rather than danger. Audre Lorde calls for the recognition of difference among women in terms that should apply to all human difference:

> As a tool of social control, women have been encouraged to recognize only one area of human difference as legitimate, those differences which exist between women and men. And we have learned to deal across those differences with the urgency of all oppressed subordinates.. . . . We have recognized and negotiated these differences, even when this recognition only continued the old dominant/subordinate mode of human relationship, where the oppressed must recognize the masters' difference in order to survive.
> But our future survival is predicated upon our ability to relate within equality.[29]

There must be choices beyond those of ignoring difference or accepting inequality. So long as difference itself is so expensive in the coin of equality, we approach the variety of human experience with blinders on. Perhaps if difference were not so costly, we, as feminists, could think about it more clearly. Perhaps if equality did not require uniformity, we, as women, could demand it less ambivalently.

II. Equality and Difference

Part I focused on the range of feminist reactions to, and attempts to work within, current equality analysis. Part II focuses on the feminist critique of equality analysis from the "outside"—that is, from a perspective that is "other" to the male construction of law and social norms. From this viewpoint, the very notion of equality as currently accepted by the culture appears phallocentric, fatally constrained by the terms of public discourse that historically have been set solely by men. In Part I, I presented the acceptance model of equality as an alternative to mainstream equality doctrine. In this part, I explain how that model derives from the feminist critique of equality and responds directly to its primary strands.

A. Feminist Critique of Equality

The phallocentricity of equality is most apparent in the extraordinary difficulty the legal system has had dealing with the fact that women (and not men) conceive and bear children. Indeed, it would not be necessary to go further than to establish that the legal system has had difficulty with this fact in order to ground the claim that equality analysis is phallocentric. It is, however, necessary to go beyond a simple recounting of the law in this area in order to lay out the particular ways in which the phallocentricity is manifested.

I have argued elsewhere[30] that the Supreme Court's decision in *Reed v. Reed*[31] marked its acceptance of the assimilationist model of sexual equality. That decision was profoundly assimilationist in that the Court rejected as "irrational" the view that women might be different from men with respect to their ability to handle the traditionally male responsibilities of estate administration.

◇ ◇ ◇

When challenges arose to pregnancy-based classifications, however, the Court was faced with a difference that it could not ignore or treat as created by irrational discrimination. In *Geduldig v. Aiello*[32] and *General Electric Co. v. Gilbert*,[33] the Supreme Court announced, apparently with a straight face, that singling out pregnancy for disadvantageous treatment was not discrimination on the basis of sex.[34] Underlying both opinions was the unarticulated assumption that pregnancy was a real difference and that equality was therefore simply inapplicable. As Justice Stewart stated in *Geduldig,* "There is no risk from which men are protected and women are not. Likewise, there is no risk from which women are protected and men are not."[35]

The Court's equality analysis could thus deal with overbroad generalizations, questions of closeness of fit, and even temporary affirmative action, but a generalization of difference between the sexes that was accurate, and permanently so, was beyond the pale. The first strand of the feminist critique of equality addresses this failing, asserting that equality analysis defines as beyond its scope precisely those issues that women find crucial to their concrete experience as women.

Legal equality analysis "runs out" when it encounters "real" difference, and only becomes available if and when the difference is analogized to some experience men can have too. Legislative overruling of *Gilbert* by the Pregnancy Discrimination Act was thus accomplished by making pregnancy look similar to something men experienced as well—disability. Given the way employment is structured, pregnancy renders a woman unable to work for a few days to a few months, just like illness and injury do for men. However, what makes pregnancy a *dis*ability rather than, say, an additional ability, is the structure of work, not reproduction. Normal pregnancy may make a woman unable to "work" for days, weeks, or months, but it also makes her able to reproduce. From whose viewpoint is the work that she cannot do "work," and the work that she is doing not work? Certainly not from hers.

Thus, the second strand of the feminist critique of equality states: Difference, which is created by the relationship of women to particular and contingent social structures, is taken as natural (that is, unchangeable and inherent), and it is located solely in the woman herself. It is not impossible to imagine a definition of "work" that includes the "labor" of childbirth, nor is it impossible to imagine a workplace setting in which pregnancy would not be disabling.

Analogizing pregnancy to disability has created new difficulties for a legal system trying to apply an assimilationist model of equality. In *California Federal Savings & Loan Association v. Guerra*,[36] an employer challenged a mandatory pregnancy leave statute, arguing that the law could be regarded as equal treatment, rather than a special bonus for women, only where men already have a right to disability leave for other reasons. Underlying the employer's argument was the assumption that the workplace is itself a gender-neutral institution that must treat all workers evenhandedly. Evenhanded treatment requires treating each worker the same as her coworkers, which means extending leave to all workers, regardless of cause, or denying leave to all. This reasoning falls prey to the second strand of the critique by assuming that if women have other needs for disability leave, it is because they are different.

It also gives rise to a third objection: that an institution structured so that women are inevitably disadvantaged by its facially neutral policies is itself phallocentric. Thus, the third strand of the critique challenges the assumed gender neutrality of social institutions, as well as the notion that practices must distinguish themselves from "business as usual" in order to be seen as unequal.

The inability of traditional equality analysis to cope with difference is not limited to biological differences in the workplace. Purporting to follow state constitutional equal rights amendments, many state courts have visited severe hardship on women in marital dissolution proceedings. In case after case, women who have spent most of the marriage as full-time homemakers and mothers are treated as "equal" to their male partners who have spent those years developing a career. In setting alimony awards, courts have refused even to consider the possibility that the woman might find herself at a competitive disadvantage in the job market—a disadvantage directly related to the work she performed during the marriage. Instead, the parties are treated "equally," and any prior disadvantaging of the woman vis-à-vis the workplace is completely ignored.[37]

To summarize, from a feminist viewpoint, current equality analysis is phallocentrically biased in three respects: (1) it is inapplicable once it encounters "real" difference; (2) it locates difference in women, rather than in relationships; and (3) it fails to question the assumptions that social institutions are gender neutral and that women and men are therefore similarly related to those institutions. What the three strands of this critique share is their focus on "difference." A reconstructed equality analysis—one that seeks to eliminate, or at least reduce, the phallocentrism of the current model—must at some point deal with each strand of the critique. Thus, from a theoretical standpoint, symmetrical equality models, with their insistence that difference be ignored, eradicated, or dissolved, are not responsive to the feminist critique of equality.

◇ ◇ ◇

C. Equality as Acceptance

The model of equality as acceptance responds to the first strand of the feminist critique of equality by insisting that equality can in fact be applied across difference. It is not, however, a "leveling" proposal. Rather, equality as acceptance calls for equalization across only those differences that the culture has encoded as gendered complements. The theory of comparable worth provides one example of this, and the field of athletics yields another.

Most proponents of comparable worth have defined the claim along the following lines: Jobs that call for equally valuable skills, effort, and responsibility should be paid equally, even though they occur in different combinations of predominantly female and predominantly male occupations.[38] Thus, when an employer has defined two job classifications as gendered complements, the employer should pay the same to each. Equality as acceptance makes the broader claim that all behavioral forms that the culture (not just the employer) has encoded as male and female counterparts should be equally rewarded. Acceptance would thus support challenges to the overvaluation of "male" skills (and corresponding undervaluation of "female" ones) by employers, rather than limiting challenges to unequal application of an existing valuation or to the failure to make such a valuation.

In the sphere of athletics, equality as acceptance would support an argument that equal resources be allocated to male and female sports programs, regardless of whether the sports themselves are "similar." In this way, women's equality in athletics would not depend on the ability of individual women to assimilate themselves to the particular sports activities traditionally engaged in by men.

Under the model of equality as acceptance, equality analysis does not end at the discovery of a "real" difference. Rather, it attempts to assess the "cultural meaning" of that difference and to determine how to achieve equality despite it. This formulation responds to the second strand of the feminist critique by locating difference in the relationship between women and men rather than in women alone, as accommodation arguably does. Acceptance would thus provide little support for the claim that traditionally male sports (such as football) should be modified so as to accommodate women (or vice versa). Equality as acceptance does not prescribe the superiority of socially female categories, nor even the superiority of androgynous categories. It does, however, affirm the equal validity of men's and women's lives.

Finally, equality as acceptance responds to the third strand of the feminist critique by acknowledging that women and men frequently stand in asymmetrical positions to a particular social institution. It recognizes that women are frequently disadvantaged by facially neutral practices and insists that such asymmetries be reflected in resource allocation. To carry forward the athletics example, equality as acceptance would support an equal division of resources between male and female programs rather than dividing up the available sports budget per capita. Since women and men do not stand symmetrically to the social institution of athletics, per capita distribution would simply serve to perpetuate the asymmetry, diverting more resources to male programs, where the participation rate has traditionally been high, and away from female programs, where the participation rate has been depressed both by women's exclusion from certain sports and by the subordination of those activities women have developed for themselves.

It may be apparent from the preceding paragraphs that equal acceptance as a legal norm does not automatically produce one and only one "right answer" to difficult questions of equality. Instead, it provides support for new remedial strategies as well as a method of uncovering deeper layers of inequality.

D. Acceptance, Not Accommodation

Asymmetrical equality theorists have usually been taken to mean that male institutions should take account of women's differences by accommodating those differences. "Reasonable accommodation" can be asked of a court (although the people usually being asked to be reasonable are those asking for accommodation), and if the choice truly is between accommodation and nothing, "half a loaf" is better than none.

The problem with accommodation, however, is that it implicitly accepts the prevailing norm as generally legitimate, even as it urges that "special circumstances" make the norm inappropriate for the particular individual or class seeking accommodation.[39] In addition, it falls prey to the feminist critique of equality by labeling women as deviant from the norm, thus locating the difference in women. Assimilated women are particularly vulnerable to this misperception and are all too often persuaded to drop valid demands for inclusion on their own terms by the response that they are asking for "an exception."[40]

The distinction between accommodation and acceptance may be illustrated by a rather commonplace example. I remember a feminist lawyer walking up to a podium to deliver a speech. The podium was high enough that she could not reach the microphone. While arrangements were being modified, she pointedly noted, "Built for a man!" Accommodation is a step platform brought for her to stand on. Acceptance is a podium whose height is adjustable.

III. Difference and the System of "Male" Power

The model of equality as acceptance attempts to be responsive both to the feminist critique of equality (as phallocentric) and to the feminist critique of society (as male dominated). Part III addresses the latter by describing the double nature of male dominance that results in both oppression and subordination of women and by showing how equality as acceptance responds to this second feminist critique.

A. Oppression and Subordination

Marilyn Frye uses the metaphor of a birdcage to explain the difference between individual acts of oppression, which may be perpetrated against members of either sex, and the systematic oppression that allows us to refer to one sex as an "oppressed class."

> Consider a birdcage. If you look very closely at just one wire in the cage, you cannot see the other wires. . . . [E]ven if, one day at a time, you myopically inspected each wire, you still could not see why a bird would have trouble going past the wires to get anywhere. There is no physical property of any one wire, *nothing* that the closest scrutiny could discover, that will reveal how a bird could be inhibited or harmed by it except in the most accidental way. It is only when you step back, stop looking at the wires one by one, microscopically, and take a macroscopic view of the whole cage, that you can see why the bird does not go anywhere.[41]

Frye's metaphor does capture the nature of systematic oppression but fails to capture the nature of systematic subordination. While it is true that women are systematically oppressed, it is nonetheless also true that "the female," a "social" category that often overlaps the biological category of women, is systematically subordinated.

Sex as a social category carries the social meaning of what might otherwise be an empirical designation of anatomy, and this conflation of empirical designation with social meaning infringes the liberty of both women and men. The weight of the infringement, however, is not necessarily symmetrical. For example, consider the range of acceptable male body size as compared with the range of acceptable female body size,[42] consider also Bem's and Bem's point that predictions of women's primary occupations are much easier to make than predictions of men's primary occupations.[43] It is true that both women and men are constrained by an acceptable range, but that range is significantly different for the two sexes. In this sense, Frye's use of the term *oppression* is appropriate.

> The root of the word "oppression" is the element "press." . . . Presses are used to mold things or flatten them or reduce them in bulk. . . . Something pressed is something caught between or among forces and barriers which are so related to each other that jointly they restrain, restrict or prevent the thing's motion or mobility. Mold. Immobilize. Reduce.[44]

The inequality of women in their lived-out experience, however, is not limited to the relatively greater constraints on their liberty to "opt out" of their assigned sex role. Rather, there is a more direct equality interest at stake: full membership, belonging, and participation—acceptance as full human beings. This equality interest is infringed by having everything that is associated with women defined as less valuable, less necessary to consider, less important.

To illustrate, in *Corning Glass Works v. Brennan*,[45] an early case involving the Equal

Pay Act,[46] the Supreme Court upheld a challenge to an employer's practice of setting higher pay rates for night-shift inspectors than for day-shift ones. At the time the night shift was instituted, women were prohibited by state law from working at night, but the higher rates were continued beyond the introduction of women into the night shift. The Court noted in passing that "there is also some evidence in the record that additional compensation was necessary because the men viewed inspection jobs as 'demeaning' and as "women's work.'"[47] There is no indication in the case that the work was "demeaning" for any reason other than that it was "women's work." In a similar vein, the job of "secretary" was, when performed almost exclusively by men, one of high status as well as a primary route into management. When the job became female dominated, it somehow lost status, relative pay, and upward mobility.[48] Anthropologists spent decades trying to fit our knowledge of human evolution into a pattern of the needs of "man the hunter"[49] without even considering the needs of "woman the gatherer" or "woman the child rearer,"[50] much less the needs of "woman for herself."

We can read such examples as simply more evidence that oppression and subordination are systematic—that is, that they occur with such frequency as to become almost invisible. But the feminist critique of male power does not stop there. Rather, it questions whether in addition male power is systemic. This question is explored below.

B. Male Power as a System

How can feminism speak of "male" power in the face of countless examples of men lacking power—the soldier who does not choose his target, the assembly-line worker who does not control the product of his labor, the father who does not choose his absence from his children's lives, the lover who does not choose the image in his head that makes him so critical of his mate's shortcomings? Even if male dominance operates in the interest of all men, it certainly does not operate equally for all men. While some forms of male power (such as the ability to physically or psychologically intimidate women) is shared broadly, other forms (such as the ability to deny women access to certain jobs and careers) are more narrowly concentrated.

Feminist critique argues that individual or class differences among men in the degree of power they hold over women are not directly relevant to the issue of male power as a system. Rather, the form of male power that constructs male dominance as a social system rather than as a systematic assertion of dominance by particular men can be viewed as concentrated in the hands of a few men who are at or near the top of intersecting hierarchies of sex, race, and class, reserved to those in what I will call the *club*. The constitutive form of male power exercised by the club is the power to set the terms by which all forms of human activity are given social meaning and social value. The power to define what is and is not a right, a legal interest, equality, justice, or law itself is power that constitutes a system. It is the power to construct reality itself; it is the power to "speak the world."

This club is "male" not because of some biological essence that only men possess. Institutions created from the socially male perspective do not depend on biological males to sustain them. It is true that the apparent intractability of male institutions (especially the institution of rape)[51] gives rise to some feminist suspicion as to their contingency and thus leads some to posit a necessary link between biological sex and social sex. However, at least in this chapter, I am concerned with maleness in the cultural and not the biological sense.

I identify the power exercised by the club as male power, as opposed to power per se, for two reasons. First, as I have argued in this chapter, and as numerous other feminists have demonstrated in the work on which I have drawn, the power of the club operates against individual women to a greater extent than against individual men. Even if no account is taken of the way in which the socially female is devalued, that biological women are significantly deprived economically might lead one to suspect that it is not female power that is at work here.

Second, feminist scholars have demonstrated distinct differences between the ways in which women and men may conceive of and exercise "power" itself. Carol Gilligan's germinal work *In a Different Voice* has given a vocabulary to previously unarticulated nuances in women's use of the term *power.* "While men represent powerful activity as assertion and aggression, women in contrast portray acts of nurturance as acts of strength."[52] While again noting that male–female differences in this area are matters of degree rather than absolutes, the way in which an apparently neutral term such as *power* takes on gendered ambiguity on close analysis is instructive. In referring to the power that sets the terms and limits of social valuation as *male power,* I mean to refer to power as control over others, as opposed to power as ability to help. To call the former male and the latter female is not to say that women are never controlling or that men are never interested in helping; rather, it is to recognize the ways in which social typing both reflects and helps to shape statistical tendencies.

The club, then, exercises male power to the extent that it defines for others what is to be aspired to, rather than helping others to articulate aspirations or to achieve the aspirations so articulated. The perceived privileges of membership in the club consist in the ability to see one's actions mirrored in the world—to have one's point of view accepted, not as a point of view, but as simple reality. For example, until Gilligan's critique emerged, Kohlberg's theory of moral development was viewed not just as a model of the moral development of adolescent males but as the way all people developed morally. In this system, women appeared to be stunted, "inexplicably" stuck at the lower stages of Kohlberg's hierarchy. Likewise, Catharine MacKinnon's work on rape points out the way in which rape law's ostensibly neutral inquiry into objective fact—Was it rape?—can be viewed as reflecting only the male actor's perspective. "When the reality is split—a woman is raped [her experience] but not by a rapist [his experience]—the law tends to conclude that a rape *did not happen.'*[53] His experience becomes truth.

Club members themselves are not free from the system their words, actions, hopes, and fears create. They may "speak the world," but the world thus spoken has negative consequences for the speaker as well. Nevertheless, the power thus to speak is apparently hard to give up. Moreover, in response to challenges to its power, the club is more likely to extend the illusion of possible membership that to abandon its practices. The terms of such admission are simple: "Outsiders" may join the club one at a time, in the same way that Boy Scouts become Eagle Scouts, by earning the right number and combination of merit badges.

Women who are "privileged" in racial and class terms seem more vulnerable to the false promise of individual acceptance into the club, probably because the promise is held up so tantalizingly close. "We're just like you," we have shouted at the clubhouse doors. "Look at our merit badges: We've gone to your schools, learned your language, copied your work styles. Let us in." And our badges got us in. However, the power we've earned as socially male club members has not earned us the right to speak in our own voices. Our club membership is contingent on our willingness to either speak in a male voice or remain silent. And since speech as it is used by the club is the power to silence others, we must agree to use our voices to silence other women.

As women, neither option is "better" than the other. Power as it is wielded by the club is not the kind of power that women want for ourselves; it is male power. Thus, assimilation ultimately fails on two levels. As the plaintiff in *Hopkins v. Price Waterhouse*[54] experienced, socially male women are always at risk of being "discovered" as biological women. And, as Kathryn Powers points out, the "success" of a few aspirational women justifies a system that excludes and subordinates *most* women.[55] When those of us with culturally male credentials speak on behalf of all women, we walk the tightrope between losing our place in the male social world and silencing other women whose experiences differ from our own.

This view of male power as a system may not be the only explanation for women's situation, but it is the one most plausible to me right now. It "fits" the observable data and provides some rationale for why "difference" is so troubling to current equality analysis. Differences in biology, moral reasoning, or social experience should result in inequality only if the society is concerned with maintaining the club. The perpetuation of that club requires the eradication of difference from candidates for membership before the granting of equality, so that those who enter the gates—be they biologically male, female, hermaphrodite, white, black, brown, yellow, or red and be they materially possessed of much or little—will enter as socially male, white, and upwardly mobile.

C. Responding to the Critique of Male Power

Theoretically, society could abolish the value hierarchy ordained by the club and replace it with a new hierarchy of human values. It could calculate new, unbiased values for primary education, child rearing, and housecleaning. It could, in the words of one of my colleagues, turn these questions into "social issues." However, while such ostensibly "neutral" revaluation has a great deal of surface appeal, it ignores the long-standing devaluation of behaviors, concerns, and occupations associated with women.

Rethinking the social value of child rearing, for instance, without simultaneously revaluing all "women's work" could hardly avoid replicating much of the current skewed value hierarchy. Additionally, the construction, through public debate and struggle, of a new social value hierarchy must include the voices of those who have been unheard within traditional policy discourse, including social women. Without some separate strategy to include these voices, public debate will continue to be male, even though some of its participants will be biological women.

Alternatively, if I am right that the maintenance of the club depends on equality's meaning sameness, then each reduction in inequality across difference will make the next step easier and more accessible to critique. Though it may take a long time, we can rescue equality and destroy the club by accepting difference, by making sex difference not make a difference in equality, by making difference "costless" (or at least cost less) in one context after another.

The model of equality as acceptance makes difference less costly by equalizing the resources "merited" by gendered complements—that is, by related male and female attributes or actions. The choice of which resources to equalize is contingent, and has been made, on pragmatic, rather than theoretical, grounds. For the present, the model will hold constant the coin in which gendered complements are to be measured—money, status, and access to decision making.

These measures and their application are themselves subject to feminist critique. First, both the value of money and the meaning of status are artifacts of a phallocentric culture. Given the choice, women might choose to value things in nonmonetary form or to define status in a radically different way. Positing alternative currency, however, will have to await a time when women have equal access to the mint. Second, my insistence that male and female job categories be equally paid implicitly accepts the validity of commodification of many forms of labor, which feminists have critiqued in other contexts as arising from a phallocentric desire for control. Finally, the model of equality as acceptance also envisions application within, as well as across, spheres of human activity. But from a radical feminist perspective, even that is problematic. For example, a feminist might argue that equalizing across difference only among workers legitimizes the socially constructed division between professional and personal, paid and unpaid, public and private work—a division strongly contested by feminists.

Symmetrical equality theorists have argued that because biological sex is no longer a strong predictor of social sex, it is harder to maintain the fiction that biological males are "naturally" better at such things as legal practice. Acceptance goes further, holding that once the social sex of a worker no longer accurately predicts that worker's pay, status, or access to decision making, it will become harder and harder to maintain the fiction that socially male behaviors are "naturally" more valuable than their socially female counterparts. This in turn will make it harder to ignore the value of socially female labor in the "private sphere" while at the same time allowing massive infusion of "private" sphere interests into the "public" arena of employment.

In this respect, then, it does not matter that some elements of the acceptance model reflect the phallocentrism of our culture (as they inevitably must do). If socially male pay scales, status, and access to decision-making processes are open, not only to socially male women, but also to socially female women and men, women's voice as it is now will be admitted to the dialogue that constructs social meaning. To whatever extent women's voice is not yet authentically our own, the dialogue will still be "tilted," but the frame around it will have moved significantly.

IV. Making Difference Costless

I have thus far constrained this speculative exercise to respond to equality's legal tradition, feminist critique of equality, and feminist critique of male power as a system. However, I also recognize the need to account for "different kinds of sexual difference." Thus, although I do not claim to offer a blueprint for specific application, I will attempt in this part to lay out the foundation for the house that a reconstructed sexual equality may someday build.

A. Differently Gendered Complements

The problem of identifying gendered complements lies along two axes of difference. One axis measures the "source" of differences, ranging from the clearly biological to the clearly social (with a great deal of controversy in between). The other measures the degree of overlap between the sexes and runs from more-or-less differences on one end to yes-or-no differences on the other.

For gender differences that are more or less, there is a significant degree of overlap between the sexes. Height is one of these. Not all women would have been disaffirmed by the too-high podium that was "built for a man," and not all men would have been affirmed by it. But more women than men in this society would have had the feminist lawyer's experience. Additionally, differences of the more-or-less variety are easier to deny, since there is always some woman over six feet or some man under five, and a great number of both in between. These differences are also easier to "match" because shorter and taller are both measures of the same concededly shared human characteristic of height.

For yes-or-no gender differences, there is no overlap at all. The primary example of this is, of course, pregnancy. No man can become pregnant, and most women can. However, women who have never had the capacity for pregnancy are not thereby made either biologically or socially male, even when the dominant culture has tended to view them as "not women." Thus, although it is useful for purposes of analysis to separate yes-or-no differences from more-or-less ones, they represent two poles of the same spectrum.

Disparate treatment analysis under Title VII allows individuals who are exceptions to the "rule" of their biological sex to be socially classed with the other sex. Thus, tall women must be treated the same as tall men, and short men the same as short women. As the podium example demonstrates, phallocentrism in such cases usually involves setting the norm by reference to the center of the male bell curve. When the norm is set by reference to the female bell curve, the same analysis applies; men who can type must be allowed into socially female secretarial positions.

To establish a prima facie case of discrimination under disparate treatment analysis, a plaintiff must show

> (i) that [the plaintiff] belongs to a racial minority [or is a woman]; (ii) that he [or she] applied and was qualified for a job for which the employer was seeking applicants; (iii) that, despite [plaintiff's] qualifications, he [or she] was rejected; and (iv) that, after [plaintiff's] rejection, the position remained open and the employer continued to seek applicants from persons of complainant's qualifications.[56]

Requiring a female complainant to establish "qualifications" for a traditionally male job is to require her to establish that she is socially male, at least in this context.

Disparate impact analysis, on the other hand, allows socially female women to bring equality claims if the job qualification containing the gendered norm is irrelevant to the applicant's ability to perform the job. No showing of direct intent to discriminate is required. Under disparate impact doctrine, then, a woman can establish discrimination by demonstrating that women as a class are more severely affected than men by a facially neutral employment practice, such as a height requirement. The employer can, however, justify the discriminatory impact by demonstrating that the practice is "job related" or necessary to the employer's business.[57] Moreover, the relevance of the practice is tested solely by reference to the way the job is already structured. Thus, even disparate impact analysis—as currently practiced—does not allow for challenges to male bias in the structure of businesses, occupations, or jobs.

Equality as acceptance would support challenges to government and employer policies and practices that use male norms even when such norms are considered job related, necessary to the business, or "substantially related to an important governmental interest." Unlike the more radical version of the model of androgyny referred to above, however, acceptance would not necessarily require the elimination of such norms. Acceptance could instead be achieved by inventing complementary structures containing female norms. For example, assume an employer successfully defends its 5'9" minimum height requirement as necessary to the job of sorting widgets as they pass on a conveyor belt. Equality as acceptance could be achieved by restructuring the job itself—in this case, by changing the height of the conveyor belt or by adding a second belt. Alternatively, the employer could defend the requirement by demonstrating that equal job opportunities exist in the plant for applicants shorter than 5'9". Acceptance would thus permit de facto sex segregation in the workplace, but only if the predominantly male and predominantly female jobs have equal pay, status, and opportunity for promotion into decision-making positions.

Yes-or-no differences do not yield so readily to matching. This has helped focus the "equal treatment/special treatment" debate on pregnancy—specifically, on the question of whether requiring employers to grant pregnancy leaves for women violates the equal rights of men, who can never take advantage of such leaves. If pregnancy were a more-or-less difference, such as disabling heart trouble or child care responsibility, it would be easy for the current legal system to answer this question. Since it is a yes-or-no difference, however, the legal system runs in circles: The Supreme Court in *Geduldig v. Aiello*[58] said pregnancy is different, so women can be punished for it; the federal district court in *Cal. Fed.*[59] said pregnancy is not different, so women should not benefit from it; the Supreme Court, affirming the Ninth Circuit in *Cal. Fed.*,[60] said pregnancy is different, so men are not hurt by taking account of it.

I think that the appropriate unit of analysis in yes-or-no cases is interaction of the sexes rather than comparison. Even with rapidly developing reproductive technology, it is still necessary for some part of a woman to interact with some part of a man to produce a pregnancy. In that interaction, the gendered complements are pregnancy for the woman and fewer sperm cells for the man. Since pregnancy almost always results in some period of disability for the woman, making the sex difference costless with respect to the workplace requires that money, status, and opportunity for advancement flow equally to the womb-donating woman and the sperm-donating man (himself an equal contributor to the procreative act).

Both average height and pregnancy lie near the biological pole of the source axis; these differences are clearly biological. Their existence and degree of overlap are less problematic as an empirical matter than differences lying closer to the cultural pole. The clearly cultural differences, on the other hand, are more problematic, primarily because they are even more likely than biological differences to give rise to stereotypes that harm women. Arguments for ignoring difference are also more plausible with reference to the cultural axis. Because these differences are acquired, they can presumably be done away with, if not for us then for our children or grandchildren. This combination of danger and plausibility has led several sex equality theorists to place themselves toward the middle of the symmetrical-versus-asymmetrical debate.[61] I am, however, either brave or foolhardy enough to believe that even cultural differences can be made accessible to equality analysis.

◊ ◊ ◊

Matching gendered complements in order to equalize across cultural differences may sound like marching directly into the valley of the stereotypes. Those who consider Carol Gilligan's discovery of "a different voice" sexist are not likely to find this appealing. Nevertheless, allow me to make two disclaimers. First, almost all cultural differences are, or could easily be, "more or less." Lots of biological men exhibit socially female characteristics (for which they are all too often punished); at least as many biological women exhibit socially male ones (for which they are often rewarded, although they are simultaneously punished for not having the biological form to match); and many more women and men fall in the middle, exhibiting no readily identifiable male or female behavior patterns. Second, what is objectionable about stereotypes is not that they are never true but, rather, that they are not always true. Demonstrating that not every woman with children is primarily responsible for their care may help those women who do not have such responsibility to compete for certain jobs, but it does little to help those women struggling to hold down two jobs, only one of which is paid.

Disclaimers aside, what is relevant for this exercise is not the accuracy or inaccuracy of any set of gendered complements but, rather, how the complements reward or punish those who are perceived to fall on one side or the other. Studies of sex-segregated work places tend to show that there is a high correlation between employer perceptions of gender differences and the segregation patterns themselves. These perceived gender differences, such as lifting strength and small-muscle dexterity, are of the more-or-less type and tend to fall toward the middle of the "source" axis. Requiring individual testing alleviates segregation to some extent, but it only helps those women who do not fit the female stereotype (at the expense, of course, of those men who do not fit the male stereotype). However, the main problem with sex segregation is that promotion patterns and pay scales are determined by entry-level job classifications. Thus, those women who do fit the female stereotype (of, say, low lifting strength and high small-muscle dexterity) are stuck. They are not harmed by the "female" job classification as such; they are harmed by the disparity in pay and opportunity for promotion that goes along with it. And the disparity in promotion opportunities continues the cycle of overvaluation of male characteristics and undervaluation of female ones, because employers will continue to select those biological men and women who are socially male.

If, alternatively, both male and female entry-level positions paid the same and offered the same promotion opportunities, individual testing would not matter so much. Indeed, assuming proportionate numbers of openings, applicants might well self-select into the classification that better utilizes their particular strenghts and minimizes their particular weaknesses. If so, the segregation pattern would gradually break down unless employers actively and, legally speaking, "intentionally" sought to maintain it. Moreover, even if self-selection by individual skills did not occur, a better sex mix at the management level would eventually have a significant impact throughout the firm.

As Frances Olsen sets forth in *The Sex of Law,* we tend to think in dichotomies, and those dichotomies are both sexualized (with one side masculine and the other feminine) and hierarchicized (with one side in each pair superior).[62] She argues that the sexualization and hierarchicization should be attacked simultaneously, to the end of deconstructing the dichotomies themselves. While I do not disagree with this goal, I do think Olsen's strategy is impractical. Dichotomies that purport to describe gender differences are, I think, only likely to fall apart once they no longer accurately describe differences in pay scales, hiring patterns, or promotion ladders. Additionally, since we presently think in these dichotomies, we may as well use them to help us in our struggle to discard them.

The rigidity of sexualized dichotomies does appear to be gradually breaking down in many areas. Whether the strategy I am suggesting would impede that breakdown is discussed below. With regard to the practical problem of implementation, however, the true breakdown of any particular male–female dichotomy is not a problem but a benefit. It puts us one step closer toward eliminating them entirely.

B. Reifying Gender

The theoretical problem of the above discussion is, of course, the danger that using gendered complements overtly (I remain convinced that we use them covertly all the time) will strengthen the gender divide. This danger seems real, although perhaps overstated if the rest of my analysis holds. As I have urged throughout this chapter, it is not gender difference but the difference gender makes, that creates a divide. Instead of division, there might easily be a continuum stretching beyond the current poles—the "polymorphous perversity" that Jeff Goldstein posits in the erotic arena[63] or the "reds and greens and blues" that Frances Olsen imagines within a liberated androgyny.[64] If the status of "victim" were not so debilitating in socially real terms, we would be able to laugh at the argument that the Minneapolis antipornography ordinance paints women as victims of male violence.[65] Similarly, if the location of a person, action, or characteristic on the "female" side of the divide did not entail her/his/its immediate devaluation, then the mere identification of a law's beneficiaries as "women" would not divert us from a deeper and more practical analysis of its relative advantages and disadvantages.

There is yet another layer, however, to the critique of reifying gender. Not only is the socially female a constructed category, but that social construction was historically created in the absence of women, or at least without their participation. Therefore, runs the criticism, the socially female cannot be claimed as truly belonging to women, because it has been men who have done the defining. How, then, can I claim it as valuable on behalf of women?

I am not claiming that women's authentic voice would value everything that has been assigned to us by social definition. I literally do not know what I would say about my selfhood had I not been raised in a phallocentric culture—and neither does anyone else. However, as long as identification with socially female attributes is more "expensive" than identification with socially male ones—when taking parental leave shunts you off the partnership track, crying in a meeting shuts off the discussion, breast feeding makes you unacceptable at the restaurant table—we are not ever going to be in a position to find out what women would value for themselves.

The social construction of "woman" has not just been a matter of men taking the best for themselves and assigning the rest to women. It has also been a matter of perceiving the "worst" as being whatever women were perceived to be. This interaction can be disrupted either by revaluing what women have been perceived to be or by reassigning the attributes that comprise the social sexes, or both. However, I am making a claim for one form of disruption rather than the other, based on my analysis of male power as a system, presented in Part III. So long as equality analysis takes place in s system defined by the club, reassignment of social sex attributes must itself operate unequally. My claim is also based on the quasi-empirical observation that women are willing to pay an increasingly heavy price to maintain at least some socially female modes of being and that men are unwilling, or unasked, to pay a similar price to take them on. To take one example, reassigning child care has not thus far meant assigning it to men or even sharing it with them; it has meant assigning it to poorer women. Despite a rapid increase in the number of married women in the full-time labor force, men's contributions to household tasks have remained astonishingly low. For the sexual dialectic to yield anything transformative, we have got to take our social finger off one end of the scale.

As indicated above, making gender difference costless, even in the skewed terms by which we now measure "cost," seems just as likely to decrease the overlap between biological and social sex as ignoring what we perceive as gender difference in the hope that it will disappear or be "transformed." If it costs most men and women the same to stay home with the baby, parenting is more likely to be shared. (Currently, women have less to lose than men by foregoing paid employment for unpaid child care, since both women's salaries and expectations are generally lower.) And if the social rewards of child rearing are closer to those of what we now think of as employment, making the two compatible can proceed from two directions instead of one.

It is, of course, possible that "social transvestitism" will not occur to any great extent, even if it becomes relatively costless. Perhaps biological or cultural imperatives do play a larger role than power and economics. I doubt it. But if it does turn out that, given a flat cost curve, most biological women opt for social womanhood and most biological men opt for social manhood and very few explore new modes of social existence, I'm not sure I'd care very much. The modernists may enjoy mixing things up for its own sake; me, I'm only in it for the equality.

◇ ◇ ◇

Conclusion

In this chapter, I have outlined the model of equality as acceptance. The claims I have made for this model are both modest and immodest: modest, in that I do not claim that even full implementation would automatically result in full sexual equality; immodest, in that I claim that even partial implementation would allow both theorists and policy-makers to see new ground for equality that is obscured now. Acceptance would, at the very least, loosen the grip that hierarchical ordering by sex has kept on our lives and on our imaginations.

As I look back on the argument made here on behalf of the model of acceptance, I perceive these major points: (1) In order to be faithful to feminist critique, a reconstructed equality norm must be capable of application across or beyond difference; (2) although no reconstruction undertaken under conditions of inequality can claim to be completely free from phallocentric bias, a reconstruction can increase equality and invite later, freer reconstructions by shifting the frame and moving the margin into the picture; (3) making difference costless (or even cost less) will shift the frame, allowing us to see ever more subtle forms of phallocentric bias while reducing the danger that difference will be used to recreate inequality; (4) the model of costless difference can be applied within contexts without impeding later efforts to apply it across contexts; and (5) much of the model's usefulness can be realized now, without waiting for major legislative or cultural change.

The enormity of the project that remains, however, should not be underestimated. We know very little about difference in its liberatory potential, and much about its potential to divide and oppress. However, if the answers we discover about difference can increase equality rather than decrease it, I am confident we will find them.

Notes

This chapter has benefited from an enormous number of people and organizations. Research funding was provided by the University of California Academic Senate and the Institute of Industrial Relations at UCLA. In addition to general research assistance from Annette DeMichele and Steven Susoeff, I have been fortunate to have had the unusually thorough and able help of Jane Newman. The ideas were developed through presentations of various papers to the Feminist Critical Legal Studies Conference, both the West and the East Coast Feminist Critical Legal Scholars, and the UCLA Faculty Research Seminar on Women, all of whose members provided helpful criticism and support. Of the many colleagues and friends who read endless drafts, the following deserve special thanks: Richard Abel, Alsion Anderson, Grace Blumberg, Jon Davidson, Herma Hill Kay, Kenneth Karst, Sheila McIntyre, Carrie Menkel-Meadow, and Sylvia Walby.

1. U.K. LeGuin, Always Coming Home 313 (1985).

2. C. Gilligan, In a Different Voice (1982).

3. *Id.* at 18. Kohlberg's theory identified six different stages of human moral reasoning from childhood to adulthood. The theory was based on an empirical survey of eighty-four boys whose development Kohlberg studied for more than twenty years.

4. *See* Gauthier, *Is There Such A Thing as Women's Writing?,* in French Feminisms, at 161-64.

5. The transformation of sexual harassment from an unmentioned and unmentionable problem of working women into a legal claim of sex discrimination is the clearest example.

6. A. Lorde, *The Master's Tools Will Never Dismantle the Master's House,* in Sister Outsider 110 (1984) (comments at "The Personal and the Political Panel," Second Sex Conference. New York, September 29, 1979).

7. Williams, *The Equality Crisis.* 7 Women's Rts. L. Rep. 196 (1982)

8. *But see* Project, *Law Firms and Lawyers with Children: An Empirical Analysis of Family/ Work Conflict,* 34 Stan. L. Rev. 1263, 1300 (1982) (finding an "increased willingness" among private law firms to consider flexible work arrangements for women, but "little evidence" for accommodating men as coequal parents). *Cf.* Taub, *From Parental Leaves to Nurturing Leaves.* 13 N.Y.U. Rev. L. & Soc. Change 381, 381 (1985).

9. *See, e.g.,* Rossi, *Sex Equality: The Beginnings of Ideology,* in Beyond Sex-Role Seterotypes, 80, 87 (A. Kaplan and J. Bean eds. 1976); Taub, *passim* (suggesting a restructuring of the way academic progress is measured).

10. Some feminists hold out an ideal of asymmetrical androgyny. *See, e.g.,* Olsen, *The Family and the Market: A Study of Ideology and Legal Reform,* 96 Harv. L. Rev. 1497, 1578 (1983) (androgyny as "reds and greens and blues" rather than undifferentiated gray). Shifting to an asymmetrical framework, however, changes the ideal of androgyny into the ideal of equal acceptance.

11. *See, e.g.,* Rostker v. Goldberg, 453 U.S. 57 (1981); Michael M. v. Superior Court, 450 U.S. 464 (1981).

12. E. Wolgast, Equality and the Rights of Women 61-63 (1980) at 122, 167.

13. Law, *Rethinking Sex and the Constitution,* 132 U. Pa. L. Rev. 955, 1007-13 (1984).

14. Kay, *Equality and Difference: The Case of Pregnancy.* I Berkeley Women's L.J. 1, 27-37 (1985).

15. *See* Lemons v. City & County of Denver, 17 Fair Empl. Prac. Cas. (BNA) 906 (I) (Apr. 17, 1978) (rejecting a comparable worth claim that paying nurses less that real estate appraisers violates Title VII).

16. *See* C. Gilligan, In a Different Voice (1982).

17. 107 S. Ct. 683 (1987).

18. Cal. Gov't. Code §§ 12900-12996 (West 1980 & Supp. 1987).

19. 42 U.S.C. §§ 2000e-10 to -17 (1982).

20. *Cal. Fed.,* 107 S. Ct. at 688, 692.

21. Brief for the ACLU as *amicus curiae, Cal. Fed.,* 107 S. Ct. 683 (1987) (No. 85-494).

22. Brief for Equal Rights Advocates as amicus curiae, *Cal. Fed.* 107 S. Ct. 683 (1987) (No. 85-494).

23. Brief for the Coalition for Reproductive Equality in the Workplace (CREW) as amicus curiae, *Cal Fed,* 107 S. Ct. 683 (1987) (no. 85-494). I was the attorney of record for CREW, and the principal author of the CREW *amicus* brief.

24. *Id.* at 36-37.

25. The *Cal Fed* opinion, authored by Justice Marshall, does much to bring together the asymmetrical and symmetrical equality arguments. As alternative holdings, the opinion first defends the California law as consistent with equal employment opportunity. "By 'taking pregnancy into account,' California's pregnancy disability leave statute allows women, as well as men, to have families without losing their jobs" (107 S. Ct. at 694). The Court then states that the employer can satisfy both California law and demands for symmetry by providing leave for all forms of disability. *Id.* at 694-95.

26. This model has been articulated most fully by Catharine MacKinnon and draws heavily on the work of radical feminist theorists such as Andrea Dworkin. *See* MacKinnon, *Feminism, Marxism, Method and the State: Toward Feminist Jurisprudence,* 8 SIGNS 635 (1983) (examining how traditional theories of "the state" perpetuate male power to exclude women's perspective); A. DWORKIN, OUR BLOOD 96–111; A. DWORKIN, PORNOGRAPHY: MEN POSSESSING WOMEN 13-24 (1979).

27. *Feminist Discourse,* 34 Buffalo L. Rev. 11, (1985) at 27.

28. A. Allen, C. Littleton, and C. Menkel-Meadow, Law in a Different Voice, 15th National Conference on Women and the Law, Address by C. Menkel-Meadow (March 31, 1984) (tape on file with the author).

29. A. LORDE. *Age, Race, Class and Sex: Women Redefining Difference,* in SISTER OUTSIDER, at 114, 122.

30. Note, 95 HARV. L. REV. 502-3 (1981).

31. 404 U.S. 71 (1971).

32. 417 U.S. 484 (1974).

33. 429 U.S. 125 (1976).

34. In *Geduldig,* a state disability plan that paid benefits to workers unable to work for any reason except normal pregnancy was challenged as violating women's right to equal protection under the Constitution. In *General Electric,* an employee insurance plan that covered all medical conditions except normal pregnancy was challenged under Title VII, the federal Equal Employment Opportunity Law. 12 USC § 2000e-2(a) (1982).

35. 417 U.S. at 496-97.

36. 107 S. Ct. 683 (1987).

37. Weitzman's findings indicate that one year after divorce, the standard of living of male ex-spouses rises 43 percent while the standard of living of female ex-spouses falls 73 percent. Weitzman, *The Economics of Divorce: Social and Economic Consequences of Property, Alimony, and Child Support.* 28 UCLA L. REV. 1181, 1251 (1980). She blames this economic disaster not on the concept of "no fault" divorce itself, but on the state legislature's failure to take into account that male and female partners to marriage usually stand in asymmetrical positions with respect to the job market. *See* Stix, *Disasters of the No-Fault Divorce. Los Angeles Times,* November 7, 1985, § V, at 3, col. 1.

38. Note, *Comparable Worth—A Necessary Vehicle for Pay Equity,* 68 MARQ. L. REV. 93, 98, n.33 (1984). *See generally* COMMITTEE ON OCCUPATIONAL CLASSIFICATION & ANALYSIS, ASSEMBLY OF BEHAVIORAL & SOCIAL SCIENCES NAT'L. RESEARCH COUNCIL, WOMEN, WORK, AND WAGES: EQUAL PAY FOR JOBS OF EQUAL VALUE (1981).

39. It is, I think, the assumption that all asymmetrical equality theorists advocate accommodation that leads symmetrists to accuse us of asking for "special treatment" rather than "equal treatment."

40. It is invalidating, on some deep level, to be treated as an exception, and asking for an accommodation under current conditions is asking for an exception. Not only do such requests fail to challenge the "rule," but they often stick in our throats.

41. M. FRYE, The Politics of Reality (1983), at 4-5.

42. *See, e.g.,* K. CHERNIN, THE OBSESSION: REFLECTIONS ON THE TYRANNY OF SLENDERNESS 122 (1981).

43. Bem and Bem, *Homogenizing the American Woman: The Power of an Unconscious Ideology,* in FEMINIST FRAMEWORKS 6, 6-8 (1978).

44. M. FRYE, at 2; *see also* Taub, *Keeping Women in Their Place: Stereotyping per Se as a Form of Employment Discrimination,* 21 B.C.L. REV. 345 (1980).

45. 417 U.S. 188 (1974).

46. The Equal Pay Act provides in relevant part:

> No employer having employees subject to [the act] shall discriminate, within any establishment in which such employees are employed, between employees on the basis of sex by paying wages to employees in such establishment at a rate less than the rate at which he pays wages to employees of the opposite sex in such establishment for equal work on jobs the performance of which requires equal skill, effort, and responsibility, and which are performed under similar working conditions.

29 U.S.C. § 206(d)(1) (1982).

47. *Brennan,* 417 U.S. at 191-92, n.3.

48. *See* S. ROTHMAN, WOMAN'S PROPER PLACE 48-52 (1978).

49. *See, e.g.,* D. MORRIS, THE NAKED APE (1967) (explaining human evolution from the perspective of male "hunter").

50. *See* E. MORGAN, THE DESCENT OF WOMAN (1972) (suggesting that Desmond Morris ignored other available theories of human evolution).

51. Rape ceases to be an individual act and becomes an institution at the point that the freedom of all women is restricted and controlled by its prevalence. *See, e.g.,* S. BROWNMILLER, AGAINST OUR WILL (1975). "From prehistoric times to the present, I believe, rape has played a critical function. It is nothing more or less than a conscious process of intimidation by which *all men* keep *all women* in a state of fear" (id. at 15).

52. C. GILLIGAN, at 167-68 (discussing David McClelland's work on the different ways men and women tend to fantasize power).

53. MacKinnon, *Toward Feminist Jurisprudence,* 26 at 651.

54. 618 F. Supp. 1109 (D.D.C. 1985).

55. Powers, *Sex, Segregation and the Ambivalent Directions of Sex Discrimination Law,* 1979 WM I. REV. 55, 91-93.

56. McDonnell-Douglas Corp. v. Green, 411 U.S. 792, 802 (1973). The disparate treatment criteria are exactly the same for race or sex, *see* Texas Dept. of Community Affairs v. Burdine, 450 U.S. 248 (1981) (sex discrimination claim based on disparate treatment), and are intended to be applied flexibly, so as to serve the same purposes in different contexts. *Id.* at 253-54, n.6. Thus, in claims of disparate treatment in promotion, the criterion of "the job remained open" is replaced by "the job was filled by a person of the other sex."

57. Griggs v. Duke Power Co., 401 U.S. 424 (1971).

58. 417 U.S. 484 (1974).

59. California Fed. Sav. & Loan Ass'n v. Guerra 758 F.2d 390 (9th Cir. 1985), *aff'd.* 107 S. Ct. 683 (1987).

60. 107 S. Ct. 683 (1987).

61. *See, e.g.,* Kay; Law, 13 (both advocating a symmetrical model as the norm, with some area of asymmetry).

62. Olsen, (1984) at 1-4, unpublished manuscript on file with author.

63. Goldstein, *Pornography and Its Discontents,* Village Voice, October 16, 1984, at 19, 44.

64. Olsen, at 1578.

65. *See, e.g.,* Vance, *Pleasure and Danger: Toward a Politics of Sexuality,* in PLEASURE AND DANGER: EXPLORING FEMINIST SEXUALITY 7 (C. Vance ed. 1984) ("If women increasingly view themselves entirely as victims through the lens of the oppressor and allow themselves to be viewed that way by others, they become enfeebled and miserable.").

II

On Justice and Harm: Battery, Harassment, and Rape

What constitutes an injury is central to legal action. It has long been a truism that justice and law require interpersonal respect, at least to the extent that we may not intentionally harm or interfere with the freedom of other individuals. Since at least the time of Immanuel Kant, fundamental principles of morality have required respect for the individual dignity of all human beings. John Stuart Mill provided an eloquent defense on utilitarian grounds for the proposition that the one purpose for which state power can clearly be used to limit individual freedom is to prevent one individual from harming another. Virtually all moral and legal theories agree that this is the core of interpersonal responsibility. One person's freedom ends with the freedom and bodily integrity of another. Any individual's rights are limited by the basic rights of all other persons. Thus, without question, coercion, intimidation, harassment, and bodily injury are prohibited by justice and law.

Given the level of agreement on the correctness and centrality of the prohibition against the unauthorized use of force and the intentional infliction of harm, there are some surprising limits on the enforcement and even the conceptualization of these minimal prohibitions. If assault is prohibited, why are husbands not prosecuted for beating their wives? If exploitation is wrong, why are employers not prosecuted for pressuring their employees into sexual relations? If rape is illegal, why are men not prosecuted if they are aquainted with the women they rape? One answer is that some men are prosecuted for these offenses, but not many. Why so few? Examining the complexities of this question will provide further glimpses into the pervasive effect of patriarchy on law.

There are two basic questions to ask about the limits to the legal prevention of coercion and harm. First, what counts as a harm? What is and what should be recognized as coercion, exploitation, harassment, or injury? These may sound like odd questions to ask, as the answers may seem obvious. One might think that anyone could recognize coercion, harassment, injury, and the rest. But on the contrary, these are not observations of fact but normative judgments that vary with time and place. For example, children who were forced to work long hours in mines and factories in the eighteenth and nineteenth centuries were not considered exploited. Rather, they were considered employed. For many centuries, slavery was not widely considered a harm, as it was thought that slaves were not fit to do anything else. Until well into the 1900s, reasonable chastisement of one's wife (i.e., beating with a stick no thicker than one's thumb) was considered appropriate and necessary discipline, and appropriate and necessary discipline is not a harm. So slavery, wife beating, and child labor (not to mention beating children and slaves) were not always considered harmful. And many other acts that we now consider harms were not always viewed in that way and are not viewed in that way now in other places.

Sometimes, therefore, the law will not intervene because no harm is recognized—the situation is considered natural, normal, inevitable, or ordinary. That means that the "victim" (the plaintiff or complainer) is not a "real" victim at all but, rather, someone who is unusually sensitive, touchy, vengeful, or at least out of step with the norm. Obviously,, everyone who claims to be a victim is not necessarily a victim. There may be no harm in some cases; there may be only a person who cannot deal with ordinary life. Remember, however, on the other hand, that the norms of ordinary life in societies throughout history have always victimized some of their members without recognizing it. We can see it only in retrospect, as is illustrated by the examples of slavery, wife beating, and child labor. Thus it may be worth noting that cases of "unrecognized" harm or disputed claims of harm are not raised until social norms are already changing. Victims will not often see themselves as victims if their treatment is typical and thus normal. They will simply think that life is hard or that they themselves are deficient. And even if the victims manage to see the wrong, if the norms are settled, a claim outside the norm has no chance of being recognized. Keep in mind that recognizing a harm is not a trivial matter; it is not like recognizing a tree or a rock; it is not an observable fact presented to us by nature; instead, it requires judgment.

Harm has been analyzed as the impairment of an interest. If you are harmed, it means that something that is a concern of yours, something in which you have a stake, something that matters to you or to your life has been impaired. But what your legitimate interests are or what is in your interest varies with time and place. A slave had no legitimate interest in freedom, nor for many centuries did a woman. In fact, for most of history, slaves and women did not have any interests of their own, especially not interests that conflicted with the interests of their masters, the men who owned them. Even today the freedom of many women is highly restricted, but it is not seen as an impairment of their interests, although other women would certainly find it so. In many Arab countries, for example, women are not allowed to vote, to drive, or to show themselves in public without covering their faces or heads. American and European women would find such restrictions offensive and harmful, but Arabs do not believe that they are offending or harming their women. They believe that their way of life is natural, ordinary, normal, perhaps inevitable, and, in many cases, ordained by God. In other words, they believe very much the same thing that we believe about the way we live. What happens all the time feels like what is normal, and so it requires imagination and judgment to decide that what feels normal may not be what is right.

The point is that what counts as a harm depends crucially on social attitudes toward what counts as an interest, and these various social attitudes can put certain members of any given society at a great disadvantage without even the possibility of recognizing that disadvantage as a harm. We thus have good reason to examine carefully what we recognize or, even more importantly, what we do not recognize as harmful and whether we have good and legitimate reasons to support our views.

The second question to ask about the limits to preventing coercion and harm is— even if we recognize something as a harm—when the law should intervene to prevent it. The law does not and cannot address all harms. If I am a competitor who manages to undercut your prices and drive you out of business, I have certainly caused you harm. I may even have intended to do so. But the law does not protect people from honest competition (at least not in the United States at this time) even if it causes great harm. How, then, do we decide which harms the law will or should address?

One factor that is relevant to legal intervention is the protection of rights. Some harms are also wrongs, that is, they violate rights. Some people say that the law will not protect you from competition in business because you have no right to eliminate competition. But that is not very helpful. To say that the law will not protect you and that you have no legal right are just two ways of saying the same thing. It does not explain when you should have a right (or be legally protected). It does not help to suggest that the law should protect your moral rights, because the law docs not (and clearly should not) protect all moral rights. Lying, for example, is a harm and a moral wrong (the violation of a moral right), but the law will not correct it unless additional factors are present that transform simple lying into fraud, slander, breach of contract, or perjury. For instance, if you simply promise to meet me for dinner and do not show up, the law will not do anything about it, even if you had no excuse and did it intentionally to hurt me. Some moral rights are backed by law, and others are not. Some harms are prohibited, but others are not. The question is, Which ones should be? There is no single answer to that question and no simple or absolute formula for obtaining answers.

One significant factor that should provide at least some notion of appropriate state protection is the widely accepted idea that a basic function of a state is to assume a monopoly on force. At a bare minimum, the state is supposed to preserve the peace among its citizens, and citizens are supposed to settle their differences peacefully, that is, without violence. So one sort of harm that clearly should be handled by the state is violent harm. This will not take us very far, as there are many harms that are not violent that the state prohibits, and so violence does not explain those prohibitions. Nevertheless, the prevention of violence provides a clear minimum.

Yet even in cases of violence, the law is reluctant to intervene among family members, or even friends or aquaintances, if the conflict takes place in a private place. Why is this? There is a long-standing respect for individual privacy, which is assumed to support the view that private parties are entitled to settle their differences (and live their lives) with as little interference by the state as possible. This view is especially strong with regard to families. It has much to commend it, but it also has some drawbacks. In particular, in private situations involving unequal parties—husbands and wives, parents and children, young and old, well and sick—it leaves the weaker at the mercy of the stronger, and the state has done little to prevent spouse abuse, child abuse, or abuse of the old or the infirm. Even when violent actions would clearly be prohibited among strangers, the state hesitates to intervene in family and personal relations. This has been a particular problem for woman, and in fact it is a way of reinforcing patriarchal notions of male supremacy in the family.

In sum, not all harms are addressed; not all rights are protected; and not all violence is prevented. All state interference is limited by a commitment to individual freedom. This leaves private parties vulnerable to one another, which is sometimes fair and sometimes not. It takes a decision to determine when the state should intervene and when it should permit individuals to settle their differences by themselves. There is no magic formula for making this decision. It requires a judgment based on many factors and a thoughtful consideration of diverse individual circumstances.

The first set of issues that we will consider in Part II is associated with the claim of sexual harassment, which is a good example of an act that has only recently been recognized as a harm, and as a harm it is still controversial. Many people consider sexual harassment a joke, mere flirtation, or simply the way of the world. As Catharine MacKinnon points out, until recently there was no term for sexual harassment, no words designated to describe it. It simply was not recognized as a harm. If a woman were unhappy about it, she needed to learn to deal with the world better. If she managed to see herself as a victim, it was rather like being a victim of cancer or heart disease, a victim of the inequality of nature, a victim of misfortune, not injustice. But now sexual harassment is recognized as a harm by the law and by many individual people as well.

What is sexual harassment? The term can be used to describe a variety of circumstances that may differ substantially in certain respects. For the most part, such circumstances fall in two major divisions, although these divisions are not as clearly demarcated as I will draw them.

One kind of sexual harassment may be explained as follows: A woman goes to work in a traditionally male work environment, such as a warehouse or shop, and finds herself unwelcome there. The response to her is hostile because she is a woman. She is subjected to abusive language, sexual innuendos and epithets, pornographic pictures and graffiti. The point of all this is to drive her out, to make her quit, or, failing that, at least to make it clear to her that she does not belong there. It can be made clear to her that she is out of place by demonstrating graphically what a rough, profane, offensive, "all-male" environment it is. The object is to make her miserable by declaring her inferiority and sexualizing her status. The harassing behavior is overtly and aggressively hostile. It is the intentional infliction of mental distress, and in that respect is like ordinary, traditional harassment, except that it focuses on her as a woman rather than as an individual or a member of a particular race, nationality, or religion. For convenience, we can call this form of harassment *antagonism*.

There are many variations on this theme. For example, there is the "all in good fun" or "boys will be boys" version, in which a woman is treated as a sex object. She may be patted, fondled, or propositioned. She may be the object of whistles, cat calls, and stories. The point is to ridicule her, not to take her seriously. The situation is a joke, and she is the butt of it. Variations like this show how antagonism can fade into the other form of sexual harassment, which I call *exploitation*.

Exploitation is not ordinarily intended to be hostile in the way that antagonism is. The clear case of exploitive sexual harassment is the case of a superior (e.g., an employer or teacher) who uses a position of power to pressure a subordinate into sexual relations. It is propositioning a person who is not in a position to refuse, at least not without risking her job, grade, promotion, career, or some other significant part of her future. It is coercion by means of the illicit exercise of power.

These two forms of sexual harassment differ either in purpose or in execution. The first is intended to antagonize a woman, to make her miserable by means of constant, overt, hostile acts that are sexual in focus. The second is intended to secure sexual gratification by means of an illicit and usually secret exercise of power. The second may be the more pernicious of the two, and it is certainly the harder to prove. Either situation discriminates against women by using their sex to their disadvantage. Both involve illegitimate attempts at coercion, but until recently, nothing whatever could be done about it.

Today, any of these circumstances are formally recognized as sexual harassment, which is a ground for legal action if it can be proved. The problem is that although this harm is formally recognized by law, many persons still discount it, and many of them are in positions of power and authority. In case after case, feminist scholars and lawyers have shown that judges do not perceive the victims of sexual harassment as real victims. These judges reflect the general attitudes and experience of men, and consequently sexual harassment is not perceived as a serious threat or a real harm. It is frivolous.

In her ground-breaking work on sexual harassment, Catharine MacKinnon confronts and challenges such attitudes. Arguing that sexual harassment is a violation of women's civil rights, she points out that the perceptions of men may be quite different from those of women who perceive themselves as victims of sexual harassment. That is, it does not follow that no harassment occurred if none was intended, nor is there good reason to assume the position of male perceptions rather than female perceptions as objective or neutral representations of factual reality. Furthermore, the systematic domination of women by men in a sexual hierarchy should not be overlooked or ignored in favor of an (erroneous) assumption of neutral social structures as the context in which sexual harassment occurs. Through the work of MacKinnon and others, questions regarding sexual injury, adequacy of remedy, standards of credibility at trial, and the scope of liability have begun to be addressed in the context of sexual harassment. But even though formal recognition is a good beginning, even a legally recognized harm will not be addressed unless judges, juries, and prosecutors recognize the harm as genuine and serious.

In Chapter 7 Susan Estrich discusses the legal schizophrenia regarding rape. Unlike sexual harassment, rape has always been considered a serious offense and a genuine harm, but only in certain circumstances. These are the circumstances that characterize what Estrich calls "real rape," or traditional rape, for example, a woman coerced into sexual intercourse outside her own home by a stranger using force. Any case that meets this description is recognized by most people as the harm of rape. Any case that deviates from this, however, is questionable, suspicious, probably not "real rape," and therefore not a real harm.

As Estrich points out, most cases of coerced sexual intercourse deviate from the clear case in at least one respect. Perhaps no physical injury was inflicted, or the level of force was questionable, or no weapon was used. Perhaps the woman said no but did not fight, or the setting was not an alley but a bedroom, or the threats were unclear or inarticulate. Perhaps the initial contact was not a kidnapping but a date or a meeting; perhaps the two know each other. In such cases the law tends to rule that no crime has taken place, that no clear harm has occurred, and that if there is blame it resides with the woman. So in all these cases, often called *acquaintance rape* or *date rape,* harm is regularly denied.

Estrich contends that by ruling that such "nontraditional" rapes are not only not criminal but also that women are responsible for them, the law is reflecting, legitimizing, and reinforcing societal attitudes that approve male aggressiveness and punish female passivity. She considers the ways in which rape has been defined differently from other crimes, focusing especially on the unusual definitions of force and consent, and asks what those differences tell us about legal attitudes toward men, women, and sex. Rape law, Estrich suggests, should be formulated to prohibit false claims and threats to procure sex, in the same way that extortion, fraud, and false pretenses are prohibited as means to secure money. Some reforms could make a difference, but before any reform can be effective, acquaintance rape must be recognized as "real rape"; that is, it must be recognized as a genuine harm.

The final chapter in Part II addresses the problem of spouse abuse or wife battering. Attitudes toward this problem were once remarkably similar to those toward sexual harassment and acquaintance rape. Somehow, even battery can be dismissed as not constituting a genuine harm. This amazing phenomenon can be traced to historical attitudes: A man was responsible for and was head of his household. He was entitled to beat his slaves, punish his children, and chastise his wife, all for more or less the same reason; that is, he owned them, but more importantly, he was in charge of them. They were his subordinates and dependents, and therefore, it was his right and possibly his duty to keep them in line, so to speak. The relationships were overtly hierarchical, and so insubordination could not be tolerated. As William Blackstone noted in his influential commentaries on the common law, because a husband was legally responsible for his wife, it was "reasonable to entrust him with the power of restraint by domestic chastisement."

Beating is less acceptable than it once was, but discipline for insubordination is commonplace, and it is not considered a harm. It is, rather, undesirable treatment inflicted by someone in authority in order to teach the "errant" a lesson so that he or she will do better in the future. Punishment is undesirable treatment inflicted by someone in authority, as "payment" or deserved response for unacceptable behavior or crime. Neither rationale can justify wife battering today. A husband no longer has such officially recognized authority; his wife is no longer his legal subordinate. Furthermore, beating is no longer acceptable as discipline. But discipline was recognized at one time as justification for wife battering, and the attitude that once supported it is far from dead. Men are still supposed to be in charge, and women are still supposed to be subordinate according to widely held, pervasive cultural standards. As long as those standards are maintained, wife beating will not be unthinkable.

The sources of wife battering are complex, and so are the responses to it. Kathleen Waits considers the legal response to battering and some possible solutions to the problem. Although domestic violence is widely disregarded or underrated, it is not that the battered woman is considered unharmed. Rather, it is believed that although she is harmed, the law should stay out of it. We should not clutter up court dockets with personal squabbles. Judges, police, and prosecutors are often unsympathetic to the claims of battered wives. It is her own fault, judges seem to say. She provoked it. Or even if she did not, it is her own fault if she stays with the batterer. Even though domestic violence accounts for more injuries to women than any other cause and for one-third of all female homicide victims, restraining orders are often not available or unenforced; offenders usually receive lenient treatment, minimal fines, suspended sentences, or dismissals; and complaints are regularly disregarded.

This shows that although a harm may be recognized, it may be felt that it should be settled privately. Theoretically, these sorts of problems are supposed to be those that are not too serious and that occur in private disputes among generally equal parties. In fact, however, the main focus of the hands-off policy toward recognized harms is the family, which is not a relationship of equals in many respects, certainly not in respect to size or strength.

Waits describes the problem of wife battering and attempts to provide a better understanding of the participants and their relationships. She then argues that this is an area appropriate for legal action and suggests what she takes to be reasonable legal goals. Believing that the current legal problems are largely due to the pursuit of incorrect goals, such as reconciliation, she reviews the present state of the law and suggests changes needed for an effective criminal justice response to battering.

These three chapters represent areas of great social change and legal progress. The very fact that such chapters are being written and read, that such topics as rape, battery, and harassment are being publicly discussed, is the first sign of social progress. Nonetheless, we have far to go before women are recognized as entitled to bodily integrity that cannot be coercively usurped by men who know them. Statistical surveys clearly indicate that women are harmed much more often by men who know them than by any other cause. Women are harassed, beaten, raped, and killed by men who know them far more often than by strangers. Yet these offenses, with the exception of killing, are still largely unprosecuted, because we the peopee excuse it.

The pervasiveness of these abusive practices attests to the worst features of the continuing sexism of our society. Physical coercion and violence remain last-resort options for male domination in personal relations and the failure to prosecute attests to the continuing sexism of our law. This will not change significantly until police and prosecutors, judges and juries recognize such injuries as serious harms and stop making excuses for them. But police and prosecutors, judges and juries by and large reflect the attitudes of the general public. As long as overpowering one's date is not the same as raping a stranger; beating one's wife is not as serious as assaulting someone on the street; and pressuring one's secretary into having sex is one of the perks of executive privilege, the physical integrity of women cannot be determined by their own choices. Thus, many women today are still dominated by physical force, denied the most basic protections of justice by a society and a legal system that pretends that some physical coercion is not a real harm, not a serious harm to women so long as it is perpetrated against them by men who know them. That is patriarchy, alive and well, but at least finally exposed to public scrutiny.

6

Sexual Harassment: Its First Decade in Court

CATHARINE A. MACKINNON

Sexual harassment, the event, is not new to women. It is the law of injuries that it is new to. Sexual pressure imposed on someone who is not in an economic position to refuse it became sex discrimination in the mid-1970s,[1] and in education soon afterward.[2] It became possible to do something legal about sexual harassment because some women took women's experience of violation seriously enough to design a law around it, as if what happens to women matters. This was apparently such a startling way of proceeding that sexual harassment was protested as a feminist invention. Sexual harassment, the event, was not invented by feminists; the perpetrators did that with no help from us. Sexual harassment, the legal claim—the idea that the law should see it the way its victims see it—is definitely a feminist invention. Feminists first took women's experience seriously enough to uncover this problem and conceptualize it and pursue it legally. That legal claim is just beginning to produce more than a handful of reported cases. Ten years later, "it may well be that sex harassment is the hottest present day Title VII issue."[3] It is time for a down-the-road assessment of this departure.

The law against sexual harassment is a practical attempt to stop a form of exploitation. It is also one test of sexual politics as feminist jurisprudence, of possibilities for social change for women through law. The existence of a law against sexual harassment has affected both the context of meaning within which social life is lived and the concrete delivery of rights through the legal system. The sexually harassed have been given a name for their suffering and an analysis that connects it with gender. They have been given a forum, legitimacy to speak, authority to make claims, and an avenue for possible relief. Before, what happened to them was all right. Now it is not.

This matters. Sexual abuse mutes victims socially through the violation itself. Often the abuser enforces secrecy and silence; secrecy and silence may be part of what is so sexy about sexual abuse. When the state also forecloses a validated space for denouncing and rectifying the victimization, it seals this secrecy and reinforces this silence. The harm of this process, a process that utterly precludes speech, then becomes all of a piece. If there is no right place to go to say, this hurt me, then a woman is simply the one who can be treated this way, and no harm, as they say, is done.

In point of fact, I would prefer not to have to spend all this energy getting the law to recognize wrongs to women as wrong. But it seems to be necessary to legitimize our injuries as injuries in order to delegitimize our victimization by them, without which it is difficult to move in more positive ways. The legal claim for sexual harassment made the events of sexual harassment illegitimate socially as well as legally for the first time. Let me know if you figure out a better way to do that.

At this interface between law and society, we need to remember that the legitimacy [that] courts give they can also take. Compared with a possibility of relief where no possibility of relief existed, since women started out with nothing in this area, this worry seems a bit fancy. Whether the possibility of relief alters the terms of power that gives rise to sexual harassment itself, which makes getting away with it possible, is a different problem. Sexual harassment, the legal claim, is a demand that state authority stand behind women's refusal of sexual access in certain situations that previously were a masculine prerogative. With sexism, there is always a risk that our demand for self-determination will be taken as a demand for paternal protection and will therefore strengthen male power rather than undermine it. This seems a particularly valid concern because the law of sexual harassment began as case law, without legislative guidance or definition.

Institutional support for sexual self-determination is a victory; institutional paternalism reinforces our lack of self-determination. The problem is, the state has never in fact protected women's dignity or bodily integrity. It just says it does. Its protections have been both condescending and unreal, in effect strengthening the protector's choice to violate the protected at will, whether the protector is the individual perpetrator or the state. This does not seem to me a reason not to have a law against sexual harassment. It is a reason to demand that the promise of "equal protection of the laws" be delivered upon for us, as it is when real people are violated. It is also part of a larger political struggle to value women more than the male pleasure of using us is valued. Ultimately, though, the question of whether the use of the state for women helps or hurts can be answered only in practice, because so little real protection of the laws has ever been delivered.

The legal claim for sexual harassment marks the first time in history, to my knowledge, that women have defined women's injuries in a law. Consider what has happened with rape. We have never defined the injury of rape; men define it. The men who define it, define what they take to be this violation of women according to, among other things, what they think they don't do. In this way rape becomes an act of a stranger (they mean black) committed upon a woman (white) whom he has never seen before. Most rapes are intraracial and are committed by men the women know.[4] Ask a woman if she has ever been raped, and often she says, "Well . . . not really." In that silence between the well and the not really, she just measured what happened to her against every rape case she ever heard about and decided she would lose in court. Especially when you are part of a subordinated group, your own definition of your injuries is powerfully shaped by your assessment of whether you could get anyone to do anything about it, including anything official. You are realistic by necessity, and the voice of law is the voice in power. When the design of a legal wrong does not fit the wrong as it happens to you, as is the case with rape, that law can undermine your social and political as well as legal legitimacy in saying that what happened was an injury at all—even to yourself.

It is never too soon to worry about this, but it may be too soon to know whether the law against sexual harassment will be taken away from us or turn into nothing or turn ugly in our hands. The fact is, this law is working surprisingly well for women by any standards, particularly when compared with the rest of sex discrimination law. If the question is whether a law designed from women's standpoint and administered through this legal system can do anything for women—which always seems to me to be a good question—this experience so far gives a qualified and limited yes.

It is hard to unthink what you know, but there was a time when the facts that amount to sexual harassment did not amount to sexual harassment. It is a bit like the injuries of pornography until recently. The facts amounting to the harm did not socially "exist," had no shape, no cognitive coherence; far less did they state a legal claim. It just happened to you. To the women to whom it happened, it wasn't part of anything, much less something big or shared like gender. It fit no known pattern. It was neither a regularity nor an irregularity. Even social scientists didn't study it, and they study anything that moves. When law recognized sexual harassment as a practice of sex discrimination, it moved it from the realm of "and then he . . . and then he . . .," the primitive language in which sexual abuse lives inside a woman, into an experience with a form, an etiology, a cumulativeness—as well as a club.

The shape, the positioning, and the club—each is equally crucial politically. Once it became possible to do something about sexual harassment, it became possible to know more about it, because it became possible for its victims to speak about it. Now we know, as we did not when it first became illegal, that this problem is commonplace. We know this not just because it has to be true, but as documented fact. Between a quarter and a third of women in the federal work force report having been sexually harassed, many physically, at least once in the last two years.[5] Projected, that becomes 85 percent of all women at some point in their working lives. This figure is based on asking women, "Have you ever been sexually harassed?"—the conclusion—not "Has this fact happened? Has that fact happened?" which usually produces more. The figures for sexual harassment of students are comparable.[6]

When faced with individual incidents of sexual harassment, the legal system's first question was, is it a personal episode? Legally, this was a way the courts inquired into whether the incidents were based on sex, as they had to be to be sex discrimination. Politically, it was a move to isolate victims by stigmatizing them as deviant. It also seemed odd to me that a relationship was either personal or gendered, meaning that one is not a woman personally. Statistical frequency alone does not make an event not personal, of course, but the presumption that sexual pressure in contexts of unequal power is an isolated idiosyncrasy to unique individual victims has been undermined both by the numbers and by their division by gender. Overwhelmingly, it is men who sexually harass women, a lot of them. Actually, it is even more accurate to say that men do this than to say that women have this done to them. This is a description of the perpetrators' behavior, not of the statisticians' feminism.

Sexual harassment has also emerged as a creature of hierarchy. It inhabits what I call hierarchies among men: arrangements in which some men are below other men, as in employer/employee and teacher/student. In workplaces, sexual harassment by supervisors of subordinates is common; in education, by administrators of lower-level administrators, by faculty of students. But it also happens among coworkers, from third parties, even by subordinates in the workplace, men who are women's hierarchical inferiors or peers. Basically, it is done by men to women regardless of relative position on the formal hierarchy. I believe that the reason sexual harassment was first established as an injury of the systematic abuse of power in hierarchies among men is that this is power men recognize. They comprehend from personal experience that something is held over your head if you do not comply. The lateral or reverse hierarchical examples[7] suggest something beyond this, something men don't understand from personal experience because they take its advantages for granted: Gender is also a hierarchy. The courts do not use this analysis, but some act as though they understand it.[8]

Sex discrimination law had to adjust a bit to accommodate the realities of sexual harassment. Like many other injuries of gender, it wasn't written for this. For something to be based on gender in the legal sense means it happens to a woman as a woman, not as an individual. Membership in a gender is understood as the opposite of, rather than part of, individuality. Clearly, sexual harassment is one of the last situations in which a woman is treated without regard to her sex; it is because of her sex that it happens. But the social meaning attributed to women as a class, in which women are defined as gender female by sexual accessibility to men, is not what courts have considered before when they have determined whether a given incident occurred because of sex.

Sex discrimination law typically conceives that something happens because of sex when it happens to one sex but not the other. The initial procedure is arithmetic: Draw a gender line and count how many of each are on each side in the context at issue, or alternatively, take the line drawn by the practice or policy and see if it also divides the sexes. One by-product of this head-counting method is what I call the *bisexual defense.*[9] Say a man is accused of sexually harassing a woman. He can argue that the harassment is not sex based because he harasses both sexes equally, indiscriminately as it were. Originally it was argued that sexual harassment was not a proper gender claim because someone could harass both sexes. We argued that this was an issue of fact to be pleaded and proven, an issue of did he do this, rather than an issue of law, of whether he could have. The courts accepted that, creating this *kamikaze* defense. To my knowledge, no one has used the bisexual defense since.[10] As this example suggests, head counting can provide a quick topography of the terrain, but it has proved too blunt to distinguish treatment whose meaning is based on gender from treatment that has other social hermeneutics, especially when only two individuals are involved.

Once sexual harassment was established as bigger than personal, the courts' next legal question was whether it was smaller than biological. To say that sexual harassment was biological seemed to me a very negative thing to say about men, but defendants seemed to think it precluded liability. Plaintiffs argued that sexual harassment is not biological in that men who don't do it have nothing wrong with their testosterone levels. Besides, if murder were found to have biological correlates, it would still be a crime. Thus, although the question purported to be whether the acts were based on sex, the implicit issue seemed to be whether the source of the impetus for doing the acts was relevant to their harmfulness.

Similarly structured was the charge that women who resented sexual harassment were oversensitive. Not that the acts did not occur but, rather, that it was unreasonable to experience them as harmful. Such a harm would be based not on sex but on individual hysteria. Again shifting the inquiry away from whether the acts are based on sex in the guise of pursuing it, away from whether they occurred to whether it should matter if they did, the question became whether the acts were properly harmful. Only this time it was not the perpetrator's drives that made him not liable but the target's sensitivity that made the acts not a harm at all. It was pointed out that too many people are victimized by sexual harassment to consider them all hysterics. Besides, in other individual injury law, victims are not blamed; perpetrators are required to take victims as they find them, so long as they are not supposed to be doing what they are doing.

Once these excuses were rejected, then it was said that sexual harassment was not really an employment-related problem. That became hard to maintain when it was her job the woman lost. If it was, in fact, a personal relationship, it apparently did not start and stop there, although this is also a question of proof, leaving the true meaning of the events to trial. The perpetrator may have thought it was all affectionate or friendly or fun, but the victim experienced it as hateful, dangerous, and damaging. Results in such cases have been mixed. Some judges have accepted the perpetrator's view; for instance, one judge held queries by the defendant such as "What am I going to get for this?" and repeated importunings to "go out" to be "susceptible of innocent interpretation."[11] Other judges, on virtually identical facts, for example, "When are you going to do something nice for me?"[12] have held for the plaintiff. For what it's worth, the judge in the first case was a man, in the second a woman.

That sexual harassment is sex-based discrimination seems to be legally established, at least for now.[13] In one of the few recent cases that reported litigating the issue of sex basis, defendants argued that a sex-based claim was not stated when a woman worker complained of terms of abuse directed at her at work such as "slut," "bitch," and "fucking cunt" and "many sexually oriented drawings posted on pillars and at other conspicuous places around the warehouse" with plaintiffs' initials on them, presenting her having sex with an animal.[14] The court said: "The sexually offensive conduct and language used would have been almost irrelevant and would have failed entirely in its crude purpose had the plaintiff been a man. I do not hesitate to find that but for her sex, the plaintiff would not have been subjected to the harassment she suffered."[15] "Obvious" or "patently obvious" they often call it.[16] I guess this is what it looks like to have proven a point.

Sexual harassment was first recognized as an injury of gender in what I called incidents of quid pro quo. Sometimes people think that harassment has to be constant. It doesn't; it's a term of art in which once can be enough. Typically, an advance is made, rejected, and a loss follows.[17] For a while it looked as if this three-step occurrence was in danger of going from one form in which sexual harassment can occur into a series of required hurdles. In many situations the woman is forced to submit instead of being able to reject the advance. The problem has become whether, say, being forced into intercourse at work will be seen as a failed quid pro quo or as an instance of sexual harassment in which the forced sex constitutes the injury.

I know of one reported case in employment and one in education in which women who were forced to submit to the sex brought a sexual harassment claim against the perpetrator; so far only the education case has won on the facts.[18] The employment case that lost on the facts was reversed on appeal. The pressures for sex were seen to state a claim without respect to the fact that the woman was not able to avoid complying.[19] It is unclear if the unwanted advances constitute a claim, separate and apart from whether or not they are able to be resisted, which they should; or if the acts of forced sex would also constitute an environmental claim separate from any quid pro quo, as it seems to me they also should. In the education case, the case of Paul Mann, the students were allowed to recover punitive damages for the forced sex.[20] If sexual harassment is not to be defined only as sexual attention imposed upon someone who is not in a position to refuse it, who refuses it, women who are forced to submit to sex must be understood as harmed not less, but as much or more, than those who are able to make their refusals effective.

Getting recoveries for women who have actually been sexually violated by the defendant will probably be a major battle. Women being compensated in money for sex they had violates male metaphysics because in that system sex is what a woman is for. As one judge concluded, "There does not seem to be any issue that the plaintiff did not desire to have relations with [the defendant], but it is also altogether apparent that she willingly had sex with him."[21] Now what do you make of that? The woman was not physically forced at the moment of penetration, and since it is sex she must have willed it, is about all you can make of it. The sexual politics of the situation is that men do not see a woman who has had sex as victimized, whatever the conditions. One dimension of this problem involves whether a woman who has been violated through sex has any credibility. Credibility is difficult to separate from the definition of the injury, since an injury in which the victim is not believed to have been injured *because she has been injured* is not a real injury, legally speaking.

The question seems to be whether a woman is valuable enough to hurt, so that what is done to her is a harm. Once a woman has had sex, voluntarily or by force—it doesn't matter—she is regarded as too damaged to be further damageable, or something. Many women who have been raped in the course of sexual harassment have been advised by their lawyers not to mention the rape because it would destroy their credibility! The fact that abuse is long term has suggested to some finders of fact that it must have been tolerated or even wanted, although sexual harassment that becomes a condition of work has also been established as a legal claim in its own right.[22] I once was talking with a judge about a case he was sitting on in which black teenage girls alleged that some procedures at their school violated their privacy. He told me that with their sexual habits they had no privacy to lose. It seemed he knew what their sexual habits were from evidence in the case, examples of the privacy violations.

The more aggravated an injury becomes, the more it ceases to exist. Why is incomprehensible to me, but how it functions is not. Our most powerful moment is on paper, in complaints we frame, and our worst is in the flesh in court. Although it isn't much, we have the most credibility when we are only the idea of us and our violation in their minds. In our allegations we construct reality to some extent; face to face, their angle of vision frames us irrevocably. In court we have breasts, we are black, we are (in a word) women. Not that we are ever free of that, but the moment we physically embody our complaint, and they can see us, the pornography of the process starts in earnest.

I have begun to think that a major reason that many women do not bring sexual harassment complaints is that they know this. They cannot bear to have their personal account of sexual abuse reduced to a fantasy they invented, used to define them and to pleasure the finders of fact and the public. I think they have a very real sense that their accounts are enjoyed, that others are getting pleasure from the first-person recounting of their pain, and that is the content of their humiliation at these rituals. When rape victims say they feel raped again on the stand, and victims of sexual harassment say they feel sexually harassed in the adjudication, it is not exactly metaphor. I hear that they—in being publicly sexually humiliated by the legal system, as by the perpetrator—are pornography. The first time it happens, it is called freedom; the second time, it is called justice.

If a woman is sexually defined—meaning all women fundamentally, intensified by previous sexual abuse or identification as lesbian, indelible if a prostitute—her chances of recovery for sexual abuse are correspondingly reduced. I'm still waiting for a woman to win at trial against a man who forced her to comply with the sex. Suppose the male plaintiff in one sexual harassment case who rented the motel room in which the single sexual encounter took place had been a woman, and the perpetrator had been a man. When the relationship later went bad, it was apparently not a credibility problem for *him* at trial that he had rented the motel room. Nor was *his* sexual history apparently an issue. Nor, apparently, was it said when he complained he was fired because the relationship went bad, that he had "asked for" the relationship. That case was reversed on appeal on legal grounds, but he did win at trial.[23] The best one can say about women in such cases is that women who have had sex but not with the accused may have some chance. In one case the judge did not believe the plaintiff's denial of an affair with another coworker but did believe that she had been sexually harassed by the defendant.[24] In another, the woman plaintiff actually had "linguistic intimacy" with another man at work, yet when she said that what happened to her with the defendant was sexual harassment, she was believed.[25] These are miraculous. A woman's word on these matters is usually indivisible. In another case a woman accused two men of sexual harassment. She had resisted and refused one man to whom she had previously submitted under pressure for a long time. He was in the process of eliminating her from her job when the second man raped her. The first man's defense was that it went on so long, she must have liked it. The second man's defense was that he had heard that she had had sexual relations with the first man, so he felt this was something she was open to.[26] This piggyback defense is premised on the class definition of woman as whore, by which I mean what men mean: one who exists to be sexually done to, to be sexually available on men's terms, that is, a woman. If this definition of women is accepted, it means that if a woman has ever had sex, forced or voluntary, she can't be sexually violated.

A woman can be seen in these terms by being a former rape victim or by the way she uses language. One case holds that the evidence shows "the allegedly harassing conduct was substantially welcomed and encouraged by plaintiff. She actively contributed to the distasteful working environment by her own profane and sexually suggestive conduct."[27] She swore, apparently, and participated in conversations about sex. This effectively made her harassment proof. Many women joke about sex to try to defuse men's sexual aggression, to try to be one of the boys in hopes they will be treated like one. This is to discourage sexual advances, not to encourage them. In other cases, judges have understood that "the plaintiffs did not appreciate the remarks and ... many of the other women did not either."[28]

The extent to which a woman's job is sexualized is also a factor. If a woman's work is not to sell sex, and her employer requires her to wear a sexually suggestive uniform, if she is repeatedly sexually harassed by the clientele, she may have a claim against her employer.[29] Similarly, although "there may well be a limited category of jobs (such as adult entertainment) in which sexual harassment may be a rational consequence of such employment," one court was "simply not prepared to say that a female who goes to work in what is apparently a predominantly male workplace should reasonably expect sexual harassment as part of her job."[30] There may be trouble at some point over what jobs are selling sex, given the sexualization of anything a woman does.

Sexual credibility, that strange amalgam of whether your word counts with whether or how much you were hurt, also comes packaged in a variety of technical rules in the sexual harassment cases; evidence, discovery, and burden of proof. In 1982 the EEOC held that if a victim was sexually harassed without a corroborating witness, proof was inadequate as a matter of law.[31] (Those of you who wonder about the relevance of pornography, get this: If nobody watched, it didn't happen.) A woman's word, even if believed, was legally insufficient, even if the man had nothing to put against it other than his word and the plaintiff's burden of proof. Much like women who have been raped, women who have experienced sexual harassment say, "But I couldn't prove it." They mean they have nothing but their word. Proof is when what you say counts against what someone else says—for which it must first be believed. To say as a matter of law that the woman's word is per se legally insufficient is to assume that with sexual violations uniquely, the defendant's denial is dispositive, is proof. To say a woman's word is no proof amounts to saying a woman's word is worthless. Usually all the man has is his denial. In 1983 the EEOC found sexual harassment on a woman's word alone. It said it was enough, without distinguishing or overruling the prior case.[32] Perhaps they recognized that women don't choose to be sexually harassed in the presence of witnesses.

The question of prior sexual history is one area in which the issue of sexual credibility is directly posed. Evidence of the defendant's sexual harassment of other women in the same institutional relation or setting is increasingly being considered admissible, and it should be.[33] The other side of the question is whether evidence of a victim's prior sexual history should be discoverable or admissible, and it seems to me it should not be. Perpetrators often seek out victims with common qualities or circumstances or situations—we are fungible to them so long as we are similarly accessible—but victims do not seek out victimization at all, and their nonvictimized sexual behavior is no more relevant to an allegation of sexual force than is the perpetrator's consensual sex life, such as it may be.

So far the leading case, consistent with the direction of rape law,[34] has found that the victim's sexual history with other individuals is not relevant, although consensual history with the individual perpetrator may be. With sexual harassment law, we are having to deinstitutionalize sexual misogyny step by step. Some defendants' counsel have even demanded that plaintiffs submit to an unlimited psychiatric examination,[35] which could have a major practical impact on victims' effective access to relief. How much sexual denigration will victims have to face to secure their right to be free from sexual denigration? A major part of the harm of sexual harassment is the public and private sexualization of a woman against her will. Forcing her to speak about her sexuality is a common part of this process, subjection to which leads women to seek relief through the courts. Victims who choose to complain know they will have to endure repeated verbalizations of the specific sexual abuse they complain about. They undertake this even though most experience it as an exacerbation, however unavoidable, of the original abuse. For others, the necessity to repeat over and over the verbal insults, innuendos, and propositions to which they have been subjected leads them to decide that justice is not worth such indignity.

Most victims of sexual harassment, if the incidence data are correct, never file complaints. Many who are viciously violated are so ashamed to make that violation public that they submit in silence, although it devastates their self-respect and often their health, or they leave the job without complaint, although it threatens their survival and that of their families. If, on top of the cost of making the violation known, which is painful enough, they know that the entire range of their sexual experiences, attitudes, preferences, and practices are to be discoverable, few such actions will be brought, no matter how badly the victims are hurt. Faced with a choice between forced sex in their jobs or schools on the one hand and forced sexual disclosure for the public record on the other, few will choose the latter. This cruel paradox would effectively eliminate much progress in this area.[36]

Put another way, part of the power held by perpetrators of sexual harassment is the threat of making the sexual abuse public knowledge. This functions like blackmail in silencing the victim and allowing the abuse to continue. It is a fact that public knowledge of sexual abuse is often worse for the abused than the abuser, and victims who choose to complain have the courage to take that on. To add to their burden the potential of making public their entire personal life, information that has no relation to the fact or severity of the incidents complained of, is to make the law of this area implicitly complicit in the blackmail that keeps victims from exercising their rights and to enhance the impunity of perpetrators. In effect, it means open season on anyone who does not want her entire intimate life available to public scrutiny. In other contexts such private information has been found intrusive, irrelevant, and more prejudicial than probative.[37] To allow it to be discovered in the sexual harassment area amounts to a requirement that women be further violated in order to be permitted to seek relief for having been violated. I also will never understand why a violation's severity, or even its likelihood of occurrence, is measured according to the character of the violated, rather than by what was done to them.

In most reported sexual harassment cases, especially rulings on law more than on facts, the trend is almost uniformly favorable to the development of this claim. At least, so far. This almost certainly does not represent social reality. It may not even reflect most cases in litigation.[38] And there may be conflicts building, for example, between those who value speech in the abstract more than they value people in the concrete. Much of sexual harassment is words. Women are called "cunt," "pussy," "tits";[39] they are invited to a company party with "bring your own bathing suits (women, either half)";[40] they confront their tormenter in front of their manager with, "You have called me a fucking bitch," only to be answered, "No, I didn't. I called you a fucking cunt."[41] One court issued an injunction against inquiries such as "Did you get any over the weekend?"[42] One case holds that where "a person in a position to grant or withhold employment opportunities uses that authority to attempt to induce workers and job seekers to submit to sexual advances, prostitution, and pornographic entertainment, and boasts of an ability to intimidate those who displease him," sexual harassment (and intentional infliction of emotional distress) is pleaded.[43] Sexual harassment can also include pictures; visual as well as verbal pornography is commonly used as part of the abuse. Yet one judge found, apparently as a matter of law, that the pervasive presence of pornography in the workplace did not constitute an unreasonable work environment because, "For better or worse, modern America features open displays of written and pictorial erotica. Shopping centers, candy stores and prime time television regularly display naked bodies and erotic real or simulated sex acts. Living in this milieu, the average American should not be legally offended by sexually explicit posters."[44] She did not say she was offended, she said she was discriminated against based on her sex. If the pervasiveness of an abuse makes it nonactionable, no inequality sufficiently institutionalized to merit a law against it would be actionable.

Further examples of this internecine conflict have arisen in education. At the Massachusetts Institute of Technology, pornography used to be shown every year during registration.[45] Is this *not* sexual harassment in education, as a group of women complained it was, because attendance is voluntary, both sexes go, it is screened in groups rather than individually, nobody is directly propositioned, and it is pictures and words? Or is it sexual harassment because the status and treatment of women, supposedly secured from sex-differential harm, are damaged, including that of those who do not attend, which harms individuals and undermines sex equality; therefore pictures and words are the media through which the sex discrimination is accomplished?

For feminist jurisprudence, the sexual harassment attempt suggests that if a legal initiative is set up right from the beginning, meaning if it is designed from women's real experience of violation, it can make some difference. To a degree women's experience can be written into law, even in some tension with the current doctrinal framework. Women who want to resist their victimization with legal terms that imagine it is not inevitable can be given some chance, which is more than they had before. Law is not everything in this respect, but it is not nothing either.[46] Perhaps the most important lesson is

that the mountain can be moved. When we started, there was absolutely no judicial precedent for allowing a sex discrimination suit for sexual harassment. Sometimes even the
law does something for the first time.

Notes

The original version of this chapter was part of a panel on sexual harassment shared with Karen
Haney, Pamela Price, and Peggy McGuiness at Stanford University, Stanford, California, April 12,
1983. It thereafter became an address to the Equal Employment Opportunities Section of the American Bar Association, New Orleans, Louisiana, May 3, 1984, and to a workshop for the national
conference of the National Organization for Women, Denver, Colorado, June 14, 1986. The ideas
developed further when I represented Mechelle Vinson as cocounsel in her U.S. Supreme Court case
in the spring of 1986. I owe a great deal to my conversations with Valerie Heller.

   1. The first case to hold this was Williams v. Saxbe, 413 F. Supp. 654 (D. D.C. 1976), followed
by Barnes v. Costle, 561 F.2d 983 (D.C. Cir. 1977).

   2. Alexander v. Yale University, 459 F. Supp. 1 (D. Conn. 1977), aff'd, 631 F.2d 178 (2d Cir.
1980).

   3. Rabidue v. Osceola Refining, 584 F. Supp. 419, 427 n.29 (E.D. Mich. 1984).

   4. See data at "Rally against Rape," notes 1–3.

   5. U.S. Merit System Protection Board, Sexual Harassment in the Federal Workplace: Is It a
Problem? (1981).

   6. National Advisory Council on Women's Education Programs, Department of Education,
Sexual Harassment: A Report on the Sexual Harassment of Students (1980); Joseph DiNunzio and
Christina Spaulding, Radcliffe Union of Students, Sexual Harassment Survey (Harvard/Radcliffe)
20–29 (1984); 32 percent of tenured female faculty, 49 percent of nontenured female faculty, 42
percent of female graduate students, and 34 percent of female undergraduate students report some
incident of sexual harassment from a person with authority over them; one-fifth of undergraduate
women report being forced into unwanted sexual activity at some point in their lives. The Sexual
Harassment Survey Committee, A Survey of Sexual Harassment at UCLA (185), finds 11 percent
of female faculty (N = 86), 7 percent of female staff (N = 650), and 7 percent of female students
(N = 933) report being sexually harassed at UCLA.

   7. If a superior sexually harasses a subordinate, the company and the supervisor are responsible if the victim can prove it happened. 29 C.F.R. 1604.11(c). With coworkers, if the employer
can be shown to have known about it or should have known about it, the employer can be held
responsible. 29 C.F.R. 1604.11(d). Sexual harassment by clients or other third parties is decided on
the specific facts. See 29 C.F.R. 1604.11(e).

   8. The EEOC's requirement that the employer must receive notice in coworker cases suggests
that they do not understand this point. 29 C.F.R. 1604.11(d). One reasonable rationale for such a
rule, however, is that a co-worker situation does not become hierarchical, hence actionable as
employment discrimination, until it is reported to the workplace hierarchy and condoned through
adverse action or inaction.

   In one inferior-to-superior case, staff was alleged to have sexually harassed a woman manager
because of an interracial relationship. Moffett v. Gene B. Glick Co., Inc., 621 F. Supp. 244 (D.Ind.
1985). An example of a third-party case that failed of "positive proof" involved a nurse bringing a
sex discrimination claim alleging she was denied a promotion that went to a less qualified female
nurse because that other nurse had a sexual relationship with the doctor who promoted her. King
v. Palmer, 598 F. Supp. 65, 69 (D.D.C. 1984). The difficulty of proving "an explicit sexual relationship between [plaintiff] and [defendant], each of whom vigorously deny it exists or even occurred,"
id., is obvious.

   9. Catharine A. MacKinnon, Sexual Harassment of Working Women 203 (1979).

10. Dissenters from the denial of rehearing en banc in Vinson v. Taylor attempted a revival, however. *Vinson v. Taylor,* 760 F.2d 1330, 1333 n.7 (Circuit Judges Bork, Scalia, and Starr).

11. Scott v. Sears & Roebuck, 605 F. Supp. 1047, 1051, 1055 (N.D. Ill. 1985).

12. Coley v. Consolidated Rail, 561 F. Supp. 647, 648 (1982).

13. Meritor Savings Bank, FSB v. Vinson, 106 S.Ct. 2399 (1986); Horn v. Duke Homes, 755 F.2d 599 (7th Cir. 1985); Crimm v. Missouri Pacific R.R. Co., 750 F.2d 703 (8th Cir. 1984); Simmons v. Lyons, 746 F.2d 265 (5th Cir. 1984); Craig v. Y & Y Snacks, 721 F.2d 77 (3d Cir. 1983); Katz v. Dole, 709 F.2d 251 (4th Cir. 1983); Miller v. Bank of America, 600 F.2d 211 (9th Cir. 1979); Tomkins v. Public Service Electric & Gas Co., 568 F.2d 1044 (3d Cir. 1977); Barnes v. Costle, 561 F.2d 983 (D.C. Cir. 1977); Bundy v. Jackson, 641 F.2d 934 (D.C. Cir. 1981); Henson v. City of Dundee, 682 F.2d 897 (11th Cir. 1982) (sexual harassment, whether quid pro quo or condition of work, is sex discrimination under Title VII). The court in *Rabidue* was particularly explicit on the rootedness of sexual harassment in the text of Title VII. Rabidue v. Osceola Refining, 584 F. Supp. 419, 427–29 (E.D. Mich. 1984). Woerner v. Brzeczek, 519 F. Supp. 517 (E.D. Ill. 1981) exemplifies the same view under the equal protection clause. Gender has also been found to create a class for a 42 U.S.C. § 1985(3) claim if the injury is covered by the Fourteenth Amendment. Scott v. City of Overland Park, 595 F. Supp. 520, 527–529 (D. Kansas 1984). *See also* Skadegaard v. Farrell, 578 F. Supp. 1209 (D.N.J. 1984). An additional question has been whether sexual harassment is intentional discrimination. Courts have been unimpressed with intent-related defenses like, he did it but "it was his way of communicating." French v. Mead Corporation, 333 FEP Cases 635, 638 (1983). Or, I did all of those things, but I am just a touchy person. Professor Sid Peck, in connection with the sexual harassment action brought against him by Ximena Bunster and other women at Clark University, reportedly stated that he exchanged embraces and kisses as greetings and to establish a feeling of safety and equality. *Worcester Magazine,* Dec. 3, 1980, at 3; *Boston Phoenix,* Feb. 24, 1981, at 6. *But see* Norton v. Vartanian, where Judge Zobel finds, inter alia, that the overtures were never sexually intended, so no sexual harassment occurred. 31 FEP Cases 1260 (D. Mass. 1983). The implicit view, I guess, is that the perpetrator's intent is beside the point of the harm, that so long as the allegations meet other requirements, the perpetrator does not need to intend that the sexual advances be discriminatory or even sex-based for them to constitute sex discrimination. Katz v. Dole holds that a showing of "sustained verbal sexual abuse" is sufficient to prove "the intentional nature of the harassment." 709 F. 2d, 255–56 esp. 256 n.7. As I understand it, this means that so long as the harassment is not credibly inadvertent, acts of this nature are facially discriminatory. Intentionality is inferred from the acts; the acts themselves, repeated after indications of disinclination and nonreceptivity, show the mental animus of bias. In short, the acts may not be intentionally discriminatory, yet still constitute intentional discrimination. The upshot seems to be that sexual harassment allegations are essentially treated as facial discrimination.

14. Zabkowicz v. West Bend Co., 589 F. Supp. 780, 782–83 (E.D. Wisc. 1984).

15. 589 F. Supp., 784.

16. Henson v. City of Dundee, 29 FEP Cases 787, 793 (11th Cir. 1983). In Huebschen v. Dept. of Health, 32 FEP Cases 1582 (7th Cir. 1983), the facts were found not gender-based on a doctrinally dubious rationale. There a man was found to have been sexually harassed by his female superior. This result was reversed on the partial basis that it did not present a valid gender claim. Basically the court said that the case wasn't gender-based because it was individual. I remember this argument: the events were individual, not gender-based, because there was no employment problem until the relationship went sour. In my view, if the defendant is a hierarchical superior and the plaintiff is damaged in employment for reasons of sexual pressure vis a vis that superior, especially if they are a woman and a man, a claim is stated. It is one thing to recognize that men as a gender have more power in sexual relations in ways that may cross-cut employment hierarchies. This is not what the court said here. This case may have been, on its facts, a personal relationship that went bad, having nothing to do with gender. But these are not the facts as found at trial. The Court of Appeals did suggest that this plaintiff was hurt as an individual, not as a man, because the employment situation was fine so long as the sexual situation was fine—that is, until it wasn't. After which, because

of which, the man was fired. Maybe men always stay individuals, even when women retaliate against them through their jobs for sexual refusals. But, doctrinally, I do not understand why this treatment does not state a gender-based claim. Not to, seems to allow employment opportunities to be conditional on the *continuing* existence of an undesired sexual relationship, where those opportunities would never be allowed to be conditioned on such a relationship's *initial* existence. Women have at times been gender female personally: "As Walter Scott acknowledges, he 'was attracted to her as a woman, on a personal basis. Her femaleness was a matter of attraction.'" Estate of Scott v. deLeon, 37 FEP Cases 563, 566 (1985).

17. *Barnes v. Costle* is the classic case. All of the cases in note 13 above are quid pro cases except *Vinson, Katz, Bundy,* and *Henson.* Note that the distinction is actually two poles of a continuum. A constructive discharge, in which a woman leaves the job because of a constant condition of sexual harassment, is an environmental situation that becomes quid pro quo.

18. In Vinson v. Taylor, 23 FEP Cases 37 (D.D.C. 1980), plaintiff accused defendant supervisor of forced sex; the trial court found, "If the plaintiff and Taylor did engage in an intimate or sexual relationship . . . [it] was a voluntary one by plaintiff." At 42. Vinson won a right to a new trial for environmental sexual harassment. Meritor Savings Bank, FSB v. Vinson, 106 S. Ct. 2399 (1986). *See also* Cummings v. Walsh Construction Co., 561 F. Supp. 872 (S.D. Ga. 1983) (victim accused perpetrator of consummated sex); Micari v. Mann, 481 N.Y.S.2d 967 (Sup. Ct. 1984) (students accused professor of forced sex as part of acting training; won and awarded damages).

19. Vinson v. Taylor, 753 F.2d 141 (D.C. Cir. 1985), *aff'd* 106 S. Ct. 2399 (1983).

20. Micari v. Mann, 481 N.Y.S.2d 967 (Sup. Ct. 1984).

21. Cummings v. Walsh Construction Co., 31 FEP Cases 930, 938 (S. D. Ga. 1983).

22. *Bundy* and *Henson,* note 13 above, establish environmental sexual harassment as a legal claim. Both that claim and the plaintiff's credibility in asserting it, since she was abused for such a long time, were raised in Vinson v. Taylor before the U.S. Supreme Court.

23. Huebschen v. Department of Health, 547 F. Supp. 1168 (W.D. Wisc. 1982).

24. Heelan v. Johns-Manville, 451 F. Supp. 1382 (D. Colo. 1978). *See also* Sensibello v. Globe Security Systems, 34 FEP Cases 1357 (E.D. Pa. 1964).

25. Katz v. Dole, 709 F.2d 251, 254 n.5 (4th Cir. 1983) ("A persons private and consensual sexual activities do not constitute a waiver of his or her legal protections against unwelcome and unsolicited sexual harassment").

26. An attorney discussed this case with me in a confidential conversation.

27. Gan v. Kepro Circuit Systems, 28 FEP Cases 639, 641 (E.D. Mo. 1982). *See also* Reichman v. Bureau of Affirmative Action, 536 F. Supp. 1149, 1177 (M.D. Penn. 1982).

28. Morgan v. Hertz Corp., 542 F. Supp. 123, 128 (W.D. Tenn. 1981).

29. EEOC v. Sage Realty, 507 F. Supp. 599 (S.D.N.Y. 1981).

30. Pryor v. U.S. Gypsum Co., 585 F. Supp. 311, 316 n.3 (W.D. Mo. 1984). The issue here was whether the injuries could be brought under worker's compensation. The suggestion is that women who work in adult entertainment might be covered under that law for sexual harassment on their jobs.

31. EEOC Decision 82-13, 29 FEP Cases 1855 (1982).

32. Commission Decision 83-1, EEOC Decisions (CCH) 6834 (1983).

33. Koster v. Chase Manhattan, 93 F.R.D. 471 (S.D.N.Y. 1982).

34. Priest v. Rotary, 32 FEP Cases 1065 (N.D. Cal. 1983) is consistent with congressional actions in criminal rape, Fed. R. Evid., Rule 412, 124 *Cong. Rec.* H11944–11945 (daily ed. Oct. 10, 1978) and 124 *Cong. Rec.* S18580 (daily ed. Oct. 12, 1978) (evidence of prior consensual sex, unless with defendant, is inadmissible in rape cases) and with developments in civil rape cases. Fults v. Superior Court, 88 Cal. App. 3d 899 (1979).

35. Vinson v. Superior Court, Calif. Sup. SF 24932 (rev. granted, Sept. 1985).

36. A further possibility—more political fantasy than practical—might be to insist that if the plaintiff's entire sexual history is open to inspection, the defendant's should be also: all the rapes,

peeping at his sister, patronizing of prostitutes, locker-room jokes, use of pornography, masturbation fantasies, adolescent experimentation with boyfriends, fetishes, and so on.

37. *See, e.g.,* U.S. v. Kasto, 584 F.2d 268, 271–72 (8th Cir. 1978), *cert. denied,* 440 U.S. 930 (1979); State v. Bernier, 491 A.2d 1000, 1004 (R.I. 1985).

38. Another reason women do not bring claims is fear of countersuit. The relationship between sexual harassment and defamation is currently unsettled on many fronts. *See, e.g.,* Walker v. Gibson, 604 F. Supp. 916 (N.D. Ill. 1985) (action for violation of First Amendment will not lie against employer Army for hearing on unwarranted sexual harassment charge); Spisak v. McDole, 472 N.E.2d 347 (Ohio 1984) (defamation claim can be added to sexual harassment claim); Equal Employment Opportunity Commission v. Levi Strauss & Co., 515 F. Supp. 640 (N.D. Ill. 1981) (defamation action brought allegedly in response to employee allegation of sexual harassment is not necessarily retaliatory, if brought in good faith to vindicate reputation); Arenas v. Ladish Co., 619 F. Supp. 1304 (E.D. Wisc. 1985) (defamation claim may be brought for sexual harassment in the presence of others, not barred by exclusivity provision of worker's compensation law); Ross v. Comsat, 34 FEP Cases 261 (D. Md. 1984) (man sues company for retaliation in discharge following his complaint against woman at company for sexual harassment). Educational institutions have been sued for acting when, after investigation, they find the complaints to be true. Barnes v. Oody, 28 FEP Cases 816 (E.D. Tenn. 1981) (summary judgment granted that arbitrators' holding for women who brought sexual harassment claim collaterally estops defamation action by sexual harassment defendant; immunity applies to statements in official investigation). Although it is much more difficult to prove defamation than to defeat a sexual harassment claim, threats of countersuit have intimidated many victims.

39. Rabidue v. Osceola Refining, 584 F. Supp. 423 (E.D. Mich. 1984).

40. Cobb v. Dufresne-Henry, 603 F. Supp. 1048, 1050 (D. Vt. 1985).

41. McNabb v. Cub Foods, 352 N.W. 2d 378, 381 (Minn. 1984).

42. Morgan v. Hertz Corp., 27 FEP Cases at 994.

43. Seratis v. Lane, 30 FEP 423, 425 (Cal. Super. 1980).

44. Rabidue v. Osceola Refining, 584 F. Supp. 419, 435 (E.D. Mich. 1984). This went to whether the treatment was sex-based. Note that the plaintiff did not say that she was offended but that she was discriminated against.

45. Women students at MIT filed a sexual harassment claim under Title IX, which was dismissed for lack of jurisdiction. Baker v. M.I.T., U.S. Dept. Education Office of Civil Rights #01–85–2013 (Sept. 20, 1985).

46. Particularly given the formative contribution to the women's movement of the struggles against racial and religious stigma, persecution, and violence, it is heartening to find a Jewish man and a black man recovering for religious and racial harassment, respectively, based on sexual harassment precedents. Weiss v. U.S., 595 F. Supp. 1050 (E.D. Va. 1984) (pattern of anti-Semitic verbal abuse actionable based on *Katz* and *Henson*); Taylor v. Jones, 653 F.2d 1193, 1199 (8th Cir. 1981) (*Bundy* cited as basis for actionability of environmental racial harassment under Title VII).

7

Rape

SUSAN ESTRICH

1. Introduction

Eleven years ago, a man held an ice pick to my throat and said: "Push over, shut up, or I'll kill you." I did what he said, but I couldn't stop crying. A hundred years later, I jumped out of my car as he drove away.

I ended up in the back seat of a police car. I told the two officers I had been raped by a man who came up to the car door as I was getting out in my own parking lot (and trying to balance two bags of groceries and kick the car door open). He took the car, too.

They asked me if he was a crow. That was their first question. A crow, I learned that day, meant to them someone who is black.

They asked me if I knew him. That was their second question. They believed me when I said I didn't. Because, as one of them put it, how would a nice (white) girl like me know a crow?

Now they were on my side. They asked me if he took any money. He did, but while I remember virtually every detail of that day and night, I can't remember how much. But I remember their answer. He did take money; that made it an armed robbery. Much better than a rape. They got right on the radio with that.

We went to the police station first, not the hospital, so I could repeat my story (and then what did he do?) to four more policemen. When we got there, I borrowed a dime to call my father. They all liked that.

By the time we went to the hospital, they were really on my team. I could've been one of their kids. Now there was something they'd better tell me. Did I realize what prosecuting a rape complaint was all about? They tried to tell me that "the law" was against me. But they didn't explain exactly how. And I didn't understand why. I believed in "the law," not knowing what it was.

Late that night, I sat in the police headquarters looking at mug shots. I was the one who insisted on going back that night. My memory was fresh. I was ready. They had four or five to "really show" me; being "really shown" a mug shot means exactly what defense attorneys are afraid it means. But it wasn't any one of them. After that, they couldn't help me very much. One shot looked close until my father realized that the man had been the right age ten years before. It was late. I didn't have a great description of identifying marks, or the like: No one had ever told me that if you're raped, you should not shut your eyes and cry for fear that this really is happening. You should keep your eyes open focusing on this man who is raping you so you can identify him when you survive. After an hour of looking, I left the police station. They told me they'd be back in touch. They weren't.

A clerk called me one day to tell me that my car had been found minus tires and I should come sign a release and have it towed—no small matter if you don't have a car to get there and are slightly afraid of your shadow. The women from the rape crisis center called me every day, then every other day, then every week. The police detectives never called at all.

I learned, much later, that I had "really" been raped. Unlike, say, the woman who claimed she'd been raped by a man she actually knew and was with voluntarily. Unlike, say, women who are "asking for it" and get what they deserve. I would listen as seemingly intelligent people explained these distinctions to me and marvel; later I read about them in books, court opinions, and empirical studies. It is bad enough to be a "real" rape victim. How terrible to be—what to call it—a "not real" rape victim.

Even the real rape victim must bear the heavy weight of the silence that surrounds this crime. At first, it is something you simply don't talk about. Then it occurs to you that people whose houses are broken into or who are mugged in Central Park talk about it all the time. Rape is a much more serious crime. If it isn't my fault, why am I supposed to be ashamed? If I shouldn't be ashamed, if it wasn't "personal," why look askance when I mention it?

As this introduction makes clear, I talk about it. I do so very consciously. Sometimes, I have been harassed as a result. More often, it leads women I know to tell me that they too are victims, and I try to help them. I cannot imagine anyone writing an article on prosecutorial discretion without disclosing that he or she had been a prosecutor. I cannot imagine myself writing on rape without disclosing how I learned my first lessons or why I care so much.

The rapes that I examine in this chapter are, like my own, the rapes of adult, competent women by men. I have simply excluded from my consideration the additional problems presented when young girls or unconscious women are raped; it is enough for me to try to understand the application of the law to women who are not special or different in these ways. I have put almost as far to one side the issue of race as a dominant theme. The history of rape, as the law has been enforced in this country, is a history of both racism and sexism. One could write an article of this length dealing only with the racism. I address it in places—for its influence is pervasive—but I cannot do justice to both. My focus is sexism.

In recent years, rape has emerged as a topic of increasing research and attention among feminists, in both popular and scholarly journals.[1] But much of the feminist writing is not focused on an analysis of the *law* of rape, and some that is so focused is not very firmly grounded in the criminal law. At the same time, much of the writing about rape in the more traditional criminal law literature, with the exception of some recent articles (primarily student notes),[2] does little more than mirror the condescension and misunderstanding, if not outright hostility to women, that have made rape a central part of the feminist agenda.[3]

This chapter examines rape within the criminal law tradition in order to expose and understand that tradition's attitude toward women. It is, first and foremost, a study of rape law as an illustration of sexism in the criminal law. A second purpose is to examine the connections between the law as written by legislators, as understood by courts, as acted upon by victims, and as enforced by prosecutors. Finally, this chapter is an argument for an expanded understanding of rape in the law.

To examine rape within the criminal law tradition is to expose fully the sexism of the law. Much that is striking about the crime of rape—and revealing of the sexism of the system—emerges only when rape is examined relative to other crimes, which the feminist literature by and large does not do. For example, rape is most assuredly not the only crime in which consent is a defense, but it is the only crime that has required the victim to resist physically in order to establish nonconsent. Nor is rape the only crime where prior relationship is taken into account by prosecutors in screening cases; yet we have not asked whether considering prior relationship in rape cases is different, and less justifiable, than considering it in cases of assault.

Sexism in the law of rape is no matter of mere historical interest; it endures even where some of the most blatant testaments to that sexism have disappeared. Corroboration requirements unique to rape may have been repealed, but they continue to be enforced as a matter of practice in many jurisdictions. The victim of rape may not be required to resist to the utmost as a matter of statutory law in any jurisdiction, but the definitions accorded to force and consent may render "reasonable" resistance both a practical and a legal necessity. In the law of rape, supposedly dead horses continue to run.

The study of rape as an illustration of sexism in the criminal law also raises broader questions about the way conceptions of gender and the different backgrounds and perspectives of men and women should be encompassed within the criminal law. In one of his most celebrated essays, Oliver Wendell Holmes explained that the law does not exist to tell the good man what to do, but to tell the bad man what not to do. Holmes was interested in the distinction between the good and bad man; I cannot help noticing that both are men. Most of the time, a criminal law that reflects male views and male standards imposes its judgment on men who have injured other men. It is "boys' rules" applied to a boys' fight. In rape, the male standard defines a crime committed against women, and male standards are used not only to judge men but also to judge the conduct of women victims. Moreover, because the crime involves sex itself, the law of rape inevitably treads on the explosive ground of sex roles, of male aggression and female passivity, of our understandings of sexuality—areas where differences between a male and a female perspective may be most pronounced.

The criminal law defines rape in at least three places. The way most of us teach "law" is by focusing on the common law tradition: cases from appellate courts and leading commentary. That is what I do in Part II of this chapter.[4] In Part III, I look at the law of statutes by examining two very different and very influential statutory schemes which were intended, and which have served, as models of "reform." Finally, in Part IV of this chapter, my focus is on how the criminal justice system defines and understands rape.*

In considering each area, my questions are essentially the same: How have the limits on the crime of rape been formulated? What do those limits signify? What makes it rape, as opposed to sex? In what ways is rape defined differently from other crimes? What do those differences tell us about the law's attitudes toward women, men, sex, and sexuality?

The answers I have found are strikingly consistent in each area of the "law." At one end of the spectrum is the "real" rape, what I will call the traditional rape: A stranger puts a gun to the head of his victim, threatens to kill her or beats her, and then engages in intercourse. In that case, the law—judges, statutes, prosecutors, and all—generally

*[Only Parts I, II, and V are reprinted here.—Ed.]

acknowledge that a serious crime has been committed. But most cases deviate in one or many respects from this clear picture, making interpretation far more complex. Where less force is used or no other physical injury is inflicted, where threats are inarticulate, where the two know each other, where the setting is not an alley but a bedroom, where the initial contact was not a kidnapping but a date, where the woman says no but does not fight, the understanding is different. In such cases, the law, as reflected in the opinions of the courts, the interpretation, if not the words, of the statutes, and the decisions of those within the criminal justice system, often tell us that no crime has taken place and that fault, if any is to be recognized, belongs with the woman. In concluding that such acts— what I call, for lack of a better title, *nontraditional* rapes—are not criminal, and worse, that the woman must bear any guilt, the law has reflected, legitimized, and enforced a view of sex and women which celebrates male aggressiveness and punishes female passivity. And that vision, while under attack in recent years, continues to be a dominant force in our society and in the law of rape.

Finally, this chapter is an argument that the law can make a difference—and that it should. But the answer is not to write the perfect statute. While some statutes invite a more restrictive application than others, there is no "model statute" solution to rape law, because the problem has never been the words of the statutes as much as our interpretation of them. A typical statute of the 1890s—punishing a man who engages in sexual intercourse "by force" and "against the will and without the consent" of the woman— may not be all that different from the "model" statute we will enforce in the 1990s. The difference must come in our understanding of "consent" and "will" and "force."

Some of those who have written about rape from a feminist perspective intimate that nothing short of political revolution can redress the failings of the traditional approach to rape, that most of what passes for "sex" in our capitalist society is coerced, and that no lines can or should be drawn between rape and what happens in tens of millions of bedrooms across America.

So understood, this particular feminist vision of rape shares one thing with the most traditional sexist vision: the view that nontraditional rape is not fundamentally different from what happens in tens of millions of bedrooms across America. According to the radical feminist, all of it is rape; according to the traditionalist, it is all permissible sex and seduction. In policy terms, neither is willing to draw lines between rape and permissible sex. As a result, the two visions, contradictory in every other respect, point to the same practical policy implications.

My own view is different from both of these. I recognize that both men and women in our society have long accepted norms of male aggressiveness and female passivity which lead to a restricted understanding of rape. And I do not propose, nor do I think it feasible, to punish all of the acts of sexual intercourse that could be termed coerced. But lines can be drawn between these two alternatives. The law should be understood to prohibit claims and threats to secure sex that would be prohibited by extortion law and fraud or false pretenses law as a means to secure money. The law should evaluate the conduct of "reasonable" men, not according to a *Playboy*-macho philosophy that says "no means yes," but by according respect to a woman's words. If in 1986 silence does not negate consent, at least crying and saying "no" should.

Traditionally, the law has done more than reflect the restrictive and sexist views of our society it has legitimized and contributed to them. In the same way, a law that rejected those views and respected female autonomy might do more than reflect the changes in our society; it might even push them forward a bit.

II. The Definition of Rape: The Common Law Tradition

The traditional way of defining a crime is by describing the prohibited act (*actus reus*) committed by the defendant and the prohibited mental state (*mens rea*) with which he must have done it. We ask: What did the defendant do? What did he know or intend when he did it?

The definition of rape stands in striking contrast to this tradition, because courts, in defining the crime, have focused almost incidentally on the defendant—and almost entirely on the victim. It has often been noted that traditionally at least, the rules associated with the proof of a rape charge—the corroboration requirement, the requirement of cautionary instructions, and the fresh complaint rule—as well as the evidentiary rules relating to prior sexual conduct by the victim, placed the victim as much on trial as the defendant.[5] Such a reversal also occurs in the course of defining the elements of the crime. *Mens rea*, where it might matter, is all but eliminated; prohibited force tends to be defined according to the response of the victim; and nonconsent—the sine qua non of the offense—turns entirely on the victim's response.

But while the focus is on the female victim, the judgment of her actions is entirely male. If the issue were what the defendant knew, thought, or intended as to key elements of the offense, this perspective might be understandable; yet the issue has instead been the appropriateness of the woman's behavior, according to male standards of appropriate female behavior.

To some extent, this evaluation is but a modern response to the long-standing suspicion of rape victims. As Matthew Hale put it three centuries ago: "Rape is . . . an accusation easily to be made and hard to be proved, and harder to be defended by the party accused, tho never so innocent."[6]

But the problem is more fundamental than that. Apart from the woman's conduct, the law provides no clear, working definition of rape. This rather conspicuous gap in the law of rape presents substantial questions of fair warning for men, which the law not so handily resolves by imposing the burden of warning them on women.

At its simplest, the dilemma lies in this: If nonconsent is essential to rape (and no amount of force or physical struggle is inherently inconsistent with lawful sex), and if no sometimes means yes, and if men are supposed to be aggressive in any event, how is a man to know when he has crossed the line? And how are we to avoid unjust convictions?

This dilemma is hardly inevitable. Partly it is a product of the way society (or at least a powerful part of it) views sex. Partly it is a product of the lengths to which the law has gone to enforce and legitimize those views. We could prohibit the use of force and threats and coercion in sex, regardless of "consent." We could define consent in a way that respected the autonomy of women. Having chosen neither course, however, we have created a problem of fair warning, and force and consent have been defined in an effort to resolve this problem.

Usually, any discussion of rape begins (and ends) with consent. I begin instead with *mens rea*, because if unjust punishment of the blameless man is our fear (as it was Hale's), then *mens rea* would seem an appropriate place to start addressing it. At least a requirement of *mens rea* would avoid unjust convictions without adjudicating the "guilt" of the victim. It could also be the first step in expanding liability beyond the most traditional rape.

Without *mens rea*, the fair warning problem turns solely on the understanding of force and consent. To the extent that force is defined apart from a woman's reaction, it has been defined narrowly, in the most schoolboyish terms. But most of the time, force has been defined according to the woman's will to resist, judged as if she could and should fight like a man. Thus defined, force serves to limit our understanding of rape even in cases where a court might be willing to say that this woman did not consent.

Rape is not a unique crime in requiring nonconsent. But it is unique in the definition given to nonconsent. As it has been understood, the consent standard denies female autonomy; indeed, it even denies that women are capable of making decisions about sex, let alone articulating them. Yet consent, properly understood, has the potential to give women greater power in sexual relations and to expand our understanding of the crime of rape. That is, perhaps, why so many efforts have been made to cabin the concept.

A. *Mens Rea*

It is difficult to imagine any man engaging in intercourse accidentally or mistakenly. It is just as difficult to imagine an accidental or mistaken use of force, at least as force is conventionally defined. But it is not at all difficult to imagine cases in which a man might claim that he did not realize that the woman was not consenting to sex. He may have been mistaken in assuming that no meant yes. He may not have bothered to inquire. He may have ignored signs that would have told him that the woman did not welcome his forceful penetration.

In doctrinal terms, such a man could argue that his mistake of fact should exculpate him because he lacked the requisite intent or *mens rea* as to the woman's required nonconsent. American courts have altogether eschewed the *mens rea* or mistake inquiry as to consent, opting instead for a definition of the crime of rape that is so limited that it leaves little room for men to be mistaken, reasonably or unreasonably, as to consent. The House of Lords, by contrast, has confronted the question explicitly and, in its leading case, has formally restricted the crime of rape to men who act recklessly, a state of mind defined to allow even the unreasonably mistaken man to avoid conviction.

This section argues that the American courts' refusal to confront the *mens rea* problem works to the detriment of the victim. In order to protect men from unfair convictions, American courts end up defining rape with undue restrictiveness. The English approach, while doctrinally clearer, also tends toward an unduly restricted definition of the crime of rape.

While the defendant's attitude toward consent may be considered either an issue of *mens rea* or a mistake of fact, the key question remains the same. In *mens rea* terms, the question is whether negligence suffices, that is, whether the defendant should be convicted who claims that he thought the woman was consenting, or didn't think about it, in situations where a "reasonable man" would have known that there was not consent. In mistake-of-fact terms, the question is whether a mistake as to consent must be reasonable in order to exculpate the defendant.

In defining the crime of rape, most American courts have omitted *mens rea* altogether. In Maine, for example, the supreme judicial court has held that there is no *mens rea* requirement at all for rape.[7] In Pennsylvania, the superior court held in 1982 that even a reasonable belief as to the victim's consent would not exculpate a defendant charged with rape.[8] In 1982 the Supreme Judicial Court of Massachusetts left open the question whether it would recognize a defense of reasonable mistake of fact as to consent, but it rejected the defendant's suggestion that any mistake, reasonable or unreasonable, would be sufficient to negate the required intent to rape; such a claim was treated by the court as bordering on the ridiculous.[9] The following year the court went on to hold that a specific intent that intercourse be without consent was not an element of the crime of rape,[10] that decision has since been construed to mean that there is no intent requirement at all as to consent in rape cases.[11]

To treat what the defendant intended or knew or even should have known about the victim's consent as irrelevant to his liability sounds like a result favorable to both prosecution and women as victims. But experience makes all too clear that it is not. To refuse to inquire into *mens rea* leaves two possibilities: turning rape into a strict liability offense where, in the absence of consent, the man is guilty of rape regardless of whether he (or anyone) would have recognized nonconsent in the circumstances; or defining the crime of rape in a fashion that is so limited that it would be virtually impossible for any man to be convicted where he was truly unaware or mistaken as to nonconsent. In fact, it is the latter approach which has characterized all of the older, and many of the newer, American cases. In practice, abandoning *mens rea* produces the worst of all possible worlds: The trial emerges not as an inquiry into the guilt of the defendant (Is he a rapist?) but of the victim (Was she really raped? Did she consent?). The perspective that governs is therefore not that of the woman, nor even of the particular man, but of a judicial system intent upon protecting against unjust conviction, regardless of the dangers of injustice to the woman in the particular case.

The requirement that sexual intercourse be accompanied by force or threat of force to constitute rape provides a man with some protection against mistakes as to consent. A man who uses a gun or knife against his victim is not likely to be in serious doubt as to her lack of consent, and the more narrowly force is defined, the more implausible the claim that he was unaware of nonconsent.

But the law's protection of men is not limited to a requirement of force. Rather than inquire whether the man believed (reasonably or unreasonably) that his victim was consenting, the courts have demanded that the victim demonstrate her nonconsent by engaging in resistance that will leave no doubt as to nonconsent. The definition of nonconsent as resistance—in the older cases, as utmost resistance,[12] while in some more recent ones, as "reasonable" physical resistance[13]—functions as a substitute for *mens rea* to ensure that the man has notice of the woman's nonconsent.

The choice between focusing on the man's intent or focusing on the woman's is not simply a doctrinal flip of the coin.

First, the inquiry into the victim's nonconsent puts the woman, not the man, on trial. Her intent, not his, is disputed, and because her state of mind is key, her sexual history may be considered relevant (even though utterly unknown to the man).[14] Considering consent from *his* perspective, by contrast, substantially undermines the relevance of the woman's sexual history where it was unknown to the man.

Second, the issue for determination shifts from whether the man is a rapist to whether the woman was raped. A verdict of acquittal thus does more than signal that the prosecution has failed to prove the defendant guilty beyond a reasonable doubt; it signals that the prosecution has failed to prove the woman's sexual violation—her innocence—beyond a reasonable doubt. Thus, as one dissenter put it in disagreeing with the affirmance of a conviction of rape: "The majority today . . . declares the innocence of an at best distraught young woman."[15] Presumably, the dissenter thought the young woman guilty.

Third, the resistance requirement is not only ill conceived as a definition of nonconsent but is an overbroad substitute for *mens rea* in any event. Both the resistance requirement and the *mens rea* requirement can be used to enforce a male perspective on the crime, but while *mens rea* might be justified as protecting the individual defendant who has not made a blameworthy choice, the resistance standard requires women to risk injury to themselves in cases where there may be no doubt as to the man's intent or blameworthiness. The application of the resistance requirement has not been limited to cases in which there was uncertainty as to what the man thought, knew or intended; it has been fully applied in cases where there can be no question that the man knew that intercourse was without consent.[16] Indeed, most of the cases that have dismissed claims that *mens rea* ought to be required have been cases where both force and resistance were present and where there was no danger of any unfairness.

Finally, by ignoring *mens rea*, American courts and legislators have imposed limits on the fair expansion of our understanding of rape. As long as the law holds that *mens rea* is not required and that no instructions on intent need be given, pressure will exist to retain some form of resistance requirement and to insist on force as conventionally defined in order to protect men against conviction for "sex." Using resistance as a substitute for *mens rea* unnecessarily and unfairly immunizes those men whose victims are afraid enough, or intimidated enough, or, frankly, smart enough, not to take the risk of resisting physically. In doing so, the resistance test may declare the blameworthy man innocent and the raped woman guilty.

While American courts have unwisely ignored the entire issue of *mens rea* or mistake of fact, the British courts may have gone too far in the other direction. To their credit, they have squarely confronted the issue, but their resolution suggests a highly restrictive understanding of criminal intent in cases of sexual assault. The focal point of the debate in Great Britain and the Commonwealth countries was the House of Lords' decision in *Director of Public Prosecutions v. Morgan*,[17] in which the certified question was: "Whether in rape the defendant can properly be convicted, notwithstanding that he in fact believed that the woman consented, if such belief was not based on reasonable grounds."[18] The majority of the House of Lords answered the question in the negative.[19]

The Heilbron Committee was created to review the controversial *Morgan* decision. The committee's recommendation, ultimately enacted in 1976, retained the *Morgan* approach in requiring that at the time of intercourse the man knew or at least was aware of the risk of nonconsent but provided that the reasonableness of the man's belief could be considered by the jury in determining what he in fact knew.[20] In situations where a "reasonable man" would have known that the woman was not consenting, most defendants will face great difficulty in arguing that they were honestly mistaken or inadvertent as to consent. Thus, in *Morgan* itself, the House of Lords, although holding that negligence was not sufficient to establish liability for rape, upheld the convictions on the ground that no properly instructed jury, in the circumstances of that case, could have concluded that the defendants honestly believed that their victim was consenting. Still, in an English case decided shortly after *Morgan*, on facts substantially similar (a husband procuring a buddy to engage in sex with his crying wife), an English jury concluded that the defendant had been negligent in believing, honestly but unreasonably, in the wife's consent. On the authority of *Morgan*, the court held that the defendant therefore deserved acquittal.[21]

My view is that such a "negligent rapist" should be punished, albeit—as in murder—

less severely than the man who acts with purpose or knowledge, or even knowledge of the risk. First, he is sufficiently blameworthy for it to be just to punish him. Second, the injury he inflicts is sufficiently grave to deserve the law's prohibition.

The traditional argument against negligence liability is that punishment should be limited to cases of choice, because to punish a man for his stupidity is unjust and, in deterrence terms, ineffective. Under this view, a man should only be held responsible for what he does knowingly or purposely, or at least while aware of the risks involved. As one of *Morgan's* most respected defenders put it:

> To convict the stupid man would be to convict him for what lawyers call inadvertent negligence—honest conduct which may be the best that this man can do but that does not come up to the standard of the so-called reasonable man. People ought not to be punished for negligence except in some minor offences established by statute. Rape carries a possible sentence of imprisonment for life, and it would be wrong to have a law of negligent rape.[22]

If inaccuracy or indifference to consent is "the best that this man can do" because he lacks the capacity to act reasonably, then it might well be unjust and ineffective to punish him for it. But such men will be rare, and there was no evidence that the men in *Morgan* were among them, at least as long as voluntary drunkenness is not equated with inherent lack of capacity. More common is the case of the man who could have done better but didn't; could have paid attention, but didn't; heard her say no, or saw her tears, but decided to ignore them. Neither justice nor deterrence argues against punishing this man.

Certainly, if the "reasonable" attitude to which a male defendant is held is defined according to a "no means yes" philosophy that celebrates male aggressiveness and female passivity, there is little potential for unfairness in holding men who fall below *that* standard criminally liable. Under such a low standard of reasonableness, only a very drunk man could honestly be mistaken as to a woman's consent, and a man who voluntarily sheds his capacity to act and perceive reasonably should not be heard to complain here— any more than with respect to other crimes—that he is being punished in the absence of choice.

But even if reasonableness is defined—as I argue it should be—according to a rule that "no means no," it is not unfair to hold those men who violate the rule criminally responsible, provided that there is fair warning of the rule. I understand that some men in our society have honestly believed in a different reality of sexual relations and that many may honestly view such situations differently than women. But it is precisely because men and women may perceive these situations differently and because the injury to women stemming from the different male perception may be grave that it is necessary and appropriate for the law to impose a duty upon men to act with reason and to punish them when they violate that duty.

In holding a man to such a standard of reasonableness, the law signifies that it considers a woman's consent to sex to be significant enough to merit a man's reasoned attention. In effect, the law imposes a duty on men to open their eyes and use their heads before engaging in sex—not to read a woman's mind but to give her credit for knowing her own mind when she speaks it. The man who has the inherent capacity to act reasonably but fails to do so has made the blameworthy choice to violate this duty. While the injury caused by purposeful conduct may be greater than that caused by negligent acts, being negligently sexually penetrated without one's consent remains a grave harm, and being treated like an object whose words or actions are not even worthy of consideration adds insult to injury. This dehumanization exacerbates the denial of dignity and autonomy which is so much a part of the injury of rape, and it is equally present in both the purposeful and negligent rape.

By holding out the prospect of punishment for negligence, the law provides an additional motive for men to "take care before acting, to use their faculties and draw on their experience in gauging the potentialities of contemplated conduct."[23] We may not yet have reached the point where men are required to ask verbally. But if silence does not negate consent, at least the word *no* should, and those who ignore such an explicit sign of nonconsent should be subject to criminal liability.

Securing the protection of the criminal law is not, however, simply a matter of forcing courts or legislatures to focus on *mens rea* or mistake. First, it would require acknowledging an understanding of consent quite at odds with the "no means yes" philosophy which has characterized the common law tradition. Such a shift would require an awareness of the extent to which distrust of women has pervaded rape law. Second, criminal prohibition would require a move away from the traditionally narrow understanding of the force required, in addition to nonconsent, to define intercourse as rape. Those are the subjects of the next two subsections.

B. Force and Threats

This section examines two views of force in human relations. The first understands force as most schoolboys do on the playground: Force is when he hits me; resistance is when I hit back. That is the definition of force traditionally enforced in rape cases. A second understanding of force, not acknowledged in the law of rape, recognizes that bodily integrity means more than freedom from the force of fists, that power can be exercised without violence, and that coercion is not limited to what boys do in schoolyards.

Virtually every jurisdiction has traditionally made "force" or "threat of force" an element of the crime of rape. Where a defendant threatens his victim with a deadly weapon, beats her, or threatens to hurt her, and then proceeds immediately to have sex, few courts have difficulty finding that force is present. These facts fit the schoolboy definition of force. But when some time elapses between the force and intercourse, when the force is more of the variety considered "incidental" to sex, or when the situation is threatening but no explicit threat of harm is communicated, "force" as defined and required by the criminal law may not be present at all. In such cases, the law fails to recognize, let alone protect, a woman's interest in bodily integrity.

In *Mills v. United States,* in 1897, the defendant seized his victim at gunpoint, told her he was a notorious train robber named Henry Starr, threatened to kill her, and proceeded to have intercourse with her twice. The trial court instructed the jury:

> The fact is that all the force that need be exercised, if there is no consent, is the force incident to the commission of the act. If there is non-consent of the woman, the force, I say, incident to the commission of the crime is all the force that is required to make out this element of the crime.[24]

The jury convicted, and the defendant appealed on the ground that this instruction was in error as to the amount of force necessary to constitute rape. The Supreme Court agreed and reversed the conviction:

> In this charge we think the court did not explain fully enough so as to be understood by the jury what constitutes in law non-consent on the part of the woman, and

what is the force, necessary in all cases of non-consent, to constitute the crime. . . . But the charge in question . . . covered the case where no threats were made; where no active resistance was overcome; where the woman was not unconscious, but where there was simply non-consent on her part and no real resistance whatever. . . . More force is necessary when that is the character of non-consent than was stated by the court to be necessary to make out that element of the crime. That kind of non-consent is not enough, nor is the force spoken of then sufficient, which is only incidental to the act itself.[25]

The requirement of force is not unique to the law of rape. But rape is different in two critical respects. First, unlike theft, if "force" is not inherent in noncriminal sex, at least physical contact is. Certainly, if a person stripped his victim, flattened that victim on the floor, lay down on top, and took the other person's wallet or jewelry, few would pause before the conclusion of a forcible robbery. Second, rape does not involve "one person" and "another person." It involves, in practice if not everywhere by definition, a male person using "force" against a female person. The question of whose definition of "force" should apply, whose understanding should govern, is therefore critical.

The distinction between the "force" incidental to the act of intercourse and the "force" required to convict a man of rape is one commonly drawn by courts.[26] Once drawn, however, the distinction would seem to require the courts to define what additional acts are needed to constitute prohibited rather than incidental force. This is where the problems arise. For many courts and jurisdictions, "force" triggers an inquiry identical to that which informs the understanding of consent. Both serve as substitutes for a *mens rea* requirement. Force is required to constitute rape, but force—even force that goes far beyond the physical contact necessary to accomplish penetration—is not itself prohibited. Rather, what is required, and prohibited, is force used to overcome female nonconsent. The prohibition is defined in terms of a woman's resistance. Thus, "forcible compulsion" becomes the force necessary to overcome reasonable resistance. When the woman does not physically resist, the question becomes then whether the force was sufficient to overcome a reasonable woman's will to resist. Prohibited force turns on the judge's evaluation of a reasonable woman's response.

In *State v. Alston,* Mr. Alston and the victim had been involved in a "consensual" relationship for six months. That relationship admittedly involved "some violence" by the defendant and some passivity by the victim. The defendant would strike the victim when she refused to give him money or refused to do what he wanted. As for sex, the court noted that "she often had sex with the defendant just to accommodate him. On those occasions, she would stand still and remain entirely passive while the defendant undressed her and had intercourse with her."[27] This was their "consensual" relationship. It ended when, after being struck by the defendant, the victim left him and moved in with her mother.

A month later, the defendant came to the school which the victim attended, blocked her path, demanded to know where she was living, and when she refused to tell him, grabbed her arm, and stated that she was coming with him. The victim told the defendant she would walk with him if he released her arm. They then walked around the school and talked about their relationship. At one point, the defendant told the victim he was going to "fix" her face; when told that their relationship was over, the defendant stated that he had a "right" to have sex with her again. The two went to the house of a friend. The defendant asked her if she was "ready," and the victim told him she did not want to have sexual relations. The defendant pulled her up from the chair, undressed her, pushed her legs apart, and penetrated her. She cried.[28]

The defendant was convicted of rape, and his conviction was affirmed by the intermediate court of appeals. On appeal, the North Carolina Supreme Court agreed that the victim was not required to resist physically to establish nonconsent: The victim's testimony that she did not consent was "unequivocal," and her testimony provided substantial evidence that the act of sexual intercourse was against her will.[29]

But the North Carolina Supreme Court nonetheless reversed on the ground that even viewing the evidence in the light most favorable to the state, the element of force had not been established by substantial evidence. The victim did not "resist"—physically, at least. And her failure to resist, in the court's evaluation, was not a result of what the defendant did before penetration. Therefore, there was no "force."[30]

The force used outside the school and the threats made on the walk, "although they may have induced fear," were considered to be "unrelated to the act of sexual intercourse."[31] Indeed, the court emphasized that the victim testified that it was not what the defendant said that day but her experience with him in the past that made her afraid. Such past experience was deemed irrelevant.

> Although [the victim's] general fear of the defendant may have been justified by his conduct on prior occasions, absent evidence that the defendant used force or threats to overcome the will of the victim to resist the sexual intercourse alleged to have been rape, such general fear was not sufficient to show that the defendant used the force required to support a conviction of rape.[32]

The undressing and the pushing of her legs apart—presumably the "incidental" force—were not even mentioned as factors to be considered.

State v. Alston is not a unique case, but it is an unusual one. Rape cases between individuals who have had what passes in the law for a "consensual" sexual relationship are rare in the system. In some sense, the supreme court here simply did what is usually done by the women (who don't press charges), by the police (who unfound them), or by the prosecutors (who dismiss them). But it did so to greater legal effect.

Later in 1984, the North Carolina Court of Appeals applied *Alston* to another case where the defendant and the victim knew each other and had had previous sexual relations. In this case, however, the parties were not "boyfriend" and "girlfriend." They were a father and his fifteen-year-old daughter.

The defendant in *State v. Lester*[33] was the father of three daughters and a son. Prior to the parents' divorce, the defendant frequently beat the children's mother in their presence. He also beat his girlfriend and his son. He had a gun and on one occasion pointed it at his children. He engaged in sexual activity with all three of his daughters. He first had sexual relations with the daughter whose rape was at issue when she was eleven years old. Her mother found out and confronted the defendant. He swore never to touch her again and then threatened to kill both mother and daughter if they told anyone of his actions. On both of the occasions in question, the victim initially refused her father's demand to take her clothes off and "do it." In both cases, she complied when the demand was repeated and she sensed that her father was becoming angry. The court held that the defendant could be convicted of incest, but not of rape:

> In the instant case there is evidence that the acts of sexual intercourse between defendant and his fifteen-year-old daughter . . . were against her will. There is no evi-

dence, however, that defendant used either actual or constructive force to accomplish the acts with which he is charged. As *Alston* makes clear, the victim's fear of defendant, however justified by his previous conduct, is insufficient to show that defendant *forcibly* raped his daughter on 25 November and 18 December.[34]

A digression is in order. Some people have suggested that I make these cases up. I don't. Others suggest that they must be rare. Such abuse of teenagers is not rare. Some suggest that even if these cases are not rare, decisions such as *Lester* must be, or must only happen in North Carolina, or must in some other easy and convenient way be sufficiently distinguishable as to be an unsuitable basis for either analysis or anxiety. I don't think so. Just a year before *Lester,* the Pennsylvania appellate court was confronted with a father who used a different approach to the same end with his seventeen-year-old daughter. Over a one-year period, the defendant had sex with her on several occasions. She "did so because her father told her that the Bible said that 'if the mother could no longer provide as a mother, it was up to the oldest daughter, and if she could no longer do it, it would go right down to the last daughter in the family.'"[35] The defendant also told his daughter that if she reported these incidents to anyone, he would show people pictures he had taken of her in the nude. His conviction for rape, like Mr. Lester's, was reversed:

> The record clearly shows that defendant never used or threatened to use force in inducing his daughter to participate in sexual intercourse. Rather, he asserted a biblical basis for the intercourse and assured his daughter's silence by threats, not of force, but of humiliation. Although this conduct is reprehensible, it is not the conduct proscribed by section 3121 of the Crimes Code, which forbids intercourse by threat of *forcible compulsion.*[36]

Decisions such as *Lester* and *Alston* are vulnerable to attack on traditional doctrinal grounds. The courts' unwillingness to credit the victim's past experience of violence at the hands of the defendant stands in sharp contrast to the black letter law that a defendant's knowledge of his attacker's reputation for violence or ownership of a gun is relevant to the reasonableness of his use of deadly force in self-defense.

That these decisions depart so straightforwardly from established criminal law doctrine is noteworthy but not unusual in the law of rape. More interesting is the apparent paradox that they create. In each case, the court says—and this is explicit, not implicit—that sex was without the woman's consent. It also says that there was no force. In other words, the woman was not forced to engage in sex, but the sex she engaged in was against her will.

Such a paradox is almost inevitable if one adopts, and then enforces, the most traditional male notion of a fight as the working definition of "force." In a fight, you hit your assailant with your fists or your elbows or your knees. In a fight, the one attacked fights back. In these terms, there was no fight in *Alston.* Therefore, there was no force.

I am not at all sure how the judges who decided *Alston* would explain the victim's simultaneous refusal to consent and failure to resist. For myself, it is not at all difficult to understand that a woman who had been repeatedly beaten, who had been a passive victim of both violence and sex during the "consensual" relationship, who had sought to escape from the man, who is confronted and threatened by him, who summons the courage to tell him their relationship is over only to be answered by his assertion of a "right" to sex— a woman in such a position would not fight. She wouldn't fight; she might cry. Hers is the reaction of "sissies" in playground fights. Hers is the reaction of people who have already been beaten, or who never had the power to fight in the first instance. Hers is, from my reading, the most common reaction of women to rape. It certainly was mine.

To say that there is no "force" in such a situation is to create a gulf between power and force and to define the latter solely in schoolboy terms. Mr. Alston did not beat his victim—at least not with his fists. He didn't have to. She had been beaten—physically and emotionally—long before. But that beating was one that the court was willing to go to great lengths to avoid recognizing.

That the law prohibiting forced sex understands force in such narrow terms is frustrating enough for its women victims. Worse, however, is the fact that the conclusion that no force is present may emerge as a judgment not that the man did not act unreasonably, but as a judgment that the woman victim did.

Pat met Rusk at a bar. They talked briefly. She announced she was leaving, and he asked for a ride. She drove him home. He invited her up. She declined. He asked again. She declined again. He reached over and took the car keys. She followed him to his room. He went to the bathroom. She didn't move. He told her to remove her slacks and his clothing. She did. After they undressed:

> I said, "you can get a lot of other girls down there, for what you want," and he just kept saying "no" and then I was really scared, because I can't describe, you know, what was said. It was more the look in his eyes; and I said, at that point—I didn't know what to say; and I said, "If I do what you want, will you let me go without killing me?" Because I didn't know, at that point, what he was going to do; and I started to cry; and when I did, he put his hands on my throat, and started lightly to choke me; and I said, "If I do what you want, will you let me go?" And he said, yes, and at that time, I proceeded to do what he wanted me to.[37]

After sex, the defendant walked her to her car and asked if he could see her again.

How does a court respond to facts like this? Is "force" established by the "look in his eyes," by light choking (her description)/heavy caresses (his description), or by taking the car keys of an adult woman? Is the latter force or motor vehicle larceny? If we accept Pat's testimony, as the jury did, then it is established that she was overcome. Is that enough?

Rusk's case was heard *en banc* by both the Maryland Court of Special Appeals and the Maryland court of Appeals. The court of special appeals reversed the conviction, eight to five. The Maryland Court of Appeals reinstated it, four to three.[38] All told, twenty-one judges, including the trial judge, considered the sufficiency of the evidence. Ten concluded that Rusk was a rapist. Eleven concluded that he was not.

Those who considered the evidence insufficient focused nearly all their attention not on what Mr. Rusk did or did not do but on how the woman victim should have responded. Prohibited force was defined according to a hypothetical victim's resistance: The defendant's words or actions must create in the mind of a victim a reasonable fear that if she resisted, he would have harmed her, or that faced with such resistance, he would have used force to overcome her. The intermediate court majority found unpersuasive the argument that an honest fear was sufficient where there is nothing whatsoever to indicate that the victim was "anything but a normal, intelligent, twenty-one year old, vigorous female."[39] Of course, the question remains as to what is "reasonably" expected of such a female faced with a man who frightens her, in an unfamiliar neighborhood, without her car keys. To the Maryland Court of Appeals dissenters, the answer was clear:

> While courts no longer require a female to resist to the utmost or to resist where resistance would be foolhardy, they do require her acquiescence in the act of inter-

course to stem from fear generated by something of substance. She may not simply say, "I was really scared," and thereby transform consent or mere unwillingness into submission by force. These words do not transform a seducer into a rapist. She must follow the natural instinct of every proud female to resist, by more than mere words, the violation of her person by a stranger or an unwelcomed friend. She must make it plain that she regards such sexual acts as abhorrent and repugnant to her natural sense of pride. She must resist unless the defendant has objectively manifested his intent to use physical force to accomplish his purpose.[40]

In the dissenters' view, Pat was not a "reasonable" victim, or even a victim at all. Instead of fighting, she cried. Instead of protecting her virtue, she acquiesced. Far from having any claim that her bodily integrity had been violated, she was adjudged complicit in the intercourse of which she complained. She was "in effect, an adulteress."

In a very real sense, the "reasonable" woman under the view of the eleven judges who would reverse Mr. Rusk's conviction is not a woman at all. Their version of a reasonable person is one who does not scare easily, one who does not feel vulnerability, one who is not passive, one who fights back, not cries. The reasonable woman, it seems, is not a schoolboy "sissy." She is a real man.

The court of appeals majority ultimately affirmed the conviction on the narrowest possible ground. The court stated that "generally . . . the correct standard" is that the victim's fear must "be reasonably grounded in order to obviate the need for either proof of actual force on the part of the assailant or physical resistance on the part of the victim."[41] Was this victim's fear reasonable? The court strove to avoid the question. The fundamental error of the intermediate court was its violation of the principle of appellate restraint; the question of reasonableness was a question of fact to be left to the jury. Still, the court of appeals could not avoid entirely the obligation to review the sufficiency of the evidence. Thus, "considering all of the evidence in the case, *with particular focus upon the actual force applied by Rusk to Pat's neck,* we conclude that the jury could rationally find that the essential elements of second degree rape had been established."[42]

The emphasis on the light choking/heavy caresses is, perhaps, understandable: It is the only "objective" (as the supreme court dissent put it) force in the victim's testimony; it is certainly the only "force" that a schoolboy might recognize. As it happens, however, that force was not applied until the two were already undressed and in bed. Whatever it was—choking or caressing—was a response to the woman's crying as the moment of intercourse approached. It was not, it seems fairly clear, the only force that produced that moment.

Unable to understand force as the power one need not use (at least physically), courts are left either to emphasize the "light choking" or to look for threats of force. Technically, these threats of force may be implicit as well as explicit.[43] But implicit to whom? That a woman feels genuinely afraid, that a man has created the situation that she finds frightening, even that he has done it intentionally in order to secure sexual satisfaction may not be enough to constitute the necessary force or even implicit threat of force which earns bodily integrity any protection under the law of rape.

In *Goldberg v. State,*[44] a high-school senior working as a sales clerk was "sold a story" by the defendant that he was a free-lance agent and thought she was an excellent prospect to become a successful model. She accompanied him to his "temporary studio" where she testified that she engaged in intercourse because she was afraid. Her reasons for being afraid, according to the appellate court which reversed the conviction, were: "(1) she was alone with the appellant in a house with no buildings close by and no one to help her if she resisted, and (2) the appellant was much larger than she was."[45] According to the appellate court, "in the complete absence of any threatening words or actions by the appellant, these two factors, as a matter of law, are simply not enough to have created a reasonable fear of harm so as to preclude resistance and be 'the equivalent of force.'"[46]

The New York Supreme Court, sitting as the trier of fact in a rape case, reached a similar conclusion with respect to the threatening situation facing an "incredibly gullible, trusting, and naive" college sophomore. In *People v. Evans,* the defendant posed as a psychologist conducting a sociological experiment, took the woman to a dating bar to "observe" her, and then induced her to come to an apartment he used as an "office." When she rejected his advances, he said to her: "'Look where you are. You are in the apartment of a strange man. How do you know that I am really who I say I am? How do you know that I am really a psychologist? . . . I could kill you. I could rape you. I could hurt you physically.'"[47] The trial court found his conduct "reprehensible," describing it as "conquest by con job." But it was not criminal; the words were ambiguous, capable of communicating either a threat to use ultimate force or the chiding of a "foolish girl."[48] While acknowledging that the victim might be terrified, the court was not persuaded beyond a reasonable doubt that the guilt of the defendant had been established.[49]

In both *Goldberg* and *Evans,* a woman finds herself alone and potentially stranded in a strange place with a man who is bigger than she. One need not be "incredibly gullible" to find oneself in this situation; one need only, as did the woman in *Rusk,* agree to give an average man (who is bigger than an average woman) a ride home. There are at least four possible doctrinal approaches to these threatening situations, even accepting the courts' understanding that "force" can only be understood in relation to a woman's resistance. It is noteworthy that all the decisions discussed above adopt the approach that not only makes conviction most difficult but also operates to place guilt most squarely on the victim.

The simplest approach would be to ask whether this woman's will to resist was in fact overcome by this defendant's actions. Is she lying, or did she submit because she was truly frightened? If she is not lying—and none of the courts suggested that any of the women in these cases were actually lying—then affirm the conviction. But what about the poor man who didn't realize that the woman was overcome by fear of him, rather than desire for him? Properly regarded, such a man lacks *mens rea* as to force or consent.

A second approach resolves that problem without relying explicitly on *mens rea.* It asks instead: Were the defendant's acts and behavior intended to overcome this woman's will to resist? Under such a standard, at least Mr. Lester, Mr. Alston, Mr. Goldberg, and Mr. Evans—if not Mr. Rusk as well—will have a hard time claiming that they didn't mean to succeed and that success was not defined as creating a situation that would frighten the woman into submission.[50]

A third approach probes whether the defendant's acts and statements were calculated to overcome the will of a reasonable woman. This standard, very close to the "reasonable calculation" standard actually used in earlier decisions in Maryland and elsewhere,[51] obviously allows men greater freedom than the second approach. It tolerates their exploitation of naive and gullible women by claiming that in their "reasonableness calculation," the tactics should not have been threatening enough. Even at its best, the "reasonably calculated" standard creates something of a paradox: If most women have a different understanding of force than most men, then the reasonable calculation standard is one that asks how a reasonable man understands the mind of a reasonable woman. But at least it focuses primarily on the defendant's actions and thoughts and makes his guilt or innocence the center of the trial.

The final approach doesn't even do that. It judges the woman, not the man. It asks—as did the court in each of these cases—whether the will of the reasonable woman would have been overcome given the circumstances. The focus is on women generally and on the victim as she compares (poorly) to the court's assessment of the reasonable woman. The court then proceeds to conclude that a reasonable woman's will would not have been overcome in those circumstances, because there is no "force" as men understand it.

Such an approach accomplishes two things. First, it ensures broad male freedom to "seduce" women who feel powerless, vulnerable, and afraid; the force standard guarantees men freedom to intimidate women and exploit their weaknesses, as long as they don't "fight" with them. Second, it makes clear that the responsibility and blame for such seductions belong with the woman. Because the will of a reasonable woman by definition would not have been overcome, a particular woman's submission can only mean that she is subpar as women go or that she was complicitous in the intercourse.

It is one thing to argue that none of the men in these cases should be considered in the same category (in terms of their blameworthiness, their dangerousness, or the harm caused by their actions) as the man who puts a gun to his victim's head and threatens to kill her if she refuses to have sex. It is quite another to argue that these men have committed no crime.

Most striking about these cases is the fact that had these men been seeking money instead of sex, their actions would plainly violate traditional state criminal prohibitions. Had Mr. Goldberg used his modeling-agent story to secure money rather than sex, his would be a case of theft by deception or false pretenses. As for Mr. Evans, had he sought money rather than sex as part of his "sociological test," he too could have been found guilty of theft. Neither Goldberg nor Evans could have escaped liability on the ground that a "reasonable person" would not have been deceived, any more than a victim's leaving his front door unlocked or his keys in the automobile ignition serves as a defense to burglary or larceny. Had Mr. Rusk simply taken the woman's car keys, he would have been guilty of larceny or theft. And had Mr. Lester threatened to expose the nude pictures were he not paid, he might well have been guilty of state law extortion.

Lying to secure money is unlawful theft by deception or false pretenses, a lesser crime than robbery but a crime nonetheless. Yet lying to secure sex is old-fashioned seduction—not first-degree rape, not even third-degree rape. A threat to expose sexual information has long considered a classic case of extortion, if not robbery itself. But securing sex itself by means of a threat short of force has, in many jurisdictions, been considered no crime at all.

To the argument that it is either impossible or unwise for the law to regulate sexual "bargains" short of physical force, the law of extortion stands as a sharp rebuke: It has long listed prohibited threats in fairly inclusive terms. While extortion may be a lesser offense than robbery, it is nonetheless prohibited.

It is almost certainly impossible to expect that the law could address all of the techniques of power and coercion which men use against women in sexual relations. I am not suggesting that we try.[52] Rather, I am suggesting that we do something that is actually quite easy—prohibit fraud to secure sex to the same extent we prohibit fraud to secure money, and prohibit extortion to secure sex to the same extent we prohibit extortion to secure money. Many states already have criminal coercion or fraud provisions that are worded with sufficient breadth (e.g., "engage in conduct") to be applied to prohibit such coerced sex. But cases enforcing such prohibitions are relatively rare, and the results have been divided. The broad reach of such statutes not only invites overbreadth challenges and claims of lack of warning but fails to make clear that loss of bodily integrity is a different and greater injury than loss of money and thus merits greater punishment. Criminal coercion statutes are, at best, poor substitutes for an expanded understanding of the "force" that makes sex rape.

C. Consent

This section will examine what has long been viewed as the most important concept in rape law—the notion of female consent. Nonconsent has traditionally been a required element in the definition of a number of crimes, including theft, assault and battery. Thus rape may be the most serious crime to encompass a consent defense, but it is certainly not the only one.

Rape is unique, however, in the definition which has been accorded to consent. That definition makes all too plain that the purpose of the consent rule is not to protect female autonomy and freedom of choice, but to assure men the broadest sexual access to women. In matters of sex, the common law tradition views women ambivalently at best: Even when not intentionally dishonest, they simply cannot be trusted to know what they want or to mean what they say. While the cases that engendered this tradition date from the 1870s and 1880s, the law reviews of the 1950s and 1960s and the appellate cases of the 1970s and 1980s have perpetuated it.

The justification for the central role of consent in the law of rape is that it protects women's choice and women's autonomy in sexual relations. Or, as one leading commentator put it: "In all cases the law of rape protects the woman's discretion by proscribing coitus contrary to her wishes."[53] Not exactly. As discussed in the preceding section, the law does not protect the woman from "coitus contrary to her wishes" when there is no "force." Secondly, the definition of nonconsent requires victims of rape, unlike victims of any other crime, to demonstrate their "wishes" through physical resistance.

A 1906 Wisconsin case, *Brown v. State,* provides an example of the classic definition of nonconsent in rape as it was applied for most of this century. In a modified form, it continues to apply in some courts and jurisdictions. The victim in *Brown,* a sixteen-year-old (and a virgin), was a neighbor of the accused. She testified at trial that on a walk across the fields to her grandmother's home, she greeted the accused. He at once seized her, tripped her to the ground, and forced himself upon her. "I tried as hard as I could to get away. I was trying all the time to get away just as hard as I could. I was trying to get up; I pulled at the grass; I screamed as hard as I could, and he told me to shut up, and I didn't, and then he held his hand on my mouth until I was almost strangled."[54] Whenever he removed his hand from her mouth she repeated her screams. The jury found the defendant guilty of rape.

On appeal, the Supreme Court of Wisconsin did not reverse Brown's conviction on the ground that the force used was insufficient to constitute rape. Nor did the court conclude that the defendant lacked the necessary *mens rea* for rape. Rather, the court reversed the conviction on the ground that the victim had not adequately demonstrated her nonconsent:

> Not only must there be entire absence of mental consent or assent, but there must be the most vehement exercise of every physical means or faculty within the woman's

power to resist the penetration of her person, and this must be shown to persist until the offense is consummated.[55]

Here, the victim failed to meet that standard: She only once said "let me go", her screams were considered "inarticulate", and her failure to actually "resist," to use her "hands and limbs and pelvic muscles"—obstacles which the court noted that "medical writers insist . . . are practically insuperable"—justified reversal of the conviction.[56] Indeed, the court noted that "when one pauses to reflect upon the terrific resistance which the determined woman should make," the victim's absence of bruises and torn clothing was "well-nigh incredible."[57]

Brown is almost eighty years old. But the problem it illustrates is not merely of historical interest. Virtually every jurisdiction has eliminated the requirement of "utmost resistance" to establish nonconsent. But by statute and inpractice, many courts continue to inquire into the victim's "earnest resistance" to establish that she did not consent to intercourse.

The 1981 case of *State v. Lima*[58] is, like the *Rusk* case discussed in the preceding section, an example of the sort of rape case that is causing concern and division in the appeals courts today. As in *Rusk*, the intermediate and highest appeals courts took different views of what was acknowledged to be a difficult case.

Lima, like *Brown*, involved an alleged rape in an open field involving no weapons and two individuals who knew each other. In *Lima*, the defendant had agreed to give his wife's fourteen-year-old cousin a ride home and stopped at a park on the way. Once there, he pinned her shoulder to the ground with his left hand and moved his right hand inside of her blouse to her breast. When she told him to remove his hand, he told her to "shut up" and began to unbutton her shorts. She protested, "Willy, why are you doing this to me, you're my cousin," and began to cry.

Both the court of appeals and the supreme court viewed the key issue in *Lima* as whether, on these facts, the prosecution had established the "earnest resistance" of the victim required by Hawaii law. The court of appeals answered the question in the negative, because the "only resistance shown by the record are the victim's pleas to appellant to stop and an attempt to push appellant off of her."[59] In reversing, the Supreme Court of Hawaii made much of this "push" in its interpretation of nonconsent, much as the Maryland court in *Rusk* emphasized the light choking/heavy caresses in its interpretation of force. The court affirmed the conviction on the ground that the victim "did not simply lie supine and unresisting while the respondent had his way with her." Thus, it could not be said, as a matter of law, that "the complainant here did not exhibit a 'genuine physical effort' to resist."[60] Presumably, in Hawaii, to say no, cry, and then "simply lie supine and unresisting while [a man] ha[s] his way" is to consent to sex.

Hawaii is not unique in holding that a victim must do more than say no, at least in the absence of deadly force. In *Goldberg v. State*, where the defendant brought a would-be modeling prospect to his fictitious and deserted "temporary studio," his conviction of rape was reversed both on the ground that the force used was insufficient and on the ground that the victim had failed to offer "real resistance." On the latter point, the court drew a bright line between verbal and physical resistance: "It is true that she *told* the appellant she 'didn't want to do that [stuff].' But the resistance that must be shown involves not merely verbal but *physical* resistance 'to the extent of her ability at the time.'"[61]

No similar effort is required of victims of other crimes for which consent is a defense.

In trespass, for example, the posting of a sign or the offering of verbal warnings generally suffices to meet the victim's burden of nonconsent; indeed, under the Model Penal Code, the offense of trespass is aggravated where a defendant is verbally warned to desist and fails to do so. A defendant's claim that the signs and the warnings were not meant to exclude him normally goes to his *mens rea* in committing the act, not to the existence of consent.

In robbery, claims that the victim cooperated with the taking of the money or eased the way, and thus consented, have generally been unsuccessful. Only where the owner of the property actively participates in planning and committing the theft will consent be found. Mere "passive submission" or "passive assent" does not amount to consent[62]— except in the law of rape.

That the law puts a special burden on the rape victim to prove through her actions her nonconsent (or at least to account for why her actions did not demonstrate "nonconsent"), while imposing no similar burden on the victim of trespass, battery, or robbery, cannot be explained by the oft-observed fact that consensual sex is part of everyday life. Visiting (trespass with consent) is equally everyday, as is philanthropy (robbery with consent), and surgery (battery with consent). Instinctively, we may think it is easier in those cases to tell the difference between consent and nonconsent. But if so, it is only because we are willing to presume that men are entitled to access to women's bodies (as opposed to their houses or their wallets), at least if they know them, and to accept male force in potentially "consensual" sexual relations.

Were the purpose of the consent requirement really to afford autonomy to women, there is no reason why a simple but clearly stated "no" would not suffice to signify nonconsent. Viewing women as autonomous human beings would mean treating them as persons who know what they want and mean what they say. A woman who wanted sex would say yes; a woman who did not would say no; and those verbal signals would be respected.

From a woman's point of view, the danger in this position is that many women who say "yes" are not in fact choosing freely but are submitting because they feel a lack of power to say "no." From some men's point of view, the problem is that some women who say "no" would be willing to say "yes," or at least to "go along," if properly pressured. The "no means yes" philosophy, from this perspective, affords sexual enjoyment to those women who desire it but will not say so—at the cost of violating the integrity of all those women who say "no" and mean it.

A system of law that has traditionally celebrated female chastity and frowned upon sex outside of marriage might be expected to err on the side of less sex and to presume nonconsent in the absence of evidence to the contrary. But if ours has now become a society in which women have been "liberated" to say yes, that provides all the more reason—if more were needed—to respect a no. If the stigma attached to saying yes has been eliminated, then so have the grounds for claiming that no means yes. That we treat women in sexual encounters more like spectators at sporting events (where consent is presumed) than like owners of property (who are merely required to post a sign or verbally communicate nonassent) is only partly explained by the fact that rape is a more serious offense than trespass. It also reflects a view of women as lacking in autonomy, if not integrity, and secures the priority of men's sexual satisfaction.

In the 1950s and 1960s, the leading law journals in this country provided detailed explanations of why women could not be relief upon to know what they wanted or mean what they said; how it was that many women enjoyed physical struggle as a sexual stimulant; and how unfair it would be to punish men who realized that "no" means "yes," only to have their ambivalent partners lie after the fact.[63] According to a student author published in the *Stanford Law Review:*

> Although a woman may desire sexual intercourse, it is customary for her to say, "no, no, no" (although meaning "yes, yes, yes") and to expect the male to be the aggressor. . . . It is always difficult in rape cases to determine whether the female really meant "no.". . . The problem of determining what the female "really meant" is compounded when, in fact, the female had no clearly determined attitude—that is, her attitude was one of ambivalence. Slovenko explains that often a woman faces a "trilemma"; she is faced with a choice among being a prude, a tease, or an "easy lay." Furthermore a woman may note a man's brutal nature and be attracted to him rather than repulsed.[64]

In order to remedy these problems, the author concluded that the resistance standard must be "high enough to assure that the resistance is unfeigned and to indicate with some degree of certainty that the woman's attitude was not one of ambivalence or unconscious compliance and that her complaints do not result from moralistic afterthoughts," but must be "low enough to make death or serious bodily injury an *unlikely outcome* of the event."[65] That death or serious bodily injury remains a possible result of ignoring a woman's words is apparently not too great a cost to pay.

Perhaps the most influential of all such commentary was the often and still-cited *Yale Law Journal* Note on what women want.[66] Relying on Freud, the author pointed out that it is not simply that women lie, although there is an "unusual inducement to malicious or psychopathic accusation inherent in the sexual nature of the crime." Even the "normal girl" is a confused and ambivalent character when it comes to sex. Her behavior is not always an accurate guide to her true desires; it may suggest resistance when in fact the woman is enjoying the physical struggle:

> When her behavior looks like resistance although her attitude is one of consent, injustice may be done the man by the woman's subsequent accusation. Many women, for example, require as part of preliminary "love play" aggressive overtures by the man. Often their erotic pleasure may be enhanced by, or even depend upon, an accompanying physical struggle. The "love bite" is a common, if mild, sign of the aggressive component in the sex act. And the tangible signs of struggle may survive to support a subsequent accusation by the woman.[67]

And if women are ambivalent toward sex, it follows that it would be unfair to punish the man who was not acting entirely against her wishes:

> A woman's need for sexual satisfaction may lead to the unconscious desire for forceful penetration, the coercion serving neatly to avoid the guilt feelings which might arise after willing participation. . . .
>
> Where such an attitude of ambivalence exists, the woman may, nonetheless, exhibit behavior which would lead the factfinder to conclude that she opposed the act. To illustrate. . . . [T]he anxiety resulting from this conflict of needs may cause her to flee from the situation of discomfort, either physically by running away, or symbolically by retreating to such infantile behavior as crying. The scratches, flight, and crying constitute admissible and compelling evidence of non-consent. But the conclusion of rape in this situation may be inconsistent with the meaning of the consent standard and unjust to the man. . . . [F]airness to the male suggests a conclusion of not guilty, despite signs of aggression, if his act was not contrary to the woman's formulated wishes.[68]

In short, the problem is not only that some women lie but that many women do not in fact know what they want, or mean what they say—at least when they say no. And the presence of force does not even prove rape, because many women enjoy and depend on force. According to this view, insisting that women do more than simply say no to sex is an essential means of protecting the man who exercises his judgment to ignore a woman's words of protestation.

◊   ◊   ◊

IV. Conclusion

The conduct that one might think of as "rape" ranges from the armed stranger who breaks into a woman's home to the date she invites in who takes silence for assent. In between are literally hundreds of variations: The man may be a stranger, but he may not be armed; he may be armed, but he may not be a stranger; he may be an almost, rather than a perfect, stranger—a man who gave her a ride or introduced himself through a ruse; she may say yes, but only because he threatens to expose her to the police or the welfare authorities; she may say no, but he may ignore her words.

In 1985, the woman raped at gunpoint by the intruding stranger should find most of the legal obstacles to her complaint removed. That was not always so: As recently as ten years ago, she might well have faced a corroboration requirement, a cautionary instruction, a fresh complaint rule, and a searing cross-examination about her sexual past to determine whether she had nonetheless consented to sex. In practice, she may still encounter some of these obstacles, but to the extent that the law communicates any clear message, it is likely to be that she was raped.

But most rapes do not as purely fit the traditional model, and most victims do not fare as well. Cases involving men met in bars (*Rusk*) or at work (*Goldberg*) or in airports (*Evans*), let alone cases involving ex-boyfriends (*Alston*), still lead some appellate courts to enforce the most traditional views of women in the context of the less traditional rape. And in the system, considerations of prior relationship and the circumstances of the initial encounter, as well as force and resistance and corroboration, seem to reflect a similarly grounded if not so clearly stated view of the limits of rape law.

In thinking about rape, it is not as difficult to decide which rapes are more serious or which rapists deserving of more punishment: Weapons, injury, and intent—the traditional grading criteria of the criminal law—are all justifiable answers to these questions. Most jurisdictions that have reformed their rape laws in the last ten years have focused on creating degrees of rape—aggravated and unaggravated—based on some combination of the presence of weapons and injury. While *mens rea* or mistake needs to be addressed more clearly in some rape laws, and bodily injury more carefully defined in others, these are essentially problems of draftsmanship which are hardly insurmountable.

The more difficult problem comes in understanding and defining the threshold for liability—where we draw the line between criminal sex and seduction. Every statute still uses some combination of "force," "threats," and "consent" to define the crime. But in giving meaning to those terms at the threshold of liability, the law of rape must confront the powerful norms of male aggressiveness and female passivity which continue to be adhered to by many men and women in our society.

The law did not invent the "no means yes" philosophy. Women as well as men have viewed male aggressiveness as desirable and forced sex as an expression of love, women as well as men have been taught and have come to believe that when a woman "encourages" a man, he is entitled to sexual satisfaction. From the sociological surveys to prime time television, one can find ample support in society and culture for even the most oppressive views of women and the most expansive notions of seduction enforced by the most traditional judges.

But the evidence is not entirely one sided. For every prime time series celebrating forced sex, there seems to be another true confession story in a popular magazine detailing the facts of a date rape and calling it "rape." College men and women may think that the typical male is forward and primarily interested in sex, but they no longer conclude that he is the desirable man. The old sex manuals may have lauded male sexual responses as automatic and uncontrollable, but some of the newer ones no longer see men as machines and even advocate sensitivity as seductive.

We live, in short, in a time of changing sexual mores—and we are likely to for some time to come. In such times, the law can cling to the past or help move us into the future. We can continue to enforce the most traditional views of male aggressiveness and female passivity, continue to adhere to the "no means yes" philosophy and to the broadest understanding of seduction, until and unless change overwhelms us. That is not a neutral course, however; in taking it, the law (judges, legislators, or prosecutors) not only reflects (a part of) society but legitimates and reenforces those views.

Or we can use the law to move forward. It may be impossible—and even unwise—to try to use the criminal law to change the way people think, to push progress to the ideal. But recognition of the limits of the criminal sanction need not be taken as a justification for the status quo. Faced with a choice between reenforcing the old and fueling the new in a world of changing norms, it is not necessarily more legitimate or neutral to choose the old. There are lines to be drawn short of the ideal: The challenge we face in thinking about rape is to use the power and legitimacy of law to reinforce what is best, not what is worst, in our changing sexual mores.

In the late eighteenth and early nineteenth centuries, the judges of England waged a successful campaign against duelling. While "the attitude of the law" was clear that killing in a duel was murder, the problem was that for some, accepting a challenge remained a matter of "honour," and juries would therefore not convict. "Some change in the public attitude toward duelling, coupled with the energy of judges in directing juries in strong terms, eventually brought about convictions, and it was not necessary to hang many gentlemen of quality before the understanding became general that duelling was not required by the code of honour."[69]

There has been "some change in the public attitude" about the demands of manhood in heterosexual relations, as in duelling. If the "attitude of the law" is made clearer—and that is, in essence, what this chapter is about—then it may not be necessary to prosecute too many "gentlemen of quality" before the understanding becomes general that manly honor need not be inconsistent with female autonomy.

In a better world, I believe that men and women would not presume either consent or nonconsent. They would ask, and be certain. There is nothing unromantic about showing the kind of respect for another person that demands that you know for sure before engaging in intimate contact. In a better world, women who said yes would be saying so from a position of equality, or at least sufficient power to say no. In a better world, fewer women would bargain with sex because they had nothing else to bargain with; they would be in at least as good a position to reject demands for sexual access as men are to reject demands for money.

If we are not at the point where it is appropriate for the law to presume nonconsent from silence, and the reactions I have received to this chapter suggest that we are not, then at least we should be at the point where it is legitimate to punish the man who ignores a woman's explicit words of protestations. I am quite certain that many women who say yes—whether on dates or on the job—would say no if they could; I have no doubt that women's silence is sometimes the product not of passion and desire but of pressure and pain. But at the very least the criminal law ought to say clearly that women who actually say no must be respected as meaning it; that nonconsent means saying no; that men who proceed nonetheless, claiming that they thought no meant yes, have acted unreasonably and unlawfully.

So, too, for threats of harm short of physical injury and for deception and false pretenses as methods of seduction. The powerlessness of women and the value of bodily integrity are great enough to argue that women deserve more comprehensive protection for their bodies than the laws of extortion or fraud provide for money. But if going so far seems too complicated and fraught with difficulty, as it does to many, then we need not. For the present, it would be a significant improvement if the law of rape in any state prohibited exactly the same threats as that state's law of extortion and exactly the same deceptions as that state's law of false pretenses or fraud.[70]

In short, I am arguing that "consent" should be defined so that "no means no." And the "force" or "coercion" that negates consent ought be defined to include extortionate threats and deceptions of material fact. As for *mens rea,* unreasonableness as to consent, understood to mean ignoring a woman's words, should be sufficient for liability: Reasonable men should be held to know that no means no, and unreasonable mistakes, no matter how honestly claimed, should not exculpate. Thus, the threshold of liability—whether phrased in terms of "consent," "force" or "coercion," or some combination of the three, should be understood to include at least those nontraditional rapes where the woman says no or submits only in response to lies or threats which would be prohibited were money sought instead.[71] The crime I have described would be a lesser offense than the aggravated rape in which life is threatened or bodily injury inflicted, but it is, in my judgment, "rape." One could, I suppose, claim that as we move from such violent rapes to "just" coerced or nonconsensual sex, we are moving away from a crime of violence toward something else. But what makes the violent rape different—and more serious—than an aggravated assault is the injury to personal integrity involved in forced sex. That same injury is the reason that forced sex should be a crime even when there is no weapon or no beating. In a very real sense, what does make rape different from other crimes, at every level of the offense, is that rape is about sex and sexual violation. Were the essence of the crime the use of the gun or the knife or the threat, we wouldn't need—and wouldn't have—a separate crime.

Conduct is labeled as criminal "to announce to society that these actions are not to be done and to secure that fewer of them are done."[72] As a matter of principle, we should be ready to announce to society our condemnation of coerced and nonconsensual sex and to secure that we have less of it. The message of the substantive law to men, and to women, should be made clear.

That does not mean that this crime will, or should, be easy to prove. The constitutional requirement of proof beyond a reasonable doubt may well be difficult to meet in cases where guilt turns on whose account is credited as to what was said. If the jury is in doubt, it should acquit. If the judge is uncertain, he should dismiss.

The message of the substantive law must be distinguished from the constitutional standards of proof. In this as in every criminal case, a jury must be told to acquit if it is in doubt. The requirement of proof beyond a reasonable doubt rests on the premise that it is better that ten guilty should go free than that one innocent man should be punished. But if we should acquit ten, let us be clear that the we are acquitting them not because they have an entitlement to ignore a woman's words, not because what they allegedly did was right or macho or manly, but because we live in a system that errs on the side of freeing the guilty.

Notes

My thanks to the many people who provided comments, criticism, support and friendship along the way: Clare Dalton, Alan Dershowitz, Martha Field, Phil Heymann, John Kaplan, Marty Kaplan, Virginia Kerr, Sylvia Law, Dan Meltzer, Martha Minow, Charlie Nesson, Richard Parker, Michael Smith, Larry Tribe, Nancy Tompkins, Jim Vorenberg, Lloyd Weinreb, and Zipporah Wiseman. My thanks as well to all of my students in Gender and the Criminal Law, who have taught me as much as I taught them. Finally, my thanks to the best friend and colleague anyone could have, Kathleen M. Sullivan.

1. *See, e.g.,* S. Brownmiller, Against Our Will: Men, Women and Rape (1975); N. Gager & C. Schurr, Sexual Assault: *CONFRONTING* Rape in America (1976); A. Medea & K. Thompson, Against Rape (1974); D. Russell, The Politics of Rape: The Victim's Perspective (1975); Griffin, *Rape: The All American Crime,* Ramparts, September 1971, at 26–36; MacKinnon, *Feminism, Marxism, Method, and the State,* 8 Signs 635 (1983).

2. *See e.g.,* Berger, *Man's Trial, Woman's Tribulation: Rape Cases in the Courtroom,* 77 Colum. L. Rev. 1 (1977); Note, *Recent Statutory Developments in the Definition of Forcible Rape, 61 Va.* L. Rev. 1500 (1975). Note, *The Rape Corroboration Requirement: Repeal not Reform,* 81 Yale L.J. 1365 (1972) Comment, *Towards a Consent Standard in the Law of Rape,* 43 U. Chi. L. Rev. 613 (1976).

3. For instance, "major" articles in the late nineteenth and early twentieth century discussed the problems of consent in the law of rape. But these articles are not concerned with the consent of adult, competent women: Rather, what fascinated Professors Beale and Puttkammer, the leading authors, was whether there is "consent" when a snake oil salesman convinces a woman that he is really her husband and that sex is really a physical examination of her wooden leg. I am kidding, but just a very little. *See* Beale, *Consent in the Criminal Law,* 8 Harv. L. Rev. 317 (1895); Puttkammer, *Consent in Rape,* 19 Ill. L. Rev. 410 (1925). Freud has exercised a major influence as well; although he did not invent the fear of lying women complainants, he gave the fear a solid foundation and an aura of reasoned elaboration that is evidenced in the law review writings of the 1950's and 1960's. *See, e.g.,* Note, *Corroborating Charges of Rape,* 67 Colum. L. Rev. 1137 (1967); Note, *The Resistance Standard in Rape Legislation,* 18 Stan. L. Rev. 680 (1966); Note, *Forcible and Statutory Rape: An Exploration of the Operation and Objectives of the Consent Standard,* 62 Yale L.J. 55 (1952).

4. The cases I have chosen to examine date primarily from the last decade; they state rules which continue to have force. While I am far more interested in slaying real dragons than straw men, these cases are admittedly unrepresentative in the same way that all appellate cases are unrepresentative of the criminal justice system. The overwhelming majority of all rape cases—and certainly most of the closest and most difficult among them—never reach the appellate courts or result in written opinions. They are dismissed or plea bargained.

5. *See, e.g.,* Berger at 6–11; S. Katz & M. Mazur, Understanding THE Rape Victim 199 (1979); Note, *The Victim in a Forcible Rape Case: A Feminist View,* 11 Am. Crim. L. Rev. 335 (1973).

6. I.M. HALE. THE H*ISTORY OF THE* PLEAS OF THE CROWN 635 (1778). This statement is the usual basis for the "cautionary" instructions traditionally given in rape cases.

7. State v. Reed, 479 A.2d 1291, 1296 (Me. 1984).

8. Commonwealth v. Williams, 294 Pa. Super. 93, 99–100, 439 A.2d 765, 769 (1982).

9. Commonwealth v. Sherry, 437 N.E.2d 224, 386 Mass. 682 (1982).

10. Commonwealth v. Grant, 391 Mass. 645, 464 N.E.2d 33 (1984).

11. In Commonwealth v. Lefkowitz, 20 Mass. App. Ct. 513, 481 N.E.2d 227, 230, *review denied,* 396 Mass. 1103, 485 N.E.2d 224 (1985).

12. *See, e.g.,* King v. State, 210 Tenn. 150, 158, 357 S.W.2d 42, 45 (1962); Moss v. State, 208 Miss. 531, 536, 45 So. 2d 125, 126 (1950); Brown v. State, 127 Wis. 193, 199, 106 N.W. 536, 538 (1906); People v. Dohring, 59 N.Y. 374, 386 (1874).

13. *See, e.g.,* Satterwhite v. Commonwealth, 201 Va. 478, 482, 111 S.E.2d 820, 823 (1960); Goldberg v. State, 41 Md. App. 58, 68, 395 A.2d 1213, 1218–19 (1979); State v. Lima, 64 Hawaii 470, 476–77, 643 P.2d, 536, 540 (1982).

14. *See, e.g.,* Government of the Virgin Islands v. John, 447 F.2d 69 (3d Cir. 1971) (holding victim's reputation for chastity relevant to consent); Packineau v. United States, 202 F.2d 681, 687.

15. State v. Rusk, 289 Md. 230, 256, 424 A.2d 720, 733 (1981) (Cole, J., dissenting).

16. *See, e.g.,* Goldberg v. State, 41 Md. App. 58, 68, 395 A.2d 1213 (1979); *see also* State v. Lima, 64 Hawaii 470, 643 P.2d 536 (1982).

17. Director of Pub. Prosecutions v. Morgan, 1976 A.C. 182, 2 All E.R. 347, [1975] 2 W.L.R. 913 (H.L.).

18. *Id.* at 205, [1975] 2 All E.R. at 354.

19. Mr. Morgan and his three codefendants had been convicted of the rape of Mr. Morgan's wife. The four men had been drinking together and when they failed in their efforts to "find some women," Mr. Morgan invited the three home to have intercourse with his wife. According to the three codefendants, Morgan told them not to be surprised if his wife struggled, since she was "kinky" and this was the only way she could get "turned on." All four were convicted, Mr. Morgan for aiding and abetting, and their convictions had been affirmed by the court of appeals. *Id.* at 182, 206 [1975] 2 All E.R. at 347, 355.

20. The Sexual Offences (Amendment) Act, § 1(1976). *See generally* Smith, *The Heilbron Report,* 1976 CRIM. L. REV. 97, 98–105.

21. The most striking difference between that case, Regina v. Cogan, 2 All E.R. 1059, [1975] 3 W.L.R. 316 (C.A.), and *Morgan* is the number of "buddies" involved. In the law of rape, numbers often assume major significance in a court's approach to the facts.

22. Professor Glanville Williams in a letter to THE TIMES (London), May 8, 1975, at 15, col. 6.

23. MODEL PENAL CODE § 2.02 comment at 126–27 (Tent. Draft No. 4, 1955). The Model Penal Code commentators thus recognized the deterrence rationale of negligence liability in justifying its inclusion as a potential basis for criminal liability (albeit for a limited number of crimes, not including rape).

24. 164 U.S. 644 (1897) at 647.

25. *Id.* at 647–48.

26. *See* R. PERKINS & R. BOYCE CRIMINAL LAW 211 (3d ed. 1982).

27. 310 N.C. 399, 312 S.E.2d 470 (1984), at 271.

28. *Id.* at 401–03, 312 S.E.2d at 471–73.

29. 310 N.C. at 408, 312 S.E. 2d at 475.

30. *Id.* at 408, 312 S.E.2d at 476.

31. *Id.*

32. *Id.* at 409, 312 S.E.2d at 476 (emphasis omitted).

33. State v. Lester, 70 N.C. App. 757, 321 S.E.2d 166 (1984), *aff'd,* 313 N.C. 595, 330 S.E.2d 205 (1985).

34. *Id.* at 761, 321 S.E.2d at 168 (emphasis in original).

35. Commonwealth v. Biggs, 320 Pa. Super. 265, 267, 467 A.2d 31, 32 (1983).

36. *Id.* at 268, 467 A.2d at 32 (emphasis in original).

37. Rusk v. State, 43 Md. App. 476, 478–79, 406 A.2d 624, 626 (1979) (en banc), *rev'd,* 289 Md. 230, 424 A.2d 720 (1981).

38. State v. Rusk, 289 Md. 230, 424 A.2d 720 (1981).

39. 43 Md. App. at 482, 406 A.2d at 627.

40. 289 Md. at 255, 424 A.2d at 733 (Cole, J., dissenting).

41. 289 Md. at 244, 424 A.2d at 727 (footnote omitted).

42. *Id.* at 246–47, 424 A.2d at 728 (emphasis added). On facts substantially similar to those in *Rusk,* the Wyoming Supreme Court in 1973 reversed a conviction entered by a trial judge sitting without a jury on the ground that the judge had failed to consider the reasonableness of the victim's fear. In Gonzales v. State, 516 P.2d 592 (Wyo. 1973), as in *Rusk,* the victim and the defendant met in a bar, and he requested a ride home. The victim refused, but the defendant got into the car anyway. After unsuccessfully refusing him again, she started driving; he asked her to turn down a road and, according to the supreme court:

> He asked her to stop "to go to the bathroom" and took the keys out of the ignition, telling her she would not drive off and leave him. She stayed in the car when he "went to the bathroom" and made no attempt to leave. When he returned he told her he was going to rape her and she kept trying to talk him out of it. He told her he was getting mad at her and then put his fist against her face and said, "I'm going to do it. You can have it one way or the other."

Id. at 593. The trial judge, in finding Mr. Gonzalez guilty of rape, reasoned that a victim "does not have to subject herself to a beating, knifing, or anything of that nature. As long as she is convinced something of a more serious nature will happen, she is then given by law the right to submit." *Id.* at 594 (quoting unreported trial court opinion). Not, however, according to the Wyoming Supreme Court, which found the trial judge's standard to be in error "because it would place the determination solely in the judgement of the prosecutrix and omit the necessary element of a reasonable apprehension and reasonable ground for such fear; and the reasonableness must rest with the fact finder." *Id.*

What is stunning about *Gonzalez* is not so much the Wyoming court's statement of the proper standard—it very much resembles that of the other courts noted here—as the fact that the court thought application of that standard to these facts could conceivably lead to a different verdict. The error, in the court's view, was far from harmless: "The evidence of the nature and sufficiency of the threat to justify nonresistance is far from overwhelming in this case." *Id.* The reasonable woman in Wyoming, apparently, is not simply a man, but Superman.

43. *See, e.g.,* People v. Flores, 62 Cal. App. 2d 700, 703, 145 P.2d 318, 320 (Dist. Ct. App. 1944) ("A threat may be expressed by acts and conduct as well as by words."); Hazel v. State, 221 Md. 464, 469, 157 A.2d 922, 925 (1960) ("acts and threats" may create in victim's mind real apprehension of imminent bodily harm); State v. Lewis, 96 Idaho 743, 760, 536 P.2d 738, 745 (1975) ("Threats or force can come in forms other than verbalized threats or displays of weaponry.").

44. 41 Md. App. 58, 395 A.2d 1213 (Ct. Spec. App. 1979).

45. *Id.* at 69, 395 A.2d at 1219.

46. *Id.* (citation omitted).

47. 85 Misc. 2d 1088, 379 N.Y.S.2d 912 (Sup. Ct. 1975), *aff'd,* 55 A.D. 2d 858, 390 N.Y.S.2d 768 (1976) at 917.

48. *Id.* at 1095, 379 N.Y.S.2d at 920.

49. *Id.* at 1096, 379 N.Y.S.2d at 921. Since the *Evans* decision, New York has amended its statute. Historically, New York had strictly enforced a standard of utmost resistance, which required a victim to resist "until exhausted or overpowered." People v. Dohring, 59 N.Y. 374, 386 (1874). By the time of *Evans,* the words of the law had changed to require earnest resistance; following

Evans, the New York legislature amended the statute to make clear that the earnest resistance standard was *not* to be equated with the utmost resistance requirement. 1977 N.Y. Laws ch. 692. The 1977 version, however, still required "reasonable" earnest resistance. *Id.* § 2.

In 1982, the New York legislature again amended the law. 1982 N.Y. Laws ch. 560. The new law prohibits the use of actual physical force or "a threat, express or implied, which places a person in fear of immediate death or physical injury to himself, herself or another person, or in fear that he, she or another person will immediately be kidnapped." N.Y. Penal Law § 130.000(8) (Consol. 1984). *See generally* Note, *Elimination of the Resistance Requirement and Other Rape Law Reforms: The New York Experience,* 47 Albany L. Rev. 871, 872–74 (1983). New York law also includes a misdemeanor provision entitled "sexual misconduct," which occurs when a male "engages in sexual intercourse with a female without her consent." N.Y. Penal Law § 130.20(1) (Consol. 1984).

Many states continue to follow New York's earlier definition of "forcible compulsion," and the requirement of "actual physical force" or a threat which *the court* understands to place the victim in fear may continue to protect con-men like Mr. Evans, although it need not.

50. This is precisely the standard applied to men who engage in theft by false pretenses; gullibility is no defense if the defendant's acts were intended to prey on that gullibility. *See* W. LaFave & A. Scott, Criminal Law 669 (1972); Clarke v. People, 64 Colo. 164, 171 P. 69 (1918); State v. Foot, 100 Mont. 33, 48 P.2d 1113 (1935).

51. *See* Hazel v. State, 221 Md. 464, 469, 157 A.2d 922, 925 (1960).

52. Nor am I arguing that these cases must of necessity be considered in the same category as first-degree, armed and brutal rape. I am more than willing to treat them as a lesser degree of "rape" and to impose lighter punishment in the same way that the unarmed robber, or the blackmailer, is treated as a less serious offender than the one who uses a deadly weapon in a robbery.

53. Note, *Forcible and Statutory Rape,* at 71; *see also* Model Penal Code § 213.1 comment 4, at 301 (1980).

54. 127 Wis. at 196, 106 N.W. at 537.

55. *Id.* at 199, 106 N.W. at 538.

56. *Id.* at 199–200, 106 N.W. at 538. According to the court, a woman is equipped to interpose most effective obstacles by means of hands and limbs and pelvic muscles. Indeed, medical writers insist that these obstacles are practically insuperable in absence of more than the usual relative disproportion of age and strength between man and woman, though no such impossibility is recognized as a rule of law.

Id. The latter qualification is, by the court's own opinion and holding, open to question. The view that an unwilling woman physically could not be raped was not limited to Wisconsin or to the nineteenth century. It provided support for insisting that the least women should do was resist to the utmost. *See* East, *Sexual Offenders—A British View,* 55 Yale L.J. 527, 543 (1946).

57. 127 Wis. at 201, 106 N.W. at 539.

58. 2 Hawaii App. 19, 624 P.2d 1374 (1981), *rev'd,* 64 Hawaii 470, 643 P.2d 536 (1982).

59. 2 Hawaii App. at 22, 624 P.2d at 1377.

60. 643 P.2d at 541. *See also State v. Jones:*

"Earnest resistance" . . . is a relative term and whether or not the statutory requirement was satisfied must be measured by the circumstances surrounding the alleged assault. Among the factors to be considered are the relative strength of the parties, the age of the female, her physical and mental condition, and the nature and degree of the force used by the assailant. Resistance may appear to be useless, and may eventually prove to be unavailing, but *there must have been a genuine physical effort on the part of the complainant to discourage and to prevent her assailant from accomplishing his intended purpose.*

62 Hawaii 572, 574, 617 P.2d 1214, 1217 (1980) (citation omitted) (emphasis added).

61. 41 Md. App. at 68, 395 A.2d at 1219 (citation omitted). *See also* Hazel v. State, 221 Md. 464, 469–70, 157 A.2d 922, 925 (1960):

The authorities are by no means in accord as to what degree of resistance is necessary to establish the absence of consent. However, the generally accepted doctrine seems to be that a female—who was conscious and possessed of her natural, mental and physical powers when the attack took place—must have resisted to the extent of her ability at the time, unless it appears that she was overcome by numbers or was so terrified by threats as to overpower her will to resist.

62. *See* Carnes v. State, 134 Tex. Crim. 8, 10, 113 S.W.2d 542, 544 (Tex. Crim. App. 1938); Alford v. Commonwealth, 240 Ky. 513, 42 S.W.2d 711, 712–13 (Ct. App. 1931) People v. Teicher, 52 N.Y.2d 638, 649, 439 N.Y.S.2d 846, 851, 422 N.E.2d 506, 511 (1981).

63. Similar concerns led leading commentators to advocate special rules of proof in rape cases. Professor Wigmore, for example, thought all women rape victims to be sufficiently suspect to argue that the complainant be examined by a psychiatrist and that no case go to the jury unless such an examination had been performed and the physician had testified as to her personal history and mental health. According to Professor Wigmore:

[Rape complainants'] psychic complexes are multifarious, distorted partly by inherent defects, partly by diseased derangements or abnormal instincts, partly by bad social environment, partly by temporary physiological or emotional conditions. . . . the unchaste . . . mentality finds incidental but direct expression in the narration of imaginary sex incidents of which the narrator is the heroine or the victim. On the surface the narration is straightforward and convincing.

3A J. WIGMORE, EVIDENCE § 924a, at 736 (Chadbourn rev. ed. 1970). *See also* Note, *Corroborating Charges,* at 1138:("Surely the simplest, and perhaps the most important, reason not to permit conviction for rape on the uncorroborated word of the prosecutrix is that that word is very often false.") (footnote omitted).

64. Note, *Resistance Standard,* at 682 (footnotes omitted) (quoting Slovenko, *A Panoramic Overview: Sexual Behavior and the Law,* in SEXUAL BEHAVIOR AND THE LAW 5, 51 (Slovenko ed. 1965)).

65. Note, *Resistance Standard,* at 685 (emphasis added).

66. Note, *Forcible and Statutory Rape.* This note is cited, and its influence apparent, not only in the Model Penal Code provisions adopted in the 1950s, but in the comments to them edited in the 1970s and published in 1980.

67. Note, *Forcible and Statutory Rape,* a at 66 (footnotes omitted).

68. *Id.* at 67–68 (footnotes omitted).

69. Williams, *Consent and Public Policy,* 9 CRIM. L. REV. 74, 154 (1962) (pts. 1 & 2); at 77.

70. To the difficult hypothetical, there is thus an easy answer: Resolve it as if money were involved, and I will gladly apply that resolution in the context of rape. Drawing lines between bargains and threats is not always easy. Deciding which misstatements are material is not always automatic. But I have never heard either problem offered as a reason for the repeal of the laws against blackmail, extortion, deception, or false pretenses. And in practice, there are likely to be more than enough easy cases for victims, prosecutors, and judges who are so inclined.

71. That the problem is more one of understanding than of draftsmanship is amply demonstrated by the statute in the state of Washington. In Washington, rape in the third degree, a felony punishable by up to five years imprisonment, occurs where a persons engage in sexual intercourse:

(a) Where the victim did not consent . . . to sexual intercourse with the perpetrator and such lack of consent was clearly expressed by the victim's words or conduct, or (b) Where there is a threat of substantial unlawful harm to property rights of the victim.

WASH. REV. CODE ANN. § 9A.44.050 (West. Supp. 1986). The provision as to threats, limited as it is to unlawful action and to property rights, is potentially narrower than the Model Penal Code's crime of gross sexual imposition and certainly narrower than traditional prohibitions of extortion.

The provision as to consent, on the other hand, is potentially quite broad; it could be read to criminalize all those cases where force is difficult to prove in traditional terms but the woman said no. That is how I would read it. Others read it differently. Professor Loh of the University of Washington, perhaps the key commentator on the Washington rape statute, and certainly the expert on its practical impact, reads this provision as adding absolutely nothing to a statute which, in the first two degrees of the offense, explicitly requires force and does not mention consent: "The definitions of the first two degrees preempt the content of rape 3 and render its prosecution difficult." Loh, at 552.

72. H.L.A. HART. PUNISHMENT AND RESPONSIBILITY 152–54 (1968) at 6.

8

♦

The Criminal Justice System's Response to Battering: Understanding the Problem, Forging the Solutions

KATHLEEN WAITS

I. Introduction

Women have been battered for centuries, but only recently has America been willing to acknowledge and address the plight of abuse victims. During the past fifteen years there have been significant changes in public perceptions of the battered woman and her abusive mate. The legal system's response to wife abuse has also significantly advanced. These changes in the legal system have come from two sources. First, the written law is different: The batterer's actions, once condoned by the law, are now largely condemned. Second, both old and new laws are being implemented more effectively, as police officers, prosecutors, and judges have altered their attitudes and responses toward domestic violence.

Despite a decade of progress, much work remains to be done to eradicate this personal and social tragedy. Misconceptions about the nature of the battering relationship are still prevalent in society and among law enforcement officials. The law's dedication to the elimination of the problem is still often halfhearted, and its reaction often misguided.

Powerful social forces permit and even encourage abuse. These forces continue to influence legal institutions and personnel and undermine the legal system's desire and ability to combat the problem. Even if these forces were purged from the legal system, they would probably continue to operate in society at large. As long as social forces and attitudes condone battering, the legal system alone can never provide a complete solution to battering. Nevertheless, the law, especially the criminal law, can play a critical role in reducing domestic violence.

This chapter will focus on the appropriate criminal justice response to battering. Part II describes the nature of the problem of wife beating. It first discusses the extent of abuse in America to demonstrate the seriousness of the problem and the urgent need for solutions. The remainder of Part II looks at the issue on a more individual basis. It examines the battered woman, the batterer, the battering relationship, and the effects of abuse on the couple's children. An understanding of the participants and their relationship, unencumbered by the many myths that surround battering, is essential to creating effective legal remedies.

Part III argues that the law must take a stand against wife abuse. The arguments for legal intervention against abuse may seem obvious, since spousal assault has been a crime for over a century. Nevertheless, the legal system remains reluctant to use its powers against batterers. Rationalizations offered for this reluctance range from alleged interests in protecting family privacy to the asserted ineffectiveness of the law in dealing with the problem. This chapter rejects these rationalizations because their effect is to condone wife beating. The law is not a panacea for domestic violence, but that does not mean it can or should do nothing.

Part IV enumerates the appropriate goals of a legal program to reduce battering. This enumeration is necessary for two reasons. First, one cannot determine whether any law is desirable without considering its purported objectives. Second, the flaws in the legal system's traditional answers to abuse are largely attributable to the pursuit of incorrect goals, such as the reconciliation of the partners.

With proper goals in mind, including protecting the victim and deterring the batterer, we can proceed to evaluate the legal system's response to battering. Part V examines the present state of the law and the change necessary for an effective criminal justice response.

The first section of Part V sets out an overall approach to the problem and distinguishes between situations in which battering should and should not be treated the same as violent crimes between strangers. The remaining sections of Part V describe appropriate responses from police, prosecutors, and judges. Particular attention is devoted to the police, because as initiators of the criminal process, they play a crucial role in reducing spouse abuse. Moreover, their actions have historically been deficient, and those deficientcies exemplify defects found elsewhere in the criminal justice system.

This chapter suggests various legislative changes. Although many state have recently enacted a number of enlightened statutes directed against battering, most jurisdictions need additional legislation. Proposed statutory modifications include mandatory arrest of batterers by police, guidelines for the use of pretrial diversion of abusers to counseling, and increased sentencing of convicted abusers. Most of these proposals would be unnecessary if legal officials understood wife beating and used their discretion wisely to stop it. Unfortunately, ignorance about the nature of battering is so widespread among police, prosecutors, and judges that the legal system's response has generally been ineffective. The legislature must therefore take the lead, establish standards for these officials, and compel them to wield their power properly. If adopted, the suggested reforms would reduce domestic violence and would prevent another generation of American children from growing up believing that the marriage license is a "hitting license."

II. The Nature of the Problem

A. The Scope of Wife Abuse

It is impossible to know the extent of wife abuse in our society. For many years, the problem was largely ignored, and the available information was so incomplete and disorganized that it was functionally useless. More recently, there have been some serious efforts to compile data,[1] and the results are shocking. The battering of women is both widespread and dangerous. In any given year, at least one-tenth to one-fifth of American women are beaten by a man with whom they are intimately involved.[2] This translates into some six million battered women in America each year.[3] One woman in four will suffer abuse during the entire course of a given relationship.[4]

Violence between partners is often serious and even fatal. Five to 10 percent of women report severe beatings or use of a weapon such as a gun or knife.[5] Fatalities from abuse are all too common: The batterer may finally kill his victim;[6] she may kill him;[7] or one or the other of them may commit suicide in order to escape an unbearable situation.[8] The grim picture does not end with the damage to the couple. Domestic disputes are also time-consuming[9] and hazardous for the police.[10]

The personal and social costs of wife abuse are staggering. Further, they are perpetuated because family violence is transmitted from generation to generation. As if this were not enough, the depressing portrait presented above is, if anything, too optimistic. All experts agree that the available statistics underestimate the extent of abuse.[11] There are myriad reasons why all forms of violence between intimates including wife beating, are systematically underreported. First is the belief that what happens within the family is a private matter that should not be discussed with outsiders. Second is the taboo nature of the subject: people are often ashamed to admit that they have violated what is considered the norm of a happy, nonviolent homelife. Finally, before people can admit the existence of battering to a researcher, they must first admit it to themselves. Such an admission is difficult for both partners in an abusive relationship, who typically lie to themselves about the existence and degree of the violence.

It is important to emphasize that wife abuse is prevalent throughout our society. Recently collected data merely confirm what people working with victims have long known: Battering occurs in all social and economic groups.[12] It is a myth that abuse is a problem only among poor people and minorities. It is true that battered women who are also poor are more likely to come to the attention of governmental officials than are middle- and upper-class counterparts. However, this phenomenon is caused more by the lack of alternative resources and the intrusiveness of the welfare state than by any significantly higher incidence of violence among lower-class families.

B. Overview of the Battering Relationship

The preceding section provides ample evidence of the seriousness of the problem of wife beating. In addition, more and more citizens are asserting that the legal system must take some responsibility for punishing and preventing abuse. However, in this area, as elsewhere, the law will be effective only if it is tailored to fit the situation. In other words, before we can fashion sensible laws to deal with abuse, we must understand the people involved and the nature of their relationship.

The most important facts about battering are (1) the abused woman cannot control the batterer; (2) the violence will only cease through intervention; and (3) the sooner intervention comes after the couple's first violent incident, the better the prognosis for ending the abuse permanently and keeping the family together.[13] The first fact is a specific instance of the more general observation that external forces—the victim's behavior, job pressures, alcohol—only trigger abuse; they do not cause it. The necessity of intervention arises from the batterer's refusal to accept responsibility for his actions. Not only do abusers minimize the extent of their violence or even deny it altogether, they also blame circumstances or other people for their violent behavior. Wife beaters will change, if at all, only if they are forced to face the consequences of what they have done. The legal system can play an important role in confronting and motivating batterers.

The importance of prompt intervention is perhaps the least surprising, since it arises from the power of inertia in human relations. Once two people have established a certain behavior pattern, changing that pattern is very difficult. The longer the pattern persists, the more difficult change becomes. For this reason, couples with a long history of battering usually cannot stay together and become violence free.[14] As will be described below, both the batterer's aggression and the woman's victimization are learned responses. The longer these responses persist, the harder they are to unlearn.

Despite the horrors of the battering relationship, powerful psychological and social forces bind the abusive couple together. These forces include the cyclical nature of battering and the fact that both parties blame the victim and not the perpetrator for the violence. As a result of these forces, abused women have great difficulty taking any action, either legal or personal, against their partners. Further, batterers, using both fear and manipulation, know how to deter their victims from leaving them and are especially adept at persuading or coercing their partners, if they have left, to return and give the relationship another try.

The picture is not entirely bleak, however. With the support, encouragement, and understanding of others, many battered women have escaped their abusive situations and have rebuilt their own lives and those of their children. Some batterers have also gotten help and have ended their abuse. With increased efforts by legal personnel and others, more victims could be saved and more assailants stopped.

C. The Battered Woman—Why Does She Stay?

So many myths[15] surround the issue of wife beating that only detailed information can dispel the ignorance of policymakers and the public. A good place to start is with a portrait of the battered woman.

The most important question about the abused woman is also the most obvious: Why does she stay? Why would anyone subject herself to repeated, severe beatings? Why would anyone remain in a relationship that carries an ever-present threat of injury and even death? And why, as so often happens, would a battered woman repeatedly leave her husband, only to return again and again to face inevitable beatings?

The traditional psychiatric answer to these questions has been that the battered woman is a masochist who stays because she enjoys being beaten.[16] In modern times, people who have actually dealt with battered women emphatically reject this answer.[17] In fact, the explanation for the abused woman's behavior is far more complex and arises from a tragic combination of social and personal forces.

Certain of the victim's traits may predate the battering. For instance, the battered woman usually subscribes to traditional opinions about proper male and female roles. Even if she works outside the home, she believes that what really counts for a woman is success as a wife and mother. She takes upon herself all responsibility for the happiness of her husband and family and believes that if she just performs her wifely duties properly, all family conflict will disappear. She thinks it her duty to accommodate all her husband's demands, no matter how irrational or inconsistent, and may even believe that he has the right to "discipline" her through violence if she fails to satisfy him.[18] She is unrealistic about her relationship with the batterer because she clings to the myth that she can control his violence and prevent the battering. Thus, when he abuses her, she blames herself rather than her mate.

The battered woman's traditionalist views on sex roles also help explain her response once the pattern of violence has begun. Because she feels that the beatings are her own fault, she may deny their existence or severity, even to herself. She is also likely to be too ashamed to tell others about the abuse, including those who might help her to assess the situation objectively. Further, because she is a traditionalist, she may place a premium on keeping the family intact. She may feel that the stigma of divorce and depriving her children of their father are worse than the continuation of the abuse against her. Her fear of separation and divorce may, of course, be even greater if she is economically dependent on her husband. Even if she is not economically dependent, she will be emotionally dependent, feeling that she cannot live without "her man" or that he cannot continue without her.[19]

By the time the battered woman has been through the battering cycle a number of times, she suffers from low self-esteem. To make matters worse, the repeated traumas of the beatings have left her in a state of "learned helplessness." While she continues to take responsibility for the batterer's behavior—which she cannot control—she is unable to take responsibility for that which she *could* control, her ability to flee the relationship. She is oblivious to means of escape because her problem-solving abilities have been literally beaten out of her. She may even appear to accept her victimization passively.[20] Inside, however, she is filled with rage, not only against her abuser, but also against herself. Subconsciously, she has probably come to recognize the need for flight and is likely to blame herself for being unable to leave. Thus, a destructive psychological spiral is established: The beatings lead to lowered self-esteem and learned helplessness, which in turn make her unable to escape; her inability to escape makes her feel even more inadequate and helpless and also leaves her in a relationship which will lead to further beatings, which will further decrease her self-esteem.

In many cases, the victim sees little point in attempting to escape. She may feel that the batterer will eventually kill her regardless of whether she leaves or stays.[21] Her fears are well founded: A batterer usually becomes even more abusive if his partner makes any attempt to assert control over her life. She may have tried to leave him before, only to have him threaten violence against her or others if she did not return. A battered woman has every reason to believe that he is capable of carrying out that threat. Under such conditions, she may decide to stay, either hoping he will change or giving up hope altogether, especially if outsiders are offering her no assistance or protection.

It cannot be emphasized enough that the battered woman's learned helplessness or her other psychological problems are the results of battering and not its cause. In other words, battered women have problems because they have been battered. They are not battered because they have problems.[22]

The characteristics of the batterer and the battering relationship reinforce the battered woman's helplessness and inability to view her situation realistically. However, the pressures to remain in the abusive relationship extend beyond the couple's own relationship. The social forces that condone battering keep victims trapped in abusive relationships. In addition, friends, family, and other outsiders may exacerbate the situation by refusing to acknowledge the symptoms of abuse or by disbelieving her when she finally summons up the courage to reveal the horrible truth. These reactions may push her further into isolation and denial. Even if outsiders admit that she is being battered, they may foster her self-blame by focusing on what she has done to "provoke" her husband. They may advise her to accede to his every demand, thereby encouraging her delusion that he will stop beating her if only she does enough to please him. Other people may impair her ability to escape (already diminished because of learned helplessness) by emphasizing possible economic hardship and stigmatization rather than stressing the advantages of increased personal safety and self-respect.[23]

At the other end of the spectrum, friends and family can hurt the battered woman by being judgmental and by insisting that she leave the abusive relationship. Condemning her for failing to extricate herself is harmful rather than helpful because it increases the victim's self-hatred and her fears that she is crazy.[24] It may also drive her into greater secrecy and shame. Excess judgmentalism also runs counter to the battered woman's long-term interests. The decision of whether and when to change her life must be hers, for both moral and practical reasons. Morally, she has an adult's right of self-determination. Practically, like other human beings, she is unlikely to adhere to a decision forced on her.

The proper role of outsiders in assisting abused women thus involves a delicate middle ground. Outsiders cannot force the victim to assume responsibility for her own safety, but they can show her the way out. They can encourage her to stop blaming herself for her partner's behavior and to start taking control of her own life. They can help her to look at her situation realistically and assess her alternatives. By being understanding and nonjudgmental, outsiders can raise her self-esteem and thereby move her toward self-reliance and away from learned helplessness. Even with sympathetic and knowledgeable support and guidance, the battered woman will find leaving her husband and home difficult. Without such support, escape may be impossible.

D. Characteristics of the Batterer—Why Does He Beat the Woman He Loves?

Because many battered women have survived and have had the courage to tell their stories, we have a solid understanding of their characteristics and motivations. We have also become aware of the best ways to help the victims of abuse. Our knowledge about batterers is less extensive but has grown considerably in the last several years. We now know a great deal about why certain men beat their wives, although we are less confident that we know how to make them permanently nonviolent.

At first blush, the batterer's actions seem as inexplicable as the victim's. Like hers, his behavior springs from a complex web of personal and social factors. Indeed, the batterer is in many ways a tragic mirror image of his wife. He, too, is a strong traditionalist when it comes to sex roles. He believes that a man should be "the master" of the house and that it is the woman's job to satisfy all his needs and wants. Additionally, he often believes that he has the right to use violence against her in order to enforce his will.[25]

While the abuser has a tremendous need to dominate and control his wife and may project a macho exterior, inside he is filled with doubt and insecurity. He may resort to battering because physical intimidation is the only way he is confident of getting his way with her. His low self-esteem manifests itself in other ways as well. He is usually emotionally isolated from everyone except his wife, and he is therefore extremely dependent on her. His dependence and fears of inadequacy typically translate into pathological jealousy. He must have sole possession of her, and not only to the exclusion of other men. He also tries to drive away her relatives and friends and is even jealous of their own children. Unfortunately, the battered woman usually yields to his demands and isolates herself from all outsiders, because she perceives his possessiveness as a sign of love rather than insecurity or just because she wants to keep the peace.

The batterer's jealousy is but one symptom of his infantile personality. Like a child, he is both impulsive and easily frustrated. This combination of traits makes him danger-ous: When he feels frustrated, he impulsively responds by lashing out at his wife. In deal-ing with her, he has not learned to separate his emotions from his actions.[26]

Although the abuser may give some signs of his impulsiveness and low frustration threshold in other aspects of his life, he is rarely violent in other relationships. In fact, with people outside the family, he is generally charming. He is violent at home because he has a bully's "sure winner" mentality. He beats his wife because he can win a physical battle with her and because he can get away with it, as long as society does not intervene. In contrast, he doesn't beat his boss or his male acquaintances, not because he is never angry at them, but because the price of such behavior is too great.[27]

Even with this information about the batterer's psyche, his conduct may still mystify us. If he loves his wife—and he will loudly proclaim that he does—how can he justify his brutality toward her? Even if he believes that "slapping her around" is all right, how can he possibly rationalize beating her senseless or threatening her with a weapon? The answer consists of two related elements. First, battering is learned behavior which, for all his remorse, does "work" for the batterer. Second, the batterer is able to delude himself about his abuse and thereby avoid taking responsibility for it.

One piece of evidence pointing to battering as a learned response is that most batterers were themselves beaten as children or saw their fathers beat their mothers, or both. Bat-terers learn from their violent homes that hurting loved ones is normal and that strong family members, be they parents or husbands, have the right to use force against weak ones. Once they become adults and start beating their wives, batterers learn (although usually not consciously) that battering "helps" them deal with their problems. Their childhood experiences leave abusers with a bottomless rage, and battering temporarily dissipates their anger. By using physical violence rather than other methods, the abuser may also succeed in getting what he wants from his wife, whether it is having her stay with him and cutting herself off from other people, or handing over her earnings to him, or preparing dinner the way he likes it.

For all the "rewards" that their violence brings, batterers could not live with them-selves and maintain their patterns without a variety of self-deceptive psychological tricks. Denial and minimization are crucial defense mechanisms for the batterer, because they allow him to evade accountability for his actions. By refusing to believe that any problem exists, he thus feels no need to change.[28] Even when confronted with undeniable evidence of his violence, he will minimize its severity. Batterers are also quite remarkable in their ability to externalize and rationalize their acts. The most obvious and frequent target of blame is, of course, his victim. Naturally, his blame feeds right into her guilt. Conse-quently, they *both* blame *her* for the battering. Even when the batterer does not blame his wife, he attributes his behavior to other forces. He will say that he cannot control his tem-per, even though his actions belie this excuse.

Perhaps the most common excuse, and one worthy of special mention, is alcohol. Many batterers have serious problems with alcohol and/or drug abuse. Both the couple and outsiders often think that the husband's alcoholism creates the violence. This expla-nation is unconvincing: Beatings typically occur not only when the alcoholic batterer is drunk but also when he is sober. His drinking may well facilitate his battering, but it is *not* its cause.[29]

The false link between alcoholism and battering is only one example of the tendency to confuse the triggers for battering with its underlying causes. In the violent household, the events that arouse the abuser's anger and "lead to" a beating are almost always trivial.

A batterer has learned how to set himself off.[30] Once he has reached the point in the battering cycle when he is ready to abuse the woman severely, the victim's behavior becomes largely irrelevant. He attributes negative motives to her behavior and reacts violently to whatever she does.

So far, we have painted a monstrous picture of the abusive man. Does this mean that batterers are all hopelessly ill individuals who can never change? The experts say no; they believe that many batterers can be helped. Most batterers are not antisocial personalities who feel no remorse for their violence. Ironically, it is the very depth of their guilt that causes them to search so vigorously for external explanations for their behavior. In his own way, an abuser usually does love his wife and children, and it may ultimately be possible to use this love to effectuate changes in his actions.[31]

Such changes will not occur, however, until the wife beater takes responsibility for the battering *and* is punished for his behavior. Unhappily, third parties often encourage his continued denial of responsibility. Every time someone takes the attitude that "she brought it on herself," or "I know it's the alcohol which made you do it," or "I'll let you off this time if you promise never to do it again," that person only succeeds in making it easier for the batterer to persist in his behavior.

E. The Battering Cycle

We have focused primarily on the traits of the batterer and his victim as individuals. As with all couples, however, the dynamic between the partners is as important as the pre-existing characteristics they bring to the relationship. The battering relationship reinforces many of the most negative personality traits of both the abused wife and her husband. Additionally, over time the battering itself comes to dominate their relationship and exacts a toll from the victim, making her escape increasingly difficult.

Even for the most violent batterer, severe beatings are not an everyday occurrence. There is an identifiable battering cycle, consisting of three definable phases: (1) the tension-building phase, (2) the acute battering incident, and (3) the contrite, loving phase.[32]

During the tension-building phase there are battering incidents, but the victim views them as minor. During this phase, the battered woman works very hard to keep her mate calm and under control. She gives in to his demands, no matter how unreasonable. She also tries to control and manipulate other possible sources of friction (in-laws, children), hoping to prevent the battering from escalating. Indeed, during the tension-building phase, the victim may have occasional, limited control over the situation; the batterer may appear to respond to her appeasing attitude. All the while, though, with each minor battering incident, tension on both sides builds. The beatings occur more frequently and are more serious. He becomes ever more possessive of her, and the level of his verbal and psychological abuse of her rises. He often abuses her sexually as well. For her part, the abused woman continues in her efforts to satisfy his increasingly irrational and inconsistent demands. Naturally, she feels tremendous anger at his actions and her growing inability to control them. She denies this anger, however, or works to keep him from seeing it. She is likely to withdraw, hoping thereby to avoid an explosion, but this only causes him to bear down on her even harder. He scrutinizes her every action, and whatever she does is interpreted negatively.[33] When the strain becomes unbearable, the severe battering incident (Phase 2) will occur.

Usually, an outside event or the boiling rage within the abuser triggers the severe beating, although with some couples the victim's behavior may set off this phase. The severe battering incident typically lasts for two to twenty-four hours. When it begins, no one except the couple and possibly their children are present. The major destructiveness which occurs during this phase is regarded as serious even by the battering couple. It is difficult for such severe violence to go unheeded, so most police intervention into the battering relationship occurs during the acute battering phase.[34]

During the severe battering incident, the batterer is enraged by whatever his victim does. If she is passive, he beats her harder; if she tries to defend herself, he retaliates until she submits. Both of them believe that he is out of control during this period, although they later display vastly different powers of recall concerning events during the acute phase. She remembers his behavior vividly, although she may be less specific about her own actions. He remembers little of what happened, although he tries to justify his brutality by blaming either his wife or external forces such as alcohol.[35] One thing is clear: the victim has absolutely no control over the aggressor during the second phase of the battering cycle. The violence stops only if he exhausts himself or the two of them are separated for a substantial period.

Once the severe battering incident is over, both partners react with shock, disbelief, and denial of the seriousness of the violence. The relationship then enters the third phase, characterized by the batterer's contrite, loving behavior. During this phase, the batterer is a generous and loving husband. He feels remorse for what he has done and promises never to hurt her again. Without some break in the battering cycle, however, the batterer lacks both the motivation and psychological tools to change his deeply seated violent pattern. Without rapid action to force him to confront his behavior and get help, his need to evade responsibility for his actions quickly asserts itself and he will regress to denial and externalization.[36]

Because her mate is no longer threatening her physically, the period immediately following an acute battering incident is when the battered woman is most likely to seek outside help or even flee the abusive relationship. If she does, he will often succeed in manipulating her to come back, appealing to her guilt and her sense of responsibility to him and their children. His considerate, normal behavior during this period helps both of them to delude themselves that the change is permanent, but it is not.[37] If she returns to him without his receiving therapy, the loving phase inevitably ends, and the battering cycle will begin again.

The battering cycle explains much of the couple's behavior and thus provides many clues to the appropriate legal response to battering. The victim's belief that she can control her abuser's violence is randomly reinforced during the tension-building phase. That is, at times it appears she can stop him or limit the violence and at other times she cannot. Such reinforcement creates great dependency and hope, because it leads her to believe that she could control him this time, if only she could learn to "push the right buttons" on the batterer. Her acquiescence to his demands is also understandable, once we perceive it as her attempt to avoid an acute battering incident and to keep the violence at "tolerable," Phase 1 levels.

The batterer's rage and seeming lack of control during the explosive battering episode explain why a brief "cooling off" of the parties will not alleviate the crisis. Even if the abuser appears calm and rational to law enforcement officials, if he is left in the house with the victim, he continues to beat her once the authorities leave. She knows this, too, and so may not cooperate with the police, hoping that her display of loyalty will persuade the batterer to stop.

The contrite, loving phase acts as a powerful cement between the batterer and the victim. She may be best able to leave him during this period, and yet this is precisely the time when she gets the most benefit from their relationship. This is why a battered woman nearly always leaves and returns to her husband several times before taking permanent steps to end the abuse. She recognizes and internalizes the intractability of his behavior only after she has repeatedly experienced the resumption of the battering cycle following the loving phase.

◊ ◊ ◊

G. The Most Innocent Victims—The Effects of Abuse on Children

The abusive relationship not only affects its direct participants; it can also destroy the couple's children, who are innocent bystanders. Even when the children are not physically abused themselves, they are emotionally scarred by witnessing their fathers beat their mothers. Such children, especially boys, are far more likely to become involved in abusive relationships as adults than are children from nonviolent families.[38]

In many families where wife abuse occurs, the children are also beaten by one of their parents. Children in this category are the most damaged of all. Child abuse is highly correlated with all forms of violent crimes and mental illness. Children who are abused and who observe violence between their parents are particularly likely to participate in family violence later in life, whether as perpetrators or victims of battering or as abusers of their own children.[39]

The proven tendency of family violence to be transferred from generation to generation makes the search for solutions all the more pressing. Further, the harm inflicted upon children of battering couples should dissuade anyone from approving a laissez-faire approach toward wife abuse. Even if our society is willing to stand by and let the battered woman "take her lumps," the same cavalier attitude toward children is unthinkable.

III. The Need for Legal Intervention

Having described the seriousness of the abuse and some of its causes and consequences, I will now address the issue of whether the law is an appropriate device to combat the problem. That it is even necessary to consider this question shows how tolerant American society is of family violence. In any other context, irrefutable evidence of such severe physical and psychological damage would cause an outraged demand for legal action. Ignorance, a refusal to accept unpleasant facts and flat-out condonation[40] all contribute to the public's apathy about battering. Ignorance and denial can be diminished through education, but condonation is less tractable. Many people who take a "law and order" approach to violence outside the family take a "hands off" approach to violence within it.

Most legal officials condemn abuse in theory, but their actions usually belie their words. Full-scale, vigorous legal response to battering remains the exception and not the rule. When asked to defend this pattern, legal personnel proffer a variety of sophisticated and superficially plausible reasons to explain their inaction. These reasons, because they are so widely accepted among police officers, prosecutors, and judges, are major obstacles to effective legal remedies for wife beating. Therefore, before correct legal solutions can be devised, these "reasons" must be exposed for what they are: justifications for unjustifiable neglect. The need to refute these rationalizations should not be interpreted in any way as conceding their validity. Given the harm caused by battering, the burden of proof clearly rests on those who oppose strong legal action.

Deference to family privacy has been asserted as a basis for nonintervention. However, legal doctrines that limit governmental interference with the family are grounded on reasons that do not apply to battering. First, the law respects decisions on intrafamily arrangements because we assume that family members will reach mutually beneficial and satisfactory answers based on their love for each other. Since abuse is so obviously harmful, the assumption is inaccurate and the rationale fallacious in the battering context. Second, many areas of family life entail controversial value judgments, where the superiority of one set of values over another is unprovable. We therefore permit pluralistic choices. By contrast, society should not hesitate to condemn family violence. Finally, policies favoring family autonomy may reflect a lack of confidence in governmental wisdom: We may allow families to make poor decisions for fear that governmental decisions would often be even worse. This reason makes no sense when family behavior—such as battering—is catastrophic and not merely questionable.

Another excuse for the law's indifference may be a perception of wife beating as a victimless crime. When children are present in the violent home, this perception is clearly absurd. Even when they are not, the perception is fallacious, based upon inaccurate assumptions about the victim's motivations.

Those who cannot defend nonintervention on a purely theoretical level may argue that legal involvement is ineffective and therefore impractical. This assertion is, at best, unproven: How can we tell whether batterers can be stopped until we try? If anything, the evidence shows that batterers can be stopped.

This "shrug of the shoulders" attitude evinces an eagerness to distinguish between battering and other dangerous conduct. The law may not eliminate battering, any more than it has eliminated murder, but that does not mean it should do nothing. Legal officers are constantly frustrated by the law's inability to create a utopia, but they do not usually offer that as a reason to surrender to lawlessness. Simply because the law will never stop all abusers does not mean it cannot stop some. With respect to other crimes, we assume that vigilant enforcement will usually result in both general and specific deterrence and incapacitation; since very few abusers are indeterrable antisocial personalities, the same assumption seems reasonable here. Finally, do-nothing arguments ignore the symbolic value of the law—that the law can lead as well as follow. By taking unequivocal action against battering, the legal system can eventually make inroads against the social forces that condone abuse.

Three variations on the ineffectiveness theme deserve mention. The first, and most outrageous, is that the cost of stopping wife abuse outweighs the benefits.[41] This idea suffers from the same fallacies as its parent theme of the law's powerlessness. In addition, it depends on a tacit assumption that the welfare of battered women and their children is unimportant compared to the time and safety of legal officials. The cost–benefit excuse may also be a tacit acknowledgment of the pervasiveness of abuse. The fear is that if the law started to take battering seriously, it would be overwhelmed by abuse cases.[42] Society must reject this reasoning on both practical and moral levels. Practically, ignoring the problem will only compound it for future generations; any laissez-faire policy is therefore shortsighted. Morally, we should not accept the sacrifice of victim's lives as a fair price for the legal system's convenience.

A more sophisticated excuse is that legal institutions are ill equipped to deal with complex social and psychological problems like battering and should thus avoid them.[43] This rationalization is really a *post hoc* justification for in action rather than a sound reason for restraint. When the stakes are high enough and when the alternatives to legal intervention are inadequate, the legal system does not hesitate to intercede in the resolution of complex issues. Of course, battering involves difficult and sensitive issues, and legal personnel need training on how best to cope with the violent home. It is equally clear, however, that someone must move against abuse and that no other social institution has the legal system's clout to protect victims and to force batterers to face the consequences of their transgressions. The best approach is for the legal system to emphasize the similarities rather than the differences between abusers and other violent criminals.

The final reason for nonintervention, ironically, sometimes comes from people who feel sympathetic toward the battered woman. Such people may argue that intervention will often anger the batterer further and that as a result he may well retaliate against the victim. Therefore, the argument continues, the law should not exacerbate a bad situation. The premise of this argument is sound: Batterers often react violently to any outside interference. But the conclusion, given what we know about battering, is absurd. Abuse continues and probably increases if intervention does not occur. It will not disappear if treated with "benign neglect." While legal officials must be sensitive to the problem of retaliation, they must not use it as an excuse for inaction. The correct responses are to protect and support the victim and to deter the assailant. These are not perfect answers, but they are preferable to leaving the victim at her husband's mercy.

The rationalizations for legal in action will endure as long as the myths of battering endure. But the need to defend against the naysayers should never blunt the positive message: The law can curtail wife abuse, and it must.

IV. Goals of a Program to Combat Battering

Having established the appropriateness of legal action, we should now delineate the goals of a program to stop battering. Only then can we propose and evaluate the specific components of such a program.

The most important goals should be to ensure both the short- and long-term safety of the battered woman. In the short term, the law must take forceful measures to protect the victim, especially during severe battering incidents. A long-range solution demands much more, for the victim will not be safe until the battering cycle is broken. The legal system must do everything it can to encourage the victim to say "no" to further abuse. This means that it should support her in every act that reduces her isolation and promotes her safety and self-esteem. At the same time, the legal system must understand why she finds it so hard to assess her situation realistically and to take control of her life. It must never shift blame from the abuser to the victim, nor should it misinterpret her struggles as masochistic enjoyment of the beatings.

The victim represents only half of the battering equation, of course, and the law must be equally sure of its goals in dealing with the batterer. The primary goal of legal action should be to force him to stop his abuse permanently. In order to have any chance of accomplishing this, the law must present the abusive man with the unambiguous message that his conduct is criminal and will not be tolerated. Legal personnel must confront his denial and externalization, emphasizing that he will be held accountable for his behavior. The law should facilitate his efforts to change if he can show that his motivations are genuine, but legal personnel must not be taken in by his charm and manipulativeness. If he does not respond satisfactorily to lesser means, the full coercive powers of the law must be used against him, including a jail sentence, if necessary. Finally, the law itself must take responsibility for deterring the abuser and must relieve the victim of this burden. This does not mean that legal officials should ignore her wishes or fail to consider her interests. Naturally, these elements should be considered as important factors in legal decision making. However, the government has an independent duty to protect its citizens, especially when they have difficulty in protecting themselves. Violence against any person is a violation of society's rules; control and reduction of such violence is society's responsibility and not the victim's.

The law must also recognize the needs of the children of the battering couple. Physical or sexual abuse of the children must be prevented. Even when direct abuse is not present, the law must strive to protect children against the emotional and psychological damage of observing parental violence.

Saving the battering couple's relationship at the expense of the victim's safety is *not* an appropriate legal goal. Protecting the battered woman must be the top priority, a priority that cannot be achieved if the law focuses primarily on keeping the family together. Establishing the victim's protection as the law's number one goal inevitably implies a value judgment that it is better for her to be safe and on her own than to remain in a dangerous relationship. Furthermore, the goal of deterring the batterer may be undermined by an emphasis on family unity. For most abusers, their wife's departure is one of the few events that may motivate them to get help. Second, it is impossible for most long-term battering relationships to ever become violence free. Lastly, because of the abuser's denial and the victim's guilt, efforts aimed at the couple, rather than at the batterer, will nearly always miss the mark by concentrating on her actions rather than his.

With the nature of the problem, the need for legal action, and the correct goals in mind, we are now prepared to outline an antibattering program for the criminal law.

V. A Criminal Law Program to Stop Abuse

This part will describe how the criminal justice system should respond to battering. First, an overall approach, devised in light of the characteristics of the battering relationship and proper legal goals, will be articulated. This overview will provide a framework for the remaining three subsections, which set forth specific proposals for police, prosecutorial, and judicial action. For each component of the criminal justice system, the discussion will (1) recommend steps to curtail abuse; (2) explain why these steps are appropriate, given what we currently know about the abuser and his victim; and (3) suggest ways to implement the proposals made.

◇ ◇ ◇

A. General Approach

Two overriding principles should guide the law's approach to wife beating. First, the legal system should constantly and consistently convey the message that abuse is unacceptable conduct. Second, legal officials must treat battering as a serious criminal offense for which the batterer is responsible and which the legal system has an obligation to deter. In responding to abuse, the law should emphasize the nature of the harm done and not the relationship between the parties. While it is proper to stress the similarities between domestic violence and crimes between strangers when dealing with the batterer, the law must recognize the difference between the two when dealing with the victim. Because of her relationship with the perpetrator, the battered woman will find it difficult to pursue legal remedies against him, much more difficult than does the victim who has not been rendered helpless by the criminal. Noncooperation from the abused victim impedes the goals of ensuring her safety and deterring her assailant. The law must therefore devise special strategies to overcome her reluctance to become involved in the batterer's prosecution.

The battering victim presents other problems for legal officials. One of the most important questions is the proper weight to give her expressed wishes. Although the legal system should act independently from the battered woman, this does not mean it should freely disregard her desires on how the case should be handled. A good rule is that her views should be accorded great deference when she wants the law to take action against the batterer but should be given less weight when she says she wants to protect him. Several reasons support the distinction. First, because the law has a duty to deter batterers and to protect their wives and children, it follows that it sometimes has an obligation to act even when the victim refuses to assist the legal process. Second, when the battered woman is taking legal steps against the batterer, her actions are consistent with the goals of the law and should be supported and encouraged. The opposite is true when she is protecting him. Third, because of learned helplessness and because she is not a masochist, any expressions of disinterest in deterring him are far less likely to represent the true state of her feelings than when she claims the converse. Fourth, a battered woman is far more likely to minimize her husband's brutality than exaggerate it; she therefore has more credibility when she is making charges against him than when she is refusing to complain. Finally, the law should defer to her when she seeks harsh penalties against the abuser because her personal safety probably rests on the outcome: If he is not stopped, she is the likely target of his renewed violence.

In dealing with the abused woman, the law's top priority should be support. Ideally, with enough understanding and encouragement, the battered woman will assess her situation realistically, start to unlearn her helplessness, and will agree to help the legal system as a witness against her husband. Even if legal officials were to offer the victim their unqualified assistance, however, her actions would often fall short of the ideal, due to the psychological glue which binds her to her mate. When, despite their best efforts, legal personnel find that the victim cannot yet take control of her life, they face difficult choices between solutions which undermine batterer deterrence and solutions which further victimize the victim or increase her jeopardy.

The law's treatment of batterers must be aimed at deterrence, and its approach geared to strength. A tough approach is proper when dealing with abusers, because it is the only way to break down their psychological walls of denial and externalization. Still, different batterers will present different situations. Thus, an overall policy of toughness may express itself in different legal responses, depending on the circumstances. Regardless of the means used in particular cases, the focus should always be on the batterer's deeds and not his words. Legal personnel must maintain a skeptical attitude toward the batterer's promises of rehabilitation, less they fall prey to his manipulation and self-delusion.

When a batterer does not respond to lesser measures, the law must react as it does with other undeterred criminals: escalate the punishment. Increased sanctions may convince the abuser to reform, and even if they do not, at least he cannot beat his wife from a jail cell.

With proper goals and approaches firmly in mind, we can now turn to specific proposals for criminal justice action. We start where the system starts, with a call to the police.

B. Law Enforcement Response

1. Arrest of the Batterer

Effective response by law enforcement officials is the cornerstone of any program designed to reduce wife beating. The goals of safety for victims and long-term change in batterers' behavior patterns are unattainable without appropriate police intervention.

The police are frequently called to the scene of domestic violence, usually during an acute battering incident. Although law enforcement officials never come into contact with many abusive couples, the more severe the abuse, the more likely it is that police assistance will be sought. Thus, the police are in a crucial frontline position to confront battering. The potential impact (for good or ill) of law enforcement response is magnified further by the crisis setting in which police intervention typically occurs.

Arrest of the batterer is the central element of an effective police response. Arrest advances the goal of victim safety (both short- and long-term) and abuser deterrence. The victim's short-term safety is enhanced because, at least if the batterer is held long enough following his arrest, the acute battering phase will be terminated. If the spouses are not separated and the husband's rage is not given time to dissipate, the beating may continue after the police have left. The violence may even be intensified by the abuser's anger of police "intrusion" into his "private life." The ongoing danger to the woman exists even if the batterer appears calm in the presence of the police or she herself requests that he not be taken away. The former is symptomatic merely of the batterer's manipulative respect for authority, while the latter arises from the victim's trauma-induced canfusion and her feelings of helplessness, guilt, fear, and dependence.

Arrest also increases the chances that the victim will begin to take the steps essential to her long-term well-being. The time away from her abuser may give her the breathing room to do an objective assessment of her options, particularly if the police provide her with information on where she can receive counseling, shelter, and other services. More importantly, arrest is a strong support signal to the victim. It communicates to her that the legal system does not blame her for the abuse and that she will not have to tolerate it. If followed up properly by prosecutor and judge, arrest is the first of a series of messages saying that legal officials will help her resolve the problem, that the burden of curbing the abuser will not fall exclusively on her.

Arrest conveys a similar message to the batterer. It signifies that society condemns his conduct and will hold him accountable for it. Arrest thus thwarts denial and evasion of responsibility. When he is taken into custody, it may also be the first time the wife beater has suffered external negative consequences from his violence. When succeeded by similarly strict measures from other criminal justice personnel, arrest begins a process under which the batterer faces both the carrot and the stick: If he changes his actions, he will be rewarded; if he doesn't, he will be punished. Arrest during or soon after a severe beating incident also benefits from good timing: With an opportunity to cool off away from his wife, the batterer will probably move into the contrite, loving phase. The legal system will then have a grip on him at precisely the time when he is the least defensive and the most motivated to change.

The advantages of arresting the batterer are not just theoretical and speculative: Arrest has been shown to be an effective deterrent to further abuse. An assertive attitude toward batterers also reduces the dangers that police themselves face in responding to domestic disturbances. Unfortunately, police attitudes and actions toward abuse remain backward and wrongheaded. Consequently, society cannot rely on them to use their discretion wisely in battering cases. Because of this intransigence, statutory change is the only means likely to achieve our stated goals.

◇ ◇ ◇

2. Other Improvements in Police Procedures

Arrest of the abuser is the linchpin of an effective police response, but other actions would also be beneficial. Better record keeping and evidence-collecting procedures would help protect both officers and victims and should be legislatively mandated. So should training for police on the nature of abuse and how to handle battering calls. As has been demonstrated, much work needs to be done to overcome police ignorance about wife beating. While many law enforcement officials may be so biased as to be unreachable, others may be less resistant, especially if issues such as police safety and protection of children are emphasized. To be effective, training cannot be designed by the police alone. Instead, it must be developed in conjunction with experts in battering, such as abuse shelter directors.

Labeling the batterer a criminal is important, but so is assisting his victim. Police should take an active interest in the welfare of the battered woman. They should inquire about her needs for medical treatment, shelter, and counseling and should be able to direct her to appropriate community agencies. The police are also in an ideal position to launch the victim in the painful but crucial process of objectively assessing her life with the batterer. The abused woman must realize that the police alone cannot stop the violence. Trained and sympathetic police officers can help her recognize that the batterer's behavior is outside her control and that she should focus her energy on taking steps to ensure her own safety.

3. Postarrest Restrictions on Batterers

Once in custody, batterers need time for the rage of the severe battering phase to subside. The objective of victim safety cannot be achieved if abusers are released too quickly after their arrest. States should adopt a law that provides that batterers can be held for twenty-four hours or over the weekend without bail being set. Additionally, in setting bail, judges should treat wife beating as seriously as they would a similar assault between strangers.

After the batterer is released, the legal system must restrain him from misusing his freedom to harrass and reinjure his wife. Unless she wants to resume her relationship, his bail should be conditioned on his staying away from her. If he violates this condition, bail should be revoked.

C. Prosecutorial Response

The police can only activate the legal process. In order to break the cycle of violence permanently, prosecutors and judges must use their power to cancel the batterer's "hitting license." Like the police, these legal officers have erred in their historical reactions to abuse.[44] This subsection will detail proper prosecutorial conduct.

Once prosecutors accept the serious, criminal nature of battering, they should conclude that the state has a duty to pursue wife-beating cases.[45] Under this view, the victim is not the leader of prosecutorial efforts; rather, she is a witness whose participation the state must support and encourage. In order to provide that support and encouragement, prosecutors must understand the special relationship between victim and accused in the family violence context; however, that special relationship does not excuse a lack of prosecutorial initiative. Indeed, assertiveness from the state's attorney is even more necessary in abuse cases than in crimes between nonintimates. A neutral prosecutorial stance—one that gives the victim great freedom to choose not to pursue criminal action—may have merit when the victim's decisions are reached freely. However, when the accused has great emotional and physical influence over the victim, the state should exert more of its authority on behalf of the victim.

A commitment by the state's attorney to assume responsibility for prosecution of wife abuse must be translated into concrete policies and procedures. The first such policy is one that strongly favors the filing of charges in battering cases.[46] The level of proof required to support the filing of charges should be no greater than that required in incidents between strangers, nor should the prosecutor refuse to file based on a general assumption that abused women will not be willing to testify against their husbands.

Prosecutors' offices must make pursuit of battering cases a priority, and must have trained staff who are experts in dealing with the problem. If these staff members sympathize with the abused woman's dilemma and take time to explain to her the advantages of testifying, they can greatly enhance the chances of her cooperation and the abuser's conviction.[47]

Perhaps the toughest question for the prosecutor comes when despite his or her best efforts, a battered woman insists that she wishes the charges against her husband dropped. In response to this problem, some prosecutors' offices have instituted "no-drop" policies in abuse cases. Where such policies exist, the prosecutors will decline to drop charges based merely on the victim's request. In at least one case, an overly zealous prosecutor went one step further by using the court's subpoena power to compel the victim's testimony and jailing her for contempt of court when she refused to testify.[48]

The basic theory behind no-drop policies is sound, since it constitutes a strong statement of societal responsibility for deterring batterers. Additionally, such policies rob the abuser of much of his coercive power against the victim. However, except perhaps in cases of severe violence or recidivism, battered women should not be further victimized by being held in contempt if they remain staunch in their unwillingness to testify. The prosecutor should first consider whether the charges can be proved without the victim's testimony. Failing that, the state's attorney should delay dropping charges, perhaps for a period of thirty days or so. During this period, the contrite phase may (unfortunately) pass, and the victim may again be prepared to cooperate.

If the prosecutor decides to go forward, he or she must next determine whether a case is appropriate for pretrial diversion. Such diversion should occur as soon as possible after the batterer's arrest and should emphasize counseling for the batterer, rather than couples counseling or family mediation. Diversion can be advantageous but also treacherous. On the positive side, diversion can be accomplished more swiftly than full-scale prosecution, thus taking advantage of the batterer's high motivation during the contrite, loving phase. Under these circumstances, there exists a greater likelihood that counseling will succeed in changing the abuser so much that he can stop his violent behavior. Diversion also permits him to earn a living so he can support his family and even maintain a relationship with his wife, if that's what she wants. The dangers of pretrial diversion to counseling include its possible misuse by prosecutors who do not want to be bothered with what they perceive as trivial cases and its being used as a haven for abusers who merely want to avoid going to trial.

Safeguards must be established so that the benefits of counseling can be reaped and its pitfalls avoided. The first safeguard is to set selection criteria for which batterers will be allowed to choose diversion to counseling. Batterers who are charged with inflicting serious injury or those who have previously participated in a diversion program should be excluded. The former group should not be diverted, at least at the pretrial phase, because diversion is not a strong enough message that their conduct is socially intolerable. The latter group consists of men whose past history shows that counseling has not altered their behavior. Consequently, they must be forced to pay a greater price for their violence in the hope that an increased penalty will result in increased motivation to change.

◇ ◇ ◇

D. Judicial Response

The judiciary is the final element of the criminal justice system. Because police and prosecutors have usually siphoned off battering cases from criminal treatment, judicial attitudes are largely untested. Still, what information is available is not encouraging. Operating on ignorant assumptions judges often inquire into victim provocation and abuser excuses, and may consider both as mitigating factors. Even if the batterer is convicted, his penalty may be no more than a stern lecture from the judge, perhaps ending with the extraction of a promise that the abuser will not hurt his wife again. Judges have been unduly reluctant to sentence batterers to jail, often deferring excessively to the victim's wishes or overemphasizing family unity. Even supervised probation or court-ordered counseling have only recently become alternatives.

Many factors, including age, limited turnover, inclination toward traditional attitudes, and male domination of the profession, make a sharp turnaround in judicial attitudes toward battering unlikely. However, prosecutors can help transform judicial perceptions. They can educate judges about the true nature of the abusive relationship—including the uselessness of "the lecture" as a deterrent—and steer judges away from such false issues as provocation. Further, if state's attorneys seek appropriate punishment for abusers, judges may defer to the prosecutor's judgment. Legislatively, we need firm and strict sentencing guidelines for batterers, guidelines that treat recidivism harshly. There should be statutory safeguards to ensure that judges do not seek refuge in knee-jerk referrals to counseling. When counseling is an appropriate alternative, the legal system's interest in permanent deterrence must be protected. This can be accomplished by incorporating the counseling component into a supervised probation program, under which battering, harassment of the victim, or failure to comply with counseling criteria will result in automatic revocation of probation. Legislation should also encourage the imaginative use of judicial discretion. Judicial power does not need expansion, but judges need to be reminded of their ability to order a wide range of alternatives in dealing with battering cases. Because the discretion of the criminal sentencing judge is so vast, judges should use this discretion to ensure protection of victims and their children, as well as to deter abusers.

VI. Conclusion

The roots of battering run deep in American society. For every person—whether police officer, prosecutor, judge, legislator, or citizen—who has come to understand wife abuse, there are many more who remain ignorant. For every person who is willing to face up to the problem, there are many more who want to pretend that it doesn't exist or that it only happens to other people.

We have made a start. As Gloria Steinem noted, it is a measure of progress that today we have a term for battering. "A few years ago, [it was] just called *life*."[49] We must continue to strive on all fronts to destroy the weed of family violence. The job will not be finished easily or soon. The law cannot do the job alone, but it can help. If we want a less violent future for our children, we cannot afford complacency. Legal reforms can bring us closer to the day when "you can't beat a woman" is a reality and not just a slogan on a button.

Notes

1. Two broad-based studies of domestic violence have been conducted in the past six years. Their results are reported in M. STRAUS, R. GELLES, AND S. STEINMETZ, BEHIND CLOSED DOORS: VIOLENCE IN THE AMERICAN FAMILY 40 (1980); and M. SCHULMAN, A SURVEY OF SPOUSAL VIOLENCE AGAINST WOMEN IN KENTUCKY (1981). The findings of the two studies are similar. *See* KENTUCKY SURVEY, at 59 (comparison table). *See also* UNITED STATES DEPARTMENT OF JUSTICE, BUREAU OF JUSTICE STATISTICS, INTIMATE VICTIMS: A STUDY OF VIOLENCE AMONG FRIENDS AND RELATIVES (1980). For a discussion of the methodologies employed in each study, see BEHIND CLOSED DOORS, at 24–28; KENTUCKY SURVEY, at 1, 10–11; INTIMATE VICTIMS, at 47–48.

2. *See* BEHIND CLOSED DOORS, at 32–33 (16 percent of married couples reported at least one violent incident during the past year); KENTUCKY SURVEY, at 1 (of representative telephone sample of Kentucky women, 10 percent had experienced violence from a male partner during the previous twelve months); INTIMATE VICTIMS, at 3 (3.8 million crimes between intimates between 1973 and 1976).

3. *Wife Beating: The Silent Crime, Time,* September 5, 1983, at 23 (cover story). Given the tremendous underreporting of family violence, the figure could be many times higher. Whatever the actual statistics, it is conceded that battering causes more injuries to women than any other cause, including automobile accidents, rapes, and muggings. *The Silent Crime. See also* KENTUCKY SURVEY, at 1–2 (while 10 percent of the sample reported having experienced violence at home, fewer than 3 percent had experienced similar violence outside the home during the same year-long period); BUREAU OF JUSTICE STATISTICS, UNITED STATES DEPARTMENT OF JUSTICE, CRIMINAL VICTIMIZATION IN THE UNITED STATES, 1981 at 71 (1983); (violent crimes against women are perpetrated by "nonstrangers" 50.9 percent of the time, as opposed to 38.4 percent for men).

4. KENTUCKY SURVEY, at 1 (21 percent of the women surveyed reported having experienced violence at some time from their partners); BEHIND CLOSED DOORS, at 32–33 (28 percent of couples still married to each other admitted to some violence during the course of their marriage).

5. KENTUCKY SURVEY, at 1.

6. *The Silent Crime,* at 23, estimates that two thousand to four thousand women are killed each year as a result of family violence. *See also* Stephens, *Domestic Assault: The Police Response,* in BATTERED WOMEN: A PSYCHOSOCIOLOGICAL STUDY OF DOMESTIC VIOLENCE 164, 168–69 (M. Roy ed. 1977) (study showed that 33.6 percent of homicides in Kansas City occured in domestic disturbance situations); FEDERAL BUREAU OF INVESTIGATION UNIFORM CRIME REPORTS,

UNITED STATES DEPARTMENT OF JUSTICE, CRIME IN THE UNITED STATES 1979 10–11 (1980) (40 percent of female homicide victims are killed by family members or boyfriends).

7. Note, *Defense Strategies for Battered Women Who Assault Their Mates:* State v. Curry, 4 HARV. WOMEN'S L. J. 161 (1981); (according to an estimate from Cook County, Illinois, 40 percent of all women held there on homicide charges were accused of killing a man who had battered them).

8. A major metropolitan hospital estimated that one quarter of all female suicide attempts it encountered were women who had experienced battering. *The Silent Crime,* at 24. *See also* NATIONAL CLEARINGHOUSE ON DOMESTIC VIOLENCE, WIFE ABUSE IN THE MEDICAL SETTING: AN INTRODUCTION FOR HEALTH PERSONNEL 20 (1981).

9. Police spend about one-third of their time on domestic disturbance calls. *The Silent Crime,* at 23.

10. In 1980, 33 percent of all assaults on police officers and 11.5 percent of all police deaths occurred during responses to "disturbance" calls. FEDERAL BUREAU OF INVESTIGATION UNIFORM CRIME REPORTS, UNITED STATES DEPARTMENT OF JUSTICE, CRIME IN THE UNITED STATES 1980, at 333, 339 (1981).

11. *See, e.g.,* Steinmetz, *Wifebeating, Husbandbeating—A Comparison of the Use of Physical Violence Between Spouses to Resolve Marital Fights,* in BATTERED WOMEN: A PSYCHOSOCIOLOGICAL STUDY OF DOMESTIC VIOLENCE 63, 65 (M. Roy ed. 1977) (only 1 in 270 incidents of spouse abuse are reported); CRIMINAL VICTIMIZATION 1981.

12. KENTUCKY SURVEY, at 17; BEHIND CLOSED DOORS, at 126–52.

13. *See* UNITED STATES COMMISSION ON CIVIL RIGHTS, UNDER THE RULE OF THUMB: BATTERED WOMEN AND THE ADMINISTRATION OF JUSTICE 5–11 (1982).

14. L. WALKER, THE BATTERED WOMAN (1979), at 28–29.

15. For an excellent discussion of myths concerning battering see L. Walker, at 18–31. Walker's book, a brilliant and readable piece of original scholarship, is the best single source for one seeking to understand the psychological dynamic of wife abuse. Drawing from nothing more than her own experiences working with battered women, she developed a portrait of the abusive couple that subsequent research has consistently affirmed.

The opinion of Chief Justice Wilentz of the New Jersey Supreme Court in State v. Kelly, 97 N.J. 178, 478 A.2d 364 (1984), which draws extensively on the work by Walker and others, is the most detailed and sympathetic judicial treatment of the "battered woman's syndrome."

16. *See, e.g.,* Snell, Rosenwald & Robey, *The Wifebeater's Wife: A Study of Family Interaction,* 11 ARCHIVES GEN. PSYCHIATRY 107 (1964).

17. L. WALKER, at 20. *See also* Dutton & Painter, *Traumatic Bonding: The Development of Emotional Attachments in Battered Women and Other Relationships of Intermittent Abuse,* 6 VICTIMOLOGY: AN INT'L J. 139 (1981) (analogizing battered women's behavior to that of prisoners of war).

18. *Cf.* L. WALKER, at 12 Roy, *A Current Survey of 150 Cases,* in BATTERED WOMEN: A PSYCHOSOCIOLOGICAL STUDY OF DOMESTIC VIOLENCE 25, 31–32 (M. Roy ed. 1977).

19. *See* Roy, at 31; L. WALKER, at 68.

20. L. WALKER, at 31.

21. *Id.* at 75, 105.

22. *Id.* at 229. After all, many American women believe in traditional sex roles. If they are not battered, however, they do not develop learned helplessness, depression, and the like. This view is further reinforced by the fact that battered women who receive beneficial intervention rarely form a second battering relationship (*id.* at 28).

23. *See, e.g.,* S. SCHECTER, WOMEN AND MALE VIOLENCE: THE VISIONS AND STRUGGLES OF THE BATTERED WOMEN'S MOVEMENT 214 (1982), at 26 (judges may discourage victim from pursuing legal remedies). Batterers often enlist the aid of family and friends to encourage victims to stay in the abusive relationship. *See* L. WALKER, at 92.

24. *See* L. WALKER, at 20, 31.

25. L. WALKER, at 12.

26. A. Ganley, Participant's Manual, Court Mandated Counseling for Men Who Batter: A Three-Day Workshop for Mental Health Professionals (1981), at 78.

27. *The Silent Crime,* at 26.

28. A. Ganley, at 28.

29. *See* D. Martin, Battered Wives (1976). L. Walker, at 25.

30. *See* D. Martin, at 49–50.

31. *See The Silent Crime,* at 26 A. Ganley, at 45.

32. L. Walker, at xv, 55–70. *See also* State v. Kelly, 97 N.J. 178, 478 A.2d 364, 371–72 (1984).

33. *See* L. Walker, at 59.

34. *Id.* at 64.

35. *Id.* at 62;

36. *See* A. Ganley, at 28 L. Walker, at 66.

37. *Id. See also* Roy, at 31, Figures 7 and 32.

38. Behind Closed Doors, at 99–101.

39. Behind Closed Doors, at 100.

40. A significant number of Americans accept and even approve of family violence, with men more likely than women to condone domestic abuse. *See* Behind Closed Doors, at 47 (couples were asked what they thought about partners slapping each other around; over 8 percent of the men and slightly over 4 percent of the women thought it was "necessary"; over 15 percent of the men and almost 9 percent of the women related it as "good"; it was considered "normal" by 28 percent of the men and over 23 percent of the women): Yllo & Straus, *Interpersonal Violence Among Married and Cohabiting Couples,* 30 Fam. Rel. 339, 339 (1981) (public perceives marital violence as less serious than violence between strangers).

41. *See* Rule of Thumb, at 13.

42. *See* Parnas, *Police Discretion and Diversion of Incidents of Intra-Family Violence,* 36 Law & Contemp. Probs. 539, 539 (1971).

43. *See* N. Loving, Responding to Spouse Abuse and Wife Beating: A Guide for Police xiii (1980).

44. *See, e.g.,* Rule of Thumb, at 93 (prosecutors have often treated the victims of abuse as if they were the criminals).

Ellis, *Prosecutorial Discretion to Charge in Cases of Spousal Assault: A Dialogue,* 75 J. Crim. L. & Crim. 56 (1984) is a fascinating treatment of the subject of prosecutorial attitudes toward battering. Ellis constructs an imaginary conversation between a "Questioner," who wants to know why prosecutors so often fail to press charges in domestic violence cases and an all-too-realistic "Prosecutor," whose rationalizations for this failure include the perceived nonseriousness of many spousal assaults, *id.* at 62–70, the supposed inappropriateness of state intervention into "private" family disputes, *id.* at 70–76, and the perception of the victim as not credible, as having provoked the assault, or as unwilling to cooperate with the prosecution, *id.* at 76–95.

45. *See* Los Angeles City Attorney Criminal Branch Trial Manual, chap. 5, *quoted in* Lerman, *Elements and Standards for Criminal Justice Programs on Domestic Violence,* in Response to Violence in the Family 9, 9 (November–December, 1982), at 13: "The decision to prosecute a criminal case is the responsibility of a public prosecution agency, not the victim of the offense."

Prosecutors also play an important "middleman" role in the criminal justice system: they are in a unique position to educate and influence both police and judges. *See* Belsky, *On Becoming and Being a Prosecutor,* 78 Nw. U.L. Rev. 1485, 1512–13 (1984). Prosecutors can improve judicial performance by recommending appropriate dispositions for abuse cases. They can help the police by communicating their commitment to vigorous enforcement of antidomestic violence laws. Such a commitment encourages both arrest of batterers and better evidence-collection procedures.

46. Rule of Thumb, at 94. Prosecutor's offices that have adopted such policies include those in Los Angeles, California, and Duluth, Minnesota, *The Silent Crime,* at 26. The filing guidelines

adopted by the King County, Washington (Seattle) Prosecuting Attorney's Office, *reprinted in* Lerman, PROSECUTION OF SPOUSE ABUSE, (1981), at 169–85, are particularly well done.

47. *See, e.g., The Silent Crime,* at 26 (conviction rate in Duluth increased from 20 percent in 1979 to 82 percent in 1983); PROSECUTION OF SPOUSE ABUSE, at 34 (victim cooperation increased dramatically in Santa Barbara, Los Angeles, and Seattle, and in some places is now comparable to cooperation rates for victims of stranger to stranger crimes).

48. *Spouse-Abuse Victim Jailed After No-Drop Policy Invoked,* NAT'L L.J. August 22, 1983, at 4, cols 3 and 4.

49. G. STEINEM, OUTRAGEOUS ACTS AND EVERYDAY REBELLIONS 149 (1983).

III

---◆---

On Adjudication: Patriarchy, Neutrality, and Judicial Reasoning

Impartiality is the highest ideal toward which judges can aspire. It is also the minimum required by justice, the best that judges can offer and also the least they can do. Every person is entitled to fair and impartial consideration in a court of law. But how can impartiality be produced? And if it cannot be guaranteed, how can it be encouraged or facilitated?

Most nations in the Anglo-American legal tradition have put their faith in the idea of detached judges constrained in their power of decision making by overarching neutral processes that determine cases in a principled way. It is thought that because individuals are susceptible to bias and even to the malicious abuse of power, the safest route to impartiality—the best way to facilitate fair judgments—is through neutral processes that can keep any one person from being able to exercise too much power in individual cases. Neutral rules should guarantee that like cases will be treated alike no matter what the judge's personal biases may be. The only problem is that new cases do not always fit within old rules.

In what has often been taken to be the definitive statement of the American judicial process, Edward Levi tried to account for the apparently incompatible requirements of consistency and innovation in adjudication by describing the law as a "moving classification system": In law, the classification changes each time a classification is made. It is a three-step process. First a similarity is noted between the case to be decided and an earlier case. Next the rule of law in the prior case is declared, and last the rule of law is applied to the new case. That is how cases are to be decided according to the rule of precedent, which is the foundation of American common law. This model makes it look as though the system rather than the judge decides the cases, and indeed that is a common conceit of the common law.

No one knows whether Levi is right or whether it is possible to decide any cases as he suggests, but many lawyers and judges assume that this sort of analogical reasoning is a good description of what judges do and/or what they should do. Thus, the traditional view of adjudication generally posits as an ideal a detached and dispassionate judge arriving at objective conclusions through the application of neutral rules. But there are some problems with this model, even as an ideal.

It is not clear whether it is always possible to be detached, and if it is possible, it is not clear if or when detachment produces justice. Furthermore, it is not obvious what *objective* means in the context of legal decision making. If it simply means unprejudiced, then that certainly is the fundamental goal of good adjudication. If it means something like scientific judgments determined by external data, as Levi's analysis suggests, it is highly questionable whether such judgments are possible in the context of law. Finally, feminists and other critics have made it quite clear that legal rules cannot be presumed to be neutral. This is the lesson of the first two chapters. In fact, the first two chapters show us that there are three major problems in adjudication that create barriers to obtaining fair and impartial treatment, particularly within the context of sexism.

The first problem is one of administration. That is, because law is administered by people, it will reflect the biases of those people in its application. And there is no reason to think that judges, juries, prosecutors, or police will be less biased than the general public is; at least there is no evidence that they will be. This problem is well illustrated, for example, in the discussions of sexual harrassment and battery.

The second problem is that the content of the law may be unfair or discriminatory. Even if the judge is detached and impartial, the application of the rule of the prior case to the present case will simply perpetuate the injustice if the first case has been decided unjustly. There is no room in the traditional model for the judge to evaluate the rule itself. That, we are told, is a legislative matter, and to some extent this is true. But it certainly does not produce justice, nor does it help the victim of the discriminatory rule. In fact, the traditional model tends to divest the judge of responsibility for the content of the rules. It views judges rather like middle-level bureaucrats: They do not make policy; they just carry it out—a rather thin notion of responsibility for people invested with the level of power that is entrusted to judges in any common-law country.

The third problem is that the very process of law may be sexist. For example, as long as equal protection is judged according to male norms, the game is rigged at the outset. The very foundation of equal protection law is sexist, so it produces the dilemma of assimilation or special accommodation: two unfair choices. This cannot be fixed without changing the foundation.

Judges adhering to the traditional model of adjudication are ill equipped to deal with such problems, as is well illustrated by much of the Supreme Court's analysis of equal protection in the context of sexism. The judicial system, as it now stands, cannot deal with systemic injustice. Judges are supposed to settle disputes by applying the rules of the system. The law does not invite innovation or self-examination; indeed, common law is based on *stare decisis,* the rule of following precedent. The ideal has been to remove the judge from the decision and let the system decide the case. In that way, the decision would be objective because it would have been determined by external factors—the rules of the prior cases—and not the subjective biases of human judges. That's the theory.

The possibility of arriving at objective conclusions through neutral processes has always been a central question for theories of judicial reasoning. Fairness, it has been thought, presupposes the possibility of objectivity: Adjudication should be conducted as science is, using the cases as data from which to draw objective conclusions. That is the argument, but the analogy is strained. It is not clear what objectivity means in the context of judicial review or whether objective truth is a realistic goal in law. Although there is no single unified feminist position on the nature of truth and knowledge in law, the feminist intellectual movement, like many postmodern movements, regards the truth of all propositions relating to society and certainly to law as depending on context, perspective, and situation. Every perspective is just that, a perspective.

This position (which, of course, is hardly new) in many ways reflects the legal realist position, but because it focuses on patriarchy, it has a vantage point that the legal realists never had. Furthermore, with the benefit of history, feminists are now in a better position to make the case against objectivity in law that the legal realists attempted forty years ago. The point of the denial of objectivity (in both the legal realist and the feminist agendas) is to focus on the problem of impartiality or neutrality.

In a certain sense, impartiality is an impossible goal to achieve, and in law, of course, that is a central and significant problem. Legal realists like Jerome Frank did a good job demonstrating just how impossible that ideal is and how far we are from approximating it in our legal decisions and processes. In *Law and the Modern Mind* he explained the inevitability of personal bias and the inability of the legal process to prevent it. This is an uncomfortable thesis, however, and so we did the best we could to forget it as quickly as possible. Soon we turned to the security of more formalized theoretical structures from scholars like Herbert Weschler, A. M. Bickel, or H. L. A. Hart. Legal positivism is a much more comfortable theory, at least because (as in the case of Hart, for example) it simply focuses on what is certain rather than what is uncertain in law (without denying uncertainty but without addressing it, either). The effects of this attitude have been compounded by "strict constructionists" like Chief Justice William Rehnquist and Judge Robert Bork (not to mention former Attorney General Edwin Meese) who argue on other grounds (the balance of power) that any twentieth-century problems that were not addressed by the Founding Fathers must be relegated to the legislature, thereby implying that this would eliminate uncertainty and bias in the courts.

Feminism, however, continues to maintain that bias still exists, that objectivity is still an illusion, and that this is so not only in individual decision making (as the realists argued) but in the structure of institutions and processes themselves. Feminists point out that social, economic, legal, and political structures regularly operate from unstated norms that reflect the assumptions, attitudes, needs, and, in general, the perspective of certain privileged white males who form, develop, and maintain those structures. The more powerful and pervasive the unstated norm is, the more likely it is to remain unnoticed and unrecognized, and the more likely it is that it will be mistaken for objectivity or neutrality. It will be regarded, to use Thomas Nagel's phrase, as the "view from nowhere," the perspectiveless vision of the ideal observer, a true picture of "reality."

A good example of the feminist treatment of these issues is Martha Minow's chapter, "Justice Engendered." Analyzing the Supreme Court term of 1986, Minow observes that every year the Court faces problems evaluating what particular differences among people ought to mean in regard to gender, race, ethnicity, religion, or handicap. Conflicting social, economic, and legal claims reveal what she calls "dilemmas of difference" that arise from unstated assumptions about whose view matters and what is given. The idea of difference, Minow explains, is meaningful only as a comparison. *Difference* is a relative term. Furthermore, language contains assumptions of comparison in (legal) categories that bury prespective, make choice look like necessity, and thus render power unaddressable. But, she argues, what looks objective from one view does not from another. A difference may be significant only because dominant institutional arrangements have been designed without it. Institutional arrangements define whose reality is the norm, and power is most effective when it is invisible.

Some examples will illustrate Minow's points. Women judges have sometimes been requested to remove themselves from sex discrimination cases, implying that men are sexless. Similarly, black judges have been asked to remove themselves from racial discrimination cases. Apparently, white men are raceless as well; if not, who would be qualified to hear such cases, only a raceless, sexless person? The point is that the norm for judges is white and male, and this norm is mistaken for perspectiveless objectivity.

Language collaborates to make our natural egocentric assumptions even more biased, making many terms appear perfectly neutral when they are not. Consider the word *mother.* Surely this is a neutral descriptive term. But it can be combined with other words to form more judgmental descriptions, such as *working mother* and *unwed mother.* These terms show that the word *mother* really assumes the norm of married housewife who does not work outside the home for pay. Of course, there can be exceptions, but exceptions arc, after all, exceptional. Notice that we never hear the terms *unwed father* or *working father.*

Our institutions, including our legal institutions, are no better. The workplace, for example, assumes an able-bodied male who either has no personal life or attachments or whose attachments and personal life are taken care of by someone else. This attitude then causes difficulty whenever personal problems impinge on regular work routines, such as when a parent has to care for a sick child. Many businesses and governmental offices also assume the leisure of a nonworking public, that is, housewives who can run errands in the daytime, and this in the face of massive evidence that the work force and consuming public no longer match these assumptions. Yet challenging the assumptions often surprises those who hold them, which is almost everyone. It just doesn't occur to us that the world and our organizations could be vastly different than they are. For example, whether including pregnancy benefits in insurance or unemployment schemes is outside the norm and therefore imposes an unfair burden on nonpregnant persons depends on who comprises the norm, how we describe the category, or for whom the insurance scheme was established. Whose perspective or whose life do we have in mind? If the working world had initially been composed of women, insurance schemes would naturally include pregnancy. Similarly, if cities and workplaces had initially been planned or built with the handicapped or the old in mind, we would have different physical facilities that would reduce the significance of many handicaps to a much lesser importance. For example, we would not build street corners with curbs or buildings with steps rather than ramps or elevators. But what makes one set of physical conditions the norm? It is not majority rule, as one might think. Most cities, workplaces, and legal institutions do not accommodate the poor or even the average in any convenient way. Did you ever notice how hard it is for a parent to get around and function in public places (let alone work) while taking care of children? Our society is not set up for families. It accommodates children even less than it does the handicapped or the poor, because it is based on unstated, unexamined norms assumed by a few powerful, privileged white males who have someone else to take care of their family matters while they work without interruption. And these norms are perpetuated by a privileged few who enact them into law and public policy. This is not to say that any of this is conscious. Rather, it is traditional and likely to be unconscious and thus unquestioned.

One of the greatest contributions of feminist jurisprudence has been to point out examples of the repeated use of these unstated norms to challenge supposedly neutral assumptions. Feminists are in a particularly good position to do this well, precisely because they are outsiders. Like an excluded minority, feminists have a greater chance of being able to operate from different assumptions and perspectives than those embedded in patriarchal structures. Feminists, however, like any group outside the mainline power centers and arguing against the status quo, have the burden of pursuading the insiders that the status quo is wrong. This formidable task is, furthermore, plagued by problems associated with the denial of objectivity. If all categories are arbitrary in the sense that they are optional, and they are chosen in preference over some other possible categories, what should the criteria of selection be? If no view is objective, then whose view should prevail? As Martha Minow has observed, institutional arrangements define whose reality is the norm. It makes a difference whose assumptions form the basis of our social structures. But even if we recognize this, what can we do about it? Minow suggests that a judge's first task is to elicit multiple perspectives. Instead of assuming that they are neutral, judges should recognize that their perspectives are partial and should encourage the expression of a variety of views.

Lynn Henderson takes this idea further in Chapter 10, arguing that the traditional dichotomy between legality and empathy, or law and feeling, is mistaken and that legal reason already (secretly but unavoidably) includes, and could be greatly enhanced by, a recognition of empathy. Using controversial cases, Henderson shows how those left out of the system can be included in it, by allowing their stories to be told and by accepting them on their own terms. Henderson's idea is to use empathy to increase the possibility of understanding, to expand the tools available to judges for dealing with problems of systemic injustice. It is a way of facilitating the ideal that all who have cause to complain are entitled to their day in court. Everyone is entitled to be heard. Empathy, Henderson suggests, might enhance our hearing.

Finally, in the last chapter in Part III, Judy Scales-Trent provides an excellent test case for Minow's and Henderson's theories. Scales-Trent is concerned about how the courts handle the intersection of race and sex in providing equal protection of the law; how the analysis should be structured to protect minority women, who suffer double discrimination; and how our present standards of adjudication can allow the most disadvantaged classes to fall through the cracks of law supposedly designed specifically to help them.

All three essays are concerned with how judges should deal with outsiders. The overall point is that law is enacted by legislators and adjudicated by judges in terms of a norm that functions as though society were homogeneous—as though all people were like judges and legislators—which everyone knows is not true. That assumption slants law and adjudication, and disadvantages everyone outside the norm. The question raised by feminists is that if the law should apply equally to all, how can judges begin to approximate this ideal of impartiality in a pluralistic society?

9

Justice Engendered

MARTHA MINOW

I. Introduction

A. What's the Difference

The use of anesthesia in surgery spread quickly once discovered. Yet the nineteenth-century doctors who adopted anesthesia selected which patients needed it and which deserved it. Both the medical literature and actual medical practices distinguished people's need for painkillers based on race, gender, ethnicity, age, temperament, personal habits, and economic class. Some people's pain was thought more serious than others; some people were thought to be hardy enough to withstand pain. Doctors believed that women, for example, needed painkillers more than men and that the rich and educated needed painkillers more than the poor and uneducated. How might we, today, evaluate these examples of discrimination? What differences between people should matter, and for what purposes?

The endless variety of our individualism means that we suffer different kinds of pain and may well experience pain differently. But when professionals use categories like gender, race, ethnicity, and class to presume real differences in people's pain and entitlement to help, I worry. I worry that unfairness will result under the guise of objectivity and neutrality. I worry that a difference assigned by someone with power over a more vulnerable person will become endowed with an apparent reality, despite powerful competing views. If no one can really know another's pain, who shall decide how to treat pain, and along what calculus? These are questions of justice, not science. These are questions of complexity, not justifications for passivity, because failing to notice another's pain is an act with significance.

B. The Problem and the Argument

Each term, the Supreme Court and the nation confront problems of difference in this heterogeneous society. The cases that present these problems attract heightened media attention and reenact continuing struggles over the meanings of subgroup identity in a nation committed to an idea called equality. The drama of these cases reveals the enduring grip of "difference" in the public imagination, and the genuine social and economic conflicts over what particular differences come to mean over time. During the 1986 term, litigators framed for the Court issues about the permissible legal meanings of difference in the lives of individuals, minority groups, and majority groups in cases involving gender, race, ethnicity, religion, and handicap.

Uniting these questions is the dilemma of difference. The dilemma of difference has three versions. The first version is the dilemma that we may recreate difference either by noticing it or by ignoring it. Decisions about employment, benefits, and treatment in society should not turn on an individual's race, gender, religion, or membership in any other group about which some have deprecating or hostile attitudes. Yet refusing to acknowledge these differences may make them continue to matter in a world constructed with some groups, but not others, in mind. If women's biological differences from men justify special benefits for women in the workplace, are women thereby helped or hurt? Are negative stereotypes reinforced, and does that matter? Focusing on differences poses the risk of recreating them. Especially when used by decision makers who award benefits and distribute burdens, traits of difference can carry meanings uncontrolled and unwelcomed by those to whom they are assigned. Yet denying those differences undermines the value they may have to those who cherish them as part of their own identity.

The second version of the dilemma is the riddle of neutrality. If the public schools must remain neutral toward religion, do they do so by balancing the teaching of evolution with the teaching of scientific arguments about divine creation—or does this accommodation of a religious view depart from the requisite neutrality? Governmental neutrality may freeze in place the past consequences of differences. Yet any departure from neutrality in governmental standards uses governmental power to make those differences matter and thus symbolically reinforces them.

The third version of the dilemma is the choice between broad discretion, which permits individualized decisions, and formal rules that specify categorical decisions for the dispensing of public—or private—power. If the criminal justice system must not take the race of defendants or victims into account, is this goal achieved by granting discretion to prosecutors and jurors, who can then make individualized decisions but may also introduce racial concerns, or should judges impose formal rules specifying conditions under which racial concerns must be made explicit to guard against them? By granting discretion to officials or to private decision makers, legislators and judges disengage themselves from directly endorsing the use of differences in decisions; yet this grant of discretion also allows those decision makers to give significance to differences. Formal rules constrain public or private discretion, but their very specificity may make differences significant.

I believe these dilemmas arise out of powerful unstated assumptions about whose point of view matters and about what is given and what is mutable in the world. "Difference" is only meaningful as a comparison. I am no more different from you than you are from me. A short person is different only in relation to a tall one. Legal treatment of difference tends to take for granted an assumed point of comparison: Women are compared to the unstated norm of men, "minority" races to whites, handicapped persons to the able-bodied, and "minority" religions to "majorities." Such assumptions work in part through the very structure of our language, which embeds the unstated points of comparison inside categories that bury their perspective and wrongly imply a natural fit with the world. The term *working mother* modifies the general category *mother*, revealing that the general term carries some unstated common meanings (that is, a woman who cares for her children full time without pay), which, even if unintended, must expressly be modified. Legal treatment of difference thus tends to treat as unproblematic the point of view from which difference is seen, assigned, or ignored, rather than acknowledging that the problem of difference can be described and understood from multiple points of view.

Noticing the unstated point of comparison and point of view used in assessments of difference does not eliminate the dilemma of difference; instead, more importantly, it links problems of difference to questions of vantage point. I will argue that what initially may seem to be an objective stance may appear partial from another point of view. Furthermore, what initially appears to be a fixed and objective difference may seem from another viewpoint like the subordination or exclusion of some people by others. Regardless of which perspective ultimately seems persuasive, the possibility of multiple viewpoints challenges the assumption of objectivity and shows how claims to knowledge bear the imprint of those making the claims.

Difference may seem salient not because of a trait intrinsic to the person but instead because the dominant institutional arrangements were designed without that trait in mind. Consider the difference between buildings built without considering the needs of people in wheelchairs and buildings that are accessible to people in wheelchairs. Institutional arrangements define whose reality is to be the norm and make what is known as different seem natural. By asking how power influences knowledge, we can address the question of whether difference was assigned as an expression of domination or as a remedy for past domination. In so doing, we can determine the risks of creating a new pattern of domination while remedying unequal power relationships.

The commitment to seek out and to appreciate a perspective other than one's own animates the reasoning of some Supreme Court justices, some of the time. It is a difficult commitment to make and to fulfill. Aspects of language, social structure, and political culture steer in the opposite direction: toward assertions of absolute categories transcending human choice or perspective. It is not only that justice is created by, and defeated by, people who have genders, races, ethnicities, religions—people who are themselves situated in relation to the differences they discuss. It is also the case that justice is made by people who live in a world already made. Existing institutions and language already carve the world and already express and recreate attitudes about what counts as a difference and who or what is the relevant point of comparison. Once we see that any point of view, including one's own, *is* a point of view, we will realize that every difference we see is seen in relation to something already assumed as the starting point. Then we can expose for debate what the starting points should be. The task for judges is to identify vantage points, to learn how to adopt contrasting vantage points, and to decide which vantage points to embrace in given circumstances.

A difficulty here, as always, is who is "we." Writing not just for judges, but for all who judge, I mean to invoke a broad array of people in the exploration of justice. Yet the perspective I advance cannot escape my own critique of the partiality of every perspective. The very focus on the "difference" problem selects that problem rather than others (for example, the loss of coherence and tradition in society) as the point of discussion. My use of "we," then, represents an invitation to the reader to assent, to disagree, but above all, to engage with this focus. I use "we," moreover, to emphasize the human authorship of the problems and solutions at hand, and to avoid locutions that eliminate human pronouns.

In Part II, I explore three versions of the dilemma of difference, illustrating how they arose in the contexts of religion, ethnicity, race, gender, and handicapping conditions in cases before the Supreme Court during the 1986 term. Next, in Part III, I turn to the influence in these cases of unstated assumptions about points of reference and starting points for analysis, assumptions that are continually reinforced by established modes of thought, language, and patterns of legal reasoning.

In Part IV, I first identify how members of the Court periodically challenge these assumptions by seeking the perspective of individuals and groups unlike themselves. Unfortunately, the justices are not always successful in their efforts. Feminist scholars have done much to reveal the persistence of these assumptions, particularly the assumption that men—their needs and experiences—are the standard for individual rights, and in Part IV I go on to develop and pursue this basic feminist insight. In so doing, I also explore ways in which some feminist analyses have recreated the problems they sought to address, elaborating the idea of "woman's experience," leaving unstated the race, ethnicity, religion, and bodily condition presumed in the identification of woman's point of view.

What, then, is to be done? In Part V, I urge the judiciary to make a perpetual commitment to approach questions of difference by seeking out unstated assumptions about difference and typically unheard points of view. There will not be a rule, a concept, a norm, or a test to apply to these problems. The very yearning for simple and clear solutions is part of the difference problem. The allure of this simplicity reflects our dangerous tendency to assign differences, to pretend that they are natural, and to use categorical solutions to cut off rather than to promote understanding. Instead of a new solution, I urge struggles over descriptions of reality. Litigation in the Supreme Court should be an opportunity to endow rival vantage points with the reality that power enables, to redescribe and remake the meanings of difference in a world that has treated only some vantage points on difference as legitimate.

Far from being unmanageable, this approach describes what happens already in the best practices of justice. Justice, in this view, is not abstract, universal, or neutral. Instead, justice is the quality of human engagement with multiple perspectives framed by, but not limited to, the relationships of power in which they are formed. Decisions, then, can and must be made. Despite the distortions sometimes injected by a language of objectivity and neutrality, the Supreme Court has "engendered" justice in many cases. These cases show the commitment in contemporary statutory and constitutional law to give equality meaning for people once thought to be "different" from those in charge. From the work of this term, which is the last for Justice Powell, the first for Justice Scalia, and the first for Chief Justice Rehnquist as head of the Court, I hope to demonstrate how our common humanity wins when the Court struggles with our differences.

II. A Case of Differences

Arguments before the Supreme Court engage all three versions of the difference dilemma and cut across cases otherwise differentiated by doctrine and contexts. The dilemma arises in both equality and religion cases, and in statutory and constitutional contexts. This section explicitly draws connections across these seemingly disparate cases and explores the dilemma in cases decided in the 1986 term.

A. The Dilemma of Recreating Difference
Both by Ignoring It and by Noticing It

California Federal Savings & Loan Association v. Guerra (Cal Fed)[1] presented in classic form the dilemma of recreating difference through both noticing and ignoring it. Petitioners, a collection of employers, argued that a California statute[2] mandating a qualified right to reinstatement following an unpaid pregnancy disability leave amounted to special preferential treatment, in violation of Title VII's prohibition of discrimination on the basis of pregnancy.[3] Writing an opinion announcing the judgment for the Court, Justice Marshall transformed the question presented by the plaintiffs: Instead of asking whether the federal ban against discrimination on the basis of pregnancy precluded a state's decision to require special treatment for pregnancy, the majority asked whether the state could adopt a minimum protection for pregnant workers while still permitting employers to avoid treating pregnant workers differently by extending similar benefits to nonpregnant workers. Framing the problem this way, the majority ruled that "Congress intended the PDA to be 'a floor beneath which pregnancy disability benefits may not drop—not a ceiling above which they may not rise.'"[4] The majority acknowledged the risk that recognizing the difference of pregnancy could recreate its stigmatizing effects, but noted that "a State could not mandate special treatment of pregnant workers based on stereotypes or generalizations about their needs and abilities."[5] Thus, despite the federal antidiscrimination requirement, the majority found that states could direct employers to take the sheer physical disability of the pregnancy difference into account, but not any stereotyped views associated with that difference. The majority gave two responses to the problem of difference: First, accommodating pregnant workers would secure a workplace that would equally enable both female and male employees to work and have a family; second, the federal and state statutes should be construed as inviting employers to provide the same benefits to men and women in comparable situations of disability.[6]

Writing for the dissenters, Justice White maintained that the California statute required disability leave policies for pregnant workers even in the absence of similar policies for men. It thus violated the PDA, which "leaves no room for preferential treatment of pregnant workers."[7] In the face of this conflict, the federal statute must preempt the state law. The commands of nondiscrimination prohibit taking differences into account, Justice White argued, regardless of the impact of this neglect on people with the difference. Justice White acknowledged the majority's argument that preferential treatment would revive nineteenth-century protective legislation, perpetuating sex role stereotypes and "imped[ing] women in their efforts to take their rightful place in the workplace."[8] For Justice White, however, such arguments were irrelevant, because the Court's role was restricted to interpreting congressional intent and thus would not permit consideration of the arguments about stereotyping. Yet to some extent, the issue of stereotypes was unavoidable: The dilemma in the case, from one point of view, was whether women could secure a benefit that would eliminate a burden connected with their gender, without at the same time reactivating negative meanings about their gender.

In two other cases in the 1986 term, the Court confronted the dilemma of recreating difference in situations in which individuals claimed to be members of minority races in order to obtain special legal protections. By claiming an identity in order to secure some benefit from it, the individuals faced the dilemma that they might fuel negative meanings of that identity, meanings beyond their control. Although racial identification under federal civil rights statutes provides a means of legal redress, it also runs the risk of recreating stigmatizing associations, thereby stimulating prejudice.

In *Saint Francis College v. Al-Khazraji*,[9] a man from Iraq who had failed to secure tenure from his employer, a private college, brought a claim of racial discrimination under 42 U.S.C. section 1981. His case foundered, however, when the lower courts rejected his claim that his Arab identity constituted racial membership of the sort protected by the federal statute.

In *Shaare Tefila Congregation v. Cobb*,[10] members of a Jewish congregation whose synagogue was defaced by private individuals alleged violations of the federal guarantee against interference with property rights on racial grounds. The difference dilemma appeared on the face of the complaint: The petitioners argued that Jews are not a racially distinct group, and yet they claimed that Jews should be entitled to protection against racial discrimination because others treat them as though they were distinct. The petitioners thus demonstrated their reluctance to have a difference identified in a way that they themselves could not control, while simultaneously expressing their desire for protection against having that difference assigned to them by others. To gain this protection, the petitioners had to identify themselves through the very category they rejected as a definition of themselves. Both the district court and the court of appeals refused to allow the petitioners to be included in the protected group on the basis of the attitudes of others, without some proof of well-established traits internal to the group. The court of appeals reasoned:

> Although we sympathize with appellant's position, we conclude that it cannot support a claim of racial discrimination solely on the basis of defendants' perception of Jews as being members of a racially distinct group. To allow otherwise would permit charges of racial discrimination to arise out of nothing more than the subjective, irrational perceptions of defendants.[11]

In contrast, one member of the appeals panel, dissenting on this point, argued: "Misperception lies at the heart of prejudice, and the animus formed of such ignorance sows malice and hatred wherever it operates without restriction."[13]

Is the cause of individualized treatment advanced by allowing groups to claim legal protections by dint of group membership, however erroneously assigned by others? Conversely, may denying these claims of legal protection against assigned difference allow the Supreme Court to avoid addressing the dilemma and thereby reenact it? In both *Shaare Tefila* and *Saint Francis,* the Court asked only whether the legislators adopting the antidiscrimination legislation shortly after the Civil War viewed Jews and Arabs as distinct races. The Court answered the question affirmatively in both cases but based its conclusion on a review of the legislative histories and contemporaneous dictionaries and encyclopedias instead of tackling the difference dilemma directly.

The Court's historical test for membership in a minority race effectively revitalized not just categorical thinking in general, but the specific categorical thinking about race prevailing in the 1860s, despite considerable changes in scientific and moral understandings of the use of abstract categories to label people and solve problems. Whether the issue is gender, religion, or race, reviving old sources for defining group difference may reinvigorate older attitudes about the meanings of group traits. Denying the presence of those traits, however, and their significance in society, deprives individuals of protection against discrimination due to outmoded or unsubstantiated conceptions of group difference.

B. Neutrality and Nonneutrality: The Dilemma of Government Embroilment in Difference

The dilemma of difference appears especially acute for a government committed to acting neutrally. Neutral means might not produce neutral results, given historic practices and social arrangements that have not been neutral. For example, securing neutrality toward religious differences is the explicit goal of both the First Amendment's ban against the establishment of religion and its protection of the free exercise of religion. Thus to be truly neutral, the government must walk a narrow path between promoting or endorsing religion and failing to make room for religious exercise. Accommodation of religious practices may look nonneutral, but failure to accommodate may also seem nonneutral by burdening the religious minority whose needs were not built into the structure of mainstream institutions.

The "creation science" case, *Edwards v. Aguillard*,[13] raised the question of how the government, in the form of public schools, can respect religious differences while remaining neutral toward them. In *Edwards*, parents and students claimed that a Louisiana statute requiring public schools to teach creation science whenever they taught the theory of evolution violated the establishment clause. Community members subscribing to fundamentalist religious beliefs, however, have argued that public school instruction in evolution alone is not neutral, because it gives a persuasive advantage to views that undermine their own religious beliefs. Relying on similar arguments, the state avowed a neutral, nonreligious purpose for its statute.[14]

The majority, in an opinion by Justice Brennan, concluded that the legislation was actually intended to "provide persuasive advantage to a particular religious doctrine that rejects the factual basis of evolution in its entirety."[15] By contrast, the dissenting opinion by Justice Scalia, which was joined by Chief Justice Rehnquist, expressly tangled with the neutrality problem, noting the difficult tensions between antiestablishment and free exercise concerns and between neutrality through indifference and neutrality through accommodation. In the end, the dissent was moved by the state's attempt to avoid undermining the different views of fundamentalist Christian students, while the majority was persuaded that the statute gave an illegal preference to a particular religious view. For both sides, however, the central difficulty was how to find a neutral position between these two risks.

In a second case, *Hobbie v. Unemployment Appeals Commission*,[16] the neutrality problem arose when the Court reviewed a state's decision to deny unemployment benefits to a woman under an apparently neutral scheme. Hobbie was discharged from her job when she refused to work during her religious Sabbath. The state argued that Hobbie's refusal to work amounted to misconduct related to her work and rendered her ineligible for unemployment benefits under a statute limiting compensation to persons who become "unemployed through no fault of their own."[17] The Court rejected this emphasis on the cause of the conflict, because the "salient inquiry" was whether the denial of unemployment benefits unlawfully burdened Hobbie's free exercise right. The Court also rejected the state's claim that making unemployment benefits available to Hobbie would unconstitutionally establish religion by easing eligibility requirements for religious adherents.[18] By requiring accommodation for free exercise, despite charges of establishing religion, the Court's solution thus framed a dilemma of neutrality: How can the government's means be neutral in a world that is not itself neutral?

A facially neutral state policy on unemployment compensation also figured in *Wimberly v. Labor & Industrial Relations Commission*.[19] Wimberly had taken a pregnancy leave from her job with no guarantee of reinstatement, and upon her return the employer told her that there were no positions available. Her application for unemployment benefits was denied under a state law disqualifying applicants unless their reasons for leaving were directly attributable to the work or to the employer. Wimberly argued that a federal statute forbidding discrimination in unemployment compensation "solely on the basis of pregnancy or termination of pregnancy[20] required accommodation for women who leave work because of pregnancy.

The Supreme Court unanimously rejected Wimberly's claim that this denial of benefits contravened the federal statute. The Court found that the state had not singled out pregnancy as the reason for withholding unemployment benefits; instead, pregnancy fell within a broad class of reasons for unemployment unrelated to work or to the employer. The Court interpreted the federal statute to forbid discrimination but not to mandate preferential treatment. In the Court's eyes, then, it was neutral to have a general rule denying unemployment benefits to anyone unemployed for reasons unrelated to the workplace or the employer.[21]

In essence, the Court interpreted the federal statutory scheme as granting discretion to state legislatures to define their own terms for disqualification from eligibility for benefits. Although many states provide unemployment benefits for women who leave their jobs because of pregnancy, subsuming it under terms like "good cause," along with other compelling personal reasons, injury, illness, or the federal ban against refusing benefits "solely on the basis of pregnancy" does not, according to the Court, compel such coverage. A state choosing to define its unemployment eligibility narrowly enough to disqualify not just those who leave work due to pregnancy but also those who leave work for good cause, illness, or compelling personal reasons may thus do so without violating federal law.

The Court in *Wimberly* rejected the argument that ignoring the difference of pregnancy produces illicit discrimination under an apparently neutral unemployment benefits rule. In *Hobbie,* on the other hand, the Court embraced the view that ignoring a religious difference produces illicit discrimination under an apparently neutral unemployment benefits rule. In both cases, the Court grappled with the dilemma of whether to give meaning to neutrality by recognizing or not recognizing difference.

C. Discretion and Formality: The Dilemma of Using Power to Differentiate

The Court's commitment to the rule of law often leads it to specify, in formal terms, the rules that govern the decisions of others. This practice can secure adherence to the goals of equality and neutrality by ensuring that differences are not taken into account except in the manner explicitly specified by the Court. Although likely to promote accountability, this solution of formal rules has drawbacks. Making and enforcing specific rules engages the Court in the problem of reinvesting differences with significance by noticing them. Specifically requiring the Court to articulate permissible and impermissible uses of difference may enshrine categorical analysis and move further away from the ideal of treating persons as individuals. One way for the Court to resolve the difference dilemma is to grant or cede discretion to other decision makers. Then the problems from both noticing and ignoring difference, and from risking nonneutrality in means and results, are no longer problems for the Court but, instead, matters within the discretion of other private or public decision makers. This approach simply moves the problem to another forum, allowing the decision maker with the discretion to take difference into account in an impermissible manner. The tension between formal, predictable rules and individualized judgments under discretionary standards thus assumes heightened significance in dilemmas of difference.

This dilemma of discretion and formality most vividly occupied the Court in *McCleskey v. Kemp,*[22] in which the Court evaluated charges of racial discrimination in the administration of the death penalty in Georgia's criminal justice system. A statistical study of over two thousand murder cases in Georgia during the 1970s, submitted by the defendant and assumed by the Court to be valid, demonstrated that the likelihood of a defendant's receiving the death sentence was correlated with the victim's race and, to a lesser extent, the defendant's race. According to the study, black defendants convicted of killing white victims "have the greatest likelihood of receiving the death penalty." Should the Court treat a sentencing "discrepancy that appears to correlate with race" as a defect requiring judicial constraints on prosecutorial and jury discretion, or as an unavoidable consequence of such discretion? In making this choice, the majority and the dissenters each latched onto opposing sides of the dilemma about discretion and formality.

Justice Powell, for the majority, began by asserting that the discretion of the jury is critical to the criminal justice system and operates to the advantage of criminal defendants because it permits individualized treatment rather than arbitrary application of rules. Because of the importance of discretion, unexplained racial discrepancies in the sentencing process should not be assumed to be invidious or unconstitutional. In the majority's view, recognizing claims such as McCleskey's would open the door "to claims based on unexplained discrepancies that correlate to membership in other minority groups, and even to gender" or physical appearance. This argument, perhaps meant in part to trivialize the dissent's objections by linking physical appearance with race, sex, and ethnicity, implied that discrepancies in criminal sentences are random and too numerous to control. Furthermore, in the majority's view, any attempt to channel discertion runs the risk of undermining it altogether: "It is difficult to imagine guidelines that would produce the predictability sought by the dissent without sacrificing the discretion essential to a humane and fair system of criminal justice."[23]

Justice Brennan, in dissent, approached the problem of discretion and formality from the other direction. Like the majority, Justice Brennan asserted that imposition of the death penalty must be based on an "individualized moral inquiry." To Justice Brennan, however, the statistical correlation between death sentences and the race of defendants and victims showed that participants in the state criminal justice system had, in fact, considered race and produced judgments "completely at odds with [the] concern that an individual be evaluated as a unique human being." Justice Brennan argued that "discretion is a means, not an end" and that, under the circumstances, the Court must monitor the discretion of others. Justice Brennan also responded to the majority's fear of widespread challenges to all aspects of criminal sentencing: "Taken on its face, such a statement seems to suggest a fear of too much justice. . . . The prospect that there may be more widespread abuse than McCleskey documents may be dismaying, but it does not justify complete abdication of our judicial role."[24]

Justice Stevens, also in dissent, argued that there remains a middle road between forbidding the death penalty and ignoring, in the name of prosecutorial and jury discretion, the correlation between the death penalty and the defendant's and victim's races. He urged a specific rule: The class of defendants eligible for the death penalty should be narrowed to the category of cases, identified by the study, in which "prosecutors consistently seek, and juries consistently impose, the death penalty without regard to the race of the victim or the race of the offender."[25]

For the majority in *McCleskey,* constricting prosecutorial and jury discretion would push toward so regulated a world that the criminal justice system would no longer pro-duce particularized, individualized decisions about defendants. For the dissenters, the Court's acquiescence in unmonitored prosecutorial and jury discretion, in the face of sen-tencing disparities correlated with race, condoned and perpetuated racial discrimination and thereby allowed racial stereotyping to be substituted for individualized justice.

Debate among the justices last term in an entirely different context exposed a similar tension between rules and discretion. In *Corporation of the Presiding Bishop of the Church of Jesus Christ of Latter-Day Saints v. Amos (Presiding Bishop)*,[26] the Court con-sidered whether the federal statute exempting religious organizations from nondiscrimi-nation requirements in their employment decisions arising out of nonprofit activities vio-lated the establishment clause. The Court's majority endorsed the legislative grant of discretion to religious organizations while rejecting the discharged engineer's claims that such state accommodation unconstitutionally promotes religion.

The opinions in the case clearly illustrate the dilemma of discretion. The majority reasoned that under the exemption the preference for religion was not exercised by the government but, rather, by the church. Justice O'Connor, however, pointed out in her concurring opinion that allowing discretion to the private decision maker to use religion in his decisions inevitably engaged the government in that differentiation. The Court could not, simply by protecting the discretion of religious organizations, escape consid-eration of the tension between the constitutional command against promoting religion and the constitutional demand for free exercise of religion. Instead, Justice O'Connor argued, in distinguishing constitutional accommodation of religion from unconstitu-tional assistance to religious organizations, the Court must evaluate the message of the government's policy as perceived by an "objective observer."[27]

Justice Brennan's separate opinion also treated this tension as unavoidable. Yet Justice Brennan focused on the risk that case-by-case review by the Court would chill the very freedom assured to religious organizations. He therefore endorsed a categorical exemption from the ban against religious discrimination in employment for the non-profit activities of religious organizations but argued for reserving judgment as to profit-making activities. Like Justice Stevens in *McCleskey,* Justice Brennan searched for a for-mal rule that could preserve discretion for other decision makers while also implementing the Court's special commitment to protect individuals from categorical, discriminatory treatment.

D. The Dilemmas in Sum

Other cases before the Court have raised one or more aspects of the difference dilemma. The Court's voluntary affirmative action cases, during the 1986 term and earlier, directly present dilemmas about recreating difference, risking nonneutral means to transform nonneutral ends, and choosing between rules and discretion in an effort to avoid cate-gorical decisions. Decisions about handicapped persons also raise perplexing issues about when the Court should permit public and private decision makers to make the difference of handicap matter. The Court comes down one way or another in each case, but the splits between majority and minority views persist and recreate the dilemmas. The next section argues that assumptions buried within the dilemmas make them seem more difficult than they need be. The task, then, is to articulate those assumptions and to evaluate the choices that remain for decision makers.

III. Behind and Beyond the Dilemma

The dilemma of difference appears unresolvable. The risk of nonneutrality—the risk of discrimination—accompanies efforts both to ignore and to recognize difference in equal treatment and special treatment; in color blindness or gender blindness and in affirmative action; in governmental neutrality and in governmental preferences; and in decision makers' discretion and in formal constraints on discretion. Yet the dilemma is not as intractable as it seems. What makes it seem so difficult are unstated assumptions about the nature of difference. Once articulated and examined, these assumptions can take their proper place among other choices about how to treat difference. I will explore here the assumptions underlying the dilemma of difference, assumptions that usually go without saying.

◊ ◊ ◊

A. The Five Unstated Assumptions

1. Assumption 1: Difference Is Intrinsic, Not Relational

> [M]any of us have never conceived of ourselves only as somebody's other.
>
> Barbara Christian[28]

Can and should the questions about who is different be resolved by a process of discovering intrinsic differences? Is difference an objective, verifiable matter rather than something constructed by social attitudes? By posing legal claims through the difference dilemma, litigants and judges treat the problem of difference as what society or a given decision maker should do about the "different person"—a formulation that implicitly assigns the label of difference to that person.

The difference inquiry functions by pigeonholing people into sharply distinguished categories based on selected facts and features. Categorization helps people cope with complexity and understand each other. The legal analyst tends to treat the difference question as one of discovery rather than of choice. The judge asks: "Into what category does a given person or feature belong?" The categories then determine the significance of the persons or features situated within them. The distinguishing features behind critical perceptions and behind the categories themselves appear natural rather than chosen. It is hard, if not impossible, to find commonalities across differences and to argue for the same treatment across difference. Responsibility for the consequences of identifying difference, then, is dispersed through the process of perception and categorization, even as the process of categorization itself can create new perceptions and realities.

◊ ◊ ◊

2. Assumption 2: The Unstated Norm

> Anyone who deviates from the official norm, whatever that is, anyone who fails to bear a likeness to the Standard Product, is simply not viewed as fully human, and then becomes at best invisible, at worst a threat to the national security.
>
> Giles Gunn[29]

To treat someone as different means to accord them treatment that is different from treatment of someone else; to describe someone as "the same" implies "the same as" someone else. When differences are discussed without explicit reference to the person or trait on the other side of the comparison, an unstated norm remains. Usually, this default reference point is so powerful and well established that it need not be specified.

Some remedial statutes explicitly state the norm: In 42 U.S.C. section 1981, the norm is "white citizens"—with an emphasis on both terms, implicitly establishing the terms of sameness and difference in this very statement of the norm. Claimants invoking the statute must show themselves to be relatively similar to "white citizens." Hence, these cases focus on whether the claimant is a member of a race.

When women argue for rights, the implicit reference point used in discussions of sameness and difference is the privilege accorded some males. This reference point can present powerful arguments for overcoming the exclusion of women from activities and opportunities available to men. For example, reform efforts on behalf of women during both the nineteenth and the twentieth centuries asserted women's fundamental similarities to privileged, white men as a tactic for securing equal treatment. Unfortunately for the reformers, embracing the theory of "sameness" meant that any sign of difference between women and men could be used to justify treating women differently from men. Men remained the unstated norm.

⬦ ⬦ ⬦

Jerome Bruner wrote, "There is no seeing without looking, no hearing without listening, and both looking and listening are shaped by expectancy, stance, and intention."[30] Unstated reference points lie hidden in legal discourse, which is full of the language of abstract universalism. Legal language seeks universal applicability, regardless of the particular traits of an individual. Yet abstract universalism often "takes the part for the whole, the particular for the universal and essential, the present for the eternal."[31] Making explicit the unstated points of reference is the first step in addressing this problem; the next is challenging the presumed neutrality of the observer who in fact sees from an unacknowledged perspective.

3. Assumption 3: The Observer Can See Without a Perspective

> Inevitably, "seeing" entails a form of subjectivity, an act of imagination, a way of looking that is necessarily in part determined by some private perspective. Its results are never simple "facts," amenable to "objective" judgments, but facts or pictures that are dependent on the internal visions that generate them.
>
> Evelyn Fox Keller[32]

If differences are intrinsic, then anyone can see them; if there is an objective reality, then any impartial observer can make judgments unaffected and untainted by his or her own perspective or experience. Once rules are selected, regardless of disputes over the rules themselves, a distinct aspiration is that they will be applied evenhandedly. This aspiration to impartiality, however, is just that—an aspiration rather than a description—because it may suppress the inevitability of the existence of a perspective and thus make it harder for the observer, or anyone else, to challenge the absence of objectivity.

What interests us, given who we are and where we stand, affects our ability to perceive. Philosophers such as A. J. Ayer and W. V. Quine note that although we can alter the theory we use to frame our perceptions of the world, we cannot see the world unclouded by preconceptions. The impact of the observer's perspective may be crudely oppressive. Yet we continue to believe in neutrality.

⬦ ⬦ ⬦

Judges often see difference in relation to some unstated norm or point of comparison and fail to acknowledge their own perspective and its influence on the assignment of difference. This failure prevents us from discovering who is doing the labeling, but it does not negate the effect of the labeling of difference itself. Veiling the standpoint of the observer conceals its impact on our perception of the world. This leads to the next unstated assumption: that all other perspectives are either presumptively identical to the observer's own or are irrelevant.

4. Assumption 4: The Irrelevance of Other Perspectives

> We have seen the blindness and deadness to each other which are our natural inheritance.
>
> William James[33]

Glimpsing contrasting perspectives helps resolve problems of difference. Several of the justices have tried, on different occasions, to glimpse the point of view of a minority group or a person quite different from themselves; some have articulated eloquently the difficulty or even impossibility of knowing another's perspective and have developed legal positions that take into account this difficulty. Others have rejected as irrelevant or relatively unimportant the experience of "different" people and have denied their own partiality, often by using stereotypes as though they were real.

◊ ◊ ◊

Thus, some justices, on some occasions, have tried to see beyond the dominant perspective and reach an alternative construction of reality. In many other instances, however, the justices presume that the perspective they adopt is either universal or superior to others. A perspective may go unstated because it is so powerful and pervasive that it may be presumed without defense; it may also go unstated because it is so unknown to those in charge that they do not recognize it as a perspective. Presumptions about whose perspective matters ultimately may be embedded in the final, typically unstated assumption: When in doubt, the status quo is preferred and is indeed presumed natural and free from coercion.

5. Assumption 5: The Status Quo Is Natural, Uncoerced, and Good

> To settle for the constitutionalization of the status quo is to bequeath a petrified forest.
>
> Aviam Soifer[34]

Connected with many of the other assumptions is the idea that critical features of the status quo—general social and economic arrangements—are natural and desirable. From this assumption follow three propositions: First, the goal of governmental neutrality demands the status quo because existing societal arrangements are assumed to be neutral. Second, governmental actions that change the status quo have a different status than omissions, or failures to act, that maintain the status quo. Third, prevailing social and political arrangements are not forced on anyone. Individuals are free to make choices and to assume responsibility for those choices. These propositions are rarely stated, both because they are deeply entrenched and because they view the status quo as good, natural, and freely chosen. At times, however, the justices have engaged in debate that exposes the status quo assumption.

◊ ◊ ◊

For the most part, unstated assumptions work in subtle and complex ways. Assumptions fill the basic human need to simplify and to make our world familiar and unsurprising. Yet, by their very simplification, assumptions exclude contrasting views. Moreover, they contribute to the dilemma of difference by frustrating legislative and constitutional commitments to change the treatment of differences in race, gender, ethnicity, religion, and handicap. Before justice can be done, judges need to hear and understand contrasting points of view about the treatment of difference.

IV. Perspectives on Perspectives

The difference dilemma seems paralyzing if framed by the unstated assumptions described in Part III. Those assumptions so entrench one point of view as natural and orderly that any conscious decision to notice or to ignore difference breaks the illusion of a legal world free of perspective. The assumptions make it seem that departures from unstated norms violate commitments to neutrality. Yet adhering to the unstated norms undermines commitments to neutrality—and to equality. Is it possible to proceed differently, putting these assumptions into question?

I will suggest that it is possible, even if difficult, to move beyond the constricting assumptions. At times in the past term, members of the Court have employed the most powerful device to expose and challenge the unstated assumptions: looking at an issue from another point of view. By asking how a member of a religious group might experience a seemingly neutral rule or how a nonmember might experience the discretion of a religious group, Justices O'Connor, Brennan, and White made an effort in several cases to understand a different perspective.[35] Justice Marshall and the majority in *Cal Fed* tried to assume the perspective of pregnant women by considering how treatment of pregnancy affects women's abilities to work outside the home while having a family. The dissenting justices in *McCleskey* asked how defendants would react to the statistical disparity in capital sentencing by race, breaking out of the tendency to see the challenge only as a threat to the discretion and manageability of the criminal justice system. In *Saint Francis College, Shaare Tefila,* and *Arline,* members of the Court struggled over whose perspective should count for purposes of defining a race and a handicap, reaching conclusions that refused to take the usual answers for granted.

Efforts to adopt or imagine alternate perspectives are also reflected in opinions from previous terms. For example, Justice Stevens assessed an equal protection challenge to a zoning restriction burdening mentally retarded people by expressing sensitivity to a point of view other than his own: "I cannot believe that a rational member of this disadvantaged class could ever approve of the discriminatory application of the city's ordinance in this case."[36] Still earlier, Justice Douglas invited inquiry into the experience of non-English-speaking students sitting in a public school classroom conducted entirely in English.[37] Similarly, litigants have sometimes tried to convince the Court to adopt their perspective. Justice Harlan's dissent in *Plessy v. Ferguson*[38] may have been assisted by Homer Plessy's attorney, who had urged the justices to imagine themselves in the shoes of a black person:

> Suppose a member of this court, nay, suppose every member of it, by some mysterious dispensation of providence should wake to-morrow with a black skin and curly hair ... and in traveling through that portion of the country where the "Jim Crow Car" abounds, should be ordered into it by the conductor. It is easy to imagine what would be the result ... What humiliation, what rage would then fill the judicial mind![39]

It may be ultimately impossible to take the perspective of another completely, but the effort to do so may help us recognize that our perspective is partial and that the status quo is not inevitable or ideal. After shaking free of these unstated assumptions and developing a sense of alternative perspectives, judges must then choose. The process of looking through other perspectives does not itself yield an answer, but it may lead to an answer different from the one that the judge would otherwise have reached. Seen in this light, the difference dilemma is hard but not impossible.

◊ ◊ ◊

Historians have described how a conception of reality, when it triumphs, convinces even those injured by it of its actuality. Accordingly, political and cultural success itself submerges the fact that conceptions of reality represent a perspective of some groups, not a picture of reality free from any perspective. At the turn of the century, for example, a new middle class justified industrialism and the control of immigrants by spreading understandings of science, technology, and bureaucracy as neutral and progressive.[40] Similarly, studies have shown how groups with relatively little social and economic power internalize the views of those with more power—often at the cost of personal conflict and damaged self-respect.[41] The work listener actually tries to reach beyond the assumption of one reality, one version of the truth. There is no neutrality, no escape from choice. But it is possible to develop better abilities to name and grasp competing perspectives and to make more knowing choices thereafter. In the next section, I suggest that efforts along these lines are central to the challenge of engendering justice.

V. Engendering Justice

> The problem of freedom is the problem of how to divest our categories of their halo of eternal truth.
>
> Mary Douglas[42]

> The truth is that we are all responsible, even if we are not to blame.
>
> Sarah Burns[43]

The nineteenth-century American legal system recognized only three races: "white," "Negro," and "Indian." Californian authorities faced an influx of Chinese and Mexicans and were forced to confront the now complicated question of racial categorization. They solved the problem of categorizing Mexicans by defining them as "whites" and by according them the rights of free white persons. Chinese, however, were labeled "Indian" and denied the political and legal rights of white persons. Similarly, in 1922, a unanimous Supreme Court concluded that Japanese persons were not covered by a federal naturalization statute applicable to "free white persons," "aliens of African nativity," and "persons of African descent."[44]

In retrospect, these results seem arbitrary. The legal authorities betrayed a striking inability to reshape their own categories for people who did not fit. Of course, it is impossible to know what might have happened if some piece of history had been otherwise. Still, it is tempting to wonder: What if the California legal authorities had changed their racial scheme, rather than forcing the Chinese and Mexican applicants into it? The officials then might have noticed that nationality, not race, distinguished these groups. What if these officials and the justices in 1922 had tried to take the point of view of the people they were labeling? Perhaps, from this vantage point, the justices would have realized the need for reasons—beyond racial classification—for granting or withholding legal rights and privileges.

In this chapter, I have argued that trying to take seriously the point of view of people labeled *different* is a way to move beyond current difficulties in the treatment of differences in our society. This last statement, like much of the chapter, is addressed to people in positions of sufficient power to label others *different* and to make choices about how to treat difference. If you have such power, you may realize the dilemma of difference: By taking another person's difference into account in awarding goods or distributing burdens, you risk reiterating the significance of that difference and, potentially, its stigma and stereotyping consequences. But if you do not take another person's difference into account—in a world that has made that difference matter—you may also recreate and reestablish both the difference and its negative implications. If you draft or enforce laws, you may worry that the effects of the laws will not be neutral whether you take difference into account or you ignore it. If you employ people, judge guilt or innocence, or make other decisions affecting lives, you may want and need the discretion to make an individualized assessment, free from any focus on categorical differences. But if that discretion is exercised without constraint, difference may be taken into account in a way that does not treat that person as an individual—and in a way that disguises this fact from view.

These dilemmas, I have argued, become less paralyzing if you try to break out of unstated assumptions and take the perspective of the person you have called *different*. Once you do that, you may glimpse that your patterns for organizing the world are both arbitrary and foreclose their own reconsideration. You may find that the categories you take for granted do not well serve features you had not focused upon in the past. You may see an injury that you had not noticed or take more seriously a harm that you had otherwise discounted. If you try to take the view of the other person, you will find that the "difference" you notice is part of the relationship on comparison you draw between that person and someone else, with reference to a norm, and you will then get the chance to examine the reference point you usually take for granted. Maybe you will conclude that the reference point itself should change. Employers do not have to treat pregnancy and parenthood as a disability, but instead as a part of the lives of valued workers. You may find that you had so much ignored the point of view of others that you did not realize that you were mistaking your point of view for reality. Perhaps you will find that the way things are is not the only way things could be—that changing the way you classify, evaluate, reward, and punish may make the differences you had noticed less significant, or even irrelevant, to the way you run your life.

I have also argued, however, that we often forget how to take the perspective of another. We forget even that our point of view is not reality and that our conceptual schemes are simplifications, serving some interests and uses rather than others. We forget because our minds—and probably our hearts—cannot contain the whole world, and so we reduce the world to shorthand that we can handle. Our shorthand—because it is our shorthand—reflects what we thought we needed, where we stood, and who we are. We treat our divisions of the world as though they were real and universal. We do not see that they embody our early experiences of discovering how we are both the same as and different from our parents. We forget how we learned from them to encode the world into the same classifications they used to serve their own needs. We forget that things may appear frightful only because they are unfamiliar. We look at people we do not know and think they are different from us in important ways. We forget that even if they are different, in a way that matters to them, too, they also have a view of reality, and ours is as different from theirs as theirs is from ours.

We think we know what is real, what differences are real, and what really matters, even though sometimes we realize that our perceptions and desires are influenced by others. Sometimes we realize that television, radio, classes we had in school, or the attitudes of people who matter to us, affect our inclinations. Every time we wear an item of clothing that we now think is fashionable but used to think was ugly, we brush up against the outside influences on what we think inside. Yet we think that we think independently. We forget that widely held beliefs may be the ones most influenced from the outside.

The more powerful we are, the less we may be able to see that the world coincides with our view precisely because we shaped it in accordance with those views. That is just one of our privileges. Another is that we are able to put and hear questions in ways that do not question ourselves. In contrast, the more marginal we feel from the world, from the groups we know, the more likely we are to glimpse a contrast between some people's perceptions of reality and our own. Yet we still may slip into the worldview of the more powerful, because it is more likely to be validated. We prefer to have our perceptions validated; we need to feel acknowledged and confirmed. But when we fail to take the perspective of another, we deny that very acknowledgment and confirmation in return.

If we want to preserve justice, we need to develop a practice for more knowing judgments about problems of difference. We must stop seeking to get close to the "truth" and instead seek to get close to other people's truths. The question is, how do we do this? In this section, I argue that we must persuade others as much as they must persuade us about the reality we should construct. Justice can be impartial only if judges acknowledge their own partiality. Justice depends on the possibility of conflicts among the values and perspectives that justice pursues. Courts, and especially the Supreme Court, provide a place for the contest over realities that govern us—if we open ourselves to the chance that a reality other than our own may matter. Justice can be engendered when we overcome our pretended indifference to difference and instead people our world with individuals who surprise one another about difference.

A. Impartiality and Partial Truths

It is a paradox. Only by admitting our partiality can we strive for impartiality. Impartiality is the guise partiality takes to seal bias against exposure. It looks neutral to apply a rule denying unemployment benefits to anyone who cannot fulfill the work schedule, but it is not neutral if the work schedule was devised with one religious Sabbath, and not another, in mind. The idea of impartiality implies human access to a view beyond human experience, a "God's eye" point of view. Not only do humans lack this inhuman perspective, but humans who claim it are untruthful, trying to exercise power to cut off conversation and debate. Doris Lessing argues that a single absolute truth would mean the end of human discourse but that we are happily saved from that end because any truth, once uttered, becomes immediately one truth among many, subject to more discourse and dispute. If we treat other points of view as irritants in the way of our own vision, we are still hanging on to faulty certainty. Even if we admit the limits of our view, while treating those limits as gaps and leaving the rest in place, we preserve the pretense that our view is sufficiently rooted in reality to resist any real change prompted by another.

Acknowledging partiality may cure the pretense of impartiality. But unless we have less capacity to step outside our own skins than I think we do, we then have a choice of which partial view to advance or accept. Whose partial view should resolve conflicts over how to treat assertions of difference, whether assigned or claimed? Preferring the standpoint of an historically denigrated group can reveal truths obscured by the dominant view, but it can also reconfirm the underlying conceptual scheme of the dominant view by focusing on it. Similarly, the perspective of those who are labeled *different* may offer an important challenge to the view of those who imposed the label, but it is a corrective lens, another partial view, not absolute truth.[45] We then fight over whether to prefer it. "Standpoint theories" may also deny the multiple experiences of members of the denigrated group and create a new claim of essentialism.

Instead of an impartial view, we should strive for the standpoint of someone who is committed to the moral relevance of contingent particulars.[46] Put in personal terms, if I pretend to be impartial, I hide my partiality; however, if I embrace partiality, I risk ignoring you, your needs, and your alternative reality—or, conversely, embracing and appropriating your view into yet another rigid, partial view. I conclude that I must acknowledge and struggle against my partiality by making an effort to understand your reality and what it means for my own. I need to stop seeking certainty and acknowledge the complexity of our shared and colliding realities, as well as the tragic impossibility of all prevailing at once. It is this complexity that constitutes our reciprocal realities, and it is the conflict between our realities that constitutes us, whether we engage in it overtly or submerge it under a dominant view.

Moral action, then, takes place in a field of complexity, and we act ethically when we recognize what we give up as well as what we embrace. The solution is not to adopt and cling to some new standpoint but, instead, to strive to become and remain open to perspectives and claims that challenge our own. Justice, like philosophy, ought

> to trust rather to the multitude and variety of its arguments than to the conclusiveness of any one. Its reasoning should not form a chain which is no stronger than its weakest link, but a cable whose fibers may be ever so slender, provided they are sufficiently numerous and intimately connected.[47]

We who judge should remove the removal of ourselves when we either ignore or notice a difference. We can and should confront our involvement in and responsibility for what happens when we act in a reality we did not invent but still have latitude to discredit or affirm. We should have the humility and the courage to act in each situation anew, rather than applying what we presume to know already, as though each case were merely a repetition of an episode from the past.

◇ ◇ ◇

Two exercises can help those who judge to glimpse the perspectives of others and to avoid a false impartiality. The first is to explore our own stereotypes, our own attitudes toward people we treat as different—and, indeed, our own categories for organizing the world. Audre Lorde put it powerfully: "I urge each one of us here to reach down into that deep place of knowledge inside herself and touch that terror and loathing of any difference that lives there. See whose face it wears. Then the personal as the political can begin to illuminate all our choices."[48] This is a call for applying "strict scrutiny" not just to a defendant's reasons for burdening a protected minority group but also to ourselves when we judge those reasons. It is a process that even we who see ourselves as victims of oppression need to undertake, for devices of oppression are buried within us. We must also examine and retool our methods of classification and consider how they save us from questioning our instincts, ourselves, and our existing social arrangements. Putting ourselves in the place of those who look different can push us to challenge our ignorance and fear and to investigate our usual categories for making sense of the world. This is an opportunity to enlarge judges' understanding and abilities to become better practitioners in the business of solving problems.

The second exercise is to search out differences and celebrate them by constructing new bases for connection. We can pursue the possibilities of difference behind seeming commonalities and seek out commonalities across difference, thereby confronting the ready association of sameness with equality and difference with inferiority. One route is to emphasize our common humanity, despite our different traits. Another tack is to disentangle difference from the allocation of benefits and burdens in society—a tack that may well require looking at difference to alter how people use it. The Court's effort to ensure equality for women and men in the conjunction of work and family life in *Cal Fed* represents such an effort to disentangle institutional arrangements from the difference they create. A third approach is to cherish difference and welcome anomaly. Still another is to understand that which initially seems strange and to learn about sense and reason from this exercise—just as philosophers, anthropologists and psychologists have urged us to take seriously the self-conceptions and perceptions of others. In the process of trying to understand how another person understands, we may even remake our categories of understanding. Other persons may not even define "self" the same way we do, and glimpsing their "self-concepts" thus challenges us to step beyond our operating assumptions. A further skill to practice is to recognize commonality in difference itself: in the relationships within which we construct difference and connect and distinguish ourselves from one another.

These exercises in taking the perspective of the other will deepen and broaden anyone's perspective. For judges, who debate the use of the coercive forces of the law in relation to issues of difference, these exercises are critical. Judges can and should act as representatives, standing in for others and symbolizing society itself. Judicial acts of representation must also be responsive to the demands of the people they govern, in order to secure apparent legitimacy and, ultimately, to remain effective. One judge explained that law's coercive power must be applied to ensure "the viability of a pluralistic democracy," which "depends upon the willingness to accept all of the 'thems' as 'us'" Whether the motives of the framers be considered moralistic or pragmatic, the structure of the Constitution rests on the foundational principle that successful self-governance can be achieved only through public institutions following egalitarian policies.[49]

This exhortation—that we must take the perspective of another while remembering that we cannot really know what another sees and must put our own categories up for challenge, without ceding the definition of reality over to others—sounds quite complicated. What do we do with the sense of complexity?

B. Complexity, Passivity, and the Status Quo:
The Problem of Deference

We are mistaken when we hold onto simple certainties. Yet complexity seems both over-whelming and incapacitating. By bearing into complexity rather than turning away from it, by listening to the variety of voices implicated in our problems, we may lose a sense of ready solutions and steady certainties. But clear answers have been false gods, paid hom-age to in the coinage of other people's opportunities, and also at cost to our own character. We harden ourselves when we treat our categories as though they were real, closing off responses to new facts and to challenges to how we live and think. Our certainties also leave unresolved conflicts among incompatible but deeply held values. In the face of com-plexity, "the politics of difference can all too easily degenerate into the politics of 'mutual indifference'"[50] If we care about justice, the biggest mistake would be to respond to com-plexity with passivity. That response is not impartial; it favors the status quo, those ben-efited by it, and the conception of reality it fosters.

1. Forms of Passivity. Four forms of judicial passivity may be tempting in the face of complexity: deference, intent requirements, reliance on apparent choices or concessions of the parties, and reliance on doctrine. I will consider each in turn.

Respect for other institutions and persons is a critical part of judging, but there are particular risks when the Court, while acknowledging the complexity of a problem of dif-ference, defers to other branches or levels of government, to private actors, or even to the parties before the Court. One risk is that the Court will pretend that it has no power over or responsibility for what results. When the Court defers to Congress, the executive, a state government, or a private actor, the justices are saying, Let's not make a decision, let's leave it to others, or let's endorse the freedom or respect the power of others. It is surely important for the justices to understand their relationship with other people or institutions with interests in a matter, but such understanding is quite different from ced-ing responsibility for what ensues. This principle is important for everybody, but espe-cially for a judicial body, which has parties with genuine conflicts before it. As Frank Michelman put it, "Attention [to other branches of government] cannot mean deference, or talismanic invocation of authority. The norm of justice to parties itself commands that no other norm should ever take a form that preempts questions or exempts from reason-giving."[51]

Problems also arise when the Court takes on the second form of passivity: focusing on the intentions of the parties before it. When the Court demands evidence of inten-tional discrimination before upholding a plaintiff's charges, the justices are deferring to and thereby entrenching the perspective of the defendant, thus rejecting the perspective of the plaintiff-victim. Asking only about the sincerity of the motive behind a statute whose effect is challenged is also an act that takes sides, defines which reality will govern, and avoids the real challenge of responding to the perspective of the plaintiff.

It is equally problematic for the Court, in a third form of passivity, to point to appar-ent choices made by plaintiffs, victims, or members of minority groups, as Justice Scalia did in *Johnson*[52] as a justification for holding against them. The Court may presume incorrectly that the choices are free and uncoerced, or the Court may wrongly attribute certain meanings to a choice. Similarly, judicial references to litigants' concessions during litigation, including during oral argument, are not without risk. Although the Court may be trying to take the perspective of others seriously, its reliance on litigants' concessions as the peg for a judicial decision may also be the Court's way of reducing the task of deciding on its own. Reliance on concessions of the lawyer may be especially troubling in cases involving the rights of minorities, because it is unclear for whom the lawyer speaks at that moment: the client, the cause, or others unrepresented there who will be affected in the future by the Court's ruling.

The fourth form of passivity is perhaps one of the most effective circumventions of responsibility: the Court's reliance on its own doctrinal boundaries and categories to resolve the cases before it. This chapter has demonstrated that the difference dilemma poses similar problems in a wide variety of contexts, including cases involving religion, gender, race, and sexual preference. Yet when the Court takes the boundaries between doctrines as given, filling the doctrines with operative tests and lines of precedent, it obscures these potential similarities across contexts. By the time a case reaches an appellate court, the adversary process has so focused on specific issues of doctrinal disagreement that the competing arguments have come under one framework, not under competing theories. Legal analogy is typically inseparable from precedential reasoning, telescoping the creative potential of a search for surprising similarities into a narrow focus on prior rulings that could "control" the instant case. The Court's practice vividly demonstrates how fabricated categories can assume the status of immutable reality. Of course, law would be overwhelming without doctrinal categories and separate lines of precedent. Yet by holding to rigid categories, the Court denies the existence of tensions and portrays a false simplicity amid a rabbit warren of complexity. The Court's strict segregation of doctrine also cloisters lines of thought and insights, thereby restricting the Court's ability to use larger frames of judgment.

2. Avoiding Passivity. Besides resisting tempting forms of passivity—which do not lessen judicial responsibility—the Court can and should challenge rigid patterns of thought. What if litigants argued more emphatically across contexts and reminded members of the Court, "You have seen something like this before?" Litigants can help the Court to avoid the dangers of complacency and complexity by searching out analogies and developing unfamiliar perspectives. At the same time, litigants may gain a tactical advantage, because they may persuade a member of the Court of their point of view by analogizing to something the justice has glimpsed elsewhere. This practice also has some support in epistemology. The difficulties each of us has in seeing around the bend of our own thought can be eased with the help of insights from others who are positioned differently. Given the relationship between knowledge and power, those with less privilege may well see better than those with more.

Surprisingly, traditional legal techniques actually provide fruitful starting points for avoiding passivity. One noted feature of the legal system that can be used to mount this challenge is analogical reasoning.[53] The existence of encrusted practices and categories, however, frustrates the full use of these tools. Litigants and judges should search out unexpected analogies to scrape off barnacles of thought and to challenge views so settled that they are not thought to be views. This process may persuade particular judges, in particular cases, to see a different angle on a problem. It also holds promise as a method for finding surprising commonalities that can nudge us all to reassess well-established categories of thought.

The promise of reasoning by analogy is lost if it becomes an arid conceptualist enterprise. Yet when immersed in the particulars of a problem, we sometimes are able to think up analogies that break out of ill-fitting conceptual schemes. As one observer of creative processes in art, science, and philosophy has commented, "In the history of human thinking the most fruitful developments frequently take place at those points where two different lines of thought meet."[54] By seeing something in a new light, seeing its similarity to something else once thought quite different, we are able to attribute different meanings and consequences to what we see. A glimpse of difference in one context may enable litigants and judges better to appreciate it in another context.

The adversarial process is another feature of the legal system that, with some modification, can be used to challenge judicial complacency. In fact, the values of thinking through analogies bear a striking similarity to the virtues of reasoning in dialogue. The dialogue form puts the student in a position to follow the connections and divergences in argument and invent for herself ways to think anew, rather than simply internalizing the monologue of inherited knowledge. Barbara Johnson notes that "learning seems to take place most rapidly when the student must respond to the contradiction between *two* teachers. And what the student learns in the process is both the power of ambiguity and the non-innocence of ignorance."[55] Similarly, dialogue in legal briefs and courtroom arguments can stretch the minds of listeners, especially if they are actively forming their own position and not simply picking between the ones before them.

The introduction of additional voices may enable adversary dialogue to expand beyond a stylized, either/or mode, prompting new and creative insights. Consequently, the Court can, and should seek out alternative views in *amicus* briefs. Inventive approaches can bring the voices of those who are not present before the Court, as in the recent brief filed with the Court that collected the autobiographical accounts of men and women who believed their lives had been changed by the availability of legalized abortion.[56] Similarly, the famous "Brandeis brief" in *Muller v. Oregon*[57] marked a creative shift for the Court, introducing the use of vivid, factual detail as a way to break out of the formalist categories dominating the analysis. Seeking unusual perspectives enables justices to avail themselves of the "partial superiority" of other people's views and to reach for what is unfamiliar and perhaps suppressed under the dominant ways of seeing. Bringing in a wider variety of views can also make the so-called countermajoritarian Court more "democratic."

Besides seeking out unfamiliar perspectives and analogies new to the law, all judges should also consider the human consequences of their decisions in difference cases, rather than insulating themselves in abstractions. Such engagement encourages the judge to fill in textual gaps based on his or her own experiences. It may seem paradoxical to urge those who judge to bring their own experiences to the problems before them, after identifying the dangerous ways in which we all confuse our own perceptions and interests for reality. In the process of personal reflection, however, the judge may stretch faculties for connection while engaging in dialogue with the parties over their legal arguments and analogies. I petition all judges to open up to the chance that someone may move them—the experience will not tell them what to do, but it may give them a way outside routinized categories to forge new approaches to the problem at hand.

This call to be open, to canvas personal experience, applies to all legal controversies, but it is especially important in the context of cases that present the dilemma of difference. Here the judicial mainstays of neutrality and distance prove most risky, for they blind judges to their own involvement in recreating the negative meanings of difference. Yet the dangers of making differences matter also argue against categorical solutions. By struggling to respond humanly to the dilemma in each particular context, the judge can supply the possibility of connection otherwise missing in the categorical treatments of difference.

C. Choosing Among Divergent Demands

Urging judges to allow themselves to be moved by the arguments may seem misguided. A judge who identifies with every perspective may simply feel indecisive and overburdened. Would feeling the tugs in all directions render us powerless to choose? It may be just this fear that explains our attachment to simplifying categories, stereotypes, and fixed ways of thought. Some of us may fear being overwhelmed by the world, others fear being too moved by it, others fear being powerless before it. Challenging familiar categories and styles of reasoning may threaten the search for order, decisiveness, and manageability that maintain the predictability in our lives. But there are other ways to hold things together than the methods we have used in the past.

Some may aspire to a jurisprudence of individualism, never treating any individual as a member of a group. Yet, resonant as it is with many American traditions, individualization is a myth: Because our language is shared and our categories communally invented, any word I use to describe your uniqueness draws you into the classes of people sharing your traits. Even if ultimately I produce enough words so that the intersection of all classes you belong in contains only one member—you—we understand this through a language of comparison with others. This language, however, seems to embroil us in the dilemma of difference.

What could we do instead? I believe we should welcome complexity and challenge complacency—and stop fearing that we will be unable to make judgments. We can and do make judgments all the time, in a way committed to making meaning, rather than recreating or ignoring difference. We make commitments when we make decisions; we reconfirm or remake current understandings by reflecting so deeply and particularly about a new situation that we challenge presumptive solutions. Instead of trying continually to fit people into categories, and to enforce or deny rights on that basis, we can and do make decisions by immersing in particulars to renew commitments to a fair world.

◊ ◊ ◊

Thus, one reason we can still decide, amid powerfully competing claims, is that immersion in particulars does not require the relinquishment of general commitments. The struggle is not over the validity of principles and generalizations—it is over which ones should prevail in a given context. The choice from among principles, in turn, implicates choices about which differences, and which similarities, should matter. These are moral choices, choices about which voices should persuade those who judge.

Even when we understand them, some voices will lose. The fundamentalist Christians who supported the Balanced Treatment Act in Louisiana deserve respect and understanding: Their view of the world may well be threatened by the curriculum taught to their children in the public schools. However, this is what the fight is about. Whose view of reality should prevail in public institutions? This deep conundrum involves the conflicts between the worldview animating any rule for the entire society, and the worldviews of subgroups who will never share the dominant views. I am tempted to propose a seemingly "neutral" rule, such as a rule that judges interpreting the commitment to respect difference should make the choice that allows difference to flourish without imposing it on others. If exclusion of their worldview from the biology curriculum creates an intolerable choice for the fundamentalists, they do and they must have the choice to establish their own educational institutions, and their own separate community. Yet this seemingly "neutral" position is a comfortable view for a nonfundamentalist like myself, who cannot appreciate the full impact of the evolution science curriculum as experienced by at least some fundamentalists. Rather than pretending to secure a permanent solution through a "neutral" rule, I must acknowledge the tragedy of nonneutrality—and admit that our very commitment to tolerance yields intolerance toward some views. If the fundamentalists lose in this case, they can continue to struggle to challenge the meaning of the commitment to separate church and state, and they may convince the rest of us in the next round. Although it may be little solace for the minority group, its challenge achieves something even when it loses, by reminding the nation of our commitment to diversity, and our inability, thus far, to achieve it fully.

Thus, choices from among competing commitments do not end after the Court announces its judgment. Continuing skepticism about the reality endorsed by the Court—or any source of governmental power—is the only guard against tyranny.

The continuing process of debate over deeply held but conflicting commitments is both the mechanism and the promise of our governmental system. Within that system, the Supreme Court's power depends upon persuasion. As Hannah Arendt wrote: "The thinking process which is active in judging something is not, like the thought process of pure reasoning, a dialogue between me and myself, but finds itself always and primarily, even if I am quite alone in making up my mind, in an anticipated communication with others with whom I know I must finally come to some agreement."[58] The important question is, with whom must you come to agreement? In a society of diversity with legacies of discrimination, within a polity committed to self-governance, the judiciary becomes a critical arena for demands of inclusion. I see the judicial arena as a forum for contests over competing realities. The question remains, however, whose definitions of realities will govern in a given case and over time.

Court judgments endow some perspectives, rather than others, with power. Judicial power is least accountable when judges leave unstated—and treat as a given—the perspective they select. Litigation before the Supreme Court sometimes highlights individuals who otherwise seldom imprint their perspective on the polity. In eliciting these perspectives and accepting their challenge to the version of reality the justices otherwise would take for granted, the Court advances the fundamental constitutional commitment to require reasons before exercises of power, whether public or private. Growing from our history, wrought from many struggles, is the tradition we have invented, and it is a tradition that declares that the status quo cannot be immune from demands for justification. Litigation over the meanings of difference represents demands for such accountability. By asking how power influences knowledge, the Court can address whether a "difference" has been assigned through past domination or as a remedy for past domination. In this way, the Court can solicit information about contrasting views of reality without casting off the moorings of historical experience, and in this inquiry, the Court can assess the risk of creating new patterns of domination while remedying inequalities of the past. As we compete for power to give reality to our visions, we confront tragic limits in our abilities to make meaning together. Yet we must continue to seek a language to speak across conflicting affiliations.

We need settings in which to engage in the clash of realities that breaks us out of settled and complacent meanings and creates opportunities for insight and growth. This is the special burden and opportunity for the Court: to enact and preside over the dialogue through which we remake the normative endowment that shapes current understandings.

When the Court performs these roles, it engenders justice. Justice is engendered when judges admit the limitations of their own viewpoints, when judges reach beyond those limits by trying to see from contrasting perspectives, and when people seek to exercise power to nurture differences, not to assign and control them. Rather than securing an illusory universality and objectivity, law is a medium through which particular people can engage in the continuous work of making justice. The law "is part of a distinctive manner of imagining the real."[59] Legal decisions engrave upon our culture the stories we tell to and about ourselves, the meanings that constitute the traditions we invent. Searching for words to describe realities too multiple and complex to be contained by their language, litigants and judges struggle over what will be revealed and what will be concealed in the inevitable partiality of human judgment. Through deliberate attention to our own partiality, we can begin to acknowledge the dangers of pretended impartiality. By taking difference into account, we can overcome our pretended indifference to difference, and people our worlds with those who can surprise and enrich one another. As we make audible, in official arenas, the struggles over which version of reality will secure power, we disrupt the silence of one perspective, imposed as if universal. Admitting the partiality of the perspective that temporarily gains official endorsement may embolden resistance to announced rules. But only by admitting that rules are resistible—and by justifying to the governed their calls for adherence—can justice be done in a democracy. "It is only through the variety of relations constructed by the plurality of beings that truth can be known and community constructed."[60] Then we constitute ourselves as members of conflicting communities with enough reciprocal regard to talk across differences. We engender mutual regard for pain we know and pain we do not understand.

Notes

For resolving any doubts about the possibility that people can take the perspective of another, the author thanks Joe Singer, Karol Dean, David Fernandez, Mary Joe Frug, Maura Kelley, Catharine Krupnick, Frank Michelman, Peter Rubin, Elizabeth Schneider, Avi Soifer, Elizabeth Spelman, Kathleen Sullivan, Cass Sunstein, and Stephen Wieder.

1. 107 S. Ct. 683 (1987).

2. California Fair Employment and Housing Act, CAL. GOV'T CODE ANN. § 12945(b)(2) (West 1980).

3. *See* 107 S. Ct. at 691. In the Pregnancy Discrimination Act of 1978 (PDA), Pub. L. No. 95-555, 92 Stat. 2076 (1978) (codified at 42 U.S.C. § 2000e(k) (1978)), Congress amended Title VII to include discrimination on the basis of pregnancy, rejecting the Supreme Court's contrary ruling in General Electric Co. v. Gilbert. 429 U.S. 125 (1976).

4. 107 S. Ct. at 692 (quoting *Cal Fed,* 758 F.2d 390, 396 (9th Cir. 1985)).

5. *Id.* at 691, n.17. In *Cal Fed,* the Court tried to avoid the problems of stereotyping by characterizing pregnancy solely as a physical disability—ignoring alternative characterizations that analogize women's role in pregnancy to veterans' role in national defense—a role justifying preferential treatment in employment. *See* Littleton, *Reconstructing Sexual Equality,* 75 CALIF. L. REV. 201 (forthcoming 1987).

6. *See* 107 S. Ct. at 694.

7. 107 S. Ct. at 698 (White, J., dissenting). The dissent rejected the claim that employers could comply with both statutes by providing benefits to both women and men in comparable situations, because that approach would extend the scope of the state statute beyond its express language and because the federal statute did not require programs where none currently existed. *See id.* at 701.

8. *Id.* at 700. *See* 107 S. Ct. at 694 (opinion of the Court).

9. 107 S. Ct. 2022 (1987).

10. 107 S. Ct. 2019 (1987).

11. 785 F.2d 523, 527 (4th Cir. 1986).

12. *Id.* at 529 (Wilkinson, J., concurring in part and dissenting in part). Judge Wilkinson explained: "It is an understatement to note that attempts to place individuals in distinct racial groups frequently serve only to facilitate continued discrimination and postpone the day when all individuals will be addressed as such" (*id.* at 533).

13. 107 S. Ct. 2573 (1987).

14. *See* 107 S. Ct. at 2576; *id.* at 2600–5 (Scalia, J., dissenting).

15. *Id.* at 2582; *accord id.* at 2587 (Powell, J., concurring).

16. 107 S. Ct. 1046 (1987).

17. *Id.* at 1048 (quoting FLA. STAT. § 443.021 (1985)).

18. *See* 107 S. Ct. at 1051 and n.11.

19. 107 S. Ct. 821 (1987).

20. 26 U.S.C. § 3304(a)(12) (1982).

21. 107 S. Ct. at 825.

22. 107 S. Ct. 1756 (1987).

23. 107 S. Ct. at 1778, n.37.

24. *Id.* at 1791; *accord id.* at 1806 (Stevens, J., dissenting); *id.* at 1805 (Blackmun, J., dissenting) ("If a grant of relief to [McCleskey] were to lead to a closer examination of the effects of racial considerations throughout the criminal-justice system, the system, and hence society, might benefit.").

25. *Id.* at 1806 (Stevens, J., dissenting).

26. 107 S. Ct. 2862 (1987).

27. 107 S. Ct. at 2874 (O'Connor, J., concurring in the judgment).

28. Christian, *The Race for Theory,* CULTURAL CRITIQUE, Spring 1987, at 51, 54.

29. G. GUNN, THE INTERPRETATION OF OTHERNESS: LITERATURE, RELIGION, AND THE AMERICAN IMAGINATION 177 (1979).

30. J. BRUNER, *supra* note 116, at 110 (paraphrasing Robert Woodworth). Similarly, Albert Einstein said. "It is the theory which decides what we can observe." D. BELL. THE COMING OF POST-INDUSTRIAL SOCIETY 9 (1973) (quoting Einstein).

31. Gould, *The Woman Question: Philosophy of Liberation and the Liberation of Philosophy,* in WOMEN AND PHILOSOPHY: TOWARD A THEORY OF LIBERATION 21 (C. Gould and M. Wartofsky eds. 1976).

32. E. KELLER. A FEELING FOR THE ORGANISM: THE LIFE AND WORK OF BARBARA MCCLINTOCK 150 (1983).

33. W. JAMES, *What Makes a Life Significant,* in ON SOME OF LIFE'S IDEALS, at 49, 81.

34. Soifer, at 409.

35. It is not clear whether Justice Scalia looked at the Balanced Treatment Act in *Edwards* from the vantage point of fundamentalist parents, or instead from the vantage point of state legislators.

36. City of Cleburne v. Cleburne Living Center, 473 U.S. 432, 455 (1985) (Stevens, J., concurring).

37. *See* Lau v. Nichols, 414 U.S. 563, 566 (1974).

38. 163 U.S. 537, 552 (1896) (Harlan, J., dissenting).

39. Brief for the Plaintiff, *Plessy v. Ferguson, reprinted in* CIVIL RIGHTS AND THE AMERICAN NEGRO 298, 303–4 (A. Blaustein and R. Zangrando eds. 1968).

40. *See* R. WIEBE, THE SEARCH FOR ORDER, 1877–1920, at 111–13 (1967).

41. *See, e.g.,* Castaneda v. Partida, 430 U.S. 482, 503 (1977) (Marshall, J., concurring)

42. M. DOUGLAS, IMPLICIT MEANINGS: ESSAYS IN ANTHROPOLOGY 224 (1975).

43. Burns, *Apologia for the Status Quo* (Book Review), 74 GEO. L.J. 1791, 1819 (1986).

44. *See* Ozawa v. United States, 260 U.S. 178 (1922).

45. *See, e.g.,* C. GILLIGAN. In a Different Voice (1982), at 151–74 (linking a visionoof maturity

to a complementary and productive tension between (feminine) ethos of care and a (masculine)ethic of rights).

46. *See* M. NUSSBAUM, The Fragility of Goodness (1986), at 314. Nussbaum adds that the someone should be committed to "the value of the passions, and the incommensurability of the values that will tend to approve of this particular sort of judge as a guide" (*id* at 311). The point is that a judge must have a plurality of attachments and do justice in the tension among them (*id.* at 314).

47. 5 C.S. PEIRCE, *Some Consequences of Four Incapacities,* in COLLECTED PAPERS at 157 (C. Hartshorne and P. Weiss eds. 1931).

48. Lorde, *The Master's Tools Will Never Dismantle the Master's House,* in THIS BRIDGE CALLED MY BACK: WRITINGS BY RADICAL WOMEN OF COLOR 98 (C. Moraga and G. Anzaldua eds. 1981). This is not sympathy, tolerance, or even compassion, each of which leaves the viewer's understanding fundamentally unchanged.

49. Keyes v. School Dist. No. 1, 576 F. Supp. 1503, 1520 (D. Colo. 1983) (Matsch. J.).

50. Cornell, *The Poststructuralist Challenge to the Ideal of Community, 8 Cardozo L.R. 989–90 (1987).*

51. Michaelman, The Supreme Court, 1985 Term—Foreward 100 HARV. L.R. 1, at 76 (1986).

52. Johnson v. Transportation Agency 107 S. CT. 1442 (1987). In Hobble v. Unemployment Appeals Commission, 107 S. Ct. 1046, 1051 (1987), however, the Court's majority was sympathetic about constraints on choice, arguing that it is unlawful coercion to force an employee to choose between fidelity to religious beliefs and continued employment.

53. *See* E. LEVI, An Introduction to Legal Reasoning (1972), at 8.

54. F. CAPRA, THE TAO OF PHYSICS xii (1984) (quoting Werner Weisenberg); *cf.* S. HARDING, at 235: "Analogies are not aids to the establishment of theories; they are an utterly essential part of theories, without which theories would be completely valueless and unworthy of the name" (quoting N. CAMPBELL, PHYSICS, THE ELEMENTS (1920)).

55. B. JOHNSON, A World of Difference (1987). at 83 (emphasis in original).

56. *See* Brief Amici Curiae, of National Abortion Rights Action League et al., Thornburgh v. American College of Obstetricians & Gynecologists, 476 U.S. 747 (1986) (no. 84–495 and 84–1379).

57. 208 U.S. 412 (1908).

58. H. ARENDT, BETWEEN PAST AND FUTURE 220 (1961).

59. C. GERTZ, LOCAL KNOWLEDGE (1983), at 184.

60. N. HARSOCK, at 254 (describing the view of Hannah Arendt), Money, Sex, & Power: Toward a Feminist Historical Materialism (1983).

10

Legality and Empathy

LYNNE N. HENDERSON

I. Introduction

> It is perfectly proper for judges to disagree about what the
> Constitution requires. But it is disgraceful for an
> interpretation of the Constitution to be premised upon
> unfounded assumptions about how people live.
>
> Justice Thurgood Marshall[1]

In 1976, John Noonan's *Persons and Masks of the Law*[2] appeared. In the first chapter, Noonan alluded to the unhinging of the law from human experience as well as the relationship of love to power and emotion to law. He conceded the need for the Rule of Law for social control—the alternative apparently being the war of all against all—but he also sought wistfully to incorporate human beings into legal thinking, stating, "Abandonment of the rules produces monsters; so does neglect of persons."[3] Yet Noonan, like others troubled by the lack of humane responses in the law, could do no more than raise a cry against legality's denial of persons. He never developed a coherent approach to help us avoid the tendency of legality to abstract the problems of persons to the point of denying persons altogether.

The troubling phenomenon produced by fidelity to the Rule of Law in legal theory and practice is captured in the quotation of Justice Marshall's dissent in *Kras:* Legal decisions and lawmaking frequently have nothing to do with understanding human experiences, affect, suffering—how people do live.[4] And feeling is denied recognition and legitimacy under the guise of the "rationality" of the Rule of Law. Incorporating experiential understanding of persons or groups into an ideological system based on a reductionist concept of reason, a system that at times seems to have a fetish for predictability and control under the Rule of Law, raises terrifying specters of destabilization, chaos, and anarchy. Accordingly, the emotional, physical, and experiential aspects of being human have by and large been banished from the better legal neighborhoods and from explicit recognition in legal discourse (although they sometimes get smuggled in as "facts" in briefs and opinions). Ironically, while emotion may generate laws via "politics," once those laws meet whatever criteria are necessary to constitute legitimacy in a system, they are cleansed of emotion under this vision of the Rule of Law. The law becomes not merely a human institution affecting real people but, rather, The Law.

A scholar or a judge may react to the pain and anguish caused actual human beings by a given law or doctrine, but she will seldom point to the painful or existential consequences of that law as reason to change it. This is because the ideological structures of legal discourse and cognition block affective and phenomenological argument: The "normal" discourse of law disallows the language of emotion and experience. The avoidance of emotion, affect, and experiential understanding reflects an impoverished view of reason and understanding—one that focuses on cognition in its most reductionist sense. This impoverished view stems from a belief that reason and emotion are separate, that reason can and must restrain emotion, that law-as-reason can and must order, rationalize, and control.

As a result, an entire mode of understanding and interpreting is seemingly foreclosed by legal discourse—or, more likely, it rumbles underground, much like the Freudian unconscious, seldom explicitly breaking through. That mode of understanding is best captured by the word *empathy,* a word that at first seems counterintuitive in a world defined as legal. Yet empathy is a form of understanding, a phenomenon that encompasses affect as well as cognition in determining meanings; it is a rich source of knowledge and approaches to legal problems—which are, ultimately, human problems. Properly understood, empathy is not a "weird" or "mystical" phenomenon, nor is it "intuition." Rather, it is a way of knowing that can explode received knowledge of legal problems and structures, that reveals moral problems previously sublimated by pretensions to reductionist rationality, and that provides a bridge to normatively better legal outcomes.

◊ ◊ ◊

This chapter argues that an understanding of the phenomenon of empathic knowledge has enormous explanatory power. It does so by examining from the perspective of empathy the stories of the Supreme Court's decisions in *Brown v. Board of Education (I),*[5] *Shaprio v. Thompson,*[6] *Roe v. Wade,*[7] and *Bowers v. Hardwick.*[8] The chapter argues that *Brown I* can best be explained by empathy, that *Shapiro* again manifests the breakthrough of empathic understanding, and that *Roe v. Wade* and its progeny demonstrate the Court's failure to hear certain empathic narratives. Finally, the chapter examines the recent case of *Bowers v. Hardwick* as an example of the complete failure of empathy in a legal decision.

II. Legality, Empathy, and Moral Choice

A. What Empathy Means

Empathy has become a favorite word in critical and feminist scholarship. Unfortunately, it is never defined or described—it is seemingly tossed in as a "nice" word in opposition to something bad or undesirable. Because I argue that empathy is a phenomenon that exists to expand understanding of others, I may or may not be writing in the traditions characterized as "critical" or "feminist." But I share the concerns of these traditions about the lack of humanistic response in legal thinking and have drawn on them to shape my own thinking.

◊ ◊ ◊

Thus it is necessary to develop an explanation of what I mean by *empathy.* While the word often appears to be used interchangeably with *love, altruism,* and *sympathy,* it actually encompasses specific psychological phenomena. Although the literature of empathy manifests disagreement about what is or is not *empathy,* rather than projection, sympathy, or what have you, there are three basic phenomena captured by the word: (1) feeling the emotion of another; (2) understanding the experience or situation of another, both affectively and cognitively, often achieved by imagining oneself to be in the position of the other; and (3) action brought about by experiencing the distress of another (hence the confusion of empathy with sympathy and compassion). The first two forms are ways of knowing, the third form a catalyst for action.

◊   ◊   ◊

As originally coined, empathy simply meant a physical reaction to something; for example, people observing the Leaning Tower of Pisa tend to lean with the building. It also meant grimacing when someone else hit her thumb with a hammer—feeling the physical sensation of pain. This meaning quickly expanded to include the empathic response to emotions. Empathy thus captured the concept of feeling globalized emotions from others—anger, fear, joy, love—or understanding the affect of a communication by "tuning in to the feelings of another." Globalized emotional reactions alert a person to the presence of emotion in an interaction or in another; however, these reactions may be misinterpreted or the emotion mislabeled. For example, because the physiological discomforts created by anger are virtually the same as those created by fear, cognitive attribution of "anger" or "fear" as the emotional state may be incorrect. Yet the detection of the strong emotional experience of another is a part of the meaning of an interaction or a phenomenon. Interpretation of that meaning, however, takes patience and sorting through, in order to understand the emotional state and what it means to the person experiencing it. Moreover, it is quite possible to misattribute causal explanations or interpretations to an emotion, which can lead to inaccurate empathy.

The second common meaning of empathy is the one often referred to in psychotherapeutic literature: the understanding of the situation of another. "The function of empathy is to help one understand and relate to another person."[9] It is embodied in the idealized vision of the field anthropologist or participant-observer sociologist who understands totally, through empathic "magic," the meanings, concepts, and way of being of a culture or group. Total understanding may be unachievable because of the social learning and cultural baggage the ethnographer, sociologist, or psychotherapist carries with her, yet it is an important mode of understanding the Other. This second form of empathy is the foundation of what philosophers refer to as "intersubjectivity."

An early developmental form of empathy as understanding the situation of the Other exists in what has been termed *conceptual perspective taking*—the capacity to perceive others as having their own goals, interests, and affects. Without empathy developed minimally, we would have the war of all against all or sociopathy. But beyond minimal conceptual perspective taking, empathy of this second type becomes historical, experiential, emotional, and cognitive. It illuminates the situations of others. This form of empathy is not a dissolution of "ego boundaries" or absorption of self by other—it is a means of relating to another or making another intelligible. A form of this kind of empathy is imaginative experiencing of the situation of another. It is not the same as "getting it," as the "aha" experience, but it gives important clues to understanding. A means of imaginative experiencing is to analogize from similar experiences of one's own (something, by the way, at which one would expect lawyers to be adept given their use of analogy in argument and reasoning).

The third meaning of empathy that is commonly used is that of sympathy, care, or compassion, captured in Hoffman's notion of "an empathic distress response"—"an aversive [e.g., uncomfortable] affect that can result from the discrepancy between some desired state of welfare of an object . . . and perceived/cognized reality.[10] This distress can lead to action in order to help or alleviate the pain of another. It is this form of empathy that is linked to action and altruistic behavior. Yet, "the relationship between action and the sharing of feelings is obviously not a simple or direct one,"[11] and while empathy may lead to helping behavior, it does not necessarily do so. Indeed, a person feeling the distress of another may find ways of blocking the experienced distress by thinking of other things, rationalizing nonaction by rules or limits, or withdrawal. Thus there is not a direct causal relationship between empathy and helping behavior, but a connection between empathy and helping or altruistic behavior does exist.

◇ ◇ ◇

Empathic responses are most likely to occur in situations of direct relationship to another, where concrete interaction occurs and incentive for understanding exists. This is not to say that they cannot occur where no relationship exists—the distress of a stranger may trigger an empathic distress response, for example. With a stranger, however, it is more likely that the individual experiencing the aversive response will minimize it "through various cognitive mechanisms . . . such as thinking about something else."[12] Individuals also can be desensitized to empathic distress, and studies have shown individuals will have reduced empathic distress if they are instructed to view a victim in a detached way. Moreover, empathic distress is unlikely to occur if the one in distress is not seen as a human or like oneself.

Empathic experiencing of emotion is probably influenced by cultural messages about which nonverbal and even verbal cues manifest particular emotions. Thus emotions are misunderstood cross-culturally. A Japanese woman may giggle when frightened—which to an American Caucasian conveys entirely the wrong emotional message. Finally, affect plus cognition—empathy as a means of understanding and relating to another—is undoubtedly less difficult in instances of shared cultural experiences than in unfamiliar ones. As Geertz has noted, however, that does not mean an ethnographer, for example, should not strive to understand the experiences of those in a culture: only that she should recognize that understanding will always be only partial.[13]

While these definitions and uses of empathy may initially sound foreign to us as members of the legal culture because of law's concern with social control and its commitment to rationality, predictability, and generalizability, empathy occasionally does surface in legal decisions. But before turning to some examples, it is necessary to examine the aspects of the legal culture that may delegitimate empathic knowledge.

B. Legality

Legality, laws, and legal actors can and do respond to human pain at times, as I shall argue in the discussions of *Brown* and *Shapiro*. In fact, legal doctrine can be placed in service to empathy, as happened in the area of desegregation once the Court abandoned *Plessy v. Ferguson*[14] and developed the doctrine that separation of the races violated the equal protection clause. I do not question that law can serve to promote individual freedom and worth under some circumstances. But in this section I am concerned to show the myriad ways in which notions of the Rule of Law and legality provide a way to avoid empathic understanding and a way to deny moral choice in legal decision-making.

Much in the nature of legality can block empathic understanding. The structures and beliefs about law that constitute "legality" may allow legal decision makers to be relatively unreflective about their choice to ignore empathic phenomena. A value of legality in American culture is that the Rule of Law opposes some Hobbesian free-for-all. The Rule of Law is the reification of rules governing rights and duties to which we pay homage: thus, this is a "government of laws, not men"; the Rule of Law transcends humans and is superior to them. The virtue of the Rule of Law is that it is ostensibly neutral and prevents abuse of persons. The neutrality and generality of the Rule of Law seek to serve the goals of protecting individuals from arbitrary treatment and of respecting people as autonomous and equal. As such it is not in direct opposition to empathy. Yet to the extent the concern is with perpetuating the Rule of Law for its own sake, the importance of empathic understanding can disappear.

◇ ◇ ◇

An example of the effect of bureaucratic legal formality on empathic communication is contained in Professor Simon's critique of welfare reform.[15] Simon argues that the creation of a formalized, rule-bound approach to eligibility determination for the Aid to Families with Dependent Children (AFDC) program created "indifference, impersonality, and irresponsibility." While the formalization of AFDC rules and procedures "seem[s] to have reduced the claimant's experience of oppressive and punitive moralism, of invasion of privacy, and of dependence on idiosyncratic personal favor . . . [it] also [has] reduced their experience of trust and personal care and [has] increased their experience of bewilderment and opacity."[16] Front-line eligibility workers view the people they are to serve as threats or nuisances; applicants are burdened with chasing down documentation from multiple bureaucracies and undoubtedly feel unheard and powerless. An effect of the formality is to render assistance "less sensitive to the circumstances of the applicant" than under the earlier, less formal system. There is little understanding of clients by workers or workers by clients. As a result, empathic understanding is lost, and many suffer denials of assistance, even though they are indeed eligible for it, because they fail to jump through the necessary "bureaucratic hoops." The form of abuse in the administration of AFDC that existed before the institution of legalistic and formalized standards and procedures has been replaced by another form of abuse: an unreflective reliance on rules.[17]

Similarly, the doctrinal development of the procedures for imposing the death penalty offers the opportunity to avoid empathic understanding by resorting to rules, as suggested in an article by Professor Weisberg. In California, at least, prosecutors take "full advantage of the doctrinal formality of the penalty trial to make the case for death in the most lawyerly, legalistic, dispassionate form. The prosecutor often reinforces the judge's instructions that if the formula of fact-finding produces a certain result, the jury has a duty to vote for death."[18] Thus, formalistically, all a jury need do is add up aggravating circumstances and subtract mitigating ones; the law then tells the jury whether death is the logical penalty. Professor Weisberg correctly observes that this formalistic discourse places the defense at a disadvantage and gives the jury a convenient way to avoid or escape the moral choice of whether to sentence the defendant to death. While the defense will seek to have the jury empathize with the defendant, the defense narrative—unattached to legal form—is a difficult one to convey, and the legalistic formula can provide sanctuary from moral anxiety.[19]

Apart from these particularized examples of legality's ability to provide refuge from empathy, more general characteristics of the legal actor's belief system can serve to block empathic understanding and moral choice. Fidelity to rules and to the autonomy of a legal system, and belief in its internal coherence, can support a judicial decision maker's avoidance of empathy and of his responsibility for human pain caused by law. As the late Professor Cover noted in his study of judicial responses to slavery:

> The judicial conscience is an artful dodger and rightfully so. Before it will concede that a case is one that presents a moral dilemma, it will hide in the nooks and crannies of the professional ethics, run to the cave of role limits, seek the shelter of separation of powers.[20]

In other words, legality gives judges a number of ways to block human pain and escape responsibility. Thus, a judge who believed himself to have chosen "fidelity to law" as a "higher value" could discount any moral concern about enforcing fugitive slave laws. Mechanistic application of the law—applying "the law and the law alone"—was a "retreat to formalism" that sheltered the judge from recognizing the horror of keeping human beings in bondage. Personal responsibility for choice was subsumed under strict adherence to the law as literally interpreted or as coming from a higher authority, with the decision maker serving as a mere conduit: "I do not make law, I follow it." Displacing responsibility for the decision to another decision maker was attractive as well, enabling the decision maker to retreat behind "separation of powers."[21] Thus, the problem of fugitive slave laws was for the people, or the legislature, or the executive to solve. Cover also described the "judicial can't"—the judge's claim that he simply did not have the power to avoid enforcing an evil law—as a way around moral choice and perhaps empathic understanding. While it is possible that judges made a moral choice in favor of legality, it is equally probable that legality, that the doctrine of persons-as-property, foreclosed their consideration of the moral issues. And because abolitionist lawyers did their best to portray their clients as humans with human stories, it is highly probable that many judges did revert to legality to avoid facing the moral dimensions of the problem.[22]

Fidelity to doctrine can justify caution as well. Because legal decisions have consequences, because they do at times affect behavior beyond that of the parties to the dispute and because people do rely on judgments, constantly changing the rules would be deeply destabilizing. Yet the reassurance of predictability of outcome provided by consistent adherence to doctrine over time is perhaps more illusory than real. While doctrine can and does provide grounding and boundaries for decisions, it is not immutable.

Legal categories—whether created by doctrine, statute, or constitution—will define legal discourse, will indicate what is relevant and what is not. Thus, legal discourse determined by category will often foreclose the narrative of experience of outgroups affected by a legal rule or doctrine. A stereotype—a belief that "acts both as a justificatory device for categorical acceptance or rejection of a group, and as a screening or selective device to maintain simplicity in perception and in thinking"[23]—embodied in a legal category can most certainly block empathic knowledge.

These characteristics of legality provide ample opportunity for "not hearing" the story of the Other, but they do not inexorably compel that result. They may submerge or mask awareness of moral choice and discourage reflexivity in the dialogue of law, but they need not do so. While abstract legal categories can strip persons of their very humanity, the narrative of that humanity often can also find a place in a legal category. For example, the categories of equal protection analysis have demonstrated this receptivity—or lack of it—to the particular narratives of blacks, the poor, women, and gays.

It may seem intuitively obvious that empathy can take place at the lower levels of the legal system—say, in the attorney/client relationship or in trials. But empathy, by nature of its very concreteness, seems out of place in the appellate court world. The connection to persons and concrete situations that leads to empathic response does grow more attenuated at the appellate level. But this does not mean that appellate courts and even the Supreme Court do not occasionally show evidence in their opinions that empathy has been operative in their decisions: The language of empathic understanding, of feeling the feelings of the people affected by a case, occasionally surfaces. Whether empathic responses helped an appellate judge reach a decision that is then justified in terms of legal discourse is often difficult to know: Of all the powerful decision-making agents in American political life, a judge's decision-making process is the least understood. But there may be some truth in Edmond Cahn's observation that "if you wish a judge to overturn a settled and established rule of law, you must convince both his mind and his emotions, which together in indissociable blend constitute his sense of injustice."[24]

The argumentative steps taken to convey human situations to a judge might be described as creating affective understanding by use of a narrative that includes emotion and description ("thick" description, if you will)[25] of a human situation created by, resulting from, or ignored by legal structures, and consciously placing that narrative within a legal framework. I shall refer to such arguments as *empathic narratives* in the remainder of this chapter. Empathic narrative, as I hope to demonstrate, includes descriptions of concrete human situations and their meanings to the persons affected in the context of their lives. It is contextual, descriptive, and affective narrative, although it need not be emotional in the pejorative sense of overwrought. It is, instead, the telling of the stories of persons and human meanings, not abstractions; it is a phenomenological argument.

The following discussion of three Supreme Court decisions in which signs of empathy may be found, or where the footprints of empathic narratives that evoke empathic responses exist, illustrates the (theoretically unrecognized) role that empathy has had in what could be considered politically and legally volatile situations. The fourth Supreme Court case provides an illustration of the effect of absence of empathic understanding. The discussion of these cases relies heavily on the narratives contained in the briefs and oral arguments, with particular reliance on quotation rather than paraphrase in order to recapture the stories and nuances as accurately as possible. The nuances of wording, the rhythm of discourse, the tones of the oral arguments cannot be reproduced directly, nor did I view the actual arguments, yet it is important to try to represent faithfully the narratives used in order to convey the presence or absence of empathic phenomena at the time the cases were argued and decided.

III. Examples of Empathic Narrative: The Discourse of "Otherness"

. . .

A. *Brown v. Board of Education*

Richard Kluger's study, *Simple Justice,*[26] the arguments, and the language of the *Brown* opinion itself provide extensive evidence of the affective message presented in the case—

and the resulting understanding of the meaning of being black in a racist American culture—that led the Court to reverse *Plessy* in principle, if not in literal terms. *Brown v. Board of Education (I)* may seem to be overworked as an example of the good in constitutional adjudication (a cynic might say it is the only example); from the ambivalent perspective of the 1980s, *Brown I* may appear trite, or the product of a simpler age, or so clear-cut that no other result would be conceivable. Yet none of these particular objections is valid given the context of the decision. *Brown I* was remarkable, and it remains so, in large part because it is a human opinion responding to the pain inflicted on outsiders by the law. In *Brown,* legality in its many forms clashed with empathy, and empathy ultimately transformed legality. The Supreme Court justices' understanding of racism was radically illuminated; as a result, the Court subsequently delegitimatized segregation in a series of decisions known as "the per curiams."

Moreover, the Court's opinion itself speaks of feeling, of human pain, and of moral evil. The recognition of human experience and pain—of feeling—is obvious: "To separate [schoolchildren] from others of similar age and qualifications solely because of their race generates a feeling of inferiority as to their status in the community that may affect their hearts and minds in a way unlikely ever to be undone."[27]

The opinion, varying as it did from the established form, was immediately and repeatedly attacked by legal scholars and the legal and political communities. The favorite criticism was trashing the social scientific evidence that segregation stigmatized and harmed black children; there were also cries for "neutral principles" against "judicial legislation" and attacks on the opinion's departure from established form.[28] Yet *Brown I* as a symbol of human dignity, of law as agent for the good, can hardly be questioned. The Court understood the experience of being black in a racist culture, and even if it quickly backed away from the obvious implications of that understanding, the case transformed American constitutional law.

There were three sets of arguments in *Brown,* two on the substantive issue of the constitutional legitimacy of segregated schools and one on the issue of the remedy. After the first set of arguments in 1952, the Court, in a delaying maneuver inspired by Felix Frankfurter, set the cases for reargument on five questions in 1953, in 1955 the Court heard arguments on remedies. While the NAACP's tone changed from an empathic narrative to a more legalistic argument through the course of the three sets of arguments, those favoring the upholding of school segregation shifted from almost purely legal to consequentialist and emotional appeals. The counterpoint of legality and empathy that appeared starkly in 1952 began to blur in 1953, but in 1955 it reemerged.

In the 1952 argument of the *Brown* Case itself, for example, counsel for Kansas made a purely "legal" argument. He urged the Court to ignore the district court's eighth finding of fact because it was "legally insignificant" and immaterial "so far as the issues in this case are concerned."[29] This was prescient, to say the least, for it was finding of fact number eight that found its way into the final opinion:

> Segregation of white and colored children in public schools has a detrimental effect upon the colored children. The impact is greater when it has the sanction of the law; for the policy of separating the races is usually interpreted as denoting the inferiority of the negro group. A sense of inferiority affects the motivation of a child to learn. Segregation with the sanction of law, therefore, has a tendency to [retard] the educational and mental development of negro children.[30]

Counsel for Kansas argued that because the physical facilities of the schools were equal, that ended the matter under the law. The psychological reaction to segregation "is something which is something apart from the objective components of the school system, and something that the state does not have within its power to confer upon the pupils therein."[31] Counsel essentially argued that legality precluded empathy.

Because the arguments of Thurgood Marshall for the NAACP and John W. Davis for the state of South Carolina provide the greatest contrast in narratives, the remainder of the discussion of *Brown* will focus on their arguments. Having laid the groundwork in the Court before *Brown,* the NAACP, and particularly Thurgood Marshall, repeatedly in their arguments emphasized the narrative of the painful experience of being black in American society. Although Philip Elman has derogated the NAACP project and has claimed that "Thurgood Marshall could have stood up there and recited 'Mary had a little lamb,' and the result would have been exactly the same," the historical evidence and the arguments in the *Brown* case contradict his assertions.[32] At oral argument, it was Marshall who returned repeatedly to the experience of segregation, the story of racism and its contradictions, and the human pain inflicted by the law. In 1952, in 1953, and even in 1955, Marshall spoke not in conventional modes of legal argumentation (indeed, in 1953, he failed miserably in that discourse) but instead used the narrative of the experience, the harm, the evil, and the irrationality of racism. As Yale Kamisar has observed, "If [John W.] Davis the mastercraftsman told the Court *how* to write an opinion reaffirming *Plessy,* Marshall, spokesman for an oppressed race, never let the Justices forget *why* they had to overrule it."[33]

In 1952 Marshall, arguing in *Briggs v. Elliot,* quickly summarized the procedural posture of the case and stated the language of the South Carolina statutory and constitutional provisions mandating segregated schools. He then moved to the story of the South Carolina case, pointing out that the state had conceded at the first hearing that physical facilities were unequal but that notwithstanding the concession, appellants were arguing about something more than physical equality. Although the state had remedied the physical inequalities, Marshall took the position "that these statutes were unconstitutional in their enforcement because they not only produced these inevitable inequalities in physical facilities, but that evidence would be produced by expert witnesses to show that the governmentally imposed racial segregation in and of itself was also a denial of equality."[34] The NAACP's experts had testified that there was no real difference between the ability of black and white children to learn, but that

> segregation deterred the development [of black children's personalities]. . . . [I]t destroys their self-respect. . . . [I]t denies them full opportunity for democratic social development. . . . [I]t stamps [the child] with a badge of inferiority.
>
> The summation of the testimony is that the Negro children have road blocks put up in their minds as a result of this segregation, so that the amount of education that they take in is much less.[35]

Marshall went on to say that the district court had ignored evidence of the harm caused by segregation, that

> we have positive testimony from Dr. Clark that the humiliation that these children have been going through is the type of injury to the minds that will be permanent as long as they are in segregated schools, not theoretical injury, but actual injury.[36]

Marshall in his opening argument fudged whether the Court had to overrule *Plessy,* but he returned frequently to the fact that children were harmed by the law of separate-but-equal to argue: "But my emphasis is that all we are asking for is to take off this state-imposed segregation. It is the state-imposed part of it that affects the individual children."[37]

John Davis began with three points, all tied to settled legal doctrines. He argued, first, that since the county had complied with the injunction to equalize the physical facilities, the case was moot; second, that the South Carolina laws did not violate the Fourteenth Amendment, and finally, that the evidence produced by the NAACP "deals entirely with legislative policy, and does not tread on constitutional right." Davis used analogy to attempt to take the bite out of racial separation by pointing to "reasonable" separations—sex, age, and "mental capacity"—thus illustrating the reasonableness of segregation. Davis told the Court that it need not decide the case, having "so often and so recently dealt with this subject that it would be a work of supererogation to remind you of the cases . . . or to argue with you, the authors, the meaning and scope of the opinions you have emitted."[38] And later, in response to Justice Frankfurter's questioning about the openness of the language of the equal protection clause, Davis stated that "certainly this Court has spoken in the most clear and unmistakable terms to the effect that this segregation is not unlawful," *Sweatt* and similar cases having been decided solely on the basis of physical inequality. He argued that "it is a little late, . . . after this question has been presumed to be settled for ninety years—it is a little late to argue that the question is still at large."[39] This appeal to settled law, doctrine, and precedent captured the issues of predictability and control that justify legality and that offered the Court an escape.

Davis attacked the expert testimony Marshall had relied on, mocking social science in general and attacking Dr. Kenneth Clark in particular. He pointed to the unfamiliarity of several witnesses with the South and argued that history and other experts supported segregated schools. He effectively, if misleadingly and out of context, quoted from W. E. B. DuBois to support his claim that "if this question is a judicial question . . . certainly it cannot be said that the testimony will be all one way."[40] He argued that if anything, segregation of schools was a local, legislative matter, and his closing statements hinted at the Court's institutional incompetence to decide the issue. Having stated at the beginning of his argument that the question of segregation was solely one of legislative policy—a separation of powers argument reminiscent of those relied on by judges upholding fugitive slave laws—he returned to that point in closing.

In his rebuttal to Davis, Marshall observed:

> So far as the appellants are concerned in this case, at this point it seems to me that the significant factor running through all these arguments up to this point is that for some reason, which is still unexplained, Negroes are taken out of the main stream of American life in these states.[41]

He followed up this assertion with an image to convey a meaning of segregation's impact to the Court, to anchor it in the Court's reality and experience:

> On this question of the will of the people of South Carolina, if Ralph Bunche [the Nobel laureate] were assigned to South Carolina, his children would have to go to a Jim Crow school. No matter how great anyone becomes, if he happens to have been born a Negro . . . he is relegated to that school.[42]

◇ ◇ ◇

During Marshall's rebuttal, Justice Reed questioned him about the purpose of segregation. Had the legislatures in the South instituted segregation in order "to avoid racial friction"? Marshall's reply drew on his knowledge and experience, and it answered both the question of the legitimacy of overriding legislative policy and whether, in fact, racial friction was an issue for the children involved. His reply also underscored what it meant to be black in the United States, to be excluded, to be disempowered: "But I think, considering the legislatures, that we have to bear in mind that I know of no Negro legislator in any of these states, and I do not know whether they consider the Negro's side or not." And:

> I know in the South where I spent most of my time, you will see white and colored kids going down the road together to school. They separate and go to different schools, and they come out and they play together. I do not see why there would necessarily be any trouble if they went to school together.[43]

In 1953, the tone of argument for the prosegregation position changed somewhat. Counsel for Delaware characterized the NAACP's arguments as appeals to emotion and underscored the legalistic view that such an argument had no place in the Court:

> If I may borrow from a statement made by the venerable Mr. John W. Davis . . . he said: "An emotional approach to this question is a poor substitute for a rational discussion of the problem at hand, which is to be judged by the application of well-settled principles governing the effect of the Fourteenth Amendment on the police power of the state."
>
> The arguments . . . such as I have heard in this courtroom for three days by our adversaries, have great emotional appeal, *but they belong in* an entirely different forum and in a different setting.
>
> Any change in state policy is for the legislature.[44]

John W. Davis, on the other hand, while perhaps regarding the case "as a strictly legal matter" and while arguing effectively that the history of the Fourteenth Amendment supported separate-but-equal segregated schools, became "emotionally overwrought." Davis effectively evoked empathy for whites by using a counterimage of 295 white children in Clarendon County being overwhelmed in the classroom by the nearly 2,800 black children. He made an indirect appeal to racial prejudice by mentioning miscegenation statutes and stated ominously that "the result [of a desegregation order] would not be pleasing." He argued that the state "is convinced that the happiness, the progress and the welfare of these children is best promoted in segregated schools" and invoked a fable in saying, "Here is equal education, not promised, not prophesied, but present. Shall it be thrown away on some fancied question of racial prestige?"[45]

Marshall retorted:

> This [argument] that Mr. Davis and Mr. Moore both relied on, these horrible census figures, the horrible number of Negroes in the South—and I thought at some stage it would be recognized by them that it shows that in truth and in fact in this country . . . two-thirds of the Negroes are compelled to submit to segregation.[46]
>
> I understand them to say that it is just a little feeling on the part of Negroes, they don't like segregation. As Mr. Davis said yesterday, the only thing . . . the Negro has been trying to get [is] what was recognized in *Strauder v. West Virginia,* which is the same status as anybody else regardless of race.[47]
>
> There is no way you can repay lost school years.[48]

◇ ◇ ◇

In *Brown* and its companion cases, the Court was directly facing the Other, who was telling his own story: All but one of the lawyers arguing for ending segregation were black. Thurgood Marshall, who had participated in fifteen cases before the Court, often departed from the usual forms of oral argument to "testify" as a black and to include his own observations of segregation in the South. He humanized the story, using specific examples and illustrations, and he expressed moral outrage as well: "We charge that these are Black Codes." The Other was in Court, and he was telling the justices what it was like to be the Other. The Court heard from the very humans it would have to rule for or against. Whether this affected the justices would be hard, if not impossible, to know; Justice Burton in 1952 appears to have considered it relevant to note "beside the name of each NAACP lawyer in *Brown*" the word "colored."

According to Kluger, the justices who could be said to have been most dedicated to the ideology of legality and the Rule of Law, Jackson and Frankfurter, had the most trouble reconciling any empathic response with their perceived roles in deciding *Brown I*. Justice Jackson, fully aware of the horrible effects of racial prejudice from his experience as chief prosecutor at the Nuremberg trials, indicated that "he did not doubt that segregation was painful to Negroes."[49] But he rejected the narrative presented by the NAACP lawyers as "sociological" and believed that the Court could not incorporate into law "these elusive psychological and subjective factors." Jackson considered the matter "political," not legal, despite the blunt fact that law was heavily implicated in the perpetuation of segregation. On the other hand, "as a political decision, he could go along with" striking down segregation.[50]

During the arguments in *Brown,* Justice Frankfurter manifested some discomfort with and resistance to the narrative presented. At one point in 1952 he stated that the testimony in the trial courts about the harmful effects of segregation was "irrelevant" to the question of the remedy. At another point, however, Frankfurter manifested concern with reconciling the narrative with legality (and, one may assume, cultural reality), by noting that "nothing would be worse than for this Court . . . to make an abstract declaration that segregation is bad and then have it evaded by tricks."[51] A justice who could be said to have "worshipped the law" and legality, he also had been advisory counsel to the NAACP and was a member of a group subjected to the worst forms of racism, prejudice, and torture throughout history: He was a Jew who had tried to assimilate and who had only partially succeeded. The pain of the experience of being Jewish could not help but resonate even if only slightly to the pain of another oppressed minority.

Frankfurter typically struggled to deny his "merely personal views" condemning racism while at the same time recognizing that "writ[ing] into the Constitution a belief in the Negro's natural inferiority or [a] personal belief in the desirability of segregat[ion] " was equally repugnant.[52] He very much wanted to strike down the school segregation statutes but ultimately found little help in the forms of legality in which he strongly believed. The history of the Fourteenth Amendment gave him no help. His commitment to separating the power of the federal government from that of state governments and his belief that the Court, as an unrepresentative decision-making body in a democracy, had very little power to change the law created seemingly insurmountable obstacles to striking down school segregation. A memo written by Frankfurter indicates, however, that he finally concluded that "law must respond to transformation of views as well as to that of outward circumstances"; this declaration served as a justification for striking down segregation because "the effect of changes in men's feelings for what is right and just" was "relevant in determining whether a discrimination denies the equal protection of the laws."[53]

Frankfurter may have empathized with blacks, but the explanation may also lie elsewhere: One of Frankfurter's biographers has noted that, because of Frankfurter's own experience, public education had utmost value for him. In a footnote, Hirsch observed that "a fragment among his files suggests that the personal value [he] attached to the importance of public schools as a means of integration into American society contributed significantly to his willingness to agree with the Court's revolutionary decision" in *Brown*. The fragment noted: "If the negro is to make his due contribution . . . he must have the knowledge, the training and the skill which only good schools can vouchsafe." Hirsch concluded that the words "'good schools' . . . helped trigger in Frankfurter a willingness to ignore judicial self-restraint."[54]

Other justices seemed to have had little trouble accepting the narrative, drawing on their own experiences and perhaps on imaginative placement of self in the black's shoes. According to Kluger, Justice Black, a native of Alabama who had briefly belonged to the Klan, "did not need scholars or philosophers to tell him what the purpose of segregation was." Having lived in the South, Black knew "its purpose . . . was to discriminate against Negroes in the belief that they were inferior beings."[55] Justice Minton thought that although *Plessy* had given segregation an "aura of legitimacy," it was unconstitutional; all that could support racial separation was a belief in black inferiority,[56] and this was a message that he was not willing to accept.

Chief Justice Warren, who as attorney general of California had indulged in racism against Americans of Japanese descent by playing an instrumental role in the internment of Japanese Californians,[57] had no doubt that segregation existed simply to perpetuate "a belief in the inferiority of the Negro."[58] "On the merits, the natural, the logical, and practically the only way the case could be decided was clear. The question was *how* the decision was to be reached." Empathy probably did play a role in Warren's decision to strike down school segregation laws, for the chief justice was frequently to decide cases by "putting himself 'in the other's shoes' . . . to 'get to the essence of the case.'" Apparently, Warren was not especially concerned about the obstacles presented by legality, whether characterized by apparent congressional approval of segregation, the attitudes and laws of the South, or the long existence of the doctrine of *Plessy* and its progeny. Instead, to Warren, "the injustice of an enforced separation of human beings based on their color was apparent." In the Court's first conference after the 1953 arguments, Warren implied that the defenders of *Plessy* were white supremacists; he used "the argument to induce shame" to persuade the justices to support striking down school segregation.[59]

Reed appears to have been the only justice who failed to be touched by the story of pain caused by segregation: "He did not accept the position that segregation was necessarily an act of discrimination."[60] Reed had written the opinions in *Smith v. Allwright*[61] and *Morgan v. Virginia*,[62] important decisions invalidating whites-only primary elections and segregation on interstate buses, respectively. But he was "an austere and very proper Southern gentleman." He had had difficulty with a case holding segregated restaurants in the District of Columbia unlawful, because he did not like the notion that "a nigra [*sic*] can walk into the restaurant at the Mayflower Hotel and sit down . . . right next to Mrs. Reed."[63] In 1952, he apparently took the position that "separation of races is for benefit of both." In 1953, after Warren's veiled moral challenge, Reed replied that "no one had suggested . . . that segregation was permissible because the Negro belonged to an inferior race," although he offered no other justification for continuing segregation.[64] One could argue that Reed failed to empathize with blacks but did empathize with white southerners; he could imagine Mrs. Reed's discomfort at having a black sitting next to her in a restaurant but couldn't imagine the discomfort caused the black by being excluded. At best, he engaged in unreflective empathy, empathizing with those like him; at worst, he was guilty of a racial prejudice that blocked his ability to hear the NAACP narrative and empathize with blacks. Racial stereotypy and prejudice seem to have rendered him deaf to the message of pain and stigma so powerfully presented in *Brown*. Reed was finally swayed by Warren with appeals to his conscience about the effect of a dissent.

All three types of empathy seem to have been present in *Brown I:* Feeling the distress of the blacks, understanding the painful situation created by segregation, and responding to the cry of pain by action:

> We conclude that in the field of public education the doctrine of "separate but equal" has no place. Separate educational facilities are inherently unequal. Therefore, we hold that the plaintiffs and others similarly situated . . . are . . . deprived of the equal protection of the laws guaranteed by the Fourteenth Amendment.[65]

The narrative was one of the pain of segregation, the legal framework was the equal protection clause, the action was the de facto overruling of *Plessy*.

◊ ◊ ◊

After *Brown I*, however, the justices were out on a limb. "The white-supremacists of the South were swift and shrill in their outcry." The governor of Virginia declared, "I shall use every legal means at my command to continue segregated schools in Virginia."[66] The Eisenhower administration remained mute in the face of public outcry. *Brown I*, by postponing the issue of remedy, increased the opportunity for second thoughts: Almost a year passed between the decision of May 17, 1954, and the arguments of April 11, 1955, a year in which southern resistance, congressional criticism, and executive inaction may have reminded the justices to stick to "legality."

B. Making the Empathic Point for Poor People: *Shapiro v. Thompson*

Shapiro v. Thompson arguably is just the "right to travel" case. Certainly the more expansive hope that it would institute a doctrine of special protection for the poor was dashed in subsequent cases. Yet it provides an excellent example of the interweaving of empathic strategies and legal principles by Archibald Cox. Not involved in the first round of briefing and argument, Cox and Howard Lesnick entered the case when the Court set the matter for reargument.[67]

In terms of the existing law and legal ideology, the original plaintiffs in *Shapiro* had to lose. As in *Brown*, Congress and state legislatures had spoken; unlike *Brown*, there was no issue of explicit racial categorization. Choices about how to spend money were legislative, not judicial. And attempts to fit the claim that one-year residency requirements for welfare eligibility were unconstitutional into existing doctrine were strained. Unless the Court declared classifications based on wealth suspect, there was little doctrine or precedent to support striking down residency requirements. Indeed, the state of Connecticut's brief in the case was smug, because the legal issues were so obviously settled. The *amicus* briefs filed by other states were less smug in tone, yet they made full use of the doctrines and beliefs about legal structure to tell the Court, essentially, that it had no reason to get involved. Spending was a legislative matter. The states and Congress were doing their best with limited funds; the one-year requirement was necessary to protect the funds for longer-term residents of the states, to enable legislatures to budget money, and to prevent opportunism and fraud.[68]

The states all conceded a constitutional right to travel from state to state and either denied that the residency requirement infringed that right or asserted that no right to "subsidized" travel existed. A story of starving people would not have helped the states, so they exploited stories supportive of stereotypes and prejudices regarding the "undeserving poor." Thus, in its brief the state of Connecticut did all it could to portray Vivian Thompson, the original plaintiff, as a stereotypical welfare parasite. Thompson was "a 19 year old unwed mother of a minor child" who "was pregnant and later gave birth to another child." "There is nothing in the record . . . to show that either the appellee or her children suffered from poor health or had any other special problem . . . which kept her out of the labor market." Moreover, the brief and counsel for Connecticut at the first oral argument strongly implied Thompson had moved to the state simply to take advantage of its "generous" benefits. Rather than establishing a claim that Connecticut harshly allowed women and children to starve, Thompson's "real claim . . . is that Connecticut discriminates against a poor applicant who has no desire to enter the labor market."[69]

The initial briefs filed for the persons denied welfare, as well as the argument for the named appellee, Thompson, were legally weak and failed to present a concrete picture of the persons affected that could rebut the stereotypical portraits painted by the states. The brief on behalf of Thompson did make her a more sympathetic figure than the state had claimed—she had moved to Connecticut to be with her mother, a Connecticut resident for eight years, but her mother ultimately was unable to support her. Her pregnancy made her unable to work or get job training. She and her two children subsisted on the $31.60 a week contributed by Catholic Family Services after she was denied AFDC by the state. But then she disappeared from the brief, which continued in the most general terms to a description of poverty in America and general legal arguments.[70]

It was not until reargument that the human issue—that poor people who moved to a new state could very well starve for a year—became clear. In the Supplemental Brief for Appellees on Reargument, the Summary of Argument made the Cox–Lesnick strategy apparent:

> Abstractly stated, therefore, the question presented by all three cases is whether this discrimination [in AFDC benefits] on the basis of length of residence in a State violates the Fifth and Fourteenth Amendments.
>
> But this abstract statement conceals the flesh, blood and heart of the true questions. The facts of these cases make three points clear that frame—and limit—the constitutional issue.[71]

Just as the abolitionist lawyers stressed the persons affected by the fugitive slave laws, Cox and Lesnick in the brief and Cox at oral argument returned again and again to the individuals involved. Cox's argument used their names and their stories to make his points. The plaintiffs were "going back home"; "they are mothers of dependent children without present husbands who moved into the new jurisdiction either to go back home . . . , or rejoin their families, or to get help from some person, or perhaps to get a job; and then who are left absolutely destitute when misfortune occurs." With the one-year residency requirement for eligibility, a woman who left Pennsylvania to help aging grandparents and was absent a few years before returning to Pennsylvania was denied AFDC;

Vera Barley, a woman committed to St. Elizabeth's Hospital in the District of Columbia for "20-odd years" and who became competent to be released had not been a "resident" for one year in the District of Columbia and was forced to remain in the hospital. Families not eligible for AFDC would be separated: In the case of Juanita Smith, who had virtually grown up in Pennsylvania and who had returned home from Delaware after an absence of "a few years," the residency requirement left her with the alternative of going back to Delaware or losing custody of her children: "Well . . . we'll take your children away from you and provide institutional care which might run anywhere from six months to two years. And this, at least, will provide them with shelter."[72]

Cox, having set a descriptive stage of the personal realities of those denied benefits solely by virtue of failing to meet a one-year residency requirement then tied the narrative to the legal arguments.

◇ ◇ ◇

What is difficult to capture is the total ease with which Cox wove the individual stories into the legal arguments; to break out one or the other fails to convey the manner in which he made the stories and the legal points one. For example, in rebutting the state's proferred justifications for the rationality of the residency requirements, he observed:

> The additional point that I would make is that while I think no discrimination can be justified on the assumption that the higher relief payment operates as a magnet . . . I do suggest to the Court that even if it be assumed that a state might deal with this problem in an appropriate way, that *this* way of dealing with it is unconstitutional. . . . I point out that it's excessively broad in a number of respects.
>
> First, the one-year residency requirement applies even to people . . . who come from states with higher or equal benefit levels. . . .
>
> Second, it applies to people who come for reasons that demonstrably are unrelated to the benefit level; and the *facts* of these cases are the best evidence of that. *Five out of seven were coming back to where they'd lived before.* Another five out of seven were coming to join families. And of course most people move for hoped-for jobs.[73]

Against these narratives, skillfully and at times movingly spoken, interwoven with cases and legal doctrines, the legalistic arguments of counsel for the states and the District of Columbia appeared to be unresponsive. More "emotional" appeals, which might better be characterized as appeals to stereotyped beliefs about the poor, also seemed unresponsive to the narrative Cox used. Iowa as *amicus* claimed that the need to "know, within one year, who wants to contribute, who are our people, who wants to live here and contribute, and [who] we want to help" justified the one-year requirement. Connecticut argued that "an adverse decision by this Court would have the effect of penalizing every liberal welfare benefit state, by putting a premium on the poor benefit states to encourage their needy and dependent to migrate to greener pastures" and claimed that its welfare rolls already had been "skyrocketing." Counsel for the District of Columbia argued that the residency requirement was a "mere discouragement" to the right to travel. The states and the District of Columbia also stressed that because of limited funding, budget increases or cuts in grants to all recipients would be necessary—implying that a decision to find for Thompson would cause greater hardship for the poor.[74]

Some members of the Court appeared during oral argument to hold stereotyped beliefs or concerns about poor people (and probably worse, about that creature, the Welfare Mother). Justice Black apparently assumed that spending six months in Massachusetts and six months in Florida is "a very common thing" and "doubt[ed]" Cox's assertion that it was not common "in relation to the types of people we're talking about here."[75] Chief Justice Warren was very concerned with the figures for AFDC migrants to California, "some of the Western states and Florida." He sharply disputed Cox's assertion that the places most affected were New York City and the District of Columbia based on the fact that the "flow of migration of the people who end up with ADC care is, for the most part, from the rural areas and very largely from the South." The chief justice pushed for information about increases for "states like California, Arizona, and Florida"[76] from Cox, who finally offered to prepare a memo on the subject.

On the other hand, other members of the Court sharply disputed the government lawyers' claims. One justice skeptically engaged counsel for Connecticut: "And my other question is: Do you think they can just not eat for a year?" And: "You want to convince me that Connecticut is one of the few states in the Union that has no unemployment?"[77]

The majority opinion itself could have been written only by a Court that heard the stories the indigent persons had presented—indeed, it reads like Cox and Lesnick's brief and Cox's oral argument. It begins with stories of the individuals:

> Appellee Vivian Marie Thompson . . . was a 19-year-old unwed mother . . . [who had moved to Connecticut] to live with her mother. . . . Because of her pregnancy, she was unable to work or enter a work training program.

> Appellee Minnie Harrel, now deceased, had moved with her three children from New York to Washington. . . . She suffered from cancer and moved to be near members of her family who lived in Washington.
> Appellee Barley . . . returned to the District in March 1941 and was committed a month later to St. Elizabeth's Hospital as mentally ill. . . . She was deemed eligible for release in 1965, and a plan was made to transfer her. . . . The plan depended, however, upon Mrs. Barley's obtaining welfare assistance. . . . Her application . . . was denied because her time spent in the hospital did not count in determining compliance with the one-year requirement.

◊ ◊ ◊

The opinion by Justice Brennan continued: "There is weighty evidence that exclusion from the jurisdiction of the poor who need or may need relief was the specific objective of these provisions"; "the purpose of deterring the in-migration of indigents cannot serve as a justification . . ., since that purpose is constitutionally impermissible"; and "none of the statutes [was] tailored to serve [the] objective" of discouraging "those indigents who would enter the State solely to obtain larger benefits."[78] The implication that the poor were somehow less deserving was wrong: "Surely such a mother is no less deserving than a mother who moves into a particular State in order to take advantage of its better educational facilities."

◊ ◊ ◊

The dissents took a "fact"-less tack insofar as the story of those individuals portrayed by the arguments and the majority opinion was concerned: If there was any understanding of the situation of the people involved on the part of Chief Justice Warren and Justices Black and Harlan, it is not readily apparent. Warren's dissent, joined by Black, includes among other things an odd essay on the commerce clause in which congressional power to regulate and tax airlines and common carriers and Congress's interest in enhancing the flow of commerce is somehow equated with refusing to provide food, clothing, and shelter for the poor. In a peculiar footnote, with a "let them eat cake" ring to it, Warren stated,

"All of the appellees in these cases found alternative sources of assistance after their disqualification."[79]

◇ ◇ ◇

Justice Harlan's dissent is thorough, careful, and very legalistic; he was honest in stating his underlying objection to the majority opinion as a violation of his belief that "it is an essential function of this Court to maintain the constitutional divisions between state and federal authority and among the three branches of the Federal Government."[80] Harlan was principled in his adherence to what he believed the proper role of the Court should be; what he failed to acknowledge implicitly or explicitly in his opinion were the human realities underlying the case. His only reference to the narrative of the poor people was his agreement with the plaintiff's claim that the one-year residency requirement had only a "minuscule" effect on the choice to move; he interpreted this as having an "indirect impact" on the right to travel, rather than as an indication that several of the original plaintiffs were returning to their home state, or rejoining their families, or migrating for reasons other than increased benefits. His list of "legitimate reasons" for imposing the one-year residency requirement favored predictability and control, as well as endorsed a rather xenophobic approach to legislative allocation of resources: The residency requirement "will make more funds available for those whom the legislature deems more worthy of subsidy" and who have "recently made some contribution to the state's economy."[81] This was the "our people" argument of the state of Iowa. It was a singularly unempathic response, legality at its best and worst, disembodied principles, and an underlying political belief system that limited the Court's role in addressing apparent injustices created by more "democratic" political bodies. Harlan never recognized the human beings affected in his dissent, perhaps because to have done so while reaffirming the one-year residency requirement would have entailed a "let them eat cake" dismissal of the narrative. His not unjustified reticence to dictate spending programs to Congress or the states was undermined by the facts of the cases in *Shapiro:* It was more expensive to keep Barley at St. Elizabeth's; foster or institutional care for children was more expensive than AFDC. Harlan, troubled by the Court's fundamental rights analysis, argued that "rights such as" "the right to pursue a particular occupation," "to receive greater or smaller wages or to work more or less hours," and "the right to inherit property" were "in principle indistinguishable from those involved here." He protested "the Court's cryptic suggestion . . . that the 'compelling interest' test is applicable *merely* because the result of the classification may be to deny the appellees 'food, shelter, and other necessities of life'." If one is talking about the requisites for existing at all, however, it seems that Harlan's failure to see a principled distinction between a law depriving the poor of having food to eat and a law making it unlawful to supply lenses without a prescription written by an ophthalmologist or optometrist[82] is almost deliberate obtuseness. Harlan's dissent highlighted the tension between devotion to legality and use of empathy as ways of seeing the world.

C. Abortion

Professor Sylvia Law has written, "Nothing the Supreme Court has ever done has been more concretely important for women"[83] than its decision to permit them access to abortions in *Roe v. Wade* and *Doe v. Bolton.* However true that statement may be, one must recognize that *Roe* has been as severely criticized as *Brown I,* if not more so. Perhaps even more than they had in the race cases, many members of the Court and the legal academy have shown a rather peculiar flight from the reality of women in the abortion cases. Thus, even though *Roe* was a victory for American women, the nature of the victory has rendered it vulnerable. In *Brown,* the Court saw the pain and stigma of being black in America; in the abortion cases, the Court has arguably failed to see the pain, despair, and stigma of women with unwanted pregnancies and unwanted children. (The two frequently go together; as a social fact, it is women who have responsibility for child rearing.) In part, perhaps, members of the Court have been unable to identify with women facing disastrous pregnancies. Perhaps because the narrative of unwanted pregnancy and its effect on women was underdeveloped when *Roe* was decided, the Court lacked appreciation of the human issues involved. Justice Powell, after his retirement from the Court in 1987, said, "I don't think I'd ever really thought about [abortion] seriously before."[84] Perhaps members of the Court did feel some empathy and concern for women but did not have a way to articulate it. Perhaps the Court's failure was because of the enormous moral complexities of empathizing with fetuses—recharacterized as human infants—and women simultaneously.

The briefs and the tapes of the oral arguments in *Roe* patently reveal that an empathic narrative about fetuses was developing. An appeal to emotional identification with the fetus was obviously present in the brief for the state of Texas: The brief contained pictures of human development, together with a narrative humanizing the fetus, making the fetus capable of "conscious experience" and, indeed, making it "autonom[ous]." Women, in contrast, warranted only a two-page discussion in the Texas brief of their "interests"; they had a limited "right of privacy" versus the "right of the child to life."[85] An *amicus* brief filed by dissenting members of the American College of Obstetrics and Gynecology argued that "the unborn child is as much a patient as is the mother." They declared:

> The unheard voices of these little ones are our concern, and we deplore this violent trend which is turning the healing art of medicine into a source of efficient swift and sure destruction of human life. A trend which will yield a "body count" unlike any we have seen in our nation's history [*sic*].[86]

The use of the words *child* and *mother* in the brief cannot have been accidental—any more than the allusion to "body counts" at a time when the war in Vietnam was causing increased consternation. *Mother* and *child* evoke an image of caring and need for protection, respectively; only a mother who is evil would kill her child, and she is unworthy of empathy.

Roe v. Wade was not well argued—counsel for both sides, none experienced advocates before the Court, seemed unprepared to answer questions, did not respond to questions, did not have facts at their disposal. According to *The Brethren,* Justice Blackmun, the author of the opinion in *Roe,* thought the presentations "poor" and felt that the "abortion issue deserved a better presentation."[87] Yet during oral arguments in *Roe v. Wade* in 1971, counsel for the state of Texas rather movingly referred to a Texas case that "held that the State had a compelling interest because of the protection of fetal life—of fetal life protection. They [the Texas court that upheld the statute] recognized the humanness of the embryo, or the fetus, and they said we have an interest in protecting fetal life." In 1972, a different lawyer arguing for Texas immediately asserted: "But it is the position of the State of Texas that, upon conception, we have a human being." And in a slowly paced summary of the "rights of the unborn child," counsel stated:

> This Court has been diligent in protecting the rights of the minority . . . .—a silent minority—the true silent minority. Who is speaking for these children? Where is the

counsel for these unborn children whose life is being taken? Where is the safeguard of the right to trial by jury? Are we to place this power in the hands of a mother, and a doctor [said dismissively]—all of the constitutional rights?[88]

These are *children*, not "fertilized eggs," "blastocysts," "fetuses," "blobs of protoplasm," or even "babies." In other words, the image is recognizably human. The Court in its questioning reflected a great concern with the argument that fetuses were children, grasping for historical, medical, and legal meanings of "person." Indeed, at one point, a member of the Court remarked that if fetuses were persons within the meaning of the Constitution, "you can sit down, you've won your case."[89] And Justice Stewart in questioning counsel for Roe, stated, "Well, if—if it were established that an unborn fetus is a person, within the protection of the Fourteenth Amendment, you would have almost an impossible case here, would you not?" To which she replied, with a laugh(!): "I would have a very difficult case."[90] (This concession returned to haunt women in the Court's opinion.)

On the other hand, the Court appeared to be singularly unable to hear the narrative of unwanted pregnancy. *Unwanted* may be an unfortunate word here, but I do not know of another word that captures the situation better. But unwanted seems to cover a continuum from an inconvenient pregnancy that was wanted but not at the particular time to a pregnancy resulting from rape or incest or a life-threatening pregnancy. Thus, it leaves the issue of choosing to have an abortion vulnerable to a male assumption that such choices can be or are frivolously or odiously made. While the brief for Jane Roe was strikingly lacking in facts or narrative about the pain and anguish of unwanted pregnancy, some of the *amicus* briefs did discuss the issue of women, of their pain, their reality; they developed a partial narrative. And in 1971, during oral argument, counsel for Jane Roe did try to tell the narrative of women faced with unwanted pregnancy:

> Texas . . . would not allow any relief at all, even in situations where the mother would suffer perhaps serious physical and mental harm. . . . If the pregnancy would result in the birth of a deformed or defective child, she has no relief. Regardless of the circumstances of conception, whether it was because of rape, incest, whether she is extremely immature, she has no relief.
>
> I think it's without question that pregnancy to a woman can completely disrupt her life. Whether she's unmarried; whether she's pursuing an education; whether she's pursuing a career; whether she has family problems; all of the problems of personal and family life, for a woman, are bound up in the problem of abortion.[91]

After listing the consequences of pregnancy for women—abandonment of education because they were forced, by the schools themselves, to quit school, loss of jobs and support because they were forced to leave employment and were ineligible for unemployment compensation or welfare, the lack of a duty for employers to rehire women who had to "drop out" because of pregnancy, and the emotional investment in raising a child—counsel argued:

> So, a pregnancy to a woman is perhaps one of the most *determinative* aspects of her life. It disrupts her body. It disrupts her education. It disrupts her employment. And it often disrupts her entire family life. And we feel that, because of the impact on the woman, this certainly . . . is a matter which is of such *fundamental* and basic concern to the woman involved that *she* should be allowed to make the choice as to whether to continue or to terminate her pregnancy.

Very shortly thereafter, a member of the Court interjected:

> Mrs. Weddington, so far on the merits, you've told us about the important impact
> of this law, and you made a very eloquent policy argument against it. And I trust you
> are going to get to what provisions of the Constitution you rely on. Sometimes the
> Court—we would like to, sometimes—but we cannot here be involved simply with
> matters of policy, as you know.[92]

Was Mrs. Weddington's argument a "mere" policy argument—unlike the arguments of counsel for Texas—or was she describing an important experiential truth about unwanted pregnancies that the Court chose to avoid? True, the need to hook up the narrative to a legal category was there, but there was also an apparent discomfort with the narrative that subsequently squelched the story. The argument shifted to legalism, standing, and the rights of unborn children.

In the reargument of the case, counsel concentrated on standing and mootness, supporting the claims with fairly conclusory statements that the injury of unwanted pregnancy was irreparable. The Court then asked counsel if she agreed "that one of the important factors that has to be considered in this case is what rights, if any, does the unborn fetus have?" Counsel tried to argue, "It seems to me that it is critical, first, that we prove this is a fundamental interest on behalf of the woman, that it is a constitutional right.[93] But she had no answer to "balancing" the questions raised if the Court were to determine the fetus was a person. Moreover, she never returned to the facts of unwanted pregnancy and failed to weave any narrative of women's experience back into her legal points.

At least some members of the Court apparently have lacked empathy when it comes to the experience of pregnant women. Furthermore, few indications exist that any of the justices experienced—imaginatively or from knowing women faced with the choice—what it means to be a woman with an unwanted pregnancy. Empathy for fetuses—particularly third-trimester fetuses that look like human infants—was much more present in *Roe.* Counsel for Roe herself stated, "Obviously I have a much more difficult time saying that the State has no interest in late pregnancy. . . . I think that's more the emotional response to a late pregnancy." Women were not the explicit concern of the justices, although the argument of counsel for Texas that any choice about pregnancy the woman makes is "prior to the time she becomes pregnant," prompted a justice to ask about the woman who is raped: "And such a woman wouldn't have had a choice, would she?" In the final arguments on rebuttal, when Roe's counsel attempted to bring women back into the picture, the Court's questions shifted to doctors and medical judgments.

The opinion by Justice Blackmun in *Roe v. Wade,* while beginning with an anguished tone ("We forthwith acknowledge our awareness of the sensitive and emotional nature of the abortion controversy"), quickly invoked the words of legality: "Our task, of course, is to resolve the issue by constitutional measurement, free of emotion and predilection."[94] The opinion was virtually free of the story of women. The story of unwanted pregnancy received comparatively short shrift, a paragraph in an opinion that is fifty-one pages long. The story of women appeared toward the end of the opinion, and it began with some emphasis placed on medical harm, concern for unwanted children, and a passing acknowledgment that "maternity, or additional offspring, may force upon the woman a distressful life and future. Psychological harm may be imminent. Mental and physical health may be taxed by child care. . . . [T]he additional difficulties and continuing stigma of unwed motherhood may be involved." But "the pregnant woman cannot be isolated in her privacy. She carries an embryo, later, a fetus, if one accepts the medical definitions of the developing young in the human [*sic*] uterus."[95] The story of women was almost non-existent; the story of the law of abortion, of medical knowledge, and of doctors took its place. The focus was less on women, and more on fetuses, fetal life, and the responsibility of physicians and their "right" to administer treatment. In truth, *Roe* can be characterized as the "case of the Incredible Disappearing Woman."[96] Even though the opinion stated that "the word 'person,' as used in the Fourteenth Amendment, does not include the unborn," it also stated that "if [the] suggestion of personhood is established, the appellant's case, of course, collapses. . . . The appellant conceded as much on reargument."[97]

The standard—or at least easy—explanation for the opinion of the Court in *Roe* is that its author, Justice Blackmun, having been general counsel for the Mayo clinic, was more concerned with the "rights" of doctors than of women. Yet this fails to explain why the other justices who joined the opinion would "empathize" with doctors rather than women to the extent that Blackmun's opinion would suggest. And in retrospect, it fails to explain why Justice Blackmun's subsequent opinions have increasingly articulated the story of women. According to *The Brethren,* Brennan, Marshall, and Douglas all supported an opinion based on "broad grounds of women's constitutional rights." Brennan reportedly felt the Blackmun opinion "focused on the rights of the doctor and the rights of the state. [But] the most important party, the woman, had been largely neglected. Her rights were the ones that needed to be upheld."[98] Stewart, however, believed Douglas's rationale in a 1971 case—that abortion was a professional medical judgment—was the proper approach. Stewart was the justice who insisted that the opinion state the "fetus was not . . . a person. If [it] were a person, it had rights. . . . Weighing two sets of rights would be dangerous." Stewart allegedly was relieved that the first conference on *Roe* and *Doe* "focused on the professional rights of a doctor . . ., rather than on the rights of a woman trying to obtain" an abortion.[99] Justice Powell apparently relied on his own knowledge of well-to-do women going away to Switzerland or New York for abortions, and horror stories about back-alley abortionists from his in-laws who were obstetricians, to conclude the antiabortion laws were "atrocious." He has recently indicated that he also "had been shocked that the Texas law . . . appeared to bar abortion even in cases of rape and that he had been moved by arguments" that the constitutional right of "liberty" included reproductive choices. Powell apparently also was persuaded by a lower court's rationale that the moral decision to have an abortion was a judgment people couldn't "'impose upon others by force of law'."[100]

It is difficult to ascertain whether there was much empathy for women from this limited information. Certainly, seven justices lent their authority to a ruling virtually excluding the story of women and framing the legal issues more in terms of medical information and decision making. At the time the Court decided *Roe,* the women's movement was noticeably active, and concern with world overpopulation was on the political agenda. But recognition of the singular impact of pregnancy on one-half the population was not well articulated in the narratives given the Court or in the language of the opinion.

Another possible explanation for the opinion is that the justices resolved the issues by denying the humanity of fetuses and women simultaneously. In the frequently if–then world of legality, if fetuses are persons, the state has an obligation to protect their lives by banning abortions. If they are not persons, they have no more "right to life" than plants. If women are not persons, then their bodies and lives may be strictly controlled as well. (Doctors, who at the time the Court reached its decision were predominantly male, were full-fledged human beings whose "rights" merited protection from prosecution, however.) The if–then structure of legality could create an either/or that had to be suppressed or denied; alternatively, any simultaneous empathy for fetuses and women could arguably also have led to decisional paralysis.

But as Donald Regan later put it, "Anyone who attempts simply to deny that there is an intrinsic horror to unwanted pregnancy lacks either imagination or compassion."[101] Imagination and compassion, empathic understanding of women with unwanted pregnancies or compassion for them leading to action to help them, seem strangely lacking in *Roe* and in subsequent criticisms of the opinion, given that there was some effort to tell the story of the effect of unwanted pregnancy on women in *amicus* briefs and at oral argument. The state has an interest in protecting "potential life": Is not the woman an "existing life" or at a minimum also a potential life? Perhaps the failure of empathy for women who somehow find themselves pregnant became evident in the reargument of *Roe,* when one justice posed the question of choosing which life to protect: "Well, what would you choose? Would you choose to kill the *innocent* one, or what?" The implication seemed to be that women who "get themselves" pregnant are somehow blameworthy. By failing to see that forcing women with unwanted pregnancies to bear children causes the women great harm and suffering, calls upon them to endure physical and mental torment in a way we do not ask of any Good Samaritan, and chains them to serve other human wishes, the Court created a doctrine extremely vulnerable to antiabortionist attack and unintelligible in its development since *Roe* was decided. Not only had the Court engaged in the sin of "Lochnering," but it had done so badly.

◇ ◇ ◇

A bare majority of the Court staved off an attempt to have *Roe v. Wade* overruled in *Thornburgh*[102] in 1986. The Reagan administration had joined the case as *amicus* to urge the overruling of *Roe,* and given the original weakness of the doctrine, together with the absence of recognition of the experience of women, *Roe* was vulnerable. But in *Thornburgh* a bare majority upheld *Roe*—and the majority opinion acknowledged explicitly the actual meaning of the experience for women.

In a running battle with the courts since *Roe,* the state of Pennsylvania had enacted laws in 1974, 1978, and 1982 to restrict abortion in a number of ways, including requiring spousal consent, abolishing advertisements for abortion clinics, and limiting funding for abortions. The 1982 legislation, titled the "Abortion Control Act," was designed to limit abortions; it was patterned after an antiabortion organization's model statute.[103] In *Thornburgh,* physicians, clergy, counselors, and others had sought declaratory and injunctive relief under section 1983 and had obtained a preliminary injunction against enforcement of the statute. *Inter alia,* the Pennsylvania law required "informed consent" for the abortion, which included requiring a doctor to tell the woman that "medical assistance benefits may be available for prenatal care, childbirth, and neonatal care" and that the father would be liable to assist in supporting a child. As part of "informed consent," a woman had to be told:

> There are many public and private agencies willing and able to help you carry your child to term, and to assist you and your child . . . whether you choose to keep your child or place her or him for adoption. The Commonwealth of Pennsylvania strongly urges you to contact them before making a final decision about abortion.[104]

In addition, a woman had to read materials printed and supplied by Pennsylvania that had to describe "the probable anatomical and physiological characteristics of the unborn child [*sic*] at two-week gestational increments . . . including any relevant information on the possibility of the unborn child's [*sic*] survival."

The perception of the majority was of a law meant to intimidate women into having children, no matter what the cost to those women. The perception of the dissenters was that *Roe* was bad law and, essentially, that the fetus, not the woman, was the state's legitimate concern. Women were just not "present" in the dissents, while they were very present in Blackmun's opinion. Acknowledging the Court's running battle with the states after the *Roe* decision, Justice Blackmun's majority opinion made reference to the resistance to school desegregation by quoting *Brown v. Board of Education II:* "'It should go without saying that the vitality of these constitutional principles cannot be allowed to yield simply because of disagreement with them.' The States are not free, under the guise of protecting maternal health or potential life, to intimidate women into continuing pregnancies."

The opinion by Justice Blackmun stated that the "informed consent" requirements and materials

> seem . . . to be nothing less than an outright attempt to wedge the Commonwealth's message discouraging abortion into the privacy of the informed-consent dialogue between a woman and her physician. . . . [I]t may serve only to confuse and punish her and to heighten her anxiety, contrary to accepted medical practice. . . .
>
> The requirements.. . . . that the woman be advised that medical assistance benefits may be available, and that the father is responsible for financial assistance in the support of the child similarly are poorly disguised elements of discouragement for the abortion decision. . . . For a patient with a life-threatening pregnancy, the "information" in its very rendition may be cruel as well as destructive of the physician–patient relationship. As any experienced social worker or counsellor knows, theoretical financial responsibility often does not equate with fulfillment. And a victim of rape should not have to hear gratuitous advice that an unidentified perpetrator is liable for support if she continues the pregnancy to term.[105]

These observations by Blackmun appear to illustrate an empathic understanding of the experience of women who have an unwanted—disastrous—pregnancy.

The majority opinion in *Thornburgh* also reflected some of the narrative of women with unwanted pregnancies that had been largely untold in *Roe* and its progeny; it rescued abortion as a fundamental right from the clutches of the *Harris v. McRae* majority's denigration of that right. The conclusion of the majority opinion in *Thornburgh* stated,

> Our cases long have recognized that the Constitution embodies a promise that a certain private sphere of individual liberty will be kept largely beyond the reach of government. That promise extends to women as well as men. Few decisions are more personal and intimate, more properly private, or more basic to individual dignity and autonomy, than a woman's decision—with the guidance of her physician and within the limits specified in *Roe*—whether to end her pregnancy. A woman's right to make that choice freely is fundamental. Any other result, in our view, would protect inadequately a central part of the sphere of liberty that our law guarantees equally to all.[106]

The National Abortion Rights Action League (NARAL) had submitted an *amicus* brief in *Thornburgh* "to place the realities of abortion in women's lives before this Court and to urge this Court to reaffirm *Roe*. . . . The circumstances of women's lives and women's compelling reasons for choosing to have abortions elucidate the strong Constitutional foundations for [*Roe*]." The brief consisted largely of excerpts from letters written by women who, although remaining anonymous perhaps because of fear of retaliation by "the anti-choice people," do tell the stories of their own abortion experiences and make concrete the reality of women. The narratives do seem directed toward appealing to the justices' possible visions of family planning and the central role of the family, which Professor Grey had posited earlier as the real reason behind the privacy decisions.[107] Of the thirty-eight excerpted stories of abortion, it is evident that in twelve the women was married and the question of abortion was a family-planning matter; in several other stories, the women had subsequently married and become mothers. Nevertheless, the stories do support NARAL's claim that "the condition of the law determines the condition of women's lives,"[108] and they illustrate the reality of those lives.

NARAL's narratives first established the effect of laws prohibiting or restricting abortion on women wanting one:

> I remember Tijuana. I remember bugs crawling on walls as I waited for the "second part" of my abortion to take place. The first part was done in comparatively clean surroundings—"a clinic"—but I was too far along for the abortion to be done in one procedure, so I was sent to a "hotel" to wait three hours—a stinking cesspool of urine, sweat, filthy sheets and bugs. . . . Where else could I have gone in 1963? A name from a hairdresser passed through the underground grapevine by other desperate women seeking a life of dignity and choice.
>
> Having an abortion in Illinois in 1957 was a demeaning experience. I had to lie, two doctors who did not know me had to lie, and my own doctor had to lie. . . . No matter that I had had a miscarriage one month previously, and my uterus looked like chopped liver, and I was in a great deal of pain.[109]

Next, the brief argued for upholding *Roe* on the basis of the due process rights of privacy and liberty relied upon in *Roe.* "The right to choose to have an abortion is so personal and so essential to women's lives and well-being that without this right women cannot exercise other fundamental rights and liberties guaranteed by the Constitution." The rights and liberties were those mentioned in *Meyer v. Nebraska;*[110] the brief tied the narratives to

> the right of the individual . . . to engage in any of the common occupations of life, to acquire useful knowledge, to marry, establish a home and bring up children, to worship God according to the dictates of his [*sic*] own conscience, and generally to enjoy those privileges . . . essential to the orderly pursuit of happiness by free men [*sic*].[111]

The brief included narrative that told how *actual* women would have had to leave their jobs, quit their schooling, marry. They would have exhausted themselves in trying to meet responsibilities to family members, bowed to religious beliefs not their own, and surrendered control of their lives and destinies had they not had abortions. No longer anonymous abstractions, women became concrete—if unnamed—human beings. These women were not moral idiots; they had carefully considered their choice.

◇ ◇ ◇

The dissenters attacked both *Roe* and the majority opinion in *Thornburgh.* Justice White urged overruling *Roe,* by implication making it synonymous with two constitutional horror stories, *Lochner* and *Plessy.* White, agreeing "that a woman's ability to choose an abortion is a species of 'liberty,'" denied that it is so "'fundamental' that restrictions upon it call into play anything more than the most *minimal* judicial scrutiny." White concentrated on the fetus: "The governmental interest at issue is in protecting those who will be citizens if their lives are not ended in the womb. . . . [T]he state's interest, if compelling after viability, is equally compelling before viability." Therefore, permitting the legislature to enact a broad range of limitations on or outright prohibition of abortion would be a "highly desirable" result "from the standpoint of the Constitution." "Such issues, in our society, are to be resolved by the will of the people."[112]

The women's side of the story never appeared in Justice White's opinion: Because abortion was "a hotly contested moral and political issue," states presumably could ignore the pain inflicted on women as a result of forcing them to bear children. White dismissed the majority's concern for the pain women would experience in receiving Pennsylvania's information as "primarily rhetorical," rather than an acknowledgment of the experience of women. (Since when did rhetoric, a perfectly good method of argument, become a pejorative?) White narrowed his analysis to "maximization of choice," missing entirely the larger issue: the coercive aspects of the Pennsylvania law and its effect on women. Instead, he found "legitimate" state interests present, denied that the effect of unwanted pregnancy could be devastating for women, and denied the existence of any fundamental privacy interest. The accepted story for White was exclusively that of the human fetus.

D. The Power of Prejudice: *Bowers v. Hardwick*

I have endeavored to illustrate how narratives of feeling and the meaning of human experience may lead to empathic understanding of the human dimensions of a legal problem and, accordingly, to a redefinition of the legal issues. By grasping the human dimensions, the decision maker is faced with a moral dimension as well. That law can have moral consequences is inescapable; to decide responsibly requires awareness of those consequences. The strong claim for empathic understanding is that the moral decision, the moral result, will be closer to the good than it otherwise would be. When empathic knowledge fails, or is not even attempted, the resulting decision can be appalling in human terms. A recent extreme example of the point may be found in the Supreme Court's majority opinions in *Bowers v. Hardwick. Hardwick* bristles with emotion, to be sure, but it is the emotion of hate, not that of empathy. The majority opinions powerfully manifest the phenomena of prejudice, stereotype, blind categorization, and denial of the humanity of a group of people. As a result, the question of whether the state may invade a person's home to monitor his or her sexual practices appears to have been answered in the affirmative, and at least 10 percent of the population may be persecuted because of their sexual practices. (While one author might call the majority's reaction "contrast empathy," I prefer to omit that term from the lexicon, because it appears to encompass something other than a perversion of empathy.)

Michael Hardwick had been cited for drinking in public by an officer concerned by "big city 'garbage'."[113] He missed his first court appearance, and a warrant for his arrest was issued and given to the citing officer. Hardwick learned that the officer had come by his home with the warrant, raced down to the courthouse, paid his fine, and forgot about it. The issuing court never recalled the warrant, and the officer never found out that Hardwick had paid his fine. He appeared with the warrant at Hardwick's home one afternoon. A house guest admitted the officer, who found Hardwick engaging in oral sex with another man in his own bedroom. The officer also saw some marijuana in the room.

Hardwick said he had paid his fine, but the officer had seen him committing a felony under Georgia law and arrested him on the warrant and the felony committed in his presence.

The ACLU found the case to be a "dream" for challenging the Georgia sodomy law. "Hardwick, a bartender whose activism was limiting to marching in the Gay Pride parade," was in his own bedroom with another male adult. The case was not one which involved someone who had also been charged with a serious violent crime. Hardwick chose to challenge the Georgia sodomy statute after having been contacted by the ACLU; he lost his job as a result. His neighbor came to the preliminary hearing and congratulated the officer for cracking down, reportedly fed up with "the naked sunbathing, the wild parties."[114]

Hardwick had had a brush with heroin when he was a teenager, had been rehabilitated, and had counseled other kids. At twenty-one, he realized he was gay, moved to Atlanta, and "melted into the gay world." At one point "a good-time guy," according to his ex-lover, Hardwick now is serious, active in gay rights, and active in publicizing the meaning of the sodomy statutes to heterosexuals as well.[115]

Mr. Hardwick never appeared in the briefs or arguments as a human being. Except for one paragraph at the beginning of the Eleventh Circuit's opinion, stating that he was arrested "because he had committed the crime of sodomy with a consenting male adult in the bedroom of his own home," the courts' opinions contain no clue as to who the man was. He became another disembodied person onto whom fears, prejudices, and false beliefs could be projected.

The Georgia statute by its terms covered all "sodomy"—defined as both oral and anal sex—committed by heterosexuals or homosexuals. Yet the state argued the statute was meant to apply only to homosexuals, despite a legislative history indicating that it also covered heterosexuals. Moreover, a married couple who had joined in the suit had been declared to have no standing to challenge the statute. The focus of the case for Georgia became homosexual sodomy. And by focusing on homosexual sodomy, the Georgia briefs and oral arguments, together with the briefs filed in support of the statute, were left free to smuggle in a homophobic message and appeals to prejudice—something that would have been far more difficult if the arguments had also been against permitting married couples to engage in oral sex in their own homes in the 1980s. At oral argument, counsel for Georgia returned again and again to homosexual sodomy.[116]

The stereotypes of homosexuals as dangerous, perverted, and child molesters, coupled with the fear of AIDS, were fully exploited by the state of Georgia and *amici.* Georgia's opening brief argued:

> If morality is a legitimate state purpose, the identification of that morality, "the widely held values" of the people, should be voiced through their representatives. The legislative process is acutely [*sic*] designed for this purpose, whereas the judiciary may be inclined to make determinations upon more empirical evidence, to which this area is not particularly amenable. . . . For example, it should be permissible for the General Assembly to find as legislative fact that homosexual sodomy leads to other deviate practices such as sado-masochism, group orgies, or transvestism, to name only a few. Homosexual sodomy is often practiced outside the home such as in public parks, rest rooms, "gay baths," and "gay bars," and is marked by the multiplicity and anonymity of sexual partners, a disproportionate involvement with adolescents, and, indeed a possible relationship to crimes of violence. Similarly, the legislature should be permit-

ted to draw conclusions concerning the relationship of homosexual sodomy in the transmission of [AIDS], . . . anorectal gonorrhea, Hepatitis . . . enteric protozoal diseases, and Cytomegalovirus. . . .

But perhaps the most profound legislative finding that can be made is that homosexual sodomy is the anathema of the basic units of our society—marriage and the family. . . .

. . . If the legal distinctions between the intimacies of marriage and homosexual sodomy are lost, it is certainly possible to make the assumption . . . that the order of society, our way of life, could be changed in a harmful way.[117]

Sodomy, bestiality, incest, and adultery are mentioned in the same breath. Children and teenagers would fall prey to all sorts of sexual perversions, abuses, and exploitation if the Court struck down a sodomy statute directed at all but allegedly enforced only against same-sex offenders.

"Concerned Women for America" filed an *amicus* brief proclaiming, "We oppose any laws designed to grant special legal protection to those who engage in homosexuality. Such laws are an affront to public morality and our dedication to family life." The brief argued that the history of sodomy laws compelled a finding of constitutionality. Another *amicus* brief raised the specter of AIDS, "as counsel [for Georgia] indicated that they would probably not raise the public health concerns before this Court." But the brief went beyond the issue of AIDS and argued that "in responding to the current health crisis, a state legislature should be free to conclude that there is a need for reinforcement of traditional sexual mores." Moreover, the brief condoned the questionable use of criminal sanctions to prevent AIDS.

Historical hatred, the terror of AIDS, and stereotypes of gays as child molesters and criminals haunt these briefs. Stereotypy blocks empathy, and in the case of an outgroup so characterized solely because of sexual orientation, prejudices and irrationality about human sexuality also block an ability to understand.[118]

What of the "other side"? Michael Hardwick is a real human being, but his particular story was absent in the Supreme Court. The story of gays was largely absent as well. Professor Lawrence Tribe's brief responded to Georgia's claims about homosexuals and morality by arguing that "the only issue is the relevant standard of [constitutional scrutiny], *not* the validity" of the statute. Only at trial "may the untried questions of fact to which Georgia alludes in its brief become relevant." This was an argument of legality, not empathy, and it failed to provide the Court a way to understand homosexuality beyond the effective appeals to prejudice contained in the petitioner's brief. As a legal tactic, it may have made sense to attempt to give the Court a narrow way out of having to decide whether the statute violated constitutional principles. But the brief only perfunctorily rebutted Georgia's claims that the statute could prevent the transmission of disease (particularly AIDS) or could "deter its citizens from defecting to a homosexual lifestyle," nor did it seriously deal with whether the statute deterred at all. These issues took up only a page at the end of the brief, hardly enough to counter the appeal to prejudice. Only in a footnote did the respondent's brief explicitly confront Georgia's appeal to prejudice:

Even if the State's imaginative recasting of the 30 million Americans who comprise our homosexual population as a furtive criminal underclass. . . had the slightest basis in fact, rather than in irrational fear and prejudice . . . , the State appears to have missed the point that nothing in Respondent's argument claims any special protection for [public] sexual activity.[119]

Both in the respondent's opening brief and in many of the *amicus* briefs, there was much discussion of heterosexuals. This was not "wrong," because the statute was extremely vulnerable to attack as invalid on its face, and the right-to-privacy decisions which were being relied on to argue for a right to noninterference with sexual intimacy involved heterosexuals. But again the brief failed to tell the story of the actual plaintiff and of gay people, thus leaving the stereotype unanswered. Because the heterosexual married couple's attack on the statute was coopted early, when the state admitted it would not enforce the statute against married couples and stressed that it was homosexual sodomy it sought to prevent, the state challenged Hardwick's lawyers to answer the sterotype, and they failed to respond.

Surely it was a good, reasonable approach to argue that the Georgia sodomy statute did not just punish "them" but also punished fine, upstanding husbands and wives. Moreover, the likelihood of at least some of the Supreme Court's justices being more at ease with the notion of married heterosexuals engaging in these particular sexual practices would seem to aid the challenge to the statute on the grounds of its facial invalidity. Yet the focus in the Georgia brief and the briefs in support of the statute was on the Other, and the fact that Hardwick was a homosexual and that the stress was on homosexuality seems to demand a response narrative about the Other. The vision of the macho, leather-clad, gay male or the drag queen was never dispelled. That gays are members of Congress, stockbrokers, lawyers, doctors, truck drivers, authors, athletes—in other words, human beings—never appeared in the briefs or arguments.

◊ ◊ ◊

Many of the *amicus* briefs attempted to argue gays were no different than heterosexuals in their sexual practices, but the focus on sex alone may have been unfortunate. Ironically, the rubric of privacy does not appear to have curbed explicit discussion of human sexual functioning. At times the briefs read more like sex manuals than life stories of human beings who happen to be attracted to the same gender. The *amicus* brief filed by the Lesbian Rights Project et al. noted that "the overwhelming majority of persons engaging in sexual activities that would violate Georgia's law, then, are persons of heterosexual orientation." While the brief also forthrightly characterized Georgia's arguments as "homophobic,"[120] it relied on examples of heterosexual sexual practices as well to illustrate, time and again, that homosexuals were essentially no different in their mode of sexual expression.

◊ ◊ ◊

The briefs and arguments by Georgia and its supporters found a receptive audience in a majority of the Supreme Court justices. The majority opinion of Justice White was as poorly crafted legally as was the opinion in *Roe* and arguably the opinion in *Brown*. Perhaps the appeal to, or at least the availability of, prejudice explains the hostility of Justice White's and Chief Justice Burger's opinions to Hardwick's claim. In an opinion "so lacking in legal craft that it makes one wonder what was going on,"[121] Justice White relied on the "ancient roots" of prohibitions against sodomy. "To claim that a right to engage in such conduct is 'deeply rooted in this Nation's history and tradition' or 'implicit in the concept of ordered liberty,'" he declared, "is, *at best,* facetious." White equated permitting consenting adult homosexuals to engage in oral or anal sex in their homes with allowing adultery, incest, "and other sexual crimes" to be committed in the home.[122] But the horror at adultery seems false, and rape, forcible oral copulation, or forcible sodomy—possible "other sexual crimes"—do not, by their definitions, involve consenting adults. Incest, technically a crime of blood relation, is horrible because it frequently involves sexual abuse of children and adolescents who do not "consent." White's vision of sexual perfidy blinded him to the very real distinctions and harms among these acts. Incest is not a "sexual" crime; neither is rape, even if they are primarily crimes of gender that involve sex organs. Rather, as Professor Tribe had pointed out, these are all crimes of violence, domination, and exploitation.[123] Against a rational-basis challenge to the statute, White dismissively wrote, "The law . . . is constantly based on notions of morality, and if all laws representing essentially moral choices are to be invalidated under the Due Process Clause, the courts will be very busy indeed."[124] He entirely ignored Ninth Amendment, equal protection, and Eighth Amendment claims, despite the fact that Professor Tribe explicitly made reference to the Ninth Amendment in his oral argument, Justice Powell specifically considered the Eighth Amendment in his concurrence, and equal protection was implicated by the singling out of homosexuals for prosecution under the Georgia statute and was explicitly raised in the NOW brief.

Chief Justice Burger dwelt even more obsessively on the "crime against nature," essentially quoting verbatim from the state of Georgia's brief. Indeed, Burger appeared to agree with Blackstone that "sodomy" was "an offense of 'deeper malignity' than rape"[125]—demonstrating an apparent lack of empathy for gays and women simultaneously, a real *tour de force.* While it is true that "taunting a conservative Reagan court with a homosexual case in a Falwellian era of Rambo, Eastwood and AIDS" may have meant a foregone conclusion, one cannot help but wonder if at least one of the justices who joined the majority might have been open to another narrative had it been more available.

The dissenters saw the human issues. Justice Blackmun's opinion was singularly undisturbed by the subject of sex or homosexuality:

> the fact that individuals define themselves in a significant way through their intimate sexual relationships with others suggests, in a Nation as diverse as ours, that there may be many "right" ways of conducting those relationships, and that much of the richness of a relationship will come from the freedom an individual has to *choose* the form and nature of these intensely personal bonds.[126]

Blackmun observed: "The Court claims that its decision today merely refuses to recognize a fundamental right to engage in homosexual sodomy; what the Court really has refused to recognize is the fundamental interest all individuals have in controlling the nature of their intimate associations with others."

Blackmun agreed with Justice Holmes that

> it is revolting to have no better reason for a rule of law than that so it was laid down in the time of Henry IV. It is still more revolting if the grounds upon which it was laid down have vanished long since, and the rule simply persists from blind imitation of the past.[127]

In rebuttal to the claim that "the majority" abhorred the conduct, Blackmun stated, "it is precisely because the issue raised by this case touches *the heart of what makes individuals what they are* that we should be especially sensitive to the rights of those whose choices upset the majority." "A State can no more punish private behavior because of religious intolerance than it can punish such behavior because of racial animus." There was no interference with the rights of others, "for the mere knowledge that other individuals do not adhere to one's value system cannot be a legally cognizable interest . . . let alone an interest that can justify invading the houses, hearts, and minds of citizens who choose to live their lives differently."[128] Blackmun concluded:

> I can only hope . . . the Court soon will reconsider its analysis and conclude that depriving individuals of the right to choose for themselves how to conduct their intimate relationships poses a far greater threat to the values most deeply rooted in our Nation's history than tolerance of nonconformity could ever do.[129]

◊ ◊ ◊

There simply was no reason for Justice White's venomous attack or for Burger's thundering about the Judeo-Christian tradition other than prejudice and lack of empathic understanding. Even legality went by the wayside as a result: It would have been perfectly plausible within the realm of legality to write an opinion upholding the statute. (Justice Powell recently suggested such an approach, indicating that his fear of abusing substantive due process analysis strongly influenced his vote in *Hardwick*.) Perhaps it was less disingenuous that these justices did not mask their dislike of an outgroup through a rhetoric of "balancing" or "legal principles" that would have more effectively disguised empathic failure. Their revulsion certainly is not open to the accusation of being "liberal," namby-pamby, toothless, pluralistic tolerance such as that advocated by Blackmun's dissent. To assert that Blackmun was unprincipled, however, is to miss the point of his dissent entirely. Blackmun was speaking for humans and for the positive values of a liberal state—respect for human freedom from oppression and tyranny.

E. Summary

The purpose of the foregoing discussion has been to demonstrate that empathic narrative is a part of legal discourse and that empathic understanding can play a role in legal decision making. The discussion is admittedly ahistorical, confined as it is to the particular narratives rather than any broader cultural or historical influence that affected the Court's decisions in these cases. Because of the ahistorical approach, among other things, the cases may seem too easily to be characterized as "obvious" examples of good guys having empathy on their side and bad guys not. But *Brown, Shapiro,* and *Roe,* at least, did raise issues of empathy on both sides, the strongest example being *Roe.* The foregoing discussion might also be characterized as wildly optimistic or ambitious about the prospects of empathic knowledge: As "everyone" knows, *Brown II* canceled *Brown I, Dandridge*[130] and *Kras*[131] canceled *Shapiro,* and *Roe* will disappear now that Justice Powell has resigned. And, as everyone "knows," distrust of others and xenophobia are an inevitable part of human nature; the argument that empathy had anything to do with the outcome of *Brown* or *Shapiro,* for example, may seem to be merely the wishful thinking of a frustrated "liberal" academic, longing for a "liberal" Court. Another possible objection to my interpretation is that empathy is an unstable phenomenon, with no "staying power" or transformative potential; arguably, it is quickly overwhelmed by dominant, unreflective ideologies and beliefs. Dominant modes of discourse won't be shaken; they are too resilient. Besides, people just don't want to hear these narratives—at least not for very long. Understanding the Other takes too much work and is too disturbing to keep up.

Yet these criticisms would overlook the fact that the result in *Brown* came from an understanding that segregation, no matter how it was rationalized, caused human beings pain; the change in doctrine facilitated empathic understanding of blacks, by forcing whites to acknowledge their humanity. Racism persists, but many whites by virtue of becoming accustomed to being with blacks rather than separated have recognized our common humanity; while "contact . . . cannot always overcome the personal variable in prejudice," people "with a normal degree of prejudice" will become less prejudiced as a result of "equal status contact between majority and minority groups in the pursuit of common goals."[132] Unfortunately, empathy for the poor has not continued, perhaps because the poor can trigger so many prejudices—racial, ethnic, and sexual. Empathy for the poor also conflicts with the work ethic of capitalism and the belief that poverty is never inescapable. Empathic understanding of the experience of women seems to wax and wane; with an administration bent on appointing justices with a definite opposition to abortion, the issue of openness to empathic narrative in that area may in the immediate future be moot.

IV. Conclusion

The tentative conclusions that can be drawn about legality and empathy are that empathic understanding is possible and that empathic narrative can and should be a proper and influential part of legal discourse. Empathic narrative need not be fulsome rhetoric—the argument of Archibald Cox in *Shapiro* was simply phrased and the stories were told in a matter-of-fact tone. Appeals to emotion are not necessarily appeals for empathy: The emotional argument of the state in *Bowers v. Hardwick* opposed empathy. But to be effective, empathic narrative does seem to require concrete human stories rather than simple abstract appeals to legal principles. And the presence or absence of empathic understanding does help us to understand why the four cases studied were decided the way they were.

To the extent that "horror stories" dominate our emotional grasp of an experience, might the resulting decision be skewed if we were to encourage empathic knowledge? I have argued elsewhere that the parade of horrible stories of criminal victimization has led to some destructive laws. Is this not inevitable? Horror stories, however, do not constitute all of empathic understanding. Because they work at the level of affect in the hearer, they evoke emotional response. Yet frequently that emotional response is not empathic because it is not the perception of the emotion or experience of another but, rather, one's own response. One's own emotional response is certainly something to explore or consider, but it is not empathy.

How to determine if the component of emotional response in empathy is one's own or a resonation with the Other is not quickly answered. The psychological phenomenon of projection—attributing one's own mental or emotional state to another—complicates things further. This is, of course, part of the larger problem of empathic accuracy—the ability not only to empathize but to understand correctly what another is experiencing. It may not be possible to empathize totally with another from a completely different culture, for example, and it is not always possible to interpret correctly the empathic messages received. As Kennedy notes, you may be wrong.[133] But these concerns neither disprove the existence of empathy nor excuse a decision maker from considering empathic narratives. Instead, as with attaining other forms of knowledge and understanding, these concerns indicate that empathic understanding takes practice and work. Part of that practice can be accomplished in the form of questioning whether the received message is the correct one or asking for clarification. Part of it can be accomplished through attentiveness to empathic narrative.

In *The Wrongs of Victim's Rights*,[134] I attempted to demonstrate that the so-called Victims' Rights Movement largely ignored the phenomenological dimension of a crime victim's experience and that, accordingly, laws passed ostensibly in the crime victim's name may have worsened conditions for victims. Undoubtedly, the victims' rights movement evoked an empathic response in at least some voters and legislators, and that response led to action to remedy perceived injustices. Yet the genuine empathic response seemed quickly to be sublimated into existing ideological debates about the criminal process. Certainly, I have argued, many of the laws passed in the name of victims often seemed to be anything but altruistic or caring toward those victims. The stories of victims were expropriated; few, if any, empathic narratives were developed in the public discourse about victims' rights laws. Instead, "advocates" paraded horror stories before legislators and the public; the need for counseling, support services, and understanding of the experience of victims of violent crime as perhaps the most appropriate response to the distress of crime victims was lost in the shuffle. Another possible explanation for the divergence of empathic response and actual outcome was that the empathic response to crime victims was inaccurate or incomplete. For example, the unreflective translation of the anger of victims into a desire for retaliatory retribution might have been inaccurate. Furthermore, the initial empathic response to the stories of victims may have been so distressing that the listener avoided empathizing further and, instead, withdrew from victims, recharacterized the story, or stopped listening—all characteristic reactions to empathic distress. Finally, the existing structures of legality in the criminal process may have provided refuge from empathic response, so that those structures and debates about them replaced the very real debate over the pain a crime victim experiences and how the legal system might address that pain.

In other instances, empathy for victims may have so dominated thinking that empathy for other actors in the criminal justice system was obliterated. As Professor Lawrence Becker has accurately noted, "incompleteness in the range of empathic powers can produce moral error."[135] This is not, however, an argument that eliminates the usefulness of empathy as a morally relevant mode of understanding, as Becker appears to assume. Absence of empathy produces moral error as well. It is simply a caution that selective empathy or unreflective empathy can mask moral choice. This is especially likely in the case of something like affirmative action, where a white decision maker unreflectively empathizes with whites to the exclusion of minorities and reaches a decision in favor of whites. As a result, patterns of covert discrimination are legitimated and become more entrenched; this, I would argue, constitutes "moral error."

Becker and others also imply that empathizing with morally "relevant 'types' of people" can be "disabling." Does empathy with all concerned create decisional paralysis? The affirmative action problem and the problem of abortion, for example, seem to present insoluble dilemmas if one empathizes with both—or all—affected. If legality—in the form of categories, accepted analogies, rules, habits—provides a solution to the dilemma by negating one side or another of the moral choice, it will perhaps overcome the moral paralysis we assume would follow. But ducking of moral choice via refuge in legality is irresponsible. Moreover, the view that decisional paralysis necessarily will follow is based on a kind of Manichaeism—the belief that there is one, and only one, "right" answer. Empathy may enable the decision maker to see other "right" answers, or a continuum of answers. Or it may simply make the decision maker aware that what once seemed like no choice or a clear choice is instead a tragic one. To mask the tragedy of choice by taking refuge in rules does not negate the tragedy.

Empathy cannot necessarily tell us what to do or how to accomplish something, but it does alert us to moral choice and responsibility. It also reminds us of our common humanity and responsibility to one another. We could do worse—indeed we have done worse—than to employ the knowledge empathy imparts to us.

Notes

Robin L. West and Paul Brest provided me with support, encouragement, criticism, and nudging throughout this project. My colleagues Jim Wilson and Mickey Davis were very helpful and conscientious readers of various drafts. I owe thanks to Robert Weisberg and Mark Tushnet for some special assistance and to Joyce Sterling, Bill Simon, and Deborah Rhode for their help and interest. Mistakes that remain are mine.

1. United States v. Kras, 409 U.S. 434, 460 (1973) (dissenting opinion).

2. J. Noonan, Persons and Masks of the Law (1976).

3. *Id.* at 18.

4. *Kras* involved a challenge to the $50 filing fee required to institute bankruptcy proceedings. The majority decision distinguished Boddie v. Connecticut, 401 U.S. 371 (1971), which had held that due process required waiver of court fees for indigents seeking dissolution of marriage, on the grounds that the interests in the marital relationship and association were "fundamental" under the Constitution. Bankruptcy, the *Kras* majority said, involved no such fundamental interest. 409 U.S. at 443 (1973).

5. 347 U.S. 483 (1954).

6. 394 U.S. 618 (1969).

7. 410 U.S. 113 (1973).

8. 106 S. Ct. 2841 (1986).

9. D. Westen, *Self & Society,* 51–94 (1985).

10. *Id.* at 39–94.

11. E. Stotland, S. Sherman & K. Shaver, *Empathy and Birth Order* 2 (1971).

12. Westen, at 35.

13. C. Geertz, *Local Knowledgeat* 70 (1983).

14. 163 U.S. 537 (1896).

15. Simon, "Legality, Bureaucracy, & Class in the Welfare System", 92 YALE L.J. 1198, 1225–40 (1983).

16. *Id.* at 1198–1221.

17. *Id.* at 1204–22.

18. Weisberg, "Deregulating Death", 1983 *Sup. Ct. Rev.,* 305–75.

19. *Id.* at 379–95.

20. R. Cover, *Justice Accused,* 201 (1975).

21. *Id.* at 229–36.

22. *Id.* at 216.

23. G. Allport, *The Nature of Prejudice,* 192 (1954).

24. E. Cahn, *The Predicament of Democratic Man,* 129 (1961).

25. C. Geertz, *The Interpretation of Cultures,* 6–28 (1973).

26. R. Kluger, *Simple Justice* (1976).

27. 347 U.S. at 494.

28. Kluger, at 711.

29. Argument (L. Friedman ed. 1969) at 33.

30. 347 U.S. at 494 (interpolation by the Court).

31. Argument, at 33.

32. Elman, The Solicitor General's Office, Justice Frankfurter, and Civil Rights Litigation, 1946–1960: An Oral History, 100 HARV.L.REV. 817 (1987).

33. Kamisar, "The School Desegration Cases in Retrospect", in Argument at xvi.

34. Argument, at 36–37.

35. *Id.* at 38.

36. *Id.* at 42.

37. *Id.* at 49.

38. *Id.* at 51–58.

39. *Id.* at 57.

40. *Id.* at 60–61.

41. *Id.* at 61–62.

42. *Id.*

43. *Id.*

44. *Id.* at 319.

45. Argument, at 216.

46. *Id.* at 234.

47. *Id.* at 237.

48. *Id.* at 238.

49. Kluger, at 689.

50. *Id.* at 681.

180 ARGUMENT, at 48–64. Frankfurter questioned or interrupted Marshall 46 times, while asking John W. Davis only seven questions.

51. R. KLUGER, at 596, 599.

52. R. KLUGER, at 684–85.

53. *Id.* at 599–602, 653–55, 683–85.

54. H. N. HIRSCH, The Enigma of Felix Frankfurter 195–96 (1981).

55. R. KLUGER, at 592–93.

56. *Id.* at 613–82.

57. *See* E. WARREN, at 145–50; *see also* G.E. WHITE, EARL WARREN: A PUBLIC LIFE 68–75, 161–62 (1982) (describing Warren's personal bias against Japanese as well as his personal responsibility for the internment camps).

58. R. KLUGER, at 680. G. E. WHITE, at 162, indicates Warren had made strong public statements for civil rights for blacks and had encouraged antidiscrimination legislation for blacks when he was attorney general, although he was not entirely free of racist sentiments.

59. G.E. WHITE, at 165; R. KLUGER, at 680.

60. R. KLUGER, at 595.

61. 321 U.S. 649 (1944).

62. 328 U.S. 373 (1946).

63. R. KLUGER, at 595.

64. *Id.* at 680.

65. 347 U.S. at 495.

66. R. KLUGER, at 710, 714.

67. Shapiro v. Thompson, 392 U.S. 920 (1968).

68. Brief for Iowa at 4; Brief for Delaware as Amicus Curiae at 4; Brief for Appellant at 10.

69. Brief for Appellant at 2–5.

70. Brief for Appellee at 2, 3.

71. Supplemental Brief for Appellees on Reargument at 3.

72. Transcript of Reargument, in 68 LANDMARK BRIEFS, Kurland and Caspar eds. 1975); at 382–84.

73. *Id.* at 405 (emphasis on tape recording of reargument; wording conforms to tape rather than transcript).

74. *Id.* at 358–59 (counsel for Connecticut); *id.* at 367 (counsel for the District of Columbia).

75. *Id.* at 394.

76. *Id.* at 403.

77. *Id.* at 360, 361.

78. 394 U.S. at 628–32.

79. 394 U.S. at 650, n.5.

80. 394 U.S. at 677.

81. 394 U.S. at 672–74.

82. 394 U.S. at 661, n.11 (citing Williamson v. Lee Optical Co., 348 U.S. 483 (1955)).

83. Law, *Rethinking Sex and the Constitution,* 132 U. PA. L. REV. 955, 981 (1984).

84. Taylor, *Powellon His Approach: Doing Justice Case by Case, New York Times,* July 12, 1987, at 1, col. 3.

85. Brief for Appellee at 28–59, Roe v. Wade, 410 U.S. 113 (1973) (no. 70–18).

86. Motion and Brief Amicus Curiae of Certain Physicians, Professors, and Fellows of the American College of Obstetrics and Gynecology in Support of Appellees at 31, 46.

87. B. WOODWARD AND S. ARMSTRONG, THE BRETHREN 167 (1979) (Woodward and Armstrong's words, not Blackmun's).

88. Transcript of Oral Argument, in 75 LANDMARK BRIEFS, at 800.

89. *Id.* at 822.

90. *Id.* at 817. Counsel earlier had suggested some form of "balancing" the "rights" of fetuses and women if fetuses were persons; *id.* at 813.

91. Transcript of Oral Argument, in 75 LANDMARK BRIEFS, at 786–87.

92. *Id.* at 787–88 (emphasis on tape recording).

93. Transcript of Reargument, in 75 LANDMARK BRIEFS, at 811–13.

94. 410 U.S. at 116 (emphasis added).

95. 410 U.S. at 153–59.

96. I am indebted to Professor George Alexander for this characterization.

97. 410 U.S. at 156–58.

98. B. WOODARD AND S. ARMSTRONG, at 169,231.

99. B. WOODWARD AND S. ARMSTRONG at 169,233 (Woodward and Armstrong's words, not Stewart's).

100. B. WOODWARD AND S. ARMSTRONG at 230. The statement quoted by Woodward and Armstrong is found in Abele v. Markle, 351 F. Supp. 224, 231 (D.Conn. 1972)(Newman J.).

101. Regan, *Rewriting* Roe v. Wade, 77 MICH. L. REV. 1569, 1617 (1979).

102. Thornburgh v. American College of Obstetricians, 106 S. Ct. 2169 (1986).

103. *See Thornburgh,* 106 S. Ct. at 2173–74.

104. 106 S. Ct. at 2179.

105. 106 S. Ct. at 2179–80.

106. 106 S. Ct. at 2184–85 (citations omitted), for the National Abortion Rights Action League, at 5.

107. Grey, *Eros, Civilization and the Burger Court,* LAW & CONTEMP. PROBS., Summer 1980, at 83.

108. 358. Brief for the National Abortion Rights Action League, et al. as Amici Curiae in support of Appellees, Thornburgh v. American College of Obstetricians, 106 S. Ct. 2169 (1986) (nos. 84–495 & 84–1379), at 8–30.

109. *Id.* at 8–10.

110. 262 U.S. 390, 399 (1923).

111. Brief for the National Abortion Rights Action League, at 22–23 (quoting Meyer v. ebraska, 262 U.S. 390, 399 (1923)).

112. 106 S. Ct. at 2194–97.

113. Harris, *The New Symbol of Gay Rights, Cleveland Plain Dealer,* September 7, 1986, at 1G, col. 1, 2G, col. 1.

114. *Id.* at 2G, cols. 2, 3.

115. *Id.* at 1G, cols. 1–2, 6.

116. 106 S. Ct. at 2857; Brief of Petitioner Michael J. Bowers, Attorney General of Georgia at 6, 20, *passim;* Official Transcript Proceedings Before the Supreme Court of the United States at 5. 9–10, Bowers v. Hardwick (no. 85–140).

117. Brief of Petitioner Michael H. Bowers at 36–38.

118. G. ALLPORT, at 192, 434–46. Stereotypy "acts both as justificatory device for categorical acceptance or rejection of a group, and as a screening or selective device to maintain simplicity in perception and in thinking" (*id.* at 192). The difficulties encountered in trying to cut through a common stereotype of homosexuals are illustrated by the following exchange between Senator Strom Thurmond and Jeffrey Levi, executive director of the National Gay and Lesbian Task Force, during the hearings on the appointment of Justice Rehnquist as Chief Justice:

> Mr. Thurmond: Does your organization advocate any kind of treatment for gays and lesbians to see if they can change them and make them normal like other people?
>
> Mr. Levi: Well, Senator, we consider ourselves to be quite normal. . . .
>
> Mr. Thurmond: You don't think gays and lesbians are subject to change or you don't think they could? . . .
>
> Mr. Levi: No more so, Senator, than . . .
>
> Mr. Thurmond: . . . don't think they could be converted so they'd be like other people, in some way?
>
> Mr. Levi: Well, we . . . think we are like other people with one small exception. And unfortunately it's the rest of society that makes a big deal out of that exception.
>
> Mr. Thurmond: A small exception? It's a pretty big exception, isn't it?
>
> Mr. Levi: Unfortunately, society makes it a big exception. We wish it wouldn't and we would—that's why our organization exists.
>
> Mr. Thurmond: Well, we thank you all for coming and testifying, and you're now excused. *Required Reading: Thurmond on Homosexuality, New York Times,* August 2, 1986, at 6, col. 4.

119. *See* Brief for Respondent at 27–28; 22 n.38.

120. Brief Amicus Curiae for Lesbian Rights Project at 6, 12–13.

121. *See* Brest, *Supreme Court Proscribes a View of Privacy, Los Angeles Times,* July 13, 1986, § V, at 2, col. 5. Professor Brest pointed out that "had the Court invalidated the statute as written, the legislature might have responded with a law that punished only homosexuals." This certainly provided an "excuse" for the Court to preempt future challenges. Brest's further point that the legislature "likely. . . would have let the matter rest—for political, moral or humanitarian reasons"— seems optimistic given the fear of AIDS as a "gay" plague.

122. 106 S. Ct. at 2844–46.

123. Official Transcript, at 21–22.

124. 106 S. Ct. at 2846.

125. 106 S. Ct. at 2847 (quoting 2 W. BLACKSTONE, COMMENTARIES *216).

126. 106 S. Ct. at 2851 (Blackmun, J., dissenting) (emphasis in original).

127. 106 S. Ct. at 2848 (quoting Holmes, *The Path of the Law,* 10 HARV. L. REV. 457, 469 (1897)).

128. 106 S. Ct. at 2856 (citation omitted).

129. 106 S. Ct. at 2856.

130. Dandridge v. Williams, 397 U.S. 471 (1970).

131. United States v. Kras, 409 U.S. 434 (1973).

132. G. ALLPORT, at 280–81.

133. Kennedy, 41 MD. L. Rev. 639 (1982).

134. Henderson, *The Wrongs of Victim's Rights,* 37 STAN. L. REV. 937 (1985).

135. L. BECKER, RECIPROCITY 159 (1986).

11

Black Women and the Constitution: Finding Our Place, Asserting Our Rights

JUDY SCALES-TRENT

◊ ◊ ◊

I. Black Women as a Discrete Group

Status is a term which sociologically identifies one's position in society. Each status carries a set of norms, defined as a pattern of behavior expected of persons of that particular status. Status is frequently used as a means of ranking one's social position or role.

Black women possess two statuses which derive from attributes over which they have no control: membership in the black race and membership in the female sex. The combination of these two statuses creates a new status, and because it is a combination of two degraded statuses, black and female, the new status is a particularly low-ranking one. In order to support this degraded status, society has created a system of mythology and misinterpretations about black women which further limits the life opportunities of black women.

In a society which sees as powerful both whiteness and maleness, black women posess no characteristic which is associated with power. They are therefore treated by society in a manner which reflects a status different from, and lower than, both black men (who have the status ascribed to maleness) and white women (who enjoy the status ascribed to whiteness).[1] This is in no way inconsistent with the fact that black women are often treated badly along with black men solely because of their race or because of their sex along with white women. A study on wages in New York State, conducted for the National Committee on Pay Equity in 1986, confirms this disparity in the treatment of black women.[2] The researchers found that the wages of white women, minority men, and minority women in job categories which were composed largely of members of those groups, were systematically depressed. The studies further showed that the wages for women of color were depressed further than those of both men of color and white women. For example, in New York State, job titles with high concentrations of minority men were devalued by 1.59 salary grades, while those with a high concentration of white women were devalued by 1.95 grades. The devaluation rate for women of color, however, was 2.77 grades. Two of the myths supporting the degraded status of black women are that they do not need money and are not worth money. Thus both of these myths are perpetuated by the economic structure of American society.

Since black women share a negative group label imposed from the outside, they feel a need to come together for mutual protection. This "perceived need to band together in defense against domination or hostility" is one major source of cultural identity.[3] Although at one level it seems bizarre to request that "black women" be identified as a group with degraded social status, only through acceptance and utilization of this status will the group be able to work to defeat limitations imposed on its members from the outside. The Constitution protects both the choice to turn inward to the cultural group and the choice to use that group identity to participate fully in the institutions of the wider society.

One example of how black women have asserted themselves as a group within the legal system is the litigation they have initiated under Title VII of the Civil Rights Act of 1964,[4] alleging employment discrimination. We examine these cases in order to show why black women want to bring these claims as a distinct group. We also consider how the courts have addressed the issue of "multiple status" discrimination under this federal statute. We then explore the extent to which issues and problems raised under Title VII are transferable to the context of the Constitution.

A. Claims of Race/Sex (Dual Status) Discrimination Under Title VII

Title VII of the Civil Rights Act of 1964 prohibits discrimination in employment based on race, sex, religion, national origin, or color.[5] All public and private employers with more than fifteen employees are required to treat all present and prospective employees in a nondiscriminatory manner. An aggrieved individual proves a case of individual or class disparate treatment by comparing herself to similarly situated employees of a different race, sex, or national origin and by showing that she received less favorable treatment than that person (or class of persons) due to her group status. A group of employees may also prove discrimination under Title VII by showing that a facially neutral employment practice has an adverse impact on that group and cannot be justified as a business necessity.

When groups allege employment discrimination based upon group status, often that discrimination is based upon one characteristic, such as religion, sex, or race. However, employers who discriminate do not always do so in such neat categories. Just as widespread discrimination against black women as a class has always existted in American society, widespread employment discrimination against the class has existed as well. Since the enactment of Title VII, black women have gone to court claiming discrimination, as individuals and as a group, based on their distinct identity as black women. In 1980, the Fifth Circuit became the first court of appeals to rule on the issue of whether black women are protected as a discrete class under Title VII, in *Jefferies v. Harris Cty. Community Action Association*.[6] The court held that they are so protected, noting that discrimination against black females can exist even in the absence of discrimination against black men or white women. The court further stated:

> In the absence of a clear expression by Congress that it did not intend to provide protection against discrimination directed especially toward black women as a class separate and distinct from the class of women and the class of blacks, we cannot condone a result which leaves black women without a viable Title VII remedy.[7]

The *Jefferies* court found further support for this position in the Supreme Court's holdings and analysis in the "sex plus" cases. In those cases the Court found that discrimination against certain subclasses of women violated Title VII. Since then, every court which has ruled on the issue has agreed that black women can claim, as a distinct group, Title VII protection against discrimination based on the race/sex dual status.[8]

While so holding, several courts nonetheless expressed concern as to how such claims would be proved and defended within the traditional evidentiary framework.[9] As one district court noted, "The prospect of the creation of new classes of protected minorities, governed only by the mathematical principles of permutation and combination, clearly raises the prospect of opening the hackneyed Pandora's box."[10] For this reason, the court in *Judge v. Marsh* interpreted the *Jefferies* holding as limited to employment decisions based on two protected characteristics such as race and sex.[11] Such a limitation would, of course, permit black women to press their group claims under Title VII.

Black women have sought to claim this distinct status in court because it is often the only way that they can prove that they have been victims of remediable harm. The facts of the *Jefferies* case provide one example of the importance of how the claimant presents herself and her claim. In that case, Jefferies alleged that the employer discriminated in failing to promote her to the position of field representative in a county agency. The person who was promoted into the job she sought was a black man.[12] Jefferies was therefore not able to prove race discrimination. Moreover, since statistical proof showed that one of the previous field representatives had been a woman and that almost half of the supervisory positions within the agency were held by women, the plaintiff could not prove sex discrimination. However, the evidence showed that every position for which she had applied had been filled either by men or white women. Therefore, she could logically claim that the employer had been discriminating against black women as a class. Thus Jeffries was able to focus the proof of discrimination on the harm committed against her as a black woman. Similarly, in *Lewis v. Bloomsburg Mills*,[13] the plaintiffs were able to show a hiring rate of black women in the range of five to eight standard deviations below the "expected" level.[14] They were able, therefore, to make a prima facie showing of discrimination. If, however, they had been required to commingle their statistical hiring data with the hiring data for either black men or white women, the standard deviation might well have been lower, thereby masking the harm they had suffered, and making their argument weaker.

Title VII and the Equal Protection Clause of the Fourteenth Amendment to the United States Constitution are similar in that both are used by disfavored groups to gain equal treatment by society. Title VII and the Constitution are dissimilar, however, in many ways, such as coverage, burden of proof and remedies. The major difference, for the purposes of this chapter, between Title VII and the Constitution is that under Title VII, protected groups are always treated in the same manner. Whether alleging discrimination because they are Jews, Mexican Americans, women, or Asians, those covered by the statute receives the same level of protection, regardless of their group affiliation. A failure to hire claim raised by a group of women (sex discrimination) is assessed in the same way as one raised by a group of Mexican Americans (national origin discrimination). Even a group which presents itself with a race and sex claim under Title VII, for example, black women, receives the same level of protection as all other groups covered by the statute. The Equal Protection Clause differs from Title VII in that the level of protection changes depending upon which group is presenting the equal protection claim and depending upon how much protection the Court thinks is warranted based on that group's social and historical status. Thus, under Title VII, black women assert their rights as a separate group in order to focus the evidence on the particular harm where that harm is to black women as a class. Under an equal protection analysis, black women might proceed as a separate group not only to focus the evidence with particularity on the harm done to black women but also in order to get the court to assess the evidence within a framework which offers more protection to black women than it might to white women or to black men. It is because of this difference between Title VII and the Constitution that a new analysis is required to situate the group "black women" within the Equal Protection Clause and to consider how this group should be treated by the courts.

II. The Equal Protection Clause

The way in which a group is defined for purposes of the Equal Protection Clause both describes how that group is viewed by the larger society, and defines how that group should be viewed. The Court must see how the group has been treated historically by the larger society before it decides what level of protection it will provide the group. For example, in *City of Cleburne v. Cleburne Living Center*,[15] the Court had to decide whether a zoning ordinance which excluded group homes for the mentally retarded violated the Equal Protection Clause. In order to do this, the Court had to determine whether a classification based on mental retardation reflected "prejudice and antipathy" by society, "an outmoded notion" of the capabilities of the mentally retarded, or whether the mentally retarded have "distinguishing characteristics relevant to interests the State has the authority to implement." The court determined that the classification made by legislators based on mental retardation reflected not prejudice but a concern for the real differences in ability to function, and therefore it refused to presume that even those legislative actions which disadvantaged the retarded were constitutionally invalid. Thus, the perception of the Court and society of the mentally retarded determined the level of constitutional protection the group was to be afforded.

A. The Framework for Group Protection Under the Equal Protection Clause

The groups possessing the clearest definition, and therefore the highest level of protection under the Constitution, are racial and ethnic minorities. As the Court noted in *Korematsu v. U.S.*, "legal restrictions which curtail the civil rights of a single racial group are immediately suspect."[16] Such laws are subject to strict scrutiny and will be sustained only if they serve a compelling state interest. Thus, black Americans, both male and female, are entitled to the highest level of protection under the Constitution when confronted with state action which restricts them due to their race.

Women, along with several other groups, come after racial and ethnic minorities in this hierarchy of protection. The Court has determined that a classification which has a negative effect on women is not "immediately suspect," although it is subject to a heightened standard of review. The government need only show that the classification is substantially related to an important government objective for it to be held constitutionally permissible under the Equal Protection Clause.

The third category of groups is those which have been defined by the Court as not needing and therefore not entitled to any heightened level of scrutiny. The Court will defer to the legislative body in cases of classifications based on age, out-of-state persons, new residents in the state, or the mentally retarded, as long as the classification is "rationally related" to a legitimate state interest.

Given this schema, black women can find specific protection under the Equal Protection Clause as either blacks or as women and, in fact, have already done so. Surely black women were protected as blacks in, for example, *Gomillion v. Lightfoot,*[17] which involved racial gerrymandering for voting purposes. Black women were granted protection as women, along with white women, in *Califano v. Westcott,*[18] which involved the use of a gender-based classification to allocate benefits to families with dependent children. If, however, a group of black women makes the claim that it is being denied the equal protection of the laws because its members are both black and women, it is not clear what kind of constitutional protection this group will be provided. Should the scrutiny level be "strict" because the women are black, or should it be the lesser, heightened level of scrutiny because these blacks are women, or is the answer to acknowledge that black women constitute a discrete group in American culture whose position in society should be analyzed separately to determine what level of scrutiny should attach to state action which adversely affects them?

It is unlikely that a statutory classification which explicitly limits the opportunities of black women can be found today, although such classifications did exist in the past. It is not unlikely, however, that there are statutory classifications which place an overwhelming burden on black women.

The Court has held that facially neutral laws, which impose heavier burdens on a suspect class, do not alone violate the Equal Protection Clause.[19] That type of discriminatory impact is insufficient; plaintiffs must be able to show discriminatory intent. Although such discriminatory intent may be inferred from the totality of the relevant facts, a statistical showing of adverse impact on the protected group, standing alone, is not equivalent to proof of a constitutional violation. The question then becomes whether black women can prove an intent to discriminate against them, specifically, as a class. As the Court noted in *Hunter v. Underwood,* statistical proof of harm plus historical testimony tending to show an intent to discriminate would be sufficient to make out a constitutional violation.[20]

Such a prima facie showing could be made as follows: In 1952, when 70 percent of all of the mothers with one or more illegitimate children in Georgia were black, a Georgia legislator proposed a bill making it a misdeameanor for women to give birth to an illegitimate child.[21] If one were to transport this situation to the present, black women could show that the law imposes a substantially heavier burden upon them than upon any other group. Also, given statements by the state welfare director that he wanted to limit aid to the children of unwed black mothers, the plaintiffs could make a credible equal protection argument.

B. The Protection of Black Women as a Class Within the Framework of the Equal Protection Clause

There are three possible ways to protect black women within the equal protection framework. The first is to treat black women as a subset of blacks or of women and to grant their claims the level of protection accorded that group under the current tripartite analysis of the Court. The second is to treat black women as a discrete group seeking protection under the Constitution and to assess that group on its own merits to determine the level of protection it should be afforded. One might analyze the situation of black women in this society as that of a "discrete and insular" minority which is unable to enjoy the benefits of full citizenship and thus entitled to strict scrutiny protection under the Equal Protection Clause. Third, one might argue that since black women carry the burden of membership in the black group, which is already entitled to strict scrutiny protection, and in the disfavored female group, they should be entitled to more than strict scrutiny protection by the courts.

1. The Subset Theory

How are black women to be subclassified: in the black group or in the female group? This question is important because the level of protection granted black women will differ depending upon whether they are placed in the black group or the female group. Yet the notion that the level of protection would change depending upon which way they are classified is bizarre, since black women are always both black and women. To the extent that they are always burdened by both classifications, the level of protection should be constant. Moreover, since black women are always stigmatized by the race classification, they should always be provided the highest level of protection available under the Constitution. If we accept the Court's formulation that race classifications are inherently more suspect than sex classifications, we must therefore conclude that the Court considers the status of racial minorities to be "lower" than the status of women. Thus if black women are provided only intermediate scrutiny, as women, a portion of the burden they carry will have gone completely unaddressed by the legal system. As long as race is part of the group identity, any classification which limits their opportunities should be reviewed under the highest level of scrutiny.

2. The "Discrete and Insular Minority" Theory

The second possibility is to treat black women as a discrete group seeking protection under the Constitution and to assess the group on its own merits to determine the level of protection it should be afforded. Black women are entitled to the greatest constitutional protection under the Equal Protection Clause because they can be viewed just as the Court has viewed other groups which have sought the same level of protection. In making this determination, the Court has traditionally looked at several criteria to determine if a group is a "discrete and insular" minority[22] and thus unable to enjoy the benefits of full citizenship. The basic criteria are whether or not the group is defined by immutable characteristics,[23] whether or not there has been historical prejudice against the group,[24] and the extent to which the group is politically powerless.[25] A classification which reflects deep-seated prejudice against a particular group would be equally suspect.[26]

   a. Immutable Characteristics. Race, gender, national origin, mental retardation, and (il)legitimacy are all immutable characteristics which often adversely affect the way certain people are treated in our society. Hence, the Court is more likely to see a group as one needing protection if one of these characteristics is part of its social group identity. This category has not been applied consistently or rigorously, however. Some groups classified on the basis of their immutable characteristics, such as mentally retarded citizens, have not been given the highest level of protection, whereas other groups defined by mutable characteristics, such as alienage, have been granted such protection. Despite this confusion, clearly race and sex are immutable characteristics, and black women thus satisfy this prong of the test.

b. Historical Prejudice. The role of history is critical in the determination of what level of protection a group receives. As Justice Holmes has noted, in determining which groups are "discrete and insular," "a page of history is worth a volume of logic."[27] Justice Marshall has further stated on this point that

> the lessons of history and experience are surely the best guide as to when, and with respect to what interests, society is likely to stigmatize individuals as members of an inferior caste or view them as not belonging to the community. Because prejudice spawns prejudice, and stereotypes produce limitations that confirm the stereotype on which they are based, a history of unequal treatment requires sensitivity to the prospect that its vestiges endure.[28]

History proves that black women suffered a dual degradation, both as black slaves and as women. Although black women did not suffer any more than black men as a result of slavery, it is fair to say that they suffered differently, because they were women. As blacks they were exploited for their physical strength in the production of crops; as women, they performed a reproductive function which was crucial to the economic interests of the slaveholders.[29] As one historian notes, "Blacks constituted a permanent labor force and metaphor that were perpetuated through the Black woman's womb."[30] The reproductive function became especially important after 1801, when it became illegal to import slaves from Africa into the United States.[31]

Black slave women were sexually exploited for other than reproductive reasons. Their objectification as sexual beings also served the function of demonstrating power, and of terrorizing the entire slave community. Rape and the constant threat of rape were not only means of crushing attempts at resistance by black women but were also means of humiliating and symbolically attacking black men.[32]

Statutes enacted during the pre–Civil War period legitimated this power relationship. For example, statutes in Virginia simultaneously provided that it was not unlawful for a white man to have sex with a black female slave; it was a crime for whites to marry blacks; and the status of a child was based on the mother's status. These laws encouraged the exploitation of black women by white men and discouraged the legitimation of their sexual relationships by marriage.[33]

During this period, black women, unlike white women, were often grouped along with white and black men as persons who were to till the soil. A 1643 Virginia statute, for example, stated that "tithable persons"—those who worked the ground, whether slave or free—included all adult men and black women. Maryland enacted a similar statute in 1664.[34]

After the Civil War, both the states and the federal government acted in ways inimical to the interests of black women, treating them, again, differently from white women and black men. Guidelines created by the Freedman's Bureau required that black women receive lesser wages than black men, based on their sex. Agents of the bureau also gave less monetary support to former slave families with female heads of households than to those with male heads of households.[35]

The subsequent history of black women as workers followed slave history by reinforcing the view of black women as either domestic servants or manual laborers.[36]

After the Civil War, black women worked largely in rural areas in the South as sharecroppers or in urban areas as domestics in white households. Since the image of black women was limited to that of a domestic and not, for example, worker in the cotton mills, domestic jobs were "reserved" for black women. Therefore, black women, unlike the women of any other group, replaced the men in their families as primary breadwinners while still bearing responsibility for the traditional "wifely" duties. The exploitation of black women as domestics was not a regional phenomenon, however. Despite the fact that the black women who migrated to the North tended to be younger and better educated than those left behind in the South, by 1905 90 percent of all the black women working in New York City were domestics. Black women were completely excluded from sales and clerical work.[37]

During the Depression, southern black women returned to farm work and migratory labor camps; in the North, domestic servants were forced to look for jobs through "slave markets." Wages dropped drastically. A survey of wages of domestics in Mississippi showed that the average weekly pay was less than two dollars per week. In Philadelphia in 1932, domestics earned between five and twelve dollars per week. Despite the overall benefits of the public works projects of the 1930s that were initiated by the Roosevelt administration, many job training and job referral opportunities were closed to black women. This was directly attributable to southern whites' concern that helping black women find better jobs would eliminate an important source of cheap labor for white households and for the fields. Thus, public works officials in the South manipulated wages and job assignments to preserve racial and sexual inequities.[38]

These inequities were maintained throughout World War II, as black women moved into jobs in industry. There they were assigned to the most dangerous, backbreaking tasks in segregated job categories. Black women were routinely assigned to jobs that required them to stand in rooms filled with toxic fumes. White women, on the other hand, were given the jobs which allowed them to sit in well-ventilated rooms. Black women were also routinely assigned to work the night shift. The armed forces discriminated against black women by forcing them to maintain the role of domestic. Army records disclose that in at least one instance, black women were court-martialed for refusing to accept kitchen assignments, a job to which white women in the army were not assigned.[39]

Within the past twenty years, the relative economic status of those black women with jobs has improved, in large part due to the increased convergence of their job structures with those of white women. This convergence only underscores the fact that black women are moving into essentially low-status, dead-end jobs. Despite this convergence, black women are still the lowest-paid group when compared to white women, black men, or white men. Even with the improvements, black women still face significantly higher unemployment rates than any other group. For example, black female unemployment rates have been twice those of white women throughout the past decade.[40]

The history of dual oppression which has operated and continues to operate in the marketplace thus continues to limit the life opportunities of black women. The effects on the black community are devastating. In 1970, 56 percent of all poor black families were maintained by women; by 1981, that figure had jumped to 70 percent. In 1981, there were 22.1 maternal deaths per 100,000 live births to black women, compared to 6.5 maternal deaths per 100,000 births for white women.[41]

c. Political Powerlessness. The political powerlessness of black women is best illustrated by their struggle for the right to vote. As members of two disenfranchised groups, they were forced to struggle twice, both as blacks and as women, to gain a meaningful franchise. Moreover, as the least powerful members within both the black and the female groups, black women have had to fight to make their voices heard at all. Thus the heaviest burden in terms of improving their social condition has fallen on, and continues to fall on, the group occupying the weakest political position.

During the debates on whether the franchise should be extended to black men through the Fifteenth Amendment, some black women hesitated to support the measure because they were not sure they could count on black men for protection. Sojourner Truth, for example, opposed the amendment, fearing the even greater oppression of black women.[42] In the formal political conventions held by blacks during this period, there were no reported women delegates.

Many white women worked hard for the passage of the Fifteenth Amendment, hoping that they could link the issues of black suffrage and women's suffrage. This, however, did not prove possible.[43]

After passage of the Fifteenth Amendment, social reformers turned to considering whether or not the franchise should be extended to women through the Nineteenth Amendment to the Constitution. At this time, black women suffragists struggled for their enfranchisement in black women's organizations or in segregated chapters of white women's organizations; they marched for their enfranchisement in segregated suffrage parades. However, many powerful forces in the country were convinced that extending the franchise to black women posed considerable risks. White women in the women's movement were concerned that requesting extension of the franchise to black women would damage their chances of gaining the vote for themselves. Southern states were concerned about what the extension of the vote to black women would mean for their way of life. In 1914, for example, in South Carolina there were 100,000 more blacks than whites and the largest group of potential voters was black women. Senator Smith of South Carolina voiced concern about this fact when he stated: "If it was a crime to enfranchise the male half of this race, why is it not a crime to enfranchise the other half? . . . [I]t was perfectly competent for the legislatures. . . . to so frame their laws as to preserve our civilization without entangling legislation involving women of the black race."[44] This concern about extending the vote to black women was not limited to the South. For example, in 1914, after enfranchising women, the Illinois state legislature attempted to eliminate black women from the rolls. On the federal level, while the suffrage bill was in the southern-dominated Senate, several congressmen proposed amendments which would have limited the scope of the amendment to white women.

When black women finally obtained the vote under the Nineteenth Amendment, whites harassed them with the intention of rendering that vote useless. In various states black women were subject to tax and property requirements imposed on them exclusively, were given special "educational tests," or were forced to wait to register to vote until after white women had registered.[45]

The history of political powerlessness of black women becomes even more apparent when examining the number of group members who are elected officials on the local, state, and federal government levels. If one's power be determined by the ability to elect representatives who are members of one's group and who are therefore more likely to represent that group's interests, the statistics for black women tell a tale of little power. In 1985, there were 392 black elected officials in the legislative bodies of forty-two states and the Virgin Islands. Of that number, only 74 were black women. Of the 20 black congressmen at the federal level, only 1 was a black woman. Of the 26 black mayors of cities with a population over 50,000, only 1 was a black woman.[46]

If political power is determined by wealth, all indicators again point to black women as a group without power. Black women are overrepresented among the poor. For example, although the incidence of poverty among all women with children under age eighteen is high, the poverty rate for black mothers is approximately three times that of white mothers. Even controlling for age and education, the poverty rates for black women are generally two to four times higher than the rates for white women. Their poverty rate is also higher than that of black men. For example, 28 percent of all black women who have finished high school are poor, compared to 16 percent of black male graduates.

Analyses of social indicators for political alienation also demonstrate that black women feel politically powerless. A 1972 study by the Center for Political Studies showed that black women are "polarized in a set of attitudes different from those of black men and whites": a set of attitudes exemplified by a sense of powerlessness and lack of control over their lives; a sense of being forced to live "unsatisfying and insecure lives." Black women, compared to white women and black and white men, were shown to have the lowest levels of trust in the political process and the lowest feelings of political efficacy. A 1976 study of the quality of American life reinforced this finding. The analysts discovered that black women were more negative in their overall sense of well-being and satisfaction than black men or whites and concluded that "the quality of life of the black female appears less positive than that of any of the other segments of the population."[47] Thus, both history and social science demonstrate that black women, a group defined by two immutable characteristics, have suffered over the centuries from prejudice based on their group characteristics. As a result, black women have suffered, and continue to suffer, from political powerlessness within our society. Therefore, black women clearly belong to a group which is entitled to be classified as "discrete and insular" for purposes of determining the level of scrutiny applicable to equal protection claims.

3. The "More Than Strict Scrutiny" Theory

The final possibility is that black women—who are burdened by the double stigma of race and sex—are entitled to more than even the "strict scrutiny" level of review accorded when there is a state action which harms based on race. If the race stigma alone is sufficient to trigger strict scrutiny review, the race stigma plus an additional stigma (sex) should entitle the group to an even higher level of scrutiny and protection by the Court. As noted above, these double burdens are at least additive. In some instances, the dual burdens create a level of harm even greater than the sum of the parts.

How could a court provide more than a "strict scrutiny" level of review? It could ease the burden of proof in equal protection cases brought by black women by lessening the requirement for a showing of intent, for example. By so doing, a court would, in effect, be taking judicial notice of the double burdens carried by black women and the likelihood that the group identity continues to operate to their detriment. Similarly, in an employment discrimination case it could require a lesser showing of harm before requiring a state employer to engage in affirmative action for black women. There are many ways a court could recognize that "race plus another burden" should be protected at the level of "strict scrutiny plus more." In analytical terms, such a step is a logical extension of the equal protection framework created by the Court. Realistically, however, it seems unlikely that the Court will break ground for a group that it barely acknowledges as a separate class. Nonetheless, it is a logical next step for a court brave enough to take it.

III. Further Questions

This chapter argues that black women can be viewed as a subset of blacks and are therefore entitled to the highest level of constitutional protection by virtue of their membership in the black class. It further argues that based on their history and position in society, black women can be seen as a discrete group which can be assessed on its own for purposes of determining the level of protection it should receive under the Equal Protection Clause. These conclusions raise new questions about the further direction of developments under the Equal Protection Clause, questions which are addressed in this section.

The first question concerns the theory that black women are a subset of the black group and therefore qualify for the highest level of protection based on that status. If this theory applies, does it follow that other subsets of black groups, with secondary characteristics which do not warrant the highest level of protection (i.e., aged, retarded), merit the same consideration as black women? That is, should the black aged and the black retarded also be treated as the black female group?

The answer is yes. Subsets, such as the black aged and the black retarded, are in the same analytical position as black women for purposes of the Equal Protection Clause and should be treated the same way. Since the stigma of race always exists in these instances, the level of protection accorded the race group must also be granted to subsets of that group.

In its decision on "dual discrimination" claims brought under Title VII of the Civil Rights Act of 1964, the Fifth Circuit maintained, in dicta, that such claims should be limited to those groups sharing two immutable traits, such as race and sex.[48] That analysis applied here would distinguish between, on the one hand, black women or the black retarded (all immutable traits), and on the other, the black aged (age, though irreversible, is not immutable). Such distinctions could be made but would make no analytical sense.

One way of thinking about this question is to ask why, in any given case, the Court declined to extend heightened review to a particular group. What did the group lack that made the Court feel comfortable about giving it a lesser level of protection? In the case of the aged, the Court reasoned that the aged "have not experienced a 'history of purposeful unequal treatment' or been subjected to unique disabilities on the basis of stereotyped characteristics not truly indicative of their abilities."[49] This void, however, is filled by adding membership in the black group, a group which has experienced such a history and has been subjected to such disabilities. Thus, the combined category "black aged" possesses the indications of other groups which qualify for "strict scrutiny" protection. Owing to the force of the race stigma in this society, any group which is part of the black group must be granted the highest level of protection available under the Constitution.

A second issue is raised by the argument that black women can be considered a discrete group for purposes of the Equal Protection Clause. If this is true, what about Asian women and Hispanic women? Where do these double categories stop?

In *Judge v. Marsh* the district court allowed a group of black women to bring a Title VII claim based on their status as black women but expressed concern that creating such subgroups turned the statute into a "many-headed Hydra."[50] The court was concerned that subgroups for every possible combination of race, color, sex, national origin, and religion could be created and wondered "whether any employer could make an employment decision under such a regime without incurring a volley of discrimination charges."[51] The concern, then, is with the "slippery slope": What are we letting ourselves in for if we start down this path? In a recent case which raised similar "slippery slope" concerns, the Court stated that the petitioner lost the case because there was "no limiting principle" to the type of challenge he brought to the Court.[52] The task here, then, is to see if there is a "limiting principle" to the notion that groups may define themselves in different ways for purposes of constitutional protection.

In reality, because of the way the Equal Protection Clause has developed, it is already self-limiting. A group demanding recognition and protection from the Court must show that it is discrete, insular, and powerless. It must show as well that this group definition is causing it to be denied the equal protection of the laws. To the extent that other "dual" groups—Asian women, for example—could show a group identity and harm to the group based on that identity, it is hard to see why they should not be equally protected. There is no way to read the language of the Equal Protection Clause to limit the scope of its protection to a small number of groups.

Another approach to the "many-headed Hydra" problem would be to imagine the worst possible scenario if this type of group redefinition were permitted. Again, it is instructive to look at the concerns raised by courts under Title VII as a starting point. In *Judge v. Marsh,* the court was concerned that an employer would not be able to make any employment decision at all without fear of facing a discrimination claim if the claims of subgroups were allowed. Despite the court's concern about the future, this statement reflects today's reality. The Supreme Court has already decided that Title VII's prohibition of race discrimination protects white workers as well as black and that its prohibition against sex discrimination protects male workers as well as female.[53] If an employer is covered by Title VII, it is true at present that she cannot make any employment decision at all without considering the possibility of a Title VII charge. Similarly, every citizen is protected by the Equal Protection Clause. Ultimately, any "dual discrimination" claim raises issues of proof. The question then becomes whether the group alleging harm will be allowed to focus the proof on the harm caused them by their dual status and thus be able to receive a remedy.[54]

Conclusion

This chapter presents a way to view "new" groups which have reconstituted themselves from groups formally recognized and granted particular constitutional status by the Court. A group may either define itself as a subset of one of the groups or as a new, discrete group created by a unique history and place in society. Because all "persons" are protected by the Equal Protection Clause and because there is no reason to limit the number of groups protected thereunder, how aggrieved persons form themselves into groups should present no problems to a court.

This chapter also discusses the level of constitutional protection which should be granted to black women, a group which can claim membership in two groups—blacks and women, each of which has been viewed differently by the Court. It argues that whether viewed as a subset of the black group or as a distinct group in itself, black women are entitled to the "strict scrutiny" level of constitutional protection. Although the subset argument might well be the stronger one, due to the clarity of the Court's recognition of race as a particularly unjustifiable mode of classification, this chapter maintains that black women also have a strong argument that they are a "discrete and insular" minority, that they are the object of historical prejudice and stereotypes, and that this prejudice and insularity affect their ability to use the political processes to protect their interests. From the colonial period to the present, various state and private actors have singled them out for treatment different than that meted out to white women or black men. This has resulted in the creation of a group which is overrepresented among those living in poverty and underrepresented among those who influence the political process. It is a group which carries the degraded statuses of both blacks and women and finds its life chances thereby doubly limited. Any state action which burdens this group should be subject to at least strict scrutiny under the Equal Protection Clause. This chapter suggests that because black women are stigmatized by race plus another stigma (sex), they should be entitled to a strict scrutiny level of review (race) plus additional protection in the form of, for example, an eased burden of proof.

The Constitution was never intended by its framers to provide protection to black Americans or women Americans.[55] Certainly there was no intention of protecting black women. Only since the passage of the Fourteenth Amendment, with its statement that all citizens are entitled to the equal protection of the laws, has the Constitution afforded such protection. Black women clearly have not been granted the "equal protection of the laws" in the past. It is only by demanding the highest level scrutiny from the courts that they will receive such protection in the future.

◊ ◊ ◊

Notes

I am indebted to the many colleagues who read earlier drafts of this chapter and offered encouragement, suggestions, and hard questions. Among that group, special thanks go to Isabelle Marcus, Bob Belton, and Betty Mensch. My appreciation also goes to Colleen Blair for her excellent research assistance.

1. The fact that society as a whole sees black women as powerless, however, should not obscure the very real strengths and contributions of black women. For the contributions of black women in American history, *see generally* J. Jones, Labor of Love, Labor of Sorrow: Black Women, Work and the Family, from Slavery to the Present (1985); P. Giddings, When and Where I Enter: The Impact of Black Women on Race and Sex in America (1984); Black Women in Nineteenth Century American Life (1976); Black Women in White America: A Documentary History (1972). In fact, it has been argued that the very perception of the group as powerless has worked to the advantage of certain group members. *See, e.g.,* Epstein, *The Positive Effects of the Multiple Negative,* at 7. *But see* Fulbright, *The Myth of Double Advantage: Black Female Managers* in Slipping Through the Cracks: The Status of Black Women (Simms and Malveaux eds. 1986) (rejecting Epstein's hypothesis as "mathematically sound but intuitively illogical").

2. National Committee on Pay Equity, Pay Equity: An Issue of Race, Ethnicity and Sex (1987).

3. Karst, *Paths to Belonging: The Constitution and Cultural Identity,* 64 N.C.L. Rev. 304 (1986).

4. 42 U.S.C. § 2000e.

5. *See* Civil Rights Act of 1964 § 703, as amended, 42 U.S.C. §§ 2000–2002 (1983).

6. 615 F.2d 1025 (5th Cir. 1980).

7. *Id.* at 1032.

8. Hicks v. Gates Rubber Co., 833 F.2d 1406 (10th Cir. 1987); Judge v. Marsh, 649 F. Supp. 770, 779–80 (D.D.C. 1986); Chambers v. Omaha Girls' Club, 629 F. Supp. 925, *aff'd* 834 F.2d 697 (8th Cir. 1987); Graham v. Bendix, 585 F. Supp. 1036, 1047 (D. Ind. 1984); Carter v. Dialysis Clinic, 28 FEP Cases 268, 269 (D. Ga. 1981). Other courts have accepted the class claims put forward by black women without specifically addressing the issue. *See, e.g.,* Lewis v. Bloomsburg Mills, 773 F.2d 561 (4th Cir. 1985); Wright v. Missouri Dept., 512 F. Supp. 729 (E.D. Mo. 1981). *But see* DeGraffenreid v. General Motors Corp., 413 F. Supp. 142, 143 (E.D. Mo. 1976) (black women not special Title VII class), *aff'd in part, rev'd in part on other grounds,* 558 F.2d 480, 484 (8th Cir. 1977) (suggesting disagreement with district court's reasoning rejecting claim of race/sex discrimination).

9. *See, e.g.,* Jefferies v. Harris Cty. Community Association, 615 F.2d 1025, 1034 (5th Cir. 1980).

10. *DeGraffenreid,* 413 F. Supp. at 145.

11. 649 F. Supp. at 780. *See also* Shoben, *Compound Discrimination: The Interaction of Race and Sex in Employment Discrimination,* 55 N.Y.U.L. Rev. 793, 821 (1980) (suggesting courts should reduce the danger of statistical manipulation in compound discrimination cases by limiting the "compounding" to two protected characteristics).

12. *Jefferies,* 615 F.2d at 1029–31.

13. 773 F.2d 561 (4th Cir. 1985).

14. *Id.* at 568–69. The probability that such a disparity could be explained by chance alone is approximately one in a thousand.

The Lawyer's Committee for Civil Rights Under Law has filed numerous lawsuits against southern textiles companies, such as Bloomsburg Mills, alleging failure to hire black women. Seymour, *A Point of View: Why Executive Order 11246 Should Be Preserved,* 11 Emp. Rel. L.J. 568, 575 (1986). Lawyers for the Committee discovered an industrywide pattern wherein "white men and white women were hired for desirable jobs, black men were hired for low-paying, undesirable jobs, and black women were simply not hired at all."

15. 473 U.S. 432 (1985), at 441–48.

16. 323 U.S. 214, 216 (1944).

17. 364 U.S. 339 (1960).

18. 443 U.S. 76 (1979).

19. Washington v. Davis, 426 U.S. 229 (1976).

20. 471 U.S. 222 (1985).

21. W. Bell, Aid to Dependent Children 81 (1965), at 67.

22. U.S. v. Carolene Products Co., 304 U.S. 144, 152, n.4 (1937).

23. *See, e.g.,* Frontiero v. Richardson, 411 U.S. 677 (1973).

24. *See, e.g.,* San Antonio v. Rodriguez, 411 U.S. 1, 28 (1973).

25. *See, e.g.,* Mass. Board of Retirement v. Murgia, 427 U.S. 307, 313 (1976); Graham v. Richardson, 403 U.S. 365, 372 (1971).

26. *See, e.g.,* Mississippi Univ. v. Hogan, 458 U.S. 718 (1982); Plyler v. Doe, 457 U.S. 202, 216 (1982).

27. New York Trust Co. v. Eisner, 256 U.S. 345, 349 (1921).

28. City of Cleburne v. Cleburne Living Center, 473 U.S. 432, (1985) (Marshall, J., concurring).

29. J. Jones, at 11–12; Hine and Wittenstein, *Female Slave Resistance: The Economics of Sex,* in The Black Woman Cross-Culturally 296 (F. Steady ed. 1981).

30. Giddings, at 39.

31. Hine, at 296.

32. Davis, *Reflections on the Black Woman's Role in the Community of Slaves,* 12 Black Scholar 3, 12–14 (1981).

33. A.L. Higginbotham, In the Matter of Color: Race and the American Legal Process: The Colonial Period 43 (1978). For a similar discussion of the laws of Georgia and Pennsylvania, see *id.* at 58 and 251.

Anna Julia Cooper, born a slave, spoke poignantly of the struggle of black women to protect themselves and their daughters from sexual exploitation:

> Yet all through the darkest period of the colored women's oppression in this country her yet unwritten history is full of heroic struggle, a struggle against fearful and overwhelming odds, that often ended in a horrible death, to maintain and protect that which woman holds dearer than life. The painful, patient, and silent toil of mothers to gain a fee simple title to the bodies of their daughters, the despairing fight, as of an entrapped tigress, to keep hallowed their own persons, would furnish material for epics.

Black Women in Nineteenth Century American Life, at 329 (statement made by Cooper in 1893 to the Congress of Representative Women, on the status of black women).

34. Giddings, at 36–37; W. Jordan, White over Black: American Attitudes Toward the Negro, 1550–1812, at 77 (1968).

35. Jones, at 62.

36. The subsequent history also followed slave history by reinforcing the view of black women as sexually available and unprotected from sexual exploitation or attack. Black Women in White America, at 149–63; Ellis, *Sexual Harassment and Race: A Legal Analysis of Discrimination,* 8 Notre Dame J. of Leg. 30, 39–41 (1981). *See also* Gruber and Bjorn, *Blue-Collar Blues: The Sexual Harassment of Women Autoworkers,* 9 Work and Occupation 271, 284–85 (1982) (black women harassed more frequently and more severely than white women). The dynamic which encourages the sexual exploitation of black women workers also exists outside the work environment and influences the likelihood of sexual attack. Black women are between two to three times more likely to be raped than white women. The profile of the most frequent rape victim in this country is a young woman, divorced or separated, poor, and black. A. Karmen, Introduction to Part II, Women Victims of Crime, in The Criminal Justice System and Women 188 (Price and Sokoloff eds. 1982).

37. Giddings, at 135–78.

38. Jones, at 216–21.

39. *Id.* at 240–53.

40. Jones, *Black Women and Labor Force Participation: An Analysis of Sluggish Growth Rates,* in Slipping Through the Cracks, at 17.

41. Headen and Headen, *General Health Conditions and Medical Insurance Issues Concerning Black Women* in Slipping Through the Cracks, at 187.

42. Giddings, at 64–65.

43. The anger of white women suffragists at losing this issue often took on racist tones, showing once again the political division between black and white women. Elizabeth Cady Stanton, a cofounder of the American Equal Rights Association, "made derogatory references to 'Sambo' and to the enfranchisement of Africans, Chinese, and all the ignorant foreigners the moment they touch our shores." E. Flexner, Century of Struggle 147 (1975). Almost one hundred years later, during the legislative debates on Title VII, Rep. Martha Griffiths drew on this history and this anger when she stated, in discussing the possibility that Congress would prohibit employment discrimination based on race, but not on sex:

> It would be incredible to me that white men would be willing to place white women at such a disadvantage except that white men have done this before . . . your great grandfathers were willing as prisoners of their own prejudice to permit ex-slaves to vote, but not their own white wives.

E.E.O.C., Legislative History of Title 7 & 9 at Civil Rights Act of 1964, at 3219.

44. Flexner, at 314.

45. Giddings, at 159.

46. Joint Center for Political Studies, Black Elected Officials: A National Roster 2, 19–20 (1985).

47. A. Campbell, P.E. Converse, and W.L. Rodgers, The Quality of American Life: Perceptions, Evaluations, and Satisfactions 464–65 (1976). *Cf.* A. Lorde, Sister Outsider: Essays and Speeches 145 (1984). ("Every black woman in America lives her life somewhere along a wide curve of ancient and unexpressed angers.")

48. Jefferies v. Harris City Community Action Association, 615 F.2d 1025, 1033–34 (5th Cir. 1980).

49. Mass. Board of Retirement v. Murgia, 427 U.S. 307, 313 (1976).

50. 649 F. Supp. 770, 780 (D.D.C. 1986).

51. *Id.* at 780.

52. McClesky v. Kemp, 481 U.S. 279, 283 (1987).

53. *See Newport News v. EEOC,* 462 U.S. 669 (1983) (men protected against sex discrimination); McDonald v. Sante Fe Trail Transportation Co., 427 U.S. 273 (1976) (whites protected

against race discrimination). It should also be noted that when white men have alleged sex/race bias in "reverse discrimination" suits, courts have assumed without discussion that the dual category "white males" is protected by Title VII. Shoben, *supra* note 39, at 798.

54. An alternative approach to this problem would be to balance the burden of the employer against the burden carried by black women. Note that the district court in *Judge v. Marsh* was concerned with the problems an employer might have to face if confronted with this "many-headed Hydra." Surely, if weighed in the balance, the rights of black women to be free from employment discrimination are stronger than the right of the employer to be able to make employment decisions without thinking through the consequences of those decisions on protected classes.

55. *See* Justice Marshall, *Reflections on the Bicentennial of the United States Constitution,* 101 Harv. L. Rev. 1 (1987).

IV

---◆---

On Freedom: Restriction, Regulation, and Reproductive Autonomy

It might be said that if the Western liberal tradition stands for anything it stands for freedom, especially the protection of individual freedom against the intrusion and interference of state power. Indeed, the United States was founded on this ideal. Generations of Americans have pledged their allegiance to a country that stands for liberty and justice for all. All citizens are considered equal, and especially, all citizens are equally free. That is what we believe, and that is what we say.

In practice, however, there have always been qualifications and limits, even contradictions, to our stated ideals. We instituted slavery in the same breath as we declared all men created equal. We established poll taxes that disenfranchised the poor and reservations that imprisoned Native Americans. And we relegated half our population, all women, to second-class status, to which not all the rights of citizenship applied, including the rights to vote, to make independent contracts, to own property, or to do anything that contradicted the will of their husbands.

Women were never granted equal freedom. There has always been a double standard. Men are entitled to freedom, whereas women are entitled to protection. But the interesting point is that protection has always meant restriction. Women were "protected" from legal practice, for example, by being banned from it. They were "protected" from jury duty in the same way. They were "protected" from the rigors of business life by being denied licenses and union memberships, and they were "protected" from the dangers of education by being relegated to women's schools, dedicated for the most part until recently to producing charming and compliant wives and mothers. They were not, however, protected from hard labor in sweatshops and fields, from poverty and exploitation, or from abusive husbands.

Feminists have fought for equal freedom for women since this country was founded and gradually, right by right, have won the formal protection of equal freedom for women in many areas. Legal barriers have been removed from educational institutions, businesses, and professions. Women can now legally own property, execute contracts, serve on juries, and hold office. Yet the idea of equal freedom for women—the idea that women themselves should be in control of their own lives, just as men are—has been and continues to be a matter of great controversy. For example, the equal rights amendment (ERA) to the Constitution failed after long months of emotional and highly visible debate, which made clear that the controversy over equal freedom for women is not between men and women but between traditionalists and progressives. One might wonder how women themselves could be opposed to their own equal rights, but many women objected to the ERA, claiming that equal rights would eliminate special protections. The fact that any such special protections are meager indeed mattered very little but sent the debate spiraling to irrational topics like the threat of unisex toilets in an equal society. What the ERA debate really revealed was the fear of traditionalist men and women that their way of life—a way of life that features a male breadwinner and a female homemaker existing in separate spheres of endeavor that together make a whole traditional life—would disappear if women had equal rights.

Debates concerning reproductive freedom are similar to those regarding the ERA. The legal debate pertains to who should be entitled to decide the moral issues of procreation, contraception, and abortion. Should such matters be decided by state legislatures, or are they matters of individual choice and personal conscience? Although state legislatures had traditionally decided public policy regarding such issues, in 1942 the Supreme Court declared procreation to be a fundamental right that could not be taken away by the state, meaning that the state could not inflict sterilization as a punishment for certain crimes. Over time the idea that choices regarding marriage, procreation, and family matters were a private concern, and not to be decided by the state, developed into a doctrine of the Court that came to be called the *right to privacy.*

The development of the right to privacy reflects both the liberals' concern for protecting individual freedom and the state's reluctance in granting it. For instance, until the controversial case of *Griswold v. Connecticut,* which established the constitutional right to privacy, was decided in 1965, state legislatures could ban the use of contraceptive devices, even by married couples.

According to the Court in *Griswold,* constitutional protection against government intrusion is found indirectly in several amendments, for example, in the Third and Fourth amendments, prohibiting the forced quartering of soldiers in private homes and unwarranted searches and seizures on private property. These have sometimes been interpreted as the protection of privacy, although privacy is not mentioned by name in the Constitution.

In the early 1920s the Supreme Court interpreted the due process clause of the Fourteenth Amendment as protecting certain private decisions from government interference. At that time the rationale was called *substantive due process,* and its major effect was on labor law and contracts. Yet, certain cases decided on the basis of due process provided the precedent for what would be called the *constitutional right to privacy* in the case of *Griswold v. Connecticut. Griswold* is one of the most controversial and important cases ever decided in American law. It is important because it lays the basis for restricting governmental regulation of individual choices regarding personal and family life. It is controversial because it does not have a clear and explicit foundation in the Constitution. *Griswold* and the cases following it are activist decisions, accused of being judicial legislation, analogous to the now-discredited doctrine of substantive due process.

Griswold is controversial in the way that *Brown v. Board of Education* is controversial. That is, both cases have generated a great deal of intellectual debate and criticism (as well as defense) concerning the grounds or constitutional foundations that might provide legal legitimacy through analytical certainty or defensibility. But in a certain sense this is simply intellectual carping or gamesmanship; in practical terms, it is highly unlikely that either case would ever be overturned. These cases protect fundamental interests of significant community commitment. They are expressions of common values. Equal protection and the right to privacy are here to stay. What is much less clear is the scope of these rights, especially the right to privacy as applied to the right to choose abortion as set out in *Roe v Wade*. Unlike *Griswold* and *Brown, Roe* does not represent uncontroversial, settled values, although it does probably represent a majority view.

Like *Griswold, Roe v. Wade* is one of the most important and controversial cases ever decided by the Supreme Court. In it the Court determined that the right to privacy—that is, the right to make private decisions regarding marriage, procreation, and family life, as stated in *Griswold*—was broad enough to encompass a woman's right to decide whether to continue or terminate her pregnancy. According to the Court, three competing interests were at stake: the woman's right to privacy, the state's right to protect maternal health, and the state's right to protect potential life. These three interests were balanced as follows: In the first trimester of pregnancy, the woman's right was said the be the strongest, and the state's rights the weakest. During that time the state was not to interfere with the decision to have an abortion, which was considered a private matter between a woman and her doctor. In the second trimester the state could regulate abortion decisions to protect maternal health, and in the third trimester the state could ban abortions outright in order to protect both the mother's health and the potential life of the fetus.

Roe was decided in 1973, and since then it has probably become the most famous and controversial case in the legal history of this country, surpassing even *Brown v. Board of Education* and the infamous *Dred Scott* case, which upheld slavery. There are basically three broad views of the legitimacy of *Roe v. Wade,* although there are also variations within each view.

First is a broad coalition of views that support the legitimacy of *Roe.* This group tends to favor women's rights, or individual rights in general; that is, feminists support the decision as protecting women's rights, and liberals support it as protecting individual rights, from the intrusion of government. Many agree that *Roe* was correctly decided on privacy grounds but may differ over details of the decision (such as the trimester balancing of competing interests); some think it should have been decided on equal protection grounds. All support the result because they think that abortion decisions should be made by individual women or their families, and not by state legislatures. They see the right protected in *Roe* as analogous to other freedoms protected by the Bill of Rights, such as speech and religion, which should not be decided by majority rule. This group calls itself *prochoice.*

A second coalition of views includes a substantial number of people who hold a natural-law religious view that life begins at conception and that therefore abortion is murder and should be prohibited as such. This group also includes antifeminists and traditionalists who think that allowing women to control their own reproductive capacities tends to destroy values associated with traditional views of the home and family and of women as homemakers and mothers. All these people disagree with *Roe* because they disagree with the result, which in their view legalizes murder or destroys the family. It is not that they believe that whatever the state legislature says is fine or that abortion is a majority rule issue. Rather, they would prefer a constitutional amendment that prohibits abortion nationally. This group calls itself *prolife.*

The third position is a technical legal view held by some conservative legal scholars and jurists. This group (which is actually very small) opposes *Roe* because, they believe, it lacks adequate constitutional foundation. These people have concerns about the right to privacy as a constitutional doctrine and therefore are highly skeptical of its expansion in any respect, including its expansion in *Roe*. They do not necessarily oppose the result—a legal right to have an abortion—rather, they feel that the Court is overstepping its rightful jurisdiction. Because there are not adequate constitutional grounds for making the decision in *Roe*, the Court is deciding a legislative question. This, they think, is a matter that should be left to majority rule in the state legislatures.

According to several opinion polls, the vast majority of the American population subscribes to the first or second view. That is, most people agree or disagree with *Roe* because their view of abortion is compatible or incompatible with the result. Those who agree with *Roe* do so because they think abortion should be a private decision. Those who disagree with *Roe* do so because they think that abortion should be prohibited by the state. The third view is probably held by 1 or 2 percent of the population, but it has been used by conservative politicians to promote the second view (or block the first view) and thus gain the conservative popular vote. It is also the prevailing view of the Supreme Court, because during the Reagan and Bush administrations the justices have been chosen specifically with an eye to overturning *Roe*. If *Roe* is overturned, the legality of abortion will be determined state by state.

One problem presented in the abortion controversy is that the plight of women does not apparently lend itself to brief formulation in abstract principles that can easily be translated into legal rules. If the rights of women are to be balanced or pitted against the right of the state to protect potential life, how are we to characterize these rights? How are we to explain the disadvantage and hardship of an unplanned child or the distress and trauma of an unwanted pregnancy? Accounts of unwanted pregnancy seemed to cause discomfort rather than sympathy among the Supreme Court justices. The interests of women, sometimes labeled as *convenience* (e.g., by Justice White) have been made to appear trivial when compared with the life of the fetus, especially when the fetus is characterized as an unborn child, at any stage of development. Explaining the needs and interests of women means explaining the quality of life for real people, which makes little sense abstracted in the form of legal rules. To be convincing, it requires a context.

In Chapter 12, Deborah Rhode provides some of this context by tracing the history of law and social attitudes toward women's roles and reproductive freedom and noting that these attitudes have fluctuated over time and place, even within the Catholic church. Weighing the possible foundations for a right to reproductive freedom (particularly in *Roe*), she continues the argument that such issues must be viewed in a social context rather than by appeal to abstract rights. Rhode suggests that the test of legal legitimacy should be whether legal policy creates a special disadvantage for women. If it does, it should be held to violate equal protection.

Laurie Nsiah-Jefferson describes in Chapter 13 some of the special hardships that are created for poor women and women of color by imposing limits and restrictions on reproductive freedom. Shortly after *Roe* guaranteed reproductive autonomy to women, Congress eliminated the funding of abortions through Medicaid. In the case of *Harris v. McRae* the Supreme Court upheld the restriction, even though its effect was to deny poor women access to abortion and even though it had a disproportionate impact on disadvantaged minority women. There is no constitutional right to benefits, the Court noted, and consequently no right to equal access to abortion funding, even if the denial of funds effectively eliminates the choice to have an abortion. Poverty is not a suspect classification for purposes of equal protection of the law. The poor are not entitled to special protection by the Court, even though they tend not to be well represented in the legislatures. Rather, majority rule should determine the treatment of the poor. Nsiah-Jefferson criticizes this current policy toward poor and minority women, describing its effects and recommending steps that would respect their freedom and rights to fair treatment.

In her chapter, "Unraveling Compromise," Frances Olsen points out that if the Court legally recognizes two fundamentally incompatible interests—on the one hand, the state's interest in protecting potential life and, on the other, the interest of all women in directing their own lives and controlling their own bodies—then the best we can hope for is a compromise that fairly considers both sides. Contending that *Roe* is already a compromise decision that cannot be improved upon by some other compromise, she criticizes recent cases like *Webster v. Reproductive Health Services* that erode the effectiveness of the compromise arrived at in *Roe*. After considering the possible bases for the *Roe* decision—specifically on grounds of privacy or of equal protection, and the limits of these grounds—Olsen argues that despite their limits, both privacy and equal protection can provide a legitimate foundation for the constitutional protection of women's reproductive freedom. The implications of the value that the Court places on potential life are directly applicable to the value it places on the lives and freedom of women. That is, the conceptualization of the nature of the fetus or embryo is directly connected to the evaluation of the function and role of women. This is an important but difficult point that is commonly ignored or misunderstood.

Finally, in Chapter 15, Sylvia Law focuses on the issue of equal protection. Law argues that antiabortion laws have been central to enforcing the inferior status of women, by imposing on women burdens that men do not have to bear, specifically by impairing women's control over their own lives and reproductive capacities. It is not a woman's reproductive function in itself that prevents women from being equal and free; it is the fact that control over their own bodies is taken from them and that special social burdens are imposed on them in connection with their reproductive function. Thus, it is not nature, as is so often argued by traditionalists and patriarchs, but society that oppresses women.

The Supreme Court recently decided the case of *Planned Parenthood of S.E. Pennsylvania v. Casey*, which upheld *Roe v. Wade* in principle but rejected the trimester formula for balancing the woman's right to terminate her pregnancy against the state's interest in protecting potential life. The new test for validity of a state regulation regarding abortion before viability is whether it creates an *undue burden* on a woman's free choice. Using this test the Court upheld a Pennsylvania statute requiring parental consent for minors, the availability of certain information, and a 24-hour waiting period but invalidated a requirement of spousal notification. Both sides are vocally unhappy with this decision, which erodes *Roe* but does not overturn it. This case moots the old trimester formula for balancing competing interests but does not change the basic issue which, as Olsen specifically points out, is how to legally recognize two fundamentally incompatible interests. Controversy over this issue remains intense.

It should not be surprising that the debate over reproductive freedom for women should be so hostile. As Law points out, it is the core issue of women's equality and freedom, and it is also intimately connected with traditional views that support patriarchy as the law of nature. It is no accident that some religions view women as vessels ordained for the sacred mission of motherhood above all else and with or without her consent. Indeed, the Catholic church still opposes contraception, not only abortion.

Feminists believe that women are entitled to and are responsible for making their own decisions and running their own lives, just as men are. If we have the technological capacity to control our procreation, then it is not nature but the state that prevents us from doing so. State decisions are not issued from nature, but from centers of political power, and it is the task of feminists to protect the freedom of all women from the abuse of that power.

12

Reproductive Freedom

DEBORAH L. RHODE

Birth control techniques have been in existence for over four millennia, but only during the last two centuries has their use prompted intense public controversy and organized political activity. Although few issues are more central to women's self-determination and sexual expression, it was not until the 1960s that the feminist movement began to attach high priority to reproductive freedom. Moreover, as with the equal rights amendment, the campaign for reproductive freedom has provoked heated opposition from those whose freedom is at stake. Questions surrounding abortion and reproductive technology have acquired deep symbolic significance for women on both sides of the contemporary debate. At issue are fundamental concerns about individual liberty and sexual equality.

The Historical Legacy

Cultures have varied considerably in their attitudes toward controlling fertility, but few have invested the practice with the kind of moral significance that it began to acquire in the mid-nineteenth century. Most ancient societies, including Greece and Rome, were reasonably tolerant of abortion and contraception, and folk wisdom about different techniques has been passed down over centuries. Since many of the more effective preventive strategies required male cooperation or technical knowledge that was not widely available until the 1900s, abortion remained of critical significance. Although early Christian theologians generally condemned birth control, they disputed abortion's moral status. Between the eleventh and thirteenth centuries the controversy abated as a consensus formed around the doctrine of quickening. According to that theory, the fetus did not acquire a soul until it "quickened," that is, moved, in the woman's body. Prior to that point, abortion was permissible. Early English and American common law followed the view.[1]

This doctrinal development had practical as well as spiritual underpinnings. Until the point of fetal movement, medical knowledge was not sophisticated enough to determine whether a woman was definitely pregnant. The first American statutes, enacted between 1820 and 1840, typically codified case law and prohibited only postquickening abortions. Although a second wave of legislation between 1840 and 1860 was more inclusive, enforcement remained lax. Since early court decisions placed high burdens of proof on prosecutors, even statutes that did not distinguish in theory between early and late abortions often did so in practice.[2]

Various cultural trends that began in the mid-nineteenth century contributed to a more stringent regulatory climate. Increased advertising of birth control and abortion made these practices more visible; expanded opportunities for women outside the domestic sphere made such techniques more desirable. The shift from rural to urban industrial society meant that large numbers of children were no longer an economic asset but, rather, an impediment to a family's rising standard of living. As middle-and upper-middle class Protestant wives increasingly turned to abortion and contraception as a means of limiting fertility, the resulting decline in birthrates sparked widespread concern. At the end of the century, estimates suggest that almost three-quarters of women practiced some method of fertility control and that the ratio of abortions to live births was between one to three and one to five. As a result, the birthrate was about half what it had been in 1800.[3]

Opposition to these abortion and contraceptive practices reflected various concerns. Some critics feared that any separation of sex from procreation would result in increased venereal disease, psychological "derange[ment]," and social instability. The decline in fertility among the "better" classes, coupled with substantial population growth among immigrants, prompted fears of "race suicide." According to one nineteenth-century observer, nature "fortunately kills off the woman who shirks motherhood, but unfortunately it takes her a generation to do it." Meanwhile, some of civilization's "best breeding stock," who had married these shirkers, would lose out in the evolutionary struggle.[4]

In addition to concerns about the decline of their own class, leaders of the organized medical profession had special reasons for mobilizing against abortion. The issue provided doctors with a means of asserting technical, ethical, and social superiority over their competitors, particularly midwives and other practitioners who had not graduated from approved educational programs. Licensed physicians could claim special knowledge of the continuity of fetal development, special commitment to preserving human life, and adherence to the Hippocratic Oath, part of which forbids abortion. In the process, they could promote their own authority and economic monopoly. By lobbying for statutes that prohibited abortions unless necessary to save the life of the mother, the organized medical profession could criminalize much of its competition.[5]

This crusade was largely effective. Physicians' efforts coincided with those of other moral reformers interested in restricting all forms of birth control and obscene materials. In 1873 Congress passed the Comstock law, which prohibited dissemination of information about abortion or contraception. Over the next several decades, all but one state made abortion a felony, and such statutes remained largely unchanged until the late 1960s. These developments were ironic in several respects. Although physicians often justified their campaign in terms of protecting maternal health, their success occurred just as medical advances had reduced the risks of abortion, making it substantially safer than childbirth. While many physicians presented the issue in moral and spiritual terms, religious leaders were relatively uninterested in the crusade. During the latter part of the nineteenth century, the Catholic church did revise its position and began condemning abortion at all stages of fetal development irrespective of the risks to the mother or her potential child. The theory, as one bishop put it, was that two deaths were preferable to one murder. Yet despite that theological shift, the Catholic church was not a major participant in the nineteenth-century American abortion campaign.[6]

Nor did the feminist movement actively support abortion reform despite the obvious

significance of the issue for women's independence. To some movement leaders, reproductive issues were "too narrow . . . and too sordid." For others, they were too threatening. Legalizing contraception appeared to reduce the risks of extramarital sex and thus
to jeopardize traditional domestic relationships. For the vast majority of late nineteenth-
and early twentieth-century women, marriage and motherhood were the best sources of
economic security and social status. Any threat to the family was not worth provoking,
particularly if the major gain was to license sexual activity that many women had experienced as duty rather than pleasure. In the view of feminist leaders such as Carrie Chapman Catt, "to make indulgence safe is not enough." Continence, not contraception, was
their solution. Although most of these leaders were committed to "voluntary motherhood," they wished to ensure it through abstinence rather than "degrading" birth control
methods.[7]

As a result, the initial struggle for reproductive freedom remained largely independent
of the organized women's movement. Margaret Sanger, founder of the early twentieth-
century birth control campaign, began with feminist principles, but they became less visible as her campaign intensified. Her first manifesto emphasized women's right to control
their own bodies, and her early socialist affiliations reflected sympathy toward issues of
class as well as gender. According to Sanger's autobiography, the catalyst for her crusade
was the death of an impoverished East Side New Yorker from a self-induced abortion.
For that woman, the only medical advice available about how to avoid a life-threatening
pregnancy was to have her husband sleep on the roof.[8]

Yet as Sanger attempted to broaden her movement's appeal, her feminist arguments
faded, her class sympathies diminished, and her emphasis shifted to eugenics. "More children from the fit and less from the unfit—that is the chief issue of birth control," she
asserted in 1919. Although Sanger was generally careful to avoid explicit racist or ethnic
slurs, her definition of unfit was highly inclusive and encompassed illiterates, epileptics,
unemployables, and "dope fiends." Many of her disciples were even less restrained, and
their publications often stressed the usefulness of contraception in reducing welfare
expenditures and social deviance through selective breeding. In order to enlist support
from the medical profession, the movement focused on strategies that gave physicians
control over the distribution of birth control materials. Sanger and her followers also dis-
avowed any support for abortion and presented their preventive approach as a sufficient
alternative. The growing conservatism of the movement was exemplified in its embrace
of the term *family planning* in the 1940s. As Linda Gordon has noted, that terminology
shifted focus from women's autonomy to family hygiene and carried as few sexual or
feminist connotations as possible.[9]

In many ways, the evolution of the early reproductive rights movement paralleled that
of the suffrage campaign. In broadening their political appeal, birth control advocates
narrowed their social vision. Moreover, appeals to eugenics helped fuel the campaign for
sterilization practices that resulted in involuntary fertility control for thousands of slightly
retarded or impoverished women, particularly among minority groups. During the
1890s, the development of reasonably safe surgical techniques laid the foundations for a
wave of compulsory sterilization laws, which received Supreme Court blessing in 1927.
In *Buck v. Bell,* the Court permitted the sterilization of Carrie Buck, an institutionalized
and assertedly "feeble-minded" daughter of a feeble-minded mother, after the daughter
had given birth to an illegitimate feeble-minded child. Writing for the majority, Justice
Holmes concluded that "three generations of imbeciles are enough." Subsequent evidence exposed the risks of such decision making. Carrie Buck does not appear to have

been mentally deficient; she was institutionalized to hide a pregnancy resulting from rape by one of her foster relatives.[10]

In the late 1930s and 1940s, the eugenic sterilization movement began to decline, partly in response to scientific evidence undermining its premises, and partly to the lessons of Nazi Germany. Without overruling *Buck,* the Supreme Court cast doubt on its reasoning and limited its application in a subsequent decision that invalidated mandatory sterilization laws for habitual criminals. However, family planners, public hospital administrators, and welfare officials continued to condition assistance on "consent" to sterilization by poor and minority women, who were assumed to lack competence or motivation for other techniques. Coercive and uninformed sterilization remained a major problem until the 1980s, when highly publicized litigation and the promulgation of federal regulations finally began to curb abuses.[11]

Throughout the early twentieth century, the birth control movement reflected both class and racial biases. Fertility control emerged as a right for the privileged and a duty for the poor. Strategies that repudiated abortion and emphasized physicians' authority over contraceptive distribution had the effect of restricting access for many women who needed it most. The movement's earliest legal victories involved reinterpretations of federal statutes to permit prescription and distribution of birth control materials where permissible under state law (for example, in order to prevent disease). The result was that women who could afford a sympathetic private physician usually could obtain contraceptives. Similarly, those with sufficient resources were sometimes able to establish a physical or psychological justification for a legal abortion. Alternatively, they could afford a relatively safe illegal one, or travel to a more permissive jurisdiction. For the poor, uneducated, or unsophisticated, the options were far more limited. Misconceptions about conception, as well as deaths from self-induced abortions, were common.[12]

Legal restraints on birth control gradually weakened in response to various cultural forces. As was true with liquor, official prohibition of contraceptives was ineffective in curbing sales. The military's distribution of condoms to prevent venereal disease during World War I increased the supply and ultimately the demand for such products. Liberalization of sexual mores in the post–World War I era further expanded the market. Other factors contributed to that trend: opportunities for nonmarital sexual contacts in automobiles, dance halls, and the like during the 1920s; greater economic pressures to curtail fertility during the Depression in the 1930s; and increased female labor force participation in the 1940s and 1950s. After 1960 the availability of an oral contraceptive helped liberalize public attitudes and practices, and concerns about global overpopulation had similar effects. Although President Eisenhower declared in 1959 that he could imagine no subject that was less a matter for government involvement than birth control, just eight years later federal agencies were spending close to $30 million on contraceptive programs at home and abroad.[13]

Beginning in the mid-1960s, the Supreme Court issued a series of decisions that reflected and reinforced these trends. In *Griswold v. Connecticut* (1965), a majority of justices interpreted the due process clause to protect private use of contraceptives by married couples. Decisions in 1972 and 1977 extended that right to unmarried minors. Although the justices' reasoning differed, a majority found constitutional grounding for a right of privacy in matters related to procreation. That right in turn provided the doctrinal foundation for some of the Court's most significant and contested decisions—decisions involving abortion.[14]

Abortion

During the 1960s, many of the same forces underlying liberalized contraception policy also encouraged abortion law reform. Women's increasing sexual activity and labor force participation increased the number of unwanted pregnancies. As improvements in medical technology reduced the circumstances in which abortion was necessary to preserve a mother's life, the rigidity of existing statutes became more apparent. Physicians faced growing pressure to evade both the letter and spirit of the law, and that pressure was reflected in abortion rates. By the 1960s, most estimates indicated that about a million abortions were occurring annually: one abortion for every three to four live births. At the close of the decade, projections suggested that a quarter of American women would have an abortion, few of them legally. Abortion was the most frequent form of criminal activity after gambling and narcotics, and its perpetrators were also its victims. Procedures could be quite painful and dangerous if performed hastily by unskilled practitioners. Somewhere between one thousand and ten thousand individuals died each year as a result of botched abortions, and more suffered permanent physical or psychological injuries. Predictably, those most at risk were poor and minority women. These human costs were a catalyst of reform activity.[15]

Other forces were also at work. The 1960s witnessed a new consciousness about population control and women's rights, and activists in both campaigns placed high priority on liberalized abortion laws. In their view, a certain number of unwanted pregnancies were unavoidable. Fear, ignorance, lack of planning, or pressure from male partners made many females, particularly teenagers, ineffective contraceptive users. Side effects deterred some women from taking the pill, and other devices had significant failure rates. Neither individual nor societal interests would be well served by coercing birth in such cases. For many women, the consequences of an unwanted pregnancy could be devastating. Lost employment and educational opportunities or the stigma of out-of-wedlock birth often had permanent repercussions. Given the enormous physical, psychological, and socioeconomic consequences of an unwanted child, abortion was crucial to women's control over their own destiny. During the 1960s the issue assumed increasing importance. "Men don't get pregnant, they just pass the laws," became a rallying cry within the women's movement.[16]

Growing concern about fetal deformities also expanded public support for abortion reform. During the early 1960s, defects resulting from the use of thalidomide, an antidepressant drug, and a German-measles epidemic crystalized sympathy for women who terminated abnormal pregnancies and for the doctors who provided illegal assistance. Capitalizing on such sympathies, feminists increased their lobbying and litigation campaigns against restrictive abortion laws.

Changes in public sentiment were apparent both in state legislative initiatives and in national opinion surveys. Reform bills began to surface in 1961, usually modeled on an American Law Institute (ALI) proposal that allowed abortion in certain compelling circumstances: where the physical or mental health of the mother might be seriously impaired, where the child might have grave physical or mental defects, or where the pregnancy resulted from rape, incest, or felonious intercourse. In the five years preceding the Supreme Court's 1973 landmark abortion decision, *Roe v. Wade,* one-third of the states had liberalized their statutes. However, on the eve of that decision, half the states still prohibited termination of pregnancy except where necessary to preserve maternal life, even though substantial evidence indicated that such restrictive statutes were out of step with public opinion.[17]

Although polls on abortion are unusually difficult to interpret, given the way slight changes in wording or question sequence affect results, it is clear that attitudes changed significantly during the 1960s. In the decade prior to *Roe v. Wade,* the number of individuals who approved of abortion in the most compelling circumstances—rape, incest, fetal abnormalities, or threats to maternal health—climbed to between 80 and 90 percent. Public support for termination of pregnancy in other cases   such as where the mother was unmarried, the family was poor, or the couple did not want further children— increased to around 50 percent. In 1972, just prior to *Roe,* two national surveys reported that between 50 and 57 percent of Americans thought abortion decisions should be left to a woman and her physician.[18]

So the Supreme Court held, at least with respect to the first trimester of pregnancy. *Roe v. Wade* involved the constitutionality of a statute prohibiting abortion except to save the life of the mother. A companion case, *Doe v. Bolton,* raised similar challenges to legislation modeled on the ALI proposal. Speaking for the majority in *Roe,* Justice Blackmun concluded that the Fourteenth Amendment's guarantee of personal liberty implied a fundamental right of privacy "broad enough to encompass a women's decision whether or not to terminate her pregnancy." Restrictions on that fundamental right required justification by a compelling state interest. In the Court's view, one such interest, protecting maternal health, became compelling only after the first trimester, the point at which mortality rates from abortion became higher than mortality rates from childbirth. As to the state's interest in protecting fetal life, the compelling point was at viability, when the fetus had the capability of meaningful life outside the womb. After that point, which generally occurred in the third trimester, the state could prohibit abortion except when necessary to protect the health or life of the mother.[19]

The *Roe* decision set off some of the most strident and sustained criticism that the American judiciary has ever experienced. Objections came from all points of the political spectrum. To most conservatives, the decision appeared utterly without moral foundation; many moderates found it lacking in constitutional justifications; and the left complained that the Court had offered the wrong justifications.

Part of the controversy stemmed from the Court's explicit attempt to avoid "resolving the difficult question of when life begins." Yet in determining that the fetus was not entitled to legal protection prior to viability, the Court necessarily concluded that the unborn were not "persons" within the meaning of the Constitution. This conclusion was unacceptable to many individuals, particularly Catholics and Fundamentalists, who believed that life begins at conception. In their view, as Ronald Reagan expressed it, society could not "diminish the value of one category of human life—the unborn" without devaluing all life. In addition, many critics who did not personally subscribe to this "right to life" position nonetheless believed that the Court gave it too little recognition in *Roe* and thereby provided a strong impetus for the antiabortion campaign. According to these scholars, had the Court proceeded more cautiously in *Roe* and given more latitude to legislatures, much of the hostility that resulted from *Roe* could have been averted or directed at other targets.[20]

To some of these commentators the Supreme Court's holding was equally problematic on doctrinal grounds. Critics frequently contended that *Roe* was without support in the Constitution's history, text, or structure, or in principles derived from them. From this perspective, not only was *Roe* bad constitutional law, it was "not constitutional law at all." Of particular concern was the Court's trimester framework. In these commentators' view, *Roe* provided insufficient justification for why viability should be the "magic moment" at which abortion could be prohibited. Nor did the Court adequately explain what viability meant. What constituted a reasonable likelihood of survival outside the womb? Ten percent? Fifty percent? Why should individual physicians have authority to determine which probability was reasonable? And why should the likelihood of fetal survival, which depended on the technology and resources available in a particular locality, be granted overwhelming moral or constitutional significance?[21]

Even those who supported the result in *Roe* were critical of a framework that made women's privacy interest depend on an unstable technological rationale. Within a decade after *Roe,* medical advances were calling into question its trimester framework; viability was occurring earlier and abortions were safer than the decision had envisioned. What would happen if, as Justice O'Connor predicted in a subsequent case, medical advances permitted fetal survival much earlier in a woman's pregnancy, even during the first trimester? So too, by the mid-1980s abortion was safer than childbirth through the twenty-second, not the twelfth week, of pregnancy. Such developments eroded the maternal health justification for restrictions on abortion during the second trimester. Yet once the Court had allowed such restrictions, it had difficulty retreating from that position. As a result, the justices remained enmeshed in controversies over regulations designed to deter abortions while purporting to offer maternal health protections, such as consent requirements, waiting periods, bans on outpatient clinics, and limitations on the type of procedures available. Related disputes arose concerning mandatory testing for fetal viability and use of public funds and facilities for abortion-related services.[22]

In assessing criticisms of *Roe,* it is important to focus on the context in which the litigation arose. Whether a more cautious approach by the Supreme Court would have reduced the conflict surrounding abortion or resulted in a more defensible accommodation of competing interests is by no means clear. To some religious groups, the issue implicates fundamental moral principles that permit no compromise. Also, for many conservatives, legalized abortion, like the proposed equal rights amendment, has come to assume profound symbolic significance. As Kristin Luker's study suggests, right-to-life advocates perceive any move toward liberalization as an assault on traditional family values and gender roles. To this constituency, abortion undermines marriage, morality, and motherhood. Given the uncompromising intensity of their convictions, antiabortion activists can disproportionately influence a pluralist political process. Moreover, the groups that suffer most from restrictive legislative policies have little power in legislative arenas: poor, nonwhite, and adolescent women.[23]

One critical function of judicial review is to safeguard the interests of such minorities. A primary reason for granting federal judges life tenure and entrusting them with the interpretation of broad constitutional provisions is to ensure some protection for evolving principles of liberty and equality. Control over reproduction implicates both of these principles, and its importance for women has long been undervalued by majoritarian political processes. If these concerns are taken seriously, the difficulty in *Roe* is not the result but the rationale. The problem rests in the Court's failure adequately to define the interests at issue and establish some coherent accommodation.

Neither of the primary governmental interests surrounding abortion can justify *Roe's* trimester framework. The state's first concern, protecting maternal health, is both broader and narrower than the Court has acknowledged. It surely exists prior to the point at which abortion is riskier than childbirth. Yet now that abortion is safer than childbirth until the third trimester of pregnancy, the original health justification for distinguishing first and second trimester procedures has disappeared.

As to the state's second concern, preserving fetal life, the viability–nonviability distinction is similarly problematic. With some modification, however, it seems preferable to the commonly suggested alternatives. From a technological standpoint, the distinction is by no means as vulnerable as some critics have asserted. Contrary to Justice O'Connor's suggestion, most experts do not anticipate imminent medical advances that will sustain fetal life outside the womb at substantially earlier points. Certainly there is no immediate prospect of developing artificial wombs that could preserve embryos during the first trimester of pregnancy, when over 90 percent of all abortions occur.[24]

From an ethical standpoint, the viability–nonviability distinction is by no means as arbitrary as is sometimes supposed. Nor do preferable alternatives suggest themselves. If as many conservative critics argue, life begins at conception and abortion is murder, it becomes impossible to justify procedures that the vast majority of Americans find morally defensible: abortion in cases of rape, incest, or jeopardy to maternal health; and contraceptive methods that prevent implantation of a fertilized egg. Similarly, the position that life does not begin until birth fails to capture what most individuals find to be an intuitively important moral distinction. In postviability procedures, where removing a fetus from the womb does not entail its extinction, the process of deliberately allowing death seems much closer to infanticide than does abortion prior to viability. Society's interest in affirming the value of human life and minimizing physical and psychological complications argues for ensuring that abortions occur before the point of fetal survival, except under limited extenuating circumstances. Those interests have been furthered by the viability framework. By the mid-1980s, 99 percent of all abortions occurred in the first twenty weeks; only 0.01 percent occurred after twenty-four weeks, the point at which a fetus has a substantial chance of surviving outside the womb.[25]

Aside from viability, the only alternative position between conception and birth that has commanded substantial support is fetal brain consciousness. Such a standard would have the advantage of symmetry with contemporary standards for determining death, now defined as the absence of brain activity. Yet that approach would present other problems. The development of brain consciousness, unlike its cessation, is a continuous process, occurring most rapidly between the nineteenth and thirtieth week of pregnancy. Singling out any particular stage as the point at which abortion becomes impermissible would be more arbitrary than maintaining the viability distinction.[26]

Yet one difficulty with the viability distinction as currently formulated involves its application to a small category of cases involving gross fetal defects that cannot be diagnosed prior to viability. Supreme Court decisions have allowed states to prohibit abortions whenever the fetus is capable of "meaningful" life, unless the mother's life or health is in danger. What constitutes "meaningful" or a substantial risk to health remains unclear. Surely it would not diminish our commitment to life to recognize that in some instances, a life is likely to be so bleak, and to exact such a heavy toll on the immediate family, that artificial support should be withdrawn. What sorts of fetal defects fall into that category is a complex question, but one that cannot be resolved by any rigid viability–nonviability distinction, or by an abstract appeal to women's "privacy." Once a fetus can survive outside the womb, other public interests are obviously implicated.

A more fundamental difficulty with the *Roe* framework lies in its doctrinal foundations. Privacy is too limited a concept to capture what is at stake for women, either as individuals or as a group. What critics too seldom acknowledge and the Court failed adequately to explain is the fundamental importance of reproductive choice in shaping individual destiny and promoting gender equality. The principal harm of abortion restrictions has little to do with those emphasized in *Roe:* invading the privacy of doctor–patient or family relationships. Rather, as Sylvia Law and Robin West have suggested, the primary harm involves "invading the physical boundaries of the body and the psychic boundaries of a life." At issue is not simply intimacy but identity—women's capacity to define the terms of their existence. To deny individuals that capacity would impose a burden unique in its combination of physical intrusiveness, psychological trauma, and career impairment. From this perspective, the moral issue of "when life begins" becomes less critical. Even if the fetus were assumed to be a person, it would not follow that its interests must assume primary importance. Just as we do not compel individuals to serve as Good Samaritans in other contexts, we ought not to expect women at all stages of pregnancy to sacrifice their own destiny to embryonic life. State efforts to coerce childbirth do violence to the values of care and commitment that should underpin mother–infant attachments. If the due process clause is to play an adequate role in safeguarding basic values "implicit in the concept of ordered liberty," reproductive freedom must rank among the protected concerns.[27]

Moreover, access to abortion implicates equal protection interests as well. Although only two of many *amici* briefs argued the point in *Roe,* equality concerns were central to a number of earlier lower court cases and emerged clearly in subsequent Supreme Court litigation. The issue is not simply individual rights but social roles. Unless women are able to control their childbearing capacity, they can never assume positions of full equality. By casting abortion issues solely in terms of individual autonomy, the Court has obscured their collective implications, and reaffirmed the public–private dichotomy that feminism challenges.

The focus on privacy also has helped rationalize the Supreme Court's subsequent decisions upholding withdrawal of public funds for abortion services. In 1977, in *Maher v. Roe,* a majority of justices affirmed the right of states to deny Medicaid funding for nontherapeutic abortions, while fully subsidizing childbirth. Three years later, in *Harris v. McRae,* the Court extended its reasoning to uphold Congress's ban on federal support even for abortions necessary to protect the mother's health, unless her life was in danger or she was the victim of rape or incest. Underlying those decisions was a revived form of the much discredited distinction between benefits and burdens. In the view of a majority of justices, the state had "place[d] no obstacles—absolute or otherwise—in the pregnant woman's path to an abortion. . . . By making childbirth a more attractive alternative, the state may have influenced a woman's decision but it has imposed no restriction on access to abortion that was not already there. Although government may not place obstacles in the path of a woman's exercise of her freedom of choice, it need not remove those not of its own creation. . . . The financial constraints that restrict an indigent woman's ability to enjoy the full range of constitutionally protected freedom of choice are the product not of governmental restrictions on access to abortions, but rather of her indigency."[28]

This reasoning is problematic on several levels. The notion that the state has played no role in creating economic constraints on choice suggests an extraordinary degree of myopia: welfare, education, employment, tax, and innumerable other public policies have contributed to cycles of poverty. It is of course true that indigency limits the exercise of many fundamental rights. Yet it is also the case that the right at stake in *Maher* and *Harris* was as significant as others for which the Court has required state assistance, such as court costs in divorce proceedings or free transcripts for defendants in criminal cases. Moreover, the usual justification for the government's failure to provide such assistance—conserving scarce resources—was unavailable in *Maher* and *Harris*. When those cases arose, the average cost of subsidizing childbirth was close to ten times that of underwriting abortions. Since many indigents' children would also require continuing welfare support, the statutes in question were inexplicable as revenue-saving measures. Rather, the government had sought to accomplish indirectly what it could not do directly: coercing women into completing unwanted pregnancies.[29]

The targets of such coercion were women least able to protect themselves through conventional political channels and least able to provide adequate support for an additional child. Although in the aftermath of *Maher* and *Harris* the vast majority of indigent women continued to receive some funding through state or private sources, surveys indicate that a significant number were unable to afford abortions. Another substantial percentage of low-income individuals could do so only at extraordinary sacrifice, often with extended delays that increased physical risk and psychological trauma. At the time of the Court's funding decisions, the average expense of an abortion exceeded the average monthly welfare payment to an entire family, and in some states it was three to four times greater. When questioned about the justice of this selective attempt to coerce childbirth, then-President Jimmy Carter replied that "life's unfair." However true, that observation was utterly unresponsive to concerns about the government's complicity in such unfairness. As this line of cases evolved, it illustrated the inadequacy not only of the Court's privacy framework, but also of a liberal rights-oriented approach to gender equality. The bottom line has been that, in Catharine MacKinnon's phrase, "women with privileges get rights."[30]

A decade after the *Roe* decision, some 1.5 million legal abortions were occurring annually in the United States, yet women's reproductive liberty remained at risk. Threats emerged from varied sources: proposed constitutional amendments to prohibit abortion; state, local, and hospital restrictions on access; funding cutoffs; bans on abortion counseling by publicly funded agencies; repeated terrorism against clinics; and new appointments to the Supreme Court. Potential curtailment of constitutional protections threatens to return the issue to the states and expose women to the dangers of the pre-*Roe* era. In this climate it has become increasingly crucial to reconceptualize the abortion question, in both political and legal terms. As with other issues, we need less preoccupation with abstract rights and more concern with the context in which they are exercised. It has been a mistake to allow the debate over abortion to proceed under *prolife* and *prochoice* labels. The issue must be reframed to encompass not only the fetus's abstract entitlement to life but also the quality of that life and of the lives of those surrounding it. Conservatives who seek to compel childbirth but who oppose adequate social services for children and their parents are not prolife. Feminists must reappropriate that label and claim abortion as a means of ensuring the quality of existence for women and their children.

This claim to abortion cannot rest with some narrow abstract understanding of a "right to choice." No adequate notion of reproductive freedom can exclude the public benefits essential for its exercise. Nor can feminists who advocate choice limit their claims to abortion on demand. Their objectives must encompass broader societal support for contraceptive research, education, counseling, and distribution that will make abortion less necessary. Experimentation is currently under way with a new French drug that might prove to be a safe abortifacient; funding for further innovations could yield important advances. As cross-cultural and historical comparisons make clear, abortion rates are much more closely related to the availability of birth control information and techniques than to repressive laws.[31]

Removing barriers to abortion, although critical, will not make women's choices truly free. Just as some individuals are unable to afford abortion, others are unable to afford childbirth. American society provides woefully inadequate health services, maternity policies, childcare, welfare assistance, and related family support structures. The decision whether to terminate a pregnancy still remains heavily constrained. Our public and private choices are interrelated, and we should not lose sight of the entire range of social conditions that must change before reproductive liberty is possible.

Adolescent Pregnancy

Teenage pregnancy raises similar issues. Traditional policy approaches were punitive, and current strategies still reflect this legacy. Prior to the 1960s, out-of-wedlock births resulted in ostracism and public sanctions. Many schools excluded unwed mothers, although not fathers, a practice ultimately discontinued after judicial challenges in the late 1960s and early 1970s. At that point, the rate of adolescent sexual activity and single parenthood was increasing sharply. By the late 1980s the United States had the highest teen pregnancy rate in the developed world. Approximately 45 percent of adolescent females were sexually active before marriage, and a substantial number of them used contraceptives intermittently or ineffectively. The result was about a million teen pregnancies each year, and around four-fifths were unintentional. An estimated four out of every ten female adolescents were becoming pregnant at least once before age twenty; about half of that group were carrying their pregnancy to term, and half of those who did so were unmarried.[32]

If such trends continue, all but a tiny percentage of these adolescent mothers will keep their children, and the costs of that decision will be substantial. For most women, the price of teenage pregnancy has been disrupted education, reduced employment opportunities, increased likelihood of poverty, and heightened medical risks. Although some recent longitudinal data suggest that the vast majority of teen mothers are eventually able to obtain a high-school education, secure full-time employment, and avoid welfare dependency, a significant number experience enduring poverty, and many face prolonged periods of severe hardship. The consequence for children of adolescent mothers has been a greater likelihood of physical, psychological, cognitive, and educational problems, as well as a greater possibility of becoming teenage parents themselves. These risks have been especially pronounced among minorities. Contemporary studies have found that the rate of teen childbirth among blacks is almost two and a half times greater than among whites; among Hispanics the rates are almost twice as great. Over a quarter of single black women have had at least one child by the age of eighteen.[33]

Adolescent pregnancy has prompted increasing national concern but no coherent policy. As with other gender-related issues, much of the problem stems from dispute over the nature of the problem. Is the primary issue morality, fertility, or poverty? Although most liberals "begin with the premise that teenagers should not have babies, [most conservatives] begin with the premise that single teenagers should not have sex." Policymakers generally fault unmarried mothers for wanting "too much too soon" in a sexual relationship, but counselors in the field generally fault government for offering those mothers "too little too late": too little reason to stay in school, too little opportunity for child care or decent jobs, and too little information about contraception, abortion, and the costs of single parenting.[34]

These disputes have resulted in a patchwork of programs with conflicting social signals. One representative survey found that three-quarters of all high schools and junior high schools offered some sex education, but only about a fifth identified reducing adolescent motherhood as an objective. In 1978, Congress amended an earlier family-planning act to require that federally funded contraceptive services (excluding abortion) be available to adolescents. Three years later, however, the first federal legislation specifically designed to deal with adolescent pregnancy, the Adolescent Family Life Act (AFLA), placed emphasis on encouraging "sexual self-discipline" rather than providing contraceptive services and banned any use of federal funds for abortion counseling. Many of the programs receiving AFLA funds have been religious. Their instruction has included distribution of pamphlets on "Reasons to Wait"—with reasons such as "God wants us to be pure." Despite substantial evidence of church–state entanglement, a 1988 Supreme Court decision sustained the act.[35]

Parental consent policies have reflected similar conservatism. A 1981 regulation by the Department of Health and Human Services required parental notification for adolescents seeking contraceptives in all federally funded clinics. Although lower federal courts enjoined enforcement of that "squeal rule," subsequent surveys indicated that about a fifth of hospitals and well over a third of private physicians voluntarily have required parental consent before prescribing contraception. Some states and localities have similarly mandated parental involvement for all unemancipated minors seeking abortions, while over a third of hospitals and about a fifth of surveyed clinics have voluntarily adopted comparable rules.[36]

Legal challenges to parental notification and consent policies have resulted in compromises that make little long-term sense. In a series of cases during the late 1970s and early 1980s, the Supreme Court held that states could require parental consent or notification for abortion services to unemancipated minors on one condition: that an adjudicative procedure be available to permit bypassing such requirements under certain circumstances. An adolescent should be able to avoid parental involvement by establishing in court either that she is sufficiently mature and well informed to make an independent decision concerning abortion or that even if she is immature, the abortion would be in her best interest.[37]

On a symbolic level, this resolution is understandable. It affirms the value of parental involvement in matters that call for mature guidance. It also acknowledges that in some instances, such involvement may result in punitive or otherwise counterproductive measures and that birth control services may be clearly appropriate. Yet on a practical level, this compromise has been unworkable. Given the absence of standards for determining maturity, courts are generally hard pressed to deny abortions to minors willing and able to navigate bypass procedures. They have been equally reluctant to identify circumstances under which an immature minor's best interest involves having a child that she does not want. Not surprisingly, the limited data available suggest that virtually all bypass petitions are granted. However, these legal obstacles impose considerable costs, particularly among young, minority, low-income, and unsophisticated adolescents. Consent requirements for abortion result in additional psychological trauma, life-endangering delays, and, according to at least one major study, increased risks of an unwanted child.[38]

These limitations on adolescent reproductive rights reflect two primary concerns. Conservatives typically argue that providing birth control for teenagers undermines parental authority and legitimates sexual promiscuity. According to Senators Orrin Hatch and Jeremiah Denton, "the most effective oral contraceptive yet devised is the word 'no.'" In their view, any outreach program designed to prevent pregnancy rather than sex is counterproductive; it encourages the activity that creates the problem. Available research, however, suggests that the issue is far more complicated. Making contraceptive services less accessible discourages contraception, not sex. Studies of birth control programs find no evidence that their availability has increased sexual activity. The vast majority of adolescents seek assistance only after they are engaging in such activity. Comparative data underscore the point. Many European countries have rates of adolescent sexual relations similar to those in the United States, but substantially lower rates of adolescent pregnancy and abortion.[39]

That is not to deny the indirect influence that birth control programs may have on adolescent attitudes. Nor is it to suppose that more vigorous outreach programs would leave sexual mores unaffected. Few adolescents in their early teens have been adequately prepared to deal with the consequences of sexual intercourse, and it is difficult to prevent materials designed for older adolescents from filtering down to their younger counterparts. But granting that risk, it nonetheless makes sense to attempt more effective birth control programs than have been available to date. Even if it were clear that the absence of such programs has helped deter some teens from sexual activity, the price has been too great. To reduce the enormous personal and social costs that flow from adolescent pregnancy, we need a different strategy.

A critical first step is to direct more systematic research and social resources to teen parenting. As a special panel of the National Research Council noted, there has been little reliable evaluation of existing programs, including contraceptive services, school-based clinics, peer counseling, media outreach, sex education, and mentoring strategies. Nor have sufficient resources been available for those programs that appear most effective in preventing unplanned pregnancy or providing assistance for adolescent parents. Education, employment, health, child care, welfare, and related services could do much to minimize the costs that early parenthood now exact. We cannot respond effectively to teenage motherhood without responding also to the broader range of social problems that make motherhood seem to be a teen's best option.[40]

In designing more effective programs for adolescents, it is critical to include both sexes. One of the striking deficiencies in most research and policy is the inattention to male attitudes and behavior. Too little work focuses on the roles and dynamics of adolescent fatherhood, or the social initiatives necessary to encourage greater contraceptive and parental responsibility among young men. While the AIDS epidemic has underscored the need for better sex education programs for males, it should not obscure the broader role that such education must serve. Encouraging men to exercise greater responsibility in sexual relationships from an early age is a crucial part of reproductive freedom for women.[41]

Given the disproportionately high rates of adolescent childbearing among women of color, it is essential to focus on issues of race and ethnicity as well as gender. Although some of the differentials in teen fertility and family stability among whites and nonwhites are decreasing and some appear attributable to relative economic disadvantage, significant disparities persist, even controlling for class and other demographic variables. More work is necessary to explain the interaction of race and other factors and to develop counseling programs and other social initiatives responsive to minority needs.[42]

Finally, and most fundamentally, an adequate response to adolescent pregnancy requires broader changes in our cultural landscape. Few if any societies exhibit a more perverse combination of permissiveness and prudishness in their treatment of sexuality. The United States tolerates pervasive sexual appeals in entertainment, literature, music, fashion, arts, and advertising. Sex sells everything from automobiles to laundry detergent. Yet we have been unable to deal frankly with the consequences of such messages among our nation's adolescents. Coherent policies on teenage pregnancy require a more searching analysis of adult values and priorities, one that encompasses men's attitudes as well as women's rights.

Notes

1.   The oldest known abortifacient was recorded between 2732 and 2696 B.C. in China. For historical overviews of abortion, see William P. Hawkinson, "Abortion: An Anthropological Overview," in Abdel R. Omran, ed., *Liberalization of Abortion Laws* (Chapel Hill: University of North Carolina Press, 1976), p. 124; Rosalind Pollack Petchesky, *Abortion and Woman's Choice: The State, Sexuality and Reproductive Freedom* (New York: Longman, 1984); Anthony Nathan Cabot, "History of Abortion Law," *Arizona State Law Journal,* 67 (1980): 73, 74–83.

2.   James C. Mohr, *Abortion in America: The Origins and Evolution of National Policy, 1800–1900* (New York: Oxford University Press, 1978), pp. 18–43; Petchesky, *Abortion,* p. 73–78.

3.   For estimates on the frequency of abortion and the decline of the birthrate, see Linda Gordon, *Woman's Body, Woman's Right: A Social History of Birth Control in America* (New York: Grossman, 1976), pp. 45–53; David M. Kennedy, *Birth Control in America* (New Haven: Yale University Press, 1970), pp. 49–51. For estimates of contraceptive practices, see Barbara Bergman, *The Economic Emergence of Women* (New Year: Basic Books, 1986), p. 42, n.5.

4.   See James Reed, *From Private Vice to Public Virtue: The Birth Control Movement and American Society Since 1830)* (New York; Basic Books, 1978), pp. 40, 188 (quoting Alexander Skeene); A. Laphorn Smith, "Higher Education of Women and Race Suicide," (1905), reprinted in Louise Michele Newman, *Men's Ideas, Women's Realities* (New York: Pergamon, 1985), p. 147.

5.   See Kristin Luker, *Abortion and the Politics of Motherhood* (Berkeley: University of California Press, 1984), pp. 27–28; Gordon, *Women's Right,* pp. 59–60; Mohr, *Abortion,* pp. 32–33, 47—70.

6.   Cabot, *Abortion,* pp. 85–86; Petchesky, *Abortion,* p. 80; Luker, *Motherhood,* pp. 58–59 (quoting Bishop Kenrick); Luker, *Abortion,* p. 15.

7.   Gordon, *Woman's Right,* pp. 109–111, 238 (quoting Carrie Chapman Catt); Reed, *Private Vice,* p. 32 (quoting Catt). See also Petchesky, *Abortion,* p. 45; Mohr, *Abortion,* p. 111; congressional testimony of Marguerita A. Stewart, reprinted in Robert Bremner et al., eds., *Children and Youth in America: A Documentary History* (Cambridge, Mass.: Harvard University Press, 1971), II, 161–65. Of course, not all women's experience of sexuality was negative; see John D'Emilio and Estelle B. Freedman, *Intimate Matters: A History of Sexuality in America* (New York: Harper & Row, 1987).

8.   Margaret Sanger, *Women and the New Race, and My Fight for Birth Control* (New York: Farrar and Reinhart, 1931).

9.   See Kennedy, *Birth Control,* pp. 115–21 (quoting Sanger); Angela Davis, *Women, Race and Class* (New York, Vintage Books, 1981), pp. 210–19, and Petchesky, *Abortion,* pp. 87–93, for quotations from Sanger and discussions of sterilization; Gordon, *Woman's Right,* p. 344.

10.   Buck v. Bell, 274 U.S. 200 (1927). See Petchesky, *Abortion,* pp. 130, 180; Thomas Shapiro, *Population Control Politics: Woman, Sterilization and Reproductive Choice* (Philadelphia: Temple University Press, 1985). J. Ralph Lindgren and Nadine Taub, *The Law of Sex Discrimination* (St. Paul: West, 1988), p. 413 (discussing Stephen Jay Gould's analysis of *Buck*).

11. Petchesky, *Abortion,* pp. 130, 159, 179–80; Lindgren and Taub, *Sex Discrimination,* pp. 413–18; Skinner v. Oklahoma, 316 U.S. 535 (1942); Hyman Rodman, Betty Sarvis, and Joy Walker Bona, *The Abortion Question* (New York: Columbia University Press, 1987), p. 74 (describing medical services conditioned on agreement to sterilization); Patricia J. Williams, "On Being the Object of Property," *Signs,* 14 (1988): 5, 7–8, n. 5.

12. Davis, *Class,* p. 210; Luker, *Abortion,* pp. 36–39. Petchesky, *Abortion,* pp. 45–50; Rodman, Sarvis, and Boner, *Abortion,* p. 154.

13. See generally Gordon, *Woman's Right;* Kennedy, *Birth Control,* viii, 218–71.

14. Griswold v. Connecticut, 381 U.S. 479 (1965), Eisenstadt v. Baird, 405 U.S. 438 (1972), Carey v. Population Services International, 431 U.S. 678 (1977).

15. Luker, *Abortion,* pp. 55–76; Kennedy, *Birth Control,* pp. 36–51; National Association for Repeal of Abortion Laws, in Gerda Lerner, *The Female Experience, An American Documentary* (Indianapolis: Bobbs-Merrill, 1977); Lawrence Lader, *Abortion II: Making the Revolution* (Boston: Beacon, 1973), p. 2; Frederick S. Jaffe, Barbara Lindheim, and Philip R. Lee, *Abortion Politics: Private Morality and Public Policy* (New York: McGraw-Hill, 1981), p. 24; D'Emilio and Freedman, *Intimate Matters,* pp. 253–55.

16. Kristin Luker, *Taking Chances: Abortion and the Decision Not to Contracept* (Berkeley: University of California Press, 1975); Sylvia A. Law, "Rethinking Sex and the Constitution," *University of Pennsylvania Law Review,* 132 (1984): 955, 1017, n. 221. Lader, *Abortion II,* p. 219.

17. Kennedy, *Birth Control,* p. 41; Raymond Tatalovich and Byron W. Daynes, *The Politics of Abortion: A Study of Community Conflict in Public Policy Making* (New York: Praeger, 1981), pp. 24–76; Barbara Hayes, "Abortion," *Signs,* 5 (1979): 307.

18. Jeffe et al., *Abortion Politics,* pp. 101–3; Judith Blake, "The Abortion Decision: Judicial Review and Public Opinion on Abortion; New Directions for Policy Studies," in Edward Manier et al., *Abortion* (Notre Dame, Ind.: University of Notre Dame Press, 1977); Lader, *Abortion II,* p. 186.

19. Roe v. Wade, 410 U.S. 113 (1973); Doe v. Bolton, 410 U.S. 179 (1973).

20. Roe v. Wade, 410 U.S. at 156–160; Ronald Reagan, "Abortion and the Conscience of the Nation," reprinted in J. Douglas Butler and David F. Walbert, *Abortion, Medicine, and the Law* (New York: Facts on File Publications, 1986), pp. 352–53. For discussion of more cautious alternatives, see Guido Calabresi, *Ideals, Beliefs, Attitudes and the Law* (Syracuse, N.Y.: Syracuse University Press, 1985); Paul Freund, "Storms over the Supreme Court," *American Bar Association Journal,* 69 (1983): 1474, 1480; Laurence H. Tribe, "The Abortion Funding Conundrum: Inalienable Rights, Affirmative Duties, and the Dilemma of Dependence," *Harvard Law Review,* 99 (1985): 330, 342.

21. John Hart Ely, "The Wages of Crying Wolf: A Comment on *Roe v. Wade,*" *Yale Law Journal,* 82 (1973): 920–49. For discussion of the physician's role in determining viability, see Planned Parenthood of Central Missouri v. Danforth, 428 U.S. 52 (1976), and Colautti v. Franklin, 439 U.S. 379 (1979). For difficulties with the Court's trimester approach, see Ely, "Crying Wolf"; Thornburgh v. American College of Obstetricians and Gynecologists, 476 U.S. 747 (1986) (White, J., dissenting); Nancy K. Rhoden, "Trimesters and Technology: Revamping *Roe v. Wade,*" *Yale Law Journal,* 95 (1986): 639–97.

22. City of Akron v. Akron Center for Reproductive Health, Inc. 462 U.S. 416 (1983) (O'Connor, J., dissenting); Rhoden, "Trimesters," p. 668; Reproductive Health Service v. Webster, 851 F.2d 1071 (8th Cir. 1988) *cert.* granted-U.S.-(1988). For a summary of post-*Roe* restrictions, see Albert M. Pearson and Paul M. Kurtz, "The Abortion Controversy: A Study in Law and Politics," in Butler and Walbert, *Abortion,* pp. 107–36.

23. See Luker, *Abortion,* and Patrick J. Sheeran, *Women, Society, the State, and Abortion: A Structural Analysis* (New York: Praeger, 1987), pp. 125–27 (discussing right-to-life activists), Laurence Tribe, *American Constitutional Law* (Mineola, N.Y.: Foundation Press, 1978), p. 929 (discussing problems in the political process).

24. See Law, "Rethinking Sex," p. 1023, n. 245 (summarizing skepticism of experts concerning early fetal survival, including those cited by O'Connor); Petchesky, *Abortion,* p. 347 (92 to 96 percent of abortions at first trimester).

25. See commentary in Lindgren and Taub, *Sex Discrimination,* pp. 409–10; Stanley K. Henshaw et al., "A Portrait of American Women Who Obtain Abortions," *Family Planning Perspectives,* 17 (1985): 90, 91.

26. Note, "Technological Advances and *Roe v. Wade:* The Need to Rethink Abortion Law," *UCLA Law Review,* 29 (1982): 1194–1215; Robert N. Wennberg, *Life in the Balance: Exploring the Abortion Controversy* (Grand Rapids, Mich.: William B. Eerdmans, 1985).

27. Robin West, "Jurisprudence and Gender," *University of Chicago Law Review,* 55 (1988): 1; Sylvia Law, "Rethinking Sex," p. 1020; Palko v. Connecticut, 302 U.S. 319, 325 (1937). This is not to suggest that Good Samaritan analogies provide a wholly satisfying approach to the abortion issue. It is morally unsettling to defend women's right to abort a previable fetus on the same grounds that one would defend her refusal to risk physical injuries in aid of an existing child. It is also the case that most Americans do not extend Good Samaritan principles to exempt individuals from other life-threatening obligations, most notably the draft. Still, philosophers such as Judith Thompson and Donald Regan have made a persuasive case that such principles have some force in assessing abortion. Donald Regan, "Rewriting *Roe v. Wade,*" *Michigan Law Review,* 77 (1979): 1569; Judith Jarvis Thompson, "Rights and Deaths," *Philosophy and Public Affairs,* 2 (1972): 146. For discussion of maternal bonds, see Robert D. Goldstein, *Mother Love and Abortion: A Legal Interpretation* (Berkeley: University of California Press, 1988).

28. Maher v. Roe, 432 U.S. 464, 474 (1977); Harris v. McRae, 448 U.S. 297, 316 (1980).

29. See dissenting opinions in *Maher* and *Harris;* Jaffe et al., *Abortion Politics,* pp. 143–45; Michael J. Perry, "Why the Supreme Court Was Plainly Wrong in the Hyde Amendment Case: A Brief Comment on *Harris v. McRae,*" *Stanford Law Review,* 32 (July 1980): 1113; Tribe, *Constitutional Law,* p. 932, n. 77.

30. Jaffe et al., *Abortion,* pp. 143–46; Jimmy Carter, quoted in Law, "Rethinking Sex," p. 1016, n. 219; Brief for the National Abortion Rights Action League et al., in Thornburgh v. American College of Obstetricians and Gynecologists (1985), p. 14 (and sources cited therein); Laura Jefferson, "Reproductive Laws, Women of Color and Low-Income Women," in Sherrell Cohen and Nadine Taub, eds., *Reproductive Law for the 1990s* (Clifton, N.J.: Humana Press, 1988) (race); Catharine MacKinnon, "*Roe v. Wade:* A Study in Male Ideology," in Jay L. Garfield and Patricia Hennessey, *Abortion: Moral and Legal Perspectives* (Amherst: University of Massachusetts Press, 1984), pp. 45, 52.

31. See Mary Ann Glendon, *Abortion and Divorce in Western Law* (Cambridge, Mass.: Harvard University Press, 1987); Rodman, Sarvis, and Bona, *Abortion,* p. 59; Gina Kolata, "Any Sale in U.S. of Abortion Pill Still Years Away," *New York Times,* October 30, 1988, p. 1 (noting U.S. companies' lack of investment in new birth-control technology because of high research and liability costs and potential profits).

32. Karen DeCrow, *Sexist Justice* (New York: Vintage, 1977), pp. 268–79; Elise F. Jones et al., "Teenage Pregnancy in Developed Countries: Determinants and Policy Implications," *Family Planning Perspectives,* 17 (1985): 53; Cheryl Hayes, ed., *Risking the Future: Adolescent Sexuality, Pregnancy, and Childbirth. Report of the Panel on Adolescent Pregnancy and Childbirth of the National Research Council, Final Report* (Washington, D.C.: National Academy Press, 1987), p. 1.2, 2.20–2.30; Janet Benshoof and Harriet Pilpel, "Minors' Right to Confidential Abortions: The Evolving Legal Scene," in Butler and Walbert, *Abortion,* p. 144.

33. DeCrow, *Sexist Justice,* pp. 268–79; Hayes, *Risking the Future,* pp. 2.3–2.20; Frank Furstenberg, Jr., J. Brooks-Gunn, and S. Phillip Morgan, *Adolescent Mothers in Later Life* (Cambridge: Cambridge University Press, 1987); Children's Defense Fund, *Teenage Pregnancy: An Advocate's Guide to the Numbers* (Washington, D.C.: January 1988); Dorothy J. Height, "What Must Be Done About Children Having Children," *Ebony* (March 1985), p. 77.

34. See Carole Joffe, *The Regulation of Sexuality,* (Philadelphia: Temple University Press,

1986), p. 45 (quoting Connaught Marshner); Sharon Thompson, "Search for Tomorrow: On Feminism and the Reconstruction of Teen Romance," in Carole Vance, ed., *Pleasure and Danger* (Boston: Routledge & Kegan Paul, 1984).

35. Hayes, *Risking the Future,* 6-5, 5-5; 42 U.S.C. Section 3003; Bowen v. Kenrick, 108 S. Ct. 2562 (1987).

36. Hayes, *Risking the Future,* 1.9 1.11; Bershoof and Pilpel, p. 152, n. 60; Brigid Rentoul, "Cognitus Interruptus: The Courts and Minor's Access to Contraceptives," *Yale Law and Policy Review,* 5 (1986): 212; Planned Parenthood Federation of America v. Schweiker, 559 F.Supp. 658, (D.D.C.) *aff'd,* 712 F.2d 650 (D.C. Cir. 1983); *Accord,* State of N.Y. v. Heckler, 719 F.2d 1191 (2d Cir. 1983).

37. Belloti v. Baird, 443 U.S. 622 (1979); H.L. Matheson, 450 U.S. 398 (1981); Planned Parenthood of Central Missouri v. Danforth, 428 U.S. 52 (1976).

38. See studies cited in Bershoof and Pilpel, *Minor's Rights,* pp. 144–145; Nanette Dembitz, "The Supreme Court and a Minor's Abortion Decision," *Columbia Law Review,* 80 (1980): 1251, 1255–58; Robert M. Mnookin, "Belloti v. Baird: A Hard Case," in Robert H. Mnookin, *In the Interests of Children* (New York, Freeman, 1985).

39. Petchesky, *Abortion,* p. 270 (quoting Holder and Denton); Rentaul, "Cognitus Interruptus," n. 113; Ann L. Harper, "Teenage Sexuality and Public Policy: An Agenda for Gender Education," in Irene Diamond, *Families and Public Policy: A Feminist Dialogue on Women and the State* (New York: Longman, 1983); Eve Paul and Dana Lassel, "Minor's Right to Confidential Contraceptive Services: The Limits of State Power" *Women's Rights Law Reporter,* 10 (1987); 1; Hayes, *Risking the Future,* 6.60, 7.7; Harrell R. Rodgers, Jr., *Poor Women, Poor Families: The Economic Plight of America's Female-headed Households* (Armonk, N.Y.: Sharpe, 1987), pp. 92–93.

40. Hayes, *Risking the Future,* pp. 17–18; Chapter 6; Kristin Luker, *Taking Chances: Abortion and the Decision Not to Contracept* (Berkeley: University of California Press, 1975); Maris A. Vinovskis, *An Epidemic of Adolescent Pregnancy: Some Historical and Policy Considerations* (New York: Oxford University Press, 1988), pp. 36–39, 194–203.

41. Catharine Chilman, "Feminist Issues in Teen Parenting," *Child Welfare,* 64 (1985): 225; Robert L. Barret and Bryan E. Robinson, "Tennage Fathers: Neglected Too Long," *Social Worker,* 27 (1982): 484; Vinovskis, *Epidemic,* pp. 166–68.

42. Marian Wright Edelman, *Families in Peril: An Agenda for Social Change* (Cambridge, Mass.: Harvard University Press, 1987); Kristin A. Moore, Margaret C. Simns, and Charles L. Betsey, *Choice and Circumstance: Racial Differences in Adolescent Sexuality and Fertility* (New Brunswick, N.J.: Transaction, 1986); Children's Defense Fund, *Advocate's Guide;* Jefferson, "Reproductive Laws."

13

Reproductive Laws, Women of Color, and Low-Income Women

LAURIE NSIAH-JEFFERSON

Introduction

Reproductive rights, like other rights, are not just a matter of abstract theory. How these rights can be exercised and which segments of the population will be allowed to exercise them must be considered in light of existing social and economic conditions. Therefore, concerns about the effects of race, sex, and poverty, as well as law and technology, must be actively integrated into all work and discussions addressing reproductive health policy.

This chapter concerns the six areas identified by the Project on Reproductive Laws for the 1990s[1] as they affect low-income and women of color. Many, though not all, women of color are poor. Women of color are not all one group, just as women of color and poor women are not one group. They have different needs, behaviors, and cultural and social norms. One thing they do share is having been left out of the decision-making process concerning reproductive rights. Although my experience is as a black woman, I will attempt to identify issues that appear to be nearly universal to both women of color and poor women and point out instances where their perspectives might differ.

There is little information available about the reproductive needs of women of color. In general, the demographic data about non-Caucasian women are clustered together under the heading "nonwhite," as if there were only two racial groups, white and non-white. For example, published abortion statistics are broken down only into two ethnic categories—white and black. As a result of this dichotomization, understanding of the experience of specific groups such as Native American, Asian/Pacific Islander, and Latina women is inadequate. This dichotomization is itself evidence of the pressing need for more precise data gathering on issues concerning women of color. The information that is available generally fails to consider the obvious cultural and social differences related to differences in ethnicity and national heritage. In many cases, this has made it difficult to define and address particular problems and to make recommendations about their solutions.

For many women of color, taking control over their reproduction is a new step and involves issues never before considered. The reason for this is that women of color have not always had access to the prochoice movement. In the past, it has been difficult for many middle-class white feminists to understand and include the different perspectives and experiences of poor and minority women. Thus, it is particularly important that adequate information on the needs and experiences of all women be made available now.

The broader economic and political structures of society impose objective limitations on reproductive choice, that is, decisions as to when, whether, and under what conditions to have a child. Very simply, women of color and poor women have fewer choices than other women. Basic health needs often go unmet in these communities. Poor women and women of color have a continuing history of negative experiences concerning reproduction, including their use of birth control pills, the IUD, and contraceptive injections of Depo-Provera;[2] sterilization abuse,[3] impeded access to abortion, coercive birthing procedures and hysterectomy,[4] and exposure to workplace hazards.[5]

Thus, the primary reproductive rights issues for poor women and women of color include access to health services and information, and the ability to give informed consent or informed refusal; access to financial resources; an end to discrimination relating to class and race, which creates the potential for abuse of the new technology; development of new policies and programs geared toward their needs; medical experimentation; and the need to explore and promote the extended family concept and alternative family structures. Given the history and circumstances of these groups, there are two overarching concerns. One is the desire to make reproductive services, including new technologies, broadly accessible. The other is the need to safeguard against abuse.

After considering each of the six topics, this chapter makes policy recommendations relating to the needs of poor women and women of color. These recommendations are designed to ensure

1. Access to quality prenatal care.
2. The birth of healthy, wanted children.
3. Protection against sterilization abuse.
4. Protection against occupational and environmental conditions harmful to fertility and health.
5. Protection from pharmaceutical experimentation and unnecessary medical procedures.
6. Access to accurate information about sex, conception, and contraception.
7. Access to safe, affordable abortion.

In light of the structural nature of the limitations on the exercise of reproductive choice by poor women and women of color, the recommendations often focus on affirmative policy initiatives rather than legal restraints.

Time Limits on Abortion

Poor women and women of color often live under circumstances that make it difficult for them to obtain early abortions. For instance, in 1971, nearly one in three nonwhite women of reproductive age lived below the poverty level. It is therefore important to develop affirmative programs that improve access to early procedures and, even more importantly, that reduce the risk of unwanted pregnancy. Unfortunately, however, such affirmative programs cannot totally obviate the need for late abortions. Thus, it is important to understand that laws restricting late abortions will continue to have a particular impact on poor women and women of color.

The Disproportionate Need for Post-First-Trimester Abortions

A significantly higher percentage of nonwhite women who get abortions do so after the first trimester, or first twelve weeks, of pregnancy. Of all abortions obtained by white women in 1983, 8.6 percent took place in the thirteenth week or later, but 12.0 percent of nonwhite women having abortions obtained them in that period. These figures represent the numbers of women who actually succeeded in obtaining post-first-trimester procedures, and they may seriously understate actual demand. Financial, geographical, and other barriers to access are likely to have a greater impact on nonwhite women, whose overall abortion rate is more than twice that of whites.

There is little information directly concerning very late abortions. Available data on women who obtain abortions after the first trimester, however, demonstrate that financial factors are very important. The enactment and implementation of the Hyde amendment terminating federal Medicaid funding for abortions has caused many poor women to delay having abortions while they raise the necessary funds. A study of a St. Louis clinic, for example, showed that in 1982, 38 percent of the Medicaid-eligible women interviewed who sought abortions after the tenth week attributed the delay between receiving the results of their pregnancy tests and obtaining their abortions to financial problems. Yet Medicaid-eligible women were not significantly later in obtaining abortions than other women before the Hyde amendment went into effect. Even where state Medicaid funding is in theory still available for abortions, it is often not available in practice. Welfare workers and other state officials do not always inform Medicaid recipients of their right to obtain Medicaid-funded abortions. Not all abortion providers are aware that reimbursement is available from Medicaid. Some providers who are aware are unwilling to except Medicaid, inpart because doctors are reluctant to assert that the abortions they perform fall within the particular categories being funded in their states and in part because Medicaid reimbursement rates are so low.[6]

Difficulty in locating abortion services also causes delay. In 1984, there were no abortion providers identified in 82 percent of the counties in the United States—that is, where 30 percent of all women of reproductive age lived. The availability of abortion services also varies considerably by state. Because abortion facilities are concentrated in metropolitan areas, access to abortion services is particularly difficult for rural women. In 1984, 79 percent of all nonmetropolitan women lived in counties that had no abortion facilities.[7] Although geographic access may not pose a significant problem for women of color from northern states who are concentrated in inner cities, it is a concern for women of color in southern states.

Not only are Native American women who live on reservations denied federal funding for abortions, but no Indian Health Service clinics or hospitals may perform abortions even when payment for those procedures is made privately. The Indian Health Service may be the only health care provider within hundreds of miles of the reservation, and as a result the impact of the regulations can be quite severe.

Women in prison, who are disproportionately poor and of color, may also have great difficulty in gaining access to abortion facilities. Abortion services are rarely available at the prison, and prison authorities are unwilling to release inmates for treatment. Recently adopted federal regulations specifically deny abortion services to federal prisoners.[8]

Even where abortion services exist, lack of information about them deters early abortion. Language barriers and the absence of culturally sensitive bilingual counselors and educational materials make gaining information about abortion services a special problem for Asian/Pacific and Hispanic women. This information gap would be severely exacerbated by the Reagan administration's proposed new Title I regulations, which would prohibit family planning services receiving federal monies under the Title X program from giving any information about the abortion option.[9]

Three factors have been identified as especially important in accounting for very late abortions: youth, medical conditions, and fetal anomalies. At least two of these, youth and medical problems, are likely to have disproportionate significance in the case of women of color. The significance of the problem of fetal anomalies for poor women and women of color is discussed below in the section on prenatal screening.

In 1981 (the latest year for which data are available), 43 percent of all abortions performed after the twentieth week of pregnancy were performed on teenagers. Women under fifteen years of age are most likely to obtain the latest abortions (those at twenty-one weeks or more gestation). Their delay is understandable in terms of the difficulties very young women experience in obtaining abortions. These difficulties include the parental notice and consent requirements in effect in some states, as well as the financial and information problems already discussed. Teenagers of color often have particular difficulty in obtaining an abortion. One study found that four out of ten black teenagers were unable to obtain a desired abortion, as compared to two out of ten white teenagers.[10]

Medical problems are also a factor in late abortions, including very late abortions. A major reason for very late abortions is the onset or worsening of certain diseases. Given the nature of their health problems, poor women and women of color are particularly vulnerable to such developments. For example, black women have higher rates of diabetes, cardiovascular disease, cervical cancer, and high blood pressure[11] than other women and may therefore be in greater need of late abortions. Similarly, the lack of prenatal and general health care that results from poverty may mean that serious health problems arise during pregnancy for many poor women.

Different Forms of Time Limits

The limits on abortion may be imposed by various laws. Currently, there is concern about statutes that impose prohibitions on postviability abortions or seek to compel the use of the method most likely to preserve fetal life unless the woman's health would be jeopardized. Poor women and women of color bear the brunt of such laws because women with money and power can find ways to circumvent the law, just as they did prior to the legalization of abortion. Affluent women can either travel to a place where a procedure is legal or find a doctor who will certify that their health is at stake. Poor women who do not have such options are denied autonomy because, as the experience with Medicaid provisions allowing reimbursement only for health-threatening situations suggests, few doctors are willing to risk prosecution under these statutes.

Time limits on abortion may result from a provider's decision not to perform procedures past a certain point in pregnancy. Poor women and women of color today have limited access to facilities that provide abortions after the first trimester. Public hospitals are a major source of health care for poor women, yet only 17 percent of all public hospitals report performing abortions in 1985. Even where the lack of access does not result in an outright denial of abortion, it may cause women further delay that subjects them to increased health risks.[12]

Because most poor women must get abortions where they can find them, they may be severely limited in their choice of method. Although abortions done by the dilatation and evacuation (D & E) technique, are safer and less upsetting for women, D & Es are not universally available. To obtain a D & E, a woman may be required to pay for a private gynecologist or travel to a facility where the procedure is done. The problem of obtaining an abortion after the twentieth week is even more acute. Because such a limited number of providers perform this procedure, locating a facility, scheduling the procedure, and traveling can all impose serious burdens on poor women.[13]

The question of abortions very late in pregnancy pits the well-being of the pregnant woman and other people against that of the unborn fetus. Although there is no consensus among poor women and women of color that the woman's interests are paramount, there is widespread appreciation of the circumstances that bring women to late abortions and a general sense that the state must not make the decision for the woman. Compelling the use of abortion methods that lead to fetal survival raises serious questions. How would the fate of a surviving fetus be determined? If a fetus were born alive, who would be responsible for its care? What if the mother did not want it? Who would be responsible for financial support? Where would the unwanted fetus be sent? Could it be experimented on? Given their economic circumstances and their history of being subjected to experimentation, poor women and women of color have valid fears about the intentions of the state toward an unwanted fetus.

Family Planning and Life Choices

The number of abortions needed can be drastically reduced by teaching men and women how to prevent unintended pregnancy, but the process may not be simple. When members of a community are denied their rights, how can they know what those rights are, much less learn to assert them? To be effective, family planning services must present information and services in culturally appropriate ways, involving bilingual materials and personnel. Family-planning programs must also take account of cultural attitudes and biases about birth control. Some women of color have been unwilling to limit their reproduction in order to redress past population decreases that resulted from war, famine, infant mortality, or genocide. Thus, such programs must make women of color aware of how the ability to take control of reproductive decisions will benefit their lives.

Another important aspect of providing family-planning services is helping teenagers make life-enhancing decisions despite the many barriers for young people in our society today. Many teenagers, faced with an empty future, believe that becoming a parent will stabilize their lives. Teenagers need information services, decision-making skills, opportunities for success, and help in building their skills and interests regarding both school and work. They also need family life and life-planning education, and adolescent health services staffed by concerned adults.

Recommendations

Family Planning

1. Information must be made available to young people and adults, on sex, pregnancy, contraception, and abortion and on how to make choices about them in ways that are culturally appropriate and targeted to the needs of specific communities. Interpreters should be available where necessary. Television, magazines, newspapers, and radio should help provide this information in a variety of languages.

2. Comprehensive job-skill development programs for young people and adults should be available in schools and community programs. In addition to providing needed job training and workplace skills, this type of training can build self-confidence and encourage men and women to make appropriate childbearing choices.
3. Expanded funding should be available to enable sexually active youngsters and teenagers to obtain family-planning services. If more young people and adults learned how to prevent unwanted pregnancies, there would be savings in the Aid to Families with Dependent Children and Medicaid programs. Knowledge about spacing pregnancies and education about prenatal care could also reduce the incidence of low–birth weight babies and associated medical costs.
4. Prochoice groups should develop stronger alliances with those concerned about teenage pregnancy.
5. Statistical data should be gathered regarding Latina, Asian, and Native American, as well as black and white, populations.
6. The Hyde amendment should be repealed.
7. In states funding abortions, Medicaid should offer more realistic and prompter reimbursement to encourage more providers to accept Medicaid patients without insisting on cash payments.
8. Where abortion funding is available, information clarifying abortion payment policies should be disseminated to health care providers. Welfare workers and hospital and clinic staff should be trained to know what Medicaid pays for. Community-based nongovernmental organizations should assist in disseminating information and in monitoring the information provided by public agencies.
9. Family-planning services must be able to provide abortion information and referrals.
10. Adequate services must be available at all stages of gestation.

Postviability Abortions
11. There should be no laws compelling completion of a pregnancy under any circumstances.
12. Responsibility for determining the fate of a live-born fetus must lay with the woman who bore it.
13. Fetal health should be secondary to that of the mother.

◊ ◊ ◊

Fetus as Patient

The topic of fetus as patient involves attempts by medical and legal authorities to compel women to follow doctors' orders and accept particular medical procedures while pregnant and when they give birth. For example, doctors and hospitals may seek court orders forcing women to undergo surgery on the fetus or to submit to cesarean sections rather than to give birth vaginally. Women may also be subject to criminal prosecution for "fetal abuse" or to civil suit by their children for their behavior while pregnant.

Medical and legal actions in the name of fetal rights raise many issues for poor women and women of color. A basic question is whether it is right to hold individual women responsible for poor outcomes at birth when many women are not able to live under healthful conditions. This topic thus implicates the general socioeconomic conditions poor women and women of color experience that result in their lack of access to basic prenatal care and advanced prenatal, perinatal, and neonatal technologies. Holding individual women responsible under present circumstances is morally unjust, and it diverts attention from the need to correct the serious inequities that permeate today's society.

Liability for Poor Reproductive Outcomes

There is good reason to believe that poor women and women of color will be especially vulnerable to prosecutors' attempts to hold mothers responsible for bad reproductive outcomes. As a general matter, their children experience greater rates of infant mortality and low birth weight, which can result in physical and neurological illness. Infant mortality and morbidity among mothers who live below the poverty line are greatly increased, sometimes to as much as twice the rate experienced by other women.[14]

Although the data differentiated by racial and ethnic group are sparse and not standardized, they generally show that infant mortality rates for minority groups are disproportionately high. In 1982, for example, infant mortality rates for black infants were almost twice those of white infants. The infant mortality rates for Native Americans are also extremely high. Hispanics present a complex picture. Puerto Ricans generally have the highest infant mortality rates of any Hispanic group. Although the neonatal mortality rate for Mexican-Americans is considered low by some analysts, most studies suggest that the low death rate is the result of underreporting. Recent studies have shown that Mexican-Americans have a higher neonatal mortality rate in all birth weight categories than do blacks. Cuban-Americans have low infant mortality and high birth weights compared to other Hispanics. This is not surprising, given the higher socioeconomic status of Cuban-Americans compared to the other groups. The Asian population in the United States is quite diverse, and available data are inadequate. In general, perinatal outcomes for Asians in the United States are good, with relatively low incidence of low birth weight. Southeast Asian refugees, however, present a different picture with respect to perinatal outcomes, as a result of lower economic status and early childbearing.[15]

Socioeconomic conditions are an important element in these poor reproductive outcomes. Low-income women and women of color lack access to prenatal and neonatal care. In addition, many suffer from general ill health, broken families, and lack of social supports. They are more likely to be exposed to environmental hazards where they live or work. When poor women and women of color lack the resources necessary to help them bring healthy babies into the world, it does not make sense to hold them responsible for poor reproductive outcomes. Is it fair, for example, to say that an indigent woman is responsible for the consequences of deficiencies in her diet when Medicaid does not pay for vitamins? Similarly, is it fair to say an indigent woman is responsible for bearing a disabled fetus if Medicaid does not pay for abortion? It may be more just morally, if less feasible legally and politically to hold the state responsible for the high incidence of infant mortality and disability among the babies born to low-income women and women of color.

Compulsory High-Tech Procedures

Recent evidence suggests that hospital authorities' efforts to force pregnant women to accept high-tech procedures will be aimed disproportionately at low-income women and women of color. In 1987, the *New England Journal of Medicine* published a report on the incidence of court-ordered obstetrical interventions, including forced cesarean sections and intrauterine transfusions. The report revealed that 81 percent of the women subjected to such court orders were black, Hispanic, or Asian; 44 percent were not married; 24 percent were not native English speakers; and none were private patients. Attempts to compel submission to procedures such as cesarean section, fetal monitoring, and other technologies presuppose that they have been adequately explained and that the pregnant woman has no good reason for refusing the procedure. Neither assumption may be warranted.

Health professionals report that most women, irrespective of color or education, do not question a doctor's orders. Indeed they stress that the major problem is unquestioning acceptance rather than rejection of prescribed procedures, particularly among low-income women. Some women who do question high-tech procedures may do so because doctors have not been able to clearly explain the risks and benefits. Others may refuse because they have personally had related negative experiences in the past or heard of others' bad experiences. Despite their failure to question the authority of a physician, poor women and women of color might have good reason to do so. They have been the subjects of experimentation in public hospitals and public health care services. In teaching hospitals, unnecessary procedures are known to have been performed to give experience to doctors in training.[16] Individual legal actions directed at women who do resist doctor's orders may divert attention from these problems and encourage other women to submit to unnecessary and risky procedures. Genuine informed consent could be an important tool in addressing these problems. Women need relevant information in a form they can understand and a supportive environment in which to consider it. It is questionable whether our informed consent laws concerning these technologies and procedures work now. What can informed consent mean today when the informer and the person being informed are on the opposite sides of education, class, race, gender, language, and culture lines? We must develop mechanisms that will really allow women to decide what treatment they want and that will protect women against being pressured into accepting tests and procedures they either do not want or whose implications they do not understand.

Technology and Resource Allocation

The overuse of sophisticated technology has inflated the cost of providing routine obstetrical care for all women. Perinatal regionalization schemes, with other high-cost equipment and personnel, focus on end-stage care for mothers and babies with medical complications. Little or no attention is paid to organizing a system that ensures that every pregnant woman receive basic prenatal care in her community and an adequate diet—an investment in preventing complicated pregnancies. More children are likely to benefit from prenatal care than from high-tech therapies. Although greater emphasis on preventive care is important for all segments of the population, it is especially important for the traditionally disadvantaged. Those concerned with the fetus as patient should focus on these needs rather than question the behavior of individual women.

A change in focus from end-stage high-tech procedures aimed at individuals to broadly aimed basic prenatal care programs will make existing resources go further. When good prenatal care and other health and social interventions are not available, the results are more difficult deliveries and more low–birth weight babies needing expensive technologies. With fewer pregnancy complications, it should be easier to arrange for all those who need high-tech services to get them.

Recommendations

1. State and local record keeping relating to prenatal care and reproductive outcomes for all women of color should be improved by maintaining separate statistics for black, Hispanic, Asian, and Native American women.
2. Private insurance coverage of maternity benefits should be mandated, and all payment caps should be removed. Where insurance is employment related, costs should be shared by employers and employees.
3. States should make every effort to enroll all eligible pregnant low-income women in prenatal programs funded by Medicaid. Eligibility standards should be modified to make more low-income women eligible for Medicaid. States should establish a payer of last resort system for situations where neither Medicaid nor private insurance provide maternity coverage.
4. Services available to low-income women should be increased by expanding existing programs for women, children, and families in underserved areas. Such services should be culturally appropriate and multilingual.
5. States should continue efforts to increase the numbers of obstetricians, gynecologists, family practitioners, and mid-level health professionals accepting Medicaid patients by use of incentive programs or legal mandate, if necessary.
6. Medicaid recipients should have the opportunity to use mid-level health professionals such as midwives, nurse practitioners, and physicians' assistants who offer cost-effective prenatal and infant care.
7. Legislation ensuring informed consent regarding the use of fetal monitoring, cesarean sections, ultrasound and similar procedures, and certain drugs should be enacted. Such legislation should be modeled on the present federal and state sterilization regulations, which are designed to ensure that the patient has adequate knowledge and is not making her decision under pressure.
8. Legal remedies should be available for overuse of technology, just as malpractice suits currently result in recoveries for underuse of technology.
9. Attempts should be made to identify and prohibit experimental procedures that are potentially harmful. All other experimentation should have rigorous standards of informed consent.
10. Legislation should be enacted to make more resources available for prenatal care by regulating the amount of resources spent on high-tech care.
11. Statistical information regarding the frequency of use of high-tech procedures, including the races and income levels of the recipients, should be published for each health care facility.

Reproductive Hazards in the Workplace

The reproductive health of minority and poor women may be impaired directly, through job-related hazards, or indirectly, as a consequence of having low-paying jobs without benefits. Thus, their reproductive health, like their general health, is affected by their status as workers, as members of a minority group, and as women. Women of color and poor women often have the most hazardous jobs, risking physical, chemical, and psychological injury. Their low income may restrict their access to health care, and force them to live in neighborhoods contaminated by environmental pollutants and to exist on inadequate diets. Many work in positions with low pay and long hours, without benefits such as health insurance, maternity leave, vacation time, or sick pay.[17] Moreover, poverty and discrimination increase stress. Women who are heads of households are particularly likely to suffer hardships.

Poor women and women of color generally have limited recourse when their rights are violated. They have been excluded from trade unions that could have improved their circumstances in the past, and they are afraid to unionize now for fear of losing their jobs.

Large numbers of low-income women and women of color are employed in the health, textile, and apparel industries and in cleaning services. For example, 30 percent of all ancillary, auxiliary, and service workers in the health service industry are female, and of this 30 percent, 84 percent are black. Women working in low-income jobs in the health field are exposed to heavy lifting and to chemical hazards such as sterilizing gases, anesthetic gases, X-rays, and drugs. As a result, black hospital workers suffer an even higher rate of primary and secondary infertility than black people generally. Similarly, although little research has been done specifically on reproductive hazards encountered by minority or other hospital workers, nonprofessional hospital workers may be at elevated risk for certain types of cancers (especially breast cancer) because of exposure to radiation and various chemical agents. Cancer-causing agents usually also cause spontaneous abortion.[18]

The textile industry is another source of danger to poor women and women of color. For example, in 1980, nationally over 20 percent of all operatives were black women. In New York City, where the bulk of the garment industry is located, approximately 25 percent are Puerto Rican. Sweatshops located in Chinatown and staffed overwhelmingly by Asian women are responsible for a significant share of production. Workers in this industry often work in high-dust areas, spaces in which picking and carding operations take place. They are exposed to chemicals, dyes, arsenic, heat, cold, inadequate ventilation, and excessive noise, all of which affect women's general reproductive health as well as the health of a fetus.[19] Most sweatshops are located in dilapidated storefronts or badly ventilated lofts, to the detriment of the women's reproductive and general health. There are approximately five hundred sweatshops in New York City, with unsafe and unhealthy conditions. There are no benefits, and the compensation is too low to allow women to pay for or take time off for prenatal care. Most women who work in such jobs are afraid to complain for fear of being fired or reported to immigration authorities as illegal aliens.[20]

Women of color are also found in laundry and cleaning establishments. In 1980, 40 percent of all clothing ironers and pressers, and 23 percent of all laundry and dry cleaning operatives were black. Jobs in this sector also pose serious health risks. The National Cancer Institute found a higher mortality rate among laundry and dry cleaning workers than among the general population as a whole and found that women in these jobs, particularly women of color, contracted cancer of the lung, cervix, uterus, and skin at excessive rates.[21]

Many minorities, especially blacks and Chicanos, work in agriculture. Of the estimated five million migrant and seasonal workers, 75 percent are Chicano, and 20 percent are black. These workers are exposed to pesticides that cause liver, renal, and reproductive damage.[22]

For some poor women and women of color, the financial precariousness of their work poses the greatest hazard. Women in low-paying positions, whether in agriculture or as domestics in private homes, tend to have no health or other benefits, such as sick leave or vacation. As a result, many women are forced to work throughout their pregnancies and to return to work immediately after giving birth irrespective of the risks to their health. For example, some jobs require women to stand on their feet all day, although continuous standing can cause complications during pregnancy.[23] Moreover, many of these jobs pay just enough to prevent women from being eligible for Medicaid and the prenatal care services it covers.

Conclusion

Poor women and women of color have pressing needs for health services, including reproductive health services. They also have a history of maltreatment by the health care delivery system. For such women, making existing rights a reality and meeting the challenges posed by new modes of reproduction and reported advances in prenatal and perinatal technology are crucially related to these needs and history. Reproductive laws and policies for the 1990s must respond to the concerns of all women. The laws for the next decade must

1. Widen the dissemination of education and information concerning reproductive health.
2. Augment private and public funding to allow financial access to health services.
3. Bar unnecessary and forced medical and surgical treatments.
4. Prohibit discriminatory and eugenicist bias or practices in health care delivery.
5. Ensure confidentiality in health care records.
6. Protect the patient's right to informed consent and informed refusal.
7. Broaden education about reproductive health hazards in the workplace.
8. Facilitate the delivery of culturally appropriate health services to ensure effective health care.
9. Enhance the recruitment of people of color to train as health care providers.
10. Guarantee equity of access to all new reproductive technologies, accompanied by equal protection against abuses of these technologies.
11. Mandate the collection of data on local, state, and federal levels on the reproductive health status of women of color, including Hispanics, Asians, blacks, and Native Americans.
12. Increase preventive health care measures to counter the health problems caused by structural socioeconomic determinants, so that there will be less need to resort to high-tech therapies as solutions.

To bring about the enactment of such laws, more information regarding the views, the life experiences, and the circumstances of poor women and women of color must be made available. Most importantly, poor women and women of color must be included in the decision-making process, so that more attention will be paid to their needs.

Notes

1. The areas are time limits on abortion, prenatal screening, fetus as patient, reproductive hazards in the workplace, interference with reproductive choice, and alternative modes of reproduction.

2. Adele Clarke, "Subtle Forms of Sterilization Abuse: A Reproductive Rights Analysis," in *Test-Tube Women*; R. Arditti, R. D. Klein, and S. Minden, eds. (1984), p. 199; "Birth Control Blamed for Health Problems," Intern Extra (April 7, 1983), p. 60. The United States Indian Health Service continues to give Depo-Provera to mentally retarded native American women in this country although it has been banned for contraceptive use in the United States since 1984. "Native Americans Given Depo-Provera," Listen Real Loud 8:1 (Spring 1987), p. A-7.

3. Judith Levin, and Nadine Taub, "Reproductive Rights," in Women and the Law; Carol Lefcourt, ed. (1987), pp. 10A-27-28.

4. Charles B. Arnold, "Public Health Aspects of Contraceptive Sterilization," in Behavioral–Social Aspects of Contraceptive Sterilization; S. H. Newman and Z. E. Klein, eds. (1978).

5. Leith Mullings, "Women of Color and Occupational Health," in Double Exposure; Wendy Chavkin, ed. (1984).

6. Stanley K. Henshaw, J. D. Forrest, and Elaine Blaine, "Abortion Services in the United States, 1981 and 1982," Family Planning Perspectives 16:3 (May/June 1984), p. 127. Of the providers in five states surveyed (Connecticut, Maryland, Massachusetts, New Jersey, and Pennsylvania), 10 percent were unaware that reimbursement was available.

7. Henshaw et al., "Abortion Services in the United States, 1984 and 1985," p. 65.

8. See 28 C.F.R. § 551.23 (December 30, 1986) providing that during fiscal year 1987 the Bureau of Prisons may pay for an abortion only where the life of the mother would be endangered if the fetus were carried to term or if the pregnancy is the result of rape.

9. "Rule on Abortion Counseling Is Blocked," *New York Times,* February 17, 1988, p. A10. Centers for Disease Control, Abortion Surveillance 1981 (November 1985), Table 14, p. 37.

10. Alan Guttmacher Institute, Teenage Pregnancy: The Problem That Hasn't Gone Away (1981) (an analysis of data from 1970).

11. U.S. Department of Health and Human Services, Report of Secretary's Task Force on Black and Minority Health, Executive Summary, vol. I (August 1985), p. 71.

12. W. Cates, Jr., and D. A. Grimes, "Morbidity and Mortality in the United States," in Abortion and Sterilization; Jane Hodgson, M.D., ed. (1983), pp. 158–59.

13. Boston Women's Health Book Collective, The New Our Bodies, Ourselves (1986), p. 303.

14. George C. Cunningham, former chief of Child and Maternal Health, California Department of Health Services, telephone conversation, January 25, 1987.

15. Report of Secretary's Task Force on Black and Minority Health, vol. I, pp. 180–81.

16. Gena Corea, The Hidden Malpractice: How American Medicine Mistreats Women (1985), pp. 200–3; Diana Scully, Men Who Control Women's Health; The Miseducation of Obstetrician–Gynecologists (1980), pp. 120–40 (see discussion of women as "teaching material").

17. U.S. Commission on Civil Rights, Health Insurance Coverage and Employment Opportunities for Minorities and Women, Clearinghouse Publication 72 (September 1982).

18. Joanna Brown, and Ronnie Scheir, "Workplace May Be Hazardous to Health of Blue Collar Minorities," The Chicago Reporter 10:3 (March 1981), p. 1.

19. Mullings, p. 129.

20. Ibid.

21. A. Blair, P. DeConfle, and D. Grassman, "Causes of Death Among Laundry and Dry Cleaning Workers," American Journal of Public Health 69:5 (May 1979), pp. 508–11.

22. F. W. Kutz, A. R. Yobs, and S. C. Strassman, "Stratification of Organochlorine Insect Residues in Human Adipose Tissue," Journal of Occupational Medicine 19:9 (1977), pp. 619–22; Mor-

ris Davis, "The Impact of Workplace Health and Safety on Black Workers: Assessment and Prognosis," Labor Law Journal 31:12 (December 1980), p. 724.

23. Richard Naeye, and Ellen Peters, "Working During Pregnancy: Effects on the Fetus," Pediatrics 69:6 (June 1982), pp. 724–27.

14

Unraveling Compromise

FRANCES OLSEN

While legal scholars across the United States ponder whether *Roe v. Wade*[1] should be reaffirmed, modified, or overruled, the decision in *Webster v. Reproductive Health Services*[2] has made many women consider burning down the Supreme Court Building. On an immediate and practical level, the *Webster* case is likely to have the greatest impact on relatively poor or otherwise disadvantaged women, but on a political level the case has threatened women across class and racial lines. *Webster* is mobilizing more prochoice people than any previous Supreme Court case on abortion.

What was actually decided in *Webster* would seem to be minimal.[3] The case upheld portions of the latest in a series of foot-dragging statutes enacted by Missouri to limit access to abortion. The lawyers defending the legislation argued that most of the provisions had little or no meaning and little or no effect on abortion practice or women's access to abortion. The Court allowed states to require that doctors check that a fetus is not viable before they perform an abortion. The Court also expanded its holding in *Harris v. McRae*[4] and upheld a ban on the use of public facilities and employees as well as public funds for performing abortions.

The Reagan administration had intervened in the *Webster* case to ask the Court to overrule *Roe v. Wade*. Acting Solicitor General Charles Fried, on behalf of the succeeding Bush administration, suggested at oral argument that the government did not seek to unravel all of the right to privacy, but merely to pull one thread.[5] Like a tennis player responding to a high lob, Frank Susman, the opposing attorney, replied, "It has always been my personal experience that when I pull a thread, my sleeve falls off."[6]

Although fallen-off sleeves may be less hackneyed than slippery slopes, they are no more intrinsically convincing. As long as the Court upholds the basic principle of judicial review and does not overrule *Marbury v. Madison*,[7] it must make distinctions that cannot be justified on purely logical or linguistic bases. Whether the Court overrules *Roe v. Wade* and whether it unravels more of privacy doctrine depend not upon any kind of abstract logic but upon political policy choices. *Webster* has begun to unravel not so much the right to privacy but rather the political, legal, and social compromise represented by *Roe v. Wade*.

Roe v. Wade was a compromise. The case legalized most abortions, but it did not grant the plaintiffs everything they wanted; states were allowed to control women's bodies and limit some of their procreative choices. Even during the first trimester of pregnancy, the case "medicalized" abortion and, at least in theory, placed it in the control of doctors. Moreover, the case allowed states to regulate second-trimester abortions in ways "reasonably related" to protecting women's health. During the third trimester, *Roe v. Wade* invited states to restrict abortion to cases in which a doctor determines that the woman's life or health would be threatened. *Roe* repeatedly emphasized that it was not recognizing or granting women a right to control their bodies.

Webster did not overrule *Roe v. Wade,* but a three-justice plurality strongly suggested that the Court might accept the government's invitation and begin to unravel *Roe.*[8] By examining some of the many ways that the abortion debate implicates the role and status of women in our society, this chapter undertakes an unraveling of a different sort—an unraveling of the sexual politics underlying the abortion controversy. Whether abortion is thought to involve sexual morality or reproductive responsibility and whether it is analyzed as a question of a woman's right to privacy, of sex equality, or of state protection of potential life, issues of gender inequality and of the devaluation of women pervade the entire field in ways that have not been adequately examined.

Part I examines the traditional analysis that a degree of freedom to choose abortion is a right protected by the privacy guarantees implicit in the due process clause of the Fourteenth Amendment. This analysis is both appealing to and problematic for those concerned with improving the role and status of women. The *Webster* case illustrates some of the weaknesses of the due process approach. Part II considers the main alternative analysis, which would ground women's rights regarding abortion in the equal protection clause of the Fourteenth Amendment. A sex equality analysis raises the issue whether equal protection necessarily requires comparing women to men or whether sex equality should mandate an end to the subordination of women to men. Recognizing that any constitutional rights women have regarding abortion, whether derived from a privacy analysis or an equality analysis, could be overcome by a finding that the state has a "compelling" interest in preventing abortion, Part III discusses the definition of that interest by examining the implications of valuing fetal and prefetal life, including the life of eggs and sperm. The value we place on new life, and when we confer that value, reflects and shapes the relative value we place on men's and women's activities. Part IV draws conclusions and looks to the future.

I. Due Process and Privacy

Ronald Dworkin recently presented the conventional liberal argument in support of *Roe v. Wade* in what is perhaps its most elegant form to date.[9] He argued that the Supreme Court rather than individual states must decide a key issue: whether a fetus is legally a person. Those who would leave the abortion issue to the state legislatures implicitly accept *Roe*'s decision that the fetus is not a constitutional person, Dworkin argued, for otherwise state policies allowing abortion would be unconstitutional. Acceptance of the premise that a fetus is not a constitutional person makes *Roe*'s decision to protect the rights of women, who are full constitutional persons, "largely persuasive." Dworkin argued that the Supreme Court in a series of "privacy" cases has recognized what he refers to as a "general right, based in the Fourteenth Amendment's guarantee of due process of law, [for individuals] to decide for themselves ethical and personal issues arising from marriage and procreation."[10]

> The Court's previous privacy decisions can be justified only on the assumption that decisions affecting marriage and childbirth are so important, so intimate and personal, so crucial to the development of personality and sense of moral responsibility, and so closely tied to religious and ethical convictions protected by the First Amendment, that people must be allowed to make these decisions for themselves, consulting their own conscience, rather than allowing society to thrust its collective decision on them. The abortion decision is at least as much a private decision in that sense as any other the Court has protected. In many ways it is more private, because the decision involves a woman's control not just of her own connections to others, but of the use of her own body, and the Constitution recognizes in a variety of ways the special intimacy of a person's connection to her own physical integrity.[11]

This right to privacy analysis appeals to women insofar as women have long been "oppressed by [the] moralistic controls society places on women's sexual expression."[12] Because antiabortion laws limit women's ability to control their procreation, they constrain women's ability to enjoy sex freely and inhibit women from fully exploring sexuality as a realm of pleasure or as an expression of intimacy. By inhibiting women more directly and severely than they do men, restrictions on abortion also reinforce the double standard of sexual morality, which divides women into two classes—"good" and "bad"—and oppresses both of them. The Court's privacy analysis thus appeals to women's desire for equality and for sexual freedom.

An additional positive aspect of the privacy analysis is its ability to place abortion in the broader context of everyone's interest in controlling his or her own reproductive capacity. This context reestablishes the connection between birth control and abortion and helps to counteract the tendency to treat abortion as an isolated act, rather than to evaluate it as an aspect of an overall program of women's control over their reproductive capacity. Instead of considering only pregnant women and asking whether they should be allowed to abort rather than being forced to carry their pregnancies to term, we should begin with women as a group and ask what limits, if any, the state may put upon their efforts to control their reproductive capacity. If birth control is constitutionally protected, what, if anything, removes abortion from constitutional protection? Because even the most carefully employed contraceptive periodically fails, abortion may be a necessary part of controlling one's procreative power. Many women may be in no position (physically, socially, emotionally, or economically) to have a child and face a choice between practicing a form of birth control that poses relatively serious long-term health risks but is unlikely to fail or one that is quite safe but has a somewhat higher failure rate. For these women, the abortion question becomes whether society has an interest in forcing or coercing them to use the more dangerous method of birth control rather than the physically safer form, with early abortion as a backup option should the safer birth control fail.

A right to privacy analysis is also unappealing to women, however, insofar as women have been "oppressed by [the] violence and sexual aggression that society [has] allow[ed] in the name of sexual freedom."[13] Much of privacy doctrine is based on the assumption that "so long as the public does not interfere [with private life], autonomous individuals interact freely and equally." Yet, in so many aspects of life, certainly including sexuality, most women are not actually autonomous individuals able to interact freely and equally with men. To change this situation "will require intervention, not abdication." Under present conditions, "when the law of privacy restricts intrusions into intimacy, it bars change in control over that intimacy."[14] Privacy doctrine tends to shield from public scrutiny the abuse of women that takes place within the "private realm of family life."[15]

Feminist criticism of the ideology of women's "separate sphere" is a criticism of the public/private dichotomy that privacy doctrine "reinforces [and which] is at the heart of the structures that perpetuate the powerlessness of women."[16] As I have argued elsewhere,[17] the public/private dichotomy is false—the state is implicated in the "private" sphere. Created by the "public," the "private" suffers from a serious power imbalance.

The abortion-funding cases highlight further limitations of the privacy analysis. A number of commentators have blamed the privacy rationale of *Roe v. Wade* for the decision in *Harris v. McRae*[18] to deny public funding of abortion. "Having won abortion rights in *Roe v. Wade* in the name of abstract personal privacy," writes Laurence Tribe, "women were poorly situated in *Harris v. McRae* to demand public funds for the exercise of such rights."[19]

The decision in *Webster* underscores this problem with a privacy analysis of abortion. Issuing five different opinions, a splintered Court upheld four provisions regulating abortion—(1) the preamble, which asserted that life in Missouri begins at conception; (2) a ban on the use of public funds for abortion counseling; (3) a ban on the use not only of public funds but also of public facilities and public employees to assist in abortion; and (4) a viability-testing requirement, which required doctors to perform tests to determine the fetus's age, weight, and lung maturity to assess fetal viability before performing an abortion at or after twenty weeks. The state officials defending the statute attributed relatively innocuous meanings to the first two provisions. The third and fourth are more controversial and pertinent to this discussion.

With respect to the ban on public facilities and public employees, Chief Justice Rehnquist, writing for the Court, found the restriction "considerably less burdensome"[20] than indigency, which the Court accepted as a limit on access to abortions in *Harris v. McRae*. The Court argued that "it is difficult to see how any procreational choice is burdened by the State's ban on the use of its facilities or employees for performing abortions"[21] in that prior to the ban no state subsidy to abortion, direct or indirect, had been provided. Chief Justice Rehnquist suggested that the ban restricted a woman's ability to obtain an abortion only "to the extent that she chooses to use a physician affiliated with a public hospital" and that this circumstance could be more "easily remedied"[22] than the circumstance of indigency at issue in *Harris v. McRae*.

In a portion of his opinion joined only by Justices Kennedy and White, Chief Justice Rehnquist concluded that Missouri's interest in protecting viable fetuses justified the viability-testing requirement, although he acknowledged that the tests would regulate the attending physician's discretion and, when the fetus was not viable, increase the costs of some second-trimester abortions. Suggesting a certain tension between *Webster* and post-*Roe* decisions such as *Akron v. Akron Center for Reproductive Health, Inc.*[23] and *Colautti v. Franklin*,[24] the plurality concluded that the conflict arose not due to a flaw in the Missouri statute but, rather, because the "rigid" *Roe* trimester framework created a "Procrustean bed." The plurality asserted that it would leave the holding of *Roe* "undisturbed" but "would modify and narrow *Roe* and succeeding cases."[25] Justice Scalia concurred in upholding the Missouri statute because he would overrule *Roe* entirely.

Justice O'Connor, whose concurrence is at present crucial to the Court majority, concurred in Chief Justice Rehnquist's decision to deny the appellees' facial challenge to the public facilities and public employees ban. She argued that "some quite straightforward applications" of the ban would be constitutional under *Harris v. McRae* and the Court's other funding precedents, which she interpreted to hold that a state regulation of abortion is constitutional "'unless it unduly burdens the right to seek an abortion.'"[26]

Justice O'Connor, while agreeing with the outcome of the plurality, saw no occasion to reconsider any prior precedents. The Missouri viability-testing provision "would be contradictory nonsense" were it to require anything more than a prudent medical determination of viability which would increase the cost of an abortion "marginally, if at all." She added, however, that she continued to consider "*Roe's* trimester framework . . . problematic."[27]

The plurality's decision limiting, though not overruling, *Roe* suggests a weakness of the privacy analysis of abortion. Abortion becomes a private right that women enjoy if they are privileged enough to have private access to it. Because of the influence that the "public" has on the "private," however, no clear line distinguishes a state's refusal to assist poor women and its interference with wealthier women, a difficulty reflected in Justice O'Connor's concept of "undue burden." In a sense, *Webster* turns *Harris* upside down. *Harris* began from the idea that the right to abortion was a private right and concluded that deprivation of public funding was constitutional;[28] the *Webster* plurality and Justice O'Connor began from the premise that deprivation of funding is constitutional to conclude that less burdensome restrictions on abortion—even burdens not related to funding, such as viability testing—are constitutional as well.[29]

Despite the problems with and the debate surrounding privacy doctrine in general, it would be problematic to exclude from the "right to privacy" a woman's interest in choosing to have an abortion. As long as our society is generally committed to a public/private distinction and an individual-rights approach to legal issues, the importance of extending that privacy doctrine equally to women does not depend upon a resolution of the question of whether privacy doctrine is wrongheaded or has a negative impact upon women in general. Women might be better off without a privacy doctrine, but they would seem to be clearly worse off with a privacy doctrine applied in a sexually discriminatory manner. If men are said to have certain rights or immunities because of the private or intimate nature of an activity, the denial of similar rights and immunities to women has a significantly negative impact and social meaning. Thus, the Court should extend "privacy" doctrine to women, even as we pursue efforts to dismantle the false dichotomies underlying it.

II. The Growing Shift to an Equality Analysis

In the years since *Roe v. Wade*, the Court has shown an increasing awareness that the abortion debate has a "gender dimension." That is, although not yet fully recognizing the significance that the social and economic inequality between men and women has, or should have, for abortion law,[30] the Court has begun to acknowledge that abortion law has something to do with the role and status of women. For example, the *Thornburgh* Court referred to the "promise that a certain private sphere of individual liberty will be kept largely beyond the reach of government" and asserted that this "promise extends to women as well as to men."[31] Justice Blackmun, dissenting in *Webster* and expressing his fears for the future, wrote of his fears "for the liberty and equality of . . . women."[32] Even Chief Justice Rehnquist's suggestion that "in a [n]ation where more than half of our population is women," the dissent in *Webster* "does scant justice" to state legislators and the people who elected them when it suggests that states might "enact abortion regulation[s] reminiscent of the dark ages,"[33] illustrates a recognition—conscious or unconscious— that restrictive abortion laws have something to do with women's relative lack of power.

Commentators have also shown increasing interest in the gender dimension of abortion, and a number have argued that restrictions on abortion violate the equal protection clause of the Fourteenth Amendment. Antiabortion laws have been criticized for denying women equal treatment with men and for preventing women from enjoying substantive equality with men.[34] Equal protection could require laws to accommodate women's as well as men's reality, to eliminate the vestiges of discrimination against women, and to value women's lives equally with men's. Sex equality doctrine could be developed to require an end to the subordination of women.[35] If the Court were to overrule its decision in *Roe v. Wade,* it would have to examine these equal protection arguments, which have not been fully explored while courts have invalidated antiabortion laws on the basis of privacy doctrine.

Just as privacy analysis places abortion in the context of birth control generally, so equality analysis needs to place abortion within the context of sexual politics generally. Beyond treating women differently from men and leaving women involuntarily pregnant and unable to act in the world as freely as men do, antiabortion laws reflect and broadly reinforce the subordination of women. It is misleading to consider gender equality the norm in our society and to expect sex discrimination law to redress the exceptional situations where women are still not treated as equals. Instead, one should recognize antiabortion laws as part of the systematic oppression and devaluation of women. As women struggle to defend their right to reproductive choice, they should also question the conditions under which they exercise their "choice" at the present time.

Antiabortion rhetoric and policies are antiwoman in a number of regards. The rhetoric's focus on abstract rights and on a characterization of the issue as a conflict between the pregnant woman and the fetus can be considered "masculinist." Treating a fetus as morally equivalent to a child obscures the active role that mothers play in procreation and is yet another example of society's tendency to devalue the work that women do. Prohibiting abortion denigrates women as moral decision makers, and it reinforces their role as sexual objects by undermining their ability to act as sexual agents. It further reduces the limited power that women are allowed to exercise over their bodies and their sexuality in our society.

A. Equality and the Barriers to Understanding

Although generally when a large portion of American society considers something important it is treated with deference, society consistently undervalues women's reproductive freedom. When many Americans forfeit their lives for a symbol, such as the U.S. flag, or a practice or idea, such as democracy, society usually respects the symbol, idea, or practice. The idea and practice of reproductive freedom, for which many women have knowingly risked their lives,[36] seems to be an exception.

This undervaluation derives in part from men's inability to empathize with women. As Madam Justice Wilson of the Canadian Supreme Court suggested:

> It is probably impossible for a man to respond, even imaginatively, to [the] dilemma [of unwanted pregnancy] not just because it is outside the realm of his personal experience (although this is, of course, the case) but because he can relate to it only by objectifying it, thereby eliminating the subjective elements of the female psyche which are at the heart of the dilemma.[37]

Nevertheless, men describe the moral dilemma of abortion from their point of view—and consider that subjective, partial description to be the objective truth. Unfortunately, to the extent that they have the power to describe and to name, what they describe and name becomes the truth. Their partial reality becomes the only reality "we" as a society share.

Decisions about the legality of abortion have been made primarily by men for whom pregnancy, to say nothing of abortion, is literally beyond their experience.[38] Even the women who have been involved in the decision-making processes have rarely, if ever, been in the situation of so many less privileged women. Virtually all these decisionmakers have had to depend upon observation, empathy, and listening to others in order to gain any understanding of the questions that they have been and are being called upon to answer.

The limits of this approach were demonstrated in 1976, when Congress enacted a version of the "Hyde amendment" that terminated all Medicaid funding for any abortions not necessary to save a woman's life, including abortions for victims of rape or incest.[39] What misperceptions could have produced such a result? Did the members of Congress who voted for this amendment really believe that a fourteen-year-old girl should have to carry her father's baby to term? Surely they did not believe that fathers would suddenly stop abusing their daughters. Did they think rape victims should be denied an abortion? Or was the funding cutoff just an unprincipled attempt to appease the antiabortion lobby at the expense of large numbers of relatively powerless people? Members of Congress must know that many of these girls and women will obtain abortions anyway: They will get the money from somewhere, or perhaps they will induce an abortion themselves, or perhaps they will die trying. In the meantime, Congress might save some money,[40] and maybe poor pregnant women will feel ashamed or guilty about their abortions. Do the members of Congress realize that even if poor women do manage somehow to scrape up the money for an abortion, the funding cutoff can delay an abortion for weeks or even months? By some religious standards, this delay could make the difference between abortion prior to or after ensoulment.[41] It may delay the abortion until after quickening. Certainly the delay increases the medical risks of abortion. And where will desperate women get money in a hurry? They may have to give up food or other necessities, sell drugs or sex, beg or borrow.

Supreme Court justices must also rely on observation and empathy rather than experience in trying to understand unwanted pregnancy. Not only are most justices male, but they also come from a socioeconomic class that has long been able to obtain abortions, a class that has never faced statutes injuring their procreative choice. Anyone in the justices' families could obtain abortions by traveling outside the country or by using family influence to obtain a safe illegal abortion from a leading American doctor. These facts may contribute to some justices' unrealistic and sometimes callous opinions on abortion.[42]

The antiabortion movement puts women into the position of having to fight for something they need rather than want. As an analogy, suppose some group believed that begging and sleeping out of doors or under bridges were immoral. The homeless and their supporters would find themselves having to fight for the right to sleep under bridges and beg in the streets. Instead of simply fighting to end homelessness, advocates would have to divert their attention to protecting the rights of people to live as homeless people.

In these ways, men's failure to understand women's needs reinforces the subordination and devaluation of women and women's reproductive freedom. The political and

social domination of women by men, and the freedom this domination gives men to misunderstand women, are crucial elements of the sexual politics of abortion.

B. The Sexual Politics of the Abortion Debate

The abortion debate keeps women off balance and less able to struggle against the unreasonable conditions that make unwanted pregnancy so common an occurrence. By making women defensive about the expression of their sexuality, antiabortionists make it
more difficult for women to object effectively to the ways in which that expression is limited and in which women's efforts to understand their sexuality are exploited. By threatening criminalization of a common and all too necessary practice, antiabortion pressure
denies women the leeway to express the ambivalence and grief they sometimes feel about
their abortions.

Participants in the abortion debate often seem to assume that women, in all but the
rarest cases, exercised a free autonomous choice regarding sexual intercourse; this
assumption overlooks the level of force and coercion that governs the lives of many
women. The "moderate" antiabortionist position that there are good and bad reasons for
abortion illustrates problems with this assumption. Many might agree, for example, that
a twelve-year-old rape victim with German measles should not have to carry a pregnancy
to term but that a woman whose father-in-law wagered that his first grandchild would be
a boy should not abort when amniocentesis indicates she is pregnant with a healthy girl
baby. Few people would wish to require any rape victim to carry a pregnancy to term,
and many people would wish to discourage an abortion sought for frivolous reasons.

However, the expected frequency of occurrence of such polar possibilities provides an
important basis for disagreement regarding abortion law.[43] Despite the evidence and statistics to the contrary, many people—perhaps especially men—consider rape to be
uncommon.[44] Other people—especially women—consider rape to be all too common. In
addition to rape by a brutal stranger on the street or who has broken into the victim's
home, there is the acquaintance who brutally rapes his "friend," the gang rape of a
retarded woman or a sorority sister, and date rape or the war in the back seat—often lost
by the woman afraid she might be *raped* if she refuses. There is also the obedient daughter
who does not know how to say no to her father, the student who cannot imagine saying
no to her teacher, the patient manipulated out of saying no to her psychiatrist, and the
marginal worker afraid to say no to her boss.

Restricting abortion in general but making exceptions for women who were forced or
coerced to have sexual intercourse would present numerous difficulties. Victims do not
report most of these rapes or "seductions" to the police for a variety of reasons. If these
victims have become pregnant, should they have to carry their pregnancies to term? Or,
when they discover they are pregnant, should they be allowed to report the rape then and
have an abortion? And what kind of extended interrogation might take place at that time?
How many details do we force the victims to relive; how much do we make them squirm
before we decide they do not have to carry their pregnancies to term?

Many prochoice advocates acknowledge the possibility of abortions for trivial
grounds but consider such to be a very small exception. Moreover, many would question
the practicability of devising any means by which even the worst of these exceptional
cases could be detected and prevented. For example, stories circulate in the West about
relatively wealthy women in India having amniocentesis tests and aborting female
fetuses. Such unjustified abortions strikingly illustrate women's lack of power and status.

However horrible it is to consider the feelings of women coerced or brainwashed into selectively aborting pregnancies that would result in new members of their own sex, forbidding such abortions does not solve the underlying problem: a society that devalues women. State policies should minimize any pressures on women to abort in such cases, but efforts to regulate this behavior directly run the risk of further oppressing women. At best, simply forbidding such abortions would lead to the birth of more unwanted girls, but what really need to change are the conditions that make girls unwanted.

The content that the Supreme Court gives to equality is a political question, not a kind of puzzle to be solved by some clever theorist. Advances for women are not obtained simply through a logical working out of the meaning of equality. Rather, the constitutional meaning of equality emerges from the process of political struggle. Only through such struggle will either legislators or judges recognize that restrictions on abortion implicate equal protection.

III. The Politics of Valuing Fetal and Prefetal Life

Whether one finds that abortion restrictions violate due process or equal protection rights of women, constitutional doctrine would allow states to infringe those rights in order to serve a compelling state interest. Thus, supporters of abortion rights must counter the argument, raised by Justice O'Connor in her *Akron* dissent and by the plurality in *Webster,* that laws against abortion serve a compelling state interest.

If women were not devalued, a pregnant woman's control over reproduction would seem natural and inevitable. Most people simply would not conceptualize an early fetus as a baby or as a person with interests separate from and potentially hostile to those of its mother.[45] Nevertheless, under the present conditions of women's subordination, antiabortionists have argued with some success that the state has a compelling interest in protecting human life from its earliest stages. In *Webster,* Chief Justice Rehnquist discussed the state's interest in protecting "potential human life," and quoted from Justice White's *Thornburgh* dissent that "'the State's interest, if compelling after viability, is equally compelling before viability.'"[46] An evaluation of the discretion [that] society exercises in defining its interest in preserving life requires consideration not only of fetuses or embryos but also of eggs and sperm. Like fetuses and embryos, eggs and sperm are surely alive, and they are not merely animal or plant life, but human. Indisputably eggs and sperm are "potential human life." To paraphrase Justice White, if the state's interest is compelling before viability, why is it not equally compelling before implantation or before conception?

Arguments that accept contraception but oppose abortion presuppose both that the state may properly value the embryo or fetus inside a woman—quite apart from her own choice regarding its valuation—and that the state has in fact done so. I challenge both of these premises: The state must not place a value on *in utero* life against the wishes of the pregnant woman, and in fact society has not in any consistent way placed such a value on embryos or fetuses.

A. Rethinking Assumptions

Some antiabortionists espouse the theory that potential human life has equal legal significance at all gestational stages. This refusal to distinguish between embryos, fetuses, and newborn babies is simplistic and untrue to the experience and common sense of most women and men. An early miscarriage is very different from a stillbirth. Birth control that prevents implantation of a blastocyst is different from a first trimester abortion. Most people experience the loss suffered from a miscarriage as less severe than the death of a newborn baby. No one would comfort herself with the thought that the embryo got to grow into a fetus and the fetus was able to live for some months: It enjoyed its fetushood. If a child is not going to be born, it is preferable to prevent the child's development as early as possible. An early abortion is preferable to a later abortion; preventing conception or implantation is preferable to aborting after implantation. To most women, the emotional impact of each of these possibilities will be different.

Absent an appeal to an external authority, any determination of the beginning of human life can be criticized as arbitrary. The scientific answer to the question of the beginning of life is that life began some three billion years ago and human life began at least four million years ago. Our life develops from prior life. As an antiabortion leaflet puts it:

Did you "come from" a human baby? No! You once were a baby.
Did you "come from" a human fetus? No! You once were a fetus.
Did you "come from" a fertilized ovum? No! You once were a fertilized ovum.
A fertilized ovum? Yes! You were then everything you are today.
Nothing has been added to the fertilized ovum who you once were except nutrition.[47]

I would add, "Did you 'come from' an egg and sperm? No! You once were an egg and a sperm. Nothing was added to the egg and sperm you once were except nutrition." The value of the fetus is not a quality of the fetus itself—spontaneous, "scientific," and inherent, independent of the social relations which create it, and uncontrolled by the power that requires women to carry fetuses. The question is not simply when human life begins but, rather, what value fetal (or embryonal, oval, spermal) life has as human life. To some people, this is a matter of religious faith; to others, a question of moral and political values. It is also inevitably a constitutional question.

The value of life is not a simple attribute of any particular life form, something that can be discovered. Culturally created, the value of life rests on social meanings and, importantly, on sexual politics. Fetal life has value when people with power value it. Thus, inquiry into the value of potential life cannot objectively resolve the question of abortion. The value of potential life is itself shaped by the answer given to the abortion question. The value of fetal life is a social attribute that arises from the totality of social relations regarding reproduction.

Although in some sense arbitrary, the culturally defined value of fetal life reflects the relative value assigned to men's and women's lives. The life of sperm is not valued because it would be considered "impossible" or "too impractical" to try to preserve it. Yet surely sperm are alive; indeed, they are human life. The only reason society does not consider it "impossible" or "too impractical" to try to preserve all or most early fetuses is that society has not sufficiently valued women's lives. The possibility of valuing fetal life from an early stage exists because of the systematic undervaluation of women's lives. If women were taken seriously, early fetal life would not be valued by society at large unless and until the woman carrying the fetus valued it.

The "moment" of conception, which is actually a process over time, may seem to be a practical cutoff point, at least to men. In fact, however, the law has treated fetuses as "rights bearers" only when it has been convenient for men to do so. For example, we do not count fetuses in the census or allow tax deduction for fetuses.

Scientifically, each egg and each sperm is alive, has a complete haploid of chromosomes, and struggles to survive.[48] Despite the absence of a principled distinction between the lives of sperm and ova and the lives of zygotes and fetuses, society has been willing to intrude upon women in serious and sometimes health-threatening ways in order to protect fetuses.

In contrast, society has not placed as many restrictions on men's sexuality. How would men react to a law that forbad them to ejaculate outside a fertile woman's vagina? While most heterosexual men would probably prefer to ejaculate into a vagina, the idea that they could not ejaculate anywhere else would probably come to seem oppressive and absurd to them. Yet such a law would seem to promote a state interest in potential life, as well as a state interest in the life of sperm. To avoid overbreadth, the law could provide that if a man does ejaculate where he is not allowed to, he could avoid criminal liability by collecting as many of the sperm as possible and rushing them to a sperm bank. At the sperm bank, he would have to register the sperm along with relevant genetic information about himself; nothing unduly personal would be required, just enough that the sperm have a reasonable chance of being chosen by a woman trying to save the life of her egg.

Of course, the burden such a law would place upon men is nothing like the burden that antiabortion laws place upon women. Many men would not be affected at all; other men would simply have to make periodic trips to sperm banks. Such periodic trips would impose a minimal burden, even on the men who have to make them. They would disrupt no one's life, disturb no long-range plans. The trips would be even less disruptive than a woman's menstrual period, so really no one could properly complain. Perhaps some disgruntled men, whose real complaint might be that they were born male, might object. Their objection, however, should be lodged against mother nature, not against the law— a law reasonably drafted to maximize a man's freedom, consistent with the state's obligation to preserve life.

Many people would consider this example silly, but this putative silliness reflects the value that society places upon men's lives and their freedom. Only convenience prevents us from valuing sperm. In fact, if men rather than women needed sperm to reproduce, some would argue that the state could not constitutionally deny men access to women's sperm.[49]

If one accepts a state goal to reduce abortion, there are alternative means to consider, apart from limiting access. The most obvious are for the state to provide more social support for pregnant women and for children, to facilitate access to birth control, and to eliminate rape and other forms of male domination that disable women from preventing conception. A less obvious, but heuristically important, means to reduce abortion would be for the state to outlaw the act of impregnating women who do not wish to become pregnant. States could require a man to obtain informed consent from a woman before he risked impregnating her and could consider whether to impose a mandatory waiting period before such consent would become effective. This approach would seem no less practical than banning abortions, except for the male domination of our society.

The notion that women should produce children for adoption reveals additional unconscious assumptions that devalue women. Perceptions of the potential alternatives to abortion influence attitudes toward abortion. A childless couple, considering the possibility of a pregnant woman carrying her pregnancy to term and giving them the child to raise, may perceive abortion as a tragic loss. Some adoptive parents say that they thank God that their adopted child was not aborted, but should they not also thank God that the natural father and mother failed to use effective birth control or that their child's natural mother was denied a meaningful opportunity to refuse intercourse? An adopted child conceived as the result of violent rape would have died as an egg and a sperm, never allowed to join or to be born, had the rape not taken place. Should the adoptive parents be glad that their child's natural father had not been sent to jail for an earlier rape or that the arrival of a police officer had not prevented the rape that "saved" their adoptive daughter? The hope that a woman will continue an unwanted pregnancy disregards her interests almost as much as does the hope that she become pregnant against her wishes. To coerce or force a woman to continue an unwanted pregnancy reflects the same kind of unconcern for her wishes as it does to coerce or force her to engage in unwanted intercourse.

B. Choosing Values

Failing an external, authoritative determination of the beginning of life, it seems clear that society chooses some period when it decides to attribute human life to its future members. The decision is not arbitrarily made by an individual, but it is socially arrived at through a complex set of negotiations. And whatever is decided comes to seem increasingly "true."

Ultimately, the struggle is not about what status fetal life *does* have but what status it *will* have. Antiabortion laws combine legitimation with force. Antiabortionists present a view of reality—the fetus as person—that they hope will construct reality. The same could be said of their opponents. If powerful people successfully assert that the fetus is not just the same as a person, this stance too will construct a reality. Under this reality, the fetus will not have significant value as a person until the woman carrying the fetus instills it with such value. Although some might complain that this reality deprives fetal life of its value, the correct question this putative loss of value raises is whether society would suffer from such a loss.

Antiabortionists sometimes express the fear that widespread, legal abortion will dehumanize society. Many people, including strongly prochoice people, view a fetus as sharing our humanity in a very important way, especially late in pregnancy. Many hope that abortion will never seem to be an easy decision for the women who choose it. Some worry that if we ever change our perceptions of when human life matters—for example, if we too thoroughly overcome our qualms about third-trimester abortions—we will come to consider infanticide with equanimity. Former Surgeon General C. Everett Koop, for example, has expressed fear that society's toleration of abortion contributes to society's toleration of "euthanasia" of seriously defective newborns. Comparing the failure of the German medical profession to cry out in opposition to Hitler's euthanasia in 1939 with the failure of Americans to protest abortion, he has warned of a "slide to Auschwitz."[50] The comparison seems ill drawn because, in fact, the Nazi practice regarding abortion was the harshest and most restrictive anywhere in Europe. The Nazis took an antiabortion law that had been in place but not widely enforced during the Weimar Republic and enforced it brutally, especially against women. They also significantly increased the penalty, even to capital punishment in aggravated cases, and they actually put a number of people to death for performing abortions.[51]

The search for a simple formula for discovering when life begins and a simple formula for avoiding dehumanization is misguided. Although some thoughtful, well-meaning people may oppose abortion in the hope that protecting fetal and prefetal life ensures against the devaluation of any human life, they fail to realize that the act of forbidding abortion is itself brutal and dehumanizing. In opposing abortion, one cooperates with the devaluation of women's lives and paves the way for further devaluation of life. Rather than prudently preserving from the devil even a little finger, these people have already given the devil an arm and a leg.

The devaluation of women implicated in antiabortion laws and policies leads to a multitude of coercive policies against women. For example, women who are denied access to drug rehabilitation programs have been prosecuted for the effects of drugs on their newborn children, and doctors have imposed particular obstetrical treatments upon women against the women's wishes and judgment.[52]

Generally, laws against abortion do not save fetal life but merely make abortions less safe and make women criminals. If antiabortionists were to succeed in making abortions not only illegal but unavailable, the resulting population problem could become so severe that society would begin pressuring or forcing women to abort. Some Chinese attribute the "one-child" pressure now considered necessary to control their overpopulation to an earlier pronatal policy.[53] Unless we work to improve the overall status of women, one abusive measure could lead to another.

IV. Conclusion

The *Webster* case threatens to unravel not only the compromise of *Roe* but also the compromise of women's accepting the legitimacy of law by accepting that the law is neutral and objective. Many view *Webster* as a clearly political case that harms women.

Justice Scalia's opinion most directly and crudely reflects the politics of law. He would have overturned *Roe* but asserted that because the Court refused to do so, he "need not set forth" his reasons, "some" of which have been set forth in his colleagues' dissents to *Thornburgh, Akron,* and *Roe* itself. Unlike some of his colleagues for whom abortion is a "'complex problem'" that presents "hard questions," Justice Scalia has an easy answer to the abortion question: "Anyone who can read and count"[54] knows that with three retirements (Chief Justice Burger and Justices Douglas and Stewart) and three appointments (Justices Scalia, Kennedy, and O'Connor) to join the two *Roe v. Wade* dissenters (Justice White and then Justice Rehnquist), provided no one defects, the five of them finally have the power to overrule *Roe v. Wade*. Impatient to exercise that power, Justice Scalia directed his anger against Justice O'Connor, who insisted upon waiting and refused to overrule *Roe v. Wade*. He referred to her opinion as "irrational" and asserted that it "cannot be taken seriously."[55]

Implicitly criticizing Justice Scalia's cynicism, Justice Blackmun asserted in dissent, "I fear for the integrity of, and public esteem for, this Court." Justice Blackmun did not limit his criticism to Justice Scalia. He charged that, in the plurality opinion, "bald assertion masquerades as reasoning. The object, quite clearly, is not to persuade but to prevail."[56]

Although judicial review requires the Court to make policy choices that are necessarily "political," reflection and persuasion should play a significant role in judicial decision making. The institutional setting of the federal courts is intended to provide for an independent judiciary. Although the possibility of and benefits from an independent judiciary could certainly easily be overestimated, many federal judges played courageous and honorable roles in the early days of school desegregation. One should not underestimate the possible value of having a prestigious court made up of justices who enjoy life tenure. Generally, the United States Supreme Court is not seen by its justices as a stepping-stone to any other job, and concern for their long-term reputations as jurists has often in the past seemed to be a more significant motivating factor than hope for any more immediate gain or loss. Such an institutional setting may encourage thoughtful reflection.

In this regard, Justice Scalia's apparent suggestion that the Court should shrink from any unpopular or controversial decision that might make it "the object of the sort of organized public pressure" experienced by elected officials "to the great damage of the Court,"[57] seems particularly muddleheaded. The Court has never been able to avoid decisions that have a political impact. Were the Court to overrule *Roe v. Wade,* a substantial portion of the American population would inevitably believe that the Court was bowing to political pressure. To think otherwise, as Justice Scalia seems to do, is fanciful.

In some sense the Court is "running up the flagpole" the idea of overruling *Roe v. Wade.* If no one salutes or if the response is too negative, then perhaps down comes the flag. *Webster* would not stand in the way. A possible benefit of this approach is that as the Court considers future abortion cases and is inundated with briefs, perhaps the quality of the eventual decision will improve. Some of the briefs provide useful analyses, supply important information, and correct factual misunderstandings.

For example, in *Akron,* Justice O'Connor clearly articulated the notion that the point of fetal "viability" was moving earlier into the second and perhaps eventually the first trimester, while the period during which abortions are safer than childbirth was extending later into the second trimester. She suggested that *Roe v. Wade* was on a "collision course" with itself—a proposition that may well have influenced many critics of *Roe,* regardless of their ability to identify or articulate their concern. Once clearly articulated, the notion could be laid to rest. Briefs submitted by *amici* cleared up a good deal of confusion felt by much of the public about neonatal advances: Mechanical wombs are not on the horizon, nor is viability about to occur within the first twenty weeks of gestation, when 99 percent of the abortions performed in the United States take place.[58] This concern, as a result, appears to have dropped out of the Court decisions in a way that might have been impossible had Justice O'Connor not openly articulated the concern in her *Akron* dissent.

Similarly, government briefs enthusiastically advanced Mary Ann Glendon's thesis[59] that European abortion laws are significantly different from and superior to American laws. When an *amicus* brief submitted by international women's health organizations thoroughly rebutted the Glendon thesis, it quietly dropped out of the discourse. Professor Glendon's book was not cited by the Court.

Former Surgeon General Koop, noted for his conservatism on social issues, including abortion, had the honesty—despite his lack of life tenure—to look at the job before him and protect public health even when that meant discussing homosexuality and sex education in an AIDS pamphlet or reporting that the evidence did not establish that abortions were bad for women who chose to have them.[60] A question remains whether the justices of the Court—also chosen in part for their political and religious views but entitled to life tenure—will show intellectual honesty and integrity. Although no amount of honesty and integrity will eliminate the political nature of any choice the Court makes, an open acknowledgment of the gender politics involved will make it harder for a society that considers itself moral and humane to restrict women's access to abortion.

Notes

For a variety of help, I would like to thank Joanne Conaghan, Duncan Kennedy, Susan Prager, Kenneth Karst, Ruth Roemer, and Robert Goldstein. I am especially grateful to Mary Joe Frug and Walter Weyrauch, who generously read and commented upon multiple drafts.

1. 410 U.S. 113 (1973).

2. 109 S. Ct. 3040 (1989).

3. Often, however, popular perception of what the Court has ruled may be more important than the legal community's judgment of what the Court has actually ruled. Within Missouri, the *Webster* decision has led public and private hospitals to refuse to allow abortions and one state university to bar talk of abortion (Southwest Missouri State University).

4. 448 U.S. 297 (1980). *Harris* upheld the constitutionality of the "Hyde amendment," a series of amendments to congressional appropriation bills. The amendment eliminated federal Medicaid funding for abortions but allowed certain exceptions, for example, in circumstances in which the woman's life would be in danger if the pregnancy were carried to term. The Hyde amendment encouraged state after state to eliminate all public funding for abortion. The funding cutoff made it difficult or impossible for many poor women to obtain an abortion. Moreover, the funding cutoff endangered women's health insofar as it was sometimes extended to medically necessary abortions—cases where a woman's health but not life was threatened by the pregnancy. *See, e.g.,* Pub. L. 94–439, §209, 90 Stat. 1434; *see also Harris,* 448 U.S. 297, 354 (Stevens, J., dissenting) (stating that the *Harris* Court "exclu[ded] benefits in 'instances where severe and long-lasting physical health damage'" may result from failure to abort pregnancy).

5. *Transcript of Oral Arguments Before Court on Abortion Case, New York Times,* April 27, 1989, at B12, col. 1.

6. *Id.* at B13, col. 1. Susman spelled out the argument explicitly: "There is no stopping."

7. 5 U.S. (1 Cranch) 137 (1803).

8. No alternative compromise to *Roe* is likely to settle the abortion issue. If the lines drawn in *Roe* can be criticized as arbitrary, no other line is likely to be accepted as less arbitrary. The conflict will continue: Not only will the prochoice side settle for no less than *Roe,* but also some antiabortionists claim they will continue their struggle until all abortion, therapeutic as well as elective, and most forms of birth control are outlawed. A number of antiabortionists, including former President Ronald Reagan, oppose even abortions necessary to protect "the life and health of the mother"; they equate this standard, which *Roe v. Wade* adopted with respect to abortions performed during the third trimester, *see Roe,* 410 U.S. at 163–64, with abortion on demand. *See* R. REAGAN, ABORTION AND THE CONSCIENCE OF THE NATION 15 (1984) (referring to a "nationwide policy of abortion-on-demand through all nine months of pregnancy" instituted by *Roe v. Wade*). Some antiabortionists oppose only "abortifacient" forms of birth control, which prevent pregnancy by preventing the implantation of the blastocyst, while others oppose virtually all forms of birth control.

Moreover, any determined effort actually to enforce a ban on abortion could require more and more intrusive regulation. For example, before *Roe v. Wade,* states prosecuted some newspapers for advertising out-of-state abortion clinics, *see* Bigelow v. Virginia, 421 U.S. 809 (1975) (holding that a statute banning such advertisements was an unconstitutional infringement on free speech), and travel agents for arranging out-of-state travel for pregnant women seeking abortion, *see* Brief Amicus Curiae on Behalf of 608 State Legislatures from 32 States at 14, *Webster* (No. 88–605).

Hungarian lawyers report that efforts to enforce antiabortion laws in Romania, a historic foe of Hungary with a large Hungarian minority, have included gynecological police who regularly test women of childbearing years to detect pregnancy and require an explanation for any termination of the pregnancy. *See* Discussion with Biró Gáspár, Hungarian lawyer with experience practicing in Romania (March 29, 1989). Pregnant women in Romania die at a strikingly higher rate than do pregnant women in any other European nation, a maternal death rate generally attributed to

Romania's stringent antiabortion policies. *See* C. Tietze, Induced Abortion: A World Review, 1983, at 102 (5th ed. 1983).

9. *See* Dworkin, *The Great Abortion Case,* 36 N.Y. Rev. Books, June 29, 1989, at 49; *see also* Dworkin, *The Future of Abortion,* N.Y. Rev. Books, September 8, 1989, at 47 (responding to the *Webster* decision).

10. *Id.* at 50–51.

11. *Id.*

12. Olsen, *Statutory Rape: A Feminist Critique of Rights Analysis,* 63 Tex. L. Rev. 387, 388 (1984).

13. Olsen, at 388.

14. C. MacKinnon, Feminism Unmodified 99 (1987) at 100, 101.

15. *Griswold,* 381 U.S. at 495.

16. Law Rethinking Sex and the Constitution, 132, U. Pa. L. Rev. (1984) at 1020. *See also* C. MacKinnon, at 93 ("Privacy doctrine reaffirms and reinforces . . . the public/private split").

17. *See* Olsen, *The Family and the Market: A Study of Ideology and Legal Reform,* 96 Harv. L. Rev. 1497 (1983); Olsen, *The Myth of State Intervention in the Family,* 18 U. Mich. J.L. Ref. 835, 842–44, 862 n.73 (1985).

18. 448 U.S. 297 (1980).

19. L. Tribe, American Constitutional Law, § 15–10, at 1353 (citations omitted).

20. *See* 109 S. Ct. at 3052.

21. *Id.* The Missouri statute, however, defines "public facility" very broadly to include "any public institution, public facility, public equipment, or any physical asset owned, leased, or controlled by this state or any agency or political subdivisions thereof." Mo. Rev. Stat. § 188.200(2) (1986). It forbids an abortion in any such facility even when performed by a private doctor and paid for privately. Recently a middle-class woman who discovered, at twenty-two weeks, that her fetus was anencephalic was unable to find any hospital in Missouri to perform an abortion because of the *Webster* decision. *See Los Angeles Times,* September 28, 1989, at 1, col. 1.

22. *See* 109 S. Ct. at 3052.

23. 462 U.S. 416 (1983).

24. 439 U.S. 379 (1979).

25. 109 S. Ct. at 3056, 3058.

26. *Id.* at 3063 (O'Connor, J., concurring in part and concurring in the judgment) (quoting *Akron,* 462 U.S. at 453).

27. *Id,* at 3060, 3063.

28. *See* 448 U.S. at 312–18.

29. *See* 109 S. Ct. at 3051–53 (O'Connor, J., concurring in part and concurring in the judgment) (citing *Harris*).

30. As recently as 1961, the Court justified a blanket exemption of women from the state jury lists on the basis that a "woman is still regarded as the center of home and family life." Hoyt v. Florida, 368 U.S. 57, 62 (1961). In Reed v. Reed, 404 U.S. 71 (1971), the Court unanimously backed away from such extreme deference to sexist political judgments and opened the way for judicial scrutiny of legislation and social practices that subordinate women to men. As the women's movement forced society to reexamine its assumptions about women, the Court began to strike down laws based on "outmoded stereotypes" and recognized behaviors once considered natural and respectful to be subordinating and illegal. In Frontiero v. Richardson, 411 U.S. 677 (1973), decided shortly after *Roe v. Wade,* a four-justice plurality opinion warned against laws based on "romantic paternalism," which operated to "put women, not on a pedestal, but in a cage." *Id.* at 684.

Nonetheless, few thought to consider mandatory childbearing a subordinating practice or to challenge abortion laws as sex discrimination. *See* Brief for the National Coalition Against Domestic Violence as Amicus Curiae Supporting Appellees at 5, *Webster* (no. 88-605) (noting the relatively undeveloped state of sex discrimination law at the time that *Roe v. Wade* was decided).

31. Thornburgh v. American College of Obstetricians & Gynecologists, 476 U.S. 747, 772 (1986). Again, perhaps with gender in mind, the Court referred to "the sphere of liberty that our law guarantees equally to all." *Id.*

32. 109 S. Ct. at 3067 (Blackmun, J., concurring in part and dissenting in part).

33. 109 S. Ct. at 3058.

34. In support of the majority opinion in the Canadian *Morgentaler* case, Madam Justice Wilson made an equality argument that deserves lengthy quotation:

> The history of the struggle for human rights . . . has been the history of men struggling to assert their dignity and common humanity against an overbearing state apparatus. The more recent struggle for women's rights has been a struggle . . . to achieve a place for women in a man's world, to . . . place women in the same position as men. It has *not* been a struggle to define the rights of women in relation to their special place in the societal structure and in relation to the biological distinction between the two sexes. . . . The right to reproduce or not to reproduce which is in issue in this case is one such right and is properly perceived as an integral part of modern woman's struggle to assert *her* dignity and worth as a human being.

Morgentaler v. Regina, 1 S.C.R. 30, 172 (Can. 1988) (Wilson, J.) (citation omitted).

35. The Women's Legal Education and Action Fund (LEAF) of Canada has submitted *amicus* briefs in Canadian abortion cases which carry the equality analysis further than American feminists have. While LEAF's argument may not directly apply to cases in the United States because of differences between our Bill of Rights and Fourteenth Amendment and the Canadian Charter of Rights and Freedoms, it can and should inform the American debate on abortion.

LEAF argues that women's reproductive capacity has been wrongly used to limit women's options in the public domain. Factum of the Women's Legal Education and Action Fund (LEAF) at 10, Borowski v. Attorney General, no. 20411 (Can. March 9, 1989). The social custom that allocates to women primary responsibility for the intimate care of children harms even women who voluntarily undertake child rearing. Failure to allocate public resources to childbearing and the care of children further aggravates this harm (*see id.* at 16). State-sanctioned interference with women's full development as human beings and with their physical well-being and authority to make prenatal decisions violates constitutional guarantees of sex equality *(see id.)*. When the state bars abortion, it is coercing women into motherhood. "Access to abortion is necessary as a means for women to survive in their unequal circumstances" (*id.* at 17). A deprivation of this reproductive control through the banning of abortion "would further women's historical relegation to social subordination and second class citizenship"*(id.)*.

36. Though commentators dispute the total number of women who have died trying to control their reproduction, all agree that a considerable number died as a result of illegal abortions prior to 1973. One should add to that number the women who have died from various forms of unsafe birth control.

37. Morgentaler v. Regina, 1 S.C.R. 30, 171 (Can. 1988) (Wilson, J.).

38. As of 1984, two-thirds of all federal district courts had no female judges, and thirty-two states had no women sitting on their highest court. As of 1985, only six states—Maine, Vermont, New Hampshire, Montana, Colorado, and Washington—had more than 22 percent female representation in their legislatures. In addition, three states had no women in the upper house of their legislature. Missouri, the state in which *Webster* originated, had but twenty-one female legislators—the fewest of any state in the nation. *See* A. GIBSON & T. FAST, THE WOMEN'S ATLAS OF THE UNITED STATES 214, 217 (1986).

39. *See* Pub. L. No. 94-439, § 209, 90 Stat. 1418, 1434 (1976) (applicable for fiscal year 1977).

40. *But see* R. Roth, C. Korenbrot, M. Tervalon, and C. Brindis, Abortion and the Role of Medicaid Funding: Lessons for California 53–56 (July 1988) (Center for Population and Reproductive Health Policy, University of California, San Francisco) (examining the overall cost increase of denying public funding for abortion).

41. *See* SACRED CONGREGATION FOR THE DOCTRINE OF THE FAITH, DECLARATION ON ABORTION 6 (1975), *cited in* Brief for Catholics for a Free Choice, Chicago Catholic Women, National Coalition of American Nuns, Women in Spirit of Colorado Task Force, as *amici curiae* in support of Appellees at 16–17, *Webster* (no. 88–605). For centuries, Catholic theologians, including Thomas Aquinas, maintained that "the human soul was infused into the body only when the latter began to show a human shape or outline and possessed the basic human organs." Donceel, *A Liberal Catholic's View,* in ABORTION AND CATHOLICISM: THE AMERICAN DEBATE 48 (P. Jung & T. Shannon eds. 1988), *quoted in* CFC Brief, at 13. Moreover, some "modern Catholic theologians believe that adequate brain development is the necessary component of human form for ensoulment" (*id.* at 18).

42. For example, Justice White's characterization in Doe v. Bolton, 410 U.S. 179 (1973), of the woman's choice to have an abortion as based on "convenience, whim or caprice" (*see id.* at 221) (White, J., dissenting), illustrates both a lack of understanding and a devaluation of women. The statement begins from the assumption that women naturally have babies—that having babies is what women are for—and that their choice not to procreate requires explanation.

43. Sex education over the years has been poor enough that some people actually believe that a rape victim is unlikely to become pregnant; such people may take the very occurrence of pregnancy to be evidence of the woman's consent because, if a woman really sought to reject the rapist's assault, her egg would somehow have had more success in resisting his sperm. *See The 1988 Equal Rites Award Winners,* Newsday, August 26, 1988, at 88 (New York City ed.) (citing statement by Pennsylvania State Representative Stephen Freind).

44. For a discussion and analysis of men's attitudes toward rape, see T. BENEKE, MEN ON RAPE (1982).

45. *See* R. GOLDSTEIN, MOTHER-LOVE AND ABORTION (1988).

46. 109 S. Ct. at 3057 (quoting Thornburgh v. American College of Obstetricians & Gynecologists, 476 U.S. 747, 795 (1986) (White, J., dissenting)).

47. J. Willke, Did You Know? (antiabortion pamphlet) (on file at the Harvard Law School Library).

48. Like the controversial antiabortion movie entitled "Silent Scream," which presented the fetus as a person struggling to survive, one can imagine an equally compelling film that could humanize the sperm and show its efforts to live and grow.

49. Consider, for example, the argument advanced with apparent seriousness by the lower court judge in the *Baby M.* case. He argued that men with infertile wives had a constitutional right barring state interference with "surrogacy contracts" by which they could requisition fertile women to bear children for them. *See In re* Baby M., 217 N.J. Super. 313, 384–87, 525 A.2d 1128, 1163–65 (Ch. Div. 1987), *aff'd in part and rev'd in part,* 109 N.J. 396, 537 A.2d 1227 (1988).

50. *See* Koop, *The Slide to Auschwitz,* in R. REAGAN, ABORTION AND THE CONSCIENCE OF THE NATION, at 41–73.
See id. at 68–70.

51. *See* David, Fleischhacker, and Höhn, *Abortion and Eugenics in Nazi Germany,* 14 POPULATION & DEV. REV. 81, 93 (1988).

52. *See* Gallagher, *Prenatal Invasions & Interventions: What's Wrong with Fetal Rights,* 10 HARV. WOMEN'S L.J. 9, 9–12 (1987).

53. *See* P. KANE, THE SECOND BILLION 53–102 (1987).

54. 109 S. Ct. at 3065 (Scalia, J., concurring in part and concurring in the judgment).

55. *Id.* at 3064.

56. *Id.* at 3064, 3067.

57. 109 S. Ct. at 3064 (Scalia, J., concurring in part and concurring in the judgment).

For further expression of concern on this topic, apparently much influenced by Justice O'Connor's opinion in *Akron,* see Rhoden, *Trimesters and Technology: Revamping* Roe v. Wade, 95 YALE L.J. 639 (1986).

58. *See* Brief of the American Medical Association et al., as *amici curiae* in Support of Appellees at 7–8, *Webster* (no. 88–605).

59. *See* M. GLENDON, ABORTION AND DIVORCE IN WESTERN LAW (1987).

60. *See* Letter from C. Everett Koop to Ronald Reagan (January 9, 1989), *cited in* Brief for Amicus Curiae American Psychological Association in Support of Appellees at 18, n.46, *Webster* (no. 88–605).

15

Rethinking Sex and
the Constitution

SYLVIA A. LAW

Introduction

This chapter attempts to articulate a stronger constitutional concept of sex-based equality than that which currently exists. The central thesis is that the development of modern constitutional sex equality doctrine has suffered from a lack of focus on biological reproductive differences between men and women. The reality of sex-based physical differences poses a significant problem for a society committed to ideals of individual human freedom and equality of opportunity.

To the extent that constitutional doctrine shapes culture and individual identity, an equality doctrine that denies the reality of biological difference in relation to reproduction reflects an idea about personhood that is inconsistent with people's actual experience of themselves and the world. The constitutional ideal alienates people from their own experience. Given our history in which the idea of "man" is the linguistic and legal equivalent of "person," a concept of equality that denies biological difference has particularly adverse effects upon women.

The central biological difference between men and women is that only women have the capacity to create a human being. For many people, the decision to bear a child is jointly made by a man and a woman and is the occasion for joyous commitment to one another, to the child, and to the future. But it is not always so. Only women can grow a human being, and although sperm is also needed, it is easily obtainable. The power to create people is awesome. Men are profoundly disadvantaged by the reality that only women can produce a human being and experience the growth of a child in pregnancy. Pregnancy and childbirth are also burdensome to health, mobility, independence, and sometimes to life itself, and women are profoundly disadvantaged in that they alone bear these burdens. And although men may be disadvantaged by their relatively minor role in reproduction, we have constructed a society in which men are advantaged, relative to women, in important material and spiritual ways.

◇ ◇ ◇

The relationship between constitutional concepts and culture is reciprocal. The rise of the women's movement in the early 1970s provided impetus for Supreme Court revision of constitutional standards applicable to laws controlling reproduction and incorporating sex-based classifications. The ideas of equality reflected both in Supreme Court decisions under the Fourteenth Amendment and in the recently defeated equal rights amendment in turn generate more general thought about sex-based equality. Contemporary ideas of equality are also reciprocal in relation to our past in two significant ways. First, historically, biology provided a central justification for the subjugation of women. That history partially explains the lack of focus on reproductive difference in contemporary equality doctrine and also suggests the need for close attention to such differences in developing new ideas of equality. Second, "protection" of women—construction of the pedestal/cage—was a core mechanism for oppression of women. Contemporary feminists are hence rightly skeptical of measures that protect women by providing them with special treatment.

At various periods the law has embodied different ideas about sex-based differences. Prior to the mid-nineteenth century, culture and religion required women to marry, and the law declared the married woman dead.[1] The law denied married women both identity and power.[2] With the enactment of the married women's property acts in the late 1800s, the law recognized women's existence. But two legal constructs enforced the subservience of women and the dominance of men in the home and wage market: first, the creation of separate spheres for men and women and, second, enactment of limits on women's power to control reproductive capacity.

Assumptions about biological difference and destiny provided the prime justification for creating a separate, inferior legal status for women. The law denied women equal opportunity for wage work and participation in public life. It reinforced social and religious commitment to family-centered child rearing. Women were required, by law and custom, to care for men and children. Although women and children were and are entitled to look to men for financial support, that expectation was and is not theoretically enforceable during an ongoing marriage or, as a practical matter, when marriage ends.

For most of the twentieth century, the law also preserved the dominance of men by creating obstacles to women's ability to control their reproductive capacity. Beginning in the mid-1800s the law restricted access to contraception and abortion.[3] Sex outside of marriage was condemned, by society and the law, much more harshly and consistently for women than for men.[4] If an unmarried woman became pregnant, she needed to persuade a man to marry her. The law did not compel a man to take responsibility for the pregnancy he had helped to cause or the child he had helped to create. The law condemned the child as a bastard and subjected the child to significant legal disabilities.[5] Laws disfavoring the children of an unmarried woman encouraged her sexual purity and made the social and economic status of both the child and mother "ultimately dependent upon the male."

Legal structures that support the dominance of men and subservience of women are fundamentally inconsistent with constitutional ideals of individual worth and equality of opportunity. It is crucial to understand, then, why contemporary constitutional sex equality doctrine evidences a lack of concern about the implications of state regulations that are based on biological differences and have been prominent in establishing and perpetuating the inequality of women. The next two sections explore first the conceptual and then the historical factors that may indicate why our present equality doctrine carefully scrutinizes explicit sex-based classifications while essentially ignoring laws governing sex-based biological differences. This history also demonstrates that the development of sex equality doctrine that excludes concern for sex-specific biology occurred at the same time the Supreme Court recognized a privacy-based right of reproductive freedom. The result of this history is that we have been virtually blinded to the relevance of equality notions when evaluating state limitations on a woman's access to abortion.

The third section of the chapter discusses another consequence of the Court's failure to focus on the myth and reality of biological differences: The Supreme Court now justifies deferential scrutiny of explicit sex-based classifications that raise significant problems of sex equality by finding that the laws are based on "real" differences between men and women.*

Section IV presents may central thesis that sex equality doctrine must confront squarely the reality of categorical biological differences between men and women. To reconcile the ideal of human equality with the reality of biological difference, we must (1) begin to distinguish clearly between laws that classify on the basis of sex and laws that govern reproduction; (2) recognize that laws governing reproduction implicate equality concerns; and (3) establish a test that can determine when laws governing reproduction violate constitutional equality norms. The test proposed here will then be applied to a variety of governmental policies, including limits on access to abortions. This application indicates the value of a unified approach to sex equality.

I. Visions of Sex-based Equality

Legal concepts of equality are informed by social vision. A growing literature attempts to give concrete content to social visions of sexual equality. In legal doctrine the dominant vision of sex equality is an assimilationist one, which conceives of a society in which sex would be a wholly unimportant characteristic of individuals, having no greater significance than eye color has in our own society. The assimilationist ideal posits that some characteristics—race, sex, eye color—do not describe differences that should ever be allowed to matter in any significant way. Even in the most personal social relations, an individual who selected friends on the basis of eye color would be regarded as idiosyncratic. The assimilationist vision asserts that it is unjust to distribute rights or responsibilities on the basis of distinctions that do not ever describe relevant differences—sex, race, or eye color. This vision is best developed in relation to race. The assimilationist view of sex equality is attractive to constitutional lawyers because it builds upon analogies between race- and sex-based discrimination.

The analogies between race- and sex-based discrimination are powerful. Blacks and women share a similar history of oppression; prior to the Civil War the laws defining the status of blacks and women borrowed freely from one another.[6] Sex, like race, is an immutable and highly visible characteristic. Women, like blacks, continue to occupy a position of economic inferiority. Indeed, as compared to white men, women are more economically disadvantaged than blacks, and black women are doubly disadvantaged.[7] Although women are not a minority, they were denied the franchise until 1920, and today women exercise limited political power.[8] Finally, and most importantly, sex, like race, "frequently bears no relation to ability to perform or contribute to society."[9]

Although these factors support the conclusion that classifications based on sex, like those based on race, should be regarded as constitutionally suspect, there are also impor-

*[Only sections I, IV, and V are included here; however, Part 1 addresses the constitutional history of equal protection law.—Ed.]

tant points of difference between sex- and race-based discrimination. There is no reason to believe that black and white people are inherently different in any way that should ever be allowed to matter in the law. Men and women, by contrast, are different in significant sex-specific physical ways. Most differences between men and women are like differences between blacks and whites: statistical generalizations, which are more or less true in the aggregate but untrue in relation to particular individuals. Accurate statistical differences between men and women that are false in individual cases include weight, height, longevity, mathematical aptitude, aggression, capacity for nurturance, and physical strength. There are, however, other categorical differences between men and women that are not simply statistical generalizations but, rather, sex-based physical differences relating to reproductive capacity. By categorical sex-based differences, what is meant, and all that is meant, is that most women and no men possess the capacity to reproduce the species. This concept of categorical sex-based differences is not merely definitional but is grounded in physical reality.

The assimilationist presumption that sex-based differences are always insignificant is false. Although both law and culture exaggerate the significance of biological differences, changes in social, cultural, and legal arrangements could not make these differences disappear. Absent development of a practical means to reproduce people outside a woman's body, a technological development not now on the horizon, it is implausible to suggest that sex-based biological differences are wholly insignificant. An assimilationist vision that ignores differences between men and women does not help us to reconcile the ideal of equality with the reality of difference.

A second vision of a sexually equal society recognizes differences in the life experience of men and women, in relation to biology, psychology, and moral development. The social reality that children are raised by women means that the process of psychological maturation is different for boys and girls. Socially developed concepts of gender define different expectations and value different qualities in males and females. Carol Gilligan, for example, describes differences in the moral character of men and women. Often, for men, "leaving childhood means renouncing relationships in order to protect [their] freedom of self-expression, . . . [while for women] 'farewell to childhood' means relinquishing the freedom of self-expression in order to protect others and preserve relationships."[10] Men tend to be concerned with rights, hierarchical relationships, and personal achievement, while women are concerned with caring and personal relationships.

> The images of hierarchy and web, drawn from the texts of men's and women's fantasies and thoughts, convey different ways of structuring relationships and are associated with different views of morality and self. . . . As the top of the hierarchy becomes the edge of the web and as the center of a network of connection becomes the middle of a hierarchical progression, each image marks as dangerous the place which the other defines as safe. Thus, the images of hierarchy and web inform different modes of assertion and response: the wish to be alone at the top and the consequent fear that others will get too close; the wish to be at the center of connection and the consequent fear of being too far out on the edge. These disparate fears of being stranded and being caught give rise to different portrayals of achievement and affiliation, leading to different modes of action and different ways of assessing the consequences of choice.[11]

The strength of a vision of differences is that it recognizes the social importance of traditional female virtues of nurturing, responsibility to others, and concern with relationships. In a society dominated by traditional male values, "assimilation" seems often to mean assimilation to a male norm. A vision of equality that incorporates respect for differences between men and women hence places a higher value on women's traditional virtues and work.

People have attempted to articulate a constitutional sexual equality doctrine that would value traditional female characteristics. For example, Elizabeth Wolgast advocates a constitutional idea of sex-based equality grounded on diversity and tolerance that would recognize the significance of sex-based differences and allow those differences to be institutionalized and valued. At the same time, her theory would attempt to mitigate the oppressive aspects of existing sex roles.[12] This vision borrows from the ideals of tolerance embodied in the First Amendment's religion clauses. Catharine MacKinnon advocates a standard that would ask simply whether laws challenged as sex discriminatory empower women and enable them to participate as full members of the society.[13]

The difficulty with an ideal of a sexually equal society that respects psychological and moral differences between men and women is that many of these differences are socially created. Gilligan recognizes that the differences she describes are "not absolute. . . . Clearly, these differences arise in a social context where factors of social status and power combine with reproductive biology to shape the experience of males and females."[14] There is a great danger that affording legal respect to presumed sex-based differences will perpetuate those differences. Furthermore, general rules premised on assumptions of universal sex-based difference are unjust in relation to the individual men and women who do not fit the presumed norm.

A constitutional theory based on either the assimilationist vision or the respect-for-difference vision presumes that it is possible to answer the question, "Are men and women essentially similar?" with a simple yes or no. The assimilationist principle answers the question "yes" and condemns laws that treat people differently. The respect-for-difference principle emphasizes that at least under present social conditions, the situations of men and women are not essentially similar, and it would evaluate laws affecting men and women differently by asking whether they empower and respect women.

A third vision, and the one that informs this chapter, assumes that it is not possible to give a single answer to the question whether men and women are essentially similar. We know that there are biological differences between men and women in relation to reproduction. These differences have been used to justify sex-based legal and cultural limitations on human potential that do not reflect any real difference between men and women and that enforce the inferiority of women and the dominance of men. The vision of equality advocated here suggests that the appropriate function of the law is not to enforce a general vision of what men and women are really like but, rather, to respect each person's authority to define herself or himself, free from sex-defined legal constraints. Our ability to develop this equality principle is enhanced by focusing on the myth and reality of differences between men and women.

Neither the assimilationist vision nor the respect-for-difference vision squarely confronts the problem of reconciling sexual equality with the reality of biological differences. The assimilationist vision denies the significance of biological differences. The vision of respect for difference underestimates the difficulty of overcoming the legal constructs that give oppressive social significance to such differences and thereby limit human liberty and equality. The development of constitutional doctrine in the past fifteen years has also failed to reconcile the idea of equality with the reality of biological difference, in part because of the failure of these dominant concepts of equality and in part because of the historical development of constitutional doctrine. A brief examination of this history reveals some of the reasons for the failure to develop a theory of sexual equality that addresses the biological differences between women and men.

◊ ◊ ◊

IV. A Proposed Approach to Sex-based Equality and Biological Difference

Before proposing a new approach to classifications based on biological differences, it is useful to identify initially how such classifications would be evaluated under several alternative approaches to sex equality. Once the advantages and limitations of these approaches are outlined, a more coherent approach will be charted.

A. Understanding Biological Differences According to Current Notions of Sex-based Equality

It is possible to construct a constitutional sex equality concept in which laws governing sex-specific physical characteristics will have one of the following three implications: (1) The laws raise no concerns about sex equality; (2) the laws are considered in the same way as laws that classify explicitly on the basis of sex; and (3) the laws are considered under a reconceptualized idea of equality that applies a new, integrated test to any sex-related classification.

The first approach is essentially the Supreme Court's notion of sex equality—one in which laws governing reproductive biology raise no sex equality concerns. As the Court stated in *Geduldig v. Aiello,* for example, "While it is true that only women can become pregnant it does not follow that every legislative classification concerning pregnancy is a sex-based classification."[15] This approach clearly denies the core reality that sex-based biological differences are related to sex. It is not easy to reconcile the ideal of sex-based equality with the reality of categorical biological difference, but the difficulty is not overcome by denying that laws governing reproductive biology are sex based. Further, because, as we have seen, it is easy for the Court to confuse real categorical biological differences with sex-based differences that are culturally imposed, an equality doctrine that exempts laws based on real physical differences from its concern is likely to be a weak one. Finally, and most importantly, in a society constitutionally committed to equality, the reality of biological difference in relation to reproduction should not be permitted to justify state action exaggerating the consequences of those differences. This is what happens when those actions escape scrutiny by courts.

The second approach to reconciling the ideal of equality with the reality of biological difference scrutinizes laws regulating reproductive differences in the same manner as laws that include explicit sex-based classifications using the Court's current gender-discrimination standard. This approach has the virtue of simplicity. It recognizes that laws based on sex-specific physical characteristics are related to sex and avoids the need to distinguish between these two types of sex-based laws.

The difficulty with this approach is that a central justification for limiting the use of explicit sex-based classifications is that they are not related to real differences between men and women. By contrast, laws governing reproductive characteristics, such as those prohibiting abortion or providing nutritional supplements for pregnant women, may be precisely related to the individual characteristics of the people they identify. The prevailing sex equality standard determines whether the sex-based classification at issue actually is responsive to real differences between men and women and rejects classifications when there are no such differences. This standard usually works in relation to explicit sex-based classifications because individual men and women escape stereotypical sex roles. The escapees disprove the judgment about men and women that motivated the explicit sex-based classification. However, because there are no escapees from biology, no pregnant men, or women sperm donors, a standard focusing solely on comparative equality does not provide a helpful tool for evaluating laws governing ways in which men and women categorically, biologically differ.

This second approach is also troubling because of a related concern. As a practical matter, it is difficult to maintain an appropriately rigorous standard for evaluating the cultural restraints of explicit sex-based classifications if the same standard is also used to judge laws governing sex-specific physical characteristics. Similarly, we have already seen how the Supreme Court's current intermediate scrutiny may become much more deferential when the Court perceives that a rule is based on "real" differences between the sexes. A better approach would consider laws based on biological differences independently of laws employing categorical sex-based classifications, thereby reducing the Court's ability to distort its intermediate scrutiny in this way.

The final approach, as advocated by Professor Catharine MacKinnon, attempts to grapple with the pervasive totality of sex-based oppression. She describes sex discrimination as a systematic construct that defines women as inferior to men and "that cumulatively disadvantages women for their differences from men, as well as ignores their similarities." She urges a constitutional equality standard that would ask simply "whether the policy or practice in question integrally contributes to the maintenance of an underclass or a deprived position because of gender status."[16]

Professor MacKinnon's approach is ambitious, but it adds unnecessary complexity to the application of sex equality doctrine in a large number of cases. The determination of what reinforces or undermines a sex-based underclass is exceedingly difficult. Professor MacKinnon may overestimate judges' capacities to identify and avoid socially imposed constraints on equality. She disregards our history, in which laws justified as protecting women have been a central means of oppressing them. Most fundamentally, her proposed standard may incorporate and perpetuate a false belief that a judicially enforced constitutional standard can, by itself, dismantle the deep structures that "integrally contribute" to sex-based deprivation.

MacKinnon discusses how sex equality doctrine can focus on an analysis of either "differences" between sexes (current doctrine) or "inequality" (her proposed doctrine). MacKinnon correctly contends that under current gender doctrine, "if the sexes can be considered relevantly the same, 'similarly situated,' or *comparable* on the dimension in question, differential treatment may be discriminatory; if not, differential treatment merely treats differences differently and is not discriminatory."[17] We have seen, and MacKinnon herself argues, that this comparative analysis leads to the conclusion that there is no sex discrimination when a law is based on real biological differences between men and women. Notwithstanding this important limitation of current equality doctrine, broad use of

an inequality approach poses tremendous risks. The very invisibility of discrimination against women makes it unlikely that the inequality approach can in fact be utilized successfully by litigators before the present judiciary. When, as in *Califano v. Goldfarb,,* . . . . . a majority of the Court cannot agree that women are discriminated against by a system of social security benefits that provides greater coverage for the dependents of male workers than it does for the dependents of female workers, there are great dangers in pressing a view that subjects discrimination against women to more exacting scrutiny than it does discrimination against men. It is all too likely that the courts will simply uphold the discrimination because they fail to see that women have been disadvantaged. Moreover, as MacKinnon herself acknowledges, "woman's 'specialness' (is) the cornerstone of that separate-but-equal logic of complementarity that has assigned her those pursuits and those qualities that are glorified as female but denigrated as human.[18]

MacKinnon's proposal is mistaken, therefore, because it would require a search for hierarchy when only a search for difference may be necessary. Her approach is helpful, however, because it provides a framework for determining when a rule classifying on the basis of biological differences is actually discriminating on the basis of sex. Such a rule is discriminatory when it "integrally contributes to the maintenance of an underclass or a deprived position because of gender status."[19]

The three approaches discussed above unsuccessfully confront the unique problem of evaluating laws based on biological differences. In articulating a new standard for evaluating such laws, I hope to incorporate the strengths while avoiding the weaknesses of these approaches.

B. A New Approach to Laws Based on Biological Differences

Professor Wendy Williams observes, "The instinct to treat pregnancy as a special case is deeply imbedded in our culture, indeed in every culture. It seems natural, and *right,* to treat it that way."[20] Yet, this wise feminist and constitutional scholar urges that we resist the temptation to see pregnancy as unique. She argues that

conceptualizing pregnancy as a special case permits unfavorable as well as favorable treatment of pregnancy. . . . [T]he same doctrinal approach that permits pregnancy to be treated *worse* than other disabilities is the same one that will allow the state constitutional freedom to create special *benefits* for pregnant women. . . . If we can't have it both ways, we need to think carefully about which way we want to have it.[21]

But pregnancy, abortion, reproduction, and creation of another human being are special—very special. Women have these experiences. Men do not. An equality doctrine that ignores the unique quality of these experiences implicitly says that women can claim equality only insofar as they are like men. Such a doctrine demands that women deny an important aspect of who they are. Such a doctrine is, to say the least, reified. Further, deny as we might, the reality remains that only women experience pregnancy. If women are to achieve fully equal status in American society, including a sharing of power traditionally held by men, and retain control of their bodies, our understanding of sex equality must encompass a strong constitutional equality guarantee that requires "radically increasing the options available to each individual, and more importantly, allowing the human personality to break out of the present dichotomized system."[22]

Because of the unique equality concerns raised by biological differences, sex equality doctrine must distinguish between laws drawing explicit sex-based lines and laws governing reproductive biology. Although both types of laws raise sex equality issues, the ground for concern are different. The problem posed by laws that classify explicitly on the basis of sex is that sex, as a proxy for some functional characteristic, is often inaccurate in relation to particular individuals. More important, even when the sex generalization is accurate in the aggregate, these generalizations tend to be self-fulfilling and oppressive to the individual who fails to fit the mold. In using explicit sex classifications the state may perpetuate arbitrary limits on human freedom and equality. Based on these concerns, scrutiny of sex-based classifications is intended to ensure that there are important governmental reasons for treating men and women differently when they are in all relevant respects the same.

Also, the equality issues raised by laws affecting reproductive biology are related, in part, to accuracy, as when the state uses the fact that women may become pregnant to justify barring all women, pregnant or not, from public life and responsible work. In addition, the laws may generate a self-fulfilling expectation, as when the fact that women bear children is used to justify an assumption that women have greater responsibility to nurture them after birth. Because these concerns are raised in a context in which men and women seem to have real differences, the inaccuracy or the stereotype may not be apparent.

Because this context may present differences between the sexes that are relevant to lawmakers, a proper concern for equality requires scrutiny that is directly focused on the impact of the rule rather than its purpose or structure. For example, programs providing material support to pregnant women are not necessarily premised on inaccurate assumptions about their need. Laws restricting or facilitating access to abortion do not inaccurately assume that only women need abortions. Neither type of law creates a culturally imposed constraint on the ability to sustain or to avoid pregnancy. Still, these laws raise equality concerns because state control of a woman's reproductive capacity and exaggeration of the significance of biological difference has historically been central to the oppression of women. When the state bars pregnant women from doing work they are able to do or denies women access to reproductive health services, the state, as well as nature, denies women equality.

If we are persuaded that the Fourteenth Amendment's equality guarantee constrains legislative authority to regulate reproductive biology and that such laws raise issues different from those raised by laws that classify explicitly on the basis of sex, we must then consider what standard is appropriate for evaluating such laws. I propose that laws governing reproductive biology should be scrutinized by courts to ensure that (1) the law has no significant impact in perpetuating either the oppression of women or culturally imposed sex role constraints on individual freedom or (2) if the law has this impact, it is justified as the best means of serving a compelling state purpose. Given how central state regulation of biology has been to the subjugation of women, the normal presumption of constitutionality is inappropriate, and the state should bear the burden of justifying its rule in relation to either proposition.

This proposed test is a substantial improvement over current sex equality doctrine and the alternative approaches discussed above. Most fundamentally, the test recognizes that laws classifying according to biological differences raise equality concerns and must therefore be tested under equality norms. The test would also be consistent with a constitutional doctrine of sex equality grounded in the ERA—the test recognizes that the legislature may sometimes have legitimate reason to take account of biological reproductive difference, even if, as under an ERA standard, explicit sex-based classifications are prohibited.

The test departs from contemporary equal protection analysis in that it does not require any comparison between allegedly similarly situated classes of people. This departure is appropriate because laws governing reproductive biology, by definition, govern ways in which men and women are not similarly situated. The requirement that similarly situated individuals be treated the same does not exhaust the idea of equality. Equality is a substantive goal, not simply a neat classification or a rational relationship between means and ends. Instead of evaluating the extent to which men and women differ in relation to a particular classification, the proposed test requires that a court consider the impact of the classification. This approach is similar to Professor MacKinnon's, but it limits the direct inquiry into a law's effect upon perpetuating inequality to those cases in which that difficult inquiry is necessary to ensure that the law is consistent with the constitutional requirement of sex equality.

The second part of the test is the compelling interest analysis. This strict scrutiny of the law is undertaken only after a court has determined that the law has a significant impact on perpetuating the inequality of women. Sometimes a law governing reproductive biology could be approved without a demonstration that it was the best means of serving a compelling state purpose, either because it had no discernable effect in oppressing women (for example, recordkeeping requirements) or because all of the effects we can discern are beneficial to women (for example, nutritional programs for pregnant women). But once we were convinced that a law governing reproductive biology oppressed women or perpetuated sex role constraints, the state should bear the burden of justifying the law as the best means of serving a compelling state purpose. In race discrimination cases the requirement of compelling justification has been "strict" in theory and "fatal" in fact. This is not surprising, given our broad cultural commitment to the assimilationist vision that explicit race classifications never accurately describe categorical differences. Since laws governing reproductive biology do accurately describe sex-based differences, we should not expect that a standard that demands a high level of justification will always be fatal in fact. Given the core importance of reproduction, laws recognizing reproductive biology might well be the best means of serving a compelling state purpose. But, once we have determined that a law governing reproductive biology oppresses women and perpetuates sex role constraints on human liberty, it is essential to require that the state demonstrate very strong justification to support its action. The demand for compelling justification for such laws is supported by our history in which biology has been so central to the subjugation of women.

The proposed two-level analysis also parallels the Supreme Court's contemporary reproductive freedom doctrine, which asks whether laws governing abortion restrict access to service and, if so, whether the legislation is supported by compelling state interests.[23] This doctrine allows the states to adopt regulations—such as record-keeping requirements—that do not impinge on access to services, without demanding that the state show compelling justification in support of such regulations. Similarly, the proposed test would subject regulations to strict scrutiny only when they restrict access to services because only those regulations have a significant impact in perpetuating oppression of women and sex role constraints. The proposed standard departs from the contemporary constitutional standard governing abortion laws in one important respect. In the abortion cases only protection of maternal health is recognized as a compelling state interest prior to fetal viability. The more general equality standard proposed here allows a compelling state interest to be established in relation to the broader substantive concerns of sex equality, including the oppression of women and the constraints of traditional sex roles.

Two criticisms of the approach advocated here deserve brief examination. First, in relation to laws governing reproductive biology, it suffers from the same inadequacies I have observed in Professor MacKinnon's suggestion that constitutional equality doctrine should ask simply whether a challenged policy or practice contributes to the oppression of women; that is, it is exceedingly difficult to determine what perpetuates sex-based deprivation, and standards that rely on judicial discretion are likely to provide weak protection. However, under the approach advocated here, the area of discretion is limited to laws governing reproductive biology; explicit sex-based classifications would continue to be evaluated under an arguably more reliable comparative standard. A second possible criticism of my suggested approach is that while it requires that equality concerns be brought to bear on laws governing biological difference, it does not allow a legislature to use explicit sex-based classifications to recognize or reward traditional women's work or supposed female virtues that are not based in biological difference. Achieving increased social valuation of women and their traditional work is a critically important enterprise. But judicial enforcement of constitutional norms seems better suited to the more modest objective of formal comparative equality, with its relatively more reliable standards.

Finally, it is important to understand that my argument that the constitutional guarantee of equality requires that courts carefully scrutinize whether laws governing reproductive biology perpetuate state-imposed restraints on sex equality is not a claim that the state has an affirmative obligation to mitigate the effects of biological difference. Analysis of the question when the state may take affirmative action to remedy race- or sex-based disadvantage is beyond the scope of this chapter. However, a clear distinction between laws using explicit sex-based classifications and those governing reproductive biology may be helpful in thinking about this issue. Affirmative action programs using explicit sex- or race-based classifications are justifiable in relation to the reality of historic oppression and the need for transitional measures to make equality of opportunity possible. But compensatory laws based explicitly on sex or race may perpetuate stereotypes of inferiority. Laws governing sex-specific physical characteristics, however, raise different issues. Special benefits for pregnant women, for example, ought to be analyzed in relation to the special needs of pregnant women, rather than as a means of providing compensation for past discrimination against women generally or pregnant women in particular. Laws governing sex-specific physical characteristics are not transitional measures enabling us to move toward sex-based equal opportunity in relation to reproductive capacity.

Now that a new approach to understanding the sex equality implications of laws that classify on the basis of biological differences has been outlined, the next part will apply the analysis to a variety of state laws related to abortion and pregnancy.

V. Sex-based Equality and Laws Governing Reproductive Biology

Applying the test developed in Section IV to laws classifying on the basis of biological differences entails several inquiries. The threshold inquiry is whether the law makes a classification that is based on biological differences. As we saw in Section II, this inquiry is not trivial—a law that implicates biological differences may actually be a categorical sex-based classification. If the law is found to be based on biological differences, the court must then consider whether the law has a substantial impact on perpetuating the inequality of women. If so, the court must engage in traditional strict scrutiny analysis to see whether the law is justified by a compelling state interest.

This part first applies the proposed test to laws restricting access to abortion. Such laws classify according to a sex-specific physical characteristic and have been central to enforcing the inferior status of women.[24] The second section applies the proposed standard to a variety of other laws that regulate according to biological differences.

A. Abortion Restrictions and the Proposed Sex-based Equality Analysis

Abortion laws present no analytic difficulty for determining whether the classification is based on biological differences. The proposed analysis clearly applies to state regulation of abortion. Only women become pregnant; only women have abortions. Technology sometimes allows human beings to transcend the limits of biology. We fly. We visit Antarctica and space. Advances in human understanding, science, and medicine allow us to control reproductive capacity and to terminate a pregnancy at minimal risk to the health or future reproductive capacity of the woman. Nature demands that women alone bear the physical burdens of pregnancy, but society, through the law, can either mitigate or exaggerate the cost of these burdens. When the state denies women access to abortion, both nature and the state impose upon women burdens of unwanted pregnancy that men do not bear.

The constitutional equality principle advocated here asks us to consider whether the state can meet the burden of proving that a law governing reproductive biology either (1) has no significant impact in perpetuating the oppression of women or culturally imposed sex role constraints on individual freedom or (2) is the best means for meeting a compelling state purpose.

The burdens of unwanted pregnancy, which laws restricting abortion impose upon women, are enormous. First, such laws enforce the invasion of women's bodies. The physical burdens of pregnancy always include minor discomfort and physical intrusion and always pose risks of permanent damage to health and life itself that are vastly greater than the risks of abortion.[25]

Second, restricting access to abortion dramatically impairs the woman's capacity for individual self-determination. When the state prohibits abortion, all women of childbearing age know that pregnancy may violently alter their lives at any time. This pervasively affects the ability of women to plan their lives, to sustain relationships with other people, and to contribute through wage work and public life. The right to equal citizenship encompasses the right "to take responsibility for choosing one's own future. . . . [T]o be a person is to respect one's own ability to make responsible choices in controlling one's own destiny, to be an active participant in society rather than an object."[26] Denying abortion denies women the capacity of responsible citizenship.

Third, the decision of whether or not to bear a child is inescapably a complex moral and practical one, requiring consideration of relations with existing people and one's capacity to care for the child or to find others who will do so. Bearing a child creates a profoundly intimate relationship between the woman and the child, even when that relationship ends shortly after birth.[27] For many women who attempt to live in accordance with mainstream Protestant and Jewish faith, religious belief informs the decision whether to bear a child.[28] For other women who are not formally religious, the choice is a conscientious one. By restricting access to abortion, the state necessarily denies the capacity of women as independent moral decisionmakers.

Finally, state action restricting access to abortion imposes a crushing restraint on the heterosexual women's capacity for sexual expression. At the heart of Sigmund Freud's central innovation in modern thought is his recognition of the pervasive imaginative force of sexuality in the life of human beings. For humans, sexual relations are invaluable expressions of love and bonding that strengthen the intimate relationships that give life meaning. More than one hundred years after Freud, "it is depressing to have to insist that sex is not an unnecessary, morally dubious self-indulgence, but a basic human need, no less for women than for men."[29]

State restrictions on access to abortion plainly oppress women. *Roe v. Wade*[30] condemns such laws as a violation of the constitutional right to privacy. The rhetoric of privacy, as opposed to equality, blunts our ability to focus on the fact that it is women who are oppressed when abortion is denied. A privacy right that demands that "the abortion decision . . . be left to the medical judgment of the pregnant woman's attending physician" gives doctors undue power by falsely casting the abortion decision as primarily a medical question. The rhetoric of privacy also reinforces a public/private dicotomy that is at the heart of the structures that perpetuate the powerlessness of women.

Although laws restricting access to abortion plainly oppress women, the standard proposed here would allow the oppressive restriction of access to abortions if the law withstood strict scrutiny. Considering the regulation of access to abortion under privacy doctrine, rather than sex equality doctrine, does not make it easier to address the difficult question of whether the state has a compelling justification for restricting women's access to abortion. The only reason seriously advanced for restricting abortion today, and the only one that could possibly justify the oppression of women under a strict scrutiny analysis, is protection of fetal life. The abortion debate is often cast as a conflict between the rights of a woman and those of a fetus. Opponents of abortion characterize it as murder. Neither equality nor privacy can support an asserted right to murder.

But even if we regard the fetus as a person, it does not necessarily follow that abortion is murder. It is "impossible to judge whether an act is murder simply by looking at the act without considering its context."[31] Ellen Willis argues that we can assume that the fetus is a person and yet support a woman's right to choose abortion as a form of self defense.

> No thoughtful pacifist would equate Hitler's murder of the Jews with the Warsaw Ghetto rebels' killing of Nazi troops. . . . However gratifying pregnancy may be to a woman who desires it, for the unwilling it is literally an invasion—the closest analogy is the difference between lovemaking and rape. . . . [A]bortion is by normal standards an act of self-defense.[32]

Similarly, Donald Regan argues that even if we think of the fetus as a person, even-handed application of the general common law principle that people are not required to aid others, particularly when aid can only be provided at significant cost and risk to the rescuer, demands respect for the woman's right to refuse to aid the fetus.[33]

The strengths of these formulations are that they come squarely to grips with the assertion that the state has an interest in protecting the fetus, and they recognize the magnitude of the injury inflicted upon women who are forced to continue an unwanted pregnancy. But these justifications for abortion are disquieting. Regan defends abortion on the same grounds we might support the legal right to refuse to throw a rope to a drowning child— as an action that is morally wrong but legally protected. Willis's self-defense formulation is equally troubling. The legalistic analogy to self-defense justifies abortion only in the limited circumstances in which the mother reasonably believes that she will suffer death or great bodily harm. Further, even if it is legally justifiable to kill an innocent person who threatens our life or well-being, the morality of such killing seems dubious. Thus both Regan and Willis characterize abortion as a conflict between the rights of the woman and the rights of the fetus. Both treat the fetus as a person and defend abortion by analogy to circumstances in which injury to or neglect of a person would be legally, if not morally, justifiable.

The view that abortion is morally suspect is inconsistent with significant currents of moral thought. A stronger defense of abortion rights must not simply assume that the fetus is a person but must, rather, directly challenge the claim that the legislature may declare fetal life to be personhood or, in the face of uncertainty, may require that the fetus be treated as a person.

Fetal life is starkly different from all other forms of human life in that the fetus is completely dependent upon the body of the woman who conceived it. It cannot survive without her. Although all human infants, and many adults, are dependent upon others for survival, that support can be provided by many people. The fetus by contrast is dependent upon a particular woman. "For a fetus, the conditions of life are such that one other human being, the pregnant woman, is in a unique position of being able to respond to its alleged right to life."[34] No other human being is in such a relationship with other humans.

This distinguishing characteristic of fetal life supports the line that *Roe v. Wade* draws between the woman's right to decide whether to abort and the state's power to protect fetal life. It is only after birth that anyone other than the mother can assume responsibility for the nurture that is indispensible to life. At the point of viability,[35] when the fetus "has the capability of meaningful life outside the mother's womb,"[36] the state may restrict abortions, except where the life or health of the mother would be endangered if the fetus were carried to term.[37]

Thus, the compelling state interest analysis leads one to conclude that once the fetus has reached the point of viability the state may restrict the availability of abortions, except in cases where the life or health of the mother would be endangered if the fetus were carried on to term. Notwithstanding this understanding of the nature of fetal life and the related strict scrutiny of the government's interest, three powerful ideas continue to fuel the effort to criminalize abortions. I believe that none of these ideas could provide the state with an interest compelling enough to justify any additional limits on access to abortions.

First, many people sincerely believe that a human being exists from the moment of conception.[38] But as Professor Laurence Tribe observes,

> The question when human life truly begins asks not for a discovery of the point at which the fetus possesses an agreed-upon set of characteristics which make it human, but rather for a decision as to what characteristics should be regarded as defining a human being. And . . . that decision in turn entails not an inference or demonstration from generally shared premises, whether factual or moral, but a statement of religious faith upon which people will invariably differ widely.[39]

In a pluralistic society,[40] religious belief cannot, by itself, justify a law imposing oppressive sex discriminatory burdens and demanding that others sacrifice their own deeply held conscientious beliefs.

Second, the right-to-life movement, as its name implies, aspires to promote an expanded respect and protection for all forms of human life. People who are dependent— infants, the poor, the elderly, and the disabled—make a strong moral claim on the resources of a society of abundance. Social values of helping and nurture are profoundly important. But the sustenance the fetus needs is not society's to give. It can only be provided by a particular pregnant woman. Forcing her to support the dependent fetus denies her capacity to decide whether that is a relationship that she can sustain and imposes enormous costs on her life, health, and autonomy. Respect for the fetus is purchased at the cost of denying the value of women.[41]

Finally, the drive to criminalize abortion is animated by an affirmation of the value of a patriarchal society. Many people believe, as a matter of revealed faith or experience, that women are and should be subordinate to men, that sex should be limited to procreation, and that the risk of unwanted pregnancy should function to discourage sex and to bind families together.[42] But application of the constitutional ideal of equality to men and women prohibits the state from using its coercive power to enforce patriarchal relations.

Control of reproduction of the sine qua non of women's capacity to live as equal people. The high place of equality in our constellation of democratic and constitutional values demands that something more compelling than traditionalist moral conviction justify state actions denying women that which is indispensibly necessary to their ability to act as moral beings and to participate in civil society. If and when it becomes technologically possible to grow children outside of a woman's body, the moral and constitutional issues we confront in relation to abortion will be categorically different than they are today. But for today, reproductive freedom is, inescapably, the core issue of women's equality and liberty.

B. Application of the Proposed Standard to Other Laws Dealing with Sex-specific Physical Characteristics

The standard proposed here asks that we first distinguish between laws governing reproductive biology and laws that classify explicitly on the basis of sex and then recognize that laws governing reproductive biology raise serious concerns about sex equality and therefore must be justified by compelling state interests if they perpetuate the inequality of women. This standard will now be applied to a number of state policies that raise concerns about sex-based equality but that would probably be subject only to minimum scrutiny under the current, flawed equality doctrine. Consider the following:

1. To protect the health of pregnant women, state policy requires that they quit public employment in the sixth month of pregnancy.
2. To protect the health of future children, state policy prohibits the employment of women of childbearing age in positions in which they may be exposed to substances that may be damaging to fetuses or future reproductive capacity.
3. To limit the cost of employee disability insurance, benefits for disabilities arising from normal pregnancy are excluded.
4. (a) Recognizing the physical burdens that pregnancy imposes upon women, a state requires that employers allow pregnant workers reasonable absences from work for medical disabilities associated with pregnancy.
   (b) Recognizing the special nutritional needs of pregnant women, the government provides supplemental food benefits for them.
5. (a) The state allows up to six months of maternity leave at half pay to women employees who are nursing infants.

   (b) The state allows all mothers, but not fathers, six months of child care leave at half pay, whether or not they are nursing.

6. In an effort to provide a social counterbalance to men's relatively minor role in reproduction and to encourage male involvement with young children, the state requires that a pregnant woman inform the man who impregnated her of the fact of pregnancy, unless she has reasonable grounds to believe that he would physically abuse her if he were informed.

The first three examples describe laws that govern reproductive biology and therefore are subject to scrutiny under the proposed standard. A requirement that women quit work once they reach the sixth month of pregnancy reflects a stereotype of incompetence that is most often inaccurate. This policy is similar to the rule that the Supreme Court struck down in *Cleveland Board of Education v. LaFleur* as an "irrebuttable presumption."[43] The sex equality analysis at the core of my proposed standard is, however, a stronger way of assessing the policy than the analysis that has grown out of the Court's limited understanding of sex equality. The law barring women from jobs that involve exposure to teratagenic chemicals stereotypes women as childbearers, a stereotype that is inaccurate in relation to the many women who cannot or intentionally do not bear children. The third example, which excludes payments for pregnancy-related disabilities from insurance plans, reflects a stereotype of women as temporary visitors to wage labor whose contributions are insignificant and for whom job continuity is unimportant.

Having determined that each of the three policies has a substantial impact upon perpetuating sex role stereotypes, each policy must be strictly scrutinized. It is clear that alternative, sex-neutral means are available to promote any of the legitimate goals that the state might hope to serve by enforcing these rules. For example, a concern that workers be physically fit can be served by a more individualized approach that encompasses non-pregnancy-related disabilities and that recognizes that many pregnant women are not disabled. Professor Wendy Williams has outlined in comprehensive detail some of the ways in which a state might limit the destructive effects of teratagenic chemicals while minimizing the damage to women's equality as wage workers.[44] There are many ways to limit the costs of employee disability programs without imposing the burdens exclusively on pregnant women.

The fourth example postulates a pair of laws, one requiring employers to allow pregnant workers reasonable absences from work without losing their jobs and the other providing special nutritional benefits to pregnant women. This type of law presents a closer case. When Montana adopted a law requiring that leave from work be allowed for pregnant women, feminists were divided in their views about whether it should be regarded as sex discriminatory. For more than a decade, the federal government has administered the Supplemental Food Program for Women, Infants, and Children (WIC), a program that provides nutritional benefits to pregnant women.

These two laws plainly govern reproductive biology. Whether they have a substantial impact upon perpetuating inequality is less clear. Such laws do not perpetuate cultural sex role stereotypes because they are tied precisely to the biological fact of pregnancy. A law providing help to pregnant women does not oppress women in an obvious way. The law requiring reasonable leave for pregnant women is dangerous, however, because the employer may decide to avoid the burden of providing the required protection by simply not hiring women who might become pregnant. Whether that danger is sufficiently real to enable one to conclude that the protective law oppresses women should, I believe, be treated as a question of fact and judgment, not as a matter of ideological preconception. It is possible that evidence would substantiate the fear that a mandatory leave rule would limit women's job opportunities.

Many issues are relevant to the assessment whether such a law oppresses women or whether it is supported by compelling state purposes. For example, can we foresee concrete ways in which the measure providing help to pregnant women can be used to hurt them? This inquiry distinguishes the WIC program from laws providing mandatory leaves for pregnant women, for it is difficult to see how the WIC program hurts women. Is the benefit provided so trivial that its primary function is to reinforce stereotypical ideas about men and women.[45] At the other extreme, is the protection mandated for pregnant women so substantial that it is likely that those required to provide it would avoid dealing with women in order to escape it? For example, a law demanding that employers provide pregnant workers four months leave with pay would very likely have an adverse effect on women's employment opportunities. It is, however, difficult to imagine facts that would support a conclusion that the law providing nutritional benefits to pregnant women enforces cultural stereotypes or is oppressive. In either case, if a court concluded that the law in fact had a substantial impact in perpetuating inequality, the law would have to be struck down. The state could employ alternative, sex-neutral means of achieving its objective of protecting against dismissal for health-related absences or of ensuring a nutritionally adequate diet.

To understand fully the difficult issue posed by these two laws, it is useful to examine the feminist opposition to them. One objection to such laws, with which I fully agree, is that they are politically divisive. "Creating special privileges of the Montana type [example 4(a)] has, as one consequence, the effect of shifting attention away from the . . . state's failure to provide important protections to all workers and focusing it upon the unfairness of protecting one class of worker and not others."[46] In developing a political strategy for the less affluent majority, it is vitally important to frame issues in ways that unite rather than divide people. But the political reality is that it is often easier to persuade a legislature to help or protection.

A second feminist objection to laws providing special protections and benefits to pregnant women rests on a view of equality that says that "conceptualizing pregnancy as a special case permits unfavorable as well as favorable treatment of pregnancy."[47] This argument has tremendous power, given our present constitutional equality doctrine that persistently confuses reproductive biology with cultural patterns and that wholly denies the applicability of equality norms to laws governing reproductive biology. But this is not necessary as a matter of nature or logic. Rather we could, as I have urged here, develop a concept of equality that distinguishes between reproductive biological difference and cultural generalizations and that prohibits regulation of reproductive biology whenever it oppresses women or reinforces cultural sex role stereotypes.

A final feminists' objection to such laws rests on an understanding of our history in which biological difference has been used to justify a separate role and world for women. Less than a century ago "doctors and scientists were generally of the view that a woman's intellect, her capacity for education, for reasoning, for public undertakings, was biologically limited."[48] This history demands profound skepticism of rules based on the fact that men and women are biologically different, but does it require that we reject any recognition of sex-based biological difference? Acknowledging the reality and importance of the reproductive biological difference does not necessarily set us on a slippery slope on which the state is allowed to exaggerate the costs of difference. Recognizing that men and women are different in relation to reproductive biology does not necessarily mean that the law can assume that we are different in relation to capacity to think, to lead, or to nurture. It is likely that courts would be less inclined to confuse biology with the social consequences of biology if a finding that a law was premised on biological differences between men and women were only the beginning and not the end of the equality inquiry. Confronting the myth and reality of biological differences may enable us to create a stronger equality concept in relation both to laws premised on cultural stereotypes and to laws that regulate reproductive biology.

The fifth example given above presents problems in relation to maternity and paternity leaves to care for young children. The policy providing child care leave to nursing mothers is one governing reproductive biology. Does the policy have a substantial impact in perpetuating inequality? It seems that it does. Either parent, or a stranger, is biologically capable of caring for a child. Limiting the child rearing to nursing women reinforces the cultural expectation that "the paramount destiny and mission of women are to fulfill the noble and benign offices of wife and mother."[49] Such a policy would have to be struck down because it could not withstand strict scrutiny; the state's interest in promoting the physical or psychic benefits of nursing is not sufficiently substantial to justify the burden upon men and women who would choose to take child care leave but who cannot nurse. Also, the oppressive effect upon women who would prefer not to nurse but are compelled to do so in order to qualify for the leave is not justified by the state's interest.

The second law presented in example 5 allows child care leave for mothers but not for fathers. This is not a law that governs reproductive biology but is instead a simple sex-based classification. A law based on what the government perceives to be the ability and willingness of certain citizens to care for children is not a law governing reproductive biology. A general maternal child care leave policy would be prohibited under the ERA and would need to be justified under the *Craig* standard as having a close relation to important government interests. The general maternal preference law would not be justifiable even under the more relaxed requirements of the *Craig* standard if challenged by a father who was able and eager to care for his child.

The final case, a statute requiring that a pregnant woman notify the man who impregnated her of the fact of the pregnancy, can be seen as a law governing reproductive biology. It addresses a problem of vital social importance—the law lends practical and symbolic force to the idea that men, as well as women, are responsible for the children they create and attempts to mitigate the effects of men's relatively minor role in relation to reproduction.

The hypothetical policy is far more sensitive to equality concerns than consent and notification requirements that are triggered by a woman's decision to have an abortion—requirements that have in the past been held unconstitutional. The hypothetical law directs the woman to provide the information, rather than imposing the requirement on a physician.[50] It excuses notification when she has reason to fear violence. It gives the man only information, not a formal right of veto. Most significantly, it is not directed solely to women who seek abortions. A requirement that men be notified only when the pregnant woman seeks an abortion powerfully reinforces the cultural stereotype that motherhood is women's destiny. A man's concrete emotional, moral, and financial interest is vastly greater when a pregnancy he has helped to create is carried to term than when it ends in abortion. Abortion-only consent and notification policies express disapprobation for abortion, regard the woman as a "mother-machine," and are indefensible as a neutral means of increasing male involvement with reproductive decision making.

But even this more sensitive notification requirement is oppressive to women. The biological reality that "it is the woman who physically bears the child and who is the more directly and immediately affected by the pregnancy"[51] must preclude the state from giving the man power over her decision whether to abort or to carry the pregnancy to term. A requirement of notification, as opposed to a formal veto, has effect only in those situations where the woman determines that communication with the man is unwise.

A man's interest in a pregnancy he has helped to create is undeniably great. But a man's interest in having children does not justify imposing the burden of pregnancy and motherhood on a particular woman. Even if that woman is his wife, the burdens of pregnancy, which the woman inescapably bears, are too great to allow the man to impose them upon her. A man's interest in terminating a pregnancy he has helped to create may also be very great. He may be emotionally and financially incapable of assuming responsibility for a child. Perhaps society should allow biological parents greater freedom to reject the rights and responsibilities of parenthood. There is a strong public interest in encouraging fathers to be more involved in the nurturing and care of their children. The notification requirement may promote this interest. While this case is, for me, a difficult one, I do not believe that even this sensitive notification policy could survive the strict scrutiny that is appropriate to an analysis of laws that oppress women through the regulation of reproductive biology. We do not now require that mothers notify fathers at the point of birth and a multitude of public policies limit, rather than enhance, the father's participation in the nurturing of children.

But parents' responsibilities to their children are not a function of reproductive biology. Such responsibilities can and should be defined in sex-neutral terms.

VI. The Future of Sex-based Equality Under the Fourteenth Amendment and the ERA

The Supreme Court's doctrine of sex-based equality under the fourteenth amendment is exceedingly unstable. This instability is manifest in the sharp divisions in analysis and result in cases such as *Parham v. Hughes*,[52] *Caban v. Mohammed*,[53] *Lehr v. Robertson*,[54] and *Michael M. v. Superior Court*.[55] The core principles of the Court's equality doctrine— the requirement that men and women be treated as individuals rather than stereotypes and the recognition that laws based on stereotypical assumptions are self-fulfilling as well as inaccurate in particular cases—are inconsistent with the approach that various members of the Court have taken in these cases. An unstable present necessarily implies an uncertain future.

The Fourteenth Amendment guarantees equal treatment under the law and recognition of the injustice of denying men and women opportunities solely on the basis of sex is broad and deep. It would be possible to achieve greater strength and stability in sexual equality doctrine through the approach advocated here, which focuses directly on the reality and myth of biological differences. The Court could draw a sharp distinction between laws creating sex-based classifications and laws regulating sex-specific physical characteristics and still recognize that laws regulating sex-specific physical characteristics implicate the core concerns of sex-based equality.

For the most part, the argument advanced here builds upon equality and privacy doctrine. Courts are skilled at the manipulation of doctrine. When doctrine develops quickly, in response to large changes in consciousness, modification in the light of experience and insight seems particularly appropriate. The analysis in cases such as *Michael M., Parham,* and *Caban* is not so compelling, nor the results so clear, that their approach need determine the way in which the Court analyzes future cases raising issues different than those resolved there. Other cases, notably *Geduldig,* are not so easily confined through the manipulation of doctrine. The Court should simply overrule *Geduldig,* recognizing it as the false step that Congress, nearly every commentator, and the Court itself have regarded it.

The equal rights amendment has been defeated, but it is certain to rise again. What is not so certain is whether we will continue to regard laws regulating reproductive biology as tangential to the constitutional guarantee of sex-based equality. The direction in which the Court will move under the Fourteenth Amendment and the vision of sex-based equality reflected in the next ERA depend in large part upon the vision of equality adopted by those who shape claims of sex-based equality and reproductive freedom under existing constitutional guarantees and those who fight for the new ERA.

The ideas developed here are simply one woman's thoughts about the meaning of sex equality, under either the Fourteenth Amendment or the ERA. Although I support the equal rights amendment, its major congressional proponents and the leaders of the struggle to enact it have expressed a different vision of sex-based equality. Strong reasons, both political and conceptual, support separation of doctrines of sex equality and reproductive freedom. The political reality is that extreme conservative religious and political groups have made opposition to abortion an organizing issue—a sine qua non political test. Although there is wide political support for equal pay for equal work and the claims of individual aspirational women seeking access to traditional male power, women's claims for control of their bodies present a more profound challenge to prevailing structures of male dominance and are less widely accepted. Conceptual support for the separation of sex-based equality and reproductive freedom rests on skepticism whether courts are able to implement, with good faith and good sense, a concept of sex equality that recognizes the reality of biological difference. Further, privacy doctrine is richly developed in relation to reproductive freedom, and a shift to sex equality analysis in these cases seems, to many, unlikely.

Nonetheless, as this chapter has attempted to demonstrate, a strong concept of sex-based equality will require that we come to grips with the reality of sex-based biological differences, either through the approach proposed here or in some other way. A political struggle that embraces recognition that men and women are both limited by biology and able to transcend it may be stronger than one that ignores the core reality of sex difference in relation to reproductive biology.

Are we locked into the road we have taken? Are the two lines of constitutional doctrine—reproductive freedom and sex-based equality—which began as a unified whole to preserve male dominance and diverged in the early 1970s, now on fixed projections that move ineluctably further apart? I think not. The law is a social creation that produced the legal structure that made biology destiny and enforced the subjugation of women. In the 1970s we began the divergent movements to create a different social construct of sex equality and reproductive freedom. We can, if we choose, move toward a more unified understanding of the ways in which the law perpetuates sex-based restraints on human equality and liberty.

Notes

Many people generously provided intellectual support and enriching criticism: Janet Benshoof, Rhonda Copelon, Peggy Davis, Norman Dorsen, Ruth Bader Ginsberg, Nan Hunter, Barry Ensminger, Nancy Erickson, Martha Field, Ken Karst, Herma Hill Kay, Cynthia Kern, Jane Levine, Susan Rotgard, Norman Redlich, David Richards, Lawrence Sager, Nancy Miller, Francis Olsen, Jane Schacter, Elizabeth Schneider, Phyllis M. Segel, Stephanie Wildman, and NYU's Law and Philosophy Group.

1. "By marriage, the husband and wife are one person in law: that is, the very being or legal existence of the woman is suspended during the marriage, or at least is incorporated . . . into that of the husband: under those wing, protection and *cover,* she performs everything." 1 W. BLACKSTONE, COMMENTARIES ON THE LAWS OF ENGLAND 430 (Oxford 1765) (footnote omitted).

2. This incorporation of legal existence gave the husband all the power: "[He] was regarded as her head and representative in the social state." Bradwell v. State, 83 U.S. (16 Wall.) 130, 141 (1872) (Bradley, J., concurring). A married woman could not bind herself by contract; her contracts were considered void, as an infant's, not just voidable. Her husband gained control and management of her real property and complete ownership of her personal property. Her services belonged to her husband. Therefore, he had sole right to any wages she earned outside the home. His domicile became hers. She could not sue or be sued; her husband had to be joined in any legal action. If any recovery was obtained through a suit, the money belonged to him. Finally, symbolic of this loss of a separate identity, the woman was required to assume her husband's name upon marriage. *See, e.g.,* Whitlow v. Hodges, 539 F.2d 582.

3. For a discussion, see Roe v. Wade, 410 U.S. 113, 138–44 (1973); Griswold v. Connecticut, 381 U.S. 479 (1965).

4. The sexual double standard creates differing sexual roles and expectations in society for men and women. Men are to be sexually aggressive; women are to have no sexual drives at all. The double standard gives women two options: to fulfill their assigned role as asexual and be revered or to accept their sexuality and endure society's condemnation. The laws reflect both choices by protecting "virginal" women and punishing women who express their sexuality.

Criminal law protects both a woman's reputation and her physical chastity. Some states penalize impugning the chastity of a woman. For example, Oklahoma makes it a crime to "orally or otherwise, falsely and maliciously . . . impute to any female, married or unmarried, a want of chastity." OKLA. STAT. ANN. tit. 21, § 779 (West 1983); *see also* FLA. STAT. ANN. § 836.04 (West 1976); WASH. REV. CODE ANN. § 9.58.110 (1977). Seduction is the crime of persuading a chaste woman to have sexual intercourse using some form of deception; some states require that there be a false promise to marry the woman. "A man who induces a woman to surrender her chastity by flattery, promises or artifice" may be guilty of seduction. 70 AM. JUR. 2D *Seduction* § 1 (1973).

Statutory rape laws traditionally punished men for consensual intercourse with a female under a certain age. The age has ranged from as young as ten to as old as twenty. *See* Comment, *The Constitutionality of Statutory Rape Laws,* 27 UCLA L. REV. 757, 762 (1980); Comment, *Forcible and Statutory Rape: An Exploration of the Operation and Objectives of the Consent Standard,* 62 YALE L.J. 55, 76 (1952). ("The law of statutory rape must intervene to prevent what is predicted will be an unwise disposition. And prevention is sought . . . by sanctioning the male, who is always assumed to be responsible for the occurrence.").

Prostitution laws provide a classic example of the law's sexual double standard. Some prostitution laws apply only to women, and facially neutral laws are enforced primarily against them. Brown, Emerson, Falk, and Freedman, *The Equal Rights Amendment: A Constitutional Basis for Equal Rights for Women,* 80 YALE L.J. 871, 962–63 (1971). Prostitution is defined as "the practice of a female offering her body to indiscriminate sexual intercourse with men," 63 AM. JUR. 2d *Prostitution* § 1 (1972) or submitting "to indiscriminate sexual intercourse which she invites or solicits" *(id.).* She "solicits" then "submits." A woman who will have sex with many men is a "common prostitute" and a criminal while a sexually active man just has a healthy sex drive.

Young women whose chastity is not "saved" through statutory rape laws may be subject to various sanctions. Until the 1970s, pregnant high-school students were commonly expelled from school. In Texas in 1971, "of 119 school districts, 105 compelled pregnant girls to withdraw from regular classes. Of those 105, 55 offered no substitute services." Comment, *Marriage, Pregnancy, and the Right to Go to School,* 50 TEX. L. REV. 1196, 1196 n.3 (1972). Boys who fathered the children were free to continue their education. Ordway v. Hargraves, 323 F. Supp. 1155 (D. Mass. 1971), held this type of school policy a possible violation of the Civil Rights Act. Title IX of the Education Amendments of 1972, Pub. L. no. 92-318, § 901, 86 Stat. 373 (1972), prohibits sex discrimination in education programs receiving federal aid; federal regulations prohibit discrimination against students on the basis of pregnancy. *See* 34 C.F.R. § 106.21(c)(2) (1983).

Young women who are sexually active may be punished through the juvenile justice system. A study of the New York system in 1974 found allegations of promiscuity, prostitution, cohabitation, and general sexual innuendo were made exlusively against females; all these allegations were grounds for a finding of "ungovernability." Note, *Ungovernability: The Unjustifiable Jurisdiction,* 83 YALE L.J. 1383, 1388–89, n.41 (1974).

The punishment of women who violate the double standard is reflected in literature as well as laws. The classic literary example is *The Scarlet Letter* by Nathaniel Hawthorne. The adulteress, Hester Prynne, was made to bear the scorn and condemnation of society symbolically displayed by a scarlet "A" for adulteress on her chest. Because she became pregnant, her indiscretion was publicly known. Her lover's identity, however, remained a secret. Hester actually may have been better off than other sexually active women in literature; she and her child both survived. Hemingway's Catherine in *A Farewell to Arms* died in childbirth after having an illicit affair; the child was also born dead. In Thomas Hardy's *Tess of the D'Urbervilles,* Tess's husband confessed to her his sexual past. She then confessed to him that after being raped she had borne a child that died. Her husband abandoned her, and she returned to a sexual relationship with the man who had raped her. Eventually she killed him and was executed for his murder. The sexual woman either lives a condemned life or dies as payment for her sexual behavior.

In recent years, the prohibition on women's sexuality has eroded. The prevalence of sexual activity among never-married American teenage women increased by 30 percent between 1971 and 1976, so that by age nineteen, 55 percent have had sexual intercourse. The increase has occurred at all ages and among all races. Zelnik and Kantner, *Sexual and Contraceptive Experience of Young Unmarried Women in the United States, 1976 and 1971,* 9 FAM. PLAN. PERSPECTIVES 55 (1977).

Change is observable in the proliferation of such works as I. KASSORLA, NICE GIRLS DO (1980); G. MASTERTON, HOW TO DRIVE YOUR MAN WILD IN BED (1976); M. SANDS, THE MISTRESS' SURVIVAL MANUAL (1982), and in the latest scenes of premarital and extramarital sex in the movies and on television. Sex is ever more explicitly used to sell books, magazines, and movies as well as perfumes, cars, and jeans.

Whether this "sexual liberation" is really liberating is a different question.

> Sexual health, measured either physically or psychologically, is in some respects deteriorating, as evidenced in spreading venereal disease, rape, and sexual encounters stripped of obligations between people as subjects. . . .
>
> The problem with the commercialization of sexual pleasure is not merely that it fosters fragmented sexual experience. These new permissive standards and practices remain fundamentally deformed by male-supremacist practices and attitudes and a heightened instrumentalism, people using one another as mere tools for personal satisfaction. . . .
>
> As men once took advantage of the sexual double standard and the enforced chastity of their wives, now they often take advantage of the mythical single standard to belittle and pressure women who resist their sexual preferences. Thus the area of sexual relationships remains . . . a major battlefield for feminists.

L. GORDON, WOMAN'S BODY WOMAN'S RIGHT 412–14 (1976).

5. The concept of illegitimacy was created to ensure male dominance. *See* H. KRAUSE, ILLE-GITIMACY: LAW AND SOCIAL POLICY 83 (1971). Krause argues that the problem of illegitimacy must be solved by maximizing paternity determinations. For a defense of the mother/child family, see Book Review, 19 UCLA L. REV. 845 (1972); *see also* Weber v. Aetna Casualty & Surety Co., 406 U.S. 164 (1972) (denial of equal recovery rights to illegitimate children violates equal protection clause); Levy v. Louisiana, 391 U.S. 68 (1967) (denial of recovery right for illegitimate children violates equal protection clause).

6. S. DEBEAUVOIR, THE SECOND SEX xxiii (1968); G. MYRDAL, AN AMERICAN DILEMMA 1073–78 (1944); Fitzhugh, *Sociology for the South,* in SLAVERY DEFENDED 34 (E. McKitrick ed. 1963).

7. In 1939 the median income of full-time full-year workers was

white men:	$1,419
white women:	863
black men:	639
black women:	327

By 1964 the relative economic positions of white women and black men had shifted:

white men:	$6,497
black men:	4,285
white women:	3,859
black women:	2,674

WOMEN'S BUREAU, U.S. DEP'T OF LABOR, OFFICE OF THE SECRETARY, FACT SHEET ON THE REL-ATIVE POSITION OF WOMEN AND MEN WORKERS IN THE ECONOMY (1981). By 1979, the gap between males and females had grown quite large:

white men:	$12,372
black men:	7,743
white women:	4,394
black women:	4,023

Sex Discrimination in the Workplace, 1981: Hearings Before the Subcommittee on Labor of the Senate Comm. on Human Resources, 97th Cong., 1st Sess. (1981).

Among year-round, full-time workers, the median income of black, male *high-school* graduates exceeds that of white female *college* graduates. BUREAU OF CENSUS, U.S. DEP'T OF COMMERCE, CURRENT POPULATION REPORTS, CONSUMER INCOME: MONEY INCOME OF HOUSEHOLDS, FAM-ILIES AND PERSONS IN THE UNITED STATES: 1980.

8. In 1982 only 6.9 percent of federal judges and 12.1 percent of state legislators were women. In the Congress there were two women in the Senate and nineteen women in the House in 1982. Statistics from Eagleton Center for the American Woman and Politics, Rutgers University, New Brunswick, N.J. The Supreme Court has recognized that sometimes a numerical majority must be treated like a minority for purposes of equal protection analysis. In Castaneda v. Partida, 430 U.S. 482 (1977), the Court held that a prima facie case of discrimination against Mexican-Americans in the selection of grand jurors was not constitutionally affected by the fact that Mexican-Americans had a "governing majority" in the affected county. Justice Marshall explained, "Social scientists agree that members of minority groups frequently respond to discrimination and prejudice by attempting to disassociate themselves from the group, even to the point of adopting the majority's negative attitudes towards the minority" *(id.* at 503 (Marshall, J., concurring). Certainly part of the reason for the second-class status of women is that they accept the stereotypes of their own inferiority.

John Ely, exploring this point, concludes, "To apply all this to the situation of women in America in 1980, . . . is to strain a metaphor past the breaking point." J. ELY, DEMOCRACY AND DIS-TRUST: A THEORY OF JUDICIAL REVIEW 166 (1980). He argues for relatively more rigorous scrutiny of sex-based laws of older vintage, enacted when women were barred from the political process, but asserts that "if women don't protect themselves from sex discrimination in the future, it won't be because they can't" *(id.* at 69). One way in which oppression is perpetuated is to assume falsely that equality has been achieved when it has not. On the other hand, recognition of the reality of oppression, particularly in the case of women, can perpetuate derogatory stereotypes. The tension between these two dangers is persistent. Ely overestimates the degree to which sex-based equality has already been achieved.

Today, every woman over thirty came to maturity in a world in which virtually no one questioned the assumption that the woman's place was in the home and her function in life was to find and keep a man. Exercise of significant ambition today demands a single-minded, egotistic devotion that is inconsistent with primary responsibility for the care of children. For all the changes in attitudes toward women since 1970, there has been little increase in male responsibility for nurturing or in the development of other forms of child care that would free women for the intense work that exercising political power demands. On the other hand, women who aspire to political office seem to be held to a very high standard to avoid the appearance of being excessively driven or lacking nurturing qualities.

9. Frontiero v. Richardson, 411 U.S. 677, 686 (1973) (plurality opinion).

10. C. GILLIGAN, In a Different Voice (1982), at 157.

12. E. WOLGAST, EQUALITY AND THE RIGHTS OF WOMEN (1980); *see also* Rutherglen, *Sexual Equality in Fringe-Benefit Plans,* 65 VA. L. REV. 199, 205–16 (1979).

13. C. MACKINNON, SEXUAL HARASSMENT OF WORKING WOMEN: A CASE OF SEX DISCRIMINATION (1979).

14. C. GILLIGAN, at 2.

15. 417 U.S. 484 (1974) at 496, n.20.

16. *See* C. MACKINNON, at 116, 117.

17. *Id.* at 110. *See also id.* at 102 ("The gender difference is lined up against the sex difference in practice, and women are compared with men, to see if the correspondences warrant the application.").

18. Taub, Book Review: *Sexual Harassment of Working Women: A Case of Sex Discrimination,* 80 COLUM. L. REV. 1686, 1691 (1980) (citation omitted).

19. C. MACKINNON, at 117.

20. Williams, *The Equality Crisis: Some Reflections on Culture, Courts, and Feminism,* 7 WOMEN'S RTS. L. REP. 175, 195 (1982).

21. *Id.*

22. Olsen, The Family and the Market, 96 HARV. L. REV. 1578 (1983).

23. *See, e.g.,* City of Akron v. Akron Center for Reproductive Health, Inc., 103 S. Ct. 2481, 2490–93 (1983).

24. After the Civil War, many states and territories enacted criminal penalties for abortion. *See* Roe v. Wade, 410 U.S. 113, 139 (1973), and sources cited therein; *see also* L. GORDON, WOMEN'S BODY, WOMEN'S RIGHT: A SOCIAL HISTORY OF BIRTH CONTROL IN AMERICA (1976); J. MOHR, ABORTION IN AMERICA: THE ORIGINS AND EVOLUTION OF NATIONAL POLICY, 1800–1900 at 200–25 (1978).

In *Roe v. Wade,* Justice Blackmun identified three justifications for the criminal abortion laws of the nineteenth century: "Victorian social concern to discourage illicit sexual conduct"; protection of the pregnant woman from medical procedures that "placed her life in serious jeopardy"; and finally, in a distinctly secondary role protection of "prenatal life." 410 U.S. at 148–50. Gordon's and Mohr's work confirm and refine this historical analysis.

Victorian social mores did not, as Justice Blackmun suggested, simply condemn "illicit sexual conduct." Gordon demonstrates that with the beginning of industrial capitalism in the first part of the nineteenth century, production drew men out of the home to socialized work places and undermined the economic basis of agrarian family unity. In reaction to this weakening of the economic basis of the traditional stability of the family structure, Victorian ideology arose to maintain family stability.

Victorian prudery was closely connected to the doctrine of a separate sphere of concerns for women. This notion that women were profoundly different from men . . . was simultaneously a description of a new reality: a male-imposed doctrine to keep women from escaping their homes and women's adaptation to their new situation.

L. GORDON, at 18.

Some women had challenged these constraints. In 1848, the first recorded women's rights convention was held in Seneca Falls, New York. The Declaration of Sentiments, adopted at this convention, discussed discrimination against women in marriage, employment, education, criminal law, and the church. *See* 1 E. STANTON, S. ANTHONY, and M. GAGE, HISTORY OF WOMAN SUFFRAGE 70–71 (1881). The next twenty years were, until the present, the most active period in the struggle for women's rights. Gordon's central thesis is that reaction to women's assertion of independence was a major factor motivating and justifying the enactment of criminal restrictions on abortion. *See* L. GORDON, at 414–18. Mohr agrees that this factor was important. *See* J. MOHR, at 168.

In the late nineteenth century the types of women seeking abortion changed (*id.* at 46–50, 86–102); L. GORDON, at 51–60. No longer were abortions sought solely because of illegitimacy or adultery; rather "respectable" women began to seek abortions to limit family size. J. MOHR, at 86–102. Nineteenth century lobbyists for criminal restrictions on abortion expressed concern with the fact the birthrates were declining among the white, Yankee Protestants relative to Catholics and non-whites (*id.* at 166–67). gordon states,

> Fears about immigrants and the poor reproducing faster than the Yankee elite had been current since before the Civil War. Physicians in particular noticed demographic patterns. Nathan Allen, a New England doctor, reported that in 1860 the foreign-born population of Massachusetts produced more children than the Yankees and that in 1877 a full 77 per cent of the births in all New England were Catholic. Another physician wrote that the birth rate was declining in "our most intelligent communities." Medical journals carried many similar articles of warning.

L. GORDON, at 138 (footnotes omitted).

Finally, the medical profession was the major group lobbying for the restrictive abortion laws. It was, however, not simply that abortions were dangerous to the woman but, rather, that abortions were generally performed by "irregulars": midwives, professional abortionists, empirical medics, herbalists, and other practitioners. The 1830s saw a blossoming of a popular health movement, dominated by women practitioners, particularly directed to women's health problems, and emphasizing education, nutrition, and self-reliance (*id.* at 162–65); *see also* B. EHRENREICH and D. ENGLISH, WITCHES, MIDWIVES, AND NURSES: A HISTORY OF WOMEN HEALERS 24–27 (1973). Mohr's central thesis is that the regular allopathic medical profession sought these restrictive laws to promote the authority of regular doctors and to restrict their irregular competitors. *See* J. MOHR, at 147–70. Gordon agrees. *See* L. GORDON, at 59–60. Mohr also argues that many physicians sincerely believed that abortion was wrong because of moral concerns about the fetus. *See* J. MOHR, at 165.

Prior to the development of antiseptic technique, abortion was extremely dangerous to the health of the woman, perhaps more dangerous than normal childbirth. But abortion was not then prohibited. At the historical moment when the development of antiseptic technique made it possible to do more good than harm through surgical procedures, abortion was prohibited. *Compare* P. STARR, THE SOCIAL TRANSFORMATION OF AMERICAN MEDICINE 156–57 (1982) (improvements in surgery) *with* J. MOHR, *supra*, at 200–25 (criminalization of abortion). This history strongly suggests that maternal health is not the primary issue at stake in the regulation of abortion.

25. The risks of death or serious complications are at least seven times greater in childbirth than in first trimester abortion. Cates, Smith, Rochat, and Grimes, *Mortality from Abortion and Childbirth: Are the Statistics Biased?* 248 J. A.M.A. 192 (1982); LeBolt, Grimes, and Cates, *Mortality from Abortion and Childbirth: Are the Populations Comparable?* 248 J. A.M.A. 188 (1982). The

health risks of pregnancy and childbirth are greatly exacerbated when a pregnancy is unwanted. Cates, *Legal Abortion: The Public Health Record,* 215 *Sci.* 1586, 1587 (1982).

26. Karst, *The Supreme Court 1976 Term, Foreword: Equal Citizenship Under the Fourteenth Amendment,* 91 HARV. L. REV. 1, 58 (1977). Karst notes that "the abortion question was not merely a 'women versus fetuses' issue; it was also a feminist issue, an issue going to women's position in society" *(id).*

27. Although two-thirds of births to unmarried teenagers are unintended, few teenage mothers place babies for adoption or for care by friends or relatives. Ninety-six percent of unmarried teenage mothers—90 percent of white and virtually all of black mothers—keep their children. ALAN GUTT-MACHER INSTITUTE, TEENAGE PREGNANCY: THE PROBLEM THAT HASN'T GONE AWAY (1981).

28. Mainstream Protestants believe that the Bible, as interpreted through the person of Jesus Christ, imposes a duty on individuals to make deliberate decisions about childbearing, according to principles of responsible parenthood. Rev. John Philip Wagaman, dean and professor of Christian Social Ethics at Wesley Theological Seminary and past president of the American Society of Christian Ethics, explains that "nearly no aspect of life is more sacred, closer to being human in relation to God, than bringing a new life into the world to share in the gift of God's grace and God's covenant." McRae v. Califano, 491 F. Supp. 630, 700 (E.D.N.Y.), *rev'd sub. nom.* Harris v. McRae, 448 U.S. 297 (1980). The question is whether one "is bringing a life into the world under conditions which make it possible for that life to participate in God's intention . . . (and under conditions which will not) threaten to undermine the theologically understood fulfillment of already existing human beings" *(id.* at 700–1). Although in Protestant teaching the basic judgment whether to bear a child is "referred to the woman and her own religious conscience," there are circumstances in which abortion may be "mandatory as a person's responsibility before God" *(id.* at 702).

Protestant theology does not regard the fetus as a person "until that stage in development where someone has begun experience of reality." This view flows from "the covenant [that] subsists between God as the Creator of reality and those who have begun to experience the reality which God has created" *(id.* at 701).

Professor Beverly Harrison explains this prochoice theology:

> We encounter God through relationship with all that nurtures and sustains life. . . . Freedom, when understood as the power of creativity, achieves its consummate expression in deepened community. . . . To be free means possessing the power to imaginatively interact with others, to give and to receive, to act upon and to suffer (that is, to be acted upon), to participate with others in co-creating a world. . . . God is not the one who stands remotely in control, but the One who binds us and bids us to deep relationality, resulting in a radical equality motivated by genuine mutuality and interdependence.

B. HARRISON, OUR RIGHT TO CHOOSE, TOWARD A NEW ETHIC OF ABORTION 99, 100, 108 (1983). In this view "the moral life involves a process of selecting and integrating many potential values through strategic choices" *(id.* at 110). The decision to have an abortion or a child requires consideration of relations with existing people, as well as assessment of capacity to provide care for the child.

The second theme of prochoice theology focuses on the health of the mother. Jewish thought places a high value on the individual obligation to protect her own health. The biblical injunction, "Therefore, choose life," refers not to the everlasting life promised to Christians through baptism and faith but to life in this world. As Rabbi David Feldman explains, "When a woman's life or health is threatened . . . abortion . . . becomes mandatory." Abortion is "appropriate," since "the duty is to choose life." *McRae,* 491 F. Supp. at 696 (testimony of Rabbi David Feldman). Rabbi Feldman's views are also set forth in MARITAL RELATIONS, CONTRACEPTION, AND ABORTION (1976).

In Jewish thought, the fetus is not a person until it "emerges from the womb into the world, or, more exactly until the head of the infant emerges, or, in the case of a breach birth, half of the body emerges" *McRae,* 491 F. Supp. at 697. The abortion decision is nonetheless a serious moral matter because it involves potential human life. There are sharp divisions in Jewish thought, with Orthodox

Jews and some Conservatives holding that only the most serious threats to a woman's life justify abortion, while those in the Reform tradition embrace a broader definition of health, holding that the primary concern is the welfare of the mother and the final decision is the woman's *(id.)*.

29. Willis, *Abortion: Is a Woman a Person?* in POWERS OF DESIRE, (1983) at 471, 474.

30. 410 U.S. 113 (1973).

31. Willis, at 473.

32. *Id.*

33. Regan, in *Rewriting* Roe v. Wade, 77 MICH. L. REV. 1569 (1979), argues that restricting access to abortion denies equal protection of the law, not because it discriminates on the basis of sex, but rather because it excludes pregnant women from the protection of the "deeply rooted principle of American law that an individual is ordinarily not required to volunteer aid to another individual who is in danger or in need of assistance" *(id.* at 1569). Individual interests in physical integrity and nonsubordination, recognized by the common law no-duty-to-aid principle, are also constitutionally protected by the Thirteenth Amendment's prohibition of involuntary servitude and the Eighth Amendment's ban on cruel and unusual punishment. On the constitutional protection of physical integrity, see Estelle v. Gamble, 429 U.S. 97, 102–3 (1976) (denial of medical treatment for prisoners is a violation of the eighth amendment); Rochin v. California, 342 U.S. 165 (1952) (pumping the stomach of a suspect is a violation of due process). On the constitutional value of nonsubordination, see Taylor v. Georgia, 315 U.S. 25 (1942) (peonage is violation of Thirteenth Amendment); Bailey v. Alabama, 219 U.S. 219, 241 (1911) (involuntary servitude encompasses more than slavery).

Regan argues that even if we hypothesize that the fetus is a full human being, the equality guarantee nonetheless prohibits the state from singling out pregnant women and demanding that these individuals sacrifice their physical integrity to aid a person in need.

> Consider a simple burning building, with a child trapped inside. Would a court impose criminal liability on anyone, even the child's parent, who did not attempt to save the child at the risk of second-degree burns over one or two percent of his or her body? . . .
> . . . An innocent life can be saved by a physical invasion comparable to or less than pregnancy and delivery. . . . Even if the potential rescuer is specified to be the child's parent, liability is unlikely. In all other cases, the suggested imposition is unthinkable in the context of our legal system.

Regan, at 1588. Those who have advocated a legal duty to rescue would limit the duty to situations in which rescue can be effected without significant cost or physical risk to the rescuer. *See, e.g.,* Ames, *Law and Morals,* 22 HARV. L. REV. 97, 111–13 (1908); Franklin, *Vermont Requires Rescue: A Comment,* 25 STAN. L. REV. 51 (1972); Weinrib, *The Case for a Duty to Rescue,* 90 YALE L.J. 247 (1980); *see also* Rudolph, *The Duty to Act: A Proposed Rule,* 44 NEB. L. REV. 499 (1965).

34. Farrell-Smith, Rights-Conflict, Pregnancy and Abortion, in BEYOND DOMINATION 265 (C. Gould ed. 1983), at 267. *See also* Fletcher, *Abortion, Euthanasia, and the Care of Defective Newborns,* 292 NEW ENG. J. OF MEDICINE 75 (1975) (arguing that the fetal dependence upon a particular woman makes abortion morally distinct from euthanasia of defective infants).

35. Justice O'Connor, dissenting in City of Akron v. Akron Center for Reproductive Health, 103 S. Ct. 2481 (1983) asserted that, "the *Roe* framework, then, is clearly on a collision course with itself. . . . As medical science becomes better able to provide for the separate existence of the fetus, the point of viability is moved further back toward conception" *(id.* at 2507). She noted that "recent studies have demonstrated increasingly earlier fetal viability. It is certainly reasonable to believe that fetal viability in the first trimester of pregnancy may be possible in the not too distant future" *(id.)*.

The evidence offered in Justice O'Connor's footnote does not support her claims. She cites Phillips, Little, Polivy & Lucey, *Neonatal Mortality Risk for the Eighties: The Importance of Birth Weight/Gestational Age Groups,* 68 PEDIATRICS 122 (1981), for the proposition that infants "with a gestational age of less than 25 weeks and weight between 500 and 1,249 grams have a 20% chance of survival." 103 S. Ct. 2507, n.5. In fact, the data presented show that of 523 premature infants treated in a regional intensive care unit between 1976 and 1979, 5 were twenty-five weeks or less gestational age. Two of these babies weighed between 500 and 749 grams, and both died; 1 baby weighed between 750 and 999 grams and it died; 2 babies weighed between 1,000 and 1,249 grams, and 1 survived (*see id.* at 125, table 4). O'Connor observes ominously, "The aborted fetus in . . . *Simopoulos v. Virginia* . . . weighed 495 grams and was approximately 22 gestational weeks" (103 S. Ct. 2507, n.5.).

In support of the claim that fetal viability may soon be possible in the first trimester, Justice O'Connor also cites Kopelman, *The Smallest Preterm Infants: Reasons for Optimism and New Dilemmas,* 132 AM. J. DISEASES CHILDREN 461 (1978). Dr. Kopelman, Head of Neonatology at East Carolina School of Medicine, comments,

> I would respond emphatically that my article does not in any way, shape or form support such a contention. Furthermore I know of no current research which would lead me to believe that a fetus of less than 22 weeks gestation can be or soon will be able to be sustained outside the uterus. . . .
>
> Below 24 weeks gestation the fetus' lungs are simply not adequately developed to sustain oxygenation even with ventilator support.

Letter to Nan Hunter, September 12, 1983 (copy on file with the *University of Pennsylvania Law Review*)

Finally Justice O'Connor cites Stern, *Intensive Care for the Pre-Term Infant,* 26 DANISH MED. BULL. 144 (1979). Dr. Stern, Professor & Chairman of Pediatrics at Brown University, responds,

> It may well be that some of the other references quoted in the footnote have demonstrated "increasingly earlier fetal viability," but that is certainly not what I said in my article. . . . It is highly likely that the lower limit beyond which human gestation is simply incapable of survival has already been virtually reached in its entirety, at least insofar as we intend such survival to be possible without the intervention of some form of artificial extrauterine environment that could be provided by the successful creation of an artificial placenta.

Letter to Nan Hunter, August 3, 1983 (copy on file with *University of Pennsylvania Law Review*). After discussing the "extreme technical difficulties" in creating substitutes for a woman's womb, Dr. Stern observes,

> Even if such a procedure could be successfully achieved, not only are its economic costs staggering to imagine but the potential for ever being able to supply the technology in sufficiently large numbers of units to make any kind of impact on the total number of threatened or spontaneously terminated first trimester gestations would be in practical terms most unlikely.

Id. In short, the evidence does not support Justice O'Connor's claims in relation to fetal viability.

Viability is a probabalistic concept that refers to the probability that a fetus has approximately a 10 percent chance of survival outside the womb. *See* Colanti v. Franklin, 439 U.S. 379, 396, n.15 (1979). The probability of survival is affected by gestational age, fetal weight, general maternal nutrition, and the technological resources available. It is difficult to make a precise determination of gestational age even after the birth of a premature infant. Dubowitz, Dubowitz & Goldberg, *Clinical Assessment of Gestational Age in the Newborn Infant,* 77 J. PEDIATR. 1 (1970). It is even more difficult to estimate gestational age or weight in utero. Because of the inherent difficulty and uncertainty of estimating viability, the Supreme Court has held that states must "afford the physician adequate discretion in the exercise of his medical judgment." Colantti v. Franklin, 439 U.S. at 387.

36. *Roe v. Wade,* 410 U.S. at 163.

37. As *Roe v. Wade* recognizes, the fact that a fetus has some probability of survival outside of the womb does not necessarily justify state action forcing the woman to continue to support it. *See* Frost, Chudwin and Wikler, *The Limited Moral Significance of Fetal Viability,* HASTINGS CENTER REP., December 1980, at 10, 13.

As a practical matter, few abortions are performed near the point of potential fetal viability. In 1976, 95 percent of abortions were performed prior to fifteen weeks gestation. *See* McRae v. Califano, 491 F. Supp. 630, 635 (E.D.N.Y.) (presenting data from the U.S. Center for Disease Control), *rev'd sub. nom.* Harris v. McRae, 448 U.S. 297 (1980). Less than 1% of abortions are performed for women who are more than 21 weeks pregnant. *New York Times,* February 15, 1984, at B-1, B-4, col. 1.

Late-term abortions are most commonly performed for girls between ages of fifteen and nineteen, who are slow to realize or acknowledge that they are pregnant and who often have difficulty in obtaining medical services. Ten percent of abortions performed after the end of the first trimester are done for women who have amniocentesis and discover that the fetus is genetically abnormal *(id).* Testing to discover genetic defects *in utero* cannot be completed until after eighteen to twenty weeks gestation. Colanti v. Franklin, 439 U.S. 379, 389, n.8 (1979). A third group of late abortions involve women who contract a disease during pregnancy that poses a risk to their life or health or that damages the fetus. *McRae,* 491 F. Supp. at 678–80.

38. For the Roman Catholic church, the largest denomination condemning abortion, opposition is grounded on the belief that a human being exists at the moment of fertilization. Any uncertainty as to the precise moment of "ensoulment" must be resolved in favor of the fetus, in part because the concept of original sin means that unborn life is perfect, born life imperfect. McRae v. Califano, 491 F. Supp. 630, 692–93 (E.D.N.Y.) (testimony of Reverend William B. Smith), *rev'd sub. nom.* Harris v. McRae, 448 U.S. 297 (1980). The *Declaration on Abortion of the Sacred Congregation for the Doctrine of the Faith* is "the Church's most definitive and authoritative statement on the morality of direct abortion" (*see id.* at 693). Catholic teaching distinguishes "indirect" abortion, that is, "operations, treatments and medications which do not directly intend termination of pregnancy, but which have as their purpose the cure of a proportionately serious pathological condition of the mother . . . when they cannot be safely postponed until the fetus is viable" (*id.* at 694) (quoting from the 1971 Ethical and Religious Directives for Catholic Health Facilities).

Catholic doctrine also regards contraception as a form of homicide. Contraception was treated differently from abortion for the first time in the Second Vatican Council's Declaration on The Church in the Modern World. Noonan, *An Almost Absolute Value in History,* in THE MORALITY OF ABORTION 45–46 (J.T. Noonan ed. 1970). The distinction was short lived, for in 1967, the Minority Report of the Papal Panel on Birth Control, which Pope Paul VI accepted as the basis for his 1968 encyclical Humanae Vitae, described contraception as "analogous to homicide." See N. ST. JOHN-STEVAS, THE AGONISING CHOICE 254 (1971), for the view of one Catholic intellectual protesting the equation of abortion and contraception.

39. Tribe, *The Supreme Court 1972 Term, Foreword: Toward a Model of Roles in the Due Process of Life and Law,* 87 HARV. L. REV. 1, 21 (1973) (citations omitted).

40. The antichoice theologies are explicitly anti-pluralist. The self-proclaimed "moral majority" asserts that "after the Christian majority takes control, pluralism will be seen as immoral and evil and the state will not permit anybody the right to practice evil." Gary Potter, President, Catholics for Political Action, *quoted in* Greene, *The Astonishing Wrongs of the New Moral Right,* PLAYBOY, January 1981, at 118.

Some Catholics ethicists, while adhering to belief that the personhood of the fetus makes abortion a grave sin, oppose use of state power to restrict access to abortion because of respect for individual human freedom in a pluralistic society. Paper by Charles Curran, Professor of Moral Theology, Catholic University of America, presented at NYU Symposium on Abortion and the First Amendment (April 1980) (copy on file with the *University of Pennsylvania Law Review*).

41. Professor Tribe argues against policies giving men a right to veto abortion choice and discusses in moving terms the sex differential aspect of denying access to the means to control reproductive capacity.

> To give men the unreviewable power to sentence women to childbearing and childraising against their will is to delegate a sweeping and unaccountable authority over the lives of others. Any such allocation of roles would operate to the serious detriment of women as a

class, given the multitude of ways in which unwanted pregnancy and unwanted children burden the participation of women as equals in society. Even a woman who is not pregnant would inevitably be affected by her knowledge of the power relations thereby created.

Tribe, *supra* note 39, at 40–41 (footnotes omitted).

Professor Kenneth Karst observes, "Only a lawyer (a male lawyer) could regard laws [regulating pregnancy, abortion, and contraception] as sex-neutral." Karst, at 57, n.320.

42. Fundamentalist Protestant and Mormon opposition to abortion is based on belief in the biblically ordained status of women as subordinate to men. The patriarchal family is the model for all human relations, with God in command of the universe and men in command of the home. The wife must submit to the husband's leadership "and help him fulfill God's will for *his* life." Children must obey teachers; workers obey employers, and citizens obey civil authority. "The lines then descent and converge upon the 'total family'—father first, then mother, then children. The organization chart is entitled 'God's chain of command.'" FitzGerald, *A Reporter At Large: A Disciplined Charging Army,* NEW YORKER, May 18, 1981, at 74.

43. 414 U.S. 632 (1974), at 644.

44. *See generally* Williams, *Firing the Woman to Protect the Fetus: The Reconciliation of Fetal Protection with Employment Opportunity Goals under Title VII,* 69 GEO. L.J. 641, 641–43 (1981).

45. Kahn v. Shevin, 416 U.S. 351 (1974), though not involving a law governing reproductive biology, illustrates the problem. There, the Court upheld a Florida law affording women a maximum tax benefit of $15 per year to compensate them for discrimination in the job market. Taub observes that this "crude brand of compensation they purport to offer women is both inadequate and a distraction from the real problems women face." Taub, at 1692.

46. Williams, at 196.

47. *Id.*

48. *Id. See also* R. ROSENBERG, BEYOND SEPARATE SPHERES: INTELLECTUAL ROOTS OF MODERN FEMINISM (1982).

49. Bradwell v. Illinois, 83 U.S. (16 Wall.) 130, 141 (1873).

50. The abortion-only consent and notification requirements have been directed to physicians. They reflect contempt for the woman as a law-abiding citizen and impose burdens on physicians that exacerbate the shortage and, in many areas, total unavailability, of doctors willing to perform abortions. In 1980, 78 percent of all U.S. counties had no identified providers of abortion services. Henshaw, Forrest, Sullivan and Tietze, *Abortion Services in the United States, 1979 and 1980,* 14 FAM. PLAN. PERSP. 5 (1982).

51. 428 U.S. at 71.

52. 441 U.S. 347 (1979).

53. 441 U.S. 380 (1979).

54. 103 S. Ct. 2985 (1983).

55. 450 U.S. 464 (1981).

V

On Human Dignity:
Commodification and Dehumanization

The rhetoric of the market and the terminology of economics have had a pervasive effect on Western culture and scholarship. Some economists and other scholars argue that economic terminology is useful for analyzing all human interactions and activities, a point of view that commodifies all human life. That is, it conceives of all human interactions as sales, or as analogous to sales or market transactions, and of all human services as commodities or analogous to commodities. Human beings are viewed as market traders, and cost–benefit analysis is basic to evaluating all aspects of life. Science, law, politics, and even psychology and art have been interpreted through the theoretical machinery of economic analysis. The market is perhaps the most prominent metaphor of twentieth-century thought, and its effects are so widespread that we need to be reminded that it is not necessary to think in market terms, that other metaphors are possible. Before the nineteenth century, the market worldview was not so prominent. It was the heyday of Newtonian physics, when everything was a clock. The universe was a clock. God was a clock maker. Governments and businesses were urged to run like clockwork, and human thought was compared to a timepiece. Every era has its metaphor, and today we are encouraged to view the world as a market.

The commodification of human beings has been a topic of debate since the rise of capitalism and the criticism of it by Karl Marx. Marxists (and Marxist feminists) have long argued that it is not a particular kind of sale that is harmful to workers or women but a market economy in general. According to them, the commodification of all workers is inevitable in a capitalist economy. The Marxists' response to the idea of universal commodification is the ideal of universal noncommodification—the view that the market should be abolished.

Both universalist views exist in theory more than in fact. A completely commodified or completely noncommodified society has never actually existed, nor is it clear that either theory can account for all aspects of human life. From a feminist perspective (and a humanist perspective as well), a totally commodified vision of human existence provides a dismal and degrading representation of home and family life, of love and sexuality, indeed, of all personal relations. On the other hand, the Marxist perspective, whatever its virtues, does not seem adequate to capture certain significant points relevant to the condition of women. Among other things, the domination of women took place long before capitalism was a predominant world economy, and their domination continues to endure in communist and socialist countries today.

Some forms of commercial transaction are more harmful or debasing to women than others are, and so it is reasonable to distinguish among kinds of transactions and to determine whether some forms of selling are unacceptable, without condemning all forms. This is a pluralist position, a middle view.

For women, a large part of this determination pertains to selling sex in one form or another, as women have always been primarily valued for their ability to provide sexual and reproductive services. Until recently they were effectively eliminated from the public sphere and consequently were economically dependent on men. Women were not allowed to function as independent units; they always had to be part of a family. Girls were kept by their fathers until given by their fathers to husbands to reproduce sons and daughters of their own. Women were, in that sense, reproductive property.

Economically and technologically, great changes have taken place in the past eighty years or so, and women are now able to maintain independent lives, to support themselves—not necessarily well—but independently nonetheless. What this means is that women no longer have to function as sex objects and dependents (or die). In addition, for women, being a sex object is today a matter of degree or level. Certain levels are perfectly acceptable (although not to feminists) to society at large, are generally rewarded—often highly rewarded—and consequently are difficult to deny. For example, women are encouraged to dress as sex objects, even in business. They are rewarded for doing so and punished for not doing so. Although being a sex object at this level is not directly connected to selling sexual and reproductive services, it may be what makes such sales possible, or at least common.

The direct sales of sexual and reproductive services (especially in the form of prostitution and baby selling) are, however, considered unacceptable and immoral and are usually illegal, even though they are still (at least initially) rewarded. Despite their general prohibition, there is always a market for these sexual services.

At least in an indirect way therefore, virtually all women are treated as sex objects, as providers of sexual and reproductive services, and most view themselves that way as well; that is, they regard their sexual status as normal, inevitable, biological—just the way things are. How does this complex of social conditions affect attitudes toward women and their attitudes toward themselves?

What does it do to a woman to view herself as an object and to be viewed as an object for use or sale? According to existentialist Simone de Beauvoir, being objectified by men is the central problem of all women. Woman is the "Other," the object that men construct. She has always been what men have made of her; thus man is the storyteller. Woman is simply part of his story. De Beauvoir believes that women must take control of their own lives, construct their own identities, and take responsibility for themselves as subjects, despite the limits placed on them by patriarchal institutions.

Radical feminists have generalized this position, seeing the central problem of women as being that the feminine gender itself has been constructed by patriarchy, for the specific purpose of subordinating women to men. Throughout history this purpose has been achieved with such stunning success that we do not even know, nor can we imagine, what the sexes would be like if they were not constructed in a society based on domination and subordination. To be free and equal, radical feminists argue, women must reconstruct their own sexuality, avoiding the influence of patriarchy. According to them, all women are sexual commodities unless and until they consciously reject that role.

But other feminists (including some radical feminists) argue that even if women are sex objects, that does not necessarily make them commodities. Certainly the relation between being a sex object and being a commodity for sale is complex. In some instances the connection is obvious: A prostitute is a sex object for sale, but what about a fashion model? The connection between being a sex object and being a commodity is not so clear in some cases as it is in others.

The same difficulty is found in providing reproductive services. In the past, women were treated as reproductive property (and regarded legally as such), traded and controlled by men for the explicit purpose of producing offspring. But in recent years that relation has become much less clear. Men and women marry voluntarily (even though the social pressure to marry is great), and women now have much more control over procreation. Accordingly, to view all wives as merely providers of sexual and reproductive services is surely too simplistic today. On the other hand, contractual arrangements, such as surrogate mother contracts, explicitly provide reproductive services for pay.

What, if anything, should a society do about regulating or banning the sale of sexual or reproductive services? Can sexual and/or reproductive services be sold without demoralizing the person who sells them? If they are degrading, should they be banned or regulated for that reason? Is it the job of the state to monitor or in some way protect the moral character of its citizens? If so, in what way and with what limits? If not, is there some other reason for banning or regulating such activities? Are they harmful to others or to society at large? Are they the source of regular exploitation or abuse? Some feminists contend that the exploitation of any women as sex objects harms all women by commodifying and thereby dehumanizing women as a group.

In the first chapter in Part V, Margaret Jane Radin considers what factors are relevant to determining market alienability—restrictions on what can be sold. Radin considers first and rejects two universal views: a laissez-faire liberal view calling for universal commodification (i.e., that everything should be open for sale) and an opposing Marxist view for universal noncommodification (i.e., that the market should be abolished). Arguing for a middle view, she then explores and rejects two common grounds, economic analysis and liberal analysis, for distinguishing among things that may and may not be sold. An alternative theory for market inalienability is based on an ideal of human flourishing, which Radin applies to three controversial market activities: prostitution, baby selling, and surrogate motherhood. These provide test cases for principles that might be used for determining when some area of life (such as sex) is suitable for the market.

As Radin notes, the recent practice of surrogate motherhood raises issues with regard to the sale of reproductive services, especially as compared to the widely prohibited practice of baby selling. Selling babies, including commissioned adoption (which is accepting a fee to produce a baby for adoption) is almost universally illegal. Surrogate motherhood (accepting a fee to produce, by artificial insemination, a father's own genetic offspring for adoption) is generally legal. But what exactly is the difference between surrogate mother contracts and contracts to produce a child for adoption? There is no single feminist view on this, but Radin does offer a principled stance for making such evaluations.

Similar comparisons can be made between prostitution and pornography (although Radin does not make them in her article.) Prostitution is widely (although not universally) held to be illegal. Pornography, although once illegal, is now widely available. Both have been described as the provision of sexual services for pay. Both have been condemned as the exploitation of women, and defended as victimless and consensual. Should one be legal and the other illegal? Pornography, but not prostitution has been protected as a form of expression, or free speech. Does that sufficiently explain the difference?

In Chapter 17, Elizabeth Wolgast considers the advantages and disadvantages of restricting pornography and and attempts to show why John Stuart Mill's famous argument in "On Liberty" should not be considered as justifying the protection of pornography.

In the following chapter, Andrea Dworkin looks at the issue of censoring pornography in terms of the equality or exploitation of women and describes the feminist goals that underlie recent antipornography laws. A model antipornography law drafted by Dworkin and Catharine MacKinnon is attached to this chapter.

Like most of the issues raised in Part V, feminists differ in their views on the legality of pornography, and the final chapter argues that pornography should not be banned. This chapter by Nan Hunter and Sylvia Law recognizes that the censorship of pornography is well intentioned among feminists as preventing violence toward and the subordination of women. But this argument plays into the hands of traditionalists who support censorship, in order to maintain traditional male-dominated roles and a sexual double standard. For the traditionalists the censorship crusade is simply part of a larger agenda to reverse the gains of feminists toward the liberation of women, by reintroducing laws and moral standards that prohibit abortion and contraception, block lesbian and gay rights, and restrict equal opportunity in the workplace for women, thereby promoting a return to traditional roles, which they describe as the "protection of family values."

Both feminists for and against the censorship of pornography oppose violence and the subordination of women. Both also hold that the exploration of sexuality is central to the liberation of women and that sexual stereotypes are a major barrier to progress toward sexual equality. Both argue that gender is socially defined. Feminists who oppose pornography say that aggressive and degradingly explicit sexual material reflects and reinforces traditional subordinating definitions of gender and that therefore it should be prohibited as exploiting women. Feminists who oppose censorship contend that censorship precludes the exploration of sexual explicitness and the liberation of women, when the discussion has only recently begun. Although they disagree with each other, both sides challenge the traditional restriction of women, and the construction of gender by patriarchy. The question on both sides is how best to end the subordination of women. Understanding social views of the status of women as commodities, particularly as suppliers of sexual and reproductive services, is central to that task.

16

Market Inalienability

MARGARET JANE RADIN

Since the declaration of "unalienable rights" of persons at the founding of our republic, inalienability has had a central place in our legal and moral culture. Yet there is no one sharp meaning for the term *inalienable*. Sometimes inalienable means nontransferable;[1] sometimes only nonsalable.[2] Sometimes inalienable means nonrelinquishable by a right-holder;[3] sometimes it refers to rights that cannot be lost at all.[4] In this chapter I explore nonsalability, a species of inalienability I call *market inalienability*. Something that is market inalienable is not to be sold, which in our economic system means it is not to be traded in the market.

Controversy over what may be bought and sold—for example, blood or babies—pervades our news. Although some scholars have considered whether such things may be traded in markets, they have not focused on the phenomenon of market inalienability. About fifteen years ago, for example, Richard Titmuss advocated in his book *The Gift Relationship*[5] that human blood should not be allocated through the market; others disagreed.[6] More recently, Elisabeth Landes and Richard Posner suggested the possibility of a thriving market in infants,[7] yet most people continue to believe that infants should not be allocated through the market.[8] What I believe is lacking, and wish to supply, is a general theory that can illuminate these debates. Two possibilities for filling this theoretical gap are traditional liberalism and modern economic analysis, but in this chapter I shall find them both wanting.

The most familiar context of inalienability is the traditional liberal triad: the rights to life, liberty, and property. To this triad, liberalism juxtaposes the most familiar context of alienability: traditional property rights. Although the right to hold property is considered inalienable in traditional liberalism, property rights themselves are presumed fully alienable, and inalienable property rights are exceptional and problematic.

Economic analysis, growing out of the liberal tradition, tends to view all inalienabilities in the way traditional liberalism views inalienable property rights. When it does this, economic analysis holds fast to one strand of traditional liberalism, but it implicitly rejects—or at least challenges—another: the traditional distinction between inalienable and alienable kinds of rights. In conceiving of all rights as property rights that can (at least theoretically) be alienated in markets, economic analysis has (at least in principle) invited markets to fill the social universe. It has invited us to view all inalienabilities as problematic.

In seeking to develop a theory of market inalienability, I argue that inalienabilities should not always be conceived of as anomalies, regardless of whether they attach to things traditionally thought of as property. Indeed, I try to show that the characteristic rhetoric of economic analysis is morally wrong when it is put forward as the sole discourse of human life. My general view deviates not only from the traditional conception of the divide between inalienable and alienable kinds of rights but also from the traditional conception of alienable property. Instead of using the categories of economics or those of traditional liberalism, I think that we should evaluate inalienabilities in connection with our best current understanding of the concept of human flourishing. . .

I. Market Inalienability and Noncommodification

In order to focus effectively on market inalienability and its moral and social significance, it will be helpful first to have an overview of the range of meanings of inalienability, as well as an idea of the framework connecting alienability and commodification.

A. Traditional Meanings

Theorists have seldom recognized that we have no one sharp meaning of inalienability. Nevertheless, the traditional meanings of inalienability share a common core: the notion of alienation as a separation of something—an entitlement, right, or attribute—from its holder. Inalienability negates the possibility of separation. Meanings proliferate because the separation that constitutes alienation can be either voluntary or involuntary and can result in the entitlement, right, or attribute ending up in the hands of another holder, or in its simply being lost or extinguished.[9] Any particular entitlement, right, or attribute may be subject to one or more forms of inalienability.

In one important set of meanings, inalienability is ascribed to an entitlement, right, or attribute that cannot be lost or extinguished. If involuntary loss is its focus, inalienable may mean nonforfeitable or noncancelable; if voluntary loss is its focus, inalienable may mean nonwaivable or nonrelinquishable.

In another important set of meanings, inalienability is ascribed to an entitlement, right, or attribute that cannot be voluntarily transferred from one holder to another. Inalienability in these uses may mean nongiveable, nonsalable, or completely nontransferable. If something is nontransferable, the holder cannot designate a successive holder. Nongiveability and nonsalability are subsets of nontransferability. If something is inalienable by gift, it might be transferred by sale, if it is inalienable by sale, it might be transferred by gift. This nonsalability is what I refer to as market inalienability. Including sales but not gifts, market inalienability places some things outside the marketplace but not outside the realm of social intercourse.

Market inalienability negates a central element of traditional property rights, which are conceived of as fully alienable. But market inalienability differs from the nontransferability that characterizes many nontraditional property rights—entitlements of the regulatory and welfare state—that are both nongiveable and nonsalable.[10] Market inalienability also differs from the inalienability of other things, like voting rights, that seem to be moral or political duties related to a community's normative life; they are subject to broader inalienabilities that preclude loss as well as transfer. Unlike the inalienabilities attaching to welfare entitlements or political duties, market inalienability does not render something inseparable from the person but, rather, specifies that market trading may not be used as a social mechanism of separation. Finally, market inalienability differs from the inalienability of things, like heroin, that are made nontransferable in order to implement a prohibition, because it does not signify that something is social anathema. Indeed, preclusion of sales often coexists with encouragement of gifts. For example, the market inalienability of human organs does not preclude—and, indeed, may seek to foster—transfer from one individual to another by gift.

B. The Commodification Issue

Market inalienability often expresses an aspiration for noncommodification. By making something nonsalable we proclaim that it should not be conceived of or treated as a commodity.[11] When something is noncommodifiable, market trading is a disallowed form of social organization and allocation. We place that thing beyond supply and demand pricing, brokerage and arbitrage, advertising and marketing, stockpiling, speculation, and valuation in terms of the opportunity cost of production.

Market inalienability poses for us more than the binary choice of whether something should be wholly inside or outside the market, completely commodified or completely noncommodified. Some things are completely commodified—deemed suitable for trade in a laissez-faire market. Others are completely noncommodified—removed from the market altogether. But many things can be described as incompletely commodified—neither fully commodified nor fully removed from the market. Thus, we may decide that some things should be market inalienable only to a degree, or only in some aspects.

To appreciate the need to develop a satisfactory analysis of market inalienability, consider the deeply contested issues of commodification that confront us. Infants and children, fetal gestational services, blood, human organs, sexual services, and services of college athletes are some salient things whose commodification is contested. Our division over whether to place a monetary equivalent on a spouse's professional degree or homemaker services in a divorce, or on various kinds of injuries in tort actions, such as loss of consortium, is another form of contest over commodification. Monetization—commodification—of clean air and water is likewise deeply contested. Moreover, debates about some kinds of regulation can be seen as contested incomplete commodification, with the contest being over whether to allow full commodification (a laissez-faire market regime) or something less. If we see the debates this way, residential rent control, minimum wage requirements, and other forms of price regulation, as well as residential habitability requirements, safety regulation, and other forms of product-quality regulation all become contests over the issue of commodification.

How are we to determine the extent to which something ought to be noncommodified, so that we can determine to what extent market inalienability is justified? Because the question asks about the appropriate relationship of particular things to the market, normative theories about the appropriate social role of the market should be helpful in trying to answer it. We can think of such theories as ordered on a continuum stretching from universal noncommodification (nothing in markets) to universal commodification (everything in markets). On this continuum, Karl Marx's theory can symbolize the theoretical pole of universal noncommodification, and Richard Posner's can be seen as close to the opposite theoretical pole. Distributed along the continuum are theorists we may call *pluralists*—those who see a normatively appropriate but limited realm for commodification coexisting with one or more nonmarket realms. Pluralists often see one other normative realm besides that of the market and partition the social world into markets and politics, markets and rights, or markets and families; but pluralists also may envision multiple nonmarket realms. For a pluralist, the crucial question is how to conceive of the permissible scope of the market. An acceptable answer would solve problems of contested commodification.

Pluralism with its crucial question is a main focus of this chapter, because a species of pluralism has been prevalent in liberal thought, and because pluralism is a common-sense position for many people. In order to explore pluralism, both in its traditional form and as it might be reconceived to yield acceptable answers, it will first be necessary to review a modern alternative to pluralism—universal commodification in the form of economic analysis—and the critique of this alternative.

II. Universal Commodification

Under universal commodification, there is no deep question about the appropriate scope of the market, because the market is theoretically all-encompassing. From this point of view, all inalienabilities reduce to market inalienability, and market theory itself, using a market failure analysis, can determine when things should not be bought and sold.

A. The Rhetoric and Methodology of the Market

The term *commodification* can be construed narrowly or broadly. Narrowly construed, commodification describes actual buying and selling (or legally permitted buying and selling) of something. Broadly construed, commodification includes not only actual buying and selling but also market rhetoric, the practice of thinking about interactions as if they were sale transactions, and market methodology, the use of monetary cost–benefit analysis to judge these interactions. Universal commodification embraces this broad construction in its most expansive form, limiting actual buying and selling only by the dictates of market methodology, and solving problems of contested commodification by making everything in principle a commodity.

Universal commodification means that anything some people are willing to sell and others are willing to buy in principle can and should be the subject of free market exchange. Moreover, universal commodification means that everything people need or desire, either individually or in groups, is conceived of as a commodity. "Everything" includes not only those things usually considered goods but also personal attributes, relationships, and states of affairs. Under universal commodification, the functions of government, wisdom, a healthful environment, and the right to bear children are all commodities.[12]

Universal commodification is characterized by universal market rhetoric and universal market methodology. In universal market rhetoric—the discourse of complete commodification—everything that is desired or valued is conceived of and spoken of as a "good." Everything that is desired or valued is an object that can be possessed, that can be thought of as equivalent to a sum of money, and that can be alienated. The person is conceived of and spoken of as the possessor and trader of these goods, and hence all human interactions are sales.

Market methodology includes a cost–benefit analysis, evaluating human actions and social outcomes in terms of actual or hypothetical gains from trade measured in money. Under universal commodification, market trading and its outcomes represent individual freedom and the ideal for individuals and society. Unrestricted choice about what goods to trade represents individual freedom, and maximizing individual gains from trade represents the individual's ideal. All social and political interactions are conceived of as exchanges for monetizable gains. Politics reduces to "rent seeking" by logrolling selfish individuals or groups,[13] and the social ideal reduces to efficiency.

In seeking efficiency through market methodology, universal commodification posits the laissez-faire market as the rule. Laissez faire is presumptively efficient because, under universal commodification, voluntary transfers are presumed to maximize gains from trade, and all human interactions are characterizable as trades. Laissez faire also presumptively expresses freedom, because freedom is defined as free choices of the person seen as trader.

Universal commodification is an archetype, a caricature. Economic analysts do not explicitly embrace it, but some of them, some of the time, implicitly come close. Posner, for example, suggests that everything ought to be ownable and salable, and he often seems to embrace universal market rhetoric and universal market methodology. Posner speaks in market rhetoric when he says that "the prohibition against rape is to the marriage and sex 'market' as the prohibition against theft is to explicit markets in goods and services."[14] Posner uses universal market methodology to suggest that a free market in infants should replace the regulated market (adoption mechanisms) we now have and the black market engendered by evasion of it.

B. Inalienability as a Means of Correcting Market Failure

Universal commodification leads to a characteristic way of understanding inalienability in general and market inalienability in particular. First, no inalienability or restraint on alienation should exist unless market methodology itself requires it. Second, if inalienability is required, it is accounted for in market terms and described in market rhetoric. These two premises combine to produce a transaction costs model of inalienability, in which inalienability is a means of controlling externalities that prevent the market from achieving an efficient result. Third, market inalienability is not seen as a subcategory of inalienability. When one supposes, for purposes of explanation and justification, that every human interaction is a sale, then all inalienabilities collapse into nonsalability.

The transaction costs model is developed by Guido Calabresi and A. Douglas Melamed in their treatment of "inalienability rules." Even though its discussion of inalienability is limited, their article has been seminal for those who conceive of inalienability in the market mode.[15] Calabresi and Melamed divide protection of entitlements into property rules, liability rules, and inalienability. Property rules signify a scheme of free transfers between willing sellers and buyers, with no coerced transfers; liability rules signify a scheme of allowable coerced transfers at market prices set by official entities, such as courts. Calabresi and Melamed argue that property rules are prima facie efficient and therefore desirable. Liability rules are an exception to the property-rule regime, justifiable only when transaction costs of various kinds cause market failures to undermine the prima facie efficiency of property rules. Both the property-rule regime and the exception to it are generated by market methodology and the pursuit of efficiency.

Calabresi and Melamed conceive of inalienability as similarly generated by the pursuite of efficiency In their approach, alienability is prima facie correct or justified, and inalienability must be the exception that proves the rule. Their definition of inalienability collapses all inalienabilities into market inalienability by failing to distinguish between prohibiting all loss or transfer and prohibiting sale. . . .

Later writers have essentially adopted the Calabresi–Melamed analysis. According to Richard Epstein, the only sound justification for inalienability is "the practical control of externalities." As in Calabresi and Melamed's view, inalienability is the exception that proves the market rule;[16] it comes into being only to achieve what the market "would" achieve but cannot, because of various kinds of transaction costs. Epstein's analysis of vote selling as an externality problem reveals the scope of his market methodology and market rhetoric.[17] If an entrepreneur could buy the votes to put herself into public office, Epstein argues, she could then pay off the sellers with public money, thus depleting the common pool of assets for her own gain.[18] This argument relies on the universal commodification version of interest-group pluralism, conceiving of politics as rent seeking by those who put their friends and sympathizers in office in order to line their own pockets.

Although Epstein's theory purportedly rests on libertarian rights as well as economic efficiency,[19] it differs little from Calabresi and Melamed's. Epstein does not recognize distinctions between market inalienability and other forms of inalienability, because for him the only real issue is whether a market is under the circumstances self-defeating so that market results must be achieved by other means. For him, the harms caused by treating rights of persons or citizens (such as voting) as alienable commodities are market types of harm—external costs.

Susan Rose-Ackerman, another scholar who carries forward the view of Calabresi and Melamed, finds three normative rationales for inalienabilities: economic efficiency, "certain specialized distributive goals," and incompatibility of unfettered market processes with "the responsible functioning of a democratic state."[20] Unless one of these is implicated, unfettered market trading is presumptively desirable.[21] The efficiency rationale is a broadened transaction costs analysis, adding information and coordination problems to the more familiar externalities. Inalienabilities are "second-best responses" to these market failures.[22]

Rose-Ackerman does not present a normative framework for evaluating inalienabilities according to distributive justice. The rationale for inalienability based on distribution is "narrowly focused," referring to situations in which an inalienability can be used to single out recipients of a benefit. More generally, Rose-Ackerman argues that using inalienability to achieve distributive goals is unjustified "except to prevent monopoly gains"[23] and that "distributive costs" that arise when efficiency-based restrictions burden a particular group might render the restrictions unjustified.[24] Although her treatment of the distributive rationale thus seems undeveloped relative to efficiency, Rose-Ackerman's is a hybrid analysis. By raising the issue of distributive justice and and by considering the incompatibility of market processes with democratic functioning, she means to combine economic analysis "with a sensitivity to noneconomic ideas."[25] Her argument connecting certain inalienabilities (such as voting) with ideals of citizenship espouses a kind of pluralism, a separation of politics and markets. Nevertheless, it is couched almost exclusively in market rhetoric.

In order to evaluate pluralist positions that are not pluralist in rhetoric, it is necessary to consider the normative role of market rhetoric: Is commodification in rhetoric tantamount to commodification? As background for considering that question, I turn now to the critique of universal commodification.

III. The Critique of Universal Commodification

A traditional critical response to universal commodification, at least since Marx, has been a global rejection of commodification. Universal decommodification or noncommodification maintains that the market ought not to exist and that social interactions involving production and consumption should be reconceived in a nonmarket way. Even if one rejects that ideal, however, as I do because of a problem of transition, the critique of universal commodification offers a crucial insight: A world in which human interactions are conceived of as market trades is different from one in which they are not. Rhetoric is not just shaped by, but shapes, reality.

A. Universal Noncommodification

Universal noncommodification holds that the hegemony of profit-maximizing buying and selling stifles the individual and social potential of human beings through its organization of production, distribution, and consumption and through its concomitant creation and maintenance of the person as a self-aggrandizing profit- and preference maximizer. Anticommodifiers tend to assume that we are living under a regime of universal commodification, with its attendant full-blown market methodology and market rhetoric. They also tend to assume that universal commodification is a necessary concomitant of commodification in the narrower sense—the existence of market transactions under capitalism. Anticommodifiers link rhetoric and reality in their assumption that our material relationships of production and exchange are interwoven with our discourse and our understanding of ourselves and the world.

1. Alienability and Alienation: The Problem of Fetishism. For critics of the market society, commodification simultaneously expresses and creates alienation. The word *alienation* thus harbors an ironic double meaning. Freedom of alienation is the paramount characteristic of liberal property rights, yet Marx saw a necessary connection between this market alienability and human alienation. In his early writings, Marx analyzed the connection between alienation and commodity production in terms of estranged labor; later he introduced the notion of commodity fetishism.[26] In his treatment of estranged labor, Marx portrayed workers' alienation from their own human self-activity as the result of producing objects that became market commodities. By objectifying the labor of the worker, commodities create object bondage and alienate workers from the natural world in and with which they should constitute themselves by creative interaction. Ultimately, laboring to produce commodities turns the worker from a human being into a commodity, "indeed the most wretched of commodities."[27] Marx continued:

> The worker becomes an ever cheaper commodity the more commodities he creates. With the *increasing value* of the world of things proceeds in direct proportion the *devaluation* of the world of men. Labour produces not only commodities; it produces itself and the worker as a *commodity*—and does so in the proportion in which it produces commodities generally.[28]

Commodification brings about an inferior form of human life. As a result of this debasement, Marx concluded that people themselves, not just their institutions, must change in order to live without the market. To reach the postcapitalist stage, "the alteration of men on a mass scale is necessary."[29]

The fetishism of commodities represents a different kind of human subjection to commodities (or a different way of looking at human subjection to commodities).[30] By *fetishism* Marx meant a kind of projection of power and action onto commodities. This projection reflects—but disguises—human social interactions. Relationships between people are disguised as relationships between commodities, which appear to be governed by abstract market forces. I do not decide what objects to produce, rather "the market" does. Unless there is a demand for paperweights, they will have no market value, and I cannot produce them for sale. Moreover, I do not decide what price to sell them for, "the market" does. At market equilibrium, I cannot charge more nor less than my opportunity costs of production without going out of business. In disequilibrium, my price and profit are still set by "the market"; my price depends upon how many of us are supplying paperweights in relation to how many people want to buy them and what they are willing to pay for them. Thus, the market value[31] of my commodity dictates my actions, or so it seems. As Marx put it, "[producers'] own social action takes the form of the action of objects, which rule the producers instead of being ruled by them."[32]

In an analysis that has profoundly influenced many contemporary anticommodifiers, George Lukács, developing Marx's concept of commodity fetishism, found commodification to be "the central, structural problem of capitalist society in all its aspects."[33] Lukács linked the trend to commodify the worker with Weberian "rationalization" of the capitalist structure. The more efficient production becomes, the more fungible are the laborers. Moreover, fungibility becomes pervasive:

> The principle of rational mechanisation and calculability [embraces] every aspect of life. Consumer articles no longer appear as the products of an organic process within a community (as for example in a village community). They now appear, on the one hand, as abstract members of a species identical by definition with its other members and, on the other hand, as isolated objects the possession or nonpossession of which depends on rational calculations.[34]

These falsely objectified commodities are said to be reified. According to Lukács, reification penetrates every level of intellectual and social life. False objectification—false separateness from us—in the way we conceive of our social activities and environment reflects and creates dehumanization and powerlessness. The rhetoric, the discourse in which we conceive of our world, affects what we are and what our world is. For example, Lukács thought that the universal commodification of fully developed capitalism underlies physicalist reductionism in science and the tendency to conceive of matter as external and real.[35] He thought that universal commodification also underlies both our rigid division of the world into subjects versus objects ("the metaphysical dilemma of the relation between 'mind' and 'matter'"),[36] and the "Kantian dilemma" that places objective reason, purportedly the foundation of metaphysics and ethics, in the noumenal realm forever beyond our reach.[37] For Lukács, thought and reality are inextricably linked.[38]

2. Inalienability and Noncommodification: The Problem of Transition. Earlier I noted that market inalienability does not exist as a separate category for universal commodifiers, because nonsalability by definition encompasses the universe of inalienabilities. Likewise, universal noncommodifiers do not distinguish market inalienability as an analytical category. Market inalienability posits a nonmarket realm that appropriately coexists with a market realm, and this implicitly grants some legitimacy to market transactions, contrary to the noncommodifier's premise. Thus, only those who think that market and nonmarket realms legitimately coexist—pluralists—readily recognize market inalienability.

Nevertheless, some who espouse universal noncommodification for the long run might espouse pluralism in the short run, if they think that introducing piecemeal market inalienabilities is a way of making progress toward universal noncommodification. True utopian noncommodifiers, however, would oppose even this interim pluralism; for them, inalienability should be eschewed because it recognizes the legitimacy of alienability, the heart of capitalist property relationships.

I shall call these two approaches to noncommodification *evolutionary* and *revolutionary*. The revolutionary approach criticizes, as misguided and as an artifact of capitalism, the entire worldview that posits a structure of persons versus objects, and alienable versus inalienable objects. It holds that the capitalist structure permeates not only our world of social interaction and allocation of resources but also our discourse, vocabulary, and conception of human flourishing. By contrast, the evolutionary approach, interim pluralism, recognizes the necessity of working within existing market structures of capitalism to achieve universal noncommodification. It differs from the other pluralist views that seek to curtail the scope of the market only in that it does not condone the remaining market order after piecemeal inalienabilities are in place. These two approaches exemplify a pervasive dilemma for social progress: whether and how existing conceptions and structures, such as commodification, can be used now to ensure they will no longer be used in some better future. This is the problem of transition.

The evolutionary approach harbors a transition problem because it does not address how we can progress toward noncommodification using existing social structures and conceptual schemes that are thought to be artifacts of commodification. Partial decommodification in the context of a continuing implicit commitment to a dominant market order may mean that any deviations from the market order will only reinforce commodification, by being seen merely as exceptions that prove the market rule. The revolutionary approach also harbors a transition problem because it does not—indeed, cannot—suppose that we shall somehow arrive all at once in the promised land of total noncommodification. Yet if radical decommodification is attempted for less than everything, it appears evolutionary, not revolutionary, and it may wreak injustice.

The problem of transition for revolutionary decommodification can be illustrated by examining a universal decommodification argument regarding our system of damage remedies in tort law. Richard Abel advocates replacing the tort system with a system that treats people equally, regardless of whether their misfortunes are caused by their own fault, other people's fault, an unavoidable accident, an illness, or a congenital disability.[39] The system should not compensate for damages to property or individual earning power, because such compensation reaffirms and maintains inequality.[40] In addition, it should not compensate for intangible injuries, because this contributes to a cultural view of experience and love as commodities. Damages for pain and suffering "commodify our unique experience;" damages for injuries to relationships, such as loss of consortium or witnessing the injury to a loved one, "commodif[y] love."[41] Abel explains:

> Just as society pays pain and suffering damages to the injured victim who is shunned (so he can purchase the commodified care and companionship that will no longer be given out of love and obligation), so it pays damages to those who loved him, compensating them for their lost "investment" in the relationship (so they can invest in other human capital).[42]

According to Abel, we should not assume that people are willing to undergo suffering or loss for a sum of money, because we should not assume that these capacities are alienable.[43] The assumption is dehumanizing and (if one is true to Marx) a self-fulfilling prophecy, bringing about a human world in which people really are estranged from their essential human capacities. By refusing to allow recovery for these kinds of injuries, we would be saying that human life activity, or at least certain aspects of it, ought not to be traded or to be conceived of in market rhetoric or evaluated in market methodology. Abel's system is thus a revolutionary proposal to decommodify the law of personal injury.

Many people, even some who deplore commodification, will find the proposal troubling and its agenda unjust. To deny money damages, inadequate though they may be, seems to compound the injury to tort victims under the present social structure, in which we have not put into practice other measures that would take care of them in better ways or prevent their injuries in the first place. This piecemeal decommodification appears unjust in its unredeemed context because of the pervasive dilemma of transition. Abel argues that existing conceptions and structures of tort law cannot be used if we are to achieve a more humane social order, but it also seems unjust not to use them during the transition to the imagined better world. This central dilemma of social change recurs in many contexts involving decommodification. Failure to face it satisfactorily is the primary shortcoming of both revolutionary and evolutionary arguments for universal noncommodification. Revolutionary noncommodification might wreak great injustice, and interim pluralism might make no progress.

B. The Moral and Political Role of Rhetoric

Although the problem of transition gives us reason not to accept arguments for universal noncommodification, an implicit but central philosophical commitment of many universal noncommodifiers should be embraced because it plays a necessary role in pluralism as I believe it must now be reconceived. That commitment is the view that our discourse and our reality are interdependent.

"The word is not the thing," we were taught, when I was growing up.[44] Rhetoric is not reality; discourse is not the world. Why should it matter if someone conceptualizes the entire human universe as one giant bundle of scarce goods subject to free alienation by contract, especially if reasoning in market rhetoric can reach the same result that some other kind of normative reasoning reaches on other grounds? Consider three possible answers: It matters because the rhetoric might lead less-than-perfect practitioners to wrong answers in sensitive cases; it matters because the rhetoric itself is insulting or injures personhood regardless of the result; or—the implicit philosophical commitment of the anticommodifiers—it matters because there is no such thing as two radically different normative discourses reaching the "same" result.

1. Risk of Error. The rhetoric of commodification might lead imperfect practitioners to wrong answers, even if the sophisticated practitioner would not be misled. In other words, commodification talk creates a serious risk of error in certain cases. To see this, it may be helpful to compare a normative heuristic like cost–benefit analysis to a flat map of the world. Such a map is easy to use at the point of projection, but difficult and misleading at the edges. Cost–benefit analysis is not difficult when two firms deal with each other, if we define firms as profit-maximizing black boxes and no difficult externalities exist. By contrast, cost–benefit analysis involving people's subjective well-being is difficult to get right when many different people are involved and we are talking about interests they hold dear.[45] For example, the economic analysis of residential rent control could take into account not only the monetary costs to landlords and would-be tenants but also the decline in well-being of tenants who are forced to lose their homes, break up their communities, and endure the frustration, disruption, and other "costs" of moving. But in practice the analysis proceeds differently.[46] Reasoning in market rhetoric, with its characterization of everything that people value as monetizable and fungible, tends to make it easy to ignore these other "costs." Money costs and easily monetizable matters are at the center of the map, and personal and community disruption are at the edges. Because it tends to ignore "costs" that are not readily monetizable, commodification talk tends to err on the side of alienation.

2. Injury to Personhood. In some cases market discourse itself might be antagonistic to interests of personhood. Recall that Posner conceives of rape in terms of a marriage and sex market. Posner concludes that "the prevention of rape is essential to protect the marriage market . . . and more generally to secure property rights in women's persons."[47] Calabresi and Melamed also use market rhetoric to discuss rape.[48] In keeping with their view that "property rules" are prima facie more efficient than "liability rules" for all entitlements, they argue that people should hold a "property rule" entitlement in their own bodily integrity.[49] Further, they explain criminal punishment by the need for an "indefinable kicker," an extra cost to the rapist "which represents society's need to keep all property rules from being changed at will into liability rules."[50] Unlike Posner's view, Calabresi and Melamed's can be understood as pluralist,[51] but like Posner's, their view conceives of rape in market rhetoric. Bodily integrity is an owned object with a price.

What is wrong with this rhetoric? The risk-of-error argument discussed above is one answer. Unsophisticated practitioners of cost–benefit analysis might tend to undervalue the "costs" of rape to the victims. But this answer does not exhaust the problem. Rather, for all but the deepest enthusiast, market rhetoric seems intuitively out of place here, so inappropriate that it is either silly or somehow insulting to the value being discussed.

One basis for this intuition is that market rhetoric conceives of bodily integrity as a fungible object.[52] A fungible object is replaceable with money or other objects; in fact, possessing a fungible object is the same as possessing money. A fungible object can pass in and out of the person's possession without effect on the person as long as its market equivalent is given in exchange.[53] To speak of personal attributes as fungible objects— alienable "goods"—is intuitively wrong. Thinking of rape in market rhetoric implicitly conceives of as fungible something that we know to be personal, in fact conceives of as fungible property something we know to be too personal even to be personal property.[54] Bodily integrity is an attribute and not an object. We feel discomfort or even insult, and we fear degradation or even loss of the value involved, when bodily integrity is conceived of as a fungible object.

Systematically conceiving of personal attributes as fungible objects is threatening to personhood because it detaches from the person that which is integral to the person. Such a conception makes actual loss of the attribute easier to countenance. For someone who conceives bodily integrity as "detached," the same person will remain even if bodily integrity is lost, but if bodily integrity cannot be detached, the person cannot remain the same after loss. Moreover, if my bodily integrity is an integral personal attribute, not a detachable object, then hypothetically valuing my bodily integrity in money is not far removed from valuing *me* in money. For all but the universal commodifier, that is inappropriate treatment of a person.

3. The "Texture of the Human World." The difference between conceiving of bodily integrity as a detached, monetizable object and finding that it is "in fact" detached is not great because there is no bright line separating words and facts. The modern philosophical turn toward coherence or antifoundationalist theories means that we cannot be sanguine about radically different normative discourses reaching the "same" result. Even if everybody agrees that rape should be punished criminally, the normative discourse that conceives of bodily integrity as detached and monetizable does not reach the "same" result as the normative discourse that conceives of bodily integrity as an integral personal attribute. If we accept the gist of the coherence or antifoundationalist theories, facts are not "out there" waiting to be described by a discourse. Facts are theory dependent and value dependent. Theories are formed in words. Fact- and value commitments are present in the language we use to reason and describe, and they shape our reasoning and description, and the shape (for us) of reality itself. Hilary Putnam's striking parable of the super-Benthamites illustrates how a view of values can alter one's view of the facts, the discourse in which one conceives and describes both fact and value, and thus the human world.[55] Putnam asks us to suppose that the continent of Australia is inhabited by people whose sole ethical imperative is that one should always act to maximize "hedonic tone." Because they are single-minded, these people would do what appears to us to be ruthless:

> While they would not cause someone suffering for the sake of the greatest happiness of the greatest number if there were reasonable doubt that *in fact* the consequence of their action would *be* to bring about the greatest happiness of the greatest number, . . . in cases where one knows with certainty what the consequences of the actions would be, they would be willing to . . . torture small children or to condemn people for crimes which they did not commit if the result of these actions would be to increase the general satisfaction level in the long run . . . by any positive [increment], however small.[56]

Putnam says that the difference between us and the super-Benthamites is not merely a disagreement about values. Our disagreement about values will entail disagreement about facts and description of facts. For example, super-Benthamites would realize that sometimes the greatest happiness of the greatest number requires telling a lie; it would not count as dishonest in any pejorative sense to tell lies in order to maximize the general pleasure level. Nor would it be wrong to break promises that would not maximize pleasure if kept. The use of the term *honest* among super-Benthamites would be extremely different from our use of that same descriptive term. Terms like *considerate, good citizen,* or *good person* would likewise be subject to different uses. The vocabulary for describing interpersonal situations would vary greatly between us and the super-Benthamites:

> Not only will they lack, or have altered beyond recognition, many of our descriptive resources, but they will very likely invent new jargon of their own (for example, exact terms for describing hedonic tones) that are unavailable to us. The texture of the human world will begin to change. In the course of time the super-Benthamites and we will end up living in different human worlds.
>
> In short, it will not be the case that we and the super-Benthamites "agree on the facts and disagree about values." In the case of almost all interpersonal situations, the description we give of the facts will be quite different from the description they give of the facts. Even if none of the statements they make about the situation are *false,* their description will not be one that we will count as adequate and perspicuous; and the description we give will not be one that they could count as adequate and perspicuous.

> In short, even if we put aside our "disagreement about the values," we could not regard their total representation of the human world as fully rationally acceptable.[57]

Putnam concludes that the super-Benthamites' inability rightly to comprehend "the way the human world is" results from their "sick conception of human flourishing"—their inferior theory of the good for human beings.

Putnam's parable is relevant to the conceptualization of rape as theft of a property right. It suggests that a particular conception of human flourishing is advanced by this pervasive use of market rhetoric. To think in terms of costs to the victim and her sympathizers versus benefits to the rapist is implicitly to assume that raping "benefits" rapists. Only an inferior conception of human flourishing would regard rape as benefiting the rapist. As a reason for criminalizing rape, Posner blandly says, "Supposing it to be true that some rapists would not get as much pleasure from consensual sex, it does not follow that there are no other avenues of satisfaction open to them."[58] The "pleasure" and "satisfaction" of maintaining one's bodily integrity is commensurate with the "pleasure" and "satisfaction" of someone who invades it. Thus, there could be circumstances in which the satisfactions or "value" to rapists would outweigh the costs or "disvalue" to victims.[59] In those situations rape would not be morally wrong and might instead be morally commendable.

Market rhetoric, if adopted by everyone, and in many contexts, would indeed transform the texture of the human world. This rhetoric leads us to view politics as just rent seeking, reproductive capacity as just a scarce good for which there is high demand, and the repugnance of slavery as just a cost. To accept these views is to accept the conception of human flourishing they imply, one that is inferior to the conception we can accept as properly ours. An inferior conception of human flourishing disables us from conceptualizing the world rightly. Market rhetoric, the rhetoric of alienability of all "goods," is also the rhetoric of alienation of ourselves from what we can be as persons.[60]

One way to see how universal market rhetoric does violence to our conception of human flourishing is to consider its view of personhood. In our understanding of personhood we are committed to an ideal of individual uniqueness that does not cohere with the idea that each person's attributes are fungible, that they have a monetary equivalent, and that they can be traded off against those of other people. Universal market rhetoric transforms our world of concrete persons, whose uniqueness and individuality is expressed in specific personal attributes, into a world of disembodied, fungible, attributeless entities possessing a wealth of alienable, severable "objects." This rhetoric reduces the conception of a person to an abstract, fungible unit with no individuating characteristics.

Another way to see how universal market rhetoric does violence to our conception of human flourishing is to consider its view of freedom. Market rhetoric invites us to see the person as a self-interested maximizer in all respects. Freedom or autonomy, therefore, is seen as individual control over how to maximize one's overall gains. In the extreme, the ideal of freedom is achieved through buying and selling commodified objects in order to maximize monetizable wealth. As we have seen, Marx argued with respect to those who produce and sell commodities that this is not freedom but fetishism; what and how much is salable is not autonomously determined. Whether or not we agree with him, it is not satisfactory to think that marketing whatever one wishes defines freedom. Nor is it satisfactory to think that a theoretical license to acquire all objects one may desire defines freedom. . . .

IV. Pluralism: The Liberal Heritage

As this part outlines, pluralism has been a prominent tenet of traditional liberalism. Nevertheless, as this part also attempts to show, liberal pluralism has borne within it the seeds of universal commodification; indeed, universal commodification is a more coherent liberal position than pluralism. Thus, I ultimately argue that pluralism should now be reconceived.

In order to understand why liberal pluralism should be reconceived, a review of its ideological heritage is necessary. Prominent principles in liberal pluralism include negative liberty, the person as abstract subject, and a conceptual notion of property. These principles are basic to the free market and its institutions, private property and free contract. Negative liberty and the subjectivity of personhood underlie convictions that inalienable things are internal to the person and that inalienabilities are paternalistic. Conceptualism finds alienability to be inherent in the concept of property. These convictions make the case for liberal pluralism uneasy, always threatening to assimilate to universal commodification.

A. Inalienability and the Concept of Property

The legal infrastructure of capitalism—what is required for a functioning laissez-faire market system—includes not merely private property, but private property plus free contract. In order for the exhange system to allocate resources, there must be both private entitlement to resources and permission to transfer entitlements at will to other private owners. Liberal theorists have expressed or reflected this necessity with conceptualist and separatist strategies. In a conceptualist strategy, both necessary characteristics can be incorporated either into the property theory, by claiming that free alienability is inherent in the concept of property, or into the contract theory, by claiming that private entitlement is inherent in the concept of freedom of contract. In a separatist strategy, property and contract split the capitalist indicia between them.

Some writers, such as Hume, Kant, and Hegel, used a separatist strategy to justify private property and free contract. In such discussions the justifications for entitlement and alienability, although separate, are interlocking parts of the same picture. Other writers, such as Mill, used a conceptualist strategy to assert that (market) alienability is inherent in the concept of private property. This argument structure submerges the issue of alienability and makes justification of it seem less necessary: Once property is justified, the task of justifying the market is done.

The conceptualist strategy faces a problem: It cannot consistently admit any inalienabilities without denying that the objects of them are property. A conceptualist cannot admit that ownership is sometimes justified only when the object owned is beyond the reach of the market. John Stuart Mill's property theory illustrates the problem. Mill declared that "included in the idea of private property" is a right of each person "to the exclusive disposal of what he or she have produced by their own exertions, or received either by gift or by fair agreement without force or fraud, from those who produced it."[61] The right of property "includes . . . the freedom of acquiring by contract," because to prevent those who produce things from giving or exchanging them as they wish violates the producers' property rights.[62] Also "implied in property" is the right to whatever a producer can get for her products "in a fair market."[63] Taken together, these declarations establish that Mill's idea of property inherently requires contracts and markets. It would be a logical contradiction for him to postulate inalienable property.

Yet, in other passages, Mill argued for inalienabilities and for restraints on alienation. He argued that the laws of property "have made property of things which never ought to be property, and absolute property where only a qualified property ought to exist."[64] He thought that public offices, monopoly privileges, professional *brevets*—and human beings—should not be considered property. In refusing to countenance certain things as property at all, Mill was able to avoid the contradiction that inalienable property poses for his conceptualism. Saying that some things are not property is one way for a liberal to be a pluralist. But Mill also thought that people could justifiably hold only "qualified," and not "absolute," property rights in land and presumably in other natural resources.[65] Here he could not avoid the contradiction. What he said about property in land implies some inalienability (and some curtailment of the right to exclude others), thus contradicting his general conceptual vision of property.

One who thinks that some things can be "property," but not fully alienable, is a different kind of pluralist from one who holds that some things are not property at all. A conceptualist can be a pluralist by holding that some things are not property at all, but she cannot consistently be a pluralist by holding that some things that are property are not fully alienable. The logical contradiction invites a move from the latter kind of pluralism toward complete commodification: Everything that is property must be fully alienable because property is necessarily suitable for trade in a laissez-faire market. Mill's "qualified" property rights would be qualified only if necessary to avoid externalities that would otherwise create market failure. This position leads to the traditional liberal pluralist picture of a laissez-faire market domain walled off from a few exceptions that are completely removed from the market. It approximates universal commodification if the list of things that cannot be property at all is short.

B. The Subject/Object Dichotomy: The Kantian Person Versus the Thing-in-Itself

Theorists who do not adopt the conceptual strategy avoid the problem of having to view all restraints on the laissez-faire market as incompatible with property. The separatist strategy practiced by Kant and Hegel justifies property and alienability (free contract) based on their connection with freedom and actualization of the person. It asserts that only objects separate from the self are suitable for alienation. The problem confronting this separatist strategy is to distinguish things internal from things external to the person—the subject/object problem.

The subject/object dichotomy metaphysically divides the universe into opposed subjective and objective realms. Kantian personhood is the subject side of the dichotomy. Kantian persons are essentially abstract, fungible units with identical capacity for moral reason and no concrete individuating characteristics.[66] They are units of pure subjectivity acting in and upon the world of objects. Pluralism based on this conception of the person founders in trying to draw the distinction between persons and objects; once it does, it gravitates toward universal commodification. The Kantian conception of personhood makes us all interchangeable and thus facilitates liberal political equality. But by postulating such a world of fungible, subjective, autonomous units, it also facilitates conceiving of concrete personal attributes as commodified objects.

The difficulties caused by Kantian personhood can be seen by examining the German theory of property and contract, in which entitlement and alienability are separately justified, relying on the subject/object dichotomy. For Kant and Hegel, private property is necessary to realize or actualize the will of a person in order to achieve freedom.[67] The German theory posited that in order to be free and well-developed selves, we must be able to alienate external things and we must not be able to alienate internal things. For Hegel, alienability of property (both transfer and relinquishment) was not inherent in the concept of property but, rather, followed from the premise that the presence of a person's will makes something property:

> The reason I can alienate my property is that it is mine only in so far as I put my will into it. Hence I may abandon . . . anything that I have or yield it to the will of another . . . provided always that the thing in question is a thing external by nature.[68]

It followed that whatever is mine but is *not* "a thing external by nature" will be inalienable (nonrelinquishable and nontransferable). Substantive characteristics of personality are not things external by nature and are hence inalienable.[69]

In order to apply this Hegelian argument to delineate inalienabilities, then, we need to draw clearly the distinction between things external by nature and substantive constitutive elements of personality. If something is external by nature, it must be propertizable and alienable so that persons can achieve freedom and proper self-development. If something is a substantive characteristic of personality, it must be inalienable for the same reasons. Thus, inalienability is either required or proscribed, and the decision turns on the distinction between external things and substantive characteristics.

By "things external by nature," Hegel meant objects in the environment that have (or can be thought to have) an existence independent of our will.[70] The initial gulf between the abstract will of the person and the world of unowned objects expresses the dichotomy between subject and object. The gulf between subject and object creates practical problems in deciding which items belong on which side of the divide; there are cases in which it does not seem intuitively obvious even to one who thinks the subject/object dichotomy itself is intuitively obvious. . . .

If the person/thing distinction is to be treated as a bright line that divides the commodifiable from the inalienable, we must know exactly which items are part of the person and which not. The person/thing distinction and its consequences seemed obvious to Kant and Hegel, but such is not the case for many modern philosophers. One who accepts the arguments of modern writers like Kuhn and Rorty[71]—and of Lukács before them—rejects the metaphysical bright line between what is inside us, in our minds, and some realm of things-in-themselves, a mind-independent reality outside of us. Without the bright line, arguments delineating the market realm on the basis of the subject/object distinction disintegrate. If the person/thing distinction is not a sharp divide, neither is inalienability/alienability. There will be a gray area between the two, and hence the outer contours of both personhood and inalienabilities based on personhood will remain contested.

Pluralism's problematic reliance on the subject/object distinction can be submerged under universal commodification. Kantian notions of abstract personhood, particularly the conceptions of personhood as autonomous moral agency and persons as completely interchangeable units of subjective will, undergird liberal political ideals: equal treatment of persons as ends, not means; equality before the law; one person, one vote; and the rule of law.[72] These principles were the Enlightenment's great achievements, but a pull toward universal commodification seems to be the dark side of Kantian personhood. If the person is simply pure subjectivity empty of individuating characteristics and personal attributes, then these characteristics and attributes are readily conceived of as separate from the person and possessed by the person. From the view that attributes and characteristics are separate possessions, it is an easy step to conceptualize them as lying on the object side of the subject/object divide. This eliminates inalienabilities based on things internal to the person, because nothing is internal to the person considered as an abstract, subjective unit. Once individuating characteristics and personal attributes are conceptualized as possessions situated in the object realm, it is another easy step to conceive of them as separable from the person through alienation. Finally, once characteristics and attributes are seen as alienable objects, it is not difficult to see them as fungible and bearing implicit money value. Kant no doubt would have abhorred this result; nevertheless, universal commodification seems to be facilitated—though not entailed—by his definition of the person. The subject/object problem pulls pluralism toward universal commodification because there is no obvious stopping place short of that.

C. Negative Liberty

Two theories about freedom are central to the ideological framework in which we view inalienability: the notion that freedom means negative liberty[73] and the notion that (negative) liberty is identical with, or necessarily connected to, free alienability of everything in markets. The conception of freedom as negative liberty gives rise to the view that all inalienabilities are paternalistic limitations on freedom. The idea that liberty consists in alienability of everything in markets clashes with substantive requirements of personhood, making it difficult, for example, to argue against human commodification. In general, the commitment to negative liberty, like the commitment to the Kantian structure of persons versus objects, has caused confusion in liberal pluralism and has exerted a pull toward universal commodification.

Inalienabilities are often said to be paternalistic.[74] Paternalism usually means to substitute the judgment of a third party or the government for that of a person on the ground that to do so is in that person's best interests. For advocates of negative liberty, to substitute someone else's choice for my own is a naked infringement of my liberty. Freedom means doing (or not doing) whatever I as an individual prefer at the moment, as long as I am not harming other people. To think of inalienability as paternalism assumes that freedom is negative liberty—that people would choose to alienate certain things if they could but are restrained from doing so by moral or legal rules saying, in effect, that they are mistaken about what is good for them.

To say that inalienabilities involve a loss of freedom also assumes that alienation itself is an act of freedom or is freedom enhancing. Someone who holds this view and conceives of alienation as sale through free contract is deeply committed to commodification as expressive of—perhaps necessary for—human freedom. Insofar as theories of negative freedom are allied to universal commodification, so are traditional discussions of inalienability in terms of paternalism. If we reject the notion that freedom means negative liberty and the notion that liberty and alienation in markets are identical or necessarily connected, then inalienability will cease to seem inherently paternalistic. If we adopt a positive view of liberty that includes proper self-development as necessary for freedom, then inalienabilities needed to foster that development will be seen as freedom enhancing rather than as impositions of unwanted restraints on our desires to transact in markets.

Joel Feinberg's discussion of the inalienable right to life[75] illustrates the traditional

link between inalienability and paternalism, as well as the tension caused by the clash
between negative liberty and substantive requirements of personhood. Feinberg distinguishes three conceptions of the inalienable right to life, which he calls "the paternalist,"
"the founding fathers," and "the extreme antipaternalist."[76] In the view he calls paternalist, to say that the right to life is inalienable means that it is a nonrelinquishable mandatory right, one that ought to be exercised, like the right to education.[77] In contrast, the
view that Feinberg attributes to the Founding Fathers holds that the inalienable right to
life is a nonrelinquishable discretionary right. It is discretionary because the individual
may choose whether to exercise it. For example, the right to own property is a discretionary right because I may choose to own nothing; it is a nonrelinquishable discretionary
right because I cannot morally or legally renounce the right to own property even if I
choose not to own any.[78] Feinberg concludes that the nonrelinquishable right to life is
discretionary, not mandatory:

> We have a right, within the boundaries of our own autonomy, to live or die, as we
> choose. . . . [T]he basic right underlying each is the right to be one's own master, to
> dispose of one's own lot as one chooses, subject of course to the limits imposed by the
> like rights of others. . . . In exercising my own choice in these matters, I am not
> renouncing, abjuring, forswearing, resigning, or relinquishing my right to life; quite the
> contrary, I am *acting* on that right by exercising it one way or the other.[79]

This passage suggests that the right to life is discretionary because it is parasitic on negative liberty. But Feinberg does not say whether the underlying right to be one's own master is mandatory or discretionary. The omission points to an apparent contradiction in
the argument, a contradiction that stems from a commitment to negative liberty. If the
discretionary right to life is nonrelinquishable, as Feinberg claims is the Founding
Fathers' view, then we can infer that the "basic right" to have discretion—liberty—must
be mandatory: One cannot choose not to be one's own master, not to dispose of one's lot
as one chooses. But to attribute this mandatory conception of liberty to the Founding
Fathers would apparently be to attribute to them a form of positive liberty, a view that
people can be required to be free. Hence, Feinberg attributes to the Founding Fathers a
discretionary, not mandatory, view of the right to liberty. But if the right to liberty is
indeed discretionary, then it seems I could choose not to be my own master, not to dispose
of my lot as I choose, just as I could choose not to own property. And if I could choose
that, I could choose not to have any of the other parasitic nonrelinquishable rights, like
the right to life. The right to life would then be relinquishable.

  This contradiction shows why a commitment to negative liberty pulls liberal pluralists
toward universal commodification. The commitment to negative liberty usually attributed to the Founding Fathers forces those who hold it to choose between submerging a
contradiction and moving toward conceiving of everything as relinquishable. If the intellectual descendants of the Founding Fathers want to maintain a nonrelinquishable discretionary right to life, they must adopt a mandatory right to liberty: We are not free not
to be free. But adopting a mandatory right moves toward positive liberty, undermining
the negative view that generates the nonrelinquishable, but discretionary, right to life.
Holding firm to the view that liberty means negative liberty leads to a view that everything, including one's life, is relinquishable.

  In this latter view, that of Feinberg's "extreme antipaternalist," the fully informed
autonomous individual could sell herself into slavery or sell her right to life. Thus, the
antipaternalist is a universal commodifier. This appears to be a more cogent view, once

we grant that rights to life and property are parasitic upon an inalienable, but nonmandatory, right to negative liberty.

Might one hold fast to negative liberty and—contrary to the argument I have just given—still claim we are not free not to be free? This difficulty is the root of the tension between pluralism and negative liberty, and of the consequent pressure to give up pluralism.

Mill's well-known attempt to argue against freedom to sell oneself into slavery directly poses this difficulty:

> By selling himself for a slave, [a person] abdicates his liberty; he foregoes any future use of it beyond that single act. He therefore defeats, in his own case, the very purpose which is the justification of allowing him to dispose of himself. . . . The principle of freedom cannot require that he should be free not to be free. It is not freedom, to be allowed to alienate his freedom.[80]

The argument is obscure. It is hard to see why Mill thought it obvious that the principle of negative freedom could not require the "freedom not to be free"; only positive freedom clearly holds that a person must be free. In general, what in Mill's view is the connection between free alienation and freedom? (Why is alienation of freedom "not freedom"?) Most commentators have viewed Mill's argument against selling off one's freedom as a lapse into paternalism.[81]

Neither in his conception of freedom nor in his conception of alienability does Mill appear to explain why human beings are noncommodifiable. One could understand him to imply that there is an unstated divide between the realm of the market (free trade) and the realm of politics (liberty). People must be free in order for a free political order to exist; they cannot be free without such a political order; hence in the nonmarket realm they cannot, without contradiction, be free not to be free. This reconstruction makes Mill a pluralist, as indeed he apparently wished to be, but the reading is not very true to Mill in the way it relinquishes negative liberty.

Again, one way to avoid Mill's problem is to espouse universal commodification. The universal commodifier can hold on to negative liberty and avoid Mill's problem—espousing negative liberty while eschewing voluntary enslavement—because under universal commodification freedom itself is seen as monetizable and alienable. Those who tend toward universal commodification may indeed endorse voluntary enslavement.[82] Those who declare human beings noncommodifiable must do so on the ground of postulated market failure (for example, transaction costs).

We can now see why liberal pluralism should be reconceived. If we are to avoid the tendency toward universal commodification inherent in liberal pluralism, we must cease thinking that market alienability is inherent in the concept of property, and we must modify pluralism's commitments to negative liberty and Kantian personhood. In doing so, we must find a satisfactory way of deciding what market inalienabilities are justified by the need to protect and foster personhood, and a way of understanding why these inalienabilities seem to us to be freedom enhancing.

V. Toward an Evolutionary Pluralism

In this part, I develop a pluralist view that differs in significant respects from liberal pluralism. My central hypothesis is that market inalienability is grounded in noncommodification of things important to personhood. In an ideal world markets would not necessarily be abolished, but market inalienability would protect all things important to personhood. But we do not live in an ideal world. In the nonideal world we do live in, market inalienability must be judged against a background of unequal power. In that world it may sometimes be better to commodify incompletely than not to commodify at all. Market inalienability may be ideally justified in light of an appropriate conception of human flourishing and yet sometimes be unjustifiable because of our nonideal circumstances.

A. Noncommodification and the Ideal of Human Flourishing

1. Rethinking Personhood: Freedom, Identity, Contextuality. Because of the ideological heritage of the subject/object dichotomy, we tend to view things internal to the person as inalienable and things external as freely alienable. Because of the ideological heritage of negative liberty, we also tend to think of inalienabilities as paternalistic. A better view of personhood, one that does not conceive of the self as pure subjectivity standing wholly separate from an environment of pure objectivity, should enable us to discard both the notion that inalienabilities relate only to things wholly subjective or internal and the notion that inalienabilities are paternalistic.

In searching for such a better view, it is useful to single out three main, overlapping aspects of personhood: freedom, identity, and contextuality. The freedom aspect of personhood focuses on will, or the power to choose for oneself. In order to be autonomous individuals, we must at least be able to act for ourselves through free will in relation to the environment of things and other people. The identity aspect of personhood focuses on the integrity and continuity of the self required for individuation. In order to have a unique individual identity, we must have selves that are integrated and continuous over time. The contextuality aspect of personhood focuses on the necessity of self-constitution in relation to the environment of things and other people. In order to be differentiated human persons, unique individuals, we must have relationships with the social and natural world.

A better view of personhood—a conception of human flourishing that is superior to the one implied by universal commodification—should present more satisfactory views of personhood in each of these three aspects. I am not seeking here to elaborate a complete view of personhood. Rather, I focus primarily on a certain view of contextuality and its consequences: the view that connections between the person and her environment are integral to personhood. I also suggest that to the extent we have already accepted certain views of freedom, identity, and contextuality, we are committed to a view of personhood that rejects universal commodification.

Universal commodification conceives of freedom as negative liberty, indeed as negative liberty in a narrow sense, construing freedom as the ability to trade everything in free markets. In this view, freedom is the ability to use the will to manipulate objects in order to yield the greatest monetizable value. Although negative liberty has had difficulty with the hypothetical problem of free choice to enslave oneself, even negative liberty can reject the general notion of commodification of persons: The person cannot be an entity exercising free will if it is a manipulable object of monetizable value.

A more positive meaning of freedom starts to emerge if one accepts the contextuality aspect of personhood. Contextuality means that physical and social contexts are integral to personal individuation, to self-development. Even under the narrowest conception of negative liberty, we would have to bring about the social environment that makes trade possible in order to become the persons whose freedom consists in unfettered trades of commodified objects. Under a broader negative view that conceives of freedom as the ability to make oneself what one will, contextuality implies that self-development in accordance with one's own will requires one to will certain interactions with the physical and social context because context can be integral to self-development. The relationship between personhood and context requires a positive commitment to act so as to create and maintain particular contexts of environment and community. Recognition of the need for such a commitment turns toward a positive view of freedom, in which the self-development of the individual is linked to pursuit of proper social development and in which proper self-development, as a requirement of personhood, could in principle sometimes take precedence over one's momentary desires or preferences.

Universal commodification undermines personal identity by conceiving of personal attributes, relationships, and philosophical and moral commitments as monetizable and alienable from the self. A better view of personhood should understand many kinds of particulars—one's politics, work, religion, family, love, sexuality, friendships, altruism, experiences, wisdom, moral commitments, character, and personal attributes—as integral to the self. To understand any of these as monetizable or completely detachable from the person—to think, for example, that the value of one person's moral commitments is commensurate or fungible with those of another or that the "same" person remains when her moral commitments are subtracted—is to do violence to our deepest understanding of what it is to be human.

To affirm that work, politics, or character is integral to the person is not to say that persons cease to be persons when they dissociate themselves from their jobs, political engagements, or personal attributes. Indeed, the ability to dissociate oneself from one's particular context seems integral to personhood. But if we must recognize the importance of the ability to detach oneself, we must recognize as well that interaction with physical and social contexts is also integral to personhood. One's surroundings—both people and things—can become part of who one is, of the self. From our understanding that attributes and things can be integral to personhood, which stems mainly from our understanding of identity and contextuality, and from our rejection of the idea of commodification of the person, which stems mainly from our understanding of freedom, it follows that those attributes and things identified with the person cannot be treated as completely commodified. Hence, market inalienability may attach to things that are personal.

2. Protecting Personhood: Noncommodification of Personal Rights, Attributes, and Things. In my discussion of possible sources of dissatisfaction with thinking of rape in market terms, I suggested that we should not view personal things as fungible commodities. We are now in a better position to understand how conceiving of personal things as commodities does violence to personhood, and to explore the problem of knowing what things are personal.

To conceive of something personal as fungible assumes that the person and the attribute, right, or thing, are separate. This view imposes the subject/object dichotomy to create two kinds of alienation. If the discourse of fungibility is partially made one's own, it creates disorientation of the self that experiences the distortion of its own personhood. For example, workers who internalize market rhetoric conceive of their own labor as a commodity separate from themselves as persons; they dissociate their daily life from their own self-conception. To the extent the discourse is not internalized, it creates alienation between those who use the discourse and those whose personhood they wrong in doing so. For example, workers who do not conceive of their labor as a commodity are alienated from others who do because, in the workers' view, people who conceive of their labor as a commodity fail to see them as whole persons.

To conceive of something personal as fungible also assumes that persons cannot freely give of themselves to others. At best they can bestow commodities. At worst—in universal commodification—the gift is conceived of as a bargain. Conceiving of gifts as bargains not only conceives of what is personal as fungible, it also endorses the picture of persons as profit maximizers. A better view of personhood should conceive of gifts not as disguised sales but, rather, as expressions of the interrelationships between the self and others. To relinquish something to someone else by gift is to give of yourself. Such a gift takes place within a personal relationship with the recipient, or else it creates one. Commodification stresses separateness both between ourselves and our things and between ourselves and other people. To postulate personal interrelationship and communion requires us to postulate people who can yield personal things to other people and not have them instantly become fungible. Seen this way, gifts diminish separateness. This is why (to take an obvious example) people say that sex bought and paid for is not the same "thing" as sex freely shared. Commodified sex leaves the parties as separate individuals and perhaps reinforces their separateness; they only engage in it if each individual considers it worthwhile. Noncommodified sex ideally diminishes separateness; it is conceived of as a union because it is ideally a sharing of selves.

Not everything with which someone may subjectively identify herself should be treated legally or morally as personal. Otherwise the category of personal things might collapse into "consumer surplus": Anything to which someone attached high subjective value would be personal. The question whether something is personal has a normative aspect: Whether identifying oneself with something—constituting oneself in connection with that thing—is justifiable. What makes identifying oneself with something justifiable, in turn, is an appropriate connection to our conception of human flourishing. More specifically, such relationships are justified if they can form part of an appropriate understanding of freedom, identity, and contextuality. A proper understanding of contextuality, for example, must recognize that, although personhood is fostered by relations with people and things, it is possible to be involved too much, or in the wrong way, or with the wrong things.

To identify something as personal, it is not enough to observe that many people seem to identify with some particular kind of thing because we may judge such identification to be bad for people. An example of a justifiable kind of relationship is people's involvement with their homes. This relationship permits self-constitution within a stable environment. An example of an unjustifiable kind of relationship is the involvement of the robber baron with an empire of "property for power."[83] The latter is unjustified because it ties into a conception of the person we can recognize as inferior: the person as self-interested maximizer of manipulative power.[84]

There is no algorithm or abstract formula to tell us which items are (justifiably) personal. A moral judgment is required in each case. We have seen that Hegel's answer to a similar problem was to fall back on the intuition that some things are "external" and some are "internal." This answer is unsatisfactory because the categories "external" and "internal" should be the conclusion of a moral evaluation and cannot be taken as obvious premises forming its basis. First we must judge whether persons can still be persons if X is considered severable from them; if we judge that they can, we then could call X external. Hegel's solution is also unsatisfactory because (at least from our present vantage point) we can see that the external/internal distinction is a continuum and not a bright-line dichotomy. Both the tendency to take external and internal as premises rather than moral conclusions and the tendency to see a bright line between external and internal are traceable to the prevailing world view that posits persons as subjects in a world of objects. This worldview makes it seem intuitively obvious that a thing must be either purely subjective or purely objective, and intuitively obvious into which category it falls. I am suggesting that we relinquish the subject/object dichotomy and rely instead on our best moral judgment in light of the best conception of personhood as we now understand it.

B. Methods of Justifying Market Inalienabilities

If some people wish to sell something that is identifiably personal, why not let them? In a market society, whatever some people wish to buy and others wish to sell is deemed alienable. Under these circumstances, we must formulate an affirmative case for market inalienability, so that no one may choose to make fungible—commodify—a personal attribute, right, or thing. In this section, I propose and evaluate three possible methods of justifying market inalienability based on personhood: a prophylactic argument, assimilation to prohibition, and a domino theory.

The method of justification that correlates most readily with traditional liberal pluralism is a *prophylactic argument.* For the liberal it makes sense to countenance both selling and sharing of personal things as the holder freely chooses. If an item of property is personal, however, sometimes the circumstances under which the holder places it on the market might arouse suspicion that her act is coerced. Given that we cannot know whether anyone really intends to cut herself off from something personal by commodifying it, our suspicions might sometimes justify banning sales. The risk of harm to the seller's personhood in cases in which coerced transactions are permitted (especially if the thing sought to be commodified is normally very important to personhood), and the great difficulties involved in trying to scrutinize every transaction closely, may sometimes outweigh the harm that a ban would impose on would-be sellers who are in fact uncoerced. A prophylactic rule aims to ensure free choice—negative liberty—by the best possible coercion-avoidance mechanism under conditions of uncertainty.[85] This prophylactic argument is one way for a liberal to justify, for example, the ban on selling oneself into slavery. We normally view such commodification as so destructive of personhood that we would readily presume all instances of it to be coerced. We would not wish, therefore, to have a rule creating a rebuttable presumption that such transactions are uncoerced (as with ordinary contracts), nor even a rule that would scrutinize such transactions case by case for voluntariness, because the risk of harm to personhood in the coerced transactions we might mistakenly see as voluntary is so great that we would rather risk constraining the exercise of choice by those (if any) who really wish to enslave themselves.

A liberal pluralist might use a prophylactic justification to prevent poor people from selling their children, sexual services, or body parts. The liberal would argue that an appropriate conception of coercion should, with respect to selling these things, include the desperation of poverty.[86] Poor people should not be forced to give up personal things because the relinquishment diminishes them as persons, contrary to the liberal regime of respect for persons. We should presume that such transactions are not the result of free choice.

When thus applied to coercion by poverty, the prophylactic argument is deeply troubling. If poverty can make some things nonsalable because we must prophylactically presume such sales are coerced, we would add insult to injury if we then do not provide the would-be seller with the goods she needs or the money she would have received. If we think respect for persons warrants prohibiting a mother from selling something personal to obtain food for her starving children, we do not respect her personhood more by forcing her to let them starve instead. To the extent it equates poverty with coercion, the prophylactic argument requires a corollary in welfare rights. Otherwise we would be forcing the mother to endure a devastating loss in her primary relationship (with her children) rather than in the secondary one (with the personal thing) she is willing to sacrifice to protect the primary one. It is as if, when someone is coerced at gunpoint, we were to direct our moral opprobrium at the victim rather than the gun wielder, and our enforcement efforts at preventing the victim from handing over her money rather than at preventing the gun wielder from placing her in the situation where she must. Thus, this aspect of liberal prophylactic pluralism is hypocritical without a large-scale redistribution of wealth and power that seems highly improbable. Although we may nevertheless decide to ban sales of certain personal things, the prophylactic argument, insofar as it rests on equating poverty with coercion, cannot be the reason.

A second method of justifying market inalienability assimilates it to prohibition. If we accept that the commodified object is different from the "same" thing noncommodified and embedded in personal relationships, then market inalienability is a prohibition of the commodified version, resting on some moral requirement that it not exist. What might be the basis of such a moral requirement? Something might be prohibited in its market form because it both creates and exposes wealth- and class-based contingencies for obtaining things that are critical to life itself—for example, health care—and thus undermines a commitment to the sanctity of life. Another reason for prohibition might be that the use of market rhetoric, in conceiving of the "good" and understanding the interactions of people respecting it, creates and fosters an inferior conception of personhood (one allied to the extreme view of negative freedom) if we suppose people may freely choose to commodify themselves.

The prohibition argument—that commodification of things is bad in itself, or because these things are not the "same" things that would be available to people in nonmarket relationships—leads to universal noncommodification. If commodification is bad in itself, it is bad for everything. Any social good is arguably "different" if not embedded in a market society. To restrict the argument in order to permit pluralism, we have to accept either that certain things are the "same" whether or not they are bought and sold, and others are "different" or that prohibiting the commodified version morally matters only for certain things, but not for all of them. At present we tend to think that nuts and bolts are pretty much the same whether commodified or not, whereas love, friendship, and sexuality are very different; we also tend to think that trying to keep society free of commodified love, friendship, and sexuality morally matters more than trying to keep it free of commodified nuts and bolts.

A third method of justifying market inalienability, the domino theory, envisions a slippery slope leading to market domination. The domino theory assumes that for some things, the noncommodified version is morally preferable; it also assumes that the commodified and noncommodified versions of some interactions cannot coexist. To commodify some things is simply to preclude their noncommodified analogues from existing. Under this theory, the existence of some commodified sexual interactions will contaminate or infiltrate everyone's sexuality so that all sexual relationships will become commodified. If it is morally required that noncommodified sex be possible, market inalienability of sexuality would be justified. This result can be conceived of as the opposite of a prohibition: There is assumed to exist some moral requirement that a certain "good" be socially available. The domino theory thus supplies an answer (as the prohibition theory does not) to the liberal question why people should not be permitted to choose both market and nonmarket interactions: The noncommodified version is morally preferable when we cannot have both.

We can now see how the prohibition and domino theories are connected. The prohibition theory focuses on the importance of excluding from social life commodified versions of certain "goods"—such as love, friendship, and sexuality—whereas the domino theory focuses on the importance for social life of maintaining the noncommodified versions. The prohibition theory stresses the wrongness of commodification—its alienation and degradation of the person—and the domino theory stresses the rightness of noncommodification in creating the social context for the proper expression and fostering of personhood. If one explicitly adopts both prongs of this commitment to personhood, the prohibition and domino theories merge.

The argument that market inalienabilities are necessary to encourage altruism relies upon the domino theory. With regard to human blood, Richard Titmuss argues that a regime permitting only donation fosters altruism. The altruistic experience of the donor in being responsible (perhaps) for saving a stranger's life is said to bring us closer together, cementing our community in a way that buying and selling cannot.[87] The possibility of reciprocity is also a part of this cementing process, because a donor's sense of obligation could be partially founded on the recognition that she could be a recipient some day. From the recipient's perspective, it is said that knowing one is dependent on others' altruism rather than on one's own wealth creates solidarity and interdependence and that this knowledge of dependence better preserves and expresses the ideal of sanctity of life. But why do we need to forbid sales to preserve opportunities for altruism for those who wish to give? In a gifts-only regime, a donor's gift remains nonmonetized, whereas if both gifts and sales are permitted, the gift has a market value. This market value undermines our altruism and discourages us from giving, the argument runs, because our gift is now equivalent merely to giving $50 (or whatever is the market price of a pint of blood) to a stranger, rather than life or health.

The "domino" part of this argument—that once something is commodified for some it is willy-nilly commodified for everyone—posits that once market value enters our discourse, market rhetoric will take over and characterize every interaction in terms of market value. If this is true, some special things (for example, blood) must be completely noncommodified if altruism is to be possible. But the feared domino effect of market rhetoric need not be true. To suppose that it must necessarily be true seems to concede to universal commodification the assumption that thinking in money terms comes "naturally" to us. Most people would probably think the assumption false in light of their common experience. For example, many people value their homes or their work in a nonmonetary way, even though those things also have market value.

Rather than merely assuming that money is at the core of every transaction in "goods," thereby making commodification inevitable and phasing out the noncommodified version of the "same" thing (or the nonmarket aspects of sale transactions), we should evaluate the domino theory on a case-by-case basis. We should assess how important it is to us that any particular contested thing remain available in a noncommodified form and try to estimate how likely it is that allowing market transactions for those things would engender a domino effect and make the nonmarket version impossible. This might involve judging how close to universal commodification our consciousness really is and how this consciousness would affect the particular thing in question.

C. The Problem of Nonideal Evaluation

One ideal world would countenance no commodification; another would insist that all harms to personhood are unjust; still another would permit no relationships of oppression or disempowerment. But we are situated in a nonideal world of ignorance, greed, and violence, of poverty, racism, and sexism. In spite of our ideals, justice under nonideal circumstances, pragmatic justice, consists in choosing the best alternative now available to us. In doing so we may have to tolerate some things that would count as harms in our ideal world. Whatever harms to our ideals we decide we must now tolerate in the name of justice may push our ideals that much farther away. How are we to decide, now, what is the best transition toward our ideals, knowing that our choices now will help to reconstitute those ideals?

The possible avenues for justifying market inalienability must be reevaluated in light of our nonideal world. In light of the desperation of poverty, a prophylactic market inalienability may amount merely to an added burden on would-be sellers; under some circumstances we may judge it, nevertheless, to be our best available alternative. We might think that both nonmarket and market interactions can exist in some situations without a domino effect leading to a more commodified order, or we might think it is appropriate to risk a domino effect in light of the harm that otherwise would result to would-be sellers. We might find prohibition of sales not morally warranted, on balance, in some situations, unless there is a serious risk of a domino effect. These will be pragmatic judgments.

1. The Double Bind. Often commodification is put forward as a solution to powerlessness or oppression, as in the suggestion that women be permitted to sell sexual and reproductive services. But is women's personhood injured by allowing or by disallowing commodification of sex and reproduction? The argument that commodification empowers women is that recognition of these alienable entitlements will enable a needy group— poor women—to improve their relatively powerless, oppressed condition, an improvement that would be beneficial to personhood. If the law denies women the opportunity to be comfortable sex workers and baby producers instead of subsistence domestics, assemblers, clerks, and waitresses—or pariahs (welfare recipients) and criminals (prostitutes)—it keeps them out of the economic mainstream and hence the mainstream of American life.

The rejoinder is that on the contrary, commodification will harm personhood by powerfully symbolizing, legitimating, and enforcing class division and gender oppression. It will create the two forms of alienation that correlate with commodification of personal things. Women will partly internalize the notion that their persons and their attributes are separate, thus creating the pain of a divided self. To the extent that this self-conception is not internalized, women will be alienated from the dominant order that, by allowing commodification, sees them in this light. Moreover, commodification will exacerbate, not ameliorate, oppression and powerlessness, because of the social disapproval connected with marketing one's body.

But the surrejoinder is that noncommodification of women's capabilities under current circumstances represents not a brave new world of human flourishing but, rather, a perpetuation of the old order that submerges women in oppressive status relationships, in which personal identity as market traders is the prerogative of males. We cannot make progress toward the noncommodification that might exist under ideal conditions of equality and freedom by trying to maintain noncommodification now under historically determined conditions of inequality and bondage.

These conflicting arguments illuminate the problem with the prophylactic argument for market inalienability. If we now permit commodification, we may exacerbate the oppression of women—the suppliers. If we now disallow commodification—without what I have called the welfare-rights corollary, or large-scale redistribution of social wealth and power—we force women to remain in circumstances that they themselves believe are worse than becoming sexual commodity suppliers. Thus, the alternatives seem subsumed by a need for social progress, yet we must choose some regime now in order to make progress. This dilemma of transition is the *double bind.*

The double bind has two main consequences. First, if we cannot respect personhood either by permitting sales or by banning sales, justice requires that we consider changing the circumstances that create the dilemma. We must consider wealth and power redistribution. Second, we still must choose a regime for the meantime, the transition, in nonideal circumstances. To resolve the double bind, we have to investigate particular problems separately; decisions must be made (and remade) for each thing that some people desire to sell.

If we have reason to believe with respect to a particular thing that the domino theory might hold—commodification for some means commodification for all—we would have reason to choose market inalienability. But the double bind means that if we choose market inalienability, we might deprive a class of poor and oppressed people of the opportunity to have more money with which to buy adequate food, shelter, and health care in the market and hence deprive them of a better chance to lead a humane life. Those who gain from the market inalienability, on the other hand, might be primarily people whose wealth and power make them comfortable enough to be concerned about the inroads on the general quality of life that commodification would make. Yet, taking a slightly longer view, commodification threatens the personhood of everyone, not just those who can now afford to concern themselves about it. Whether this elitism in market inalienability should make us risk the dangers of commodification will depend upon the dangers of each case.

2. Incomplete Commodification. One way to mediate the dilemma is through what I shall call *incomplete commodification.* Under nonideal circumstances the question whether market inalienability can be justified is more complicated than a binary decision between complete commodification and complete noncommodification. Rather, we should understand there to be a continuum reflecting degrees of commodification that will be appropriate in a given context. An incomplete commodification—a partial market inalienability—can sometimes substitute for a complete noncommodification that might accord with our ideals but cause too much harm in our nonideal world.

Before considering examples, it may be helpful to distinguish two aspects of incomplete commodification: participant and social. The participant aspect draws attention to the meaning of an interaction for those who engage in it. For many interactions in which money changes hands, market rhetoric cannot capture this significance. In other words, market and nonmarket aspects of an interaction coexist: Although money changes hands, the interaction also has important nonmonetizable personal and social significance. The social aspect of incomplete commodification draws attention instead to the way society as a whole recognizes that things have nonmonetizable participant significance by regulating (curtailing) the free market.

Work and housing are possible examples of incomplete commodification. With respect to the participant aspect, consider that for many of us, work is not only the way we make our living but also a part of ourselves. What we hope to derive from our work, and the personal importance we attach to it, is not understandable entirely in money terms, even though we demand and accept money. These ideals about work seem to be part of our conception of human flourishing, and thus the loss of this personal aspect of work would be considered inhumane. Consider also our attachment of meaning to housing. Although a house has market value and we can express our investment in terms of dollars, there is a nonmonetizable, personal aspect to many people's relationships with their homes.

With respect to the social aspect of incomplete commodification, consider the regulation of labor. Although work has not been fully decommodified, it is incompletely commodified through collective bargaining, minimum wage requirements, maximum hour limitations, health and safety requirements, unemployment insurance, retirement benefits, prohibition of child labor, and antidiscrimination requirements. Consider also the regulation of residential tenancies. Rent control, habitability requirements, restrictions upon termination of tenancies, and antidiscrimination requirements can all be seen as indications of incomplete commodification.

When we see these regulations as reflecting incomplete commodification, we progress toward conceiving of work and housing in other than market rhetoric. In this view, work and housing are not conceived of as completely monetizable and fungible objects of exchange that are separated from persons, because to conceive of them in such a way is to adopt an inferior conception of human flourishing. These forms of regulation should instead be seen as an effort to take into account workers' and tenants' personhood, to recognize and foster the nonmarket significance of their work and housing.

Regulation of residential tenancies can be seen as connected to identity and contextuality: attempting to make possible and protect the constituting of one's personhood in one's home, and one's continuity of residence there, because the home is a justifiable kind of personal property. Regulation can be seen as attempting to ensure that tenants are not forced to move from their homes for ideological, discriminatory, or arbitrary reasons or by a sudden rise in market prices, and to ensure that rental housing is decent to live in and a decent place for family life.

Regulation of work can be seen as attempting to make more possible the realization of personal ideals about work, which are related to human flourishing: a self-conception inseparable from one's work (contextuality), continuity of work (identity), and control over one's own work (freedom). Regulation can be seen as attempting to ensure that employees are not forced to leave their jobs for ideological, discriminatory, or arbitrary reasons; to ensure that the workplace is safe, and free from sexual or racial harassment; and to ensure that employees have some say in workplace decisions, and the opportunity to understand how their work is helpful or significant to other people. Although complete decommodification of work or housing is not now possible, these incomplete commodifications can be seen as responses in out nonideal world to the harm to personhood caused by complete commodification of work and housing.

D. Evolutionary Pluralism Applied: Problems of Sexuality and Reproductive Capacity

I now offer thoughts on how the analysis that I recommend might be brought to bear on a set of controversial market inalienabilities. It is not my purpose to try to provide the detailed, practical evaluation that is needed, but only to sketch its general contours. The example I shall pursue is the contested commodification of aspects of sexuality and reproductive capacity: the issues of prostitution, baby selling, and surrogacy. I conclude that market inalienability is justified for baby selling and also—provisionally—for surrogacy but that prostitution should be governed by a regime of incomplete commodification.

Assuming that our ideal of personhood includes the ideal of sexual interaction as equal nonmonetized sharing, we might imagine that the "good" commodified sexuality ought not to exist: that sexual activity should be market inalienable. But perhaps prohibition of the sale of sexual services, if it aims to preserve sexuality as nonmonetized sharing, is not justified under current circumstances because sex is already commodified.[88] Moreover, in our nonideal world, market inalienability—especially if enforced through criminalization of sales—may cause harm to ideals of personhood instead of maintaining and fostering them, primarily because it exacerbates the double bind. Poor women who believe that they must sell their sexual services to survive are subject to moral opprobrium, disease, arrest, and violence. The ideal of sexual sharing is related to identity and contextuality, but the identity of those who sell is undermined by criminalization and powerlessness, and their ability to develop and maintain relationships is hurt by these circumstances.

Nevertheless, despite the double bind and the harms of the black market to prostitutes, fear of a domino effect could perhaps warrant market inalienability as an effort to ward off conceiving of all sexuality as fungible. Many people would say, however, that the known availability of commodified sex by itself does not render nonfungible sexual interactions impossible or even more difficult and that the prevalence of ideals of interpersonal sexual sharing in spite of the widespread association of sex and money is proof that the domino effect in rhetoric is not to be feared. But we must evaluate the seriousness of the risk if commodification proceeds. What if sex were fully and openly commodified? Suppose newspapers, radio, TV, and billboards advertised sexual services as imaginatively and vividly as they advertise computer services, health clubs, or soft drinks. Suppose the sexual partner of your choice could be ordered through a catalog, or through a large brokerage firm that has an "800" number, or at a trade show, or in a local showroom. Suppose the business of recruiting suppliers of sexual services was carried on in the same way as corporate head-hunting or training of word-processing operators. A change would occur in everyone's discourse about sex, and in particular about women's sexuality. New terms would emerge for particular gradations of market value, and new discussions would be heard of particular abilities or qualities in terms of their market value. With this change in discourse would come a change in everyone's experience. The open market might render subconscious valuation of women (and perhaps everyone) in sexual dollar value impossible to avoid. It might make the ideal of nonmonetized sharing impossible. Thus, the argument for noncommodification of sexuality based on the domino effect, in its strongest form, is that we do not wish to unleash market forces onto the shaping of our discourse regarding sexuality and hence onto our very conception of sexuality and our sexual feelings.

This domino argument assumes that nonmonetized equal sharing relationships are the norm or are at least attainable. That assumption is now contested. Some feminists argue that male–female sexual relationships that actually instantiate the ideal of equal sharing are under current social circumstances rare or even impossible.[89] According to this view, moreover, women are oppressed by this ideal because they try to understand their relationships with men in light of it and conceal from themselves the truth about their own condition. They try to understand what they are doing as giving, as equal sharing, while their sexuality is actually being taken from them. If we believe that women are deceived (and deceiving themselves) in this way, attempted noncommodification in the name of the ideal may be futile or even counterproductive. Noncommodification under current circumstances is part of the social structure that perpetuates false consciousness about the current role of the ideal. Some feminists also argue that many male–female sexual relationships are (unequal) economic bargains, not a context in which equal sharing occurs.[90] If that is true, attempted noncommodification means that prostitutes are being singled out for punishment for something pervasive in women's condition and that they are being singled out because their class or race forecloses more socially accepted forms of sexual bargaining. This returns us to the double bind.

Perhaps the best way to characterize the present situation is to say that women's sexuality is incompletely commodified. Many sexual relationships may have both market and nonmarket aspects: Relationships may be entered into and sustained partly for economic reasons and partly for the interpersonal sharing that is part of our ideal of human flourishing. Even if under current circumstances the ideal misleads us into thinking that unequal relationships are really equal, it seems that the way out of such ideological bondage is not to abandon the ideal but, rather, to pursue it in ways that are not harmful under these nonideal circumstances. Market inalienability seems harmful, not only because it might be ideologically two-edged, but also because of the double bind. Yet complete commodification, if any credence is given to the feared domino effect, may relinquish our conception of sexuality entirely.

The issue thus becomes how to structure an incomplete commodification that takes account of our nonideal world yet does not foreclose progress to a better world of more equal power (and less susceptibility to the domino effect of market rhetoric). I think we should now decriminalize the sale of sexual services in order to protect poor women from the degradation and danger either of the black market or of other occupations that seem to them less desirable. At the same time, in order to check the domino effect, we should prohibit the capitalist entrepreneurship that would operate to create an organized market in sexual services, even though this step would pose enforcement difficulties. It would include, for example, banning brokerage (pimping) and recruitment. It might also include bannig advertising. Trying to keep commodification of sexuality out of our discourse by banning advertising does have the double bind effect of failing to legitimate the sales we allow, and hence it may fail to alleviate significantly the social disapproval suffered by those who sell sexual services. It also adds "information costs" to their "product" and thus fails to yield them as great a "return" as would the full-blown market. But these nonideal effects must be borne if we really accept that extensive permeation of our discourse by commodification talk would alter sexuality in a way that we are unwilling to countenance.

A different analysis is warranted for baby selling. Like relationships of sexual sharing, parent–child relationships are closely connected with personhood, particularly with personal identity and contextuality. Moreover, poor women caught in the double bind raise the issue of freedom: They may wish to sell a baby on the black market,[91] as they may wish to sell sexual services, perhaps to try to provide adequately for other children or family members. But the double bind is not the only problem of freedom implicated in baby selling. Under a market regime, prostitutes may be choosing to sell their sexuality, but babies are not choosing for themselves that under current nonideal circumstances they are better off as commodities. If we permit babies to be sold, we commodify not only the mother's (and father's) baby-making capacities—which might be analogous to commodifying sexuality—but we also conceive of the baby itself in market rhetoric. When the baby becomes a commodity, all of its personal attributes—sex, eye color, predicted IQ, predicted height, and the like—become commodified as well. This is to conceive of potentially all personal attributes in market rhetoric, not merely those of sexuality. Moreover, to conceive of infants in market rhetoric is likewise to conceive of the people they will become in market rhetoric and to create in those people a commodified self-conception.

Hence, the domino theory has a deep intuitive appeal when we think about the sale of babies. An idealist might suggest, however, that the fact that we do not now value babies in money suggests that we would not do so even if babies were sold. Perhaps babies could be incompletely commodified, valued by the participants to the interaction in a nonmarket way, even though money changed hands. Although this is theoretically possible, it seems too risky in our nonideal world.[92] If a capitalist baby industry were to come into being, with all of its accompanying paraphernalia, how could any of us, even those who did not produce infants for sale, avoid subconsciously measuring the dollar value of our children? How could our children avoid being preoccupied with measuring their own dollar value? This makes our discourse about ourselves (when we are children) and about our children (when we are parents) like our discourse about cars. Seeing commodification of babies as an inevitable and grave injury to personhood appears rather easy. In the worst case, market rhetoric could create a commodified self-conception in everyone, as the result of commodifying every attribute that differentiates us and that other people value in us, and could destroy personhood as we know it.

I suspect that an intuitive grasp of the injury to personhood involved in commodification of human beings is the reason many people lump baby selling together with slavery.[93] But this intuition can be misleading. Selling a baby, whose personal development requires caretaking, to people who want to act as the caretakers is not the same thing as selling a baby or an adult to people who want to act only as users of her capacities. Moreover, if the reason for our aversion to baby selling is that we believe it is like slavery, then it is unclear why we do not prohibit baby giving (release of a child for adoption) on the ground that enslavement is not permitted even without consideration. We might say that respect for persons prohibits slavery but may require adoption in cases in which only adoptive parents will treat the child as a person or in the manner appropriate to becoming a person. But this answer is still somewhat unsatisfactory. It does not tell us whether parents who are financially and psychologically capable of raising a child in a manner we deem proper nevertheless may give up the child for adoption, for what we would consider less than compelling reasons. If parents are morally entitled to give up a child even if the child could have (in some sense) been raised properly by them, our aversion to slavery does not explain why infants are subject only to market inalienability. There must be another reason why baby-giving is unobjectionable.

The reason, I think, is that we do not fear relinquishment of children unless it is accompanied by market rhetoric. The objection to market rhetoric may be part of a moral prohibition on market treatment of any babies, regardless of whether nonmonetized treatment of other children would remain possible. To the extent that we condemn baby selling even in the absence of any domino effect, we are saying that this "good" simply should not exist. Conceiving of any child in market rhetoric wrongs personhood. In addition, we fear, based on our assessment of current social norms, that the market value of babies would be decided in ways injurious to their personhood and to the personhood of those who buy and sell on this basis, exacerbating class, race, and gender divisions. To the extent the objection to baby selling is not (or is not only) to the very idea of this "good" (marketed children), it stems from a fear that the nonmarket version of human beings themselves will become impossible. Conceiving of children in market rhetoric would foster an inferior conception of human flourishing, one that commodifies every personal attribute that might be valued by people in other people. In spite of the double bind, our aversion to commodification of babies has a basis strong enough to recommend that market inalienability be maintained.

The question of surrogate mothering seems more difficult.[94] I shall consider the surrogacy situation in which a couple desiring a child consists of a fertile male and an infertile female. They find a fertile female to become impregnated with the sperm of the would-be father, to carry the fetus to term, to give birth to the child, and to relinquish it to them for adoption. This interaction may be paid, in which case surrogacy becomes a good sold on the market, or unpaid, in which case it remains a gift.

Those who view paid surrogacy as tantamount to permitting the sale of babies point out that a surrogate is paid for the same reasons that an ordinary adoption is commissioned: to conceive, carry, and deliver a baby.[95] Moreover, even if an ordinary adoption is not commissioned, there seems to be no substantive difference between paying a woman for carrying a child she then delivers to the employers, who have found her through a brokerage mechanism, and paying her for an already "produced" child whose buyer is found through a brokerage mechanism (perhaps called an adoption agency) after she has paid her own costs of "production." Both are adoptions for which consideration is paid. Others view paid surrogacy as better analogized to prostitution (sale of sexual services) than to baby selling. They would say that the commodity being sold in the surrogacy interaction is not the baby itself but, rather, "womb services."[96]

The different conceptions of the good being sold in paid surrogacy can be related to the primary difference between this interaction and (other) baby selling: The genetic father is more closely involved in the surrogacy interaction than in a standard adoption. The disagreement about how we might conceive of the "good" reflects a deeper ambiguity about the degree of commodification of mothers and children. If we think that ordinarily a mother paid to relinquish a baby for adoption is selling a baby but that if she is a surrogate, she is merely selling gestational services, it seems we are assuming that the baby cannot be considered the surrogate's property, so as to become alienable by her, but that her gestational services can be considered property and therefore become alienable. If this conception reflects a decision that the baby cannot be property at all—cannot be objectified—then the decision reflects a lesser level of commodification in rhetoric. But this interpretation is implausible because of our willingness to refer to the ordinary paid adoption as baby selling. A more plausible interpretation of conceiving of the "good" as gestational services is that this conception reflects an understanding that the baby is already someone else's property—the father's. This characterization of the interaction can be understood as both complete commodification in rhetoric and an expression of gender hierarchy. The would-be father is "producing" a baby of his "own,"[97] but in order to do so he must purchase these "services" as a necessary input. Surrogacy raises the issue of commodification and gender politics in how we understand even the description of the problem. An oppressive understanding of the interaction is the more plausible one: Women—their reproductive capacities, attributes, and genes—are fungible in carrying on the male genetic line.

Whether one analogizes paid surrogacy to sale of sexual services or to baby selling, the underlying concerns are the same. First, there is the possibility of even further oppression of poor or ignorant women, which must be weighed against a possible step toward their iberation through economic gain from a new alienable entitlement—the double bind. Second, there is the possibility that paid surrogacy should be completely prohibited because it expresses an inferior conception of human flourishing. Third, there is the possibility of a domino effect of commodification in rhetoric that leaves us all inferior human beings.

Paid surrogacy involves a potential double bind. The availability of the surrogacy option could create hard choices for poor women. In the worst case, rich women, even those who are not infertile, might employ poor women to bear children for them. It might be degrading for the surrogate to commodify her gestational services or her baby, but she might find this preferable to her other choices in life. But although surrogates have not tended to be rich women, nor middle-class career women, neither have they (so far) seemed to be the poorest women, the ones most caught in the double bind.[98]

Whether surrogacy is paid or unpaid, there may be a transition problem: an ironic self-deception. Acting in ways that current gender ideology characterizes as empowering might actually be disempowering. Surrogates may feel they are fulfilling their womanhood by producing a baby for someone else, although they may actually be reinforcing oppressive gender roles.[99] It is also possible to view would-be fathers as (perhaps unknowing) oppressors of their own partners. Infertile mothers, believing it to be their duty to raise their partners' genetic children, could be caught in the same kind of false consciousness and relative powerlessness as surrogates who feel called upon to produce children for others. Some women might have conflicts with their partners that they cannot acknowledge, either about raising children under these circumstances instead of adopting unrelated children, or about having children at all. These considerations suggest that to avoid reinforcing gender ideology, both paid and unpaid surrogacy must be prohibited.

Another reason we might choose prohibition of all surrogacy, paid or unpaid, is that allowing surrogacy in our nonideal world would injure the chances of proper personal development for children awaiting adoption. Unlike a mother relinquishing a baby for adoption, the surrogate mother bears a baby only in response to the demand of the would-be parents: Their demand is the reason for its being born. There is a danger that unwanted children might remain parentless even if only unpaid surrogacy is allowed, because those seeking children will turn less frequently to adoption. Would-be fathers may strongly prefer adopted children bearing their own genetic codes to adopted children genetically strange to them; perhaps women prefer adopted children bearing their partners' genetic codes. Thus, prohibition of all surrogacy might be grounded on concern for unwanted children and their chances in life.

Perhaps a more visionary reason to consider prohibiting all surrogacy is that the demand for it expresses a limited view of parent–child bonding; in a better view of personal contextuality, bonding should be reconceived. Although allowing surrogacy might be thought to foster ideals of interrelationships between men and their children, it is unclear why we should assume that the ideal of bonding depends especially on genetic connection. Many people who adopt children feel no less bonded to their children than responsible genetic parents; they understand that relational bonds are created in shared life more than in genetic codes. We might make better progress toward ideals of interpersonal sharing—toward a better view of contextual personhood—by breaking down the notion that children are fathers'—or parents'—genetic property.[100]

In spite of these concerns, attempting to prohibit surrogacy now seems too utopian because it ignores a transition problem. At present, people seem to believe that they need genetic offspring in order to fulfill themselves; at present, some surrogates believe their actions to be altruistic. To try to create an ideal world all at once would do violence to things people make central to themselves. This problem suggests that surrogacy should not be altogether prohibited.

Concerns about commodification of women and children, however, might counsel permitting only unpaid surrogacy (market inalienability). Market inalienability might be grounded in a judgment that commodification of women's reproductive capacity is harmful for the identity aspect of their personhood and in a judgment that the closeness of paid surrogacy to baby selling harms our self-conception too deeply. There is certainly the danger that women's attributes, such as height, eye color, race, intelligence, and athletic ability, will be monetized. Surrogates with "better" qualities will command higher prices in virtue of those qualities. This monetization commodifies women more broadly than merely with respect to their sexual services or reproductive capacity. Hence, if we wish to avoid the dangers of commodification and, at the same time, recognize that there are some situations in which a surrogate can be understood to be proceeding out of love or altruism and not out of economic necessity or desire for monetary gain, we could prohibit sales but allow surrogates to give their services. We might allow them to accept payment of their reasonable out-of-pocket expenses—a form of market inalienability similar to that governing ordinary adoption.

Fear of a domino effect might also counsel market inalienability. At the moment, it does not seem that women's reproductive capabilities are as commodified as their sexuality. Of course, we cannot tell whether this means that reproductive capabilities are more resistant to commodification or whether the trend toward commodification is still at an early stage. Reproductive capacity, however, is not the only thing in danger of commodification. We must also consider the commodification of children. The risk is serious indeed because if there is a significant domino effect, commodification of some children means commodification of everyone. Yet, as long as fathers do have an unmonetized attachment to their genes (and as long as their partners tend to share it), even though the attachment may be nonideal, we need not see children born in a paid surrogacy arrangement—and they need not see themselves—as fully commodified. Hence, there may be less reason to fear the domino effect with paid surrogacy than with baby selling. The most credible fear of a domino effect—one that paid surrogacy does share with commissioned adoption—is that all women's personal attributes will be commodified. The pricing of surrogates' services will not immediately transform the rhetoric in which women conceive of themselves and in which they are conceived, but that is its tendency. This fear, even though remote, seems grave enough to take steps to ensure that paid surrogacy does not become the kind of institution that could permeate our discourse.

Thus, for several reasons market inalienability seems an attractive solution. But in choosing this regime, we would have to recognize the danger that the double bind might force simulations of altruism by those who would find living on an expense allowance preferable to their current circumstances. Furthermore, the fact that they are not being paid "full" price exacerbates the double bind and is not really helpful in preventing a domino effect. We would also have to recognize that there would probably not be enough altruistic surrogates available to alleviate the frustration and suffering of those who desire children genetically related to fathers,[101] if this desire is widespread.

The other possible choice is to create an incomplete commodification similar to the one suggested for sale of sexual services. The problem of surrogacy is more difficult, however, primarily because the interaction produces a new person whose interests must be respected. In such an incomplete commodification, performance of surrogacy agreements by willing parties should be permitted, but women who change their minds should not be forced to perform.[102] The surrogate who changes her mind before birth can choose abortion; at birth, she can decide to keep the baby.[103] Neither should those who hire a surrogate and then change their minds be forced to keep and raise a child they do not want. But if a baby is brought into the world and nobody wants it, the surrogate who intended to relinquish the child should not be forced to keep and raise it.[104] Instead, those who, out of a desire for genetically related offspring, initiated the interaction should bear the responsibility for providing for the child's future in a manner that can respect the child's personhood and not create the impression that children are commodities that can be abandoned as well as alienated.[105]

We should be aware that the case for incomplete commodification is much more uneasy for surrogacy than for prostitution. The potential for commodification of women is deeper because as with commissioned adoption, we risk conceiving of all of women's personal attributes in market rhetoric and because paid surrogacy within the current gender structure may symbolize that women are fungible baby makers for men whose seed must be carried on. Moreover, as with commissioned adoption, the interaction brings forth a new person who did not choose commodification and whose potential personal identity and contextuality must be respected even if the parties to the interaction fail to do so.

Because the double bind has similar force whether a woman wishes to be a paid surrogate or simply to create a baby for sale on demand, the magnitude of the difference between paid surrogacy and commissioned adoption is largely dependent on the weight we give to the father's genetic link to the baby. If we place enough weight on this distinction, then incomplete commodification for surrogacy, but not for baby selling, will be justified. But we should be aware, if we choose incomplete commodification for surrogacy, that this choice might seriously weaken the general market inalienability of babies, which prohibits commissioned adoptions.[106] If, on balance, incomplete commodification rather than market inalienability comes to seem right for now, it will appear so for these reasons: because we judge the double bind to suggest that we should not completely foreclose women's choice of paid surrogacy, even though we foreclose commissioned adoptions; because we judge that people's (including women's) strong commitment to maintaining men's genetic lineage will ward off commodification and the domino effect, distinguishing paid surrogacy adequately from commissioned adoptions; and because we judge that that commitment cannot be overridden without harm to central aspects of people's self-conception. If we choose market inalienability, it will be because we judge the double bind to suggest that poor women will be further disempowered if paid surrogacy becomes a middle-class option and because we judge that people's commitment to men's genetic lineage is an artifact of gender ideology that can neither save us from commodification nor result in less harm to personhood than its reinforcement would now create. In my view, a form of market inalienability similar to our regime for ordinary adoption will probably be the better nonideal solution.

VI. Conclusion

Market inalienability is an important normative category for our society. Economic analysis and traditional liberal pluralism have failed to recognize and correctly understand its significance because of the market orientation of their premises. In attempting to free our conceptions from these premises in order to see market inalienability as an important countercurrent to our market orientation, I have created an archetype, universal commodification, and tried to show how it underlies both economic analysis and more traditional liberal thinking about inalienability. As an archetype, universal commodification is too uncomplicated to describe fully any actual thinker or complex of ideas, but I believe consideration of the archetype and what it entails is a necessary corrective. The rhetoric of commodification has led us into an unreflective use of market characterizations and comparisons for almost everything people may value, and hence into an inferior conception of personhood.

I have created a contrasting archetype, universal noncommodification, to characterize the utopian vision—expressed by Marxists and other social critics of the market order—of a social world free of market relationships and market conceptions. Although this archetype, too, is an oversimplification, I believe it enables us to focus on the transition problem that always lies between us and our utopias. If decommodification of things important to personhood is provisionally the ideal of justice we should strive for, trying to bring it to pass now may sometimes be unjust. In attempting to make the hard choices in which both commodification and decommodification seem harmful—the transition problem of the double bind—we must evaluate each contested commodification in its temporal and social context, and we must learn to see in the commodification issue the same interconnection between rhetoric and reality that we have come to accept between physical reality and our paradigms of thought.

To the extent that we must not assimilate our conception of personhood to the market, market inalienabilities are justified. But market inalienabilities are unjust when they are too harmful to personhood in our nonideal world. Incomplete commodification can help us mediate this kind of injustice. To see the world of exchange as shot through with incomplete commodification can also show us that inalienability is not the anomaly that economics and more traditional liberalism conceive it to be. This perspective can also help us begin to decommodify things important to personhood—like work and housing—that are now wrongly conceived of in market rhetoric.

Market inalienability ultimately rests on our best conception of human flourishing, which must evolve as we continue to learn and debate. Likewise, market inalienabilities must evolve as we continue to learn and debate; there is no magic formula that will delineate them with utter certainty, or once and for all. In our debate, there is no such thing as two radically different normative discourses reaching the "same" result. The terms of our debate will matter to who we are.

Notes

I gratefully acknowledge the support of the University of Southern California Faculty Research and Innovation Fund in the preparation of this chapter. Earlier versions were presented to workshops at the University of Wisconsin School of Law, Northwestern School of Law, and the University of

Southern California Law Center, as well as to the Los Angeles Feminist Legal Scholars and to my spring 1987 seminar in property theory. The chapter benefited greatly from the responses of the participants. It also benefited greatly from the willingness of friends and colleagues—too numerous to name—to think and argue with me, sharing generously their time and talents. I am grateful to all of them and hope they will take up where I leave off. For making this work possible, I record my thanks to my family: Layne Leslie Britton, Wayland Jeremiah Radin, and Amadea Kendra Britton.

1. *See, e.g.,* McConnell, *The Nature and Basis of Inalienable Rights,* 3 LAW & PHIL. 25, 27 (1984)

2. *See, e.g.,* Calabresi & Melamed, *Property Rules, Liability Rules, and Inalienability: One View of the Cathedral,* 85 HARV. L. REV. 1089, 1092 (1972)

3. *See, e.g.,* Barnett, *Contract Remedies and Inalienable Rights,* 4 SOC. PHIL. & POL'Y 179, 185 (1986)

4. *See, e.g.,* D. MEYERS, INALIENABLE RIGHTS: A DEFENSE 4 (1985)

5. R. TITMUSS, THE GIFT RELATIONSHIP: FROM HUMAN BLOOD TO SOCIAL POLICY (1971).

6. *See, e.g.,* Arrow, *Gifts and Exchanges,* I PHIL. & PUB. AFF. 343 (1972).

7. *See* Landes & Posner, *The Economics of the Baby Shortage,* 7 J. LEGAL STUD. 323 (1978).

8. *See, e.g.,* Prichard, *A Market for Babies?,* 34 U. TORONTO L.J. 341, 348–57 (1984).

9. As these two variables suggest, each of four broad categories of separability might be negated by a corresponding form of inalienability: involuntary extinguishment (cancellation, forfeiture of civil rights), voluntary extinguishment (waiver, abandonment); involuntary transfer), (condemnation, adverse possession), and voluntary transfer (gift, sale).

10. Examples are entitlements to social security and welfare benefits, and many kinds of licenses.

11. As I use it here, the term *commodity* means simply something that is thought appropriate to buy and sell through a market. Later I discuss further complexities of meaning in the term *commidification.*

12. *See, e.g.,* A. ALCHIAN AND W. ALLEN, EXCHANGE AND PRODUCTION: COMPETITION, COORDINATION, AND CONTROL 17 n. 1 (3d ed. 1983). *See generally* ECONOMIC IMPERIALISM: THE ECONOMIC APPROACH APPLIED OUTSIDE THE FIELD OF ECONOMICS (G. Radnitzky and P. Bernholz eds. 1987); Hirshleifer, *The Expanding Domain of Economics,* 75 AM. ECON. REV. 53, 53 ("Special Issue" December 1985)

13. *See* J. BUCHANAN AND G. TULLOCK, THE CALCULUS OF CONSENT (1974); D. MUELLER, PUBLIC CHOICE (1979); Buchanan, *Rent Seeking and Profit Seeking,* in TOWARD A THEORY OF THE RENT-SEEKING SOCIETY 4 (J. Buchanan, R. Tollison, and G. Tullock eds. 1980)

14. Posner, *An Economic Theory of the Criminal Law,* 85 COLUM. L. REV. 1193, 1199 (1985).

15. *See, e.g.,* Epstein, *Why Restrain Alienation?* 85 COLUM. L. REV. 970 (1985); at 990.

16. *See* Epstein, at 971.

17. *See* Epstein, at 988.

18. To see the extent of Epstein's market rhetoric, consider his opinion that the most likely motive for buying votes "is to obtain control of the public machinery, in ways that allow a person to recover, at the very least, the money that was paid out to the individuals who sold their votes, with something left to compensate the buyer for the labor and entrepreneurial risk" (id. at 987–88). Someone whose rhetoric is less thoroughly market oriented might surely conceive the motive for buying votes to be advancing one's unmonetized political, social, religious, or moral ideas.

19. *See* Epstein, at 971. In earlier work, Epstein stressed libertarian rights. *See, e.g.,* Epstein, *Possession as the Root of Title,* 13 GA. L. REV. 1221 (1979). Recently he claimed that libertarian rights and utilitarian reasoning lead to the same institutional rules. *See, e.g.,* Epstein, *Past and Future: The Temporal Dimension in the Law of Property,* 64 WASH. U.L.Q. 667 (1986);

20. Rose-Ackerman, *Inalienability and the Theory of Property Rights,* 85 COLUM. L. REV. 931 (1985).

21. *See id.* at 932.

22. *See id.* at 938.

23. *Id.* at 942, 948–49.

24. *See id.* at 941.

25. *Id.* at 931.

26. For discussion of Marx's early and later treatment of alienation and its relationship to commodification, see S. AVINERI, THE SOCIAL AND POLITICAL THOUGHT OF KARL MARX 96–123 (1968); and A. GOULDNER, THE TWO MARXISMS 177–220 (1980).

27. Marx, *Economic and Philosophic Manuscripts of 1844,* in THE MARXÄENGELS READER 70 (R. Tucker 2d ed. 1984).

28. *Id.* at 71 (emphasis in original).

29. Marx, *The German Ideology: Part I, in* THE MARXÄENGELS READER at 193.

30. *See* I K. MARX, CAPITAL, 71–83 (F. Engels ed. 1894, S. Moore and E. Aveling trans.

31. What we now call market value, Marx thought of as "exchange value," which he contrasted with "use value" (the worth of something to consumers) and "value" (the amount of labor socially necessary to produce something). *See* I K. MARX, at 84–93.

32. I K. MARX, at 79;

33. G. LUKÁCS, *Reification and the Consciousness of the Proletariat,* in HISTORY AND CLASS-CONSCIOUSNESS 83 (R. Livingstone trans. 1971).

34. G. LUKÁCS, at 91.

35. *Id.* at 100, 184.

36. *Id.* at 116.

37. *See id.* at 114–17.

38. "Only by conceiving of thought as a form of reality, as a factor in the total process can philosophy overcome its own rigidity dialectically and take on the quality of Becoming" *(id.* at 203, footnote omitted).

39. *See* Abel, *A Critique of American Tort Law,* 8 BRITISH J. L. & SOC'Y 199, 207–09 (1981); Abel, *A Socialist Approach to Risk,* 41 MD. L. REV. 695 (1982); Abel, *Torts,* in THE POLITICS OF LAW 185 (D. Kairys ed. 1982).

40. *See* Abel, *A Critique of American Tort Law,* at 201–2.

41. *Id.* at 207.

42. Abel, *A Critique of American Tort Law,* at 208 (footnote omitted).

43. *See id.* at 207.

44. This slogan seems to have been popularized by Samuel Hayakawa. *See* S. HAYAKAWA, LANGUAGE IN THOUGHT AND ACTION 24–25 (4th ed. 1978).

45. *See, e.g.,* Baker, *Ideology of the Economic Analysis of Law,* 5 PHIL. & PUB. AFF. 3, 32–41 (1975); Kennedy, *Cost–Benefit Analysis of Entitlement Problems: A Critique,* 33 STAN. L. REV. 387, 401–21 (1981).

46. For example, a typical economic analysis can be found in Hirsch, *From "Food for Thought" to "Empirical Evidence" About Consequences of Landlord-Tenant Laws,* 69 CORNELL L. REV. 604 (1984).

47. R. POSNER, at 202. In the passage in which this sentence appears, Posner examines the argument that rape should not be punished criminally if there is "no market substitute for rape" because the rapist "derives extra pleasure from the coercive character of his act." (Presumably, the "market substitutes" would be marriage, dating, and prostitution.) Posner finds the argument "weak"—and is thus able to conclude that rape should be punished criminally—for three reasons: protecting the marriage market and property rights in women's persons; avoiding "wasteful expenditures" on protecting women and on overcoming the protections; and "the fact that the rapist cannot find a consensual substitute does not mean that he values the rape more than the victim disvalues it" *(id.).*

48. *See* Calabresi and Melamed, at 1124–27.

49. *See id.* at 1125–27.

50. *Id.* at 1126.

51. *Id.* at 1125–27 (emphasis in original). Recall that Calabresi and Melamed also hint at pluralism in their mention of "other justice reasons" for setting entitlements, but they find it difficult to flesh out this idea, in my view because of their commitment to market rhetoric in that article. It should be noted that Calabresi has modified his views and probably no longer conceives of rape in market rhetoric.

52. In Radin, *Property and Personhood,* 34 STAN L. REV. 957 (1982), I suggest that property may be divided into fungible and personal categories for purposes of moral evaluation. Property is personal in a philosophical sense when it has become identified with a person, with her self-constitution and self-development in the context of her environment. Personal property cannot be taken away and replaced with money or other things without harm to the person—to her identity and existence. In a sense, personal property becomes a personal attribute. On the other hand, property is fungible when there is no such personal attachment. *See id.* at 959–61, 978–79, 986–88.

53. Thus, fungible objects are commodified: trading them is like trading money. Personal things are not commodified (or have been decommodified by assimilation into the person); the effect of detaching them from the person is nonmonetizable.

54. The distinction between fungible and personal property is intended to distinguish between, on the one hand, things that are really "objects" in the sense of being "outside" the person, indifferent to personal constitution and continuity, and on the other hand, things that have become at least partly "inside" the person, involved with one's continuing personhood. The traditional subject/object dichotomy makes the notion of personal property hard to grasp, and, in the present context, poses a danger. To analogize bodily integrity to personal property may simply reintroduce the suggestion inherent in market rhetoric that I am trying to argue against: the suggestion that bodily integrity is somehow an owned object separate from personhood, rather than an inseparable attribute of personhood.

55. *See* H. PUTNAM, REASON, TRUTH AND HISTORY 139–41 (1981).

56. *See id.* at 139–40. This term *hedonic tone* referring to the aggregate level of satisfaction or pleasure, derives from the use of a hedonic calculus (like Bentham's) to judge the good.

57. *Id.* at 141 (emphasis in original).

58. Posner, at 1199.

59. *See* R. POSNER, at 202.

60. *See* M. Radin, The Rhetoric of Alienation (unpublished manuscript on file at the Harvard Law School Library).

61. J. S. MILL, PRINCIPLES OF POLITICAL ECONOMY bk. II, ch. ii, at 218 (W. Ashley ed. 1909).

62. *Id.* at 220.

63. *Id.* at 221.

64. *Id.* bk. III, ch. i, at 208.

65. J. S. MILL, at 229–30, 231.

66. *See* I. KANT, *General Introduction to the Metaphysics of Morals,* in HE PHILOSOPHY OF LAW 9, 31–32 (W. Hastie trans. 1887) (1797) ("A PERSON is a Subject who is capable of having actions *imputed* to him. Moral Personality is, therefore, nothing but the Freedom of a rational Being under Moral Laws"); G. HEGEL, PHILOSOPHY OF RIGHT § 41 (T. Knox trans. 1952) ("Personality is the first, still wholly abstract, delineation of the absolute and infinite will."); *id.* § 35 ("The universality of [the] consciously free will is abstract universality, the self-conscious but otherwise contentless and simple relation of itself to itself in its individuality, and from this point of view the subject is a person.").

67. *See* I. KANT, *The Science of Right,* in THE PHILOSOPHY OF LAW, at 61, 61–67; G. HEGEL, §§ 41–71.

68. G. HEGEL, § 65.

69. *Id.* at § 66.

70. *See* G. HEGEL, § 42.

71. *See* T. KUHN, THE STRUCTURE OF SCIENTIFIC REVOLUTIONS (2d ed. 1970). at 6, Ronty, Philosophy and The Mirror of Nature (1979).

72. *See, e.g.,* Kuflik, *The Inalienability of Autonomy,* 130 PHIL. & PUB. AFF. 271, 296–98 (1984).

73. "Negative liberty" means roughly the freedom of the individual to be let alone to do whatever she chooses as long as others are not harmed. *See* I. BERLIN, *Two Concepts of Liberty* in FOUR ESSAYS ON LIBERTY 122 (1969)

74. Calabresi and Melamed's discussion of inalienability rules illustrates a typical use of the notion of paternalism. Another illustration is Anthony Kronman's treatment of restrictions on alienation as a form of paternalism. *See* Kronman, *Paternalism and the Law of Contracts,* 92 YALE L. J. 763 (1983).

75. *See* Feinberg, *Voluntary Euthanasia and the Inalienable Right to Life,* 7 PHIL. & PUB. AFF. 93 (1978).

76. *See id.* at 120–23.

77. *See id.* at 121.

78. *See id.* at 155–16.

79. *Id.* at 121.

80. J. S. MILL, *On Liberty,* in THREE ESSAYS 126 (1975).

81. *See, e.g.,* J. FEINBERG, at 75–79.

82. Robert Nozick takes the extreme view: a "free system" will allow an individual "to sell himself into slavery." R. NOZICK, at 331.

83. The distinction between "property for use" and "property for power" appears in Hobhouse, *The Historical Evolution of Property, in Fact and in Idea,* in PROPERTY: ITS DUTIES AND RIGHTS 3, 9–11, 23 (2d ed. 1922).

84. The normative element in identifying personal things is discussed in a little more detail in Radin, *Residential Rent Control,* 15 PHIL. & PUB. AFF. 350 (1986), and in Radin.

85. A prophylactic ban on sales would thus be a risk-of-error rule based on respect for persons. *See* Radin, *Risk-of-Error Rules and Non-Ideal Justification,* in JUSTIFICATION: NOMOS XXVIII 33 (J. Pennock and J. Chapman eds. 1986).

86. *Cf.* M. WALZER, at 102.

87. *See* R. TITMUSS, at 237–46; Singer.

88. Legalized prostitution has existed in many places, and there has always been a large black market of which everyone is well aware. That those who purchase prostitutes' services are often not prosecuted seems to indicate that commodification of sexuality, at least by the purchasers, is tolerated. For various views on commodification and prostitution, see, for example, Jaggar, *Prostitution,* in THE PHILOSOPHY OF SEX (A. Soble ed. 1980); Richards, *Commercial Sex and the Rights of the Person: A Moral Argument for the Decriminalization of Prostitution,* 127 U. PA. L. REV. 1195 (1979).

89. *See, e.g.,* C. MACKINNON, FEMINISM UNMODIFIED: DISCOURSES ON LIFE AND LAW (1987); Gottlieb, *The Political Economy of Sexuality,* 16 REV. RADICAL POL. ECON. 143 (1984); Hantzis, *Is Gender Justice a Completed Agenda?* (Book Review), 100 HARV. L. REV. 690 (1987).

90. *See, e.g.,* A. JAGGAR, FEMINIST POLITICS AND HUMAN NATURE (1983); P. ROOS, GENDER AND WORK 119–54 (1985); Rubin, *The Traffic in Women,* in TOWARD AN ANTHROPOLOGY OF WOMEN 157 (R. Reiter ed. 1975).

91. *See generally* N. BAKER, BABYSELLING: THE SCANDAL OF BLACK-MARKET ADOPTIONS (1978), at 43 (suggesting that most natural mothers who give up babies for adoption on the black market are thirteen- to fourteen-year-old girls).

92. Perhaps we should separately evaluate the risk in the cases of selling "unwanted" babies and selling babies commissioned for adoption or otherwise "produced" for sale. The risk of complete commodification may be greater if we officially sanction bringing babies into the world for purposes of sale than if we sanction accepting money once they are already born. It seems such a distinction would be quite difficult to enforce, however, because nothing prevents the would-be seller from declaring any child to be "unwanted." Thus, permitting the sale of any babies is perhaps tantamount to permitting the production of them for sale.

93. It is sometimes said that baby selling violates the thirteenth amendment. *See, e.g.,* Holder, *Surrogate Motherhood: Babies for Fun and Profit,* 12 LAW, MED. & HEALTH CARE 115 (1984). For a summary of various arguments leveled against baby selling, see Prichard.

94. Surrogacy is often popularly viewed as baby selling, and the Thirteenth Amendment is invoked. *See, e.g.,* Holder, at 117. The slavery analogy is inadequate for the reasons detailed above.

95. Surrogacy appears even more like a commissioned adoption if what is important to the adopting couple is not primarily the genetic link between father and baby, but rather the opportunity to exercise control over the mother's background and genetic make-up and to monitor her pregnancy. *See, e.g., The Pain of Infertility: One Couple's Choices, Los Angeles Times,* March 22, 1987, § 6, at 12, col. 1. One adopting father remarked: "We felt, in the case of surrogates, we would be involved from the beginning: conception, monitoring the fetus." The couple said they "would have adopted had the surrogate option not been available" *(id.).*

96. *See, e.g.,* Hollinger, at 893; *see also* Note, *Baby-sitting Consideration: Surrogate Mother's Right to "Rent Her Womb" for a Fee,* 18 GONZAGA L. REV. 539, 549 (1983).

97. *See, e.g., To Serve "the Best Interest of the Child," New York Times,* April 1, 1987, § B, at 2, col. 2. ("At birth, the father does not purchase the child. It is his own biological genetically related child. He cannot purchase what is already his.") Indeed, the very label we now give the birth mother reflects the father's ownership: she is a "surrogate" for "his" wife in her role of bearing "his" child.

98. *See, e.g., Surrogate Motherhood: A Practice That's Still Undergoing Birth Pangs, Los Angeles Times,* March 22, 1987, § 6, at 12, col. 2.

99. Even if surrogate mothering is subjectively experienced as altruism, the surrogate's self-conception as nurturer, caretaker, and service giver might be viewed as a kind of gender role-oppression. *See, e.g.,* A. DALLY, INVENTING MOTHERHOOD: THE CONSEQUENCES OF AN IDEAL (1982); A. RICH, OF WOMAN BORN: MOTHERHOOD AS EXPERIENCE AND INSTITUTION (1976); Hantzis, at 696.

100. *See* Smith, *Parenting and Property,* in MOTHERING: ESSAYS IN FEMINIST THEORY 199 (J. Trebilcot ed. 1983).

101. In light of the apparent strength of people's desires for fathers' genetic offspring, the ban on profit would also be difficult to enforce. As with adoption, we would see a black market develop in surrogacy.

102. The issue of whether surrogacy agreements should be specifically performed—whether the mother who changes her mind should nonetheless be forced to hand over the baby—has received the most popular attention recently. *See, e.g., Father of Baby M Granted Custody; Contract Upheld, New York Times,* April 1987, § A, at I, col. 5. We should not think, however, that we are faced with merely a binary choice: either banning paid surrogacy arrangements or granting specific performance of them. To conceive of surrogacy as a special situation requiring specific performance seems to place undue weight on the supposed genetic interests of would-be fathers in their unique "property," and to undervalue both the personal development of unwanted children they might otherwise adopt (and become bonded to) and the personal identity of women torn between economic need and deep attachment to a baby. *But cf.* Hollinger, at 909–19. Hollinger's sensitivity to the effect of surrogacy and other new reproductive strategies on the adoption of children who are not white or middle-class, and hence are less 'desirable," and her understanding that the strength of the interest in parenthood need not be as closely tied to genetic parenthood as we have tended to view it, seem at odds with her conclusion that surrogacy contracts should be specifically performed. *See id.* at 909–12.

103. Of course, we should decide upon a reasonable time limit during which she must make up her mind, for it would be injurious to the child if her life were in limbo for very long. This could be done analogously with statutory waiting periods for adoption to become final after birth. *See, e.g.,* Surrogate Parenting Assocs. v. Kentucky *ex rel* Armstrong, 707 S.W. 2d 209, 213 (Ky. 1986) (holding that the five-day waiting period in Kentucky's termination of parental rights statute and consent to adoption statute "take[s] precedence over the parties' contractual commitments, meaning that the surrogate mother is free to change her mind"). We might wish to make the birth mother's deci-

sion to keep the child not an absolute right but only a very strong presumption, such as would be used in a custody dispute over a newborn baby in a divorce. In my view, however, adoption is the better analogy: Except in very special cases, both surrogates and others who are considering relinquishing children for adoption should be able to decide after birth to keep the child. *See, e.g., id.* (stating that if a surrogate decides to keep her child, "[s]he would be in the same position vis-a-vis the child and the biological father as any other mother with a child born out of wedlock" and that the "parental rights and obligations between the biological father and mother, and the obligations they owe the child," would be those imposed by the statutes applicable to this situation).

104. Because a pregnancy and a child's life are involved in the surrogacy interaction, rather than just one sexual encounter as with prostitution, "official" recognition of the interaction, with its contribution to commodification, will have to be tolerated, regardless of whether we choose market-inalienability or incomplete commodification. Decisions will have to be made about restitution in case of breach, about payment of the surrogate's expenses, and above all, about care for the child if all parties fail to take responsibility. Even if we choose incomplete commodification, contract remedies should be avoided. Specific performance should be avoided because of the analogy to personal service agreements, and also because we should not conceive of children as unique goods; damage remedies should be avoided because of the obvious "official" commodification involved in setting a dollar value on the loss. It is not my purpose here, however, to try to draft an appropriate statute or guidelines for courts.

105. The special dangers of commodification in the surrogacy situation should serve to distinguish it from the way we treat children generally. Perhaps a regulatory scheme should require bonding, insurance policies, or annuities for the child in case of death of the adoptive parents or reneging by them. *See* Note, *Developing a Concept of the Modern "Family": A Proposed Uniform Surrogate Parenthood Act,* at 1304. *But cf.* Hollinger, at 911 n. 174 (arguing that financial requirements for surrogate parents are unwarranted because the state does not require that "children generated by coital means be similarly protected"). Perhaps a better scheme (because less oriented to market solutions) could require that alternative adoptive parents at least be sought in advance.

106. If paid surrogacy is permitted, it can become a substitute for commissioned adoption. *Cf. supra* note 95.

17

Pornography and the Tyranny of the Majority

ELIZABETH WOLGAST

The respect that atomism accords individuals justifies the maximum degree of freedom of expression, and that freedom protects pornography from public control. But many objectors to pornography, righteously indignant, also emphasize individual respect, particularly the respect due to women as sexual partners. Thus conflicting views, on both sides fervent and moralistic, draw their support from a single atomistic root. Where does such conflict lead us?

I

"If all mankind minus one were of one opinion," John Stuart Mill wrote, "mankind would be no more justified in silencing that one person than he, if he had the power, would be justified in silencing mankind." No matter how great the majority, the very power to control opinion and expression is illegitimate, he argued. Worse, such power "is robbing the human race" of the chance to hear different sides of a question whether right or wrong, and thus does injury to the whole community.[1]

Society has no right to demand conformity to a set of beliefs, to "maim by compression, like a Chinese lady's foot, every part of human nature which stands out prominently, and tends to make the person markedly dissimilar in outline to commonplace humanity." A person needs opportunity to live as he chooses, to take up causes passionately, make mistakes, change his or her mind. Only in this way can anyone develop to the fullest potential. "Human nature is not a machine to be built after a model, and set to do exactly the work prescribed for it, but a tree, which requires to grow and develop itself on all sides, according to the tendency of the inward forces which make it a living thing."[2] Society will itself benefit when people have liberty to experiment in ideas and ways of living, Mill believed, for it is innovators, not conformists, who advance culture.

Truth also is advanced when people are allowed to express all opinions and to debate every question. And who is it argues against a popular view but a minority of dissenters? They are the ones, then, who need the most protection: "On any of the great open questions . . . if either of the two opinions has a better claim than the other, not merely to be tolerated but to be encouraged . . . it is the one which happens at the particular time and place to be in a minority. That is the one which for the time being represents the neglected interests, the side of human well-being which is in danger of obtaining less than its share."[3]

Even in the gentler form of custom, majority tyranny is as much to be feared as political tyranny, Mill believes, and maybe more. His criterion for interference is that only if harm or injury to someone results should people be restrained from acting and living as they please. There is a presumption that in the absence of proof of injury, individuals should be left alone.

I quote extensively from Mill because his language is echoed in modern discussions of free speech, particularly those related to control of pornography.[4] Control is seen as a simple case of the majority forcing others into conformity with their (puritanical) moral standard without argument. It appears a clear case of social compression, what Mill would call a "Calvinistic" demand for "Christian self-denial," aimed at stifling the virtue of "Pagan self-assertion." Similarly, Joel Feinberg refers to control as "moralistic paternalism." Other writers echo Mill's attitude.[5]

For Americans this is a powerful and seductive argument against restrictions on any published material, including pornography.[6] All the libertarian or the nonconformist minority asks of the majority is tolerance of its curious ways. What problem is there in that? Others don't have to look or buy; one person should be free to enjoy pornography even though others prefer not to, just as they are free to accept or reject escargots or dandelion wine. Passionate tastes are not a bad thing, Mill argued; they are the very "raw material of human nature," capable of both more good and more evil than ordinary feelings. "Strong impulses are but another name for energy. A person whose desires and impulses are his own—are the expression of his own nature—. . . is said to have a character."[7] And society needs people of strong character: that is the romantic message.

To understand the role of Mill's argument, it is important to recognize that he wrote long after the Bill of Rights became law and that his view of freedom was not the one that prompted the First Amendment, or even one shared by the early Americans. The idea that truth depends on a "marketplace of ideas," that freedom of expression advances the universal search for truth, that self-expression is an essential part of a person's self-development, that—most important—the only restriction rightly placed on a person's freedom is the injunction not to injure others—such ideas are those of Mill's time, not of Jefferson's. They originated with romantic philosophers of the nineteenth century, not with the political and moral thinkers of seventeenth-century England and eighteenth-century America, who stressed individual responsibility, restraint, and self-governance.[8] Such virtues Mill would probably find much too straitlaced. It is therefore a wild anachronism to use Mill's *On Liberty* as a gloss on the First Amendment. But my argument does not turn on this point. I will argue that one kind of moral issue raised by pornography overshadows and requires us to reevaluate the free speech issue. Further, once the argument against protecting pornography is spelled out, I believe Mill can be rallied to its support instead of to the libertarian side.

Two points about "harm" should be made. First, the language of injury and harm are no part of the First Amendment. The framers of that amendment did not suggest that if someone's practice of religion, for example, were to cause injury in some vague sense, the right of religious practice is restrictable. One might conclude from their terse statement that on the contrary, the right to practice religion should be very difficult to restrict. The "injury" proviso, which may originate with utilitarians, is therefore a gauntlet I do not propose to pick up. Second, Mill's single proviso that a person's exercise of freedom should not harm others places a heavy burden of proof on anyone defending pornography's restriction and sets the presumption that freedom should prevail. How can injury be shown? How can it even be understood here?[9] Who is injured when pornography is aimed at adult customers, free to decide whether they are interested in it?

To answer these questions we appear to need both a specific conception of harm and persuasive evidence of a causal connection, both of which various critics have shown to be problematic.[10] I will argue, on the contrary, that to accept this burden of proof—that harm or injury to an individual has been caused—is an error of strategy. It is to accept a difficult or even impossible challenge when a more direct and powerful moral argument is available.

II

Freedom of speech and press are commonly connected with democratic government and seen as essential to it. Tocqueville, for instance, wrote: "In the countries in which the doctrine of the sovereignty of the people ostensibly prevails, the censorship of the press is not only dangerous, but it is absurd."[11] It was a connection not lost on the framers of the Constitution, who were on their guard against the danger that government might seek to impose its will on reluctant citizens. We don't need to doubt the connection here. The question is: Does protection of free expression legitimately protect pornography?

A reasonable statement on this point is made by Ronald Dworkin, who argues that the right to have an equal voice in the political process is not denied when a person "is forbidden to circulate photographs of genitals to the public at large, or denied his right to listen to argument when he is forbidden to consider these photographs at his leisure."[12] Some other basis for protection is needed, according to him.

The Supreme Court argued along similar lines in *Roth v. United States.* What the amendment protects, it says, is the "unfettered interchange of ideas for the bringing about of political and social changes desired by the people." And pornography is "no essential part of any exposition of ideas."[13]

In my view the distinction set forth in *Roth* is important and should have been developed. But instead of developing it, the Court went on to give another reason not to protect pornography, namely, that a "social interest in order and morality" clearly "outweighed" pornography's right to protection. Such a move was plainly hazardous: If other "social interests" can "outweigh" the right to free expression, then the protection of the First Amendment has been greatly diluted. The better argument would follow along the original lines, saying that pornography isn't in the category of "expression" meant to be protected.

A knotty problem arises, however, when pornography is excluded from protection: The amendment speaks of freedom of the press. So from one angle it looks as if the amendment was meant to protect not citizens who want to read but publishers in the business of selling printed matter of whatever kind. And pornography certainly belongs in this large domain.[14]

Were the framers trying to protect one kind of business while refusing to protect others? We are helped here by remembering that the First Amendment also dealt with freedom of worship and the right to congregate. The rights to worship and congregate in public rest on the respect of one's need to commune with God on the one hand and with one's fellow citizens on the other. The latter right has something to do with the role citizens play in the whole process of government, their sense that the government is there to serve them and it is their job to monitor it. None of this suggests why publishers should be protected by a fundamental constitutional right, rather than cobblers or hotel keepers. The more plausible connection is that between protecting the press and protecting citizens from oppression through censorship. The citizens have a need to know and hear printed opinions, just as they have a need to get together and talk, if they are to do their civic duty and live by their consciences. However, this ambiguity in the language of the First Amendment, this way of speaking of the press as if publishers per se are protected and not the free exchange of opinion, seems never to have been cogently dealt with by the courts, and it perenially causes problems, as it does in the present case.

The main point here is that if the amendment is understood to protect publishers as a special form of business protection, then it has no particular moral weight; business protections and trade restrictions may change with the times and do, and a business may seek protection for some political reason or other without invoking the First Amendment or any basic constitutional values.

Another problem with the *Roth* argument is that it invites the comparison of pornography with art, thereby suggesting that good art is more entitled to protection than bad. Good art presumably should survive lack of social value; bad art shouldn't. But what validity is there in this idea? It invites the comment that the degree of badness is relative and may well be a matter of taste, that history has shown . . . and so on. A more important point is that bad literature—bad essays on politics, appealing to weak and unworthy motives of a reader—are surely protected by the First Amendment. And bad political art, too. Then why not the poor-quality stuff called pornography? The case made in *Roth* for restricting pornography is worse than unconvincing: It provides ground for a kind of moral repression that both the Constitution's framers and Mill would abhor. We still have to explain what is bad about pornography that is not bad about bad literature and bad art in general.

III

Joel Feinberg's use of pornography, he says, is "purely descriptive"; he uses the term to refer to "sexually explicit writing and pictures designed entirely and plausibly to induce sexual excitement in the reader or observer."[15] According to this definition, pornography is a genre of materials of an erotic sort, some of which may be objectionable while the rest is not. Some Japanese prints or Indian murals could be described as pornographic and still appreciated as art by this characterization, for "pornography" is used in a morally neutral way. But since we are not concerned at the moment with erotic materials that are not offensive, I propose to use pornography as a pejorative term, which is to say in the way Feinberg would speak of offensive pornography. In response to the objection that the word is (most) commonly used in a descriptive and neutral way, I suggest that many ordinary people, including many feminists, commonly use it in a pejorative way and that in much ordinary speech to call something pornographic is to say that it is offensive.[16] That is sufficient justification for using the term in this way.

It needs to be pointed out that to say that pornography is objectionable is not to demonstrate that it should be controlled. Many things that people do and say are acknowledged to be bad, including being unfaithful to one's spouse, misusing and deceiving friends, neglecting elderly parents, and lying. But we don't have laws against these things. As Feinberg says, in many respects "the Court has interpreted [the Constitution] . . . to permit responsible adults to go to Hell morally in their own way provided only they don't drag others unwillingly along with them."[17] Such interpretations constitute a formidable defense against controls.

Though pornography may be objectionable in various dimensions (and I believe it is), I will focus on only one kind of objection that I claim to have moral weight. I will substantiate the claim that there is such an objection by citing expressions of it. Then I will defend the claim that this kind of objection should carry enough legal weight to justify the control of the objectionable materials. Last, I will argue that such control is quite compatible with the Constitution and the First Amendment and, finally, John Stuart Mill.

The objections I focus on are those expressed by women against certain representations of women in sexual situations:[18] objections against representations of women "being raped, beaten or killed for sexual stimulation" and women enjoying brutal sexual treatment, usually at the hands of men. One pornography model demands censorship of "all pornography which portrays torture, murder, and bondage for erotic stimulation and pleasure."[19] What is objectionable is not just the representations but the lack of a context in which they are understood to be reprehensible and condemnable. Without some such context. the representations carry the message that such treatment of women is all right. This is one kind of objection.

Another model protests against the circulation of any representation "that reduces women to passive objects to be abused, degraded, and used in violence against women, because now every woman is for sale to the lowest bidder and to all men." She adds that a government that protects this kind of image making expresses "an ideology of women as sexual objects and nothing else."[20] A related criticism was made by Gloria Steinem: "[Pornography's] message is violence, dominance, and conquest. . . . If we are to feel anything, we must identify with conqueror or victim." It is a poor choice for women: "We can only experience pleasure through the adoption of some degree of sadism or masochism. . . . We may feel diminished by the role of conqueror, or enraged, humiliated, and vengeful by sharing identity with the victim."[21]

These quotations illustrate one general kind of objection made to pornography. That it is objectionable in these respects is an inference I make from the facts that (1) people do make vehement objections to it and (2) they see the offense as a moral one, concerning the respect due any individual.

I emphasize that although I take it for granted that pornography deals with human sexuality, I am not defining it, although many writers consider a definition crucial for a coherent argument.[22] There is a variety of erotic material that could be called pornographic, and whether we call something pornographic or not will depend in part on whether people find it seriously objectionable. But my argument isn't meant to fit all varieties of such material.[23] I am testing only one dimension of objectionability against the First Amendment defense with the claim that it has moral weight.

My partial characterization is this: Some pornography is objectionable because it is perceived as seriously degrading and demeaning to women as a group. This characterization draws on the fact that the materials are perceived by women as representing them as inferior or less-than-human beings to be used by others in sexual and sadistic ways.[24]

Now, why should we take this complaint seriously, so seriously as to control a class of printed and pictorial materials? I hold that such complaints are the stuff of a serious moral issue.

Let us see how the reasoning works. Where is the moral problem? Who is to blame that the speaker was a pornography model? Presumably she chose to be one, and her choice—*volenti,* as Feinberg argues—applies to her as well as to the consumers. But this answer is not clearly adequate. The complaint is against the role in which women are portrayed, not against the working conditions, as it were.

The perception that one is being demeaned and that sanction is given to one's mistreatment—to mistreatment as a means to sexual satisfaction here—is a complaint that touches an important moral nerve. It offends basic moral ideas, in particular the Kantian one that everyone should be treated with dignity and respect and not used as a means to another's end. The complaint or objection needs therefore to be taken seriously. That is the first inference.

But several questions leap to mind. First, what determines that this complaint justifies—or lays the foundation for justifying—control of the objectionable materials? Does just any group have the license to insist that laws be changed to improve that group's image? How is the line to be drawn so as to prevent censuring of political caricatures, for instance?

The answer to this question is complicated but contains a general point. If respect for individuals is an important community value, then complaints by any group that their members are demeaned by some vehicle or other must have some weight. Such complaints must be addressed by the community seriously, for otherwise the value of respect is immediately and automatically undermined. The message conveyed that it doesn't matter if these people—members of this group—are demeaned suggests that some people are less important than others.

Therefore the answer to the question whose complaints count is that any complaint by any group that its members are not treated with respect deserves and needs to be treated seriously. To treat such complaints seriously isn't to concede automatically that the complainers are treated with disrespect or that the changes they want should be made. But at issue is not which is the right and which the wrong side of the question; justice doesn't have to be conceived in this way. The issue is the need to deal seriously with the complaint, the need to discuss it in a serious way and then either answer it or act upon it. Ignoring it, laughing at it, and dismissing it are self-incriminating responses that tend to undermine the trust that the emphasis on respect helps to guard.

An underlying theme here is that if respect is valued and presumed to prevail in the society, then the respect given one group cannot be casually evaluated by the perception of other groups. What respect for all others amounts to cannot be defined by a single authoritative group, say the group of the majority; the relation of this point to the pornography issue is explored below. Therefore if a number of members of some group perceive their treatment as demeaning, that is prima facie evidence that there is a problem.[25] And given the seriousness of the matter, the rest of the community must take it seriously either by answering it or by making changes.

I conclude that although there may be different ways of responding to pornography and alternatives to control of such materials, this kind of complaint cannot be lightly dismissed. It needs to be handled in terms of the respect felt to be accorded the complainants by the rest of the community. One way the complaint against pornography by women is not addressed is by reference to the First Amendment and the possible "slippery slope" to censorship.

IV

Granted that there is a prima facie reason to think women are demeaned by pornographic materials, how does censorship become justified? Isn't some other means to deal with it available, and wouldn't that be preferable? The answer is that of course it's possible and other means may be preferable, for there certainly are dangers in permitting one group to control what others may read or see. It is not my thesis that censorship of pornography is the only answer to the moral complaint or that it should be invoked lightly. In fact, it might be invoked as a last resort when such moral protests are raised. But censorship is one answer, and my aim is to show that the justification for using it is not rebutted by an appeal to the First Amendment. Whatever answer is given, that answer needs to address the moral objection to the way treatment of women is represented. The establishment of guidelines for sexual representations might be a solution. Must we decide in general which kind of response is best? I propose rather that there is no theoretical and final answer but that an acceptable response will take serious account of the perceptions of the objecting group.

One has to ask, however, whether there isn't a danger in appealing to the moral standards of any one group when laws are formulated. As Mill suggests, shouldn't anyone have the right to live anyway he wishes? Isn't experimentation generally a good and not a bad thing?

One kind of answer to the libertarian would relate a society to a "moral community," showing that morals and laws must be joined together. Harry Clor and Patrick Devlin each defend such views, the former defending a restrained use of censorship, the latter a freer use.[26] The problem with such views is that they are too broad. What is the "moral community," and where is it to be found? Is it represented by the majority? If so, then surely moral constraints are worse than paternalistic: They are downright tyrannical, as Mill said.

Even though the complaint of women against pornography cannot be dismissed by appeals to freedom of the press, why shouldn't Mill's argument for freedom apply here? Why shouldn't the objection still hold that if women don't want to look at pornographic pictures or film, they shouldn't look? So long as there is "reasonable avoidability" and people can avoid pornography if they want to, where, as Feinberg argues, is the offense? "When the 'obscene' book sits on a shelf, who is there to be offended?" If pornograhy lies between "decorous covers," no one need look at it who doesn't want to. It is only when pornography produces an offense on a par with "shame, or disgust, or noisome stenches" (however they would translate in this case) that the law may justifiably interfere. That is to say, pornography should be restricted only when it becomes a nuisance difficult to avoid.[27] To restrict it on other grounds would be to engage in moral paternalism. It would be to set standards for those who enjoy pornography in order to save them from themselves.

This protest, however, misses the point. The felt insult and indignity that women protest is not like a noise or bad odor, for these are group neutral and may offend anyone, while pornography is felt to single women out as objects of insulting attention. There is a clear division in the community here, unlike the division between people who mind an odor very much and others who can ignore it. The question of how the rest of the community should respond to the perceived debasement that women feel is not analogous to the way the community should treat people particularly sensitive to and offended by certain smells. There is a democracy with respect to smells, but with pornography there is a felt hostile discrimination.

V

One way to deal with objections to pornography has been to appeal to a typical member of the community, an "average man" who can judge as a representative of the rest whether some material is sufficiently objectionable to warrant restriction.[28]

But there is an internal logical difficulty in this appeal. The "average man" is understood not to be a woman, as is clear from the way the perceptions of the average man are viewed. *Roth,* for instance, speaks of the "appeal to prurient interests," but such interests are surely interests predominantly of men, not of women. Feinberg, too, speaks to public nudity in terms of "the conflict between these attracting and repressing forces, between allure and disgust," and again leaves the impression that he is speaking of general human reactions, while those he describes are characteristically male reactions.[29] Other writers refer carelessly to the "effects" of pornography—sexual arousal or even criminal behavior—in such a way as to suggest that all people are included when in fact the effects referred to are specifically effects that pornography has on men.[30]

The premise is essential to my argument that pornographic materials may be seen differently by one group than by another. They may be felt as insulting by one group but inoffensive to another, as seriously demeaning by one and silly by another. An analogy can be drawn with the different perceptions of blacks and whites, or of Jews and Gentiles, regarding certain materials: Blacks may find demeaning an image that others think innocuous. It is crucial for my argument that such differences in perception be acknowledged as a social reality and that our understanding of what it is to treat everyone with respect allow for such differences in the perception of respect. It is important, in short, that we do not assume that there is one Everyman view, with the only question being which view that is. Only by respecting different perceptions about what is demeaning will we see that there may be a reason to limit materials that some group—even the largest—finds unobjectionable.

There is a further curious twist in the idea that there is an "average man" who can judge whether some materials are offensive and obscene, a man such as the "rational man" of English law or the "man in the jury box," as Devlin calls him, someone who expresses "the view" of the society.[31] For presumably when such a person is called upon to judge the offending material, he is to judge it from his own character and conscience. And of course his character will influence what he finds: A man of very strong character may find pornography only mildly or not at all objectionable; a man of weaker character will find it has an influence on him but not in consequence call it objectionable; an "average man" will fall somewhere in between. So sound judgment is difficult to come by.

But not only does a man's character influence his perception; the perception he expresses—his judgment as to the offensiveness of lewd materials—reflects back upon his character. Suppose he says that some materials are very provocative and could lead a viewer to do wicked things. He is testifying not only against the materials but also about his own susceptibility, and thus indirectly incriminating himself. We are told something about his own weakness if he sees pornography as dangerous. He is testifying about his character.

The result is that a bias is built into the testimony of the "average man" and particularly of the "right-minded man" regarding the offensiveness of pornography. A man—even a right-minded one—cannot judge that materials are "corrupting" without revealing his own corruptibility. And so there is pressure both on men who are strong and on men who are not so strong to find pornography harmless. On the other side, a person who objects to it is likely to be characterized as "often . . . emotionally disturbed," "propelled by [his] own neurosis," or a "Comstock."[32]

Given that there is a connection between a man's testimony about pornography and his character, should men who are weak and susceptible be consulted? That would be paradoxical: Such people can hardly be counted on to give any reliable testimony. But a particularly upright and conscientious man (say a respected judge) is not qualified either, for he may be unable to see any problem. And the ordinarily upright but susceptible man may be reluctant to reveal his weakness. Then whose judgment should be given weight? Given the lack of any "objective" or authoritative spokesman for the whole society, there's only one sensible answer.

If blacks are in a position to say what is demeaning to them, why shouldn't women's voices be heard on the pornography issue? Not because they are truly "disinterested" parties and therefore qualified as authorities. On the contrary; I have been arguing that there are no disinterested authorities, no "objective" representatives of the moral community. And if one group were acknowledged to be completely disinterested in regard to sex or disinterested in regard to heterosexuality, that would be no qualification but the contrary. The objectionability of pornography cannot be assessed in this way; there is no analogue here to the "average consumer" who might represent the whole community in judging a retailing policy.

The reason that women should be viewed as particularly qualified is their charge that pornography is an offense against them. That charge puts them in a morally authoritative position, just as blacks are in such a position in regard to racial insults and Jews in regard to anti-Semitic humiliations. Then we need only to add that a complaint of this kind demands to be addressed somehow. It does not follow what we should do.

What lies behind our invocation of an "average man" in regard to such issues is a powerful tendency to treat pornography—and other ethically colored issues—in androgynous terms. But common sense tells us that where sexuality is central, an androgynous point of view, even if there were one, would be irrelevant. Without sexuality and sexual difference, sexual attraction and sexual polarity, no pornography issue would ever arise. Therefore to treat the issue in terms of universal principles that hold objectively—atomistically—for all beings alike is to perpetrate a kind of legal comedy.[33]

VI

Feinberg questions Justice William Brennan's argument in *Roth* by asking, "What is the alleged 'state interest' that makes the unobtrusive and willing enjoyment of pornographic materials the state's business to control and prevent?"[34] What is the positive ground for interference?

This demand is legitimate, and it needs to be answered in full. Even if a moral argument such as I have outlined can be made for control of pornography, how can the moral argument be translated into constitutional terms? If controls are justified, their justification should answer Feinberg's question. The need to protect respect may be clear, but the means for protecting it are not. Is there an analogy or a precedent to guide us?

I will argue at a common-sense level, not meaning to interpret the notion of "state interest" in its technical legal sense. Given that respect for persons is an important constitutional value, I propose to show a strategy that connects respect with controls on pornography, to show that the means, the logical path, is there already and has no need to be newly cut. The connection between respect and constitutional action has been made already.

What we need here is reasoning somewhat like that in *Brown v. Board of Education.* There the Court decided that educational facilities—equal "with respect to buildings, curricula . . . and other 'tangible' factors"—might nevertheless be unequal in an important sense. And one of the reasons they might be counted unequal was (as one summary puts it) that "to separate [children] from others . . . solely because of their race generates a feeling of inferiority as to their status in the community that may affect their hearts and minds in a way unlikely ever to be undone."[35] Such an institution with the "sanction of law" which thus produces the sense of inferiority of one race is unconstitutional. Respect is not to be measured in the specifics of equipment or curriculum but in the felt implication of inferiority.

In rejecting the justice of "separate but equal" facilities, the Court specifically rejected the protest that any "badge of inferiority" supposed to be implied by segregation exists "not by reason of anything found in the act, but soley because the colored race chooses to put that construction upon it."[36] The insult perceived by blacks has priority over protests of innocence by those charged with offending. It is not crucial that they see the offense in the same way. Thus the Court answered by analogy 2 parallel argument in the pornography issue, that women shouldn't be so sensitive about pornography, for since no one intends to demean them by it, there is nothing demeaning in it. The parallel answer is that whether there was intent to demean or not is irrelevant.

The argument in *Brown* exemplifies the general form of reasoning we need: An institution that perceptibly demeans some group and represents its members as inferior impugns the claim to equality of those members; in doing so it violates the Constitution's provisions; thus it shouldn't be protected by the federal government. There is no reference here to interpretations of other provisions of the Constitution. Of course the production of pornography isn't an institution, yet insofar as pornography is felt to demean women, its protection by the government under the First Amendment cannot be easily argued.

A caveat is needed here. This argument does not imply that if some group feels demeaned—say, by advertising or institutional arrangements—then censorship is automatically justified. Considerations other than the offense taken are often relevant, some of which may also be moral, and these considerations may overbalance the initial concern for respect. Nonetheless, if what is needed is a line of reasoning that can be used to support control of pornographic materials in the face of First Amendment protections, then such a line is clearly available.

In its general conception this approach accords with Ronald Dworkin's view that absolute principles are not what is needed in much legal reasoning. Instead, we often need to balance one kind of claim or principle against others. That's the case here. The First Amendment is terribly important to us as a democracy; there's no dispute about that. But it doesn't give the last word on the question "What may a printer print, and what may a store sell?" While this approach shows a way to defeat the absolutist claim of the First

Amendment and open the possibility of censorship, I have no desire to insist that this course be taken. Other solutions may be preferable.

A number of features of the pornography issue are illuminated by its analogy with race discrimination.[37] For one thing, it would be irrelevant to argue that the demeaning of blacks causes no "injury" and therefore is harmless. What it causes is not the issue: The harm and the offense lie in the practices themselves and the felt implications for people's status, the light cast upon them as citizens, and the like. Second, just as it would be bizarre to appeal to a group of whites to determine whether racial inferiority is part of the message of segregation, it is curious to consult only men about the offense of pornography. Third, the protest that not all blacks were offended would be taken as specious. Even if many blacks denied that they felt offended, we might still acknowledge the vigorous complaints of others. The same holds for women; if some are not offended by pornography, it remains true that many are, and that they see the offense as one against women as a group.

But imagine that the Commission on Obscenity were to make the following argument: If we do nothing in the way of controls, we shall at least be doing nothing wrong.[38] And in such a doubtful matter, with something as important as First Amendment protection at issue, it is better to do nothing. The answer to this argument contains a point often overlooked. When a powerful plea for respectful treatment is addressed by some group to the government, no "neutral" or safe response is possible. Inaction is a kind of action; it signifies toleration of the practice and thus condones it, and in condoning endorses it. Thus to respond to discrimination by arguing that the rights of states and communities are sacred matters, and that one risks a slide down a "slippery slope" if one interferes with them, would be hollow and disingenuous and recognized as such. Similarly, I propose that there is also no "neutral" and safe response against pornography's demeaning of women. The issue demands to be addressed by a government that wants not to give sanction to the message carried by the images. A state that wants to ensure an atmosphere of respect for all persons has to face the issue in more decisive terms than protection of the First Amendment.

The Constitution does not lead us to believe that our first duty is to protect the First Amendment, as if its application needed no justification, as if it stood above other values, including that of respect for all persons. On the contrary, the rights of free speech, religion, and assembly are protected because of the respect due to citizens and their consequent need to be free of government control in certain ways. Freedom of speech is not a fundamental right of a certain kind of enterprise—namely, the press—but stems from a view of humans as morally autonomous.

Therefore it is curious that the Court and libertarian writers show such dedication to freedom of the press as an abstraction, as a principle taken by itself. They deal with it, so it seems to me, as with an icon of a faith whose main tenets they have forgotten. In this respect theirs is less than a high moral stand. Remarking the irony of this liberal position, one writer comments that "women may rightly ask why the Constitution must be read to value the pornographer's first amendment claim to individual dignity and choice over women's equal rights claim to their own dignity and choice."[39] It is a curious turn of thinking that asks citizens to lay down their claim to respect at the feet of this idol.

Mill warned us about the threat presented by people who think they have the "right" moral perspective and therefore the only "right" answers to serious questions. I agree; we need to beware of all sorts of tyranny, however righteous, well meaning, and scholarly. For on its side the protection of pornography also may represent a kind of tyranny of opinion, a libertarian tyranny that treats would-be censors as neurotic, misguided zealots and dismisses the moral complaint altogether.

Looked at from the perspective of women, the tolerance of pornography is hard to understand. Equally hard to understand is a point of view that sees the offense of pornography only in terms of its impact on and significance to men, as if the women of the society were irrelevant or invisible.[40] And a more political point can be added. In the light of women's increasing protests against pornography and the proliferation of defenses of it, the issue carries the hazard of generating conflict between two definable groups, roughly between libertarian men on the one hand and outraged women on the other. Given these dimensions, it seems imperative to straighten the arguments and the issue out.

VII

I wish to say something more about the claim that a definition of pornography is needed for the present argument. My argument has followed the tactic of considering certain objections to pornography without a definition of pornography or a criterion as to what objections are valid. While it focuses on objections of a certain kind, those imputing a demeaning character to pornography, it doesn't specify what kinds of things are legitimately objected to or what is really objectionable.

Where could we get a definition of pornography suitable to the role I give it, the role of materials to which a certain vague kind of objection is made? Who should define it authoritatively? Common sense does not endorse the view that legal authorities should set standards for the rest of the community, should decide about the inherent rightness or wrongness of certain pictures, for example; for there might be no strong moral objection to pictures the community calls pornographic, and in the absence of such objection the pictures are not, on my view, pornographic at all. My argument says only that the law might justifiably restrict materials that are found insulting in a sexual way, as some materials are by women.

Because the argument is so vague, however, it arouses concern. How will pornographic pictures be distinguished from sexy art, and pornography distinguished from sexy literature—Lawrence's portrayal of Constance Chatterly, for instance? The answer is that the lack of a sharp line is precisely what I allow for, as I allow for changing attitudes. If a public work of art is found insulting by some part of the community that has to look at it, then that is a reason—though only one—for restricting it in some way. If no one objects, then a definition that makes it objectionable would be superfluous and really beside the point.

The terms of the issue as I frame it require only the value of individual respect, which is part of our moral heritage, and the perceptions by members of the community about how they are respected. They therefore allow for changes in customs and tastes, allow that what is demeaning in one time may not be found so in another. When pornography is defined in terms of what is perceptibly demeaning, not what is permanently and abstractly so, there is no force to the protest that since "Grandpa was excited even by bare ankles, dad by flesh above the knee, grandson only by flimsy bikinis," no standards can be set.[41] As fashions change, their moral implications change, too. So if what was found demeaning once is not found so any longer, any problem regarding it has vanished. It is better not to define pornography for all time, or to define it at all.

VIII

One important problem involving the First Amendment still needs to be considered. Suppose we are considering a work that asserts and argues that women are inferior to men, more animal than men, and that they enjoy brutal and sadistic treatment. Imagine such a work: It asserts that there is evidence to show that women enjoy a subservient, animal, victimized role and that this is a correct and proper way to treat women, particularly with regard to sex. Some evidence or other is cited, and it is argued that "equality" is simply inappropriate for beings of this kind, belonging to an inferior level of sensibility or whatever.[42] To be sure, these ideas run directly against the moral idea that an individual, qua individual, has worth; nonetheless, we believe in free pursuit of all manner of debate, moral, scientific, and political, without government interference. So would such a work, purporting to be a scientific study, come under the protections of the First Amendment, or may it be treated like pornography and restricted on the same grounds? Does it differ from the case of hard pornographic pictures and films, and if so, how?

On this question I side with the libertarians, for the difference between pornographic pictures and such a report is a signal one for us and for the First Amendment. Mill also would recognize the difference, for he based the freedom of circulation of opinion on the possibility of refuting an opinion that is false and criticizing one that's poorly founded. In his vision an opinion or argument is at continual risk of being refuted, and so it cannot endanger a community where reason and truth are valued. We can draw the distinction by saying that the materials that say nothing are beyond this risk of refutation and therefore, by protecting them, we give them an immunity to criticism that expressions of opinion do not enjoy.[43] The argument of a work may be objectionable, but like all arguments, it is vulnerable to criticism, while pornography lacks such vulnerability.

This distinction is one I believe the framers of the Constitution would also have recognized. The need for opinions to be circulated freely is part of the respect for citizens which prompted the Bill of Rights. But protection of opinion could be distinguished then as well as now from protection of the press to print what it likes, including offensive pictures.

Defenses of pornography have often turned on leaving this distinction obscure, arguing, for example, "that pornography is intended not as a statement of fact, but as an opinion or fantasy about male and female sexuality." Taken this way, it cannot be prohibited on the ground of being false. At the same time, however, one hears that "correction of opinion depends . . . 'on the competition of other ideas'." It is a catch-22. Critics of pornography who are told that they should "compete in the marketplace of ideas with their own views of sexuality," while pornography doesn't present ideas are placed in an impossible situation.[44] The pictures don't argue for a demeaning attitude toward women in regard to sex or present a view of sexuality; at the same time they are demeaning. They don't argue that women enjoy being brutally handled; they show brutality and insinuate the victims' pleasure. While an author would be correct in saying that pornography carries an implied message that brutal treatment of women is acceptable, the fact that it is implied rather than explicit is important.[45]

With this argument I believe Mill would concur, for he consistently maintained the need for respect of differences, including different points of view, and here the differences, including different points of view, and here the difference is one relating to the two sex groups. Respect for persons in all their variety was at the heart of both his libertarianism and his ethical philosophy. However difficult they may be to understand in terms of one's own principles, people are worthy of respect: That was his repeated theme. "Man is not a machine," he wrote, and he surely did not think women are machines for sex.[46] To demean women in the way pornography is felt to do is to treat them as possessions or as servants. So in the end I think that Mill, who argued passionately for women's rights and equal worth and dignity, would find it intolerable to have his views invoked to protect pornography, as they have been.

Although the libertarian case against controls seemed clear-cut and irrefutable, appeal to atomistic ideas cannot solve such a powerfully felt moral issue. If respect for people really exists, it will appear in the way complaints of insult are handled and not only in the propositions used to rebut them. What is needed is not a vision of justice, a simple doctrinaire solution, but a carefully plotted middle way between broad and oppressive controls and reckless liberty. Such an approach will go beyond atomism and deal with injustice in a different and less theoretical way.

Notes

1. John Stuart Mill, *On Liberty* (Bungay: Penguin, 1980), p. 76.
2. Ibid., p. 135.
3. Ibid., p. 123.
4. A presidential commission formed to consider pornography and obscenity remarked that Mill's "market-place remains a correct and profound idea," relevant presumably to the defense of pornography *(United States Commission on Obscenity and Pornography, Report* [1970]. p. 55). Other references to the "marketplace of ideas" can be found in Abrams v. United States, 250 U.S. 630 (1919) (Holmes dissenting); the "competition of ideas" figures prominently in Gertz v. Robert Welch, Inc., 418 U.S. 339–40 (1974); Police Department v. Mosley, 408 U.S. 92, 96–97, refers to the importance of self-expression for personal development; and many other examples could be given.
5. See, for example, Robert Haney, *Comstockery in America: Patterns of Censorship and Control* (New York: Da Capo, 1974); Fred Berger, "Pornography, Sex, and Censorship," in *Pornography and Censorship,* ed. David Copp and Susan Wendell (Buffalo: Prometheus, 1983), esp. pp. 99–100. Mill's reference to Calvinism is in *On Liberty,* pp. 126–27; Joel Feinberg's remark is in "Pornography and the Criminal Law," in *Pornography and Censorship,* ed. Copp and Wendell, p. 133. Fred Berger also sounds very much like Mill, attributing to the moralists a stultifying influence on sexual practices. He writes: "The fact is that most sex is routinized, dull, unfulfilling, a source of neurosis, precisely because its practice is governed by the restraints the conservatives insist on. . . . Moreover, the web of shame and guilt which is spun around sex tends to destroy its enjoyment, and thus to stunt our sexual natures—our capacity for joy and pleasure through sex. The result is a society which is highly neurotic in its attitudes toward and practice of sex—all of which interferes with honest communication and self-realization" (p. 89). Robert Haney also echoes Mill's view when he writes that "cultural creativity must always be ready to stand up and fight for its existence. Societies all too frequently equate the good with the familiar" (p. 12).
6. I intentionally don't speak of "pornographic literature" in anticipation of a distinction to be made later between pornography and expressions of opinion.
7. Mill, *On Liberty,* pp. 124–25.
8. Mill cites Wilhelm von Humboldt as his source on the ultimate value of self-development. Humboldt stated his laissez-faire political theory in *The Sphere and Duties of Government (Ideen zu einem Versuch die Grenzen der Wirksamkeit des Staats zu bestimmen)* in 1791–92. But other

thinkers in Europe were working along this line in the early nineteenth century, including Alexis de Tocqueville, of whose *Democracy in America* Mill wrote a lengthy review. Later the American pragmatists William James and John Dewey gave these ideas an important place in American philosophy. But they were not ideas that Jefferson and Hamilton, Franklin and Adams connected with the need for free expression of opinion. My source here is Garry Wills, *Inventing America* (Garden City, N.Y.: Doubleday, 1978).

9. Among those who use this strategy is Helen Longino, in "Pornography, Oppression, and Freedom: A Closer Look," in *Take Back the Night*, ed. Laura Lederer (New York: Bantam, 1980), esp. p. 48. Longino, however, uses "harm" and "injury" in very broad ways, as if such latitude makes the case easier to prove. I think that, on the contrary, it makes the whole "proof of injury" argument look vague and unpersuasive.

10. The report of the presidential commission felt that the harm argument was in both respects defective. Among the many others who raise the same doubts are Haney *(Comstockery in America)* and Berger ("Pornography, Sex, and Censorship"). The question of whether the personality of an offender determines his use of pornography or vice versa is exceedingly ambiguous and seems to need a sophisticated theory of psychological causation. If the burden of devising one can be pressed on its opponents, pornography's position appears secure.

11. Alexis de Tocqueville, *Democracy in America,* trans. George Lawrence, ed. J. P. Mayer (Garden City, N.Y.: Doubleday, 1969), 1:10, 118.

12. Ronald Dworkin, "Do We have a Right to Pornography?" in *A Matter of Principle* (Cambridge: Harvard University Press, 1985), p. 336. Dworkin goes on to argue that we can value free expression and "accept a presumption against censorship" and still allow that presumption to be overcome, for example, "by some showing that the harm the activity threatens is grave, probable, and uncontroversial" (pp. 337–38). This is basically the strategy of the report of the Committee on Pornography and Obscenity.

13. Roth v. United States, 354 U.S. 481.

14. I include films in this argument, since they, like the press, deal with fiction and pornographic materials as well as with information.

15. Feinberg, "Pornography and the Criminal Law," p. 110. Ann Garry writes that couples might watch pornographic films as they watch "old romantic movies on TV" ("Pornography and Respect for Women," *Social Theory and Practice* 4 [Summer 1978]: 395–421; reprinted in *Applying Ethics,* ed. Vincent Barry [Belmont, Calif.: Wadsworth, 1985], p. 110).

16. There is a problem with using "obscenity" to do the work of "objectionable pornography." First, there is no more a generally accepted definition of obscenity than there is of pornography. But also an invocation of the broader category doesn't clarify anything and can be a positive hindrance, widening the discussion to matters that are not offensive in the same dimension and deflecting the effort to clarify the issue of why we should control pornography.

17. Feinberg, "Pornography and the Criminal Law," p. 133.

18. Certainly objections other than the demeaning of women can be raised against pornography: the exploitation of children is an important case. The argument for controlling child pornography, however, will not be patterned on the one I propose here. It is tempting to argue (as I did at first) that a symmetrical objection might be made by men against a kind of pornography that demeans them, but Christine Littleton has convinced me that against the current background, no really symmetrical situation in which men are similarly demeaned is imaginable. Their objection would therefore have to be different.

19. Diana Russell with Laura Lederer, "Questions We Get Asked Most Often," in *Take Back the Night,* ed. Lederer, p. 25. Russell adds that "pornography is detrimental to all women" (p. 29). A similar complaint from another pornography model includes this observation: "The misogyny I see today is so blatant and so accepted as a matter of fact that when we challenge it, we're seen as irrational or bad sports. . . . We're training little girls and boys to view sadomasochistic behaviour as normal. . . . To me the acceptability of pornography is the clearest statement about the accepta-

bility of women-hating and of women's real place in society" ("Then and Now: An Interview with a Former Pornography Model," in ibid., p. 70).

20. "Testimony against Pornography: Witness from Denmark," ed. Diana E. H. Russell, in *Take Back the Night,* ed. Lederer, pp. 84–85.

21. Gloria Steinem, "Erotica and Pornography: A Clear and Present Difference," in *Take Back the Night,* ed. Lederer, pp. 37–38. A similar voice is Andrea Dworkin's: In pornography, she says, "A woman's sex is appropriated, her body is possessed, she is used and she is despised: the pornography does it and the pornography proves it" *(Pornography: Men Possessing Women* [New York: Putnam, 1979], p. 223).

22. Helen Longino defines pornography as *"verbal or pictorial explicit representations of sexual behavior . . . that have as a distinguishing characteristic the degrading and demeaning portrayal of the role and status of the human female . . . as a mere sexual object to be exploited and manipulated sexually"* ("Pornography, Oppression, and Freedom," pp. 42, 43; italics are Longino's). But it turns out that Longino sees in pornography more than sexual manipulation and abuse of women; pornography, she says, contains also a recommendation that women be treated in this way. "What makes a work a work of pornography . . . is not simply its representation of degrading and abusive sexual encounters, but its implicit, if not explicit, approval and recommendation of sexual behavior that is immoral, i.e., that physically or psychologically violates the personhood of one of the participants." Andrea Dworkin traces the word's origins to "the graphic description of women as vile whores" and says that the word still has the same meaning *(Pornography,* p. 200).

23. Michael Krausz, in correspondence with me, proposes that some materials are offensive in portraying human sexuality without being demeaning to any group in particular. It isn't clear to me that such materials are pornographic, but in any case their control would rest on a different moral objection. The general question whether a definition of pornography is needed is discussed further below.

24. Edmund Cahn expresses a common response to such objections as I make here when he says that "the sense of injustice may be and frequently is applied mistakenly" *(The Sense of Injustice* [New York: New York University Press, 1949], p. 184). I would say that while our perceptions differ, people's moral objections are important moral data.

25. Such perceptions by a large number of people—by most members of the group—would certainly suggest that there is a problem, but what about a small number, what about only one? Then one may have to make a tough moral compromise, but I concede that compromise may be necessary in any case.

26. Clor argues that in the libertarian view "there is no community. Society is made up of a variety of 'communities'—the masochistic, the sadistic, . . . [etc.], which are entitled to equal social status." Such a community has lost its value, Clor thinks; the government has a clear obligation to prevent the development of such a state. It "cannot afford to be neutral toward a perception . . . which undermines its efforts to make of man something more than a creature of elemental passions and sensations." Censorship, used with restraint, is quite justifiable "for the promotion of public standards of civility which our democracy needs" *Obscenity and Public Morality.* [Chicago: University of Chicago Press, 1969], pp. 200, 242, 204). Devlin holds that "the government of a state rests upon the moral virtue of its subjects. The law cannot make people good; it can only punish them for being bad or at least discourage them." The function of the criminal law, he argues, is "to protect the citizen from what is offensive or injurious." Society "is held by invisible bonds of common thought," part of which is a common morality. "This bondage is part of the price of society; and mankind, which needs society, must pay its price" *(The Enforcement of Morals* [Oxford: Oxford University Press, 1965], pp. 83, 10).

27. Joel Feinberg, *Rights, Justice, and the Bounds of Liberty* (Princeton: Princeton University Press, 1980), pp. 87, 89.

28. This was basically the tack taken in Roth v. United States.

29. Feinberg, *Rights,* p. 87.

30. Haney, for instance, writes: "Like the [drug] addict, the man or woman who depends upon

pornography has lost control of his or her life. Like the addict, such a person is sick" *(Comstockery in America,* pp. 66–67). The phrase "his or her" does not convince us that pornography's addicts are commonly women.

31. Devlin, *Enforcement of Morals,* p. 15.

32. The first characterization comes from William Lockhart and Robert McClure, "Literature, the Law of Obscenity, and the Constitution," *Minnesota Law Review* 38 (March 1954): 320; the second is from William O. Douglas's opinion in Ginzberg v. New York, 20 L. ed. 2d 195 (1968), at 213; both are cited in Clor, *Obscenity and Public Morality,* p. 116.

33. Catherine MacKinnon writes of the bias of gender perspectives on pornography as if we should be able to accommodate the two views without difficulty: "Not a Moral Issue," *Yale Law and Policy Review* 2 (April 1984): 327–34. I argue differently in my discussion of androgyny and sex equality in *Equality and the Rights of Women* (Ithaca: Cornell University Press, 1980), chap. 1.

34. Feinberg, "Pornography and the Criminal Law," pp. 132–33.

35. This paraphrase is Gerald Gunther's, in *Constitutional Law: Cases and Materials,* 9th ed. (Mineola, N.Y.: Foundation Press, 1975), p. 715. Gunther goes on to quote an earlier decision in the Brown case which referred to the effect of segregation on a child's motivation and its "tendency to [retard] the educational and mental development of negro children." In this connection also see Edmund Cahn, "Jurisprudence," 30 *N.Y.U. Law Review* 15 (1955); he justifies the Brown decision by speaking of the humiliating treatment of any group as "morally evil."

36. Plessy v. Ferguson, 163 U.S. 537 (1896); Gunther, *Constitutional Law,* p. 709.

37. Ronald Dworkin also finds the analogy between expressions of racial hatred and pornography instructive and remarks that while British law supports the control of incitements to racial hatred, the First Amendment prevents such laws in America ("Do We Have a Right to Pornography?" p. 335).

38. In a recent federal court decision (American Booksellers Association v. Hudnut) the court took the attitude that the "state interest [in protecting women from degrading depictions that may contribute to discrimination] . . . though important and valid . . . in other contexts, is not so fundamental an interest as to warrant a broad intrusion into otherwise free expression" (quoted in "Anti-Pornography Laws and First Amendment Values," *Harvard Law Review* 98 [December 1984]: 481).

39. "Anti-Pornography Laws and First Amendment Values," p. 46.

40. The invisibility of women in much of our thinking and its connection with atomism are discussed in my *Equality and the Rights of Women,* chap. 6. Anthony Woozley argues that a law that made "publishers liable for prosecution for the publication of material which intentionally exploits sex by insulting it, and by degrading the parties to it," would have his support ("The Tendency to Deprave and Corrupt," in *Law, Morality, and Rights,* ed. M. A. Stewart [Dordrecht: Reidel, 1983], p. 221). By talking of "insulting sex" and of the genderless "parties to it," however, he defuses the impact of the feminists' complaint, namely, that it is demeaning of them in particular. That is to say, someone who argued, as Fred Berger does in "Pornography, Sex, and Censorship," that it isn't demeaning of sex or of the male participants would still not have dealt with the main objection.

41. Feinberg, "Pornography and the Criminal Law," p. 122.

42. Works that assert women's genetic inferiority include Aristotle's *Politics,* Schopenhauer's essay "On Women," and Otto Weininger's *Sex and Character (Geschlecht und Charakter);* none, however, goes so far as my fictional author.

43. Others have made suggestions along this line. See, for example, Frederick Schauer, "Speech and 'Speech'—Obscenity and 'Obscenity': An Exercise in the Interpretation of Constitutional Language," *Georgetown Law Journal* 67 (April 1979): 899–933. So far as I know, however, none have used this distinction together with the value of respect as an argument for control while leaving the First Amendment protection intact.

44. "Anti-Pornography Laws and First Amendment Values," p. 471.

45. Longino argues that pornography is a particular kind of speech but that "speech has functions other than the expression of ideas" ("Pornography, Oppression, and Freedom," p. 52). In treating pornography as a form of defamation or libel, I think, she uses a mistaken paradigm and makes the case against pornography less persuasive.

46. One needs only to read Mill's essay *The Subjection of Women* (Cambridge: Harvard University Press, 1970) to see a heavy irony in using his arguments to defend pornography from controls. See particularly pp. 42–44, 59.

18

Against the Male Flood: Censorship, Pornography, and Equality

ANDREA DWORKIN

To say what one thought—that was my little problem—against the prodigious Current; to find a sentence that could hold its own against the male flood.

Virginia Woolf

I want to say right here, that those well-meaning friends on the outside who say that we have suffered these horrors of prison, of hunger strikes and forcible feeding, because we desired to martyrise ourselves for the cause, are absolutely and entirely mistaken. We never went to prison in order to be martyrs. We went there in order that we might obtain the rights of citizenship. We were willing to break laws that we might force men to give us the right to make laws.

Emmeline Pankhurst

I. Censorship

Censorship is a real thing, not an abstract idea or a word that can be used to mean anything at all.

In ancient Rome, a censor was a magistrate who took the census (a count of the male population and an evaluation of property for the purpose of taxation done every fifth year), assessed taxes, and inspected morals and conduct. His power over conduct came from his power to tax. For instance, in 403 B.C., the censors Camillus and Postimius heavily fined elderly bachelors for not marrying. The power to tax, then as now, was the power to destroy. The censor, using the police and judicial powers of the state, regulated social behavior.

At its origins, then, censorship had nothing to do with striking down ideas as such; it had to do with acts. In my view, real state censorship still does. In South Africa and the Soviet Union, for instance, writing is treated entirely as an act, and writers are viewed as persons who engage in an act (writing) that by its very nature is dangerous to the continued existence of the state. The police in these countries do not try to suppress ideas. They are more specific, more concrete, more realistic. They go after books and manuscripts (writing) and destroy them. They go after writers as persons who have done something that they will do again, and they persecute, punish, or kill them. They do not worry about what people think—not, at least, as we use the word *think:* a mental event, entirely internal, abstract. They worry about what people do: And writing, speaking, even as evidence that thinking is going on, are seen as things people do. There is a quality of immediacy and reality in what writing is taken to be. Where police power is used against writers systematically, writers are seen as people who by writing do something socially real and significant, not contemplative or dithering. Therefore, writing is never peripheral or beside the point. It is serious and easily seditious. I am offering no brief for police states when I say that virtually all great writers, cross-culturally and transhistorically, share this view of what writing is. In countries like ours, controlled by a bourgeoisie to whom the police are accountable, writing is easier to do and valued less. It has less impact. It is more abundant and cheaper. Less is at stake for reader and writer both. The writer may hold writing to be a life-or-death matter, but the police and society do not. Writing is seen to be a personal choice, not a social, political, or aesthetic necessity fraught with danger and meaning. The general view in these pleasant places[1] is that writers think up ideas or words and then other people read them and all this happens in the head, a vast cavern somewhere north of the eyes. It is all air, except for the paper and ink, which are simply banal. Nothing happens.

Police in police states and most great writers throughout time see writing as act, not air—as act, not idea; concrete, specific, real, not insubstantial blather on a dead page. Censorship goes after the act and the actor: the book and the writer. It needs to destroy both. The cost in human lives is staggering, and it is perhaps essential to say that human lives destroyed must count more in the weighing of horror than books burned. This is my personal view, and I love books more than I love people.

Censorship is deeply misunderstood in the United States, because the fairly spoiled, privileged, frivolous people who are the literate citizens of this country think that censorship is some foggy effort to supress ideas. For them, censorship is not something in itself—an act of police power with discernible consequences to hunted people; instead, it is about something abstract—the suppressing or controlling of ideas. Censorship, like writing itself, is no longer an act. Because it is no longer the blatant exercise of police power against writers or books because of what they do, what they accomplish in the real world, it becomes vague, hard to find, except perhaps as an attitude. It gets used to mean unpleasant, even angry frowns of disapproval or critiques delivered in harsh tones; it means social disapproval or small retaliations by outraged citizens where the book is still available and the writer is entirely unharmed, even if insulted. It hangs in the air, ominous, like the threat of drizzle. It gets to be, in silly countries like this one, whatever people say it is, separate from any material definition, separate from police power, separate from state repression (jail, banning, exile, death), separate from devastating consequences to real people (jail, banning, exile, death). It is something that people who eat fine food and wear fine clothes worry about frenetically, trying to find it, anticipating it with great anxiety, arguing it down as if—if it were real—an argument would make it go away; not knowing that it has a clear, simple, unavoidable momentum and meaning in a cruel world of police power that their privilege cannot comprehend.

II. Obscenity

In the nineteenth and twentieth centuries, in most of Western Europe, England, and the United States, more often than not (time-out for Franco, for instance), writing has been most consistently viewed as an act warranting prosecution when the writing is construed to be obscene.

The republics, democracies, and constitutional monarchies of the West, now and then, do not smother writers in police violence; they prefer to pick off writers who annoy and irritate selectively with fairly token prosecutions. The list of writers so harassed is elegant, white, male (therefore the pronoun *he* is used throughout this discussion), and remarkably small. Being among them is more than a ceremonial honor. As Flaubert wrote his brother in 1857:

> My persecution has brought me widespread sympathy. If my book is bad, that will serve to make it seem better. If, on the other hand, it has lasting qualities, that will build a foundation for it. There you are!
>
> I am hourly awaiting the official document which will name the day when I am to take my seat (for the crime of having written in French) in the dock in the company of thieves and homosexuals.[2]

A few months later that same year, Baudelaire was fined three hundred francs for publishing six obscene poems. They also had to be removed from future editions of his book. In harder, earlier days, Jean-Jacques Rousseau spent eight years as a fugitive after his *Émile* was banned and a warrant was issued for his arrest. English censors criminally prosecuted Swinburne's *Poems and Ballads* in 1866. They were particularly piqued at Zola, even in translation, so his English publisher, seventy years old, went to jail for three months. In 1898, a bookseller was arrested for selling Havelock Ellis's work and received a suspended sentence. This list is representative, not exhaustive. While prosecutions of writers under obscenity laws have created great difficulties for writers already plagued with them (as most writers are), criminal prosecutions under obscenity law in Europe and the United States are notable for how narrowly they reach writers, how sanguine writers tend to be about the consequences to themselves, and how little is paid in the writer's lifeblood to what D. H. Lawrence (who paid more than most modern Western writers) called the "censor-moron."[3] In South Africa, one would hardly be so flip. In our world, the writer gets harassed, as Lawrence did; the writer may be poor or not—the injury is considerably worse if he is, but the writer is not terrorized or tortured, and writers do not live under a reign of terror as writers because of what they do. The potshot application of criminal law for writing is not good, nice, or right, but it is important to recognize the relatively narrow scope and marginal character of criminal prosecution under obscenity law in particular—especially compared with the scope and character of police-state censorship. Resisting obscenity law does not require hyperbolic renderings of what it is and how it has been used. It can be fought or repudiated on its own terms.

The use of obscenity laws against writers, however haphazard or insistent, is censorship, and it does hold writing to be an act. This is a unique perception of what writing is, taking place, as it does, in a liberal context in which writing is held to be ideas. It is the obscene quality of the writing, the obscenity itself, that is seen to turn writing from idea into act. Writing of any kind or quality is idea, except for obscene writing, which is act. Writing is censored, even in our own happy little land of Oz, as act, not idea.

What is obscenity, such that it turns writing, when obscene, into something that actually happens—changes it from internal wind somewhere in the elevated mind into a genuinely offensive and utterly real fart, noticed, rude, occasioning pinched fingers on the nose?

There is the legal answer and the artistic answer. Artists have been consistently pushing on the boundaries of obscenity because great writers see writing as an act, and in liberal culture, only obscene writing has that social standing, that quality of dynamism and heroism. Great writers tend to experience writing as an intense and disruptive act; in the West, it is only recognized as such when the writing itself is experienced as obscene. In liberal culture, the writer has needed obscenity to be perceived as socially real.

What is it that obscenity does? The writer uses what the society deems to be obscene because the society then reacts to the writing the way the writer values the writing: as if it does something. But obscenity itself is socially constructed; the writer does not invent it or in any sense originate it. He finds it, knowing that it is what society hides. He looks under rocks and in dark corners.

There are two possible derivations of the word *obscenity:* the discredited one, "what is concealed," and the accepted one, "filth." Animals bury their filth, hide it, cover it, leave it behind, separate it from themselves: so do we, going way way back. Filth is excrement, from down there. We bury it or hide it; also, we hide where it comes from. Under male rule, menstrual blood is also filth, so women are twice dirty. Filth is where the sexual organs are and because women are seen primarily as sex, existing to provide sex, women have to be covered, our naked bodies being obscene.

Obscenity law uses both possible root meanings of *obscene* intertwined: It typically condemns nudity, public display, lewd exhibition, exposed genitals or buttocks or pubic areas, sodomy, masturbation, sexual intercourse, excretion. Obscenity law is applied to pictures and words: The artifact itself exposes what should be hidden; it shows dirt. The human body and all sex and excretory acts are the domain of obscenity law.

But being in the domain of obscenity law is not enough. One must feel alive there. To be obscene, the representations must arouse prurient interest. *Prurient* means "itching" or "itch"; it is related to the Sanskrit for "he burns." It means sexual arousal. Judges, lawmakers, and juries have been, until very recently, entirely male: Empirically, *prurient* means "causes erection." Theologians have called this same quality of obscenity "venereal pleasure," holding that

> if a work is to be called obscene it must, of its nature, be such as actually to arouse or
> calculated to arouse in the viewer or reader such venereal pleasure. If the work is *not*
> of such a kind, it may, indeed, be vulgar, disgusting, crude, unpleasant, what you will—
> but it will *not* be, in the strict sense which Canon Law obliges us to apply, obscene.[4]

A secular philosopher of pornography isolated the same quality when he wrote: "Obscenity is our name for the uneasiness which upsets the physical state associated with self-possession."[5]

Throughout history, the male has been the standard for obscenity law: Erection is his venereal pleasure or the uneasiness which upsets the physical state associated with his self-possession. It is not surprising, then, that in the same period when women became jurors, lawyers, and judges—but especially jurors, women having been summarily excluded from most juries until perhaps a decade ago—obscenity law fell into disuse and disregard. In order for obscenity law to have retained social and legal coherence, it would have had to recognize as part of its standard women's sexual arousal, a more subjective standard than erection. It would also have had to use the standard of penile erection in a social environment that was no longer sex segregated, an environment in which male sexual arousal would be subjected to female scrutiny. In my view, the presence of women in the public sphere of legal decision making has done more to undermine the efficacy of obscenity law than any self-conscious movement against it.

The act that obscenity recognizes is erection, and whatever writing produces erection is seen to be obscene—act, not idea—because of what it makes happen. The male sexual response is seen to be involuntary, so there is no experientially explicable division between the material that causes erection and the erection itself. That is the logic of obscenity law used agiinst important writers who have pushed against the borders of the socially defined obscene because they wanted writing to have that very quality of being a socially recognized act. They wanted the inevitability of the response—the social response. The erection makes the writing socially real from the society's point of view, not from the writer's. What the writer needs is to be taken seriously, by any means necessary. In liberal societies, only obscenity law comprehends writing as an act. It defines the nature and quality of the act narrowly—not writing itself, but producing erections. Flaubert apparently did produce them; so did Baudelaire, Zola, Rousseau, Lawrence, Joyce, and Nabokov. It's that simple.

What is at stake in obscenity law is always erection: under what conditions, in what circumstances, how, by whom, by what materials men want it produced in themselves. Men have made this public policy. Why they want to regulate their own erections through law is a question of endless interest and importance to feminists. Nevertheless, that they do persist in this regulation is simple fact. There are civil and social conflicts over how best to regulate erection through law, especially when caused by words or pictures. Arguments among men notwithstanding, high culture is phallocentric. It is also, using the civilized criteria of jurisprudence, not infrequently obscene.

Most important writers have insisted that their own uses of the obscene as socially defined are not pornography. As D. H. Lawrence wrote: "But even I would censor genuine pornography, rigorously. It would not be very difficult. . . . [Y]ou can recognize it by the insult it offers, invariably, to sex, and to the human spirit."[6] It was also, he pointed out, produced by the underworld. Nabokov saw in pornography "mediocrity, commercialism, and certain strict rules of narration. . . . [Ac]tion has to be limited to the copulation of clichés. Style, structure, imagery should never distract the reader from his tepid lust."[7] They knew that what they did was different from pornography, but they did not entirely know what the difference was. They missed the heart of an empirical distinction because writing was indeed real to them but women were not.

The insult pornography offers, invariably, to sex is accomplished in the active subordination of women: the creation of a sexual dynamic in which the putting down of women, the suppression of women, and ultimately the brutalization of women, is what sex is taken to be. Obscenity in law, and in what it does socially, is erection. Law recognizes the act in this. Pornography, however, is a broader, more comprehensive act because it crushes a whole class of people through violence and subjugation, and sex is the vehicle that does the crushing. The penis is not the test, as it is in obscenity. Instead, the status of women is the issue. Erection is implicated in the subordinating, but who it reaches and how are the pressing legal and social questions. Pornography, unlike obscenity, is a discrete, identifiable system of sexual exploitation that hurts women as a class by creating inequality and abuse. This is a new legal idea, but it is the recognition and naming of an old and cruel injury to a dispossessed and coerced underclass. It is the sound of women's words breaking the longest silence.

III. Pornography

In the United States, it is an $8-billion trade in sexual exploitation.

It is women turned into subhumans, beaver, pussy, body parts, genitals exposed, buttocks, breasts, mouths opened and throats penetrated, covered in semen, pissed on, shitted on, hung from light fixtures, tortured, maimed, bleeding, disemboweled, killed.

It is some creature called female, used.

It is scissors poised at the vagina and objects stuck in it, a smile on the woman's face, her tongue hanging out.

It is a woman being fucked by dogs, horses, snakes.

It is every torture in every prison cell in the world, done to women and sold as sexual entertainment.

It is rape and gang rape and anal rape and throat rape, and it is the woman raped, asking for more.

It is the woman in the picture to whom it is really happening and the women against whom the picture is used, to make them do what the woman in the picture is doing.

It is the power men have over women turned into sexual acts men do to women, because pornography is the power and the act.

It is the conditioning of erection and orgasm in men to the powerlessness of women: our inferiority, humiliation, pain, torment; to us as objects, things, or commodities for use in sex as servants.

It sexualizes inequality and in doing so creates discrimination as a sex-based practice.

It permeates the political condition of women in society by being the substance of our inequality however located—in jobs, in education, in marriage, in life.

It is women, kept a sexual underclass, kept available for rape and battery and incest and prostitution.

It is what we are under male domination; it is what we are for, under male domination.

It is the heretofore hidden (from us) system of subordination that women have been told is just life.

Under male supremacy, it is the synonym for what being a woman is.

It is access to our bodies as a birthright to men: the grant, the gift, the permission, the license, the proof, the promise, the method, how-to; it is us accessible, no matter what the law pretends to say, no matter what we pretend to say.

It is physical injury and physical humiliation and physical pain: to the women against whom it is used after it is made; to the women used to make it.

As words alone, or words and pictures, moving or still, it creates systematic harm to women in the form of discrimination and physical hurt. It creates harm inevitably by its nature because of what it is and what it does. The harm will occur as long as it is made and used. The name of the next victim is unknown, but everything else is known.

Because of it—because it is the subordination of women perfectly achieved—the abuse done to us by any human standard is perceived as using us for what we are by nature: Women are whores; women want to be raped; she provoked it; women like to be hurt; she says no but means yes because she wants to be taken against her will, which is not really her will because what she wants underneath is to have anything done to her that violates or humiliates or hurts her; she wants it because she is a woman, no matter what it is, because she is a woman; that is how women are, what women are, what women are for. This view is institutionally expressed in law. So much for equal protection.

If it were being done to human beings, it would be reckoned an atrocity. It is being done to women. It is reckoned fun, pleasure, entertainment, sex, somebody's (not something's) civil liberty no less.

What do you want to be when you grow up? *Doggie Girl? Gestapo Sex Slave? Black Bitch in Bondage?* Pet, bunny, beaver? In dreams begin responsibilities,[8] whether one is the dreamer or the dreamed.

IV. Pornographers

Most of them are small-time pimps or big-time pimps. They sell women: the real flesh-and-blood women in the pictures. They like the excitement of domination; they are greedy for profit; they are sadistic in their exploitation of women; they hate women, and the pornography they make is the distillation of that hate. The photographs are what they have created live, for themselves, for their own enjoyment. The exchanges of women among them are part of the fun, too: so that the fictional creature "Linda Lovelace," who was the real woman Linda Marchiano, was forced to "deep-throat" every pornographer her ownerpornographer wanted to impress. Of course, it was the woman, not the fiction, who had to be hypnotized so that the men could penetrate to the bottom of her throat and who had to be beaten and terrorized to get her compliance at all. The finding of new and terrible things to do to women is part of the challenge of the vocation: So the inventor of "Linda Lovelace" and "deepthroating" is a genius in the field, a pioneer. Or as Al Goldstein, a colleague, referred to him in an interview with him in *Screw* several years ago: a pimp's pimp.

Even with written pornography, there has never been the distinction between making pornography and the sexual abuse of live women that is taken as a truism by those who approach pornography as if it were an intellectual phenomenon. The Marquis de Sade, as the world's foremost literary pornographer, is archetypal. His sexual practice was the persistent sexual abuse of women and girls, with occasional excursions into the abuse of boys. As an aristocrat in a feudal society, he preyed with near impunity on prostitutes and servants. The pornography he wrote was an urgent part of the sexual abuse he practiced: not only because he did what he wrote, but also because the intense hatred of women that fueled the one also fueled the other: not two separate engines, but one engine running on the same tank. The acts of pornography and the acts of rape were waves on the same sea: that sea, becoming for its victims however it reached them, a tidal wave of destruction. Pornographers who use words know that what they are doing is both aggressive and destructive: Sometimes they philosophize about how sex inevitably ends in death, the death of a woman being a thing of sexual beauty as well as excitement. Pornography, even when written, is sex because of the dynamism of the sexual hatred in it; and for pornographers, the sexual abuse of women as commonly understood and pornography are both acts of sexual predation, which is how they live.

One reason that stopping pornographers and pornography is not censorship is that pornographers are more like the police in police states than they are like the writers in police states. They are the instruments of terror, not its victims. What police do to the powerless in police states is what pornographers do to women, except that it is entertainment for the masses, not dignified as political. Writers do not do what pornographers do. Secret police do. Torturers do. What pornographers do to women is more like what police do to political prisoners than it is like anything else; except for the fact that it is watched with so much pleasure by so many. Intervening in a system of terror where it is vulnerable to public scrutiny to stop it is not censorship; it is the system of terror that stops speech and creates abuse and despair. The pornographers are the secret police of male supremacy: keeping women subordinate through intimidation and assault.

V. Subordination

In the amendment to the Human Rights Ordinance of the City of Minneapolis written by Catharine A. MacKinnon and myself,[9] pornography is defined as the graphic, sexually explicit subordination of women whether in pictures or in words that also includes one or more of the following: Women are presented dehumanized as sexual objects, things, or commodities; or women are presented as sexual objects who enjoy pain or humiliation; or women are presented as sexual objects who experience sexual pleasure in being raped; or women are presented as sexual objects tied up or cut up or mutilated or bruised or physically hurt; or women are presented in postures of sexual submission; or women's body parts are exhibited, such that women are reduced to those parts; or women are presented being penetrated by objects or animals; or women are presented in scenarios of degradation, injury, abasement, torture, shown as filthy or inferior, bleeding, bruised, or hurt in a context that makes these conditions sexual.

This statutory definition is an objectively accurate definition of what pornography is, based on an analysis of the material produced by the $8-billion-a-year industry and also on extensive study of the whole range of pornography extant from other eras and other cultures. Given the fact that women's oppression has an ahistorical character—a sameness across time and cultures expressed in rape, battery, incest, and prostitution—it is no surprise that pornography, a central phenomenon in that oppression, has precisely that quality of sameness. It does not significantly change in what it is, what it does, what is in it, or how it works, whether it is, for instance, classical or feudal or modern, Western or Asian; whether the method of manufacture is words, photographs, or video. What has changed is the public availability of pornography and the numbers of live women used in it because of new technologies, not its nature. Many people note what seems to them a qualitative change in pornography—that it has gotten more violent, even grotesquely violent, over the last two decades. The change is only in what is publicly visible: not in the range or preponderance of violent pornography (e.g., the place of rape in pornography stays constant and central, no matter where, when, or how the pornography is produced); not in the character, quality, or content of what the pornographers actually produce; not in the harm caused; not in the valuation of women in it or the metaphysical definition of what women are; not in the sexual abuse promoted, including rape, battery, and incest; not in the centrality of its role in subordinating women. Until recently, pornography operated in private, where most abuse of women takes place.

The oppression of women occurs through sexual subordination. It is the use of sex as the medium of oppression that makes the subordination of women so distinct from racism or prejudice against a group based on religion or national origin. Social inequality is created in many different ways. In my view, the radical responsibility is to isolate the material means of creating the inequality so that material remedies can be found for it.

This is particularly difficult with respect to women's inequality because that inequality is achieved through sex. Sex as desired by the class that dominates women is held by that class to be elemental, urgent, necessary, even if or even though it appears to require the repudiation of any claim women might have to full human standing. In the subordination of women, inequality itself is sexualized, made into the experience of sexual pleasure, essential to sexual desire. Pornography is the material means of sexualizing inequality, and that is why pornography is a central practice in the subordination of women.

Subordination itself is a broad, deep, systematic dynamic discernible in any persecution based on race or sex. Social subordination has four main parts. First, there is *hierarchy,* a group on top and a group on the bottom. For women, this hierarchy is experienced both socially and sexually, publicly and privately. Women are physically integrated into the society in which we are held to be inferior, and our low status is both put in place and maintained in the sexual usage of us by men, and so women's experience of hierarchy is incredibly intimate and wounding.

Second, subordination is *objectification.* Objectification occurs when a human being, through social means, is made less than human, turned into a thing or commodity, bought and sold. When objectification occurs, a person is depersonalized, so that no individuality or integrity is available socially or in what is an extremely circumscribed privacy (because those who dominate determine its boundaries). Objectification is an injury right at the heart of discrimination: Those who can be used as if they are not fully human are no longer fully human in social terms; their humanity is hurt by being diminished.

Third, subordination is *submission.* A person is at the bottom of a hierarchy because of a condition of birth; a person on the bottom is dehumanized, an object or commodity; inevitably, the situation of that person requires obedience and compliance. That diminished person is expected to be submissive; there is no longer any right to self-determination because there is no basis in equality for any such right to exist. In a condition of inferiority and objectification, submission is usually essential for survival. Oppressed groups are known for their abilities to anticipate the orders and desires of those who have power over them, to comply with an obsequiousness that is then used by the dominant group to justify its own dominance: The master, not able to imagine a human like himself in such degrading servility, thinks the servility is proof that the hierarchy is natural and that the objectification simply amounts to seeing these lesser creatures for what they are. The submission forced on inferior, objectified groups precisely by hierarchy and objectification is taken to be the proof of inherent inferiority and subhuman capacities.

Fourth, subordination is *violence.* The violence is systematic, endemic enough to be unremarkable and normative, usually taken as an implicit right of the one committing the violence. In my view, hierarchy, objectification, and submission are the preconditions for systematic social violence against any group targeted because of a condition of birth. If violence against a group is both socially pervasive and socially normal, then hierarchy, objectification, and submission are already solidly in place.

The role of violence in subordinating women has one special characteristic congruent with sex as the instrumentality of subordination: The violence is supposed to be sex for the woman, too—what women want and like as part of our sexual nature; it is supposed to give women pleasure (as in rape); it is supposed to mean love to a woman from her point of view (as in battery). The violence against women is seen to be done not just in accord with something compliant in women but in response to something active in and basic to women's nature.

Pornography uses each component of social subordination. Its particular medium is sex. Hierarchy, objectification, submission, and violence all become alive with sexual energy and sexual meaning. A hierarchy, for instance, can have a static quality, but pornography, by sexualizing it, makes it dynamic, almost carnivorous, so that men keep imposing it for the sake of their own sexual pleasure—for the sexual pleasure it gives them to impose it. In pornography, each element of subordination is conveyed through the sexually explicit usage of women: pornography in fact is what women are and what women are for and how women are used in a society premised on the inferiority of women. It is a metaphysics of women's subjugation: our existence delineated in a definition of our nature; our status in society predetermined by the uses to which we are put. The woman's body is what is materially subordinated. Sex is the material means through which the subordination is accomplished. Pornography is the institution of male dominance that sexualizes hierarchy, objectification, submission, and violence. As such, pornography creates inequality, not as artifact, but as a system of social reality; it creates the necessity for and the actual behaviors that constitute sex inequality.

VI. Speech

Subordination can be so deep that those who are hurt by it are utterly silent. Subordination can create a silence quieter than death. The women flattened out on the page are deathly still, except for *hurt me*. *Hurt me* is not women's speech. It is the speech imposed on women by pimps to cover the awful, condemning silence. The Three Marias of Portugal went to jail for writing this: "Let no one tell me that silence gives consent, because whoever is silent dissents."[10] The women say the pimp's words: The language is another element of the rape; the language is part of the humiliation; the language is part of the forced sex. Real silence might signify dissent, for those reared to understand its sad discourse. The pimps cannot tolerate literal silence—it is too eloquent as testimony—so they force the words out of the woman's mouth. The women say pimp's words, which is worse than silence. The silence of the women not in the picture, outside the pages, hurt but silent, used but silent, is staggering in how deep and wide it goes. It is a silence over centuries: an exile into speechlessness. One is shut up by the inferiority and the abuse. One is shut up by the threat and the injury. In her memoir of the Stalin period, *Hope Against Hope,* Nadezha Mandelstam wrote that screaming

> is a man's way of leaving a trace, of telling people how he lived and died. By his screams he asserts his right to live, sends a message to the outside world demanding help and calling for resistance. If nothing else is left, one must scream. Silence is the real crime against humanity.[11]

Screaming is a man's way of leaving a trace. The scream of a man is never misunderstood as a scream of pleasure by passersby or politicians or historians, or by the tormentor. A man's scream is a call for resistance. A man's scream asserts his right to live, sends a message; he leaves a trace. A woman's scream is the sound of her female will and her female pleasure in doing what the pornographers say she is for. Her scream is a sound of celebration to those who overhear. Women's way of leaving a trace is the silence, centuries' worth: the entirely inhuman silence that surely one day will be noticed; someone will say that something is wrong, some sound is missing, some voice is lost; the entirely inhuman silence that will be a clue to human hope denied, a shard of evidence that a crime has occurred, the crime that created the silence; the entirely inhuman silence that is a cold, cold condemnation of hurt sustained in speechlessness, a cold, cold condemnation of what those who speak have done to those who do not.

But there is more than the *hurt me* forced out of us, and the silence in which it lies. The pornographers actually use our bodies as their language. Our bodies are the building blocks of their sentences. What they do to us, called speech, is not unlike what Kafka's Harrow machine—"'The needles are set in like the teeth of a harrow and the whole thing works something like a harrow, although its action is limited to one place and contrived with much more artistic skill'"[12]—did to the condemned in *In the Penal Colony:*

> "Our sentence does not sound severe. Whatever commandment the prisoner has disobeyed is written upon his body by the Harrow. This prisoner, for instance"—the officer indicated the man—"will have written on his body: HONOR THY SUPERIORS!"[13]
>
> ". . . The Harrow is beginning to write; when it finishes the first draft of the inscription on the man's back, the layer of cotton wool begins to roll and slowly turns the body over, to give the Harrow fresh space for writing. . . . So it keeps on writing deeper and deeper."[14]

Asked if the prisoner knows his sentence, the officer replies: "'There would be no point in telling him. He'll learn it on his body.'"[15]

This is the so-called speech of the pornographers, protected now by law.

Protecting what they "say" means protecting what they do to us, how they do it. It means protecting their sadism on our bodies, because that is how they write: not like a writer at all, like a torturer. Prttecting what they "say" means protecting sexual exploitation, because they cannot "say" anything without diminishing, hurting, or destroying us. Their rights of speech express their rights over us. Their rights of speech require our inferiority and that we be powerless in relation to them. Their rights of speech mean that *hurt me* is accepted as the real speech of women, not speech forced on us as part of the sex forced on us but originating with us because we are what the pornographers "say" we are.

If what we want to say is not *hurt me,* we have the real social power only to use silence as eloquent dissent. Silence is what women have instead of speech. Silence is our dissent during rape unless the rapist, like the pornographer, prefers *hurt me,* in which case we have no dissent. Silence is our moving, persuasive dissent during battery unless the batterer, like the pornographer, prefers *hurt me.* Silence is a fine dissent during incest and for all the long years after.

Silence is not speech. We have silence, not speech. We fight rape, battery, incest, and prostitution with it. We lose. But someday someone will notice: that people called women were buried in a long silence that meant dissent and that the pornographers—with needles set in like the teeth of a harrow—chattered on.

VII. Equality

To get that word, male, out of the Constitution, cost the women of this country fifty-two years of pauseless campaign; 56 state referendum campaigns; 480 legislative campaigns to get state suffrage amendments submitted; 47 state consti-

tutional convention campaigns; 277 state party convention campaigns; 30
national party convention campaigns to get suffrage planks in the party plat-
forms; 19 campaigns with 19 successive Congresses to get the federal amendment submitted, and the final ratification campaign.

Millions of dollars were raised, mostly in small sums, and spent with economic care. Hundreds of women gave the accumulated possibilities of an entire
lifetime, thousands gave years of their lives, hundreds of thousands gave constant interest and such aid as they could. It was a continuous and seemingly
endless chain of activity. Young suffragists who helped forge the last links of that
chain were not born when it began. Old suffragists who helped forge the first
links were dead when it ended.

Carrie Chapman Catt

Feminists have wanted equality. Radicals and reformists have different ideas of what
equality would be, but it has been the wisdom of feminism to value equality as a political
goal with social integrity and complex meaning. The Jacobins also wanted equality, and
the French Revolution was fought to accomplish it. Conservatism as a modern political
movement actually developed to resist social and political movements for equality, beginning with the egalitarian imperatives of the French Revolution.

Women have had to prove human status before having any claim to equality. But
equality has been impossible to achieve, perhaps because, really, women have not been
able to prove human status. The burden of proof is on the victim.

Not one inch of change has been easy or cheap. We have fought so hard and so long
for so little. The vote did not change the status of women. The changes in women's lives
that we can see on the surface do not change the status of women. By the year 2000,
women are expected to be 100 percent of this nation's poor.[16] We are raped, battered, and
prostituted: These acts against us are in the fabric of social life. As children, we are raped,
physically abused, and prostituted. The country enjoys the injuries done to us and spends
$8 billion a year on the pleasure of watching us being hurt (exploitation as well as torture
constituting substantive harm). The subordination gets deeper: We keep getting pushed
down further. Rape is an entertainment. The contempt for us in that fact is immeasura-
ble, yet we live under the weight of it. Discrimination is a euphemism for what happens
to us.

It has plagued us to try to understand why the status of women does not change. Those
who hate the politics of equality say they know: We are biologically destined for rape; God
made us to be submissive unto our husbands. We change, but our status does not change.
Laws change, but our status stays fixed. We move into the marketplace only to face there
classic sexual exploitation, now called sexual harassment. Rape, battery, prostitution,
and incest stay the same in that they keep happening to us as part of what life is; even
though we name the crimes against us as such and try to keep the victims from being
destroyed by what we cannot stop from happening to them. And the silence stays in place
too, however much we try to dislodge it with our truths. We say what has happened to us,
but newspapers, governments, the culture that excludes us as fully human participants,
wipe us out, wipe out our speech by refusing to hear it. We are the tree falling in the desert.
Should it matter; they are the desert.

The cost of trying to shatter the silence is astonishing to those who do it: the women,
raped, battered, prostituted, who have something to say and say it. They stand there even
as they are erased. Governments turn from them; courts ignore them; this country disa-

vows and dispossesses them. Men ridicule, threaten, or hurt them. Women jeopardized by them—silence being safer than speech—betray them. It is ugly to watch the complacent destroy the brave. It is horrible to watch power win.

Still, equality is what we want, and we are going to get it. What we understand about it now is that it cannot be proclaimed; it must be created. It has to take the place of subordination in human experience, physically replace it. Equality does not coexist with subordination, as if it were a little pocket located somewhere within it. Equality has to win. Subordination has to lose. The subordination of women has not even been knocked loose, and equality has not materially advanced, at least in part because the pornography has been creating sexualized inequality in hiding, in private, where the abuses occur on a massive scale.

Equality for women requires material remedies for pornography, whether pornography is central to the inequality of women or only one cause of it. Pornography's antagonism to civil equality, integrity, and self-determination for women is absolute; and it is effective in making that antagonism socially real and socially determining.

The law that Catharine A. MacKinnon and I wrote making pornography a violation of women's civil rights recognizes the injury that pornography does, how it hurts women's rights of citizenship through sexual exploitation and sexual torture both.

The civil rights law empowers women by allowing women to civilly sue those who hurt us through pornography by trafficking in it, coercing people into it, forcing it on people, and assaulting people directly because of a specific piece of it.

The civil rights law does not force the pornography back underground. There is no prior restraint or police power to make arrests, which would then result in a revivified black market. This respects the reach of the First Amendment, but it also keeps the pornography from getting sexier—hidden, forbidden, dirty, happily back in the land of the obscene, sexy slime oozing on great books. Wanting to cover the pornography up, hide it, is the first response of those who need pornography to the civil rights law. If pornography is hidden, it is still accessible to men as a male right of access to women; its injuries to the status of women are safe and secure in those hidden rooms behind those opaque covers; the abuses of women are sustained as a private right supported by public policy. The civil rights law puts a flood of light on the pornography, what it is, how it is used, what it does, those who are hurt by it.

The civil rights law changes the power relationship between pornographers and women; it stops the pornographers from producing discrimination with the total impunity they now enjoy, and gives women a legal standing resembling equality from which to repudiate the subordination itself. The secret-police power of the pornographers suddenly has to confront a modest amount of due process.

The civil rights law undermines the subordination of women in society by confronting the pornography, which is the systematic sexualization of that subordination. Pornography is inequality. The civil rights law would allow women to advance equality by removing this concrete discrimination and hurting economically those who make, sell, distribute, or exhibit it. The pornography, being power, has a right to exist that we are not allowed to challenge under this system of law. After it hurts us by being what it is and doing what it does, the civil rights law would allow us to hurt it back. Women, not being power, do not have a right to exist equal to the right the pornography has. If we did, the pornographers would be precluded from exercising their rights at the expense of ours, and since they cannot exercise them any other way, they would be precluded, period. We come to the legal system beggars, though in the public dialogue around the passage of this civil rights law we have the satisfaction of being regarded as thieves.

The civil rights law is women's speech. It defines an injury to us from our point of view. It is premised on a repudiation of sexual subordination which is born of our experience of it. It breaks the silence. It is a sentence that can hold its own against the male flood. It is a sentence on which we can build a paragraph, then a page.

It is my view, learned largely from Catharine MacKinnon, that women have a right to be effective. The pornographers, of course, do not think so, nor do other male supremacists, and it is hard for women to think so. We have been told to educate people on the evils of pornography; before the development of this civil rights law, we were told just to keep quiet about pornography altogether; but now that we have a law we want to use, we are encouraged to educate and stop there. Law educates. This law educates. It also allows women to do something. In hurting the pornography back, we gain ground in making equality more likely, more possible—someday it will be real. We have a means to fight the pornographers' trade in women. We have a means to get at the torture and the terror. We have a means with which to challenge the pornography's efficacy in making exploitation and inferiority the bedrock of women's social status. The civil rights law introduces into the public consciousness an analysis of what pornography is, what sexual subordination is, what equality might be. The civil rights law introduces a new legal standard: These things are not done to citizens of this country. The civil rights law introduces a new political standard: These things are not done to human beings. The civil rights law provides a new mode of action for women through which we can pursue equality and because of which our speech will have social meaning. The civil rights law gives us back what the pornographers have taken from us: hope rooted in real possibility.

Appendix A:
Model Antipornography Law

Section 1. Statement of Policy

Pornography is sex discrimination. It exists in [PLACE], posing a substantial threat to the health, safety, peace, welfare, and equality of citizens in the community. Existing [state and] federal laws are inadequate to solve these problems in [PLACE].

Pornography is a systematic practice of exploitation and subordination based on sex that differentially harms women. The harm of pornography includes dehumanization, sexual exploitation, forced sex, forced prostitution, physical injury, and social and sexual terrorism and inferiority presented as entertainment. The bigotry and contempt it promotes, with the acts of aggression it fosters, diminish opportunities for equality of rights in employment, education, property, public accommodations and public services; create public and private harassment, persecution and denigration; promote injury and degradation such as rape, battery, child sexual abuse, and prostitution and inhibit just enforcement of laws against these acts; contribute significantly to restricting women in particular from full exercise of citizenship and participation in public life, including in neighborhoods; damage relations between the sexes; and undermine women's equal exercise of rights to speech and action guaranteed to all citizens under the Constitutions and laws of the United States and [PLACE, INCLUDING STATE].

Section 2. Definitions

1. *Pornography* is the graphic sexually explicit subordination of women through pictures and/or words that also includes one or more of the following: (i) women are presented dehumanized as sexual objects, things, or commodities; or (ii) women are presented as sexual objects who enjoy pain or humiliation; or (iii) women are presented as sexual objects who experience sexual pleasure in being raped; or (iv) women are presented as sexual objects tied up or cut up or mutilated or bruised or physically hurt; or (v) women are presented in postures or positions of sexual submission, servility, or display; or (vi) women's body parts—including but not limited to vaginas, breasts, or buttocks—are exhibited such that women are reduced to those parts; or (vii) women are presented as whores by nature; or (viii) women are presented being penetrated by objects or animals; or (ix) women are presented in scenarios of degradation, injury, torture, shown as filthy or inferior, bleeding, bruised, or hurt in a context that makes these conditions sexual.

2. The use of men, children, or transsexuals in the place of women in (1) above is pornography for purposes of this law.

Section 3. Unlawful Practices

1. *Coercion into pornography:* It shall be sex discrimination to coerce, intimidate, or fraudulently induce (hereafter, "coerce") any person, including transsexual, into performing for pornography, which injury may date from any appearance or sale of any product(s) of such performance(s). The maker(s), seller(s), exhibitor(s), and/or distributor(s) of said pornography may be sued for damages and for an injunction, including to eliminate the product(s) of the performance(s) from the public view.

Proof of one or more of the following facts or conditions shall not, without more, negate a finding of coercion: (i) that the person is a woman; or (ii) that the person is or has been a prostitute; or (iii) that the person has attained the age of majority; or (iv) that the person is connected by blood or marriage to anyone involved in or related to the making of the pornography; or (v) that the person has previously had, or been thought to have had, sexual relations with anyone, including anyone involved in or related to the making of the pornography; or (vi) that the person has previously posed for sexually explicit pictures with or for anyone, including anyone involved in or related to the making of the pornography at issue; or (vii) that anyone else, including a spouse or other relative, has given permission on the person's behalf; or (viii) that the person actually consented to a use of the performance that is changed into pornography; or (ix) that the person knew that the purpose of the acts or events in question was to make pornography; or (x) that the person showed no resistance or appeared to cooperate actively in the photographic sessions or in the events that produced the pornography; or (xi) that the person signed a contract, or made statements affirming a willingness to cooperate in the production of pornography; or (xii) that no physical force, threats, or weapons were used in the making of the pornography; or (xiii) that the person was paid or otherwise compensated.

2. *Trafficking in pornography:* It shall be sex discrimination to produce, sell, exhibit, or distribute pornography, including through private clubs.

(i) City, state, and federally funded public libraries or private and public university and college libraries in which pornography is available for study, including on open shelves but excluding special display presentations, shall not be construed to be trafficking in pornography.

(ii) Isolated passages or isolated parts shall not be actionable under this section.

(iii) Any woman has a claim hereunder as a woman acting against the subordination of women. Any man, child, or transsexual who alleges injury by pornography in the way women are injured by it also has a claim.

3. *Forcing pornography on a person:* It shall be sex discrimination to force pornography on a person, including a child or transsexual, in any place of employment, education, home, or public place. Only the perpetrator of the force or responsible institution may be sued.

4. *Assault of physical attack due to pornography:* It shall be sex discrimination to assault, physically attack, or injure any person, including child or transsexual, in a way that is directly caused by specific pornography. The perpetrator of the assault or attack may be sued for damages and enjoined where appropriate. The maker(s), distributor(s), seller(s), and/or exhibitor(s) may also be sued for damages and for an injunction against the specific pornography's further exhibition, distribution, or sale.

Section 4. Defenses

1. It shall not be a defense that the defendant in an action under this law did not know or intend that the materials were pornography or sex discrimination.

2. No damages or compensation for losses shall be recoverable under Sec. 3(2) or other than against the perpetrator of the assault or attack in Sec. 3(4) unless the defendant knew or had reason to know that the materials were pornography.

3. In actions under Sec. 3(2) or other than against the perpetrator of the assault or attack in Sec. 3(4), no damages or compensation for losses shall be recoverable against maker(s) for pornography made, against distributor(s) for pornography distributed, against seller(s) for pornography sold, or against exhibitor(s) for pornography exhibited, prior to the effective date of this law.

Section 5. Enforcement[17]

1. *Civil action:* Any person aggrieved by violations of this law may enforce its provisions by means of a civil action. No criminal penalties shall attach for any violation of the provisions of this law. Relief for violation of this act may include reasonable attorney's fees.

2. *Injunction:* Any person who violates this law may be enjoined except that:

(i) In actions under Sec. 3(2), and other than against the perpetrator of the assault or attack under Sec. 3(4), no temporary or permanent injunction shall issue prior to a final judicial determination that the challenged activities constitute a violation of this law.

(ii) No temporary or permanent injunction shall extend beyond such material(s) that, having been described with reasonable specificity by the injunction, have been determined to be validly proscribed under this law.

Section 6. Severability

Should any part(s) of this law be found legally invalid, the remaining part(s) remains valid. A judicial declaration that any part(s) of this law cannot be applied validly in a particular manner or to a particular case or category of cases shall not affect the validity of that part(s) as otherwise applied, unless such other application would clearly frustrate the [LEGISLATIVE BODY'S] intent in adopting this law.

Section 7. Limitation of Action

Actions under this law must be filed within one year of the alleged discriminatory acts.

Notes

I thank all of the women who talked to me about how pornography has been used on them over all the years when there was nothing we could do. I thank Jeanne Barkey in particular for her stunning work in organizing the first Minneapolis hearings on pornography; and Charlee Hoyt, for being the driving force behind getting the legislation written and enacted. I thank Van White for cosponsoring the bill and conducting the hearings. I thank everyone who testified in behalf of the legislation at the first hearings and later in subsequent hearings, and also those who talked to the press about sexual abuse at great cost to themselves. I thank the people who organized and now run the Pornography Resource Center in Minneapolis, especially for their work in organizing victims. I especially thank Therese Stanton for her extraordinary personal courage in testifying at the first Minneapolis hearings and for her untiring work in behalf of victims. I thank Steve Jevning for his tenacity, courage, and astuteness in working for the legislation and for initiating the political process that led to both the legislation and a new kind of grassroots organizing. I especially thank my colleague, Catharine MacKinnon, for the honor of the intellectual and political dialogue we have had in conceiving and drafting the legislation and for her indomitable will to stop the pornographers from hurting women. I thank John Stoltenberg for his many contributions to the politics of equality on which the legislation and this essay are built. All of these people contributed in both knowledge and faith to the writing of this chapter. I dedicate this chapter to all those resolute and brave people who worked to accomplish the passage of the first Minneapolis antipornography civil rights bill. Thank you.

1. "Well, you know, it amazes me," says dissident South African writer Nadine Gordimer in an interview. "I come to America, I go to England, I go to France . . . nobody's at risk. They're afraid of getting cancer, losing a lover, losing their jobs, being insecure. . . . It's only in my own country that I find people who voluntarily choose to put everything at risk—in their personal life." *Nadine Gordimer*, WRITERS AT WORK: THE PARIS REVIEW INTERVIEWS 261 (G. Plimpton ed. 6th ser. 1984).

2. G. FLAUBERT, LETTERS 94 (J.M. Cohen trans. 1950).

3. Letter from D.H. Lawrence to Morris Ernst, *quoted in* H. Moore, *Introduction* to D.H. LAWRENCE, SEX, LITERATURE AND CENSORSHIP 9 (1959).

4. H. GARDINER, CATHOLIC VIEWPOINT ON CENSORSHIP 65 (1958).

5. G. BATAILLE, DEATH AND SENSUALITY 12 (1969).

6. D. H. LAWRENCE, at 69.

7. V. NABOKOV, *Afterword* to LOLITA 284 (1977).

8. The actual line is "In dreams begins responsibility," quoted by Yeats as an epigram to a collection of his poetry. W. B. YEATS, RESPONSIBILITIES AND OTHER POEMS (1916).

9. *Editor's note:* The first antipornography law drafted by Dworkin and MacKinnon was proposed as an amendment to Minneapolis, Minn., Code of Ordinances Relating to Civil Rights tit. 7, chs. 139 & 141. Extensive hearings on the proposed bill, which included testimony from expert witnesses and victims of sexual abuse, were held on December 12 and 13, 1983. The Minneapolis City Council passed the ordinance on December 30, 1983; Mayor Donald Fraser vetoed it on January 5, 1984. The city council, with several newly elected members, passed a slightly revised form of the bill on July 13, 1984, and Mayor Fraser again vetoed it.

The Indianapolis City Council passed a similar bill on April 23, 1984; it was signed into law by Mayor William H. Hudnut, III. Gen'l Ordinance no. 24 (May 1, 1984) (amending Indianapolis & Marion County, Ind., Code ch. 16). The ordinance was later amended by Gen'l Ordinance no. 35 (June 15, 1984), to bring it into closer conformity with the Minneapolis prototype.

The Indianapolis ordinance was immediately challenged on first amendment grounds by media trade groups with support from civil liberties organizations. On November 19, 1984, Judge Sarah Evans Barker held the ordinance unconstitutional. *See* American Booksellers Ass'n, Inc. v. Hudnut, 598 F. Supp. 1316 (S.D. Ind. 1984), *appeal docketed,* No. 84-3147 (7th Cir. Dec. 21, 1984).

10. M.I. Barreno, M.T. Horta, and M. Velho da Costa, The Three Marias: New Portuguese Letters 291 (H. R. Lane trans. 1976).

11. N. Mandelstam, Hope Against Hope 42–43 (M. Hayward trans. 1978).

12. F. Kafka, *In the Penal Colony,* in The Penal Colony 194 (W. Muir and E. Muir trans. 1965).

13. *Id.* at 197.

14. *Id.* at 203.

15. *Id.* at 197.

16. For a comprehensive analysis of how the feminization of poverty brutally impacts on people of color in the United States, see *The Coming Gynocide,* in A. Dworkin, Right-Wing Women 147, 162–73 (1983).

17. In the event that this law is amended to a preexisting human-rights law, the complaint would first be made to a Civil Rights Commission. Any injunction issued under Sec. 3(2), the trafficking provision, would require trial *de novo* (a full court trial after the administrative hearing).

19

Brief *Amici Curiae* of Feminist Anticensorship Task Force et al., in *American Booksellers Association v. Hudnut*

NAN D. HUNTER
SYLVIA A. LAW

I. The Ordinance Suppresses Constitutionally Protected Speech in a Manner Particularly Detrimental to Women

Although appellants argue that the ordinance is designed to restrict images which legitimate violence and coercion against women, the definition of pornography in the ordinance is not limited to images of violence or of coercion or to images produced by women who were coerced. Nor is it limited to materials which advocate or depict the torture or rape of women as a form of sexual pleasure. It extends to any sexually explicit material which an agency or court finds to be "subordinating" to a claimant acting on behalf of women and which fits within one of the descriptive categories which complete the definition of pornography.

For purposes of the trafficking cause of action, the ordinance defines pornography as the "graphic sexually explicit subordination of women, whether in pictures or in words, that also includes one or more" of the depictions described in six categories.[1] The violent and brutal images which appellants use as illustrative examples[2] cannot obscure the fact that the ordinance authorizes suppression of material that is sexually explicit but in no way violent. The language of the definition mixes phrases that have clear meanings and thus ascertainable applications (e.g., "cut up or mutilated") with others which are sufficiently elastic to encompass almost any sexually explicit image that someone might find offensive (e.g., "scenarios of degradation" or "abasement"). The material that could be suppressed under the latter category is virtually limitless.

While the sweep of the ordinance is breathtaking, it does not address (nor would *amici* support state suppression of) the far more pervasive commercial images depicting women as primarily concerned with the whiteness of their wash, the softness of their toilet tissue, and whether the lines of their panties show when wearing tight slacks. Commercial images, available to the most impressionable young children during prime time, depict women as people interested in inconsequential matters who are incapable of taking significant, serious roles in societal decision making.

The constitutionality of the ordinance depends on the assumption that state agencies and courts can develop clear legal definitions of terms like "sexually explicit subordination," "sexual object," and "scenarios of degradation" and "abasement." In truth, these terms are highly contextual and of varying meanings. Worse, many of their most commonly accepted meanings would, if applied in the context of this ordinance, reinforce rather than erode archaic and untrue stereotypes about women's sexuality.

A. *Historically the Law Has Incorporated a Sexual Double Standard Denying Women's Interest in Sexual Expression*

Traditionally, laws regulating sexual activity were premised upon and reinforced a gender-based double standard which assumed.

> that women are delicate, that voluntary sexual intercourse may harm them in certain circumstances and that they may be seriously injured by words as well as deeds. The statutes also suggest that, despite the generally delicate nature of most women, there exists a class of women who are not delicate or who are not worthy of protection. [By contrast, the law's treatment of male sexuality reflected] the underlying assumption that only males have aggressive sexual desires [and] hence they must be restrained. . . .
> The detail and comprehensiveness of [such] laws suggest that men are considered almost crazed by sex.[3]

The Indianapolis ordinance is squarely within the tradition of the sexual double standard. It allows little room for women to openly express certain sexual desires and resurrects the notion that sexually explicit materials are subordinating and degrading to women. Because the "trafficking" cause of action allows one woman to obtain a court order suppressing images which fall within the ordinance's definition of pornography, it implies that individual women are incapable of choosing for themselves what they consider to be enjoyable, sexually arousing material without being degraded or humiliated.

The legal system has used many vehicles to enforce the sexual double standard which protected "good" women from both sexual activity and explicit speech about sex. For example, the common law of libel held that "an oral imputation of unchastity to a woman is actionable without proof of damage. . . . Such a rule never has been applied to a man, since the damage to his reputation is assumed not to be as great.[4]

The common law also reinforced the image of "good" women as asexual and vulnerable by providing the husband, but not the wife, remedies for "interference" with his right to sole possession of his wife's body and services. The early writ of "ravishment" listed the wife with the husband's chattels. To this day, the action for criminal conversation allows the husband to maintain an action for trespass, not only when his wife is raped

> but also even though the wife had consented to it, or was herself the seducer and had invited and procured it, since it was considered that she was no more capable of giving a consent which would prejudice the husband's interests than was his horse.[5]

While denying the possibility that "good" women could be sexual, the common law dealt harshly with the "bad" women who were. Prostitution laws often penalized only the woman, and not the man, and even facially neutral laws were and are enforced primarily against women.[6] Prostitution is defined as "the practice of a female offering her body to indiscriminate sexual intercourse with men" or submitting "to indiscriminate sexual intercourse which she invites or solicits."[7] A woman who has sexual relations with many men is a "common prostitute" and a criminal, while a sexually active man is considered normal.

The sexual double standard is applied with particular force to young people. Statutory rape laws often punished men for consensual intercourse with a female under a certain age.[8] Such laws reinforce the stereotype that in sex the man is the offender and the woman the victim and that young men may legitimately engage in sex, at least with older people, while a young woman may not legally have sex with anyone.

The suppression of sexually explicit material most devastating to women was the restriction on dissemination of birth control information, common until 1971. In that year, the Supreme Court held that the constitutional right to privacy protects an unmarried person's right to access to birth control information.[9] To deny women access to contraception "prescribe[s] pregnancy and the birth of an unwanted child as punishment for fornication.[10] For the previous century, the federal Comstock law, passed in 1873, had prohibited mailing, transporting or importing "obscene, lewd or lascivious" items, specifically including all devices and information pertaining to "preventing contraception and producing abortion."[11] Women were jailed for distributing educational materials regarding birth control to other women because the materials were deemed sexually explicit in that they "contain[ed] pictures of certain organs of women" and because the materials were found to be "detrimental to public morals and welfare."[12]

The Mann Act also was premised on the notion that women require special protection from sexual activity.[13] It forbids interstate transportation of women for purposes of "prostitution, debauchery, or any other immoral purposes" and was enacted to protect women from reportedly widespread abduction by bands of "white slavers" coercing them into prostitution. As the legislative history reveals, the act reflects the assumption that women have no will of their own and must be protected against themselves.[14] Like the premises underlying this ordinance, the Mann Act assumed

> that women were naturally chaste and virtuous, and that no woman became a whore unless she had first been raped, seduced, drugged or deserted. [Its] image of the prostitute . . . was of a lonely and confused female. . . . [Its proponents] maintained that prostitutes were the passive victims of social disequilibrium and the brutality of men. . . . [Its] conception of female weakness and male domination left no room for the possibility that prostitutes might consciously choose their activities.[15]

The Mann Act initially defined a "white slave" to include "only those women or girls who are literally slaves—those women who are owned and held as property and chattels . . . those women and girls who, if given a fair chance, would, in all human probability, have been good wives and mothers," H.R. Rep. no. 47, 61st Cong.,2d Sess., at 9-10 (1910). Over the years, the interpretation and use of the act changed drastically to punish voluntary "immoral" acts even when no commercial intention or business profit was involved.[16]

> The term "other immoral acts" was held to apply to a variety of activities: the interstate transportation of a woman to work as a chorus girl in a theatre where the woman was exposed to smoking, drinking, and cursing; a dentist who met his young lover in a neighboring state and shared a hotel room to discuss her pregnancy; two students at the University of Puerto Rico who had sexual intercourse on the way home from a

date; and a man and woman who had lived together for four years and traveled around the country as man and wife while the man sold securities.[17]

Society's attempts to "protect" women's chastity through criminal and civil laws have resulted in restrictions on women's freedom to engage in sexual activity, to discuss it publicly, and to protect themselves from the risk of pregnancy. These disabling restrictions reinforced the gender roles which have oppressed women for centuries. The Indianapolis ordinance resonates with the traditional concept that sex itself degrades women, and its enforcement would reinvigorate those discriminatory moral standards which have limited women's equality in the past.

◇ ◇ ◇

C. The Ordinance Is Unconstitutionally Vague Because Its Central Terms Have No Fixed Meaning, and the Most Common Meanings of These Terms Are Sexist and Damaging to Women

The ordinance's definition of pornography, essential to each cause of action, is fatally flawed. It relies on words often defined in ways that reinforce a constricted and constricting view of women's sexuality. Thus *amici* fear that experimentations in feminist art which deal openly and explicitly with sexual themes will be easily targeted for suppression under this ordinance.

The central term *sexually explicit subordination* is not defined.[18] Appellants argue that *subordination* means that which "places women in positions of inferiority, loss of power, degradation and submission, among other things."[19] The core question, however, is left begging: What kinds of sexually explicit acts place a woman in an inferior status? Appellants argued in their brief to the district court that "the mere existence of pornography in society degrades and demeans all women."[20] To some observers, any graphic image of sexual acts is "degrading" to women and hence would subordinate them. To some, the required element of subordination or "positions of . . . submission" might be satisfied by the image of a woman lying on her back inviting intercourse, while others might view the same image as affirming women's sexual pleasure and initiative. Some might draw the line at acts outside the bounds of marriage or with multiple partners. Others might see a simple image of the most traditional heterosexual act as subordinating in presenting the man in a physical position of superiority and the woman in a position of inferiority.

In any of these contexts, it is not clear whether the ordinance is to be interpreted with a subjective or an objective standard. If a subjective interpretation of subordination is contemplated, the ordinance vests in individual women a power to impose their views of politically or morally correct sexuality upon other women by calling for repression of images consistent with those views. The evaluative terms—subordination, degradation, abasement—are initially within the definitional control of the plaintiff, whose interpretation, if colorable, must be accepted by the court. An objective standard would require a court to determine whether plaintiff's reaction to the material comports with some generalized notion of which images do or do not degrade women. It would require the judiciary to impose its views of correct sexuality on a diverse community. The inevitable result would be to disapprove those images that are least conventional and privilege those that are closest to majoritarian beliefs about proper sexuality.

Whether subjective or objective, the inquiry is one that plainly and profoundly threatens First Amendment freedoms and is totally inconsistent with feminist principles, as they are understood by *amici.* Sexuality is particularly susceptible to extremely charged emotions, including feelings of vulnerability and power. The realm of image judgment opened by the ordinance is too contested and sensitive to be entrusted to legislative categorization and judicial enforcement.

The danger of discrimination is illustrated by the probability that some women would consider any explicit lesbian scene as subordinating, or as causing "[their] dignity [to] suffer."[21] Appellants plainly intend to include same-sex depictions, since their carefully selected trial court exhibits include such materials.[22] Lesbians and gay men[23] encounter massive discrimination based on prejudice related to their sexuality.[24] The trafficking provision of the ordinance virtually invites new manifestations of this prejudice by means of civil litigation against the erotica of sexual minorities.

The six subsections of the definition applicable to a trafficking complaint provide no clarification. The term *sexual object,* for example, appears frequently in the definition. Appellants are confident that "the common man knows a sex object when he sees one."[25] Yet, although *sex object* may be a phrase which has begun to enjoy widened popular usage, its precise meaning is far from clear. Some persons maintain that any detachment of women's sexuality from procreation, marriage, and family objectifies it, removing it from its "natural" web of association and context. When sex is detached from its traditional moorings, men allegedly benefit and women are the victims.[26] Feminists, on the other hand, generally use the term *sex object* to mean the absence of any indicia of personhood, a very different interpretation.

Appellants argue that the meaning of *subordination* and *degradation* can be determined in relation to "common usage and understanding."[27] But as we have seen, the common understanding of sexuality is one that incorporates a sexual double standard. Historically, virtually all sexually explicit literature and imagery has been thought to be degrading or abasing or humiliating, especially to women.

The interpretation of such morally charged terms has varied notoriously over time and place. A state supreme court thirty years ago ruled that the words "obscene, lewd, licentious, indecent, lascivious, immoral, [and] scandalous" were "neither vague or indefinite" and had "a meaning understood by all."[28] A Florida obscenity statute which declared it to be "unlawful to publish, sell[, etc.] any obscene, lewd, lascivious, filthy, indecent, immoral, degrading, sadistic, masochistic or disgusting book"[29] was found to be no longer adequate after the decision in *Roth v. United States,* absent both a contemporary definition of those terms and a standard based on the materials' overall value and not just their explicitness.[30] After *Roth* and subsequent decisions, the statute was amended three times to incorporate these additional elements.[31] Upon amending the statute in 1961, the word *degrading* was dropped. Words like *degradation, abasement,* and *humiliation* have been used in the past synonymously with subjective, moralistic terms. There is no reason to believe that the language in this ordinance will be magically resistant to that kind of interpretation.

The First Amendment prohibits any law regulating expression which would of necessity result in such unpredictable and arbitrary interpretations. This ordinance transgresses all three of the measures of impermissible vagueness. A person of ordinary intelligence would be at a loss to predict how any of a huge range of sexually explicit materials would be interpreted by a court.[32] Protected expression would be chilled because the makers, distributors, and exhibitors of sexually explicit works would be induced to practice self-censorship rather than risk potentially endless lawsuits under this ordinance.[33] Lastly, the absence of reasonably clear guidelines for triers of fact would open the door to arbitrary and discriminatory enforcement of the ordinance.[34]

The ordinance requires enforcement of "common understandings" of culturally loaded terms. It perpetuates beliefs which undermine the principle that women are full, equal, and active agents in every realm of life, including the sexual.

◊ ◊ ◊

II. The Ordinance Unconstitutionally Discriminates on the Basis of Sex and Reinforces Sexist Stereotypes

The challenged ordinance posits a great chasm—a categorical difference—between the makeup and needs of men and of women. It goes far beyond acknowledgment of the differences in life experiences which are inevitably produced by social structures of gender inequality. The ordinance presumes women as a class (and only women) are subordinated by virtually any sexually explicit image. It presumes women as a class (and only women) are incapable of making a binding agreement to participate in the creation of sexually explicit material. And it presumes men as a class (and only men) are conditioned by sexually explicit depictions to commit acts of aggression and to believe misogynist myths.

Such assumptions reinforce and perpetuate central sexist stereotypes; they weaken, rather than enhance, women's struggles to free themselves of archaic notions of gender roles. In so doing, this ordinance itself violates the equal protection clause of the Fourteenth Amendment. In treating women as a special class, it repeats the error of earlier protectionist legislation which gave women no significant benefits and denied their equality.

A. The District Court Erred in Accepting Appellants' Assertion That Pornography Is a Discriminatory Practice Based on Sex

The ordinance is predicated on a finding that

> pornography is a discriminatory practice based on sex which denies women equal opportunities in society. Pornography is central in creating and maintaining sex as a basis for discrimination. . . . [It harms] women's opportunities for equality of rights in employment, education, access to and use of public accommodations, and acquisition of real property; promote[s] rape, battery, child abuse, kidnapping and prostitution and inhibit[s] just enforcement of laws against such acts.[35]

The district court accepted that finding but held that First Amendment values outweighed the asserted interest in protecting women.[36]

Amici dispute the city's and county's "finding" that "pornography is central in creating and maintaining sex as a basis for discrimination." There was no formal, or indeed informal, legislative fact-finding process leading to this conclusion. Rather, legislators who had previously opposed obscenity on more traditional and moralistic grounds adopted a "model bill" incorporating this finding.[37] The model bill was in turn based on legislative hearings, held in Minneapolis, which did not, in fairness, reflect a reasoned attempt to understand the factors "central" in maintaining "sex as a basis for discrimination."[38]

It is true that sex discrimination takes multiple forms, which are reflected in the media. But the finding that "pornography is central in creating and maintaining sex as a basis for discrimination" does not represent our best understanding of the complex, deep-seated, and structural causes of gender inequality. In the past decade, many people have grappled with the question of causation. Feminist law professors and scholars have published and revised collections of cases and materials.[39] The factors they find most significant include the sex-segregated wage labor market; systematic devaluation of work traditionally done by women; sexist concepts of marriage and family, inadequate income maintenance programs for women unable to find wage work, lack of day care services and the premise that child care is an exclusively female responsibility, barriers to reproductive freedom, and discrimination and segregation in education and athletics.[40] Numerous feminist scholars have written major works tracing the cultural, economic, and psychosocial roots of women's oppression.[41]

Misogynist images, both those which are sexually explicit and the far more pervasive ones which are not, reflect and may help to reinforce the inferior social and economic status of women. But none of these studies and analyses identifies sexually explicit material as the central factor in the oppression of women. History teaches us that the answer is not so simple. Factors far more complex than pornography produced the English common law treatment of women as chattel property and the enactment of statutes allowing a husband to rape or beat his wife with impunity. In short, the claim that "pornography is central in creating and maintaining sex as a basis of discrimination" is flatly inconsistent with the conclusions of most who have studied the question.

Amici also dispute the "finding" that pornography, as defined by the ordinance, is "a discriminatory practice . . . which denies women equal opportunities." Images and fictional text are not the same thing as subordinating conduct. The ordinance does not target discriminatory actions denying access to jobs, education, public accommodations, or real property. It prohibits images. Although ideas have impact, images of discrimination are not the discrimination.

Further, the ordinance is cast in a form very different from the traditional antidiscrimination principles embodied in the Constitution and federal civil rights laws. Antidiscrimination laws demand equality of treatment for men and women, blacks and whites. The ordinance, by contrast, purports to protect women. It assumes that women are subordinated by sexual images and that men act uncontrollably if exposed to them. Sexist stereotypes are thus built into its very premises, and, as we demonstrate, its effect will be to reinforce those stereotypes.

Hence, the district court misperceived this case as one requiring the assignment of rank in a constitutional hierarchy. It is not necessary to rule that either gender equality or free speech is more important. The ordinance is fatally flawed not only because it authorizes suppression of speech protected by the First Amendment but also because it violates the constitutional guarantee of sex-based equality.

B. The Ordinance Classifies on the Basis of Sex and Perpetuates Sexist Stereotypes

The ordinance defines pornography in gender specific terms as "the graphic sexually explicit subordination of women" that also presents "women" in particular ways proscribed by the law. The district court found the Ordinance seeks to protect adult women, as a group, from the diminution of the legal and sociological status as women, that is from the discriminatory stigma which befalls women as women as a result of "pornography."[42]

The heart of the ordinance is the suppression of sexually explicit images of women, based on a finding of "subordination," a term which is not defined. The ordinance implies that sexually explicit images of women necessarily subordinate and degrade women and perpetuates stereotypes of women as helpless victims and people who could not seek or enjoy sex.

The ordinance also reinforces sexist stereotypes of men. It denies the possibility that graphic sexually explicit images of a man could ever subordinate or degrade him. It provides no remedy for sexually explicit images showing men as "dismembered, truncated or fragmented" or "shown as filthy or inferior, bleeding, bruised or hurt."

The stereotype that sex degrades women, but not men, is underscored by the proviso that "the use of men, children, or transsexuals in the place of women . . . also constitutes pornography."[43] The proviso does not allow men to claim that they, as men, are injured by sexually explicit images of them. Rather, men are degraded only when they are used "in place of women." The ordinance assumes that in sexuality, degradation is a condition that attaches to women.[44]

The ordinance authorizes any woman to file a complaint against those trafficking in pornography "as a woman acting against the subordination of women." A man, by contrast, may obtain relief only if he can "prove injury in the same way that a woman is injured."[45] Again the ordinance assumes that women as a class are subordinated and hurt by depictions of sex, and men are not.

The ordinance reinforces yet another sexist stereotype of men as aggressive beasts. Appellants assert:

> By conditioning the male orgasm to female subordination, pornography . . . makes the subordination of women pleasurable and seemingly legitimate. Each time men are sexually aroused by pornography, they learn to connect a woman's sexual pleasure to abuse and a woman's sexual nature to inferiority. They learn this in their bodies, not just their minds, so that it becomes a natural physiological response. At this point pornography leaves no more room for further debate than does shouting "kill" to an attack dog.[46]

Men are not attack dogs but morally responsible human beings. The ordinance reinforces a destructive sexist stereotype of men as irresponsible beasts, with "natural physiological responses" which can be triggered by sexually explicit images of women, and for which the men cannot be held accountable. Thus, men are conditioned into violent acts or negative beliefs by sexual images; women are not. Further, the ordinance is wholly blind to the possibility that men could be hurt and degraded by images presenting them as violent or sadistic.

The ordinance also reinforces sexist images of women as incapable of consent. It creates a remedy for people "coerced" to participate in the production of pornography. Unlike existing criminal, tort, and contract remedies against coercion, the ordinance provides

> proof of the following facts or conditions shall not constitute a defense: that the person actually consented . . .; or, knew that the purpose of the acts or events in question was to make pornography; or demonstrated no resistance or appeared to cooperate actively in the photographic sessions or in the sexual events that produced the pornography; or

. . . signed a contract, or made statements affirming a willingness to cooperate in the production of pornography.[47]

In effect, the ordinance creates a strong presumption that women who participate in the creation of sexually explicit material are coerced.[48] A woman's manifestation of consent—no matter how plain, informed, or even self-initiated—does not constitute a defense to her subsequent claim of coercion. Women are judged incompetent to consent to participation in the creation of sexually explicit material and condemned as "bad" if they do so.

Appellants argue that this provision is justified by Supreme Court precedent allowing suppression of sexually explicit material involving children. They assert that women, like children, "are incapable of consenting to engage in pornographic conduct, even absent a showing of physical coercion and therefore require special protection. . . . The coercive conditions under which most pornographic models work make this part of the law one effective address to the industry."[49]

This provision does far more than simply provide a remedy to women who are pressured into the creation of pornography which they subsequently seek to suppress. It functions to make all women incompetent to enter into legally binding contracts for the production of sexually explicit material. When women are legally disabled from making binding agreements, they are denied power to negotiate for fair treatment and decent pay. Enforcement of the ordinance would drive production of sexually explicit material even further into an underground economy, where the working conditions of women in the sex industry would worsen, not improve.

C. The Ordinance Is Unconstitutional Because It Reinforces Sexist Stereotypes and Classifies on the Basis of Sex

In recent years, the Supreme Court has firmly and repeatedly rejected gender-based classifications, such as that embodied in the ordinance. The constitutionally protected right to sex-based equality under law demands that

> the party seeking to uphold a statute that classifies individuals on the basis of their gender must carry the burden of showing an "exceedingly persuasive justification" for the classification. . . . The burden is met only by showing at least that the classification serves "important governmental objectives and that the discriminatory means employed" are "substantially related to the achievement of those objectives."[50]

The sex-based classifications embodied in the statute are justified on the basis of stereotypical assumptions about women's vulnerability to sexually explicit images and their production and men's latent uncontrollability. But the Supreme Court has held that "[this standard] must be applied free of fixed notions concerning the roles and abilities of males and females. Care must be taken in ascertaining whether the statutory objective itself reflects archaic and stereotypic notions."[51] Gender-based classifications cannot be upheld if they are premised on "'old notions' and 'archaic and overbroad' generalizations" about the roles and relative abilities of men and women."[52]

The ordinance damages individuals who do not fit the stereotypes it embodies. It delegitimates and makes socially invisible women who find sexually explicit images of women "in positions of display" or "penetrated by objects" to be erotic, liberating, or educational. These women are told that their perceptions are a product of "false consciousness" and that such images are so inherently degrading that they may be suppressed by the state.

At the same time, it stamps the imprimatur of state approval on the belief that men are attack dogs triggered to violence by the sight of a sexually explicit image of a woman. It delegitimates and makes socially invisible those men who consider themselves gentle, respectful of women, or inhibited about expressing their sexuality.

Even worse, the stereotypes of the ordinance perpetuate traditional social views of sex-based difference. By defining sexually explicit images of woman as subordinating and degrading to them, the ordinance reinforces the stereotypical view that "good" women do not seek and enjoy sex.[53] As applied, it would deny women access to sexually explicit material at a time in our history when women have just begun to acquire the social and economic power to develop our own images of sexuality. Stereotypes of hair-trigger male susceptibility to violent imagery can be invoked as an excuse to avoid directly blaming the men who commit violent acts.

Finally, the ordinance perpetuates a stereotype of women as helpless victims, incapable of consent, and in need of protection. A core premise of contemporary sex equality doctrine is that if the objective of the law is to "'protect' members of one gender because they are presumed to suffer from an inherent handicap or to be innately inferior, the objective itself is illegitimate."[54] We have learned through hard experience that gender-based classifications protecting women from their own presumed innate vulnerability reflect "an attitude of 'romantic paternalism' which, in practical effect, puts women not on a pedestal but in a cage."[55]

The coercion provisions of the ordinance "protect" by denying women's capacity to voluntarily agree to participate in the creation of sexually explicit images. The trafficking provisions "protect" by allowing women to suppress sexually explicit speech which the ordinance presumes is damaging to them. The claim that women need protection and are incapable of voluntary action is familiar. Historically, the presumed "natural and proper timidity and delicacy" of women made them unfit "for many of the occupations of civil life," and justified denying them the power to contract.[56]

Until quite recently, the law commonly provided women special protections against exploitation. In 1936, the Supreme Court upheld a law establishing minimum wages for women saying, "What can be closer to the public interest than the health of women and their protection from unscrupulous and overreaching employers?"[57] In 1948, the Court approved a law banning women from work as bartenders as a legitimate measure to combat the "moral and social problems" to which bartending by women might give rise.[58] The protectionist premise of these cases is now discredited and their holdings repudiated.

Women were, and continue to be, in a position of social and economic vulnerability that inhibits their ability to negotiate fair terms and conditions of wage labor. Further, the pervasive sexism and violence of our culture make women vulnerable to exploitation and inhibit their ability to enter into sexual or other relationships on a free and voluntary basis.

Slavery and free self-actualization are opposite poles on a continuum. Both free agency and response to external pressure are simultaneous aspects of human action. In the 1930s, employers challenged minimum wage-and-hour laws saying that laborers "freely consented" to work twelve hours a day, under dangerous and harmful conditions, for wages that did not provide minimal subsistence. We understand today that this concept of voluntary consent is self-serving and empty. Similarly, many women engage in sex or in the production of sexually explicit materials in response to pressures so powerful that it would be cynical to characterize their actions as simply voluntary and consensual.

Still, the laws that "protected" only women from exploitation in wage labor hurt them.[59] Many employers responded by barring women from the best-paying jobs with the greatest opportunity for advancement. Further, the protective labor laws reinforced general beliefs about women's vulnerability and incompetence. Similarly here, the protection of the ordinance reinforces the idea that women are incompetent, particularly in relation to sex.

The pervasive sexism and violence of our culture create a social climate—in the home, workplace, and street—that *is* different for women than for men. But even accurate generalizations about women's need for help do not justify sex-based classifications such as those in this ordinance. It is also true that women generally are still the ones who nurture young children. Yet we understand that laws giving mothers an irrebuttable "tender years" presumption for custody, or offering child rearing leaves only to mothers but not to fathers, ultimately hurt women and are unconstitutional.[60]

Some of the proponents of the ordinance believe that it will empower women, while others support it for more traditional, patriarchal reasons.[61] But many gender-based classifications are premised on a good faith intent to help or protect women. Good intent does not justify an otherwise invidious gender-based law. "Our nation has had a long and unfortunate history of sex discrimination."[62] The clearest lesson of that history is that sex-based classifications hurt women.

Thus, the district court was correct to reject appellants' claim that women are like children who need special protection from sexually explicit material. The court found that

> adult women as a group do not, as a matter of public policy or applicable law, stand in need of the same type of protection which has long been afforded children. . . . Adult women generally have the capacity to protect themselves from participating in and being personally victimized by pornography.[63]

The gender-based classification embodied in the ordinance is unconstitutional because it assumes and perpetuates classic sexist concepts of separate gender-defined roles, which carry "the inherent risk of reinforcing the stereotypes about the 'proper place' of women and their need for special protection."[64]

◇ ◇ ◇

III. Conclusion

Sexually explicit speech is not per se sexist or harmful to women. Like any mode of expression, it can be used to attack women's struggle for equal rights, but it is also a category of speech from which women have been excluded. The suppression authorized by the Indianapolis ordinance of a potentially enormous range of sexual imagery and texts reinforces the notion that women are too fragile, and men too uncontrollable, absent the aid of the censor, to be trusted to reject or enjoy sexually explicit speech for themselves. By identifying "subordination of women" as the concept that distinguishes sexually explicit material which is tolerable from that to be condemned, the ordinance incorporates a vague and asymmetric standard for censorship that can as readily be used to curtail feminist speech about sexuality or to target the speech of sexual minorities, as to halt hateful speech about women. Worse, perpetuation of the concept of gender-determined roles in regard to sexuality strengthens one of the main obstacles to achieving real change and ending sexual violence.

Notes

1. 1. Women are presented as sexual objects who enjoy pain or humiliation; or
    2. Women are presented as sexual objects who experience sexual pleasure in being raped; or
    3. Women are presented as sexual objects tied up or cut up or mutilated or bruised or physically hurt, or as dismembered or truncated or fragmented or severed into body parts; or
    4. Women are presented being penetrated by objects or animals; or
    5. Women are presented in scenarios of degradation, injury, abasement, torture, shown as filthy or inferior, bleeding, bruised, or hurt in a context that makes these conditions sexual; or
    6. Women are presented as sexual objects for domination, conquest, violation, exploitation, possession, or use, or through postures or positions of servility or submission or display.

Indianapolis, Ind., Code § 16-3(q) (1984).

2. By the use of highly selected examples, Appellants and supporting *amici* convey the impression that the great majority of materials considered pornographic are brutal. Although most commercial pornography, like much of all media, is sexist, most is not violent. A study of pictorials and cartoons in *Playboy* and *Penthouse* between 1973 and 1977 found that, by 1977, about 5 percent of the pictorials were rated as sexually violent. "No significant changes in the percentage of sexually violent cartoons were found over the years"; Malamuth and Spinner, *A Longitudinal Content Analysis of Sexual Violence in the Best-Selling Erotic Magazines,* 16 J. Sex. Research 226, 237 (1980). The Women Against Pornography (W.A.P.) *amicus* brief, in particular, totally mischaracterizes content analyses of pornography. It asserts, at p. 8, n.14, that one study found the depictions of rape in "adults only" paperbacks had doubled from 1968 to 1974, a statement which is simply false. The study found that the amount of explicit sexual content had doubled, but also "that the plots, themes, and stories have remained much the same in these books throughout the years measured in this study"; Smith, *The Social Content of Pornography,* 26 J. Comm. 16, 23 (1976). The brief then cites a study finding that depictions of bondage and domination in Times Square pornography stores "had increased dramatically in frequency by 1982," but neglects to mention that the increase was to 17.2 percent. The same study also concluded that "many bondage and domination magazines do not depict suffering or bodily injury"; Dietz and Evans, *Pornographic Imagery and Prevalence of Paraphilia,* 139 Am. J. Psychiatry 1493, 1495 (1982). That some pronography would be found by *amici* on both sides to be offensive to women does not support this legislative approach to curtailing that pornography, which is overbroad and dependent on suppression of speech.

3. K. Davidson, R. Ginsburg, and H. Kay, *Sex-based Discrimination* 892 (1st ed. 1974).

4. W. Prosser, *Law of Torts,* 759–60 (1971).

5. *Id.* at 874–77.

6. *See, e.g.,* Jennings, *The Victim as Criminal: A Consideration of California's Prostitution Law,* 64 Calif. L. Rev. 1235 (1976).

7. 63 Am. Jur. 2d *Prostitution* § 1 (1972).

8. Comment, *The Constitutionality of Statutory Rape Laws,* 27 UCLA L. Rev. 757, 762 (1980).

9. *Eisenstadt v. Baird,* 405 U.S. 438 (1972).

10. *Id.* at 448.

11. 18 U.S.C.A. §§ 1461-1462 (West 1984); 19 U.S.C.A. § 1305 (West 1980 & Supp. 1984); *see United States v. One Obscene Book Entitled "Married Love",* 48 F.2d 821 (S.D.N.Y. 1931); *United States v. One Book Entitled "Contraceptions",* 51 F.2d 525 (S.D.N.Y. 1931) (prosecution for distribution of books by Marie Stopes on contraception); *United States v. Dennett,* 39 F.2d 564 (2d Cir. 1930) (prosecution of Mary Ware Dennett for publication of pamphlet explaining sexual physiology and functions to children); and *Bours v. United States,* 229 F. 960 (7th Cir. 1915) (prosecu-

tion of physician for mailing a letter indicating that he might perform a therapeutic abortion). It was not until 1971 that an amendment was passed deleting the prohibition as to contraception, Pub. L. No. 91-662, 84 Stat. 1973 (1971); and the ban as to abortion remains in the current codification of the law.

12. *People v. Byrne,* 99 Misc. 1, 6, (N.Y. 1917).

13. 35 Stat. 825 (1910), 18 U.S.C. §§ 2421-2422.

14. *See* H.R.Rep. no. 47, 61st Cong., 2d Sess. (1910), at 10-11.

15. Note, *The White Slave Traffic Act: The Historical Impact of a Criminal Law Policy on Women,* 72 Geo. L.J. 1111 (1984).

16. *See Caminetti v. United States,* 242 U.S. 470 (1917); *Cleveland v. United States,* 329 U.S. 14 (1946).

17. Note, at 1119.

18. To define *pornography* as that which subordinates women, and then prohibit as pornographic that which subordinates, makes the claim that pornography subordinates either circular or logically trivial.

19. Appellants' brief at 26.

20. Defendants' memorandum at 10.

21. Appellants' brief at 36.

22. *See, e.g.,* appellants' Exhs. N., M., and W. These exhibits, like most commercial pornography which depicts sex between women, were not produced by or primarily for lesbians. Yet part of the shock value of such images in contemporary society may be attributable to their depiction of sexual explicitness between women. When the door is opened to suppress "scenarios of degradation," for example, there is no guarantee that this shock value of any graphic depiction of homosexual acts will not spill over to images and texts which authentically express lesbian sexuality.

23. The provision that "the use of men . . . in the place of women . . . shall also constitute pornography" makes clear that same-sex male images and texts could fall within the scope of the ordinance, especially so, one supposes, if one male partner is depicted as effeminate.

24. *See, e.g., Baker v. Wade,* 553 F. Supp. 1121 (N.D. Tex. 1982), on appeal; *People v. Onofre,* 51 N.Y.2d 476 (1980), *cert. denied,* 451 U.S. 987 (1980); *National Gay Task Force v. Board of Educ.,* 729 F.2d 1270 (10th Cir. 1984), *aff'd per curiam,* 53 U.S.L.W. 4408 (U.S. Mar. 26, 1985).

25. Appellants' brief at 40.

26. *See, e.g.,* G. Gilder, *Sexual Suicide* (1973).

27. Appellants' brief at 33.

28. *State v. Becker,* 364 Mo. 1079, 1087, 272 S.E.2d 283, 288 (1954). *See also Winters v. New York,* 333 U.S. 507, 518 (1948). In *Kansas v. Great American Theatre Co.,* the court accepted as a definition for "prurient interest," "an unhealthy, unwholesome, morbid, degrading, and shameful interest in sex," 227 Kan. 633, 633, 608 P.2d 951, 952 (1980).

29. Act of June 20, 1957 ch. 57-779, § 1, 1957 Fla. Laws vol. 1, pt. 1, 1102, 1103-04 (amending Fla. Stat. § 847.01) (amended 1959, repealed 1961).

30. *See State v. Cohen,* 125 So. 2d 560 (Fla. 1960); *State v. Reese,* 222 So. 2d 732 (Fla. 1969); and *Rhodes v. State,* 283 So. 2d 351 (Fla. 1973).

31. *See* Act of May 5, 1961, ch. 61-7, 1961 Fla. Laws vol. 1, pt. 1, 13; Act of June 3, 1969, ch. 69-41, 1969 Fla. Laws vol. 1, pt. 1, 164; Act of June 7, 1973, ch. 73-120, 1973 Fla. Laws 185.

32. *Grayned v. City of Rockford,* 408 U.S. 104, 108 (1972); *Smith v. Goguen,* 415 U.S. 566, 572-73 (1974); *Kolender v. Lawson,* 461 U.S. 352, 357 (1983).

33. *Buckley v. Valeo,* 424 U.S. 1, 41 (1976); *Smith v. Goguen,* 415 U.S. at 573.

34. *Id.;* Grayned v. City of Rockford, 408 U.S. at 108; *Kolender v. Lawson,* 461 U.S. at 358; *Papachristou v. City of Jacksonville,* 405 U.S. 156, 168-69 (1972).

35. Indianapolis, Ind., Code § 16-1(a)(2).

36. *American Booksellers Ass'n v. Hudnut,* 598 F. Supp. 1316, 1335-37 (S.D. Ind. 1984).

37. Duggan, *Censorship in the Name of Feminism,* Village Voice, October 16, 1984, at 15, col. 1.

38. See appellants' brief at 15, n. 6. Courts may not defer to legislative determination of fact when the supposed "facts" are marshaled to suppress free speech or to justify sex discrimination. "Deference to a legislative finding cannot limit judicial inquiry when First Amendment rights are at stake"; *Landmark Communications, Inc. v. Virginia,* 435 U.S. 829, 843 (1978). *See also Craig v. Boren,* 429 U.S. 190 (1976).

39. K. Davidson, R. Ginsberg, and H. Kay, (1974 & 2d ed. 1981); B. Babcock, A. Freedman, E. Norton, and S. Ross, *Sex Discrimination and the Law: Causes and Remedies* (1974 & Supp. 1978).

40. *See also* U.S. Commission on Civil Rights, *Women and Poverty* (1974); *Women Still in Poverty* (1979); and *Child Care and Equal Opportunity for Women* (1981) and National Advisory Council on Economic Opportunity, *Final Report: The American Promise: Equal Justice and Economic Opportunity* (1981).

41. *See, e.g., Toward an Anthropology of Women* (R. Reiter ed. 1975); M. Rosaldo and L. Lamphere, *Women, Culture and Society* (1974); M. Ryan, *Womanhood in America: From Colonial Times to the Present* (1979); N. Chodorow, *The Reproduction of Mothering: Psychoanalysis and the Sociology of Gender* (1978); D. Dinnerstein, *The Mermaid and the Minotaur: Sexual Arrangements and Human Malaise* (1976); J. Mitchell, *Women's Estate* (1972).

42. *American Booksellers Ass'n v. Hudnut,* 598 F. Supp. at 1335.

43. Indianapolis, Ind., Code § 16-3(q).

44. Appellants explain that the proviso is needed because "without it, pornographers could circumvent the ordinance by producing the exact same material using models other than adult biological females, i.e., men, children, and transsexuals, to portray women"; appellants' brief at 45.

45. Indianapolis, Ind., Code § 16-17(a)(7)(b).

46. Appellants' brief at 21.

47. Indianapolis, Ind., Code § 16-3.(5)(A) VIII-XI.

48. The provisions negating common law defenses to coercion are cast in facially neutral terms. But since "pornography" is defined in gender specific terms, the provisions abrogating defenses to coercion also apply to women or to others used "in the place of women."

49. Appellants' brief at 17.

50. *Mississippi Univ. for Women v. Hogan,* 458 U.S. 718, 724-25 (1982).

51. *Id.*

52. *Califano v. Goldfarb,* 430 U.S. 199, 217 (1977).

53. Perpetuating the stereotype that "good girls" do not enjoy sex, and suppressing images of women's sexuality, is particularly tragic for teenagers. A recent study by the prestigious Alan Guttmacher Institute identifies factors explaining why teenagers in the United States experience unwanted pregnancy at rates significantly higher than those in any other developed nation. This extensive study found that the single most important factor associated with low rates of unwanted pregnancy is "openness about sex (defined on the basis of four items: media presentations of female nudity, the extent of nudity on public beaches, sales of sexually-explicit literature and media advertising of condoms)." The researchers conclude:

> American teenagers seem to have inherited the worst of all possible worlds regarding their exposure to messages about sex: Movies, music, radio and TV tell them that sex is romantic, exciting, titillating. . . . Yet, at the same time, young people get the message good girls should say no. Almost nothing that they see or hear about sex informs them about contraception or the importance of avoiding pregnancy. . . . Such messages lead to an ambivalence about sex that stifles communication and exposes young people to increased risk of pregnancy, out-of-wedlock births and abortions.

Jones, Forrest, Goldman, Heusbaw, Livecloer, Rosoff, Westoff, and Wolf, *Teenage Pregnancy in Developed Countries: Determinants and Policy Implications,* 17 Family Plan. Persp., March–April 1985, at 53, 61.

54. *Mississippi Univ. for Women v. Hogan,* 458 U.S. at 725.

55. *Frontiero v. Richardson,* 411 U.S. 677, 684 (1973).

56. *Bradwell v. Illinois,* 83 U.S. (16 Wall.) 130, 141-42 (1872).

57. *West Coast Hotel v. Parrish,* 300 U.S. 379, 398 (1936).

58. *Goesaert v. Cleary,* 335 U.S. 464, 466 (1948).

59. B. Babcock, A. Freedman, E. Norton, and S. Ross, at 48, 191-217.

60. On the dangers and unconstitutionality of a blanket "tender years" presumption, see *Devine v. Devine,* 398 So. 2d 686 (Ala. 1981); *Developments in the Law: The Constitution and the Family,* 93 Harv. L. Rev. 1156, 1334-38 (1980); S. Ross & A. Barcher, *The Rights of Women* 229-30 (1983). On the danger and illegality of a mother-only child-rearing leave, see *Danielson v. Board of Higher Educ.,* 358 F. Supp. 22 (S.D.N.Y. 1972). *See also Phillips v. Martin Marietta Corp.,* 400 U.S. 542 (1971) (company policy prohibiting the hiring of mothers, but not fathers, of preschool-aged children violates section 703(a) of Title VII of the Civil Rights Act of 1964). Williams, *Reflections on Culture, Courts and Feminism,* 7 Women's Rts. L. Rep. 175, 198 (1982).

61. Duggan, *Censorship.*

62. *Frontiero v. Richardson,* 411 U.S. at 684.

63. *American Booksellers Ass'n v. Hudnut,* 598 F. Supp. at 1333–34.

VI

On Law and Jurisprudence: Feminism and Legal Theory

The philosophical discipline that examines the fundamental nature or elements of law is called jurisprudence. The idea of jurisprudence in common usage today can be divided into a broad and a narrow sense. Broadly speaking, jurisprudential theories are political theories that have legal ramifications. For example, liberal, Marxist, and socialist political theories spawn jurisprudential views that follow from and reflect their implications. Much feminist jurisprudence is an application of one or more of these political theories to the many facets of women's oppression as implied in law. For example, liberal feminists have always argued that liberal values should be applied equally to women; Marxist feminists argue that Marxist class analysis applies equally to gender; and socialist feminists argue that socialist principles should be used to alleviate the oppression of sexism. That is, all these feminist theories point to the omission of women or the presence of gender discrimination within the general political theories with which they are associated.

Other feminist theories that are primarily epistemological or psychological, rather than explicitly political, also tend to be associated with various jurisprudential views. For example, pragmatic feminists tend to identify with a legal realist view of jurisprudence, and postmodern and many radical feminists (insofar as radical feminist views can be categorized) often translate their views into a jurisprudence closely associated with another postmodern movement, called *critical legal studies.* In other words, there is no single feminist jurisprudence, no single political theory associated with feminism. Yet all of these views fit within the broad sense of jurisprudence, which is the sense that informs most feminist work and most of the chapters in this volume.

There is also a narrow or technical sense of jurisprudence that is sometimes equated with all jurisprudence. That is, the legitimacy of the broad sense of jurisprudence is sometimes questioned, and that may be considered a basis for denying that feminist jurisprudence is "really" jurisprudence. It does not fit the narrow sense of jurisprudence. But the narrow sense of jurisprudence—at least in the form that denies the legitimacy of feminist jurisprudence—is itself open to question.

The narrow sense of jurisprudence is primarily concerned with the question, What is the law? That is, what is distinctive about law? What are its defining features? Trying to answer these questions, philosophers have focused on the concept of law as such, on legal concepts and relations, and on legal functions, particularly legal reasoning. Three major theories have been advanced toward this end.

The oldest, called *natural law,* commonly defined law as a precept of reason, promulgated for the common good by those in authority to do so. Natural law holds that there is a necessary connection between law and morality, and so an immoral law is invalid or not binding.

A second view, called *legal positivism,* objected to the natural law view as confusing what law is with what law ought to be and attempted to construct a value-neutral definition of its own. Positivists today generally define law as a system of rules promulgated by authorized procedures, recognized as binding by officials, and obeyed by the bulk of the population.

A third theory, *legal realism,* objected to the natural law approach as too obscure and metaphysical and to the positivist approach as too rigid, abstract, and static. Instead, the realists defined law roughly as a method of settling disputes by appealing to the authority of an office; or, to put it more succinctly, they claimed that law is what judges say it is. All three theories continue to debate the fundamental nature of law and the appropriate function of jurisprudence to this day.

If we were to attempt to situate feminist jurisprudence among these theories, it would be easy to see that it would be impossible to fit all feminist views under any one of them (although the pragmatic, concrete, antiessentialist tendencies of much feminism would push it in the direction of legal realism). If I were to create a feminist definition of law, more or less comparable to those of the other three theories, I think that it would have to be something like the following: Law is a system of binding norms or rules created by, reflecting, and perpetuating patriarchy. Something on this order would be necessary, I think, to capture the focus and thrust of feminism. But there are a number of important differences between this definition and the others. To examine these differences we should first look more closely at the traditional theories of jurisprudence and their interactions through history.

Natural Law

The oldest legal philosophy (or jurisprudence) is natural law theory. According to St. Thomas Aquinas, one of the greatest systematizers of the doctrine of natural law, "law is nothing else than an ordinance of reason, for the common good, promulgated by him who has the care of the community." This statement sets out the basic elements of natural law theory.

First, natural law is a set of absolute or objective moral principles—thought by Aquinas and some others to be implanted by God in the minds of man—but in any case discoverable by reason. Thus, natural law is moral law.

Second, human law (the rules of human society) is valid or legitimate if, and only if, it accords with the demands of natural law. Thus, to be valid, law must be moral. There are many different versions and interpretations of this requirement. For example, a strong interpretation is that an unjust law is a contradiction in terms. It is not only not binding; it is a conceptual confusion that is contrary to the very nature and meaning of law. (This strong version is what is particularly criticized by both positivists and realists.) A weaker version holds that to be valid or legitimate, a legal system must be moral overall, or more moral than not, or at least not fundamentally immoral. In any case, these two elements point to the basic question raised by the natural law theory: What is the connection between law and morality?

Aquinas's theory reflects the ancient view of law as the enforcement of right; with ancient Jewish law as perhaps the best-known example. Other ancient civilizations, such as those of the Greeks, the Romans, and the Egyptians, also considered those in power—the lawgivers—to be backed by the authority of deities and morality. While many subtleties have developed in natural law theory since ancient times, its salient feature is still that there is a necessary connection between law and morality. Although there were always skeptical attacks on the theory (e.g., by the Sophists), it was unquestionably the predominant view of law until a new theory, legal positivism, became prominent in the seventeenth century.

Legal Positivism

The theory of legal positivism was first systematically articulated by John Austin in his lectures on jurisprudence (originally published in 1832), but its roots reach back at least to Hobbes in the 1600s. In its broadest sense, positivism is also conventionalism, in that it concentrates on the conventions of actual legal systems in order to make its observations about the nature of law. In this regard it provides a sharp contrast—and, indeed, served as an explicit objection—to natural law theory.

Against the natural law view, Austin (and other legal positivists) argued that although law ought to be both rational and moral, it often is neither. It is, in fact, a serious conceptual error to assume a necessary connection between law and morality. Although an immoral law may be a bad thing, it is not self-contradictory. This can easily be seen by comparing an immoral law with the idea of an illegal law, which is self-contradictory. Thus, the positivists argued, the natural law theorists were confusing what law is with what law ought to be. They were conflating the project of description (what is) with the project of evaluation (what ought to be), and according to the positivists, these two projects should be carried out by different theories.

So positivists, and in particular Austin, undertook to formulate a value-neutral, descriptive theory of law. Austin believed that the essential feature of law was not its moral quality, but its coerciveness or power. According to Austin, law is the command of the sovereign. The sovereign is the established ultimate power in a state who is habitually obeyed by the bulk of the people, but is not in the habit of obeying anyone else. In this way Austin could distinguish one state as independent from another, explain the hierarchy of authority or chain of command in a given state, and identify legal rules by their origin (i.e., by tracing them to the sovereign) rather than by evaluating their (moral) content.

This enabled Austin to answer a number of questions. For example, where do laws come from? They are promulgated by the sovereign. How can they be identified or distinguished from nonlegal rules, such as the rules of etiquette, morality, or social custom? They can be identified by their source in the legal system. They can be traced ultimately to sovereign enactment or indirectly to sovereign power, whether express or tacit. The character of legal rules is imperative; that is, they are commands. Austin defined a command as the expression of a wish or desire coupled with the threat of sanction for disobedience. The idea of this element is to capture the obligatory nature of law and its essential connection to sovereign power.

This theory has many attractive features. It clarifies much about the basic nature of law, though there have been many objections to it as well. In 1961, H. L. A. Hart provided a modern version of the positivist theory, focusing on law as a system of rules rather than as the command of a sovereign. Hart reformulates the Austinian theory into the form most commonly accepted by legal positivists today. His general view is that although Austin's command theory is inadequate as a comprehensive description of law, the general principles of positivism are basically correct. Thus, Hart argues, if we discard the narrow command theory and replace it with an understanding of law as a hierarchy of certain sorts of rules that can be identified by tracing their source in the legal system, we can account for all conceptual elements of law.

Even though the specifics of Austin's theory (the command theory) are no longer widely held, its basic principles and motivations, with Hart's friendly revisions, remain the same for legal positivists today. All positivists basically agree on the following:

First, law is essentially a system of rules.

Second, these rules are to be identified formally, that is, by reference to their source or origin in the legal system (and not by their content or subject matter). What makes a legal rule legal is its source.

Third, because law can be so identified formally, it can and should be distinguished from morality. What law is (description) should not be confused with what law ought to be (evaluation). An unjust law is neither self-contradictory nor illegal; it is immoral. To conflate the two is both innaccurate and misleading.

Given this history, we can see that traditional jurisprudence was not always divided but has long been divided (or supposedly divided) into two major subcategories: normative and descriptive (the latter often being called *analytical* jurisprudence. This division was initiated by Austin, who dedicated his famous lectures to "determining the province of jurisprudence, properly so called." According to Austin, the proper domain of jurisprudence was the descriptive analysis of the positive law, its basic concepts and relations. A normative analysis of law, he thought, was the proper domain of legislation, not jurisprudence, and the two should not be confused.

The powerful influence of this view can be seen in the official definition of jurisprudence found in *Black's Law Dictionary:*

> [It is] that science of law which has for its function to ascertain the principles on which legal rules are based, so as not only to classify those rules in their proper order . . . but also to settle the manner in which doubtful cases should be brought under the appropriate rules. Jurisprudence is more a formal than a material science. It has no direct concern with questions of moral or political policy, for they fall under the province of ethics and legislation.

The interesting thing about this definition is that it settles the long and continuing controversy between positivists and natural law theorists, making positivism true by definition. Unfortunately, philosophical questions cannot be answered so easily, and presumably those who find natural law plausible and positivism deficient will not have their questions answered by *Black's Law Dictionary.* Nevertheless, the dictionary entry does show the power of positivist influence in American legal thought, as well as the problems with the approach taken by Austin to define natural law out of jurisprudence. According to *Black's Law Dictionary,* natural law theory is not jurisprudence, and so perhaps feminists should not be disturbed if their theory is not considered to be jurisprudence for the same reasons.

Ironically, there is another problem that actually points to a commonality, a shared deficiency of natural law theory and legal positivism, that becomes the focus of the subsequent critique by legal realists: Positivists criticize natural law theorists for conflating morality with law, but positivists never claimed that either morality or law could not be conceptually determined. Two implications of natural law theory are that human life and law are rational and ultimately can be rationally determined. That is, in principle, there is a single right answer to legal and moral questions, and we could determine what it is by means of rational analysis if our information and analytical powers were great enough. Positivists make no such extensive claims, but they do make a related one. An implication of positivist theory is that legal cases can (at least most of the time) be rationally determined by the language of preexisting legal rules. So, although the conceptual presuppositions of natural law are more extensive than those of positivism, both theories share a commitment to the conceptual or logical determination of legal questions. It is that possibility that the legal realists challenged.

Legal Realism

Legal realism is a twentieth-century phenomenon. It arose largely in the United States and Scandanavia, but there are proponents in many other countries as well. Oliver Wendell Holmes was a forerunner of this intellectual movement, and some of his comments in "The Path of Law" point to the direction that realism would later take. In that essay, Holmes challenged the pretensions of conceptualism and suggested that a better way to approach law is simply as a prediction of what judges will decide. He urged legal theorists and lawyers to regard the law as the ordinary person on the street would regard it, and not as a "brooding omnipresence in the sky." Another legal analyst, John Chipman Gray, in *The Nature and Sources of Law* set out what came to be central ideas of legal realism. Gray's focus (like Holmes's and that of all later realists) is on the function of the courts. Gray believes that the last person authorized to interpret the law is the lawgiver, and thus, the opinions of the courts are the law. All else (statutes, ordinances, etc.) should be considered sources of law. Ultimately, the law is what the judges decide.

Legal realists, like existentialists and radical feminists, form a rather ragged group of rugged individualists. No one's view is quite like anyone else's. Nevertheless, we can characterize their theory as having roughly the following attributes:

First, like positivists, realists separate law from morality. For realists, however, this is not to say that moral evaluation is irrelevant or inappropriate to legal analysis, but only that it is unhelpful to claim that immoral law is invalid; this is metaphorical language that is misleading in the long run. Instead, realists, like positivists, recognize law as an exercise of power.

Second, unlike positivists, realists distrust the judicial technique of seeming to deduce legal conclusions from legal rules. Rather, realists want to emphasize the indeterminacy of legal rules and legal language and to point out the wide range of judicial discretion and consequently the inevitable influence of the personal attitudes, backgrounds, and biases of judges and other officials. This is sometimes called *rule skepticism.* Because of the indeterminacy of rules, law is fundamentally political.

Third, realism is functional. It focuses on the process of law, emphasizing its fluid, dynamic, evolutionary character. The study of day-to-day interactions, the everyday working of officials, is what will provide insight into and understanding of the nature and substance of law. Thus, realism is sociological or behavioral, rather than conceptual, in its approach to legal analysis. Law should be approached as a science, not a natural science, but a social science. Law is after all, a social institution that affects and is affected by other institutions and individuals inside it and outside it.

Recent Developments

We now have a three-way debate among traditional jurisprudential theories:

Natural law assumes that (1) morality is objective and rationally ascertainable in principle and (2) that law is necessarily connected to morality, so that its validity depends on its morality.

Positivism denies point 2, arguing that it conflates law and morality, or what law is with what law ought to be, and instead (3) focuses on producing a properly value-neutral definition of law.

Realism denies point 2 and the possibility of point 3, contending that (4) because legal rules are indeterminate, law is fundamentally political and should be recognized and evaluated as such.

The effect of the realist critique in the 1930s and 1940s was in some ways liberating but in other ways devastating. On the one hand, it revealed some groundless pretensions to objectivity in legal analysis and opened up some rigid legal structures to broader bases for legal decision making. On the other hand, the critique destroyed the traditional grounds for judicial authority and legitimacy. Traditionally, judicial analysis was thought to be rational and objective, not political or subjective.

The response in the 1950s (oversimplifying a bit for brevity) was what might be termed a positivist retreat, particularly in jurisprudence or legal theory. Theorists were concerned with establishing the foundations of authority or the justification of legal legitimacy, as evidenced by the influencial legal process materials by Henry Hart and Albert Sachs, or the powerful defense of legal positivism in H. L. A. Hart's *Concept of Law,* or Alexander Bickel's recommendations for a restrained Supreme Court in *The Least Dangerous Branch,* among others.

The foundations of legitimacy in judicial review has continued to be the focus of legal theory and jurisprudence in treatises like Lawrence Tribe's *American Constitutional Law* and John Hart Ely's *Democracy and Distrust,* but the realist challenge never disappeared completely, nor was it ever satisfactorily answered. In the late 1960s a postmodern movement called *critical legal studies* (often called CLS) revived and refined the realist critique, attacking what was termed *liberal jurisprudence,* by which was meant either the positivist or the natural law pretensions to the conceptual determination of law on objective, neutral, impersonal, and apolitical grounds. Using techniques of critical theory (such as deconstruction), CLS debunks many apparently coherent theories of law and denies the usefulness of Grand Theory, or the possibility of arriving at objective, universal solutions to practical social or moral problems by means of abstract conceptual or logical analysis.

The critique by CLS has been effective, but like the challenge of legal realism, it provides no viable positive alternative to the mainstream liberal jurisprudence that it undermines. So the problem, and the debate, continues. Are law and jurisprudence neutral, or not? Is it possible to be neutral, or not? If the realists and the critical legal theorists are right, the approach to adjudication that is most conducive to fairness and impartiality (which is, after all, the basis of the value of neutrality or objectivity in law) is likely to be quite different from what seems to follow from the positivist or the natural law assumptions of objectivity.

Where Does Feminist Jurisprudence Fit?

As we have already noted, feminist jurisprudence may fall in line with any of the traditional jurisprudential theories. There are as many feminist approaches as there are political approaches. But all feminist approaches are political in the sense that they all advocate a political agenda (the liberation of women). It is also worth remembering that feminists hold that all traditional jurisprudential and legal theories are also political in that they are patriarchal. That would seem to put all feminists in the realist/CLS camp, which claims that all law is political. However, though that claim may be true of many feminists, it is a bit too strong to be true of all feminists.

A feminist can believe, and some do, that law can be conceptually determined by either reference to objective morality or preexisting legal standards but that as it currently stands, it is unjust and discriminatory because it is patriarchal. That is, it is perfectly coherent to hold that law may be objectively determinable by means of preexisting standards (either legal or moral) and also hold that the actual determinations that have been made in the past have been made wrongly. Very few feminists think that it is conceptually necessary that law be patriarchal. Most regard patriarchy as a historical truth or a social fact of monumental proportions that pervasively affects the basic structure as well as the substance of law. Some believe that it affects the substance of law only. But these positions (except the conceptual position) are compatible with any traditional theory of jurisprudence.

These positions also point to a difference between feminist theories and all the traditional theories (although not necessarily CLS), which is that feminist theories pertain to the material condition of law rather than to its conceptual implications as such. This difference is reflected in the definition that I offered as representative of the feminist project. Thus, feminist jurisprudence is concrete; it tends to be problem driven; it is concerned with the material condition of law and its consequences in the lives of actual people. It does not aim to answer the question "What is law?" in terms of immutable or necessary logical characteristics. Instead, it challenges that approach to jurisprudence altogether. Like legal realism and CLS, it focuses on the everyday functions and effects of law; not to describe law, however, but to correct its injustices. Does that disqualify it as jurisprudence? If we go by *Black's Law Dictionary,* feminist jurisprudence is not "real" jurisprudence, but then neither is legal realism, CLS, or even natural law. Perhaps that definition is a bit too narrow.

If, on the other hand, jurisprudence includes the moral, political, or otherwise normative evaluation or critique of legal concepts, processes, and institutions, then all the traditional theories of jurisprudence are included in the concept, and so is feminist jurisprudence. Thus, because of its diversity, feminist jurisprudence may be aligned with any traditional theory of jurisprudence, but because of its focus on the material condition of law—law's actual function in daily adjudication and concrete impact on the lives of real people—feminist jurisprudence tends to be drawn in the direction of legal realism, pragmatism, or CLS. It is essentially critical and normative, and it insists that traditional jurisprudence is normative as well because it is patriarchal. Its one common focus is the rejection of patriarchy and the liberation of women, which puts it at odds with mainstream jurisprudence but does not make it not jurisprudence.

The chapters in Part VI are intended to represent the wide range, the diversity, of feminist jurisprudence, but they also illustrate the common focus. The first chapter, by Robin West, draws on several theoretical traditions to explain why traditional jurisprudence and law cannot address the needs of women, why, in effect, traditional law and jurisprudence write women out of legal existence.

West's thesis is that the concept of human being assumed in legal theory and law excludes the concept of woman as described by feminists, causing severe problems for any supposedly universal jurisprudence. Tracing the principal divisions in legal theory and feminist theory, West arrives at the following differences: According to liberal legal theory and critical legal theory, humans value autonomy and fear annihilation while also longing for community and dreading alienation. According to relational feminists and radical feminists, women value intimacy and fear separation while also longing for individuation and dreading invasion. All four views embody human contradictions and contradict one another. But, they are not mirror images; they cannot be reduced to one another. Although the values, fears, and contradictions of the male experience are reflected in both law and jurisprudence, the values, fears, and contradictions of the female experience are reflected in neither. Thus, traditional jurisprudence is not universal or neutral; it is masculine. The feminist task is to analyze patriarchal jurisprudence and to reconstruct descriptions of concepts like harm and human being in a way that is true to women's experience. We must imagine a postpatriarchal world, West urges, to transform the images or concepts as well as the power structure of law, so that masculine jurisprudence may become humanist jurisprudence.

Toward this end, in "Deconstructing Gender," Joan Williams offers, from a liberal feminist point of view, a devastating critique of biological essentialism and the relational feminist's glorification of domesticity. She challenges the description of gender advocated by Carol Gilligan, which West uses, arguing that it is less a description of female psychology than an attempt to attribute to women two critiques of Western culture: the critique of Western "formalist" epistemology and the critique of possessive individualism. Pointing to the dangers of returning to a "separate spheres" mentality, Williams contends that the greatest strength of feminism is its ability to challenge male norms. But this can be done, she claims, without a celebration of feminine domesticity. Williams, like the socialist feminists, argues for a focus on economic structure to alleviate oppressive social institutions that perpetuate inequality and discriminate against women.

In "The Pragmatist and the Feminist," Margaret Jane Radin offers a pragmatic middle view between the two poles of feminist debate, as well as between feminist legal theory and traditional legal thought. Tracing similarities between feminist and pragmatist theories, she suggests that the two theories may be combined to provide a further common ground for a feminist middle way. Such a middle way might incorporate the best of many other theories, for example, utilizing both the ethic of care and the ethic of justice that Carol Gilligan talks about. Radin also argues that this middle way may help create alternative descriptions of reality that more fairly and accurately represent a truly pluralistic society. The special contribution of feminism to legal theory, she believes, is that it stresses the importance and legitimacy of the perspective of the oppressed. In this respect, feminism can go beyond the original issue of women's oppression to represent oppression in general.

Regina Austin discusses in "Sapphire Bound!" the diversity among women. We have no reason to think that even as feminists we can understand, let alone represent, the needs and views of women unlike ourselves. The problems of professional women differ from those of working women, and the problems of whites differ from those of blacks. Because minority women tend to be left out of feminist legal critiques, if feminists profess to represent the voice of the oppressed, then they should structure their legal procedures to include the needs of black and other minority women.

In Chapter 24 Deborah Rhode charts the interrelations among CLS, feminist jurisprudence, and critical race theory, focusing on feminist critical theories. She shows that although there are similarities in their objectives and methods, there also are attributes of feminist critical theory that distinguish it from CLS and make it feminist. As Rhode points out, feminist critical theories share three central commitments. Politically, they seek to promote equality between men and women. Substantively, they make gender their framework of analysis, aiming to reconstitute legal practice to include women's concerns. Methodologically, they aspire to describe the world to reflect women's experience and to identify the social transformations necessary for equality. These features are shared by all feminist legal theories; what distinguishes feminist critical theories from other feminist legal theories are those features shared with CLS or critical theory. Feminist critical theories build on postmodern and poststructuralist social theories that suggest the social construction of knowledge and deny the possibility of universal foundations for critique.

In the final chapter, Catharine MacKinnon sets out a radical feminist thesis of law and jurisprudence. Confronting Austinian positivism, she states that "a jurisprudence is a theory about the relation between life and law." MacKinnon is concerned with the transformation of belief into reality. Law, she points out, is crucial to this transformation. Virtually all societies, she notes, are organized in social hierarchies that subordinate women to men on the basis of sex and subordinate certain people to others on the basis of race and class. These facts of social organization, which institutionalize social power, are embodied in the organization of states as law. That is, through law, social domination is made both legitimate and invisible. It becomes reality, "just the way things are." Positivist jurisprudence buries the embodiment of patriarchal domanance even further by insisting that the proper domain of jurisprudence is descriptive, not evaluative or normative.

> Liberal legalism [i.e., legal positivism] is thus a medium for making male dominance both invisible and legitimate by adopting the male point of view in law at the same time as it enforces that view on society. . . . Through legal mediation, male dominance is made to seem a feature of life, not a one-sided construct imposed by force for the advantage of a dominant group. To the degree it succeeds ontologically, male dominance does not look epistemological: control over being produces control over consciousness. . . . Dominance reified becomes difference. Coercion legitimated becomes consent. . . . In the liberal state, the rule of law—neutral, abstract, elevated, pervasive—both institutionalizes the power of men over women and institutionalizes power in its male form.

The question is how to find cracks in the picture of reality that institutionalizes patriarchy and makes it normal. How can the legal norm be challenged? MacKinnon argues that the law of equality provides an opportunity to challenge the inequality of law on behalf of women. Equality in law is now understood formally, and so it is generally assumed that by and large women already have it. But it is up to feminists to make equality law meaningful for women, by defining it in terms of the concrete reality of women's lives and challenging the male forms of power affirmatively embodied as rights in law. MacKinnon recognizes that equality does not refer to character traits or even human nature, to "sameness and difference," but to domination and subordination. Equality and inequality pertain to the distribution of power. To confront that distribution of power, recognizing it for what it is, and to remove the mask of legitimacy raised by its legalization are the critical tasks of feminist jurisprudence.

20

Jurisprudence and Gender

ROBIN WEST

Introduction

What is a human being? Legal theorists must, perforce, answer this question: Jurisprudence, after all, is about human beings. The task has not proven to be divisive. In fact, virtually all modern American legal theorists, like most modern moral and political philosophers, either explicitly or implicitly embrace what I will call the "separation thesis" about what it means to be a human being: A "human being," whatever else he is, is physically separate from all other human beings. I am one human being and you are another, and that distinction between you and me is central to the meaning of the phrase *human being*. Individuals are, in the words of one commentator, "distinct and not essentially connected with one another."[1] We are each physically "boundaried"—this is the trivially true meaning of the claim that we are all individuals. In Robert Nozick's telling phrase, the "root idea" of any acceptable moral or political philosophy is that "there are individuals with separate lives."[2] Although Nozick goes on to derive from this insight an argument for the minimal state, the separation thesis is hardly confined to the libertarian right. According to Roberto Unger, premiere spokesperson for the communitarian left, "to be conscious is to have the experience of being cut off from that about which one reflects: it is to be a subject that stands over against its objects. . . . The subjective awareness of separation . . . defines consciousness."[3] The political philosopher Michael Sandel has recently argued that most (not all) modern political theory is committed to the proposition that "what separates us is in some important sense prior to what connects us—epistemologically prior as well as morally prior. We are distinct individuals first, and then we form relationships and engage in co-operative arrangements with others; hence the priority of plurality over unity."[4] The same commitment underlies virtually all of our legal theory. Indeed, Sandel's formulation may be taken as a definitive restatement of the "separation thesis" that underlies modern jurisprudence.

The first purpose of this chapter is to put forward the global and critical claim that by virtue of their shared embrace of the separation thesis, all of our modern legal theory—by which I mean "liberal legalism" and "critical legal theory" collectively—is essentially and irretrievably masculine. My use of "I" above was inauthentic, just as the modern, increasing use of the female pronoun in liberal and critical legal theory, although well intended, is empirically and experientially false. For the cluster of claims that jointly constitute the "separation thesis"—the claim that human beings are, definitionally, distinct from one another, the claim that the referent of "I" is singular and unambiguous, the claim that the word *individual* has an uncontested biological meaning, namely, that we are each physically individuated from every other, the claim that we are individuals "first," and the claim that what separates us is epistemologically and morally prior to what connects us—while "trivially true" of men, are patently untrue of women.

◇ ◇ ◇

Indeed, perhaps the central insight of feminist theory of the last decade has been that woman are "essentially connected," not "essentially separate," from the rest of human life, both materially, through pregnancy, intercourse, and breast feeding, and existentially, through the moral and practical life. If by human beings legal theorists mean women as well as men then the separation thesis is clearly false. If, alternatively, by human beings they mean those for whom the separation thesis is true, then women are not human beings. It's not hard to guess which is meant.

Parts I and II of this chapter will contrast the "human being" constructed and described by (nonlegal) feminist theory, with the human being constructed, described, or simply assumed by masculine jurisprudence. I will try to show that the human being sometimes explicated, and most often simply assumed, by our modern legal theory contrasts in every particular with the "woman" sometimes assumed but more often carefully constructed by modern feminist theory.

◇ ◇ ◇

The third part of the chapter discusses the possibility for, the promise of, the obstacles to, and the present status of a truly feminist jurisprudence, which I define as a jurisprudence built upon feminist insights into women's true nature, rather than upon masculine insights into "human" nature. The gap between the description of human nature assumed or explicated by legal theory and the description of women explicated by feminist theory reflects a very real political obstacle to the development of a "feminist jurisprudence": Feminists take women's humanity seriously, and jurisprudence does not because the law does not. Until that fact changes, feminist jurisprudence is a political impossibility. The virtual abolition of patriarchy—a political structure that values men more than women—is the political precondition of a truly ungendered jurisprudence. But the gap between legal theory's descriptions of human nature and women's true nature also presents a conceptual obstacle to the development of feminist jurisprudence: Jurisprudence must be about the relationship of human beings to law, and feminist jurisprudence must be about women. Women, though, are not human beings. Until that philosophical fact changes, the phrase feminist jurisprudence is a conceptual anomaly. Nevertheless, it does not follow that there is no such thing as feminist jurisprudence, any more than it follows from the dominant definition of a human being that there is no such thing as women. The second purpose of this chapter is to explore and improve upon the feminist jurisprudence we have generated to date, in spite of patriarchy and in spite of the masculinity of mainstream jurisprudence. Part II aims to schematize, review, and, to some extent, redirect that jurisprudence.

Finally, the conclusion suggests how a humanist jurisprudence might evolve and how feminist legal theory can contribute to its creation.

I. Masculine Jurisprudence and Feminist Theory

The by now very well publicized split in masculine jurisprudence between legal liberalism and critical legal theory can be described in any number of ways. The now standard way to describe the split is in terms of politics: "Liberal legal theorists" align themselves with a liberal political philosophy which entails, among other things, allegiance to the Rule of Law and to Rule of Law virtues, while "critical legal theorists," typically left wing and radical, are skeptical of the Rule of Law and the split between law and politics which the Rule of Law purportedly delineates. Critical legal theorists are potentially far more sensitive to the political underpinnings of purportedly neutral legalistic constructs than are liberal legalists. I think this traditional characterization is wrong for a number of reasons: Liberal theorists are not necessarily politically naive, and critical theorists are not necessarily radical. However, my purpose is not to critique it. Instead, I want to suggest another way to understand the divisions in modern legal theory.

An alternative description of the difference (surely not the only one) is that liberal legal theory and critical legal theory provide two radically divergent phenomenological descriptions of the paradigmatically male experience of the inevitability of separation of the self from the rest of the species, and indeed from the rest of the natural world. Both schools, as we shall see, accept the separation thesis; they both view human beings as materially (or physically) separate from each other, and both view this fact as fundamental to the origin of law. But their accounts of the subjective experience of physical separation from the other—an individual other, the natural world, and society—are in nearly diametrical opposition. Liberal legalists, in short, describe an inner life enlivened by freedom and autonomy from the separate other and threatened by the danger of annihilation by him. Critical legal theorists, by contrast, tell a story of inner lives dominated by feelings of alienation and isolation from the separate other and enlivened by the possibility of association and community with him. These differing accounts of the subjective experience of being separate from others, I believe, are at the root of at least some of the divisions between critical and liberal legal theorists. I want to review each of these experiential descriptions of separation in some detail, for I will ultimately argue that they are not as contradictory as they first appear. Each story, I will suggest, constitutes a legitimate and true part of the total subjective experience of masculinity.

I will start with the liberal description of separation, because it is the most familiar and surely the most dominant. According to liberal legalism, the inevitability of the individual's material separation from the "other" entails, first and foremost, an existential state of highly desirable and much valued freedom: Because the individual is separate from the other, he is free of the other. Because I am separate from you, my ends, my life, my path, my goals are necessarily my own. Because I am separate, I am "autonomous." Because I am separate, I am existentially free (whether or not I am politically free). And, of course, this is true not just of me, but of everyone: It is the universal human condition. We are each separate and we are all separate, so we are each free and we are all free. We are, that is, equally free.

This existential condition of freedom in turn entails the liberal's conception of value. Because we are all free and we are each equally free, we should be treated by our government as free and as equally free. The individual must be treated by his government and by others in a way that respects his equality and his freedom. The government must honor at the level of politics the existential claim made above: that my ends are my ends; that I cannot be forced to embrace your ends as my own. Our separation entails our freedom which in turn entails our right to establish and pursue our own concept of value, independent of the concept of value pursued or favored by others. Ronald Dworkin puts the point in this way:

> What does it mean for the government to treat its citizens as equals? That is . . . the same question as the question of what it means for the government to treat all its citizens as free, or as independent, or with equal dignity. . . . [To accord with this demand, a government must] be neutral on what might be called the question of the good life. . . . [P]olitical decisions must be, so far as is possible, independent of any particular conception of the good life, or of what gives value to life. Since the citizens of a society differ in their conceptions, the government does not treat them as equals if it prefers one conception to another, either because the officials believe that one is intrinsically superior, or because one is held by the more numerous or more powerful group.[5]

Because of the dominance of liberalism in this culture, we might think of autonomy as the "official" liberal value entailed by the physical, material condition of inevitable separation from the other: separation from the other entails my freedom from him, and that in turn entails my political right to autonomy. I can form my own conception of the good life and pursue it. Indeed, any conception of the good which I form, will necessarily be my conception of the good life. That freedom must be respected. Because I am free, I value and have a right to autonomy. You must value it as well. The state must protect it. This in turn implies other (more contested) values, the most important of which is (or may be) equality. Dworkin continues:

> I now define a liberal as someone who holds . . . [a] liberal . . . theory of what equality requires. Suppose that a liberal is asked to found a new state. He is required to dictate its constitution and fundamental institutions. He must propose a general theory of political distribution. . . . He will arrive initially at something like this principal of rough equality: resources and opportunities should be distributed, so far as possible, equally, so that roughly the same share of whatever is available is devoted to satisfying the ambitions of each. Any other general aim of distribution will assume either that the fate of some people should be of greater concern than that of others, or that the ambitions or talents of some are more worthy, and should be supported more generously on that account.[6]

Autonomy, freedom, and equality collectively constitute what might be called the "up side" of the subjective experience of separation. Autonomy and freedom are both entailed by the separation thesis, and autonomy and freedom both feel very good. However, there's a "down side" to the subjective experience of separation as well. Physical separation from the other entails not just my freedom; it also entails my vulnerability. Every other discrete, separate individual—because he is the "other"—is a source of danger to me and a threat to my autonomy. I have reason to fear you solely by virtue of the fact that I am me and you are you. You are not me, so by definition my ends are not your ends. Our ends might conflict. You might try to frustrate my pursuit of my ends. In an extreme case, you might even try to kill me—you might cause my annihilation.

Annihilation by the other, we might say, is the official harm of liberal theory, just as autonomy is its official value. Hobbes, of course, gave the classic statement of the terrifying vulnerability that stems from our separateness from the other:

Nature hath made men so equall, in the faculties of body, and mind; as that though there bee found one man sometimes manifestly stronger in body, or of quicker mind then [*sic*] another; yet when all is reckoned together, the difference between man, and man, is not so considerable, as that one man can thereupon claim to himself any benefit, to which another may not pretend, as well as he. For as to the strength of body, the weakest has strength enough to kill the strongest, either by secret machination, or by confederacy with others, that are in the same danger with himselfe. . . . From this equality of ability, ariseth equality of hope in the attaining of our Ends. And therefore if any two men desire the same thing, which neverthelesse they cannot both enjoy, they become enemies; and in the way to their End, (which is principally their owne conservation, . . .) endeavour to destroy, or subdue one an other. And from hence it comes to passe, that where an Invader hath no more to feare, than another mans single power; if one plant, sow, build, or possesse a convenient Seat, others may probably be expected to come prepared with forces united, to dispossesse, and deprive him, not only of the fruit of his labour, but also of his life, or liberty. And the Invader again is in the like danger of another.[7]

◊ ◊ ◊

Thus, according to liberal legalism, the subjective experience of physical separation from the other determines both what we value (autonomy) and what we fear (annihilation). We value and seek societal protection of our autonomy: The liberal insists on my right to define and pursue my own life, my own path, my own identity, and my own conception of the good life free of interference from others. Because I am me and you are you, I value what I value, and you value what you value. The only value we truly share, then, is our joint investment in autonomy from each other: We both value our right to pursue our lives relatively free of outside control. We can jointly insist that our government grant us this protection. We also share the same fears. I fear the possibility—indeed the likelihood—that our ends will conflict, and you will frustrate my ends and in an extreme case cause my annihilation, and you fear the same thing about me. I want the right and the power to pursue my own chosen ends free of the fear that the you will try to prevent me from doing so. You, of course, want the same.

We can call this liberal legalist phenomenological narrative the "official story" of the subjectivity of separation. According to the official story, we value the freedom that our separateness entails, while we seek to minimize the threat that it poses. We do so, of course, through creating and then respecting the state. Whether or not Robert Nozick is right that the minimal state achieves the liberal's ideal, he has nevertheless stated that liberal ideal well in the following passage:

> The minimal state treats us as inviolate individuals . . . ; it treats us as persons having individual rights with the dignity this constitutes. . . . [This treatment] allows us, individually or with whom we choose, to choose our life and to realize our ends and our conception of ourselves, insofar as we can, aided by the voluntary cooperation of other individuals possessing the same dignity. How *dare* any state or group of individuals do more. Or less. . . . [T]here is no *social entity* with a good that undergoes some sacrifice for its own good. There are only individual people, different individual people, with their own individual lives. Using one of these people for the benefit of the others, uses him and benefits others. Nothing more.[8]

Now, critical legal theory diverges from liberal legalism on many points, but one striking contrast is this: Critical theorists provide a starkly divergent phenomenological description of the subjective experience of separation. According to our critical legal theorists, the separate individual is indeed, in Sandel's phrase, "epistemologically prior to the collective." Like liberal legalists, critical legal theorists also view the individual as materially separate from the rest of human life. But according to the critical theorist, what that material state of separation existentially entails is not a perpetual celebration of autonomy but, rather, a perpetual longing for community, or attachment, or unification, or connection. The separate individual strives to connect with the "other" from whom he is separate. The separate individual lives in a state of perpetual dread not of annihilation by the other, but of the alienation, loneliness, and existential isolation that his material separation from the other imposes upon him. The individual strives through love, work, and government to achieve a unification with the other, the natural world, and the society from which he was originally and continues to be existentially separated. The separate individual seeks community—not autonomy—and dreads isolation and alienation from the other—not annihilation by him. If we think of liberalism's depiction of the subjectivity of separation as the official story, then, we might think of this alternative description of the subjectivity of separation as the unofficial story. It is the subterranean, unofficial story of the unrecognized and—at least by liberals—slightly detested subjective craving of lost individuals.

Thus, there is a vast gap, according to critical theory, between the "official value" of liberal legalism—autonomy—and what the individual truly subjectively desires, which is to establish a true connection with the other. Similarly, there is a vast gap between the "official harm" of liberal legalism—annihilation by the other—and what the individual truly subjectively dreads, which is not annihilation by him, but isolation and alienation from him. According to the critical theorist, while the dominant liberal culture insists we value autonomy and fear the other, what the individual truly desires, craves, and longs to establish is some sort of connection with the other, and what the individual truly dreads is alienation from him.[9]

◊ ◊ ◊

Indeed, the individual longs to reestablish connection with the other in spite of the very real possibility (acknowledged by most if not all critical theorists) that that other might, at any moment, frustrate his ends, threaten his autonomy, or annihilate him. But this longing for community survives in the face of an even more powerful source of resistance. The longing for attachment to the other persists in spite of the dominant liberal culture's adamant denial of the desire's existence.[10]

◊ ◊ ◊

In another sense, though, the longing for connection persists not so much "in spite of" the dominant culture's valuation of autonomy but because of that value. The value we place on autonomy, according to some critical legal theorists, aggravates our alienation, isolation and loneliness.[11]

◊ ◊ ◊

The longing for connection with the other, and the dread of alienation from him, according to the critical theorists, is in a state of constant "contradiction" with the official value and official harm that flow from separation—autonomy from the other and annihilation by him. Nevertheless, in spite of that tension, both the dread of alienation and the desire for connection are constantly there. The dominant culture insists we value autonomy from the other and fear annihilation by him. But subjectively, the individual lives with a more or less unrealized desire to connect with the other, and a constant dread or fear, of becoming permanently alienated, isolated—lost—from the other.

To summarize: According to liberal legalism, each of us is physically separate from every other, and because of that separation, we value our autonomy from the other and fear our annihilation by him. I have called these our officially recognized values and harms. Critical legal theory tells the unofficial story. According to critical legal theory, we are indeed physically separate from the other, but what that existentially entails is that we dread the alienation and isolation from the separate other and long for connection with him. While liberal culture officially and publicly claims that we love our autonomy and fear the other, subjective life belies this claim. Subjectively and in spite of the dominant culture's insistence to the contrary, we long to establish some sort of human connection with the other in order to overcome the pain of isolation and alienation which our separateness engenders.

⋄ ⋄ ⋄

Let me now turn to feminist theory. Although the legal academy is for the most part unaware of it, modern feminist theory is as fundamentally divided as legal theory. One way to characterize the conflict—the increasingly standard way to characterize the conflict—is that while most modern feminists agree that women are different from men and agree on the importance of the difference, feminists differ over which differences between men and women are most vital. According to one group of feminists, sometimes called *cultural feminists,* the important difference between men and women is that women raise children and men don't. According to a second group of feminists, now called *radical feminists,* the important difference between men and women is that women get fucked and men fuck: "Women," definitionally, are "those from whom sex is taken," just as workers, definitionally, are those from whom labor is taken. Another way to put the difference is in political terms. Cultural feminists appear somewhat more "moderate" when compared with the traditional culture: From a mainstream nonfeminist perspective, cultural feminists appear to celebrate many of the same feminine traits that the traditional culture has stereotypically celebrated. Radical feminists, again from a mainstream perspective, appear more separatist and, in contrast with standard political debate, more alarming. They also appear to be more "political" in a sense which perfectly parallels the critical theory–liberal theory split described above: Radical feminists appear to be more attuned to power disparities between men and women than are cultural feminists.

I think this traditional characterization is wrong on two counts. First, cultural feminists no less than radical feminists are well aware of women's powerlessness vis-à-vis men, and second, radical feminism, as I will later argue, is as centrally concerned with pregnancy as it is with intercourse. But again, instead of arguing against this traditional characterization of the divide between radical and cultural feminism, I want to provide an alternative. My alternative characterization structurally (although not substantively) parallels the characterization of the difference between liberal and critical legalism. Underlying both radical and cultural feminism is a conception of women's existential state that is grounded in women's potential for physical, material connection to human life, just as underlying both liberal and critical legalism is a conception of men's existential state that is grounded in the inevitability of men's physical separation from the species. I will call the shared conception of women's existential lives the *connection thesis.* The divisions between radical and cultural feminism stem from divergent accounts of the subjectivity of the potential for connection, just as what divides liberal from critical legal theory are divergent accounts of the subjectivity of the inevitability of separation.

The connection thesis is simply this: Women are actually or potentially materially connected to other human life. Men aren't. This material fact has existential consequences. While it may be true for men that the individual is "epistemologically and morally prior to the collectivity," it is not true for women. The potential for material connection with the other defines women's subjective, phenomenological, and existential state, just as surely as the inevitability of material separation from the other defines men's existential state. Our potential for material connection engenders pleasures and pains, values and dangers, and attractions and fears, which are entirely different from those which follow, for men, from the necessity of separation. Indeed, it is the rediscovery of the multitude of implications from this material difference between men and women which has enlivened (and divided) both cultural and radical feminism in this decade (and it is those discoveries which have distinguished both radical and cultural feminism from liberal feminism). As Carol Gilligan notes, this development is somewhat paradoxical: During the same decade that liberal feminist political activists and lawyers pressed for equal (meaning same) treatment by the law, feminist theorists in nonlegal disciplines rediscovered women's differences from men.[12] Thus, what unifies radical and cultural feminist theory (and what distinguishes both from liberal feminism) is the discovery, or rediscovery, of the importance of women's fundamental material difference from men. As we shall see, neither radical feminists nor cultural feminists are entirely explicit in their embrace of the connection thesis. But both groups, implicitly if not explicitly, adhere to some version of it.

If both cultural and radical feminists hold some version of the connection thesis, then one way of understanding the issues that divide radical and cultural feminists, different from the standard account given above, is that while radical and cultural feminists agree that women's lives are distinctive in their potential for material connection to others, they provide sharply contrasting accounts of the subjective experience of the material and existential state of connection. According to cultural feminist accounts of women's subjectivity, women value intimacy, develop a capacity for nurturance, and an ethic of care for the "other" with which we are connected, just as we learn to dread and fear separation from the other. Radical feminists tell a very different story. According to radical feminism, women's connection with the "other" is above all else invasive and intrusive: Women's potential for material "connection" invites invasion into the physical integrity of our bodies, and intrusion into the existential integrity of our lives. Although women may "officially" value the intimacy of connection, we "unofficially" dread the intrusion it inevitably entails and long for the individuation and independence that deliverance from that state of connection would permit. Paralleling the structure above, I will call these two descriptions feminism's official and unofficial stories of women's subjective experience of physical connection.

In large part due to the phenomenal success of Carol Gilligan's book *In a Different Voice,* cultural feminism may be the most familiar of these two feminist strands, and for that reason alone, I call it feminism's *official story.* Cultural feminism (in this country and among academics) is in large part defined by Gilligan's book. Defined as such, cultural feminism begins not with a commitment to the "material" version of the connection thesis (as outlined above) but, rather, with a commitment to its more observable existential and psychological consequences. Thus limited, we can put the cultural feminist point this way: Women have a "sense" of existential "connection" to other human life which men do not. That sense of connection in turn entails a way of learning, a path of moral development, an aesthetic sense, and a view of the world and of one's place within it which sharply contrasts with men's. To reverse Sandel's formulation, for women, connection is "prior," both epistemologically and, therefore, morally, to the individual. One cultural feminist—Suzanna Sherry—calls this women's view of the world a "feminine" rather than "feminist" perspective. She summarizes the "feminine perspective" in this way:

> The feminine perspective views individuals primarily as interconnected members of a community. Nancy Chodorow and Carol Gilligan, in groundbreaking studies on the development of self and morality, have concluded that women tend to have a more intersubjective sense of self than men and that the feminine perspective is therefore more other-directed.... The essential difference between the male and female perspectives [is that] ... "the basic feminine sense of self is connected to the world, the basic masculine sense of self is separate." Women thus tend to see others as extensions of themselves rather than as outsiders or competitors.[13]

Why are men and women different in this essential way? The cultural feminist explanation for women's heightened sense of connection is that women are more "connected" to life than are men because it is women who are the primary caretakers of young children. A female child develops her sense of identity as "continuous" with her caretaker's, while a young boy develops a sense of identity that is distinguished from his caretaker's. Because of the gender alignment of mothers and female children, young girls "fuse" their growing sense of identity with a sense of sameness with and attachment to the other, while because of the gender distinction between mothers and male children, young boys "fuse" their growing sense of identity with a sense of difference and separation from the other. This turns out to have truly extraordinary and far reaching consequences, for both cognitive and moral development. Nancy Chodorow explains:

> [This means that] [g]irls emerge from this period with a basis for "empathy" built into their primary definition of self in a way that boys do not. . . . [G]irls come to experience themselves as less differentiated than boys, as more continuous with and related to the external object-world and as differently oriented to their inner object-world as well.[14]

Women are therefore capable of a degree of physical as well as psychic intimacy with the other which greatly exceeds men's capacity. Carol Gilligan finds that

> the fusion of identity and intimacy . . . [is] clearly articulated . . . in [women's] . . . self-descriptions. In response to the request to describe themselves, . . . women describe a relationship, depicting their identity *in* the connection of future mother, present wife, adopted child, or past lover. Similarly, the standard of moral judgment that informs their assessment of self is a standard of relationship, an ethic of nurturance, responsibility, and care . . . [In] women's descriptions, identity is defined in a context of relationship and judged by a standard of responsibility and care. Similarly, morality is seen by these women as arising from the experience of connection and conceived as a problem of inclusion rather than one of balancing claims.[15]

◊ ◊ ◊

Thus, according to Gilligan (and her subjects), women view themselves as fundamentally connected to, not separate from, the rest of life. This difference permeates virtually every aspect of our lives. According to the vast literature on difference now being developed by cultural feminists, women's cognitive development, literary sensibilty, aesthetic taste, and psychological development, no less than our anatomy, are all fundamentally different from men's, and are different in the same way: Unlike men, we view ourselves as connected to, not separate from, the other. As a consequence, women's ways of knowing are more "integrative" than men's; women's aesthetic and critical sense is "embroidered" rather than "laddered", women's psychological development remains within the sphere of "attachment" rather than "individuation."

The most significant aspect of our difference, though, is surely the moral difference. According to cultural feminism, women are more nurturant, caring, loving, and responsible to others than are men. This capacity for nurturance and care dictates the moral terms in which women, distinctively, construct social relations: Women view the morality of actions against a standard of responsibility to others, rather than against a standard of rights and autonomy from others. As Gilligan puts it:

> The moral imperative . . . [for] women is an injunction to care, a responsibility to discern and alleviate the "real and recognizable trouble" of this world. For men, the moral imperative appears rather as an injunction to respect the rights of others and thus to protect from interference the rights to life and self-fulfillment.[16]

Cultural feminists, to their credit, have reidentified these differences as women's strengths, rather than women's weaknesses. Cultural feminism does not simply identify women's differences—patriarchy too insists on women's differences—it celebrates them. Women's art, women's craft, women's narrative capacity, women's critical eye, women's ways of knowing, and women's heart, are all, for the cultural feminist, redefined as things to celebrate. Quilting, cultural feminism insists, is not just something women do; it is art, and should be recognized as such. Integrative knowledge is not a confused and failed attempt to come to grips with the elementary rules of deductive logic; it is a way of knowledge and should be recognized as such. Women's distinctive aesthetic sense is as valid as men's. Most vital, however, for cultural feminism is the claim that intimacy is not just something women do, it is something human beings ought to do. Intimacy is a source of value, not a private hobby. It is morality, not habit.

To pursue my structural analogy to masculine legal theory, then, intimacy and the ethic of care constitute the entailed values of the existential state of connection with others, just as autonomy and freedom constitute the entailed values of the existential state of separation from others for men. Because women are fundamentally connected to other human life, women value and enjoy intimacy with others (just as because men are fundamentally separate from other human life men value and enjoy autonomy). Because women are connected with the rest of human life, intimacy with the "other" comes naturally. Caring, nurturance, and an ethic of love and responsibility for life is second nature. Autonomy, or freedom from the other, constitutes a value for men because it reflects an existential state of being: separate. Intimacy is a value for women because it reflects an existentially connected state of being.

Intimacy, the capacity for nurturance, and the ethic of care constitute what we might call the "up side" of the subjective experience of connection. It's all good. Intimacy feels good, nurturance is good, and caring for others morally is good. But there's a "down side" to the subjective experience of connection. There's danger, harm, and fear entailed by the state of connection as well as value. Whereas men fear annihilation from the separate other (and consequently have trouble achieving intimacy), women fear separation from the connected other (and consequently have trouble achieving independence). Gilligan makes the point succinctly: "Since masculinity is defined through separation while femininity is defined through attachment, male gender identity is threatened by intimacy while female gender identity is threatened by separation."[17] Separation, then, might be regarded as the official harm of cultural feminism. When a separate self must be asserted, women have trouble asserting it.

◇ ◇ ◇

Separation, and the fear of separation, can lead to real harm, especially in later life. In her final chapter, Gilligan elaborates:

> Because women's sense of integrity appears to be entwined with an ethic of care, so that to see themselves as women is to see themselves in a relationship of connection, the major transitions in women's lives would seem to involve changes in the understanding and activities of care. Certainly the shift from childhood to adulthood witnesses a major redefinition of care. . . .
>
> In the same vein, however, the events of mid-life—the menopause and changes in family and work—can alter a woman's activities of care in ways that affect her sense of herself. If mid-life brings an end to relationships, to the sense of connection on which she relies, as well as to the activities of care through which she judges her worth, then the mourning that accompanies all life transitions can give way to the melancholia of self-deprecation and despair.[18]

Now, while Gilligan is undoubtedly explaining a real experiential phenomenon—I don't know of any woman who hasn't recognized herself somewhere in this book—her material explanation of that phenomenon is incomplete. Which is not to say it isn't true: It seems quite plausible that women are more psychically connected to others in just the way Gilligan describes and for just the reason she expounds. Mothers raise children, and as a consequence girls, and not boys, think of themselves as continuous with, rather than separate from, that first all-important "other"—the mother. But this psychological and developmental explanation just raises—it does not answer—the background material question: Why do women, rather than men, raise, nurture, and cook for children? What is the cause of this difference?

Although Gilligan doesn't address the issue, other cultural feminists have, and their explanations converge, I believe, implicitly if not explicitly, on a material, or mixed material–cultural, and not just a cultural answer: women raise children—and hence raise girls who are more connected and nurturant and therefore more likely to be nurturant caretakers themselves—because it is women who bear children. Women are not inclined to abandon an infant they've carried for nine months and then delivered. If so, then women are ultimately more "connected"—psychically, emotionally, and morally—to other human beings because women, as children were raised by women and women raise children because women, uniquely, are physically and materially "connected" to those human beings when the human beings are fetuses and then infants. Women are more empathic to the lives of others because women are physically tied to the lives of others in a way which men are not. Women's moral voice is one of responsibilty, duty, and care for others because women's material circumstance is one of responsibility, duty, and care for those who are first physically attached, then physically dependent, and then emotionally interdependent. Women think in terms of the needs of others rather than the rights of others because women materially, and then physically, and then psychically, provide for the needs of others. Lastly, women fear separation from the other rather than annihilation by him, and "count" it as a harm, because women experience the "separating" pain of childbirth and more deeply feel the pain of the maturation and departure of adult children.

◇ ◇ ◇

In *Caring: A Feminine Approach to Ethics and Moral Education,*[19] Stanford philosopher and cultural feminist Nel Noddings endorses a biological and material explanation of women's different moral voice:

> Clearly, mothering and caring are deeply related. Several contemporary writers have raised a question that seems odd at first glance: Why is it that women in our society do the mothering? . . . The biological view holds that women, having given birth and entered lactation, are naturally nurturant toward their infants. The socialization view denies arguments for nature, instinct, and natural nurturance and insists that mothering is a role—something learned. Finally, the psychological view suggested by Nancy Chodorow holds that the tendency for girls to want to mother, and to actually engage in mothering, is the result of deep psychological processes established in close and special relationships with their own mothers.
>
> The socialization view, as an explanatory theory, seems nonsense. We are not nearly so successful at socializing people into roles as we are at reproducing mothering in women. Mothering is not a role but a relationship. The psychological view, however, seems very strong. . . . One difficulty [with it] is that those endorsing psychological views have felt the need to set aside or minimize biological arguments. It is true that a woman's natural inclination to mother a newborn does not explain why she continues to mother a child into adolescence or why she mothers other people's half-grown children. But it may well be that a completely adequate theory will have to embrace both biological and psychological factors.[20]

Whether we embrace a material or a purely developmental explanation of women's heightened connection with the other, however, the "story" of women's relationship with the other as told by cultural feminists contrast in virtually every particular with the story of men's relationship to the other as told by liberals. First, men, according to the Hobbesian account, are by nature equal. "Nature hath made men so equall, in the faculties of body, and mind; as that though there bee found one man sometimes manifestly stronger in body . . . ; yet when all is reckoned together, the difference between man, and man, is not so considerable, as that one man can thereupon claim to himselfe any benefit. . . . [T] he weakest has strength enough to kill the strongest."[21] Women, by contrast, are not "equal" in strength to the most important "other" they encounter: the fetus and then the newborn child. Rather, the fetus and the woman and later the infant and the mother occupy what might be called a natural, hierarchical web of inequality, not a natural state of equality: Whereas men may be "by nature equal" women are "by nature stronger" than those who are most important to them and most dependent upon them. The natural physical equality between self and other on which Hobbes insists is simply untrue of women's natural state. Second, according to Hobbes, "men" are naturally inclined to aggress against those they perceive as the vulnerable other. Again, women are not: Infants are dependent upon mothers and vulnerable to them, yet the natural mother does not aggress against her child, she breast-feeds her. And lastly, men respond to the vulnerability of natural equality by developing a morality and a civil state that demand respect for the equality, rights, and freedom of the other. Women do not. Women respond to their natural state of inequality by developing a morality of nurturance that is responsible for the well-being of the dependent, and an ethic of care that responds to the greater needs of the weak. Men respond to the natural state of equality with an ethic of autonomy and rights. Women respond to the natural state of inequality with an ethic of responsibility and care.

We might summarize cultural feminism in this way: Women's potential for a material connection to life entails (either directly, as I have argued, or indirectly, through the reproduction of mothering) an experiential and psychological sense of connection with other human life, which in turn entails both women's concept of value, and women's concept of harm. Women's concept of value revolves not around the axis of autonomy, individuality, justice, and rights, as does men's but, instead, around the axis of intimacy, nurturance, community, responsibility, and care. For women, the creation of value and the living of a good life therefore depend upon relational, contextual, nurturant, and affective responses to the needs of those who are dependent and weak, while for men the creation of value and the living of the good life depend upon the ability to respect the rights of independent coequals, and the deductive, cognitive ability to infer from those rights rules for safe living. Women's concept of harm revolves not around a fear of annihilation by the other but around a fear of separation and isolation from the human community on which she depends and which is dependent upon her. If, as I have suggested, cultural feminism is our dominant feminist dogma, then this account of the nature of women's lives constitutes the official text of feminism, just as liberal legalism constitutes the official text of legalism.

These two official stories sharply contrast. Whereas according to liberal legalism, men value autonomy from the other and fear annihilation by him, women, according to cultural feminism, value intimacy with the other and fear separation from her. Women's sense of connection with others determines our special competencies and special vulnerabilities, just as men's sense of separation from others determines theirs. Women value and have a special competency for intimacy, nurturance, and relational thinking and a special vulnerability to and fear of isolation, separation from the other, and abandonment, just as men value and have a special competency for autonomy and a special vulnerability to and fear of annihilation.

Against the cultural feminist backdrop, the story that radical feminists tell of women's invaded, violated lives is "subterranean" in the same sense that against the backdrop of liberal legalism, the story critical legal theorists tell of men's alienation and isolation from others is subterranean. According to radical feminism, women's connection to others is the source of women's misery, not a source of value worth celebrating. For cultural feminists, women's connectedness to the other (whether material or cultural) is the source, the heart, the root, and the cause of women's different morality, different voice, different "ways of knowing," different genius, different capacity for care, and different ability to nurture. For radical feminists, that same potential for connection—experienced materially in intercourse and pregnancy but experienced existentially in all spheres of life—is the source of women's debasement, powerlessness, subjugation, and misery. It is the cause of our pain and the reason for our stunted lives. Invasion and intrusion, rather than intimacy, nurturance, and care, is the "unofficial" story of women's subjective experience of connection.

Thus, modern radical feminism is unified among other things by its insistence on the invasive, oppressive, destructive implications of women's material and existential connection to the other. So defined, radical feminism (of modern times) begins not with the 1980s' critique of heterosexuality but, rather, in the late 1960s with Shulamith Firestone's angry and eloquent denunciation of the oppressive consequences for women of the physical condition of pregnancy. Firestone's assessment of the importance and distinctiveness of women's reproductive role parallels Marilyn French's.[22] Both view women's physical connection with nature and with the other as in some sense the "cause" of patriarchy. But their analyses of the chain of causation sharply contrast. For French, women's reproductive role—the paradigmatic experience of physical connection to nature, to life, and to the other and thus the core of women's moral difference—is also the cause of patriarchy, primarily because of men's fear of and contempt for nature. Firestone has a radically different view. Pregnancy is indeed the paradigmatic experience of physical connection, and it is indeed the core of women's difference, but according to Firestone, it is for that reason alone the cause of women's oppression. Male contempt has nothing (at first) to do with it. Pregnancy itself, independent of male contempt, is invasive, dangerous and oppressive; it is an assault on the physical integrity and privacy of the body. For Firestone, the strategic implication of this is both clear and clearly material. The technological separation of reproduction from the female body is the necessary condition for women's liberation.[23]

In a moment, I will turn to heterosexual intercourse, for it is intercourse, rather than pregnancy, which consumes the attention of the modern radical feminism of our decade. But before doing so it's worth recognizing that the original radical feminist case for reproductive freedom did not turn on rights of "privacy" (either of the doctor–patient relationship, or of the marriage, or of the family), or rights to "equal protection," or rights to be free of "discrimination." It did not turn on rights at all. Rather, the original feminist argument for reproductive freedom turned on the definitive radical feminist insight that pregnancy—the invasion of the body by the other to which women are distinctively vulnerable—is an injury and ought to be treated as such. Pregnancy connects us with life, as the cultural feminist insists, but that connection is not something to celebrate; it is that very connection that hurts us. This argument, as I will argue later, is radically incommensurate with liberal legal ideology. There's no legal category that fits it. But it is nevertheless the radical argument—that pregnancy is a dangerous, psychically consuming, existentially intrusive, and physically invasive assault upon the body which in turn leads to a dangerous, consuming, intrusive, invasive assault on the mother's self-identity—that best captures women's own sense of the injury and danger of pregnancy, whether or not it captures the law's sense of what an unwanted pregnancy involves or why women should have the right to terminate it.

The radical feminist argument for reproductive freedom appears in legal argument only inadvertently or surreptitiously, but it does on occasion appear. It appeared most recently in the phenomenological descriptions of unwanted pregnancies collated in the *Thornburgh amicus* brief recently filed by the National Abortion Rights Action League (NARAL).[24] The descriptions of pregnancy collated in that peculiarly nonlegal legal document are filled with metaphors of invasion—metaphors, of course, because we lack the vocabulary to name these harms precisely. Those descriptions contrast sharply with the "joy" that cultural feminists celebrate in pregnancy, childbirth, and child raising. The invasion of the self by the other emerges as a source of oppression, not a source of moral value.

"During my pregnancy," one women explains, "I was treated like a baby machine— an incubator without feelings."[25] "Then I got pregnant again," another woman writes,

> This one would be only 13 months younger than the third child. I was faced with the
> unpleasant fact that I could not stop the babies from coming no matter what I did. . . .

You cannot possibly know what it is like to be the helpless pawn of nature. I am a 71 year old widow.[26]

"Almost exactly a decade ago," writes another, "I learned I was pregnant. . . . I was sick in my heart and I thought I would kill myself. It was as if I had been told my body had been invaded with cancer. It seemed that very wrong."[27]

One woman speaks directly, without metaphor: "On the ride home from the clinic, the relief was enormous. I felt happy for the first time in weeks. I had a future again. I had my body back."[28]

According to these women's self-descriptions, when the unwanted baby arrives, the injury is again one of invasion, intrusion, and limitation. The harm of an unwanted pregnancy is that the baby will elicit a surrender (not an end) of the mother's life. The fear of unwanted pregnancy is that one will lose control of one's individuated being (not that one will die). Thus, one woman writes, "I was like any other woman who had an unintended pregnancy, I was terrified and felt as though my life was out of my control."[29]

This danger, and the fear of it, is gender specific. It is a fear which grips women, distinctively, and it is a fear about which men, apparently, know practically nothing. Another woman writes:

> I was furiously angry, dismayed, dismal, by turns. I could not justify an abortion on economic grounds, on grounds of insufficient competence or on any other of a multitude of what might be perceived as "legitimate" reasons. But I kept being struck by the ultimate unfairness of it all. I could not conceive of any event which would so profoundly impact upon any man. Surely my husband would experience some additional financial burden, and additional "fatherly" chores, but his whole future plan was not hostage to this unchosen, undesired event. Basically his life would remain the same progression of ordered events as before.[30]

◇ ◇ ◇

Conversely, women who had abortions felt able to form their own destiny. One woman wrote: "Personally legal abortion allowed me the choice as a teenager living on a very poor Indian Reservation to finish growing up and make something of my life."[31] And another:

> I was not glad that I was faced with an unwanted, unplanned pregnancy, however I am glad that I made the decision to have an abortion. The experience was a very positive one for me. It helped me learn that I am a person and I can make independent decisions. Had I not had the abortion I would have probably ended up a single mother struggling for survival and dealing with a child that I was not ready for."[32]

As noted above, radical feminism of the 1980s has focused more on intercourse than on pregnancy. But this may represent less of a divergence than it first appears. From the point of view of the connection thesis, what the radical feminists of the 1980s find objectionable, invasive, and oppressive about heterosexual intercouurse, is precisely what the radical feminists of the 1960s found objectionable, invasive, and oppressive about pregnancy and motherhood. According to the 1980s radical critique, intercourse, like pregnancy, blurs the physical boundary between self and other, and that blurring of boundaries between self and other constitutes a profound invasion of the self's physical integrity. That invasion—the "dissolving of boundaries"—is something to condemn, not celebrate. Andrea Dworkin explains:

◇ ◇ ◇

A human being has a body that is inviolate; and when it is violated, it is abused. A woman has a body that is penetrated in intercourse: permeable, its corporeal solidness a lie. The discourse of male truth—literature, science, philosophy, pornography—calls that penetration *violation*. This it does with some consistency and some confidence. *Violation* is a synonym for intercourse. At the same time, the penetration is taken to be a use, not an abuse; a normal use; it is appropriate to enter her, to push into ("violate") the boundaries of her body. She is human, of course, but by a standard that does not include physical privacy. She is, in fact, human by a standard that precludes physical privacy, since to keep a man out altogether and for a lifetime is deviant in the extreme, a psychopathology, a repudiation of the way in which she is expected to manifest her humanity.[33]

◇ ◇ ◇

Although Dworkin herself does not draw the parallel, for both Dworkin and Firestone, women's potential for material connection with the other—whether through intercourse or pregnancy—constitutes an invasion upon our physical bodies, an intrusion upon our lives, and consequently an assault upon our existential freedom, whether or not it is also the root of our moral distinctiveness (the claim cultural feminism makes on behalf of pregnancy) or the hope of our liberation (the claim sexual liberationists make on behalf of sex). Both intercourse and pregnancy are literal, physical, material invasions and occupations of the body. The fetus, like the penis, literally occupies my body. In their extremes, of course, both unwanted heterosexual intercourse and unwanted pregnancy can be life-threatening experiences of physical invasion. An unwanted fetus, no less than an unwanted penis, invades my body, violates my physical boundaries, occupies my body, and can potentially destroy my sense of self. Although the culture does not recognize them as such, the physical and existential invasions occasioned by unwanted pregnancy and intercourse are real harms. They are events we should fear. They are events which any sane person should protect herself against. What unifies the radical feminism of the 1960s and 1980s is the argument that women's potential for material, physical connection with the other constitutes an invasion which is a very real harm causing very real damage and which society ought to recognize as such.

The material, sporadic violation of a woman's body occasioned by pregnancy and intercourse implies an existential and pervasive violation of her privacy, integrity, and life projects. According to radical feminists, women's longings for individuation, physical privacy, and independence go well beyond the desire to avoid the dangers of rape or unwanted pregnancy. Women also long for liberation from the oppression of intimacy (and its attendant values) which both cultural feminism and most women officially, and wrongly, overvalue. Intimacy, in short, is intrusive, even when it isn't life threatening (perhaps especially when it isn't life threatening). An unwanted pregnancy is disastrous, but even a wanted pregnancy and motherhood are intrusive. The child intrudes, just as the fetus invades.

Similarly, while unwanted heterosexual intercourse is disastrous, even wanted heterosexual intercourse is intrusive. The penis occupies the body and "divides the woman" internally, to use Andrea Dworkin's language, in consensual intercourse no less than in rape. It preempts, challenges, negates, and renders impossible the maintenance of physical integrity and the formation of a unified self. The deepest unofficial story of radical feminism may be that intimacy—the official value of cultural feminism—is itself oppressive. Women secretly, unofficially, and surreptitiously long for the very individuation that cultural feminism insists women fear: the freedom, the independence, the individuality, the sense of wholeness, the confidence, the self-esteem, and the security of identity which can only come from a life, a history, a path, a voice, a sexuality, a womb, and a body of one's own. Dworkin explains:

> In the experience of intercourse, she loses the capacity for integrity because her body— the basis of privacy and freedom in the material world for all human beings—is entered and occupied; the boundaries of her physical body are—neutrally speaking—violated. What is taken from her in that act is not recoverable, and she spends her life—wanting, after all to have something—pretending that pleasure is in being reduced through intercourse to insignificance. . . . She learns to eroticize powerlessness and self-anni-hilation. The very boundaries of her own body become meaningless to her, and even worse, useless to her. The transgression of those boundaries comes to signify a sexually charged degradation into which she throws herself, having been told, convinced, that identity, for a female, is there—somewhere beyond privacy and self-respect.[34]

Radical feminism, then, is unified by a particular description of the subjectivity of the material state of connection. According to that description, women dread intrusion and invasion and long for an independent, individualized, separate identity. While women may indeed "officially" value intimacy, what women unofficially crave is physical pri-vacy, physical integrity, and sexual celibacy—in a word, physical exclusivity. In the moral realm, women officially value contextual, relational, caring, moral thinking but secretly wish that everyone would get the hell out of our lives so that we could pursue our own projects—we loathe the intrusion that intimacy entails. In the epistemological and moral realms, while women officially value community, the web, the spinning wheel, and the weave, we privately crave solitude, self-regard, self-esteem, linear thinking, legal rights, and principled thought.

◊ ◊ ◊

Finally, then, we can schematize the contrast between the description of the human being that emerges from modern legal theory and the description of women that emerges from modern feminism.

	The Official Story (Liberal legalism and cultural feminism)		The Unofficial Story (Critical legalism and radical femininsm)	
	Value	Harm	Longing	Dread
Legal Theory (human beings)	Autonomy	Annihilation; Frustration	Attachment; Connection	Alienation
Feminist Theory (women)	Intimacy	Separation	Individuation	Invasion; Intrusion

As the diagram reveals, the descriptions of the subjectivity of human existence told by feminist theory and legal theory contrast at every point. There is no overlap. First, and most obviously, the official descriptions of human beings' subjectivity and women's sub-jectivity contrast rather than compare. According to liberal theory, human beings respond aggressively to their natural state of relative physical equality. In response to the great dangers posed by their natural aggression, they abide by a sharply antinaturalist morality of autonomy, rights, and individual spheres of freedom, which is intended to and to some extent does curb their natural aggression. They respect a civil state that enforces those rights against the most egregious breaches. The description of women's subjectivity told by cultural feminism is much the opposite. According to cultural feminism, women inhabit a realm of natural inequality. They are physically stronger than the fetus and the infant. Women respond to their natural inequality over the fetus and infant not with aggression but with nurturance and care. That natural and nurturant response evolves into a naturalist moral ethic of care which is consistent with women's natural response. The substantive moralities consequent to these two stories, then, unsurprisingly, are also diametrically opposed. The autonomy that human beings value and the rights they need as a restriction on their natural hostility to the equal and separate other are in sharp contrast to the intimacy that women value, and the ethic of care that represents not a limitation upon, but an extension of, women's natural nurturant response to the dependent, connected other.

The subterranean descriptions of subjectivity that emerge from the unofficial stories of radical feminism and critical legalism also contrast rather than compare. According to the critical legalists, human beings respond to their natural state of physical separateness not with aggression, fear, and mutual suspicion, as liberalism holds, but with longing. Men suffer from a perpetual dread of isolation and alienation and a fear of rejection and harbor a craving for community, connection, and association. Women, by contrast, according to radical feminism, respond to their natural state of material connection to the other with a craving for individuation and a loathing for invasion. Just as clearly, the subterranean dread men have of alienation (according to critical legalism) contrasts sharply with the subterranean dread that women have of invasion and intrusion (according to radical feminism).

The responses of human beings and women to these subterranean desires also contrast in substance, although, interestingly, the responses are structurally similar. According to both critical legalism and radical feminism, human beings and women, respectively, for the most part deny the subterranean desires that permeate their lives. Instead, they collaborate, to some degree, in the official culture's elaborate attempt to deny while partially accommodating the intensity of those felt needs. Both do so for the same reason: Both human beings and women deny their subterranean desires because of a fear—legitimately grounded—that the subterranean need, if asserted, will be met by either violence or rejection by the dominant culture. The dominant male culture condemns as aberrant the man who needs others, just as the dominant female culture condemns the woman who wants to exist apart from others. Thus, men deny their need for attachment and women deny their need for individuation. The mechanisms by which the two groups effect the denial are fundamentally opposed in substance, albeit structurally parallel. According to critical theory, human beings deny their need for attachment primarily through the distancing and individuating assertion of individual rights. It is the purpose and content of those rights to largely deny the human need for attachment and communion with the other. According to radical feminism, women deny their need for individuation through the "intimating" mechanisms of romance, sentiment, familial ideology, the mystique of motherhood, and commitment to the false claims of affective attachment. It is the purpose and content of romance and familial ideology to largely deny women's need for individuation, separation, and individual identity. . . .

Somewhat less obviously, the unofficial description of subjectivity provided by each side is not simply the equivalent of the official description of the other, although they are often mistaken as such. The mistaken belief that they are is responsible, I think, for the widespread and confused claim that critical legal studies already is feminist because the critical scholars' description of subjectivity converges with the cultural feminists' description of subjectivity, and the less widespread but equally confused claim that radical feminism is "just" liberalism, for the parallel reason.

First, the subjectivity depicted by critical legalism—the craving for connection and the dread of alienation—is not the subjectivity depicted by cultural feminism—the capacity for intimacy, the ethic of care, and the fear of separation. It is not hard to see the basis for the confused claim that cultural feminism's depiction of feminine subjectivity mirrors critical conceptions of the subjective experience of masculinity, though. There are two reasons for this confused identification. First, as Duncan Kennedy correctly notes, liberalism is indeed the rhetoric of the status quo. The description of subjectivity upon which critical legalists insist—"withdrawn selves" who cringe from autonomy and secretly crave community—contrasts sharply with the description of subjectivity endorsed by dominant, mainstream liberal ideology. The critics' description of subjective life is not well regarded by people in power, to put the point lightly. Indeed, it is somewhat despised. Vis-à-vis liberal ideology, it is truly radical. It is underground. Similarly, women and women's values, to put the point lightly, are underground, despised, opposed, or at best undervalued by people in power. Vis-à-vis feminism, cultural feminism may be "dominant," but vis-à-vis liberalism, cultural feminism is at least as deeply underground and disapproved as critical legalism, if not more so. Cultural feminism and critical legalism share the outsider's status.

Further, the potential for connection which women naturally have and which cultural feminism celebrates, is in a sense the goal of critical legalism's alienated hero. For that reason, perhaps, the critical description of subjectivity may be confusedly identified as feminist. Nevertheless, the identification is overstated. Unger explains the human being's natural goal of connection, or "natural harmony," in this way:

> In what sense and to what extent can . . . natural harmony be achieved by man? Take first the problem of reconciliation to the nonhuman world. The moral, artistic, and religious traditions of many cultures emphasize the persistence of men's desire to see themselves as members of a community of natural, and, above all, of living things.
>
> Because of its sexual aspect, love helps man overcome the distinction between self and nature within his own person. As a conscious and indeterminate being, he is distinguished by his relative freedom from the instincts or natural inclinations. These inclinations are the natural element within him. Insofar as he undergoes them, he is a natural being, and, insofar as he is free from them, he is more than a natural being. The natural inclinations, like the drives for food and sex, appear as a tyrannical fate; they impose limits and demands on what consciousness can accomplish.
>
> But in love, the union of persons, which represents an ideal of the relation between self and others, is consummated through the natural inclination of sex. It is not the case in love that the more a man is a natural being, the less is he distinctively human. On the contrary, the gap between mind and natural disposition is bridged. By satisfying the ideal of his relation with others and thereby becoming more human, he also becomes more completely natural.[35]

But Unger's explanation reveals the difference, not the sameness, between the intimacy women value and the "connection" that men seek. Women do not value love and intimacy because it "helps us overcome the distinction between self and nature." On the contrary, women value love and intimacy because they express the unity of self and nature within our own selves. More generally, women do not struggle toward connection with others, against what turn out to be insurmountable obstacles. Intimacy is not something which women fight to become capable of. We just do it. It is ridiculously easy. It is also, I suspect, qualitatively beyond the pale of male effort. The difference might be put pictorially: The intimacy women value is a sharing of intersubjective territory that preexists the effort made to identify it. The connection that I suspect men strive for does not preexist the effort, and it is not a sharing of space; at best it is an adjacency. Gilligan inadvertently sums the difference between the community critical legal studies insists that men surreptitiously seek, and the intimacy that cultural feminism insists that women value: "The discovery now being celebrated by men in mid-life of the importance of intimacy, relationships, and care is something that women have known from the beginning."[36]

Similarly, the dread of alienation that (according to critical legal studies) permeates men's lives is not the same as the fear of isolation and separation from the other that characterizes women's lives. The fear of separation, for women, is fundamental, physical, economic, empathic, and psychological, as well as psychic. Separation from one's infant will kill the infant to whom the mother has been physically and then psychically connected, and therefore a part of the mother will die as well; separation from one's community may have similarly life-threatening consequences. The alienation men dread is not the fear that oneself or the one with whom one is in symbiosis will be threatened. The alienation that men dread is a sorrow over a fundamental, basic, "first" existential state of being. The longing to overcome alienation is a socially constructed reaction against the natural fact of individuation. More bluntly—love, for men, is an acquired skill; separation (and therefore autonomy) is what comes naturally. The separation that endangers women, by contrast, is what is socially constructed—attachment is natural. Separation, and the dread of it, is the response to the natural (and pleasant) state of connection.

Second, the description of women's subjective nature, aspirations, and fears drawn by radical feminism is not the same as the description of "human nature" employed by liberalism. It is not hard, however, to see the basis for this confusion. Both radical feminism and liberalism view the other as a danger to the self: Liberalism identifies the other as a threat to autonomy and to life itself; radical feminism identifies the other as a threat to individuation and to physical integrity. It is hardly surprising, then, that radical feminists borrow heavily from liberalism's protective armor of rights and distance. From the radical feminist point of view, "liberal rights-talk," so disparaged by critical legalists, is just fine, and it would be even better if it protected women against the dangers that characterize their lives, as well as protecting men against the dangers that characterize their lives.

The structural similarity ends there, though. The invasion and intrusion that women dread from the penetrating and impregnating potential of the connected other is not the same as the annihilation and frustration by the separate other than men fear. Men's greatest fear is that of being wiped out—of being killed. The fear of sexual and fetal invasion and intrustion that permeates women's lives is not the fear of annihilation or frustration. The fear of sexual and fetal invaison is the fear of being occupied from within, not annihilated from without; of having one's self overcome, not ended; of having one's own physical and material life taken over by the pressing physical urgency of another, not ended by the conflicting interests of another; of being, in short, overtaken, occupied, displaced, and invaded, not killed. Furthermore, the intrusiveness of less damaging forms of intimacy—"wanted" intimacy—is not equivalent to the lesser form of annihilation liberalism recognizes: having one's ends frustrated by the conflicting ends of the other. I do not fear having my "ends" frustrated; I fear having my ends "displaced" before I even formulate them. I fear that I will be refused the right to be an "I" who fears. I fear that my ends will not be my own. I fear that the phrase "my ends" will prove to be (or already is) oxymoronic. I fear I will never feel the freedom, or have the space, to become an ends-making creature.

Similarly, the individuation prized by radical feminism is not the same as the autonomy liberalism heralds, although it may be a precondition of it. The "autonomy" praised by liberalism is one's right to pursue one's own ends. "Individuation," as understood by radical feminism, is the right to be the sort of creature who might have and then pursue one's "own" ends. Women's longing for individuation is a longing for a transcendent state of individuated being against that which is internally contrary, given, fundamental, and first. Autonomy is something which is natural to men's existential state and which the state might protect. Individuation, by contrast, is the material precondition of autonomy. Individuation is what you need to be before you can even begin to think about what you need to be free.

These, then, are the differences between the "human beings" assumed by legal theory and women, as their lives are now being articulated by feminist theory. The human being, according to legal theory, values autonomy and fears annihilation, while at the same time he subjectively dreads the alienation that his love of autonomy inevitably entails. Women, according to feminist theory, value intimacy and fear separation, while at the same time longing for the individuation which our fear of separation precludes and dreading the invasion which our love of intimacy entails. The human being assumed or constituted by legal theory precludes the woman described by feminism.

II. Fundamental Contradictions

In Part III of this chapter, I will explore the implications of the conclusion just offered—that the human being assumed by legal theory precludes the women described by feminism—for the development of feminist jurisprudence. Before doing so, however, I want to pursue the structural comparison of the descriptions of subjectivity offered by legal theory and feminist theory one step further. Both theories appear to offer internally contradictory descriptions of men and women's subjectivity respectively. The official story of subjectivity proffered by liberal legalism conflicts with the account of the subjectivity of separation put forward by critical legal theory, just as the official story of cultural feminism conflicts with radical feminists' contrasting account of the subjectivity of connection. Neither cultural feminism nor liberal legalism has generated explanations of the apparently contradictory accounts of subjectivity offered by radical feminism and critical legalism, respectively. Both should do so. Radical feminism and critical legalism, however, have addressed the issue and at considerable length. I want now to explore those explanations and try to improve on them.

◇ ◇ ◇

The first explanation for the contradiction between official value and subjective life that recurs in both critical legal theory and in radical feminism centers on the psychoanalytic concept of "denial" and its political corollary, "collaboration." Thus, both Andrea Dworkin and Catharine MacKinnon (and numerous other radical feminists) have argued that the high regard in which women hold physical, heterosexual intimacy constitutes a form of denial, bad faith, and, ultimately, collaboration with patriarchy. Dworkin presents the argument in its greatest detail. Women claim to find intimacy in intercourse, Dworkin argues, because women must, after all, "have something." Women claim to enjoy intercourse (and mislabel it as *intimacy* because women have become "alienated from freedom" as a result of our fear of self-assertion. This fear is not ground-less—it is based for the most part on all-too-accurate memories of either threatened or actual violent reactions to an attempted asserting of sexual independence. But it is nev-ertheless a form of cowardice. Women who claim to value heterosexual intimacy deny their desire for freedom because they fear a reenactment of a primary, and extremely painful, experience of violent, sexual oppression. In a word, they collaborate:

> There is the initial complicity, the acts of self-mutilation, self-diminishing, self-recon-struction, until there is no self, only the diminished, mutilated reconstruction. It is all superficial and unimportant, except what it costs the human in her to do it: except for the fact that it is submissive, conforming, giving up an individuality that would with-stand object status or defy it. Something happens inside; a human forgets freedom; a human learns obedience; a human, this time a woman, learns how to goose-step the female way. . . . So the act goes beyond complicity to collaboration; but collaboration requires a preparing of the ground, an undermining of values and vision and dignity, a sense of alienation from the worth of other human beings—and this alienation is fundamental to females who are objectified because they do not experience themselves as human beings. . . . Being an object for a man means being alienated from other women—those like her in status, in inferiority, in sexual function. Collaboration by women with men to keep women civilly and sexually inferior has been one of the hall-marks of female subordination; we are ashamed when Freud notices it, but it is true.[37]

Critical theorist Peter Gabel has given a perfectly parallel explanation of the attraction of autonomous, rights-focused, individuated liberal values in spite of the acutely painful longing for connection which in fact permeates men's lives. Gabel's argument structur-ally compares with Dworkin's, although it contrasts with it substantively. Thus, whereas Dworkin argues that women deny their desire for freedom and distance themselves from it through a false commitment to intimacy, Gabel argues that human beings deny their craving for attachment with the other and distance themselves from it through a false commitment to rights. As women deny their desire for freedom because of a fear that by asserting that desire they risk violent invasion, so human beings, according to Gabel, deny their desire for attachment because they fear that by exposing their deeper and truer need for connection, they will leave themselves vulnerable to the pain of rejection. This fear is rooted in an unconsciously embedded memory from infancy, just as women's fear of their own desire for freedom is rooted in a memory of male violence. At some point in early infancy, according to Gabel, the other (read: the mother) rejected him. That rejec-tion was painful and humiliating. The individual denies his need for connection because he refuses to risk the reenactment of such a painful, humiliating, and embarrassing rejec-tion, just as the woman denies her need for physical individuation because she refuses to risk the reenactment of rape. So instead he creates a false self defined by liberal "rights." In a word, he collaborates.

◊ ◊ ◊

As Gabel by now must surely be aware, his account of the source of "our" alienation from the other is deeply gendered.[38] The story he tells of attachment, separation, longing, rejection, repression, humiliation, and then alienation is a story of male development, not female. But structurally, his argument is not at all gendered. Dworkin's and Gabel's arguments employ precisely the same logical structure. Dworkin, like Gabel, argues that women engage in massive denial, identification, and collaboration with the powers that cause their alienation. In fact, Gabel's account of male denial of the need for attachment is the structural mirror, although the substantive negative, of Dworkin's account of women's denial of the need for individuation.

Both Gabel's and Dworkin's explanations, I believe, are ultimately unsatisfying, and although they are exploring substantively opposed phenomena, they are unsatisfying for the same reason. Both claims fail to do justice to the complexity of the phenomenology that they are seeking to explain. Others have argued, and I think persuasively, that Gabel's explanation of the disempowered's "collaborative" embrace of rights fails to capture the phenomenological experience of rights as an empowering and even communitarian tool for disempowered peoples.[39] I will not pursue that argument here. I do want to argue, though, that Dworkin's parallel insistence that women's enjoyment of heterosexual intercourse constitutes a form of collaboration fails to capture the phenomenological experience of intercourse as one of positive intimacy, rather than an experience that is inevitably destructive of "all that is creative within us." Women often, and perhaps increasingly, experience heterosexual intercourse as freely chosen intimacy, not invasive bondage. A radicalism that flatly denies the reality of such a lived experience runs the risk of making itself unintelligible and irrelevant to all people, not to mention the audience that matters most: namely, those women for whom intercourse is not free, not chosen, and anything but intimate, and who have no idea that it either could be or should be both.

This "critique of the intimacy critique" can easily be misconstrued—as can the "critique of the rights critique." I am not denying that heterosexuality is compulsory in this culture or that women as a consequence of that compulsion become alienated from their desire for freedom. It is indeed true, as the lesbian-feminist poet Adrienne Rich argued some time ago, that both heterosexuality and heterosexual intercourse are compulsory. But heterosexuality is compulsory because of the institutions that render it compulsory, not because of the nature of the act. The same is true of motherhood and pregnancy. Because they are compulsory, motherhood and heterosexuality are tremendously constraining, damaging, and oppressive. It is indeed true that the institutions which render them such need to be, ought to be, and will be destroyed. But it does not follow from any of this that either motherhood or intercourse themselves will be, need to be, or ought to be destroyed. As Rich has argued of mothering,

> To destroy the institution is not to abolish motherhood. It is to release the creation and sustenance of life into the same realm of decision, struggle, surprise, imagination, and conscious intelligence, as any other difficult, but freely chosen, work.[40]

Similarly, to destroy the "institution" of heterosexual intercourse is not to abolish intercourse. Rather, it is to "release" it into the same realm of decision, struggle, surprise, imagination, and conscious intelligence as any other freely chosen "form"—not of work, as is the case of motherhood—but of intimacy, love, and play.

Now, it is also true—emphatically true—that neither motherhood nor intercourse have been "released" from patriarchy. Until they are, there is no project more vital to our understanding of women's present oppression than the description of the subjective experience of motherhood, and of intercourse, within the patriarchical institutions that render those activities compulsory. This is the importance of Rich's multitextured work on compulsory motherhood and heterosexuality and of Dworkin's passionate but disappointingly unidimensional work on intercourse. We need to be aware—to be made aware—of those institutions as institutions that constrain as they define the act. But as Rich clearly saw with respect to mothering, that is not all we need to understand. Feminists also need to understand what it means to mother and to enjoy intercourse within aspirational conditions of freedom, for it is those conditions which potentially and increasingly, for many of us, define the nature of those events. When we reach this understanding, or at least strive for it, we will have a better understanding of what noninstitutional and nonpatriarchal intercourse and motherhood might be and might ultimately become.

Of course, to again borrow from Rich, to catch even a glimpse of mothering or intercourse within a nonpatriarchal culture requires a "quantum leap" of imagination. It requires, most of all, the ability to imagine ourselves in a society in which women are in full possession of our bodies:

> The "quantum leap" [of imagination] implies that even as we try to deal with backlash and emergency, we are imagining the new: a future in which women are powerful, full of our own power, not the old patriarchal power-over but the power-to-create, power-to-think, power-to-articulate and concretize our visions and transform our lives and those of our children. I believe . . . that this power will begin to speak in us more and more as we repossess our own bodies, including the decision to mother or not to mother, and how, and with whom, and when. For the struggle of women to become self-determining is rooted in our bodies, and it is an indication of this that the token woman artist or intellectual or professional has so often been constrained to deny her female physicality in order to enter realms designated as male domain.[41]

Yet we make small versions of these "quantum leaps" every day. We continue to mother and to want to mother in spite of the compulsory nature of institutional motherhood. We also make small versions of the same "quantum leap" with respect to intercourse. Women do, increasingly, freely engage in heterosexual intercourse in spite of the compulsory nature of the institution of intercourse. Increasingly, we have a sense of what intercourse feels like when "released" from compulsory heterosexuality. Explanations that rest on denial of the possibility that equality and freedom can define intercourse and motherhood fail to incorporate real glimpses that we increasingly have of a world without the present oppresive institutions. They consequently endanger the seriousness and the truth of the radical feminist insight that many women, indeed most women, define their intimate relationships within the confines of necessity rather than possibility and within the dictates of compulsion, rather than choice.

The second possible explanation of contradiction between the official story and true subjectivity centers on the Gramscian and Marxist concept of legitimation and apology. Thus, Catharine MacKinnon argues that "intimacy" simply legitimates invasion, and that cultural feminism's celebration of intimacy is, in essence, simply apology for patriarchy:

> For women to affirm difference, when difference means dominance, as it does with gender, means to affirm the qualities and characteristics of powerlessness. . . .
>
> So I am critical of affirming what we have been, which necessarily is what we have been permitted, as if it is women's, ours, possessive. . . .
>
> I do not think that the way women reason morally is morality "in a different voice." I think it is morality in a higher register, in the feminine voice. Women value care because men have valued us according to the care we give them, and we could

probably use some. Women think in relational terms because our existence is defined in relation to men. . . . All I am saying is that the damage of sexism is real, and reifying that into differences is an insult to our possibilities.[42]

This explanation has a parallel in critical legal theory. According to critical legalists, the dominant class legitimates the oppressive reality of alienation by relabeling alienation as freedom, just as cultural feminism, according to MacKinnon, relabels invasion as intimacy. Indeed, it is a recurrent claim in critical legal theory that the rhetoric of autonomy and freedom found in nineteenth-century contract law, like the rhetoric of good faith and fulfilled expectations in twentieth-century contract law, all operate to deny the true human need for connection and collectivity:

> The legitimating image of classical contract law in the nineteenth century was the ideal of free competition as the consequence of wholly voluntary interactions among many private persons, all of whom were in their nature free and equal to one another. . . . [T]his was denial and apology. It did not take account of the practical limitations on market freedom and equality arising from class position or unequal distribution of wealth. It also ignored other meanings of freedom and equality having to do with the realization of human spirit and potential through work and community. The legitimation of the free market was achieved by seizing upon a narrow economic notion of freedom and equality, and fusing it in the public mind with the genuine meaning.[43]

> The central point to understand from this is that contract law today constitutes an elaborate attempt to conceal what is going on in the world. . . . Contemporary capitalism is a coercive system of relationships. . . . [O]ur narrow functional roles produce isolation, passivity, unconnectedness and impotence. Contract law, like the other images constituted by capitalism, is a denial of these painful feelings and an apology for the system that produces them.[44]

Again, both MacKinnon's argument and the parallel critical legal claim are unsatisfying, and for the same reason. Both claims fail to do justice to the complexity of the opposing vision they attack. For while it is true that liberalism's commitment to individualism echoes capitalism's legitimating myth of market freedom, this doesn't come anywhere near the whole story. The commitment to individualism that pervades part of liberalism and of liberal culture exists in spite of capitalism's actual disdain for true individualism, not because of capitalism's false claim to freedom. Liberalism has always had a radical commitment to a true individualism which is not in any sense apologist; liberal individualism in at least some of its historical and modern forms undercuts, rather than relegitimates, capitalist superstructure. Similarly, women's ethic of care, and commitment to the value of nurturance and intimacy celebrated by cultural feminism, exists in spite of patriarchy's contempt for and undervaluation of those values, not because of their false claim to honor women's separate sphere. While it is of course true that cultural feminism's celebration of women's ethic of care echoes patriarchy's celebration of separate spheres, the former is hardly an apology for the latter. The differences between cultural feminism and patriarchy are the all-important ones: Patriarchy devalues women, and cultural feminism does not. Patriarchy celebrates women's different sphere in order to reinforce women's powerlessness. Cultural feminism does not.

Critical legal theorists have developed a third account of the contradiction between liberal values and subjective desire: The contradiction is based on a real, lived contradiction grounded in material, unreconstructed reality. I believe this explanation is the strongest of the three, though, as far as I know, it has no parallel in feminist theory. Both

Roberto Unger and Duncan Kennedy have argued, with considerable force, that the "contradiction" between liberalism's claim that human beings value autonomy and fear the other, and critical theory's opposing claim that they desire connection with the other and dread their alienation from him, reflects a real contradiction in our subjective, material, and natural lives. It is not then (solely) the product of either psychoanalytic denial or Gramscian legitimation. The contradiction is an experiential contradiction, not a logical contradiction. The difference is important.

According to Kennedy, we value both autonomy and connection, and fear both annihilation by the other and alienation from him, and all for good reason. The other is both necessary to our continued existence and a threat to that continued existence. While it is true that the dominant liberal story of autonomy and annihilation serves to perpetuate the status quo, it does not follow from that fact that the subjective desires for freedom and security which those liberal values reify are entirely false. Rather, Kennedy argues, collectivity is both essential to our identity and an obstacle to it. We have contradictory desires and values because our essential human condition—physical separation from the collectivity which is necessary to our identity—is itself contradictory. It is that essential human condition which carries the seeds of our twin fears of alienation and annihilation, as well as our twin desires for autonomy and attachment:

> Here is an initial statement of the fundamental contradiction: ... Others (family, friends, bureaucrats, cultural figures, the state) are necessary if we are to become persons at all—they provide us the stuff of our selves and protect us in crucial ways against destruction. Even when we seem to ourselves to be most alone, others are with us, incorporated in us through processes of language, cognition and feeling that are, simply as a matter of biology, collective aspects of our individuality. Moreover, we are not always alone. We sometimes experience fusion with others, in groups of two or even two million, and it is good rather than a bad experience.
>
> But at the same time that it forms and protects us, the universe of others (family, friendship, bureaucracy, culture, the state) threatens us with annihilation and urges upon us forms of fusion that are quite plainly bad rather than good. ... Numberless conformities, large and small abandonments of self to others, are the price of what freedom we experience in society. And the price is a high one.[45]

◊ ◊ ◊

This third explanation of the contradiction between liberal ideology and critical descriptive claims might, of course, just be wrong. The value the individual places on autonomy and the fear he claims to have of annihilation may reflect only the effectiveness of legitimation and apology, or the thoroughness of psychoanalytic denial. But if Kennedy is wrong, he is wrong in a way that is shared by the practicing legal culture itself. For as any good law student knows, on an empirical level Kennedy is clearly right: Our legal doctrine, or at least our legal ideology, does indeed reflect the contradictory fundamental urges that Kennedy has identified. Any sufficiently rich statement of any area of legal doctrine quite explicitly reflects both the "official" story of our values as told by liberal legalism and the "unofficial" story of a sharply contrasting subjectivity as told by critical theory.

◊ ◊ ◊

The strength of Duncan Kennedy's work is that he has not just asserted the existence of this fundamental contradiction but has shown its permeation through a remarkably wide range of legal materials. The structurally parallel claim in feminist theory that I think radical feminists should explore, is that women "officially" value intimacy (and fear separation) in spite of subjective desires to the contrary not (solely) because of the legitimating power of patriarchal ideology or (solely) because of the power of denial but, rather, because women's existential and material circumstance is itself one of contradiction. The potentiality for physical connection with others that uniquely characterizes women's lives has within it the seeds of both intimacy and invasion, and therefore women rightly value the former while we dread and fear the latter, just as the necessity of physical separation, for men, carries within it the seeds of both intimacy and alienation, and men rightly value the former and dread the latter. If this is right, then all four accounts of human experience—liberal legalism, critical legalism, cultural feminism, and radical feminism—are saying something true about human experience. Liberal legalism and critical legalism both describe something true about male experience, and cultural feminism and radical feminism both describe something true about female experience. If Kennedy is right, then men simply live with an experiential contradiction. In a parallel fashion, cultural feminism and radical feminism may both be true although contradictory. The contradiction between them may be experiential rather than logical. Women may both value intimacy and dread the intrusion and invasion which intimacy implies, and women may both fear separation and long for the individualization which separation would bring.

Although Adrienne Rich has argued something like this with respect to motherhood, no radical feminist has, to my knowledge, advanced this claim with respect to intercourse. Nor has anyone advanced the claim with respect to the fear of invasion and the value of intimacy generally.

◇ ◇ ◇

Minimally, I want to suggest that feminists should think about the possibility that the notion of a "fundamental" experienced contradiction, grounded in the material and existential state of connection with the other, might help us explain women's subjective lives, as well as close the broadening gap between cultural and radical feminist theory. The presence of such a contradiction, for example, explains why some women see the possibility of intimacy in pornographic depictions of female sexual submission while others see the threat of invasion (and it would explain why many ?? and have always known but have never been able to claim as my own moral vision, and what parts of that vision I share with women generally. When I read Andrea Dworkin's book, I had the same unequivocal shock of recognition. What Dworkin is saying about intercourse is important, transformative, empowering, exciting, liberating, enlivening, and most fundamentally, it is simply true. It is true of me, was true of my mother, and is true of my sisters. She is describing how I have been debased, victimized, intruded, invaded, harmed, damaged, injured, and violated by intercourse. Yet it also seems undeniably true to me that these two feminist visions of my subjective life rest on flatly contradictory premises.

This realization—if it is shared—presents us with a choice. We can assume that the contradictions in feminist descriptions of our lives are conceptual, in which case we must look for flawed arguments—we cannot and ought not believe contradictory things. Alternatively, we can start to think about the possibility that the contradiction in women lives is experientially felt and materially based. Kennedy's account of the dilemma that contradiction poses for the legal theorist, I believe, is equally true of the dilemma that the very different contradiction in women's lives now poses for feminism:

> The acknowledgment of contradiction does not abate the moral and practical conflict, but it does permit us to make some progress in characterizing it. At an elementary level, it makes it clear that it is futile to imagine that moral and practical conflict will yield to analysis in terms of higher level concepts. The meaning of contradiction at the level of abstraction is that there is no metasystem that would, if only we could find it, key us into one mode or the other as circumstances "required." Second, the acknowledgment of contradiction means that we cannot "balance" individualist and altruist values or rules against equitable standards. . . . The imagery of balancing presupposes exactly the kind of more abstract unit of measurement that the sense of contradiction excludes. The only kind of imagery that conveys the process by which we act and act and act in one direction, but then reach the sticking point, is that of existentialist philosophy. We make commitments, and pursue them. The moment of abandonment is no more rational than that of beginning, and equally a moment of terror.[46]

Of course, there is a major difference between the presence of contradiction in legal theory and the presence of contradiction in feminist theory. Even if it is true that women, like men, live within the parameters of a contradiction, women live within the parameters of this fundamental contradiction within the oppressive conditions of patriarchy. Men don't (although men do live within the parameters of the oppressive conditions of capitalism). Therefore, feminists need to develop not just an examination of the experience of the contradiction between invasion and intimacy to which our potential for connection gives rise but also a description of how patriarchy effects, twists, perverts, and surely to some extent causes that contradiction. We also need, however, to imagine how the contradiction would be felt outside of patriarchy, and we need to reflect on our own experiences of nonpatriarchal mothering, intercourse, and intimacy to generate such imaginings. For while women's bodies may continue to be "materially connected" to others as long as they are women's bodies, they need not forever be possessed by others. Our connection to the other is a function of our material condition; our possession by the other, however, is a function of patriarchy. We need to imagine both having power over our bodies and power over our contradictory material state. We need to imagine how this fundamental contradiction would feel outside of the context of the dangers and fears that patriarchy requires.

◊ ◊ ◊

III. Feminist Jurisprudence

By the claim that modern jurisprudence is "masculine," I mean two things. First, I mean that the values, the dangers, and what I have called the *fundamental contradiction* that characterize women's lives are not reflected at any level whatsoever in contracts, torts, constitutional law, or any other field of legal doctrine. The values that flow from women's material potential for physical connection are not recognized as values by the Rule of Law, and the dangers attendant to that state are not recognized as dangers by the Rule of Law.

First, the Rule of Law does not value intimacy—its official value is autonomy. The material consequence of this theoretical undervaluation of women's values in the material world is that women are economically impoverished. The value women place on intimacy reflects our existential and material circumstance; women will act on that value whether it is compensated or not. But it is not. Nurturant, intimate labor is neither valued by liberal legalism nor compensated by the market economy. It is not compensated in the home, and it is not compensated in the workplace—wherever intimacy is, there is no compensation. Similarly, separation of the individual from his or her family, community, or children is not understood to be a harm, and we are not protected against it. The Rule of Law generally and legal doctrine in its particularity are coherent reactions to the existential dilemma that follows from the liberal's description of the male experience of material separation from the other: The Rule of Law acknowledges the danger of annihilation, and the Rule of Law protects the value of autonomy. Just as assuredly, the Rule of Law is not a coherent reaction to the existential dilemma that follows from the material state of being connected to others, and the values and dangers attendant to that condition. It neither recognizes nor values intimacy and neither recognizes nor protects against separation.

Nor does the Rule of Law recognize, in any way whatsoever, muted or unmuted, occasionally or persistently, overtly or covertly, the contradiction which characterizes women's, but not men's, lives: while we value the intimacy we find so natural, we are endangered by the invasion and dread the intrusion in our lives which intimacy entails, and we long for individuation and independence. Neither sexual nor fetal invasion of the self by the other is recognized as a harm worth bothering with. Sexual invasion through rape is understood to be a harm, and is criminalized as such, only when it involves some other harm: Today, when it is accompanied by violence that appears in a form men understand (meaning a plausible threat of annihilation); in earlier times, when it was understood as theft of another man's property. But marital rape, date rape, acquaintance rape, simple rape, unaggravated rape, or as Susan Estrich wants to say "real rape"[47] are either not criminalized, or if they are, they are not punished—to do so would force a recognition of the concrete, experiential harm to identity formation that sexual invasion accomplishes.

Similarly, fetal invasion is not understood to be harmful, and therefore the claim that I ought to be able to protect myself against it is heard as nonsensical. The argument that the right to abortion mirrors the right of self-defense falls on deaf ears for a reason: The analogy is indeed flawed. The right of self-defense is the right to protect the body's security against annihilation liberally understood, not invasion. But the danger an unwanted fetus poses is not to the body's security at all but, rather, to the body's integrity. Similarly, the woman's fear is not that the she will die but that she will cease to be or never become a self. The danger of unwanted pregnancy is the danger of invasion by the other, not of annihilation by the other. In sum, the Rule of Law does not recognize the danger of invasion, nor does it recognize the individual's need for, much less entitlement to, individuation and independence from the intrusion which heterosexual penetration and fetal invasion entails. The material consequence of this lack of recognition in the real world is that women are objectified—regarded as creatures who can't be harmed.

The second thing I mean to imply by the phrase *masculine jurisprudence* is that both liberal and critical legal theory, which is about the relation between law and life, is about men and not women. The reason for this lack of parallelism, of course, is hardly benign neglect. Rather, the distinctive values women hold, the distinctive dangers from which we suffer, and the distinctive contradictions that characterize our inner lives are not reflected in legal theory because legal theory (whatever else it's about) is about actual, real life, enacted, legislated, adjudicated law, and women have, from law's inception, lacked the power to make law protect, value, or seriously regard our experience. Jurisprudence is masculine because jurisprudence is about the relationship between human beings and the laws we actually have, and the laws we actually have are masculine both in terms of their intended beneficiary and in authorship. Women are absent from jurisprudence because women as human beings are absent from the law's protection: Jurisprudence does not recognize us because law does not protect us. The implication for this should be obvious. We will not have a genuinely ungendered jurisprudence (a jurisprudence "unmodified," so to speak) until we have legal doctrine that takes women's lives as seriously as it takes men's. We don't have such legal doctrine. The virtual abolition of patriarchy is the necessary political condition for the creation of nonmasculine feminist jurisprudence.

It does not follow, however, that there is no such thing as feminist legal theory. Rather, I believe what is now inaccurately called feminist jurisprudence consists of two discrete projects. The first project is the unmasking and critiquing of the patriarchy behind purportedly ungendered law and theory, or, put differently, the uncovering of what we might call patriarchal jurisprudence from under the protective covering of jurisprudence. The primary purpose of the critique of patriarchal jurisprudence is to show that jurisprudence and legal doctrine protect and define men, not women. Its second purpose is to show how women—that is, people who value intimacy, fear separation, dread invasion, and crave individuation—have fared under a legal system which fails to value intimacy, fails to protect against separation, refuses to define invasion as a harm, and refuses to acknowledge the aspirations of women for individuation and physical privacy.

The second project in which feminist legal theorists engage might be called *reconstructive jurisprudence*. The last twenty years have seen a substantial amount of feminist law reform, primarily in the areas of rape, sexual harassment, reproductive freedom, and pregnancy rights in the workplace. For strategic reasons, these reforms have often been won by characterizing women's injuries as analogous to, if not identical with, injuries men suffer (sexual harassment as a form of "discrimination"; rape as a crime of "violence"), or by characterizing women's longing as analogous to, if not identical with, men's official values (reproductive freedom—which ought to be grounded in a right to individuation—conceived instead as a "right to privacy," which is derivative of the autonomy right). This misconceptualization may have once been a necessary price, but it is a high price and, as these victories accumulate, an increasingly unnecessary one. Reconstructive feminist jurisprudence should set itself the task of rearticulating these new rights in such a way as to reveal, rather than conceal, their origin in women's distinctive existential and material state of being. The remainder of this article offers a schematization and criticism of the feminist jurisprudence we have generated to date under the umbrella concept described above, in spite of patriarchy and in spite of the masculinity of legal theory. I then suggest further lines of inquiry.

A. The Critique of Patriarchal Jurisprudence

Structurally, the feminist attempt to describe and critique patriarchal jurisprudence by necessity tracks the methodological divisions in masculine jurisprudence, so I need to make one further diversion. Masculine jurisprudence is divided internally by a methodological issue which is as definitive and foundational as the substantive issues that divide liberal from critical legalism. Some legal theorists practice what might be called a *narrative* and *phenomenological* jurisprudential method (hereinafter, simply narrative), and some practice what might be called an *interpretivist* method. Narrative and interpretive methodology have adherents in both liberal and critical legal literature. Thus, if we look at both substance and method (instead of just substance), there are not two but four major jurisprudential traditions in legal scholarship. Liberal legalism can be either interpretive or narrative, as can critical legal theory. Put differently, a narrative methodology can be either critical or liberal, as can interpretivism.

Narrative legal theory, whether it be liberal or critical, moves methodologically from a description of justice, the state of nature, or of the human being which aims for some degree of generality if not universality and then tells either a narrative story about how human beings thus described come to agree on the Rule of Law, or, alternatively, a phenomenological description of how it feels to be a person within a legal regime. To the narrative and phenomenological legal theorists (whether critical or liberal), the person, the natural state, and the demands of justice are first, both historically and phenomenologically. Human beings create the Rule of Law from the state of nature to comply with the demands of justice, and the narrative theorist tells how and why. Interpretive jurisprudence, whether liberal or critical, moves methodologically in the opposite direction. Interpretive theorists begin with an interpretation of law, or of a body of legal doctrine, or of the idea of law itself, and derive from that interpretation an account of justice. The methodological assumption of interpretive jurisprudence is that the legal text not only reflects, but to some degree even defines, what justice requires and hence what a person is. It is the purpose of interpretive jurisprudence to provide the best interpretation of the "justice" that the legal text has defined. Thus, the interpretivist tells the story of justice from the point of view of the Rule of Law, rather than the story of the emergence of "law" from the point of view of human beings under the constraints of justice. While to the narrative theorist, "we" create legal texts, to the interpretivists, the texts "create" as they define our moral commitments and hence our view of ourselves, and it is the theorist's special role to show exactly who it is that the texts have created.

Putting together substance and method, we can generate a four-boxed matrix: narrative liberal legalism, interpretive liberal legalism, narrative critical theory, and interpretive critical theory. . . .

1. The Narrative and Phenomenological Critique. By the critique of patriarchal jurisprudence I mean four distinct projects. . . . First, *narrative* critical jurisprudence aims to provide, in a Hobbesian (or Ungerian) manner, the material, internal, phenomenological, subjective story of women's experience of the emergence and present reality of the Rule of Law. That story goes something like this: Prior to the advent of the "Rule of Law," we might hypothesize, women bore, breast-fed, nurtured, and protected children. Women did the nurturant work. As described above, women lived in a "natural web of hierarchy": They were profoundly unequal to the infants they raised. While men responded to their condition of natural equality with mutual aggression, women responded to their condition of natural inequality with nurturance and an ethic of care. Women were at the same time profoundly unequal to men. Prior to the Rule of Law, women, and only women, were vulnerable to sexual invasion. As Catharine MacKinnon suggests, on the only "first day that matters," and this day occurred long before the signing of the social contract, men established sexual power over women.[48] Thus, inequality vis-à-vis both children and men, an ethic of care for the weak and sexual vulnerability to the male, was women's natural state, while equality, mutual fear and suspicion was men's.

Then, on day two, came the Rule of Law. According to the Hobbesian story, the Rule of Law significantly improved the quality of men's lives: Men's lives became longer, less nasty, less brutish (even if somewhat more alienated), and more productive. But not so for women: The same Rule of Law left women's natural lives intact, worsened her material condition, and reified her sexual vulnerability into a male right of access. The Rule of Law changed the conditions that uniquely pertained to women in the state of nature, but the change was for the worse: After the Rule of Law, women are still uniquely capable of intimacy but newly unrecognized for their nurturant activity in a world that values autonomy and compensates individuated labor. Similarly, women remain uniquely vulnerable to invasion but newly unprotected against that injury in a world that protects against other injuries. The narrative and phenomenological task for the critique of patriarchal jurisprudence is to tell the story and phenomenology of the human community's commitment to the Rule of Law from women's point of view. We need to show what the exclusion of women from law's protection has meant to both women and law, and we need to show what it means for the Rule of Law to exclude women and women's values.

The way to do this—the only way to do this—is to tell true stories of women's lives. The Hobbesian "story" of deliverance from the state of nature to the Rule of Law, as both liberal and radical legal scholars are fond of pointing out, does not purport to be history. But that doesn't make it fantasy. The Hobbesian story of the state of nature (and the critical story of alienation as well) is a synthesis of umpteen thousands of personal, subjective, everyday, male experiences. Images are generated from that synthesis, and those images, sometimes articulate, sometimes not, of what it means to be a human being then become the starting point of legal theory. Thus, for example, the Hobbesian, liberal picture of the "human being" as someone who treasures autonomy and fears annihilation from the other comes from men's primary experiences, presumably, of school-yard fights, armed combat, sports, games, work, big brothers, and fathers. Similarly, the critical picture of the human being as someone who longs for attachment and dreads alienation comes from the male child's memory of his mother, from rejection experiences painfully culled from his adolescence, and from the adult male's continuing inability to introspect, converse, or commune with the natural world, including the natural world of others. When Peter Gabel says "Let me start by making a descriptive assertion [about human beings] . . . which seems to me . . . [to be] self-evidently true;"[49] and then what follows is a descriptive statement which is self-evidently untrue of women, he is not simply "mistaken," he is mistaken in a particular (male) way and for a particular (male) reason. When Hobbes, Ackerman, Dworkin, Rawls, and the rest of the liberal tradition describe the natural human predicament as one of natural equality and mutual antagonism and describe human beings as inevitably separate and mutually self-interested, thus definitionally excluding pregnant women and breast-feeding mothers from the species, they also are mistaken in a particular way and for a particular reason. Gabel has confused his male experience of separation and alienation with "human" experience, and liberals have confused their male experiences of natural equality, mutual suspicion, fear of annihilation, and pervasive, through-and-through selfishness with "human" experience, and they have done so because women have not made clear that our day-to-day, lived experience—of intimacy, bonding, separation, sexual invasion, nurturance and intrusion—is incommensurable with men's. We need to flood the market with our own stories until we get one simple point across: Men's narrative story and phenomenological description of law are not women's story and phenomenology of law. We need to dislodge legal theorists' confidence that they speak for women, and we need to fill the gap that will develop when we succeed in doing so.

Put phenomenologically, instead of narratively, feminist legal theorists need to show through stories the value of intimacy—not just to women, but to the community—and the damage done—again, not just to women, but to the community—by the law's refusal to reflect that value. Indeed, I can't imagine any project more crucial, right now, to the survival of this species than the clear articulation of the importance of love to a well-led public life. We not only need to show that these values are missing from public life and not rewarded in private life, but we also need to show how our community would improve if they were valued. We need to show (as Suzanna Sherry,[50] Lynne Henderson,[51] Martha Minow,[52] and others have begun to do) that a community and a judiciary that relies on nurturant, caring, loving, empathic values rather than exclusively on the rule of reason will not melt into a murky quagmire or sharpen into the dreaded spector of totalitarianism.

On a more local level, we need to show that a law school which employs, protects, and even compensates for these competencies will be a better law school. We need to show (as Martha Fineman has done in the area of custody decisions[53]) that a legal and economic system which values, protects, and rewards nurturant labor in private life will make for a better community. We need to show that community, nurturance, responsibility, and the ethic of care are values at least as worthy of protection as autonomy, self-reliance, and individualism. We must do that, in part, by showing how those values have affected and enriched our own lives. Similarly, we need to show—and again, I think we need to do it with stories—how the refusal of the legal system to protect those values has weakened this community as it has impoverished our lives.

From a radical point of view, we also need to explain through stories how physical invasion and intrusion harm women and how they harm women distinctively. We need to explain, as Susan Estrich, Lynn Henderson, and Diana Russell have begun to do, the danger and the harm of rape that is not seen as rape: invasive marital intercourse and invasive intercourse with "dates."[54] We need to explain how it feels to live entirely outside the protection of rape law: how it feels to be a wife in a state which defines rape as the "nonconsensual sexual intercourse by a man with a woman not his wife"; how it feels to be the person that another person has a legal right to invade without your consent. We need to provide stories rich enough to show that this harm is not the harm of annihilation protected by the Rule of Law, although it may accompany it. We need to show that the harm of invasive intercourse is real even when it does not look like the kind of violence protected by the Rule of Law. We need to show that invasive intercourse is a danger even when it cannot be analogized in any way whatsoever to male experience.

Similarly, we need to explain, as the National Abortion Rights Action League has begun to do, the harms and dangers of invasive pregnancy. We need to explain that this harm has nothing to do with invading the privacy of the doctor–patient relationship, or the privacy of the family, or the privacy of the marriage but that, rather, it has to do with invading the physical boundaries of the body and the psychic boundaries of a life. Finally, we need to provide phenomenological accounts of those ameliorative institutions, ideologies, and psychic constructs that purport to make the invasiveness and intrusiveness of our lives tolerable. Romance, for example, is one such cluster: Just as liberal rights mediate the gulf between the liberal value of autonomy and the subjective craving for connection in liberal legalism, so romance mediates the gulf between the feminine value of intimacy and the subjective craving for individuation. The mystique of femininity is surely another, and the pornographic imagination is a third. With the exception of MacKinnon and Dworkin's work on pornography, we haven't done much of this sort of jurisprudence, and we need to do a lot more.

2. The Interpretive Critique. The purpose of the interpretive critique of patriarchal jurisprudence complements that of the narrative critique. As the narrative critique explores the Rule of Law from women's point of view, the interpretive critique aims to explore women from the point of view of the Rule of Law. The interpretive critique shows how patriarchal doctrine constructs, defines, and delimits women, just as interpretive masculine jurisprudence, both liberal and critical, aims to provide accounts of how doctrine constructs, defines, and delimits the human being. For although women—people who value intimacy and are harmed by invasion—have not been accorded the protection of the Rule of Law, we have hardly been ignored. Women are not constructed as human within this system, but we are nevertheless constructed as something else: as valueless, as objects, as children, or as invisible. The interpretive critique should aim to articulate what that something else might be. The interpretive critique is a lot like shining a light on darkness or proving a negative—it involves looking at what lies between the images of legalism instead of looking directly at legalism. The interpretive critique must deconstruct the images that authoritatively diminish women, sometimes down to nothing.

On the cultural side of the substantive divide, this means showing how legalism devalues women, by not valuing what women value. To name just a few examples, Martha Fineman has tried to show who and what a "mother" is understood to be in a legal system where nurturant labor is neither recognized nor valued in custody disputes.[55] Other interpretive cultural feminists have tried to show what it means, objectively, not to be paid for housework, for child raising, and for relational work in the workplace. On the radical side, this means showing what it means to be objectified. Again, to take just a few examples, Andrea Dworkin has begun to show who the "woman" is defined to be by the pornographer, and Catharine MacKinnon has begun to show how the First Amendment has defined the pornographer's definition of the woman.[56] Susan Estrich, Diana Russell, and others have begun to show what a "wife" is in a legal system which defines rape as the nonconsensual intercourse by a man with a woman not his wife.[57] We need, I think, to do more of this: Most notably, we need to understand how laws criminalizing abortion construct "motherhood" and how *Roe v. Wade*[58]—which constructs the right to abortion as the product of a need to balance medicinal privacy rights of doctors and patients against the right to life of a fetus—constructs the female. Henderson has done some of this work.[59]

◇ ◇ ◇

B. Reconstructive Jurisprudence

The goal of reconstructive feminist jurisprudence is to render feminist reform rational. We must change the fact that from a mainstream point of view, arguments for feminist legal reform efforts are (or appear to be) invariably irrational. The moral questions feminist reforms pose are always incommensurable with dominant moral and legal categories. Let me put it this way: Given present moral categories, women's issues are crazy issues. Arguments for reproductive freedom, for example, are a little insane: Prochoice advocates can't explain the difference between reproductive freedom and infanticide, or how this right can possibly be grounded in the Constitution, or how it is that women can claim to be "nurturant" and at the same time show blatant disregard for the rights and feelings of fetuses. In fact, my sense, drawn from anecdotal evidence only, is that the abortion issue is increasingly used in ethics as well as constitutional law classrooms to exemplify the "irrationality" of individual moral commitment. Rape reform efforts that aim to expand the scope of the defined harm are also perceived, I believe, as insane. Why would anyone possibly object to nonviolent sex? Isn't sex always pleasurable? Feminist pornography initiatives are viewed as irrational, and the surrogate motherhood issue is no better. There's an air of irrationality around each of these issues.

That air of irrationality is partly real and partly feigned. The reason for the air of irrationality around particular, substantive feminist legal reform efforts, I believe, is that feminist legal reforms are by necessity advocated in a form that masks rather than reflects women's true subjective nature. This is hardly surprising: Language, of course, constrains our descriptive options. But whether or not surprising, the damage is alarming, and we need to understand its root. Arguments for reproductive freedom, for example, are irrational because the categories in which such arguments must be cast are reflective of men's, not women's, nature. This culture thinks about harm and violence and therefore self-defense in a particular way, namely, a Hobbesian way, and a Hobbesian conception of physical harm cannot possibly capture the gender-specific subjective harm that constitutes the experience of unwanted pregnancy. From a subjective, female point of view, an abortion is an act of self-defense (not the exercise of a "right of privacy"), but from the point of view of masculine subjectivity, an abortion can't possibly be an act of self-defense: The fetus is not one of Hobbes's "relatively equal" natural men against whom we have a right to protect ourselves. The fetus is unequal and above all else dependent. That dependency and inequality is the essence of fetus-hood, so to speak. Self-defense doctrine, with its Hobbesian background and overlay, simply doesn't apply to such dependent and unequal "aggressors"; indeed, the notion of aggression itself does not apply to such creatures.

Rape reform efforts to criminalize simple rape are also irrational, as Susan Estrich has discovered, and for the same reason: Subjectively, "simple rapes" are harms, but from the point of view of masculine subjectivity, nonviolent acts that don't threaten annihilation or frustration of projects can't possibly be "harmful." In both cases, we have tried to explain feminist reform efforts through the use of analogies that don't work and arguments that are strained. The result in both cases is internally inconsistent, poorly reasoned, weak, and ultimately vulnerable legal doctrine.

"Reconstructive feminist jurisprudence," I believe, should try to explain or reconstruct the reforms necessary to the safety and improvement of women's lives in direct language that is true to our own experience and our own subjective lives. The dangers of mandatory pregnancy, for example, are invasion of the body by the fetus and the intrusion into the mother's existence following childbirth. The right to abort is the right to defend against a particular bodily and existential invasion. The harm the unwanted fetus does is not the harm of annihilation nor anything like it: It is not an assault or a battery or a breached contract or an act of negligence. A fetus is not an equal in the state of nature, and the harm a fetus can do is not in any way analogous to that harm. It is, however, a harm. The fetus is an "other," and it is perfectly sensible to seek a liberal sounding "right" of protection against the harm the fetus does.

We need, though, to be more accurate in our description of the harm. Unwanted intercourse is "harmful" because it is invasive, not because it is (necessarily) violent. For that reason alone, the harm of intercourse is descriptively incommensurate with liberal concepts of harm. But it is not incommensurate with women's lives. The goal of reconstructive feminist jurisprudence should be to provide descriptions of the "human being" underlying feminist legal reforms that will be true to the conditions of women's lives. Our jurisprudential constructs—liberalism and critical theory—might then change as well to account for true descriptions of women's subjectivity.

Conclusion: Toward a Jurisprudence Unmodified

The separation thesis, I have argued, is drastically untrue of women. What's worth noting by way of conclusion is that it is not entirely true of men either. First, it is not true materially. Men are connected to another human life prior to the cutting of the umbilical cord. Furthermore, men are somewhat connected to women during intercourse, and men have openings that can be sexually penetrated. Nor is the separation thesis necessarily true of men existentially. As Suzanna Sherry has shown, the existence of the entire classical republican tradition belies the claim that masculine biology mandates liberal values.[60] More generally, as Dinnerstein, Chodorow, French, and Gilligan all insist, material biology does not mandate existential value: Men can connect to other human life. Men can nurture life. Men can mother. Obviously, men can care and love and support and affirm life. Just as obviously, however, most men don't. One reason that they don't, of course, is male privilege. Another reason, though, may be the blinders of our masculinist utopian visionary. Surely one of the most important insights of feminism has been that biology is indeed destiny when we are unaware of the extent to which biology is narrowing our fate, but that biology is destiny only to the extent of our ignorance. As we become increasingly aware, we become increasingly free. As we become increasingly free, we, rather than biology, become the authors of our fate. Surely this is true both of men and women.

On the flip side, the connection thesis is also not entirely true of women, either materially or existentially. Not all women become pregnant, and not all women are sexually penetrated. Women can go through life unconnected to other human life. Women can also go through life fundamentally unconcerned with other human life. Obviously, as the liberal feminist movement firmly established, many women can and do individuate, speak the truth, develop integrity, pursue personal projects, embody freedom, and attain an atomistic liberal individuality. Just as obviously, most women don't. Most women are indeed forced into motherhood and heterosexuality. One reason for this is utopian blinders: Women's lack of awareness of existential choice in the face of what are felt to be biological imperatives. But that is surely not the main reason. The primary reason for the stunted nature of women's lives is male power.

Perhaps the greatest obstacle to the creation of a feminist jurisprudence is that feminist jurisprudence must simultaneously confront both political and conceptual barriers to women's freedom. The political barrier is surely the most pressing. Feminists must first and foremost counter a profound power imbalance, and the way to do that is through law and politics. But jurisprudence—like law—is persistently utopian and conceptual as well as apologist and political: Jurisprudence represents a constant and at least at times a sincere attempt to articulate a guiding utopian vision of human association. Feminist jurisprudence must respond to these utopian images, correct them, improve upon them, and participate in them as utopian images, not just as apologies for patriarchy. Feminism must envision a postpatriarchal world, for without such a vision we have little direction. We must use that vision to construct our present goals, and we should, I believe, interpret our present victories against the backdrop of that vision. That vision is not necessarily androgynous; surely in a utopian world the presence of differences between people will be cause only for celebration. In a utopian world, all forms of life will be recognized, respected, and honored. A perfect legal system will protect against harms sustained by all forms of life and will recognize life affirming values generated by all forms of being. Feminist jurisprudence must aim to bring this about, and to do so, it must aim to transform the images as well as the power. Masculine jurisprudence must become humanist jurisprudence, and humanist jurisprudence must become a jurisprudence unmodified.

Notes

I would like to thank Mike Kelly, Paul Brest, Lynne Henderson, Robert B. Green, Jana Singer, Peter Quint, Cass Sunstein, Richard Posner, Erin Enright, Quincie Hopkins, Tom Grey, the participants in the Wisconsin 1987 Feminism and Legal Theory Summer Workshop, and the Georgetown Feminist Legal Theory Workshop for their comments on early drafts of this chapter. I am also indebted to Marcy Wilder (Stanford Law School '88) for helping me to clarify and develop the critique of the critical legal scholarship discussed in this chapter.

1. Naomi Scheman, Individualism and the Objects of Psychology, in Sandra Harding and Merrill B. Hintikka, eds., Discovering Reality 225, 237 (1983).

2. Robert Nozick, Anarchy, State, and Utopia 33 (1974).

3. Roberto Mangabeira Unger, Knowledge and Politics 200 (1975) (citation omitted).

4. Sandel, Liberalism and the Limits of Justice (1982).

5. Ronald Dworkin, A Matter of Principle 191 (1985)(capitalization omitted).

6. Id. at 192–93 (capitalization omitted).

7. Thomas Hobbes, Leviathan 183–84 (C. B. Macpherson, ed. 1968).

8. Nozick, Anarchy, State, and Utopia at 333–34, 32–33 (emphasis in original).

9. Unger, Knowledge and Politics at 201.

10. Peter Gabel, The Phenomenology of Rights-Consciousness and the Pact of the Withdrawn Selves, 62 Tex.L.Rev. 1563, 1566–67 (1984)(citation omitted).

11. Duncan Kennedy, Form and Substance in Private Law Adjudication, 89 Harv.L.Rev. 1685, 1774 (1976).

12. Carol Gilligan, In a Different Voice 6–8 (1982).

13. Suzanna Sherry, Civic Virtue and the Feminine Voice in Constitutional Adjudication, 72 Va.L.Rev. 543, 584–85 (1986) (citations omitted).

14. Nancy Chodorow, The Reproduction of Mothering 167 (1978).

15. Gilligan, In a Different Voice at 159–60.

16. Id. at 100.

17. Id. at 8.

18. Id. at 171.

19. Nel Noddings, Caring (1984).

20. Id. at 128.

21. Hobbes, Leviathan at 183.

22. M. French, Beyond Power (1985).

23. Shulamith Firestone, The Dialectic of Sex (1970).

24. Amicus Brief for the National Abortion Rights Action League et al., Thornburgh v. American College of Obstetricians and Gynecologists, nos. 84-495 and 84-1379 ("NARAL Amicus Brief")(on file at The University of Chicago Law Review). For the Supreme Court opinion, see 476 U.S. 747 (1986).

25. NARAL *Amicus* Brief at 13.

26. Id. at 19.

27. Id. at 28.

28. Id. at 29.

29. Id. at 29.

30. Id. at 29.

31. Id. at 29.

32. Id.

33. Id. at 122.

34. Id. at 137–38.

35. Unger, Knowledge and Politics at 205–6.

36. Gilligan, In a Different Voice at 17.

37. Dworkin, Intercourse at 141–42.

38. Gabel briefly alludes to, but then dismisses, an alternative feminist explanation; see footnote 1, 62 Tex.L.Rev. at 1568. Conversations with Marcy Wilder and Toni Fitzpatrick (Stanford Law School '88) have helped me see the gender bias in Gabel's work.

39. See, e.g., Patricia Williams, Alchemical Notes: Reconstructed Ideals from Deconstructed Rights, 22 Harv.Civ.Rts.–Civ.Liberties Law Review 401 (1987); and Richard Delgado, The Ethereal Scholar: Does Critical Legal Studies Have What Minorities Want? 22 Harv.Civ.Rts.–Civ.Liberties Law Review 301 (1987).

40. Rich, On Lies, Secrets, and Silence at 272.

41. Id. at 271–72.

42. Catharine A. MacKinnon, Feminism Unmodified 39 (1987).

43. Peter Gabel and Jay M. Feinman, Contract Law as Ideology, in David Kairys, ed., The Politics of Law 172, 176 (1982)(citation omitted).

44. Id. at 183.

45. Duncan Kennedy, The Structure of Blackstone's Commentaries, 28 Buffalo L.Rev. 209, 211–12 (1979).

46. Kennedy, 89 Harv.L.Rev. at 1775.

47. Susan Estrich, Real Rape (1987).

48. MacKinnon, Feminism Unmodified at 40.

49. Gabel, 62 Tex.L.Rev. at 1566.

50. Sherry, 72 Va.L.Rev. at 584; Suzanna Sherry, The Gender of Judges, 4 Law & Inequality 159 (1986).

51. Henderson, Legality and Empathy, 85 Mich.L.Rev. 1574 (1987).

52. Martha Minow, Foreword: Justice Engendered, 101 Harv.L.Rev. 10 (1987).

53. Martha L. Fineman and Anne Opie, The Uses of Social Science Data in Legal Policymaking: Custody Determination at Divorce, 1987 Wisc.L.Rev. 107; Martha L. Fineman, A Reply to David Chambers, 1987 Wisc.L.Rev. 165; Martha L. Fineman, Dominant Discourse, Professional Language and Legal Change, 101 Harv.L.Rev.   (forthcoming 1988).

54. Estrich, Real Rape; Henderson, Book Review,   Berkeley Women's L.J.   ; Diana E. H. Russell, Rape in Marriage (1982).

55. Martha L. Fineman, Dominant Discourse: The Professional Appropriation of Child Custody Decision-Making, Institute for Legal Studies, Working Papers Series 2 (April 1987).

56. MacKinnon, Feminism Unmodified at 206–13.

57. Estrich, Real Rape; Russel, Rape in Marriage.

58. 410 U.S. 113 (1973).

59. Henderson, 85 Mich.L.Rev. 1574 (1987).

60. Sherry, 72 Va.L.Rev. at 584.

21

Deconstructing Gender

JOAN C. WILLIAMS

Introduction

I start out, as have many others, from the deep split among American feminists between "sameness" and "difference." The driving force behind the mid-twentieth-century resurgence of American feminism was an insistence on the fundamental similarity of men and women and, hence, their essential equality. Betty Friedan comes to mind as an enormously influential housewife whose focus on men and women as individuals made her intensely hostile to gender stereotyping.[1]

Mid-century feminism, now often referred to somewhat derisively as *assimilationism*, focused on providing opportunities to women in realms traditionally preserved for men. In the 1980s two phenomena have shifted feminists' attention from assimilationists' focus on how individual women are like men to a focus on gender differences, on how women as a group differ from men as a group. The first is the feminization of poverty, which dramatizes the chronic and increasing economic vulnerability of women. Feminists now realize that the assimilationists' traditional focus on gender neutrality may have rendered women more vulnerable to certain gender-related disabilities that have important economic consequences. The second phenomenon that plays a central role in the current feminist imagination is that of career women "choosing" to abandon or subordinate their careers so they can spend time with their small children. These phenomena highlight the fact that deep-seated social differences continue to encourage men and women to make quite different choices with respect to work and family. Thus, "sameness" scholars are increasingly confronted by the existence of gender differences.

Do these challenges to assimilationism prove that we should stop trying to kid ourselves and admit the "real" differences between men and women, as the popular press drums into us day after day and as the "feminism of difference" appears to confirm? Do such phenomena mean that feminists' traditional focus on gender neutrality is a bankrupt ideal? I will argue no on both counts, taking an approach quite different from that ordinarily taken by feminists on the sameness side of the spectrum. "Sameness" feminists usually have responded to the feminists of difference by reiterating their basic insight that individual men and women can be very similar. While true, this is not an adequate response to the basic insight of "difference" feminists: that gender exists, that men and women differ as groups. In this chapter, I try to speak to feminists of difference on their own terms. While I take gender seriously, I disagree with the description of gender provided by difference feminists.

I begin in Part I by challenging the widely influential description of gender advocated by Carol Gilligan. I suggest that Gilligan's description of "women's voice" is less a description of women's psychology than an attempt to attribute to women two influential critiques of contemporary Western culture. One is the critique of traditional Western epistemology. I argue that it is incorrect as a matter of intellectual history to claim, as have Gilligan and others, that the twentieth century's shift to a more contextualizing, antiformalist, and relativizing form of discourse constitutes a rejection of absolutist "male" epistemology in favor of "women's voice." The second critique Gilligan claims for women, the critique of possessive individualism, presents more subtle issues. Unlike the critique of traditional epistemology, the critique of possessive individualism has traditionally been associated with women. Gilligan's description of gender differences reclaims this critique for women through an updated version of the Victorian ideology of domesticity, whose attraction for modern feminists lies in its perceived potential "to transform our polity and its underlying assumptions [away] from the alienated world of atomistic competition.[2] This critique of individualism is one well worth exploring. But its power is undermined when modern feminists adopt domesticity's peculiarly domesticated version of the critique. The perils of modern domesticity become apparent in an analysis of the recent Title VII case of *Equal Employment Opportunity Commission (EEOC) v. Sears, Roebuck & Co.*[3] This case provides ample evidence of how domesticity's critique of possessive individualism serves to marginalize both women and the critique itself.

While Part I challenges the description of gender differences offered by Gilligan feminists, it does not deny the existence of gender differences. Gender differences do exist: That is, men as a group differ from women as a group not only on the basis of biological "sex" differences but on the basis of social "gender" differences.[4] What I reject is Gilligan's description of gender differences, which I think is inaccurate and potentially destructive.

The chief strength of the feminism of difference is its challenge to what have been called male norms. Part II demonstrates how these norms can be challenged without resort to domesticity. I begin from Catharine MacKinnon's description of gender as a system of power relations. While MacKinnon focuses on sexuality, I return to a more traditional topic: the relationship between work and family responsibilities. I argue that these issues are at the core of the contemporary gender system, which systematically enriches men at the expense of women and children. Problems such as the feminization of poverty stem in substantial part from a wage-labor system premised on an ideal worker with no family responsibilities. Experiences of the past decade have shown that women can only enter the labor force without insisting on a redefinition of the ideal worker at the expense of failing to meet the ideal.

Yet the gendered structure of wage labor is not being challenged. More astonishing, difference feminists celebrate a women's culture that encourages women to "choose" economic marginalization and celebrate that choice as a badge of virtue. The notion that women "choose" to become marginalized (nonideal) workers clouds the fact that all workers currently are limited to two unacceptable choices: the traditional male life pattern or women's traditional economic vulnerability. Wage labor does not have to be structured in this way. Changing it should be a central thrust of a feminist program.

In Part III, I continue to develop this alternative vision of gender. I first discuss the rejection by MacKinnon and others of the traditional feminist goal of gender neutrality. Its critics have argued that gender neutrality mandates a blindness to gender realities and so inhibits attempts to help women victimized by gender. I redefine the traditional goal, which in fact does not require neutrality, or blindness, with respect to gender but, rather, advocates a consistent refusal to institutionalize a correlation between gender roles and biological sex differences. Thus redefined, the traditional goal has continuing validity, since institutionalizing a correlation between gender and sex necessarily reinforces gender stereotypes and the oppressive gender system as a whole. Moreover, the traditional goal does not preclude helping women disadvantaged by their adherence to gender roles, since such women can be protected in a sex-neutral fashion by protecting all people (regardless of biology) who are victimized by gender.

The article concludes by detailing the limitations of Gilligan's description of gender differences. This discussion responds to comments from some who have heard my analysis and then assumed that I cannot really be denying women's "different voice." I stress that though I am not denying the existence of gender, I am denying the validity of the description of women's voice that Gilligan has provided. In particular I reject Gilligan's core claim that women are focused on relationships, while men are not. To the extent this claim pinpoints actual gender differences, I argue it merely reflects the oppressive realities of the current gender system. Beyond that, Gilligan's claim is inaccurate and serves to perpetuate our traditional blindness to the ways in which men are nurturing and women are competitive and power seeking.

I. The Feminism of Difference

A. Introduction

The most influential source for the feminism of difference is Carol Gilligan's book, in which Gilligan argues that women speak "in a different voice."[5] Women are portrayed as nurturers, defined by their relationships and focused on contextual thinking; men are depicted as abstract thinkers, defined by individual achievement. We should listen to women's "voice," argue Gilligan and her followers, because women's culture offers the basis for a transformation of our society, a transformation based on the womanly values of responsibility, connection, selflessness, and caring, rather than on separation, autonomy, and hierarchy.[6]

One reason why the feminism of difference has proved so persuasive is that it has claimed for women two of the central critiques of twentieth-century thought. In a strain of argument particularly popular in law reviews, feminists characterize traditional Western epistemology as "male" and identify the twentieth-century critique of that epistemology as an integral part of "women's voice."[7] Gilligan and her followers also identify with women a critique of possessive individualism whose implications have been spelled out in *EEOC v. Sears.*

B. The New Epistemology as Women's Voice

Gilligan's description is often presented as a rediscovery of obvious differences between men and women we knew about all along. In fact, even feminists of difference disagree about what are the "obvious" differences between men and women. Gilligan's description of women has been so widely adopted that it is easy to overlook the fact that other feminists of difference have offered a sharply different version of women's true nature. Some radical feminists, more influential ten years ago than today, have espoused a view of women dramatically different from Gilligan's. Often using witch imagery, they stress women's intuition, their sexual power, and their alliance with deep forces of irrationality.[8]

This portrait of woman as id derives largely from the premodern stereotype of woman as the "weaker vessel."[9] Before the mid-eighteenth century, women were viewed not only as physically weaker than men; their intellectual and moral frailty meant they needed men's guidance to protect them from the human propensity for evil. Women's intense sexuality and their fundamental irrationality meant they were in need of outside control, because women in their weakness could be easily tempted. The darkest expression of the traditional view that women unsupervised quickly slipped into collusion with evil was the persecution (during some periods, massive in scale) of women as witches.[10]

This traditional stereotype of women crystallized after the early modern period into some traditional truths about women. As the *philosophes* of the Enlightenment celebrated logic and reason, women's intellectual inferiority came to be expressed as an inability to engage in rigorous, abstract thinking. The Enlightenment also celebrated reason over emotion, and women's premodern alliance with the devil was transmuted into the view that women's limited ability for rational thought meant they were fundamentally emotional creatures.

These stereotypes have provided the link for many feminists of difference between women and the critique of traditional Western epistemology.[11] This critique, which I have elsewhere called the new epistemology,[12] consists of a broad and diverse intellectual movement that rejects a range of long-standing Western verities, some dating to the Enlightenment and others all the way back to Plato. Perhaps the core element of the new epistemology is its rejection of an absolute truth accessible through rigorous, logical manipulation of abstractions. Feminists of difference have characterized the new epistemology with women's voice, noting that women traditionally have been thought to eschew abstraction for sensitivity to context and to eschew logic for a faith in emotion and intuition as tools of thought.

On closer inspection, however, the traditional stereotype of women as overly emotional and incapable of rational, abstract thought is quite different from the critique proffered by the new epistemology: Feminists are being highly selective in the aspects of the traditional stereotype they choose to stress. It is true there are some similarities between the traditional stereotype of women and the new epistemology. Both share a sense of the limitations of pure logic and a faith in contextual thinking. But feminists of difference submerge the fact that the thinkers who have developed the new epistemology have, by and large, been cerebral and detached in the extreme. Neither they nor the new epistemology fits the traditional stereotype of women as too emotional for sustained rational thought. What the new epistemologists are talking about is a new kind of rationality, one not so closely tied to abstract, transcendental truths, one that does not exclude so much of human experience as Western rationality traditionally has done. The ideal they propose represents a broadening of traditional intellectual life, whereas the traditional caricature of women as emotional and irrational represents a formal marginalization of those characteristics of human personality that the Western tradition has devalued.[13]

Thus, this attempt to rehabilitate traditional stereotypes as "women's voice" and to associate women's voice with the new epistemology fails to come to terms with the extent to which the gender stereotypes were designed to marginalize women. These stereotypes no doubt articulated some values shunted aside by Western culture. But the circumstances of their birth mean they presented a challenge to predominant Western values that was designed to fail and to marginalize women in the process.

At a simpler level, the attempt to claim the new epistemology for women is unconvincing simply because the new epistemology has been developed largely by men. These include philosophers from Frederick Nietzsche and the American pragmatists to Martin Heidegger and Ludwig Wittgenstein, all of whom helped develop the movement's critique of absolutes. Important figures in developing the new epistemology's view of truths as necessarily partial and contextual include the fathers of post-Newtonian physics (Albert Einstein and Max Planck), the linguists Benjamin Whorf and Ferdinand de Saussure, and Wittgenstein, who rejected the "picture theory" that Truth is an objective picture of reality in favor of the view that a multiplicity of truths exists as an integral part of culture and context.

Note that all these scholars, and most others who were seminal in articulating the basic outlook of the new epistemology, are male. This history is no news to relational feminists, who regularly cite Wittgenstein and others as sources of inspiration.[14] In what sense, then, is this vast epistemological shift "feminist" or even "feminine"? The simple answer is that the new epistemology is not in any meaningful way "women's voice."

C. Women's Voice and the Critique of Possessive Individualism

1. The Feminism of Difference as a Resurgence of Domesticity

The traditional stereotype of women, designed to justify women's subservience in a society that saw hierarchies as natural and desirable, came during the course of the eighteenth century to seem inconsistent with the emerging political philosophy of liberalism, which held all men as equal. Gradually a new gender ideology, the ideology of domesticity, developed in which women continued to be viewed as weaker than men physically and intellectually but were newly extolled as more moral than men.[15]

Gilligan echoes domesticity's "discovery" of women's higher morality. Unlike the Victorians, Gilligan does not argue explicitly that women's morality is of a higher order: She articulates her ideal as a "dialectic mixture" of the male and female "voices." Yet commentators have noted the striking resemblance between Gilligan's ideal morality and her description of female emotional maturity. An emotionally mature woman, it seems, will reach Gilligan's ideal moral state automatically, while men will attain it only through a fundamental restructuring of their gender identity.

A close analysis of the traits Gilligan attributes to women suggests that she and other scholars who share her view of women offer domesticity with a difference. These "relational feminists,"[16] as they have been aptly called, reclaim the compliments of Victorian gender ideology while rejecting its insults. Thus, relational feminists agree with the Victorians that women are more nurturing than men ("focused on relationships"), less tied to the questionable virtues of capitalism, and ultimately more moral than men. But they disagree with the Victorians' view that women are also more passive than men, less competent, more timid, and naturally demure.

Relational feminism has had a pervasive impact on women's history, and it is a historian of women who has best illustrated its relation to the ideology of domesticity. One of the major achievements of relational feminism in women's history is Suzanne Lebsock's subtle and persuasive study of a small Virginia town before the Civil War. In *The Free Women of Petersburg,* Lebsock summarizes her conclusions about women's values in the pre–Civil War period as follows:

Here, in one list, are the documentable components of a women's value system. Women, more than men, noticed and responded to the needs and merits of particular persons. This showed in their tendency to reward favorite slaves and to distribute their property unevenly among their heirs. It also showed in their ability to make independent judgments about their own fitness to administer estates. Women were particularly sensitive to the interests of other women and to their precarious economic position; this was demonstrated in favoritism toward female heirs and in the establishment of separate estates. As their real estate and credit transactions suggest, women wanted financial security for themselves as well as for others. Beyond that they were not as ego-invested as were men in the control of wealth. Our list grows a bit longer if we add the more ambiguous evidence derived from women's vanguard action in providing relief to the poor and in promoting religion. Women as a group were more invested than were men in Christian communities and the life of the spirit. And in their efforts to give assistance to the poor, both personalism and regard for other women surfaced again; the poor were mainly women and children, most of whom cannot have "deserved" their poverty.

The people who wrote the antebellum period's popular literature have been trying to tell us all along that women were different from men, better than men in some respects. Perhaps it is time we took their message more seriously.[17]

Lebsock's book, published shortly after Gilligan's, comes to some strikingly similar conclusions. Both authors conclude that women are more focused on relationships than are men, and both suggest that women's is a higher morality. But Lebsock differs from Gilligan and from most other relational feminists in her awareness that she is reclaiming stereotypes from domesticity. Unlike scholars who have glossed over the Victorians' negative characterizations of women, Lebsock confronts them directly, and her conclusions are instructive. She asserts that women were not uniformly inept; many were active and competent as executors of their husbands' estates. Nor were they passive as investors; only risk averse. When it comes to the positive attributes of Victorian gender stereotypes, Lebsock's conclusions differ. She concludes that women were characterized by a "personalism" that made them more sensitive to slaves, the poor, and vulnerability in other women, less involved in capitalist values, and (consequently?) more moral than men.

Lebsock thus rejects the insults of Victorian gender ideology but embraces those elements complimentary to women. So do most feminists of difference, though few make their selectivity so clear. Moreover, relational feminists often seem unaware of their own selectivity. "Perhaps it is time we took [the antebellum] message more seriously," Lebsock argues, forgetting the half of the antebellum message she rejects. In this she is joined by the majority of relational feminists.

Given the decision to rehabilitate domesticity's gender stereotypes, it is not surprising that relational feminists choose domesticity's compliments over its insults. But this veils the deeper question: Why return to domesticity at all?

In answer let us start with a telling exchange between Carol Gilligan and Catharine MacKinnon in the 1984 "conversation" held at the Buffalo School of Law. In a discussion of Jake, Gilligan's typical male, and Amy, her typical female, Gilligan argued that her goal was to assimilate Amy's voice into the mainstream of society. MacKinnon responded that her goal was more to have Amy develop a new voice, one that "would articulate what she cannot now, because his foot is on her throat." Gilligan's Amy, said MacKinnon, "is articulating the feminine. And you are calling it hers. That's what I find infuriating." "No," replied Gilligan, "I am saying she is articulating a set of values which are very positive."[18]

Note Gilligan's assumption that because what she has found is "very positive," she cannot have found "the feminine"—that is, conventional gender stereotypes derived from domesticity. MacKinnon is right that what Gilligan has found is femininity; Gilligan is right that there is something positive there.

2. Domesticity as a Critique of Possessive Individualism

The conventional wisdom among the "sameness" contingent is that relational feminists in their celebration of women's voice are simply basking in self-congratulation. I think this misses the mark. Relational feminists' interest in "the feminine" stems from its transformative potential. Relational feminists find enshrined in domesticity "female" values that, they believe, will enable women to achieve equality not by buying into the male world on male terms but by transforming the world in women's image. Thus Kathy Ferguson in *The Feminist Case Against Bureaucracy* asserts that feminist theory "can provide for a reconceptualization of some of the most basic terms of political life."[19] Carrie Menkel-Meadow, a leading disciple of Gilligan within the legal community, hopes to restructure the legal system to express the values of "Portia's" voice.[20] Robin West recommends a new focus on connectedness and intimacy.[21] Other relational feminists go further and argue that women's voice is the best hope for the future of the planet. But Suzanne Lebsock, as usual, says it best: "If we find that all along women have managed to create and sustain countercultures, then the chances increase that as women come to power, a more humane social order will indeed come with them."[22]

For all these feminists, this "more humane social order" entails a new ethic of care[23] based on a focus on relationships, not competition; on negotiation, not combat; on community, not individual self-interest. "What is needed," concludes the early and influential feminist of difference Elizabeth Wolgast, "is another model. . . . We need a model that acknowledges . . . other kinds of interest than self-interest."[24] A more recent legal feminist echoes this thought, noting his aspiration "to transform our polity and its underlying assumptions from the alienated world of atomistic competition to an interconnected world of mutual cooperation."[25] The model being rejected is possessive individualism.

If we examine the transformation proposed by relational feminists, we uncover a critique of this model that dates back to the original version of domesticity. Historians have long known that domestic ideology presented a challenge to the capitalist mainstream of American society. Said Daniel Scott Smith in 1973:

> Instead of postulating woman as an atom in competitive society, [the Victorians] viewed women as a person in the context of relationships with others. By defining the family as a community, this ideology allowed women to engage in something of a critique of male, materialistic, market society and simultaneously proceed to seize power within the family.[26]

In 1977, historian Nancy Cott worked out in detail the way domesticity functioned as an internal critique of capitalism. She linked the invention of domestic ideology with changes in work patterns that accompanied the industrial revolution. Cott argued that domesticity developed in conjunction with the shift from traditional "task-oriented" work, which mixed labor and leisure, to modern "time-disciplined" wage labor, which isolates work both temporally and geographically from family life. She argued that domestic ideology set up the home as a haven from the heartless world of nineteenth-century capitalism.

> In accentuating the split between "work" and "home" and proposing the latter as a place of salvation, the canon of domesticity tacitly acknowledged the capacity of modern work to desecrate the human spirit. Authors of domestic literature, especially the female authors, denigrated business and politics as arenas of selfishness, exertion, embarrassment, and degradation of soul. These rhetoricians suggested what Marx's analysis of alienated labor in the 1840s would assert, that "the worker . . . feels at ease only outside work, and during work he is outside himself. He is at home when he is not working and when he is working he is not at home." The canon of domesticity embodied a protest against that advance of exploitation and pecuniary values.[27]

Cott's description of domesticity as a *"cri de coeur* against modern work relations" suggests that domesticity has from the beginning functioned as an internal critique of Western capitalism. Gilligan and her followers carry on this tradition in their visions of the future that extol connection, cooperation, and community (the "values of the web") and aspire to overcome competition and self-interest.

Gilligan picks up not only domesticity's claim that women offer an alternative to capitalism, but also its stereotype of men as capitalists par excellence. "For men," Gilligan asserts, "the moral imperative appears . . . as an injunction to respect the rights of others and thus to protect from interference the rights to life and self-fulfillment.[28] By labelling as "male" the "morality of rights and noninterference," Gilligan links men with the liberal ideology that underlies American capitalism. Gilligan also attributes to men the liberal premise that the world is one of "people standing alone," arguing in effect that men accept liberalism's vision of society as a set of preconstituted individuals who choose to associate for limited purposes. Hence Jake, Gilligan's typical male, is "concerned with limiting interference" and places a high value on separation and autonomy. Gilligan associates the male voice with the pursuit of self-interest, and, therefore, with capitalism's central tenet that this pursuit will benefit society as a whole.[29]

Relational feminism is better understood as a critique of possessive individualism than as a description of what men and women are actually like. Gilligan herself acknowledges this when she refuses to associate her "voices" with males and females.[30] Yet Gilligan appears not to heed her own warnings on this point, for in the remainder of her book she invariably associates men with one voice and women with the other, and often makes sweeping statements about the way men and women "are." Gilligan's inconsistent signals about whether she is talking about women or "the feminine" have left relational feminism with the potential to be used as a weapon against women. As evidence of this, I next turn to the *Sears* case, a clear example of the perils of modern domesticity.

3. *EEOC v. Sears:* The Perils of Modern Domesticity

In *EEOC v. Sears, Roebuck & Co.,*[31] Sears argued successfully that women were underrepresented in its relatively high-paying commission sales positions not because Sears had discriminated against them but because women lacked "interest" in commission sales. Sears used the language of relational feminism to support its core argument that women's focus on relationships at home and at work makes them choose to sacrifice worldly advancement in favor of a supportive work environment and limited hours that accommodate their devotion to family.[32] An unmistakable undertone is Sears's subtle intimation that women's sacrifice is limited, since their "different voice" makes the fast track unappealing. Women's "ethic of care" enables them to rise above the fray, so they are not truly hurt when they are excluded from high-powered, competitive jobs in commission sales.[33]

The brilliance of Sears's lawyers lies in their success in enshrining gender stereotypes at the core of Title VII.[34] *Sears* provides a dramatic illustration of the power of relational feminism to provide a respectable academic language in which to dignify traditional stereotypes. The case holds the potential to transform Title VII law in a way that pits gender discrimination plaintiffs against stereotypes in a battle the stereotypes are designed to win, for in effect *Sears* establishes a legal assumption that all women fit gender stereotypes and imposes on plaintiffs a burden to disprove that assumption as part of their prima facie case. Understanding the potential impact of *Sears* requires some background in Title VII law.

The usual focus of a Title VII class action lawsuit is on statistics comparing the proportion of women in a given job category with the proportion of women in the relevant labor market. Statistics are direct proof that a facially neutral hiring policy has a disparate impact on a group protected under Title VII.[35] Statistics also are evidence of intent, as is illustrated by the "billiard ball" example. Say one begins with a barrel containing fifty black and fifty white billiard balls. If balls were removed in a random fashion, one would expect half black and half white balls to be chosen. The further the results are from a fifty/ fifty split, the greater the likelihood some other factor is at work. Because defendants who discriminate are rarely open about it, the law helps plaintiffs through a presumption that the "other factor" involved is discrimination. Thus, courts have required only evidence of a statistically significant disparity by a plaintiff to establish a prima facie case of discrimination. Thereafter, the burden shifts to the defendant to articulate some nondiscriminatory reason for the disparity documented.

In contrast to courts prior to *Sears,* both the trial and appellate *Sears* courts required the EEOC to prove not only statistical disparities but also men's and women's "equal interest." Under *Sears,* therefore, a class of gender discrimination plaintiffs cannot prove their prima facie case simply by proving a disparity between the proportion of women in the relevant labor market and the proportion of women in the jobs at issue. Instead they have the additional burden of establishing what percentage of women in the otherwise relevant labor market was truly "interested" in the jobs at issue.

Sears based its argument first upon testimony of managers, one of whom made the now famous claim that women did not want commission sales jobs because such salesmen were required to work outside the store and women do not like to go out when "it's snowing or raining or whatever."[36] The managers' testimony was bolstered by a sociologist who testified about a survey of Sears employees, by a writer on women's issues, and by historian Rosalind Rosenberg, who cited Gilligan and other relational feminists to support her assertion that the EEOC's "assumption that women and men have identical interests and aspirations regarding work is incorrect. Historically, men and women have had different interests, goals and aspirations regarding work."[37]

To support this statement, Rosenberg offered portraits of men and women that closely echoed Gilligan's. Women she depicted as "humane and nurturing," focused on relationships, and averse to capitalist virtues such as competition. Again echoing Gilligan, she painted men as competitive and motivated by self-interest: possessive individualists par excellence.[38]

Sears proceeded to use against women the gender stereotypes rehabilitated by relational feminism. The implication of Sears's successful use of domesticity's insults is that relational feminists delude themselves if they think they can rehabilitate domesticity's compliments without its insults. To relational feminists, the key point of domesticity may be women's higher morality; to Sears managers it was that women are weak and dependent, delicate and passive.

A closer look at the trial transcript dramatizes the power of these stereotypes once unleashed, for it shows how Sears systematically used stereotypes to override information about the desires and the aspirations of actual women. The most obvious example of this occurs in the testimony of Joan Haworth, Sears's major statistical witness, who argued that even female applicants who appeared to be interested in commission sales, in fact, were not interested. When the EEOC challenged this statement, Haworth chose three applications that indicated background and experience in commission sales and explained how she knew none was truly interested.[39] The EEOC located two of the three women Haworth discussed, both of whom testified they had in fact been seeking jobs in commission sales.[40] The trial judge glossed over this rebuttal in his opinion.

Sears also systematically discounted interests expressed by female applicants in "male" jobs such as auto sales. Haworth, who argued that those applicants were puffing up their interest, guarded against this by "normalizing" the scores of female applicants. Her methodology functioned to ensure that sales applicants who indicated interest in working both in "male" areas such as auto sales and in "female" areas such as the baby department had their "male" interests systematically discounted.[41]

Sears's attorneys had help from the trial judge in policing gender stereotypes. Judge John A. Nordberg, a Reagan appointee, played an active role in shaping the evidence to support his eventual holdings that women lack interest in "male" jobs. Whenever EEOC witnesses made statements about women's commitment to the home and their lack of commitment to wage labor that contradicted gender stereotypes, Nordberg insisted they specify the precise percentage of women whose interests diverged from those of women in general (i.e., from gender stereotypes). Here's one example from the testimony of historian Alice Kessler-Harris, who countered Rosenberg's testimony by arguing that women generally have taken higher paying jobs when they became available despite the mandates of domesticity.

> Could I just interrupt for one second, Dr. Harris, or Kessler-Harris. This is what I have said to others, and if you had sat through all the testimony, you would understand the reason for my saying this. One of the difficulties in analyzing and dealing with the evidence in the case is a tendency of witnesses to use the phrase "men and women" as though it is 100 percent of men or 100 percent of women. I think that the testimony makes it clear that there are a range of personalities, interests, experiences, achievements, and everything in both sexes. . . . And what this case in a sense is getting down to, because of the statistical nature of the case, is percentages. It would be very helpful to me during the course of your testimony to try to quantify the percentage or the proportion or possible number that you are dealing with in any particular thing that you say. I [know] it is hard, because you are, in a sense, seeking to generalize. But it makes it very difficult when it is asserted that either women so and so or men so and so, when we all know that it isn't 100 percent correct.[42]

Judge Nordberg repeated the same point as a constant refrain to the testimony of EEOC witnesses. Women behave like this, they testified. What percentage, Nordberg asked again and again. When Sears witnesses made generalized statements about women that confirmed stereotypes derived from domesticity, Nordberg's concern for quantification evaporated. I found no instance in which Nordberg felt the need for this type of quantification from Sears witnesses. Nordberg's opinion shows why: He adopted the argument advanced by Sears (through Rosalind Rosenberg) that women who did not fit conventional stereotypes were a marginal group of (uppity?) college women. No statistical evidence supported this assertion.

Nordberg's insistence on quantification in effect required plaintiffs to specify the precise percentage of women interested in nontraditional jobs such as commission sales. By not requiring Sears to provide equivalent proof of the specific percentage of women who fit gender stereotypes, the *Sears* district court opinion in effect establishes a legal presumption that all women fit traditional gender stereotypes. The Seventh Circuit opinion wholeheartedly adopted this approach.[43]

Sears's doctrinal innovation clashes at a fundamental level with the thrust of Title VII. *Sears* allows information about gender, about women as a group, to be used to establish a legal presumption about individual plaintiffs consolidated into a class. This is inappropriate because Title VII is designed to protect women who do not fit gender stereotypes, who want to work as physicists or in auto sales. Title VII's underlying goal is to protect women who want nontraditional work. Establishing a legal presumption that every class of female plaintiffs conforms to gender stereotypes frustrates this goal.

Sears is thus a dramatic reversal of existing Title VII law and should be overruled. From a theoretical standpoint, *Sears* shows the power of gender stereotypes to overshadow evidence about actual women. *Sears* also shows how relational feminism's critique of possessive individualism serves to marginalize both women and the critique itself.

Unlike the critique of capitalism from traditional radical discourse, domesticity's critique does not compel its followers to confront capitalist practice and to change it. Instead, an abiding tenet of domesticity is that women's aversion to capitalist virtues makes them "choose" home and family. This is an argument that encourages women to "choose" economic marginalization and celebrate that choice as a badge of virtue. This analysis of domesticity as an ideology designed to enlist women in their own oppression will be more fully developed later. For now the important thing is how Sears mobilized domesticity's critique of possessive individualism against women.

One can see how domesticity's compliments add up to its critique: Women reject crass competition; they favor a friendly, cooperative, working environment over mere material advancement; they value their commitments to family over career success. Sears's argument demonstrates how domesticity's critique of possessive individualism rests on a claim that women are psychologically unsuited to the economic mainstream. All Sears did was pick this up and use it to argue that women are psychologically unsuited to work in commission sales.

Sears thus illustrates how domesticity's gendered critique of possessive individualism functions to marginalize the women who espouse it. It also shows that domesticity's power derives from its ability to make arguments about women's "choice" vaguely complimentary instead of clearly insulting. When defendants prior to *Sears* tried to mobilize the interest argument, they met with little success because their "interest" arguments so clearly mobilized racist or sexist insults. For example, the assertion in a 1976 race discrimination case that blacks lacked interest in law enforcement evidently smacked too much of a claim that blacks are lazy and shiftless or inherently not law abiding.[44] In another case, the defendant's argument that women did not need the vocational training available to men, since women choose unskilled jobs anyway also struck a jarring note.[45] In both cases, the interest argument evidently struck the courts as a blatant attempt to use against minorities the insulting stereotypes to which they traditionally have been sub-jected. Sears's lawyers succeeded because they used against women not the insults but the compliments of domesticity. Once the interest argument was linked with women's vir-tues, the trial judge and the conservative Seventh Circuit found it easier to frame com-plimentary holdings asserting that women choose their relative poverty, while framing their argument as a paean to female virtue.

If *Sears* contains some disturbing messages for relational feminists, it also contains a comforting one: that by giving up domesticity's critique of possessive individualism, they are abandoning a singularly ineffective critique. A key source of the attraction of "wom-en's voice" for feminists and other progressive thinkers is that in a society where radicals have had trouble being taken seriously, relational feminism offers a critique of capitalism that avoids the perceived stridency of traditional radical discourse. It is Marxism you can take home to mother.[46] But as *Sears* shows, this strength is also a weakness, for what domesticity offers is a singularly "domesticated" critique that accepts the notion that any-one who rejects the values of contemporary capitalism freely chooses to eschew the spoils of capitalist endeavor. As traditional radical discourse makes clear, the whole point of critiquing capitalism is to challenge the way in which wealth is created and distributed. Domesticity's critique is designed to evade the central issue of whether society should be transformed.

D. Conclusion

Lebsock offered a balanced assessment of relational feminism when she noted that the "emphasis on gender differences has great promise and great strategic risks. The risks derive from the difficulty we have in thinking in genuinely egalitarian terms. . . . The promise lies farther off."[47] With *Sears,* the risks associated with relational feminism have been played out. Moreover, I have argued that the promise of relational feminism, its critique of possessive individualism, is fundamentally flawed. Plenty of less dangerous, nongendered critiques exist to help progressives in their search for words against the resurgence of classical economic liberalism: The ongoing fascination with republicanism offers a possible alternative. Neither this approach nor traditional radical discourse—nor, for that matter, standard New Deal rhetoric—holds the pitfalls of relational feminism. Instead of rehabilitating inherently loaded stereotypes, contemporary feminists should follow through domesticity's insights into the gendered structure of American capitalism to their logical conclusion. This following section begins that process.

II. Challenging the Gendered Structure of Wage Labor

The challenge to "male norms" offered by the feminism of difference is comprised of two quite different elements. The first is the critique of "male" behavior and values, which in essence is the critique of possessive individualism. A second element is the critique of men's traditional life patterns. Like the first, this second critique has traditionally been linked with domesticity, but it need not be. In this section, I present an analysis that chal-lenges the desirability of men's traditional life patterns without linking the critique to domestic ideology.

A rejection of men's traditional life patterns entails a fundamental challenge to the structure of wage labor. In articulating such a challenge, I begin from Catharine Mac-

Kinnon's analysis of gender as a system of power relations.[48] While I disagree with many of MacKinnon's conclusions, her initial premise is a powerful one: that inequalities of power are the core feature of the gender system as we know it. MacKinnon and her followers have explored the implications of this insight primarily in the context of sexuality. Here I turn to a more conventional topic and analyze the Western wage labor system as a system of power relations that leaves women economically and socially vulnerable.

Western wage labor is premised on an ideal worker with no child care responsibilities. In this system men and women workers are allocated very different roles. Men are raised to believe they have the right and the responsibility to perform as ideal workers. Husbands as a group therefore do far less child care, and earn far more, than their wives. Women are raised with complementary assumptions. They generally feel that they are entitled to the pleasure of spending time with their children while they are small. Moreover, even upon their return to work, the near-universal tendency is to assume that women's work commitment must be defined to accommodate continuing child care responsibilities.

This gender system results in the impoverishment of women, since it leads mothers systematically to "choose" against performing as ideal workers in order to ensure that their children receive high-quality care. The phenomena that comprise the gender system today are often noted, but the way the system functions as a coherent whole remains largely hidden. The following analysis will show how the impoverishment of women upon divorce, the feminization of poverty, and, to some extent, the wage gap between men and women are all parts of a dynamic that leads to the systematic impoverishment of women.

Before the Industrial Revolution, both men and women engaged in economic production, and though women were viewed as inferior, a certain fluidity existed between men's and women's roles.[49] This situation changed with the shift from task-oriented to time-disciplined labor in the late eighteenth century. By the nineteenth century, men's and women's roles were sharply differentiated. Under the new gender system, married women ordinarily experienced utter financial dependence on their husbands, though a divorceless society protected wives from destitution so long as they stayed with their husbands and—perhaps more to the point—their husbands stayed with them.

This gendered division of labor had a certain logic during the colonial era, when the average white woman got pregnant once every twenty-four months, and had an average of more than seven live births. In addition, childbirth was hazardous and frequently incapacitated women for substantial periods. Marriage made biological reproduction a full-time job for most married women, even assuming that the household did not produce what it consumed, which many households did.[50] Under these conditions the blanket assumption that married women were not suitable for life-long careers of time-disciplined labor may not have been far from the truth.

Since colonial times, childbirth has become safer and birthrates have fallen precipitously, yet the structure of wage labor remains unchanged. Meanwhile, divorce rates have risen at an astonishing rate. In 1870, 8 percent of marriages ended in divorce; today, 48 percent of all marriages do, and half of all American children will experience family disruption by age eighteen.[51] This has created a new dynamic within the traditional gender system that makes the system more repressive than at any other time in its history. While women are keeping their side of the gender bargain, by "choosing" to marginalize themselves economically in order to allow their husbands to perform as ideal workers, many men no longer are honoring their commitment to support their mates and children. Divorced men in massive numbers pay little or no alimony or child support. Under these conditions, women's choice to eschew "ideal worker" status for the sake of their children often leads to impoverishment of their children as well as themselves.

The impoverishment of previously married women parallels the pattern among single mothers. With the breakdown of sexual taboos, increasing numbers of mothers are never married to the fathers of their children. These unwed fathers tend to play even less of a role in financial support of their children than do divorced fathers.

The wage gap, a third crucial element in the feminization of poverty, also appears to stem in part from the gendered distribution of wage labor and child care responsibility.[52] Economists employing "human capital" theory have argued that the wage gap is attributable not to discrimination but to women's choices.[53] One study has estimated that roughly half of the wage gap between men and women is attributable to factors that, upon inspection, relate to women's child care responsibilities. These factors include differences in work experience, work continuity, and ability to work full time and during illnesses of the worker or other family members. (Note that even were we to agree that women "choose" disproportionate child care responsibilities, human capital theorists themselves implicitly acknowledge that such choices cannot account for all of the wage gap. Their own estimates leave 55 percent of the wage gap unexplained. This percentage may reflect discrimination.[54]

In fact, both discrimination against women and women's "choices" must be seen as elements of an integrated system of power relations that systematically disadvantages women. Women's choices show the system's success in persuading women to buy into their own economic marginalization. Openly discriminatory treatment based on the notion that "women should stay at home" shows how gender ideology serves to police the gender system by eliminating options that would loosen the grip of gender roles. In sum, women's choices show how women perpetuate the gender system themselves; discrimination shows how others join them in policing the gender system.

The impoverishment of women that results from the current gender system has been well documented. Lenore Weitzman has shown that women experience a 73 percent decline in their standard of living in the year after divorce; men experience a concomitant 42 percent rise in living standards.[55] Statistics on the feminization of poverty also are well known. Three out of every five people with incomes below the poverty line are women.[56] Three-fourths of all black families below the poverty line are headed by women. Two out of every three poor elderly people are women.[57] Almost one in three female-headed households is poor; only about one in eighteen male-headed households is.[58] The average income of female-headed families is less than half that of male-headed families. Moreover, families composed of women and children are ten times more likely to stay poor than are families where a male is present.

The feminization of poverty reflects the way the gendered labor system invented at the time of the Industrial Revolution has adapted to modern conditions. In a world where many more women than ever before are raising children without significant financial assistance from men, the gender system has taken on a more repressive dynamic than at any time since its invention.

Why is this so difficult to see? In large part because of the ideology that women's disadvantaged position results from choices made by women themselves. Alexis de Tocqueville offered an early version of this argument over a century ago.

> In America, a woman loses her independence forever in the bonds of matrimony. While there is less constraint on girls there than anywhere else, a wife submits to stricter

obligations. For the former, her father's house is a home of freedom and pleasure; for the latter, her husband's is almost a cloister.

... [Yet, the American woman] herself has freely accepted the yoke. She suffers her new state bravely, for she has chosen it.[59]

The modern form of this argument is the contemporary celebration of women who either subordinate their careers or abandon them altogether because they "know their own priorities." "A woman shouldn't have to apologize for her priorities," said Betty Friedan in a recent interview on "sequencing," that is, women dropping out of professional life for the period when their children are young.[60] News articles on "sequencing" seem invariably to point to women such as Jeane J. Kirkpatrick, Sandra Day O'Connor, and D.C. Circuit Chief Judge Patricia Wald, each of whom took from five to fifteen years off to stay home with young children. Only occasionally do these articles note that such women are the exception. I suspect most women would take years off their careers if they could be guaranteed that upon their return they could become an ambassador to the United Nations, a Supreme Court Justice, or a D.C. Circuit Court Judge—just as many men (and women) would take time off for a stint as an artist, a carpenter, or a ski bum if they could be offered the same assurance. But most "sequencers" are not so lucky. In the words of one company executive, "From a total career standpoint, anyone has to realize the realities of a big hiatus in their career—that it is certainly going to slow it down."[61] (And this executive worked for a company that is actively seeking to hire reentering women—what do the executives of companies say who refuse to hire such women?)

There is growing evidence that a career hiatus, at least in some professions, does not merely slow women down but places them permanently in a second-class, relatively low-paid "mommy track." This development has received particular attention in the law. One recent article notes the "frightening possibility" that law firms will evolve into institutions "top-heavy with men and childless women, supported by a pink-collar ghetto of mommy-lawyers," often with permanent associate status.[62]

The professional who removes herself from the fast track is only part of the syndrome by which women systematically "choose" economic marginalization. Probably the more important aspect of the phenomenon is the tendency among women to select jobs that will allow them to fulfill their "family responsibilities," even if such jobs pay less and offer less opportunity for advancement.

These two phenomena are an integral part of the economic marginalization of women. Decoded, the current talk about women's priorities is a translation into new language of domesticity's old argument that women's values lead them to make different choices. The persistence of this classic argument makes it imperative for feminists to analyze why the argument has abiding persuasiveness. The approach most useful to an analysis of women's "choice" is Antonio Gramsci's concept of cultural hegemony.[63] Gramsci painted a complex picture of how the dominant culture rules with the consent of the governed by shaping a "hegemony" of values, norms, perceptions, and beliefs that "helps mark the boundaries of permissible discourse, discourages the clarification of social alternatives, and makes it difficult for the dispossessed to locate the source of their unease, let alone remedy it."[64]

Gramsci's thought suggests that feminists can approach women's culture as a system of cultural hegemony. Marxist feminists have long argued that domesticity is a capitalist tool to privatize the costs of workers at the expense of women for the benefit of the employers. Gramsci's analysis offers needed subtlety by focusing on the complexities surrounding women's consent. For Gramsci consent is a complex state fraught with ambiguities, a "'contradictory consciousness' mixing approbation and apathy, resistance and resignation."[65]

Gramsci's analysis of consent suggests that feminists must come to terms with the ways in which women's culture has served to enlist women's support in perpetuating existing power relations. As historian T. J. Jackson Lears has expressed it:

> The idea that less powerful folk may be unwitting accomplices in the maintenance of existing inequalities runs counter to much of the social and cultural historiography of the last fifteen years, which has stressed the autonomy and vitality of subordinate cultures. Discovering nearly inexhaustible resources for resistance to domination, many social historians have been reluctant to acknowledge the possibility that their subjects may have been muddled by assimilation to the dominant culture—perhaps even to the point of believing and behaving against their own best interests.[66]

Women's historians and other feminists have illustrated this reluctance. In their effort to do justice to the dignity of women, they resoundingly rejected the image of women as victims, and instead have celebrated women's "nearly inexhaustible resources for resistance." Now that this refusal to see women as victims has been transposed into a blame-the-victim argument through the rhetoric of choice, there is an acute need for a more balanced view of women's culture. A balanced perspective could be achieved by synthesizing two distinct periods of women's history that thus far have remained remarkably resistant to such synthesis.

Before the mid-1970s, many women's historians concentrated on documenting how domesticity cramped women's lives. This early focus on how domesticity oppressed women was replaced after 1975 by a revisionist movement initiated by Carroll Smith-Rosenberg's influential article entitled *The Female World of Love and Ritual: Relations Between Women in Nineteenth-Century America.*[67] Smith-Rosenberg's article began a celebration of nineteenth-century women's culture, as historians explored the close emotional ties as well as the empowering aspects of women's separate sphere. This literature, which developed simultaneously with Gilligan's feminism and echoed its celebration of women's different voice, takes on new meaning when it is combined with the earlier literature documenting the oppressive aspects of nineteenth-century women's culture. To put it bluntly, women's rich emotional relationships in their disempowered sphere and the seductive compliments of domesticity—in particular, the notion that women were more moral than men—encouraged women to "choose" their own repression. This analysis need not deny the positive elements of women's culture. But it does demonstrate the need to assess how those positive elements sought to enlist women in their own oppression, and the extent to which that effort has been successful. *Sears* showed how traditionalist judges can use women's culture against women. The more troubling question is the extent to which women use it against themselves, as they do every time a woman "chooses" to subordinate her career "for the good of the family" and congratulates herself on that choice as a mature assessment of her own "priorities."

Feminists need to arm women to resist the argument that women's economic marginalization is the product of their own choice. Challenging this argument should be easy, since, in fact, in our deeply gendered system men and women face very different choices indeed. Whereas women, in order to be ideal workers, have to choose not to fulfill their "family responsibilities," men do not. The question women ask themselves is this: Should

I make professional sacrifices for the good of my children? In order for the wife's "choice" to be equivalent to her husband's, she would first have to be in a position to ask herself whether or not she would choose to be an ideal worker if her husband would choose to stay home with the children. Second, she would have to pose the question in a context where powerful social norms told her he was peculiarly suited to raising children. When we speak of women's "choices" to subordinate their careers, we are so blinded by gender prescriptions that we can forget that the husband's decision to be an ideal worker rests upon the assumption that his wife will choose not to be in order to allow him that privilege. This is true whether the wife eschews a career altogether or whether (in the modern pattern) she merely subordinates her career to child care responsibilities. The point is that the husband is doing neither. Women know that if they do not sacrifice, no one will, whereas men assume that if they do not, women will.

Thus women do not enjoy the same choices as men. But the underlying point is a deeper one: that society is structured so that everyone, regardless of sex, is limited to two unacceptable choices—men's traditional life patterns or economic marginality. Under the current structure of wage labor, people are limited to being ideal workers, which leaves them with inadequate time to devote to parenting, and being primary parents condemned to relative poverty (if they are single parents) or economic vulnerability (if they are currently married to an ideal worker). Wage labor does not have to be structured in this way.

The increasing onerousness of the gender system makes a challenge to the structure of wage labor a priority of the highest order. Moreover, a historic opportunity exists for a challenge: the current revolution in wage labor itself.

This revolution is not that women work; women have always worked. The change is that the majority of mothers now engage in wage labor. In 1890, only 2.5 percent of married white women did so, but 59 percent of married women do today, including 51 percent of those with children under three, and 54 percent of those with children under six.[68] Not only have married women gone out to work, but the social taboos against such work, a crucial policing mechanism of domestic ideology, also are disappearing. The shift in the traditional assumption that mothers will not work outside the home is encapsulated in the recent welfare reforms.[69]

This massive shift in the gendered distribution of wage labor has produced intense pressures to challenge the assumption that the ideal worker has no child care responsibilities. But this pressure is being evaded by a cultural decision to resolve the conflicts between home and work where they have always been resolved: on the backs of women. In the nineteenth century, married women "chose" total economic dependence in order to fulfill family responsibilities. Today, many women with children continue to make choices that marginalize them economically in order to fulfill those same responsibilities, through part-time work, "sequencing," the "mommy track," or "women's work." In each case, the career patterns that accommodate women's child care responsibilities often are ones that hurt women's earning potential.

Day care, widely assumed to be the key to incorporating mothers into the labor force, is part of the emerging gender system that reinforces women's traditional condemnation to the margins of economic life, for even mothers with day care cannot truly perform as ideal workers. The ideal worker is one who can work a minimum of forty hours a week and has no career interruptions (such as time out for childbirth, infant care, or care of the sick) and who can do the things required for "normal" career advancement—which frequently include the ability to work overtime and the willingness to travel and (for white-collar jobs) to be transferred to a different city. Employers are taught they can expect this, but mothers cannot fulfill this career profile even with most types of day care—the single exception may be the mother with a full-time housekeeper, a solution available only to the relatively rich.

The child care options available to the great bulk of workers often require someone to take time from work when the child or the caretaker is sick or for other appointments that must take place during business hours. Moreover, many day care centers and many family care situations offer sharply limited hours that do not accommodate many employers' requirements for overtime work. So long as mothers systematically take up the slack, the traditional gender system will not change: Mothers will remain at the margins of economic life. And 85 percent of all working women are likely to become mothers during their working years.

Women can work without insisting on a redefinition of the ideal worker, but most can do so only at the cost of failing to fulfill the ideal. This is not happening. Consequently, what we are seeing today is the adjustment of the gender system to these new conditions in a way that ensures women's continued relegation to the margins of economic life. We are living through a reinvention of the gender system, when we as feminists should be proposing a paradigm shift that entails a redesign of wage labor to take parenting activities into account. There are three basic options for changing the status quo. One is for each individual woman to rebel against the traditional demand that she sacrifice in order for her husband to be an ideal worker. But what will that mean: that she will become the ideal worker and he will play the supportive role? This is an alternative most men would find unthinkable because they are socially conditioned to believe that the option to be an ideal worker is their birthright. Most women, moreover, would find this option unattractive because society has nourished in them the belief that it is their birthright to be able to take time off the grind and enjoy their children while they are small.

A second alternative is for both men and women to give a little, so that they share the family responsibilities that preclude ideal worker status. But then neither husband nor wife functions as an ideal worker—a risky strategy in an age of economic uncertainty.

The only remaining alternative is to challenge the structure of wage labor. Since the current structure, and the gender system of which it is a part, increasingly condemns women to poverty, this should be at the core of a feminist program.

Such a program would build upon many reforms that currently exist. These include programs such as day care, flex time, and four-day workweeks, organized labor contracts that provide for unconditional personal days that can be used for care of sick children, as well as paid maternity leave (for the physical disability associated with childbirth) and parental leave. More sweeping proposals are those offered by noted child care specialists Benjamin Spock and Penelope Leach[70] and by noted economist Heidi Hartmann, who advocates a six-hour workday for all workers.[71]

Feminists' goal must be to redesign wage labor to take account of reproduction. Such a goal today seems utopian—but then the eight-hour work day seemed utopian in the mid-nineteenth century. The notion that the wage-labor system should take account of the human life cycle has always faced the argument that such "private costs" as aging or raising children are of no concern to employers. Even in the United States, this view has been successfully challenged: Old age is now acknowledged as a reality, and wage-labor expectations have been modified accordingly. That, too, once seemed a utopian goal. But expectations change: Hegemony is never complete. Feminists should begin to work both toward cultural change and toward the kind of small, incremental steps that will gradually modify the wage-labor system to acknowledge the reality of society's reproductive needs.

III. Refocusing the Debate

This section pursues two themes that will be crucial in refocusing the debate within feminism away from the destructive battle between "sameness" and "difference" toward a deeper understanding of gender as a system of power relations. I first argue that despite the force of Catharine MacKinnon's insight that gender involves disparities of power, her rejection of the traditional feminist ideal of gender neutrality rests on misconceptions about this traditional goal, whose core aim is to oppose rules that institutionalize a correlation between gender and sex. Thus the traditional goal is not one of gender blindness; the goal instead is to deinstitutionalize gender, a long and arduous process that first requires us to see through the seductive descriptions of men and women offered by domesticity. I conclude the chapter by arguing that to the extent these descriptions offer an accurate description of gender differences, they merely reflect the realities of the oppressive gender system. Beyond that, the description is unconvincing.

A. From Gender Neutrality to Deinstitutionalizing Gender

"Sameness" feminists' focus on the similarities between individual men and individual women led them to advocate "gender-neutral" categories that do not rely on gender stereotypes to differentiate between men and women. Recent feminists have challenged the traditional goal of gender neutrality on the grounds that it mandates a blindness to gender that has left women in a worse position than they were before the mid-twentieth-century challenge to gender roles.

This argument has been made in two different ways. Scholars such as Martha Fineman have argued that liberal feminists' insistence on gender neutrality in the formulation of "no-fault" divorce laws has led to courts' willful blindness to the ways in which marriage systematically helps men's, and hurts women's, careers.[72] Catharine MacKinnon has generalized this argument. She argues that because women are systematically disadvantaged by their sex, properly designed remedial measures can legitimately be framed by reference to sex.[73]

MacKinnon's "inequality approach" would allow for separate standards for men and women so long as "the policy or practice in question [does not] integrally contribute[] to the maintenance of an underclass or a deprived position because of gender status."[74] The strongest form her argument takes is that adherence to gender roles disadvantages women: Why let liberal feminists' taboo against differential treatment of women eliminate the most effective solution to inequality?

This debate is graced by a core truth and massive confusion. The core truth is that an insistence on gender neutrality by definition precludes protection for women victimized by gender.

The confusion stems from the use of the term *gender neutrality*. One could argue that problems created by the gendered structure of wage labor, or other aspects of the gender system, should not be remedied through the use of categories that identify the protected group by reference to the gender roles that have disadvantaged them. For example, one could argue that workers whose careers were disadvantaged by choices in favor of child care should not be given the additional support they need to "catch up" with their former spouses, on the grounds that the group protected inevitably would be mostly female, and this could reinforce the stereotype that women need special protections. Yet I know of no feminist of any stripe who makes this argument, which would be the position of someone committed to gender neutrality.

Traditionally, feminists have insisted not upon a blindness to gender, but on opposition to the traditional correlation between sex and gender. MacKinnon's crucial divergence is that she accepts the use of sex as a proxy for gender. Thus MacKinnon sees nothing inherently objectionable about protecting workers who have given up ideal worker status due to child care responsibilities by offering protections to women. Her inequality approach allows disadvantages produced by gender to be remedied by reference to sex. This is in effect an acceptance and a reinforcement of the societal presumption that the social role of primary caretaker is necessarily correlated with possession of a vagina.

MacKinnon's approach without a doubt would serve to reinforce and to legitimize gender stereotypes that are an integral part of the increasingly oppressive gender system. Let's focus on a specific example. Scholars have found that the abolition of the maternal presumption in child custody decisions has had two deleterious impacts on women.[75] First, in the 90 percent of the cases where mothers received custody, mothers often find themselves bargaining away financial claims in exchange for custody of the children. Even if the father does not want custody, his lawyer often will advise him to claim it in order to have a bargaining chip with which to bargain down his wife's financial claims. Second, the abolition of the maternal preference has created situations where a father who wants custody often wins even if he was not the primary caretaker prior to the divorce— on the grounds that he can offer the children a better life because he is richer than his former wife. In these circumstances, the ironic result of a mother's sacrifice of ideal worker status for the sake of her children is that she ultimately loses the children.

While these results are no doubt infuriating, do they merit a return to a maternal presumption, as MacKinnon's approach seems to imply? No: The deconstruction of gender, by highlighting the chronic and increasing oppressiveness of the gender system, demonstrates the undesirability of the inequality approach, which would reinforce the gender system in both a symbolic way and a practical one. On a symbolic level, the inequality approach would reinforce and legitimize the traditional assumption that childrearing is "naturally" the province of women. MacKinnon's rule also would reinforce gender mandates in a very concrete way. Say a father chose to give up ideal worker status in order to undertake primary child care responsibility. MacKinnon's rule fails to help him because the rule is framed in terms of biology, not gender. The result: a strong message to fathers that they should not deviate from established gender roles. MacKinnon's rule operates to reinforce the gender system.

What we need, then, is a rule that avoids the traditional correlation between gender and sex, a rule that is sex- but not gender neutral. The traditional goal, properly understood, is really one of sex neutrality, or, more descriptively, one of deinstitutionalizing gender. It entails a systematic refusal to institutionalize gender in any form. This approach mandates not an enforced blindness to gender but, rather, a refusal to reinforce the traditional assumption that adherence to gender roles flows "naturally" from biological sex. Reinforcing that assumption reinforces the grip of the gender system as a whole.

For an example that highlights the distinction between gender neutrality and deinstitutionalization, let us return to our "divorce revolution" example. It is grossly unfair for courts suddenly to pretend that gender roles within marriage do not exist once a couple enters the courtroom, and the deinstitutionalization of gender does not require it. What is needed is not a gender-neutral rule but one that avoids the traditional shorthand of addressing gender by reference to sex.

This analysis shows that the traditional commitment, which is really one to deinstitutionalizing gender rather than to gender neutrality, need not preclude rules that protect people victimized by gender. People disadvantaged by gender can be protected by properly naming the group: in this case, not mothers but anyone who has eschewed ideal worker status to fulfill child care responsibilities. One court, motivated to clear thinking by a legislature opposed to rules that addressed gender disabilities by reference to sex, has actually framed child custody rules in this way.[76]

The traditional goal is misstated by the term *gender neutrality*. The core feminist goal is not one of pretending gender does not exist. Instead, it is to deinstitutionalize the gendered structure of our society. There is no reason why people disadvantaged by gender need to be suddenly disowned. The deconstruction of gender allows us to protect them by reference to their social roles instead of their genitals.

B. Deconstructing Difference

How can this be done? Certainly the hardest task in the process of deconstructing gender is to begin the long and arduous process of seeing through the descriptions of men and women offered by domesticity. Feminists need to explain exactly how the traditional descriptions of men and women are false. This is a job for social scientists, for a new Carol Gilligan in reverse, who can focus the massive literature on sex stereotyping in a way that dramatizes that Gilligan is talking about metaphors, not actual people. Nonetheless, I offer some thoughts on Gilligan's central imagery: that women are focused on relationships, while men are not. As I see it, to the extent this is true, it is merely a restatement of male and female gender roles under the current gender system. Beyond that, it is unconvincing.

This is perhaps easiest to see from Gilligan's description of men as empty vessels of capitalist virtues—competitive and individualistic and espousing liberal ideology to justify this approach to life. Gilligan's description has an element of truth as a description of gender: It captures men's sense of entitlement to ideal worker status and their gendered choice in favor of their careers when presented with the choice society sets up between child care responsibilities and being a "responsible" worker.

Similarly, Gilligan's central claim that women are more focused on relationships reflects gender verities. It is true in the sense that women's lives are shaped by the needs of their children and their husbands—but this is just a restatement of the gender system that has traditionally defined women's social existence in terms of their husbands' need to eliminate child care and other responsibilities that detract from their ability to function as ideal workers. And when we speak of women's focus on relationships with men, we also reflect the underlying reality that the only alternative to marriage for most women— certainly for most mothers—has traditionally been poverty, a state of affairs that continues in force to this day.

The kernel of truth in Gilligan's "voices," then, is that Gilligan provides a description of gender differences related to men's and women's different roles with respect to wage labor and child care under the current gender regime. Yet we see these true gender differences through glasses framed by an ideology that distorts our vision. To break free of traditional gender ideology, we need at the simplest level to see how men nurture people and relationships and how women are competitive and powerful. This is a task in which we as feminists will meet considerable resistance, both from inside and outside the feminist movement.

Our difficulty in seeing men's nurturing side stems in part from the word *nurture.* Although its broadest definition is "the act of promoting development or growth,"[77] the word derives from nursing a baby, and still has overtones of "something only a mother can do." Yet men are involved in all kinds of relationships in which they promote another's development in a caring way: as fathers, as mentors, as camp counselors, as boy scout leaders. These relationships may have a somewhat different emotional style and tone than do those of women and often occur in somewhat different contexts: That is the gender difference. But a blanket assertion that women are nurturing while men are not reflects more ideology than reality.

So does the related claim that women's voice involves a focus on relationships that is lacking in men. Men focus on relationships, too. How they can be said not to in a culture that deifies romantic love as much as ours does has always mystified me. Perhaps part of what resonates in the claim that men do not focus on relationships is that men as a group tend to have a different style than do women: Whereas women tend to associate intimacy with self-disclosure, men tend not to.[78] This may be why women forget about the role that relationships play in men's lives, from work relationships, to solidarity based on spectator sports, to time spent "out with the boys." These relationships may not look intimate to women, but they are often important to men.

Ideology not only veils men's needy side, it also veils the competitive nature of many women who want power as avidly as men. "Feminists have long been fiercely critical of male power games, yet we have often ignored or concealed our own conflicts over money, control, position, and recognition. . . . It is time to end the silence.[79] The first step, as these authors note, is to acknowledge the existence of competition in women's lives. Women's desire for control may be exercised in running "a tight ship" on a small income, in tying children to apron strings, or in nagging husbands—the classic powerplay of the powerless. Note how these examples tend to deprecate women's desire for power. These are the stereotypes that come to mind because they confirm the ideology that "real" women don't need power. These are ways women's yearning for power has been used as evidence against them, as evidence they are not worthy as wives, as mothers, or as women. Feminists' taboo against competition has only reinforced the traditional view that real women don't need power. Yet women's traditional roles have always required them to be able to wield power with self-confidence and subtlety. Other cultures recognize that dealing with a two-year-old is one of the great recurring power struggles in the cycle of human life. But not ours. We are too wrapped up in viewing child rearing as nurturing, as something opposed by its nature to authoritative wielding of power, to see that nurturing involves a sophisticated use of power in a hierarchical relationship. The differences between being a boss and a mother in this regard are differences in degree as well as in kind.

Moving ever closer to the bone, we need to reassess the role of power in relationships based on romantic love. The notion that a marriage involves complex ongoing negotiations over power may seem shocking. But if we truly are committed to a deconstruction of traditional gender verities, we need to stop blinding ourselves to nurturing outside the home and to power negotiations within it.

Conclusion

The first message of this chapter is that feminists uncomfortable with relational feminism cannot be satisfied with their conventional response: "When we get a voice, we don't all say the same thing." The traditional focus on how individuals diverge from gender stereotypes fails to come to terms with gender similarities of women as a group. I have tried to present an alternative response. By taking gender seriously, I have reached conclusions very different from those of the relational feminists. I have not argued that gender differences do not exist; only that relational feminists have misdescribed them.

Relational feminism, I have argued, can best be understood as encompassing two critiques: the critique of possessive individualism and the critique of absolutes. Both are better stated in nongendered terms, though for different reasons. Feminists are simply incorrect when they claim the critique of absolutes as women's voice, since that critique has been developed by men and its ideal is different from the traditional stereotype of women as emotional and illogical.

Relational feminism's linkage of women to the critique of possessive individualism is trickier. If all relational feminists claim is that elite white men are disproportionately likely to buy more completely into the ideology that controls access to wealth, in one sense this is true. I would take it on faith that a higher proportion of elite white males buy into possessive individualism than do black males, working-class and poor males, or women of all groups. Indeed, in the last twenty years writers have documented that these marginalized groups have developed their own cultures that incorporate critiques of mainstream culture. "One very important difference between white people and black people is that white people think you are your work," a black informant told an anthropologist in the 1970s. "Now a black person has more sense than that."[80] Marginalized groups necessarily have maintained a more critical perspective on possessive individualism in general, and the value of wage labor in particular, than did white males who had most to gain by taking the culture's dominant ideology seriously. Moreover, the attitude of white women towards wage labor reflects their unique relationship with it. Traditionally, married white women, even many working-class women, had a relationship to wage labor that only a very few leisured men have ever had: These women viewed wage labor as something that had to prove its worth in their lives because the option not to work remained open to them psychologically (if, at times, not economically).

Fewer blacks and women have made the virtues of possessive individualism a central part of their self-definition, and this is a powerful force for social change. But blacks as a group and women as a group have these insights not because they are an abiding part of "the" black family or of women's "voice." These are insights black culture and women's culture bring from their history of exclusion. We want to preserve the insights but abandon the marginalization that produced them: to become part of a mainstream that learns from our experience. The *Sears* case shows how these insights' transformative potential can easily backfire if the critiques can be marginalized as constitutive of a semipermanent part of the black or female personality.

Relational feminists help diffuse the transformative potential of the critique of possessive individualism by championing a gendered version of that critique. The simple answer is that they should not say they are talking about women if they admit they aren't. Once they admit they are talking about gender, they have to come to terms with domesticity's hegemonic role in enlisting women in their own oppression.

The approach of deconstructing gender requires women to give up their claims to special virtue. But it offers ample compensation. It highlights the fact that women will be vulnerable until we redesign the social ecology, starting with a challenge to the current structure of wage labor. The current structure may not have been irrational in the eighteenth century, but it is irrational today. Challenging it today should be at the core of a feminist program.

The message that women's position will remain fundamentally unchanged until labor is restructured is both a hopeful and a depressing one. It is depressing because it shows that women will remain economically vulnerable in the absence of fundamental societal change. Yet it is hopeful because if we heed it, we may be able to unite as feminists to seize the opportunity offered by mothers' entry into the work force, instead of frittering it away rediscovering traditional (and inaccurate) descriptions of gender differences.

Notes

Special thanks to James X. Dempsey and Suzanne Lebsock, and to others who have read and commented on drafts of this chapter: Ann E. Freeman, Wendy W. Williams, Lena S. Zezulin, and the members of the Maryland/D.C. Feminist Theory Reading Group. Thanks also for the comments offered when the chapter was presented at the Georgetown University Law Center Faculty Speaker Series. Finally, I would like to thank Thomas Grasso, Rosemarie Kelley, Doris Masse, and Daphne Srinivasin for expert research assistance and the editors of the Michigan Law Review. I would also like to acknowledge the help given me by Alice Kessler-Harris, Rosalind Rosenberg, the law firm of Morgan Associates, Chartered, and by Karen Baker and James Scanlon of the Equal Employment Opportunity Commission.

1. B. FRIEDAN, THE FEMININE MYSTIQUE (1963). For a discussion of the breadth of the resurgence of feminism in the 1960s, see THE NEW FEMINISM IN TWENTIETH-CENTURY AMERICA (J. Sochen ed. 1971). It should be noted that Friedan has substantially changed her focus. *See* B. FRIEDAN, THE SECOND STAGE 38–41, 83–87 (1981).

2. Comments of Paul J. Spiegelman, *James McCormick Mitchell Lecture: Feminist Discourse, Moral Values, and the Law—A Conversation,* 34 BUFFALO L. REV. 36 (1985).

3. 628 F. Supp. 1264 (N.D. Ill. 1986), *affd.,* 839 F.2d 302 (7th Cir. 1988).

4. Some influential feminists have denied the importance of the distinction between sex and gender by arguing in effect that most (or all) of the important differences between men and women are biological as opposed to social.

5. C. GILLIGAN, IN A DIFFERENT VOICE 24–63 (1982). Gilligan is only the most famous of the scholars who have defined gender in psychological terms. Her findings parallel, and presumably were influenced by, the work of Jean Baker Miller, *see* J. B. MILLER, TOWARD A NEW PSYCHOLOGY OF WOMEN (2d ed. 1986); *see also* N. CHODOROW, THE REPRODUCTION OF MOTHERING: PSYCHOANALYSIS AND THE SOCIOLOGY OF GENDER (1978). All three authors focus in different ways on "connectedness" as a crucial (if not the crucial) gender difference. *See* C. GILLIGAN, at 8–9; J. B. MILLER, at 83, 148, n.1; N. CHODOROW, at 90–91, 167–70, 178–79. But only Chodorow seems clearly to recognize that what she is talking about is the psychological construction of gender and its costs for women *(id.* at 213–19).

It is important to place Gilligan's work into historical context. Though I take issue with her conclusions about women's voice, I endorse her fundamental motivation, namely, to reverse the previous practice of ignoring women altogether or treating any differences between men and women as reflecting women's inadequacy. Gilligan's primary contribution was to articulate a modern challenge to "male norms."

6. *See* C. GILLIGAN, at 19–21, 64–66, 70–71, 82–83.

7. *See, e.g.,* Scales, *The Emergence of Feminist Jurisprudence: An Essay,* 95 YALE L.J. 1373 (1986); Matsuda, *Liberal Jurisprudence and Abstracted Visions of Human Nature: A Feminist Critique of Rawls' Theory of Justice,* 16 N. MEX. L. REV. 613 (1986).

8. *See, e.g.,* M. DALY, PURE LUST xii, 4–7 (1984); M. DALY, GYN/ECOLOGY 220–22 (1978). The French feminists combine elements of domesticity with elements of this earlier image of women. *See, e.g.,* L. IRIGARAY, THIS SEX WHICH IS NOT ONE 29, 208–11 (1985).

9. For an introduction, see A. FRASER, THE WEAKER VESSEL 1–6 (1984); N. COTT, THE BONDS OF WOMANHOOD: "WOMAN'S SPHERE" IN NEW ENGLAND, 1780–1835, at 201–4 (1977).

10. C. KARLSEN, THE DEVIL IN THE SHAPE OF A WOMAN 154–81 (1987); J. DEMOS, ENTERTAINING SATAN 60–64, 197–209, 394–95 (1982);

11. *See generally* A. JAGGAR, FEMINIST POLITICS AND HUMAN NATURE 364–84 (1983); A FEMINIST PERSPECTIVE IN THE ACADEMY (E. Langland and W. Gove eds. 1981); S. HARDING, THE SCIENCE QUESTION IN FEMINISM (1986); C. MCMILLAN, WOMEN, REASON, AND NATURE (1982); Vickers, *Memoirs of an Ontological Exile: The Methodological Rebellions of Feminist Research,* in FEMINISM IN CANADA: FROM PRESSURE TO POLITICS (G. Ginn and A. Miles eds. 1982).

12. *See* Williams, *Critical Legal Studies: The Death of Transcendence and the Rise of the New Langdells,* 62 N.Y.U. L. REV. 429 (1987).

13. The most sophisticated of the feminist scholars who link traditional rationalism with males is the historian of science (a scientist herself) Evelyn Fox Keller. *See* E. F. KELLER, REFLECTIONS ON GENDER AND SCIENCE 61–65 (1985). Keller convincingly argues that the ideology of science developed as part and parcel of a new gender system in the early modern era. But this does not establish, as she and others seem to assume, that the new epistemology (which is a critique of that system of science in the sense that science built upon the tenets of traditional epistemology) is "female" in any meaningful sense.

14. *See, e.g.,* Scales, at 1374, n.3.

15. *See* Baker, *The Domestication of Politics: Women and American Political Society, 1780–1920,* 89 AM. HIST. REV. 620 (1984); N. COTT.

16. Offen, *Defining Feminism: A Comparative Approach,* 14 SIGNS: J. WOMEN CULTURE & SOCY. 119, 135 (1988).

17. S. LEBSOCK, THE FREE WOMEN OF PETERSBURG: STATUS AND CULTURE IN A SOUTHERN TOWN, 1784–1860 (1984), at 142–43. Lebsock won the prestigious Bancroft Prize for this work.

18. Conversation between Carol Gilligan and Catharine MacKinnon, Mitchell Lecture Series, State University of New York at Buffalo School of Law (Nov. 20, 1984), *reprinted in A Conversation,* at 11.

19. K. FERGUSON, The Feminist Case Against Bureaucracy 56 (1984).

20. Menkel-Meadow, Portia in a Different Voice, 1 BERK. W.L.J. 43 (1985).

21. *See* West, *Jurisprudence and Gender,* 55 U. Chi. L. Rev. 1 (1988) at 65.

22. S. LEBSOCK, at 144.

23. *See* N. NODDINGS, caring (1984).

24. E. WOLGAST, Equality and The Rights of Women 156 (1980).

25. Comments of Paul J. Spiegelman, *A Conversation,* at 36.

26. Smith, *Family Limitation, Sexual Control, and Domestic Feminism in Victorian America,* in A HERITAGE OF HER OWN, at 222, 238–39.

27. N. COTT, at 67–68; *see also* C. LASCH, HAVEN IN A HEARTLESS WORLD: THE FAMILY BESIEGED (1977).

28. C. GILLIGAN, at 17, 62–63, 100.

29. *Id.* at 35, 79.

30. *Id.* at 2. This is a standard disclaimer. *See, e.g.,* Menkel-Meadow, at 41. But the disclaimer does not solve the underlying problem.

31. 628 F. Supp. 1264 (N.D. Ill. 1986), *aff'd.,* 839 F.2d 302 (7th Cir. 1988).

32. This argument was made most clearly through the testimony of Rosalind Rosenberg. *See* Offer of Proof Concerning the Testimony of Dr. Rosalind Rosenberg at paras. 11, 16–22, *EEOC v. Sears* (no. 79-C-4373). Sear's testimony at times made it seem that all women prefer part-time work.

33. *See id.* at paras. 16–22. Another Title VII defendant successfully used a similar interest argument in EEOC v. General Tel. Co. of Northwest, Inc., 40 Fair Empl. Prac. Cas. (BNA) 1533 (W.D. Wash. 1985), *affd.,* 45 Fair Empl. Prac. Cas. (BNA) 1888 (9th Cir. 1988) (unpublished opinion).

34. 42 U.S.C. §§ 2000e–2000e-17 (1982).

35. I'm simplifying for clarity. In individual cases, of course, what the relevant labor market is can be a subject of hot contention. *See* D. BALDUS and J. COLE, STATISTICAL PROOF OF DISCRIMINATION 44–49, 102–41 (1980).

36. Trial Transcript at 8439, Testimony of Ray Graham, EEOC v. Sears, Roebuck & Co., 628 F. Supp. 1264 (N.D. Ill. 1986) (no. 79-C-4373), *affd.,* 839 F.2d 302 (7th Cir. 1988). Graham, Sear's corporate director of equal opportunity, repeatedly expressed the opinion that some jobs (hardware, for example) have "natural appeal" for men, *id.* at 8435, while others (draperies) are "a natural" for women, *id.* at 8432. His assessments were based on assertions that women are averse to competition, *id.* at 8433, and pressure, *id.* at 8434–35.

37. Offer of Proof Concerning the Testimony of Dr. Rosalind Rosenberg, at para. 1, *EEOC v. Sears* (no. 79-C-4373).

38. *Id.* at paras. 16–22.

39. Trial Transcript at 14625–29, Testimony of Joan Haworth, *EEOC v. Sears* (no. 79-C-4373). Haworth was analyzing applications that provided a single box marked "sales" for applicants to check, without a breakdown into commission and noncommission sales. The EEOC's analysis incorporated the assumption that female applicants who checked sales and had background and experience in commission sales were interested in commission sales positions. Sears challenged this assumption by putting Haworth on the stand to testify that such women were not in fact interested in commission sales.

40. One stated, "Commission sales is exactly what I was looking for and was the reason I came to Sears and put in an application." Written Testimony of Lura L. Nader at 1, *EEOC v. Sears* (no. 79-C-4373). *See also* Written Testimony of Alice Howland at 4.

41. This arose in Sear's lawyers' analysis of Sear's Applicant Interview Guides (AIGs), in which applicants were asked to rate their interest in selling various categories of items from one to five in terms of interest, experience, and skill. In Judge Nordberg's words, "The scores were normalized to take into account that some applicants might inflate their scores to increase their chances of being hired" (628 F. Supp. at 1322). Normalization is a commonly used statistical technique, but two of EEOC's experts testified they had never seen it used as Dr. Haworth used it.

42. Trial Transcript at 16501-02, *EEOC v. Sears* (no. 79-C-4373).

43. *See* 839 F.2d at 320–21.

44. Castro v. Beecher, 334 F. Supp. 930, 936 (D. Mass. 1971).

45. Glover v. Johnson, 478 F. Supp. 1075, 1086–88 (E.D. Mich. 1979), *affd. sub nom.* Cornish v. Johnson, 774 F.2d 1161 (6th Cir. 1985), *cert. denied,* 478 U.S. 1020 (1986).
See EEOC v. Sears, 628 F. Supp. 1264, 1307–08 (N.D. Ill. 1986); 839 F.2d 302, 320–21 (7th Cir. 1988).

46. This phrase was first applied to Antonio Gramsci. *See* Romano, *But Was He a Marxist?* (Book Review), VILLAGE VOICE, March 29, 1983, at 41, *quoted in* Lears, *The Concept of Cultural Hegemony: Problems and Possibilities.* 90 AM. HIST. REV. 567 (1985).

47. S. LEBSOCK, at 144.

48. *See, e.g.,* C. MACKINNON, SEXUAL HARASSMENT OF WORKING WOMEN—A CASE OF SEX DISCRIMINATION 92, 101–29, 215–21 (1979); C. MACKINNON, FEMINISM UNMODIFIED 32–42 (1987).

49. *See* L. ULRICH, Good Wives 14–50. (1980).

50. The first figure is for women in New England. *See New England: The Little Commonwealth,* in THE LEGACIES BOOK: A COMPANION VOLUME TO THE AUDIOCOURSE LEGACIES: A HISTORY

OF WOMEN AND THE FAMILY IN AMERICA, 1607–1870, at 32 (E. Pleck and E. Rothman eds. 1987). The second figure is for all American white women. *See* J. LEAVITT, BROUGHT TO BED 14 (1986). Leavitt points out that the standard statistic refers to live births, which implies a substantially greater number of pregnancies to account for stillbirths and miscarriages.

51. L. WEITZMAN, THE DIVORCE REVOLUTION 215 (1985); U.S. DEPT. OF COMMERCE, BUREAU OF THE CENSUS, STATISTICAL ABSTRACT OF THE UNITED STATES (108th ed. Supp. 1988); U.S. DEPT. OF COMMERCE AND LABOR, BUREAU OF THE CENSUS, MARRIAGE AND DIVORCE: 1867–1906, at 13 (1909).

52. *See* WOMEN AND THE WORKPLACE: THE IMPLICATIONS OF OCCUPATIONAL SEGREGATION (M. Blaxall and B. Reagan eds. 1976); SEX SEGREGATION IN THE WORKPLACE: TRENDS, EXPLANATIONS, REMEDIES (B. Reskin ed. 1984).

53. *See* C. LLOYD and B. NIEMI, THE ECONOMICS OF SEX DIFFERENTIALS 88–150 (1979).

54. *See id.* at 204–5. *See also* R. TSUCHIGANE and N. DODGE, ECONOMIC DISCRIMINATION AGAINST WOMEN IN THE UNITED STATES 35–45 (1974).

55. L. WEITZMAN, at 337–56. *See also* Burtless, *Comments on Income for the Single Parent: Child Support, Work, and Welfare,* in GENDER IN THE WORKPLACE 263 (C. Brown and J. Pechman eds. 1987).

56. Eisenstein, *The Sexual Politics of the New Right: Understanding the "Crisis of Liberalism" for the 1980s, reprinted in* FEMINIST THEORY: A CRITIQUE OF IDEOLOGY 77 (1981).

57. Eisenstein, at 91.

58. Figures for households not headed by females are from the National Advisory Council in Economic Opportunity study, which reported that 39 percent of all female-headed households live under the poverty line. *See* Blair, at 40.

59. A. DE TOCQUEVILLE, DEMOCRACY IN AMERICA 568 (J. Mayer and M. Lerner eds. 1966).

60. *See* Rimer, Sequencing: Putting Careers on Hold, *New York Times,* September 23, 1988, at A21, col. 1.

61. Rimer.

62. Hickey, The Dilemma of Having It All, Wash. Law, May–June 1988, at 59.

63. Good introductions to Gramsci are A. GRAMSCI, SELECTIONS FROM THE PRISON NOTEBOOKS (Q. Hoare and G. Smith eds. & trans. 1971); W. ADAMSON, HEGEMONY AND REVOLUTION: A STUDY OF ANTONIO GRAMSCI'S POLITICAL AND CULTURAL THEORY (1980); J. CAMMETT, ANTONIO GRAMSCI AND THE ORIGINS OF ITALIAN COMMUNISM (1967).

64. Lears, at 569–70.

65. *Id.* at 570.

66. *Id.* at 573 (footnote omitted).

67. Smith-Rosenberg, *The Female World of Love and Ritual: Relations Between Women in Nineteenth-Century America, reprinted in* A HERITAGE OF HER OWN, at 311.

68. U.S. DEPT. OF COMMERCE, BUREAU OF THE CENSUS, STATISTICAL ABSTRACT OF THE UNITED STATES 383 (1987).

69. *See* Stevens, *The Welfare Consensus, New York Times,* June 22, 1988, at 4, col. 5.

70. "Go after our industries!" advises Dr. Spock. He recommends more flexibility in hours, six-hour work days and subsidized day care. Both Penelope Leach, a psychology Ph.D., and Dr. T. Barry Brazelton believe that current trends have potentially adverse psychological consequences for today's families. Brazelton has stressed the need for improved pay for day care workers; Leach advocates extensive paid maternity leave (six months) and part-time work by both parents (next eighteen months). *See Work and Families,* WASHINGTON PARENT 1, 3, 5, (November 1988) (report of a panel discussion in Boston, April 1988). *See also* Brazelton, *Stress for Families Today,* INFANT MENTAL HEALTH J., Spring 1988, at 65.

71. *See* Hartmann, *Achieving Economic Equity for Women,* in WINNING AMERICA: IDEAS AND LEADERSHIP FOR THE 1990s, 99 (M. Raskin and C. Hartman, eds. 1988).

72. Fineman, *Implementing Equality: Ideology, Contradiction and Social Change,* 1983 WIS. L. REV. 789, 791; Levin, at 55. *See also* Finley, at 1148–63.

73. SEXUAL HARASSMENT, at 100–41 (discussing Phillips v. Martin Marietta Corp., 400 U.S. 542 (1971); FEMINISM UNMODIFIED, at 35–36.

74. SEXUAL HARASSMENT, at 117. *See* Taub, Book Review, 80 COLUM. L. REV. 1686 (1980).

75. *See* Polikoff, *Why Mothers Are Losing: A Brief Analysis of Criteria Used in Child Custody Determinations,* 7 WOMEN'S RTS. L. REP. 235 (1982); L. WEITZMAN, at 217, 310–18.

76. *See* Garska v. McCoy, 278 S.E.2d 357, 360–63 (W. Va. 1981), *cited in* Williams, *The Equality Crisis: Some Reflections on Culture, Courts, and Feminism,* 7 WOMEN'S RTS. L. REP. 175, 190, n.80 (1982).

77. THE AMERICAN HERITAGE DICTIONARY (William Morris ed. 1970).

78. *See* Rubin and Shenker, *Friendship, Proximity, and Self-disclosure,* 46 J. PERSONALITY 1–22 (1978).

79. COMPETITION: A FEMINIST TABOO? 1 (V. Miner and H. Longino eds. 1987).

80. J. L. GWALTNEY, DRYLONGSOUL: A SELF-PORTRAIT OF BLACK AMERICA 173–74 (1981), *quoted in* S. Harley, "When Your Work Is Not Who You Are": The Development of a Working-Class Consciousness Among Afro-American Women, Paper given at the Conference on Women in the Progressive Era, sponsored by the American Historical Association in conjunction with the National Museum of American History (March 10–12, 1988).

22

The Pragmatist and the Feminist

MARGARET JANE RADIN

I want to discuss pragmatism and feminism. I undertake this project not because I have read everything considered feminist or pragmatist by its writers or readers, although I wish I had, but, rather, because I have discovered that in my own work I am speaking both of pragmatism and feminism. I desire to explore how pragmatism and feminism cohere, if they do, in my own thought, and I write with the hope that what I find useful will be useful for others as well.

I offer four interlinked short essays in which I think I am "doing" both pragmatism and feminism.* Actually writing pragmatist–feminist analysis is one way to explore the question I pose, and perhaps it is the way most in the pragmatic spirit, or at least closest to the practice side of pragmatism. There is a theory side of pragmatism too, however, and I am interested in suggesting a broader theoretical connection between feminism and pragmatism as well.

◇ ◇ ◇

II. The Perspective of Domination and the Problem of Bad Coherence

> Women's standpoint is not an ossified truth that some feminist academicians have chiseled in stone for all women to worship; rather, it is a kaleidoscope of truths, continually shaping and reshaping each other, as more and different women begin to work and think together.
>
> Rosemarie Tong[1]

> It was when I said,
> "There is no such thing as the truth,"
> That the grapes seemed fatter.
> The fox ran out of his hole.
>
> You . . . You said,
> "There are many truths,
> But they are not parts of a truth."

*[Essays II, III, and IV are reprinted here—Ed.]

> Then the tree, at night, began to change,
> Smoking through green and smoking blue.
>
> Wallace Stevens[2]

Over the past few years I have been continually struck with some points of resonance between the methodology and commitments of many who call themselves feminists and those of certain important figures in the new wave of pragmatism.[3] It now seems to me that the points of resonance between feminism and pragmatism are worthy of some exploration.

I begin with an awareness that there is something problematic about my ambition to talk theoretically about pragmatism and feminism together. I want to avoid the type of exercise that tries to define two "isms" and then compare and contrast them. Insomuch as they are lively, these "isms" resist definition. There are a number of pragmatisms. At least there are distinctive strains stemming from Peirce, James, and Dewey, and the new wave may be considered a fourth pragmatism. There are also a number of feminisms. One recent survey of feminist thought lists them as liberal, Marxist, radical, socialist, psychoanalytic, existentialist, and postmodern.[4]

One way to frame the investigation I have in mind would be to start with the question, Is feminism "really" pragmatism? (Or is pragmatism "really" feminism?) If this is the question, one way to respond to it—a way I think would be both unpragmatic and unfeminist—is to ask what commitments or characteristics are common to all the pragmatisms we are certain are pragmatisms and ask what commitments or characteristics are common to all the feminisms we are certain are feminisms. We would then see whether the feminist list includes both the necessary criteria for being pragmatist and enough or important enough criteria to be sufficient for being pragmatist or whether the pragmatist list includes the necessary and sufficient criteria for being feminist. This definitional response is a blueprint of conceptualist methodology, an abstract exercise in reification that promises little of interest to a pragmatist or a feminist.

In a more pragmatic and feminist spirit of inquiry, we might ask instead another question. Of what use might it be to think of feminism and pragmatism as allied, as interpenetrating each other? . . . I will pursue this question in various ways. In order to do so I still have to engage in some problematic cataloguing, but at least it will be easier to deal with the inescapable incompleteness of that way of seeing matters. I can explore how in some ways it might be useful to consider pragmatism and feminism together, without having to have a definite answer to the (to a pragmatist inapposite) question of what pragmatism and feminism "really are." Feminism and pragmatism are not things; they are ways of proceeding.

The pragmatists were famous for their theory of truth without the capital T—their theory that truth is inevitably plural, concrete, and provisional. John Dewey wrote, "Truth is a collection of truths; and these constituent truths are in the keeping of the best available methods of inquiry and testing as to matters-of-fact."[5] Similarly, William James wrote:

> Truth for us is simply a collective name for verification processes, just as health, wealth, strength, etc., are names for other processes connected with life, and also pursued because it pays to pursue them. Truth is *made,* just as health, wealth and strength are made, in the course of experience.[6]

Pragmatism and feminism largely share, I think, the commitment to finding knowledge in the particulars of experience.[7] It is a commitment against abstract idealism, transcendence, foundationalism, and atemporal universality and in favor of immanence, historicity, concreteness, situatedness, contextuality, embeddedness, narrativity of meaning.

If feminists largely share the pragmatist commitment that truth is hammered out piecemeal in the crucible of life and our situatedness, they also share the pragmatist understanding that truth is provisional and ever changing. Too, they also share the pragmatist commitment to concrete particulars. Since the details of our life are connected with what we know, those details matter. Thus, the pragmatist and the feminist both arrive at an embodied perspectivist view of knowledge.

It is not surprising that pragmatists have stressed embodiment more than other philosophers, or that feminists have stressed it even more. Once we understand that the details of our embodiment matter for what the world is for us (which in some pragmatist views is all the world is), then it must indeed be important that only one half of humans directly experience menstruation, pregnancy, birth, and lactation. So it is no wonder that feminists write about prostitution, contract motherhood, rape, child care, and the PMS defense. It is not just the fact that these are women's issues that makes these writings feminist—they are after all human issues—but specifically the instantiation of the perspective of female embodiment.

Another pragmatist commitment that is largely shared by feminists is the dissolution of traditional dichotomies. Pragmatists and feminists have rejected the dichotomy between thought and action or between theory and practice. John Dewey especially made this his theme, and he also rejected the dichotomies of reason and feeling, mind and body, nature and nurture, connection and separation, and means and ends.[8] In a commitment that is not, at least not yet, shared by modern pragmatists, feminists have also largely rejected the traditional dichotomy of public (man) and private (woman). For these feminists, the personal is political.[9]

One more strong resonance between the pragmatist and the feminist is in concrete methodology. The feminist commitment to learning through consciousness raising in groups can be regarded as the culmination of the pragmatist understanding that for consciousness to exist at all, there must be shared meaning arising out of shared interactions with the world. A particularly clear statement of this pragmatist position is found in Dewey's *Experience and Nature.* Dewey's treatment is suffused with the interrelationship of communication, meaning, and shared group experience. In one representative passage, Dewey says:

> The heart of language is not "expression" of something antecedent, much less expression of antecedent thought. It is communication; the establishment of cooperation in an activity in which there are partners, and in which the activity of each is modified and regulated by that partnership.[10]

The modern pragmatists' stress on conversation or dialogue stems from the same kind of understanding.

The special contribution of the methodology of consciousness raising is that it makes new meaning out of a specific type of experience, the experience of domination and oppression. In order to do so, it must make communication possible where before there was silence. In general, rootedness in the experiences of oppression makes possible the distinctive critical contribution that feminism can make to pragmatism. Feminist methodology and perspective make it possible to confront the problem of bad coherence, as I will now try to explain.

Pragmatists have tended toward coherence theories of truth and goodness.[11] Coherence theories tend toward conservativism, in the sense that when we are faced with new experiences and new beliefs, we fit them into our web with as little alteration of what is already there as possible. James said that "in this matter of belief we are all extreme conservatives." According to James, we will count a new idea as true if we can use it to assimilate a new experience to our old beliefs without disturbing them too much.

> That new idea is truest which performs most felicitously its function of satisfying our double urgency. It makes itself true, gets itself classed as true, by the way it works; grafting itself then upon the ancient body of truth, which thus grows much as a tree grows by the activity of a new layer of cambium.[12]

James also said that truth is what is good in the way of belief,[13] meaning that we should, and do, believe those things that work best in our lives.

To those whose standpoint or perspective—whose embodied contextuality—is the narrative of domination and oppression, these coherence theories raise a question that is very hard for the pragmatist to answer. It is possible to have a coherent system of belief and have that system be coherently bad?[14] Those who have lived under sexism and racism know from experience that the answer must be yes. We know we cannot argue that any given sexist decision is wrong simply because it does not fit well with all our history and institutions, for the problem is more likely that it fits only too well. Bad coherence creates the double bind. Everywhere we look we find a dominant conception of gender undermining us.

But how can the pragmatist find a standpoint from which to argue that a system is coherent but bad if pragmatism defines truth and good as coherence? Inattention to this problem is what makes pragmatism seem complacent, when it does. One answer to the problem of bad coherence, which the pragmatist will reject, is to bring back transcendence, natural law, or abstract idealism. Another answer, which the pragmatist can accept, is to take the commitment to embodied perspective very seriously indeed, and especially the commitment to the perspective of those who directly experience domination and oppression.

What this leads to, first, is either an expansive view of coherence that leaves room for broad critique of the dominant understandings and the status quo, or else, perhaps, to denial that pragmatism espouses coherence theory. Its other consequences need exploring. It seems that a primary concomitant of the commitment to perspectivism might be a serious pluralism. "We" are looking for coherence in "our" commitments, but the most important question might be, Who is "we"? A serious pluralism might begin by understanding that there can be more than one "we." One "we" can have very different conceptions of the world, selves, communities, than another. Perhaps, at least practically speaking, each "we" can have its own coherence. Dominant groups have tended to understand themselves without question as the only "we," whereas oppressed groups, simply by virtue of recognizing themselves as an oppressed group, have understood that there can be plural "we's." Perhaps, then, we should understand the perspective of the oppressed as making possible an understanding that coherence can be plural.

A serious pluralism must also find a way to understand the problem of transition, as the "we" of an oppressed group seeks to change dominant conceptions in order to make possible its own empowerment.[15] One important problem of transition is false consciousness. If the perspective of the oppressed includes significant portions of the dominant conception of the world, and of the role of the oppressed group in it, then the oppressed perspective may well be incoherent, rather than a separate coherence to be recognized as a separate "reality." If this is a useful way to view the matter, then we can say that the perspective of the oppressed struggles to make itself coherent in order to make itself real.

What leads some pragmatists into complacency and overrespect for the status quo is partly the failure to ask, Who is "we"? And what are "our" material interests? Why does it "work" for "us" to believe this? It is not necessary for pragmatists to make this mistake. Dewey, especially, understood the connection between truth, goodness, and liberation. He argued cogently that many of philosophy's earlier errors, such as belief in eternal abstract forms, were expressions of the social position of philosophers as an elite leisure class.[16] But the mistake is tempting for a pragmatist whose perspective is that of a member of the dominant group, because from that perspective it seems that one has "the" perspective. I suggest that feminism, in its pragmatic aspect, can correct this complacent tendency. The perspective of domination, and the critical ramifications it must produce once it is taken seriously, seems to be feminism's important contribution to pragmatism.

III. A Mediating Way of Thinking?

In *Pragmatism: A New Name for Some Old Ways of Thinking,*[17] William James asked us to recognize a distinction between two opposing philosophical temperaments or ways of construing the world. He labeled these characteristic habits of thought as *tender-minded* and *tough-minded.* In *In a Different Voice: Psychological Theory and Women's Development,*[18] Carol Gilligan asks us to recognize a distinction between two opposing conceptions of morality or paths of moral development. She labels these characteristic moral personalities as ethics (or ideologies) of *care* and of *justice.* Gilligan associates the ethic of care with the moral development of mature women, and the ethic of justice with the moral development of mature men. The ethic of care is the "different voice" of women.

For those who are struck with the parallels between pragmatist and feminist thought, it is tempting to associate feminism with the tender-minded prong of James's dichotomy. It is also tempting, in view of Gilligan's striking findings and our subsequent reflection upon women's culture, to associate feminism with the ethic of care prong of Gilligan's dichotomy. Both of these tempting assimilations are mistaken. Moreover, there is a great deal to be learned from understanding the way in which they are mistaken.

In order to see why it is tempting to think of feminist thought as tender-minded, consider how we might schematically understand the characteristics of the moral conceptions labeled caring and justice. The following list probably summarizes the way we think of the distinction:

Ethic of Care	*Ethic of Justice*
nonviolence	equality
needs, interests	fairness, rights
contextual	universal
responsibility, nurture	desert, rights
attachment, connection, community	separation, autonomy, individualism
interdependence	independence
cooperation	competition

concrete, embedded, perspectival	abstract, universal, principled
narrative	systematic
intuitive	logical
emotional	rational
web	hierarchy

Concentrate for a moment on the part of the justice list that characterizes this conception as abstract, universal, principled, systematic, logical. In contemporary intellectual culture we are inclined to regard logic as cold and hard and to regard universal, systematic, all-encompassing structures as intellectually rigorous and appropriately rational. Those who associate the justice list with men would say that this inclination reflects the fact that contemporary intellectual culture is masculine. On the other hand, important aspects of the care list—feeling, responsiveness to needs and interests, nurturing, interconnectedness, intuition—are regarded as soft, mushy, unrigorous, and sentimental in contemporary intellectual culture. Cold, hard, rigorous: in other words, tough. Soft, sentimental, nurturing: in other words, tender.

If this is what James meant by tough-minded and tender-minded, Kant and Rawls would be the quintessential examples of tough-minded thinkers. Perhaps G. E. Moore, or perhaps Kierkegaard or Sartre, would be tender-minded. If this is what James meant, it is easy to see the correlation between tough-mindedness and the conventionally masculine, and tender-mindedness and the conventionally feminine. We would be tempted to add other ways of thought to the tough, masculine list, such as market rhetoric, cost-benefit analysis, rigid entitlements, and going by rules rather than situated judgment. Richard Posner would be tough because he can countenance baby selling if it enhances efficiency,[19] and Richard Epstein would be tough because he can countenance abject poverty and homelessness for the same reasons.[20] Robert Nozick would be tough because he can countenance one person dying of thirst if water rights are owned by another.[21]

But this is not at all what James meant. In the intellectual culture in which he drew up his lists, he meant to contrast idealist rationalism with skeptical empiricism. Here are the opposing traits as James presented them:

The Tender-Minded	*The Tough-Minded*
Rationalistic (going by "principles"),	Empiricist (going by "facts"),
Intellectualistic,	Sensationalistic,
Idealistic,	Materialistic,
Optimistic,	Pessimistic,
Religious,	Irreligious,
Free-willist,	Fatalistic,
Monistic,	Pluralistic,
Dogmatical.	Skeptical.[22]

For James, the tender-minded are those who need the reassurance of a systematic, all-encompassing ideal structure. They need the security of believing that the world is one; that it is, and must necessarily be, good; that there is a perfect, absolute reality behind the imperfect appearances in which we live; and that all things necessarily tend toward perfection and the salvation of the world. The tender-minded need formal systems, principles, a priori reality, and complete rationality. The tough-minded, on the other hand, do not need to postulate a better and more unified world above, beyond, or beneath the messy and conflicting particulars in which we live—the facts as we know them. The tough-minded have the temperamental wherewithal to live with incompleteness, openness, uncertainty, skepticism, and the nonideal. For us today, universal logic and systematicity are cold, hard, and crystalline. But for James, they—that is, the need for them—evidenced vulnerability and tenderness.

It is evident that the quintessential tender-minded thinker to which James opposed his radical empiricism must be Hegel. Indeed, he mentioned two contemporary turn-of-the-century strands of tender-minded philosophy, the more important of which is "the so-called transcendental idealism of the Anglo-Hegelian school."[23] Among its exponents he included T. H. Green, Edward and John Caird, Bernard Bosanquet, and Joseph Royce.

If we try to be true to James, perhaps the foremost tender-minded thinker of today would be Roberto Unger. His work is thoroughly systematic, and it is neo-Hegelian. Even though John Rawls is not a transcendental idealist and is neo-Kantian rather than neo-Hegelian, we would probably also have to think of Rawls as tender-minded rather than tough-minded, because neo-Kantianism, no less than neo-Hegelianism, tries to find all-encompassing first principles and to build ideal theories systematically upon them. Perhaps indeed James's distinction would lead us to consider tender-minded all theorists who need universal, ideal, abstract, algorithmic structure.

What we have seen so far is that our current philosophical culture, perhaps including a conventionally accepted complex of traits divided into the masculine and feminine, tempts us to misunderstand what James meant by his distinction between tough-minded and tender-minded theories and temperaments. Although it is important to understand this, it is more important to understand that James introduced the distinction not to embrace one of its prongs but, rather, to try to dissolve it or bridge it.

James offered pragmatism as a "mediating way of thinking."[24] Pragmatism is a way of understanding our simultaneous commitments to optimism and pluralism, to concrete empiricism and principles, to an incomplete and dynamic universe and to the possibility of perfection that our ideals impel us unceasingly to hope for and work for. It was important for James that pragmatism allow us to retain a religious commitment, though not the kind of religion characteristic of the tender-minded. Indeed, although James's sympathies are in many ways with the tough-minded—he is interested foremost in the pluralistic and incomplete nature of the world, the never-ending variety and criss-crossing conflict and interconnectedness of facts—he tells us that pragmatism must include all ideas that prove best for people to hold (the most useful, the ones that work the best). This means that pragmatism includes some of the commitments of tender-mindedness:

> One misunderstanding of pragmatism is to identify it with positivistic tough-mindedness, to suppose that it scorns every rationalistic notion as so much jabber and gesticulation, that it loves intellectual anarchy as such and prefers a sort of wolf-world absolutely unpent and wild and without a master or a collar to any philosophic classroom product, whatsoever. I have said so much in these lectures against the overtender forms of rationalism, that I am prepared for some misunderstanding here, [but] I have simultaneously defended rationalistic hypotheses so far as these re-direct you fruitfully into experience.[25]

Pragmatism does not prefer a wolf-world because that is not a world that would be good for human beings. That is not a human world, not a conception of the world that works for us, and not one that makes us flourish as best we can. For James pragmatism is capacious:

> On pragmatic principles we cannot reject any hypothesis if consequences useful to life flow from it. Universal conceptions, as things to take account of, may be as real for pragmatism as particular sensations are. They have indeed no meaning and no reality if they have no use. But if they have any use they have that amount of meaning. And the meaning will be true if the use squares well with life's other uses.
>
> Well, the use of the Absolute is proved by the whole course of men's religious history. The eternal arms are then beneath.[26]

So James finds that we have used the idea of the absolute because we need to fall back and float upon the eternal arms.

James's own solution does not favor any such floating. His religion of pragmatism is neither optimistic (tender-minded: The world's salvation is inevitable, and we need do nothing about it) nor pessimistic (tough-minded: There is no salvation and we cannot do anything about it). Instead, it is "melioristic"—the world's salvation is possible, and it depends upon what we do about it. Whether or not we follow James and choose to think of it as religious, this is one of the deepest commitments of pragmatism, its commitment to the interconnection, indeed the inseparability, of theory (vision) and action (practice). "In the beginning was the Act,"[27] wrote Goethe at the dawn of the romantic era, and perhaps this commitment of pragmatism to the significance of our actions is what it retains of romanticism. It seems so in passages such as this:

> Does our act then *create* the world's salvation . . . ? Here I take the bull by the horns, and in spite of the whole crew of rationalists and monists, of whatever brand they be, I ask *why not?* Our acts, our turning-places, where we seem to ourselves to make ourselves and grow, are the parts of the world to which we are closest, the parts of which our knowledge is the most intimate and complete. Why should we not take them at their face-value? Why may they not be the actual turning-places and growing-places which they seem to be, of the world—why not the workshop of being, where we catch fact in the making, so that nowhere may the world grow in any other kind of way than this?[28]

The optimism of pragmatism is not the static and secure optimism of the world in which everything is already fixed, could we but know or understand it, but, rather, the dynamic and risky optimism of a "workshop of being" in which reality is always incomplete and always dependent upon our practice.

James did not argue that we should accept pragmatism because it is a more rational system. Rather, he argued pragmatically that we should be pragmatists because when we look at our various commitments and practices we should recognize that pragmatism fits them best, that pragmatism will work best for us. If we accept everything on either the tender-minded or the tough-minded list, we are forced to deny, for the sake of supposed philosophical consistency, things on the other list that are very real and important to us.

When we see feminism in its pragmatic aspect, I think it will be easy to conclude that feminists should not easily relinquish what are important attributes of the ethic of justice because of the present conventional association with a version of masculinity that needs to be transcended. When we see feminism pragmatically, we may be impelled, rather, to affirm both lists, suitably metamorphosed. Perhaps feminism, as well as earlier pragmatism, can be a middle way.

In the wake of Gilligan's work, many feminists did affirm that there is something essentially female about the moral structure characterized in the care list. These feminists also affirmed that this female morality is good, indeed that women's "different voice" is not just different from, but better than, male morality and should be the guide to moral and political progress.[29] It did not take long for other feminists to point out, however, that this simple identification with the care list might be a bad mistake.[30]

Rather than a window into an essentially female form of character and development or female kind of knowing and acting, the ethic of care in our current world might be an artifact of coping with oppression. It might be the expression of what is most useful for a group that exists in bondage, in victimhood.[31] If so, it is the expression of "femininism,"[32] not feminism, and its moral significance is complex. Its traits will be a mixture of cooptation with defiance, and sycophantism with subtle subversion. It will not be something either to affirm wholeheartedly or to reject out of hand.

Certainly, it seems that male ideology invented the polarities of rationality and just deserts versus emotions and nurturing and then found the rational pole to be dominant, suitable for the market and the public world, and the emotional pole to be subordinate, suitable for the family and the private world. Much of the eighteenth- and nineteenth-century rhetoric about the nature of womanhood makes this clear. To exalt the ethic of care leaves the polarities intact. It just reverses their signs. As others have pointed out, a group that seeks liberation from a dominating system of thought should be very suspicious of adopting its categories.[33]

What would a feminist middle way look like? It might recommend that all of us, women and men, are morally inclined toward both care and justice and that neither women nor men should impoverish themselves with the conventional categories of femininity and masculinity. The feminist middle way would not want to relinquish the concrete knowledge that women have gained through living, working, creating, and surviving under male domination. This is a perspective that is unique and important for humanity. The actions and commitments of those who struggle to find room for themselves, and ultimately to free themselves, in a world whose formulating conceptions are not of their making, are indeed indispensable in the pragmatic "workshop of being." As I argued earlier, this perspective is the best way for pragmatism to confront the complacent tendency to be satisfied with coherence with the past. But neither would the feminist middle way want to deny women the right or the ability to engage in the theoretical joys of cold, hard logic and of rational system building, nor to deny women the practical power of standing at the top of a hierarchy, in a position of authority, and meting out just deserts.

The feminist middle way cannot be understood, however, as some kind of synthesis between the two lists. It would be unpragmatic, and perhaps incoherent, to seek some overarching universal conception or set of principles that could harmonize "attachment, connection, community" with "separation, autonomy, individualism," or "cooperation" with "competition," or the concrete with the abstract, or the intuitive with the logical, or the narrative with the systematic. Instead, the pragmatist middle way recommends two things for feminism: (1) We should recognize that sometimes one of the opposing modes of thought is appropriate, and sometimes the other, and no theory—only situated judgment—will tell us which one to adopt and when; (2) we should recognize that the traditional conceptions of the modes of thought on each list are inadequate insofar as they are part of a universal worldview that denies the modes on the other list.

It could be that both the ethic of care and the ethic of justice are caricatures of morality. These caricatures have seemed plausible because to some extent they fit with contemporary conventions of femininity and masculinity. It could be that human beings, whether male or female, need both ethics to function morally. If we are pragmatists, we will reject static, timeless conceptions of reality. We will prefer contextuality, expressed in the commitment of Dewey and James, to facts and their meaning in human life, and narrative, expressed in James's unfolding "epic" universe and Dewey's historicism. If we are pragmatists, we will recognize the inescapability of perspective and the indissolubility of thought and action. Indeed, as I have said, these pragmatist commitments are shared by many feminists, and they make it useful to think of many forms of feminism as sharing a great deal with pragmatism.

These pragmatic commitments nevertheless do not compel us to affirm the ethic of care and deny the ethic of justice, even if the realities of the narrative epic as it has so far unfolded have produced these contrasting ethics as the salient conventions of our day. James thought that if we reflected hard and honestly about our experiences and ideals, and our hopes and commitments, we would be neither tender-minded nor tough-minded but would find a middle way that is truer to ourselves. So too today, it may be that we need not exalt either the characteristics of conventional femininity or conventional masculinity but, rather, that we can define a middle way that is truer to ourselves, including what we hope to become.

IV. The Struggle over Descriptions of Reality and Its Consequences for Legal Discourse

One useful consequence of putting pragmatism and feminism together is that we need not deny that certain philosophical commitments are distinctively feminist just because they seem to be pragmatist too. Joan Williams writes that "the attempt to claim the new epistemology for women is unconvincing simply because the new epistemology has been developed largely by men."[34] By "the new epistemology," Williams means the "view of truths as necessarily partial and contextual," which she associates with "philosophers from Frederick [*sic*] Nietzsche and the American pragmatists to Martin Heidegger and Ludwig Wittgenstein." I think Williams moves too quickly here. Of course, it is correct that pragmatism, with its commitment to perspectivism, is not the exclusive province of females. But I have argued that the commitment to perspectivism finds its concrete payoff in the perspective of feminism and in the perspectives of oppressed people generally. Rather than affirming that there is no specific feminist perspective because men have espoused perspectivism, it is pragmatically better, as I have argued above, to affirm that the standpoint of people who have themselves been dominated and oppressed makes it possible to see and confront the problem of bad coherence. Their standpoint therefore assumes a crucial importance.

For the legal actor who accepts the significance of the perspective of the oppressed, the important issues must be (1) How can we recognize bad coherence in our legal institutions? and (2) How can we use this recognition to change those institutions? In order to approach these issues for pragmatist–feminist legal theory, I suggest we can start with a distinction between two kinds of coherence. Like all pragmatic distinctions, I do not mean this one to be hard and fast.

There seem to be two ways to construe coherence, which I will call *conceptual* and *institutional.* If traditional pragmatism is best understood as expressing a coherence theory, its thrust is primarily conceptual. James's conservatism about belief was connected with what conceptions we should hold to be true, especially in light of recalcitrant experience (to use Quine's later phrase). On the other hand, complacent pragmatists are tempted to focus on existing institutions and not just conceptions. These different ways of construing coherence have ramifications for the problem of bad coherence. As I shall explain, dominant forms of legal pragmatism have been especially conservative because they have embraced institutional—not just conceptual—coherence.

If our worldview exhibits bad coherence at the conceptual level, then we are unable to formulate and think about any opposing views. Indeed, it does not make any sense to speak of bad coherence at the time, for we can only see it in retrospect, if we change our conceptions and come to see our past understandings as bad. This might have been the situation with slavery in the ancient world. It might have been unthinkable to conceive of human beings in such a way that there could be any plausible argument that all people are equal and that slavery is wrong. Some pragmatists might say that in this situation we have no standpoint from which to say that slavery is bad, and hence that it is meaningless, except in retrospect, to think of this situation as "bad" coherence. Pragmatists who adopt conceptual coherence as the test of truth need not be conservative about all institutions.[35] Nor need the conceptual meaninglessness be static. The methodology of consciousness raising is one way people can emerge from the unthinkable (silence) to an alternative conception of the world (voice). Perhaps that is the point at which it becomes meaningful to speak of bad coherence.

With institutional bad coherence, the situation may be different. If our social world exhibits bad coherence at the institutional level but not at the conceptual level, then our institutions uniformly exhibit the bad conception of things, but it is possible for at least some of us to conceive that things might be otherwise. This might have been the situation in the last days of coverture. All our legal institutions treated women as subordinate to their husbands, yet it was possible for some women to think of themselves otherwise and to envision a legal regime that would recognize their changed self-conception. If bad coherence exists only at the institutional level, then the possibility of transition opens up. How can a newly conceivable alternative conception find the power to make inroads into the coherent legal order held in place by the dominant conception of the world?

The problem of institutional bad coherence is the point where the enlightened pragmatist, the pragmatist-feminist, can make the most significant contribution to legal theory. The unenlightened, complacent pragmatist tends to argue that since "truth" about the world is found in conceptual coherence, legal "truth" should be discerned by reference to institutional coherence. The enlightened pragmatist must counter this conservative non sequitur by finding a way to transform alternative conceptual possibilities into legal realities. She must find a way that "the law" can be understood to include the conceptions of the oppressed as they are coming to be, even if the weight of legal institutions coherently excludes them. In other words, the transition problem in this guise is how to make thinkable alternatives into institutional commitments.

Dworkin's Hercules can be understood as a complacent pragmatist judge.[36] This reading of Dworkin might not represent his real views, if we were to ask him. Yet I think it is a fair picture of how a reader might understand his work, taken as a whole. Although Dworkin confusingly, and I think irresponsibly, gerrymanders the word *pragmatism* to mean "crass instrumentalism,"[37] it is clear that he is a pragmatist of sorts. Pragmatism is reflected in his commitment to the ubiquity of interpretation, and his concomitant commitment to finding meaning in assembling concrete events (institutional coherence and fit), rather than to measuring correspondence with abstract truth or justice.

Hercules is conservative because Dworkin accepts the flawed analogy between truth as conceptual coherence and legal truth as institutional coherence. Hercules, the ideal interpreter, must find the interpretation that coheres best with all that has gone before in the legal system. He is not allowed to say that the web of previous precedent is coherently wrong or, in his chain novel analogy, that the narrative to which he must add is a bad story so far.[38]

Of course, Hercules is allowed to find that some of our institutional history, as embodied in concrete decisions, is mistaken. Any adherent of coherence theory must allow some of the old commitments to be given up when confronted with a new problem. Dworkin argues conservatively that the proper theory of mistake is to give up as little as possible. He does not even provide any serious discussion about how every once in awhile a paradigm shift must come about, to parallel the avenue pursued by conceptual pragmatists in science.

For the oppressed this means the status quo must change very slowly, if at all. For example, how would Hercules deal with *Plessy v. Ferguson?*[39] Dworkin argues that at the time of *Brown v. Board of Education,*[40] *Plessy* should not have been treated as compelling precedent, but he stops short of arguing that *Plessy* was wrong at the time it was decided. Nor could he do so, it seems, since he admits that *Plessy* cohered well with its contemporary institutional legal, moral, and political universe. Toward the end of *Law's Empire,* Dworkin makes a distinction between the integrity required by justice and the integrity required by all of the virtues that the legal system must balance.[41] Perhaps he might argue that the integrity of justice would have recommended that *Plessy* was wrong at the time, even though institutionally coherent with its surroundings. Since Dworkin appears in the end to measure justice by the same kind of institutional coherence, it seems to me that such an argument would fail.

Of course, Dworkin does argue that things have changed and that it was coherently right by 1954 to ignore *Plessy.* But how did things change? Not, it appears, with any help from the legal system. In Dworkin's conservative theory, the legal system was required to hold fast to the old description of the world, composed by the dominant order and expressed in its institutions, until extralegal forces dislodged it. Moreover, if Dworkin cannot argue that *Plessy* was wrong at the time it was decided because in his theory there is no foothold from which to argue that the system was institutionally coherently bad, then he has no room to admit the possibility that in some ways our system is coherently bad today. All he can say is that some of the coherent things we are doing today will probably seem wrong in retrospect, not that they are wrong now. That is small consolation to the oppressed.

In contrast to complacent legal pragmatists are the legal writers who have stressed the crucial importance of the perspective of the oppressed and its consequences for a serious pluralism. These writers, such as Robert Cover, Frank Michelman, and Martha Minow,[42] are essentially at work on the particular transition problem posed by institutional bad coherence—that is, the problem of institutional bad coherence in the context of excluded but conceivable alternatives.

In his resolutely antistatist view of law, Cover wanted to make us aware of how in our commitments we create and inhabit a *nomos.* He wanted to make us concretely aware of the way meaning, including legal meaning, is inseparable from commitment and action. Reversing the old positivist slogan that judges should apply, not make, the law, Cover argued that the role of judges, like the roles of all who interpret authoritative texts for those who are committed to them, is rightly "jurisgenerative." Cover drew attention in particular to the "hermeneutic of resistance,"[43] because he wanted us to see the deep and all-encompassing significance of the standpoint of those who are dominated and oppressed.

In many ways consonant with the work of Cover, both Minow and Michelman plead with us to drop the prevalent conception of the judicial role as one in which our hands are tied by abstract rules laid down.[44] Minow and Michelman urge that the best role for the judge in our legal system is to try to grasp the world from the perspective of the dominated, to hear the outsiders who have been silent and are now trying to speak, and to make concrete our deepest ideals of inclusion when the conventions of our day—"our" dominant perspective—run counter to them. In other words, Minow and Michelman ask us to allow the transitional possibilities opened up by the developing perspectives of the oppressed to infiltrate the dominant institutional coherence.

Minow "links problems of difference to questions of vantage point." In "urg[ing] struggles over descriptions of reality,"[45] Minow echoes James's call for a workshop of being but adds the perspective that only concrete participation in struggle can give. Michelman argues that pluralism is necessary for the evolutionary self-reflection appropriate to our best self-development, and that pluralism depends upon listening to the perspectives of the oppressed. He also argues that "judges perhaps enjoy a situational advantage over the people at large in listening for voices from the margins."[46] If they are willing to be sympathetic, judges, with their concrete knowledge of legal history and institutions and their malleable character,

> are perhaps better situated to conduct a sympathetic inquiry into how, if at all, the readings of history upon which those voices base their complaint can count as interpretations of that history which, however re-collective or even transformative, remain true to that history's informing commitment to the pursuit of political freedom through jurisgenerative politics.[47]

Minow and Michelman embrace pluralism through taking seriously the perspective of the oppressed. This allows them to find, unlike Dworkin, that courts can take the lead sometimes in the search for better justice. Dworkin's Hercules does not admit the perspective of the oppressed. He cannot, because his task is to find coherence with existing institutions, and the oppressed have not made those institutions. They are outsiders. Perhaps through consciousness raising or through struggle over descriptions of reality, they have created a thinkable perspective, but their perspective is not represented in the institutional artifacts of the power structure.

Even without the search for the excluded perspectives, Hercules would be truer to the critical spirit of pragmatism if Dworkin were attentive to the ways pluralism is built into our system of legal interpretation. Hercules has no colleagues in making his decisions, and this picture is quite untrue to our practice. After all, as Michelman points out, there is a reason why appellate courts decide things in groups, why they deliberate, and why they issue plural opinions even when their deliberation is done.[48] The reason is that conversation and dialogue in appellate decisionmaking represent judges' interaction in the context of commitment, for the decisions of courts matters to people's lives, and no judge is unaware of this. This judicial interaction is crucial to our idea of what might be the best result.

A serious pluralism makes possible an understanding of the deep role of discourse in the way conceptions and practices are made and remade, and thus makes possible a commitment to dialogue among alternative conceptions. Even the occasional conceptual paradigm shift can only find the old dominant description of the world to be wrong in retrospect. It cannot help us find that today's dominant description is wrong. For that, we must realize that another perspective is always possible. The best critical spirit of pragmatism recommends that we take our present descriptions with humility and openness and accept their institutional embodiments as provisional and incompletely entrenched. Pragmatism recommends this openness in the only way pragmatism can—because it seems to work best for human beings. It is time for the openness and critical spirit of pragmatism to infiltrate pragmatist legal theory. Feminism can lead the way.

Notes

1. R. Tong, Feminist Thought: A Comprehensive Introduction 193 (1989).

2. W. Stevens, *On the Road Home,* in The Collected Poems of Wallace Stevens 203 (1954).

3. Joseph Singer and I gave a dialogue presentation entitled "The Feminist Turn in Moral Philosophy" at the Critical Legal Studies Feminist Conference in 1985. The title was intended to be provocative: We were discussing Hilary Putnam and Richard Rorty.

4. R. Tong, at 1. *Cf.* A. Jaggar, Feminist Politics and Human Nature 8, 10 (1983) (categorizing feminisms as liberal, Marxist, radical, and socialist).

5. J. Dewey, Experience and Nature 410 (2d ed. 1929).

6. W. James, Pragmatism 104 (1975).

7. There is a strain of essentialist feminism that might be an exception. Some feminists, often labeled as "radical," tend to think there is a real nature of women, linked to female biology, which has been obscured but not shaped by the patriarchy. *See, e.g.,* A. Jaggar, at 93–98. I believe Robin West's writing tends in this essentialist direction, especially her apparent claim that morality rests on some kind of primeval womanhood that is prelinguistic. West, *Feminism, Critical Social Theory and Law,* 1989 U. Chi. Legal F. 59, 80–82.

8. As Dewey says in the preface to the second edition of *Experience and Nature.*

9. *See, e.g.,* C. MacKinnon, Toward a Feminist Theory of the State 191 (1989).

10. J. Dewey, at 179.

11. This statement is subject to dispute. Hilary Putnam, for example, espouses "internal realism" or "pragmatic realism." *See* H. Putnam, The Many Faces of Realism 17 (1987).

12. W. James, at 35, 36.

13. *Id.* at 42.

14. If the notion of coherent badness causes philosophical difficulties, then we could speak here of integrity in badness or merely consistency in badness. The point is that we can experience a situation in which almost everything about the status quo—our language, our social priorities, our law—reflects and expresses racism or sexism. We need a way to recognize that this situation is bad or unjust, indeed worse or more unjust than a situation that is on the whole just and has only small pockets of injustice that can be seen to lack coherence (or integrity, or consistency) with the whole.

15. Indeed, there is a transition problem in the very commitment to take seriously the perspective of oppressed groups, because attention to the group qua group risks reinforcing the old categories of subordination. *See* Brewer, *Pragmatism, Oppression, and the Flight to Substance,* 63 S. Cal. L. Rev. 1753 (1990); *Afterword,* 63 S. Cal. L. Rev. 1911, 1922–24 (1990).

16. *See* J. Dewey, at 119–20. "The conception that contemplative thought is *the* end in itself was at once a compensation for inability to make reason effective in practice, and a means for perpetuating a division of social classes. A local and temporal polity of historical nature became a metaphysics of everlasting being" *(id.* at 119).

17. W. JAMES, at 13.

18. C. GILLIGAN, IN A DIFFERENT VOICE: PSYCHOLOGICAL THEORY AND WOMEN'S DEVELOPMENT (1982).

19. *See, e.g.,* Posner, *The Regulation of the Market in Adoptions,* 67 B.U.L. REV. 59 (1987).

20. *See* R. EPSTEIN, TAKINGS 315–23 (1985).

21. *See* R. NOZICK, ANARCHY, STATE AND UTOPIA 180–81 (1972).

22. W. JAMES, at 13.

23. *Id.* at 16.

24. *Id.* at 26.

25. *Id.* at 128.

26. *Id.* at 131.

27. *"Im Anfang war die Tat."* GOETHE, FAUST PT. I In. 1237 (C. Thomas ed. 1892). This is to be understood, of course, as countervailing the Gospel of St. John, "In the beginning was the Word." Pragmatists traditionally are wary of emphasis on words without action or without commitment to actual results in the world. Perhaps Richard Rorty's stress on conversation or dialogue can prove uncomfortable for pragmatism if conversation becomes a category apart from practical action.

28. W. JAMES, at 138.

29. *See, e.g.,* Ruddick, *Preservative Love and Military Destruction: Some Reflections on Mothering and Peace,* in J. TREBILCOT, MOTHERING: ESSAYS IN FEMINIST THEORY 231 (1983).

30. *See, e.g.,* Williams, *Deconstructing Gender,* 87 MICH. L. REV. 797 (1989).

31. *See, e.g.,* Hantzis, *Is Gender Justice a Completed Agenda?* (Book Review), 100 HARV. L. REV. 690, 700–3 (1987).

32. I learned this word from Kathleen M. Sullivan. *Femininism* connotes the misunderstanding of today's conventional femininity as some kind of real woman's nature.

33. A. LORDE, *The Master's Tools Will Never Dismantle the Master's House,* in SISTER OUTSIDER 112 (1984).

34. Williams, at 806.

35. Conceptual coherence may be an expansive view of coherence in the sense discussed above. When coherence includes all our ideals and critical visions, many existing institutions may be found wanting.

36. Ronald Dworkin introduces Hercules, "a lawyer of superhuman skill, learning, patience and acumen," to represent the ideal judge. R. DWORKIN, TAKING RIGHTS SERIOUSLY 81, 104–5 (1978). Hercules plays the same role in *Law's Empire,* described there as "an imaginary judge of superhuman intellectual power and patience who accepts law as integrity." R. DWORKIN, LAW'S EMPIRE 239 (1986).

37. *See* R. DWORKIN, LAW'S EMPIRE, at 95, 151–64.

38. R. DWORKIN, LAW'S EMPIRE, at 115–18, 228–32. Dworkin compares judging to writing a chain novel, each writer interpreting the previous chapters in order to write a new chapter that fits with what has gone before.

39. 163 U.S. 537 (1896).

40. 73 U.S. 1 (1952).

41. R. DWORKIN, LAW'S EMPIRE, at 379–89, 404–7.

42. I think of these writers because of my own situatedness in the discourse of legal theory. It is equally important to think in this context of "critical race theory." *See* Bell, *Foreword: The Civil Rights Chronicles,* 99 HARV. L. REV. 4 (1985); Delgado, *When a Story Is Just a Story: Does Voice Really Matter?,* 76 VA. L. REV. 95 (1990); Matsuda, *Looking to the Bottom,* 22 HARV. C.R.–C.L. L. REV. 323 (1987); Matsuda, *Public Response to Racist Speech: Considering the Victim's Story,* 87 MICH. L. REV. 2320 (1989). We should also look to the emerging perspective of gay and lesbian writers. *See, e.g.,* Cain, *Feminist Jurisprudence,* 1989 BERKELEY WOMEN'S L.J. 191 (arguing that feminist jurisprudence ignores the lesbian perspective).

43. Cover, *Foreword: Nomos and Narrative,* 97 HARV. L. REV. 4 (1983) at 48–53.

44. Michelman, *Foreword: Traces of Self-Government* 100 HARV. L. REV. 4, 32–33 (1986); Michelman, *Law's Republic* 97 YALE L.J. 1493, 1532–37 (1988); Minow, *Foreword: Justice Engendered,* 101 HARV. L. REV. 10, 70–95 (1987).

45. Minow, at 13–16.

46. Michelman, *Law's Republic,* at 1537.

47. *Id.*

48. Michelman, *Traces,* at 16–17.

23

Sapphire Bound!

REGINA AUSTIN

I. "Write-ous" Resistance

I grew up thinking that Sapphire was merely a character on the "Amos 'n' Andy" program, a figment of a white man's racist/sexist comic imagination.[1] Little did I suspect that Sapphire was a more generally employed appellation for the stereotypical BLACK BITCH—tough, domineering, emasculating, strident, and shrill.[2] Sapphire is the sort of person you look at and wonder how she can possibly stand herself. All she does is complain. Why doesn't that woman shut up?

Black bitch hunts are alive and well in the territory where minority female law faculty labor. There are so many things to get riled about that keeping quiet is impossible. We really cannot function effectively without coming to terms with Sapphire. Should we renounce her, rehabilitate her, or embrace her and proclaim her our own?

There are a whole host of situations that minority female instructors encounter that convey in more or less subtle ways the undesirability of looking at the world through eyes that are Sapphire's, or Maria's, or Mai Ling's. I am really just addressing the minority women at this point. When was the last time someone asked you to choose between being a woman and being a minority person or asked you to assess the hardships and the struggles of your life in terms of your being a woman on top of being black (or whatever color you are) or a black on top of being a woman, as if being a woman or being black were like icing on a cake? As if you and your kind were not an integrated, undifferentiated, complete whole with a consciousness and politics of your own. As if you should be content to be a foot soldier in someone else's army of liberation. As if the ring leader should not be a person like yourself doubly and affectively bound to the community of the oppressed. Of course, to insist on your own vision would be divisive, and you don't want to be divisive, do you?

When was the last time someone told you that your way of approaching problems, be they legal or institutional, was all wrong? You are too angry, too emotional, too subjective, too pessimistic, too political, too anecdotal, and too instinctual. I never know how to respond to such accusations. How can I "legitimate" my way of thinking? I know that I am not just flying off the handle, seeing imaginary insults and problems where there are none. I am not a witch solely by nature, but by circumstance and choice as well. I suspect that what my critics really want to say is that I am being too self-consciously black (brown, yellow, red) and/or female to suit their tastes and should "lighten up" because I am making them feel very uncomfortable, and that is not nice. And I want them to think that I am nice, don't I?

When was the last time you had a student who wanted to write a paper on a topic having to do with the legal problems of minority women, and you had precious little to offer in the way of legal articles or commentary that might be on point?[3] You especially regretted your limited ability perhaps to challenge her bourgeois orientation and to acquaint her with alternative nationalistic or feminist perspectives. And your next response was to curse the powers that be. Toni Morrison,[4] Alice Walker,[5] Louise Erdrich,[6] and Maxine Hong Kingston[7] write about the lives of minority women and manage to sell books, whereas minority female legal scholars have every reason to believe that almost no one is interested in the legal problems of minority women, certainly not enough to reward scholarly investigations of them with tenure, promotions, and such. If you did attempt to do it, who could help you, and if you actually did pull it off, who would evaluate it favorably?

Suppose that at last you actually got around to considering the impact of law on the lives of minority women. You would have to decide whether you too will portray them as helpless, powerless, troubled souls, woefully in need of legal rights and remedies. You know that is not the entire story. Minority women as the "pathology of the society" does not capture the dignity, righteous resistance, and practical endurance that are ingrained in our cultures. Minority women do amazing things with limited resources, are powerful in their own communities and, not unlike Sapphire, can mount scathing critiques of the sources of their oppression.[8] Yet, the enormity of the task of capturing the complexity of their legal status and of translating their concerns into those that the legal scholarly community recognizes makes it an unrealistic endeavor for you, given the demands on your time and talent. Somehow other people are always setting your agenda—either by making positive requests that you just cannot refuse or by provoking you to act in defense of yourself, your students, your colleagues, or your entire race. With your commitments, a manual of ten thousand ways to say "no" would not be of much help. After all, you want to do what you really feel you must do, don't you?

Well, I think the time has come for us to get truly hysterical, to take on the role of "professional Sapphires" in a forthright way, to declare that we are serious about ourselves, and to capture some of the intellectual power and resources that are necessary to combat the systematic denigration of minority women. It is time for Sapphire to testify on her own behalf, in writing, complete with footnotes.

"To testify" means several different things in this context: to present the facts, to attest to their accuracy, and to profess a personal belief or conviction. The minority feminist legal scholar must be a witness in each of these senses. She must document the material legal existences of minority women. Her work should explore their concrete problems and needs, many of which are invisible even to minority lawyers because of gender and class differences. Moreover, a synthesis of the values, traditions, and codes that bind women of the same minority group to one another and that fuel their collective struggle is crucial to the enterprise. The intellectual product of the minority feminist scholar should incorporate in a formal fashion the ethical and moral consciousnesses of minority women, their aspirations, and their quest for liberation. Her partisanship and advocacy of a minority feminist jurisprudence should be frankly acknowledged and energetically defended. Because her scholarship is to be grounded in the material and ideological realities of minority women and in their cultural and political responses, its operative premises must necessarily be dynamic and primarily immanent: As the lives of minority women change, so too should the analysis.

Finally, the experiential is not to be abandoned by the minority female legal scholar. She must be guided by her life, instincts, sensibility, and politics. The voice and vision reflected in her work should contain something of the essence of the culture that she has lived and learned. Imagine, if you can, writing a law review article embodying the spontaneity of jazz, the earthiness of the blues, or the vibrancy of salsa.

I have given some thought to the tenets that a black feminist or "womanish" legal jurisprudence might pursue or embrace. Other approaches are imaginable, and I hope that this chapter will encourage or provoke their articulation. "Misty humanism" and "simplistic assertions of a distinguishable . . . cultural and discursive practice" are not adequate.[9] Begging won't get it either: I am not sappy and do not care whether white men love me. I can think of nothing more debilitating than thinking ourselves dependent upon the goodwill and civility of those in a position to oppress us. While it is important to build coalitions with whites of both sexes and other people of color, black women will not prosper from them if we entirely muffle our indignation and negotiate as mere supplicants. Oh, no! We have paid our dues, done more than our share of the doing and the dying, and are entitled to prosper with everyone else.

We must write with an empowered and empowering voice. The chief sources of our theory should be black women's critiques of a society that is dominated by and structured to favor white men of wealth and power. We should also find inspiration in the modes of resistance black women mount, individually and collectively, on a daily basis in response to discrimination and exploitation. Our jurisprudence should amplify the criticism and lend clarity and visibility to the positive transformative cultural parries that are overlooked unless close attention is given to the actual struggles of black women. In addition, our jurisprudence should create enough static to interfere with the transmission of the dominant ideology and jam the messages that reduce our indignation, limit our activism, misdirect our energies, and otherwise make us the (re)producers of our own subordination. By way of an alternative, a black feminist jurisprudence should preach the justness of the direct, participatory, grass-roots opposition black women undertake despite enormous material and structural constraints.

A thoroughly critical stance, high standards, and a sharp focus are absolutely essential to our scholarly mission. Whatever we do must be analytical and rigorously researched and reasoned, not to convince and please those who have the power to control our professional advancement, but to repay the debt we owe our grandmothers, mothers, and sisters whose invisibility and marginality we aim to ameliorate. Although critiques of the racism of white feminists and the sexism of male "race persons" are useful, to my way of thinking they can be an abdication of the responsibility to shape an affirmative agenda that makes the lives of real black women the central focus. Our scholarship must be accessible to an audience of black female law students, legal scholars, practitioners, and nonlegal activists. They are likely to be both sources of politically pragmatic criticism and programmatic grounding, and informants as to the authentic, spontaneous, imaginative counterhegemonic moves being made by black women fighting racial, sexual, and class oppression on the front lines of their everyday lives. As scholars, we in turn can aid their political mobilization with lucid analyses that offer broad and cogent perspectives of the structural constraints that produce their subordination and the material openings that must be exploited if further freedom is to be achieved.

It is imperative that our writing acknowledge and patently reflect that we are not the voices of a monolithic racial/sexual community that does not know class divisions or social and cultural diversity. This recognition should check the basically conservative impulse to rely on generalizations about racism and sexism that are the product of our own experiences. It should also make us vigilant about lapsing into outrageous themes which suggest that black people are united by biological essences that produce in all of us a refined instinctive sense of justice. Our positions as "scholars" set us apart to some extent from the women about whom we write, and our work would be better if we acknowledged the distance and attempted to bridge it. For a start, we must accept that there is skepticism about both the law and intellectual pursuits in our communities. It accordingly behooves us to eschew the role of self-anointed spokespersons for our race and sex and instead take our lead as teachers and scholars from the ongoing liberation politics of black women.

Moreover, we must be responsive to the attacks that are leveled against us as well-paid, relatively assimilated professionals. As we are validly critiqued, so should we critique. We are obliged, therefore, to look at the needs and problems of black women to determine the role black elites (male and female) have played in their creation or perpetuation. Similarly, in seeking jurisprudential reference points in the wisdom of black women at the bottom of the status hierarchy, we must reject the romanticization of their "difference." It is patronizing, tends to support our position as intermediaries, and ignores the role that state-tolerated violence, material deprivation, and the dominant ideology play in minority cultural production. We must not be deterred from maintaining a critical stance from which to assess what black women might do to improve their political and economic positions and to strengthen their ideological defenses. At the same time, however, we must scrupulously avoid the insensitive disparagement of black women that ignores the positive, hopeful, and life-affirming characteristics of their actual struggles and thereby overlooks the basis for more overt political activity.

Our contributions will not be divisive to the cause of the liberation of minority peoples and women if our scholarship is based on the concrete, material conditions of black women. Antiracist or antisexist scholarship that is overinclusive and abstract is dangerous because it misconceives the often knotty structural nature of the conditions that are its subject. In addition, such scholarship frequently reflects the assumption that oppressed groups are pitted against one another in a competition for scarce attention and resources, with the victory going to the most downtrodden. (I call this phenomenon *the running of the oppression sweepstakes.*) For example, the much-touted concept of the "feminization of poverty" would be fine if it did not obscure the reality that poverty varies with race, has a class dimension, and in many minority communities afflicts both sexes.[10] Black women in particular have much to gain from efforts to understand the complexity of the interaction of race, sex (including sexual orientation), and class factors in the creation of social problems.

The mechanics of undertaking a research project based on the concrete material and legal problems of black women are daunting. The research is hard to do, but I believe it can be done. I have twice embarked on such projects. My first effort concerned industrial insurance, the rip-off life insurance with the small face amounts that my mother and grandmother purchased.[11] I was stymied because of a lack of information going beyond my own experience regarding the motivations that prompt poor black people to spend so much for essentially burial protection. I have more nexus with, respect for, and intellectual curiosity about the cultures of poor black people than to mount a scholarly project on the assumption that the women in my family are typical of the whole. The second project grew out of my interest in the causes of excess death in minority communities or what is the unacknowledged genocide of the poor black, brown, and red peoples of America.[12] I decided to start with the problem of infant mortality. The infant mortality rate for blacks was 18.2 per 1,000 live births in 1985, as compared with 9.3 per 1,000 live births for whites.[13] I thought that I would begin by examining the extent to which the vilification of the cultural modes and mores of low-income minority females affects the prenatal care they receive. The inquiry would then extend to the role the law might play in curbing the mistreatment or nontreatment of pregnant women of color. I have not entirely abandoned this one.

The problems these projects involve are difficult because they do not begin with a case and will not necessarily end with a new rule. The world with which many legal scholars deal is that found within the four corners of judicial opinions. If the decisions and the rubrics they apply pay no attention to race, sex, and class (and the insurance and malpractice cases generally do not), then the material conditions of minority females are nowhere to be found, and the legal aspects of the difficulties these conditions cause are nearly impossible to address as a matter of scholarly inquiry. It is thus imperative that we find a way to portray, almost construct for a legal audience, the contemporary reality of the disparate groups of minority women about whom we write. We really cannot do this without undertaking field research or adopting an interdisciplinary approach, relying on the empipirical and ethnographic research of others. The latter route is the one that I have taken in this chapter and elsewhere.[14]

Interdisciplinary research provides additional benefits. It gets one out of the law school and among scholars who are supportive and receptive to modes of analysis that are not Eurocentric or patriarchal. I have found that academics from other parts of the university where I teach supply the intellectual community, stimulation, and encouragement that are essential to doing research. Furthermore, black scholars from other disciplines have provided me with useful strategies for dealing with the hostility my intellectual agenda might evoke.

Looking at legal problems against the context of nonlegal perspectives has its dangers. The legal scholar's obligation to take the law seriously generally requires that her writing be legalistic—that she show the inadequacy of the existing rules and either propose clever manipulations of the doctrine that overcome the weaknesses exposed by her critique or draft model legislation. This approach tends to collapse the inquiries into what black people need and want and what they are likely to get, into one. The conservatism that is an inherent part of traditional doctrinal legal analysis can be a stifling handicap for the black female researcher. Speculation concerning proposals that are not rule bound and lawyer controlled (like, for example, strategies by which poor women might increase their power to shape the gynecological services provided by health care facilities ostensibly serving them)[15] seems beyond the pale. That is utopian politics, not law or legal scholarship. Of course, black people get almost nowhere in terms of gaining and enforcing legal entitlements without also exercising their political clout or scaring white people. (Truly powerless people do not "get" rights on account of their helplessness, and the rights they do "get" are protected only so long as they are backed up by the threat of disruption.) Thus, the black feminist legal scholar must be able to think political and talk legal if need be. Her pedagogical mission should extend to educating black women about the political sig-

nificance of their ordinary lives and struggles. She must translate their frustrations and
aspirations into a language that both reveals their liberatory potential and supports the
legal legitimacy of their activism and their demands.

The remedies we contemplate must go beyond intangibles. We must consider
employing the law to create and sustain institutions and organizations that will belong to
black women long after any movement has become quiescent and any agitation has died.
Full utilization of the economic, political, and social resources that black women represent cannot depend on the demand of a society insincerely committed to an ethic of integration and equal opportunity.

Implementation of an agenda for black feminist legal scholarship and expanded study
of the legal status of minority women in general will require the right sort of environmental conditions, such as receptive or at least tolerant nonminority publishers and a
network of established academics engaged in similar pursuits. We minority female scholars must devote a bit of our sass to touting the importance of the perspective of minority
women and the significance of their concerns to any list of acceptable law review topics.
If anyone asks you to talk or write about anything related to your race or your sex, turn
the opportunity into one for exploring the legal concerns of women of color.

This chapter, for example, grew out of an invitation I received to address a conference
for women in law teaching on the subject of my experiences as a black female legal academic. The talk was listed under the general topic "Double Binds: Managing Your Several Roles." The term *double binds* evokes images of multiple restraints, redundant bondage, a no-win situation. It is not one that I as a black woman in America can lightly
associate with myself. Our history is one of struggle and resistance, and the fight continues. *Bound,* however, has many meanings that better capture my actions, attitudes, and
aspirations than *tied down:* to be attached or devoted to, to move by leaps, to be on the
way, to be under a legal or moral obligation, and to secure within the covers of a book. I
am not a Pollyanna, and I am as pessimistic and cynical as can be. I simply refuse to be
doubly or triply bound in the negative sense of the term by a racist, sexist, and class-strat-
ified society without its hearing from me.

II. A Sapphire Named Crystal

The task of articulating and advancing distinctive minority feminist jurisprudential
stances will become easier as those of us interested in the status of minority women begin
to analyze concrete cases and legal problems. To substantiate my point that a black feminist perspective can and must be made manifest, I have attempted to apply the rough,
tentative thesis I advance above to the examination of a particular decision, *Chambers v.
Omaha Girls Club.*[16]

The plaintiff, Crystal Chambers, was employed by the defendant Girls Club of Omaha
(the Club) as an arts and crafts instructor at a facility where approximately 90 percent of
the program participants were black. Two years later, Chambers, an unmarried black
woman in her early twenties, was discharged from her job when she became pregnant.
Her dismissal was justified by the Club's so-called negative role model rule, which provided for the immediate discharge of staff guilty of "negative role modeling for Girls Club
Members," including "such things as single parent pregnancies."[17]

In her lawsuit, Crystal Chambers attacked the role model rule on several grounds. In
her Title VII claims, for example, she maintained that the rule would have a disparate

impact on black women because of their significantly higher fertility rate. She further asserted that her discharge constituted per se sex discrimination barred by the Pregnancy Discrimination Act of 1978. Although the soundness of these arguments was acknowledged, they were effectively countered by the business necessity and the bona fide occupational qualification defenses.[18]

The district court ruled against Crystal Chambers because it concluded that the Club's role model rule was the product of its dedication to the goal of "helping young girls reach their fullest potential." Programmatic concerns provided adequate support for the rule. According to the findings, the Club's activities were characterized by a "high staff to member ratio," "extensive contact," and "close relationships" between the staff and members, and an "open, comfortable atmosphere."[19] "Model" behavior by the staff and imitation by the members were essential to the Club's agenda:

> Those closely associated with the Girls Club contend that because of the unique nature of the Girls Club's operations, each activity, formal or informal, is premised upon the belief that the girls will or do emulate, at least in part, the behavior of staff personnel. Each staff member is trained and expected to act as a role model and is required, as a matter of policy, to be committed to the Girls Club philosophies so that the messages of the Girls Club can be conveyed with credibility.[20]

The Club's goal was to expose its members "to the greatest number of available positive options in life." "Teenage pregnancy [was] contrary to this purpose and philosophy" because it "severely limit[s] the available opportunities for teenage girls." Citing plaintiff's expert, the court stated that "teenage pregnancy often deprives young women of educational, social and occupational opportunities, creating serious problems for both the family and society."[21] The Club had several programs that related to pregnancy prevention.

In the opinion of the district court, the Club "established that it honestly believed that to permit single pregnant staff members to work with the girls would convey the impression that the Girls Club condoned pregnancy for the girls in the age group it serves." Furthermore, "while a single pregnant working woman may, indeed, provide a good example of hard work and independence, the same person may be a negative role model with respect to the Girls Club objective of diminishing the number of teenage pregnancies." The Club pointed to the reaction of two members to the earlier pregnancies of other single staffers in accounting for the genesis of the rule. In one case, a member who stated "that she wanted to have a baby as cute" as that of a staff member became pregnant shortly thereafter. In the second, a member became upset upon hearing of the pregnancy of an unmarried staff member.[22]

As painted by the court, there were numerous indications that the operative animus behind the role model rule was paternalistic, not racist or sexist. The North Omaha facility was "purposefully located to better serve a primarily black population." Although the Club's principal administrators were white, the girls served were black, the staff was black, and Crystal Chambers's replacements were black. "Great sensitivity" was shown to the problems of the staff members, including those who were black, pregnant, and unmarried. Plaintiff was even offered help in finding other employment after she was fired.[23]

The district court concluded its opinion as follows:

> This Court believes that the policy is a legitimate attempt by a private service organization to attack a significant problem within our society. The evidence has shown that the Girls Club did not intentionally discriminate against the plaintiff and that the

policy is related to the Girls Club's central purpose of fostering growth and maturity of young girls. . . . The Court emphasizes, however, that this decision is based upon the *unique* mission of the Girls Club of Omaha, the age group of the young women served, the geographic locations of the Girls Club facilities, and the comprehensive and historical methods the organization has employed in addressing the problem of teenage pregnancy.[24]

There were dissenting views among the Eighth Circuit judges who considered the case. In opposing the judgment in the Club's favor, Judge McMillian demanded hard evidence to support the legality of the negative role model rule:

> Neither an employer's sincere belief, without more, (nor a district court's belief), that a discriminatory employment practice is related and necessary to the accomplishments of the employer's goals is sufficient to establish a BFOQ or business necessity defense. The fact that the goals are laudable and the beliefs sincerely held does not substitute for data which demonstrate a relationship between the discriminatory practice and the goals.[25]

◊ ◊ ◊

The Club is not alone in leveling the charge of "negative role modeling" against unmarried black adult pregnant women and mothers who are said to be adversely affecting adolescent black females. For example, at a congressional hearing on pregnancy among black teenagers, Marian Wright Edelman of the Children's Defense Fund suggested that consideration should be given to the conduct of (black and white) entertainment celebrities and nonteenagers who have children out of wedlock. Said Edelman, "We must also remember the majority, two-thirds, of out-of-wedlock births in this Nation are to women over 20. Young women see the older generation do it. I think we need better moral examples."[26] Liz Walker, an unmarried black news anchorwoman in Boston, was extensively criticized for becoming pregnant and giving news interviews announcing her pregnancy in order to preempt speculation about her changing physical appearance. The *New York Times* reported that "many of the critics . . . said, that as a black woman, Ms. Walker had a special responsibility as a role model for black teen-agers, who are responsible for a disproportionately large share of out-of-wedlock births."[27] Carl Rowan, in a nationally syndicated column, mentioned the controversy, labeled teen parenthood "a national social tragedy," and concluded that he could not "see how a TV anchorwoman in Boston or anyplace else would feel comfortable adding to it."[28]

Thus, the motherhood of unmarried adult black women is being treated as if it were a social problem inextricably linked with, if not causally responsible for, teenage pregnancy. Both the adolescents and the adults have in common the degeneracy of engaging in intercourse that produces babies that other people think they should not have. But beyond their shared profligate sexuality, it is not entirely clear what connects single adult mothers and pregnant women with the conduct of their teenage counterparts. The concern may be that unmarried adult pregnancies and motherhood prompt teens to believe that sex before marriage is morally acceptable. The Club, however, denied that its discharge of Crystal Chambers was based upon her "premarital sexual activity."[29] Moreover, workers who were unwed mothers prior to the role model rule's promulgation were not subjected to punitive sanctions. It would be foolish, in any event, to expect abstinence on the part of all teens. Urging adolescents simply to say "no" may work just fine with respect to drugs; it is too much to think that the admonition will have as much efficacy when applied to premarital teenage sex.

Black adolescent pregnancy is considered more problematic today because teen mothers are less likely to be married at the time that they give birth than ever before and the families of single black females are generally poorer than those of either wage-earning black males or dual wage-earning black couples.[30] In addition to moral and social tenets that prescribe marriage as a prerequisite to motherhood, economic concerns suggest that young black women should be discouraged from becoming pregnant because of their singleness. It may be thought that condemning unwed pregnancy in general will foster increased wedlock on the part of teenss and adults alike, with a resulting improvement in the financial resources of black households. The goal is unlikely to be achieved with regard to teens, however, given the economic prospects of young black males. Moreover, marriage for pregnant adolescents is correlated with dropping out of school, having more babies, and ultimately being divorced or separated. A more reasonable alternative response to the impoverishment of black single-parent families would involve bolstering the earning capacity and economic well-being of black female heads of households.

Finally, the culture of poor black teens assigns a positive value to being pregnant[31] and tends to underestimate the emotional and physical perils of motherhood and the economic hardships of parenting. Perhaps it is assumed that if the cultural ethos more generally and strongly deprecated pregnancy unconnected with matrimony, unwed pregnancy would lose its attractive status, and the number of babies born to black teenagers would dramatically decline. Of course, a campaign directed against teenage pregnancy without regard to marital status might have the same effect. And as suggested above, the mechanisms of teen culture are too complex to justify the belief that denouncing single motherhood will translate into a change in adolescents' assessments of their own behavior.

In any event, the condemnation of black unwed motherhood is so deeply embedded in mainstream thought that its invocation in connection with teenage pregnancy may be considered uncontroversial. Single black mothers get blamed for so much that there is little reason not to blame them for teenage pregnancy as well. The accusation of negative role modeling on the part of black single mothers represents an extension of long-standing indictments that are the product of the unique variants of patriarchy that apply to black women alone. Poor and low-income black females who have children, maintain families of their own, and for whatever reason (whether because of choice or necessity) head households of their own have been labeled *matriarchs.*[32] In the mid-1960s, Daniel Patrick Moynihan argued that "the matriarchal structure" of the black family was an aspect of the "tangle of pathology" gripping the "Negro community" because it "seriously retards the progress of the group as a whole, and impsses a crushing burden on the Negro male and, in consequence, on a great many Negro women as well."[33] After "the Moynihan Report," the term *matriarch* became a slur even among blacks, an accusation that a woman was both antimale and antiblack. Matriarchs are disloyal to the black men with whom they share the common experience of racial oppression because they deny the men the opportunity to assert a semblance of masculine supremacy in a context that white people theoretically do not control. In addition, matriarchs are traitors to the cause of black liberation, the success of which depends on black males, first before others, securing parity of status with white men.

More contemporary appraisals of black single motherhood also pit black women against black men as well as each other and continue to leave black women hard pressed to articulate satisfactory justifications for their solo family formation. For example, the reality of the demographics of the black community suggest that there is a limited pool of eligible men for black women to marry. In 1986, there were 100,000 more black females between the ages of twenty and twenty-four than there were black males, and the ratio of males to females declined for each succeeding cadre at a faster rate than it did for whites.[34] Social scientists have concluded that there is a qualitative disparity between the socioeconomic status of black women and men which exacerbates the quantitative difference that the gross numbers reflect. In *The Truly Disadvantaged,* William Julius Wilson and Kathryn Neckerman hypothesize that the shortage of employed and, in their assessment, "marriageable" males is the principal factor accounting for the increased percentage of black female-headed families. Low-income men with jobs are more likely to marry the mothers of their children than those without work. Increasing rates of unemployment coupled with high male mortality and incarceration rates reduce the number of black males who are available and capable of supporting a family and thereby reduce the options of black women with regard to family structure.[35]

The emphasis on the "marriageability" of black men or their financial usefulness to a nuclear family exposes black women to attack on the grounds that they are insufficiently concerned about what racism and economic exploitation do to black men (their brothers, sons, and lovers) who, unemployed, incarcerated, or dead, are not of much use to themselves. Moreover, stressing the worsening economic position of black males as the prime reason for the increase in female-headed families is too often taken to be an endorsement of patriarchy as a normative ideal. As a result, changes in the socioeconomic status of black males are gauged in terms of their parity with black females, as opposed to more favorably situated white males, and advances by black women are seen as being at black men's expense.[36]

Other analyses of black single motherhood set up a conflict along both gender and class lines. The current hysteria over negative role modeling extends the stigma of unwed pregnancy and motherhood that has long plagued black women of the lower classes to those who are older (arbitrarily over twenty-four), "highly educated," and middle-class. Their economic security and emotional maturity, however, arguably make it reasonable for them to undertake the responsibilities of single parenthood. The ratio of males to females is particularly low if educational attainment is considered. Moreover, because unwed motherhood has become a more acceptable option for white middle-class women, comparably situated black females have reason to resent restrictions on their reproductive choices.

Denigrators espousing a supposedly "black" perspective should have a ready response to each of these points, inasmuch as the indictment of middle-class blacks who remain single applies equally well to middle-class black women who become unwed mothers. The single female parents too can be accused of assimilating white values that are not in keeping with the needs of the race. The black community cannot possibly "develop when its most educated members fail to marry." Moreover, it is doubtful that individualistic singlehood and parenthood are a "luxury" that "an oppressed racial minority can afford." Black children need to be reared and socialized in strong nuclear families.[37] If middle-class women cannot find suitable mates, it is likely that they are being too choosy, since black women have historically selected as partners men who do not possess comparable academic credentials.[38]

Those of us who are concerned about class cleavages among black women would also rebut the claim that middle-class females are entitled to a special exemption from criticism for their parenting choices. An assessment of single motherhood which emphasizes socioeconomic standing is no less offensive or divisive than blanket reproach. The notion of a means test for black motherhood is repulsive. It would be tantamount to delegating to economic forces hostile to the community the decision of who should have black children and who should not. The critique of the distribution of wealth which decidedly favors whites over blacks applies to some extent to the means by which middle-class blacks achieve their superior socioeconomic standing. Bourgeois black women should be no more privileged to bring children into the world than poor ones. What proof is there that middle-class black women are better mothers than poorer ones? Material convenience is not a moral necessity with regard to raising children.

Poor black women are not total captives of their material circumstances or strangers to the mores of the dominant society. Even though their options are limited, black women might still ask themselves what is the magic of having a husband. The support of an extended family has proven to be more reliable in some cases than marriage relationships.[39] Additionally, in situations where disappointed trust and misplaced reliance carry a high psychological and economic price, flexible relationships with lovers and boyfriends can be an asset.[40]

If we are to stake out an ethical black feminist position on single motherhood, it cannot be dependent on socioeconomic status. Furthermore, professional success and economic security do not buy black women freedom from other folks' ideas of their obligations to their race, their sex, and their class. Rather than trying to distinguish ourselves from one another, the general condemnation of black unwed pregnancy and female-headed families should be taken as proof that to some extent black women of all classes share a common ideological straitjacket insofar as motherhood and marriage are concerned.

At bottom, unmarried black woman workers who have babies are being accused of carrying on like modern-day Jezebels when they should be acting like good revisionist Mammies. Though not totally divorced from reality, Jezebel and Mammy were largely ideological constructs that supported slavery. Each pertained to black female slaves' intertwined roles as sexual beings and workers. Each justified the economic and sexual exploitation of black female slaves by reference to their character traits, rather than to the purposes of the masters. Jezebel was the wanton, libidinous black woman whose easy ways excused white men's abuse of their slaves as sexual "partners" and bearers of mulatto offspring. Jezebel was both "free of the social constraints that surrounded the sexuality of white women," as to whom she represented a threat, and "isolated from the men of her own community."[41]

In contrast, Mammy was "asexual," "maternal," and "deeply religious." Her principal tasks were caring for the master's children and running the household. Mammy was said to be so enamored of her white charges that she placed their welfare above that of her own children. Mammy was "the perfect slave—a loyal faithful, contented, efficient, conscientious member of the family who always knew her place; and she gave the slaves a white-approved standard of black behavior."[42] She was "the personification of the ideal slave, and the ideal woman. . . . an ideal symbol of the patriarchal tradition. She was not just a product of the 'cultural uplift' theory [*sic*] [which touted slavery as a means of civilizing blacks], but she was *also* a product of the forces that in the South raised motherhood to sainthood."[43]

Commentators have emphasized the negative implications of the Mammy stereotype. Writes Elizabeth Fox-Genovese:

> If implicitly the idea of the Mammy referred to motherhood and reproduction, it also claimed those privileges for the masters rather than for the slaves themselves. Just as Buck signaled the threat [to] master–slave relations, Mammy signaled the wish for organic harmony and projected a woman who suckled and reared white masters. The image displaced sexuality into nurture and transformed potential hostility into sustenance and love. It claimed for the white family the ultimate devotion of black women, who reared the children of others as if they were their own. Although the image of the Mammy echoed the importance that black slaves attached to women's roles as mothers, it derived more from the concerns of the master than from those of the slave.[44]

Bell Hooks sounds a similar theme:

> The mammy image was portrayed with affection by whites because it epitomized the ultimate sexist–racist vision of ideal black womanhood—complete submission to the will of whites. In a sense whites created in the mammy figure a black woman who embodied solely those characteristics they as colonizers wished to exploit. They saw her as the embodiment of woman as passive nurturer, a mother figure who gave all without expectation of return, who not only acknowledged her inferiority to whites but who loved them.[45]

Unsurprisingly, there have been efforts to redeem Mammy, I suppose, because the role in part praises black women's maternal qualities. For example, historian Eugene Genovese has concluded that while the black slave woman who actually occupied the position of Mammy "absorbed the paternalistic ethos" of her master's society, she also acquired "courage, compassion, dignity, and self-respect and might have provided a black model for these qualities among people who needed one, had not the constricting circumstances of her own development cut her off . . . from playing that role." Genovese continues, more ambivalently, "Her tragedy lay, not in her abandonment of her own people, but in her inability to offer her individual power and beauty to black people on terms they could accept without themselves sliding further into a system of paternalistic dependency."[46]

The critique of the images of black women whites have historically promoted is relevant to the assessment of the treatment accorded contemporary role models. Role models are supposed to forgo the vices of Jezebel and exhibit the many virtues of Mammy. The case of Crystal Chambers illustrates this quite well. When Crystal Chambers refused to subordinate her interest in motherhood to the supposed welfare of the Club girls, she essentially rejected the Club's attempt to impose upon her the "positive" stereotype of the black female as a repressed, self-sacrificing, nurturing woman whose heart extends to other people's children because she cannot (or should not) have kids of her own. Instead, like a Jezebel, Crystal Chambers "flaunted" her sexuality and reproductive capacity, but unlike her counterpart in slavery, she did so in furtherance of her own ends, in defiance of her white employers, and in disregard of a rule that forbade her from connecting with a man outside of the marriage relationship.

As if to resemble the role model Genovese says Mammy could have been, Crystal Chambers was supposed to expose the young Club members, the beneficiaries of white benevolence, to images congruent with traditional notions of patriarchy that were not entirely consistent with the norms of the black community. She was supposed to be an accomplice in regulating the sexuality of other young black females, in much the same way that she was expected to tolerate the regulation of her own. The courts would have us believe that the Club acted for the good of the girls who would miss out on a host of opportunities if they became teen mothers. Yet the distinction between paternalism and oppression is hardly crisper now than it was during slavery. It may be that the young women of the Club set are not fully informed that there is an increasing demand for their labor and are misreading the material landscape. On the other hand, they could be well informed and reaching more negative assessments of their actual economic prospects. If their options are indeed no greater than they imagine, the effort to repress their fertility may stem from its being dysfunctional for the larger society. Declining to live out the myth of the modern Mammy, Crystal Chambers refused to accept the yoke of either paternalism or oppression for herself and thereby freed the Club girls, to a small extent, from manipulation of their productive and reproductive capacities. Crystal Chambers then became valueless to her employers and was in essence expelled from the big house and returned to the field.

Breaking the hold of ideological shackles that have restricted black women's sexuality and fertility will not be easy. Hortense Spillers, a black female literary critic, has argued that "sexual experience among black people . . . is so boundlessly imagined that it loses meaning and becomes, quite simply, a medium through which the individual is suspended."[47] Jezebel and Mammy, harlot and nun, "whore" and "eunuch" have "acquire[d] mystical attribution . . . , divested of specific reference and dispersed over time and space in blind disregard for the particular agents on which it lands." Spillers likens this process to a mugging. She challenges feminist literary critics to find words that embody "differentiated responsiveness," words that enable us "to imagine women in their living and pluralistic confrontation with experience."[48] Her charge is equally relevant to black feminist jurisprudes.

Some of the black women who are not married yet have babies may be young and wise; others may be poor and brave; and yet a third group may be rich and selfish. Whether they confirm or confound the stereotypes, all of them deserve a measure of freedom with regard to their sexuality that the dominant culture withholds. All of them have the potential for being guerrilla fighters in a war that is being waged on three fronts. Struggles to control sexual expression and reproduction pit the combined hegemonic power of whites, males, and the middle class against overlapping constituencies of women, peolle of color, and ordinary working folks. Black values regarding individual family formation and parenthood decisions, as befits a community under siege, should facilitate, not interfere with, the critical vision which promotes the "seeing that negotiates at every point a space for living."[49] In other words, black women who attempt to express their sexuality and control their reproduction should not have to travel through a mine field of stereotypes, clichés, and material hardships with the handicap of a restriction that they keep to the right. Black women must be permitted to exercise their judgments without fear of reprisals from patriarchal, bourgeois, and culturally repressive elements within the black community. In an interview given some fifteen months after the birth of her son, news anchor Liz Walker, whose single pregnancy attracted strong disapproval from black clergy, described how she withstood the criticism which, if heeded, would have limited her options and constricted her life:

> Suppose I let my critics make my decision for me. Suppose I let the loudest outside vocal forces tell me what to do with my life. Hideous thought! I wouldn't have had my son.

> I believe in believing in myself. Answers have to come from within. This was a test.
> I made a decision that would influence the rest of my life. It had nothing to do with
> public opinion. I knew I had made the right decision.[50]

She should not have had to struggle.

There are significant norms that bind and create a basis for a community of concern among black men and women of various classes and outlooks. They support an agenda of systemic changes to strengthen minority families. Thus, economic resources should be available to both black men and women who want to maintain families with children. Black teenagers of both sexes should be given the means and the support required to delay parenthood until the time is best for them. Everybody else should be allowed to do what they want to do with the admonition that they give their offspring the advantages of the prenatal care, schools, and health programs that an ethical society would make available to assure its future.

Far too much importance is being attached to the impact of black role models. I am not debunking the notion that black youngsters need people beyond their families whose regard for them is reinforcing of their aspirations and ambitions. A sense of connection and closeness to an adult of the same sex and race might prove a valuable addition to familial interaction and supervision. Role models who are affectively engaged with youngsters and act in sync with the concerns and values of the black community are one thing; the sorts of role models the Club envisioned are another.

It is hard to think of Crystal Chambers, arts and crafts instructor, as a role model, as powerless and vulnerable as she ultimately proved to be. Her skills and natural behavior were not particularly valued by the people running the Club. Rather than being a role model by virtue of doing her job and living her own life, Chambers was supposed to perform the role of model, play a part that was not of her own design. She was a model in the sense that a model is "something made in a [ ] pliable material ([such] as clay or wax) [that is] intended to serve as a pattern of an object or figure to be made in a more permanent material."[51] When she deviated from the Club's philosophy and engaged in a practice that was common to the community of black women from which she and the members came, she was fired.

Crystal Chambers's experience is emblematic of the political significance of the professional "black role model" (including many of us lawyers and law professors) in this, the post–civil rights, post–black power era. Blacks are deluged with role models. Our attention is constantly being directed to some black person who is, should, or wants to be a role model for others.[52] Many of these role models are black people who have achieved stature and power in the white world because they supposedly represent the interests of the entire black community. Such role models gain capital (literally and figuratively) to the extent that they project an assimilated persona that is as unthreatening to white people as it is (supposed to be) intriguing to our young. They become embodiments of the liberal image of "the successful Negro" with perhaps a bit of "cut-up" thrown in to keep them credible. By their sheer visibility, they are of service to those left behind. They are functionally useful in providing images for emulation, and their legitimacy should be unquestioned. Because the emphasis on role modeling suggests that motivation and aspirations are the cure for the problems of poor minority people, those who accept the appellation *role model* help to contain demands from below for further structural changes and thereby assist in the management of other blacks. Insofar as doing more for the poor is concerned, the service role models perform is regrettably distinguishable from mentoring or power brokering; the role models really do not have very much clout to wield on behalf of other blacks, racial and sexual discrimination and exploitation being what they are.

Fortunately, the actual impact of these so-called role models is often reduced by the critical insight of the young people who are supposed to be overwhelmed by the positive impressions. For example, the mass media repeatedly referred to University of Maryland basketball player Len Bias as a role model after he died of a drug overdose. The *New York Times* reported that some of the young urban playground males it interviewed after Bias's death took a cynical view of the hype and even questioned the amount of attention paid to Bias: "In a society with rampant cocaine use by all races, they wondered aloud why a black man had been made into a symbol. How many white youths stopped using drugs, one teen-ager asked angrily, when John Belushi [the actor] died of an overdose of cocaine and heroin?"[53]

Role models are not an adequate response to material conditions that limit the choices of young black women, both those who get pregnant and those who do not. "Pride" and "positive identities" are not substitutes for "prosperity" or "power."[54] Material conditions have to be altered in a way that gives black youngsters the hope that they can come close to being the heroines and heroes of their own lives. To the extent that material conditions remain the same, they must be the subject of a sustained and forthright critique. Role models who do not have power to affect young women's life chances and who stand between them and the means to improve their prospects might as well be the enemy.

There are conceptions of "role modeling" that are not quite so alien to the political and cultural heritage of African-American women.[55] As far as I am concerned, Crystal Chambers became more nearly a role model when she fought back, when she became a Sapphire. Her legal protest brought the Club's contempt for the values of the population it served into the open. Her behavior and her lawsuit challenged the hegemony of the Club's white, patriarchal, and middle-class orientation. Her single motherhood represented an alternative social form that one might choose deliberately, rationally, and proudly. She made manifest the critique that is "life-as-it-is-lived" by ordinary black single mothers. Refusing to go along with the program, she joined the host of nonelite black women who everyday mount local, small-scale resistance grounded in indigenous cultural values, values whose real political potential is often hidden even from those whose lives they govern.

Nonetheless, there are times when low-volume defiance must give way to all-out "mouthing off." Crystal Chambers' rebellion was ended not because Title VII doctrine could not be manipulated in her favor, but because the presiding judges did not respect her normative framework. Her position should have been "out there," vocalized affirmatively, coherently, and vehemently by black women and others, before she got to court. History suggests that black people's resort to conventional warfare on the legal terrain proceeds more smoothly when the positions underlying their claims of entitlement have achieved some positive visibility via skirmishes in the cultural and political domains. Of course, concrete legal cases that prove to be losing efforts may nonetheless provide an opportunity for lawyers and law professors to get their acts together, to engage the enemy, and to refine their arguments. Although the frontline may remain in a distant realm, ideas do percolate from one sphere to another, and those of us who are daring may move about as well. Next time we should all be better prepared.

III. For Kanti and Asia and Fatima . . . and Ruth (Which is to say, Sapphires by Another Name)

◊ ◊ ◊

The reign of President Reagan was blessed with unusual legal and political quiescence among black women, but the signs of dissent are there. I have often wondered why black women give their daughters the names they do. Names like Kanti, Asia, Fatima, Rashiah, Tamika, Latoya, Chauntel, Ebony, and DaJuvetta (for David). The mothers in naming them and the girls in being so named share a bond with other distinctively named black women that extends backward in time to slavery. Desperation born of material and political powerlessness may be operating here. Perhaps the mothers are trying to give to their daughters a mark of distinction that will otherwise be denied them because they are black and female. Uncommon names also generate hostility that can be a severe handicap.[56] I like to think that the names are in part an expression of group solidarity and self-affirmation, and not the by-product of the mothers' unfamiliarity with and isolation from the dominant culture. Whether the naming practices represent a tactic of opposition, a critique of a society that typically chooses to call its female children Ashley, Jessica, Amanda, and the like, and a form of cultural resistance, I do not know. The possibility should be fully explored. It is my fondest hope, however, that whatever their mothers' motivations, the little black girls will grow up to see the positive potential of what their mothers did and relish being Sapphires by another name.

Notes

The first part of this chapter is based on a presentation given at the American Association of Law Schools Workshop for Women in Legal Education, which was held in Washington, D.C., on October 22–24, 1987. Drafts were presented to the Ad Hoc Seminar of the University of Pennsylvania Law School. I must acknowledge the assistance I have received from a number of black female law professors, especially those of the informal Northeastern corridor collective. Susan Sturm, Michelle Fine, and Michael Schill provided particularly helpful comments. I want to thank Jacqueline Sanchez, Elise Zoli, Juan Gomez, and Margo Brodie for their research assistance. The views I express and the way I express them are, of course, my responsibility alone.

1. New Dictionary of American Slang 368 (R. Chapman ed. 1986). *Amos 'n' Andy* originated as a radio comedy program about two black males. B. Andrews and A. Juilliard, Holy Mackerel! The Amos 'n' Andy Story 15–16 (1986). It was first broadcast in 1928, and the characters were played by the program's white originators. *Id. Amos 'n' Andy* came to CBS television in 1951, *id.* at 60–61, with a cast of carefully chosen black actors, *id.* at 45–59. Various black civil rights organizations condemned the television version "as insulting to blacks" and as portraying blacks "in a stereotyped and derogatory manner." The sponsor withdrew from the show, and it was dropped by the network in 1953, *id.* at 61, 101. It lived on in syndication until 1966, *id.* at 118, 121–22.

2. B. Hooks, Ain't I a Woman: Black Women and Feminism 85-86 (1981); Scott, *Debunking Sapphire: Toward a Non-Racist and Non-Sexist Social Science, in* All the Women Are White, All the Blacks Are Men, but Some of Us Are Brave 85 (G. Hall, P. Scott, and B. Smith eds. 1982).

3. Among the most readily identifiable legal sources on the legal problems of black women are Scales-Trent, *Black Women and the Constitution: Finding Our Place, Asserting Our Rights,* 24 Harv. C.R.–C.L. L. Rev. 9 (1989); Ellis, *Sexual Harassment and Race: A Legal Analysis of Dis-*

crimination, 8 NOTRE DAME J. LEGIS. 30 (1981); and Martin, *Race, Gender, and Southern Justice: The Rosa Lee Ingram Case,* 29 AM. J. LEGAL HIST. 251 (1985).

4. *See, e.g.,* T. MORRISON, BELOVED (1987); T. MORRISON, SULA (1974); T. MORRISON, THE BLUEST EYE (1972).

5. *See, e.g.,* A. WALKER, THE COLOR PURPLE (1982); A. WALKER, MERIDIAN (1976).

6. L. ERDRICH, THE BEET QUEEN (1986); L. ERDRICH, LOVE MEDICINE (1984).

7. M. KINGSTON, THE WOMAN WARRIOR: MEMOIRS OF A GIRLHOOD AMONG GHOSTS (1976).

8. *See, e.g.,* J. ROLLINS, BETWEEN WOMEN: DOMESTICS AND THEIR EMPLOYERS 138–47 (1985); Sacks, *Computers. Ward Secretaries, and a Walkout in a Southern Hospital,* in MY TROUBLES ARE GOING TO HAVE TROUBLE WITH ME: EVERYDAY TRIALS AND TRIUMPHS OF WOMEN WORKERS 173, 180–81 (K. Sacks and D. Remy eds. 1984).

9. H. BAKER, WORKINGS OF THE SPIRIT: THE POETICS OF AFRO-AMERICAN WOMEN'S WRITING (forthcoming).

10. Alliance Against Women's Oppression, *Poverty: Not for Women Only—A Critique of the "Feminization of Poverty,"* in THE BLACK FAMILY: ESSAYS AND STUDIES 239 (R. Staples 3d ed. 1986).

11. *See* Comment, *With Insurance Like This Who Needs Enemies?: Reforming California's Industrial Life Insurance Industry,* 13 U.C. DAVIS L. REV. 273 (1980).

12. *See* U.S. DEP'T OF HEALTH AND HUMAN SERVICES, REPORT OF THE SECRETARY'S TASK FORCE ON BLACK AND MINORITY HEALTH (1985) (Vol. 1, Executive Summary).

13. *U.S. Falling Short on Its Infant Health Goals, New York Times.* July 10, 1988. § 1, at 17. col. 1.

14. *See* Austin, *Employer Abuse, Worker Resistance, and the Tort of Intentional Infliction of Emotional Distress,* 41 STAN. L. REV. 1 (1988).

15. The imperative for such theorizing is illustrated by Sandra Morgen's account of the struggle of a group of poor women in a New England city who organized to keep open a low-cost clinic providing prenatal and gynecological services. Morgen, *"It's the Whole Power of the City Against Us!": The Development of Political Consciousness in a Women's Health Care Coalition,* in WOMEN AND THE POLITICS OF EMPOWERMENT 97 (A. Bookman and S. Morgen eds. 1988). The alternative available to the women was visits to the same physicians who staffed the clinic during their private practice hours and at private practice rates, *id.* at 98. The women's commitment remained strong so long as they were engaged in direct negotiations with the representatives of the health care establishment. The representatives, however, refused their demands and directed them to file a claim with the federal Health Systems Agency (HSA), *id.* at 101. After the hospital received HSA's investigatory report before the claimants did, they were forced to file a lawsuit in order to keep pressure on the hospital and to gain access to withheld information, *id.* at 102. The suit "became more time-consuming than anticipated and entangled [the women] in legalistic, bureaucratic tasks to the increasing exclusion of grassroots activity," *id.* at 102. The hospital reopened the clinic, denied access to most of the women who fought the closing, and gave the women no credit for the decision, *id.* at 102–03. Demoralized, the group was disbanded, *id.* at 103.

16. 629 F. Supp. 925 (D. Neb. 1986), *aff'd,* 834 F.2d 697 (8th Cir. 1987), *reh'g denied,* 840 F.2d 583 (1988).

17. 834 F.2d at 699 n.2.

18. 834 F.2d at 703–5, 946–49.

19. 629 F. Supp. at 943, 928.

20. *Id.*

21. *Id.* at 928–29, 950.

22. *Id.* at 945, 950–51.

23. *Id.* at 928–46.

24. *Id.* at 951–52 (emphasis in original).

25. 834 F.2d at 708.

26. *Pregnancy Among Black Teenagers: Hearing Before the Subcommittee on Public Assistance and Unemployment Compensation of the House Ways and Means Committee* 53 (1986).

27. *Pregnant, Unmarried and Much in the Public Eye, New York Times,* July 12, 1987. § 1, at 27, col. 4.

28. Rowan, *Bostonians Are in Swivet over Role Model Behavior. Atlanta Constitution.* June 18, 1987, at 19A, col. 1.

29. 629 F. Supp. at 946.

30. W. WILSON The Truly Disadvantaged at 71–72 (1987).

31. Pregnant teens report that their relationships with parents, partners, and peers are closer than they were before they became pregnant and that they are the objects of increased attention. *See* A. Graham. Teenage Pregnancy: A Study of Pregnant and Non-Pregnant Urban Black High School Students on Personality. Societal and Family Factors 80 (1986) (doctoral dissertation, Rutgers University).

32. Hooks reminds us that black women in America are not really matriarchs, since they lack economic security, social and political power, control over their bodies, and a preference for daughters. B. HOOKS, at 71–77.

33. OFFICE OF PLANNING AND POLICY RESEARCH. U.S. DEP'T OF LABOR. THE NEGRO FAMILY: THE CASE FOR NATIONAL ACTION 29 (1965).

34. BUREAU OF THE CENSUS, U.S. DEP'T OF COMMERCE, STATISTICAL ABSTRACT OF THE UNITED STATES 17 (108th ed. 1988).

35. W. WILSON, at 81–89.

36. For example, a *New York Times* article ostensibly about the shrinking college enrollment of black males had as its theme the concern that because of the decline, black women would wind up with better educations, more prestigious jobs, higher incomes, and a larger share of the leadership roles, and the resulting social and economic imbalance between black men and women would "undermine black institutions." Daniels, *Experts Foresee a Social Gap Between Sexes Among Blacks,* N.Y. *New York Times,* February 5, 1989, § 1, at 1, col. 5.

37. Staples, *Beyond the Black Family: The Trend Toward Singlehood,* in THE BLACK FAMILY, at 99, 101, 105.

38. Spanier and Glick, *Mate Selection Differentials Between Whites and Blacks in the United States,* in THE BLACK FAMILY, at 114, 123–25.

39. *See* McAdoo, *Strategies Used by Black Single Mothers Against Stress,* in SLIPPING THROUGH THE CRACKS: THE STATUS OF BLACK WOMEN, at 153; H. McADOO, CHANGES IN THE FORMATION AND STRUCTURE OF BLACK FAMILIES: THE IMPACT ON BLACK WOMEN 19–22 (Wellesley College Center for Research on Women Working Paper no. 182, 1988).

40. *See* C. WILLIE, A NEW LOOK AT BLACK FAMILIES 54–57, 149–56 (2d ed. 1981).

41. E. FOX-GENOVESE, WITHIN THE PLANTATION HOUSEHOLD: BLACK AND WHITE WOMEN OF THE OLD SOUTH 292 (1988).

42. E. GENOVESE, ROLL, JORDAN, ROLL: THE WORLD THE SLAVES MADE 353–56 (1972), at 356–57.

43. D. WHITE, AR'N'T I A WOMAN? FEMALE SLAVES IN THE PLANTATION SOUTH 46, 58, 61 (1985).

44. E. FOX-GENOVESE, at 291–92.

45. B. HOOKS, at 84–85.

46. E. GENOVESE, at 360–61.

47. Spillers, *Interstices: A Small Drama of Words.* in PLEASURE AND DANGER, at 73, 85.

48. *Id.* at 94.

49. *Id.* at 84.

50. Christy, *Liz Walker Talks About Her "Real Riches,"* Boston Globe, March 22, 1989, at 75, 77, col. 1.

51. WEBSTER'S THIRD NEW INTERNATIONAL DICTIONARY 1451 (1981).

52. *See, e.g.,* B. REYNOLDS, AND STILL WE RISE: INTERVIEWS WITH 50 BLACK ROLE MODELS (1988).

53. Freedman, *From Playgrounds, Observations on Len Bias, New York Times,* June 29, 1986, § 1, at 1, 28, col. 3.

54. C. VALENTINE, CULTURE AND POVERTY 151 (1968).

55. *See* Gilkes, *Successful Rebellious Professionals: The Black Woman's Professional Identity and Community Commitment,* 6 PSYCHOLOGY OF WOMEN Q. 289 (1982).

56. *See* Jackson, *Names "Can" Hurt,* ESSENCE, April 1989, at 134 (an assimilationist attack by a black woman on the naming practices of poor, young black mothers); Reynolds, *Making Names for Themselves. Boston Globe,* April 7, 1989, at 33. col. 4 (reporting on the debate among "African Americans" regarding distinctive names).

24

Feminist Critical Theories

DEBORAH L. RHODE

Heidi Hartmann once described the relation between Marxism and feminism as analogous to that of husband and wife under English common law: "Marxism and feminism are one, and that one is Marxism." In Hartmann's view, "Either we need a healthier marriage or we need a divorce."[1] Responding to that metaphor, Gloria Joseph underscored the exclusion of black women from the wedding and redescribed the interaction between Marxist, feminist, and minority perspectives as an "incompatible ménage à trois."[2]

The relations between critical legal studies (CLS) and feminism have provoked similar concerns. The origins of this article are a case in point. The piece grows out of an invitation to offer a feminist perspective for an anthology on critical legal studies.[3] Such invitations are problematic in several respects. Almost any systematic statement about these two bodies of thought risks homogenizing an extraordinarily broad range of views. Moreover, providing some single piece on the "woman question" perpetuates a tradition of tokenism that has long characterized left political movements.

Whatever the risks of other generalizations, one threshold observation is difficult to dispute: Feminism takes gender as a central category of analysis, while the core texts of critical legal studies do not. To be sure, many of these texts make at least some reference to problems of sex-based subordination and to the existence (if not the significance) of feminist scholarship. Yet most critical legal theory and the traditions on which it relies have not seriously focused on gender inequality. Why then should feminists continue participating in enterprises in which their perspectives are added but not integrated, rendered separate but not equal?

Efforts to provide the "woman's point of view" also risk contributing to their own marginalization. In effect, feminists are invited to explain how their perspectives differ from others associated with critical legal studies or with more mainstream bodies of legal theory. Such invitations impose the same limitations that have been characteristic for women's issues in conventional legal ideology. Analysis has fixated on how women are the same or different from men; men have remained the unstated standard of analysis.

In recent years, these concerns have increasingly emerged within the critical legal studies movement. During the last decade, issues of gender as well as race and ethnicity dominated the agendas of several national CLS conferences, and feminist theorists organized regional groups around common interests. A growing body of feminist and critical race scholarship also developed along lines that paralleled, intersected, and challenged critical legal theory.[4]

This chapter charts relationships among these bodies of work. Although no brief overview can adequately capture the range of scholarship that coexists under such labels, it is at least possible to identify some crosscutting objectives, methodologies, and concerns. The point of this approach is neither to develop some unifying Grand Theory nor simply to compare feminism with other critical frameworks. Rather, it is to underscore the importance of multiple frameworks that avoid universal or essentialist claims and that yield concrete strategies for social change.

The following discussion focuses on a body of work that may be loosely identified as feminist crticial theories. Although they differ widely in other respects, these theories share three central commitments. On a political level, they seek to promote equality between women and men. On a substantive level, feminist critical frameworks make gender a focus of analysis; their aim is to reconstitute legal practices that have excluded, devalued, or undermined women's concerns. On a methodological level, these frameworks aspire to describe the world in ways that correspond to women's experience and that identify the fundamental social transformations necessary for full equality between the sexes. These commitments are, for the most part, mutually reinforcing, but they occasionally pull in different directions. This essay explores various ways that feminists have sought to fuse a political agenda that is dependent on both group identity and legalist strategies with a methodology that is in some measure skeptical of both.

What distinguishes feminist critical theories from other analysis is both the focus on gender equality and the conviction that it cannot be obtained under existing ideological and institutional structures. This theoretical approach partly overlaps and frequently draws upon other critical approaches, including CLS and critical race scholarship. At the most general level, these traditions share a common goal: to challenge existing distributions of power. They also often employ similar deconstructive or narrative methodologies aimed at similar targets—certain organizing premises of conventional liberal legalism. Each tradition includes both internal and external critiques. Some theorists focus on the inadequacy of conventional legal doctrine in terms of its own criteria for coherence, consistency, and legitimacy. Other commentators emphasize the role of legal ideology in legitimating unjust social conditions. Yet these traditions also differ considerably in their theories about theory, in their critiques of liberal legalism, in their strategies for change, and in their alternative social visions.

I. Theoretical Premises

Critical feminism, like other critical approaches, builds on recent currents in social theory that have made theorizing increasingly problematic. Postmodern and poststructural traditions that have influenced left legal critics presuppose the social construction of knowledge.[5] To varying degrees, critics within these traditions deny the possibility of any universal foundations for critique. Taken as a whole, their work underscores the cultural, historical, and linguistic construction of human identity and social experience.[6]

Yet such a theoretical stance also limits its own aspirations to authority. For feminists, this postmodern paradox creates political as well as theoretical difficulties. Adherents are left in the awkward position of maintaining that gender oppression exists while challenging our capacity to document it.[7] Such awkwardness is, for example, especially pronounced in works that assert as unproblematic certain "facts" about the pervasiveness of sexual abuse while questioning the possibility of any objective measure.[8]

To take an obvious illustration, feminists have a stake both in quantifying the frequency of rape and in questioning the conventional definitions on which rape statistics are based. Victims of sexual assault by acquaintances often respond to questions such as, "Have you ever been raped?" with something like, "Well . . . not exactly." What occurs in the pause between "well" and "not exactly" suggests the gap between the legal understanding and social experience of rape, and the ways in which data on abuse are constructed, not simply collected.

Although responses to this dilemma vary widely, the most common feminist strategies bear mention. The simplest approach is to decline to address the problem—at least at the level of abstraction at which it is customarily formulated. The revolution will not be made with slogans from Lyotard's *Postmodern Condition,* and the audiences that are most in need of persuasion are seldom interested in epistemological anxieties. Critiques of existing ideology and institutions can proceed under their own standards without detailed discussions of the philosophy of knowledge. Yet even from a purely pragmatic view, it is helpful to have some self-consciousness about the grounding for our claims about the world and the tensions between our political and methodological commitments.

Critical feminism's most common response to questions about its own authority has been reliance on experiential analysis. This approach draws primarily on techniques of consciousness raising in contemporary feminist organizations but also on pragmatic philosophical traditions. A standard practice is to begin with concrete experiences, integrate these experiences into theory, and rely on theory for a deeper understanding of the experiences. One distinctive feature of feminist critical analysis is, as Katharine Bartlett emphasizes, a grounding in practical problems and a reliance on "practical reasoning."[9] Rather than working deductively from abstract principles and overarching conceptual schemes, such analysis builds from the ground up. Many feminist legal critics are also drawn to narrative styles that express the personal consequences of institutionalized injustice.[10] Even those commentators most wedded to broad categorical claims usually situate their works in the lived experience of pornography or sexual harassment rather than, for example, in the deep structure of Blackstone's *Commentaries* or the fundamental contradictions in Western political thought.[11]

In part, this pragmatic focus reflects the historical origins and contemporary agenda of feminist legal theory. Unlike critical legal studies, which began as a movement within the legal academy and took much of its inspiration from the Grand Theory of contemporary Marxism and the Frankfurt school, feminist legal theories emerged against the backdrop of a mass political movement. In America, that struggle has drawn much of its intellectual inspiration not from overarching conceptual schemes but from efforts to provide guidance on particular substantive issues. As Carrie Menkel-Meadow has argued, the strength of feminism "originates" in the experience of "*being* dominated, not just in thinking about domination" and in developing concrete responses to that experience.[12] Focusing on women's actual circumstances helps reinforce the connection between feminist political and analytic agendas, but it raises its own set of difficulties. How can critics build a unified political and analytical stance from women's varying perceptions of their varying experiences? And what entitles that stance to special authority?

The first question arises from a long-standing tension in feminist methodology. What gives feminism its unique force is the claim to speak from women's experience. But that experience counsels sensitivity to its own diversity across such factors as time, culture, class, race, ethnicity, sexual orientation, and age. As Martha Minow has noted, "cognitively we need simplifying categories, and the unifying category of 'woman' helps to organize experience, even at the cost of denying some of it."[13] Yet to some constituencies, particularly those who are not white, heterosexual, and economically privileged, that cost appears prohibitive, since it is their experience that is most often denied.

A variation of this problem arises in discussions of "false consciousness." How can feminists wedded to experiential analysis respond to women who reject feminism's basic premises as contrary to their experience? In an extended footnote to an early article, Catharine MacKinnon noted:

> Feminism aspires to represent the experience of all women as women see it, yet criticizes antifeminism and misogyny, including when it appears in female form. . . . [Conventional response treat] some women's views as unconscious conditioned reflections of their oppression, complicitous in it. . . . [T]his approach criticizes the substance of a view because it can be accounted for by its determinants. But if both feminism and antifeminism are responses to the condition of women, how is feminism exempt from devaluation by the same account? That feminism is critical, and antifeminism is not, is not enough, because the question is the basis on which we know something is one or the other when women, all of whom share the condition of women, disagree.[14]

Yet having raised the problem, MacKinnon declined to pursue it. As a number of feminist reviewers have noted, MacKinnon has never reconciled her unqualified condemnation of opponents with her reliance on experiential methodology.[15]

The issue deserves closer attention, particularly since contemporary survey research suggests that the vast majority of women do not experience the world in the terms that most critical feminists describe.[16] Nor do these feminists agree among themselves about which experiental accounts of women's interests should be controlling in disputes involving, for example, pornography, prostitution, surrogate motherhood, or maternity leaves.

A related issue is how any experiential account can claim special authority. Most responses to this issue take one of three forms. The first approach is to invoke the experience of exclusion and subordination as a source of special insight. According to Menkel-Meadow, the "feminist critique starts from the experiential point of view of the oppressed, dominated, and devalued, while the critical legal studies critique begins—and, some would argue, remains—in a male-constructed, privileged place in which domination and oppression can be described and imagined but not fully experienced."[17] Yet such "standpoint" theories, if left unqualified, present their own problems of privilege. There remains the issue of whose standpoint to credit, since not all women perceive their circumstances in terms of domination and not all who share that perception agree on its implications. Nor is gender the only source of oppression. Other forms of subordination, most obviously class, race, ethnicity, and sexual orientation, can yield comparable and, in some instances competing, claims to subjugated knowledge. To privilege any single trait risks impeding coalitions and understating other forces that constitute our identities.

A second feminist strategy is to claim that women's distinctive attributes promote a distinctive form of understanding. Robin West has argued, for example, that there is surely no way to know with any certainty whether women have a privileged access to a way of life that is more nurturant, more caring, more natural, more loving, and thereby more moral than the lives which both men and women presently pursue in the public sphere, including the legal sphere of legal practice, theory, and pedagogy. But it does seem that whether by reason of sociological role, psychological upbringing or biology, women are *closer* to such a life.[18]

Such claims occur in more muted form in much of the legal scholarship that draws on relational strands of feminist theory. This line of analysis, popularized by Carol Gilligan, argues that women tend to reason in "a different voice"; they are less likely than men to privilege abstract rights over concrete relationships and are more attentive to values of care, connection, and context.[19] The strength of this framework lies in its demand that values traditionally associated with women be valued and that legal strategies focus on altering societal structures, not just assimilating women within them. Such an approach can yield theoretical and political cohesiveness on initiatives that serve women's distinctive needs.

Yet such efforts to claim an authentic female voice illustrate the difficulty of theorizing from experience without essentializing or homogenizing it. There is no "generic woman,"[20] or any uniform "condition of women."[21] To divide the world solely along gender lines is to ignore ways in which biological constraints are experienced differently by different groups under different circumstances. If, as critical feminists generally maintain, women's experience has been shaped through culturally contingent patterns of subordination, no particular experience can claim universal authentic status. Moreover, to emphasize only the positive attributes traditionally associated with women is to risk overclaiming and oversimplifying their distinctive contributions. Most empirical work on moral reasoning and public values discloses less substantial gender differences than relational frameworks generally suggest.[22] These frameworks also reinforce dichotomous stereotypes—such as males' association with abstract rationality and females' with empathetic nurturance—that have restricted opportunities for both sexes.

Such concerns underpin those strands of critical feminism that focus on challenging rather than celebrating sex-based difference. The virtue of their approach lies in revealing how legal ideology has misdescribed cultural constructions as biological imperatives. Yet the strengths of this framework also suggest its limitations. Affirmations of similarity between the sexes may inadvertently institutionalize dominant social practices and erode efforts to build group solidarity. Denying difference can, in some contexts, reinforce values that critics seek to change.

A more promising response to the "difference dilemma," and to more general questions about feminist epistemology, is to challenge the framework in which these issues are typically debated. The crucial issue becomes not difference, but the difference difference makes. In legal contexts, the legitimacy of sex-based treatment should not depend on whether the sexes are differently situated. Rather, analysis should turn on whether legal recognition of gender distinctions is likely to reduce or reinforce gender disparities in power, status, and economic security. Since such issues cannot be resolved in the abstract, this strategy requires contextual judgments, not categorical choices. It asks which perspective on difference can best serve particular theoretical or practical objectives and recognizes that there may be trade-offs between them. Such an approach demands that feminists shift self-consciously among needs to acknowledge both distinctiveness and commonality between the sexes and unity and diversity among their members.

On the more general question of what validates any particular feminist claim, the first step is to deconstruct the dualistic framework of truth and falsehood in which these issues are often discussed. As postmodernist theorists remind us, all perspectives are partial, but some are more incomplete than others. To disclaim objective standards of truth is not to disclaim all value judgments. We need not become positivists to believe that some accounts of experience are more consistent, coherent, inclusive, self-critical, and so forth. Critical feminism can illuminate the process by which claims about the world are constituted as well as the effects of marginalizing women and other subordinate groups in that process. Such a framework can subject traditional forms of argument and criteria of relevance to sustained scrutiny. It can challenge exclusionary institutions in which knowledge is constructed. And it can press for social changes that would encourage deeper understanding of our experience and the forces that affect it.

Although critical feminists by no means speak with one voice on any of these issues, part of our strength lies in building on our differences as well as our commonalities. Precisely because we do not share a single view on this, or other more substantive concerns, we need theories but not Theory. Our objective should be multiple accounts that avoid privileging any single universalist or essentialist standpoint. We need understandings that can resonate with women's shared experience without losing touch with our diversity. The factors that divide us can also be a basis for enriching our theoretical perspectives and expanding our political alliances. Any framework adequate to challenge sex-based oppression must simultaneously condemn the other forms of injustice with which it intersects.

What allies this method with other critical accounts is its skepticism toward everything, including skepticism. Critical feminist theories retain a commitment to locate judgment within the patterns of social practice, to subject that judgment to continuing critique, and to promote gender equality as a normative ideal. Those commitments may take us in multiple directions, but as Martha Minow maintains, they are unifying commitments nonetheless.[23]

II. Liberal Legalism

For CLS theorists, the most frequent unifying theme is opposition to a common target: the dominance of liberal legalism and the role law has played in maintaining it.[24] On this issue, critical feminism offers more varied and more ambivalent responses. This diversity in part reflects the diversity of perspectives within the liberal tradition. The target appearing in many critical legal studies accounts and in some critical feminist analyses is only one version of liberal legalism, generally the version favored by law and economics commentators. Under a more robust framework, many inequalities of greatest concern to feminists reflect limitations less in liberal premises than in efforts to realize liberalism's full potential.

From both a philosophical and pragmatic standpoint, feminist legal critics have less stake in the assault on liberalism than CLS. Their primary target is gender inequality, whatever its pedigree, and their allies in many concrete political struggles have come as often from liberal as from radical camps. Thus, when critical feminist theorists join the challenge to liberal legalism, they often do so on somewhat modified grounds. Their opposition tends to focus on the particular form of liberalism embodied in existing legal and political structures and on the gender biases it reflects.

Although they differ widely in other respects, liberal theorists generally begin from the premise that the state's central objective lies in maximizing individuals' freedom to pursue their own objectives to an extent consistent with the same freedom for others. Implicit in this vision are several assumptions about the nature of individuals and the subjectivity of values. As conventionally presented, the liberal state is composed of autonomous, rational individuals. Their expressed choices reflect a stable and coherent understanding of their independent interests. Yet while capable of full knowledge of their own preferences, these liberal selves lack similar knowledge about others. Accordingly, the good society remains as neutral as possible about the meaning of the good life: It seeks simply to provide the conditions necessary for individuals to maximize their own preferences through voluntary transactions. Although liberal theorists differ widely about what those background conditions entail, they share a commitment to preserving private zones for autonomous choices, free from public intervention.[25]

Critical feminist theorists have challenged this account along several dimensions. According to theorists such as West, these liberal legalist selves are peculiarly masculine constructs—peculiarly capable of infallible judgments about their own wants and peculiarly incapable of empathetic knowledge about the wants of others.[26] Classic liberal frameworks take contractual exchanges rather than affiliative relationships as the norm. Such frameworks undervalue the ways social networks construct human identities and the ways individual preferences are formed in reference to the needs and concerns of others. For many women, a nurturing, giving self has greater normative and descriptive resonance than an autonomous, egoistic self.[27]

Critical feminists by no means agree about the extent, origins, or implications of such gender differences. Some concept of autonomy has been central to the American women's movement since its inception, autonomy from the constraints of male authority and traditional roles. How much emphasis to place on values of self-determination and how much to place on values of affiliation have generated continuing controversies that cannot be resolved at the abstract level on which debate has often foundered. Even critical feminists who agree about the significance of difference disagree about its causes and likely persistence. Disputes center on how much importance is attributable to women's intimate connection to others through childbirth and identification with primary caretakers, how much to cultural norms that encourage women's deference, empathy, and disproportionate assumption of nurturing responsibilities, and how much to inequalities in women's status and power.

Yet despite these disagreements, most critical feminists share an emphasis on the importance of social relationships in shaping individual preferences. From such a perspective, no adequate conception of the good society can be derived through standard liberal techniques, which hypothesize social contracts among atomistic actors removed from the affiliations that give meaning to their lives and content to their choices.

This feminist perspective points up a related difficulty in liberal frameworks, which critical theorists from a variety of traditions have noted. The liberal assumption that individuals' expressed preferences can be taken as reflective of genuine preferences is flatly at odds with much of what we know about human behavior. To a substantial extent, our choices are socially constructed and constrained; the desires we develop are partly a function of the desires our culture reinforces. As long as gender plays an important role in shaping individual expectations and aspirations, expressed objectives cannot be equated with full human potential. Women, for example, may "choose" to remain in an abusive relationship, but such choices are not ones most liberals would want to maximize. Yet a liberal legalist society has difficulty distinguishing between "authentic" and "inauthentic" preferences without violating its own commitments concerning neutrality and the subjectivity of value.

Similar problems arise with the legal ideology that underpins contemporary liberal frameworks. In its conventional form, liberal legalism assumes that appropriate conduct can be defined primarily in terms of adherence to procedurally legitimate and determinate rules, that law can be separated from politics, and that spheres of private life can be insulated from public intrusion.[28] Critical feminism challenges all of these assumptions on both empirical and normative levels.

The feminist critique joins other CLS work in denying that the rule of law in fact offers a principled, impartial, and determinate means of dispute resolution. Attention has centered both on the subjectivity of legal standards and the gender biases in their application. By exploring particular substantive areas, feminists have underscored the law's fluctuation between standards that are too abstract to resolve particular cases and rules that are too specific to result in principled, generalizable norms.[29] Such explorations have also revealed sex-based assumptions that undermine the liberal legal order's own aspirations.

These limitations in conventional doctrine are particularly apparent in the law's consistently inconsistent analysis of gender difference. Decision makers have often reached identical legal results from competing factual premises. In other cases, the same notions about sexual distinctiveness have yielded opposite conclusions. Identical assumptions about woman's special virtues or vulnerabilities have served as arguments for both favored and disfavored legal treatment in criminal and family law and for both including and excluding her from public roles such as professional occupations and jury service. For example, although courts and legislatures traditionally assumed that it was "too plain" for discussion that sex-based distinctions in criminal sentencing statutes and child custody decisions were appropriate, it was less plain which way those distinctions cut. Under different statutory schemes, women received lesser or greater punishments for the same criminal acts and in different historical periods were favored or disfavored as the guardians of their children.[30]

The law's traditional approach to gender-related issues has not only yielded indeterminate interpretations; it has allowed broad mandates of formal equality to mask substantive inequality. Part of the problem with "difference" as an organizing principle is that legal decision makers do not always seem to know it when they see it. One of the most frequently noted illustrations is the Supreme Court's 1974 conclusion that pregnancy discrimination did not involve gender discrimination or even "gender a such"; employers were simply distinguishing between "pregnant women and non-pregnant persons."[31] So too, although most contemporary divorce legislation promises "equal" or "equitable" property distributions between spouses, wives have in practice received neither equality nor equity. In the vast majority of cases, women end up with far greater caretaking responsibilities and far fewer resources to discharge them.[32]

Such indeterminacies and biases also undermine the liberal legalist distinction between public and private spheres. From a critical feminist view, the boundary between state and family is problematic on both descriptive and prescriptive grounds. As an empirical matter, the state inevitably participates in determining what counts as private and what forms of intimacy deserve public protection. Governmental policies concerning child care, tax, inheritance, property, welfare, and birth control have all heavily influenced family arrangements. As Fran Olsen and Clare Dalton have noted, the same legal decisions regarding intimate arrangements often can be described either as intervention or nonintervention, depending on the decision makers' point of view. For example, a refusal to enforce unwritten cohabitation agreements can be seen as a means of either preserving or intruding on intimate relationships.[33]

Conventional public/private distinctions present normative difficulties as well. Contrary to liberal legalist assumptions, the state's refusal to intervene in private matters has not necessarily expanded individual autonomy; it has often simply substituted private for public power. Courts' failure to recognize unwritten agreements between cohabitants or to enforce support obligations and rape prohibitions in ongoing marriages has generally enlarged the liberties of men at the expense of women.[34]

Critical feminism does not, however, categorically renounce the constraints on state power that liberal legalism has secured. Rather, it denies that conventional public/private dichotomies provide a useful conceptual scheme for assessing such constraints. As the following discussion of rights suggests, judgments about the appropriate scope of state intervention require a contextual analysis, which takes account of gender disparities in existing distributions of power. In this, as in other theoretical contexts previously noted, we need less reliance on abstract principles and more on concrete experience.

A similar point emerges from one final challenge to liberal legalism. Building on the work of moral theorists such as Carol Gilligan, Annette Baier, and Sarah Ruddick, some commentators have questioned the primacy that this culture attaches to formal, adversarial, and hierarchical modes of dispute resolution.[35] A legal system founded on feminist priorities—those emphasizing trust, care, and empathy—should aspire to less combative, more conciliatory, procedures.

Yet as other feminist critics have noted, an appeal to empathetic values leaves most of the difficult questions unanswered. With whom should legal decision making empathize when individual needs conflict?[36] And what procedural protections should be available to monitor those judgments? One risk is that conciliation between parties with unequal negotiating skills, information, and power can perpetuate those inequalities. Judicial systems that have aspired to more nurturing processes, such as juvenile and family courts, have often reinforced patriarchal assumptions and sexual double standards.[37] Norms appropriate to our vision of justice in an ideal state may not be the best way to get us there.

Here again, a critical feminist approach to procedural values demands contextual judgment. To further the substantive objectives that critical feminism seeks, its greatest challenge lies at the pragmatic level; its taks is to design frameworks more responsive to the experiences of subordinate groups. A crucial first step is to deconstruct the apparent dichotomy between formalism and informalism that has traditionally structured debate over alternative dispute resolution processes. Since neither approach has adequately responded to women's experiences and concerns, we cannot rest with debunking both possibilities or choosing the least objectionable alternative. Rather, as is true with debates over substantive rights, we need to reimagine the range of procedural options and to challenge the broader system of sex-based subordination that constrains their exercise.

III. Rights

One central difference between critical feminism and other critical legal theory involves the role of rights. Although both bodies of work have challenged liberal legalism's reliance on formal entitlements, feminist accounts, like those of minority scholars, have tended more toward contextual analysis than categorical critique.

Most CLS scholarship has viewed rights-based strategies as an ineffective and illusory means of progressive social change. While sometimes acknowledging the importance of basic political liberties in preserving opportunities for dissent, critical legal theorists have generally presented the liberal rights agenda as a constraint on individual consciousness and collective mobilization. Part of the problem arises from the indeterminacy noted earlier. Feminist commentators such as Fran Olsen have joined other critical theorists in noting that rights discourse cannot resolve social conflict but can only restate it in somewhat abstract, conclusory form. A rights-oriented framework may distance us from necessary value choices and obscure the basis on which competing interests are accommodated.[38]

According to this critique, too much political energy has been diverted into battles that cannot promise significant gains. For example, a decade's experience with state equal rights amendments reveals no necessary correlation between the standard of constitutional protection provided by legal tribunals and the results achieved. It is unlikely that a federal equal rights amendment would have ensured the vast array of substantive objectives that its proponents frequently claimed. Supporters' tendencies to cast the amendment as an all-purpose prescription for social ills—the plight of displaced homemakers, the feminization of poverty, and the gender gap in earnings—have misdescribed the problem and misled as to the solution.[39]

A related limitation of the liberal rights agenda involves its individualist premises and restricted scope. A preoccupation with personal entitlements can divert concern from collective responsibilities. Rights rhetoric too often channels individuals' aspirations into demands for their own share of protected opportunities and fails to address more fundamental issues about what ought to be protected. Such an individualistic framework ill serves the values of cooperation and empathy that feminists find lacking in our current legal culture.

Nor are mandates guaranteeing equality in formal rights adequate to secure equality in actual experience as long as rights remain restricted to those that a predominately white upper-middle-class male judiciary has been prepared to regard as fundamental. No legal structure truly committed to equality for women would end up with a scheme that affords extensive protection to the right to bear arms or to sell violent pornography but not to control our reproductive lives.

In a culture where rights have been defined primarily in terms of "freedoms from" rather than "freedoms to," many individuals lack the resources necessary for exercising rights to which they are formally entitled. Such problems are compounded by the costs and complexities of legal proceedings and the maldistribution of legal services available to enforce formal entitlements or prevent their curtailment. By channeling political struggles into legal disputes, rights-based strategies risk limiting aspirations and reinforcing dependence on legal decisionmakers.

Yet while acknowledging these limitations, critical feminism has also emphasized certain empowering dimensions of rights strategies that other CLS work discounts. As theorists including Kimberlé Crenshaw, Christine Littleton, Elizabeth Schneider, and Patricia Williams have argued, legal rights have a special resonance in our culture.[40] The source of their limitations is also the source of their strength. Because claims about rights proceed within established discourse, they are less readily dismissed than other progressive demands. By insisting that the rule of law make good on its own aspirations, rights-oriented strategies offer a possibility of internal challenge that critical theorists have recognized as empowering in other contexts.

So too, critiques that focus only on the individualist premises of rights rhetoric obscure its collective dimensions. The dichotomies often drawn between rights and relationships or rights and responsibilities are highly exaggerated. Rights not only secure personal autonomy; they also express relationships between the individual and the community. Just as rights can impose responsibilities, responsibilities can imply rights. Often the concepts serve identical ends: A right to freedom from discrimination imposes a responsibility not to engage in it. Discarding one form of discourse in favor of another is unlikely to alter the foundations of our legal culture. Moreover, for subordinate groups, rights-based frameworks have supported demands not only for individual entitlements but also for collective selfhood. For example, women's right to reproductive autonomy is a prerequisite to their social equality; without control of their individual destinies, women cannot challenge the group stereotypes and role constraints that underpin their subordinate status. Claims of right can further advance collective values by drawing claimants within a community capable of response and demanding that its members take notice of the grievances expressed.[41]

For critical feminism, the most promising approach is both to acknowledge the indeterminate nature of rights rhetoric and to recognize that in particular circumstances, such rhetoric can promote concrete objectives and social empowerment. Too often, rights have been abstracted from their social context and then criticized as abstract. Yet however manipulable, the rubric of autonomy and equality have made enormous practical differences in the lives of subordinate groups. Undermining the conceptual foundations of rights like privacy, on which women's reproductive choice has depended, involves considerable risks. Even largely symbolic campaigns, such as the recent ERA struggle, can be highly important, less because of the specific objective they seek than because of the political mobilization they inspire. Like the suffrage movements a half-century earlier, the contemporary constitutional battle offered women invaluable instruction in both the limits of their own influence and the strategies necessary to expand it.

Whatever its inadequacies, rights rhetoric has been the vocabulary most effective in catalyzing mass progressive movements in this culture. It is a discourse that critical feminists are reluctant to discard in favor of ill-defined or idealized alternatives. The central problem with rights-based frameworks is not that they are inherently limiting but that they have operated within a limited institutional and imaginative universe. Thus, critical feminism's central objective should be not to delegitimate such frameworks but, rather, to recast their content and recognize their constraints. Since rights-oriented campaigns can both enlarge and restrict political struggle, evaluation of their strategic possibilities requires historically situated contextual analysis.

On this point, feminists join other critical theorists in seeking to build on the communal, relational, and destabilizing dimensions of rights-based arguments.[42] Claims to self-determination can express desires not only for autonomy but also for participation in the communities that shape our existence. If selectively invoked, the rhetoric of rights can empower subordinate groups to challenge the forces that perpetuate their subordination.

IV. Alternative Visions

One final issue on which critical feminism often parts company with other critical theory involves the construction of alternative visions of the good society. Although both traditions reflect considerable ambivalence about the value of such projects, the focus of concern varies. Most critical theory that has attempted to construct alternative visions assumes away the problems with which feminists have been most concerned or opens itself to the same challenges of indeterminacy that it has directed at other work. Partly for these reasons, feminist legal critics have devoted relatively little attention to idealized programs. Rather, their efforts have centered on identifying the values that must be central to any affirmative vision and the kinds of concrete legal and institutional transformations that such values imply.

A recurrent problem with most progressive utopian frameworks involves their level of generality. Objectives are often framed in terms of vague, seemingly universal aspirations—such as Roberto Unger's appeal to a world free "from deprivation and drudgery, from the choice between isolation from other people and submission to them."[43] Such formulations leave most of the interesting questions unanswered. How are such ideals to be interpreted and implemented under specific circumstances; how are interpretive disputes to be resolved; and how are gender relations to be reconstructed?

In response to such questions, a standard critical strategy is to specify conditions under which answers would be generated. Habermas's ideal speech situation has been perhaps the most influential example. Under his theory, beliefs would be accepted as legitimate only if they could have been acquired through full uncoerced discussion in which all members of society participate. Some critical feminists, including Drucilla Cornell and Seyla Benhabib, draw on similar conversational constructs.[44]

Such strategies are, however, problematic on several levels. One difficulty involves the level of abstraction at which the ideals are formulated. It is not self-evident how individuals with diverse experiences, interests, and resources will reach consensus or how their agreements can be predicted with enough specificity to provide adequate heuristic frameworks. Strategies emphasizing uncoerced dialogue have often assumed away the problems of disparate resources and capacities that parties bring to the conversation. Given the historical silencing of women's voices, many critical feminists have been unsatisfied by approaches that are themselves silent about how to prevent that pattern from recurring.

A related difficulty stems from idealists' faith in dialogue as the primary response to social subordination. Alternative visions that proceed as if the central problem were our inability to imagine such alternatives often understate the material conditions that contribute to that inability. Many feminists have no difficulty imagining a world without pervasive sexual violence or the feminization of poverty; the difficulty lies in commanding support for concrete strategies that would make that vision possible. It is, of course, true that we cannot be free from coercive institutional structures as long as we retain an ideology that legitimates them. But neither can we rid ourselves of that ideology as long as such structures limit our ability to challenge it.

In response to this dilemma, critical feminism has tended to focus on particular issues that implicate both material and ideological concerns. Rather than hypothesizing some universal utopian program, feminist legal critics have generally engaged in more concrete analysis that challenges both structural inequalities and the normative assumptions that underlie them. In evaluating particular strategies, critical feminism focuses on their capacity to improve women's social and economic status; to reach those women most in need; and to enhance women's self-respect, power, and ability to alter existing institutional arrangements.

For example, the struggle for comparable pay for jobs of comparable worth presents direct opportunities to increase women's financial security. The campaign has helped reveal the cultural undervaluation of "women's work," has exposed gender and racial bias in employers' own criteria for compensation, and has aided workplace organizing efforts.[45] Pay equity initiatives have also raised broader questions about market principles and social priorities. How should we reward various occupational and worker characteristics and how should those decisions be made? Are we comfortable in a society that pays more to parking attendants than child care attendants, whatever the gender composition of those positions? The struggle for comparable worth could spark a rethinking of the scope of inequality and the ideologies that sustain it.

The feminist focus on concrete issues has avoided an idealized vision that must inevitably change in the course of change. Feminist legal critics have been less interested in predicting the precise role that gender would play in the good society than in undermining its role in this one. Whether sex would ultimately become as unimportant as eye color or whether some sex-linked traits and affiliations would endure is not an issue on which more speculation seems fruitful. Since what is now problematic about gender relations is the disparity in power, we cannot fully anticipate the shape of those relations in an ideal world where, by definition, such disparities do not exist. At utopian as well as practical levels, critical feminism is unwilling to remain trapped in debates about women's commonality with or difference from men. Its commitment is neither to embrace nor to suppress difference but to challenge the dualism and make the world safe for differences.

Although we cannot know a priori what the good society will be, we know more than enough about what it will not be to provide a current agenda. It will not be a society with sex-based disparities in status, power, and security. Nor will it be a society that denies many of its members substantial control over the terms of their daily existence. To realize its full potential, feminism must sustain a vision concerned not only with relations between men and women, but also with relations among them. The commitment to sexual equality that gave birth to the women's movement is necessary but not sufficient to realize the values underlying it. Those values place critical feminism in both tension and alliance with aspirations that other critical legal theory expresses.

Notes

The comments of Peter Chadwick, Katharine Bartlett, Thomas Grey, Regenia Gagnier, Henry Greely, Mark Kelman, Christine Littleton, Frances Olsen, Robert Post, Carol Sanger, Reva Siegel, William Simon, and John Stick are gratefully acknowledged.

1. Heidi Hartmann, *The Unhappy Marriage of Marxism and Feminism: Toward a More Progressive Union,* in WOMAN AND REVOLUTION 2, 2 (L. Sargent ed. 1981).

2. Gloria Joseph, *The Incompatible Ménage à Trois: Marxism, Feminism and Racism,* in WOMAN AND REVOLUTION, at 91.

3. Deborah Rhode, *Feminist Critical Theories,* in CRITICAL LEGAL THEORY (J. Stick ed. 1990).

4. *See* Menkel-Meadow, Feminist Legal Theory–Critical Legal Studies, *Minority Critiques of the Critical Legal Studies Movement,* 22 HARV. C.R.–C.L. L. REV. 297 (1987); *Voices of Experience: New Responses to Gender Discourse,* 24 HARV. C.R.–C.L. L. REV. 1 (1989).

5. Critics such as Francois Lyotard invoke the term *postmodernism* to describe the present age's collapse of faith in traditional Grand Narratives. Since the Enlightenment, these metanarratives have sought to develop principles of objective science, universal morality, and autonomous art. For discussion of postmodernism's denial that categorical, noncontingent, abstract theories derived through reason or human nature can serve as the foundation for knowledge, see JEAN-FRANÇOIS LYOTARD, THE POSTMODERN CONDITION (1984); POST-ANALYTIC PHILOSOPHY (J. Rajchmand and C. West eds. 1985); Nancy Fraser and Linda Nicholsen, *Social Criticism Without Philosophy: An Encounter Between Feminism and Postmodernism,* in UNIVERSAL ABANDON?: THE POLITICS OF POSTMODERNISM 83 (A. Ross ed. 1988); Sandra Harding, *The Instability of the Analytical Categories of Feminist Theory,* 11 SIGNS 645 (1986); David Luban, *Legal Modernism,* 84 MICH. L. REV. 1656 (1986); Robin West, *Feminism, Critical Social Theory and Law,* 1989 U. CHI. LEGAL F. 59.

Poststructuralism, which arises from and contributes to this postmodern tradition, refers to theories of interpretation that view meaning as a cultural construction mediated by arrangements of language or symbolic form. What distinguishes poststructuralism from other interpretive schools is the premise that these arrangements are unstable and contradictory, and that readers create rather than simply discover meaning. For a useful overview, see CHRISTOPHER NORRIS, DECONSTRUCTION: THEORY AND PRACTICE (1982); Peter Fitzpatrick and Alan Hunt, *Critical Legal Studies: Introduction,* 14 J.L. & SOC'Y 1 (1987); David Kennedy, *Critical Theory, Structuralism and Contemporary Legal Scholarship,* 21 NEW ENG. L. REV. 209 (1986).

6. J. F. LYOTARD; Jane Flax, *PostModernism and Gender Relations in Feminist Theory,* 12 SIGNS 621 (1987). Critical legal studies scholars have responded in varying ways, ranging from Roberto Unger's and Jürgen Habermas's continued embrace of universalist claims, to Duncan Kennedy's reliance on deconstructive technique. *Compare* ROBERTO MANGABEIRA UNGER, KNOWLEDGE AND POLITICS (1975) *and* JÜRGEN HABERMAS, LEGITIMATION CRISIS (1975) *with* Peter Gabel and Duncan Kennedy, *Roll over Beethoven,* 36 STAN. L. REV. 1 (1984).

7. As Nancy Cott notes, "in deconstructing categories of meaning, we deconstruct not only patriarchal definitions of 'womanhood' and 'truth' but also the very categories of our own analysis—'woman' and 'feminism' and 'oppression'" *(quoted in* France E. Macia-Lees, Patricia Sharpe, and Colleen Ballerino Cohen, *The Postmodernist Turn in Anthropology: Cautions from a Feminist Perspective,* 15 SIGNS 7, 27 (1989)).

8. *Compare* C. MACKINNON, Feminism Unmodified (1987), at 81–92 (discussing the social construction of rape and sexual violence) *with id.* at 23 (asserting "facts" about its prevalence). *See also* CATHARINE A. MACKINNON, TOWARD A FEMINIST THEORY OF THE STATE 100 (1989) (acknowledging without exploring the difficulty).

9. See, for example, the work of Amelie Rorty, discussed in Katharine T. Bartlett, *Feminist Legal Methods,* 103 HARV. L. REV. 829 (1990); Margaret Jane Radin, *The Pragmatist and the Feminist,* 63 S. CAL. L. REV 1699 (1990).

10. *See, e.g.,* Patricia Williams, *Spirit Murdering the Messenger: The Discourse of Fingerpointing as the Law's Response to Racism,* 42 U. MIAMI L. REV. 127 (1987); Mari J. Matsuda, *Public Response to Racist Speech: Considering the Victim's Story,* 87 MICH. L. REV. 2320 (1989); Robin L. West, *The Difference in Women's Hedonic Lives: A Phenomenological Critique of Feminist Legal Theory,* 3 WIS. WOMEN'S L.J. 81 (1987).

11. *See* Duncan Kennedy, *The Structure of Blackstone's Commentaries,* 28 BUFFALO L. REV. 205 (1979); R. M. UNGER.

12. Menkel-Meadow, at 61.

13. Martha Minow, *Feminist Reason: Getting It and Losing It,* 38 J. LEGAL EDUC. 47, 51 (1988).

14. MacKinnon, Feminism, Marxism, Method & State, 7 SIGNS (1982), at 637, n. 5.

15. *See* West, at 117–18.

16. *See, e.g.,* D. RHODE, JUSTICE AND GENDER, at 66 (1989); Lisa Belkin, *Bars to Equality of Sexes Seen as Eroding Slowly, New York Times,* August 20, 1989, at 1, 16 (61 percent of wives felt husbands did less than fair share of house work; 70 percent of women with full-time jobs felt women had an equal or better chance of promotion than men where they worked; and only 39 percent of black women and 22 percent of white women believed organized women's groups had made their lives better); *Rosy Outlook Among Women Ages 18 to 44, San Francisco Examiner,* August 23, 1988, at A7, col. 3 (finding that nearly 90 percent of women of childbearing ages are satisfied with their lives). For more qualitative research, see SPOUSE, PARENT, WORKER: ON GENDER AND MULTIPLE ROLES (F. Crosby ed. 1987).

17. Menkel-Meadow, at 61.

18. West, at 48.

19. *See* CAROL GILLIGAN, IN A DIFFERENT VOICE (1982); MARY FIELD BELENKY, BLYTHE MC VICKAR CLINCHY, NANCY RULE GOLDBERGER & JILL MATTUCK TARULE, WOMEN'S WAYS OF KNOWING (1986); Carrie Menkel-Meadow, *Portia in a Different Voice: Speculations on a Women's Lawyering Process,* 1 BERKELEY WOMEN'S L.J. 39 (1985).

20. The phrase is Elizabeth V. Spelman's in INESSENTIAL WOMAN: PROBLEMS OF EXCLUSION IN FEMINIST THOUGHT 187 (1988). *See also* ADRIENNE RICH, *Disloyal to Civilization: Feminism, Racism, Gynephobia,* in ON LIES, SECRETS AND SILENCE 275 (1979).

21. MacKinnon, at 637, n. 5.

22. D. RHODE, JUSTICE AND GENDER, at 311–12.

23. Martha Minow, *Beyond Universality,* 1989 U. CHI. LEGAL F. 115.

24. Robert W. Gordon, *New Developments in Legal Theory,* in THE POLITICS OF LAW: A PROGRESSIVE CRITIQUE, at 281; A. Hutchinson, *Introduction* to CRITICAL LEGAL STUDIES (A. Hutchinson ed. 1989).

25. *See* JOHN RAWLS, A THEORY OF JUSTICE (1971); Ronald Dworkin, *Liberalism,* in PUBLIC AND PRIVATE MORALITY 113 (S. Hampshire ed. 1978); BRUCE ACKERMAN, SOCIAL JUSTICE IN THE LIBERAL STATE (1980). *See generally* Steven Shiffrin, *Liberalism, Radicalism, and Legal Scholarship,* 30 UCLA L. REV. 1103 (1983).

26. Robin West, *Economic Man and Literary Woman: One Contrast,* 39 MERCER L. REV. 867 (1988).

27. A. JAGGAR, at 21–22; Virginia Held, *Feminism and Moral Theory,* in WOMEN AND MORAL THEORY 111 (E. Kittay and D. Meyers eds. 1987); Susan Moller Okin, *Humanist Liberalism,* in LIBERALISM AND THE MORAL LIFE 39 (N. Rosenblum ed. 1989); Robin West, *Jurisprudence and Gender,* 55 U. CHI. L. REV. 1 (1988).

28. *See* JUDITH N. SHKLAR, LEGALISM (1964); Duncan Kennedy, *Legal Formality,* 2 J. LEGAL STUD. 351, 371–72 (1973); Karl Klare, *Law-Making as Praxis,* 40 TELOS 123, 132 (1970).

29. *See* Clare Dalton, *An Essay in the Deconstruction of Contract Doctrine,* 94 YALE L.J 997, 1106–8 (1985).

30. Territory v. Armstrong, 28 Haw. 88 (1924) (upholding greater statutory penalties for males than females convicted of adultery); Wark v. Maine, 266 A.2d 62, 64–65 (Me. 1970) (upholding greater statutory penalties for males than females convicted of escape from penal institutions), *cert. denied,* 400 U.S. 952 (1970); *Ex parte* Gosselin, 141 Me. 412, 421, 44 A.2d 882, 885–86 (1945) (upholding greater statutory penalties for females than males convicted of misdemeanors such as intoxication); Commonwealth v. Daniel, 210 Pa. Super. 156, 232 A.2d 247 (1967), *rev'd,* 430 Pa. 642, 243 A.2d 400 (1968) (invalidating statute that gave judges greater discretion to consider exonerating circumstances for males than females convicted of robbery). For changes in custody provisions, see Fran Olsen, *The Politics of Family Law,* 2 LAW & INEQUALITY 1, 12–19 (1984).

31. Geduldig v. Aiello, 417 U.S. 484, 497, n.20 (1974); *see also* General Elec. Co. v. Gilbert 429 U.S. 125 (1976).

32. LENORE J. WEITZMAN, THE DIVORCE REVOLUTION (1985); Herma Hill Kay, *Equality and Difference: A Perspective on No-Fault Divorce and Its Aftermath,* 56 U. CIN. L. REV. 1, 60–65 (1987); Deborah L. Rhode and Martha Minow, *Reforming the Questions, Questioning the Reforms: Feminist Perspectives on Divorce Reform,* in DIVORCE REFORM AT THE CROSS ROADS (S. Sugarman and H. Kay eds. 1990).

33. Dalton, at 1107; Frances E. Olsen, *The Myth of State Intervention in the Family,* 18 U. MICH. J.L. REF. 835 (1985).

34. *See* MICHAEL D.A. FREEMAN and CHRISTINA M. LYON, COHABITATION WITHOUT MARRIAGE: AN ESSAY IN LAW AND SOCIAL POLICY (1983); DIANA E.H. RUSSEL, RAPE IN MARRIAGE 17–24 (1982); Olsen, at 843–58; Marjorie Maguire Shultz, *Contractual Ordering of Marriage: A New Model for State Policy,* 70 CALIF. L. REV. 204 (1982).

35. C. GILLIGAN; Annette Baier, *Trust and Antitrust,* 96 ETHICS 231, 247–53 (1986); Sara Ruddick, *Maternal Thinking,* 6 FEMINIST STUD. 342 (1980); *see* Lynne N. Henderson, *Legality and Empathy,* 85 MICH. L. REV. 1574 (1987); Menkel-Meadow.

36. Toni Masaro, *Empathy, Legal Storytelling, and the Rule of Law,* 87 MICH. L. REV. 2104 (1989).

37. Judith Resnik, *On the Bias: Feminist Reconsiderations of the Aspirations for Judges,* 61 S. CAL. L. REV. 1877, 1926–33 (1988).

38. Olsen, Statutory Rape: A Feminist Critique of Rights, 63 Tex. L. Rev. 387 (1984); *see* Peter Gabel, *The Phenomenology of Rights-Consciousness and the Pact of the Withdrawn Selves,* 62 TEX. L. REV. 1563 (1984); Mark Tushnet, *An Essay on Rights,* 62 TEX. L. REV. 1363, 1382–84 (1984).

39. *See* D. RHODE, JUSTICE AND GENDER; 16 Catharine A. MacKinnon, *Unthinking ERA Thinking* (Book Review), 54 U. CHI. L. REV. 759 (1987).

40. Kimberlé Williams Crenshaw, *Race, Reform, and Retrenchment: Transformation and Legitimation in Antidiscrimination Law,* 101 HARV. L. REV. 1331, 1366–69 (1988); Schneider, The Dialectic of Rights & Politics, 61 N.Y.U. L. Rev. 589 (1986); Patricia J. Williams, *Alchemical Notes: Reconstructing Ideals from Deconstructed Rights,* 22 HARV. C.R.–C.L. L. REV. 401 (1987).

41. *See* Schneider; Martha Minow, *Interpreting Rights: An Essay for Robert Cover,* 96 YALE L.J. 1860, 1875–77 (1987).

42. *See* Staughton Lynd, *Communal Rights,* 62 TEX. L. REV. 1417 (1984); Roberto Mangabeira Unger, *The Critical Legal Studies Movement,* 96 HARV. L. REV. 561, 612–16 (1983).

43. *See* Unger, at 651; *see also* R. UNGER, at 18, 24.

44. *See* Seyla Benhabib, *The Generalized and the Concrete Other,* in FEMINISM AS CRITIQUE. (J. Benhabib & D. Cornell eds. 1987) at 92–94; *see also* J. HABERMAS; Richard J. Bernstein, *Philosophy in the Conversation of Mankind,* in HERMENEUTICS AND PRAXIS 54, 82 (R. Hollinger ed. 1985).

45. *See* D. RHODE, JUSTICE AND GENDER, at 368–69, 379–81. *See generally* COMPARABLE WORTH: NEW DIRECTIONS FOR RESEARCH (H. Hartmann ed. 1985).

25

Toward Feminist Jurisprudence

CATHARINE A. MACKINNON

Happy above all Countries is our Country where that equality is found, without destroying the necessary subordination.

Thomas Lee Shippen (1788)

If I fight, some day some woman will win.

Michelle Vinson (1987)

A jurisprudence is a theory of the relation between life and law. In life, "woman" and "man" are widely experienced as features of being, not constructs of perception, cultural interventions, or forced identities. Gender, in other words, is lived as ontology, not as epistemology. Law actively participates in this transformation of perspective into being. In liberal regimes, law is a particularly potent source and badge of legitimacy, and site and cloak of force. The force underpins the legitimacy as the legitimacy conceals the force. When life becomes law in such a system, the transformation is both formal and substantive. It reenters life marked by power.

In male supremacist societies, the male standpoint dominates civil society in the form of the objective standard—that standpoint which, because it dominates in the world, does not appear to function as a standpoint at all. Under its aegis, men dominate women and children, three-quarters of the world. Family and kinship rules and sexual mores guarantee reproductive ownership and sexual access and control to men as a group. Hierarchies among men are ordered on the basis of race and class, stratifying women as well. The state incorporates these facts of social power in and as law. Two things happen: Law becomes legitimate, and social dominance becomes invisible. Liberal legalism is thus a medium for making male dominance both invisible and legitimate by adopting the male point of view in law at the same time as it enforces that view on society.

Through legal mediation, male dominance is made to seem a feature of life, not a one-sided construct imposed by force for the advantage of a dominant group. To the degree it succeeds ontologically, male dominance does not look epistemological: Control over being produces control over consciousness, fusing material conditions with consciousness in a way that is inextricable short of social change. Dominance reified becomes difference. Coercion legitimated becomes consent. Reality objectified becomes ideas; ideas objectified become reality. Politics neutralized and naturalized becomes morality. Discrimination in society becomes nondiscrimination in law. Law is a real moment in the social construction of these mirror-imaged inversions as truth. Law, in societies ruled and penetrated by the liberal form, turns angle of vision and construct of social meaning into dominant institution. In the liberal state, the rule of law—neutral, abstract, elevated, pervasive—both institutionalizes the power of men over women and institutionalizes power in its male form.

From a feminist perspective, male supremacist jurisprudence erects qualities valued from the male point of view as standards for the proper and actual relation between life and law. Examples include standards for scope of judicial review, norms of judicial restraint, reliance on precedent, separation of powers, and the division between public and private law. Substantive doctrines like standing, justiciability, and state action adopt the same stance. Those with power in civil society, not women, design its norms and institutions, which become the status quo. Those with power, not usually women, write constitutions, which become law's highest standards. Those with power in political systems that women did not design and from which women have been excluded write legislation, which sets ruling values. Then, jurisprudentially, judicial review is said to go beyond its proper scope—to delegitimate courts and the rule of law itself—when legal questions are not confined to assessing the formal correspondence between legislation and the constitution, or legislation and social reality, but scrutinize the underlying substance. Lines of precedent fully developed before women were permitted to vote, continued while women were not allowed to learn to read and write, sustained under a reign of sexual terror and abasement and silence and misrepresentation continuing to the present day are considered valid bases for defeating "unprecedented" interpretations or initiatives from women's point of view. Doctrines of standing suggest that because women's deepest injuries are shared in some way by most or all women, no individual woman is differentially injured enough to be able to sue for women's deepest injuries.

Structurally, only when the state has acted can constitutional equality guarantees be invoked.[1] But no law gives men the right to rape women. This has not been necessary, since no rape law has ever seriously undermined the terms of men's entitlement to sexual access to women. No government is, yet, in the pornography business. This has not been necessary, since no man who wants pornography encounters serious trouble getting it, regardless of obscenity laws. No law gives fathers the right to abuse their daughters sexually. This has not been necessary, since no state has ever systematically intervened in their social possession of and access to them. No law gives husbands the right to batter their wives. This has not been necessary, since there is nothing to stop them. No law silences women. This has not been necessary, for women are previously silenced in society—by sexual abuse, by not being heard, by not being believed, by poverty, by illiteracy, by a language that provides only unspeakable vocabulary for their most formative traumas, by a publishing industry that virtually guarantees that if they ever find a voice it leaves no trace in the world. No law takes away women's privacy. Most women do not have any to take, and no law gives them what they do not already have. No law guarantees that women will forever remain the social unequals of men. This is not necessary, because the law guaranteeing sex equality requires, in an unequal society, that before one can be equal legally, one must be equal socially. So long as power enforced by law reflects and corresponds—in form and in substance—to power enforced by men over women in society, law is objective, appears principled, becomes just the way things are. So long as men dominate women effectively enough in society without the support of positive law, nothing constitutional can be done about it.

Law from the male point of view combines coercion with authority, policing society where its edges are exposed: at points of social resistance, conflict, and breakdown. Since there is no place outside this system from a feminist standpoint, if its solipsistic lock could be broken, such moments could provide points of confrontation, perhaps even openings for change. The point of view of a total system emerges as particular only when confronted, in a way it cannot ignore, by a demand from another point of view. This is why epistemology must be controlled for ontological dominance to succeed and why consciousness raising is subversive. It is also why, when law sides with the powerless, as it occasionally has,[2] it is said to engage in something other than law—politics or policy or personal opinion—and to delegitimate itself.[3] When seemingly ontological conditions are challenged from the collective standpoint of a dissident reality, they become visible as epistemological. Dominance suddenly appears no longer inevitable. When it loses its ground, it loosens its grip.

Thus when the Supreme Court held that racial segregation did not violate equality rights, it said that those who felt that to be segregated on the basis of race implied inferiority merely chose to place that construction upon it. The harm of forced separation was a matter of point of view.[4] When the Supreme Court later held that racial segregation violated equality rights, it said that segregation generated a feeling of inferiority in the hearts and minds of black children which was unlikely ever to be undone. Both Courts observed the same reality: the feelings of inferiority generated by apartheid. *Plessy* saw it from the standpoint of white supremacy; *Brown* saw it from the standpoint of the black challenge to white supremacy, envisioning a social equality that did not yet exist. Inequality is difficult to see when everything tells the unequal that the status quo is equality—for them. To the Supreme Court, the way black people saw their own condition went from being sneered at as a point of view within their own control, a self-inflicted epistemological harm, to being a constitutional measure of the harm a real social condition imposed upon them. Consciousness raising shifts the episteme in a simialr way, exposing the political behind the personal, the dominance behind the submission, participating in altering the balance of power subtly but totally. The question is, What can extend this method to the level of the state for women?

To begin with, Why law? Marx saw the modern state as "the official expression of antagonism in civil society."[5] Because political power in such a state could emancipate the individual only within the framework of the existing social order, law could emancipate women to be equal only within "the slavery of civil society."[6] By analogy, women would not be freed from forced sex, but freed to engage in it and initiate it. They would not be freed from reproductive tyranny and exploitation, but freed to exercise it. They would not be liberated from the dialectic of economic and sexual dominance and submission, but freed to dominate. Depending upon the substantive analysis of civil dominance, either women would dominate men, or some women (with all or some men) would dominate other women. In other words, the liberal vision of sex equality would be achieved. Feminism unmodified, methodologically post-Marxist feminism, aspires to better.

From the feminist point of view, the question of women's collective reality and how to change it merges with the question of women's point of view and how to know it. What do women live, hence know, that can confront male dominance? What female ontology can confront male epistemology; that is, what female epistemology can confront male ontology? What point of view can question the code of civil society? The answer is simple, concrete, specific, and real: women's social inequality with men on the basis of sex, hence the point of view of women's subordination to men. Women are not permitted fully to know what sex equality would look like, because they have never lived it. It is idealist, hence elitist, to hold that they do. But they do not need to. They know inequality because they have lived it, so they know what removing barriers to equality would be. Many of these barriers are legal; many of them are social; most of them exist at an interface between law and society.

Inequality on the basis of sex, women share. It is women's collective condition. The first task of a movement for social change is to face one's situation and name it. The failure to face and criticize the reality of women's condition, a failure of idealism and denial, is a failure of feminism in its liberal forms. The failure to move beyond criticism, a failure of determinism and radical paralysis, is a failure of feminism in its left forms. Feminism on its own terms has begun to give voice to and describe the collective condition of women as such, so largely composed as it is of all women's particularities. It has begun to uncover the laws of motion of a system that keeps women in a condition of imposed inferiority. It has located the dynamic of the social definition of gender in the sexuality of dominance and subordination, the sexuality of inequality: sex as inequality and inequality as sex. As sexual inequality is gendered as man and women, gender inequality is sexualized as dominance and subordination. The social power of men over women extends through laws that purport to protect women as part of the community, like the rape law; laws that ignore women's survival stake in the issue, like the obscenity law, or obscure it, like the abortion law; and laws that announce their intent to remedy that inequality but do not, like the sex equality law. This law derives its authority from reproducing women's social inequality to men in legal inequality, in a seamless web of life and law.

Feminist method adopts the point of view of women's inequality to men. Grasping women's reality from the inside, developing its specificities, facing the intractability and pervasiveness of male power, relentlessly criticizing women's condition as it identifies with all women, it has created strategies for change, beginning with consciousness raising. On the level of the state, legal guarantees of equality in liberal regimes provide an opening. Sex inequality is the true name for women's social condition. It is also, in words anyway, illegal sometimes. In some liberal states, the belief that women already essentially have sex equality extends to the level of law. From a perspective that understands that women do not have sex equality, this law means that once equality is meaningfully defined, the law cannot be applied without changing society. To make sex equality meaningful in law requires identifying the real issues, and establishing that sex inequality, once established, matters.

Sex equality in law has not been meaningfully defined for women but has been defined and limited from the male point of view to correspond to the existing social reality of sex inequality. An alternative approach to this mainstream view threads through existing law. It is the reason sex equality law exists at all. In this approach, inequality is a matter not of sameness and difference, but of dominance and subordination. Inequality is about power, its definition, and its maldistribution. Inequality at root is grasped as a question of hierarchy, which—as power succeeds in constructing social perception and social reality—derivatively becomes categorical distinctions, differences. Where mainstream equality law is abstract, this approach is concrete; where mainstream equality law is falsely universal, this approach remains specific.[7] The goal is not to make legal categories that trace and trap the status quo, but to confront by law the inequalities in women's condition in order to change them.

This alternative approach centers on the most sex-differential abuses of women as a gender, abuses that sex equality law in its sameness/difference obsession cannot confront. It is based on the reality that feminism, beginning with consciousness raising, has most distinctively uncovered, a reality about which little systematic was known before 1970: the reality of sexual abuse. It combines women's sex-based destitution and enforced dependency and permanent relegation to disrespected and starvation-level work—the lived meaning of class for women—with the massive amount of sexual abuse of girls apparently endemic to the patriarchal family, the pervasive rape and attempted rape about which nothing is done, the systematic battery of women in homes, and prostitution—the fundamental condition of women—of which the pornography industry is an arm. Keeping the reality of gender in view makes it impossible to see gender as a difference, unless this subordinated condition of women is that difference. This reality has called for a new conception of the problem of sex inequality, hence a new legal conception of it, both doctrinally and jurisprudentially.

Experiences of sexual abuse have been virtually excluded from the mainstream doctrine of sex equality because they happen almost exclusively to women and because they are experienced as sex. Sexual abuse has not been seen to raise sex equality issues because these events happen specifically and almost exclusively to women as women. Sexuality is socially organized to require sex inequality for excitement and satisfaction. The least extreme expression of gender inequality, and the prerequisite for all of it, is dehumanization and objectification. The most extreme is violence. Because sexual objectification and sexual violence are almost uniquely done to women, they have been systematically treated as the sex difference when they represent the socially situated subjection of women to men. The whole point of women's social relegation to inferiority as a gender is that this is not generally done to men. The systematic relegation of an entire people to a condition of inferiority is attributed to them, made a feature of theirs, and read out of equality demands and equality law when it is termed a *difference*. This condition is ignored entirely, with all the women who are determined by it, when only features women share with the privileged group are allowed to substantiate equality claims.

It follows that seeing sex equality questions as matters of reasonable or unreasonable classification of relevant social characteristics expresses male dominance in law. If the shift in perspective from gender as difference to gender as dominance is followed, gender changes from a distinction that is ontological and presumptively valid to a detriment that is epistemological and presumptively suspect. The given becomes the contingent. In this light, liberalism, purporting to discover gender, has discovered male and female in the mirror of nature; the left has discovered masculine and feminine in the mirror of society. The approach from the standpoint of the subordination of women to men, by contrast, criticizes and claims the specific situation of women's enforced inferiority and devaluation, pointing a way out of the infinity of reflections in law-and-society's hall of mirrors where sex equality law remains otherwise trapped.

Equality understood substantively rather than abstractly, defined on women's own terms and in terms of women's concrete experience, is what women in society most need and most do not have. Equality is also what society holds that women have already and therefore guarantees women by positive law. The law of equality, statutory and constitutional, therefore provides a peculiar jurisprudential opportunity, a crack in the wall between law and society. Law does not usually guarantee rights to things that do not exist. This may be why equality issues have occasioned so many jurisprudential disputes about what law is and what it can and should do. Every demand from women's point of view looks substantive, just as every demand from women's point of view requires change. Can women, demanding actual equality through law, be part of changing the state's relation to women and women's relation to men?

The first step is to claim women's concrete reality. Women's inequality occurs in a context of unequal pay, allocation to disrespected work, demeaned physical characteristics, targeting for rape, domestic battery, sexual abuse as children, and systematic sexual harassment. Women are daily dehumanized, used in denigrating entertainment, denied reproductive control, and forced by the conditions of their lives into prostitution. These abuses occur in a legal context historically characterized by disenfranchisement, preclusion from property ownership, exclusion from public life, and lack of recognition of sex-specific injuries.[8] Sex inequality is thus a social and political institution.

The next step is to recognize that male forms of power over women are affirmatively embodied as individual rights in law. When men lose power, they feel they lose rights. Often they are not wrong. Examples include the defense of mistaken belief in consent in the rape law, which legally determines whether or not a rape occurred from the rapist's perspective; freedom of speech, which gives pimps rights to torture, exploit, use, and sell women to men through pictures and words and gives consumers rights to buy them; the law of privacy, which defines the home and sex as presumptively consensual and protects the use of pornography in the home; the law of child custody, which purports gender neutrality while applying a standard of adequacy of parenting based on male-controlled resources and male-defined norms, sometimes taking children away from women but more generally controlling women through the threat and fear of loss of their children. Real sex equality under law would qualify or eliminate these powers of men, hence men's current "rights" to use, access, possess, and traffic women and children.

In this context, many issues appear as sex equality issues for the first time—sexual assault, for example. Rape is a sex-specific violation. Not only are the victims of rape overwhelmingly women, perpetrators overwhelmingly men, but also the rape of women by men is integral to the way inequality between the sexes occurs in life. Intimate violation with impunity is an ultimate index of social power. Rape both evidences and practices women's low status relative to men. Rape equates female with violable and female sexuality with forcible intrusion in a way that defines and stigmatizes the female sex as a gender. Threat of sexual assault is threat of punishment for being female. The state has laws against sexual assault, but it does not enforce them. Like lynching at one time, rape is socially permitted, though formally illegal. Victims of sex crimes, mostly women and girls, are thus disadvantaged relative to perpetrators of sex crimes, largely men.

A systemic inequality between the sexes therefore exists in the social practice of sexual violence, subjection to which defines women's status, and victims of which are largely women, and in the operation of the state, which *de jure* outlaws sexual violence but de facto permits men to engage in it on a wide scale. Making sexual assault laws gender neutral does nothing to address this, nothing to alter the social equation of female with rapable, and may obscure the sex specificity of the problem. Rape should be defined as sex by compulsion, of which physical force is one form. Lack of consent is redundant and should not be a separate element of the crime.[9] Expanding this analysis would support as sex equality initiatives laws keeping women's sexual histories out of rape trials[10] and publication bans on victims' names and identities.[11] The defense of mistaken belief in consent—which measures whether a rape occurred from the standpoint of the (male) perpetrator—would violate women's sex equality rights by law because it takes the male point of view on sexual violence against women.[12] Similarly, the systematic failure of the state to enforce the rape law effectively or at all excludes women from equal access to justice, permitting women to be savaged on a mass scale, depriving them of equal protection and equal benefit of the laws.

Reproductive control, formerly an issue of privacy, liberty, or personal security, would also become a sex equality issue. The frame for analyzing reproductive issues would expand from focus on the individual at the moment of the abortion decision to women as a group at all reproductive moments. The social context of gender inequality denies women control over the reproductive uses of their bodies and places that control in the hands of men. In a context of inadequate and unsafe contraceptive technology, women are socially disadvantaged in controlling sexual access to their bodies through social learning, lack of information, social pressure, custom, poverty and enforced economic dependence, sexual force, and ineffective enforcement of laws against sexual assault. As a result, they often do not control the conditions under which they become pregnant. If intercourse cannot be presumed to be controlled by women, neither can pregnancy. Women have also been allocated primary responsibility for intimate care of children yet do not control the conditions under which they rear them, hence the impact of these conditions on their own lives.

In this context, access to abortion is necessary for women to survive unequal social circumstances. It provides a form of relief, however punishing, in a life otherwise led in conditions that preclude choice in ways most women have not been permitted to control. This approach also recognizes that whatever is done to the fetus is done to a woman. Whoever controls the destiny of a fetus controls the destiny of a woman. Whatever the conditions of conception, if reproductive control of a fetus is exercised by anyone but the woman, reproductive control is taken only from women, as women. Preventing a woman from exercising the only choice an unequal society leaves her is an enforcement of sex inequality. Giving women control over sexual access to their bodies and adequate support of pregnancies and care of children extends sex equality. In other words, forced maternity is a practice of sex inequality.[13] Because motherhood without choice is a sex equality issue, legal abortion should be a sex equality right. Reproductive technology, sterilization abuse, and surrogate motherhood, as well as abortion funding, would be transformed if seen in this light.

Pornography, the technologically sophisticated traffic in women that expropriates, exploits, uses, and abuses women, also becomes a sex equality issue. The mass production of pornography universalizes the violation of the women in it, spreading it to all women, who are then exploited, used, abused, and reduced as a result of men's consumption of it. In societies pervaded by pornography, all women are defined by it: This is what a woman wants; this is what a woman is. Pornography sets the public standard for the treatment of women in private and the limits of tolerance for what can be permitted in public, such as in rape trials. It sexualizes the definition of male as dominant and female as subordinate. It equates violence against women with sex and provides an experience of that fusion. It engenders rape, sexual abuse of children, battery, forced prostitution, and sexual murder.

In liberal legalism, pornography is said to be a form of freedom of speech. It seems that women's inequality is something pornographers want to say, and saying it is protected even if it requires doing it. Being the medium for men's speech supersedes any rights women have. Women become men's speech in this system. Women's speech is silenced by pornography and the abuse that is integral to it. From women's point of view, obscenity law's misrepresentation of the problem as moral and ideational is replaced with the understanding that the problem of pornography is political and practical. Obscenity law is based on the point of view of male dominance. Once this is exposed, the urgent issue of freedom of speech for women is not primarily the avoidance of state intervention as such, but getting equal access to speech for those to whom it has been denied. First the abuse must be stopped.[14] The endless moral debates between good and evil, conservative and liberal, artists and philistines, the forces of darkness and repression and suppression and the forces of light and liberation and tolerance would be superseded by the political debate, the abolitionist debate: Are women human beings or not? Apparently, the answer provided by legal mandates of sex equality requires repeating.

The changes that a sex equality perspective provides as an interpretive lens include the law of sex equality itself. The intent requirement would be eliminated. The state action requirement would weaken. No distinction would be made between nondiscrimination and affirmative action. Burdens of proof would presuppose inequality rather than equality as a factual backdrop and would be more substantively sensitive to the particularities of sex inequality. Comparable worth would be required. Statistical proofs of disparity would be conclusive. The main question would be, Does a practice participate in the subordination of women to men, or is it no part of it? Whether statutes are sex specific or gender neutral would not be as important as whether they work to end or reinforce male supremacy, whether they are concretely grounded in women's experience of subordination or not. Discrimination law would not be confined to employment, education, and accommodation. Civil remedies in women's hands would be emphasized. Gay and lesbian rights would be recognized as sex equality rights. Since sexuality largely defines gender, discrimination based on sexuality is discrimination based on gender. Other forms of social discrimination and exploitation by men against women, such as prostitution and surrogate motherhood, would become actionable.

The relation between life and law would also change. Law, in liberal jurisprudence, objectifies social life. The legal process reflects itself in its own image, makes be there what it puts there, while presenting itself as passive and neutral in the process. To undo this, it will be necessary to grasp the dignity of women without blinking at the indignity of women's condition, to envision the possibility of equality without minimizing the grip of inequality, to reject the fear that has become so much of women's sexuality and the corresponding denial that has become so much of women's politics, and to demand civil parity without pretending that the demand is neutral or that civil equality already exists. In this attempt, the idealism of liberalism and the materialism of the left have come to much the same for women. Liberal jurisprudence that the law should reflect nature or society and left jurisprudence that all law does or can do is reflect existing social relations are two guises of objectivist epistemology. If objectivity is the epistemological stance of which women's sexual objectification is the social process, its imposition the paradigm of power in the male form, then the state appears most relentless in imposing the male point of view when it comes closest to achieving its highest formal criterion of distanced aperspectivity. When it is most ruthlessly neutral, it is most male; when it is most sex blind, it is most blind to the sex of the standard being applied. When it most closely conforms to precedent, to "facts," to legislative intent, it most closely enforces socially male norms and most thoroughly precludes questioning their content as having a point of view at all.

Abstract rights authoritize the male experience of the world. Substantive rights for women would not. Their authority would be the currently unthinkable: nondominant authority, the authority of excluded truth, the voice of silence. It would stand against both the liberal and left views of law. The liberal view that law is society's text, its rational mind, expresses the male view in the normative mode; the traditional left view that the state, and with it the law, is superstructural or ephiphenomenal expresses it in the empirical mode. A feminist jurisprudence, stigmatized as particularized and protectionist in male eyes of both traditions, is accountable to women's concrete conditions and to changing them. Both the liberal and the left view rationalize male power by presuming that it does not exist, that equality between the sexes (room for marginal corrections conceded) is society's basic norm and fundamental description. Only feminist jurisprudence sees that male power does exist and sex equality does not, because only feminism grasps the extent to which antifeminism is misogyny and both are as normative as they are empirical. Masculinity then appears as a specific position, not just the way things are, its judgments and partialities revealed in process and procedure, adjudication and legislation.

Equality will require change, not reflection—a new jurisprudence, a new relation between life and law. Law that does not dominate life is as difficult to envision as a society in which men do not dominate women, and for the same reasons. To the extent feminist law embodies women's point of view, it will be said that its law is not neutral. But existing law is not neutral. It will be said that it undermines the legitimacy of the legal system. But the legitimacy of existing law is based on force at women's expense. Women have never consented to its rule—suggesting that the system's legitimacy needs repair that women are in a position to provide. It will be said that feminist law is special pleading for a particular group and one cannot start that or where will it end. But existing law is already special pleading for a particular group, where it has ended. The question is not where it will stop but whether it will start for any group but the dominant one. It will be said that feminist law cannot win and will not work. But this is premature. Its possibilities cannot be assessed in the abstract but must engage the world. A feminist theory of the state has barely been imagined; systematically, it has never been tried.

Notes

1. In the United States, the "state action" requirement restricts review under the Fourteenth Amendment. See Lawrence Tribe, *American Constitutional Law* (Mineola, N.Y.: Foundation Press, 1978), pp. 1688–1720, for summary. In Canada, under the Canadian Charter of Rights and Freedoms, Section 32 restricts charter review to acts of government.

2. Brown v. Board of Education, 347 U.S. 483 (1954); Swann v. Charlotte–Mecklenburg Board of Education, 402 U.S. 2 (1971); Griggs v. Duke Power, 401 U.S. 424 (1971).

3. Herbert Wechsler, "Toward Neutral Principles of Constitutional Law," 73 *Harvard Law Review* 1 (1959).

4. Plessy v. Ferguson, 163 U.S. 537, 551 (1896); Wechsler, "Toward Neutral Principles," p. 33.

5. Karl Marx, *The Poverty of Philosophy* (New York: International Publishers, 1963), p. 174.

6. Karl Marx and Friedrich Engels, *The Holy Family,* trans. R. Dixon (Moscow: Progress Publishers, 1956), p. 157. See generally M. Cain and A. Hunt, *Marx and Engels on Law* (London: Academic Press, 1979).

7. Examples are Loving v. Virginia, 388 U.S. 1 (1967); Brown v. Board of Education, 347 U.S. 483 (1954); some examples of the law against sexual harassment (e.g., Barnes v. Costle, 561 F.2d 983 [D.C. Cir. 1977]; Vinson v. Taylor, 753 F.2d 141 [D.C. Cir. 1985], aff'd. 477 U.S. 57 (1986); Priest v. Rotary, 98 F.R.D. 755 [D.Cal. 1983]), some athletics cases (e.g., Clark v. Arizona Interscholastic Assn., 695 F.2d 1126 [9th Cir. 1986]), some affirmative action cases (e.g., Johnson v. Transportation Agency, Santa Clara County, 480 U.S. 616 [1987]), and California Federal Savings and Loan Association v. Guerra, 492 U.S. 272 (1987).

8. This context was argued as the appropriate approach to equality in an intervention by the Women's Legal Education and Action Fund (LEAF) in Law Society of British Columbia v. Andrews (May 22, 1987) before the Supreme Court of Canada. This approach to equality in general, giving priority to concrete disadvantage and rejecting the "similarly situated" test, was adopted by the Supreme Court of Canada in that case (1989)—DLR (3d)—.

9. See Ill. Rev. Stat. 1985, ch. 38, par. 12–14; People v. Haywood, 515 N.E.2d 45 (Ill. App. 1987) (prosecution not required to prove nonconsent, since sexual penetration by force implicitly shows nonconsent); but cf. People v. Coleman, 520 N.E.2d 55 (Ill. App. 1987) (state must prove victim's lack of consent beyond reasonable doubt).

10. This is argued by LEAF in its intervention application with several groups in Seaboyer v. The Queen (July 12, 1988) and Gayme v. The Queen (November 18, 1988), both on appeal before the Supreme Court of Canada. The rulings below are The Queen v. Seaboyer and Gayme (1986) 50 C.R. (3d) 395 (Ont. C.A.).

11. LEAF and a coalition of rape crisis centers, groups opposing sexual assault of women and children, and feminist media made this argument in an intervention in The Queen v. Canadian Newspapers Co., Ltd. The Canadian statute was upheld by a unanimous court. (1988)—D.L.R. (3d)—.

12. This is argued by LEAF intervening in The Queen v. Gayme.

13. This argument was advanced by LEAF in an intervention in Borowski v. Attorney General of Canada (October 7, 1987).

14. The Anti-Pornography Civil Rights Ordinance aims to do this. See Andrea Dworkin and Catharine A. MacKinnon, *Pornography and Civil Rights: A New Day for Women's Equality* (Minneapolis: Organizing Against Pornography, 1988).

---------------- ◆ ----------------

Suggested Readings

I On Equality

Abrams, K., "Gender Discrimination and the Transformation of Workplace Norms," Vol. 42 VAN-
DERBILT LAW REVIEW at p. 1183 (1989).

Crenshaw, K., "Race, Reform and Retrenchment: Transformation and Legitimation in antidiscrimination Law," Vol. 101 HARVARD LAW REVIEW at p. 1331 (1988).

————, "Demarginalizing the Intersection of Race and Sex," Vol. 1989 UNIVERSITY OF CHICAGO
LEGAL FORUM at p. 139 (1989).

Finley, L., "Transcending Equality Theory: A Way Out of the Maternity-Workplace Debate," Vol.
86 COLUMBIA LAW REVIEW at p. 1118 (1986).

Frug, M., "Securing Job Equality for Women: Labor Market Hostility to Working Mothers," Vol.
59 BOSTON UNIVERSITY LAW REVIEW at p. 55 (1979).

Kay, H., "Models of Equality," Vol. 1985 UNIVERSITY OF ILLINOIS LAW REVIEW at p. 39 (1985).

Krieger, L., and Cooney, P., "The Miller-Wohl Controversy: Equal Treatment, Positive Action and
the Meaning of Women's Equality," Vol. 13 GOLDEN GATE UNIVERSITY LAW REVIEW at
p. 513 (1983).

Law, S., "Women, Work, Welfare and Patriarchy," Vol. 131 UNIVERSITY OF PENNSYLVANIA LAW
REVIEW at p. 1256 (1984).

Littleton, C., "Equality and Feminist Legal Theory," Vol. 48 UNIVERSITY OF PITTSBURGH LAW
REVIEW at p. 1043 (1987).

Scott, J., "Deconstructing Equality-Versus-Difference: Or Uses of Poststructural Theory for Feminism," Vol. 14 FEMINIST STUDIES at p. 33 (1988).

Taub, N., "From Parental Leaves to Nurturing Leaves," 13 NEW YORK UNIVERSITY JOURNAL OF
LAW AND SOCIAL CHANGE at p. 381 (1985).

Williams, W., "The Equality Crisis: Some Reflections on Culture, Courts, and Feminism," Vol. 7
WOMEN'S RIGHTS LAW REPORTER at p. 175 (1982).

II On Justice and Harm

Brownmiller, S., AGAINST OUR WILL: MEN, WOMEN AND RAPE (New York: Bantam, 1976).

Clark, M., and Lewis, D., RAPE: THE PRICE OF COERCIVE SEXUALITY (Toronto: Women's Press,
1977).

Collins, E., and Blodgett, T., "Sexual Harassment: Some See It . . . Some Won't," Vol. 59 HARVARD
BUSINESS REVIEW at p. 76 (March/April, 1981).

Dobash, R., and Dobash, R., VIOLENCE AGAINST WIVES: A CASE AGAINST PATRIARCHY (New
York: Free Press, 1979).

Ellis, S., "Sexual Harassment and Race," Vol. 8 NOTRE DAME JOURNAL OF LEGISLATION at p. 30
     (1981).
Estrich, S., REAL RAPE (Cambridge: Harvard University Press, 1987).
Guberman, C., and Wolfe, M. (eds.), NO SAFE PLACE: VIOLENCE AGAINST WOMEN AND CHIL-
     DREN (Toronto: Women's Press, 1985).
Gutek, B., SEX AND THE WORKPLACE (San Francisco: Jossey-Bass, 1985).
MacKinnon, C., SEXUAL HARASSMENT OF WORKING WOMEN: A CASE OF SEX DISCRIMINATION
     (New Haven: Yale University Press, 1979).
Martin, D., BATTERED WIVES (San Francisco: Glide, 1976; rev. ed. 1981).
Russell, D., RAPE IN MARRIAGE (New York: Macmillan, 1982).
Special Issue, *Forum on Sexual Harassment,* Vol. 10 CAPITAL UNIVERSITY LAW REVIEW (1981).
Stanks, E., INTIMATE INTRUSIONS: WOMEN'S EXPERIENCES OF MALE VIOLENCE (Boston:
     Routledge, 1985).
Stark, Flitcraft and Frazier, "Medicine and Patriarchal Violence: The Social Construction of a Pri-
     vate Event," Vol. 3 INTERNATIONAL JOURNAL OF HEALTH SERVICES at p. 461 (1979).
U.S. Merit Systems Protection Board, *Harassment in the Federal Government: An Update* (Wash-
     ington DC: Government Printing Office, 1988).
Walker, L., THE BATTERED WOMAN (New York: Harper and Row, 1979).
————, THE BATTERED WOMAN SYNDROME (Berkeley: Springer Publishing Company, 1984).
Wriggins, J., "Rape, Racism, and the Law," Vol. 6 HARVARD WOMEN'S LAW REVIEW at p. 103
     (1983).

III On Adjudication

Ginsberg, R., "Some Thoughts on Autonomy and Equality in Relation to Roe vs. Wade," Vol. 63
     NORTH CAROLINA LAW REVIEW at p. 375 (1985).
Hirshman, L. R., "Bronte, Bloom, and Bork: An Essay on the Moral Education of Judges," Vol.
     137 UNIVERSITY OF PENNSYLVANIA LAW REVIEW at p. 177 (1988).
Masaro, T., "Empathy, Legal Storytelling and the Rule of Law," Vol. 87 MICHIGAN LAW REVIEW
     at p. 2104 (1989).
Minow, M., MAKING ALL THE DIFFERENCE: INCLUSION, EXCLUSION AND AMERICAN LAW (Ith-
     aca: Cornell University Press, 1991).
Resnik, J., "On the Bias: Feminist Reconsideration of the Aspirations for Judges," Vol. 61
     SOUTHERN CALIFORNIA LAW JOURNAL at p. 1877 (1988).
Schafran, "Documenting Gender Bias in the Courts: The Task Force Approach," Vol. 70 JUDI-
     CATURE at p. 280 (1987).
Sherry, S., "Civic Virtue and the Feminine Voice in Constitutional Adjudication," Vol. 72 VIR-
     GINIA LAW REVIEW at p. 543 (1986).

IV On Freedom

Allen, A., UNEASY ACCESS: PRIVACY FOR WOMEN IN A FREE SOCIETY (Totowa, NJ: Rowman and
     Littlefield, 1988).
Callahan, J., and Knight, J. PREVENTING BIRTH: CONTEMPORARY METHODS AND RELATED
     MORAL CONTROVERSIES (Salt Lake City: University of Utah Press, 1989).
Cohen, S., and Taub, N. (eds.), REPRODUCTIVE LAW FOR THE 1990s (Clifton, NJ: Humana Press,
     1984).
Douglas, J., et al., ABORTION, MEDICINE AND THE LAW (New York: Facts on File, 1986).

Garfield, J., and Hennessey, P., ABORTION: MORAL AND LEGAL PERSPECTIVES (Amherst: University of Massachusetts Press, 1984).

Gordon, L., WOMAN'S BODY, WOMAN'S RIGHT (New York: Grossman, 1976).

Kamm, F., CREATION AND ABORTION (New York: Oxford University Press, 1992).

Luker, K., ABORTION AND THE POLITICS OF MOTHERHOOD (Berkeley: University of California Press, 1984).

O'Brien, M., REPRODUCING THE WORLD (Boulder, CO: Westview Press, 1989).

Overall, C., ETHICS AND HUMAN REPRODUCTION (Boston: Unwin Hyman, 1978).

Perry, M., "Why the Supreme Court Was Plainly Wrong in the Hyde Amendment Case: A Brief Comment on Harris vs. McRae," Vol. 32 STANFORD LAW REVIEW at p. 1113 (July, 1980).

Rothman, B., RECREATING MOTHERHOOD (New York: Norton, 1989).

Tribe, L., "The Abortion Funding Conundrum: Inalienable Rights, Affirmative Duties, and the Dilemma of Dependence," Vol. 99 HARVARD LAW REVIEW at p. 330 (1985).

V On Human Dignity

Baker, N., BABYSELLING: THE SCANDAL OF BLACK-MARKET ADOPTIONS (New York: Vanguard, 1978).

Burstyn, V. (ed.), WOMEN AGAINST CENSORSHIP (Vancouver: Douglas and McIntyre, 1985).

Corea, G., THE MOTHER MACHINE (New York: Harper and Row, 1984).

Decker, J., PROSTITUTION: REGULATION AND CONTROL (Littleton, CO: Rothman, 1979).

Dworkin, A., PORNOGRAPHY: MEN POSSESSING WOMEN (New York: Dutton, 1979).

Hobsen, B., UNEASY VIRTUE: THE POLITICS OF PROSTITUTION AND THE AMERICAN REFORM TRADITION (New York: Basic Books, 1987).

Holder, A. R., "Surrogate Motherhood: Babies for Fun and Profit," Vol. 12 LAW, MEDICINE AND HEALTH CARE at p. 115 (1984).

James, J., et al., THE POLITICS OF PROSTITUTION (Seattle: Social Research Association, 1975).

Lederer, L. (ed.), TAKE BACK THE NIGHT: WOMEN ON PORNOGRAPHY (New York: Bantam, 1980).

LeMoncheck, L., DEHUMANIZING WOMEN: TREATING PERSONS AS SEX OBJECTS (Totowa, NJ: Rowman and Allanheld, 1984).

Millett, K., THE PROSTITUTION PAPERS (New York: Avon, 1973).

VI On Law and Jurisprudence

Bartlett, K., "Feminist Legal Methods," Vol. 101 HARVARD LAW REVIEW at p. 97 (1988).

Bender, L., "A Lawyer's Primer on Feminist Theory and Tort," Vol. 88 JOURNAL OF LEGAL EDUCATION at p. 3 (1988).

Cornell, D., BEYOND ACCOMMODATION: ETHICAL FEMINISM, DECONSTRUCTION AND THE LAW (New York: Routledge, 1990).

DuBois, E., Dunlap, M., Gilligan, C., MacKinnon, C., and Menkel-Meadow, C., "Feminist Discourse, Moral Values and the Law—A Conversation," Vol. 34 BUFFALO LAW REVIEW at p. 11 (1985).

Fineman, M., "Dominant Discourse, Professional Language and Legal Change," Vol. 101 HARVARD LAW REVIEW at p. 727 (1988).

Littleton, C., "Does It Still Make Sense To Talk About 'Women'?," Vol. 1, UNIVERSITY OF CALIFORNIA, LOS ANGELES, WOMEN'S LAW JOURNAL at p. 15 (1991).

MacKinnon, C., "Feminism, Marxism, Method and the State: An Agenda for Theory," Vol. 7 SIGNS at p. 515 (1982).

————, "Feminism, Marxism, Method and State: Toward Feminist Jurisprudence," Vol. 8 SIGNS at p. 635 (1983).

————, FEMINISM UNMODIFIED—DISCOURSES ON LIFE AND LAW (Cambridge: Harvard University Press, 1987).

————, TOWARD A FEMINIST THEORY OF THE STATE (Cambridge: Harvard University Press, 1989).

Polan, D., "Toward a Theory of Law and Patriarchy," in THE POLITICS OF LAW: A PROGRESSIVE CRITIQUE at p. 294, D. Kairys, ed. (New York: Pantheon Books, 1982).

Rhode, D., "The 'No-Problem' Problem: Feminist Challenges and Cultural Change," Vol. 100 YALE LAW JOURNAL at p. 1731 (1991).

Rifkin, J., "Toward a Theory of Law and Patriarchy," Vol. 3 HARVARD WOMEN'S LAW JOURNAL at p. 83 (1980).

Wishik, H., "To Question Everything: The Inquiries of Feminist Jurisprudence," Vol. 1 BERKELEY WOMEN'S LAW JOURNAL at p. 64 (1985).

VII On Rights

Littleton, C., "Equality Across Difference: Is There Room for Rights Discourse?," Vol. 3 WISCONSIN WOMEN'S LAW JOURNAL p. 189 (1987).

McGlen, N., and O'Connor, K., WOMEN'S RIGHTS: THE STRUGGLE FOR EQUALITY IN 19TH AND 20TH CENTURY AMERICA (New York: Praeger, 1983).

Minow, M., "Rights for the Next Generation: A Feminist Approach to Children's Rights," Vol. 9 HARVARD WOMEN'S LAW JOURNAL at p. 1 (1986).

Olsen, R., "Statutory Rape: A Feminist Critique of Rights Analysis," Vol. 63 TEXAS LAW REVIEW at p. 387 (1984).

Villamore, A., "The Left's Problems with Rights," Vol. 9 LEGAL STUDIES FORUM at p. 39 (1985).

Williams, P., "Alchemical Notes: Reconstructed Ideals from Deconstructed Rights," Vol. 22 HARVARD CIVIL RIGHTS/CIVIL LIBERTIES LAW REVIEW at p. 401 (1987).

————, THE ALCHEMY OF RACE AND RIGHTS (Cambridge: Harvard University Press, 1991).

Wolgast, E., EQUALITY AND THE RIGHTS OF WOMEN (Ithaca: Cornell University Press, 1980).

VIII On Crime and Punishment

Callahan, J., "Prenatal Harm as Child Abuse?," in KINDRED MATTERS, Meyers, D., et al., eds. (Ithaca: Cornell University Press, 1992).

Jordan, S., and Schneider, E., "Representations of Women Who Defend Themselves Against Physical Assault," Vol. 4 WOMEN'S RIGHTS LAW REPORTER at p. 149 (1978).

Messerschmidt, J., CAPITALISM, PATRIARCHY AND CRIME (Savage, MD: Rowman and Littlefield, 1986).

Note, "Sentencing Women: Equal Protection in the Context of Discretionary Decisionmaking," Vol. 6 WOMEN'S RIGHTS LAW REPORTER at p. 85 (1979–80).

Rapaport, E., "Some Questions About Gender and the Death Penalty," Vol. 20 GOLDEN GATE UNIVERSITY LAW REVIEW at p. 502 (1990).

Schneider, E., "Describing and Changing: Women's Self-Defense Work and the Problem of Expert Testimony on Battering," Vol. 9 WOMEN'S RIGHTS LAW REPORTER at p. 195 (1986).

Zingraff and Thompson, "Differential Sentencing of Women and Men in the USA," Vol. 12 INTERNATIONAL JOURNAL OF SOCIETY AND LAW at p. 401 (1984).

IX General

Bartlett, K., and Kennedy, R., FEMINIST LEGAL THEORY (Boulder, CO: Westview Press, 1991).

Fineman, M., and Thomadsen, N., AT THE BOUNDARIES OF LAW: FEMINISM AND LEGAL THEORY (New York: Routledge, 1991).

Kay, H., SEX-BASED DISCRIMINATION (St. Paul: West, 1988).

Lindgren, R., and Taub, N., THE LAW OF SEX DISCRIMINATION (St. Paul: West, 1988).

Rhode, D., JUSTICE AND GENDER (Harvard University Press, 1989).

Special Issue, Vol. 88 JOURNAL OF LEGAL EDUCATION (1988).

Special Issue, "Feminism in the Law: Theory, Practice and Criticism," Vol. 1989 UNIVERSITY OF CHICAGO LEGAL FORUM (1989).

Special Issue, "Women's Law Forum," Vol. 20 GOLDEN GATE LAW REVIEW (1990).

Tong, R., WOMEN, SEX AND THE LAW (Totowa, NJ: Rowman and Littlefield, 1984).

Credits